D0714829

Ceres Primary School

Alexander Pollock

Leaver 2010

Chambers
French
Mini
Dictionary

Chambers

CHAMBERS
An imprint of Chambers Harrap Publishers Ltd
7 Hopetoun Crescent, Edinburgh, EH7 4AY

Chambers Harrap is an Hachette UK company

© Chambers Harrap Publishers Ltd 2009

Chambers® is a registered trademark of Chambers Harrap Publishers Ltd

First published by Chambers Harrap Publishers Ltd 2009
Previously published as *Harrap's French Mini Dictionary* in 1999
Second edition published 2003

Database right Chambers Harrap Publishers Ltd (makers)

A CIP catalogue record for this book is available from the British Library.

ISBN 978 0550 10526 4

10 9 8 7 6 5 4 3 2 1

www.chambers.co.uk

Designed by Chambers Harrap Publishers Ltd, Edinburgh
Typeset in Cheltenham and Frutiger by Chambers Harrap Publishers Ltd,
Edinburgh
Printed and bound in Italy by Legoprint

Project Manager/Coordination éditoriale
Kate Nicholson

Editors/Rédaction
Isabelle Elkaim
Stuart Fortey
Rachel Skeet

Publishing Manager/Direction éditoriale
Anna Stevenson

Prepress/Prépresse
Becky Pickard

Trademarks

Words considered to be trademarks have been designated in this dictionary by the symbol ®. However, no judgement is implied concerning the legal status of any trademark by the presence or absence of such a symbol.

Marques déposées

Les termes considérés comme des marques déposées sont signalés dans ce dictionnaire par le symbole ®. Cependant, la présence ou l'absence de ce symbole ne constitue nullement une indication quant à la valeur juridique de ces termes.

Contents
Table des matières

Preface

This dictionary will provide all students of French at beginner and intermediate level with a reliable, comprehensive and user-friendly resource in a compact, portable form. The clear, systematic layout of information makes the dictionary an easy-to-use resource and its wide coverage of vocabulary should ensure that it becomes an invaluable tool.

With over 45,000 words and phrases, the dictionary covers all essential everyday vocabulary, making it ideal for both study and travel. As in all Chambers bilingual dictionaries, colloquial and idiomatic language is well represented, as are words from a wide range of specialized fields, such as IT, business and science.

A wealth of extra help is provided in the form of a useful supplement comprising information on French and English irregular verbs, together with sections on numbers, days of the week, months of the year and time-related phrases. In addition, a handy communication guide provides essential phrases for travel and holidays in French-speaking countries, making this the ideal pocket resource.

Préface

Ce nouveau dictionnaire a pour but de fournir aux apprenants d'anglais de niveau débutant ou intermédiaire un dictionnaire fiable et pratique sous forme compacte. La présentation claire et systématique en fait un outil d'usage facile, et grâce à son traitement du vocabulaire, il devrait s'avérer une aide précieuse pour l'utilisateur.

Avec plus de 45,000 références, le dictionnaire traite tous les mots et expressions utiles pour les situations courantes et les voyages aux pays anglo-saxons. Il contient des expressions familiers et idiomatiques, ainsi que des termes issus de domaines spécialisés variés tels que l'informatique, le sport ou la finance.

Des tableaux de prononciation se trouvent au début de livre, et le supplément central contient des informations sur les verbes irréguliers anglais et français ainsi que sur les nombres, les jours, les mois de l'année et l'heure. De plus, un guide de conversation propose des phrases essentielles pour les voyages et les vacances aux pays anglophones, faisant de l'ouvrage une ressource de poche essentielle.

Abbreviations   Abréviations

gloss	=	glose
[introduces an explanation]		[introduit une explication]
cultural equivalent	≃	équivalent culturel
[introduces a translation which has a roughly equivalent status in the target language]		[introduit une traduction dont les connotations dans la langue cible sont comparables]
abbreviation	*abbr, abrév*	abréviation
adjective	*adj*	adjectif
adverb	*adv*	adverbe
agriculture	*Agr*	agriculture
American English	*Am*	anglais américain
anatomy	*Anat*	anatomie
architecture	*Archit*	architecture
slang	*Arg*	argot
astrology	*Astrol*	astrologie
cars	*Aut*	automobile
auxiliary	*aux*	auxiliaire
aviation	*Aviat*	aviation
Belgian French	*Belg*	belgicisme
biology	*Biol*	biologie
botany	*Bot*	botanique
British English	*Br*	anglais britannique
Canadian French	*Can*	canadianisme
chemistry	*Chem, Chim*	chimie
cinema	*Cin*	cinéma
commerce	*Com*	commerce
computing	*Comptr*	informatique
conjunction	*conj*	conjonction
cooking	*Culin*	cuisine
economics	*Econ, Écon*	économie
electricity, electronics	*El, Él*	électricité, électronique
exclamation	*exclam*	exclamation
feminine	*f*	féminin
familiar	*Fam*	familier
figurative	*Fig*	figuré
finance	*Fin*	finance
geography	*Geog, Géog*	géographie
geology	*Geol, Géol*	géologie
grammar	*Gram*	grammaire
gymnastics	*Gym*	gymnastique
history	*Hist*	histoire

humorous	*Hum*	humoristique
invariable	*inv*	invariable
journalism	*Journ*	journalisme
law	*Jur*	droit
linguistics	*Ling*	linguistique
masculine	*m*	masculin
mathematics	*Math*	mathématique
medicine	*Med, Méd*	médecine
military	*Mil*	militaire
music	*Mus*	musique
noun	*n*	nom
shipping	*Naut*	nautisme
feminine noun	*nf*	nom féminin
feminine plural noun	*nfpl*	nom féminin pluriel
masculine noun	*nm*	nom masculin
masculine and feminine noun	*nmf*	nom masculin et féminin
masculine plural noun	*nmpl*	nom masculin pluriel
plural noun	*npl*	nom pluriel
computing	*Ordinat*	ordinateurs, informatique
pejorative	*Pej, Péj*	péjoratif
philosophy	*Phil*	philosophie
photography	*Phot*	photographie
physics	*Phys*	physique
plural	*pl*	pluriel
politics	*Pol*	politique
past participle	*pp*	participe passé
prefix	*pref, préf*	préfixe
preposition	*prep, prép*	préposition
pronoun	*pron*	pronom
past tense	*pt*	prétérit
* something	*qch*	quelque chose
registered trademark	®	marque déposée
rail	*Rail*	chemin de fer
religion	*Rel*	religion
somebody	*sb*	quelqu'un
school	*Sch, Scol*	domaine scolaire
Scottish English	*Scot*	anglais d'Écosse
singular	*sing*	singulier
something	*sth*	quelque chose
suffix	*suff*	suffixe
technology	*Tech*	technologie
telecommunications	*Tel, Tél*	télécommunications
theatre	*Theat, Théât*	théâtre
television	*TV*	télévision

typography, printing	*Typ*	typographie, imprimerie
university	*Univ*	domaine universitaire
verb	*v*	verbe
intransitive verb	*vi*	verbe intransitif
reflexive verb	*vpr*	verbe pronominal
transitive verb	*vt*	verbe transitif
inseparable transitive verb	*vt insep*	verbe transitif à particule inséparable [par ex.: **he looks after the children** il s'occupe des enfants]
separable transitive verb	*vt sep*	verbe transitif à particule séparable [par ex.: **she sent the present back** *or* **she sent back the present** elle a rendu le cadeau]

All other labels are written in full.
Toutes les autres indications d'usage sont données en entier.

Prononciation de l'anglais

Pour indiquer la prononciation anglaise, nous avons utilisé dans ce dictionnaire les symboles de l'API (Alphabet phonétique international). Pour chaque son anglais, vous trouverez dans le tableau ci-dessous des exemples de mots anglais, suivis de mots français présentant un son similaire. Une explication est donnée lorsqu'il n'y a pas d'équivalent en français.

Caractère API	Exemple en anglais	Exemple en français
Consonnes		
[b]	**b**a**bb**le	**b**é**b**é
[d]	**d**ig	**d**ent
[dʒ]	**g**iant, **j**ig	**j**ean
[f]	**f**it, **ph**ysics	**f**ace
[g]	**g**rey, bi**g**	**g**a**g**
[h]	**h**appy	h aspiré : à quelques rares exceptions près, il est toujours prononcé en anglais
[j]	**y**ellow	**y**aourt
[k]	**c**lay, **k**i**ck**	**c**ar
[l]	**l**ip, pi**ll**	**l**i**l**as
[m]	**mumm**y	**m**a**m**an
[n]	**n**ip, pi**n**	**n**é
[ŋ]	si**ng**	parki**ng**
[p]	**p**i**p**	**p**a**p**a
[r]	**r**ig, **wr**ite	Pas d'équivalent français : se prononce en plaçant le bout de la langue au milieu du palais
[(r)]		Seulement prononcé en cas de liaison avec la voyelle qui suit comme dans : far away; the car is blue
[s]	**s**ick, **sc**ience	**s**ilence
[ʃ]	**sh**ip, na**t**ion	**ch**èvre
[t]	**t**ip, bu**tt**	**t**artine
[tʃ]	**ch**ip, ba**tch**	a**tch**oum
[θ]	**th**ick	Son proche du /s/ français, il se prononce en plaçant le bout de la langue entre les dents du haut et celles du bas

x

Caractère API	Exemple en anglais	Exemple en français
[ð]	**th**is	Son proche du /z/ français, il se prononce en plaçant le bout de la langue entre les dents du haut et celles du bas
[v]	**v**ague, gi**v**e	**v**ie
[w]	**w**it, **wh**y	**wh**isky
[z]	**z**ip, phy**s**ics	ro**s**e
[ʒ]	plea**s**ure	**j**e
[χ]	lo**ch**	Existe seulement dans certains mots écossais. Pas d'équivalent français : se prononce du fond de la gorge, comme Ba**ch** en allemand ou la '**j**ota' espagnole.

Voyelles

[æ]	r**a**g	n**a**tte
[ɑː]	l**a**rge, h**a**lf	p**â**te
[e]	s**e**t	/e/ moins ouvert que le [ɛ] français
[ɜː]	c**ur**tain, w**er**e	h**eu**re
[ə]	**u**tter	ch**e**val
[ɪ]	b**i**g, w**o**men	/i/ bref, à mi-chemin entre les sons [ɛ] et [i] français (plus proche de 'n**e**t' que de 'v**i**te')
[iː]	l**ea**k, w**ee**	/i/ plus long que le [i] français
[ɒ]	l**o**ck	b**o**nne – mais plus ouvert et prononcé au fond du palais
[ɔː]	w**a**ll, c**o**rk	b**au**me – mais plus ouvert et prononcé au fond du palais
[ʊ]	p**u**t, l**oo**k	Son à mi-chemin entre un /ou/ bref et un /o/ ouvert
[uː]	m**oo**n	Son /ou/ prolongé
[ʌ]	c**u**p	À mi-chemin entre un /a/ et un /e/ ouverts

Diphtongues

Elles sont rares en français et sont la combinaison de deux sons.

[aɪ]	wh**y**, h**igh**, l**ie**	**aï**e
[aʊ]	h**ow**	mi**aou**, **aoû**tat – mais se prononce comme un seul son

[eə]	b**ear**, sh**are**, wh**ere**	fl**air**
[eɪ]	d**ay**, m**a**ke, m**ai**n	merv**eille**
[əʊ]	sh**ow**, g**o**	Combinaison d'un /o/ fermé et d'un /ou/
[ɪə]	h**ere**, g**ear**	Combinaison d'un /i/ long suivi d'un /e/
		ouvert bref
[ɔɪ]	b**oy**, s**oi**l	langue d'oïl
[ʊə]	s**ure**	Combinaison d'un son /ou/ suivi d'un /e/
		ouvert bref

Prononciation de l'anglais américain

L'accent américain est différent de l'accent anglais : il est facile de le constater dans la prononciation du mot **tomato** qui se dit [təˈmeɪtəʊ] en anglais américain et [təˈmɑːtəʊ] en anglais britannique. Le r, qui disparaît souvent en anglais, est toujours prononcé en américain : **mother** se dit [ˈmʌðər] aux États-Unis et [ˈmʌðə] en Grande-Bretagne.

Quelques exemples :

	Prononciation américaine	*Prononciation anglaise*
advertisement	[ædvəˈtaɪzmənt]	[ədˈvɜːtɪsmənt]
clerk	[klɜːk]	[klɑːk]
derby	[ˈdɜːbɪ]	[ˈdɑːbɪ]
leisure	[ˈliːʒər]	[ˈleʒə]
privacy	[ˈpraɪvəsɪ]	[ˈprɪvəsɪ]
schedule	[ˈskedʒʊl]	[ˈʃedjuːl]
tube	[tuːb]	[tjuːb]
vase	[veɪz]	[vɑːz]
z	[ziː]	[zed]

L'accent tonique est souvent différent : **distribute** se prononce [dɪsˈtrɪbjuːt] aux États-Unis et [ˈdɪstrɪbjuːt] en Grande-Bretagne ; **ballet** se dit [bæˈleɪ] en américain et [ˈbæleɪ] en anglais britannique.

Autres exemples :

	Prononciation américaine	*Prononciation anglaise*
Birmingham	[bɜːmɪŋˈhæm]	[ˈbɜːmɪŋəm]
laboratory	[ˈlæbrətərɪ]	[ləˈbɒrətərɪ]
fillet	[fɪˈleɪ]	[ˈfɪlɪt]
garage	[gəˈrɑːʒ]	[ˈgærɪdʒ]
pecan	[pɪˈkæn]	[ˈpiːkæn]

French Pronunciation

French pronunciation is shown in this dictionary using the symbols of the IPA (International Phonetic Alphabet). In the table below, examples of French words using these sounds are given, followed by English words which have a similar sound. Where there is no equivalent in English, an explanation is given.

IPA symbol	French example	English example
Consonants		
[b]	**b**é**b**é	**b**ut
[d]	**d**onner	**d**oor
[f]	**f**orêt	**f**ire
[g]	**g**are	**g**et
[ʒ]	**j**our	plea**s**ure
[k]	**c**arte	**k**itten
[l]	**l**ire	**l**onely
[m]	**m**a**m**an	**m**at
[n]	**n**i	**n**ow
[ŋ]	parki**ng**	singi**ng**
[ɲ]	campa**gn**e	ca**ny**on
[p]	**p**atte	**p**at
[r]	**r**a**r**e	Like an English /r/ but pronounced at the back of the throat
[s]	**s**oir	**s**it
[ʃ]	**ch**ose	**sh**am
[t]	**t**able	**t**ap
[v]	**v**aleur	**v**alue
[z]	**z**éro	**z**ero
Vowels		
[a]	ch**a**t	c**a**t
[ɑ]	**â**ge	g**a**sp
[e]	**é**t**é**	b**ay**
[ɛ]	p**è**re	b**e**d
[ə]	l**e**	**a**mend
[ø]	d**eu**x	Does not exist in English: [e] pronounced with the lips rounded

[œ]	s**eu**l	c**ur**tain
[i]	v**i**te	b**ee** – not quite as long as the English [iː]
[ɔ]	d**o**nner	c**o**t – slightly more open than the English /o/
[o]	ch**au**d	d**au**ghter – but higher than its English equivalent
[u]	t**ou**t	y**ou** – but shorter than its English equivalent
[y]	voit**u**re	Does not exist in English: [i] with lips rounded
[ã]	enf**an**t	Nasal sound pronounced lower and further back in the mouth than [ɔ̃]

Vowels

[ɛ̃]	v**in**	Nasal sound: /a/ sound pronounced letting air pass through the nose
[ɔ̃]	b**on**jour	Nasal sound: closed /o/ sound pronounced letting air pass through the nose
[œ̃]	**un**	Nasal sound: like [ɛ̃] but with lips more rounded

Semi-vowels

[w]	v**oi**r	**w**eek
[j]	**y**oyo, pai**ll**e	**y**ard
[ɥ]	n**ui**t	Does not exist in English: the vowel [y] elided with the following vowel

ENGLISH-FRENCH

Aa

A, a¹ [eɪ] *n* (a) A, a *m inv*; **5A** *(in address, street number)* 5 bis; **to go from A to B** aller du point A au point B (b) *Sch (grade)* **to get an A in French** = avoir une très bonne note en français, ≃ avoir entre 16 et 20 en français (c) *(street atlas)* **an A to Z of London** un plan de Londres

A² [ə, *stressed* eɪ]

a devient **an** [ən, *stressed* æn] devant voyelle ou h muet.

indefinite article (a) *(in general)* un, une; **a man** un homme; **an apple** une pomme; **an hour** une heure

(b) *(definite article in French)* **60 pence a kilo** 60 pence le kilo; **50 km an hour** 50 km à l'heure; **I have a broken arm** j'ai le bras cassé

(c) *(article omitted in French)* **he's a doctor/a father** il est médecin/père; **Caen, a town in Normandy** Caen, ville de Normandie; **what a man!** quel homme!; **a hundred** cent

(d) *(a certain)* **a Mr Smith** un certain M. Smith

(e) *(time)* **twice a month** deux fois par mois

aback [ə'bæk] *adv* **taken a. (by)** déconcerté (par)

abandon [ə'bændən] **1** *n* abandon *m* **2** *vt* abandonner; **to a. ship** abandonner le navire

abbey ['æbɪ] *(pl* **-eys)** *n* abbaye *f*

abbreviate [ə'briːvɪeɪt] *vt* abréger ■ **abbreviation** *n* abréviation *f*

abdicate ['æbdɪkeɪt] *vt & vi* abdiquer

abdomen ['æbdəmən] *n* abdomen *m*

abduct [æb'dʌkt] *vt (kidnap)* enlever ■ **abduction** *n* enlèvement *m*, rapt *m*

ability [ə'bɪlətɪ] *(pl* **-ies)** *n* capacité *f* **(to do sth** de faire)**; to the best of my a.** de mon mieux

ablaze [ə'bleɪz] *adj* en feu; *Fig* **a. with** *(light)* resplendissant de

able ['eɪbəl] *adj* capable; **to be a. to do sth** être capable de faire qch, pouvoir faire qch; **to be a. to swim/drive** savoir nager/conduire ■ **able-bodied** *adj* robuste

abnormal [æb'nɔːməl] *adj* anormal

aboard [ə'bɔːd] **1** *adv (on ship, plane)* à bord; **to go a.** monter à bord **2** *prep* **a. the ship/plane** à bord du navire/de l'avion; **a. the train** dans le train

abolish [ə'bɒlɪʃ] *vt* abolir ■ **abolition** [æbə'lɪʃən] *n* abolition *f*

abominable [ə'bɒmɪnəbəl] *adj* abominable

Aborigine [æbə'rɪdʒɪnɪ] *n* Aborigène *mf* (d'Australie)

abort [ə'bɔːt] **1** *vt (space flight, computer program)* avorter **2** *vi Med* faire une fausse couche ■ **abortion** *n* avortement *m*; **to have an a.** se faire avorter

ABOUT [ə'baʊt] **1** *adv* (a) *(approximately)* à peu près, environ; **at a. two o'clock** (b) *(here and there)* çà et là, ici et là; *Fig* **there's a lot of flu a.** at the moment il y a beaucoup de cas de grippe en ce moment; **there's a rumour a. (that...)** il y a une rumeur qui circule (selon laquelle...); **to look a.** regarder autour de soi; **to follow someone a.** suivre quelqu'un partout **2** *prep* (a) *(around)* **a. the garden** autour du jardin

(b) *(near to)* **a. here** par ici

(**c**) *(concerning)* au sujet de; **to talk a. sth** parler de qch; **a book a. sth** un livre sur qch; **what's it (all) a.?** de quoi s'agit-il?

(**d**) (+ *infinitive*) **a. to do** sur le point de faire; **I was a. to say…** j'étais sur le point de dire…

above [ə'bʌv] **1** *adv* au-dessus; *(in book)* ci-dessus; **from a.** d'en haut; **the floor a.** l'étage *m* du dessus
2 *prep* (**a**) *(in height, hierarchy)* au-dessus de; **he's a. me** *(in rank)* c'est mon supérieur; **she's not a. lying** elle n'est pas incapable de mentir; **he's not a. asking** il n'est pas trop fier pour demander; **a. all** surtout
(**b**) *(with numbers)* plus de ■ **above-board 1** *adj* honnête **2** *adv* sans tricherie ■ **above-mentioned** *adj* susmentionné

abreast [ə'brest] *adv* côte à côte, de front; **four a.** par rangs de quatre; **to keep a. of sth** se tenir au courant de qch

abroad [ə'brɔːd] *adv* à l'étranger; **from a.** de l'étranger

abrupt [ə'brʌpt] *adj (sudden)* brusque, soudain; *(rude)* brusque, abrupt; *(slope, style)* abrupt

abscess ['æbses] *n* abcès *m*

absence ['æbsəns] *n* absence *f*; **in the a. of** *(person)* en l'absence de; *(thing)* faute de

absent 1 ['æbsənt] *adj* absent (**from** de) **2** [æb'sent] *vt* **to a. oneself (from)** s'absenter (de) ■ **absent-minded** *adj* distrait

absentee [æbsən'tiː] *n* absent, -e *mf*

absolute ['æbsəluːt] *adj (sure)* absolu; *(proof)* indiscutable; **he's an a. fool!** il est complètement idiot!; **it's an a. disgrace!** c'est une honte! ■ **absolutely** *adv* absolument; **you're a. right** tu as tout à fait raison

absorb [əb'zɔːb] *vt (liquid)* absorber; *(shock)* amortir; **to be absorbed in sth** être plongé dans qch ■ **absorbent** *adj* absorbant

abstain [əb'steɪn] *vi Pol* s'abstenir; **to**

a. from sth/from doing sth s'abstenir de qch/de faire qch

abstract ['æbstrækt] **1** *adj* abstrait **2** *n* (**a**) *(notion)* **the a.** l'abstrait *m* (**b**) *(summary)* résumé *m*

absurd [əb'sɜːd] *adj* absurde, ridicule

abundant [ə'bʌndənt] *adj* abondant ■ **abundantly** *adv* **a. clear** parfaitement clair

abuse 1 [ə'bjuːs] *n (of power)* abus *m* (**of** de); *(of child)* mauvais traitements *mpl*; *(insults)* injures *fpl* **2** [ə'bjuːz] *vt (misuse)* abuser de; *(ill-treat)* maltraiter; *(insult)* injurier ■ **abusive** [ə'bjuːsɪv] *adj (person, language)* grossier, -ère

abysmal [ə'bɪzməl] *adj Fam (bad)* exécrable

academic [ækə'demɪk] **1** *adj* (**a**) *(year, diploma)* (*of school)* scolaire; *(of university)* universitaire (**b**) *(scholarly)* intellectuel, -elle (**c**) *(theoretical)* **the issue is of purely a. interest** cette question n'a d'intérêt que d'un point de vue théorique; **this is a. now** cela n'a plus d'importance **2** *n (teacher)* universitaire *mf*

academy [ə'kædəmɪ] *(pl* **-ies)** *n (society)* académie *f*; *(military)* école *f*

accelerate [ək'seləreɪt] **1** *vt* accélérer **2** *vi (of pace)* s'accélérer; *(of vehicle, driver)* accélérer ■ **accelerator** *n* accélérateur *m*

accent ['æksənt] *n* accent *m*

accept [ək'sept] *vt* accepter ■ **acceptable** *adj (worth accepting, tolerable)* acceptable; **to be a. to sb** convenir à qn

access ['ækses] **1** *n* accès *m* (**to sth** à qch; **to sb** auprès de qn); *Comptr* **a. provider** fournisseur *m* d'accès; **a. road** route *f* d'accès **2** *vt Comptr* accéder à ■ **accessible** *adj* accessible

accessories [ək'sesərɪz] *npl (objects)* accessoires *mpl*

accessory [ək'sesərɪ] *(pl* **-ies)** *n Law (accomplice)* complice *mf* (**to** de)

accident ['æksɪdənt] *n* accident *m*; **by a.** accidentellement; *(by chance)* par hasard ■ **accidental** *adj* accidentel, -elle ■ **accidentally** *adv* accidentellement; *(by chance)* par hasard

acclaim [ə'kleɪm] **1** *n* (critical) a. éloges *mpl* **2** *vt* (cheer) acclamer; *(praise)* faire l'éloge de

acclimatize [ə'klaɪmətaɪz] *(Am* **acclimate** ['æklə meɪt]) *vi* s'acclimater

accommodate [ə'kɒmədeɪt] *vt* (a) *(of house)* loger (b) *(oblige)* rendre service à ■ **accommodating** *adj* accommodant, obligeant

accommodation [əkɒmə'deɪʃən] *n* *(Am* **accommodations**) *(lodging)* logement *m*; *(rented room(s))* chambre(s) *f(pl)*

accompany [ə'kʌmpəni] *(pt & pp* **-ied**) *vt* accompagner

accomplice [ə'kʌmplɪs] *n* complice *mf*

accomplish [ə'kʌmplɪʃ] *vt* (task, duty) accomplir; *(aim)* atteindre ■ **accomplishment** *n* (of task, duty) accomplissement *m*; *(thing achieved)* réalisation *f*

accord [ə'kɔːd] **1** *n* accord *m*; of my own a. de mon plein gré **2** *vt* (grant) accorder ■ **accordance** *n* in a. with conformément à

according [ə'kɔːdɪŋ] **according to** *prep* selon, d'après ■ **accordingly** *adv* en conséquence

accordion [ə'kɔːdɪən] *n* accordéon *m*

accost [ə'kɒst] *vt* accoster, aborder

account [ə'kaʊnt] **1** *n* (a) (with bank or company) compte *m* (b) (report) compte rendu *m*; *(explanation)* explication *f* (c) (expressions) by all accounts au dire de tous; on a. of à cause de; on no a. en aucun cas; to take sth into a. tenir compte de qch **2** *vi* to a. for *(explain)* expliquer; *(give reckoning of)* rendre compte de; *(represent)* représenter ■ **accountable** *adj* responsable (**for/to** de/devant)

accountant [ə'kaʊntənt] *n* comptable *mf*

accounting [ə'kaʊntɪŋ] *n* comptabilité *f*

accumulate [ə'kjuːmjʊleɪt] **1** *vt* accumuler **2** *vi* s'accumuler

accuracy ['ækjʊrəsɪ] *n* exactitude *f*, précision *f*

accurate ['ækjʊrət] *adj* exact, précis

accuse [ə'kjuːz] *vt* **to a. sb (of sth/of doing sth)** accuser qn (de qch/de faire qch) ■ **accusation** *n* accusation *f*; **to make an a. against sb** lancer une accusation contre qn ■ **accused** *n Law* **the a.** l'accusé, -e *mf*

accustom [ə'kʌstəm] *vt* habituer, accoutumer ■ **accustomed** *adj* **to be a. to sth/to doing sth** être habitué à qch/à faire qch; **to get a. to sth/to doing sth** s'habituer à qch/à faire qch

ace [eɪs] *n* (a) (card, person) as *m* (b) *(at tennis)* ace *m*

ache [eɪk] **1** *n* douleur *f* **2** *vi* faire mal; **my head aches** j'ai mal à la tête

achieve [ə'tʃiːv] *vt* (result) obtenir; *(aim)* atteindre; *(ambition)* réaliser; *(victory)* remporter; **to a. success** réussir ■ **achievement** *n* (success) réussite *f*; *(of ambition)* réalisation *f*

aching [eɪkɪŋ] *adj* douloureux, -euse

acid ['æsɪd] *adj & n* acide *(m)*; **a. rain** pluies *fpl* acides

acknowledge [ək'nɒlɪdʒ] *vt* reconnaître (**as** pour); *(greeting)* répondre à ■ **acknowledg(e)ment** *n* (of letter) accusé *m* de réception; *(receipt)* reçu *m*; *(confession)* aveu *m* (**of** de)

acne ['æknɪ] *n* acné *f*

acoustics [ə'kuːstɪks] *npl* acoustique *f*

acquaint [ə'kweɪnt] *vt* **to be acquainted with** (person) connaître; *(fact)* savoir ■ **acquaintance** *n* (person, knowledge) connaissance *f*

acquire [ə'kwaɪə(r)] *vt* acquérir; *(taste)* prendre (**for** à); *(friends)* se faire

acquit [ə'kwɪt] *(pt & pp* **-tt-**) *vt* (a) *Law* **to a. sb (of a crime)** acquitter qn (b) **to a. oneself badly/well** mal/bien s'en tirer

acre ['eɪkə(r)] *n* ≃ demi-hectare *m*, acre *f*; *Fam* **acres of space** plein de place

acrimonious [ˌækrɪˈməʊnɪəs] *adj (person, remark)* acrimonieux, -euse, hargneux, -euse; *(attack, dispute)* virulent

acrobat [ˈækrəbæt] *n* acrobate *mf* ■ **acrobatics** *npl* acrobaties *fpl*

acronym [ˈækrənɪm] *n* sigle *m*

across [əˈkrɒs] **1** *prep (from side to side of)* d'un côté à l'autre de; *(on the other side of)* de l'autre côté de; *(crossways)* en travers de; **a bridge a. the river** un pont sur la rivière; **to walk or go a.** *(street, lawn)* traverser; **to run/swim a.** traverser en courant/à la nage **2** *adv* **to be a kilometre a.** *(wide)* avoir un kilomètre de large; **to get sth a. to sb** faire comprendre qch à qn

acrylic [əˈkrɪlɪk] *adj (paint, fibre)* acrylique; *(garment)* en acrylique

act [ækt] **1** *n* (a) *(deed)* acte *m*; **a. (of parliament)** loi *f*; **caught in the a.** pris sur le fait

(b) *Theatre (part of play)* acte *m*; *(in circus, cabaret)* numéro *m*; *Fig* **to get one's a. together** se secouer; *Fam* **to be in on the a.** dans le coup

2 *vt (part)* jouer; **to a. the fool** faire l'idiot

3 *vi* (a) *(take action, behave)* agir; **it's time to a.** il est temps d'agir; **to a. as secretary/etc** faire office de secrétaire/etc; **to a. (up)on** *(affect)* agir sur; *(advice)* suivre; **to a. on behalf of sb** représenter qn; *Fam* **to a. up** *(of person, machine)* faire des siennes

(b) *(in play, film)* jouer; *(pretend)* jouer la comédie ■ **acting 1** *adj (temporary)* intérimaire **2** *n (of play)* représentation *f*; *(art)* jeu *m*; *(career)* théâtre *m*

action [ˈækʃən] *n* action *f*; *(military)* combats *mpl*; *(legal)* procès *m*, action *f*; **to take a.** prendre des mesures; **to put into a.** *(plan)* exécuter; **out of a.** *(machine)* hors service; *(person)* hors de combat

active [ˈæktɪv] **1** *adj* actif, -ive; *(interest, dislike)* vif (*f* vive); *(volcano)* en activité **2** *n Gram* actif *m* ■ **activity**

(*pl* **-ies**) *n* activité *f*; *(in street)* animation *f*

actor [ˈæktə(r)] *n* acteur *m* ■ **actress** *n* actrice *f*

actual [ˈæktʃʊəl] *adj* réel (*f* réelle); *(example)* concret, -ète; **the a. book** le livre même; **in a. fact** en réalité ■ **actually** *adv (truly)* réellement; *(in fact)* en réalité, en fait

acupuncture [ˈækjʊpʌŋktʃə(r)] *n* acuponcture *f*

acute [əˈkjuːt] *adj (pain, angle)* aigu (*f* aiguë); *(anxiety, emotion)* vif (*f* vive); *(mind, observer)* perspicace; *(shortage)* grave ■ **acutely** *adv (suffer, feel)* profondément; *(painful)* extrêmement

AD [eɪˈdiː] *(abbr* **anno Domini)** apr. J.-C.

ad [æd] *n Fam (on radio, TV)* pub *f*; *(private, in newspaper)* annonce *f*; *Br* **small ad,** *Am* **want ad** petite annonce *f*

adapt [əˈdæpt] **1** *vt* adapter (**to** à); **to a. oneself to sth** s'adapter à qch **2** *vi* s'adapter ■ **adaptable** *adj (person)* souple; *(instrument)* adaptable ■ **adapter, adaptor** *n (for use abroad)* adaptateur *m*; *(for several plugs)* prise *f* multiple

add [æd] **1** *vt* ajouter (**to/that** à/que); **to a. (up or together)** *(numbers)* additionner; **to a. in** inclure **2** *vi* **to a. to** *(increase)* augmenter; **to a. up to** *(total)* s'élever à; *(mean)* signifier; *(represent)* constituer

adder [ˈædə(r)] *n* vipère *f*

addict [ˈædɪkt] *n* **drug a.** toxicomane *mf*, drogué, -e *mf*; **TV a.** fana(tique) *mf* de la télé ■ **addicted** *adj* **to be a. to drugs** être toxicomane; **to be a. to alcohol** être alcoolique; **to be a. to cigarettes** ne pas pouvoir se passer de tabac ■ **addictive** *adj (drug, TV)* qui crée une dépendance

addition [əˈdɪʃən] *n* addition *f*; *(increase)* augmentation *f*; **in a.** de plus; **in a. to** en plus de ■ **additional** *adj* supplémentaire

additive ['ædɪtɪv] n additif m

address [Br əˈdres, Am ˈædres] **1** n (on letter, parcel) adresse f; (speech) allocution f 2 [əˈdres] vt (person, audience) s'adresser à; (words, speech) adresser (**to** à); (letter) mettre l'adresse sur

adept [əˈdept] adj expert (**in** or **at** à)

adequate ['ædɪkwət] adj (enough) suffisant; (acceptable) convenable; (performance) acceptable ■ **adequately** adv (sufficiently) suffisamment; (acceptably) convenablement

adhere [ədˈhɪə(r)] vi **to a. to** adhérer à; (decision, rule) s'en tenir à ■ **adhesive** [-ˈhiːsɪv] adj & n adhésif (m)

adjacent [əˈdʒeɪsənt] adj (house, angle) adjacent (**to** à)

adjective ['ædʒɪktɪv] n adjectif m

adjoin [əˈdʒɔɪn] vt être attenant à ■ **adjoining** adj attenant

adjourn [əˈdʒɜːn] **1** vt (postpone) ajourner; (session) suspendre **2** vi suspendre la séance

adjust [əˈdʒʌst] vt (machine) régler; (machine part) ajuster, régler; (salaries, prices) (r)ajuster; (clothes) rajuster; **to a. to sth** s'adapter à qch ■ **adjustable** adj (seat) réglable

ad-lib [ædˈlɪb] vi (pt & pp **-bb-**) improviser

administer [ədˈmɪnɪstə(r)] vt administrer (**to** à) ■ **administration** n administration f; (government) gouvernement m ■ **administrator** n administrateur, -trice mf

admiral ['ædmərəl] n amiral m

admire [ədˈmaɪə(r)] vt admirer (**for** sth pour qch; **for doing sth** de faire qch) ■ **admirable** adj admirable

admit [ədˈmɪt] (pt & pp **-tt-**) **1** vt (let in) laisser entrer; (to hospital, college) admettre; (acknowledge) reconnaître, admettre (**that** que) **2** vi **a. to sth** avouer qch; (mistake) reconnaître qch ■ **admission** n (to theatre) entrée f (**to** à ou de); (to club, school) admission f; (acknowledgement) aveu m; **a. (charge)** (prix m d') entrée f ■ **admittance** n entrée f; **'no a.'** 'entrée

interdite' ■ **admittedly** [-ɪdlɪ] adv de l'aveu général

adolescent [ædəˈlesənt] n adolescent, -e mf

adopt [əˈdɒpt] vt adopter; Pol (candidate) choisir ■ **adopted** adj (child) adopté; (son, daughter) adoptif, -ive; (country) d'adoption ■ **adoptive** adj (parent) adoptif, -ive

adore [əˈdɔː(r)] vt adorer (**doing** faire) ■ **adorable** adj adorable

Adriatic [eɪdrɪˈætɪk] n **the A.** l'Adriatique f

adult ['ædʌlt, əˈdʌlt] **1** n adulte mf **2** adj (animal) adulte; **a. class/film** classe f/ film m pour adultes

adultery [əˈdʌltərɪ] n adultère m; **to commit a.** commettre l'adultère

advance [ədˈvɑːns] **1** n (movement, money) avance f; (of science) progrès mpl; **advances** (sexual) avances fpl; **in a.** (book, inform, apply) à l'avance; (pay) d'avance; (arrive) en avance **2** adj (payment) anticipé; **a. booking** réservation f **3** vt (**a**) (put forward) faire avancer (**b**) (science, one's work) faire progresser; (opinion) avancer **4** vi (go forward, progress) avancer; **to a. towards sb** s'avancer ou avancer vers qn ■ **advanced** adj (studies, level) supérieur; (course) de niveau supérieur; **a. in years** âgé

advantage [ədˈvɑːntɪdʒ] n avantage m (**over** sur); **to take a. of** (situation) profiter de; (person) exploiter; (woman) séduire; **a. Hewitt** (in tennis) avantage Hewitt

advent ['ædvent] n arrivée f, avènement m; Rel **A.** l'Avent m

adventure [ədˈventʃə(r)] **1** n aventure f **2** adj (film, story) d'aventures ■ **adventurous** adj aventureux, -euse

adverb ['ædvɜːb] n adverbe m

adverse ['ædvɜːs] adj défavorable; (effect) négatif, -ive

advert ['ædvɜːt] n Br pub f; (private, in newspaper) annonce f

advertise ['ædvətaɪz] **1** vt (commercially) faire de la publicité pour; (privately) passer une annonce pour vendre **2** vi faire de la publicité; (privately) passer une annonce (**for** pour trouver) ■ **advertising** n publicité f; **a. agency** agence f de publicité; **a. campaign** campagne f de publicité

advertisement [Br əd'vɜ:tɪsmənt, Am ædvər'taɪzmənt] n publicité f; (private or in newspaper) annonce f; (poster) affiche f; TV **the advertisements** la publicité

advice [əd'vaɪs] n conseil(s) m(pl); Com (notification) avis m; **a piece of a.** un conseil; **to ask sb's a.** demander conseil à qn; **to take sb's a.** suivre les conseils de qn

advise [əd'vaɪz] vt (**a**) (counsel) conseiller; (recommend) recommander; **to a. sb to do sth** conseiller à qn de faire qch; **to a. sb against doing sth** déconseiller à qn de faire qch (**b**) (inform) **to a. sb that...** aviser qn que... ■ **advisable** adj (action) à conseiller; **it's a. to wait** /etc il est plus prudent d'attendre/etc ■ **adviser, advisor** n conseiller, -ère mf

advocate 1 ['ædvəkət] n (of cause) défenseur m; (lawyer) avocat, -e mf **2** ['ædvəkeɪt] vt préconiser

aerial ['eərɪəl] **1** n Br antenne f **2** adj (photo) aérien, -enne

aerobics [eə'rəʊbɪks] npl aérobic m

aeroplane ['eərəpleɪn] n Br avion m

aerosol ['eərəsɒl] n aérosol m

aesthetic [Br i:s'θetɪk, Am es'θetɪk] adj esthétique

affair ['əfeə(r)] n (matter, concern) affaire f; (love) **a.** liaison f; **state of affairs** situation f

affect [ə'fekt] vt (concern) concerner; (move, pretend to have) affecter; (harm) nuire à; (influence) avoir sur; **to be deeply affected by sth** être très affecté par qch ■ **affected** adj (manner) affecté

affection [ə'fekʃən] n affection f (**for**

pour) ■ **affectionate** adj affectueux, -euse

affinity [ə'fɪnɪtɪ] (pl -ies) n affinité f

affirm [ə'fɜ:m] vt affirmer ■ **affirmative 1** adj affirmatif, -ive **2** n affirmative f; **to answer in the a.** répondre par l'affirmative

affix [ə'fɪks] vt (stamp, signature) apposer

afflict [ə'flɪkt] vt affliger (**with** de) ■ **affliction** n (misery) affliction f; (disability) infirmité f

affluent ['æfluənt] adj riche; **a. society** société f d'abondance

afford [ə'fɔ:d] vt (pay for) **I can't a. it/a new car** je n'ai pas les moyens de l'acheter/d'acheter une nouvelle voiture; **he can't a. the time (to read it)** il n'a pas le temps (de le lire); **I can a. to wait** je peux me permettre d'attendre ■ **affordable** adj (price) abordable

Afghanistan [æf'gænɪsta:n] n l'Afghanistan m

afield [ə'fi:ld] adv **further a.** plus loin

afloat [ə'fləʊt] adv (ship, swimmer, business) à flot; (awash) submergé; **to stay a.** (of ship) rester à flot; (of business) se maintenir à flot

afraid [ə'freɪd] adj **to be a.** avoir peur (**of** de); **to be a. to do** or **of doing sth** avoir peur de faire qch; **I'm a. (that) he'll fall** j'ai peur qu'il (ne) tombe; **I'm a. he's out** je regrette, il est sorti

afresh [ə'freʃ] adv de nouveau; **to start a.** recommencer

Africa ['æfrɪkə] n l'Afrique f ■ **African 1** adj africain **2** n Africain, -e mf

after ['ɑ:ftə(r)] **1** adv après; **soon/long a.** peu/longtemps après; **the month a.** le mois d'après; **the day a.** le lendemain

2 prep après; **a. three days** au bout de trois jours; **the day a. the battle** le lendemain de la bataille; **a. eating** après avoir mangé; **day a. day** jour après jour; **a. all** après tout; **it's a. five** il est cinq heures passées; Am **ten a. four** quatre heures dix; **to be a. sb/sth** (seek) chercher qn/qch

3 *conj* après que; **a. he saw you** après qu'il t'a vu ∎ **after-effects** *npl* suites *fpl*, séquelles *fpl* ∎ **afterlife** *n* vie *f* après la mort ∎ **aftermath** *n* suites *fpl* ∎ **after-sales service** *n* service *m* après-vente ∎ **aftershave** *n* (lotion *f*) après-rasage *m*, after-shave *m inv* ∎ **afterthought** *n* réflexion *f* après coup; **to add/say sth as an a.** ajouter/dire qch après coup ∎ **afterward(s)** *adv* après, plus tard

afternoon [ɑːftəˈnuːn] *n* après-midi *m ou f inv*; **in the a.** l'après-midi; **at three in the a.** à trois heures de l'après-midi; **every Monday a.** tous les lundis après-midi; **good a.!** bonjour!

again [əˈgen] *adv* de nouveau, encore une fois; *(furthermore)* en outre; **to go down/up a.** redescendre/remonter; **she won't do it a.** elle ne le fera plus; **never a.** plus jamais; **a. and a.** bien des fois; **what's his name a.?** comment s'appelle-t-il déjà?

against [əˈgenst, əˈgeɪnst] *prep* contre; **to lean a. sth** s'appuyer contre qch; **to go** *or* **be a. sth** s'opposer à qch; **the law illegal**; *Br* **a. the rules,** *Am* **a. the rule** interdit, contraire aux règlements; **the pound rose a. the dollar** la livre est en hausse par rapport au dollar

age [eɪdʒ] **1** *n* âge *m*; **(old) a.** vieillesse *f*; **what a. are you?, what's your a.?** quel âge as-tu?; **five years of a.** âgé de cinq ans; **under a.** trop jeune, mineur; *Fam* **to wait (for) ages** attendre une éternité; **a. gap** différence *f* d'âge; **a. limit** limite *f* d'âge

2 *vt & vi (pres p* **ag(e)ing)** vieillir ∎ **aged** *adj* (**a**) [eɪdʒd] **a. ten** âgé de dix ans (**b**) [ˈeɪdʒɪd] vieux (*f* vieille), âgé; **the a.** les personnes *fpl* âgées

agenda [əˈdʒendə] *n* ordre *m* du jour

agent [ˈeɪdʒənt] *n* agent *m*; *(car dealer)* concessionnaire *mf* ∎ **agency** *n* agence *f*

aggravate [ˈægrəveɪt] *vt (make worse)* aggraver; *Fam (annoy)* exaspérer

aggregate [ˈægrɪgət] **1** *adj* global **2** *n* *(total)* ensemble *m*; **on a.** au total

aggressive [əˈgresɪv] *adj* agressif, -ive

aggrieved [əˈgriːvd] *adj (offended)* blessé, froissé; *(tone)* peiné

aghast [əˈgɑːst] *adj* horrifié (**at** par)

agile [*Br* ˈædʒaɪl, *Am* ˈædʒəl] *adj* agile

agitated [ˈædʒɪteɪtɪd] *adj* agité

agnostic [ægˈnɒstɪk] *adj & n* agnostique *(mf)*

ago [əˈgəʊ] *adv* **a year a.** il y a un an; **how long a.?** il y a combien de temps (de cela)?; **long a.** il y a longtemps; **a short time a.** il y a peu de temps

agonizing [ˈægənaɪzɪŋ] *adj (pain)* atroce; *(situation)* angoissant

agony [ˈægənɪ] *(pl* **-ies)** *n (pain)* douleur *f* atroce; *(anguish)* angoisse *f*; **to be in a.** être au supplice; **a. column** *(in newspaper)* courrier *m* du cœur

agree [əˈgriː] **1** *vi (come to an agreement)* se mettre d'accord; *(be in agreement)* être d'accord (**with** avec); *(of facts, dates)* concorder; *(of verb)* s'accorder; **to a. (up)on** *(decide)* convenir de; **to a. to sth/to doing sth** consentir à qch/à faire qch

2 *vt (plan)* se mettre d'accord sur; *(date, price)* convenir de; *(approve)* approuver; **to a. to do sth** accepter de faire qch; **to a. that...** admettre que... ∎ **agreed** *adj (time, place)* convenu ∎ **agreement** *n (contract, assent) & Gram* accord *m* (**with** avec); **to be in a. with sb** être d'accord avec qn; **to come to an a.** se mettre d'accord

agreeable [əˈgriːəbəl] *adj (pleasant)* agréable; **to be a.** *(agree)* être d'accord; **to be a. to sth** consentir à qch

agriculture [ˈægrɪkʌltʃə(r)] *n* agriculture *f* ∎ **agricultural** *adj* agricole

aground [əˈgraʊnd] *adv* **to run a.** *(of ship)* (s')échouer

ahead [əˈhed] *adv (in space)* en avant; *(leading)* en tête; *(in the future)* à l'avenir; **a. of** *(in space)* devant; *(in time)* avant; **one hour/etc a. (of)** une heure/etc d'avance (sur); **to be a. of schedule** être en avance; **to go on a.**

partir devant; **to go a.** *(advance)* avancer; *(continue)* continuer; *(start)* commencer; **go a.!** allez-y!; **to think a.** prévoir

aid [eɪd] **1** *n (help)* aide *f*; *(device)* accessoire *m*; **with the a. of sb** avec l'aide de qn; **with the a. of sth** à l'aide de qch; **in a. of** *(charity)* au profit de **2** *vt* aider *(sb to do* qn à faire*)*

aide [eɪd] *n* collaborateur, -trice *mf*

AIDS [eɪdz] *(abbr* Acquired Immune Deficiency Syndrome*)* *n* SIDA *m*

ailing ['eɪlɪŋ] *adj (ill)* souffrant; *(company)* en difficulté ▪ **ailment** *n* affection *f*

aim [eɪm] **1** *n* but *m*; **to take a. (at)** viser; **with the a. of** dans le but de **2** *vt (gun)* braquer *(at* sur*)*; *(stone)* lancer *(at* à *ou* vers*)*; *(blow, remark)* décocher *(at* à*)* **3** *vi* viser; **to a. at sb** viser qn; **to a. to do sth** avoir l'intention de faire qch ▪ **aimless** *adj (existence)* sans but

air [eə(r)] **1** *n* (a) *(atmosphère)* air *m*; **in the open a.** en plein air; **by a.** *(travel)* en *ou* par avion; *(send letter, goods)* par avion; **to be** *or* **go on (the) a.** *(of person)* passer à l'antenne; *(of programme)* être diffusé; **to throw sth in(to) the a.** jeter qch en l'air; *Fig* **there's something in the a.** il se prépare quelque chose; *Aut* **a. bag** airbag *m*; **a. base** base *f* aérienne; **a. bed** matelas *m* pneumatique; **a. fare** prix *m* du billet d'avion; **a. force** armée *f* de l'air; **a. freshener** désodorisant *m* *(pour la maison)*

(b) *(appearance, tune)* air *m*; **to put on airs** se donner des airs; **with an a. of sadness** d'un air triste

2 *vt (room)* aérer; *(views)* exposer ▪ **air-conditioning** *n* climatisation *f* ▪ **aircraft** *n inv* avion *m*; **a. carrier** porte-avions *m inv* ▪ **airfield** *n* terrain *m* d'aviation ▪ **airgun** *n* carabine *f* à air comprimé ▪ **airlift** *vt* transporter par avion ▪ **airline** *n* compagnie *f* aérienne; **a. ticket** billet *m* d'avion ▪ **airmail** *n* poste *f* aérienne; **by a.** par

avion ▪ **airplane** *n Am* avion *m* ▪ **airport** *n* aéroport *m* ▪ **air-raid shelter** *n* abri *m* antiaérien ▪ **airship** *n* dirigeable *m* ▪ **airtight** *adj* hermétique ▪ **air-traffic controller** *n* contrôleur *m* aérien, aiguilleur *m* du ciel

airy ['eərɪ] *(-ier, -iest)* *adj (room)* clair et spacieux, -euse; *Fig (manner)* désinvolte

aisle [aɪl] *n (in supermarket, cinema)* allée *f*; *(in plane)* couloir *m*; *(in church)* *(on side)* nef *f* latérale; *(central)* allée *f* centrale

ajar [ə'dʒɑ:(r)] *adj & adv (door)* entrouvert

alarm [ə'lɑ:m] **1** *n (warning, fear, device)* alarme *f*; *(mechanism)* sonnerie *f* (d'alarme); **false a.** fausse alerte *f*; **a. clock** réveil *m* **2** *vt (frighten)* alarmer; *(worry)* inquiéter; **they were alarmed at the news** la nouvelle les a beaucoup inquiétés

alas [ə'læs] *exclam* hélas!

Albania [æl'beɪnɪə] *n* l'Albanie *f* ▪ **Albanian 1** *adj* albanais **2** *n* Albanais, -e *mf*

album ['ælbəm] *n (book, record)* album *m*

alcohol ['ælkəhɒl] *n* alcool *m* ▪ **alcoholic 1** *adj (person)* alcoolique; **a. drink** boisson *f* alcoolisée **2** *n (person)* alcoolique *mf*

alcove ['ælkəʊv] *n* alcôve *f*

ale [eɪl] *n* bière *f*

alert [ə'lɜ:t] **1** *adj (watchful)* vigilant; *(lively)* *(mind, baby)* éveillé **2** *n* alerte *f*; **on the a.** sur le qui-vive **3** *vt* alerter

A level ['eɪlevəl] *n Br (exam)* ≃ épreuve *f* de baccalauréat

algebra ['ældʒɪbrə] *n* algèbre *f*

Algeria [æl'dʒɪərɪə] *n* l'Algérie *f* ▪ **Algerian 1** *adj* algérien, -enne **2** *n* Algérien, -enne *mf*

alias ['eɪlɪəs] **1** *adv* alias **2** *(pl* aliases*)* *n* nom *m* d'emprunt

alibi ['ælɪbaɪ] *n* alibi *m*

alien ['eɪlɪən] **1** *adj* étranger, -ère *(to* à*)* **2** *n (from outer space)* extraterrestre *mf*; *Formal (foreigner)* étranger, -ère *m*

■ **alienate** *vt (friend, supporters, readers)* s'aliéner; **to feel alienated** se sentir exclu

alight¹ [ə'laɪt] *adj (fire)* allumé; *(building)* en feu; *(face)* éclairé; **to set sth a.** mettre le feu à qch

alight² [ə'laɪt] *(pt & pp **alighted** or **alit**)* *vi* (**a**) *Formal (from bus, train)* descendre (**from** de) (**b**) *(of bird)* se poser (**on** sur)

align [ə'laɪn] *vt* aligner

alike [ə'laɪk] **1** *adj (people, things)* semblables, pareils, -eilles; **to look** or **be a.** se ressembler **2** *adv* de la même manière; **summer and winter a.** été comme hiver

alimony [*Br* 'ælɪmənɪ, *Am* 'ælɪməʊnɪ] *n Law* pension *f* alimentaire

alit [ə'lɪt] *pt & pp of* **alight²**

alive [ə'laɪv] *adj* vivant, en vie; **to stay a.** survivre; **a. and well** bien portant; *Fam* **a.** kicking plein de vie

ALL [ɔːl] **1** *adj* tout, toute, *pl* tous, toutes; **a. day** toute la journée; **a. men** tous les hommes; **a. the girls** toutes les filles; **a. four of them** tous les quatre; **for a. his wealth** malgré toute sa fortune

2 *pron (everyone)* tous *mpl*, toutes *fpl*; *(everything)* tout; **my sisters are a. here** toutes mes sœurs sont ici; **he ate it a., he ate a. of it** il a tout mangé; **take a. of it** prends (le) tout; **a. of us** nous tous; **a. together** tous ensemble; **a. (that) he has** tout ce qu'il a; **a. in a.** à tout prendre; **anything at a.** quoi que ce soit; **if there's any wind at a.** s'il y a le moindre vent; **nothing at a.** rien du tout; **not at a.** pas du tout; *(after 'thank you')* il n'y a pas de quoi

3 *adv* tout; **a. alone** tout seul; **a. bad** entièrement mauvais; **a. over** *(everywhere)* partout; *(finished)* fini; **a. too soon** bien trop tôt; *Sport* **six a.** six partout; *Fam* **not a. there** un peu fêlé

■ **all-night** *adj (party)* qui dure toute la nuit; *(shop)* ouvert toute la nuit ■ **all-out** *adj (effort)* acharné; *(war,*

strike) tous azimuts ■ **all-purpose** *adj (tool)* universel, -elle ■ **all-round** *adj (knowledge)* approfondi; *(athlete)* complet, -ète ■ **all-time** *adj (record)* jamais battu; **to reach an a. low/high** arriver à son point le plus bas/le plus haut

allegation [ælɪ'geɪʃən] *n* accusation *f*

allege [ə'ledʒ] *vt* prétendre (**that** que) ■ **alleged** *adj (so-called) (crime, fact)* prétendu; *(author, culprit)* présumé; **he is a. to be...** on prétend qu'il est...

allegiance [ə'liːdʒəns] *n (to party, cause)* fidélité *f* (**to** à)

allergy ['ælədʒɪ] *(pl* **-ies)** *n* allergie *f* (**to** à) ■ **allergic** [ə'lɜːdʒɪk] *adj* allergique (**to** à)

alleviate [ə'liːvɪeɪt] *vt (pain, suffering)* soulager; *(burden, task)* alléger; *(problem)* remédier à

alley ['ælɪ] *(pl* **-eys)** *n* ruelle *f*; *Fam* **that's (right) up my a.** c'est mon rayon

alliance [ə'laɪəns] *n* alliance *f*

allied ['ælaɪd] *adj (country)* allié; *(matters)* lié

alligator ['ælɪgeɪtə(r)] *n* alligator *m*

allocate ['æləkeɪt] *vt (assign)* affecter (**to** à); *(distribute)* répartir

allot [ə'lɒt] *(pt & pp* **-tt-)** *vt (assign)* attribuer (**to** à); *(distribute)* répartir; **in the allotted time** dans le temps imparti ■ **allotment** *n Br (land)* jardin *m* ouvrier

allow [ə'laʊ] **1** *vt* permettre (**sb sth** qch à qn); *(give, grant)* accorder (**sb sth** qch à qn); *(request)* accéder à; **to a. sb to do** permettre à qn de faire; **to a. an hour/a metre/***etc* prévoir une heure/un mètre/*etc*; **it's not allowed** c'est interdit; **you're not allowed to go** on vous interdit de partir **2** *vi* **to a. for sth** tenir compte de qch ■ **allowable** *adj (acceptable)* admissible; *(expense)* déductible

allowance [ə'laʊəns] *n* allocation *f*; *(for travel, housing, food)* indemnité *f*; *(tax-free amount)* abattement *m*; **to make allowances for** *(person)* être indulgent envers; *(thing)* tenir compte de

alloy [ˈælɔɪ] *n* alliage *m*

all right [ɔːlˈraɪt] **1** *adj (satisfactory)* bien *inv*; *(unharmed)* sain et sauf; *(undamaged)* intact; *(without worries)* tranquille; **it's a.** ça va; **are you a.?** ça va?; **I'm a.** *(healthy)* je vais bien; *(financially)* je m'en sors; **to be a. at maths** se débrouiller en maths; **the TV is a. now** *(fixed)* la télé marche maintenant **2** *adv (well)* bien; **a.!** *(in agreement)* d'accord!; **is it a. if I smoke?** ça ne vous dérange pas si je fume?

allude [əˈluːd] *vi* **to a. to** faire allusion à ■ **allusion** *n* allusion *f*

ally 1 [ˈælaɪ] *(pl* **-ies)** *n* allié, -e *mf* **2** [əˈlaɪ] *(pt & pp* **-ied)** *vt* **to a. oneself with** s'allier à *ou* avec

almighty [ɔːlˈmaɪtɪ] **1** *adj* **(a)** *(powerful)* tout-puissant *(f* toute-puissante*)* **(b)** *Fam (enormous)* terrible, formidable **2** *n* **the A.** le Tout-Puissant

almond [ˈɑːmənd] *n* amande *f*

almost [ˈɔːlməʊst] *adv* presque; **he a. fell** il a failli tomber

alone [əˈləʊn] *adj & adv* seul; **an expert a. can...** seul un expert peut...; **I did it (all) a.** je l'ai fait (tout) seul; **to leave** *or* **let a.** *(person)* laisser tranquille; *(thing)* ne pas toucher à; **I can't afford a bike, let a. a car!** je n'ai pas les moyens de m'acheter un vélo, encore moins une voiture

along [əˈlɒŋ] **1** *prep (all)* **a.** (tout) le long de; **to walk a. the shore** marcher le long du rivage; **to walk a. the street** marcher dans la rue; **a. here** par ici; *Fig* **somewhere a. the way** à un moment donné
2 *adv* **to move a.** avancer; **I'll be** *or* **come a. shortly** je viendrai tout à l'heure; **come a.!** venez donc!; **to bring sth a.** apporter qch; **to bring sb a.** amener qn; **a.** *(all the time)* dès le début; *(all the way)* d'un bout à l'autre; **a. with** ainsi que

alongside [əlɒŋˈsaɪd] *prep & adv* à côté (de); **a. the kerb** le long du trottoir

aloof [əˈluːf] **1** *adj* distant **2** *adv* à distance

aloud [əˈlaʊd] *adv* à haute voix

alphabet [ˈælfəbet] *n* alphabet *m* ■ **alphabetical** *adj* alphabétique

Alps [ælps] *npl* **the A.** les Alpes *fpl* ■ **Alpine** *adj (club, range)* alpin; *(scenery)* alpestre

already [ɔːlˈredɪ] *adv* déjà

alright [ɔːlˈraɪt] *adv Fam* = **all right**

Alsatian [ælˈseɪʃən] *n (dog)* berger *m* allemand

also [ˈɔːlsəʊ] *adv* aussi, également; *(moreover)* de plus

altar [ˈɔːltə(r)] *n* autel *m*

alter [ˈɔːltə(r)] **1** *vt* changer; *(clothing)* retoucher **2** *vi* changer ■ **alteration** *n* changement *m* **(in** de*)*; *(of clothing)* retouche *f*; **alterations** *(to building)* travaux *mpl*

alternate 1 [ɔːlˈtɜːnət] *adj* alterné; **on a. days** tous les deux jours **2** [ˈɔːltəneɪt] *vt* faire alterner **3** [ˈɔːltəneɪt] *vi* alterner **(with** avec*)*; *El* **alternating current** courant *m* alternatif

alternative [ɔːlˈtɜːnətɪv] **1** *adj (other)* de remplacement; **an a. way** une autre façon; **a. medicine** médecine *f* douce **2** *n (choice)* alternative *f*; **she had no a. but to obey** elle n'a pas pu faire autrement que d'obéir ■ **alternatively** *adv* **(or) a.** ou alors, ou bien

although [ɔːlˈðəʊ] *adv* bien que *(+ subjunctive)*

altitude [ˈæltɪtjuːd] *n* altitude *f*

altogether [ɔːltəˈgeðə(r)] *adv (completely)* tout à fait; *(on the whole)* somme toute; **how much a.?** combien en tout?

aluminium [Br æljʊˈmɪnɪəm] *(Am* **aluminum** [əˈluːmɪnəm]*) n* aluminium *m*

always [ˈɔːlweɪz] *adv* toujours; **he's a. criticizing** il est toujours à critiquer; **as a.** comme toujours

am [æm, *unstressed* əm] *see* **be**

a.m. [eɪˈem] *adv* du matin

amalgamate [əˈmælgəmeɪt] *vt & vi* fusionner

amateur ['æmətə(r)] **1** n amateur m **2** adj (interest, sports, performance) d'amateur; **a. painter/actress** peintre m/actrice f amateur

amaze [ə'meɪz] vt stupéfier ■ **amazed** adj stupéfait (**at sth** de qch); (filled with wonder) émerveillé; **I was a. by his courage** son courage m'a stupéfié ■ **amazing** adj (surprising) stupéfiant; (incredible) extraordinaire

ambassador [æm'bæsədə(r)] n ambassadeur, -drice mf

amber ['æmbə(r)] n ambre m; **a. (light)** (of traffic signal) feu m orange m

ambiguous [æm'bɪgjʊəs] adj ambigu (f ambiguë)

ambition [æm'bɪʃən] n ambition f ■ **ambitious** adj ambitieux, -euse

ambivalent [æm'bɪvələnt] adj ambivalent

ambulance ['æmbjʊləns] n ambulance f; **a. driver** ambulancier, -ère mf

ambush ['æmbʊʃ] **1** n embuscade f **2** vt tendre une embuscade à; **to be ambushed** tomber dans une embuscade

amend [ə'mend] vt (text) modifier; Pol (law) amender

amends [ə'mendz] npl **to make a.** se racheter; **to make a. for sth** réparer qch

amenities [Br ə'miːnɪtɪz, Am ə'menɪtɪz] npl (of town) aménagements mpl; (shops) commerces mpl

America [ə'merɪkə] n l'Amérique f; **North/South A.** l'Amérique f du Nord/du Sud ■ **American 1** adj américain **2** n Américain, -e mf

amiable ['eɪmɪəbəl] adj aimable

amicable ['æmɪkəbəl] adj amical

amid(st) [ə'mɪd(st)] prep au milieu de, parmi

amiss [ə'mɪs] adv & adj **something is a.** (wrong) quelque chose ne va pas; **that wouldn't go a.** ça ne ferait pas de mal

ammunition [æmjʊ'nɪʃən] n munitions fpl

among(st) [ə'mʌŋ(st)] prep (amidst) parmi; (between) entre; **a. the crowd/** books/others/etc parmi la foule/les livres/les autres/etc; **a. friends** entre amis; **a. other things** entre autres (choses)

amoral [eɪ'mɒrəl] adj amoral

amount [ə'maʊnt] **1** n quantité f; (sum of money) somme f; (total figure of invoice, debt) montant m; (scope, size) importance f **2** vi **to a. to** (total) s'élever à; Fig **it amounts to blackmail** ce n'est rien d'autre que du chantage; **it amounts to the same thing** ça revient au même

amp [æmp] n (unit of electricity) ampère m; Br **3-a. plug** prise f avec fusible de 3 ampères

ample ['æmpəl] adj (a) (plentiful) abondant (b) (large) (woman, bosom) fort (c) (roomy) (garment) large

amplify ['æmplɪfaɪ] (pt & pp -ied) vt (essay, remarks) développer; (sound) amplifier ■ **amplifier** n amplificateur m

amputate ['æmpjʊteɪt] vt amputer; **to a. sb's hand/etc** amputer qn de la main/etc

amuse [ə'mjuːz] vt amuser; **to keep sb amused** distraire qn ■ **amusement** n amusement m, divertissement m; (pastime) distraction f; **amusements** (at fairground) attractions fpl; (gambling machines) machines fpl à sous; **a. arcade** salle f de jeux; **a. park** parc m d'attractions

an [æn, unstressed ən] see **a**

an(a)emic [ə'niːmɪk] adj anémique; **to become a.** faire de l'anémie

an(a)esthetic [ænəs'θetɪk] n (process) anesthésie f; (substance) anesthésique m; **under a.** sous anesthésie; **general/local a.** anesthésie f générale/locale

analogy [ə'nælədʒɪ] (pl -ies) n analogie f (**with** avec)

analyse ['ænəlaɪz] vt analyser ■ **analysis** (pl -yses [-əsiːz]) n analyse f ■ **analyst** n analyste mf

anarchy ['ænəkɪ] n anarchie f ■ **anarchist** n anarchiste mf

anatomy [əˈnætəmɪ] *n* anatomie *f*

ancestor [ˈænsestə(r)] *n* ancêtre *m*

anchor [ˈæŋkə(r)] **1** *n* ancre *f* **2** *vt (ship)* mettre à l'ancre **3** *vi* jeter l'ancre, mouiller

anchovy [*Br* ˈæntʃəvɪ, *Am* ænˈtʃəʊvɪ] *(pl* **-ies)** *n* anchois *m*

ancient [ˈeɪnʃənt] *adj* ancien, -enne; *(pre-medieval)* antique

and [ænd, *unstressed* ən(d)] *conj* et; **a knife a. fork** un couteau et une fourchette; **my mother a. father** mon père et ma mère; **two hundred a. two** deux cent deux; **four a. three quarters** quatre trois quarts; **nice a. warm** bien chaud; **better a. better** de mieux en mieux; **she can read a. write** elle sait lire et écrire; **go a. see** va voir; **I knocked a. knocked** j'ai frappé pendant un bon moment

anemic [əˈniːmɪk] *adj* = **anaemic**

anesthetic [ænɪsˈθetɪk] *n* = **anaesthetic**

angel [ˈeɪndʒəl] *n* ange *m* ■ **angelic** *adj* angélique

anger [ˈæŋɡə(r)] **1** *n* colère *f*; **in a., out of a.** sous le coup de la colère **2** *vt* mettre en colère

angina [ænˈdʒaɪnə] *n* angine *f* de poitrine

angle¹ [ˈæŋɡəl] *n* angle *m*; **at an a.** en biais

angle² [ˈæŋɡəl] *vi (fish)* pêcher à la ligne; *Fig* **to a. for** *(compliments)* quêter ■ **angler** *n* pêcheur, -euse *mf* à la ligne

Anglican [ˈæŋɡlɪkən] *adj & n* anglican, -e *(mf)*

Anglo- [ˈæŋɡləʊ] *pref* anglo- ■ **Anglo-Saxon** *adj & n* anglo-saxon, -onne *(mf)*

angry [ˈæŋɡrɪ] **(-ier, -iest)** *adj (person)* en colère, fâché; *(look)* furieux, -euse; **an a. letter** une lettre indignée; **a. words** des paroles indignées; **to get a. (with)** se fâcher (contre)

anguish [ˈæŋɡwɪʃ] *n* angoisse *f*

animal [ˈænɪməl] *n* animal *m*

animated [ˈænɪmeɪtɪd] *adj (lively)* animé; **to become a.** s'animer

animation [ænɪˈmeɪʃən] *n (liveliness) & Cin* animation *f*

aniseed [ˈænɪsiːd] *n (as flavouring)* anis *m*

ankle [ˈæŋkəl] *n* cheville *f*; **a. sock** socquette *f*

annex¹ [əˈneks] *vt* annexer

annex², Br annexe [ˈæneks] *n (building)* annexe *f*

anniversary [ænɪˈvɜːsərɪ] *(pl* **-ies)** *n (of event)* anniversaire *m*

announce [əˈnaʊns] *vt* annoncer; *(birth, marriage)* faire part de ■ **announcement** *n (statement)* annonce *f*; *(notice of birth, marriage, death) (in newspaper)* avis *m*; *(private letter)* faire-part *m inv* ■ **announcer** *n (on TV)* speaker, -ine *mf*

annoy [əˈnɔɪ] *vt (inconvenience)* ennuyer; *(irritate)* agacer ■ **annoyed** *adj* fâché; **to get a. (with)** se fâcher (contre) ■ **annoying** *adj* ennuyeux, -euse

annual [ˈænjʊəl] **1** *adj* annuel, -elle **2** *n (yearbook)* annuaire *m*; *(children's)* album *m*; *(plant)* plante *f* annuelle ■ **annually** *adv (every year)* tous les ans; *(per year)* par an

annul [əˈnʌl] *(pt & pp* **-ll-)** *vt (contract, marriage)* annuler

anoint [əˈnɔɪnt] *vt* oindre **(with** de)

anomalous [əˈnɒmələs] *adj* anormal ■ **anomaly** *(pl* **-ies)** *n* anomalie *f*

anonymous [əˈnɒnɪməs] *adj* anonyme

anorak [ˈænəræk] *n* anorak *m*

anorexia [ænəˈreksɪə] *n* anorexie *f* ■ **anorexic** *adj & n* anorexique *(mf)*

another [əˈnʌðə(r)] *adj & pron* un(e) autre; **a. man** *(different)* un autre homme; **a. month** *(additional)* encore un mois; **a. ten** encore dix; **one a.** l'un(e) l'autre, *pl* les un(e)s les autres; **they love one a.** ils s'aiment

answer [ˈɑːnsə(r)] **1** *n* réponse *f*; *(to problem, riddle) & Math* solution *f* (**to** de); *(reason)* explication *f*; **in a. to your letter** en réponse à votre lettre

2 vt (person, question, letter) répondre à; (prayer, wish) exaucer; **he answered yes** il a répondu oui; **to a. the door** ouvrir la porte; **to a. the phone** répondre au téléphone

3 vi répondre ▪ **answering machine** n répondeur m

ant [ænt] n fourmi f

antagonize [ænˈtægənaɪz] vt provoquer (l'hostilité de)

Antarctic [ænˈtɑːktɪk] **1** adj antarctique **2** n the A. l'Antarctique m

antenatal [æntɪˈneɪtəl] adj Br prénatal; **a. classes** préparation f à l'accouchement

antenna¹ [ænˈtenə] (pl -ae [-iː]) n (of insect) antenne f

antenna² [ænˈtenə] (pl -as) n Am (for TV, radio) antenne f

anthem [ˈænθəm] n national a. hymne m national

anthology [ænˈθɒlədʒɪ] (pl -ies) n anthologie f

anti- [Br ˈæntɪ, Am ˈæntaɪ] pref anti- ▪ **antibiotic** adj & n antibiotique (m) ▪ **anticlimax** n déception f ▪ **anticlockwise** adv Br dans le sens inverse des aiguilles d'une montre ▪ **antidote** n antidote m ▪ **antifreeze** n (for vehicle) antigel m ▪ **antihistamine** n (drug) antihistaminique m ▪ **antiperspirant** n déodorant m ▪ **anti-Semitic** adj antisémite ▪ **antiseptic** adj & n antiseptique (m) ▪ **antisocial** adj (unsociable) peu sociable

anticipate [ænˈtɪsɪpeɪt] vt (foresee) anticiper; (expect) s'attendre à, prévoir; (forestall) devancer ▪ **anticipation** n (expectation) attente f; (foresight) prévision f; **in a. of** en prévision de; **in a.** (thank, pay) d'avance

antics [ˈæntɪks] npl singeries fpl; **he's up to his a. again** il a encore fait des siennes

antiquated [ˈæntɪkweɪtɪd] adj (expression, custom) vieillot, -otte; (person) vieux jeu inv; (object, machine) antédiluvien, -enne

antique [ænˈtiːk] **1** adj (furniture) ancien, -enne; (of Greek or Roman antiquity) antique; **a. dealer** antiquaire mf; **a. shop** magasin m d'antiquités **2** n antiquité f, objet m d'époque

Antwerp [ˈæntwɜːp] n Anvers m ou f

anxiety [æŋˈzaɪətɪ] (pl -ies) n (worry) inquiétude f (**about** au sujet de); (fear) anxiété f; (eagerness) désir m (**to do** de faire; **for sth** de qch)

anxious [ˈæŋkʃəs] adj (worried) inquiet, -ète (**about** pour); (troubled) anxieux, -euse; (causing worry) angoissant; (eager) impatient (**to do** de faire)

ANY [ˈenɪ] **1** adj (a) (in questions) du, de la, des; **have you a. milk/tickets?** avez-vous du lait/des billets?

(b) (in negatives) (the slightest) aucun; **he hasn't got a. milk/tickets** il n'a pas de lait/de billets; **there isn't a. doubt/problem** il n'y a aucun doute/problème

(c) (no matter which) n'importe quel; **ask a doctor** demande à n'importe quel médecin

(d) (every) tout; **at a. moment** à tout moment; **in a. case, at a. rate** de toute façon

2 pron (a) (no matter which one) n'importe lequel; (somebody) quelqu'un; **if a. of you...** si l'un d'entre vous..., si quelqu'un parmi vous...

(b) (quantity) en; **have you got a.?** en as-tu?; **I don't see a.** je n'en vois pas

3 adv **not a.** further/happier pas plus loin/plus heureux, -euse; **I don't see him a. more** je ne le vois plus; **a. more tea?** encore un peu de thé?; **I'm not a. better** je ne vais pas mieux

anybody [ˈenɪbɒdɪ] pron (a) (somebody) quelqu'un; **do you see a.?** tu vois quelqu'un?; **more than a.** plus que tout autre (b) (in negatives) personne; **he doesn't know a.** il ne connaît personne (c) (no matter who) n'importe qui; **a. would think that...** on croirait que...

anyhow [ˈenɪhaʊ] adv (at any rate) de

toute façon; *Fam (badly)* n'importe comment

anyone ['enɪwʌn] *pron* = **anybody**

anyplace ['enɪpleɪs] *adv Am* = **anywhere**

anything ['enɪθɪŋ] *pron* (**a**) *(something)* quelque chose; **can you see a.?** tu vois quelque chose?

(**b**) *(in negatives)* rien; **he doesn't do a.** il ne fait rien; **without a.** sans rien

(**c**) *(everything)* tout; **a. you like** tout ce que tu veux; *Fam* **like a.** *(work)* comme un fou

(**d**) *(no matter what)* **a. (at all)** n'importe quoi

anyway ['enɪweɪ] *adv (at any rate)* de toute façon

anywhere ['enɪweə(r)] *adv* (**a**) *(no matter where)* n'importe où

(**b**) *(everywhere)* partout; **a. you go** où que vous alliez, partout où vous allez; **a. you like** où tu veux

(**c**) *(somewhere)* quelque part; **is he going a.?** va-t-il quelque part?

(**d**) *(in negatives)* nulle part; **he doesn't go a.** il ne va nulle part; **without a.** to put it sans un endroit où le/la mettre

apart [ə'pɑ:t] *adv* (**a**) *(separated)* **we kept them a.** nous les tenions séparés; **two years a.** à deux ans d'intervalle; **they are a metre a.** ils se trouvent à un mètre l'un de l'autre; **to come a.** *(of two objects)* se séparer; **to tell two things/people a.** distinguer deux choses/personnes (l'une de l'autre)

(**b**) *(to pieces)* **to tear a.** mettre en pièces; **to take a.** démonter

(**c**) *(to one side)* à part; **joking a.** sans blague; **a. from** *(except for)* à part

apartment [ə'pɑ:tmənt] *n* appartement *m*; *Am* **a. building, a. house** immeuble *m* (d'habitation)

apathy ['æpəθɪ] *n* apathie *f*

ape [eɪp] **1** *n* grand singe *m* **2** *vt (imitate)* singer

aperitif [əperɪ'ti:f] *n* apéritif *m*

aperture ['æpətʃʊə(r)] *n* ouverture *f*

apiece [ə'pi:s] *adv* chacun; **£2 a.** 2 livres pièce *ou* chacun

apologetic [əpɒlə'dʒetɪk] *adj (letter)* plein d'excuses; *(smile)* d'excuse; **to be a. (about)** s'excuser (de)

apology [ə'pɒlədʒɪ] *(pl* **-ies**) *n* excuses *fpl* ■ **apologize** *vi* s'excuser (**for** de); **he apologized for being late** il s'est excusé de son retard; **to a. to sb (for)** faire ses excuses à qn (pour)

apostle [ə'pɒsəl] *n* apôtre *m*

apostrophe [ə'pɒstrəfɪ] *n* apostrophe *f*

appal [ə'pɔ:l] *(Am* **appall**) *(pt & pp* **-ll-**) *vt* consterner; **to be appalled (at)** être horrifié (par) ■ **appalling** *adj* épouvantable

apparatus [æpə'reɪtəs] *n (equipment, organization)* appareil *m*; *Br (in gym)* agrès *mpl*

apparent [ə'pærənt] *adj (seeming)* apparent; *(obvious)* évident; **it's a. that...** il est clair que... ■ **apparently** *adv* apparemment; **a. she's going to Venice** il paraît qu'elle va à Venise

appeal [ə'pi:l] **1** *n (charm)* attrait *m*; *(interest)* intérêt *m*; *(call)* appel *m*; *(pleading)* supplication *f*; *(to a court)* appel *m* **2** *vt* (**a**) *(in court)* faire appel (**b**) **to a. to sb** *(attract)* plaire à qn; *(interest)* intéresser qn; *(ask for help)* faire appel à qn; **to a. to sb's generosity** faire appel à la générosité de qn; **to a. to sb for sth** demander qch à qn; **to a. to sb to do sth** supplier qn de faire qch ■ **appealing** *adj (attractive)* *(offer, idea)* séduisant; *(begging)* *(look)* suppliant

appear [ə'pɪə(r)] *vi (become visible)* apparaître; *(seem, be published)* paraître; *(on stage, in film)* jouer; *(in court)* comparaître; **it appears that...** *(it seems that)* il semble que... (+ *subjunctive or indicative)*; *(it is rumoured that)* il paraît que... (+ *indicative)* ■ **appearance** *n (act)* apparition *f*; *(look)* apparence *f*; *(of book)* parution *f*; **to put in an a.** faire acte de présence; **to keep up appearances** sauver les apparences

appendix [ə'pendɪks] (*pl* **-ixes** [-ɪksɪz] *or* **-ices** [-ɪsiːz]) *n* (*in book, body*) appendice *m*; **to have one's a. out** se faire opérer de l'appendicite ▪ **appendicitis** *n* appendicite *f*

appetite ['æpɪtaɪt] *n* appétit *m* ▪ **appetizer** *n* (*drink*) apéritif *m*; (*food*) amuse-gueule *m inv* ▪ **appetizing** *adj* appétissant

applaud [ə'plɔːd] **1** *vt* (*clap*) applaudir; (*approve of*) approuver, applaudir à **2** *vi* applaudir ▪ **applause** *n* applaudissements *mpl*

apple ['æpəl] *n* pomme *f*; *Br* **stewed apples** compote *f* de pommes; **cooking a.** pomme *f* à cuire; **eating a.** pomme *f* de dessert; **a. core** trognon *m* de pomme; **a. pie** tarte *f* aux pommes; **a. sauce** compote *f* de pommes; **a. tree** pommier *m*

appliance [ə'plaɪəns] *n* appareil *m*

applicable [ə'plɪkəbəl] *adj* (*rule*) applicable (**to** à); (*relevant*) pertinent (**to** à)

applicant ['æplɪkənt] *n* candidat, -e *mf* (**for** à)

application [æplɪ'keɪʃən] *n* (**a**) (*request*) demande *f* (**for** de); (*for job*) candidature *f* (**for** de); (*for membership*) demande *f* d'inscription; **a. (form)** (*for job*) formulaire *m* de candidature; (*for club*) formulaire *m* d'inscription (**b**) (*diligence*) application *f*

apply [ə'plaɪ] (*pt & pp* **-ied**) **1** *vt* (*put on, carry out*) appliquer; (*brake*) appuyer sur; **to a. oneself (to)** s'appliquer (à) **2** *vi* (*be relevant*) s'appliquer (**to** à); **to a. for** (*job*) poser sa candidature à; **to a. to sb (for)** (*ask*) s'adresser à qn (pour) ▪ **applied** *adj* (*maths, linguistics*) appliqué

appoint [ə'pɔɪnt] *vt* (*person*) nommer (**to a post** à un poste; **to do** pour faire); (*director, minister*) nommer; (*secretary, clerk*) engager; (*time, place*) fixer; **at the appointed time** à l'heure dite ▪ **appointment** *n* nomination *f*;

(*meeting*) rendez-vous *m inv*; (*post*) situation *f*; **to make an a. with** prendre rendez-vous avec

appraise [ə'preɪz] *vt* évaluer ▪ **appraisal** *n* évaluation *f*

appreciate [ə'priːʃɪeɪt] **1** *vt* (*enjoy, value, assess*) apprécier; (*understand*) comprendre; (*be grateful for*) être reconnaissant de **2** *vi* (*of goods*) prendre de la valeur ▪ **appreciation** *n* (**a**) (*gratitude*) reconnaissance *f*; (*judgement*) appréciation *f* (**b**) (*rise in value*) augmentation *f* (de la valeur) ▪ **appreciative** *adj* (*grateful*) reconnaissant (**of** de); (*favourable*) élogieux, -euse; **to be a. of** (*enjoy*) apprécier

apprehend [æprɪ'hend] *vt* (*seize, arrest*) appréhender

apprehensive [æprɪ'hensɪv] *adj* inquiet, -ète (**about** de *ou* au sujet de); **to be a. of** appréhender

apprentice [ə'prentɪs] *n* apprenti, -e *mf* ▪ **apprenticeship** *n* apprentissage *m*

approach [ə'prəʊtʃ] **1** *n* (*method*) façon *f* de s'y prendre; (*path, route*) voie *f* d'accès; (*of winter, vehicle*) approche *f* **2** *vt* (*draw near to*) s'approcher de; (*go up to, tackle*) aborder; **to a. sb about sth** parler à qn de qch; **he's approaching forty** il va sur ses quarante ans **3** *vi* (*of person, vehicle*) s'approcher; (*of date*) approcher ▪ **approachable** *adj* (*person*) d'un abord facile

appropriate 1 [ə'prəʊprɪət] *adj* (*place, clothes, means*) approprié (**to** à); (*remark, time*) opportun; **a. to** *or* **for** qui convient à **2** [ə'prəʊprɪeɪt] *vt* (*steal*) s'approprier; (*set aside*) affecter (**for** à)

approve [ə'pruːv] *vt* approuver; **to a. of** (*conduct, decision, idea*) approuver; **I don't a. of him** il ne me plaît pas ▪ **approval** *n* approbation *f*; **on a.** (*goods*) à l'essai

approving [ə'pruːvɪŋ] *adj* (*look*) approbateur, -trice

approximate 1 [ə'prɒksɪmət] *adj* approximatif, -ive **2** [ə'prɒksɪmeɪt] *vi* **to**

a. to sth se rapprocher de qch
apricot ['eɪprɪkɒt] *n* abricot *m*
April ['eɪprəl] *n* avril *m*; **A. fool!** poisson d'avril!
apron ['eɪprən] *n (garment)* tablier *m*
apt [æpt] *adj (remark, reply, means)* qui convient; *(word, name)* bien choisi; **to be a. to do sth** avoir tendance à faire qch ■ **aptly** *adv (described)* justement; *(chosen)* bien
aptitude ['æptɪtjuːd] *n* aptitude *f* (**for** pour); *(of student)* don *m* (**for** pour)
aquarium [əˈkweərɪəm] *n* aquarium *m*
Aquarius [əˈkweərɪəs] *n (sign)* le Verseau
aquatic [əˈkwætɪk] *adj (plant)* aquatique; *(sport)* nautique
Arab ['ærəb] **1** *adj* arabe **2** *n* Arabe *mf* ■ **Arabian** *adj* arabe ■ **Arabic** *adj & n (language)* arabe *(m)*; **A. numerals** chiffres *mpl* arabes
arbitrary ['ɑːbɪtrərɪ] *adj* arbitraire
arbitration [ɑːbɪˈtreɪʃən] *n* arbitrage *m*
arc [ɑːk] *n (of circle)* arc *m*
arcade [ɑːˈkeɪd] *n (for shops) (small)* passage *m* couvert; *(large)* galerie *f* marchande
arch [ɑːtʃ] **1** *n (of bridge)* arche *f*; *(of building)* voûte *f*, arc *m*; *(of foot)* cambrure *f* **2** *vt* **to a. one's back** *(inwards)* se cambrer; *(outwards)* se voûter
arch- [ɑːtʃ] *pref* **a.-enemy** ennemi *m* juré; **a.-rival** grand rival *m*
archaeology [ɑːkɪˈɒlədʒɪ] *n* archéologie *f* ■ **archaeologist** *n* archéologue *mf*
archaic [ɑːˈkeɪɪk] *adj* archaïque
archbishop [ɑːtʃˈbɪʃəp] *n* archevêque *m*
archeologist [ɑːkɪˈɒlədʒɪst] *n* = **archaeologist**
archeology [ɑːkɪˈɒlədʒɪ] *n* = **archaeology**
archer ['ɑːtʃə(r)] *n* archer *m*
archetype ['ɑːkɪtaɪp] *n* archétype *m*
architect ['ɑːkɪtekt] *n* architecte *mf* ■ **architecture** *n* architecture *f*

archives ['ɑːkaɪvz] *npl* archives *fpl*
archway ['ɑːtʃweɪ] *n* voûte *f*
arctic ['ɑːktɪk] **1** *adj* arctique; *(weather)* polaire, glacial **2** *n* **the A.** l'Arctique *m*
ardent ['ɑːdənt] *adj (supporter)* ardent, chaud
ardour ['ɑːdə(r)] *n* ardeur *f*
arduous ['ɑːdjʊəs] *adj* pénible, ardu
are [ɑː(r)] *see* **be**
area ['eərɪə] *n (of country)* région *f*; *(of town)* quartier *m*; Mil zone *f*; *(surface)* superficie *f*, Fig *(of knowledge)* domaine *m*; **kitchen a.** coin-cuisine *m*; **play a.** aire *f* de jeux; Am **a. code** *(in phone number)* indicatif *m*
arena [əˈriːnə] *n (for sports)* & Fig arène *f*
aren't [ɑːnt] = **are not**
Argentina [ɑːdʒənˈtiːnə] *n* l'Argentine *f*
arguable ['ɑːɡjʊəbəl] *adj* discutable
argue ['ɑːɡjuː] **1** *vt (matter)* discuter (de); *(position)* défendre; **to a. that...** soutenir que... **2** *vi (quarrel)* se disputer (**with/about** avec/au sujet de); *(reason)* raisonner (**with/about** avec/sur)
argument ['ɑːɡjʊmənt] *n (quarrel)* dispute *f*; *(debate)* discussion *f*; *(point)* argument *m*; **to have an a. with sb** *(quarrel)* se disputer avec qn ■ **argumentative** *adj (person)* querelleur, -euse
Aries ['eəriːz] *n (sign)* le Bélier; **to be A.** être Bélier
arise [əˈraɪz] *(pt* arose, *pp* arisen [əˈrɪzən]) *vi (of problem, opportunity)* se présenter; *(of cry, objection)* s'élever; *(result)* provenir (**from** de)
aristocracy [ærɪˈstɒkrəsɪ] *n* aristocratie *f* ■ **aristocrat** [Br 'ærɪstəkræt, Am əˈrɪstəkræt] *n* aristocrate *mf*
arithmetic [əˈrɪθmətɪk] *n* arithmétique *f*
ark [ɑːk] *n* **Noah's a.** l'arche *f* de Noé
arm¹ [ɑːm] *n* bras *m*; **a. in a.** bras dessus bras dessous; **with open arms** bras ouverts ■ **armband** *n* brassard

m ■ **armchair** *n* fauteuil *m* ■ **armpit** *n* aisselle *f*

arm² [ɑːm] *vt (with weapon)* armer **(with** *de)* ■ **armaments** *npl* armements *mpl*

armistice [ˈɑːmɪstɪs] *n* armistice *m*

armour [ˈɑːmə(r)] *n (of knight)* armure *f; (of tank)* blindage *m* ■ **armoured, armour-plated** [ɑːˈməplɜːtɪd] *adj (car)* blindé

arms [ɑːmz] *npl (weapons)* armes *fpl;* **the a. race** la course aux armements

army [ˈɑːmɪ] **1** *(pl* **-ies)** *n* armée *f;* **to join the a.** s'engager **2** *adj (uniform)* militaire

A road [ˈeɪrəʊd] *n Br* ≃ route *f* nationale

aroma [əˈrəʊmə] *n* arôme *m* ■ **aromatherapy** *n* aromathérapie *f* ■ **aromatic** [ærəʊˈmætɪk] *adj* aromatique

arose [əˈrəʊz] *pp of* **arise**

around [əˈraʊnd] **1** *prep* autour de; *(approximately)* environ; **to travel a. the world** faire le tour du monde **2** *adv* autour; **a.** a tout autour; **a. here** par ici; **to follow sb a.** suivre qn partout; **to rush a.** courir dans tous les sens; **is Jack a.?** est-ce que Jack est dans le coin?; **he's still a.** il est encore là; **there's a lot of flu a.** beaucoup de gens ont la grippe en ce moment

arouse [əˈraʊz] *vt (suspicion, anger, curiosity)* éveiller

arrange [əˈreɪndʒ] *vt* arranger; *(time, meeting)* fixer; **to a. to do sth** s'arranger pour faire qch ■ **arrangement** *n (layout, agreement, for music)* arrangement *m;* **arrangements** *(preparations)* préparatifs *mpl; (plans)* projets *mpl;* **to make arrangements to do sth** prendre des dispositions pour faire qch

arrears [əˈrɪəz] *npl (payment)* arriéré *m;* **to be in a.** avoir du retard dans ses paiements

arrest [əˈrest] **1** *vt (criminal, progress)* arrêter **2** *n (of criminal)* arrestation *f;* **under a.** en état d'arrestation

arrive [əˈraɪv] *vi* arriver; **to a. at** *(conclusion, decision)* arriver à, parvenir à

■ **arrival** *n* arrivée *f;* **on my a.** à mon arrivée; **new a.** nouveau venu *m,* nouvelle venue *f; (baby)* nouveau-né, -e *mf*

arrogant [ˈærəgənt] *adj* arrogant ■ **arrogance** *n* arrogance *f*

arrow [ˈærəʊ] *n* flèche *f*

arson [ˈɑːsən] *n* incendie *m* criminel

art [ɑːt] *n* art *m;* **faculty of arts, arts faculty** faculté *f* des lettres; **arts degree** ≃ licence *f* ès lettres; **a. exhibition** exposition *f* d'œuvres d'art; **a. gallery** *(museum)* musée *m* d'art; *(shop)* galerie *f* d'art; **a. school** école *f* des beaux-arts

artery [ˈɑːtərɪ] *(pl* **-ies)** *n* artère *f*

arthritis [ɑːˈθraɪtɪs] *n* arthrite *f*

artichoke [ˈɑːtɪtʃəʊk] *n (globe)* a. artichaut *m;* **Jerusalem a.** topinambour *m*

article [ˈɑːtɪkəl] *n* article *m;* **a. of clothing** vêtement *m;* **Br articles** *(of lawyer)* contrat *m* de stage

articulate 1 [ɑːˈtɪkjʊlət] *adj (person)* qui s'exprime clairement; *(speech)* clair **2** [ɑːˈtɪkjʊleɪt] *vt & vi (speak)* articuler ■ **articulation** [-ˈleɪʃən] *n* articulation *f*

artificial [ɑːtɪˈfɪʃəl] *adj* artificiel, -elle

artillery [ɑːˈtɪlərɪ] *n* artillerie *f*

artist [ˈɑːtɪst] *n* artiste *mf* ■ **artiste** *n (singer, dancer)* artiste *mf* ■ **artistic** *adj (pattern, treasure)* artistique; *(person)* artiste

artless [ˈɑːtləs] *adj* naturel, -elle

arty [ˈɑːtɪ] *adj Pej* du genre artiste

AS [æz, *unstressed* əz] **1** *adv* **(a)** *(with manner)* comme; **as promised/planned** comme promis/prévu; **as you like** comme tu veux; **such as** comme, tel que; **as much as I can** (au)tant que je peux; **as it is** *(this being the case)* les choses étant ainsi; **to leave sth as it is** le laisser qch comme ça *ou* tel quel; **it's late as it is** il est déjà tard; **as if, as though** comme si; **you look as if** *or* **as though you're tired** tu as l'air fatigué (**b**) *(comparison)* **as tall as you** aussi grand que vous; **as white as a sheet** blanc (*f* blanche) comme un linge; **as much as you** autant que vous; **as much money as** autant d'argent que; **as many people as** autant de gens que; **twice as big as** deux fois plus grand que; **the same as** le même que

2 *conj* (**a**) *(expressing time)* **as always** comme toujours; **as I was leaving, as I left** comme je partais; **as one grows older** à mesure que l'on vieillit; **as he slept** pendant qu'il dormait; **one day as...** un jour que...; **as from, as of** *(time)* à partir de

(**b**) *(expressing reason)* puisque, comme; **as it's late...** puisqu'il est tard..., comme il est tard...

(**c**) *(though)* **as clever as he is...** si intelligent qu'il soit...

(**d**) *(concerning)* **as for that** quant à cela

(**e**) *(+ infinitive)* **so as to...** de manière à...; **so stupid as to...** assez bête pour...

3 *prep* comme; **she works as a cashier** elle est caissière, elle travaille comme caissière; **dressed up as a clown** déguisé en clown; **as a teacher** en tant que professeur

asap [eɪeseɪ'piː] *(abbr* **as soon as possible)** dès que possible

ascend [ə'send] **1** *vt (throne)* accéder à; *(stairs, mountain)* gravir **2** *vi* monter ■ **ascent** *n* ascension *f* (**of** de); *(slope)* côte *f*

ascertain [æsə'teɪn] *vt (discover)* établir; *(check)* s'assurer de; **to a. that...** s'assurer que...

ash [æʃ] *n* (**a**) *(of cigarette, fire)* cendre *f*; **A. Wednesday** mercredi *m* des Cendres (**b**) *(tree)* frêne *m* ■ **ashtray** *n* cendrier *m*

ashamed [ə'ʃeɪmd] *adj* **to be/feel a. (of sth/sb)** avoir honte (de qch/qn); **to be a. of oneself** avoir honte; **to make sb a.** faire honte à qn

ashore [ə'ʃɔː(r)] *adv* à terre; **to go a.** débarquer

Asia ['eɪʃə, 'eɪʒə] *n* l'Asie *f* ■ **Asian 1** *adj* asiatique; *Br (from Indian sub-continent)* = du sous-continent indien **2** *n* Asiatique *mf*; *Br (from Indian sub-continent)* = personne originaire du sous-continent indien

aside [ə'saɪd] **1** *adv* de côté; **to take** *or* **draw sb a.** prendre qn à part; **to step a.** s'écarter; *Am* **a. from** en dehors de **2** *n (in play, film)* aparté *m*

ask [ɑːsk] **1** *vt (request, inquire about)* demander; *(invite)* inviter (**to sth** à qch); **to a. sb sth** demander qch à qn; **to a. sb about sth/sb** interroger qn sur qn/qch; **to a. (sb) a question** poser une question (à qn); **to a. sb the time/way** demander l'heure/son chemin à qn; **to a. sb for sth** demander qch à qn; **to a. sb to do** *(request)* demander à qn de faire; *(invite)* inviter qn à faire; **to a. to leave/***etc* demander à partir/*etc*

2 *vi (inquire)* se renseigner (**about** sur); *(request)* demander; **to a. for sb/sth** demander qn/qch; **to a. after** *or* **about sb** demander des nouvelles de qn; **the asking price** le prix demandé

askew [ə'skjuː] *adv* de travers

asleep [ə'sliːp] *adj* endormi; *(arm, leg)* engourdi; **to be a.** dormir; **to fall a.** s'endormir

asparagus [ə'spærəgəs] *n (plant)* asperge *f*; *(food)* asperges *fpl*

aspect ['æspekt] *n* aspect *m*; *(of house)* orientation *f*

asphyxiate [æs'fɪksɪeɪt] *vt* asphyxier

aspire [ə'spaɪə(r)] *vi* **to a. to** aspirer à ■ **aspiration** [æspɪ'reɪʃən] *n* aspiration *f*

aspirin ['æsprɪn] *n* aspirine *f*

ass [æs] *n* âne *m*

assailant [ə'seɪlənt] *n* agresseur *m*

assassin [ə'sæsɪn] *n* assassin *m* ■ **assassinate** *vt* assassiner ■ **assassination** *n* assassinat *m*

assault [ə'sɔːlt] **1** *n (military)* assaut *m*; *(crime)* agression *f* **2** *vt (attack)* agresser; **to be sexually assaulted**

être victime d'une agression sexuelle

assemble [ə'sembəl] **1** *vt* *(objects, ideas)* assembler; *(people)* rassembler; *(machine)* monter **2** *vi* se rassembler ■ **assembly** *n* *(meeting)* assemblée *f*; *(of machine)* montage *m*, assemblage *m*; *(in school)* rassemblement *m* *(avant les cours)*; **a. line** *(in factory)* chaîne *f* de montage

assent [ə'sent] **1** *n* assentiment *m* **2** *vi* consentir (**to** à)

assert [ə'sɜːt] *vt* affirmer (**that** que); *(rights)* faire valoir; **to a. oneself** s'affirmer ■ **assertion** *n* *(statement)* affirmation *f*; *(of rights)* revendication *f* ■ **assertive** *adj* *(forceful)* *(tone, person)* affirmatif, -ive; *(authoritarian)* autoritaire

assess [ə'ses] *vt* *(value, damage)* évaluer; *(situation)* analyser; *(decide amount of)* fixer le montant de; *(person)* juger ■ **assessment** *n* *(of value, damage)* évaluation *f*; *(of situation)* analyse *f*; *(of person)* jugement *m*

asset ['æset] *n* *(advantage)* atout *m*; **assets** *(of business)* avoir *m*

assign [ə'saɪn] *vt* *(give)* attribuer; *(day, time)* fixer; *(appoint)* nommer; *(send, move)* affecter (**to** à) ■ **assignment** *n* *(task)* mission *f*; *(for student)* devoir *m*

assimilate [ə'sɪmɪleɪt] **1** *vt* *(absorb)* assimiler **2** *vi* *(of immigrants)* s'assimiler

assist [ə'sɪst] *vt & vi* aider (**in doing** or **to do** à faire) ■ **assistance** *n* aide *f*; **to be of a. to sb** aider qn ■ **assistant 1** *n* assistant, -e *mf*; *Br* *(in shop)* vendeur, -euse *mf* **2** *adj* adjoint

associate 1 [ə'səʊʃɪeɪt] *vt* associer (**with sth** à *ou* avec qch; **with sb** à qn) **2** [ə'səʊʃɪeɪt] *vi* **to a. with sb** *(mix socially)* fréquenter qn **3** [ə'səʊʃɪət] *n & adj* associé, -e *(mf)* ■ **association** [-'eɪʃən] *n* association *f*

assorted [ə'sɔːtɪd] *adj* *(different)* variés; *(foods)* assortis ■ **assortment** *n* assortiment *m*; **an a. of people** des gens de toutes sortes

assume [ə'sjuːm] *vt* **(a)** *(suppose)*

supposer (**that** que); **let us a. that…** supposons que… (+ *subjunctive*) **(b)** *(take on)* *(power, control)* prendre; *(responsibility, role)* assumer; *(attitude, name)* adopter ■ **assumed** *adj* *(feigned)* faux *(f* fausse); **a. name** nom *m* d'emprunt ■ **assumption** [ə'sʌmpʃən] *n* *(supposition)* supposition *f*; **on the a. that…** en supposant que… (+ *subjunctive*)

assure [ə'ʃʊə(r)] *vt* assurer ■ **assurance** *n* **(a)** *(confidence, promise)* assurance *f* **(b)** *Br* *(insurance)* assurance *f*

asterisk ['æstərɪsk] *n* astérisque *m*

asthma [*Br* 'æsmə, *Am* 'æzmə] *n* asthme *m*

astonish [ə'stɒnɪʃ] *vt* étonner; **to be astonished (at sth)** s'étonner (de qch) ■ **astonishing** *adj* étonnant ■ **astonishment** *n* étonnement *m*

astound [ə'staʊnd] *vt* stupéfier ■ **astounding** *adj* stupéfiant

astray [ə'streɪ] *adv* **to go a.** s'égarer; **to lead a.** détourner du droit chemin

astride [ə'straɪd] **1** *adv* à califourchon **2** *prep* à cheval sur

astrology [ə'strɒlədʒɪ] *n* astrologie *f*

astronaut ['æstrənɔːt] *n* astronaute *mf*

astronomy [ə'strɒnəmɪ] *n* astronomie *f* ■ **astronomer** *n* astronome *mf*

astute [ə'stjuːt] *adj* *(crafty)* rusé; *(clever)* astucieux, -euse

asylum [ə'saɪləm] *n* asile *m*

AT [æt, *unstressed* ət] *prep* **(a)** à; **at the end** à la fin; **at school** à l'école; **at work** au travail; **at six (o'clock)** à six heures; **at Easter** à Pâques; **to drive at 10 mph** rouler à ≃ 15 km; **to buy/sell at 10 euros a kilo** acheter/vendre (à) 10 euros le kilo

(b) chez; **at the doctor's** chez le médecin; **at home** chez soi, à la maison

(c) en; **at sea** en mer; **at war** en guerre; **good at maths** fort en maths

(d) contre; **angry at** fâché contre

(e) sur; **to shoot at** tirer sur; **at my request** sur ma demande

(f) de; **to laugh at sb/sth** rire de qn/

qch; **surprised at sth** surpris de qch **(g)** (au)près de; **at the window** près de la fenêtre **(h)** par; **six at a time** six par six **(i)** *(phrases)* **at night** la nuit; **to look at** regarder; **while you're at it** tant que tu y es

ate [eɪt] *pt of* **eat**

atheist ['eɪθɪɪst] *n* athée *mf*

Athens ['æθənz] *n* Athènes *m ou f*

athlete ['æθliːt] *n* athlète *mf*; **a.'s foot** *(disease)* mycose *f* ■ **athletic** *adj* athlétique ■ **athletics** *npl Br* athlétisme *m*; *Am* sport *m*

Atlantic [ət'læntɪk] **1** *adj (coast, ocean)* atlantique **2** *n* **the A.** l'Atlantique *m*

atlas ['ætləs] *n* atlas *m*

atmosphere ['ætməsfɪə(r)] *n* atmosphère *f* ■ **atmospheric** [-'ferɪk] *adj* atmosphérique

atom ['ætəm] *n* atome *m*; **a. bomb** bombe *f* atomique ■ **atomic** *adj* atomique

atrocious [ə'trəʊʃəs] *adj* atroce ■ **atrocity** *n (cruel action)* atrocité *f*

attach [ə'tætʃ] *vt* attacher **(to** à); *(document)* joindre **(to** à); **attached to sb** *(fond of)* attaché à qn ■ **attachment** *n* **(a)** *(affection)* attachement *m* **(to sb** à qn) **(b)** *(tool)* accessoire *m* **(c)** *(to e-mail)* fichier *m* joint

attack [ə'tæk] **1** *n (military)* attaque *f* **(on** contre); *(on someone's life)* attentat *m*; *(of illness)* crise *f*; *(of fever)* accès *m* **2** *vt* attaquer; *(problem, plan)* s'attaquer à **3** *vi* attaquer ■ **attacker** *n* agresseur *m*

attain [ə'teɪn] *vt (aim)* atteindre; *(goal, ambition)* réaliser; *(rank)* parvenir à

attempt [ə'tempt] **1** *n* tentative *f*; **to make an a. to do** tenter de faire **2** *vt* tenter; *(task)* entreprendre; **to a. to do** tenter de faire; **attempted murder** tentative *f* d'assassinat

attend [ə'tend] **1** *vt (meeting)* assister à; *(course)* suivre; *(school, church)* aller à **2** *vi* assister; **to a. to** *(take care of)* s'occuper de

attendance [ə'tendəns] *n* présence *f*

(at à); *(people)* assistance *f*; **(school) a.** scolarité *f*; **in a.** de service ■ **attendant** *n* employé, -e *mf*; *(in service station)* pompiste *mf*; *Br (in museum)* gardien, -enne *mf*

attention [ə'tenʃən] *n* attention *f*; **to pay a.** faire *ou* prêter attention **(to** à); **for the a. of** à l'attention de ■ **attentive** *adj (heedful)* attentif, -ive **(to** à); *(thoughtful)* attentionné **(to** pour)

attest [ə'test] **1** *vt (certify, confirm)* confirmer **2** *vi* **to a. to** témoigner de

attic ['ætɪk] *n* grenier *m*

attitude ['ætɪtjuːd] *n* attitude *f*

attorney [ə'tɜːnɪ] *(pl* **-eys)** *n Am (lawyer)* avocat *m*

attract [ə'trækt] *vt* attirer ■ **attraction** *n (charm, appeal)* attrait *m*; *(place, person)* attraction *f*; *(between people)* attirance *f*; *Phys* attraction *f* terrestre

attractive [ə'træktɪv] *adj (house, room, person, car)* beau *(f* belle); *(price, offer)* intéressant; *(landscape)* attrayant

attribute 1 ['ætrɪbjuːt] *n (quality)* attribut *m* **2** [ə'trɪbjuːt] *vt (ascribe)* attribuer **(to** à)

aubergine ['əʊbəʒiːn] *n Br* aubergine *f*

auburn ['ɔːbən] *adj (hair)* auburn *inv*

auction ['ɔːkʃən] **1** *n* vente *f* aux enchères **2** *vt* **to a. (off)** vendre aux enchères ■ **auctioneer** *n* commissaire-priseur *m*

audacity [ɔː'dæsɪtɪ] *n* audace *f*

audible ['ɔːdɪbəl] *adj (sound, words)* audible

audience ['ɔːdɪəns] *n* **(a)** *(of speaker, musician, actor)* public *m*; *(of radio broadcast)* auditeurs *mpl*; **TV a.** téléspectateurs *mpl* **(b)** *(interview)* audience *f* **(with sb** avec qn)

audio ['ɔːdɪəʊ] *adj (cassette, system)* audio *inv*; **a. tape** cassette *f* audio ■ **audiotypist** *n* audiotypiste *mf* ■ **audiovisual** *adj* audiovisuel, -elle

audit ['ɔːdɪt] **1** *n* audit *m* **2** *vt (accounts)* vérifier

audition [ɔːˈdɪʃən] **1** *n* audition *f* **2** *vt & vi* auditionner

auditorium [ɔːdɪˈtɔːrɪəm] *n (of theatre, concert hall)* salle *f*

August [ˈɔːɡəst] *n* août *m*

aunt [ɑːnt] *n* tante *f* ■ **auntie, aunty** (*pl* **-ies**) *n Fam* tata *f*

au pair [əʊˈpeə(r)] *n* **a. (girl)** jeune fille *f* au pair

aura [ˈɔːrə] *n (of place)* atmosphère *f*; *(of person)* aura *f*

austere [ɔːˈstɪə(r)] *adj* austère ■ **austerity** *n* austérité *f*

Australia [ɒˈstreɪlɪə] *n* l'Australie *f* ■ **Australian 1** *adj* australien, -enne **2** *n* Australien, -enne *mf*

Austria [ˈɒstrɪə] *n* l'Autriche *f* ■ **Austrian 1** *adj* autrichien, -enne **2** *n* Autrichien, -enne *mf*

authentic [ɔːˈθentɪk] *adj* authentique ■ **authenticate** *vt* authentifier

author [ˈɔːθə(r)] *n* auteur *m*

authority [ɔːˈθɒrɪtɪ] (*pl* **-ies**) *n* autorité *f*; *(permission)* autorisation *f* (**to do** de faire); **to be in a.** *(in charge)* être responsable ■ **authoritarian** *adj & n* autoritaire *(mf)* ■ **authoritative** *adj (report, book)* qui fait autorité; *(tone, person)* autoritaire

authorize [ˈɔːθəraɪz] *vt* autoriser (**to do** à faire) ■ **authorization** [-ˈzeɪʃən] *n* autorisation *f* (**to do** de faire)

autistic [ɔːˈtɪstɪk] *adj* autiste

auto [ˈɔːtəʊ] (*pl* **-os**) *n Am* auto *f*

autobiography [ɔːtəʊbaɪˈɒɡrəfɪ] (*pl* **-ies**) *n* autobiographie *f*

autograph [ˈɔːtəɡrɑːf] **1** *n* autographe *m*; **a. book** album *m* d'autographes **2** *vt* dédicacer (**for sb** à qn)

automatic [ɔːtəˈmætɪk] *adj* automatique

automobile [ˈɔːtəməbiːl] *n Am* automobile *f*

autonomous [ɔːˈtɒnəməs] *adj* autonome ■ **autonomy** *n* autonomie *f*

autopsy [ˈɔːtɒpsɪ] (*pl* **-ies**) *n* autopsie *f*

autumn [ˈɔːtəm] *n* automne *m*; **in a.** en automne

auxiliary [ɔːɡˈzɪljərɪ] (*pl* **-ies**) *adj & n* auxiliaire *(mf)*; **a. (verb)** *(verbe m)* auxiliaire *m*

avail [əˈveɪl] **1** *n* **to no a.** en vain **2** *vt* **to a. oneself of** profiter de ■ **availability** *n (of object)* disponibilité *f*; *(of education)* accessibilité *f*

available [əˈveɪləbəl] *adj* disponible; **tickets are still a.** il reste des tickets; **this model is a. in black or green** ce modèle existe en noir et en vert

avalanche [ˈævəlɑːnʃ] *n* avalanche *f*

Ave *(abbr* **Avenue)** av.

avenge [əˈvendʒ] *vt* venger; **to a. oneself (on)** se venger (de)

avenue [ˈævənjuː] *n* avenue *f*; *Fig (possibility)* possibilité *f*

average [ˈævərɪdʒ] **1** *n* moyenne *f*; **on a.** en moyenne; **above/below a.** au-dessus/au-dessous de la moyenne **2** *adj* moyen, -enne **3** *vt (do)* faire en moyenne; *(reach)* atteindre la moyenne de; *(figures)* faire la moyenne de

averse [əˈvɜːs] *adj* **to be a. to doing** répugner à faire

aversion [əˈvɜːʃən] *n (dislike)* aversion *f*; **to have an a. to sth/to doing sth** avoir de la répugnance pour qch/à faire qch

avert [əˈvɜːt] *vt (prevent)* éviter; **to a. one's eyes (from)** *(turn away)* détourner les yeux (de)

aviation [eɪvɪˈeɪʃən] *n* aviation *f*

avid [ˈævɪd] *adj* avide (**for** de)

avocado [ævəˈkɑːdəʊ] (*pl* **-os**) *n* avocat *m*

avoid [əˈvɔɪd] *vt* éviter; **to a. doing** éviter de faire ■ **avoidable** *adj* évitable

await [əˈweɪt] *vt* attendre

awake [əˈweɪk] **1** *adj* réveillé, éveillé; **he's still a.** il ne dort pas encore **2** (*pt* **awoke**, *pp* **awoken**) *vi* se réveiller **3** *vt* réveiller ■ **awaken 1** *vi* se réveiller **2** *vt* réveiller

award [əˈwɔːd] **1** *n (prize)* prix *m*, récompense *f*; *(scholarship)* bourse *f* **2** *vt (money)* attribuer; *(prize)* décerner; **to a. damages** *(of judge)* accorder des dommages-intérêts

aware [ə'weə(r)] *adj* **to be a. of** *(conscious)* être conscient de; *(informed)* être au courant de; *(realize)* se rendre compte de; **to become a. of/that** se rendre compte de/que ■ **awareness** *n* conscience *f*

AWAY [ə'weɪ] *adv* (**a**) *(distant)* loin; **5 km a.** à 5 km (de distance) (**b**) *(in time)* **ten days a.** dans dix jours (**c**) *(absent, gone)* absent; **to drive a.** partir (en voiture); **to fade/melt a.** disparaître/fondre complètement (**d**) *(to one side)* **to look** *or* **turn a.** détourner les yeux (**e**) *(continuously)* **to work/talk a.** travailler/parler sans arrêt (**f**) *Br* **to play a.** *(of team)* jouer à l'extérieur

awe [ɔ:] *n* crainte *f* (mêlée de respect); **to be in a. of sb** éprouver pour qn une crainte mêlée de respect ■ **awesome** *adj (impressive)* impressionnant; *(frightening)* effrayant; *Am Fam (excellent)* super *inv*

awful ['ɔ:fəl] *adj* affreux, -euse; *(terrifying)* effroyable; *Fam* **an a. lot (of)** énormément (de); **I feel a. (about it)** j'ai vraiment honte ■ **awfully** *adv (suffer)* affreusement; *(very) (good, pretty)* extrêmement; *(bad, late)* affreusement

awkward ['ɔ:kwəd] *adj* (**a**) *(clumsy) (person, gesture)* maladroit (**b**) *(difficult)* difficile; *(cumbersome)* gênant; *(tool)* peu commode; *(time)* mal choisi; *(silence)* gêné ■ **awkwardly** *adv (walk)* maladroitement; *(speak)* d'un ton gêné; *(placed, situated)* à un endroit peu pratique

awning ['ɔ:nɪŋ] *n (of tent)* auvent *m*; *(over shop, window)* store *m*; *(canvas or glass canopy)* marquise *f*

awoke [ə'wəʊk] *pt of* **awake**

awoken [ə'wəʊkən] *pp of* **awake**

axe [æks] (*Am* **ax**) **1** *n* hache *f*; *Fig (reduction)* coupe *f* sombre; **to get the a.** *(of project)* être abandonné; *(of worker)* être mis à la porte; *Fig* **to have an a. to grind** agir dans un but intéressé **2** *vt (costs)* réduire; *(job)* supprimer; *(project)* abandonner

axis ['æksɪs] (*pl* **axes** ['æksi:z]) *n* axe *m*

axle ['æksəl] *n* essieu *m*

Bb

B, b [biː] n B, b m inv; **2B** (number) 2 ter
BA [biːˈeɪ] n (abbr **Bachelor of Arts**) to
have a BA in history ≃ avoir une licence en histoire

babble [ˈbæbəl] **1** vi (mumble) bredouiller; (of baby, stream) gazouiller
2 n inv (of voices) rumeur f; (of baby,
stream) gazouillis m

baboon [bəˈbuːn] n babouin m

baby [ˈbeɪbɪ] (pl -ies) n bébé m; **b. boy**
petit garçon m; **b. girl** petite fille f; **b.
tiger**/etc bébé-tigre/etc m; **b. clothes/
toys**/etc vêtements mpl/jouets mpl/
etc de bébé; **Am b. carriage** landau m;
b. sling kangourou m, porte-bébé m
■ **baby-sit** (pt & pp -sat, pres p -sitting)
vi faire du baby-sitting ■ **baby-sitter** n
baby-sitter mf

bachelor [ˈbætʃələ(r)] n (a) (not married) célibataire m (b) Univ **B. of
Arts/of Science** (person) ≃ licencié,
-e mf ès lettres/ès sciences; (qualification) ≃ licence f de lettres/de sciences

back [bæk] **1** n (of person, animal,
hand) dos m; (of chair) dossier m; (of
house, vehicle, train, head) arrière m;
(of room) fond m; (of page) verso m;
(of fabric) envers m; (in sport) arrière
m; **at the b. of the book** à la fin du livre; **at the b. of the car** à l'arrière de la
voiture; **at the b. of one's mind** derrière la tête; **b. to front** devant der-
rière; Fam **to get off sb's b.** ficher la paix à qn; Fam **to get sb's b.
up** braquer qn
2 adj (wheel, seat) arrière inv; **b. door**
porte f de derrière; **b. room** pièce f du
fond; **b. street** rue f écartée; **b. tooth**
molaire f

3 adv (behind) en arrière; **far b., a
long way b.** loin derrière; **a month b.**
il y a un mois; **to go b. and forth** aller
et venir; **to come b.** revenir; **he's b.** il
est de retour, il est revenu; **the journey there and b.** le voyage aller et retour

4 vt (with money) financer; (horse) parier sur; (vehicle) faire reculer; **to be
backed with** (of curtain, picture) être
renforcé de; **to back sb (up)** (support) appuyer qn; Comptr **to b. up** sauvegarder

5 vi (move backwards) reculer; **to b.
down** faire marche arrière; **to b. out**
(withdraw) se retirer; (of vehicle) sortir
en marche arrière; **to b. on to** (of
house) donner par derrière sur; **to b.
up** (of vehicle) faire marche arrière
■ **backache** n mal m de dos ■ **back-
bencher** n Br Pol député m de base
■ **backbone** n colonne f vertébrale;
(of fish) grande arête f; Fig (main support) pivot m ■ **backpack** n sac m à dos
■ **backside** n Fam (buttocks) derrière m
■ **backstage** adv dans les coulisses
■ **backstroke** n (in swimming) dos m
crawlé ■ **backup** n appui m; Am (tailback) embouteillage m; Comptr sauvegarde f ■ **backyard** n Br (enclosed
area) arrière-cour f; Am (garden) jardin m de derrière

backer [ˈbækə(r)] n (supporter) partisan m; (on horses) parieur, -euse mf;
(financial) commanditaire m

backfire [bækˈfaɪə(r)] vi (a) (of vehicle)

pétarader (**b**) *Fig* **to b. on sb** *(of plot)* se retourner contre qn

backgammon ['bækgæmən] *n* backgammon *m*

background ['bækgraʊnd] *n* fond *m*, arrière-plan *m*; *(educational)* formation *f*; *(professional)* expérience *f*; *(environment)* milieu *m*; *(circumstances)* contexte *m*; **b. music/noise** musique *f*/bruit *m* de fond

backlash ['bæklæʃ] *n* retour *m* de bâton

backlog ['bæklɒg] *n* **a b. of work** du travail *m* en retard

backward ['bækwəd] **1** *adj (person, country)* arriéré; *(glance)* en arrière **2** *adv* = **backwards** ■ **backwards** *adv* en arrière; *(walk)* à reculons; *(fall)* à la renverse; **to go** *or* **move b.** reculer

bacon ['beɪkən] *n* bacon *m*; **b. and eggs** œufs *mpl* au bacon

bacteria [bæk'tɪərɪə] *npl* bactéries *fpl*

bad [bæd] (**worse, worst**) *adj* mauvais; *(wicked)* méchant; *(sad)* triste; *(accident, wound)* grave; *(tooth)* carié; *(arm, leg)* malade; *(pain)* violent; **b. language** gros mots *mpl*; **b. cheque** chèque *m* sans provision; **to feel b.** *(ill)* se sentir mal; **to be b. at maths** être mauvais en maths; **things are b.** ça va mal; **it's not b.** pas mal; **to go b.** *(of fruit, meat)* se gâter; *(of milk)* tourner; **too b.!** tant pis! ■ **bad-mannered** *adj* mal élevé ■ **bad-tempered** *adj* grincheux, -euse

bade [bæd] *pt of* **bid**

badge [bædʒ] *n (of plastic, bearing slogan or joke)* badge *m*; *(of metal, bearing logo)* pin's *m*; *(of postman, policeman)* plaque *f*; *(on school uniform)* insigne *m*

badger ['bædʒə(r)] **1** *n (animal)* blaireau *m* **2** *vt* importuner

badly ['bædlɪ] *adv* mal; *(hurt)* grièvement; **to be b. mistaken** se tromper lourdement; **b. off** dans la gêne; **to want sth b.** avoir grande envie de qch

badminton ['bædmɪntən] *n* badminton *m*

baffle ['bæfəl] *vt (person)* laisser perplexe

bag [bæg] *n* sac *m*; **bags** *(luggage)* bagages *mpl*; *(under eyes)* poches *fpl*; *Fam Pej* **an old b.** une vieille taupe; *Fam* **in the b.** dans la poche

baggage ['bægɪdʒ] *n* bagages *mpl*; *Am* **b. car** fourgon *m*; **b. handler** *(in airport)* bagagiste *mf*; *Am* **b. room** consigne *f*

baggy ['bægɪ] (**-ier, -iest**) *adj (garment) (out of shape)* déformé; *(by design)* large

bagpipes ['bægpaɪps] *npl* cornemuse *f*

Bahamas [bə'hɑːməz] *npl* **the B.** les Bahamas *fpl*

bail [beɪl] **1** *n Law* caution *f*; **on b.** sous caution; **to grant sb b.** libérer qn sous caution **2** *vt* **to b. sb out** *Law* se porter garant de qn; *Fig* tirer qn d'affaire **3** *vi* **to b. out** *(from aircraft)* s'éjecter

bailiff ['beɪlɪf] *n (law officer)* huissier *m*; *Br (of landowner)* régisseur *m*

bait [beɪt] **1** *n* appât *m* **2** *vt* (**a**) *(fishing hook)* amorcer (**b**) *(annoy)* tourmenter

bake [beɪk] **1** *vt* (faire) cuire au four **2** *vi (of person) (make cakes)* faire de la pâtisserie; *(make bread)* faire du pain; *(of food)* cuire (au four); *Fam* **it's baking (hot)** on crève de chaleur ■ **baked** *adj (potatoes, apples)* au four; **b. beans** haricots *mpl* blancs à la tomate

baker ['beɪkə(r)] *n* boulanger, -ère *mf* ■ **bakery** *n* boulangerie *f*

baking ['beɪkɪŋ] *n* cuisson *f*; **b. powder** levure *f* chimique; **b. tin** moule *m* à pâtisserie

balaclava [bælə'klɑːvə] *n Br* passemontagne *m*

balance ['bæləns] **1** *n (equilibrium)* équilibre *m*; *(of account)* solde *m*; *(remainder)* reste *m*; *(in accounting)* bilan *m*; *(for weighing)* balance *f*; **to lose one's b.** perdre l'équilibre; **to strike a b.** trouver le juste milieu; **on b.** à tout prendre; **b. of payments** balance *f* des paiements; **b. sheet** bilan *m*

2 *vt* maintenir en équilibre (**on** sur); *(budget, account)* équilibrer; *(compare)* mettre en balance; **to b. (out)** *(compensate for)* compenser

3 *(vi of person)* se tenir en équilibre; *(of accounts)* être en équilibre, s'équilibrer; **to b. (out)** *(even out)* s'équilibrer

balcony ['bælkənɪ] *(pl* -**ies**) *n* balcon *m*

bald [bɔːld] (-**er**, -**est**) *adj* chauve; *(statement)* brutal; *(tyre)* lisse; **b. patch** *or* **spot** tonsure *f*

balk [bɔːk] *vi* reculer (**at** devant)

Balkans ['bɔːlkənz] *npl* **the B.** les Balkans *fpl*

ball¹ [bɔːl] *n* balle *f*; *(inflated, for football, rugby)* ballon *m*; *(for snooker, pool)* bille *f*; *(of string, wool)* pelote *f*; *(sphere)* boule *f*; *(of meat, fish)* boulette *f*; *Fam* **to be on the b.** *(alert)* avoir de la présence d'esprit; *(knowledgeable)* connaître son affaire; **b. bearing** roulement *m* à billes; *Am* **b. game** match *m* de base-ball; *Fig* **it's a whole new b. game** c'est une tout autre affaire

ball² [bɔːl] *n (dance)* bal *m (pl* bals)

ballad ['bæləd] *n (poem)* ballade *f*; *(song)* romance *f*

ballast ['bæləst] **1** *n* lest *m* **2** *vt* lester

ballet ['bæleɪ] *n* ballet *m* ■ **ballerina** *n* ballerine *f*

balloon [bə'luːn] *n (toy, airship)* ballon *m*; *(in cartoon)* bulle *f*

ballot ['bælət] **1** *n (voting)* scrutin *m*; **b. paper** bulletin *m* de vote; **b. box** urne *f* **2** *vt (members)* consulter (par un scrutin)

ballpoint (pen) ['bɔːlpɔɪnt(pen)] *n* stylo *m* à bille

ballroom ['bɔːlruːm] *n* salle *f* de danse

Baltic ['bɔːltɪk] *n* **the B.** la Baltique

bamboo [bæm'buː] *n* bambou *m*; **b. shoots** pousses *fpl* de bambou

ban [bæn] **1** *n* interdiction *f*; **to impose a b. on sth** interdire qch **2** *(pt & pp* -**nn**-) *vt* interdire; **to b. sb from doing sth** interdire à qn de faire qch; **to b. sb from** *(club)* exclure qn de

banal [bə'næl] *adj* banal *(mpl* -als)

banana [bə'nɑːnə] *n* banane *f*

band [bænd] **1** *n* (**a**) *(strip)* bande *f*; *(of hat)* ruban *m*; **rubber** *or* **elastic b.** élastique *m* (**b**) *(group of people)* bande *f*; *(of musicians)* (petit) orchestre *m*; *(pop group)* groupe *m* **2** *vi* **to b. together** se (re)grouper

bandage ['bændɪdʒ] **1** *n (strip)* bande *f*; *(dressing)* bandage *m* **2** *vt* **to b. (up)** *(arm, leg)* bander; *(wound)* mettre un bandage sur; **to b. sb's arm** bander le bras à qn

Band-aid® ['bændeɪd] *n Am* pansement *m* adhésif

B and B, B & B [biːənd'biː] *n (abbr* **bed and breakfast**) *(service)* ≃ chambre *f* avec petit déjeuner; **to stay at a B and B** ≃ prendre une chambre d'hôte

bandit ['bændɪt] *n* bandit *m*

bandwagon ['bændwægən] *n Fig* **to jump on the b.** prendre le train en marche

bandy¹ ['bændɪ] (-**ier**, -**iest**) *adj* **to have b. legs** avoir les jambes arquées

bandy² ['bændɪ] *(pt & pp* -**ied**) *vt* **b. about** *(story, rumour)* faire circuler

bang¹ [bæŋ] **1** *n (blow, noise)* coup *m* *(violent)*; *(of gun)* détonation *f*; *(of door)* claquement *m*

2 *vt (hit)* cogner, frapper; *(door)* (faire) claquer; **to b. one's head** se cogner la tête

3 *vi* cogner, frapper; *(of door)* claquer; **to b. into sb/sth** heurter qn/qch

4 *exclam* vlan!, pan!; **to go b.** éclater

bang² [bæŋ] *adv Br Fam (exactly)* exactement; **b. in the middle** en plein milieu; **b. on six** à six heures tapantes

banger ['bæŋə(r)] *n Br* (**a**) *Fam (sausage)* saucisse *f* (**b**) *(firecracker)* pétard *m* (**c**) *Fam* **old b.** *(car)* vieille guimbarde *f*

bangle ['bæŋgəl] *n* bracelet *m*

bangs [bæŋz] *npl Am (of hair)* frange *f*

banish ['bænɪʃ] *vt* bannir

banister ['bænɪstə(r)] *n* **banister(s)** rampe *f* (d'escalier)

banjo [ˈbændʒəʊ] (*pl* **-os** *or* **-oes**) *n* banjo *m*

bank[1] [bæŋk] **1** (*of river*) bord *m*, rive *f*; (*raised*) berge *f*; (*of earth*) talus *m*; (*of sand*) banc *m*; **the Left B.** (*in Paris*) la Rive gauche **2** *vt* to **b. (up)** (*earth*) amonceler; (*fire*) couvrir **3** *vi* (*of aircraft*) virer

bank[2] [bæŋk] **1** *n* (*for money*) banque *f*; **b. account** compte *m* en banque; **b. card** carte *f* d'identité bancaire; *Br* **b. holiday** jour *m* férié; *Br* **b. note** billet *m* de banque **2** *vt* (*money*) mettre à la banque **3** *vi* avoir un compte en banque (**with** à) ■ **banker** *n* banquier, -ère *mf*; *Br* **b.'s card** carte *f* d'identité bancaire ■ **banking 1** *adj* (*transaction*) bancaire **2** *n* (*activity, profession*) la banque

bank[3] [bæŋk] *vi* **to b. on sb/sth** (*rely on*) compter sur qn/qch

bankrupt [ˈbæŋkrʌpt] **1** *adj* **to go b.** faire faillite **2** *vt* mettre en faillite

banner [ˈbænə(r)] *n* banderole *f*; (*military flag*) *Fig* bannière *f*

banns [bænz] *npl* bans *mpl*; **to put up the b.** publier les bans

banquet [ˈbæŋkwɪt] *n* banquet *m*

banter [ˈbæntə(r)] **1** *n* plaisanteries *fpl* **2** *vi* plaisanter

baptism [ˈbæptɪzəm] *n* baptême *m* ■ **Baptist** *n & adj* baptiste (*mf*)

baptize [bæpˈtaɪz] *vt* baptiser

bar [bɑː(r)] **1** *n* (**a**) (*of metal*) barre *f*; (*of gold*) lingot *m*; (*of chocolate*) tablette *f*; (*on window*) barreau *m*; **b. of soap** savonnette *f*; **behind bars** (*criminal*) sous les verrous; *Law* **the B.** le barreau; **b. code** (*on product*) code-barres *m*
(**b**) (*pub*) bar *m*; (*counter*) bar *m*, comptoir *m*
(**c**) (*group of musical notes*) mesure *f*
2 (*pt & pp* **-rr-**) *vt* (**a**) to **b. sb's way** barrer le passage à qn; **barred window** fenêtre *f* munie de barreaux
(**b**) (*prohibit*) interdire (**sb from doing** à qn de faire); (*exclude*) exclure (**from** à)

3 *prep* (*except*) sauf; **b. none** sans exception ■ **barmaid** *n Br* serveuse *f* (de bar) ■ **barman** (*pl* **-men**) *n Br* barman *m* ■ **bartender** *n Am* barman *m*

Barbados [bɑːˈbeɪdɒs] *n* la Barbade

barbaric [bɑːˈbærɪk] *adj* barbare

barbecue [ˈbɑːbɪkjuː] **1** *n* barbecue *m* **2** *vt* cuire au barbecue

barbed wire [bɑːbdˈwaɪə(r)] *n* fil *m* de fer barbelé; (*fence*) barbelés *mpl*

barber [ˈbɑːbə(r)] *n* coiffeur *m* pour hommes

bare [beə(r)] **1** (**-er, -est**) *adj* nu; (*tree, hill*) dénudé; (*room, cupboard*) vide; (*mere*) simple; **the b. necessities** le strict nécessaire; **with his b. hands** à mains nues **2** *vt* (*arm, wire*) dénuder ■ **barefoot 1** *adv* nu-pieds **2** *adj* aux pieds nus

barely [ˈbeəlɪ] *adv* (*scarcely*) à peine; **b. enough** tout juste assez

bargain [ˈbɑːgɪn] **1** *n* (*deal*) marché *m*, affaire *f*; **a b.** (*good buy*) une occasion, une bonne affaire; **to make a b. (with sb)** faire un marché (avec qn); **into the b.** (*in addition*) par-dessus le marché; **b. price** prix *m* exceptionnel **2** *vi* (*negotiate*) négocier; (*haggle*) marchander; **to b. for** *or* **on sth** (*expect*) s'attendre à qch

barge [bɑːdʒ] **1** *n* péniche *f* **2** *vi* **to b. in** (*enter room*) faire irruption; (*interrupt*) interrompre

bark[1] [bɑːk] *n* (*of tree*) écorce *f*

bark[2] [bɑːk] **1** *n* aboiement *m* **2** *vi* aboyer

barley [ˈbɑːlɪ] *n* orge *f*; **b. sugar** sucre *m* d'orge

barn [bɑːn] *n* (*for crops*) grange *f*; (*for horses*) écurie *f*; (*for cattle*) étable *f* ■ **barnyard** *n* cour *f* de ferme

barometer [bəˈrɒmɪtə(r)] *n* baromètre *m*

baron [ˈbærən] *n* baron *m*; *Fig* (*industrialist*) magnat *m*; **press/oil b.** magnat de la presse/du pétrole ■ **baroness** *n* baronne *f*

barracks [ˈbærəks] *npl* caserne *f*

barrage [*Br* ˈbærɑːʒ, *Am* bəˈrɑːʒ] *n*

(across river) barrage *m*; *Fig* **a b. of questions** un feu roulant de questions
barrel ['bærəl] *n* (**a**) *(cask)* tonneau *m*; *(of oil)* baril *m* (**b**) *(of gun)* canon *m* (**c**) **b. organ** orgue *m* de Barbarie
barren ['bærən] *adj* (*land, woman, ideas*) stérile; *(style)* aride
barricade ['bærɪkeɪd] **1** *n* barricade *f* **2** *vt* barricader; **to b. oneself (in)** se barricader (dans)
barrier ['bærɪə(r)] *n also Fig* barrière *f*; *Br (ticket)* **b.** *(of station)* portillon *m*; **sound b.** mur *m* du son
barring ['bɑːrɪŋ] *prep* sauf
barrister ['bærɪstə(r)] *n Br* ≃ avocat *m*
barrow ['bærəʊ] *n (wheelbarrow)* brouette *f*; *(cart)* charrette *f* ou voiture *f* à bras
barter ['bɑːtə(r)] **1** *n* troc *m* **2** *vt* troquer (**for** contre)
base [beɪs] **1** *n* (**a**) *(bottom, main ingredient)* base *f*; *(of tree, lamp)* pied *m*; **b. rate** *(of bank)* taux *m* de base (**b**) *(military)* base *f* **2** *adj (dishonourable)* bas (*f* basse) **3** *vt* baser, fonder (**on** sur); **based in London** *(person, company)* basé à Londres
baseball ['beɪsbɔːl] *n* base-ball *m*
basement ['beɪsmənt] *n* sous-sol *m*
bash [bæʃ] **1** *n (bang)* coup *m*; *Br* **Fam to have a b.** *(try)* essayer un coup **2** *vt (hit)* cogner; **to b. (about)** *(ill-treat)* malmener; **to b. in** or **down** *(door, fence)* défoncer
bashful ['bæʃfəl] *adj* timide
basic ['beɪsɪk] **1** *adj* essentiel, -elle, de base; *(elementary)* élémentaire; *(pay, food)* de base; *(room, house, meal)* tout simple **2** *n* **the basics** l'essentiel *m* ■ **basically** *adv (on the whole)* en gros; *(in fact)* en fait; *(fundamentally)* au fond
basil [*Br* 'bæzəl, *Am* 'beɪzəl] *n* basilic *m*
basin [*Br* 'beɪsən, *Am* 'beɪzən] *n* (**a**) *(made of plastic)* bassine *f*; *(for soup, food)* (grand) bol *m*; *(portable washbasin)* cuvette *f*; *(sink)* lavabo *m* (**b**) *(of river)* bassin *m*

basis ['beɪsɪs] *(pl* **-ses** [-siːz]*)* *n (for discussion)* base *f*; *(for opinion, accusation)* fondement *m*; *(of agreement)* bases *fpl*; **on the b. of** d'après; **on a weekly b.** chaque semaine
basket ['bɑːskɪt] *n* panier *m*; *(for bread, laundry, litter)* corbeille *f* ■ **basketball** *n* basket(-ball) *m*
Basque [bæsk] **1** *adj* basque **2** *n* Basque *mf*
bass¹ [beɪs] **1** *n Mus* basse *f* **2** *adj (note, voice, instrument)* bas (*f* basse)
bass² [bæs] *n (sea fish)* bar *m*; *(freshwater fish)* perche *f*
bassoon [bə'suːn] *n* basson *m*
bat¹ [bæt] *n (animal)* chauve-souris *f*
bat² [bæt] *n (for cricket, baseball)* batte *f*; *(for table-tennis)* raquette *f*; **off my own b.** de ma propre initiative **2** *(pt & pp* **-tt-***)* *vt* (**a**) *(ball)* frapper (**b**) **she didn't b. an eyelid** elle n'a pas sourcillé
batch [bætʃ] *n (of people)* groupe *m*; *(of letters)* paquet *m*; *(of books)* lot *m*; *(of loaves)* fournée *f*; *(of papers)* liasse *f*
bath [bɑːθ] **1** *(pl* **baths** [bɑːðz]*)* *n* bain *m*; *(tub)* baignoire *f*; **to have** or **take a b.** prendre un bain; **b. towel** drap *m* de bain; *Br* **swimming baths** piscine *f* **2** *vt Br* baigner ■ **bathrobe** *n Br* peignoir *m* de bain; *Am* robe *f* de chambre ■ **bathroom** *n* salle *f* de bain(s); *Am (toilet)* toilettes *fpl* ■ **bathtub** *n* baignoire *f*
bathe [beɪð] **1** *vt* baigner; *(wound)* laver **2** *vi (swim)* se baigner; *Am (have bath)* prendre un bain ■ **bathing** *n* baignades *fpl*; **b. suit**, *Br* **b. costume** maillot *m* de bain
baton [*Br* 'bætən, *Am* bə'tɒn] *n (of conductor)* baguette *f*; *(of policeman)* matraque *f*; *(of soldier, drum majorette)* bâton *m*; *(in relay race)* témoin *m*
battalion [bə'tæljən] *n* bataillon *m*
batter ['bætə(r)] **1** *n* pâte *f* à frire **2** *vt (strike)* cogner sur; *(person)* frapper; *(town)* pilonner; **to b. down** *(door)* défoncer ■ **battered** *adj (car, hat)* cabossé; *(house)* délabré; *(face)*

meurtri; **b. child** enfant *m* martyr; **b. wife** femme *f* battue

battery ['bætərɪ] (*pl* **-ies**) *n* (*in vehicle, of guns, for hens*) batterie *f*; (*in radio, appliance*) pile *f*; **b. hen** poule *f* de batterie

battle ['bætəl] **1** *n* bataille *f*; (*struggle*) lutte *f*; *Fam* **that's half the b.** la partie est à moitié gagnée **2** *vi* se battre, lutter ■ **battlefield** *n* champ *m* de bataille ■ **battleship** *n* cuirassé *m*

bawl [bɔːl] *vt & vi* **to b. (out)** brailler; *Fam* **to b. sb out** engueuler qn

bay¹ [beɪ] **1** *n* (**a**) (*part of coastline*) baie *f* (**b**) (*in room*) renfoncement *m*; **b. window** bow-window *m*, oriel *m* (**c**) *Br* (*for loading*) aire *f* de chargement (**d**) **at b.** (*animal, criminal*) aux abois; **to keep** *or* **hold at b.** (*enemy, wild dog*) tenir en respect; (*disease*) juguler **2** *vi* aboyer **3** *adj* (*horse*) bai

bay² [beɪ] *n* (*tree*) laurier *m*; **b. leaf** feuille *f* de laurier

bayonet ['beɪənɪt] *n* baïonnette *f*

bazaar [bə'zɑː(r)] *n* (*market, shop*) bazar *m*; (*charity sale*) vente *f* de charité

BC [biː'siː] (*abbr* **before Christ**) av. J.-C.

BE [biː] (*present tense* **am, are, is**; *past tense* **was, were**; *pp* **been**; *pres p* **being**) **1** *vi* (**a**) (*gen*) être; **it is green/small**/*etc* c'est vert/petit/*etc*; **he's a doctor** il est médecin; **he's an Englishman** c'est un Anglais; **it's him** c'est lui; **it's them** ce sont eux; **it's three (o'clock)** il est trois heures; **it's the sixth of May,** *Am* **it's May sixth** nous sommes le six mai; **to be hot/right/lucky** avoir chaud/raison/de la chance; **my feet are cold** j'ai froid aux pieds

(**b**) (*with age, height*) avoir; **to be twenty** (*age*) avoir vingt ans; **to be 2 metres high** avoir 2 m de haut; **to be 6 feet tall** ≃ mesurer 1,80 m

(**c**) (*with health*) aller; **how are you?** comment vas-tu?; **I'm well/not well** je vais bien/mal

(**d**) (*with place, situation*) se trouver, être; **she's in York** elle se trouve *ou* elle est à York

(**e**) (*exist*) être; **the best painter there is** le meilleur peintre qui soit

(**f**) (*go, come*) **I've been to see her** je suis allé la voir; **he's (already) been** il est (déjà) venu

(**g**) (*with weather, calculations*) faire; **it's nice** il fait beau; **it's foggy** il y a du brouillard; **2 and 2 are 4** 2 et 2 font 4

(**h**) (*cost*) coûter, faire; **it's 20 pence** ça coûte 20 pence; **how much is it?** ça fait combien?, c'est combien?

2 *v aux* (**a**) **I am going** je vais; **I was going** j'allais; **I'll be staying** je vais rester; **I'm listening to the radio** je suis en train d'écouter la radio; **what has she been doing?** qu'est-ce qu'elle a fait?; **she's been there some time** elle est là depuis un moment; **he was killed** il a été tué; **I've been waiting (for) two hours** j'attends depuis deux heures; **it is said** on dit

(**b**) (*in questions and answers*) **isn't it?/aren't you?**/*etc* n'est-ce pas?, non?; **she's ill, is she?** (*in surprise*) alors, comme ça, elle est malade?; **he isn't English, is he?** il n'est pas anglais, si?

(**c**) (*+ infinitive*) **he is to come at once** (*must*) il doit venir tout de suite

(**d**) **there is/are** il y a; (*pointing*) voilà; **here is/are** voici; **there she is** la voilà; **here they are** les voici

beach [biːtʃ] *n* plage *f*

beacon ['biːkən] *n* (*for ship, aircraft*) balise *f*; (*lighthouse*) phare *m*

bead [biːd] *n* (*small sphere*) perle *f*; (*of rosary*) grain *m*; (*of sweat*) goutte *f*, gouttelette *f*; (*string of*) **beads** collier *m*

beak [biːk] *n* bec *m*

beaker ['biːkə(r)] *n* gobelet *m*

beam [biːm] **1** *n* (**a**) (*of wood*) poutre *f* (**b**) (*of light, sunlight*) rayon *m*; (*of headlight, flashlight*) faisceau *m* (lumineux) **2** *vi* (*of light*) rayonner; (*of sun, moon*) briller; (*smile broadly*) sourire largement; **to b. with pride/joy** rayonner de fierté/joie **3** *vt* (*signals, programme*) transmettre (**to** à)

bean [biːn] *n* haricot *m*; *(of coffee)* grain *m*; *Fam* **to be full of beans** être plein d'énergie

bear¹ [beə(r)] *n (animal)* ours *m*; **b. cub** ourson *m*

bear² [beə(r)] **1** *(pt* bore, *pp* borne) *vt (carry, show)* porter; *(endure)* supporter; *(resemblance)* offrir; **I can't b. him/it** je ne peux pas le supporter/supporter ça; **to b. sth in mind** *(remember)* se souvenir de qch **2** *vi* **to b. left/right** *(turn)* tourner à gauche/droite; **to b. up** tenir le coup; **b. up!** courage!

bearable ['beərəbəl] *adj* supportable

beard [biəd] *n* barbe *f*; **to have a b.** porter la barbe

bearing ['beərɪŋ] *n (relevance)* rapport *m* (**on** avec); *(posture, conduct)* port *m*; *(of ship, aircraft)* position *f*; **to get one's bearings** s'orienter

beast [biːst] *n* bête *f*; *Fam (person)* brute *f*

beat [biːt] **1** *n (of heart, drum)* battement *m*; *(of policeman)* ronde *f*; *(in music)* rythme *m* **2** *(pt* beat, *pp* beaten [biːtən]) *vt* battre; *Fam* **it beats me** ça me dépasse; *Fam* **b. it!** fiche le camp!; **to b. sb to it** devancer qn; **to b. down** *or* **in** *(door)* défoncer; **to b. sb up** tabasser qn **3** *vi* battre; *(at door)* frapper (**at** à); *Fam* **to b. about** *or* **around the bush** tourner autour du pot ■ **beating** *n (blows, defeat)* raclée *f*; *(of heart, drums)* battement *m*

beater ['biːtə(r)] *n (whisk)* fouet *m*

beautician [bjuː'tɪʃən] *n* esthéticienne *f*

beautiful ['bjuːtɪfəl] *adj (très)* beau (*f* belle); *(superb)* merveilleux, -euse

beauty ['bjuːtɪ] *(pl* -ies) *n (quality, woman)* beauté *f*; **it's a b.!** *(car, house)* c'est une merveille!; **b. parlour** *or* **salon** institut *m* de beauté; **b. spot** *(on skin)* grain *m* de beauté; *Br (in countryside)* endroit *m* pittoresque

beaver ['biːvə(r)] **1** *n* castor *m* **2** *vi* **to b. away (at sth)** travailler dur (à qch)

became [bɪ'keɪm] *pt of* become

because [bɪ'kɒz] *conj* parce que; **b. of** à cause de

beckon ['bekən] *vt & vi* **to b. (to) sb (to do sth)** faire signe à qn (de faire qch)

become [bɪ'kʌm] *(pt* became, *pp* become) *vi* devenir; **to b. a painter** devenir peintre; **to b. thin** maigrir; **what has b. of her?** qu'est-elle devenue?

becoming [bɪ'kʌmɪŋ] *adj (clothes)* seyant; *(modesty)* bienséant

bed [bed] *n* lit *m*; *(flowerbed)* parterre *m*; *(of vegetables)* carré *m*; *(of sea)* fond *m*; *(of river)* lit *m*; *(of rock)* couche *f*; **to go to b.** (aller) se coucher; **to put sb to b.** coucher qn; **in b.** couché; **to get out of b.** se lever; **to make the b.** faire le lit; **b. and breakfast** *(in hotel)* chambre *f* avec petit déjeuner; **to stay in a b. and breakfast** ≃ prendre une chambre d'hôte; *Br* **b. settee** (canapé *m*) convertible *m* ■ **bedclothes** *npl,* **bedding** *n* couvertures *fpl* et draps *mpl* ■ **bedridden** *adj* alité ■ **bedroom** *n* chambre *f* à coucher ■ **bedside** *n* chevet *m*; **b. lamp/book/table** lampe *f*/livre *m*/table *f* de chevet ■ **bedsit, bedsitter** ['bedsɪtə(r)] *n Br* chambre *f* meublée ■ **bedspread** *n* dessus-de-lit *m inv* ■ **bedtime** *n* heure *f* du coucher; **b. story** histoire *f* *(pour endormir les enfants)*

bedraggled [bɪ'drægəld] *adj (clothes, person)* débraillé et tout trempé

bee [biː] *n* abeille *f* ■ **beehive** *n* ruche *f*

beech [biːtʃ] *n (tree, wood)* hêtre *m*

beef [biːf] *n* bœuf *m* ■ **beefburger** *n* hamburger *m*

been [biːn] *pp of* be

beer [bɪə(r)] *n* bière *f*; **b. glass** chope *f*

beet [biːt] *n Am* betterave *f*

beetle ['biːtəl] *n* scarabée *m*

beetroot ['biːtruːt] *n Br* betterave *f*

before [bɪ'fɔː(r)] **1** *adv* avant; *(already)* déjà; *(in front)* devant; **the month b.** le mois d'avant *ou* précédent; **the day b.** la veille; **I've seen it b.** je l'ai déjà vu; **I've never done it b.** je ne l'ai (encore) jamais fait

2 *prep* *(time)* avant; *(place)* devant; **the year b. last** il y a deux ans; **b. my very eyes** sous mes yeux

3 *conj* avant que (ne) (+ *subjunctive*), avant de (+ *infinitive*); **b. he goes** avant qu'il (ne) parte; **b. going** avant de partir

befriend [bɪ'frend] *vt* **to b. sb** se prendre d'amitié pour qn

beg [beg] **1** *(pt & pp* **-gg-)** *vt* **to b. (for)** *(favour, help)* demander; *(bread, money)* mendier; **to b. sb to do sth** supplier qn de faire qch **2** *vi (in street)* mendier; *(ask earnestly)* supplier

began [bɪ'gæn] *pt of* **begin**

beggar ['begə(r)] *n* mendiant, -e *mf*; *Br Fam (person)* type *m*; **lucky b.** veinard, -e *mf*

begin [bɪ'gɪn] **1** *(pt* **began**, *pp* **begun**, *pres p* **beginning)** *vt* commencer; *(fashion, campaign)* lancer; *(bottle, sandwich)* entamer; *(conversation)* engager; **to b. doing** *ou* **to do sth** commencer *ou* se mettre à faire qch; **he began laughing** il s'est mis à rire **2** *vi* commencer *(with par; by doing* par faire); **beginning from** à partir de; **to b. with** *(first of all)* d'abord ■ **beginner** *n* débutant, -e *mf* ■ **beginning** *n* commencement *m*, début *m*; **in** *ou* **at the b.** au commencement

begrudge [bɪ'grʌdʒ] *vt (envy)* envier *(sb sth* qch à qn); *(reproach)* reprocher *(sb sth* qch à qn); *(give unwillingly)* donner à contrecœur; **to b. doing sth** faire qch à contrecœur

begun [bɪ'gʌn] *pp of* **begin**

behalf [bɪ'hɑːf] *n* **on b. of sb**, **on sb's b.** *(representing)* au nom de qn, de la part de qn; *(in the interests of)* en faveur de qn

behave [bɪ'heɪv] *vi* se conduire; **to b. (oneself)** se tenir bien; *(of child)* être sage ■ **behaviour** *(Am* **behavior)** *n* conduite *f*, comportement *m*; **to be on one's best b.** se tenir particulièrement bien

behind [bɪ'haɪnd] **1** *prep* derrière; *(in terms of progress)* en retard sur **2** *adv*

derrière; *(late)* en retard; **to be b. with one's work** avoir du travail en retard **3** *n Fam (buttocks)* derrière *m*

beige [beɪʒ] *adj & n* beige *(m)*

Beijing [beɪ'dʒɪŋ] *n* Beijing *m ou f*

being ['biːɪŋ] *n (person, soul)* être *m*; **to come into b.** naître

belated [bɪ'leɪtɪd] *adj* tardif, -ive

belch [beltʃ] **1** *n* renvoi *m* **2** *vi (of person)* roter **3** *vt* **to b. (out)** *(smoke)* vomir

Belgium ['beldʒəm] *n* la Belgique ■ **Belgian 1** *adj* belge **2** *n* Belge *mf*

belief [bɪ'liːf] *n (believing, thing believed)* croyance *f* (**in sb** en qn; **in sth** à *ou* en qch); *(trust)* confiance *f*, foi *f* (**in** en); *(religious faith)* foi *f*

believe [bɪ'liːv] **1** *vt* croire; **I don't b. it** c'est pas possible; **I b. I'm right** je crois avoir raison, je crois que j'ai raison **2** *vi* croire *(in sth* à qch); **to believe in God** croire en Dieu; **I b. so/not** je crois que oui/que non; **to b. in doing sth** croire qu'il faut faire qch ■ **believable** *adj* crédible ■ **believer** *n (religious)* croyant, -e *mf*; **to be a b. in sth** croire à qch

belittle [bɪ'lɪtəl] *vt* dénigrer

bell [bel] *n (large) (of church)* cloche *f*; *(small)* clochette *f*; *(in phone, mechanism, alarm)* sonnerie *f*; *(on door, bicycle)* sonnette *f* ■ **b. tower** clocher *m* ■ **bellboy**, **bellhop** *n Am* groom *m*

bellow ['beləʊ] *vi* beugler, mugir

belly ['belɪ] *(pl* **-ies)** *n* ventre *m*; *Fam* **b. button** nombril *m*; **b. dancing** danse *f* du ventre

belong [bɪ'lɒŋ] *vi* appartenir *(to* à); **to b. to a club** être membre d'un club; **that book belongs to me** ce livre m'appartient *ou* est à moi; **the cup belongs here** cette tasse se range ici ■ **belongings** *npl* affaires *fpl*

beloved [bɪ'lʌvɪd] *adj & n Literary* bien-aimé, -e *(mf)*

below [bɪ'ləʊ] **1** *prep (lower than)* audessous de; *(under)* sous; *(with numbers)* moins de; *Fig (unworthy of)* indigne de **2** *adv* en dessous; *(in text* ci-dessous; **on the floor b.** à l'étage du dessous; **it's 10 degrees b.** il fait moins 10

belt [belt] **1** n ceinture f; (in machine) courroie f; (area) zone f, région f **2** vi **to b. up** (fasten seat belt) attacher sa ceinture; Br Fam **b. up!** (shut up) boucle-la! **3** vt Fam (hit) (ball) cogner dans; (person) flanquer un gnon à

bemused [br'mju:zd] adj perplexe

bench [bentʃ] n (seat) banc m; (work table) établi m; Law **the B.** (magistrates) la magistrature (assise); (court) le tribunal; Sport **to be on the b.** être remplaçant, -e

bend [bend] **1** n courbe f; (in river, pipe) coude m; (in road) virage m; Fam **round the b.** (mad) cinglé **2** (pt & pp bent) vt courber; (leg, arm) plier; **to b. one's head** baisser la tête; **to b. the rules** faire une entorse au règlement **3** vi (of branch) plier; (of road) tourner; (of river) faire un coude; **to b. (down)** (stoop) se courber; **to b. (over or forward)** se pencher

beneath [br'ni:θ] **1** prep sous; (unworthy of) indigne de **2** adv (au-)dessous

benefactor ['benɪfæktə(r)] n bienfaiteur m ■ **benefactress** n bienfaitrice f

beneficial [benɪ'fɪʃəl] adj bénéfique

benefit ['benɪfɪt] **1** n (advantage) avantage m; (money) allocation f; **benefits** (of science, education) bienfaits mpl; **to sb's b.** dans l'intérêt de qn; **for your (own) b.** pour vous, pour votre bien; **to be of b. (to sb)** faire du bien (à qn); **b. concert** concert m de bienfaisance **2** vt faire du bien à; (be useful to) profiter à **3** vi **to b. from doing sth** gagner à faire qch

Benelux ['benɪlʌks] n Benelux m

benevolent [br'nevələnt] adj bienveillant

benign [br'naɪn] adj (kind) bienveillant; (climate) doux (f douce); **b. tumour** tumeur f bénigne

bent [bent] **1** adj (nail, mind) tordu; Fam (dishonest) pourri; **b. on doing**

sth résolu à faire qch **2** n (talent) aptitude f (**for** pour); (inclination, liking) penchant m, goût m (**for** pour) **3** pt & pp of bend

bequeath [br'kwi:ð] vt Formal léguer (**to** à)

bereaved [br'ri:vd] **1** adj endeuillé **2** npl **the b.** la famille du défunt/de la défunte ■ **bereavement** n deuil m

beret [Br 'bereɪ, Am bə'reɪ] n béret m

Berlin [bɜ:'lɪn] n Berlin m or f

Bermuda [bə'mju:də] n les Bermudes fpl

berry ['berɪ] (pl -ies) n baie f

berserk [bə'zɜ:k] adj **to go b.** devenir fou furieux (f folle furieuse)

berth [bɜ:θ] **1** n (**a**) (in ship, train) couchette f (**b**) (anchorage) poste m à quai; Fig **to give sb a wide b.** éviter qn comme la peste **2** vi (of ship) aborder à quai

beset [br'set] (pt & pp beset, pres p besetting) vt assaillir

beside [br'saɪd] prep à côté de; **that's b. the point** ça n'a rien à voir

besides [br'saɪdz] **1** prep (in addition to) en plus de; (except) excepté; **there are ten of us b. Paul** nous sommes dix sans compter Paul; **what else can you do b. singing?** que savez-vous faire à part chanter? **2** adv (in addition) en plus; (moreover) d'ailleurs

besiege [br'si:dʒ] vt (of soldiers, crowd) assiéger; Fig (annoy) assaillir (**with** de)

besought [br'sɔ:t] pt & pp of beseech

best [best] **1** adj meilleur; **my b. dress** ma plus belle robe; **the b. part of** (most) la plus grande partie de; **the b. thing is to accept** le mieux c'est d'accepter; **'b. before…'** (on product) 'à consommer avant…'; **b. man** (at wedding) témoin m

2 n **the b. (one)** le meilleur, la meilleure; **it's for the b.** c'est pour le mieux; **at b.** au mieux; **to do one's b.** faire de son mieux; **to look one's b., to be at one's b.** être à son avantage; **to the b. of my knowledge** autant que je sache; **to make the b. of** sth *(accept)* s'accommoder de qch; **to get the b. out of** sth tirer le meilleur parti de qch; **in one's Sunday b.** endimanché; **all the b.!** *(when leaving)* prends bien soin de toi!; *(good luck)* bonne chance!; *(in letter)* amicalement

3 *adv* **(the) b.** *(play, sing)* le mieux; **to like** sb/sth **(the) b.** aimer qn/qch le plus; **I think it b. to wait** je juge prudent d'attendre ■ **best-seller** *n (book)* best-seller *m*

bet [bet] **1** *n* pari *m* **2** *(pt & pp* **bet** *or* **betted,** *pres p* **betting)** *vti* parier **(on** sur; **that** que); *Fam* **you b.!** tu parles! ■ **betting** *n* paris *mpl*; *Br* **b. shop** ≃ PMU *m*

betray [bɪ'treɪ] *vt (person, secret)* trahir ■ **betrayal** *n (disloyalty)* trahison *f*; *(disclosure) (of secret)* révélation *f*

better ['betə(r)] **1** *adj* meilleur **(than** que); **I need a b. car** j'ai besoin d'une meilleure voiture; **that's b.** c'est mieux; **she's (much) b.** *(in health)* elle va *(beaucoup)* mieux; **to get b.** *(recover)* se remettre; *(improve)* s'améliorer; **it's b. to go** il vaut mieux partir; **the b. part of** *(most)* la plus grande partie de

2 *adv* mieux **(than** que); **b. dressed/known/**etc mieux habillé/connu/etc; **to look b.** *(of ill person)* avoir meilleure mine; **b. and b.** de mieux en mieux; **so much the b., all the b.** tant mieux **(for** pour); **I'd b. go** il vaut mieux que je parte; **to be b. off** *(financially)* être plus à l'aise

3 *n* **to get the b. of** sb l'emporter sur qn; **to change for the b.** *(of person)* changer en bien; *(of situation)* s'améliorer; **one's betters** ses supérieurs *mpl*

4 *vt (improve)* améliorer; *(do better than)* dépasser; **to b. oneself** améliorer sa condition; **to b. sb's results/**etc dépasser les résultats/etc de qn

between [bɪ'twiːn] **1** *prep* entre; **in b.** entre **2** *adv* **in b.** *(space)* au milieu; *(time)* dans l'intervalle

beware [bɪ'weə(r)] *vi* se méfier **(of** de); **b.!** attention!; **'b. of the dog!'** 'attention, chien méchant!'

bewilder [bɪ'wɪldə(r)] *vt* dérouter, laisser perplexe

beyond [bɪ'jɒnd] **1** *prep* **(a)** *(further than)* au-delà de; **b. reach/doubt** hors de portée/de doute; **b. belief** incroyable; **b. my/our/**etc **means** au-dessus de mes/nos/etc moyens; **it's b. me** ça me dépasse **(b)** *(except)* sauf **2** *adv (further)* au-delà

bias ['baɪəs] **1** *n* **(a)** *(inclination)* penchant *m* **(towards** pour); *(prejudice)* préjugé *m*, parti pris *m* **(towards/ against** en faveur de/contre) **(b)** *(fabric)* coupé dans le biais; **to cut on the b.** couper dans le biais **2** *(pt & pp* **-ss-** *or* **-s-)** *vt* influencer **(towards/against** en faveur de/contre) ■ **bias(s)ed** *adj* partial; **to be b. against** avoir des préjugés contre

bib [bɪb] *n (for baby)* bavoir *m*

bible ['baɪbəl] *n* bible *f*; **the B.** la Bible ■ **biblical** *adj* biblique

bibliography [bɪblɪ'ɒgrəfɪ] *(pl* **-ies)** *n* bibliographie *f*

biceps ['baɪseps] *n inv (muscle)* biceps *m*

bicker ['bɪkə(r)] *vi* se chamailler

bicycle ['baɪsɪkəl] *n* bicyclette *f*; **by b.** à bicyclette

bid¹ [bɪd] **1** *n* **(a)** *(offer)* offre *f*; *(at auction)* enchère *f* **(for** pour) **(b)** *(attempt)* tentative *f* **2** *(pt & pp* **bid,** *pres p* **bidding)** *vt (sum of money)* offrir; *(at auction)* faire une enchère de **3** *vi* faire une offre **(for** pour); *(at auction)* faire une enchère **(for** sur) ■ **bidder** *n (at auction)* enchérisseur, -euse *mf*; **to the highest b.** au plus offrant

bid² [bɪd] *(pt* **bade,** *pp* **bidden** ['bɪdən] *or* **bid,** *pres p* **bidding)** *vt Literary (command)* commander **(sb to do** à qn de faire); *(say, wish)* dire, souhaiter

bide [baɪd] *vt* **to b. one's time** attendre le bon moment

big [bɪg] **(bigger, biggest)** *adj (tall, large)* grand; *(fat)* gros *(f* grosse); *(drop, increase)* fort; **to get big(ger)**

(taller) grandir; *(fatter)* grossir; **my b. brother** mon grand frère; *Fam* **b. mouth** grande gueule f; **b. toe** gros orteil m ■ **bighead** n *Fam* crâneur, -euse mf ■ **bigshot, bigwig** n *Fam* gros bonnet m

bigot ['bɪɡət] n sectaire mf; *(religious)* bigot, -e m f ■ **bigoted** adj sectaire; *(religious)* bigot

bike [baɪk] n *Fam* vélo m; *(motorbike)* moto f

bikini [bɪ'ki:nɪ] n Bikini® m; **b. briefs** mini-slip m

bilberry ['bɪlbərɪ] *(pl -ies)* n myrtille f

bilingual [baɪ'lɪŋɡwəl] adj bilingue

bill[1] [bɪl] 1 n **(a)** *(invoice)* facture f; *(in restaurant)* addition f; *(in hotel)* note f **(b)** *Am (banknote)* billet m **(c)** *(bank draft)* effet m **(d)** *(notice)* affiche f **(e)** *Pol* projet m de loi; **B. of Rights** = les dix premiers amendements de la Constitution américaine
2 vt **(a)** **to b. sb** envoyer la facture à qn **(b)** *(publicize)* annoncer ■ **billboard** n panneau m d'affichage

bill[2] [bɪl] n *(of bird)* bec m

billiards ['bɪljədz] n billard m

billion ['bɪljən] n milliard m ■ **billionaire** n milliardaire mf

billow ['bɪləʊ] 1 n *(of smoke)* volute f 2 vi *(of smoke)* tourbillonner; *(of sea)* se soulever; *(of sail)* se gonfler

bimonthly [baɪ'mʌnθlɪ] adj *(every two weeks)* bimensuel, -elle; *(every two months)* bimestriel, -elle

bin [bɪn] 1 n *(for rubbish)* poubelle f 2 *(pt & pp -nn-)* vt *Fam* mettre à la poubelle

binary ['baɪnərɪ] adj binaire

bind [baɪnd] 1 *(pt & pp bound)* vt *(fasten)* attacher; *(book)* relier; *(fabric, hem)* border; *(unite)* lier; **to b. sb hand and foot** ligoter qn; **to be bound by sth** être lié par qch 2 n *Fam (bore)* plaie f ■ **binding 1** n *(of book)* reliure f 2 adj *(contract)* qui lie; **to be b. on sb** *(legally)* lier qn

binder ['baɪndə(r)] n *(for papers)* classeur m

binge [bɪndʒ] n *Fam* **to go on a b.** *(drinking)* faire la bringue; *(eating)* se gaver

bingo ['bɪŋɡəʊ] n ≃ loto m

binoculars [bɪ'nɒkjʊləz] npl jumelles fpl

biochemistry [baɪəʊ'kemɪstrɪ] n biochimie f

biodegradable [baɪəʊdɪ'ɡreɪdəbəl] adj biodégradable

biography [baɪ'ɒɡrəfɪ] *(pl -ies)* n biographie f

biology [baɪ'ɒlədʒɪ] n biologie f ■ **biological** adj biologique; **b. warfare** guerre f bactériologique

bird [bɜːd] n **(a)** *(animal)* oiseau m; *(fowl)* volaille f; **b. of prey** oiseau m de proie; **b.'s-eye view** perspective f à vol d'oiseau; *Fig* vue f d'ensemble **(b)** *Br Fam (girl)* nana f ■ **birdseed** n graines fpl pour oiseaux

birth [bɜːθ] n naissance f; **to give b. to** donner naissance à; **from b.** *(blind, deaf)* de naissance; **b. certificate** acte m de naissance; **b. control** limitation f des naissances; **b. rate** (taux m de) natalité f ■ **birthday** n anniversaire m; **happy b.!** joyeux anniversaire!; **b. party** fête f d'anniversaire; *Fig* **in one's b. suit** *(man)* en costume d'Adam; *(woman)* en costume d'Ève ■ **birthmark** n tache f de naissance ■ **birthplace** n lieu m de naissance; *(house)* maison f natale

biscuit ['bɪskɪt] n *Br* biscuit m, petit gâteau m; *Am* petit pain m au lait

bishop ['bɪʃəp] n évêque m; *(in chess)* fou m

bit[1] [bɪt] n **(a)** *(of string, time)* bout m; **a b.** *(a little)* un peu; **not a b.** pas du tout; **a b. of luck** une chance; **b. by b.** petit à petit; **in bits (and pieces)** en morceaux **(b)** *(coin)* pièce f **(c)** *(of horse)* mors m **(d)** *(of drill)* mèche f **(e)** *Comptr* bit m

bit[2] [bɪt] pt of **bite**

bitch [bɪtʃ] 1 n *(dog)* chienne f; *very Fam Pej (woman)* garce f 2 vi *Fam (complain)* râler (**about** après)

bite [baɪt] **1** n (**a**) (wound) morsure f; (from insect) piqûre f; Fishing touche f (**b**) (mouthful) bouchée f; **to have a b. to eat** manger un morceau **2** (pt **bit**, pp **bitten** ['bɪtən]) vt mordre; (of insect) piquer; **to b. one's nails** se ronger les ongles; **to b. sth off** arracher qch d'un coup de dents **3** vi mordre; (of insect) piquer; **to b. into sth** mordre dans qch ■ **biting** adj (cold) mordant; (wind) cinglant

bitter ['bɪtə(r)] **1** n Br (beer) = bière anglaise brune **2** adj (person, taste, irony) amer, -ère; (cold, wind) glacial; (criticism) acerbe; (shock, fate) cruel (f cruelle); (conflict) violent; **to feel b. (about sth)** être plein d'amertume (à cause de qch) ■ **bitterly** adv **to cry/regret b.** pleurer/regretter amèrement; **b. disappointed** cruellement déçu; **it's b. cold** il fait un froid de canard ■ **bittersweet** adj doux-amer (f douce-amère); Am **b. chocolate** chocolat m noir

bizarre [bɪ'zɑː(r)] adj bizarre

blab [blæb] (pt & pp **-bb-**) vi jaser

black [blæk] **1** (**-er, -est**) adj noir; **b. eye** œil m au beurre noir; **b. and blue** (bruised) couvert de bleus; Aviat **b. box** boîte f noire; Br **b. ice** verglas m; Br **b. pudding** boudin m noir; Fig **b. sheep** brebis f galeuse **2** n (colour) noir m; (person) Noir, -e mf ■ **blackberry** (pl **-ies**) n mûre f ■ **blackbird** n merle m (noir) ■ **blackboard** n tableau m (noir) ■ **blackcurrant** n cassis m ■ **blacken** vt & vi noircir ■ **blacklist** n liste f noire **2** vt mettre sur la liste noire ■ **blackmail** n chantage m **2** vt faire chanter; **to b. sb into doing sth** faire chanter qn pour qu'il/elle fasse qch ■ **blackout** n panne f d'électricité; (during war) black-out m inv; (fainting fit) évanouissement m; (**news**) **b.** black-out m inv ■ **blacksmith** n forgeron m; (working with horses) maréchal-ferrant m

▶ **black out** vi (faint) s'évanouir

bladder ['blædə(r)] n vessie f

blade [bleɪd] n lame f; **b. of grass** brin m d'herbe

blame [bleɪm] **1** n responsabilité f; (criticism) blâme m; **to lay the b. (for sth) on sb** faire porter à qn la responsabilité (de qch); **to take the b.** endosser la responsabilité de qch **2** vt rendre responsable, faire porter la responsabilité à (**for** de); **to b. sb for doing sth** reprocher à qn d'avoir fait qch; **you're to b.** c'est de ta faute ■ **blameless** adj irréprochable

blanch [blɑːntʃ] **1** vt (vegetables) blanchir **2** vi (turn pale) blêmir

bland [blænd] (**-er, -est**) adj (person) terne; (food) insipide; (remark, joke) quelconque

blank [blæŋk] **1** adj (paper, page) blanc (f blanche), vierge; (cheque) en blanc; (look, mind) vide; **b. tape** cassette f vierge **2** n (space) blanc m; (cartridge) cartouche f à blanc; **to fire blanks** tirer à blanc; **my mind's a b.** j'ai un trou

blanket ['blæŋkɪt] **1** n (on bed) couverture f; (of snow, leaves) couche f **2** adj (term, remark) général

blankly ['blæŋklɪ] adv **to look b. at sb/sth** (without expression) regarder qn/qch, le visage inexpressif; (without understanding) regarder qn/qch sans comprendre

blare [bleə(r)] **1** n (noise) beuglements mpl; (of trumpet) sonnerie f **2** vi **to b. (out)** (of radio) beugler; (of music, car horn) retentir

blasé ['blɑːzeɪ] adj blasé

blasphemous ['blæsfəməs] adj (text) blasphématoire; (person) blasphémateur, -trice

blast [blɑːst] **1** n explosion f; (air from explosion) souffle m; (of wind) rafale f; (of trumpet) sonnerie f; (**at**) **full b.** (loud) à fond **2** vt (hole, tunnel) creuser (en dynamitant); Fam (criticize) démolir **3** exclam Br Fam zut! ■ **blasted** adj Br Fam fichu ■ **blast-off** n (of spacecraft) mise f à feu

blatant ['bleɪtənt] adj (obvious) flagrant; (shameless) éhonté

blaze [bleɪz] **1** *n (fire)* feu *m; (large)* incendie *m; Fig (splendour)* éclat *m;* **a b. of colour** une explosion de couleurs; **b. of light** torrent *m* de lumière **2** *vi (of fire, sun)* flamboyer; *(of light, eyes)* être éclatant **3** *vt Fig* **to b. a trail** ouvrir la voie ■ **blazing** *adj (burning)* en feu; *(sun)* brûlant; *Fig (argument)* violent

blazer ['bleɪzə(r)] *n* blazer *m*

bleach [bliːtʃ] **1** *n (household)* (eau *f* de) Javel *f; (for hair)* décolorant *m* **2** *vt (clothes)* passer à l'eau de Javel; *(hair)* décolorer

bleak [bliːk] *(-er, -est) adj (appearance, countryside, weather)* morne; *(outlook)* lugubre; *(prospect)* peu encourageant

bleat [bliːt] *vi* bêler

bleed [bliːd] *(pt & pp bled [bled])* **1** *vi* saigner; **to b. to death** saigner à mort; **her nose is bleeding** elle saigne du nez **2** *vt (radiator)* purger

bleep [bliːp] **1** *n* bip *m* **2** *vt* appeler au bip **3** *vi* faire bip ■ **bleeper** *n (pager)* bip *m*

blemish ['blemɪʃ] **1** *n (fault)* défaut *m; (mark)* marque *f* **2** *vt Fig (reputation)* entacher

blend [blend] **1** *n* mélange *m* **2** *vt* mélanger *(with à ou avec)* **3** *vi* se mélanger; *(of styles, colours)* se marier *(with avec)* ■ **blender** *n* mixer *m*

bless [bles] *vt* bénir; **to be blessed with sth** être doté de qch; **b. you!** *(when sneezing)* à vos souhaits! ■ **blessed** *adj* (a) *(holy)* béni (b) *Fam (blasted)* fichu ■ **blessing** *n Rel* bénédiction *f; (benefit)* bienfait *m;* **it was a b. in disguise** finalement, ça a été une bonne chose

blew [bluː] *pt of* **blow²**

blind¹ [blaɪnd] **1** *adj* aveugle; **b. person** aveugle *mf;* **b. in one eye** borgne; *Fig* **to be b. to sth** ne pas voir qch; **b. alley** impasse *f;* **b. date** = rencontre arrangée avec quelqu'un qu'on ne connaît pas **2** *npl* **the b.** les aveugles *mpl* **3** *adv* **b. drunk** ivre mort **4** *vt*

(dazzle, make blind) aveugler

blind² [blaɪnd] *n Br (on window)* store *m*

blindfold ['blaɪndfəʊld] **1** *n* bandeau *m* **2** *vt* bander les yeux à **3** *adv* les yeux bandés

blindly ['blaɪndlɪ] *adv Fig* aveuglément

blink [blɪŋk] **1** *n* clignement *m; Br Fam* **on the b.** *(machine)* détraqué **2** *vt* **to b. one's eyes** cligner des yeux **3** *vi (of person)* cligner des yeux; *(of eyes)* cligner; *(of light)* clignoter

blissful ['blɪsfəl] *adj (wonderful)* merveilleux, -euse; *(very happy) (person)* aux anges ■ **blissfully** *adv (happy)* merveilleusement; **to be b. unaware that…** ne pas se douter le moins du monde que…

blister ['blɪstə(r)] **1** *n (on skin)* ampoule *f* **2** *vi* se couvrir d'ampoules

blitz [blɪts] **1** *n (air attack)* raid *m* éclair; *(bombing)* bombardement *m* aérien; *Fam (onslaught)* offensive *f* **2** *vt* bombarder

blizzard ['blɪzəd] *n* tempête *f* de neige

bloated ['bləʊtɪd] *adj (swollen)* gonflé

blob [blɒb] *n (of ink, colour)* tache *f*

block [blɒk] *n (of stone)* bloc *m; (of buildings)* pâté *m* de maisons; *(in pipe)* obstruction *f;* **b. of flats** immeuble *m; Am* **a b. away** une rue plus loin; **b. booking** réservation *f* de groupe; **b. capitals** *or* **letters** majuscules *fpl* **2** *vt (obstruct)* bloquer; *(pipe)* boucher; *(view)* cacher; **to b. up** *(pipe, hole)* boucher ■ **blockage** *n* obstruction *f* ■ **blockbuster** *n (film)* film *m* à grand spectacle

bloke [bləʊk] *n Br Fam* type *m*

blond [blɒnd] *adj & n* blond (*m*)

blonde [blɒnd] *adj & n* blonde (*f*)

blood [blʌd] *n* sang *m;* **b. bank** banque *f* du sang; **b. bath** bain *m* de sang; **b. donor** donneur, -euse *mf* de sang; **b. group** groupe *m* sanguin; **b. poisoning** empoisonnement *m* du sang; **b. pressure** tension *f* artérielle; **high b. pressure** hypertension *f;* **to**

have high b. **pressure** avoir de la tension; *Am* b. **sausage** boudin *m*; b. **test** prise *f* de sang ■ **bloodshed** *n* effusion *f* de sang ■ **bloodshot** *adj* (*eye*) injecté de sang ■ **bloodstream** *n* sang *m* ■ **bloodthirsty** *adj* sanguinaire

bloody ['blʌdɪ] **1** (-ier, -iest) *adj* (a) (*covered in blood*) ensanglanté (b) *Br very Fam* foutu; a b. **liar** un sale menteur; **you b. fool!** espèce de connard! **2** *adv Br Fam* (*very*) vachement; **it's b. hot!** il fait une putain de chaleur! ■ **bloody-minded** *adj* pas commode

bloom [blu:m] **1** *n* fleur *f*; in b. (*tree*) en fleur(s); (*flower*) éclos **2** *vi* (*of tree, flower*) fleurir; *Fig* (*of person*) s'épanouir ■ **blooming** *adj* (a) (*in bloom*) en fleur(s); (*person*) resplendissant; (*thriving*) florissant (b) *Br Fam* (*for emphasis*) sacré; **you b. idiot!** espèce d'idiot!

blossom ['blɒsəm] **1** *n* fleurs *fpl* **2** *vi* fleurir; to b. (**out**) *(of person)* s'épanouir

blot [blɒt] **1** *n* tache *f* **2** (*pt & pp* -tt-) *vt* (*stain*) tacher; (*dry*) sécher; to b. **sth out** (*obliterate*) effacer qch ■ **blotting paper** *n* (papier *m*) buvard *m*

blotch [blɒtʃ] *n* tache *f* ■ **blotchy** (-ier, -iest) *adj* couvert de taches; (*face, skin*) marbré

blouse [blaʊz] *n* chemisier *m*

blow[1] [bləʊ] *n* (*hit, setback*) coup *m*; to **come to blows** en venir aux mains

blow[2] [bləʊ] **1** (*pt* blew, *pp* blown) *vt* (*of wind*) pousser; (*of person*) (*smoke, glass*) souffler; (*bubbles*) faire; (*trumpet*) souffler dans; (*kiss*) envoyer (to à); *Br Fam* (*money*) claquer (**on sth** pour s'acheter qch); to b. a **fuse** faire sauter un plomb; to b. **one's nose** se moucher; to b. a **whistle** donner un coup de sifflet **2** *vi* (*of wind, person*) souffler; (*of fuse*) sauter; (*of papers*) (*in wind*) s'éparpiller

▸ **blow away 1** *vt sep* (*of wind*) emporter **2** *vi* (*of hat, paper*) s'envoler

▸ **blow down 1** *vt sep* (*chimney, fence*) faire tomber **2** *vi* (*fall*) tomber

▸ **blow off** *vt sep* (*hat*) emporter; (*arm*) arracher

▸ **blow out 1** *vt sep* (*candle*) souffler; (*cheeks*) gonfler **2** *vi* (*of light*) s'éteindre

▸ **blow over 1** *vt sep & vi* = **blow down 2** *vi* (*of quarrel*) se tasser

▸ **blow up 1** *vt sep* (*building*) faire sauter; (*pump up*) gonfler; (*photo*) agrandir **2** *vi* (*explode*) exploser

blow-dry ['bləʊdraɪ] **1** *n* brushing® *m* **2** *vt* to b. **sb's hair** faire un brushing® à qn

blown [bləʊn] *pp of* **blow**

blowout ['bləʊaʊt] *n* (a) (*tyre*) éclatement *m* (b) *Br Fam* (*meal*) gueuleton *m*

blowtorch ['bləʊtɔːtʃ] *n* chalumeau *m*

bludgeon ['blʌdʒən] **1** *n* gourdin *m* **2** *vt* matraquer

blue [blu:] **1** (-er, -est) *adj* bleu; *Fam* to **feel b.** avoir le cafard; *Fam* b. **movie** film *m* porno **2** *n* bleu *m*; **blues** (*music*) le blues; *Fam* **the blues** (*depression*) le cafard; **out of the b.** (*unexpectedly*) sans crier gare ■ **bluebell** *n* jacinthe *f* des bois ■ **blueberry** (*pl* -ies) *n* airelle *f* ■ **bluebottle** *n* mouche *f* de la viande ■ **blueprint** *n Fig* plan *m*

bluff [blʌf] **1** *n* bluff *m* **2** *vt & vi* bluffer

blunder ['blʌndə(r)] **1** *n* (*mistake*) gaffe *f* **2** *vi* faire une gaffe

blunt [blʌnt] **1** (-er, -est) *adj* (*edge*) émoussé; (*pencil*) mal taillé; (*question, statement*) direct; (*person*) brusque **2** *vt* (*blade*) émousser; (*pencil*) épointer

blur [blɜː(r)] **1** *n* tache *f* floue **2** (*pt & pp* -rr-) *vt* (*outline*) brouiller ■ **blurred** *adj* (*image, outline*) flou

blurb [blɜːb] *n* notice *f* publicitaire

blurt [blɜːt] *vt* to b. (**out**) (*secret*) laisser échapper; (*excuse*) bredouiller

blush [blʌʃ] **1** *n* rougeur *f* **2** *vi* rougir (**with** de)

blustery ['blʌstərɪ] *adj* (*weather*) de grand vent; (*wind*) violent

boar [bɔː(r)] *n* (**wild**) b. sanglier *m*

board¹ [bɔːd] **1** n (piece of wood) planche f; (for notices) panneau m; (for games) tableau m; (cardboard) carton m; **on b. (a ship/plane)** à bord (d'un navire/avion) **2** vt (ship, plane) monter à bord de; (bus, train) monter dans; **to b. up** (door) condamner **3** vi **flight Z001 is now boarding** vol Z001, embarquement immédiat ▪ **boarding** n (of passengers) embarquement m; **b. pass** carte f d'embarquement ▪ **boardwalk** n Am (on beach) promenade f

board² [bɔːd] n (committee) conseil m; **b. (of directors)** conseil m d'administration; **b. (of examiners)** jury m (d'examen); **across the b.** (pay increase) global; (apply) globalement; **b. room** salle f du conseil

board³ [bɔːd] **1** n (food) pension f; **b. and lodging**, Br **full b.** pension f complète; Br **half b.** demi-pension f **2** vi (lodge) être en pension (**with** chez); **boarding house** pension f de famille; **boarding school** pensionnat m ▪ **boarder** n pensionnaire mf

boast [bəʊst] **1** n vantardise f **2** vt se glorifier de **3** vi se vanter (**about** or **of** de) ▪ **boastful** adj vantard

boat [bəʊt] n bateau m; (small) canot m; (liner) paquebot m; **by b.** en bateau; Fig **in the same b.** logé à la même enseigne; **b. race** course f d'aviron

bode [bəʊd] vi **to b. well/ill (for)** être de bon/mauvais augure (pour)

bodily ['bɒdɪlɪ] **1** adj (need) physique **2** adv (lift, seize) à bras-le-corps; (carry) dans ses bras

body ['bɒdɪ] (pl -ies) n corps m; (of car) carrosserie f; (quantity) masse f; (institution) organisme m; (dead) **b.** cadavre m; **b. building** culturisme m; **b. warmer** gilet m matelassé ▪ **bodyguard** n garde du corps m ▪ **bodywork** n carrosserie f

bog [bɒg] **1** n (swamp) marécage m **2** vt **to get bogged down in** (mud, work) s'enliser (dans); (details) se perdre (dans)

bogus ['bəʊgəs] adj faux (f fausse)

boil¹ [bɔɪl] n (pimple) furoncle m

boil² [bɔɪl] **1** n **to come to the b.** bouillir; **to bring sth to the b.** amener qch à ébullition **2** vt **to b. (up)** faire bouillir; **to b. the kettle** mettre de l'eau à chauffer **3** vi bouillir; Fig **to b. down to** (of situation, question) revenir à; **to b. over** (of milk) déborder; Fig (of situation) empirer ▪ **boiled** adj bouilli; **b. egg** œuf m à la coque ▪ **boiling 1** n ébullition f; **to be at b. point** (of liquid) bouillir **2** adj **b. (hot)** bouillant; **it's b. (hot)** (weather) il fait une chaleur infernale

boiler ['bɔɪlə(r)] n chaudière f; Br **b. suit** bleus mpl de chauffe

boisterous ['bɔɪstərəs] adj (noisy) bruyant; (child) turbulent; (meeting) houleux, -euse

bold [bəʊld] (-er, -est) adj hardi

bolster ['bəʊlstə(r)] **1** n (pillow) traversin m **2** vt (confidence, pride) renforcer, consolider

bolt [bəʊlt] **1** n (a) (on door) verrou m; (for nut) boulon m (b) (dash) **to make a b. for the door** se précipiter vers la porte (c) **b. of lightning** éclair m **2** adv **b. upright** tout droit **3** vt (a) (door) verrouiller (b) (food) engloutir **4** vi (dash) se précipiter; (run away) détaler; (of horse) s'emballer

bomb [bɒm] **1** n bombe f; **b. scare** alerte f à la bombe **2** vt (from the air) bombarder; (of terrorist) faire sauter une bombe dans ou à ▪ **bombshell** n **to come as a b.** faire l'effet d'une bombe ▪ **bombsite** n zone f bombardée

bombard [bɒm'bɑːd] vt (with bombs, questions) bombarder (**with** de)

bona fide [bəʊnə'faɪdɪ] adj véritable

bond [bɒnd] **1** n (link) lien m; (agreement) engagement m; Fin obligation f **2** vt (of glue) coller (**to** à) **3** vi (form attachment) créer des liens affectifs (**with** avec)

bone [bəʊn] **1** n os m; (of fish) arête f; **b. china** porcelaine f tendre **2** vt (meat) désosser; (fish) ôter les arêtes de **3** vi

Fam **to b. up on** (*subject*) bûcher ■ **bone-dry** *adj* complètement sec (*f* sèche) ■ **bone-idle** *adj Br* paresseux, -euse

bonfire ['bɒnfaɪə(r)] *n* (*for celebration*) feu *m* de joie; *Br* (*for dead leaves*) feu *m* (de jardin)

bonkers ['bɒŋkəz] *adj Br Fam* dingue

bonnet ['bɒnɪt] *n* (*hat*) bonnet *m*; *Br* (*of vehicle*) capot *m*

bonus ['bəʊnəs] (*pl* -**uses** [-əsɪz]) *n* prime *f*; **no-claims b.** (*in motor insurance*) bonus *m*

boo [buː] **1** *exclam* (*to frighten*) hou! **2** *n* boos huées *fpl* **3** (*pt & pp* **booed**) *vt & vi* huer

boob [buːb] *Br Fam* **1** *n* (**a**) (*mistake*) gaffe *f* (**b**) **boobs** (*breasts*) nénés *mpl* **2** *vi* gaffer

booby-trap ['buːbɪtræp] **1** *n* engin *m* piégé **2** (*pt & pp* -**pp**-) *vt* piéger

book [bʊk] **1** *n* livre *m*; (*record*) registre *m*; (*of tickets*) carnet *m*; (*for exercises and notes*) cahier *m*; **books** (*accounts*) comptes *mpl*; **b. club** club *m* du livre
2 *vt* (*seat*) réserver; *Br* **to b. sb** (*for traffic offence*) dresser une contravention à qn; **fully booked** (*hotel*) complet, -ète; (*person*) pris
3 *vi* **to b. (up)** réserver des places; **to b. in** (*to hotel*) signer le registre; **to b. into a hotel** prendre une chambre dans un hôtel ■ **bookcase** *n* bibliothèque *f* ■ **bookend** *n* serre-livres *m inv* ■ **bookie** *n Fam* bookmaker *m* ■ **booking** *n* réservation *f*; **b. office** bureau *m* de location ■ **bookkeeping** *n* comptabilité *f* ■ **booklet** *n* brochure *f* ■ **bookmaker** *n* bookmaker *m* ■ **bookmark** *n* marque-page *m* ■ **bookseller** *n* libraire *mf* ■ **bookshelf** *n* étagère *f* ■ **bookshop** (*Am* **bookstore**) *n* librairie *f* ■ **bookstall** *n* kiosque *m* à journaux ■ **bookworm** *n* passionné, -ée *mf* de lecture

boom [buːm] **1** *n* (**a**) (*noise*) grondement *m* (**b**) (*economic*) boom *m* **2** *vi* (**a**) (*of thunder, gun*) gronder (**b**) (*of*

business, trade) être florissant

boor [bʊə(r)] *n* rustre *m*

boost [buːst] **1** *n* **to give sb a b.** remonter le moral à qn **2** *vt* (*increase*) augmenter; (*economy*) stimuler; **to b. sb's morale** remonter le moral à qn ■ **booster** *n* **b.** (**injection**) rappel *m*

boot[1] [buːt] **1** *n* (**a**) (*footwear*) botte *f*; (*ankle b.*) bottillon *m*; (*knee b.*) bottine *f*; *Fam* **to get the b.** être mis à la porte (**b**) *Br* (*of vehicle*) coffre *m* (**c**) **to b.** (*in addition*) en plus **2** *vt Fam* (*kick*) donner un coup/des coups de pied à; **to b. sb out** mettre qn à la porte

boot[2] [buːt] *Comptr* **1** *vt* amorcer **2** *vi* s'amorcer

booth [buːθ, buːð] *n* (*for phone, in language lab*) cabine *f*; (*at fair*) stand *m*; (*for voting*) isoloir *m*

booze [buːz] *Fam* **1** *n* alcool *m* **2** *vi* picoler ■ **boozer** *n Fam* (*person*) poivrot, -e *mf*; *Br* (*pub*) pub *m*

border ['bɔːdə(r)] **1** *n* (*of country*) *& Fig* frontière *f*; (*edge*) bord *m*; (*of garden*) bordure *f* **2** *adj* (*town*) frontière *inv* **3** *vt* (*street*) border; **to b. (on)** (*country*) avoir une frontière commune avec; (*resemble, verge on*) être voisin de

bore[1] [bɔː(r)] **1** *vt* (*weary*) ennuyer; **to be bored** s'ennuyer **2** *n* (*person*) raseur, -euse *mf*; **it's a b.** c'est ennuyeux *ou* rasoir ■ **boredom** *n* ennui *m* ■ **boring** *adj* ennuyeux, -euse

bore[2] [bɔː(r)] **1** *n* (*of gun*) calibre *m* **2** *vt* (*hole*) percer; (*rock, well*) forer, creuser **3** *vi* forer

bore[3] [bɔː(r)] *pt of* **bear**[2]

born [bɔːn] *adj* né; **to be b.** naître; **he was b. in Paris/in 1980** il est né à Paris/en 1980

borne [bɔːn] *pp of* **bear**[2]

borough ['bʌrə] *n* circonscription *f* électorale urbaine

borrow ['bɒrəʊ] *vt* emprunter (**from** à)

Bosnia ['bɒznɪə] *n* la Bosnie

bosom ['bʊzəm] *n* (*chest, breasts*) poitrine *f*; (*breast*) sein *m*; *Fig* (*heart, soul*) sein *m*

boss [bɒs] **1** n patron, -onne mf **2** vt to **b. sb around** or **about** donner des ordres à qn ■ **bossy** (**-ier, -iest**) adj Fam autoritaire

botany ['bɒtənɪ] n botanique f

botch [bɒtʃ] vt Fam to **b. (up)** (spoil) bâcler; (repair badly) rafistoler

both [bəʊθ] **1** adj les deux; **b. brothers** les deux frères

2 pron tous/toutes (les) deux; **b. of the boys** les deux garçons; **b. of us** tous les deux; **b. of them died** ils sont morts tous les deux

3 adv (at the same time) à la fois; **b. in England and in France** en Angleterre comme en France; **b. you and I know that…** vous et moi, nous savons que…

bother ['bɒðə(r)] **1** n (trouble) ennui m; (effort) peine f; (inconvenience) dérangement m **2** vt (annoy, worry) ennuyer; (disturb) déranger; (pester) importuner; (hurt, itch) (of foot, eye) gêner; to **b. doing** or to do sth se donner la peine de faire qch; **I can't be bothered** ça ne me dit rien **3** vi to **b. about** (worry about) se préoccuper de; (deal with) s'occuper de; **don't b.!** ce n'est pas la peine!

bottle ['bɒtəl] **1** n bouteille f; (for perfume) flacon m; (for baby) biberon m; **b. bank** conteneur m pour verre usagé; **b. opener** ouvre-bouteilles m inv **2** vt (milk, wine) mettre en bouteilles; to **b. up** (feeling) refouler ■ **bottle-feed** (pt & pp **-fed**) vt nourrir au biberon ■ **bottleneck** n (in road) goulot m d'étranglement; (in traffic) bouchon m

bottom ['bɒtəm] **1** n (of sea, box) fond m; (of page, hill) bas m; (of table) bout m; (buttocks) derrière m; to **be (at the) b. of the class** être le dernier/la dernière de la classe

2 adj (shelf) inférieur, du bas; **b. floor** rez-de-chaussée m; **b. gear** première vitesse f; **b. part** or **half** partie f inférieure; Fig the **b. line is that…** le fait est que… ■ **bottomless** adj (funds) inépuisable; **b. pit** gouffre m

bought [bɔːt] pt & pp of **buy**

boulder ['bəʊldə(r)] n rocher m

bounce [baʊns] **1** n rebond m **2** vt (ball) faire rebondir **3** vi (of ball) rebondir (**off** contre); (of person) faire des bonds; Fam (of cheque) être sans provision

bouncer ['baʊnsə(r)] n Fam (doorman) videur m

bound¹ [baʊnd] adj (**a**) **b. to do** (obliged) obligé de faire; (certain) sûr de faire; **it's b. to snow** il va sûrement neiger; to **be b. for** (of person, ship) être en route pour; (of train, plane) être à destination de (**b**) **b. up with** (connected) lié à

bound² [baʊnd] **1** n (leap) bond m **2** vi bondir

bound³ [baʊnd] pt & pp of **bind**

boundary ['baʊndərɪ] (pl **-ies**) n limite f

bounds [baʊndz] npl limites fpl; **out of b.** (place) interdit f

bouquet [bəʊ'keɪ] n (of flowers, wine) bouquet m

bout [baʊt] n (of fever, coughing, violence) accès m; (of asthma, malaria) crise f, (session) séance f; (period) période f; (in boxing) combat m; **a b. of flu** une grippe

boutique [buː'tiːk] n boutique f (de mode)

bow¹ [bəʊ] n (weapon) arc m; (of violin) archet m; (knot) nœud m; **b. tie** nœud m papillon ■ **bow-legged** adj aux jambes arquées

bow² [baʊ] **1** n (with knees bent) révérence f; (nod) salut m **2** vt to **b. one's head** incliner la tête **3** vi s'incliner (**to** devant); (nod) incliner la tête (**to** devant); to **b. down** (**to**) (submit) s'incliner (devant)

bow³ [baʊ] n (of ship) proue f

bowels ['baʊəlz] npl intestins mpl

bowl¹ [bəʊl] n (small dish) bol m; (for salad) saladier m; (for soup) assiette f creuse; (of toilet) cuvette f

bowl² [bəʊl] **1** n **bowls** (game) boules

box 40 **Brazil**

fpl **2** *vi* (*in cricket*) lancer la balle ▪ **bowling** *n* (*tenpin*) **b.** bowling *m*; **b. alley** bowling *m*; **b. ball** boule *f* de bowling; **b. green** terrain *m* de boules ▸ **bowl over** *vt sep* (*knock down*) renverser; *Fig* (*astound*) **to be bowled over by sth** être stupéfié par qch

box [bɒks] **1** *n* boîte *f*; (*larger*) caisse *f*; (*made of cardboard*) carton *m*; (*in theatre*) loge *f*; (*for horse, in stable*) box *m*; *Br Fam* (*television*) télé *f*; **b. office** bureau *m* de location; *Br* **b. room** (*for storage*) débarras *m*; (*bedroom*) petite chambre *f*
2 *vt* (**a**) **to b. (up)** mettre en boîte/caisse; **to b. in** (*enclose*) enfermer (**b**) **to b. sb's ears** gifler qn
3 *vi* boxer ▪ **boxing** *n* (**a**) (*sport*) boxe *f*; **b. gloves/match** gants *mpl*/combat *m* de boxe; **b. ring** ring *m* (**b**) *Br* **B. Day** le lendemain de Noël

boxer [ˈbɒksə(r)] *n* (*fighter*) boxeur *m*; (*dog*) boxer *m*

boy [bɔɪ] *n* garçon *m* ▪ **boyfriend** *n* petit ami *m*

boycott [ˈbɔɪkɒt] **1** *n* boycottage *m* **2** *vt* boycotter

bra [brɑː] *n* soutien-gorge *m*

brace [breɪs] **1** *n* (*dental*) appareil *m* dentaire; (*on leg, arm*) appareil *m* orthopédique; (*for fastening*) attache *f*; *Br* **braces** (*for trousers*) bretelles *fpl* **2** *vt* **to b. oneself for sth** (*news, shock*) se préparer à qch ▪ **bracing** *adj* (*air*) vivifiant

bracelet [ˈbreɪslɪt] *n* bracelet *m*

bracket [ˈbrækɪt] **1** *n* (*for shelves*) équerre *f*; (*in writing*) parenthèse *f*; (*group*) groupe *m*; (*for tax*) tranche *f*; **in brackets** entre parenthèses **2** *vt* mettre entre parenthèses

brag [bræg] (*pt & pp* **-gg-**) *vi* se vanter (**about** *or* **of sth** de qch; **about doing sth** de faire qch)

braid [breɪd] **1** *n* (*of hair*) tresse *f*; (*trimming*) galon *m* **2** *vt* (*hair*) tresser; (*trim*) galonner

Braille [breɪl] *n* braille *m*; **in B.** en braille

brain [breɪn] **1** *n* cerveau *m*; (*of animal, bird*) cervelle *f*; *Fam* **to have brains** être intelligent; *Fam* **to have sth on the b.** être obsédé par qch; **b. death** mort *f* cérébrale; **b. drain** fuite *f* des cerveaux **2** *vt Fam* (*hit*) assommer ▪ **brainchild** *n* trouvaille *f* ▪ **brainstorm** *n Am* (*brilliant idea*) idée *f* géniale; *Br* (*mental confusion*) aberration *f* ▪ **brainwash** *vt* faire un lavage de cerveau à ▪ **brainwave** *n* idée *f* géniale

brainy [ˈbreɪnɪ] (**-ier, -iest**) *adj Fam* intelligent

brake [breɪk] **1** *n* frein *m*; **b. light** stop *m* **2** *vi* freiner

bran [bræn] *n* son *m*

branch [brɑːntʃ] **1** *n* branche *f*; (*of road*) embranchement *m*; (*of river*) bras *m*; (*of shop*) succursale *f*; (*of bank*) agence *f*; **b. office** succursale *f* **2** *vi* **to b. off** (*of road*) bifurquer; **to b. out** (*of company, person*) étendre ses activités; (*of family, tree*) se ramifier

brand [brænd] **1** *n* (*on product, on cattle*) marque *f*; (*type*) type *m*, style *m*; **b. name** marque *f* **2** *vt* (*mark*) marquer; *Fig* **to be branded as a liar/coward** avoir une réputation de menteur/lâche

brandish [ˈbrændɪʃ] *vt* brandir

brand-new [brænd'njuː] *adj* tout neuf (*f* toute neuve)

brandy [ˈbrændɪ] (*pl* **-ies**) *n* cognac *m*; (*made with fruit*) eau-de-vie *f*

brash [bræʃ] *adj* exubérant

brass [brɑːs] *n* cuivre *m*; (*instruments in orchestra*) cuivres *mpl*; *Fam* **b. band** fanfare *f*

brat [bræt] *n Pej* (*child*) morveux, -euse *mf*; (*badly behaved*) sale gosse *mf*

brave [breɪv] (**-er, -est**) *adj* courageux, -euse **2** *n* (*native American*) brave *m* **3** *vt* (*danger*) braver ▪ **bravery** *n* courage *m*

brawl [brɔːl] **1** *n* (*fight*) bagarre *f* **2** *vi* se bagarrer

Brazil [brəˈzɪl] *n* le Brésil ▪ **Brazilian 1**

adj brésilien, -enne **2** *n* Brésilien, -enne *mf*

breach [bri:tʃ] **1** *n (of rule)* violation *f* (**of** de); **b. of contract** rupture *f* de contrat; **b. of trust** abus *m* de confiance **2** *vt (law, code)* enfreindre à; *(contract)* rompre

bread [bred] *n* pain *m*; *Fam (money)* blé *m*; **loaf of b.** pain *m*; **brown b.** pain *m* bis; **(slice** *or* **piece of) b. and butter** pain *m* beurré; **b. knife** couteau *m* à pain ■ **breadbin** *n* (*Am* **breadbox**) *n* boîte *f* à pain ■ **breadboard** *n* planche *f* à pain ■ **breadcrumb** *n* miette *f* de pain; **breadcrumbs** *(in cooking)* chapelure *f* ■ **breaded** *adj* pané ■ **breadline** *n* **on the b.** indigent ■ **breadwinner** *n* **to be the b.** faire bouillir la marmite

breadth [bretθ] *n* largeur *f*

break [breɪk] **1** *n* cassure *f*; *(in bone)* fracture *f*; *(with person, group)* rupture *f*; *(in journey)* interruption *f*; *(rest)* repos *m*; *(in activity)* pause *f*; *(at school)* récréation *f*; *(holidays)* vacances *fpl* **2** *(pt* **broke,** *pp* **broken)** *vt* casser; *(into pieces, with force)* briser; *(silence, spell, vow)* rompre; *(strike, will, ice)* briser; *(agreement, promise)* manquer à; *(law)* violer; *(record)* battre; *(journey)* interrompre; *(news)* annoncer (**to** à); *(habit)* se débarrasser de; **to b. one's arm** se casser le bras; **to b. sb's heart** briser le cœur à qn; *Fam* **to b. the sound barrier** franchir le mur du son; **to b. a fall** amortir une chute **3** *vi* se casser; *(into pieces, of heart, of voice)* se briser; *(of boy's voice)* muer; *(of spell)* se rompre; *(of weather)* changer; *(of news)* éclater; *(of day)* se lever; *(stop work)* faire la pause; **to b. in two** se casser en deux; **to b. free** se libérer; **to b. loose** se détacher ■ **breakable** *adj* fragile ■ **breakage** *n* **were there any breakages?** est-ce qu'il y a eu de la casse? ■ **breakdown** *n (of machine)* panne *f*; *(of argument, figures)* analyse *f*; *(of talks, negotiations)* échec *m*; *(of person)* dépression *f*; *Br*

▸ **break away 1** *vi* se détacher **2** *vt sep* détacher

▸ **break down 1** *vt sep (door)* enfoncer; *(resistance)* briser; *(argument, figures)* analyser **2** *vi (of machine)* tomber en panne; *(of talks, negotiations)* échouer; *(of person)* *(have nervous breakdown)* craquer; *(start crying)* éclater en sanglots

▸ **break in 1** *vi (of burglar)* entrer par effraction; *(interrupt)* interrompre **2** *vt sep (door)* enfoncer; *(horse)* dresser

▸ **break into** *vt insep (house)* entrer par effraction; *(safe)* forcer; **to b. into song/a run** se mettre à chanter/courir

▸ **break off 1** *vt sep (detach) (twig, handle)* détacher; *(relations)* rompre **2** *vi (become detached)* se casser; *(stop)* s'arrêter; **to b. off with sb** rompre avec qn

▸ **break out** *vi (of war, fire)* éclater; *(escape)* s'échapper (**of** de); **to b. out in a rash** se couvrir de boutons

▸ **break through 1** *vi (of sun, army)* percer **2** *vt insep (defences)* percer; *(barrier)* forcer; *(wall)* faire une brèche dans

▸ **break up 1** *vt sep (reduce to pieces)* mettre en morceaux; *(marriage)* briser; *(fight)* mettre fin à **2** *vi (end)* prendre fin; *(of group)* se disperser; *(of marriage)* se briser; *(from school)* partir en vacances

breakfast ['brekfəst] *n* petit déjeuner *m*; **to have b.** prendre le petit déjeuner; **b. TV** émissions *fpl* (télévisées) du matin

break-in ['breɪkɪn] *n* cambriolage *m*

breaking-point ['breɪkɪŋpɔɪnt] *n* **at b.** *(person, patience)* à bout; *(marriage)* au bord de la rupture

breakthrough ['breɪkθru:] *n (discovery)* découverte *f* fondamentale

breast [brest] *n (of woman)* sein *m*; *(chest)* poitrine *f*; *(of chicken)* blanc *m* ■ **breastfeed** *(pt & pp* **-fed)** *vt* allaiter ■ **breaststroke** *n (in swimming)* brasse *f*

breath [breθ] *n* souffle *m*; **bad b.** mauvaise haleine *f*; **out of b.** à bout de souffle; **to hold one's b.** retenir son souffle; **under one's b.** tout bas ■ **breathalyser**® *n* Alcotest® *m* ■ **breathless** *adj* hors d'haleine ■ **breathtaking** *adj* à couper le souffle

breathe [briːð] 1 *vi (of person, animal)* respirer; **to b. in** inhaler; **to b. out** expirer 2 *vt* respirer; **to b. a sigh of relief** pousser un soupir de soulagement ■ **breathing** *n* respiration *f*; *Fig* **b. space** moment *m* de repos

bred [bred] 1 *pt & pp of* **breed** 2 *adj* **well-b.** bien élevé

breed [briːd] 1 *n* race *f* 2 *(pt & pp* **bred)** *vt (animals)* élever; *Fig (hatred, violence)* engendrer 3 *vi (of animals)* se reproduire ■ **breeding** *n (of animals)* élevage *m*; *Fig (manners)* éducation *f*

breeze [briːz] *n* brise *f* ■ **breezy** *(-ier, -iest) adj (a) (weather, day)* frais *(f* fraîche), venteux, -euse *f* (b) *(cheerful)* jovial; *(relaxed)* décontracté

brew [bruː] 1 *n (drink)* breuvage *m*; *(of tea)* infusion *f* 2 *vt (beer)* brasser; *Fig (trouble, plot)* préparer 3 *vi (of beer)* fermenter; *(of tea)* infuser; *Fig (of storm)* se préparer ■ **brewery** *(pl* -ies) *n* brasserie *f*

bribe [braɪb] 1 *n* pot-de-vin *m* 2 *vt* acheter, soudoyer; **to b. sb into doing sth** soudoyer qn pour qu'il fasse qch ■ **bribery** *n* corruption *f*

brick [brɪk] *n* brique *f*; **b. wall** mur en briques ■ **bricklayer** *n* maçon *m*

bridal [ˈbraɪdəl] *adj (ceremony, bed)* nuptial; **b. suite** *(in hotel)* suite *f* nuptiale

bride [braɪd] *n* mariée *f*; **the b. and groom** les mariés *mpl* ■ **bridegroom** *n* marié *m* ■ **bridesmaid** *n* demoiselle *f* d'honneur

bridge[1] [brɪdʒ] 1 *n* pont *m*; *(on ship)* passerelle *f*; *(of nose)* arête *f*; *(on teeth)* bridge *m* 2 *vt* **to b. a gap** combler une lacune

bridge[2] [brɪdʒ] *n (game)* bridge *m*

brief[1] [briːf] *(-er, -est) adj* bref *(f*

brève); **in b.** en résumé ■ **briefly** *adv (say)* brièvement; *(hesitate, smile)* un court instant

brief[2] [briːf] 1 *n (instructions)* instructions *fpl*; *(legal)* dossier *m*; *Fig (task)* tâche *f* 2 *vt* donner des instructions à; *(inform)* mettre au courant (**on** de) ■ **briefing** *n (information)* instructions *fpl*; *(meeting)* briefing *m*

briefcase [ˈbriːfkeɪs] *n* serviette *f*

briefs [briːfs] *npl (underwear)* slip *m*

brigade [brɪˈɡeɪd] *n* brigade *f*

bright [braɪt] 1 *(-er, -est) adj (star, eyes, situation)* brillant; *(light, colour)* vif *(f* vive); *(weather, room)* clair; *(clever)* intelligent; *(happy)* joyeux, -euse; *(future)* prometteur, -euse; *(idea)* génial 2 *adv* **b. and early** de bon matin ■ **brightly** *adv (shine)* avec éclat

brighten [ˈbraɪtən] 1 *vt* **to b. (up)** *(room)* égayer 2 *vi* **to b. (up)** *(of weather)* s'éclaircir; *(of face)* s'éclairer; *(of person)* s'égayer

brilliant [ˈbrɪljənt] *adj (light)* éclatant; *(person, idea, career)* brillant; *Br Fam (fantastic)* super *inv*

brim [brɪm] 1 *n (of hat, cup)* bord *m* 2 *(pt & pp* **-mm-**) *vi* **to b. over (with)** déborder (de)

bring [brɪŋ] *(pt & pp* **brought)** *vt (person, animal, car)* amener; *(object)* apporter; *(cause)* provoquer; **it has brought me great happiness** cela m'a procuré un grand bonheur; **to b. sth to sb's attention** attirer l'attention de qn sur qch; **to b. sth to an end** mettre fin à qch

▸ **bring about** *vt sep* provoquer

▸ **bring along** *vt sep (object)* apporter; *(person)* amener

▸ **bring back** *vt sep (person)* ramener; *(object)* rapporter; *(memories)* rappeler

▸ **bring down** *vt sep (object)* descendre; *(overthrow)* faire tomber; *(reduce)* réduire; *(shoot down) (plane)* abattre

▸ **bring forward** *vt sep (in time or space)* avancer; *(witness)* produire

▸ **bring in** *vt sep (object)* rentrer;

(person) faire entrer; *(introduce)* introduire; *(income)* rapporter
▶ **bring off** *vt sep (task)* mener à bien
▶ **bring out** *vt sep (object)* sortir; *(person)* faire sortir; *(meaning)* faire ressortir; *(book)* publier; *(product)* lancer
▶ **bring round** *vt sep (revive)* ranimer; *(convert)* convaincre; **she brought him round to her point of view** elle a su le convaincre
▶ **bring to** *vt sep* **to b. sb to** ranimer qn
▶ **bring together** *vt sep (friends, members)* réunir; *(reconcile)* réconcilier; *(put in touch)* mettre en contact
▶ **bring up** *vt sep (object)* monter; *(child)* élever; *(question)* soulever; *(subject)* mentionner; *(food)* rendre
brink [brɪŋk] *n* bord *m*; **on the b. of sth** au bord de qch
brisk [brɪsk] *(-er, -est) adj (lively)* vif *(f* vive*)*; **at a b. pace** vite; **business is b.** les affaires marchent bien
bristle ['brɪsəl] **1** *n* poil *m* **2** *vi* se hérisser
Britain ['brɪtən] *n* la Grande-Bretagne ■ **British 1** *adj* britannique; **the B. Isles** les îles *fpl* Britanniques; **B. Summer Time** heure *f* d'été *(en Grande-Bretagne)* **2** *npl* **the B.** les Britanniques *mpl* ■ **Briton** *n* Britannique *mf*
Brittany ['brɪtənɪ] *n* la Bretagne
brittle ['brɪtəl] *adj* cassant
broad [brɔːd] *(-er, -est) adj (wide)* large; *(accent)* prononcé; **in b. daylight** en plein jour; **the b. outline of** *(plan)* les grandes lignes *de*; **b. bean** fève *f*; *Am Sport* **b. jump** saut *m* en longueur ■ **broad-minded** *adj (person)* à l'esprit large ■ **broad-shouldered** *adj* large d'épaules ■ **broaden 1** *vt* élargir **2** *vi* s'élargir ■ **broadly** *adv* **b. (speaking)** en gros
broadcast ['brɔːdkɑːst] **1** *n* émission *f* **2** *(pt & pp* **broadcast)** *vt* diffuser **3** *vi (of station)* émettre; *(of person)* parler à la radio/à la télévision
broccoli ['brɒkəlɪ] *n inv (plant)* brocoli *m*; *(food)* brocolis *mpl*

brochure ['brəʊʃə(r)] *n* brochure *f*
broil [brɔɪl] *vt & vi Am* griller
broke [brəʊk] **1** *pt of* **break 2** *adj Fam (penniless)* fauché ■ **broken 1** *pp of* **break 2** *adj (man, voice, line)* brisé; *(ground)* accidenté; *(spirit)* abattu; **in b. English** en mauvais anglais; **b. home** famille *f* désunie
broker ['brəʊkə(r)] *n (for shares, currency)* agent *m* de change; *(for goods, insurance)* courtier, -ère *mf*
bronchitis [brɒŋ'kaɪtɪs] *n* bronchite *f*
bronze [brɒnz] *n* bronze *m*; **b. statue** statue *f* en bronze
brooch [brəʊtʃ] *n (ornament)* broche *f*
brood [bruːd] **1** *n* couvée *f* **2** *vi (of bird)* couver; *Fig* **to b. over sth** *(of person)* ruminer qch ■ **broody** *(-ier, -iest) adj (person) (sulky)* maussade; *(dreamy)* rêveur, -euse; *Br Fam (woman)* en mal d'enfant
broom [bruːm] *n* **(a)** *(for sweeping)* balai *m* **(b)** *(plant)* genêt *m*
broth [brɒθ] *n (thin)* bouillon *m*; *(thick)* potage *m*
brothel ['brɒθəl] *n* maison *f* close
brother ['brʌðə(r)] *n* frère *m* ■ **brother-in-law** *(pl* **brothers-in-law)** *n* beau-frère *m*
brought [brɔːt] *pt & pp of* **bring**
brow [braʊ] *n* **(a)** *(forehead)* front *m* **(b)** *(of hill)* sommet *m*
brown [braʊn] **1** *(-er, -est) adj* marron *inv*; *(hair)* châtain; *(tanned)* bronzé **2** *n* marron *m* **3** *vt (food)* faire dorer **4** *vi (of food)* dorer
Brownie ['braʊnɪ] *n (girl scout)* ≃ jeannette *f*
brownie ['braʊnɪ] *n (cake)* brownie *m*
browse [braʊz] **1** *vt Comptr* **to b. the Web** naviguer sur le Web **2** *vi (in bookshop)* feuilleter des livres; *(in shop, supermarket)* regarder; **to b. through** *(book)* feuilleter
bruise [bruːz] **1** *n* bleu *m*; *(on fruit)* meurtrissure *f* **2** *vt* **to b. one's knee/ hand** se faire un bleu au genou/à la main ■ **bruised** *adj (covered in bruises)* couvert de bleus

brunch [brʌntʃ] *n* brunch *m*

brunette [bruːˈnet] *n* brunette *f*

brunt [brʌnt] *n* **to bear the b. of** *(attack, anger)* subir le plus gros de; *(expense)* assumer la plus grosse part de

brush [brʌʃ] **1** *n* *(tool)* brosse *f*; *(for shaving)* blaireau *m*; *(for sweeping)* balayette *f*; **to give sth a b.** donner un coup de brosse à qch
2 *vt* *(teeth, hair)* brosser; *(clothes)* donner un coup de brosse à; **to b. sb/sth aside** écarter qn/qch; **to b. sth away** *or* **off** enlever qch; **to b. up (on) one's French** se remettre au français **3** *vi* **to b. against sb/sth** effleurer qn/qch ▪ **brush-off** *n Fam* **to give sb the b.** envoyer promener qn

brusque [bruːsk] *adj* brusque

Brussels [ˈbrʌsəlz] *n* Bruxelles *m ou f*; **B. sprouts** choux *mpl* de Bruxelles

brutal [ˈbruːtəl] *adj* brutal; *(attack)* sauvage

brute [bruːt] **1** *n* *(animal)* bête *f*; *(person)* brute *f* **2** *adj* **by b. force** par la force

BSc [biːesˈsiː] *(Am* **BS** [biːˈes]*) (abbr* **Bachelor of Science)** *(person)* ≃ licencié, -e *mf* ès sciences; *(qualification)* ≃ licence *f* de sciences

BSE [biːesˈiː] *(abbr* **bovine spongiform encephalopathy)** *n* EBS *f*, maladie *f* de la vache folle

bubble [ˈbʌbəl] **1** *n* *(of air, soap)* bulle *f*; **b. bath** bain *m* moussant; **b. gum** chewing-gum *m* **2** *vi* *(of liquid)* bouillonner; **to b. over (with)** déborder (de)

bubbly [ˈbʌblɪ] **1** *adj* *(liquid)* plein de bulles; *(person, personality)* débordant de vitalité **2** *n Fam* champ *m*

buck [bʌk] **1** *n* **(a)** *Am Fam* dollar *m* **(b)** *(of rabbit)* mâle *m* **2** *vt Fam* **to b. sb up** remonter le moral à qn **3** *vi Fam* **to b. up** *(become livelier)* reprendre du poil de la bête; *(hurry)* se grouiller

bucket [ˈbʌkɪt] *n* seau *m*

buckle [ˈbʌkəl] **1** *n* boucle *f* **2** *vt* **(a)** *(fasten)* boucler **(b)** *(deform)* déformer **3** *vi* *(deform)* se déformer

bud [bʌd] **1** *n* *(on tree)* bourgeon *m*; *(on flower)* bouton *m* **2** *(pt & pp -dd-)* *vi* bourgeonner; *(of flower)* pousser des boutons ▪ **budding** *adj* *(talent)* naissant; *(doctor)* en herbe

Buddhist [ˈbʊdɪst] *adj & n* bouddhiste *(mf)*

buddy [ˈbʌdɪ] *(pl -ies)* *n Am Fam* pote *m*

budge [bʌdʒ] **1** *vi* bouger **2** *vt* faire bouger

budgerigar [ˈbʌdʒərɪgɑː(r)] *n Br* perruche *f*

budget [ˈbʌdʒɪt] **1** *n* budget *m* **2** *vi* dresser un budget; **to b. for sth** inscrire qch au budget

budgie [ˈbʌdʒɪ] *n Br Fam* perruche *f*

buff [bʌf] **1** *adj* **b.(-coloured)** chamois *inv* **2** *n Fam* **jazz/film b.** fanatique *mf* de jazz/de cinéma

buffalo [ˈbʌfələʊ] *(pl -oes or -o)* *n* buffle *m*; **(American) b.** bison *m*

buffer [ˈbʌfə(r)] *n* *(on train)* tampon *m*; *(at end of track)* butoir *m*; *Fig* **(safeguard)** protection *f* **(against** contre)

buffet[1] [ˈbʊfeɪ] *n* *(meal, café)* buffet *m*; **cold b.** viandes *fpl* froides; *Br* **b. car** *(on train)* wagon-restaurant *m*

buffet[2] [ˈbʌfɪt] *vt* *(of waves)* secouer; *(of wind, rain)* cingler

bug[1] [bʌg] **1** *n* **(a)** *(insect)* bestiole *f*; *(bedbug)* punaise *f*; *Fam (germ)* microbe *m* **(b)** *(in machine)* défaut *m*; *Comptr* bogue *m* **(c)** *(listening device)* micro *m* **2** *(pt & pp -gg-)* *vt (room)* installer des micros dans

bug[2] [bʌg] *(pt & pp -gg-)* *vt Fam (nag)* embêter

buggy [ˈbʌgɪ] *(pl -ies)* *n Br* **(baby) b.** *(pushchair)* poussette *f*; *Am (pram)* landau *m*

build [bɪld] **1** *n* *(of person)* carrure *f* **2** *(pt & pp* **built** [bɪlt]*) vt* construire; **to b. sth up** *(increase)* augmenter qch; *(business)* monter qch **3** *vi* **to b. up** *(of tension, pressure)* augmenter; *(of dust, snow, interest)* s'accumuler; *(of traffic)* devenir dense ▪ **builder** *n* *(skilled)* maçon *m*; *(unskilled)* ouvrier *m*; *(contractor)* entrepreneur *m* ▪ **building**

bâtiment *m*; *(flats, offices)* immeuble *m*; *(action)* construction *f*; **b. site** chantier *m*; *Br* **b. society** ≃ société *f* de crédit immobilier ▪ **build-up** *n (increase)* augmentation *f*; *(of dust)* accumulation *f*; *(for author, book)* publicité *f*

built-in [bɪlt'ɪn] *adj (cupboard)* encastré; *(part of machine)* incorporé; *Fig (innate)* inné

built-up [bɪlt'ʌp] *adj* urbanisé; **b. area** agglomération *f*

bulb [bʌlb] *n (of plant)* bulbe *m*; *(of lamp)* ampoule *f*

bulge [bʌldʒ] **1** *n* renflement *f* **2** *vi* to **b. (out)** bomber; *(of eyes)* sortir de la tête ▪ **bulging** *adj* bombé; *(eyes)* protubérant; *(bag, pocket)* to be **b. (with)** être bourré de

bulimia [bʊ'lɪmɪə] *n* boulimie *f*

bulk [bʌlk] *n inv (of building, parcel)* volume *m*; *(of person)* grosseur *f*; the **b. of sth** la majeure partie de qch; in **b.** *(buy, sell)* en gros ▪ **bulky (-ier, -iest)** *adj* volumineux, -euse

bull [bʊl] *n* **(a)** *(animal)* taureau *m* **(b)** *very Fam (nonsense)* conneries *fpl* ▪ **bullfight** *n* corrida *f*

bulldozer [ˈbʊldəʊzə(r)] *n* bulldozer *m*

bullet [ˈbʊlɪt] *n* balle *f* ▪ **bulletproof** *adj (car)* blindé; **b. glass** vitre *f* blindée; *Br* **b. jacket,** *Am* **b. vest** gilet *m* pare-balles *inv*

bulletin [ˈbʊlətɪn] *n* bulletin *m*; *Am* **b. board** panneau *m* d'affichage

bullion [ˈbʊljən] *n* **gold b.** lingots *mpl* d'or

bull's-eye [ˈbʊlzaɪ] *n (of target)* centre *m*; **to hit the b.** mettre dans le mille

bully [ˈbʊlɪ] **1** *(pl -ies)* *n* terreur *f* **2** *(pt & pp -ied)* *vt (ill-treat)* maltraiter

bum [bʌm] *Fam* **1** *n* **(a)** *(loafer)* clochard, -e *mf*; *(good-for-nothing)* bon *m* à rien, bonne *f* à rien **(b)** *Br (buttocks)* derrière *m*; **b. bag** banane *f* **2** *(pt & pp -mm-)* *vi* to **b. (around)** *(be idle)* glander; *(travel)* vadrouiller **3** *vt*

to b. sth off sb taxer qch à qn

bump [bʌmp] **1** *n (impact)* choc *m*; *(jerk)* secousse *f*; *(on road, body)* bosse *f* **2** *vt (of car)* heurter; **to b. one's head/knee** se cogner la tête/le genou; **to b. into** *(of person)* se cogner contre; *(of car)* rentrer dans; *(meet)* tomber sur ▪ **bumper 1** *n (of car)* pare-chocs *m inv* **2** *adj (crop, year)* exceptionnel, -elle

bumpy [ˈbʌmpɪ] **(-ier, -iest)** *adj (road, ride)* cahoteux, -euse

bun [bʌn] *n* **(a)** *(cake)* petit pain *m* au lait **(b)** *(of hair)* chignon *m*

bunch [bʌntʃ] *n (of flowers)* bouquet *m*; *(of keys)* trousseau *m*; *(of bananas)* régime *m*; *(of grapes)* grappe *f*; *(of people)* bande *f*

bundle [ˈbʌndəl] **1** *n* paquet *m*; *(of papers)* liasse *f*; *(of firewood)* fagot *m* **2** *vt (put)* fourrer **(into** dans); *(push)* pousser **(into** dans); **to b. up** *(newspapers, letters)* mettre en paquet **3** *vi* to **b. (oneself) up** *(bien)* se couvrir

bungalow [ˈbʌŋɡələʊ] *n* pavillon *m* de plain-pied

bungle [ˈbʌŋɡəl] **1** *vt* gâcher **2** *vi* se tromper

bunk [bʌŋk] *n (in ship, train)* couchette *f*; **b. beds** lits *mpl* superposés

bunker [ˈbʌŋkə(r)] *n Mil & Golf* bunker *m*; *(for coal)* coffre *m* à charbon

bunny [ˈbʌnɪ] *(pl -ies)* *n Fam* **b. (rabbit)** petit lapin *m*

buoy [bɔɪ] *n* bouée *f* **2** *vt Fig* to **b. up** *(support)* soutenir

buoyant [ˈbɔɪənt] *adj (in water)* qui flotte; *Fig (economy, prices)* stable; *Fig (person, mood)* plein d'allant

burden [ˈbɜːdən] **1** *n* fardeau *m* **2** *vt* charger **(with** de); *Fig* accabler **(with** de)

bureau [ˈbjʊərəʊ] *(pl -eaux* [-əʊz]*)* *n (office)* bureau *m*; *Br (desk)* secrétaire *m*; *Am (chest of drawers)* commode *f*

bureaucracy [bjʊəˈrɒkrəsɪ] *n* bureaucratie *f* ▪ **bureaucrat** *n* bureaucrate *mf*

burger [ˈbɜːɡə(r)] *n* hamburger *m*

burglar ['bɜːglə(r)] n cambrioleur, -euse mf; **b. alarm** alarme f antivol ■ **burglarize** or Am **cambrioler** ■ **burgle** vt Br cambrioler

burial ['berɪəl] **1** n enterrement m **2** adj (service) funèbre; **b. ground** cimetière m

burn [bɜːn] **1** n brûlure f **2** (pt & pp **burned** or **burnt**) vt brûler; **to b. sth down** incendier qch **3** vi brûler; **to b. down** (of house) être détruit par les flammes; (of fuse) sauter ■ **burning 1** adj en feu; (fire) allumé; Fig (fever) dévorant **2** n **a smell of b.** une odeur de brûlé

burner ['bɜːnə(r)] n (on stove) brûleur m; Fig **to put sth on the back b.** remettre qch à plus tard

burp [bɜːp] Fam **1** n rot m **2** vi roter

burrow ['bʌrəʊ] **1** n (hole) terrier m **2** vt & vi creuser

burst [bɜːst] **1** n (of shell) éclatement m, explosion f; (of laughter) éclat m; (of applause) salve f; (of thunder) coup m; (surge) élan m

2 (pt & pp **burst**) vt (bubble, balloon, boil) crever; (tyre) faire éclater; **to b. open** (door) ouvrir brusquement

3 vi (of bubble, balloon, boil, tyre, cloud) crever; (with force) (of shell, boiler, tyre) éclater; **to b. into a room** faire irruption dans une pièce; **to b. into flames** prendre feu; **to b. into tears** fondre en larmes; **to b. out laughing** éclater de rire; **to b. open** (of door) s'ouvrir brusquement

bury ['berɪ] (pt & pp **-ied**) vt (body) enterrer; (hide) enfouir; (plunge) plonger (**in** dans); **buried in one's work** plongé dans son travail

bus [bʌs] (pl **buses** or **busses**) n autobus m, bus m; (long-distance) autocar m, car m; **by b.** en bus/en car; **b. driver** chauffeur m de bus/car; **b. shelter** Abribus® m; **b. station** gare f routière; **b. stop** arrêt m de bus

bush [bʊʃ] n buisson m; **the b.** (land) la brousse ■ **bushy** (**-ier, -iest**) adj (hair, tail) touffu

bushed [bʊʃt] adj Fam (tired) crevé

business ['bɪznɪs] **1** n affaires fpl, commerce m; (shop) commerce m; (company, task, concern, matter) affaire f; **the textile/construction b.** l'industrie f du textile/de la construction; **big b.** les grosses entreprises fpl; **to go out of b.** (stop trading) fermer; **that's none of your b.!, mind your own b.!** ça ne vous regarde pas!

2 adj commercial; (meeting, trip, lunch) d'affaires; **b. card** carte f de visite; **b. hours** (office) heures fpl de bureau; (shop) heures fpl d'ouverture; **b. school** école f de commerce ■ **businessman** (pl **-men**) n homme m d'affaires ■ **businesswoman** (pl **-women**) n femme f d'affaires

bust [bʌst] **1** n (statue) buste m; (of woman) poitrine f **2** adj Fam (broken) fichu; **to go b.** (bankrupt) faire faillite **3** (pt & pp **bust** or **busted**) vt Fam (break) bousiller; (arrest) coffrer ■ **bust-up** n Fam (quarrel) engueulade f; (breakup) rupture f

bustle ['bʌsəl] **1** n animation f **2** vi **to b. (about)** s'affairer

busy ['bɪzɪ] **1** (**-ier, -iest**) adj occupé; (active) actif, -ive; (day) chargé; (street) animé; Am (phone, line) occupé; **to be b. doing** (in the process of) être occupé à faire; **to keep oneself b.** s'occuper; **the shops were very b.** il y avait plein de monde dans les magasins; Am **b. signal** sonnerie f occupé **2** vt **to b. oneself** s'occuper (**with** sth à qch; **doing** sth à faire qch) ■ **busybody** (pl **-ies**) n Fam fouineur, -euse mf

but [bʌt, unstressed bət] **1** conj mais **2** prep (except) sauf; **b. for him** sans lui; **no one b. you** personne d'autre que toi; **the last b. one** l'avant-dernier, -ère mf

butcher ['bʊtʃə(r)] **1** n boucher m; **b.'s (shop)** boucherie f **2** vt (people) massacrer; (animal) abattre

butler ['bʌtlə(r)] n maître m d'hôtel

butt [bʌt] **1** n (of cigarette) mégot m; (of

gun) crosse *f*; *Am Fam (buttocks)* derrière *m* **2** *vt (with head)* donner un coup de tête à **3** *vi* **to b. in** intervenir

butter ['bʌtə(r)] **1** *n* beurre *m*; *Br* **b. bean** = gros haricot blanc; **b. dish** beurrier *m* **2** *vt* beurrer; *Fam* **to b. sb up** passer de la pommade à qn ■ **butterscotch** *n* caramel *m* dur au beurre

butterfly ['bʌtəflaɪ] *(pl* **-ies)** *n* papillon *m*; *Fam* **to have butterflies** avoir l'estomac noué; **b. stroke** *(in swimming)* brasse *f* papillon

buttock ['bʌtək] *n* fesse *f*

button ['bʌtən] **1** *n* bouton *m*; *(of phone)* touche *f*; *Am (badge)* badge *m* **2** *vt* **to b. (up)** boutonner **3** *vi* **to b. (up)** *(of garment)* se boutonner ■ **buttonhole 1** *n* boutonnière *f* **2** *vt Fam (person)* coincer

buy [baɪ] **1** *n* **a good b.** une bonne affaire **2** *(pt & pp* **bought)** *vt* (**a**) *(purchase)* acheter (**from sb** à qn; **for sb** à ou pour qn) (**b**) *Am Fam (believe)* avaler; **I'll b. that!** je veux bien le croire! ■ **buyer** *n* acheteur, -euse *mf*

buzz [bʌz] **1** *n* (**a**) *(noise)* bourdonnement *m* (**b**) *Fam (phone call)* **to give sb a b.** passer un coup de fil à qn **2** *vt* **to b. sb** *(using buzzer)* appeler qn **3** *vi* bourdonner; *Fam* **to b. off** se tirer ■ **buzzer** *n* *(internal phone)* Interphone® *m*; *(of bell, clock)* sonnerie *f*

BY [baɪ] **1** *prep* (**a**) *(agent)* par; de; **hit/chosen by** frappé/choisi par; **surrounded/followed by** entouré/suivi de; **a book/painting by...** un livre/tableau de...

(**b**) *(manner, means)* par; en; à; de; **by**

sea par mer; **by mistake** par erreur; **by car/train** en voiture/train; **by bicycle** à bicyclette; **by moonlight** au clair de lune; **by doing** en faisant; **one by one** un à un; **day by day** de jour en jour; **by sight/day** de vue/jour; **(all) by oneself** tout seul

(**c**) *(next to)* à côté de; *(near)* près de; **by the lake/sea** au bord du lac/de la mer; **to go** *or* **pass by the bank/school** passer devant la banque/l'école

(**d**) *(before in time)* avant; **by Monday** avant lundi, d'ici lundi; **by now** à cette heure-ci; **by yesterday** (dès) hier

(**e**) *(amount, measurement)* à; **by the kilo** au kilo; **taller by a metre** plus grand d'un mètre; **paid by the hour** payé à l'heure

(**f**) *(according to)* à, d'après; **by my watch** à ma montre; **it's fine** *or* **OK** *or* **all right by me** je n'y vois pas d'objection

2 *adv* **close by** tout près; **to go** *or* **pass by** passer; **by and large** en gros

bye(-bye) ['baɪ('baɪ)] *exclam Fam* salut!, au revoir!

by-law ['baɪlɔː] *n* arrêté *m* (municipal)

bypass ['baɪpɑːs] **1** *n* rocade *f*; **(heart) b. operation** pontage *m* **2** *vt (town)* contourner; *Fig (ignore)* court-circuiter

bystander ['baɪstændə(r)] *n* passant, -e *mf*

byte [baɪt] *n* Comptr octet *m*

Cc

C, c¹ [siː] *n* C, c *m inv*

c² (*abbr* **cent(s)**) ct

cab [kæb] *n* taxi *m*; (*of lorry*) cabine *f*

cabaret ['kæbəreɪ] *n* cabaret *m*

cabbage ['kæbɪdʒ] *n* chou *m* (*pl* choux)

cabin ['kæbɪn] *n* (*on ship*) cabine *f*; (*hut*) cabane *f*; *Aviat* **c. crew** équipage *m*

cabinet¹ ['kæbɪnɪt] *n* (*cupboard*) armoire *f*; (*for display*) vitrine *f*; (**filing**) **c.** classeur *m* (*meuble*)

cabinet² ['kæbɪnɪt] *n* (*government ministers*) gouvernement *m*; **c. minister** ministre *m*

cable ['keɪbəl] **1** *n* câble *m*; **c. car** (*with overhead cable*) téléphérique *m*; **c. television** la télévision par câble **2** *vt* (*message*) câbler (**to** à)

cactus ['kæktəs] (*pl* **-ti** [-taɪ] *or* **-tuses** [-təsɪz]) *n* cactus *m*

caddie ['kædɪ] *n* Golf caddie *m*

cadet [kə'det] *n* élève *m* officier

cadge [kædʒ] *vt Fam* **to c. money from** *or* **off sb** taper qn

café ['kæfeɪ] *n* café *m*

caffeine ['kæfiːn] *n* caféine *f*

cage [keɪdʒ] **1** *n* cage *f* **2** *vt* **to c. (up)** mettre en cage

cajole [kə'dʒəʊl] *vt* enjôler

cake [keɪk] *n* gâteau *m*; (*small*) pâtisserie *f*

calamity [kə'læmɪtɪ] (*pl* **-ies**) *n* calamité *f*

calculate ['kælkjʊleɪt] *vti* calculer; **to c. that...** (*estimate*) calculer que... ▪ **calculated** *adj* (*deliberate*) délibéré; **a c. risk** un risque calculé ▪ **calculation** [-'leɪʃən] *n* calcul *m* ▪ **calculator** *n* calculatrice *f*

calendar ['kælɪndə(r)] *n* calendrier *m*; *Am* (*for engagements*) agenda *m*; **c. month** mois *m* civil

calf [kɑːf] (*pl* **calves**) *n* (**a**) (*animal*) veau *m* (**b**) (*part of leg*) mollet *m*

calibre ['kælɪbə(r)] (*Am* **caliber**) *n* calibre *m*

call [kɔːl] **1** *n* (*shout*) cri *m*; (*visit*) visite *f*; (*telephone*) **c.** appel *m* (*téléphonique*); **to make a c.** téléphoner (**to** à); **to give sb a c.** téléphoner à qn; *Br* **c. box** cabine *f* téléphonique; **c. centre** centre *m* d'appels

2 *vt* (*phone*) appeler; (*shout to*) crier; **he's called David** il s'appelle David; **to c. sb a liar** traiter qn de menteur

3 *vi* appeler; (*cry out*) crier; (*visit*) passer

▸ **call back 1** *vt sep* rappeler **2** *vi* rappeler

▸ **call by** *vi* (*visit*) passer

▸ **call for** *vt insep* (*require*) demander; (*collect*) passer prendre

▸ **call in 1** *vt sep* (*into room*) faire entrer; (*police*) appeler **2** *vi* **to c. in** (**on sb**) (*visit*) passer (chez qn)

▸ **call off** *vt sep* (*cancel*) annuler; (*strike*) mettre fin à

▸ **call on** *vt insep* (*visit*) passer voir; **to c. on sb to do** (*urge*) sommer qn de faire

▸ **call out 1** *vt sep* (*shout*) crier; (*doctor*) appeler; (*workers*) donner une consigne de grève à **2** *vi* (*shout*) crier; **to c. out to sb** interpeller qn

▸ **call round** *vi* (*visit*) passer

▶**call up** *vt sep* (*phone*) appeler; *Mil* (*recruits*) appeler (sous les drapeaux)

caller ['kɔːlə(r)] *n* visiteur, -euse *mf*; (*on phone*) correspondant, -e *mf*

callous ['kæləs] *adj* (*cruel*) insensible

calm [kɑːm] **1** (-**er**, -**est**) *adj* calme, tranquille; **keep c.!** restez calme! **2** *n* calme *m* **3** *vt* to **c.** (**down**) calmer **4** *vi* to **c. down** se calmer ▪ **calmly** *adv* calmement

calorie ['kælərɪ] *n* calorie *f*

calves [kɑːvz] *pl of* **calf**

camcorder ['kæmkɔːdə(r)] *n* camé-scope® *m*

came [keɪm] *pt of* **come**

camel ['kæməl] *n* chameau *m*

camera ['kæmrə] *n* appareil photo *m*; (*for film, video*) caméra *f*

camouflage ['kæməflɑːʒ] **1** *n* camouflage *m* **2** *vt also Fig* camoufler

camp¹ [kæmp] **1** *n* camp *m*, campement *m*; **c. bed** lit *m* de camp **2** *vi* to **c.** (**out**) camper ▪ **camper** *n* (*person*) campeur, -euse *mf*; (*vehicle*) camping-car *m* ▪ **camping** *n* camping *m*; **c. site** (terrain *m* de) camping *m* ▪ **campsite** *n* camping *m*

camp² [kæmp] *adj* (*effeminate*) efféminé

campaign [kæm'peɪn] **1** *n* (*political, military*) campagne *f*; **press/publicity c.** campagne *f* de presse/publicité **2** *vi* faire campagne (**for/against** pour/contre) ▪ **campaigner** *n* militant, -e *mf* (**for** pour)

campus ['kæmpəs] *n* (*of university*) campus *m*

CAN¹ [kæn, *unstressed* kən] (*pt* could)

Le verbe **can** n'a ni infinitif, ni géron-dif, ni participe. Pour exprimer l'infi-nitif ou le participe, on aura recours à la forme correspondante de **be able to** (he wanted to be able to speak English; she has always been able to swim). La forme négative est **can't**, qui s'écrit **cannot** dans la lan-gue soutenue.

v aux (*be able to*) pouvoir; (*know how to*) savoir; **he couldn't help me** il ne

pouvait pas m'aider; **she c. swim** elle sait nager; **he could do it tomorrow** il pourrait le faire demain; **he could have done it** il aurait pu le faire; **you could be wrong** (*possibility*) tu as peut-être tort; **he can't be dead** (*prob-ability*) il ne peut pas être mort; **c. I come in?** (*permission*) puis-je entrer?; **yes, you c.!** oui!

can² [kæn] **1** *n* (*for food*) boîte *f*; (*for beer*) can(n)ette *f* **2** (*pt & pp* -**nn**-) *vt* mettre en boîte ▪ **canned** *adj* en boîte, en conserve; **c. beer** bière *f* en can(n)ette; **c. food** conserves *fpl* ▪ **can-opener** *n* ouvre-boîtes *m inv*

Canada ['kænədə] *n* le Canada ▪ **Ca-nadian** **1** *adj* canadien, -enne **2** *n* Ca-nadien, -enne *mf*

canal [kə'næl] *n* canal *m*

canary [kə'neərɪ] (*pl* -**ies**) *n* canari *m*

cancel ['kænsəl] **1** (*Br* -**ll**-, *Am* -**l**-) *vt* (*flight, appointment*) annuler; (*goods, taxi*) décommander; (*train*) suppri-mer **2** *vi* se décommander ▪ **cancella-tion** [-'leɪʃən] *n* annulation *f*; (*of train*) suppression *f*

cancer ['kænsə(r)] *n* cancer *m*; **sto-mach/skin c.** cancer *m* de l'estomac/la peau

candid ['kændɪd] *adj* franc (*f* franche)

candidate ['kændɪdeɪt] *n* candidat, -e *mf* (**for** à)

candle ['kændəl] *n* (*made of wax*) bou-gie *f*; (*in church*) cierge *m* ▪ **candle-light** *n* **to have dinner by c.** dîner aux chandelles ▪ **candlestick** *n* bougeoir *m*; (*taller*) chandelier *m*

candy ['kændɪ] (*pl* -**ies**) *n Am* bonbon *m*; (*sweets*) bonbons *mpl*; **c. store** confi-serie *f* ▪ **candyfloss** *n Br* barbe *f* à papa

cane [keɪn] **1** *n* (*stick*) canne *f*; (*for pun-ishment*) baguette *f* **2** *vt* (*punish*) frap-per avec une baguette

canine ['keɪnaɪn] *adj* (*tooth, race*) ca-nin

canister ['kænɪstə(r)] *n* boîte *f* (en mé-tal)

cannabis ['kænəbɪs] *n* (*drug*) canna-bis *m*

cannon ['kænən] (*pl* **-s** or **cannon**) *n* canon *m*

cannot ['kænɒt] = **can not**

canoe [kə'nu:] *n* canoë *m*; (*dugout*) pirogue *f* ■ **canoeing** *n* to go c. faire du canoë-kayak

canopy ['kænəpɪ] (*pl* -ies) *n* (*awning*) auvent *m*; (*made of glass*) marquise *f*

can't [kɑ:nt] = **can not**

canteen [kæn'ti:n] *n* (*in school, factory*) cantine *f*; **c. of cutlery** ménagère *f*

canvas ['kænvəs] *n* (a) (*cloth*) (grosse) toile *f*, (*for embroidery*) canevas *m* (b) (*painting*) toile *f*

canvass ['kænvəs] *vt* (*opinions*) sonder; **to c. sb** (*seek votes*) solliciter le suffrage de qn; (*seek orders*) solliciter des commandes de qn ■ **canvassing** *n* (*for orders*) démarchage *m*; (*for votes*) démarchage *m* électoral

canyon ['kænjən] *n* cañon *m*, canyon *m*

cap¹ [kæp] *n* (a) (*hat*) casquette *f*; (*for shower, of sailor*) bonnet *m*; (*of soldier*) képi *m* (b) (*of tube, valve*) bouchon *m*; (*of bottle*) capsule *f*; (*of pen*) capuchon *m* (c) (*of child's gun*) amorce *f*

cap² [kæp] (*pt & pp* **-pp-**) *vt* (a) (*outdo*) surpasser (b) *Br* (*spending*) limiter

capable ['keɪpəbəl] *adj* (*person*) capable (**of sth** de qch; **of doing sth** de faire qch) ■ **capability** *n* capacité *f*

capacity [kə'pæsətɪ] *n* (a) (*of container*) capacité *f*; (*ability*) aptitude *f*, capacité *f* (**for sth** pour qch; **for doing sth** à faire qch); (*output*) rendement *m*; **in my c. as a doctor** en ma qualité de médecin

cape [keɪp] *n* (*cloak*) cape *f*; (*of cyclist*) pèlerine *f*

capital ['kæpɪtəl] 1 *adj* (*letter, importance*) capital; **c. punishment** peine *f* capitale 2 *n* (a) **c. (city)** capitale *f*; **c. (letter)** majuscule *f* (b) (*money*) capital *m* ■ **capitalism** *n* capitalisme *m* ■ **capitalist** *adj & n* capitaliste (*mf*) ■ **capitalize** *vi* **to c. on** tirer parti de

capsize [kæp'saɪz] 1 *vt* faire chavirer 2 *vi* chavirer

capsule [*Br* 'kæpsju:l, *Am* 'kæpsəl] *n* (*of medicine*) gélule *f*; **(space) c.** capsule *f* spatiale

captain ['kæptɪn] 1 *n* capitaine *m* 2 *vt* (*ship*) commander; (*team*) être le capitaine de

caption ['kæpʃən] *n* (*of illustration*) légende *f*; (*of film, article*) sous-titre *m*

captivate ['kæptɪveɪt] *vt* captiver

captive ['kæptɪv] *n* captif, -ive *mf* ■ **captivity** *n* **in c.** en captivité

capture ['kæptʃə(r)] 1 *n* capture *f*; (*of town*) prise *f* 2 *vt* (*person, animal*) capturer; (*escaped prisoner or animal*) reprendre; (*town*) prendre; *Fig* (*mood*) rendre

car [kɑ:(r)] *n* voiture *f*, automobile *f*; (*train carriage*) wagon *m*, voiture *f*; **c. insurance/industry** assurance *f*/industrie *f* automobile; **the c. door** la portière de la voiture; **c. crash** accident *m* de voiture; **c. ferry** ferry *m*; *Br* **c. hire** location *f* de voitures; *Br* **c. park** parking *m*; **c. phone** téléphone *m* de voiture; **c. radio** autoradio *m*; **c. rental** location *f* de voitures; **c. wash** (*machine*) = station de lavage automatique pour voitures ■ **carport** *n* abri *m* pour voiture

carafe [kə'ræf] *n* carafe *f*

caramel ['kærəməl] *n* caramel *m*

carat ['kærət] *n* carat *m*; **18-c. gold** or *m* (à) 18 carats

caravan ['kærəvæn] *n* caravane *f*; (*horse-drawn*) roulotte *f*; **c. site** camping *m* pour caravanes

carbohydrates [kɑ:bəʊ'haɪdreɪts] *npl* hydrates *mpl* de carbone; (*in food*) glucides *mpl*

carbon ['kɑ:bən] *n* carbone *m*; **c. dioxide** dioxyde *m* de carbone, gaz *m* carbonique

card [kɑ:d] *n* carte *f*; (*cardboard*) carton *m*; (*index*) **c.** fiche *f*; **to play cards** jouer aux cartes ■ **cardboard** *n* carton *m*; **c. box** boîte *f* en carton, carton *m* ■ **cardphone** *n* téléphone *m* à carte

cardigan ['kɑ:dɪɡən] *n* cardigan *m*

cardinal ['kɑ:dɪnəl] *n Rel* cardinal *m*

care [keə(r)] **1** *n* (*attention*) soin *m*; (*protection*) soins *mpl*; (*worry*) souci *m*; **to take c. to do** veiller à faire; **to take c. not to do** faire attention à ne pas faire; **to take c. of sb/sth** s'occuper de qn/qch; **to take c. of oneself** (*manage*) savoir se débrouiller tout seul; (*keep healthy*) faire attention à soi; **take c.!** (*goodbye*) au revoir!; **'c. of'** (*on envelope*) 'chez'

2 *vt* **I don't c. what he says** peu m'importe ce qu'il en dit

3 *vi* **I don't c.** ça m'est égal; **who cares?** qu'est-ce que ça peut faire?; **to c. about** (*feel concern about*) se soucier de; **to c. about** *or* **for sb** (*be fond of*) avoir de la sympathie pour qn; **to c. for sb** (*look after*) soigner qn

career [kə'rɪə(r)] **1** *n* carrière *f* **2** *vi* **to c. along** aller à vive allure

carefree ['keəfri:] *adj* insouciant

careful ['keəfəl] *adj* (*exact, thorough*) soigneux, -euse (**about** de); (*cautious*) prudent; **to be c. of** *or* **with sth** faire attention à qch; **be c.!** (*fais*) attention! ■ **carefully** *adv* (*thoroughly*) avec soin; (*cautiously*) prudemment

careless ['keələs] *adj* négligent; (*work*) peu soigné; **c. mistake** faute *f* d'étourderie ■ **carelessness** *n* négligence *f*

carer ['keərə(r)] *n* (*relative*) = personne s'occupant d'un parent malade ou âgé

caress [kə'res] **1** *n* caresse *f* **2** *vt* caresser

caretaker ['keəteɪkə(r)] *n* gardien, -enne *mf*, concierge *mf*

cargo ['kɑ:gəʊ] (*pl* **-oes** *or* **-os**) *n* cargaison *f*; **c. ship** cargo *m*

Caribbean [*Br* kærɪ'bi:ən, *Am* kə'rɪbɪən] **1** *adj* caraïbe **2 the C.** (**islands**) les Antilles *fpl*

caricature ['kærɪkətʃʊə(r)] **1** *n* caricature *f* **2** *vt* caricaturer

caring ['keərɪŋ] *adj* (*loving*) aimant; (*understanding*) très humain

carnation [kɑ:'neɪʃən] *n* œillet *m*

carnival ['kɑ:nɪvəl] *n* carnaval *m* (*pl* -als)

carol ['kærəl] *n* chant *m* de Noël

carp [kɑ:p] **1** *n inv* (*fish*) carpe *f* **2** *vi* se plaindre (**at** de)

carpenter ['kɑ:pɪntə(r)] *n* (*for house building*) charpentier *m*; (*for light woodwork*) menuisier *m* ■ **carpentry** *n* charpenterie *f*, (*light woodwork*) menuiserie *f*

carpet ['kɑ:pɪt] **1** *n* (*rug*) tapis *m*; (*fitted*) moquette *f* **2** *vt* recouvrir d'un tapis/d'une moquette

carriage ['kærɪdʒ] *n Br* (*of train*) voiture *f*, (*horse-drawn*) voiture *f*, équipage *m*; *Br* (*transport of goods*) transport *m*; (*cost*) frais *mpl*; (*of typewriter*) chariot *m* ■ **carriageway** *n Br* chaussée *f*

carrier ['kærɪə(r)] *n* (*company, airline*) transporteur *m*; *Br* **c. (bag)** sac *m* en plastique

carrot ['kærət] *n* carotte *f*

carry ['kærɪ] (*pt & pp* **-ied**) **1** *vt* porter; (*goods, passengers*) transporter; (*gun, money*) avoir sur soi; *Math* (*in calculation*) retenir **2** *vi* (*of sound*) porter

► **carry away** *vt sep* emporter; **to be** *or* **get carried away** (*excited*) s'emballer

► **carry back** *vt sep* (*thing*) rapporter; (*person*) ramener

► **carry forward** *vt sep* (*in bookkeeping*) reporter

► **carry off** *vt sep* (*take away*) emporter

► **carry on 1** *vt sep* (*continue*) continuer (**doing** à faire); (*negotiations*) mener; (*conversation*) poursuivre **2** *vi* (*continue*) continuer; *Pej* (*behave badly*) se conduire mal; **to c. on with sth** continuer qch

► **carry out** *vt sep* (*plan, promise*) mettre à exécution; (*order*) exécuter; (*repair, reform*) effectuer; (*duty*) accomplir; *Am* (*meal*) emporter

► **carry through** *vt sep* (*plan*) mener à bien

carrycot ['kærɪkɒt] *n Br* porte-bébé *m inv*

cart [kɑ:t] **1** *n* (*horse-drawn*) charrette

f; (handcart) voiture *f* à bras; *Am (in supermarket)* Caddie® *m* **2** *vt Fam* **to c. (around)** trimbaler

carton ['kɑːtən] *n (box)* carton *m; (of milk, fruit juice)* brique *f; (of cigarettes)* cartouche *f; (of cream)* pot *m*

cartoon [kɑː'tuːn] *n (in newspaper)* dessin *m* humoristique; *(film)* dessin *m* animé; **c. (strip)** bande *f* dessinée

cartridge ['kɑːtrɪdʒ] *n* cartouche *f*

carve [kɑːv] *vt (cut)* tailler (**out of** dans); *(name)* graver; *(sculpt)* sculpter; **to c. (up)** *(meat)* découper ∎ **carving 1** *adj* **c. knife** couteau *m* à découper **2** *n (wood)* **c.** sculpture *f* sur bois

cascade [kæs'keɪd] *vi* tomber en cascade

case[1] [keɪs] *n (instance, situation)* & *Med* cas *m; Law* affaire *f; Fig (arguments)* arguments *mpl*; **in any c.** en tout cas; **in c. it rains** au cas où il pleuvrait; **in c. of** en cas de

case[2] [keɪs] *n (bag)* valise *f; (crate)* caisse *f; (for pen, glasses, camera, violin, cigarettes)* étui *m; (for jewels)* écrin *m*

cash [kæʃ] **1** *n (coins, banknotes)* liquide *m; Fam (money)* sous *mpl*; **to pay (in) c.** payer en liquide; **c. box** caisse *f; Br* **c. desk** caisse *f;* **c. dispenser** *or* **machine** distributeur *m* de billets; **c. price** prix *m* (au) comptant; **c. register** caisse *f* enregistreuse **2** *vt* **to c. a cheque** *or Am* **check** *(of person)* encaisser un chèque; *(of bank)* payer un chèque

cashew ['kæʃuː] *n* **c. (nut)** noix *f* de cajou

cashier [kæ'ʃɪə(r)] *n* caissier, -ère *mf*

casino [kə'siːnəʊ] *(pl* -os) *n* casino *m*

casket ['kɑːskɪt] *n (box)* coffret *m; (coffin)* cercueil *m*

casserole ['kæsərəʊl] *n (covered dish)* cocotte *f; (stew)* ragoût *m*

cassette [kə'set] *n (audio, video)* cassette *f; (for camera)* cartouche *f;* **c. player** lecteur *m* de cassettes; **c. recorder** magnétophone *m* à cassettes

cast [kɑːst] **1** *n (actors)* acteurs *mpl;*

(list of actors) distribution *f; Med* **in a c.** dans le plâtre **2** *(pt & pp* **cast)** *vt (throw)* jeter; *(light, shadow)* projeter; *(glance)* jeter (**at** à *ou* sur); **to c. doubt on sth** jeter le doute sur qch; **c. iron** fonte *f* ∎ **cast-iron** *adj (pan)* en fonte; *Fig (alibi, excuse)* en béton

caster ['kɑːstə(r)] *n (wheel)* roulette *f; Br* **c. sugar** sucre *m* en poudre

castle ['kɑːsəl] *n* château *m; (in chess)* tour *f*

castoffs ['kɑːstɒfs] *npl* vieux vêtements *mpl*

castrate [kæ'streɪt] *vt* châtrer

casual ['kæʒjʊəl] *adj (offhand) (remark, glance)* en passant; *(relaxed, informal)* décontracté; *(conversation)* à bâtons rompus; *(clothes)* sport *inv; (careless)* désinvolte; *(employment, worker)* temporaire ∎ **casually** *adv (remark, glance)* en passant; *(informally)* avec décontraction; *(dress)* sport; *(carelessly)* avec désinvolture

casualty ['kæʒjʊəltɪ] *(pl* -ies) *n* victime *f; Br* **c. (department)** *(in hospital)* service *m* des urgences *fpl*

cat [kæt] *n* chat *m; (female)* chatte *f*

catalogue ['kætəlɒg] *(Am* **catalog) 1** *n* catalogue *m* **2** *vt* cataloguer

catalyst ['kætəlɪst] *n Chem & Fig* catalyseur *m*

catapult ['kætəpʌlt] **1** *n (toy)* lance-pierres *m inv* **2** *vt* catapulter

catastrophe [kə'tæstrəfɪ] *n* catastrophe *f*

catch [kætʃ] **1** *n (in fishing)* prise *f; (of a whole day)* pêche *f; (difficulty)* piège *m; (on door)* loquet *m*

2 *(pt & pp* **caught)** *vt (ball, thief, illness)* attraper; *(fish, train, bus)* prendre; *(grab)* prendre, saisir; *(surprise)* surprendre; *(understand)* saisir; *(garment)* accrocher (**on** à); **to c. sb's eye** *or* **attention** attirer l'attention de qn; **to c. sight of sb/sth** apercevoir qn/qch; **to c. fire** prendre feu; **to c. sb doing** surprendre qn à faire; **to c. sb out** prendre qn en défaut; **to c. sb up** rattraper qn

3 *vi* her skirt (got) caught in the door sa jupe s'est prise dans la porte; **to c. up with sb** rattraper qn ■ **catching** *adj (illness)* contagieux, -euse

catchy ['kætʃɪ] *(-ier, -iest) adj (tune, slogan)* facile à retenir

category ['kætɪgərɪ] *(pl -ies)* n catégorie *f* ■ **categorical** *adj* catégorique

cater ['keɪtə(r)] *vi (provide food)* s'occuper des repas **(for** pour); **to c. to,** *Br* **to c. for** *(need, taste)* satisfaire ■ **caterer** *n* traiteur *m* ■ **catering** *n* restauration *f*; **to do the c.** s'occuper des repas

caterpillar ['kætəpɪlə(r)] *n* chenille *f*

cathedral [kə'θiːdrəl] *n* cathédrale *f*

Catholic ['kæθlɪk] *adj & n* catholique *(mf)*

cattle ['kætəl] *npl* bétail *m*

caught [kɔːt] *pt & pp of* **catch**

cauliflower ['kɒlɪflaʊə(r)] *n* chou-fleur *m*

cause [kɔːz] **1** *n (origin, ideal) & Law* cause *f*; *(reason)* raison *f*, motif *m* **(of** de) **2** *vt* causer, occasionner; **to c. trouble for sb** créer *ou* causer des ennuis à qn

caution ['kɔːʃən] **1** *n (care)* prudence *f*; *(warning)* avertissement *m* **2** *vt (warn)* avertir; *Sport* donner un avertissement à ■ **cautious** *adj* prudent

cavalry ['kævəlrɪ] *n* cavalerie *f*

cave [keɪv] **1** *n* grotte *f* **2** *vi* **to c. in** *(of ceiling)* s'effondrer; *(of floor)* s'affaisser

cavern ['kævən] *n* caverne *f*

cavity ['kævɪtɪ] *(pl -ies)* n cavité *f*

CD [siː'diː] *(abbr* **compact disc)** *n* CD *m*; **CD player** lecteur *m* de CD

CD-ROM [siːdiː'rɒm] *(abbr* **compact disc read-only memory)** *n* Comptr CD-ROM *m inv*

cease [siːs] **1** *vt* cesser **(doing** de faire) **2** *vi* cesser ■ **cease-fire** *n* cessez-le-feu *m inv* ■ **ceaseless** *adj* incessant

cedar ['siːdə(r)] *n (tree, wood)* cèdre *m*

ceiling ['siːlɪŋ] *n (of room) & Fig (limit)* plafond *m*

celebrate ['selɪbreɪt] **1** *vt (event)* célébrer, fêter; *(mass)* célébrer **2** *vi* faire la fête ■ **celebration** [-'breɪʃən] *n (event)* fête *f*; **the celebrations** les festivités *fpl*

celebrity [sə'lebrɪtɪ] *(pl -ies)* n célébrité *f*

celery ['selərɪ] *n* céleri *m*

celibate ['selɪbət] *adj* **to be c.** ne pas avoir de rapports sexuels; *(by choice)* être chaste

cell [sel] *n* cellule *f*; *El* élément *m*

cellar ['selə(r)] *n* cave *f*

cello ['tʃeləʊ] *(pl -os)* n violoncelle *m*

cellophane® ['seləfeɪn] *n* Cellophane® *f*

cellphone ['selfəʊn] *n Am* (téléphone *m*) portable *m*

cellular ['seljʊlə(r)] *adj* cellulaire; **c. phone** téléphone *m* cellulaire

Celsius ['selsɪəs] *adj* Celsius *inv*

cement [sɪ'ment] **1** *n* ciment *m*; **c. mixer** bétonnière *f* **2** *vt also Fig* cimenter

cemetery ['semətrɪ] *(pl -ies)* n cimetière *m*

censor ['sensə(r)] **1** *n* censeur *m* **2** *vt* censurer ■ **censorship** *n* censure *f*

census ['sensəs] *n* recensement *m*

cent [sent] *n (coin)* cent *m*

centenary [*Br* sen'tiːnərɪ, *Am* sen'tenərɪ] *(pl -ies)* n centenaire *m*

center ['sentə(r)] *n Am* = **centre**

centigrade ['sentɪgreɪd] *adj* centigrade

centimetre ['sentɪmiːtə(r)] *n* centimètre *m*

central ['sentrəl] *adj* central; **C. London** le centre de Londres; **c. heating** chauffage *m* central ■ **centralize** *vt* centraliser

centre ['sentə(r)] *(Am* **center) 1** *n* centre *m*; *Football* **c. forward** avant-centre *m* **2** *vt (attention, interest)* concentrer **(on** sur)

century ['sentʃərɪ] *(pl -ies)* n siècle *m*; **in the twenty-first c.** au vingt et unième siècle

ceramic [sə'ræmɪk] *adj (tile)* en céramique

cereal ['sɪərɪəl] *n* céréale *f*; **(breakfast) c.** céréales *fpl (pour le petit déjeuner)*

ceremony ['serɪmənɪ] *(pl* **-ies)** *n (event)* cérémonie *f*

certain ['sɜːtən] *adj* (**a**) *(sure)* certain (**that** que); **she's c. to come, she'll come for c.** c'est certain qu'elle viendra; **to be c. of sth** être certain *ou* sûr de qch; **for c.** *(say, know)* avec certitude (**b**) *(particular, some)* certain; **(yes)** bien sûr ■ **certainly** *adv (undoubtedly)* certainement; *(yes)* bien sûr ■ **certainty** *(pl* **-ies)** *n* certitude *f*

certificate [sə'tɪfɪkɪt] *n* certificat *m*; *(from university)* diplôme *m*

certify ['sɜːtɪfaɪ] *(pt & pp* **-ied)** *vt (document, signature)* certifier; *Am* **certified letter** ≃ lettre *f* recommandée; *Am* **certified public accountant** expert-comptable *m*

chain [tʃeɪn] **1** *n (of rings, mountains)* chaîne *f; (of events)* suite *f; (of lavatory)* chasse *f* d'eau; **c. reaction** réaction *f* en chaîne; **c. saw** tronçonneuse *f;* **c. store** magasin *m* à succursales multiples **2** *vt* **to c. (up)** *(dog)* mettre à l'attache ■ **chain-smoker** *n* **to be a c.** fumer cigarette sur cigarette

chair [tʃeə(r)] **1** *n* chaise *f; (armchair)* fauteuil *m; Univ (of professor)* chaire *f;* **the c.** *(office of chairperson)* la présidence; **c. lift** télésiège *m* **2** *vt (meeting)* présider ■ **chairman** *(pl* **-men),** ■ **chairperson** *n* président, -e *mf*

chalet ['ʃæleɪ] *n* chalet *m*

chalk [tʃɔːk] **1** *n* craie *f* **2** *vt* marquer à la craie

challenge ['tʃælɪndʒ] **1** *n* défi *m; (task)* challenge *m,* gageure *f* **2** *vt* défier (**sb to do** qn de faire); *(question, dispute)* contester ■ **challenger** *n Sport* challenger *m*

chamber ['tʃeɪmbə(r)] *n (room, assembly, of gun)* chambre *f;* **c. music/orchestra** musique *f*/orchestre *m* de chambre ■ **chambermaid** *n* femme *f* de chambre

champagne [ʃæm'peɪn] *n* champagne *m*

champion ['tʃæmpɪən] **1** *n* champion, -onne *mf;* **c. skier, skiing c.** champion, -onne *mf* de ski **2** *vt (support)* se faire le champion de ■ **championship** *n* championnat *m*

chance [tʃɑːns] **1** *n (luck)* hasard *m; (possibility)* chance *f, (opportunity)* occasion *f; (risk)* risque *m;* **by c.** par hasard; **to have the c. to do sth** *ou* **of doing sth** avoir l'occasion de faire qch; **to give sb a c.** donner une chance à qn; **to take a c.** tenter le coup **2** *adj (remark)* fait au hasard **3** *vt* **to c. it** risquer le coup

chancellor ['tʃɑːnsələ(r)] *n Pol* chancelier *m*

chandelier [ʃændə'lɪə(r)] *n* lustre *m*

change [tʃeɪndʒ] **1** *n* changement *m; (money)* monnaie *f;* **for a c.** pour changer; **a c. of clothes** des vêtements de rechange

 2 *vt (modify)* changer; *(exchange)* échanger (**for** pour *ou* contre); *(money)* changer (**into** en); *(transform)* changer, transformer (**into** en); **to c. trains/colour/one's skirt** changer de train/de couleur/de jupe; **to c. gear** *(in vehicle)* changer de vitesse; **to c. the subject** changer de sujet; **to get changed** *(put on other clothes)* se changer

 3 *vi (alter)* changer; *(change clothes)* se changer; **to c. into sth** *(be transformed)* se changer *ou* se transformer en qch; **she changed into a dress** elle a mis une robe; **to c. over** passer (**from** de; **to** à) ■ **changeable** *adj (weather, mood)* changeant ■ **changeover** *n* passage *m* (**from** de; **to** à)

changing ['tʃeɪndʒɪŋ] *n* **c. room** vestiaire *m; (in shop)* cabine *f* d'essayage

channel ['tʃænəl] **1** *n (on television)* chaîne *f; (for boats)* chenal *m; (groove)* rainure *f; (of communication, distribution)* canal *m; Geog* **the C.** la Manche; **the C. Islands** les îles Anglo-Normandes; **the C. Tunnel** le tunnel sous la Manche 2 (Br -ll-, Am -l-) vt (energies, crowd, money) canaliser (into vers)

chant [tʃɑːnt] 1 vt (slogan) scander 2 vi (of demonstrators) scander des slogans

chaos [ˈkeɪɒs] n chaos m ■ **chaotic** adj (situation, scene) chaotique

chapel [ˈtʃæpəl] n chapelle f; (nonconformist church) temple m

chaplain [ˈtʃæplɪn] n aumônier m

chapped [ˈtʃæpt] adj (hands, lips) gercé

chapter [ˈtʃæptə(r)] n chapitre m

character [ˈkærɪktə(r)] n (a) (of person, place) caractère m; (in book, film) personnage m; (person) individu m; (unusual person) personnage m (b) (letter) caractère m ■ **characteristic** adj & n caractéristique f

charcoal [ˈtʃɑːkəʊl] n Art fusain m

charge¹ [tʃɑːdʒ] 1 n (in battle) charge f; Law chef m d'accusation; (care) garde f; to take c. of sth prendre qch en charge; to be in c. of sth être responsable de 2 vt (battery, soldiers) charger; Law (accuse) inculper (with de) 3 vi (rush) se précipiter; (soldiers) charger ■ **charger** n (for battery) chargeur m

charge² [tʃɑːdʒ] 1 n (cost) prix m; **charges** (expenses) frais mpl 2 vt (amount) demander (for pour); to c. sb faire payer qn

charity [ˈtʃærɪtɪ] (pl -ies) n (kindness, alms) charité f; (society) œuvre f de charité

charm [tʃɑːm] 1 n (attractiveness) charme m; (trinket) breloque f 2 vt charmer ■ **charming** adj charmant

chart [tʃɑːt] n (map) carte f; (table) tableau m; (graph) graphique m; (pop) **charts** hit-parade m

charter [ˈtʃɑːtə(r)] n (aircraft) charter m; c. flight vol m charter ■ **chartered accountant** n Br expert-comptable m

chase [tʃeɪs] 1 n poursuite f 2 vt poursuivre; to c. sb away or off chasser qn

3 vi to c. after sb/sth courir après qn/qch

chasm [ˈkæzəm] n also Fig abîme m, gouffre m

chassis [ˈʃæsɪ] n (of vehicle) châssis m

chaste [tʃeɪst] adj chaste

chat [tʃæt] 1 n petite conversation f; Comptr bavardage m; to have a c. causer (with avec); Comptr c. room site m de bavardage 2 (pt & pp -tt-) vi causer (with avec); Comptr bavarder 3 vt Br Fam to c. sb up draguer qn

chatter [ˈtʃætə(r)] 1 n bavardage m 2 vi (of person) bavarder; his teeth were chattering il claquait des dents

chatty [ˈtʃætɪ] (-ier, -iest) adj (person) bavard; (letter) plein de détails

chauffeur [ˈʃəʊfə(r)] n chauffeur m

chauvinist [ˈʃəʊvɪnɪst] n Pej (male) c. macho m, phallocrate m

cheap [tʃiːp] 1 (-er, -est) adj bon marché inv, pas cher (f pas chère); (rate, fare) réduit; (worthless) sans valeur; (vulgar) de mauvais goût; **cheaper** meilleur marché inv, moins cher (f moins chère) 2 adv (buy) (à) bon marché, au rabais ■ **cheaply** adv (à) bon marché

cheat [tʃiːt] 1 n (at games) tricheur, -euse mf; (crook) escroc m 2 vt (deceive) tromper; (defraud) frauder; to c. sb out of sth escroquer qch à qn 3 vi (at games) tricher

check¹ [tʃek] n c. (pattern) carreaux mpl ■ **checked** adj (patterned) à carreaux

check² [tʃek] n vérification f (on de); (inspection) contrôle m; (in chess) échec m; Am (tick) ≃ croix f; Am (receipt) reçu m; Am (restaurant bill) addition f; Am (cheque) chèque m; to keep a c. on sth contrôler qch

2 vt (examine) vérifier; (inspect) contrôler; (mark off) cocher; Am (baggage) mettre à la consigne

3 vi vérifier; to c. on sth vérifier qch; to c. on sb surveiller qn ■ **checkbook** n Am carnet m de chèques ■ **check-in** n (at airport) enregistrement m (des

bagages) ■ **checklist** n liste f de contrôle; *Aviat* check-list / ■ **checkout** n *(in supermarket)* caisse f ■ **checkpoint** n poste m de contrôle ■ **checkroom** n *Am* vestiaire m; *Am (left-luggage office)* consigne f ■ **checkup** n *(medical)* bilan m de santé; **to have a c.** faire un bilan de santé

▶ **check in 1** vt sep *(luggage)* enregistrer **2** vi *(arrive)* arriver; *(sign in)* signer le registre; *(at airport)* se présenter à l'enregistrement

▶ **check out 1** vt sep *(confirm)* confirmer **2** vi *(at hotel)* régler sa note

▶ **check up** vi vérifier

checkers ['tʃekəz] npl *Am* jeu m de dames

cheddar ['tʃedə(r)] n cheddar m *(fromage)*

cheek [tʃiːk] n joue f; *Br (impudence)* culot m ■ **cheeky** (**-ier, -iest**) adj *Br (person, reply)* insolent

cheer [tʃɪə(r)] **1** n cheers *(shouts)* acclamations fpl; *Fam* **cheers!** *(when drinking)* à votre santé!; *(thanks)* merci! **2** vt *(applaud)* acclamer; **to c. sb up** *(comfort)* remonter le moral à qn; *(amuse)* faire sourire qn **3** vi applaudir; **to c. up** reprendre courage; **c. up!** (du) courage! ■ **cheering** n *(shouts)* acclamations fpl

cheerful ['tʃɪəfəl] adj gai

cheerio [tʃɪərɪ'əʊ] exclam *Br* salut!, au revoir!

cheese [tʃiːz] n fromage m ■ **cheeseburger** n cheeseburger m ■ **cheesecake** n cheesecake m, tarte f au fromage blanc

chef [ʃef] n chef m *(cuisinier)*

chemical 1 adj chimique **2** n produit m chimique

chemist ['kemɪst] n *Br (pharmacist)* pharmacien, -enne mf; *(scientist)* chimiste mf; *Br* **c.'s (shop)** pharmacie f ■ **chemistry** n chimie f

cheque [tʃek] n *Br* chèque m; **c. card** carte f d'identité bancaire *(sans laquelle un chéquier n'est pas valable)* ■ **chequebook** n *Br* carnet m de chèques

cherry ['tʃerɪ] *(pl* **-ies)** n cerise f

chess [tʃes] n échecs mpl ■ **chessboard** n échiquier m

chest [tʃest] n *(a) (part of body)* poitrine f; *Fig* **to get it off one's c.** dire ce qu'on a sur le cœur *(b) (box)* coffre m; **c. of drawers** commode f

chestnut ['tʃestnʌt] **1** n *(nut)* châtaigne f; *(cooked)* marron m **2** adj *(hair)* châtain

chew [tʃuː] **1** vt **to c. (up)** mâcher **2** vi mastiquer; **chewing gum** chewing-gum m

chewy ['tʃuːɪ] adj *(meat)* caoutchouteux, -euse; *(sweet)* mou *(f* molle)

chick [tʃɪk] n *(chicken)* poussin m

chicken ['tʃɪkɪn] **1** n poulet m **2** vi *Fam* **to c. out** se dégonfler ■ **chickenpox** n varicelle f

chickpea ['tʃɪkpiː] n pois m chiche

chief [tʃiːf] **1** n chef m; *Fam (boss)* patron m **2** adj *(most important)* principal; *Com* **c. executive** directeur m général ■ **chiefly** adv principalement, surtout

chilblain ['tʃɪlbleɪn] n engelure f

child [tʃaɪld] *(pl* **children)** n enfant mf; **c. abuse** mauvais traitements mpl à enfant, maltraitance f; **c. care** *(for working parents)* crèches fpl et garderies fpl; *Br* **c. minder** assistante f maternelle ■ **childhood** n enfance f ■ **childish** adj puéril ■ **childlike** adj enfantin ■ **childproof** adj *(lock, bottle)* que les enfants ne peuvent pas ouvrir

children ['tʃɪldrən] pl of **child**

chill [tʃɪl] **1** n froid m; *(illness)* refroidissement m; **to catch a c.** prendre froid **2** vt *(wine, melon)* mettre au frais; *(meat)* réfrigérer

chilli ['tʃɪlɪ] *(pl* **-is** or **-ies)** n *(vegetable)* piment m; *(dish)* chili m con carne; **c. powder** ≃ chili m

chilly ['tʃɪlɪ] (**-ier, -iest**) adj froid; **it's c.** il fait (un peu) froid

chime [tʃaɪm] vi *(of bell)* carillonner; *(of clock)* sonner

chimney ['tʃɪmnɪ] *(pl* **-eys)** n cheminée f

chimpanzee [tʃɪmpæn'ziː] n chimpanzé m

chin [tʃɪn] n menton m

China ['tʃaɪnə] n la Chine ■ **Chinese 1** adj chinois **2** n inv (person) Chinois, -e mf; (language) chinois m

china ['tʃaɪnə] **1** n inv porcelaine f **2** adj en porcelaine

chink [tʃɪŋk] **1** n (slit) fente f **2** vt faire tinter

chip [tʃɪp] **1** n (splinter) éclat m; (break) ébréchure f; (counter) jeton m; Comptr puce f, **chips** Br (French fries) frites fpl; Am (crisps) chips fpl; Br **c. shop** = boutique où l'on vend du poisson pané et des frites **2** (pt & pp **-pp-**) vt (cup) ébrécher; (paint) écailler

chiropodist [kɪ'rɒpədɪst] n Br pédicure mf

chirp [tʃɜːp] vi (of bird) pépier

chisel ['tʃɪzəl] **1** n ciseau m **2** (Br **-ll-**, Am **-l-**) vt ciseler

chives [tʃaɪvz] npl ciboulette f

chlorine ['klɔːriːn] n Chem chlore m

choc-ice ['tʃɒkaɪs] n Br = glace individuelle enrobée de chocolat

chocolate ['tʃɒklɪt] **1** n chocolat m; **hot c.** chocolat m chaud; **plain c.** chocolat m à croquer **2** adj (made of chocolate) en chocolat; (chocolate-flavoured) au chocolat

choice [tʃɔɪs] n choix m; **to make a c.** choisir

choir ['kwaɪə(r)] n chœur m ■ **choirboy** n jeune choriste m

choke [tʃəʊk] **1** n (of car) starter m **2** vt (strangle) étrangler; (clog) boucher **3** vi **she choked on a fishbone** elle a failli s'étouffer avec une arête

cholesterol [kə'lestərɒl] n cholestérol m

choose [tʃuːz] **1** (pt **chose**, pp **chosen**) vt choisir; **to c. to do sth** choisir de faire qch **2** vi choisir ■ **choos(e)y** (**choosier, choosiest**) adj Fam difficile (**about** sur)

chop [tʃɒp] **1** n (of lamb, pork) côtelette f **2** (pt & pp **-pp-**) vt (wood) couper (à la hache); (food) couper en morceaux;

(finely) hacher; **to c. down** (tree) abattre; **to c. off** (branch, finger) couper; **to c. up** couper en morceaux

choppy ['tʃɒpɪ] (**-ier, -iest**) adj (sea) agité

chopsticks ['tʃɒpstɪks] npl baguettes fpl (pour manger)

choral ['kɔːrəl] adj choral

chord [kɔːd] n Mus accord m

chore [tʃɔː(r)] n corvée f; **(household) chores** travaux mpl du ménage

chorus ['kɔːrəs] n (of song) refrain m; (singers) chœur m; (dancers) troupe f

chose [tʃəʊz] pt of **choose**

chosen ['tʃəʊzən] pp of **choose**

Christ [kraɪst] n le Christ ■ **Christian** adj & n chrétien, -enne (mf); **C. name** prénom m ■ **Christianity** n christianisme m

christen ['krɪsən] vt (person, ship) baptiser ■ **christening** n baptême m

Christmas ['krɪsməs] **1** n Noël m; **at C. (time)** à Noël; **Merry** or **Happy C.!** Joyeux Noël! **2** adj (tree, card, Day, party) de Noël; **C. Eve** la veille de Noël

chrome [krəʊm], **chromium** ['krəʊmɪəm] n chrome m

chronic ['krɒnɪk] adj (disease, state) chronique

chronological [krɒnə'lɒdʒɪkəl] adj chronologique; **in c. order** par ordre chronologique

chubby ['tʃʌbɪ] (**-ier, -iest**) adj (person, hands) potelé; (cheeks) rebondi

chuck [tʃʌk] vt Fam (throw) lancer; (boyfriend, girlfriend) plaquer; Br **to c. (in** or **up)** (give up) laisser tomber; **to c. out** (throw away) balancer; (from house, school, club) vider

chuckle ['tʃʌkəl] vi rire tout bas

chug [tʃʌg] (pt & pp **-gg-**) vi **to c. along** (of vehicle) avancer lentement; (of train) haleter

chum [tʃʌm] n Fam copain m, copine f

chunk [tʃʌŋk] n (gros) morceau m

church [tʃɜːtʃ] n église f; **to go to c.** aller à l'église; **c. hall** salle f paroissiale ■ **churchyard** n cimetière m

churn [tʃɜːn] vt Pej **to c. out** (books)

pondre (en série); *(goods)* produire en série

chute [ʃuːt] *n Br (in pool, playground)* toboggan *m*; *(for rubbish)* vide-ordures *m inv*

CID [siːaɪˈdiː] *(abbr Criminal Investigation Department)* *n Br* ≃ PJ *f*

cider [ˈsaɪdə(r)] *n* cidre *m*

cigar [sɪˈɡɑː(r)] *n* cigare *m*

cigarette [sɪɡəˈret] *n* cigarette *f*; **c. end** mégot *m*

cinder [ˈsɪndə(r)] *n* cendre *f*

cinema [ˈsɪnəmə] *n (art)* cinéma *m*; *Br (place)* cinéma; *Br* **to go to the c.** aller au cinéma ■ **cinemagoer** *n Br* cinéphile *mf*

cinnamon [ˈsɪnəmən] *n* cannelle *f*

circle [ˈsɜːkəl] **1** *n (shape, group, range)* cercle *m*; *Theatre* balcon *m* **2** *vt (move round)* tourner autour de; *(surround)* entourer (**with** de) **3** *vi (of aircraft, bird)* décrire des cercles

circuit [ˈsɜːkɪt] *n (electrical path, journey, for motor racing)* circuit *m*; *El* **c. breaker** disjoncteur *m*

circular [ˈsɜːkjʊlə(r)] **1** *adj* circulaire **2** *n (letter)* circulaire *f*; *(advertisement)* prospectus *m*

circulate [ˈsɜːkjʊleɪt] **1** *vt* faire circuler **2** *vi* circuler ■ **circulation** [-ˈleɪʃən] *n (of air, blood, money)* circulation *f*; *(of newspaper)* tirage *m*

circumcised [ˈsɜːkəmsaɪzd] *adj* circoncis

circumference [sɜːˈkʌmfərəns] *n* circonférence *f*

circumstance [ˈsɜːkəmstæns] *n* circonstance *f*; **circumstances** *(financial)* situation *f* financière; **in** *or* **under the circumstances** étant donné les circonstances; **in** *or* **under no circumstances** en aucun cas

circus [ˈsɜːkəs] *n* cirque *m*

citizen [ˈsɪtɪzən] *n* citoyen, -enne *mf*; *(of city)* habitant, -e *mf*

citrus [ˈsɪtrəs] *adj* **c. fruit(s)** agrumes *mpl*

city [ˈsɪtɪ] *(pl -ies)* *n (grande)* ville *f*, cité *f*; *Br* **the C.** la City *(quartier des*

affaires de Londres); **c. centre** centre-ville *m*; *Am* **c. hall** hôtel *m* de ville

civil [ˈsɪvəl] *adj* (**a**) *(rights, war, marriage)* civil; **c. servant** fonctionnaire *mf*; **c. service** fonction *f* publique (**b**) *(polite)* civil

civilian [sɪˈvɪljən] *adj & n* civil, -e *(mf)*

civilize [ˈsɪvɪlaɪz] *vt* civiliser ■ **civilization** [-ˈzeɪʃən] *n* civilisation *f*

claim [kleɪm] **1** *n (demand) (for damages, compensation)* demande *f* d'indemnisation; *(as a right)* revendication *f*; *(statement)* affirmation *f*; *(right)* droit *m* (**to** à); *(insurance)* **c.** demande *f* d'indemnité

2 *vt (as a right)* réclamer, revendiquer; *(payment, benefit, reduction)* demander à bénéficier de; **to c. damages (from sb)** réclamer des dommages et intérêts (à qn); **to c. that...** *(assert)* prétendre que... ■ **claimant** *n Br (for social benefits, insurance)* demandeur, -euse *mf*

clam [klæm] *n* palourde *f*

clamber [ˈklæmbə(r)] *vi* **to c. up** grimper

clamour [ˈklæmə(r)] *(Am* **clamor***)* **1** *n* clameur *f* **2** *vi* **to c. for sth** demander qch à grands cris

clamp [klæmp] **1** *n (clip-like)* pince *f*; *(wheel)* **c.** *(for vehicle)* sabot *m* (de Denver) **2** *vt* serrer; *(vehicle)* mettre un sabot à **3** *vi* **to c. down on** sévir contre ■ **clampdown** *n* coup *m* d'arrêt (**on** à)

clan [klæn] *n also Fig* clan *m*

clang [klæŋ] *n* son *m* métallique

clap [klæp] *(pt & pp* **-pp-***)* *vti (applaud)* applaudir; **to c. (one's hands)** applaudir; *(once)* frapper dans ses mains ■ **clapping** *n* applaudissements *mpl*

claret [ˈklærət] *n (wine)* bordeaux *m* rouge

clarify [ˈklærɪfaɪ] *(pt & pp -ied)* *vt* clarifier ■ **clarification** [-ɪˈkeɪʃən] *n* clarification *f*

clarinet [klærɪˈnet] *n* clarinette *f*

clarity [ˈklærətɪ] *n (of expression, argument)* clarté *f*; *(of sound)* pureté *f*

clash [klæʃ] **1** *n (of interests)* conflit *m*; *(of events)* coïncidence *f* **2** *vi (of objects)* s'entrechoquer; *(of interests, armies)* s'affronter; *(of colours)* jurer (**with** avec); *(coincide)* tomber en même temps (**with** que)

clasp [klɑːsp] **1** *n (fastener)* fermoir *m*; *(of belt)* boucle *f* **2** *vt (hold)* serrer; **to c. one's hands** joindre les mains

class [klɑːs] **1** *n* classe *f*; *(lesson)* cours *m* **2** *vt* classer (**as** comme) ▪ **classmate** *n* camarade *mf* de classe ▪ **classroom** *n* (salle *f* de) classe *f*

classic ['klæsɪk] **1** *adj* classique **2** *n (writer, work)* classique *m* ▪ **classical** *adj* classique

classify ['klæsɪfaɪ] *(pt & pp -ied)* *vt* classer ▪ **classification** *n* classification *f* ▪ **classified** *adj (information, document)* confidentiel, -elle; **c. advertisement** petite annonce *f*

classy ['klɑːsɪ] *(-ier, -iest)* *adj Fam* chic *inv*

clatter ['klætə(r)] *n* fracas *m*

clause [klɔːz] *n (in sentence)* proposition *f*; *(in legal document)* clause *f*

claustrophobic [klɔːstrə'fəʊbɪk] *adj (person)* claustrophobe; *(room, atmosphere)* oppressant

claw [klɔː] **1** *n (of lobster)* pince *f*; *(of cat, sparrow)* griffe *f*; *(of eagle)* serre *f* **2** *vt (scratch)* griffer

clay [kleɪ] *n* argile *f*

clean [kliːn] **1** *(-er, -est)* *adj* propre; *(clear-cut)* net *(f* nette); *(joke)* pour toutes les oreilles; *(game, fight)* dans les règles; **to come c.** tout avouer
2 *adv (utterly)* complètement
3 *n* **to give sth a c.** nettoyer qch
4 *vt* nettoyer; *(wash)* laver; **to c. one's teeth** se brosser *ou* se laver les dents; **to c. out** *(room)* nettoyer à fond; *(empty)* vider; **to c. up** *(room)* nettoyer; *Fig (reform)* épurer
5 *vi* **to c. (up)** faire le nettoyage ▪ **cleaner** *n (in home)* femme *f* de ménage; **(dry) c.** teinturier, -ère *mf* ▪ **cleaning** *n* nettoyage *m*; *(housework)* ménage *m*; **c. woman** femme *f* de ménage ▪ **cleanly** *adv (break, cut)* net ▪ **clean-shaven** *adj (with no beard or moustache)* glabre; *(closely shaven)* rasé de près

cleanse [klenz] *vt (wound)* nettoyer; **cleansing cream** crème *f* démaquillante

clear [klɪə(r)] **1** *(-er, -est)* *adj (sky, water, sound, thought)* clair; *(glass)* transparent; *(outline, photo, skin, majority)* net *(f* nette); *(road)* libre; *(winner)* incontesté; *(obvious)* évident, clair; *(certain)* certain; **to make oneself c.** se faire comprendre; **it is c. that...** il est évident *ou* clair que...
2 *adv* **to keep** *or* **steer c. of** se tenir à l'écart de; **to get c. of** *(away from)* s'éloigner de
3 *vt (table)* débarrasser; *(road, area)* dégager; *(accused person)* disculper; *(cheque)* compenser; *(debts)* liquider; *(through customs)* dédouaner; *(for security)* autoriser; **to c. one's throat** s'éclaircir la gorge
4 *vi (of weather)* s'éclaircir; *(of fog)* se dissiper ▪ **clearing** *n (in woods)* clairière *f* ▪ **clearly** *adv (explain, write)* clairement; *(see, understand)* bien; *(obviously)* évidemment
▸ **clear away** *vt sep (remove)* enlever
▸ **clear off** *vi Fam (leave)* filer
▸ **clear out** *vt sep (empty)* vider; *(remove)* enlever
▸ **clear up 1** *vt sep (mystery)* éclaircir; *(room)* ranger **2** *vi (of weather)* s'éclaircir; *(tidy)* ranger

clearance ['klɪərəns] *n (sale)* liquidation *f*; *(space)* dégagement *m*; *(permission)* autorisation *f*

clear-cut [klɪə'kʌt] *adj* net *(f* nette)

clef [klef] *n Mus* clef *f*

clench [klentʃ] *vt* **to c. one's fist/teeth** serrer le poing/les dents

clergy ['klɜːdʒɪ] *n* clergé *m* ▪ **clergyman** *(pl -men)* *n* ecclésiastique *m*

clerical ['klerɪkəl] *adj (job)* d'employé; *(work)* de bureau

clerk [*Br* klɑːk, *Am* klɜːk] *n* employé, -e

mf de bureau; *Am (in store)* vendeur, -euse *mf*

clever ['klevə(r)] *(-er, -est) adj* intelligent; *(smart, shrewd)* astucieux, -euse; *(skilful)* habile (**at sth** à qch; **at doing** à faire); *(ingenious) (machine, plan)* ingénieux, -euse; *(gifted)* doué; **c. with one's hands** adroit de ses mains ▪ **cleverly** *adv* intelligemment; *(ingeniously)* astucieusement; *(skilfully)* habilement

cliché ['kli:ʃeɪ] *n* cliché *m*

click [klɪk] **1** *n* bruit *m* sec **2** *vi* faire un bruit sec; *Fam* **it suddenly clicked** ça a fait tilt

client ['klaɪənt] *n* client, -e *mf* ▪ **clientele** *n* clientèle *f*

cliff [klɪf] *n* falaise *f*

climate ['klaɪmɪt] *n (weather) & Fig (conditions)* climat *m*

climax ['klaɪmæks] *n* point *m* culminant; *(sexual)* orgasme *m*

climb [klaɪm] **1** *n* montée *f* **2** *vt* **to c. (up)** *(steps, hill)* gravir; *(mountain)* faire l'ascension de; *(tree, ladder)* grimper à; **to c. (over)** *(wall)* escalader; **to c. down (from)** *(wall, tree)* descendre de; *(hill)* descendre **3** *vi (of plant)* grimper; **to c. (up)** *(steps, tree, hill)* monter; **to c. down** descendre; *Fig (back down)* revenir sur sa décision ▪ **climber** *n (mountaineer)* alpiniste *mf*; *(on rocks)* varappeur, -euse *mf*; *(plant)* plante *f* grimpante ▪ **climbing** *n (mountain)* alpinisme *m*; *(rock-)c.* varappe *f*

climb-down ['klaɪmdaʊn] *n* reculade *f*

clinch [klɪntʃ] *vt (deal)* conclure

cling [klɪŋ] *(pt & pp* **clung)** *vi* s'accrocher (**to** à); *(stick)* adhérer (**to** à)

clinic ['klɪnɪk] *n Br (private)* clinique *f*; *(part of hospital)* service *m* ▪ **clinical** *adj Med* clinique

clink [klɪŋk] **1** *vt* faire tinter **2** *vi* tinter

clip [klɪp] **1** *n* (**a**) *(for paper)* trombone *m*; *(fastener)* attache *f*; *(of brooch, of cyclist, for hair)* pince *f* (**b**) *(of film)* extrait *m* **2** *(pt & pp* **-pp-)** *vt (paper)*

attacher *(avec un trombone)*; *(cut)* couper; *(hedge)* tailler; *(ticket)* poinçonner; **to c. (on)** *(attach)* attacher (**to** à) **3** *vi* **to c. together** s'emboîter ▪ **clippers** *npl (for hair)* tondeuse *f*; *(for fingernails)* coupe-ongles *m inv* ▪ **clipping** *n Am (from newspaper)* coupure *f*

clique [kli:k] *n Pej* clique *f*

cloak [kləʊk] *n* cape *f* ▪ **cloakroom** *n* vestiaire *m*; *Br (lavatory)* toilettes *fpl*

clock [klɒk] *n (large)* horloge *f*; *(small)* pendule *f*; *Br Fam (mileometer)* compteur *m*; **round the c.** vingt-quatre heures sur vingt-quatre; **to put the clocks forward/back** *(in spring, autumn)* avancer/retarder les pendules; **c. radio** radioréveil *m*; **c. tower** clocher *m* ▪ **clockwise** *adv* dans le sens des aiguilles d'une montre ▪ **clockwork 1** *adj (toy)* mécanique **2** *n* **to go like c.** marcher comme sur des roulettes

clog [klɒg] **1** *n (shoe)* sabot *m* **2** *(pt & pp* **-gg-)** *vt* **to c. (up)** *(obstruct)* boucher

cloister ['klɔɪstə(r)] *n* cloître *m*

close¹ [kləʊs] **1** *(-er, -est) adj (in distance, time, relationship)* proche; *(collaboration, resemblance, connection)* étroit; *(friend)* intime; *(contest)* serré; *(study)* rigoureux, -euse; *Br* **it's c.** *(of weather)* il fait lourd; **to be c. to** *(near)* près de, proche de; **that was a c. shave** or **call** il s'en est fallu de peu

2 *adv* **c. by, c. at hand** tout près; **we stood/sat c. together** nous étions debout/assis serrés les uns contre les autres; **to follow c. behind** suivre de près ▪ **close-fitting** *adj (clothes)* ajusté ▪ **closing** **1** *n* fermeture *f* **2** *adj (remarks)* dernier, -ère; **c. date** *(for application)* date *f* limite; **c. time** heure *f* de fermeture ▪ **close-up** *n* gros plan *m*

close² [kləʊz] **1** *n (end)* fin *f* **2** *vt (door, shop, account, book, eye)* fermer; *(road)* barrer; *(gap)* réduire; *(deal)* conclure **3** *vi (of shop)* se fermer; *(of shop)* fermer ▪ **closed** *adj (door, shop)* fermé; **c.-circuit television** télévision *f*

en circuit fermé ■ **closure** n (of business, factory) fermeture f (définitive)
► **close down 1** vt sep (business, factory) fermer (définitivement) **2** vi (of TV channel) terminer les émissions; (of business, factory) fermer (définitivement)
► **close in** vi (approach) approcher; **to c. in on sb** se rapprocher de qn
► **close up 1** vt sep fermer **2** vi (of shopkeeper) fermer; (of wound) se refermer; (of line of people) se resserrer

closet ['klɒzɪt] n Am (cupboard) placard m; (wardrobe) penderie f

clot [klɒt] **1** n (of blood) caillot m **2** (pt & pp **-tt-**) vi (of blood) (se) coaguler

cloth [klɒθ] n tissu m; (for dusting) chiffon m; (for dishes) torchon m; (tablecloth) nappe f ■ **clothing** n (clothes) vêtements mpl

clothes [kləʊðz] npl vêtements mpl; **to put one's c. on** s'habiller; **to take one's c. off** se déshabiller; **c. line** corde f à linge; Br **c. peg**, Am **c. pin** pince f à linge; **c. shop** magasin m de vêtements

cloud [klaʊd] **1** n nuage m **2** vi **to c. over** (of sky) se couvrir ■ **cloudy** (-ier, -iest) adj (weather, sky) nuageux, -euse; (liquid) trouble

clove [kləʊv] n (spice) clou m de girofle; **c. of garlic** gousse f d'ail

clover ['kləʊvə(r)] n trèfle m

clown [klaʊn] **1** n clown m **2** vi **to c. around** or **about** faire le clown

club [klʌb] **1** n (**a**) (society) club m (**b**) (nightclub) boîte f de nuit (**c**) (weapon) massue f; (in golf) club m (**d**) **clubs** (in cards) trèfle m **2** (pt & pp **-bb-**) vi Br **to c. together** se cotiser (**to buy sth** pour acheter qch)

clue [kluː] n indice m; (of crossword) définition f; Fam **I don't have a c.** je n'en ai pas la moindre idée

clump [klʌmp] n (of flowers, trees) massif m

clumsy ['klʌmzɪ] (-ier, -iest) adj maladroit

clung [klʌŋ] pt & pp of **cling**

cluster ['klʌstə(r)] **1** n groupe m **2** vi se grouper

clutch [klʌtʃ] **1** n (in car) embrayage m; (pedal) pédale f d'embrayage **2** vt tenir fermement **3** vi **to c. at** essayer de saisir

clutter ['klʌtə(r)] **1** n (objects) désordre m **2** vt **to c. (up)** (room, table) encombrer (**with de**)

cm (abbr **centimetre(s)**) cm

Co (abbr **company**) Cie

co- [kəʊ] pref co-

c/o (abbr **care of**) (on envelope) chez

coach [kəʊtʃ] **1** n (**a**) Br (train carriage) voiture f, wagon m; Br (bus) car m; (horse-drawn) carrosse m (**b**) (for sports) entraîneur, -euse mf **2** vt (sportsman, team) entraîner

coal [kəʊl] **1** n charbon m **2** adj (fire) de charbon; **c. industry** industrie f houillère ■ **coalmine** n mine f de charbon

coalition [kəʊə'lɪʃən] n coalition f

coarse [kɔːs] (-er, -est) adj (person, manners) grossier, -ère, vulgaire; (surface, fabric) grossier, -ère

coast [kəʊst] n côte f

coaster ['kəʊstə(r)] n (for glass) dessous-de-verre m inv

coat [kəʊt] **1** n manteau m; (overcoat) pardessus m; (jacket) veste f; (of animal) pelage m; (of paint) couche f; **c. hanger** cintre m **2** vt couvrir (**with** de); (with chocolate, sugar) enrober (**with de**) ■ **coating** n couche f

coax [kəʊks] vt **to c. sb to do** or **into doing sth** amener qn à faire qch par des cajoleries

cob [kɒb] n (of corn) épi m

cobbled ['kɒbəld] adj (street) pavé

cobweb ['kɒbweb] n toile f d'araignée

Coca-Cola® [kəʊkə'kəʊlə] n Coca-Cola® m

cocaine [kəʊ'keɪn] n cocaïne f

cock [kɒk] n (rooster) coq m

cockerel ['kɒkərəl] n jeune coq m

cockney ['kɒknɪ] adj & n cockney (mf) (natif des quartiers est de Londres)

cockpit ['kɒkpɪt] n (of aircraft) poste m de pilotage

cockroach ['kɒkrəʊtʃ] n cafard m

cocktail ['kɒkteɪl] n cocktail m; **fruit c.** macédoine f de fruits; **c. party** cocktail m

cocky ['kɒkɪ] (**-ier, -iest**) adj Fam culotté

cocoa ['kəʊkəʊ] n cacao m

coconut ['kəʊkənʌt] n noix f de coco

COD [siːəʊ'diː] (abbr **cash on delivery**) n Br Com paiement m à la livraison

cod [kɒd] n morue f; (as food) cabillaud m

code [kəʊd] n code m; **in c.** (letter, message) codé; **c. word** code

co-educational [kəʊedjʊ'keɪʃənl] adj (school, teaching) mixte

coerce [kəʊ'ɜːs] vt contraindre (**sb into doing** qn à faire)

coexist [kəʊɪg'zɪst] vi coexister

coffee ['kɒfɪ] n café m; **c. with milk**, Br **white c.** café m au lait; **black c.** café noir; Br **c. bar**, **c. house** café m; **c. break** pause-café f; **c. pot** cafetière f; **c. table** table f basse

coffin ['kɒfɪn] n cercueil m

cog [kɒg] n dent f

cognac ['kɒnjæk] n cognac m

cohabit [kəʊ'hæbɪt] vi vivre en concubinage (**with** avec)

coherent [kəʊ'hɪərənt] adj (logical) cohérent; (way of speaking) compréhensible, intelligible

coil [kɔɪl] n (of wire, rope) rouleau m; (contraceptive) stérilet m

coin [kɔɪn] n pièce f (de monnaie)

coincide [kəʊɪn'saɪd] vi coïncider (**with** avec) ■ **coincidence** n coïncidence f

coke [kəʊk] n (fuel) coke m; (Coca-Cola®) Coca® m inv

colander ['kʌləndə(r)] n (for vegetables) passoire f

cold [kəʊld] 1 (**-er, -est**) adj froid; **to be** or **feel c.** (of person) avoir froid; **my hands are c.** j'ai froid aux mains; **it's c.** (of weather) il fait froid; **to get c.** (of weather) se refroidir; (of food) refroidir; Fam **to get c. feet** se dégonfler; Br **c. meats**, Am **c. cuts** viandes fpl froides

2 n (**a**) (temperature) froid m (**b**) (illness) rhume m; **to have a c.** être enrhumé; **to catch a c.** attraper un rhume; **to get a c.** s'enrhumer ■ **coldness** n froideur f

coleslaw ['kəʊlslɔː] n = salade de chou cru à la mayonnaise

collaborate [kə'læbəreɪt] vi collaborer (**on** à) ■ **collaboration** [-'reɪʃən] n collaboration f

collage ['kɒlɑːʒ] n (picture) collage m

collapse [kə'læps] **1** n effondrement m; (of government) chute f **2** vi (of person, building) s'effondrer; (faint) se trouver mal; (of government) tomber

collar ['kɒlə(r)] n (on garment) col m; (of dog) collier m

colleague ['kɒliːg] n collègue mf

collect [kə'lekt] **1** vt (pick up) ramasser; (gather) rassembler; (information) recueillir; (stamps) collectionner; **to c. money** (in street, church) quêter; **to c. sb** (pick up) passer prendre qn **2** vi (in street, church) quêter (**for** pour) **3** adv Am **to call** or **phone sb c.** téléphoner à qn en PCV

collection [kə'lekʃən] n (of objects, stamps) collection f; (of poems) recueil m; (of money for church) quête f; (of mail) levée f

collector [kə'lektə(r)] n (of stamps) collectionneur, -euse mf

college ['kɒlɪdʒ] n Br (of further education) établissement m d'enseignement supérieur; Am (university) université f; **to be at c.** être étudiant

collide [kə'laɪd] vi entrer en collision (**with** avec) ■ **collision** n collision f

colloquial [kə'ləʊkwɪəl] adj familier, -ère

colon ['kəʊlən] n (**a**) (punctuation mark) deux-points m (**b**) Anat côlon m

colonel ['kɜːnl] n colonel m

colonial [kə'ləʊnɪəl] adj colonial

colony ['kɒlənɪ] (pl **-ies**) n colonie f

colossal [kə'lɒsəl] adj colosse

colour ['kʌlə(r)] (Am **color**) **1** n couleur f **2** adj (photo, television) en couleurs; (television set) couleur inv **3** vt colorer; **to c. (in)** *(drawing)* colorier ■ **coloured** *adj (person, pencil)* de couleur; *(glass)* coloré ■ **colouring** *n (in food)* colorant *m*; *(shade, effect)* coloris *m*; **c. book** album *m* de coloriages

colour-blind ['kʌləblaɪnd] *adj* daltonien, -ienne

colourful ['kʌləfəl] *adj (crowd, story)* coloré; *(person)* pittoresque

column ['kɒləm] *n* colonne *f*; *(newspaper feature)* rubrique *f*

coma ['kəʊmə] *n* **in a c.** dans le coma

comb [kəʊm] **1** *n* peigne *m* **2** *vt Fig (search)* ratisser, passer au peigne fin; **to c. one's hair** se peigner

combat ['kɒmbæt] *n* combat *m*

combination [kɒmbɪ'neɪʃən] *n* combinaison *f*; **in c. with** en association avec; **c. lock** serrure *f* à combinaison

combine [kəm'baɪn] *vt (activities, qualities, elements, sounds)* combiner; *(efforts)* joindre, unir

combustion [kəm'bʌstʃən] *n* combustion *f*

COME [kʌm] *(pt* came, *pp* come*) vi* venir **(from** de; **to** à); **to c. home** rentrer (à la maison); **to c. first** *(in race, exam)* se classer premier; **c. and see me** viens me voir; **to c. near** *or* **close to doing sth** faillir faire qch; **in the years to c.** dans les années à venir
► **come about** *vi (happen)* arriver
► **come across 1** *vi* **to c. across well/ badly** bien/mal passer **2** *vt insep (find)* tomber sur
► **come along** *vi* venir **(with** avec); *(progress) (of work)* avancer; *(of student)* progresser
► **come away** *vi (leave, come off)* partir **(from** de); **to c. away from sb/sth** *(step or move back from)* s'écarter de qn/qch
► **come back** *vi* revenir; *(return home)* rentrer
► **come by** *vt insep (obtain)* obtenir; *(find)* trouver
► **come down 1** *vi* descendre; *(of rain, temperature, price)* tomber; *(of building)* être démoli **2** *vt insep (stairs, hill)* descendre
► **come down with** *vt insep (illness)* attraper
► **come for** *vt insep* venir chercher
► **come forward** *vi (make oneself known, volunteer)* se présenter
► **come in** *vi (enter)* entrer; *(of train)* arriver; *(of money)* rentrer; **to c. in useful** être bien utile
► **come in for** *vt insep* **to c. in for criticism** faire l'objet de critiques
► **come into** *vt insep (room)* entrer dans; *(money)* hériter de
► **come off 1** *vi (of button)* se détacher; *(succeed)* réussir **2** *vt insep (fall from)* tomber de; *(get down from)* descendre de
► **come on** *vi (make progress) (of work)* avancer; *(of student)* progresser; **c. on!** allez!
► **come out** *vi* sortir; *(of sun, book)* paraître; *(of stain)* s'enlever, partir; *(of photo)* réussir; *(of homosexual)* révéler son homosexualité; **to c. out (on strike)** se mettre en grève
► **come over** *vi (visit)* passer **(to** chez); **to c. over to** *(approach)* s'approcher de
► **come round** *vi (visit)* passer **(to** chez); *(regain consciousness)* revenir à soi
► **come through 1** *vi (survive)* s'en tirer **2** *vt insep (crisis)* sortir indemne de
► **come to 1** *vi (regain consciousness)* revenir à soi **2** *vt insep (amount to)* revenir à; **to c. to a conclusion** arriver à une conclusion; **to c. to a decision** se décider
► **come under** *vt insep (heading)* être classé sous
► **come up 1** *vi (rise)* monter; *(of question, job)* se présenter **2** *vt insep (stairs)* monter
► **come up against** *vt insep (problem)* se heurter à
► **come upon** *vt insep (book, reference)* tomber sur

▸ **come up to** *vt insep (reach)* arriver jusqu'à; *(approach)* s'approcher de

▸ **come up with** *vt insep (idea, money)* trouver

comeback ['kʌmbæk] *n* **to make a c.** *(of actor, athlete)* faire un come-back

comedy ['kɒmɪdɪ] *(pl -ies)* n comédie *f* ■ **comedian** *n* comique *mf*

comet ['kɒmɪt] *n* comète *f*

comfort ['kʌmfət] **1** *n (ease)* confort *m*; *(consolation)* réconfort *m*, consolation *f* **2** *vt* consoler ■ **comfortable** *adj (chair, house)* confortable; *(rich)* aisé

comfortably ['kʌmfətəblɪ] *adv (sit)* confortablement; *(win)* facilement; **c. off** *(rich)* à l'aise financièrement

comic ['kɒmɪk] **1** *adj* comique **2** *n Br (magazine)* bande *f* dessinée, BD *f*; **c. strip** bande *f* dessinée ■ **comical** *adj* comique

coming ['kʌmɪŋ] **1** *adj (future) (years, election)* à venir; **the c. days** les prochains jours **2** *n* **comings and goings** allées *fpl* et venues *fpl*

comma ['kɒmə] *n* virgule *f*

command [kə'mɑːnd] **1** *n (order)* ordre *m*; *(authority)* commandement *m*; *(mastery)* maîtrise *f* **(of** de); *Comptr* commande *f* **2** *vt (order)* commander **(sb to do** à qn de faire) ■ **commander** *n Mil* commandant *m* ■ **commanding** *adj (authoritative)* imposant; *(position)* dominant; **c. officer** commandant *m*

commandment [kə'mɑːndmənt] *n Rel* commandement *m*

commemorate [kə'meməreɪt] *vt* commémorer ■ **commemoration** [-'reɪʃən] *n* commémoration *f*

commence [kə'mens] *vti Formal* commencer **(doing** à faire)

commend [kə'mend] *vt (praise)* louer ■ **commendable** *adj* louable

comment ['kɒment] **1** *n* commentaire *m* **(on** sur) **2** *vi* faire des commentaires **(on** sur); **to c. on** *(text, event, news item)* commenter; **to c. that...** remarquer que... ■ **commentary** *(pl -ies)* n commentaire *m*; **live c.** *(on TV or radio)*

reportage *m* en direct ■ **commentator** *n* commentateur, -trice *mf* **(on** de)

commerce ['kɒmɜːs] *n* commerce *m* ■ **commercial** [kə'mɜːʃəl] **1** *adj* commercial **2** *n (advertisement)* publicité *f*; **the commercials** la publicité

commercialize [kə'mɜːʃəlaɪz] *vt Pej (event)* transformer en une affaire de gros sous

commiserate [kə'mɪzəreɪt] *vi* **to c. with sb** être désolé pour qn

commission [kə'mɪʃən] **1** *n (fee, group)* commission *f*; *(order for work)* commande *f* **2** *vt (artist)* passer une commande à; *(book)* commander; **to c. sb to do sth** charger qn de faire qch ■ **commissioner** *n Br (police)* **c.** commissaire *m* de police

commit [kə'mɪt] *(pt & pp -tt-)* *vt (crime)* commettre; *(bind)* engager; *(devote)* consacrer; **to c. suicide** se suicider; **to c. oneself** *(make a promise)* s'engager **(to** à) ■ **commitment** *n (duty, responsibility)* obligation *f*; *(promise)* engagement *m*; *(devotion)* dévouement *m* **(to** à)

committee [kə'mɪtɪ] *n* comité *m*

commodity [kə'mɒdɪtɪ] *(pl -ies)* n *Econ* marchandise *f*, produit *m*

common ['kɒmən] **(-er, -est)** *adj (shared, vulgar)* commun; *(frequent)* courant, commun; **in c.** *(shared)* en commun **(with** avec); **to have nothing in c.** n'avoir rien de commun **(with** avec); **c. room** *(for students)* salle *f* commune; *(for teachers)* salle *f* des professeurs; **c. sense** sens *m* commun, bon sens *m* ■ **commonly** *adv* communément

commonplace ['kɒmənpleɪs] *adj* courant

Commonwealth ['kɒmənwelθ] *n Br* **the C.** le Commonwealth

commotion [kə'məʊʃən] *n (disruption)* agitation *f*

communal [kə'mjuːnəl] *adj (shared) (bathroom, kitchen)* commun; *(of the community)* communautaire

commune [n 'kɒmjuːn] *n (district)*

commune f; (group) communauté f

communicate [kə'mjuːnɪkeɪt] **1** vt communiquer **2** vi (of person) communiquer (**with** avec) ■ **communication** [-'keɪʃən] n communication f; Br **c. cord** (on train) signal m d'alarme

Communion [kə'mjuːnjən] n (Holy) C. communion f; **to take C.** communier

communism ['kɒmjʊnɪzəm] n communisme m ■ **communist** adj & n communiste (mf)

community [kə'mjuːnɪtɪ] **1** (pl -ies) n communauté f; **the student c.** les étudiants mpl **2** adj (life, spirit) communautaire; **c. centre** centre m socioculturel

commute [kə'mjuːt] vi to c. (to work) faire la navette entre son domicile et son travail ■ **commuter** n banlieusard, -e mf; **c. train** train m de banlieue

compact[1] [kəm'pækt] adj (car, crowd, substance) compact; **c. disc** ['kɒmpækt] disque m compact

compact[2] ['kɒmpækt] n (for face powder) poudrier m

companion [kəm'pænjən] n (person) compagnon m, compagne f

company ['kʌmpənɪ] (pl -ies) n (companionship) compagnie f; (guests) invités mpl, -es fpl; (business) société f, compagnie f; (theatre) **c.** compagnie f (théâtrale); **to keep sb c.** tenir compagnie à qn; **c. car** voiture f de société

comparable ['kɒmpərəbəl] adj comparable (**with** or **to** à)

comparative [kəm'pærətɪv] adj (relative) (costs, comfort) relatif, -ive ■ **comparatively** adv relativement

compare [kəm'peə(r)] **1** vt comparer (**with** or **to** à); **compared to** or **with** en comparaison de **2** vi être comparable (**with** à) ■ **comparison** [kəm'pærɪsən] n comparaison f (**between** entre; **with** avec); **by** or **in c.** en comparaison

compartment [kəm'pɑːtmənt] n compartiment m

compass ['kʌmpəs] n (**a**) (for finding direction) boussole f (**b**) (pair of) compasses compas m

compassion [kəm'pæʃən] n compassion f

compatible [kəm'pætɪbəl] adj compatible

compatriot [kəm'pætrɪət, kəm'peɪtrɪət] n compatriote mf

compel [kəm'pel] (pt & pp -ll-) vt forcer, obliger; **to c. sb to do sth** forcer qn à faire qch ■ **compelling** adj (argument) convaincant

compensate ['kɒmpenseɪt] **1** vt to c. sb (with payment, reward) dédommager qn (**for** de) **2** vi compenser; **to c. for sth** (make up for) compenser qch ■ **compensation** [-'seɪʃən] n (financial) dédommagement m; (consolation) compensation f

compère ['kɒmpeə(r)] n animateur, -trice mf

compete [kəm'piːt] vi (take part in race) concourir (**in** à); **to c. (with sb)** rivaliser (avec qn); (in business) faire concurrence (à qn); **to c. for sth** se disputer qch

competent ['kɒmpɪtənt] adj (capable) compétent (**to do** pour faire) ■ **competently** adv avec compétence

competition [kɒmpɪ'tɪʃən] n (**a**) (rivalry) rivalité f; (between companies) concurrence f (**b**) (contest) concours m; (in sport) compétition f

competitive [kəm'petɪtɪv] adj (price, market) compétitif, -ive; (person) qui a l'esprit de compétition ■ **competitor** n concurrent, -e mf

compile [kəm'paɪl] vt (list, catalogue) dresser; (documents) compiler

complacent [kəm'pleɪsənt] adj content de soi

complain [kəm'pleɪn] vi se plaindre (**to sb** à qn; **of** or **about sb/sth** de qn/qch; **that** que) ■ **complaint** n plainte f; (in shop) réclamation f; (illness) maladie f

complement ['kɒmplɪmənt] vt compléter

complete [kəm'pli:t] **1** *adj (whole)* complet, -ète; *(utter)* total; *(finished)* achevé **2** *vt (finish)* achever; *(form)* compléter ∎ **completely** *adv* complètement

complex ['kɔmpleks] **1** *adj* complexe **2** *n (feeling, buildings)* complexe *m* ∎ **complexion** [kəm'plekʃən] *n (of face)* teint *m*

complicate ['kɔmplɪkeɪt] *vt* compliquer ∎ **complication** *n* complication *f*

compliment 1 ['kɔmplɪmənt] *n* compliment *m*; **to pay sb a c.** faire un compliment à qn **2** ['kɔmplɪment] *vt* **to c. sb on sth** *(bravery)* féliciter qn de qch; *(dress, haircut)* faire des compliments à qn sur qch ∎ **complimentary** [-'mentərɪ] *adj* (**a**) *(praising)* élogieux, -euse (**b**) *(free)* gratuit; **c. ticket** billet *m* de faveur

comply [kəm'plaɪ] *(pt & pp* **-ied**) *vi* **to c. with** *(order)* obéir à; *(request)* accéder à

component [kəm'pəʊnənt] *n (of structure, furniture)* élément *m*; *(of machine)* pièce *f*

compose [kəm'pəʊz] *vt* composer; **to c. oneself** se calmer ∎ **composed** *adj* calme ∎ **composer** *n (of music)* compositeur, -trice *mf* ∎ **composition** [kɔmpə'zɪʃən] *n (in music, art, chemistry)* composition *f*

compost ['kɔmpɔst] *n* compost *m*

composure [kəm'pəʊʒə(r)] *n* sang-froid *m*

compound ['kɔmpaʊnd] **1** *n (word) & Chem (substance)* composé *m*; *(area)* enclos *m* **2** *adj (word, substance) & Fin (interest)* composé

comprehend [kɔmprɪ'hend] *vt* comprendre

comprehensive [kɔmprɪ'hensɪv] **1** *adj* complet, -ète; *(study)* exhaustif, -ive; *(knowledge)* étendu; *(insurance)* tous risques *inv* **2** *adj & n Br* **c. (school)** ≃ établissement *m* d'enseignement secondaire *(n'opérant pas de sélection à l'entrée)*

compress [kəm'pres] *vt (gas, air)* comprimer

comprise [kəm'praɪz] *vt (consist of)* comprendre; *(make up)* constituer

compromise ['kɔmprəmaɪz] **1** *n* compromis *m* **2** *vt (person, security)* compromettre **3** *vi* transiger (**on** sur)

compulsion [kəm'pʌlʃən] *n (urge)* besoin *m*; *(obligation)* contrainte *f* ∎ **compulsive** *adj (smoker, gambler, liar)* invétéré

compulsory [kəm'pʌlsərɪ] *adj* obligatoire

computer [kəm'pju:tə(r)] **1** *n* ordinateur *m* **2** *adj (program, system, network)* informatique; *(course, firm)* d'informatique; **c. game** jeu *m* électronique; **c. science** informatique *f* ∎ **computerized** *adj* informatisé

computing [kəm'pju:tɪŋ] *n* informatique *f*

con [kɔn] *Fam* **1** *n* arnaque *f*; **c. man** arnaqueur *m* **2** *(pt & pp* **-nn-***)* *vt* arnaquer; **to be conned** se faire arnaquer

conceal [kən'si:l] *vt (hide) (object)* dissimuler (**from sb** à qn); *(plan, news)* cacher (**from sb** à qn)

concede [kən'si:d] **1** *vt* concéder (à; **that** que) **2** *vi* s'incliner

conceited [kən'si:tɪd] *adj* vaniteux, -euse

conceive [kən'si:v] **1** *vt (idea, child)* concevoir **2** *vi (of woman)* concevoir; **to c. of sth** concevoir qch ∎ **conceivable** *adj* concevable; **it's c. that…** il est concevable que… (+ *subjunctive*)

concentrate ['kɔnsəntreɪt] **1** *vt* concentrer (**on** sur) **2** *vi* se concentrer (**on** sur); **to c. on doing sth** s'appliquer à faire qch ∎ **concentration** [-'treɪʃən] *n* concentration *f*; **c. camp** camp *m* de concentration

concept ['kɔnsept] *n* concept *m*

concern [kən'sɜ:n] **1** *n (matter)* affaire *f*; *(worry)* inquiétude *f*; **his c. for** son souci de; *(business)* **c.** entreprise *f* **2** *vt* concerner; **to be concerned about** *(be worried)* s'inquiéter de; **as far as I'm concerned…** en ce qui me concerne... ■ **concerned** adj (anxious) inquiet, -ète (**about/at** au sujet de); **the person c.** (in question) la personne dont il s'agit; (involved) la personne concernée ■ **concerning** prep en ce qui concerne

concert ['kɒnsət] n concert m; **c. hall** salle f de concert

concerto [kən'tʃɑːtəʊ] (pl **-os**) n concerto m; **piano c.** concerto m pour piano

concession [kən'seʃən] n concession f (**to** à)

conciliatory [kən'sɪlɪətərɪ, Am -tɔːrɪ] adj (tone, person) conciliant

concise [kən'saɪs] adj concis

conclude [kən'kluːd] **1** vt (end, settle) conclure; **to c. that...** (infer) conclure que... **2** vi (of event) se terminer (**with** par); (of speaker) conclure ■ **conclusion** n conclusion f ■ **conclusive** adj concluant

concoct [kən'kɒkt] vt (dish, scheme) concocter ■ **concoction** n (dish, drink) mixture f

concourse ['kɒŋkɔːs] n (in airport, train station) hall m

concrete ['kɒŋkriːt] **1** n béton m; **c. wall** mur m en béton **2** adj (ideas, example) concret, -ète

concur [kən'kɜː(r)] (pt & pp **-rr-**) vi (agree) être d'accord (**with** avec)

concurrently [kən'kʌrəntlɪ] adv simultanément

concussion [kən'kʌʃən] n (injury) commotion f cérébrale

condemn [kən'dem] vt condamner (**to** à); (building) déclarer inhabitable

condense [kən'dens] vt condenser ■ **condensation** [kɒndən'seɪʃən] n (mist) buée f

condescend [kɒndɪ'send] vi condescendre (**to do** à faire)

condition [kən'dɪʃən] n (stipulation, circumstance) condition f; (state) état m, condition f; (disease) maladie f; **on the c. that...** à la condition que... (+ subjunctive); **in good c.** en bon état; **in/out of c.** en bonne/mauvaise

forme ■ **conditional** adj conditionnel, -elle

conditioner [kən'dɪʃənə(r)] n (hair) c. après-shampooing m

condo ['kɒndəʊ] (pl **-os**) n Am = **condominium**

condolences [kən'dəʊlənsɪz] npl condoléances fpl

condom ['kɒndɒm] n préservatif m

condominium [kɒndə'mɪnɪəm] n Am (building) immeuble m en copropriété; (apartment) appartement m en copropriété

condone [kən'dəʊn] vt (overlook) fermer les yeux sur; (forgive) excuser

conducive [kən'djuːsɪv] adj **to be c. to** être favorable à

conduct 1 ['kɒndʌkt] n (behaviour, directing) conduite f **2** [kən'dʌkt] vt (campaign, inquiry, experiment) mener; (orchestra) diriger; (electricity, heat) conduire; **to c. oneself** se conduire; **conducted tour** (of building, region) visite f guidée

conductor [kən'dʌktə(r)] n (of orchestra) chef m d'orchestre; Br (on bus) receveur m; Am (on train) chef m de train

cone [kəʊn] n cône m; (for ice cream) cornet m; **pine** or **fir c.** pomme f de pin; Br **traffic c.** cône de chantier

confectionery [kən'fekʃənərɪ] n (sweets) confiserie f; (cakes) pâtisserie f

confederation [kənfedə'reɪʃən] n confédération f

confer [kən'fɜː(r)] (pt & pp **-rr-**) **1** vt (grant) octroyer (**on** à) **2** vi (talk together) se consulter (**on** or **about** sur); **to c. with sb** consulter qn

conference ['kɒnfərəns] n conférence f; (scientific, academic) congrès m; **press** or **news c.** conférence f de presse

confess [kən'fes] **1** vt avouer, confesser (**that** que; **to sb** à qn); Rel confesser **2** vi avouer; Rel se confesser; **to c. to sth** (crime) avouer ou confesser qch ■ **confession** n aveu m, confession f; Rel confession f; **to go to c.** aller à confesse

confetti [kən'fetɪ] n confettis mpl
confide [kən'faɪd] 1 vt confier (**to** à; **that** que) 2 vi **to c. in sb** se confier à qn
confidence ['kɒnfɪdəns] n (trust) confiance f (**in** en); (self-)c. confiance f en soi; **in c.** en confidence; **c. trick** escroquerie f ■ **confident** adj (smile, exterior) confiant; (self-)c. sûr de soi ■ **confidently** adv avec confiance
confidential [kɒnfɪ'denʃəl] adj confidentiel, -elle ■ **confidentially** adv en confidence
confine [kən'faɪn] vt (**a**) (limit) limiter (**to** à); **to c. oneself to doing sth** se limiter à faire qch (**b**) (keep prisoner) enfermer (**to/in** dans) ■ **confined** adj (space) réduit; **c. to bed** alité; **c. to one's room** obligé de garder la chambre
confirm [kən'fɜ:m] vt confirmer (**that** que) ■ **confirmation** [kɒnfə'meɪʃən] n also Rel confirmation f ■ **confirmed** adj (bachelor) endurci; (smoker) invétéré
confiscate ['kɒnfɪskeɪt] vt confisquer (**from** à)
conflict 1 ['kɒnflɪkt] n conflit m **2** [kən'flɪkt] vi (of statement) être en contradiction (**with** avec); (of dates, events, programmes) tomber en même temps (**with** que) ■ **conflicting** adj (views, theories, evidence) contradictoire; (dates) incompatible
conform [kən'fɔ:m] vi (of person) se conformer (**to** or **with** à); (of ideas, actions) être en conformité (**to** with); (of product) être conforme (**to** or **with** à)
confront [kən'frʌnt] vt (danger) affronter; (problem) faire face à; **to c. sb** (be face to face with) se trouver en face de qn; (oppose) s'opposer à qn; **to c. sb with sth** mettre qn en face de qch ■ **confrontation** [kɒnfrʌn'teɪʃən] n confrontation f
confuse [kən'fju:z] vt (make unsure) embrouiller; **to c. sb/sth with** (mistake for) confondre qn/qch avec; **to c. matters** or **the issue** embrouiller la

question ■ **confused** adj (situation, noises, idea) confus; **to get c.** s'embrouiller ■ **confusing** adj déroutant ■ **confusion** [-ʒən] n (bewilderment) perplexité f; (disorder, lack of clarity) confusion f
congested [kən'dʒestɪd] adj (street, town, lungs) congestionné; (nose) bouché ■ **congestion** [-tʃən] n (traffic) encombrements mpl; (overcrowding) surpeuplement m
congratulate [kən'grætʃʊleɪt] vt féliciter (**sb on sth** qn de qch; **sb on doing sth** qn d'avoir fait qch) ■ **congratulations** [-'leɪʃənz] npl félicitations fpl (**on** pour)
congregate ['kɒngrɪgeɪt] vi se rassembler ■ **congregation** [-'geɪʃən] n (worshippers) fidèles mpl
Congress ['kɒngres] n Am Pol le Congrès (assemblée législative américaine)
conifer ['kɒnɪfə(r)] n conifère m
conjunction [kən'dʒʌŋkʃən] n **in c. with** conjointement avec
connect [kə'nekt] 1 vt relier (**with** or **to** à); (telephone, washing machine) brancher; **to c. sb with sb** (on phone) mettre qn en communication avec qn; **to c. sb/sth with sb/sth** établir un lien entre qn/qch et qn/qch
2 vi (of train, bus) assurer la correspondance avec ■ **connected** adj (facts, events) lié; **to be c. with** (have to do with, relate to) avoir un lien avec
connection [kə'nekʃən] n (link) rapport m, lien m (**with** avec); (train, bus) correspondance f; (phone call) communication f; (between electrical wires) contact m; connections (contacts) relations fpl; **to have no c. with** n'avoir aucun rapport avec; **in c. with** à propos de
connive [kə'naɪv] vi **to c. with sb** être de connivence avec qn
connoisseur [kɒnə'sɜ:(r)] n connaisseur m
connotation [kɒnə'teɪʃən] n connotation f

conquer [ˈkɒŋkə(r)] *vt (country)* conquérir; *(enemy, habit, difficulty)* vaincre ▪ **conquest** *n* conquête *f*

cons [kɒnz] *npl* **the pros and (the) c.** le pour et le contre

conscience [ˈkɒnʃəns] *n* conscience *f*; **to have sth on one's c.** avoir qch sur la conscience

conscientious [kɒnʃɪˈenʃəs] *adj* consciencieux, -euse; **c. objector** objecteur *m* de conscience

conscious [ˈkɒnʃəs] *adj (awake)* conscient; **to make a c. effort to do sth** faire un effort particulier pour faire qch; **c. of sth** *(aware)* conscient de qch ▪ **consciously** *adv (knowingly)* consciemment ▪ **consciousness** *n* **to lose/regain c.** perdre/reprendre connaissance

conscript 1 [ˈkɒnskrɪpt] *n (soldier)* conscrit *m* **2** [kənˈskrɪpt] *vt* enrôler ▪ **conscription** [kənˈskrɪpʃən] *n* conscription *f*

consecutive [kənˈsekjʊtɪv] *adj* consécutif, -ive

consensus [kənˈsensəs] *n* consensus *m*

consent [kənˈsent] **1** *n* consentement *m* **2** *vi* consentir (**to** à)

consequence [ˈkɒnsɪkwəns] *n (result)* conséquence *f* ▪ **consequently** *adv* par conséquent

conservative [kənˈsɜːvətɪv] **1** *adj (estimate)* modeste; *(view, attitude)* traditionnel, -elle; *(person)* traditionaliste; *Br Pol* conservateur, -trice **2** *n Br Pol* conservateur, -trice *mf*

conservatory [kənˈsɜːvətrɪ] (*pl* **-ies**) *n Br (room)* véranda *f*

conserve [kənˈsɜːv] *vt (energy, water, electricity)* faire des économies de ▪ **conservation** [kɒnsəˈveɪʃən] *n (of energy)* économies *fpl*; *(of nature)* protection *f* de l'environnement

consider [kənˈsɪdə(r)] *vt (think over)* considérer; *(take into account)* tenir compte de; *(an offer)* étudier; **to c. doing sth** envisager de faire qch; **to c. that…** considérer que…; **I c. her**

(as) a friend je la considère comme une amie; **all things considered** tout bien considéré

considerable [kənˈsɪdərəbəl] *adj (large)* considérable; *(much)* beaucoup de ▪ **considerably** *adv* considérablement

considerate [kənˈsɪdərət] *adj* attentionné (**to** à l'égard de)

consideration [kənsɪdəˈreɪʃən] *n* considération *f*; **to take sth into c.** prendre qch en considération

considering [kənˈsɪdərɪŋ] **1** *prep* étant donné **2** *conj* **c. (that)** étant donné que

consignment [kənˈsaɪnmənt] *n (goods)* envoi *m*

consist [kənˈsɪst] *vi* consister (**of** en; **in** en; **in doing** à faire)

consistent [kənˈsɪstənt] *adj (unchanging) (quality, results)* constant ▪ **consistency** *n (of substance, liquid)* consistance *f* ▪ **consistently** *adv (always)* constamment; *(regularly)* régulièrement

console[1] [kənˈsəʊl] *vt* consoler ▪ **consolation** *n* consolation *f*; **c. prize** lot *m* de consolation

console[2] [ˈkɒnsəʊl] *n (control desk)* console *f*

consolidate [kənˈsɒlɪdeɪt] *vt* consolider

consonant [ˈkɒnsənənt] *n* consonne *f*

conspicuous [kənˈspɪkjʊəs] *adj (noticeable)* bien visible; *(striking)* manifeste; *(showy)* voyant

conspiracy [kənˈspɪrəsɪ] (*pl* **-ies**) *n* conspiration *f*

conspire [kənˈspaɪə(r)] *vi* conspirer (**against** contre); **to c. to do sth** comploter de faire qch

constable [ˈkʌnstəbəl] *n Br* **(police) c.** agent *m* de police

constant [ˈkɒnstənt] *adj (frequent)* incessant; *(unchanging)* constant ▪ **constantly** *adv* constamment, sans cesse

constellation [kɒnstəˈleɪʃən] *n* constellation *f*

constipated [ˈkɒnstɪpeɪtɪd] *adj* constipé

constituent [kənˈstɪtjʊənt] *n Pol (voter)* électeur, -trice *mf* ■ **constituency** (*pl* -**ies**) *n* circonscription *f* électorale; (*voters*) électeurs *mpl*

constitute [ˈkɒnstɪtjuːt] *vt* constituer ■ **constitution** *n* constitution *f*

constraint [kənˈstreɪnt] *n* contrainte *f*

construct [kənˈstrʌkt] *vt* construire ■ **construction** *n* (*building, structure, in grammar*) construction *f*; **under c.** en construction; **c. site** chantier *m* ■ **constructive** *adj* constructif, -ive

consul [ˈkɒnsəl] *n* consul *m* ■ **consulate** [-sjʊlət] *n* consulat *m*

consult [kənˈsʌlt] **1** *vt* consulter **2** *vi* **to c. with sb** discuter avec qn; *Br* **consulting room** (*of doctor*) cabinet *m* de consultation ■ **consultation** [kɒnsəlˈteɪʃən] *n* consultation *f*

consultancy [kənˈsʌltənsɪ] (*pl* -**ies**) *n* **c. (firm)** cabinet-conseil *m* ■ **consultant** *n Br* (*doctor*) spécialiste *mf*; (*adviser*) consultant *m*

consume [kənˈsjuːm] *vt* (*food, supplies*) consommer; (*of fire*) consumer; (*of grief, hate*) dévorer ■ **consumer** *n* consommateur, -trice *mf* ■ **consumption** [-ˈsʌmpʃən] *n* consommation *f*

contact [ˈkɒntækt] **1** *n* (*act of touching*) contact *m*; (*person*) relation *f*; **in c. with** en contact avec; **c. lenses** lentilles *fpl* de contact **2** *vt* contacter

contagious [kənˈteɪdʒəs] *adj* (*disease*) contagieux, -euse

contain [kənˈteɪn] *vt* (*enclose, hold back*) contenir ■ **container** *n* (*box, jar*) récipient *m*; (*for transporting goods*) conteneur *m*

contaminate [kənˈtæmɪneɪt] *vt* contaminer

contemplate [ˈkɒntəmpleɪt] *vt* (*look at*) contempler; (*consider*) envisager (**doing** de faire)

contemporary [kənˈtempərərɪ] **1** *adj* contemporain (**with** de); (*style*) moderne **2** (*pl* -**ies**) *n* (*person*) contemporain, -e *mf*

contempt [kənˈtempt] *n* mépris *m*; **to hold sb/sth in c.** mépriser qn/qch ■ **contemptible** *adj* méprisable ■ **contemptuous** *adj* méprisant; **to be c. of sth** mépriser qch

contend [kənˈtend] *vi* **to c. with** (*problem*) faire face à ■ **contender** *n* (*in sport*) concurrent, -e *mf*; (*in election, for job*) candidat, -e *mf*

content¹ [kənˈtent] *adj* (*happy*) satisfait (**with** de) ■ **contented** *adj* satisfait ■ **contentment** *n* contentement *m*

content² [ˈkɒntent] *n* (*of book, text, film*) (*subject matter*) contenu *m*; **contents** contenu *m*; (*in book*) table *f* des matières; **alcoholic/iron c.** teneur *f* en alcool/fer

contest **1** [ˈkɒntest] *n* (*competition*) concours *m*; (*fight*) lutte *f*; (*in boxing*) combat *m* **2** [kənˈtest] *vt* (*dispute*) contester ■ **contestant** [kənˈtestənt] *n* concurrent, -e *mf*; (*in fight*) adversaire *mf*

context [ˈkɒntekst] *n* contexte *m*; **in/out of c.** en/hors contexte

continent [ˈkɒntɪnənt] *n* continent *m*; **the C.** l'Europe *f* continentale; **on the C.** en Europe ■ **continental** [-ˈnentəl] *adj* (*of Europe*) européen, -enne; **c. breakfast** petit déjeuner *m* à la française

contingent [kənˈtɪndʒənt] *n* (*group*) contingent *m* ■ **contingency** (*pl* -**ies**) *n* éventualité *f*; **c. plan** plan *m* d'urgence

continual [kənˈtɪnjʊəl] *adj* continuel, -elle

continue [kənˈtɪnjuː] **1** *vt* continuer (**to do** *or* **doing** à *ou* de faire); **to c. (with)** (*work, speech*) poursuivre; (*resume*) reprendre **2** *vi* continuer; (*resume*) reprendre

continuous [kənˈtɪnjʊəs] *adj* continu; *Sch & Univ* **c. assessment** contrôle *m* continu des connaissances ■ **continuously** *adv* sans interruption

contour [ˈkɒntʊə(r)] *n* contour *m*

contraception [kɒntrəˈsepʃən] *n*

contraception *f* ■ **contraceptive** *n* contraceptif *m*

contract¹ [ˈkɒntrækt] **1** *n* contrat *m*; **to be under c.** être sous contrat; **c. work** travail *m* en sous-traitance **2** *vt* **to c. work out** sous-traiter du travail ■ **contractor** *n* entrepreneur *m*

contract² [kənˈtrækt] **1** *vt (illness)* contracter **2** *vi (shrink)* se contracter

contradict [kɒntrəˈdɪkt] *vt (person, statement)* contredire; *(deny)* démentir; **to c. oneself** se contredire ■ **contradictory** *adj* contradictoire

contraption [kənˈtræpʃən] *n Fam* machin *m*

contrary [ˈkɒntrərɪ] **1** *adj (opposite)* contraire (**to** à) **2** *adv* **c. to** contrairement à **3** *n* contraire *m*; **on the c.** au contraire; **unless you/I/etc hear to the c.** sauf avis contraire

contrast 1 [ˈkɒntrɑːst] *n* contraste *m*; **in c. to** par opposition à **2** [kənˈtrɑːst] *vt* mettre en contraste **3** [kənˈtrɑːst] *vi* contraster (**with** avec)

contravention [kɒntrəˈvenʃən] *n* **in c. of a treaty** en violation d'un traité

contribute [kənˈtrɪbjuːt] **1** *vt (time, clothes)* donner (**to** à); *(article)* écrire (**to** pour); **to c. money** to verser de l'argent à **2** *vi* **to c. to** contribuer à; *(publication)* collaborer à; *(discussion)* prendre part à; *(charity)* donner à ■ **contribution** [kɒntrɪˈbjuːʃən] *n* contribution *f* ■ **contributor** *n (to newspaper)* collaborateur, -trice *mf*; *(of money)* donateur, -trice *mf*

contrive [kənˈtraɪv] *vt* **to c. to do sth** trouver moyen de faire qch

contrived [kənˈtraɪvd] *adj* qui manque de naturel

control [kənˈtrəʊl] **1** *n* contrôle *m*; *(authority)* autorité *f* (**over** sur); **(self-)c.** la maîtrise (de soi); **the situation** *or* **everything is under c.** je/il/etc contrôle la situation; **to lose c. of** *(situation, vehicle)* perdre le contrôle de; **out of c.** *(situation, crowd)* difficilement maîtrisable; *Comptr* **c. key** touche *f* de contrôle; **c.**

panel tableau *m* de bord

2 *(pt & pp* **-ll-***)* *vt (business, organization)* diriger; *(prices, quality)* contrôler; *(emotion, reaction)* maîtriser; *(disease)* enrayer; **to c. oneself** se contrôler

controversy [ˈkɒntrəvɜːsɪ] *(pl* **-ies***)* *n* controverse *f* ■ **controversial** [-ˈvɜː- ʃəl] *adj* controversé

convalesce [kɒnvəˈles] *vi (rest)* être en convalescence

convenience [kənˈviːnɪəns] *n* commodité *f*; *Br* **(public) conveniences** toilettes *fpl*; **c. food(s)** plats *mpl* tout préparés; **c. store** magasin *m* de proximité

convenient [kənˈviːnɪənt] *adj* commode, pratique; **to be c. (for)** *(suit)* convenir (à) ■ **conveniently** *adv* **c. situated** bien situé

convention [kənˈvenʃən] *n (custom)* usage *m*; *(agreement)* convention *f*; *(conference)* convention *f*, congrès *m* ■ **conventional** *adj* conventionnel, -elle

converge [kənˈvɜːdʒ] *vi* converger (**on** sur)

conversation [kɒnvəˈseɪʃən] *n* conversation *f* (**with** avec)

convert 1 [ˈkɒnvɜːt] *n* converti, -e *mf* **2** [kənˈvɜːt] *vt (change)* convertir (**into** *or* **to** en); *(building)* aménager (**into, to** en); *Rel* **to c. sb** convertir qn (**to** à) **3** *vi (change religion)* se convertir (**to** à) ■ **conversion** *n* conversion *f*; *(of building)* aménagement *m*

convertible [kənˈvɜːtəbəl] **1** *adj (sofa)* convertible **2** *n (car)* décapotable *f*

convey [kənˈveɪ] *vt (transport)* transporter; *(communicate)* transmettre ■ **conveyor belt** *n* tapis *m* roulant

convict 1 [ˈkɒnvɪkt] *n* détenu *m* **2** [kənˈvɪkt] *vt* déclarer coupable (**of** de) ■ **conviction** [kənˈvɪkʃən] *n (for crime)* condamnation *f*; *(belief)* conviction *f* (**that** que)

convince [kənˈvɪns] *vt* convaincre (**of sth** de qch; **sb to do sth** qn de faire qch) ■ **convincing** *adj (argument,* *person)* convaincant

convoy ['kɒnvɔɪ] *n* convoi *m*

cook [kʊk] **1** *n (person)* cuisinier, -ère *mf* **2** *vt (meal)* préparer; *(food)* (faire) cuire **3** *vi (of food)* cuire; *(of person)* faire la cuisine ■ **cookbook** *n* livre *m* de cuisine ■ **cooker** *n Br (stove)* cuisinière *f* ■ **cookery** *n* cuisine *f; Br* **c. book** livre *m* de cuisine ■ **cooking** *n (activity, food)* cuisine *f; (process)* cuisson *f;* **to do the c.** faire la cuisine; **c. apple** pomme *f* à cuire

cookie ['kʊkɪ] *n Am* gâteau *m* sec

cool [ku:l] **1** **(-er, -est)** *adj (weather, place, wind)* frais *(f* fraîche); *(tea, soup)* tiède; *(calm)* calme; *(unfriendly)* froid; *Fam (good)* cool *inv; Fam (fashionable)* branché; **a (nice) c. drink** une boisson (bien) fraîche; **the weather is c., it's c.** il fait frais; **to keep sth c.** tenir qch au frais

2 *n* **to keep/lose one's c.** garder/perdre son sang-froid

3 *vt* **to c. (down)** refroidir, rafraîchir **4** *vi* **to c. (down or off)** *(of hot liquid)* refroidir; *(of enthusiasm)* se refroidir; *(of angry person)* se calmer; **to c. off** *(by drinking, swimming)* se rafraîchir ■ **cooler** *n (for food)* glacière *f*

coop [ku:p] *vt* **to c. up** *(person, animal)* enfermer

co-op ['kəʊɒp] *n* coopérative *f*

cooperate [kəʊ'ɒpəreɪt] *vi* coopérer (**in** à; **with** avec) ■ **cooperation** *n* coopération *f*

coordinate [kəʊ'ɔ:dɪneɪt] *vt* coordonner ■ **coordination** [-'neɪʃən] *n* coordination *f*

cop [kɒp] *n Fam (policeman)* flic *m*

cope [kəʊp] *vi* **to c. with** *(problem, demand)* faire face à

copier ['kɒpɪə(r)] *n (photocopier)* photocopieuse *f*

copper ['kɒpə(r)] *n (metal)* cuivre *m; Br* **coppers** *(coins)* petite monnaie *f*

copy ['kɒpɪ] **1** **(-ies)** *n (of letter, document)* copie *f; (of book, magazine)* exemplaire *m; (of photo)* épreuve *f* **2** *(pt & pp* **-ied)** *vt* copier; **to c. out or**

down *(text, letter)* copier **3** *vi* copier

coral ['kɒrəl] *n* corail *m*

cord [kɔ:d] *n* (**a**) *(of curtain, bell, pyjamas)* cordon *m; (electrical)* cordon électrique (**b**) **cords** *(trousers)* pantalon *m* en velours côtelé

cordial ['kɔ:dɪəl] **1** *adj (friendly)* cordial **2** *n Br (fruit)* **c.** sirop *m*

cordless ['kɔ:dləs] *adj* **c. phone** téléphone *m* sans fil

cordon ['kɔ:dən] **1** *n* cordon *m* **2** *vt* **to c. off** *(road)* barrer; *(area)* boucler

corduroy ['kɔ:dərɔɪ] *n* velours *m* côtelé

core [kɔ:(r)] *n (of apple)* trognon *m; (of problem)* cœur *m; (group of people)* noyau *m*

cork [kɔ:k] **1** *n (material)* liège *m; (stopper)* bouchon *m* **2** *vt (bottle)* boucher ■ **corkscrew** *n* tire-bouchon *m*

corn[1] [kɔ:n] *n Br (wheat)* blé *m; Am (maize)* maïs *m;* **c. on the cob** maïs *m* en épi, *Can* blé *m* en Inde

corn[2] [kɔ:n] *n (on foot)* cor *m*

corner ['kɔ:nə(r)] **1** *n (of street, room, page, screen)* coin *m; (bend in road)* virage *m; (in football)* corner *m;* **it's just round the c.** c'est juste au coin; **c. shop** épicerie *f* du coin **2** *vt (person, animal)* acculer

cornet ['kɔ:nɪt] *n Br (of ice cream)* cornet *m*

cornflakes ['kɔ:nfleɪks] *npl* corn flakes *mpl*

corny ['kɔ:nɪ] **(-ier, -iest)** *adj Fam (joke)* nul *(f* nulle); *(film)* tarte

coronary ['kɒrənərɪ] *(pl* **-ies)** *n Med* infarctus *m*

coronation [kɒrə'neɪʃən] *n* couronnement *m*

corporal[1] ['kɔ:pərəl] *n (in army)* caporal-chef *m*

corporal[2] ['kɔ:pərəl] *adj* **c. punishment** châtiment *m* corporel

corporate ['kɔ:pərət] *adj (decision)* collectif, -ive

corporation [kɔ:pə'reɪʃən] *n (business)* société *f*

corps [kɔ:(r), *pl* kɔ:z] *n inv Mil & Pol*

corps *m*; **the press c.** les journalistes *mpl*

corpse [kɔ:ps] *n* cadavre *m*

correct [kə'rekt] **1** *adj (accurate)* exact; *(proper)* correct; **he's c.** il a raison; **the c. time** l'heure exacte **2** *vt* corriger ■ **correction** *n* correction *f*

correspond [kɒrɪ'spɒnd] *vi* correspondre ■ **corresponding** *adj (matching)* correspondant; *(similar)* semblable

correspondence [kɒrɪ'spɒndəns] *n* correspondance *f*; **c. course** cours *m* par correspondance

corridor ['kɒrɪdɔ:(r)] *n* couloir *m*, corridor *m*

corrosion [kə'rəʊʒən] *n* corrosion *f*

corrugated ['kɒrəgeɪtɪd] *adj* ondulé

corrupt [kə'rʌpt] **1** *adj* corrompu **2** *vt* corrompre ■ **corruption** *n* corruption *f*

Corsica ['kɔ:sɪkə] *n* la Corse

cosmetic [kɒz'metɪk] **1** *adj* **c. surgery** chirurgie *f* esthétique **2** *n* produit *m* de beauté

cosmopolitan [kɒzmə'pɒlɪtən] *adj* cosmopolite

cost [kɒst] **1** *n* coût *m*; **the c. of living** le coût de la vie; **at any c., at all costs** à tout prix

2 *(pt & pp cost)* *vti* coûter; **how much does it c.?** ça coûte combien? ■ **costly** *(-ier, -iest)* *adj (expensive) (car, trip)* coûteux, -euse

costume ['kɒstju:m] *n* costume *m*; *Br* **(swimming)** **c.** maillot *m* de bain

cosy ['kəʊzɪ] **1** *(-ier, -iest)* *adj Br (house)* douillet, -ette; *(atmosphere)* intime **2** *n (tea)* **c.** couvre-théière *m*

cot [kɒt] *n Br (for child)* lit *m* d'enfant; *Am (camp bed)* lit *m* de camp

cottage ['kɒtɪdʒ] *n* petite maison *f* de campagne; **(thatched)** **c.** chaumière *f*; **c. cheese** fromage *m* blanc (maigre)

cotton ['kɒtən] *n* coton *m*; *(yarn)* fil *m* de coton; *Br* **c. wool**, *Am* **absorbent c.** coton *m* hydrophile, ouate *f*; **c. shirt** chemise *f* en coton; *Am* **c. candy** barbe *f* à papa

couch [kaʊtʃ] *n (sofa)* canapé *m*; *(for doctor's patient)* lit *m*

couchette [ku:'ʃet] *n Br (on train)* couchette *f*

cough [kɒf] **1** *n* toux *f*; **c. syrup** *or* **medicine**, *Br* **c. mixture** sirop *m* pour la toux **2** *vt* **to c. up** *(blood)* cracher **3** *vi* tousser

could [kʊd, *unstressed* kəd] *pt of* **can¹**

couldn't ['kʊdənt] = **could not**

council ['kaʊnsəl] *n* **(town/city) c.** conseil *m* municipal; *Br* **c. flat/house** ≃ HLM *f*; *Br* **c. tax** = impôt regroupant taxe d'habitation et impôts locaux ■ **councillor** *n* **(town) c.** conseiller *m* municipal

counselling ['kaʊnsəlɪŋ] *(Am* **counseling**) *n* assistance *f* psychosociale

count¹ [kaʊnt] *n (calculation)* compte *m*; **to keep c. of sth** tenir le compte de qch

2 *vt (find number of, include)* compter; *(consider)* considérer; **c. me in!** j'en suis!; **c. me out!** ne compte pas sur moi!

3 *vi* compter; **to c. against sb** jouer contre qn; **to c. on sb/sth** *(rely on)* compter sur qn/qch; **to c. on doing sth** compter faire qch ■ **countdown** *n* compte *m* à rebours

count² [kaʊnt] *n (title)* comte *m*

counter ['kaʊntə(r)] **1** *n* **(a)** *(in shop, bar)* comptoir *m*; *(in bank)* guichet *m* **(b)** *(in games)* jeton *m* **(c)** *(counting device)* compteur *m* **2** *adv* **c. to** contrairement à **3** *vt (threat)* répondre à; *(effects)* neutraliser **4** *vi* riposter **(with par)**

counter- ['kaʊntə(r)] *pref* contre-

counterattack ['kaʊntərətæk] **1** *n* contre-attaque *f* **2** *vti* contre-attaquer

counterclockwise [kaʊntə'klɒkwaɪz] *adj & adv Am* dans le sens inverse des aiguilles d'une montre

counterfeit ['kaʊntəfɪt] **1** *adj* faux (*f* fausse) **2** *vt* contrefaire

counterpart ['kaʊntəpɑ:t] *n (thing)* équivalent *m*; *(person)* homologue *mf*

countless ['kaʊntlɪs] *adj* innombrable

country ['kʌntrɪ] (*pl* **-ies**) **1** *n* pays *m*; (*opposed to town*) campagne *f*; **in the c.** à la campagne **2** *adj* (*house, road*) de campagne; **c. and western music** country *f* ■ **countryman** (*pl* **-men**) *n* (**fellow**) **c.** compatriote *m* ■ **countryside** *n* campagne *f*; **in the c.** à la campagne

county ['kaʊntɪ] (*pl* **-ies**) *n* comté *m*

coup [kuː, *pl* kuːz] *n Pol* coup *m* d'État

couple ['kʌpəl] **1** *n* (*of people*) couple *m*; **a c. of** deux ou trois; (*a few*) quelques **2** *vt* (*connect*) accoupler

coupon ['kuːpɒn] *n* (*for discount*) bon *m*; (*form*) coupon *m*

courage ['kʌrɪdʒ] *n* courage *m* ■ **courageous** [kə'reɪdʒəs] *adj* courageux, -euse

courgette [kʊə'ʒet] *n Br* courgette *f*

courier ['kʊrɪə(r)] *n* (*for tourists*) guide *mf*; (*messenger*) messager *m*

course [kɔːs] **1** *n* (**a**) (*of river, time, events*) cours *m*; (*of ship*) route *f*; **c. of action** ligne *f* de conduite; **in the c. of** au cours de; **in due c.** en temps utile (**b**) (*lessons*) cours *m* (**c**) *Med* **c. of treatment** traitement *m* (**d**) (*of meal*) plat *m*; **first c.** entrée *f* (**e**) (*for race*) parcours *m*; (*for horseracing*) champ *m* de courses; (*for golf*) terrain *m* **2** *adv* **of c.!** bien sûr!; **of c. not!** bien sûr que non!

court¹ [kɔːt] *n* (*of king*) cour *f*; (*for trials*) cour *f*, tribunal *m*; (*for tennis*) court *m*; **to go to c.** aller en justice; **to take sb to c.** poursuivre en justice ■ **courthouse** *n Am* palais *m* de justice ■ **courtroom** *n Law* salle *f* d'audience ■ **courtyard** *n* cour *f*

court² [kɔːt] **1** *vt* (*woman*) faire la cour à; (*danger*) aller au-devant de **2** *vi* **to be courting** (*of couple*) se fréquenter

courteous ['kɜːtɪəs] *adj* poli, courtois ■ **courtesy** [-təsɪ] (*pl* **-ies**) *n* politesse *f*, courtoisie *f*; **c. car** = voiture mise à la disposition d'un client par un hôtel, un garage etc

cousin ['kʌzən] *n* cousin, -e *mf*

cover ['kʌvə(r)] **1** *n* (*lid*) couvercle *m*; (*of book*) couverture *f*; (*for furniture, typewriter*) housse *f*; (*bed*) **to take c.** se mettre à l'abri; **under c.** (*sheltered*) à l'abri; **c. charge** (*in restaurant*) couvert *m* **2** *vt* couvrir (**with** or **in** de); (*include*) englober; (*treat*) traiter; (*distance*) parcourir; (*event*) (*in newspaper, on TV*) couvrir; (*insure*) assurer (**against** contre); **to c. up** recouvrir; (*truth, tracks*) dissimuler; (*scandal*) étouffer **3** *vi* **to c. for sb** (*of colleague*) remplacer qn; **to c. up for sb** cacher la vérité pour protéger qn ■ **cover-up** *n* **there was a c.** on a étouffé l'affaire

coverage ['kʌvərɪdʒ] *n* (*on TV, in newspaper*) couverture *f* médiatique

covering ['kʌvərɪŋ] *n* (*wrapping*) enveloppe *f*; (*layer*) couche *f*; **c. letter** lettre *f* jointe

cow [kaʊ] *n* vache *f*; *very Fam* (*nasty woman*) peau *f* de vache ■ **cowboy** *n* cow-boy *m*; *Br Fam Pej* (*workman*) rigolo *m*

coward ['kaʊəd] *n* lâche *mf*

cower ['kaʊə(r)] *vi* (*with fear*) trembler

cozy ['kəʊzɪ] *adj Am* = **cosy**

crab [kræb] *n* (*crustacean*) crabe *m*

crack¹ [kræk] **1** *n* (*split*) fente *f*; (*in glass, china, bone*) fêlure *f*; (*noise*) craquement *m* **2** *vt* (*glass, ice*) fêler; (*nut*) casser; (*whip*) faire claquer; (*problem*) résoudre; (*code*) déchiffrer; *Fam* (*joke*) raconter **3** *vi* se fêler; (*of branch, wood*) craquer; **to c. down on** prendre des mesures énergiques en matière de

crack² [kræk] *adj* (*first-rate*) (*driver, skier*) d'élite; **c. shot** fin tireur *m*

crack³ [kræk] *n* (*drug*) crack *m*

cracker ['krækə(r)] *n* (**a**) (*biscuit*) biscuit *m* salé (**b**) (*firework*) pétard *m*; **Christmas c.** diablotin *m*

crackle ['krækəl] *vi* (*of fire*) crépiter; (*of frying*) grésiller; (*of radio*) crachoter

cradle ['kreɪdəl] **1** *n* berceau *m* **2** *vt* bercer

craft [krɑːft] **1** *n* (*skill*) art *m*; (*job*) métier *m* **2** *vt* façonner ■ **craftsman** (*pl*

-men) *n* artisan *m* ■ **craftsmanship** *n* (*skill*) art *m*

crafty ['krɑːftɪ] (**-ier, -iest**) *adj* astucieux, -euse; *Pej* rusé

cram [kræm] (*pt & pp* **-mm-**) **1** *vt* to c. sth into (*force*) fourrer qch dans; **to c. with** (*fill*) bourrer de **2** *vi* **to c. into** (*of people*) s'entasser dans; **to c. (for an exam)** bûcher

cramp [kræmp] *n* (*pain*) crampe *f* (**in** à)

cramped [kræmpt] *adj* (*surroundings*) exigu (*f* exiguë)

crane [kreɪn] **1** *n* (*machine, bird*) grue *f* **2** *vt* **to c. one's neck** tendre le cou

crank¹ [kræŋk] *n* (*handle*) manivelle *f*

crank² [kræŋk] *n Fam* (*person*) excentrique *mf*; (*fanatic*) fanatique *mf*

crash [kræʃ] **1** *n* (*accident*) accident *m*; (*collapse of firm*) faillite *f*; (*noise*) fracas *m*; **c. course/diet** cours *m*/régime *m* intensif; **c. barrier** (*on road*) glissière *f* de sécurité; **c. helmet** casque *m*; **c. landing** atterrissage *m* en catastrophe **2** *exclam* (*of fallen object*) patatras! **3** *vt* (*car*) avoir un accident avec; **to c. one's car into sth** rentrer dans qch (avec sa voiture) **4** *vi* (*of car, plane*) s'écraser; **to c. into** rentrer dans

crate [kreɪt] *n* (*large*) caisse *f*; (*small*) cageot *m*; (*for bottles*) casier *m*

crater ['kreɪtə(r)] *n* cratère *m*; (**bomb**) **c.** entonnoir *m*

craving ['kreɪvɪŋ] *n* envie *f* (**for** de)

crawl [krɔːl] **1** *n* (*swimming stroke*) crawl *m* **2** *vi* (*of snake, animal*) ramper; (*of child*) marcher à quatre pattes; (*of vehicle*) avancer au pas; **to be crawling with** grouiller de

crayon ['kreɪən] *n* (*wax*) crayon *m* gras

craze [kreɪz] *n* engouement *m* (**for** pour)

crazy ['kreɪzɪ] (**-ier, -iest**) *adj* fou (*f* folle) (**about** de); **to drive sb c.** rendre qn fou; **to run/work like c.** courir/travailler comme un fou

creak [kriːk] *vi* (*of hinge*) grincer; (*of floor, timber*) craquer

cream [kriːm] *n* (*of milk, lotion*) crème

f; **c. of tomato soup** crème *f* de tomates; **c. cake** gâteau *m* à la crème; **c. cheese** fromage *m* à tartiner

creamy ['kriːmɪ] (**-ier, -iest**) *adj* crémeux, -euse

crease [kriːs] **1** *n* pli *m* **2** *vt* froisser **3** *vi* se froisser

create [kriː'eɪt] *vt* créer ■ **creation** *n* création *f* ■ **creative** *adj* (*person, activity*) créatif, -ive ■ **creator** *n* créateur, -trice *mf*

creature ['kriːtʃə(r)] *n* (*animal*) bête *f*; (*person*) créature *f*

crèche [kreʃ] *n Br* (*nursery*) crèche *f*

credentials [krɪ'denʃəlz] *npl* (*proof of ability*) références *fpl*

credible ['kredɪbəl] *adj* crédible ■ **credibility** *n* crédibilité *f*

credit ['kredɪt] **1** *n* (*financial*) crédit *m*; (*merit*) mérite *m*; (*from university*) unité *f* de valeur; **credits** (*of film*) générique *m*; **to buy sth on c.** acheter qch à crédit; **to be in c.** (*of account*) être créditeur; (*of person*) avoir un solde positif; **to her/his c., she** refused c'est tout à son honneur d'avoir refusé; **c. card** carte *f* de crédit **2** *vt* (*of bank*) créditer (**sb with sth** qn de qch); (*believe*) croire

credulous ['kredjʊləs] *adj* crédule

creek [kriːk] *n* (*bay*) crique *f*; *Am* (*stream*) ruisseau *m*

creep [kriːp] **1** *n Fam* **it gives me the creeps** ça me fait froid dans le dos **2** (*pt & pp* **crept**) *vi* ramper; (*silently*) se glisser (*furtively*); (*slowly*) avancer lentement ■ **creepy** (**-ier, -iest**) *adj Fam* sinistre

cremate [krɪ'meɪt] *vt* incinérer ■ **cremation** *n* crémation *f*

crematorium [kremə'tɔːrɪəm] (*pl* **-ia** [-ɪə]) (*Am* **crematory** ['kriːmətɔːrɪ]) *n* crématorium *m*

crept [krept] *pt & pp of* **creep**

crescent ['kresənt] *n* (*shape*) croissant *m*; *Br Fig* (*street*) rue *f* en demi-lune

crest [krest] *n* (*of wave, mountain, bird*) crête *f*; (*of hill*) sommet *m*; (*on seal, letters*) armoiries *fpl*

Crete [kriːt] *n* la Crète

crevice ['krevɪs] *n* (*crack*) fente *f*

crew [kruː] *n* (*of ship, plane*) équipage *m*; *Fam* (*gang*) équipe *f*; **c. cut** coupe *f* en brosse

crib [krɪb] **1** *n Am* (*cot*) lit *m* d'enfant; (*cradle*) berceau *m* **2** (*pt & pp* **-bb-**) *vti Fam* pomper

cricket[1] ['krɪkɪt] *n* (*game*) cricket *m*

cricket[2] ['krɪkɪt] *n* (*insect*) grillon *m*

crime [kraɪm] *n* crime *m*; *Law* délit *m*; (*criminal activity*) criminalité *f*

criminal ['krɪmɪnəl] *adj & n* criminel, -elle (*mf*); **c. offence** (*minor*) délit *m*; (*serious*) crime *m*; **c. record** casier *m* judiciaire

crimson ['krɪmzən] *adj & n* cramoisi (*m*)

cringe [krɪndʒ] *vi* (*show fear*) avoir un mouvement de recul; (*be embarrassed*) avoir envie de rentrer sous terre

crinkle ['krɪŋkəl] **1** *n* (*in paper, fabric*) pli *m* **2** *vt* (*paper, fabric*) froisser

cripple ['krɪpəl] **1** *n* (*lame*) estropié, -e *mf*; (*disabled*) infirme *mf* **2** *vt* (*disable*) rendre infirme; *Fig* (*nation, system*) paralyser

crisis ['kraɪsɪs] (*pl* **crises** ['kraɪsiːz]) *n* crise *f*

crisp [krɪsp] **1** (**-er, -est**) *adj* (*biscuit*) croustillant; (*apple, vegetables*) croquant **2** *npl Br* (*potato*) **crisps** chips *fpl* ■ **crispbread** *n* pain *m* suédois

criterion [kraɪ'tɪərɪən] (*pl* **-ia** [-ɪə]) *n* critère *m*

critic ['krɪtɪk] *n* (*reviewer*) critique *mf*; (*opponent*) détracteur, -trice *mf* ■ **critical** *adj* critique ■ **critically** *adv* (*examine*) en critique; **to be c. ill** être dans un état critique ■ **criticism** [-sɪzəm] *n* critique *f* ■ **criticize** [-saɪz] *vti* critiquer

croak [krəʊk] *vi* (*of frog*) croasser

Croatia [krəʊ'eɪʃə] *n* la Croatie

crockery ['krɒkərɪ] *n* vaisselle *f*

crocodile ['krɒkədaɪl] *n* crocodile *m*

crocus ['krəʊkəs] (*pl* **-uses** [-əsɪz]) *n* crocus *m*

crook [krʊk] *n* (*thief*) escroc *m*

crooked ['krʊkɪd] *adj* (*hat, picture*) de travers; (*deal, person*) malhonnête

crop [krɒp] **1** *n* (*harvest*) récolte *f*; (*produce*) culture *f* **2** (*pt & pp* **-pp-**) *vt* (*hair*) couper ras **3** *vi* **to c. up** (*of issue*) survenir; (*of opportunity*) se présenter; (*of name*) être mentionné

cross[1] [krɒs] **1** *n* croix *f*; **a c. between** (*animal*) un croisement entre; *Fig* **it's a c. between a car and a van** c'est un compromis entre une voiture et une camionnette **2** *vt* (*street, room*) traverser; (*barrier, threshold*) franchir; (*legs, animals*) croiser; (*cheque*) barrer; **to c. off** *or* **out** (*word, name*) rayer; **to c. over** (*road*) traverser **3** *vi* (*of paths*) se croiser; **to c. over** traverser

cross[2] [krɒs] *adj* (*angry*) fâché (**with** contre); **to get c.** se fâcher (**with** contre) ■ **cross-country** *adj* **c. race** cross *m*; **c. runner** coureur, -euse *mf* de fond ■ **cross-legged** *adj & adv* **to sit c.** être assis en tailleur ■ **crossroads** *n* carrefour *m* ■ **cross-section** *n* coupe *f* transversale; (*sample*) échantillon *m* représentatif ■ **crossword** (**puzzle**) *n* mots *mpl* croisés

crossing ['krɒsɪŋ] *n* (*of sea, river*) traversée *f*; *Br* (**pedestrian**) **c.** passage *m* clouté

crotch [krɒtʃ] *n* (*of garment, person*) entrejambe *m*

crouch [kraʊtʃ] *vi* **to c. (down)** (*of person*) s'accroupir; (*of animal*) se tapir

crow [krəʊ] **1** *n* corbeau *m*; **as the c. flies** à vol d'oiseau **2** *vi* (*of cock*) chanter; *Fig* (*boast*) se vanter (**about** de)

crowbar ['krəʊbɑː(r)] *n* levier *m*

crowd [kraʊd] **1** *n* foule *f*; *Fam* (*group of people*) bande *f*; **there was quite a c.** il y avait beaucoup de monde **2** *vt* (*street*) envahir; **to c. people/objects into** entasser des gens/des objets dans **3** *vi* **to c. into** (*of people*) s'entasser dans; **to c. round sb/sth** se presser autour de qn/qch; **to c. together** se serrer ■ **crowded** *adj* plein (**with**

de); *(train, room)* bondé; *(city)* surpeuplé; **it's very c.** il y a beaucoup de monde

crown [kraʊn] **1** n *(of king)* couronne f; *(of head, hill)* sommet m; **the C.** *(monarchy)* la Couronne **2** vt couronner

crucial ['kru:ʃəl] adj crucial

crucify ['kru:sɪfaɪ] *(pt & pp -ied)* vt crucifier ■ **crucifix** [-fɪks] n crucifix m

crude [kru:d] **(-er, -est)** adj *(manners, person, language)* grossier, -ère; *(painting, work)* rudimentaire; **c. oil** pétrole m brut

cruel [krʊəl] **(crueller, cruellest)** adj cruel, -elle ■ **cruelty** n cruauté f

cruise [kru:z] **1** n croisière f; **to go on a c.** partir en croisière; **c. ship** bateau m de croisière **2** vi *(of ship)* croiser; *(of vehicle)* rouler; *(of taxi)* marauder; *(of tourists)* faire une croisière

crumb [krʌm] n miette f

crumble ['krʌmbəl] **1** vt *(bread)* émietter **2** vi *(of bread)* s'émietter; *(collapse) (of resistance)* s'effondrer; **to c. (away)** *(in small pieces)* s'effriter

crumpet ['krʌmpɪt] n Br = petite crêpe grillée servie beurrée

crumple ['krʌmpəl] **1** vt froisser **2** vi se froisser

crunch [krʌntʃ] vt *(food)* croquer

crusade [kru:'seɪd] n Hist & Fig croisade f

crush [krʌʃ] **1** n *(crowd)* foule f; *(rush)* bousculade f; Fam **to have a c. on sb** en pincer pour qn **2** vt écraser; *(clothes)* froisser; *(cram)* entasser **(into** dans)

crust [krʌst] n croûte f ■ **crusty (-ier, -iest)** adj croustillant

crutch [krʌtʃ] n **(a)** *(of invalid)* béquille f **(b)** *(crotch)* entrejambe m

cry [kraɪ] **1** *(pl* **cries)** n *(shout)* cri m **2** *(pt & pp* **cried)** vt **to c. (out)** *(shout)* crier **3** vi *(weep)* pleurer; **to c. (out)** pousser un cri; **to c. for help** appeler au secours; **to c. over sb/sth** pleurer qn/qch ■ **crying** n *(weeping)* pleurs mpl

crypt [krɪpt] n crypte f

crystal ['krɪstəl] n cristal m; **c. vase** vase m en cristal

cub [kʌb] n **(a)** *(of animal)* petit m **(b)** *(scout)* louveteau m

Cuba ['kju:bə] n Cuba f

cube [kju:b] n cube m; *(of meat, vegetables)* dé m; *(of sugar)* morceau m ■ **cubic** adj **c. capacity** volume m; *(of engine)* cylindrée f; **c. metre** mètre m cube

cubicle ['kju:bɪkəl] n *(for changing clothes)* cabine f

cuckoo ['kʊku:] *(pl* **-oos)** n *(bird)* coucou m

cucumber ['kju:kʌmbə(r)] n concombre m

cuddle ['kʌdəl] **1** n câlin m; **to give sb a c.** faire un câlin à qn **2** vt *(hug)* serrer dans ses bras; *(caress)* câliner **3** vi *(of lovers)* se faire des câlins ■ **cuddly (-ier, -iest)** adj *(person)* mignon, -onne à croquer; **c. toy** peluche f

cue¹ [kju:] n *(in theatre)* réplique f; *(signal)* signal m

cue² [kju:] n **(billiard) c.** queue f de billard

cuff [kʌf] n *(of shirt)* poignet m; Am *(of trousers)* revers m; **off the c.** *(remark)* impromptu; **c. link** bouton m de manchette

cul-de-sac ['kʌldəsæk] n Br impasse f

culinary ['kʌlɪnərɪ] adj culinaire

culminate ['kʌlmɪneɪt] vi **to c. in** aboutir à

culprit ['kʌlprɪt] n coupable mf

cult [kʌlt] n culte m; **c. film** film m culte

cultivate ['kʌltɪveɪt] vt *(land, mind)* cultiver ■ **cultivated** adj cultivé

culture ['kʌltʃə(r)] n culture f ■ **cultural** adj culturel, -elle ■ **cultured** adj *(person, mind)* cultivé

cumbersome ['kʌmbəsəm] adj encombrant

cunning ['kʌnɪŋ] **1** adj *(ingenious)* astucieux, -euse; *(devious)* rusé **2** n astuce f; Pej ruse f

cup [kʌp] n tasse f; *(prize)* coupe f; **c. final** *(in football)* finale f de la coupe

cupboard ['kʌbəd] n Br armoire f;

(built into wall) placard *m*

curable [ˈkjʊərəbəl] *adj* guérissable

curate [ˈkjʊərɪt] *n* vicaire *m*

curb [kɜːb] **1** *n* (**a**) *(limit)* **to put a c. on** mettre un frein à (**b**) *Am (kerb)* bord m du trottoir **2** *vt (feelings)* refréner; *(ambitions)* modérer; *(expenses)* réduire

cure [ˈkjʊə(r)] **1** *n* remède *m* (**for** contre) **2** *vt* (**a**) *(person, illness)* guérir; **to c. sb of** guérir qn de (**b**) *(meat, fish)* *(smoke)* fumer; *(salt)* saler; *(dry)* sécher

curious [ˈkjʊərɪəs] *adj* curieux, -euse *(about* de); **to be c. to know/see** être curieux de savoir/voir ▪ **curiosity** *(pl* -ies) *n* curiosité *f (about* de)

curl [kɜːl] **1** *n (in hair)* boucle *f* **2** *vti (hair)* boucler; *(with small, tight curls)* friser **3** *vi* **to c. up** *(shrivel)* se racornir ▪ **curler** *n* bigoudi *m* ▪ **curly** (**-ier**, **-iest**) *adj (hair)* bouclé; *(having many tight curls)* frisé

currant [ˈkʌrənt] *n (dried grape)* raisin *m* de Corinthe

currency [ˈkʌrənsɪ] *(pl* -ies) *n (money)* monnaie *f*; *(foreign)* **c.** devises *fpl* (étrangères)

current [ˈkʌrənt] **1** *adj (fashion, trend)* actuel, -elle; *(opinion, use)* courant; *(year, month)* en cours; **c. account** *(in bank)* compte *m* courant; **c. affairs** questions *fpl* d'actualité **2** *n (of river, air, electricity)* courant *m* ▪ **currently** *adv* actuellement

curriculum [kəˈrɪkjʊləm] *(pl* -**la** [-lə]) *n* programme *m* scolaire; *Br* **c. vitae** curriculum vitae *m inv*

curry [ˈkʌrɪ] *(pl* -ies) *n (dish)* curry *m*, cari *m*

curse [kɜːs] **1** *n* malédiction *f*; *(swearword)* juron *m*; *(scourge)* fléau *m* **2** *vt* maudire; **cursed with sth** affligé de qch **3** *vi (swear)* jurer

cursor [ˈkɜːsə(r)] *n Comptr* curseur *m*

cursory [ˈkɜːsərɪ] *adj* superficiel, -elle

curt [kɜːt] *adj* brusque

curtail [kɜːˈteɪl] *vt (visit)* écourter

curtain [ˈkɜːtən] *n* rideau *m*; **to draw the curtains** *(close)* tirer les rideaux

curts(e)y [ˈkɜːtsɪ] **1** *(pl* -**ies** *or* -**eys**) *n* révérence *f* **2** *(pt & pp* -ied) *vi* faire une révérence (**to** à)

curve [kɜːv] **1** *n* courbe *f*; *(in road)* virage *m* **2** *vt* courber **3** *vi* se courber; *(of road)* faire une courbe ▪ **curved** *adj (line)* courbe

cushion [ˈkʊʃən] **1** *n* coussin *m* **2** *vt (shock)* amortir

cushy [ˈkʊʃɪ] (**-ier**, **-iest**) *adj Fam (job, life)* pépère

custard [ˈkʌstəd] *n* crème *f* anglaise; *(when set)* crème *f* renversée

custody [ˈkʌstədɪ] *n (of child, important papers)* garde *f*

custom [ˈkʌstəm] *n* coutume *f*; *(of individual)* habitude *f*; *(customers)* clientèle *f* ▪ **customary** *adj* habituel, -elle; **it is c. to...** il est d'usage de...

customer [ˈkʌstəmə(r)] *n* client, -e *mf*; *Pej (individual)* individu *m*

customs [ˈkʌstəmz] *npl* (**the**) **c.** la douane; **to go through c.** passer la douane; **c. officer** douanier *m*

cut [kʌt] **1** *n (mark)* coupure *f*; *(stroke)* coup *m*; *(of clothes, hair)* coupe *f*; *(in salary, prices)* réduction *f*; *(of meat)* morceau *m*

2 *(pt & pp* **cut**, *pres p* **cutting**) *vt* couper; *(meat, chicken)* découper; *(glass, diamond, tree)* tailler; *(salary, prices, profits)* réduire; **to c. sb's hair** couper les cheveux à qn; **to c. sth open** ouvrir qch avec un couteau/des ciseaux/*etc*; **to c. sth short** *(visit)* écourter qch

3 *vi (of knife, scissors)* couper

▶ **cut back** *vt sep & vi* réduire ▪ **cutback** *n* réduction *f*

▶ **cut down 1** *vt sep* (**a**) *(tree)* abattre (**b**) *(reduce)* réduire **2** *vi* réduire

▶ **cut in** *vi (interrupt)* interrompre; *(in vehicle)* faire une queue de poisson (**on sb** à qn)

▶ **cut off** *vt sep (piece, limb, hair)* couper; *(isolate)* isoler

▶ **cut out 1** *vt sep (article)* découper; *(remove)* enlever; *(eliminate)* supprimer; **to c. out drinking** s'arrêter de boire; *Fam* **c. it out!** ça suffit!; **c. out to be a doctor** fait pour être médecin **2** *vi (of car engine)* caler

▶ **cut up** *vt sep* couper en morceaux; *(meat, chicken)* découper; **to be very c. up about sth** *(upset)* être complètement chamboulé par qch

cute [kjuːt] (**-er, -est**) *adj Fam (pretty)* mignon, -onne

cutlery ['kʌtləri] *n* couverts *mpl*

cutlet ['kʌtlɪt] *n* côtelette *f*

cut-price [kʌt'praɪs] *adj* à prix réduit

cutting ['kʌtɪŋ] **1** *n (from newspaper)* coupure *f*; *(plant)* bouture *f* **2** *adj (wind, remark)* cinglant

CV [siː'viː] *(abbr* **curriculum vitae)** *n Br* CV *m*

cybercafé [saɪbə'kæfeɪ] *n* cybercafé *m*

cyberspace ['saɪbəspeɪs] *n Comptr* cyberespace *m*

cycle¹ ['saɪkəl] **1** *n (bicycle)* bicyclette *f*; **c. lane** voie *f* réservée aux vélos; **c. path** piste *f* cyclable **2** *vi* aller à bicyclette (**to** à); *(as activity)* faire de la bicyclette ■ **cycling** *n* cyclisme *m* ■ **cyclist** *n* cycliste *mf*

cycle² ['saɪkəl] *n (series, period)* cycle *m*

cylinder ['sɪlɪndə(r)] *n* cylindre *m*

cymbal ['sɪmbəl] *n* cymbale *f*

cynical ['sɪnɪkəl] *adj* cynique

Cyprus ['saɪprəs] *n* Chypre *f*

cyst [sɪst] *n Med* kyste *m*

Czech [tʃek] **1** *adj* tchèque; **the C. Republic** la République tchèque **2** *n (person)* Tchèque *mf*; *(language)* tchèque *m*

Dd

D, d [di:] *n* D, d *m inv*

dab [dæb] **1** *n* a **d. of** un petit peu de **2** (*pt & pp* **-bb-**) *vt* (*wound, brow*) tamponner; **to d. sth on sth** appliquer qch (à petits coups) sur qch

dabble ['dæbəl] *vi* **to d. in politics/ journalism** faire vaguement de la politique/du journalisme

dad [dæd] *n Fam* papa *m* ■ **daddy** (*pl* **-ies**) *n Fam* papa *m*

daffodil ['dæfədɪl] *n* jonquille *f*

daft [dɑːft] (**-er, -est**) *adj Fam* bête

dagger ['dægə(r)] *n* dague *f*

daily ['deɪlɪ] **1** *adj* quotidien, -enne; (*wage*) journalier, -ère; **d. paper** quotidien *m* **2** *adv* chaque jour, quotidiennement; **twice d.** deux fois par jour **3** (*pl* **-ies**) *n* (*newspaper*) quotidien *m*

dainty ['deɪntɪ] (**-ier, -iest**) *adj* délicat

dairy ['deərɪ] **1** (*pl* **-ies**) *n* (*factory*) laiterie *f*; (*shop*) crémerie *f* **2** *adj* laitier, -ère; **d. produce** produits *mpl* laitiers

daisy ['deɪzɪ] (*pl* **-ies**) *n* pâquerette *f*; (*bigger*) marguerite *f*

dam [dæm] *n* (*wall*) barrage *m*

damage ['dæmɪdʒ] **1** *n* dégâts *mpl*; (*harm*) préjudice *m*; **damages** (*in court*) dommages-intérêts *mpl* **2** *vt* (*object*) endommager, abîmer; (*health*) nuire à; (*eyesight*) abîmer; (*plans, reputation*) compromettre ■ **damaging** *adj* (*harmful*) préjudiciable (**to** à)

damn [dæm] **1** *n Fam* **he doesn't care** or **give a d.** il s'en fiche pas mal **2** *adj Fam* fichu **3** *adv Fam* (*very*) vachement **4** *vt* (*condemn, doom*) condamner; (*curse*) maudire; *Fam* **d. him!** qu'il aille se faire voir! **5** *exclam Fam* **d. (it)!** mince! ■ **damned** *Fam* **1** *adj* (*awful*) fichu **2** *adv* vachement

damp [dæmp] **1** (**-er, -est**) *adj* humide; (*skin*) moite **2** *n* humidité *f* ■ **damp(en)** *vt* humecter; **to d. (down)** (*enthusiasm, zeal*) refroidir

damson ['dæmzən] *n* prune *f* de Damas

dance [dɑːns] **1** *n* danse *f*; (*social event*) bal *m* (*pl* bals); **d. hall** dancing *m* **2** *vt* (*waltz, tango*) danser **3** *vi* danser ■ **dancing** *n* danse *f*

dandelion ['dændɪlaɪən] *n* pissenlit *m*

dandruff ['dændrʌf] *n* pellicules *fpl*

Dane [deɪn] *n* Danois, -e *mf*

danger ['deɪndʒə(r)] *n* danger *m* (**to** pour); **in d.** en danger; **out of d.** hors de danger; **to be in d. of doing sth** risquer de faire qch ■ **dangerous** *adj* dangereux, -euse (**to** pour)

dangle ['dæŋgəl] **1** *vt* balancer **2** *vi* (*hang*) pendre; (*swing*) se balancer

Danish ['deɪnɪʃ] **1** *adj* danois **2** *n* (*language*) danois *m*

dare [deə(r)] *vt* **to d. (to) do sth** oser faire qch; **I d. say he tried** il a essayé, c'est bien possible; **to d. sb to do sth** défier qn de faire qch ■ **daring 1** *adj* audacieux, -euse **2** *n* audace *f*

dark [dɑːk] **1** (**-er, -est**) *adj* (*room, night*) & *Fig* sombre; (*colour, skin, hair, eyes*) foncé; **it's d. at six** il fait nuit à six heures; **d. glasses** lunettes *fpl* noires **2** *n* obscurité *f*; **after d.** une fois la nuit tombée; *Fig* **to keep sb in the d.** laisser qn dans l'ignorance (**about** de)

- **dark-haired** *adj* aux cheveux bruns
- **dark-skinned** *adj* (*person*) à peau brune

darken ['dɑːkən] **1** *vt* assombrir; (*colour*) foncer **2** *vi* s'assombrir; (*of colour*) foncer

darkness ['dɑːknəs] *n* obscurité *f*

darkroom ['dɑːkruːm] *n* (*for photography*) chambre *f* noire

darling ['dɑːlɪŋ] *n* (*favourite*) chouchou, -oute *mf*; **(my) d.** (mon) chéri/(ma) chérie

darn [dɑːn] *vt* (*mend*) repriser

dart [dɑːt] **1** *n* (*in game*) fléchette *f*; **darts** (*game*) fléchettes *fpl* **2** *vi* (*dash*) se précipiter (**for** vers)

dash [dæʃ] **1** *n* (**a**) (*run, rush*) ruée *f*; **to make a d. for sth** se ruer vers qch (**b**) **a d. of sth** un petit peu de qch (**c**) (*handwritten stroke*) trait *m*; (*punctuation sign*) tiret *m* **2** *vt* (*throw*) jeter; **to d. off** (*letter*) écrire en vitesse **3** *vi* (*rush*) se précipiter; **to d. in/out** entrer/sortir en vitesse; **to d. off** *or* **away** filer ■ **dashboard** *n* (*of vehicle*) tableau *m* de bord

data ['deɪtə] *npl* informations *fpl*; *Comptr* données *fpl*; **d. base** base *f* de données; **d. processing** informatique *f*

date¹ [deɪt] **1** *n* (*day*) date *f*; *Fam* (*meeting*) rendez-vous *m inv*; *Fam* (*person*) ami, -e *mf*; **d. of birth** date *f* de naissance; **up to d.** (*in fashion*) à la mode; (*information*) à jour; (*well-informed*) au courant (**on** de); **out of d.** (*old-fashioned*) démodé; (*expired*) périmé **2** *vt* (*letter*) dater; *Fam* (*girl, boy*) sortir avec **3** *vi* (*go out of fashion*) dater; **to d. back to, to d. from** dater de

date² [deɪt] *n* (*fruit*) datte *f*

dated ['deɪtɪd] *adj* démodé

daughter ['dɔːtə(r)] *n* fille *f* ■ **daughter-in-law** (*pl* **daughters-in-law**) *n* belle-fille *f*

dawdle ['dɔːdəl] *vi* traînasser

dawn [dɔːn] **1** *n* aube *f*; **at d.** à l'aube **2** *vi* (*of day*) se lever; **it dawned on him that...** il s'est rendu compte que...

day [deɪ] *n* (*period of daylight, 24 hours*) jour *m*; (*referring to duration*) journée *f*; **all d. (long)** toute la journée; **what d. is it?** quel jour sommes-nous?; **the following** *or* **next d.** le lendemain; **the d. before** la veille; **the d. before yesterday** *or* **before last** avant-hier; **the d. after tomorrow** après-demain; **in those days** en ce temps-là; **these days** de nos jours ■ **daybreak** *n* point *m* du jour ■ **daydream 1** *n* rêverie *f* **2** *vi* rêvasser ■ **daylight** *n* (*lumière f du*) jour *m* ■ **daytime** *n* journée *f*, jour *m*

daze [deɪz] **1** *n* **in a d.** étourdi; (*because of drugs*) hébété; (*astonished*) ahuri **2** *vt* (*by blow*) étourdir

dazzle ['dæzəl] *vt* éblouir

dead [ded] **1** *adj* mort; (*numb*) (*limb*) engourdi; **the phone's d.** il n'y a pas de tonalité; **d. end** (*street*) & *Fig* impasse *f*; **a d. stop** un arrêt complet **2** *npl* **the d.** les morts *mpl* **3** *adv* (*completely*) totalement; *Fam* (*very*) très; **to stop d.** s'arrêter net

deaden ['dedən] *vt* (*shock*) amortir; (*pain*) calmer

deadline ['dedlaɪn] *n* date *f* limite; (*hour*) heure *f* limite

deadlock ['dedlɒk] *n Fig* impasse *f*

deadly ['dedlɪ] **1** (-**ier,** -**iest**) *adj* (*poison, blow, enemy*) mortel, -elle; **d. weapon** arme *f* meurtrière **2** *adv* (*pale, boring*) mortellement

deaf [def] **1** *adj* sourd; **d. and dumb** sourd-muet (*f* sourde-muette) **2** *npl* **the d.** les sourds *mpl* ■ **deafen** *vt* assourdir

deal¹ [diːl] *n* **a good** *or* **great d. (of)** (*a lot*) beaucoup (de)

deal² [diːl] *n* **1** (*in business*) marché *m*, affaire *f*; (*in card games*) donne *f*; **to make** *or* **do a d. (with sb)** conclure un marché (avec qn); **it's a d.!** d'accord!; *Ironic* **big d.!** la belle affaire! **2** (*pt & pp* **dealt**) *vt* **to d. (out)** (*cards, money*) distribuer **3** *vi* (*trade*) traiter (**with sb** avec qn); **to d. in** faire le commerce de; **to d. with** (*take care* *of)* s'occuper de; *(concern) (of book)* traiter de, parler de ■ **dealer** *n* marchand, -e *mf* (**in** de); *(for cars)* concessionnaire *mf*; *(in drugs)* revendeur, -euse *mf*; *(in card games)* donneur, -euse *mf* ■ **dealings** *npl* relations *fpl* (**with** avec); *(in business)* transactions *fpl*

dealt [delt] *pt & pp of* **deal**

dear [dɪə(r)] **1** (**-er, -est**) *adj (loved, precious, expensive)* cher (*f* chère); **D. Madam** *(in letter)* Madame; **D. Sir** Monsieur; **D. Jane** chère Jane; **oh d.!** oh là là! **2** *n* **(my) d.** *(darling)* (mon) chéri/(ma) chérie; *(friend)* mon cher/ma chère **3** *adv (cost, pay)* cher

dearly [ˈdɪəlɪ] *adv (love)* tendrement; *(very much)* beaucoup; **to pay d. for sth** payer qch cher

death [deθ] *n* mort *f*; **to be bored to d.** s'ennuyer à mourir; **to be scared to d.** être mort de peur; **to be sick to d.** en avoir vraiment marre (**of** de); **d. certificate** acte *m* de décès; **d. penalty** peine *f* de mort; **d. sentence** condamnation *f* à mort ■ **deathly** *adj (silence, paleness)* de mort

debate [dɪˈbeɪt] **1** *n* débat *m* **2** *vti* discuter ■ **debatable** *adj* **it's d. whether she will succeed** il est difficile de dire si elle réussira

debit [ˈdebɪt] **1** *n* débit *m*; **in d.** *(account)* débiteur **2** *vt* débiter (**sb with sth** qn de qch)

debris [ˈdebriː] *n (of building)* décombres *mpl*; *(of plane, car)* débris *mpl*

debt [det] *n* dette *f*; **to be in d.** avoir des dettes; **to run** *or* **get into d.** faire des dettes ■ **debtor** *n* débiteur, -trice *mf*

debut [ˈdebjuː] *n (on stage)* début *m*; **to make one's d.** faire ses débuts

decade [ˈdekeɪd] *n* décennie *f*

decadent [ˈdekədənt] *adj* décadent

decaffeinated [diːˈkæfɪneɪtɪd] *adj* décaféiné

decanter [dɪˈkæntə(r)] *n* carafe *f*

decay [dɪˈkeɪ] **1** *n (rot)* pourriture *f*; *(of tooth)* carie *f*; **to fall into d.** *(of*

building) tomber en ruine **2** *vi (go bad)* se gâter; *(rot)* pourrir; *(of tooth)* se carier

deceased [dɪˈsiːst] **1** *adj* décédé **2** *n* **the d.** le défunt/la défunte

deceit [dɪˈsiːt] *n* tromperie *f* ■ **deceitful** *adj (person)* fourbe; *(behaviour)* malhonnête

deceive [dɪˈsiːv] *vti* tromper; **to d. oneself** se faire des illusions

December [dɪˈsembə(r)] *n* décembre *m*

decent [ˈdiːsənt] *adj (respectable)* convenable; *(good)* bon (*f* bonne); *(kind)* gentil, -ille ■ **decency** *n* décence *f*; *(kindness)* gentillesse *f*

deception [dɪˈsepʃən] *n* tromperie *f* ■ **deceptive** *adj* trompeur, -euse

decide [dɪˈsaɪd] **1** *vt (outcome, future)* décider de; *(question, matter)* régler; **to d. to do sth** décider de faire qch; **to d. that...** décider que... **2** *vi (make decisions)* décider; *(make up one's mind)* se décider (**on doing** à faire); **to d. on sth** décider de qch; *(choose)* choisir qch

decimal [ˈdesɪməl] **1** *adj* décimal; **d. point** virgule *f* **2** *n* décimale *f*

decipher [dɪˈsaɪfə(r)] *vt* déchiffrer

decision [dɪˈsɪʒən] *n* décision *f*

decisive [dɪˈsaɪsɪv] *adj (action, event, tone)* décisif, -ive; *(person)* résolu

deck [dek] *n* **(a)** *(of ship)* pont *m*; **top d.** *(of bus)* impériale *f* **(b)** **d. of cards** jeu *m* de cartes **(c)** *(of record player)* platine *f* **2** *vt* **to d. (out)** *(adorn)* orner ■ **deckchair** *n* chaise *f* longue

declare [dɪˈkleə(r)] *vt* déclarer (**that** que); *(result)* proclamer ■ **declaration** *n* déclaration *f*

decline [dɪˈklaɪn] **1** *n* déclin *m*; *(fall)* baisse *f* **2** *vt (offer)* décliner; **to d. to do sth** refuser de faire qch **3** *vi (become less) (of popularity, birthrate)* être en baisse; *(deteriorate) (of health, strength)* décliner; *(refuse)* refuser

decode [diːˈkəʊd] *vt (message)* décoder ■ **decoder** *n* Comptr & TV décodeur *m*

decompose [di:kəm'pəuz] *vi (rot)* se décomposer

decor ['deɪkɔ:(r)] *n* décor *m*

decorate ['dekəreɪt] *vt (cake, house, soldier)* décorer (**with** de); *(hat, skirt)* orner (**with** de); *(paint)* peindre; *(wallpaper)* tapisser ▪ **decoration** *n* décoration *f* ▪ **decorative**, -ive *adj* décoratif, -ive ▪ **decorator** *n Br (house painter)* peintre *m* décorateur; (**interior**) **d.** décorateur, -trice *mf*

decrease 1 ['di:kri:s] *n* diminution *f* (**in** de) **2** [dɪ'kri:s] *vti* diminuer

decree [dɪ'kri:] **1** *n (by court)* jugement *m*; *(municipal)* arrêté *m* **2** *(pt & pp -eed) vt* décréter (**that** que)

decrepit [dɪ'krepɪt] *adj (building)* en ruine; *(person)* décrépit

dedicate ['dedɪkeɪt] *vt (devote)* consacrer (**to** à); *(book)* dédier (**to** à); **to d. oneself to sth** se consacrer à qch ▪ **dedicated** *adj (teacher)* consciencieux, -euse ▪ **dedication** *n (in book)* dédicace *f*; *(devotion)* dévouement *m*

deduce [dɪ'dju:s] *vt (conclude)* déduire (**from** de; **that** que)

deduct [dɪ'dʌkt] *vt* déduire (**from** de) ▪ **deductible** *adj (from income) (expenses)* déductible ▪ **deduction** *n (subtraction, conclusion)* déduction *f*

deed [di:d] *n* action *f*, acte *m*; *(feat)* exploit *m*; *(legal document)* acte *m* notarié

deep [di:p] **1** (**-er, -est**) *adj* profond; *(snow)* épais *(f* épaisse); *(voice)* grave; *(musical note)* bas *(f* basse); **to be 6 metres d.** avoir 6 mètres de profondeur; **d. in thought** plongé dans ses pensées; **d. red** rouge foncé **2** *adv* profondément ▪ **deeply** *adv* profondément

deepen ['di:pən] **1** *vt (increase)* augmenter; *(canal, knowledge)* approfondir **2** *vi (of river)* devenir plus profond; *(of mystery)* s'épaissir; *(of voice)* devenir plus grave

deep-freeze [di:p'fri:z] **1** *n* congélateur *m* **2** *vt* surgeler

deer [dɪə(r)] *n inv* cerf *m*

deface [dɪ'feɪs] *vt (damage)* dégrader; *(daub)* barbouiller

default [dɪ'fɔ:lt] *n* **by d.** par défaut; **to win by d.** gagner par forfait

defeat [dɪ'fi:t] **1** *n* défaite *f* **2** *vt (opponent, army)* vaincre; **that defeats the purpose** *or* **object** ça va à l'encontre du but recherché

defect¹ ['di:fekt] *n* défaut *m*

defect² [dɪ'fekt] *vi (of party member, soldier)* déserter

defective [dɪ'fektɪv] *adj (machine)* défectueux, -euse

defence [dɪ'fens] (*Am* **defense**) *n* défense *f* (**against** contre); **in his d.** à sa décharge

defend [dɪ'fend] *vti* défendre ▪ **defendant** *n (accused)* prévenu, -ue *mf* ▪ **defender** *n* défenseur *m*; *(of sports title)* tenant, -e *mf*

defense [dɪ'fens] *n Am =* **defence**

defensive [dɪ'fensɪv] **1** *adj* défensif, -ive; **to be d.** être sur la défensive **2** *n* **on the d.** sur la défensive

defer [dɪ'fɜ:(r)] (*pt & pp* **-rr-**) *vt (postpone)* différer

defiant [dɪ'faɪənt] *adj (person)* provocant ▪ **defiance** *n (resistance)* défi *m* (**of** à)

deficient [dɪ'fɪʃənt] *adj (not adequate)* insuffisant; *(faulty)* défectueux, -euse; **to be d. in** manquer de ▪ **deficiency** (*pl* **-ies**) *n (shortage)* manque *m*; *(in vitamins, minerals)* carence *f* (**in** de); *(flaw)* défaut *m*

deficit ['defɪsɪt] *n* déficit *m*

define [dɪ'faɪn] *vt* définir

definite ['defɪnɪt] *adj (exact) (date, plan, answer)* précis; *(clear) (improvement, advantage)* net *(f* nette); *(firm) (offer, order)* ferme; *(certain)* certain; **he was quite d.** il a été tout à fait formel; **d. article** *(in grammar)* article *m* défini ▪ **definitely** *adv* certainement; *(improved, superior)* nettement; *(say)* catégoriquement

definition [defɪ'nɪʃən] *n* définition *f*

deflect [dɪ'flekt] *vt (bullet)* faire dévier

deformed [dɪˈfɔːmd] *adj (body)* difforme

defraud [dɪˈfrɔːd] *vt (customs, State)* frauder; **to d. sb of sth** escroquer qch à qn

defrost [diːˈfrɒst] *vt (fridge)* dégivrer; *(food)* décongeler

defuse [diːˈfjuːz] *vt (bomb, conflict)* désamorcer

defy [dɪˈfaɪ] *(pt & pp -ied) vt (person, death, logic)* défier; *(efforts)* résister à; **to d. sb to do sth** défier qn de faire qch

degenerate 1 [dɪˈdʒenərət] *adj & n* dégénéré, -e *(mf)* **2** [dɪˈdʒenəreɪt] *vi* dégénérer (**into** en)

degrading [dɪˈɡreɪdɪŋ] *adj* dégradant

degree [dɪˈɡriː] *n* (**a**) *(of angle, temperature, extent)* degré *m*; **it's 20 degrees** *(temperature)* il fait 20 degrés; **to some d., to a certain d.** jusqu'à un certain point; **to such a d.** à tel point (**that** que) (**b**) *(from university)* diplôme *m*; *(Bachelor's)* ≃ licence *f*; *(Master's)* ≃ maîtrise *f*; *(PhD)* ≃ doctorat *m*

dehydrated [diːhaɪˈdreɪtɪd] *adj* déshydraté; **to get d.** se déshydrater

de-ice [diːˈaɪs] *vt (car window)* dégivrer

dejected [dɪˈdʒektɪd] *adj* abattu

delay [dɪˈleɪ] **1** *n (lateness)* retard *m*; *(waiting period)* délai *m*; **without d.** sans tarder **2** *vt* retarder; *(payment)* différer; **to d. doing sth** tarder à faire qch; **to be delayed** avoir du retard **3** *vi (be slow)* tarder (**in doing** à faire)

delegate 1 [ˈdelɪɡət] *n* délégué, -e *mf* **2** [ˈdelɪɡeɪt] *vt* déléguer (**to** à) ■ **delegation** *n* délégation *f*

delete [dɪˈliːt] *vt* supprimer

deliberate [dɪˈlɪbərət] *adj (intentional)* délibéré; *(slow)* mesuré ■ **deliberately** *adv (intentionally)* délibérément

delicate [ˈdelɪkət] *adj* délicat ■ **delicacy** *(pl -ies) n (quality)* délicatesse *f*; *(food)* mets *m* délicat

delicatessen [delɪkəˈtesən] *n (shop)* épicerie *f* fine

delicious [dɪˈlɪʃəs] *adj* délicieux, -euse

delight [dɪˈlaɪt] **1** *n (pleasure)* plaisir *m*, joie *f* **2** *vt* ravir **3** *vi* **to d. in doing sth** prendre plaisir à faire qch ■ **delighted** *adj* ravi (**with** de qch; **to do** de faire; **that** que)

delightful [dɪˈlaɪtfəl] *adj* charmant; *(meal, perfume, sensation)* délicieux, -euse

delinquent [dɪˈlɪŋkwənt] *adj & n* délinquant, -e *(mf)*

delirious [dɪˈlɪrɪəs] *adj* délirant; **to be d.** délirer

deliver [dɪˈlɪvə(r)] *vt* (**a**) *(goods)* livrer; *(letters)* distribuer; *(hand over)* remettre (**to** à) (**b**) *(rescue)* délivrer (**from** de) (**c**) **to d. a woman's baby** accoucher une femme (**d**) *(speech)* prononcer; *(warning, ultimatum)* lancer

delivery [dɪˈlɪvərɪ] *(pl -ies) n* (**a**) *(of goods)* livraison *f*; *(of letters)* distribution *f* (**b**) *(birth)* accouchement *m* (**c**) *(speaking)* débit *m*

delude [dɪˈluːd] *vt* tromper; **to d. oneself** se faire des illusions ■ **delusion** *n* illusion *f*; *(in mental illness)* aberration *f* mentale

de luxe [dɪˈlʌks] *adj* de luxe

demand [dɪˈmɑːnd] **1** *n* exigence *f*; *(claim)* revendication *f*; *(for goods)* demande *f* (**for** pour); **to be in (great) d.** être très demandé; **to make demands on sb** exiger beaucoup de qn **2** *vt* exiger (**sth from sb** qch de qn); *(rights, more pay)* revendiquer; **to d. that…** exiger que… ■ **demanding** *adj* exigeant

demeaning [dɪˈmiːnɪŋ] *adj* dégradant

demeanour [dɪˈmiːnə(r)] *(Am* **demeanor***) n (behaviour)* comportement *m*

demo [ˈdeməʊ] *(pl -os) n Fam (demonstration)* manif *f*

democracy [dɪˈmɒkrəsɪ] *(pl -ies) n*

démocratie *f* ■ **democratic** *adj (institution)* démocratique; *(person)* démocrate

demolish [dɪ'mɒlɪʃ] *vt* démolir

demon ['diːmən] *n* démon *m*

demonstrate ['demənstreɪt] **1** *vt* démontrer; *(machine)* faire une démonstration de; **to d. how to** do sth montrer comment faire qch **2** *vi (protest)* manifester ■ **demonstration** [-'streɪʃən] *n* démonstration *f*; *(protest)* manifestation *f* ■ **demonstrator** *n (protester)* manifestant, -e *mf*

demoralize [dɪ'mɒrəlaɪz] *vt* démoraliser

demote [dɪ'məʊt] *vt* rétrograder

den [den] *n (of lion, person)* antre *m*

denial [dɪ'naɪəl] *n (of rumour, allegation)* démenti *m*

denigrate ['denɪgreɪt] *vt* dénigrer

denim ['denɪm] *n* denim *m*; **denims** *(jeans)* jean *m*

Denmark ['denmɑːk] *n* le Danemark

denomination [dɪnɒmɪ'neɪʃən] *n (religion)* confession *f*; *(of coin, banknote)* valeur *f*

denote [dɪ'nəʊt] *vt* dénoter

denounce [dɪ'naʊns] *vt (person, injustice)* dénoncer (**to** à)

dense [dens] (**-er, -est**) *adj* dense; *Fam (stupid)* lourd ■ **densely** *adv* **d. populated** très peuplé

dent [dent] **1** *n (in car, metal)* bosse *f* **2** *vt* cabosser

dental ['dentəl] *adj* dentaire; **d. appointment** rendez-vous *m inv* chez le dentiste

dentist ['dentɪst] *n* dentiste *mf*; **to go to the d.** aller chez le dentiste

dentures ['dentʃəz] *npl* dentier *m*

deny [dɪ'naɪ] *(pt & pp* **-ied**) *vt* nier (**doing** avoir fait; **that** que); *(rumour)* démentir; **to d. sb sth** refuser qch à qn

deodorant [diː'əʊdərənt] *n* déodorant *m*

depart [dɪ'pɑːt] *vi* partir; *(deviate)* s'écarter (**from** de)

department [dɪ'pɑːtmənt] *n* département *m*; *(in office)* service *m*; *(in shop)* rayon *m*; *(of government)* ministère *m*; **d. store** grand magasin *m*

departure [dɪ'pɑːtʃə(r)] *n* départ *m*; **d. lounge** *(in airport)* salle *f* d'embarquement

depend [dɪ'pend] *vi* dépendre (**on** *or* **upon** de); **to d. (up)on** *(rely on)* compter sur (**for sth pour qch**) ■ **dependant** *n* personne *f* à charge ■ **dependent** *adj (relative, child)* à charge; **to be d. (up)on** dépendre de; **to be d. on sb** *(financially)* être à la charge de qn

depict [dɪ'pɪkt] *vt (describe)* décrire; *(in pictures)* représenter

deplorable [dɪ'plɔːrəbəl] *adj* déplorable

deploy [dɪ'plɔɪ] *vt (troops)* déployer

deport [dɪ'pɔːt] *vt (foreigner, criminal)* expulser

deposit [dɪ'pɒzɪt] **1** *n* (a) *(in bank)* dépôt *m*; *(part payment)* acompte *m*; *(returnable)* caution *f* (b) *(sediment)* dépôt *m*; *(of gold, oil)* gisement *m* **2** *vt (object, money)* déposer

depot [*Br* 'depəʊ, *Am* 'diːpəʊ] *n (for goods)* dépôt *m*; *Am (railroad station)* gare *f*; *Am* (**bus**) **d.** gare *f* routière

depraved [dɪ'preɪvd] *adj* dépravé

depreciate [dɪ'priːʃɪeɪt] *vi (fall in value)* se déprécier

depress [dɪ'pres] *vt (discourage)* déprimer ■ **depressed** *adj (person, market)* déprimé; **to get d.** se décourager ■ **depression** *n* dépression *f*

deprive [dɪ'praɪv] *vt* priver (**of** de) ■ **deprived** *adj (child)* défavorisé

depth [depθ] *n* profondeur *f*; **in the depths of** *(forest, despair)* au plus profond de; *(winter)* au cœur de; **in d.** en profondeur

deputy ['depjʊtɪ] *(pl* **-ies**) *n (replacement)* remplaçant, -e *mf*; *(assistant)* adjoint, -e *mf*

derailed [dɪ'reɪld] *adj* **to be d.** *(of train)* dérailler

derelict ['derɪlɪkt] *adj (building)* abandonné

derision [dɪˈrɪʒən] n dérision f
derisory [dɪˈraɪsərɪ] adj (amount) dérisoire
derive [dɪˈraɪv] **1** vt provenir (**from** de); **to be derived from** provenir de **2** vi **to d. from** provenir de ∎ **derivation** n Ling dérivation f
descend [dɪˈsend] **1** vt (stairs, hill) descendre; **to be descended from** descendre de **2** vi descendre (**from** de); **to d. upon** (of tourists) envahir; (attack) faire une descente sur; **in descending order** en ordre décroissant ∎ **descendant** n descendant, -e mf
descent [dɪˈsent] n (**a**) (of aircraft) descente f (**b**) (ancestry) origine f; **to be of Norman d.** être d'origine normande
describe [dɪˈskraɪb] vt décrire ∎ **description** n description f
desert¹ [ˈdezət] n désert m; **d. island** île f déserte
desert² [dɪˈzɜːt] **1** vt (person) abandonner; (place, cause) déserter **2** vi (of soldier) déserter ∎ **deserted** adj désert
deserve [dɪˈzɜːv] vt mériter (**to do** de faire) ∎ **deserving** adj (person) méritant; (action, cause) méritoire
design [dɪˈzaɪn] **1** n (**a**) (pattern) motif m; (sketch) plan m; (of dress, car, furniture) modèle m (**b**) (aim) dessein m; **to have designs on** avoir des vues sur **2** vt (car, building) concevoir; (dress) créer; **designed to do sth/for sth** conçu pour faire qch/pour qch ∎ **designer** n (artistic) dessinateur, -trice mf; (industrial) concepteur-dessinateur m; (of clothes) styliste mf; (well-known) couturier m; **d. clothes** vêtements mpl de marque
designate [ˈdezɪgneɪt] vt désigner
desire [dɪˈzaɪə(r)] **1** n désir m **2** vt désirer (**to do** faire) ∎ **desirable** adj désirable
desk [desk] n (in school) table f; (in office) bureau m; Br (in shop) caisse f; (reception) **d.** (in hotel) réception f; Am **d. clerk** (in hotel) réceptionniste mf

desktop [ˈdesktɒp] n Comptr bureau m; **d. computer** ordinateur m de bureau; **d. publishing** publication f assistée par ordinateur
desolate [ˈdesələt] adj (deserted) désolé; (dreary, bleak) morne, triste
despair [dɪˈspeə(r)] **1** n désespoir m; **to be in d.** être au désespoir **2** vi désespérer (**of sb** de qn; **of doing** de faire)
despatch [dɪˈspætʃ] n & vt = dispatch
desperate [ˈdespərət] adj désespéré; **to be d. for** (money, love) avoir désespérément besoin de; (cigarette, baby) mourir d'envie d'avoir ∎ **desperately** adv (ill) gravement
despicable [dɪˈspɪkəbəl] adj méprisable
despise [dɪˈspaɪz] vt mépriser
despite [dɪˈspaɪt] prep malgré
despondent [dɪˈspɒndənt] adj abattu
dessert [dɪˈzɜːt] n dessert m ∎ **dessertspoon** n Br cuillère f à dessert
destination [destɪˈneɪʃən] n destination f
destine [ˈdestɪn] vt destiner (**for** à; **to do** à faire)
destiny [ˈdestɪnɪ] (pl -ies) n destin m, destinée f
destitute [ˈdestɪtjuːt] adj (poor) indigent
destroy [dɪˈstrɔɪ] vt détruire; (cat, dog) faire piquer
destruction [dɪˈstrʌkʃən] n destruction f ∎ **destructive** adj (person, war) destructeur, -trice
detach [dɪˈtætʃ] vt détacher (**from** de) ∎ **detached** adj Br **d. house** maison f individuelle
detachable [dɪˈtætʃəbəl] adj amovible
detail [ˈdiːteɪl] n (item of information) détail m; **in d.** en détail; **to go into d.** entrer dans les détails ∎ **detailed** adj (account) détaillé
detain [dɪˈteɪn] vt (delay) retenir; (prisoner) placer en détention; (in hospital) garder ∎ **detention** n (at school) retenue f

detect [dɪ'tekt] *vt* détecter

detective [dɪ'tektɪv] *n (police officer)* ≃ inspecteur *m* de police; *(private)* détective *m* privé; **d. film/novel** film *m*/roman *m* policier

detector [dɪ'tektə(r)] *n* détecteur *m*

deter [dɪ'tɜː(r)] *(pt & pp* **-rr-***) vt* **to d. sb** dissuader qn **(from doing** de faire)

detergent [dɪ'tɜːdʒənt] *n* détergent *m*

deteriorate [dɪ'tɪərɪəreɪt] *vi* se détériorer

determine [dɪ'tɜːmɪn] *vt (cause, date)* déterminer; **to d. to do sth** décider de faire qch ■ **determined** *adj (look, person)* déterminé; **to be d. to do sth** être décidé à faire qch

deterrent [dɪ'terənt] *n* **to be a d.**, **to act as a d.** être dissuasif, -ive

detest [dɪ'test] *vt* détester **(doing** faire)

detonate ['detəneɪt] **1** *vt* faire exploser **2** *vi* exploser

detour ['diːtʊə(r)] *n* détour *m*; **to make a d.** faire un détour

detract [dɪ'trækt] *vi* **to d. from** *(make less)* diminuer

detriment ['detrɪmənt] *n* **to the d. of** au détriment de ■ **detrimental** *adj* préjudiciable **(to** à)

devaluation [diːvæljʊ'eɪʃən] *n (of money)* dévaluation *f*

devastate ['devəsteɪt] *vt (crop, village)* dévaster; *(person)* anéantir ■ **devastating** *adj (news, results)* accablant

develop [dɪ'veləp] **1** *vt (theory, argument)* développer; *(area, land)* mettre en valeur; *(habit)* contracter; *(photo)* développer **2** *vi (grow)* se développer; *(of event, crisis)* se produire; *(of talent, illness)* se manifester; **to d. into** devenir ■ **developing** *adj* **d. country** pays *m* en voie de développement

developer [dɪ'veləpə(r)] *n* **(property) d.** promoteur *m*

development [dɪ'veləpmənt] *n (growth, progress)* développement *m*; **(housing) d.** lotissement *m*; *(large)* grand ensemble *m*; **a (new) d.** *(in situation)* un fait nouveau

deviate ['diːvɪeɪt] *vi* dévier **(from** de)

device [dɪ'vaɪs] *n (instrument, gadget)* dispositif *m*; *(scheme)* procédé *m*; **explosive d.** engin *m* explosif; **left to one's own devices** livré à soi-même

devil ['devəl] *n* diable *m*; *Fam* **what/ where/why the d....?** que/où/pourquoi diable…?

devious ['diːvɪəs] *adj (mind, behaviour)* tortueux, -euse

devise [dɪ'vaɪz] *vt* imaginer; *(plot)* ourdir

devoid [dɪ'vɔɪd] *adj* **d. of** dénué *ou* dépourvu de

devote [dɪ'vəʊt] *vt* consacrer **(to** à) ■ **devoted** *adj* dévoué; *(admirer)* fervent

devotion [dɪ'vəʊʃən] *n (to friend, family, cause)* dévouement *m* **(to sb** à qn); *(religious)* dévotion *f*

devour [dɪ'vaʊə(r)] *vt (eat, engulf, read)* dévorer

devout [dɪ'vaʊt] *adj (person)* dévot

dew [djuː] *n* rosée *f*

diabetes [daɪə'biːtiːz] *n* diabète *m* ■ **diabetic** [-'betɪk] **1** *adj* diabétique **2** *n* diabétique *mf*

diagnose [daɪəg'nəʊz] *vt* diagnostiquer ■ **diagnosis** [-'nəʊsɪs] *(pl* **-oses** [-əʊsiːz]*) n* diagnostic *m*

diagonal [daɪ'ægənəl] **1** *adj* diagonal **2** *n* diagonale *f* ■ **diagonally** *adv* en diagonale

diagram ['daɪəgræm] *n* schéma *m*

dial ['daɪəl] **1** *n* cadran *m*; *Am* **d. tone** tonalité *f* **2** *(Br* **-ll-**, *Am* **-l-***) vt (phone number)* composer; *(person)* appeler ■ **dialling** *n Br* **d. code** indicatif *m*; *Br* **d. tone** tonalité *f*

dialect ['daɪəlekt] *n* dialecte *m*

dialogue ['daɪəlɒg] *(Am* **dialog**) *n* dialogue *m*

diameter [daɪ'æmɪtə(r)] *n* diamètre *m*

diamond ['daɪəmənd] *n* **(a)** *(stone)* diamant *m*; *(shape)* losange *m*; **d. necklace** rivière *f* de diamants **(b)** **diamond(s)** *(in card games)* carreau *m*

diaper ['daɪpə(r)] *n Am* couche *f*

diarrh(o)ea [daɪə'riːə] *n* diarrhée *f*;

to have d. avoir la diarrhée

diary ['daɪərɪ] (pl -ies) n Br (for appointments) agenda m; (private) journal m (intime)

dice [daɪs] n inv dé m

dictate [dɪk'teɪt] 1 vt (letter, conditions) dicter (**to** à) 2 vi dicter qn ■ **dictation** n dictée f

dictator [dɪk'teɪtə(r)] n dictateur m

dictionary ['dɪkʃənərɪ] (pl -ies) n dictionnaire m

did [dɪd] pt of **do**

die [daɪ] vi (pt & pp **died**, pres p **dying**) mourir (**of** or **from** de); Fig to be dying to do sth mourir d'envie de faire qch; **to be dying for sth** avoir une envie folle de qch; **to d. away** (of noise) mourir; **to d. down** (of storm) se calmer; **to d. out** (of custom) mourir

diesel ['diːzəl] adj & n **d. (engine)** (motor m) diesel m; **d. (oil)** gazole m

diet ['daɪət] 1 n (usual food) alimentation f; (restricted food) régime m; **to go on a d.** faire un régime 2 vi être au régime

differ ['dɪfə(r)] vi différer (**from** de); (disagree) ne pas être d'accord (**from** avec)

difference ['dɪfərəns] n différence f (**in** de); **d. of opinion** différend m; **it makes no d.** ça n'a pas d'importance

different ['dɪfərənt] adj différent (**from** de); (another) autre; (various) divers

differentiate [dɪfə'renʃɪeɪt] 1 vt différencier (**from** de) 2 vi faire la différence (**between** entre) ■ **differently** adv différemment (**from** de)

difficult ['dɪfɪkəlt] adj difficile (**to do** à faire)

difficulty ['dɪfɪkəltɪ] (pl -ies) n difficulté f; **to have d. doing sth** avoir du mal à faire qch;

dig [dɪg] 1 n (with elbow) coup de coude; Fam (remark) pique f 2 (pt & pp **dug**, pres p **digging**) vt (ground, garden) bêcher; (hole, grave) creuser; **to d. sth into sth** (push) planter qch dans qch; **to d. out** (from ground) déterrer;

Fam (find) dénicher; **to d. up** (from ground) déterrer; (road) excaver 3 vi (dig a hole) creuser

digest [daɪ'dʒest] vti digérer ■ **digestion** n digestion f

digit ['dɪdʒɪt] n (number) chiffre m ■ **digital** adj numérique; (tape, recording) audionumérique

dignified ['dɪgnɪfaɪd] adj digne ■ **dignity** n dignité f

digress [daɪ'gres] vi faire une digression

dilapidated [dɪ'læpɪdeɪtɪd] adj (house) délabré

dilemma [daɪ'lemə] n dilemme m

diligent ['dɪlɪdʒənt] adj appliqué

dilute [daɪ'luːt] vt diluer

dim [dɪm] 1 (**dimmer, dimmest**) adj (light) faible; (room) sombre; (memory) vague; (person) stupide 2 (pt & pp **-mm-**) vt (light) baisser; Am **to d. one's headlights** se mettre en code

dime [daɪm] n Am (pièce f de) dix cents mpl

dimension [daɪ'menʃən] n dimension f

diminish [dɪ'mɪnɪʃ] vti diminuer

dimple ['dɪmpəl] n fossette f

din [dɪn] n (noise) vacarme m

dine [daɪn] vi dîner (**on** or **off** de); **to d. out** aller dîner au restaurant ■ **diner** n (person) dîneur, -euse mf; Am (restaurant) petit restaurant m ■ **dining** n **d. car** (on train) wagon-restaurant m; **d. room** salle f à manger

dinghy ['dɪŋgɪ] (pl -ies) n petit canot m; **(rubber) d.** canot m pneumatique

dingy ['dɪndʒɪ] (**-ier, -iest**) adj (room) minable; (colour) terne

dinner ['dɪnə(r)] n (evening meal) dîner m; (lunch) déjeuner m; **to have d.** dîner; **d. jacket** smoking m; **d. party** dîner m; **d. plate** grande assiette f; **d. service, d. set** service m de table

dinosaur ['daɪnəsɔː(r)] n dinosaure m

dip [dɪp] 1 n (in road) petit creux m; **to go for a d.** (swim) faire trempette 2 (pt & pp **-pp-**) vt plonger; Br **to d. one's headlights** se mettre en code 3 vi (of *road)* plonger; **to d. into** *(pocket, savings)* puiser dans; *(book)* feuilleter

diploma [dɪˈpləʊmə] *n* diplôme *m*

diplomat [ˈdɪpləmæt] *n* diplomate *mf*
■ **diplomatic** *adj* diplomatique

dire [ˈdaɪə(r)] *adj (situation)* affreux, -euse; *(consequences)* tragique; *(poverty, need)* extrême; **to be in d. straits** être dans une mauvaise passe

direct [daɪˈrekt] **1** *adj (result, flight, person)* direct; *Br* **d. debit** prélèvement *m* automatique
2 *adv* directement
3 *vt (gaze, light, attention)* diriger **(at** sur); *(traffic)* régler; *(letter, remark)* adresser **(to** à); *(film)* réaliser; *(play)* mettre en scène; **to d. sb to** *(place)* indiquer à qn le chemin; **to d. sb to do sth** charger qn de faire qch

direction [daɪˈrekʃən] *n* direction *f*, sens *m*; **directions** *(orders)* indications *fpl*; **directions (for use)** mode *m* d'emploi

directly [daɪˈrektlɪ] *adv (without detour)* directement; *(exactly)* juste; *(at once)* tout de suite; **d. in front** juste devant

director [daɪˈrektə(r)] *n* directeur, -trice *mf*; *(board member)* administrateur, -trice *mf*; *(of film)* réalisateur, -trice *mf*; *(of play)* metteur *m* en scène

directory [daɪˈrektərɪ] *(pl* **-ies)** *n (phone book)* annuaire *m*; *(of addresses)* & *Comptr* répertoire *m*; **telephone d.** annuaire *m* du téléphone; *Br* **d. enquiries** renseignements *mpl* téléphoniques

dirt [dɜːt] *n* saleté *f*; *(mud)* boue *f*; *(earth)* terre *f*; *Fam* **d. cheap** très bon marché

dirty [ˈdɜːtɪ] **1 (-ier, -iest)** *adj* sale; *(job)* salissant; *(word)* grossier, -ère; **to get d.** se salir; **to get sth d.** salir qch; **a d. joke** une histoire cochonne; **a d. trick** un sale tour **2** *vt* salir

disability [dɪsəˈbɪlɪtɪ] *(pl* **-ies)** *n (injury)* infirmité *f*; *(condition)* invalidité *f*; *Fig* désavantage *m*

disabled [dɪsˈeɪbəld] **1** *adj* handicapé

2 *npl* **the d.** les handicapés *mpl*

disadvantage [ˌdɪsədˈvɑːntɪdʒ] **1** *n* désavantage *m* **2** *vt* désavantager

disagree [dɪsəˈgriː] *vi* ne pas être d'accord **(with** avec); **to d. with sb** *(of food, climate, medicine)* ne pas réussir à qn ■ **disagreement** *n* désaccord *m*; *(quarrel)* différend *m*

disagreeable [dɪsəˈgriːəbəl] *adj* désagréable

disappear [dɪsəˈpɪə(r)] *vi* disparaître ■ **disappearance** *n* disparition *f*

disappoint [dɪsəˈpɔɪnt] *vt* décevoir ■ **disappointing** *adj* décevant ■ **disappointment** *n* déception *f*

disapproval [dɪsəˈpruːvəl] *n* désapprobation *f*

disapprove [dɪsəˈpruːv] *vi* **to d. of sb/ sth** désapprouver qn/qch

disarray [dɪsəˈreɪ] *n* **in d.** *(army, political party)* en plein désarroi; *(clothes, hair)* en désordre

disaster [dɪˈzɑːstə(r)] *n* désastre *m*, catastrophe *f*; **d. area** région *f* sinistrée ■ **disastrous** *adj* désastreux, -euse

disband [dɪsˈbænd] **1** *vt* dissoudre **2** *vi* se dissoudre

disbelief [dɪsbəˈliːf] *n* incrédulité *f*

disc [dɪsk] *(Am* **disk)** *n* disque *m*; **d. jockey** disc-jockey *m*

discard [dɪsˈkɑːd] *vt (get rid of)* se débarrasser de; *(plan)* abandonner

discern [dɪˈsɜːn] *vt* discerner ■ **discerning** *adj (person)* averti

discernible [dɪˈsɜːnəbəl] *adj* perceptible

discharge 1 [ˈdɪstʃɑːdʒ] *n (of gun, electricity)* décharge *f*; *(dismissal)* renvoi *m*; *(freeing)* libération *f* **2** [dɪsˈtʃɑːdʒ] *vt (patient)* laisser sortir; *(employee)* renvoyer; *(soldier, prisoner)* libérer; *(gun)* décharger

disciple [dɪˈsaɪpəl] *n* disciple *m*

discipline [ˈdɪsɪplɪn] **1** *n (behaviour, subject)* discipline *f* **2** *vt (control)* discipliner; *(punish)* punir

disclose [dɪsˈkləʊz] *vt* révéler ■ **disclosure** [-ʒə(r)] *n* révélation *f*

disco ['dɪskəʊ] (*pl* **-os**) *n* discothèque *f*

discolour [dɪs'kʌlə(r)] (*Am* **discolor**) *vt* décolorer; (*teeth*) jaunir

discomfort [dɪs'kʌmfət] *n* (*physical*) petite douleur *f*, (*mental*) malaise *m*

disconcerting [dɪskən'sɜːtɪŋ] *adj* déconcertant

disconnect [dɪskə'nekt] *vt* (*unfasten*) détacher; (*unplug*) débrancher; (*gas, telephone, electricity*) couper

discontented [dɪskən'tentɪd] *adj* mécontent (**with** de)

discord ['dɪskɔːd] *n* (*disagreement*) discorde *f*

discotheque ['dɪskətek] *n* (*club*) discothèque *f*

discount 1 ['dɪskaʊnt] *n* (*on article*) réduction *f*, (*on account paid early*) escompte *m*; **d. store** solderie *f* **2** [dɪs'kaʊnt] *vt* (*story*) ne pas tenir compte de

discourage [dɪs'kʌrɪdʒ] *vt* décourager (**sb from doing** qn de faire)

discover [dɪs'kʌvə(r)] *vt* découvrir (**that** que) ■ **discovery** (*pl* **-ies**) *n* découverte *f*

discredit [dɪs'kredɪt] *vt* (*cast slur on*) discréditer

discreet [dɪ'skriːt] *adj* discret, -ète

discrepancy [dɪ'skrepənsɪ] (*pl* **-ies**) *n* décalage *m* (**between** entre)

discretion [dɪ'skreʃən] *n* (*tact*) discrétion *f*

discriminate [dɪ'skrɪmɪneɪt] *vi* **to d. against** faire de la discrimination envers; **to d. between** distinguer entre ■ **discrimination** [-'neɪʃən] *n* (*bias*) discrimination *f*

discus ['dɪskəs] *n Sport* disque *m*

discuss [dɪ'skʌs] *vt* discuter de ■ **discussion** *n* discussion *f*

disdain [dɪs'deɪn] *n* dédain *m*

disease [dɪ'ziːz] *n* maladie *f*

disembark [dɪsɪm'bɑːk] *vti* débarquer

disenchanted [dɪsɪn'tʃɑːntɪd] *adj* désenchanté

disfigured [dɪs'fɪɡə(r)] *adj* défiguré

disgrace [dɪs'ɡreɪs] **1** *n* (*shame*) honte *f* (**to** à) **2** *vt* déshonorer ■ **disgraceful** *adj* honteux, -euse

disgruntled [dɪs'ɡrʌntəld] *adj* mécontent

disguise [dɪs'ɡaɪz] **1** *n* déguisement *m*; **in d.** déguisé **2** *vt* déguiser (**as** en)

disgust [dɪs'ɡʌst] **1** *n* dégoût *m* (**for** *or* **at** *or* **with** de) **2** *vt* dégoûter ■ **disgusted** *adj* dégoûté (**at** *or* **by** *or* **with** de); **to be d. with sb** (*annoyed*) être fâché contre qn ■ **disgusting** *adj* dégoûtant

dish [dɪʃ] **1** *n* (*container, food*) plat *m*; **to do the dishes** faire la vaisselle **2** *vt* **to d. out** *or* **up** (*food*) servir ■ **dishcloth** *n* (*for washing*) lavette *f*, (*for drying*) torchon *m* ■ **dishtowel** *n* torchon *m* (à vaisselle) ■ **dishwasher** *n* (*machine*) lave-vaisselle *m inv*

dishevelled [dɪ'ʃevəld] (*Am* **disheveled**) *adj* (*person, hair*) ébouriffé

dishonest [dɪs'ɒnɪst] *adj* malhonnête ■ **dishonesty** *n* malhonnêteté *f*

dishonourable [dɪs'ɒnərəbəl] (*Am* **dishonorable**) *adj* déshonorant

disillusion [dɪsɪ'luːʒən] *vt* décevoir; **to be disillusioned** être déçu (**with** de)

disinclined [dɪsɪn'klaɪnd] *adj* peu disposé (**to do** à faire)

disinfect [dɪsɪn'fekt] *vt* désinfecter ■ **disinfectant** *n* désinfectant *m*

disinherit [dɪsɪn'herɪt] *vt* déshériter

disintegrate [dɪs'ɪntɪɡreɪt] *vi* se désintégrer

disinterested [dɪs'ɪntrɪstɪd] *adj* (*impartial*) désintéressé

disjointed [dɪs'dʒɔɪntɪd] *adj* (*words, style*) décousu

disk [dɪsk] *n* (**a**) *Am* = **disc** (**b**) *Comptr* disque *m*; (*floppy*) disquette *f*; **on d.** sur disque; **d. drive** unité *f* de disques ■ **diskette** *n Comptr* disquette *f*

dislike [dɪs'laɪk] **1** *n* aversion *f* (**for** *or* **of** pour); **to take a d. to sb/sth** prendre qn/qch en grippe **2** *vt* ne pas aimer (**doing** faire)

dislocate ['dɪsləkeɪt] *vt* (*limb*) démettre; **to d. one's shoulder** se démettre l'épaule

dislodge [dɪs'lɒdʒ] *vt* faire bouger, déplacer; *(enemy)* déloger

disloyal [dɪs'lɔɪəl] *adj* déloyal

dismal ['dɪzməl] *adj* lugubre ■ **dismally** *adv (fail, behave)* lamentablement

dismantle [dɪs'mæntəl] *vt (machine)* démonter; *(organization)* démanteler

dismay [dɪs'meɪ] **1** *n* consternation *f* **2** *vt* consterner

dismiss [dɪs'mɪs] *vt (from job)* renvoyer (**from** de); *(official)* destituer; *(thought, suggestion)* écarter; **to d. a case** *(of judge)* classer une affaire ■ **dismissal** *n* renvoi *m*; *(of official)* destitution *f*

dismount [dɪs'maʊnt] *vi (of person)* descendre (**from** de)

disobedient [dɪsə'biːdɪənt] *adj* désobéissant

disobey [dɪsə'beɪ] **1** *vt* désobéir à **2** *vi* désobéir

disorder [dɪs'ɔːdə(r)] *n (confusion)* désordre *m*; *(illness, riots)* troubles *mpl* ■ **disorderly** *adj (behaviour)* désordonné; *(meeting, crowd)* houleux, -euse

disorganized [dɪs'ɔːgənaɪzd] *adj* désorganisé

disorientate [dɪs'ɔːrɪənteɪt] *(Am* **disorient** [dɪs'ɔːrɪənt]) *vt* désorienter

disown [dɪs'əʊn] *vt* renier

disparaging [dɪs'pærɪdʒɪŋ] *adj (remark)* désobligeant

dispatch [dɪ'spætʃ] **1** *n (sending)* expédition *f* (**of** de); *(message)* dépêche *f* **2** *vt (send, finish off)* expédier; *(troops, messenger)* envoyer

dispel [dɪ'spel] *(pt & pp* **-ll-**) *vt* dissiper

dispensary [dɪ'spensərɪ] *(pl* **-ies**) *n (in chemist's shop)* officine *f*

dispense [dɪ'spens] **1** *vt (give out)* distribuer; *(medicine)* préparer **2** *vi* **to d. with** *(do without)* se passer de ■ **dispenser** *n (device)* distributeur *m*

disperse [dɪ'spɜːs] **1** *vt* disperser **2** *vi* se disperser

displace [dɪs'pleɪs] *vt (shift)* déplacer; *(replace)* supplanter

display [dɪ'spleɪ] **1** *n (in shop)* étalage *m*; *(of paintings, handicrafts)* exposition *f*; **d. (unit)** *(of computer)* moniteur *m*; **on d.** exposé **2** *vt (goods)* exposer; *(sign, notice)* afficher; *(emotion)* manifester; *(talent, concern, ignorance)* faire preuve de

displeased [dɪs'pliːzd] *adj* mécontent (**with** de)

disposable [dɪ'spəʊzəbəl] *adj Br (plate, nappy)* jetable; *(income)* disponible

disposal [dɪ'spəʊzəl] *n (of waste)* évacuation *f*; **at sb's d.** à la disposition de qn

dispose¹ [dɪ'spəʊz] *vi* **to d. of** *(get rid of)* se débarrasser de; *(throw away)* jeter; *(matter, problem)* régler

dispose² [dɪ'spəʊz] *vt* **to be disposed to do** être disposé à faire; **well-disposed towards** bien disposé envers

disposition [dɪspə'zɪʃən] *n (character)* tempérament *m*

dispossess [dɪspə'zes] *vt* déposséder (**of** de)

disproportionate [dɪsprə'pɔːʃənət] *adj* disproportionné

disprove [dɪs'pruːv] *(pp* **disproved,** *Law* **disproven** [-'prəʊvən]) *vt* réfuter

dispute [dɪ'spjuːt] **1** *n (quarrel)* dispute *f*; *(legal)* litige *m*; **(industrial) d.** conflit *m* social **2** *vt (claim, will)* contester

disqualify [dɪs'kwɒlɪfaɪ] *(pt & pp* **-ied**) *vt (make unfit)* rendre inapte (**from** à); *Sport* disqualifier; **to d. sb from driving** retirer son permis à qn ■ **disqualification** *n Sport* disqualification *f*

disregard [dɪsrɪ'gɑːd] **1** *n* mépris *m* (**for** de) **2** *vt* ne tenir aucun compte de

disrepair [dɪsrɪ'peə(r)] *n* **in (a state of) d.** délabré

disreputable [dɪs'repjʊtəbəl] *adj* peu recommandable; *(behaviour)* honteux, -euse

disrepute [dɪsrɪ'pjuːt] *n* **to bring sb/sth into d.** discréditer qn/qch

disrespectful [dɪsrɪ'spektfʊl] *adj*

irrespectueux, -euse (**to** envers)

disrupt [dɪsˈrʌpt] *vt (traffic, class)* perturber; *(communications)* interrompre; *(plan)* déranger ■ **disruption** *n* perturbation *f*

disruptive [dɪsˈrʌptɪv] *adj* perturbateur, -trice

dissatisfied [dɪsˈsætɪsfaɪd] *adj* mécontent (**with** de) ■ **dissatisfaction** [-ˈfækʃən] *n* mécontentement *m* (**with** devant)

dissent [dɪsˈsent] **1** *n* désaccord *m* **2** *vi* être en désaccord (**from** avec)

dissertation [dɪsəˈteɪʃən] *n* mémoire *m*

dissident [ˈdɪsɪdənt] *adj & n* dissident, -e *(mf)*

dissimilar [dɪˈsɪmɪlə(r)] *adj* différent (**to** de)

dissipate [ˈdɪsɪpeɪt] *vt (fog, fears)* dissiper; *(energy, fortune)* gaspiller

dissociate [dɪˈsəʊʃɪeɪt] *vt* dissocier (**from** de)

dissolute [ˈdɪsəluːt] *adj* dissolu

dissolve [dɪˈzɒlv] **1** *vt* dissoudre **2** *vi* se dissoudre

dissuade [dɪˈsweɪd] *vt* dissuader (**from doing** de faire)

distance [ˈdɪstəns] *n* distance *f*; **in the d.** au loin; **from a d.** de loin; **to keep one's d.** garder ses distances

distant [ˈdɪstənt] *adj* lointain; *(relative)* éloigné; *(reserved)* distant

distasteful [dɪsˈteɪstfʊl] *adj* déplaisant

distil [dɪsˈtɪl] *(pt & pp -ll-) vt* distiller; **distilled water** eau *f* déminéralisée

distinct [dɪsˈtɪŋkt] *adj* (**a**) *(clear)* clair; *(preference, improvement, difference)* net (*f* nette) (**b**) *(different)* distinct (**from** de) ■ **distinctly** *adv (see, hear)* distinctement; *(remember)* très bien; *(better, easier)* nettement

distinction [dɪsˈtɪŋkʃən] *n* distinction *f*; *(in exam)* mention *f* bien

distinctive [dɪsˈtɪŋktɪv] *adj* distinctif, -ive

distinguish [dɪsˈtɪŋgwɪʃ] *vti* distinguer (**from** de; **between** entre); **to d.**

oneself se distinguer (**as** en tant que)

distinguished [dɪsˈtɪŋgwɪʃd] *adj* distingué

distort [dɪsˈtɔːt] *vt* déformer ■ **distortion** *n (of features, sound)* distorsion *f*; *(of truth)* déformation *f*

distract [dɪsˈtrækt] *vt* distraire (**from** de) ■ **distracted** *adj* préoccupé

distraction [dɪsˈtrækʃən] *n* distraction *f*

distraught [dɪsˈtrɔːt] *adj* éperdu

distress [dɪsˈtres] **1** *n (mental)* détresse *f*; *(physical)* douleur *f* **2** *vt* bouleverser ■ **distressing** *adj* bouleversant

distribute [dɪsˈtrɪbjuːt] *vt (give out) & Com (supply)* distribuer; *(spread evenly)* répartir ■ **distribution** [-ˈbjuːʃən] *n* distribution *f*

distributor [dɪsˈtrɪbjʊtə(r)] *n (in car, of films)* distributeur *m*

district [ˈdɪstrɪkt] *n* région *f*; *(of town)* quartier *m*; *(administrative)* district *m*

distrust [dɪsˈtrʌst] **1** *n* méfiance *f* (**of** à l'égard de) **2** *vt* se méfier de

disturb [dɪsˈtɜːb] *vt (sleep, water)* troubler; *(papers, belongings)* déranger; **to d. sb** *(bother)* déranger qn; *(worry, alarm)* troubler qn ■ **disturbing** *adj (worrying)* inquiétant; *(annoying, irksome)* gênant

disturbance [dɪsˈtɜːbəns] *n (noise)* tapage *m*; **disturbances** *(riots)* troubles *mpl*

disunity [dɪsˈjuːnɪtɪ] *n* désunion *f*

disuse [dɪsˈjuːs] *n* **to fall into d.** tomber en désuétude ■ **disused** *adj (building)* désaffecté

ditch [dɪtʃ] **1** *n* fossé *m* **2** *vt Fam (get rid of)* se débarrasser de; *(plan)* laisser tomber

ditto [ˈdɪtəʊ] *adv* idem

dive [daɪv] **1** *n (of swimmer, goalkeeper)* plongeon *m*; *(of aircraft)* piqué *m* **2** *(pt* **dived,** *Am* **dove)** *vi* plonger; *(of plane)* piquer ■ **diver** *n* plongeur, -euse *mf*; *(deep-sea)* scaphandrier *m*

diverge [daɪˈvɜːdʒ] *vi* diverger (**from** de)

diverse [daɪˈvɜːs] *adj* divers ■ **diversity** *n* diversité *f* ■ **diversify** (*pt & pp* -**ied**) *vi* (*of firm*) se diversifier

diversion [daɪˈvɜːʃən] *n Br* (*on road*) déviation *f*; (*amusement*) distraction *f*; **to create a d.** faire diversion

divert [daɪˈvɜːt] *vt* (*attention, suspicions, river, plane*) détourner; *Br* (*traffic*) dévier; (*amuse*) divertir

divide [dɪˈvaɪd] *vt Math* diviser (**into** en; **by** par); (*food, money, time*) partager (**between** *or* **among** entre); **to d. sth (off) (from sth)** séparer qch (de qch); **to d. sth up** (*share out*) partager qch

divine [dɪˈvaɪn] *adj* divin

diving [ˈdaɪvɪŋ] *n* (*underwater*) plongée *f* sous-marine; **d. board** plongeoir *m*

division [dɪˈvɪʒən] *n* division *f*; (*distribution*) partage *m*; *Sport* **first d.** première division

divorce [dɪˈvɔːs] **1** *n* divorce *m* **2** *vt* (*husband, wife*) divorcer de; *Fig* (*idea*) séparer (**from** de) **3** *vi* divorcer ■ **divorced** *adj* divorcé (**from** de); **to get d.** divorcer ■ **divorcee** [dɪvɔːˈsiː, *Am* dɪvɔːrˈseɪ] *n* divorcé, -e *mf*

divulge [daɪˈvʌldʒ] *vt* divulguer

DIY [diːaɪˈwaɪ] (*abbr* **do-it-yourself**) *n Br* bricolage *m*

dizzy [ˈdɪzɪ] (-**ier**, -**iest**) *adj* **to be** *or* **feel d.** avoir le vertige; **to make sb (feel) d.** donner le vertige à qn

DJ [ˈdiːdʒeɪ] (*abbr* **disc-jockey**) *n* disc-jockey *m*

DO [duː]

Les formes négatives sont **don't/doesn't** et **didn't**, qui deviennent **do not/does not** et **did not** dans un style plus soutenu.

1 (*3rd person sing present tense* **does**, *pt* **did**, *pp* **done**, *pres p* **doing**) *v aux* **do you know?** savez-vous?; **I do not** *or* **don't see** je ne vois pas; **he did say so** (*emphasis*) il l'a bien dit; **do stay** reste donc; **you know him, don't you?** tu le connais, n'est-ce pas?; **better than I do** mieux que je ne le fais; **so do I** moi aussi;

don't! non!

2 *vt* faire; **what does she do?** (*in general*) que fait-elle qu'elle fait?, que fait-elle?; **what is she doing?** (*now*) qu'est-ce qu'elle fait?, que fait-elle?; **what have you done (with...)?** qu'as-tu fait (de...)?; **well done** (*congratulations*) bravo!; (*steak*) bien cuit; **it's over and done (with)** c'est fini; **that'll do me** (*suit*) ça m'ira; *Br Fam* **I've been done** (*cheated*) je me suis fait avoir; **to do sb out of sth** escroquer qch à qn; *Fam* **I'm done (in)** (*tired*) je suis claqué; **to do out** (*clean*) nettoyer; **to do over** (*redecorate*) refaire; **to do up** (*coat, buttons*) boutonner; (*zip*) fermer; (*house*) refaire; (*goods*) emballer

3 *vi* **do as you're told** fais ce qu'on te dit; **that will do** (*be OK*) ça ira; (*be enough*) ça suffit; **have you done?** vous avez fini?; **to do well/badly** (*of person*) bien/mal se débrouiller; **business is doing well** les affaires marchent bien; **how are you doing?** (*comment*) ça va?; **how do you do** (*introduction*) enchanté; (*greeting*) bonjour; **to make do** se débrouiller; **to do away with sb/sth** supprimer qn/qch; **I could do with a coffee** (*need, want*) je prendrais bien un café; **it has to do with...** (*relates to*) cela a à voir avec...; (*concerns*) cela concerne...

4 *n* (*pl* **dos**) *Br Fam* (*party*) fête *f*

docile [ˈdəʊsaɪl] *adj* docile

dock [dɒk] **1** *n* (**a**) (*for ship*) dock *m* (**b**) (*in court*) banc *m* des accusés **2** *vi* (*of ship*) (*at quayside*) accoster; (*in port*) relâcher

doctor [ˈdɒktə(r)] **1** *n* (*medical*) médecin *m*, docteur *m*; (*having doctor's degree*) docteur *m* **2** *vt* (*text, food*) altérer; *Br* (*cat*) châtrer ■ **doctorate** *n* doctorat *m* (**in** ès/en)

document [ˈdɒkjʊmənt] *n* document *m* ■ **documentary** [-ˈmentərɪ] (*pl* -**ies**) *n* (*film*) documentaire *m*

dodge [dɒdʒ] **1** *n* (*trick*) truc *m* **2** *vt* (*question*) esquiver; (*person*) éviter;

(pursuer) échapper à; *(tax)* éviter de payer **3** *vi (to one side)* faire un saut de côté; **to d. through** *(crowd)* se faufiler dans

Dodgems® ['dɒdʒəmz] *npl* autos *fpl* tamponneuses

dodgy ['dɒdʒɪ] **(-ier, -iest)** *adj Fam (suspect)* louche; *(not working properly)* en mauvais état; *(risky)* risqué

does [dʌz] *see* **do**

doesn't ['dʌzənt] = **does not**

dog¹ [dɒg] *n* chien *m*; *(female)* chienne *f*

dog² [dɒg] *(pt & pp* **-gg-)** *vt (follow)* suivre de près

doggedly ['dɒgɪdlɪ] *adv* obstinément

doing ['du:ɪŋ] *n* **that's your d.** c'est toi qui as fait ça

do-it-yourself [du:ɪtjə'self] *n Br* bricolage *m*; **d. store/book** magasin *m*/ livre *m* de bricolage

dole [dəʊl] *n Br* **d. (money)** allocation *f* de chômage; **to go on the d.** s'inscrire au chômage

doll [dɒl] *n* poupée *f*; *Br* **doll's house,** *Am* **dollhouse** maison *f* de poupée

dollar ['dɒlə(r)] *n* dollar *m*

dollop ['dɒləp] *n (of cream, purée)* grosse cuillerée *f*

dolphin ['dɒlfɪn] *n* dauphin *m*

domain [dəʊ'meɪn] *n (land, sphere)* domaine *m*

dome [dəʊm] *n* dôme *m*

domestic [də'mestɪk] *adj (appliance, use, tasks)* ménager, -ère; *(animal)* domestique; *(policy, flight, affairs)* intérieur

dominant ['dɒmɪnənt] *adj* dominant; *(person)* dominateur, -trice

dominate ['dɒmɪneɪt] *vti* dominer

domineering [dɒmɪ'nɪərɪŋ] *adj (person, character)* dominateur, -trice

domino ['dɒmɪnəʊ] *(pl* **-oes)** *n* domino *m*; **dominoes** *(game)* dominos *mpl*

donate [dəʊ'neɪt] **1** *vt* faire don de; *(blood)* donner **2** *vi* donner ▪ **donation** *n* don *m*

done [dʌn] *pp of* **do**

donkey ['dɒŋkɪ] *(pl* **-eys)** *n* âne *m*

donor ['dəʊnə(r)] *n* donneur, -euse *mf*

don't [dəʊnt] = **do not**

donut ['dəʊnʌt] *n Am* beignet *m*

doom [du:m] **1** *n (fate)* destin *m* **2** *vt* condamner **(to à)**; **to be doomed (to failure)** *(of project)* être voué à l'échec

door [dɔ:(r)] *n* porte *f*; *(of vehicle, train)* portière *f*; **d. handle** poignée *f* de porte ▪ **doorbell** *n* sonnette *f* ▪ **doorknob** *n* bouton *m* de porte ▪ **doorman** *(pl* **-men)** *(of hotel)* portier *m* ▪ **doormat** *n* paillasson *m* ▪ **doorstep** *n* seuil *m* ▪ **door-to-door** *adj* **d. salesman** démarcheur *m* ▪ **doorway** *n* **in the d.** dans l'embrasure de la porte

dope [dəʊp] *n Fam* **(a)** *(drugs)* drogue *f* **(b)** *(idiot)* andouille *f*

dormitory [*Br* 'dɔ:mɪtrɪ, *Am* 'dɔ:rmɪtɔ:rɪ] *(pl* **-ies)** *n* dortoir *m*; *(university residence)* résidence *f* universitaire

dosage ['dəʊsɪdʒ] *n (amount)* dose *f*

dose [dəʊs] *n* dose *f*; **a d. of flu** une grippe

dossier ['dɒsɪeɪ] *n (papers)* dossier *m*

dot [dɒt] **1** *n* point *m*; *Fam* **on the d.** à l'heure pile **2** *(pt & pp* **-tt-)** *vt (letter)* mettre un point sur; **dotted with** parsemé de; **dotted line** pointillé *m*

dote [dəʊt] *vt* **to d. on** adorer

dot-matrix [dɒt'meɪtrɪks] *n Comptr* **d. printer** imprimante *f* matricielle

double ['dʌbəl] **1** *adj* double; **a d. bed** un grand lit; **a d. room** une chambre pour deux personnes; **d. 's/'deux's; d. three four two** *(phone number)* trente-trois quarante-deux

2 *adv (twice)* deux fois; *(fold)* en deux; **he earns d. what I do** il gagne le double de moi

3 *n* double *m*; *(person)* double *m*, sosie *m*; *(stand-in film)* doublure *f*

4 *vt* doubler; **to d. sth back** *or* **over** *(fold)* replier qch; **to be doubled up with pain/laughter** être plié (en deux) de douleur/rire

5 *vi* doubler; **to d. back** *(of person)* revenir en arrière ■ **double-bass** n Br *(instrument)* contrebasse f ■ **double-check** vti revérifier ■ **double-cross** vt doubler ■ **double-decker** n d. **(bus)** autobus m à impériale ■ **double-glazing** n *(window)* double vitrage m

doubt [daʊt] **1** n doute m; **I have no d. about it** je n'en doute pas; **no d.** *(probably)* sans doute; **in d.** *(result, career)* dans la balance **2** vt douter de; **to d. whether** or **that** or **if…** douter que… *(+ subjunctive)*

doubtful ['daʊtfəl] adj *(person, future, success)* incertain; **to be d. (about sth)** avoir des doutes (sur qch); **it's d. whether** or **that** or **if…** il n'est pas certain que… *(+ subjunctive)* ■ **doubtless** adv sans doute

dough [dəʊ] n pâte f; Fam *(money)* blé m

doughnut ['dəʊnʌt] n beignet m

dove¹ [dʌv] n colombe f

dove² [dəʊv] Am pt of **dive**

Dover ['dəʊvə(r)] n Douvres m ou f

dowdy ['daʊdɪ] (**-ier**, **-iest**) adj peu élégant

DOWN [daʊn] **1** adj d. **payment** acompte m

2 adv en bas; *(to the ground)* à terre; **d. there** or **here** en bas; Fam **to feel d.** *(depressed)* avoir le cafard; **d. to** *(in series, numbers, dates)* jusqu'à; **d. under** aux antipodes, en Australie

3 prep *(at bottom of)* en bas de; *(from top to bottom of)* du haut en bas de; *(along)* le long de; **to go d.** *(hill, street, stairs)* descendre; **to live d. the street** habiter plus loin dans la rue

4 vt **to d. a drink** vider un verre ■ **down-and-out 1** adj sur le pavé **2** n clochard, -e mf ■ **downcast** adj découragé ■ **downfall** n chute f ■ **down-hearted** adj découragé ■ **downhill** adv en pente; **to go d.** descendre; *(of sick person, business)* aller de plus en plus mal ■ **down-market** adj Br *(car, furniture)* bas de gamme inv; *(neighbourhood)* populaire ■ **downpour** n averse f ■ **down-**

right 1 adj *(rogue)* véritable; *(refusal)* catégorique **2** adv *(rude, disagreeable)* franchement ■ **downstairs 1** ['daʊnsteəz] adj *(room, neighbours)* (below) d'en bas; *(on the ground floor)* du rez-de-chaussée **2** [daʊn'steəz] adv en bas; *(to the ground floor)* au rez-de-chaussée; **to come** or **go d.** descendre l'escalier ■ **down-to-earth** adj terre-à-terre inv ■ **downtown** advAm en ville; **d. Chicago** le centre de Chicago ■ **downward** adj vers le bas; *(path)* qui descend; *(trend)* à la baisse ■ **downward(s)** adv vers le bas

doze [dəʊz] **1** n petit somme m **2** vi sommeiller; **to d. off** s'assoupir

dozen ['dʌzən] n douzaine f; **a d. books/eggs** une douzaine de livres/d'œufs; Fig **dozens of** des dizaines de

Dr *(abbr Doctor)* Docteur

drab [dræb] adj terne; *(weather)* gris

draft¹ [drɑːft] **1** n (**a**) *(outline)* ébauche f, *(of letter)* brouillon m (**b**) Am *(military)* conscription f **2** vt (**a**) **to d.** *(out)* *(sketch out)* faire le brouillon de; *(write out)* rédiger (**b**) Am *(conscript)* appeler sous les drapeaux

draft² [drɑːft] nAm = **draught**

drafty ['drɑːftɪ] (**-ier**, **-iest**) adjAm = **draughty**

drag [dræg] **1** n Fam **it's a d.!** *(boring)* c'est la barbe! **2** (pt & pp **-gg-**) vt traîner; **to d. sb/sth along** (en)traîner qn/qch; **to d. sb away from** arracher qn à; **to d. sb into** entraîner qn dans **3** vi traîner; **to d. on** or **out** *(of film, day)* traîner en longueur

dragon ['drægən] n dragon m

dragonfly ['drægənflaɪ] (pl **-ies**) n libellule f

drain [dreɪn] **1** n *(sewer)* égout m; *(in street)* bouche f d'égout **2** vt *(glass, tank)* vider; *(vegetables)* égoutter; **to d. (off)** *(liquid)* faire écouler; **to feel drained** être épuisé **3** vi **to d. (off)** *(of liquid)* s'écouler ■ **draining** n d. **board** paillasse f

drainpipe ['dreɪnpaɪp] n tuyau m

d'évacuation

drama ['drɑːmə] n (event) drame m; (dramatic art) théâtre m

dramatic [drə'mætɪk] adj dramatique; (very great, striking) spectaculaire

dramatize ['dræmətaɪz] vt (exaggerate) dramatiser; (novel) adapter pour la scène/l'écran

drank [dræŋk] pt of **drink**

drape [dreɪp] vt (person, shoulders) draper (**with** de) ■ **drapes** npl Am (curtains) rideaux mpl

drastic ['dræstɪk] adj (change, measure) radical; (remedy) puissant

draught [drɑːft] (Am **draft**) n (a) (wind) courant m d'air (b) Br **draughts** (game) dames fpl (c) **d. beer** bière f (à la) pression

draughty ['drɑːftɪ] (Am **drafty**) (-ier, -iest) adj (room) plein de courants d'air

draw[1] [drɔː] 1 n Sport match m nul; (of lottery) tirage m au sort; (attraction) attraction f
2 (pt **drew**, pp **drawn**) vt (a) (pull) tirer; (pass, move) passer (**over** sur; **into** dans); **to d. up** (chair) approcher; (contract, list, plan) dresser, rédiger (b) (extract) retirer; (pistol, sword) dégainer; Fig (strength, comfort) retirer, puiser (**from** de) (c) (attract) attirer
3 vi Sport faire match nul; **to d. near (to)** s'approcher (de); (of time) approcher (de); **to d. back** (go backwards) reculer; **to d. up** (of vehicle) s'arrêter

draw[2] [drɔː] 1 (pt **drew**, pp **drawn**) vt (picture) dessiner; (circle) tracer; Fig (parallel, distinction) faire (**between** entre) 2 vi (as artist) dessiner

drawback ['drɔːbæk] n inconvénient m

drawer [drɔː(r)] n (in furniture) tiroir m

drawing ['drɔːɪŋ] n dessin m; Br **d. pin** punaise f; **d. room** salon m

drawl [drɔːl] n voix f traînante

drawn [drɔːn] 1 pp of **draw**[1,2] 2 adj **d. match** or **game** match m nul

dread [dred] 1 n terreur f 2 vt (exam) appréhender; **to d. doing sth** appréhender de faire qch

dreadful ['dredfəl] adj épouvantable; (child) insupportable; **I feel d.** (ill) je ne me sens vraiment pas bien; **I feel d. about it** j'ai vraiment honte ■ **dreadfully** adv terriblement; **to be d. sorry** regretter infiniment

dream [driːm] 1 n rêve m; **to have a d.** faire un rêve (**about** de); **a d. world** un monde imaginaire 2 (pt & pp **dreamed** or **dreamt** [dremt]) vt rêver (**that** que); **I never dreamt that...** (imagined) je n'aurais jamais songé que...; **to d. sth up** imaginer qch 3 vi rêver (**of** or **about** sb/sth de qn/qch; **of** or **about doing** de faire)

dreary ['drɪərɪ] (-ier, -iest) adj morne

drench [drentʃ] vt tremper; **to get drenched** se faire tremper (jusqu'aux os)

dress [dres] 1 n (garment) robe f; (style of dressing) tenue f; Br **d. circle** (in theatre) premier balcon m; **d. rehearsal** (in theatre) (répétition f) générale f 2 vt (person) habiller; (wound) panser; (salad) assaisonner; **to get dressed** s'habiller 3 vi s'habiller; **to d. up** (smartly) bien s'habiller; (in disguise) se déguiser (**as** en)

dressing ['dresɪŋ] n (for wound) pansement m; (seasoning) assaisonnement m; Br **d. gown** robe f de chambre; **d. room** (in theatre) loge f; (in shop) cabine f d'essayage; **d. table** coiffeuse f

drew [druː] pt of **draw**[1,2]

dribble ['drɪbəl] vi (a) (of baby) baver; (of liquid) tomber goutte à goutte (b) (of footballer) dribbler

dribs [drɪbz] npl **in d. and drabs** par petites quantités; (arrive) par petits groupes

dried [draɪd] adj (fruit) sec (f sèche); (milk, eggs) en poudre; (flowers) séché

drier ['draɪə(r)] n = **dryer**

drift [drɪft] 1 n (movement) mouvement *m*; *(of snow)* congère *f*; *(meaning)* sens *m* général **2** *vi (through air)* être emporté par le vent; *(on water)* être emporté par le courant; *(of ship)* dériver; Fig *(of person, nation)* aller à la dérive

drill [drɪl] **1** *n* (**a**) *(tool)* perceuse *f*; *(bit)* mèche *f*; *(pneumatic)* marteau *m* piqueur; *(dentist's)* roulette *f* (**b**) *(exercise)* exercice *m*; *(correct procedure)* marche *f* à suivre **2** *vt (wood)* percer; *(tooth)* fraiser **3** *vi* to d. for oil faire de la recherche pétrolière

drily [ˈdraɪlɪ] *adv (remark)* sèchement, d'un ton sec

drink [drɪŋk] **1** *n* boisson *f*; to have a d. boire quelque chose; *(alcoholic)* prendre un verre
2 *(pt* drank, *pp* drunk) *vt* boire **3** *vi* boire (out of dans); to d. up finir son verre ∎ **drink-driving** *n Br* conduite *f* en état d'ivresse ∎ **drinking** *n* **d. chocolate** chocolat *m* en poudre; **d. water** eau *f* potable

drinkable [ˈdrɪŋkəbəl] *adj (fit for drinking)* potable; *(not unpleasant)* buvable

drip [drɪp] **1** *n (drop)* goutte *f*; *(sound)* bruit *m* de l'eau qui goutte; Med to be on a d. être sous perfusion **2** *(pt & pp* -pp-) *vt (paint)* laisser tomber goutte à goutte; you're dripping water everywhere! tu mets de l'eau partout! **3** *vi (of water, rain)* goutter; *(of tap)* fuir

drive [draɪv] **1** *n (in car)* promenade *f* en voiture; *(road to private house)* allée *f*; *(energy)* énergie *f*; *(campaign)* campagne *f*; Comptr lecteur *m*; an hour's d. une heure de voiture
2 *(pt* drove, *pp* driven) *vt (vehicle, train, passenger)* conduire (to à); *(machine)* actionner; to d. sb to do sth pousser qn à faire qch; to d. sb mad or crazy rendre qn fou/folle; he drives a Ford il a une Ford
3 *vi (drive a car)* conduire; *(go by car)* rouler; to d. on the left rouler à gauche; to d. to Paris aller en voiture à Paris; to d. to work aller au travail en voiture; Fig what are you driving at?

où veux-tu en venir?
▸ **drive along** *vi (in car)* rouler
▸ **drive away 1** *vt sep (chase away)* chasser **2** *vi (in car)* partir en voiture
▸ **drive back 1** *vt sep (passenger)* ramener (en voiture); *(enemy)* repousser **2** *vi (in car)* revenir (en voiture)
▸ **drive in** *vt sep (nail)* enfoncer
▸ **drive off** *vi (in car)* partir (en voiture)
▸ **drive on** *vi (in car)* continuer sa route
▸ **drive out** *vt sep (chase away)* chasser
▸ **drive up** *vi (in car)* arriver (en voiture)

drive-in [ˈdraɪvɪn] *adj Am* d. (movie theater) drive-in *m inv*; d. (restaurant) = restaurant où l'on est servi dans sa voiture

drivel [ˈdrɪvəl] *n* idioties *fpl*

driven [ˈdrɪvən] *pp of* drive

driver [ˈdraɪvə(r)] *n (of car)* conducteur, -trice *mf*; *(of taxi, truck)* chauffeur *m*; *(train or engine)* **d.** mécanicien *m*; she's a good d. elle conduit bien; Am d.'s license permis *m* de conduire

driveway [ˈdraɪvweɪ] *n (road to house)* allée *f*

driving [ˈdraɪvɪŋ] *n (in car)* conduite *f*; d. lesson leçon *f* de conduite; Br d. licence permis *m* de conduire; d. school auto-école *f*; d. test examen *m* du permis de conduire

drizzle [ˈdrɪzəl] *vi* bruiner

droop [druːp] *vi (of flower)* se faner; *(of head)* pencher; *(of eyelids, shoulders)* tomber

drop [drɒp] **1** *n* (**a**) *(of liquid)* goutte *f*; eye/nose drops gouttes *fpl* pour les yeux/le nez
(**b**) *(fall)* baisse *f*, chute *f* (in de); *(distance of fall)* hauteur *f* de chute; *(slope)* descente *f*
2 *(pt & pp* -pp-) *vt* laisser tomber; *(price, voice)* baisser; *(bomb)* larguer; *(passenger, goods from vehicle)* déposer; *(leave out)* faire sauter, omettre;

(get rid of) supprimer; *(team member)* écarter; **to d. sb off** *(from vehicle)* déposer qn; **to d. sb a line** écrire un petit mot à qn; **to d. a hint that…** laisser entendre que…

3 *vi (fall)* tomber; *(of person)* se laisser tomber; *(of price)* baisser; **to d. back** *or* **behind** rester en arrière; **to d. by** *or* **in** *(visit sb)* passer; **to d. off** *(fall asleep)* s'endormir; *(fall off)* tomber; *(of interest, sales)* diminuer; **to d. out** *(fall out)* tomber; *(withdraw)* se retirer; *(of student)* laisser tomber ses études; **to d. round** *(visit sb)* passer

dropout ['drɒpaʊt] *n* marginal, -e *mf;* *(student)* étudiant, -e *mf* qui abandonne ses études

droppings ['drɒpɪŋz] *npl (of animal)* crottes *fpl; (of bird)* fiente *f*

drought [draʊt] *n* sécheresse *f*

drove [drəʊv] *pt of* **drive**

drown [draʊn] **1** *vt* noyer; **to d. one- self, to be drowned** se noyer **2** *vi* se noyer

drowsy ['draʊzɪ] *(-ier, -iest) adj* **to be** *or* **feel d.** avoir sommeil

drudgery ['drʌdʒərɪ] *n* corvée *f*

drug [drʌg] **1** *n (against illness)* médi- cament *m; (narcotic)* drogue *f;* **drugs** *(narcotics in general)* la drogue; **to be on drugs, to take drugs** se droguer; **d. addict** drogué, -e *mf;* **d. dealer** *(large-scale)* trafiquant *m* de drogue; *(small-scale)* petit trafiquant *m* de dro- gue, dealer *m* **2** *(pt & pp* **-gg-)** *vt* dro- guer

druggist ['drʌgɪst] *n Am* pharmacien, -enne *mf*

drugstore ['drʌgstɔ:r] *n Am* drugstore *m*

drum [drʌm] **1** *n Mus* tambour *m; (for oil)* bidon *m;* **the drums** *(of rock group)* la batterie **2** *(pt & pp* **-mm-)** *vt* **to d. sth into sb** enfoncer qch dans la tête de qn; **to d. up** *(support, interest)* recher- cher ■ **drummer** *n* tambour *m; (in rock group)* batteur *m* ■ **drumstick** *n (for drum)* baguette *f* de tambour; *(of chicken)* pilon *m*

drunk [drʌŋk] **1** *pp of* **drink 2** *adj* ivre; **to get d.** s'enivrer **3** *n* ivrogne *mf* ■ **drunkard** *n* ivrogne *mf* ■ **drunken** *adj (person) (regularly)* ivrogne; *(dri- ver) (quarrel, brawl)* d'ivrogne

dry [draɪ] **1** *(drier, driest) adj (f sè- che)* *(well, river)* à sec; *(day)* sans pluie; *(subject, book)* aride; **to wipe sth d.** essuyer qch

2 *vt* sécher; *(by wiping)* essuyer; *(clothes)* faire sécher; **to d. the dishes** essuyer la vaisselle; **to d. sth off** *or* **up** sécher qch

3 *vi* sécher; **to d. off** sécher; **to d. up** sécher; *(dry the dishes)* essuyer la vaisselle; *(of stream)* se tarir ■ **dryer** *n (for hair, clothes)* séchoir *m*

dry-clean [draɪˈkli:n] *vt* nettoyer à sec ■ **dry-cleaner** *n* **the d.'s** *(shop)* le pressing, la teinturerie

dual ['dju:əl] *adj* double; *Br* **d. carriage- way** route *f* à deux voies

dub [dʌb] *(pt & pp* **-bb-)** *vt (film)* dou- bler *(into* en)

dubious ['dju:bɪəs] *adj (offer, person)* douteux, -euse; **I'm d. about going** *or* **about whether to go** je me demande si je dois y aller

duchess ['dʌtʃɪs] *n* duchesse *f*

duck [dʌk] **1** *n* canard *m* **2** *vt (head)* baisser subitement **3** *vi* se baisser ■ **duckling** *n* caneton *m*

due [dju:] *adj (money, sum)* dû *(f* due) *(to* à); *(rent, bill)* à payer; *(fitting, prop- er)* qui convient; **he's d. (to arrive)** il doit arriver d'un moment à l'autre; **in d. course** *(when appropriate)* en temps voulu; *(eventually)* le moment venu; **d. to** par suite de, en raison de

duel ['dju:əl] **1** *n* duel *m* **2** *(Br* **-ll-,** *Am* **-l-)** *vi* se battre en duel

duet [dju:'et] *n* duo *m*

duffel, duffle ['dʌfəl] *adj* **d. coat** duf- fel-coat *m*

dug [dʌg] *pt & pp of* **dig**

duke [dju:k] *n* duc *m*

dull [dʌl] **1** *(-er, -est) adj (boring)* en- nuyeux, -euse; *(colour, character)* terne; *(weather)* maussade; *(sound,* *ache*) sourd; *(edge, blade)* émoussé **2** *vt (pain)* endormir

duly ['dju:lɪ] *adv (properly)* dûment; *(as expected)* comme prévu

dumb [dʌm] *(-er, -est) adj* muet (*f* muette); *Fam (stupid)* bête

dumbfound [dʌm'faʊnd] *vt* sidérer

dummy ['dʌmɪ] **1** *(pl -ies) n Br (of baby)* tétine *f; (for displaying clothes)* mannequin *m; (of ventriloquist)* pantin *m* **2** *adj* factice

dump [dʌmp] **1** *n (for refuse)* décharge *f; Fam Pej (town)* trou *m; Fam Pej (house)* baraque *f* **2** *vt (rubbish)* déposer; *Fam* **to d. sb** plaquer qn

dumpling ['dʌmplɪŋ] *n (in stew)* boulette *f* de pâte

dune [dju:n] *n* **(sand) d.** dune *f*

dung [dʌŋ] *n (of horse)* crottin *m; (of cattle)* bouse *f; (manure)* fumier *m*

dungarees [dʌŋgə'ri:z] *npl (of child, workman)* salopette *f; Am (jeans)* jean *m*

dunk [dʌŋk] *vt* tremper

dupe [dju:p] *vt* duper

duplex ['du:pleks] *n Am (apartment)* duplex *m*

duplicate 1 ['dju:plɪkət] *n* double *m;* **in d.** en deux exemplaires **2** ['dju:plɪkeɪt] *vt (key, map)* faire un double de; *(on machine)* photocopier

durable ['djʊərəbəl] *adj (material, shoes)* résistant

duration [djʊə'reɪʃən] *n* durée *f*

duress [djʊ'res] *n* **under d.** sous la contrainte

during ['djʊərɪŋ] *prep* pendant, durant

dusk [dʌsk] *n (twilight)* crépuscule *m*

dust [dʌst] *n* poussière *f;* **d. cover or**

sheet (for furniture) housse *f;* **d. cover** *or* **jacket** *(for book)* jaquette *f* **2** *vt (furniture)* dépoussiérer **3** *vi* faire la poussière ▪ **dustbin** *n Br* poubelle *f* ▪ **dustman** *(pl -men) n Br* éboueur *m* ▪ **dustpan** *n* pelle *f* (à poussière) ▪ **dusty** *(-ier, -iest) adj* poussiéreux, -euse

duster ['dʌstə(r)] *n* chiffon *m*

Dutch [dʌtʃ] **1** *adj* hollandais **2** *n* **(a) the D.** *(people)* les Hollandais *mpl* **(b)** *(language)* hollandais *m*

duty ['dju:tɪ] *(pl -ies) n (tax)* droit *m;* **duties** *(responsibilities)* fonctions *fpl;* **to be on/off d.** être/ne pas être de service

duty-free ['dju:tɪ'fri:] *adj (goods, shop)* hors taxe *inv*

duvet ['du:veɪ] *n Br* couette *f*

DVD [di:vi:'di:] *(abbr Digital Versatile Disk, Digital Video Disk) n Comptr* DVD *m inv,* disque *m* vidéo numérique

dwarf [dwɔ:f] *n* nain, -e *mf*

dwell [dwel] *(pt & pp* **dwelt** [dwelt]*) vi* demeurer; **to d. (up)on** *(think about)* penser sans cesse à; *(speak about)* parler sans cesse de

dwindle ['dwɪndəl] *vi* diminuer (peu à peu)

dye [daɪ] **1** *n* teinture *f* **2** *vt* teindre; **to d. sth green** teindre qch en vert

dying ['daɪɪŋ] **1** *pres p of* **die[1] 2** *adj (person, animal)* mourant; *(wish, words)* dernier, -ère **3** *n (death)* mort *f*

dynamic [daɪ'næmɪk] *adj* dynamique

dynamite ['daɪnəmaɪt] *n* dynamite *f*

dynamo ['daɪnəməʊ] *(pl -os) n* dynamo *f*

dyslexic [dɪs'leksɪk] *adj & n* dyslexique *(mf)*

Ee

E, e [iː] *n (letter)* E, e *m inv*

each [iːtʃ] **1** *adj* chaque; **e. one** chacun, -e; **e. one of us** chacun d'entre nous

2 *pron* chacun, -e; **e. other** l'un(e) l'autre, *pl* les un(e)s les autres; **to see/greet e. other** se voir/se saluer; **e. of us** chacun, -e d'entre nous

eager ['iːgə(r)] *adj (impatient)* impatient (**to do** de faire); *(enthusiastic)* plein d'enthousiasme ■ **eagerly** *adv (work)* avec enthousiasme; *(await)* avec impatience

eagle ['iːgəl] *n* aigle *m*

ear [ɪə(r)] *n* oreille *f*; **to play it by e.** improviser ■ **earache** *n* mal *m* d'oreille ■ **earphones** *npl* écouteurs *mpl* ■ **earplug** *n* boule *f* Quiès® ■ **earring** *n* boucle *f* d'oreille ■ **earshot** *n* **within e.** à portée de voix

early ['ɜːlɪ] **1** (**-ier, -iest**) *adj (first)* premier, -ère; *(death)* prématuré; *(age)* jeune; *(painting, work)* de jeunesse; *(retirement)* anticipé; **it's e.** *(on clock)* il est tôt; *(referring to meeting, appointment)* c'est tôt; **to be e.** *(ahead of time)* être en avance; **in the e. 1990s** au début des années 90; **to be in one's e. fifties** avoir à peine plus de cinquante ans

2 *adv* tôt, de bonne heure; *(ahead of time)* en avance; *(die)* prématurément; **earlier (on)** plus tôt; **at the earliest** au plus tôt

earmark ['ɪəmɑːk] *vt (funds)* assigner (**for** à)

earn [ɜːn] *vt* gagner; *(interest)* rapporter; **to e. one's living** gagner sa vie

■ **earnings** *npl (wages)* salaire *m*; *(profits)* bénéfices *mpl*

earnest ['ɜːnɪst] **1** *adj (serious)* sérieux, -euse **2** *n* **in e.** sérieusement

earth [ɜːθ] *n (ground)* sol *m*; *(soil)* terre *f*; *Br (electrical wire)* terre *f*, masse *f*; **the E.** *(planet)* la Terre; **where/what on e....?** où/que diable...? ■ **earthquake** *n* tremblement *m* de terre

ease [iːz] **1** *n (facility)* facilité *f*; **with e.** facilement; **to be at e./ill at e.** être à l'aise/mal à l'aise **2** *vt (pain)* soulager; *(mind)* calmer; *(tension)* réduire; *(restrictions)* assouplir **3** *vi* **to e. (off** or **up)** *(of pressure)* diminuer; *(of demand)* baisser; *(of pain)* se calmer

easily ['iːzɪlɪ] *adv* facilement; **the best** de loin le meilleur/la meilleure

east [iːst] **1** *n* est *m*; **(to the) e. of** à l'est de; **the E.** *(Eastern Europe)* l'Est *m*; *(the Orient)* l'Orient *m*

2 *adj (coast)* est *inv*; *(wind)* d'est; **E. Africa** l'Afrique *f* orientale

3 *adv* à l'est; *(travel)* vers l'est ■ **eastbound** *adj (traffic)* en direction de l'est; *Br (carriageway)* est *inv* ■ **easterly** *adj (direction)* de l'est ■ **eastern** *adj (coast)* est *inv*; **E. France** l'est *m* de la France; **E. Europe** l'Europe *f* de l'Est ■ **eastward(s)** *adj & adv* vers l'est

Easter ['iːstə(r)] *n* Pâques *fpl*; **Happy E.!** joyeuses Pâques!; **E. egg** œuf *m* de Pâques

easy ['iːzɪ] **1** (**-ier, -iest**) *adj (not difficult)* facile; *(solution)* simple; *(pace)* modéré; **e. chair** fauteuil *m* **2** *adv* doucement; **go e. on the salt** vas-y mollo avec le sel; **go e. on him** ne sois pas trop dur avec lui; **take it e.** *(rest)* repose-toi; *(work less)* ne te fatigue pas; *(calm down)* calme-toi; *(go slow)* ne te presse pas ■ **easygoing** *adj (carefree)* insouciant; *(easy to get along with)* facile à vivre

eat [iːt] *(pt* **ate** *[Br* et, eɪt, *Am* eɪt], *pp* **eaten** [ˈiːtən]) **1** *vt* manger; *(meal)* prendre; **to e. sth up** *(finish)* finir qch **2** *vi* manger; **to e. into one's savings** entamer ses économies; **to e. out** manger dehors ■ **eater** *n* **big e.** gros mangeur *m*, grosse mangeuse *f*

eaves [iːvz] *npl* avant-toit *m* ■ **eavesdrop** *(pt & pp* **-pp-)** *vti* **to e. (on)** écouter avec indiscrétion

ebb [eb] **1** *n* **the e. and flow** le flux et le reflux; *Fig* **to be at a low e.** *(of patient, spirits)* être déprimé **2** *vi Fig* **to e. (away)** *(of strength)* décliner

EC [iːˈsiː] *(abbr* **European Community)** *n* CE *f*

eccentric [ɪkˈsentrɪk] *adj & n* excentrique *(mf)*

ecclesiastical [ɪkliːzɪˈæstɪkəl] *adj* ecclésiastique

echo [ˈekəʊ] **1** *(pl* **-oes)** *n* écho *m* **2** *(pt & pp* **echoed)** *vt Fig (repeat)* répéter **3** *vi* résonner **(with** de)

eclipse [ɪˈklɪps] *n (of sun, moon)* éclipse *f*

ecological [iːkəˈlɒdʒɪkəl] *adj* écologique

economic [iːkəˈnɒmɪk] *adj* économique; *(profitable)* rentable ■ **economical** *adj* économique ■ **economics** **1** *n* économie *f* **2** *npl (profitability)* aspect *m* financier

economize [ɪˈkɒnəmaɪz] *vti* économiser **(on** sur)

economy [ɪˈkɒnəmɪ] *(pl* **-ies)** *n* économie *f; Av* **e. class** classe *f* économique

ecstasy [ˈekstəsɪ] *(pl* **-ies)** *n (state)* extase *f; (drug)* ecstasy *f* ■ **ecstatic** [ekˈstætɪk] *adj* fou *(f* folle) de joie; **to be e. about** s'extasier sur

edge [edʒ] **1** *n* bord *m; (of forest)* lisière *f; (of town)* abords *mpl; (of page)*

marge *f; (of knife, blade)* tranchant *m* **2** *vt (clothing)* border **(with** de) **3** *vi* **to e. forward** avancer doucement

edgeways [ˈedʒweɪz] *(Am* **edgewise** [ˈedʒwaɪz]) *adv* de côté; *Fam* **I can't get a word in e.** je ne peux pas en placer une

edgy [ˈedʒɪ] *(-ier, -iest) adj* énervé

edible [ˈedɪbəl] *adj (safe to eat)* comestible; *(fit to eat)* mangeable

edifice [ˈedɪfɪs] *n (building)* édifice *m*

Edinburgh [ˈedɪnbərə] *n* Édimbourg *m* ou *f*

edit [ˈedɪt] *vt (newspaper)* diriger; *(article)* corriger; *(prepare for publication)* préparer pour la publication; *(film)* monter

edition [ɪˈdɪʃən] *n* édition *f*

editor [ˈedɪtə(r)] *n (of newspaper)* rédacteur, -trice *mf* en chef; *(of film)* monteur, -euse *mf; Comptr (software)* éditeur *m*

educate [ˈedʒʊkeɪt] *vt (bring up)* éduquer; *(in school)* instruire ■ **educated** *adj* **(well-)e.** *(person)* instruit

education [edʒʊˈkeɪʃən] *n* éducation *f; (teaching)* enseignement *m; (training)* formation *f; (university subject)* pédagogie *f* ■ **educational** *adj (qualification)* d'enseignement; *(method, theory, content)* pédagogique; *(game, film, system)* éducatif, -ive; *(establishment)* scolaire

eel [iːl] *n* anguille *f*

eerie [ˈɪərɪ] *(-ier, -iest) adj* sinistre

effect [ɪˈfekt] **1** *n (result, impression)* effet *m* **(on** sur); **in e.** en fait; **to come into e., to take e.** *(of law)* entrer en vigueur **2** *vt (change, rescue)* effectuer

effective [ɪˈfektɪv] *adj (efficient)* efficace; *(actual)* réel *(f* réelle); **to become e.** *(of law)* prendre effet ■ **effectively** *adv (efficiently)* efficacement; *(in fact)* effectivement

efficient [ɪˈfɪʃənt] *adj* efficace; *(productive)* performant ■ **efficiently** *adv* efficacement

effort [ˈefət] *n* effort *m;* **to make an e.**

faire un effort (**to** pour) ■ **effortlessly** *adv* sans effort

e.g. [iːˈdʒiː] (*abbr exempli gratia*) p. ex.

egg¹ [eg] *n* œuf *m*; **e. timer** sablier *m* ■ **eggplant** *n Am* aubergine *f*

egg² [eg] *vt* **to e. sb on** encourager qn (**to do** à faire)

ego [ˈiːgəʊ] (*pl* -os) *n* **to have an enormous e.** avoir une très haute opinion de soi-même

egoistic(al) [iːgəʊˈɪstɪk(əl)] *adj* égoïste

Egypt [ˈiːdʒɪpt] *n* l'Égypte *f* ■ **Egyptian** [ɪˈdʒɪpʃən] **1** *adj* égyptien, -enne **2** *n* Égyptien, -enne *mf*

eight [eɪt] *adj & n* huit (*m*) ■ **eighth** *adj & n* huitième (*mf*); **an e.** (*fraction*) un huitième

eighteen [eɪˈtiːn] *adj & n* dix-huit (*m*) ■ **eighteenth** *adj & n* dix-huitième (*mf*)

eighty [ˈeɪtɪ] *adj & n* quatre-vingts (*m*); **e.-one** quatre-vingt-un; **in the eighties** dans les années 80 ■ **eightieth** *adj & n* quatre-vingtième (*mf*)

Eire [ˈeərə] *n* l'Eire *f*

either [ˈaɪðə(r), ˈiːðə(r)] **1** *adj & pron* (*one or other*) l'un(e) ou l'autre; (*with negative*) ni l'un(e) ni l'autre; (*each*) chaque; **on e. side** des deux côtés **2** *adv* **she can't swim e.** elle ne sait pas nager non plus; **I don't e.** (ni) moi non plus **3** *conj* **e.... or...** ou... ou..., soit... soit...; (*with negative*) ni... ni...

eject [ɪˈdʒekt] **1** *vt* (*troublemaker*) expulser (**from** de); (*from machine*) éjecter **2** *vi* (*of pilot*) s'éjecter

elaborate¹ [ɪˈlæbərət] *adj* (*meal*) élaboré; (*scheme*) compliqué; (*description*) détaillé; (*style*) recherché

elaborate² [ɪˈlæbəreɪt] **1** *vt* (*theory*) élaborer **2** *vi* entrer dans les détails (**on** de)

elapse [ɪˈlæps] *vi* s'écouler

elastic [ɪˈlæstɪk] **1** *adj* élastique; *Br* **e. band** élastique *m* **2** *n* (*fabric*) élastique *m*

elated [ɪˈleɪtɪd] *adj* transporté de joie

elbow [ˈelbəʊ] **1** *n* coude *m* **2** *vt* **to e. one's way** se frayer un chemin en jouant des coudes (**through** à travers)

elder [ˈeldə(r)] *adj & n* (*of two people*) aîné, -e (*mf*) ■ **eldest** *adj & n* aîné, -e (*mf*); **his/her e. brother** l'aîné de ses frères

elderly [ˈeldəlɪ] **1** *adj* âgé **2** *npl* **the e.** les personnes *fpl* âgées

elect [ɪˈlekt] *vt* (*by voting*) élire (**to** à)

election [ɪˈlekʃən] **1** *n* élection *f*; **general e.** élections *fpl* législatives **2** *adj* (*campaign*) électoral; (*day, results*) des élections

electoral [ɪˈlektərəl] *adj* électoral ■ **electorate** *n* électorat *m*

electric [ɪˈlektrɪk] *adj* électrique; **e. blanket** couverture *f* chauffante; *Br* **e. fire** radiateur *m* électrique; **e. shock** décharge *f* électrique ■ **electrical** *adj* électrique

electrician [ɪlekˈtrɪʃən] *n* électricien *m*

electricity [ɪlekˈtrɪsɪtɪ] *n* électricité *f*

electrify [ɪˈlektrɪfaɪ] (*pt & pp* -ied) *vt* (*excite*) électriser

electronic [ɪlekˈtrɒnɪk] *adj* électronique ■ **electronics** (*subject*) électronique *f*

elegant [ˈelɪgənt] *adj* élégant ■ **elegantly** *adv* avec élégance

element [ˈeləmənt] *n* (*component, chemical, person*) élément *m*; (*of heater, kettle*) résistance *f*; **the elements** (*bad weather*) les éléments *mpl*; **to be in one's e.** être dans son élément

elementary [elɪˈmentərɪ] *adj* élémentaire; *Am* (*school*) primaire

elephant [ˈelɪfənt] *n* éléphant *m*

elevate [ˈelɪveɪt] *vt* élever (**to** à)

elevator [ˈelɪveɪtə(r)] *n Am* ascenseur *m*

eleven [ɪˈlevən] *adj & n* onze (*m*) ■ **eleventh** *adj & n* onzième (*mf*)

elicit [ɪˈlɪsɪt] *vt* tirer (**from** de)

eligible [ˈelɪdʒəbəl] *adj* (*for post*) admissible (**for** à); **to be e. for sth** (*entitled to*) avoir droit à qch

eliminate [ɪ'lɪmɪneɪt] *vt* éliminer

elite [eɪ'liːt] *n* élite *f* (**of** de)

elongated ['iːlɒŋgeɪtɪd] *adj* allongé

elope [ɪ'ləʊp] *vi* (of lovers) s'enfuir (**with** avec)

eloquent ['eləkwənt] *adj* éloquent

else [els] *adv* d'autre; **somebody/anybody e.** quelqu'un/n'importe qui d'autre; **everybody e.** tous les autres; **something e.** autre chose; **anything e.?** (in shop) est-ce qu'il vous faut autre chose?; **somewhere e.,** *Am* **someplace e.** ailleurs, autre part; **nowhere e.** nulle part ailleurs; **who e.?** qui d'autre?; **or e.** ou bien, sinon ■ **elsewhere** *adv* ailleurs

elude [ɪ'luːd] *vt* échapper à ■ **elusive** *adj* (person) insaisissable

emaciated [ɪ'meɪsɪeɪtɪd] *adj* émacié

e-mail ['iːmeɪl] **1** *n* courrier *m* électronique, mél *m*; **e. address** adresse *f* électronique **2** *vt* envoyer un courrier électronique *ou* un mél à

emanate ['eməneɪt] *vi* émaner (**from** de)

emancipation [ɪmænsɪ'peɪʃən] *n* émancipation *f*

embankment [ɪm'bæŋkmənt] *n* (of path) talus *m*; (of river) berge *f*

embargo [ɪm'bɑːgəʊ] (*pl* -**oes**) *n* embargo *m*

embark [ɪm'bɑːk] *vi* (s')embarquer; **to e. on sth** s'embarquer dans qch

embarrass [ɪm'bærəs] *vt* embarrasser ■ **embarrassing** *adj* embarrassant

embassy ['embəsɪ] (*pl* -**ies**) *n* ambassade *f*

embellish [ɪm'belɪʃ] *vt* embellir

embers ['embəz] *npl* braises *fpl*

embezzle [ɪm'bezəl] *vt* (money) détourner

emblem ['embləm] *n* emblème *m*

embody [ɪm'bɒdɪ] (*pt & pp* -**ied**) *vt* (express) exprimer; (represent) incarner

embrace [ɪm'breɪs] **1** *n* étreinte *f* **2** *vt* (person) étreindre; Fig (belief) embrasser **3** *vi* s'étreindre

embroider [ɪm'brɔɪdə(r)] *vt* (cloth)

broder; Fig (story, facts) enjoliver ■ **embroidery** *n* broderie *f*

embryo ['embrɪəʊ] (*pl* -**os**) *n* embryon *m*

emerald ['emərəld] *n* émeraude *f*

emerge [ɪ'mɜːdʒ] *vi* apparaître (**from** de); (from hole) sortir; (from water) émerger

emergency [ɪ'mɜːdʒənsɪ] **1** (*pl* -**ies**) *n* (situation, case) urgence *f*; **in an e.** en cas d'urgence **2** *adj* (measure, operation, services) d'urgence; **e. exit** sortie *f* de secours; **e. landing** atterrissage *m* forcé

emigrant ['emɪgrənt] *n* émigrant, -e *mf* ■ **emigrate** [-greɪt] *vi* émigrer

eminent ['emɪnənt] *adj* éminent

emission [ɪ'mɪʃən] *n* (of gas, light) émission *f*

emit [ɪ'mɪt] (*pt & pp* -**tt**-) *vt* (light, heat) émettre

emotion [ɪ'məʊʃən] *n* (strength of feeling) émotion *f*; (individual feeling) sentiment *m*

emotional [ɪ'məʊʃənəl] *adj* (person, reaction) émotif, -ive; (speech, plea) émouvant

emotive [ɪ'məʊtɪv] *adj* (word) affectif, -ive

empathy ['empəθɪ] *n* compassion *f*

emperor ['empərə(r)] *n* empereur *m*

emphasis ['emfəsɪs] (*pl* -**ases** [-əsiːz]) *n* (in word or phrase) accent *m*; (insistence) insistance *f*

emphasize ['emfəsaɪz] *vt* (importance) souligner; (word, fact) insister sur, souligner; (syllable) appuyer sur; **to e. that...** souligner que...

emphatic [em'fætɪk] *adj* (denial, refusal) (clear) catégorique; (forceful) énergique

empire ['empaɪə(r)] *n* empire *m*

employ [ɪm'plɔɪ] *vt* (person, means) employer ■ **employee** [em'plɔɪiː] *n* employé, -e *mf* ■ **employer** *n* patron, -onne *mf* ■ **employment** *n* emploi *m*; **e. agency** bureau *m* de placement

emptiness ['emptɪnɪs] *n* vide *m*

empty ['emptɪ] **1** (-**ier**, -**iest**) *adj* vide;

(threat, promise) vain; **on an e. stomach** à jeun **2** *npl* **empties** *(bottles)* bouteilles *fpl* vides **3** *(pt & pp* **-ied)** *vt* **to e. (out)** *(box, pocket, liquid)* vider; *(objects from box)* sortir **(from** *or* **out of** de) **4** *vi (of building, tank)* se vider
■ **empty-handed** *adv* **to return e.** revenir les mains vides

emulate ['emjʊleɪt] *vt* imiter

enable [ɪ'neɪbəl] *vt* **to e. sb to do sth** permettre à qn de faire qch

enamel [ɪ'næməl] **1** *n* émail *m (pl* émaux*)* **2** *adj* en émail

enamoured [ɪ'næməd] *adj* **e. of** *(thing)* séduit par; *(person)* amoureux, -euse de

encapsulate [ɪn'kæpsjʊleɪt] *vt (ideas, views)* résumer

encase [ɪn'keɪs] *vt (cover)* envelopper **(in** dans)

enchanting [ɪn'tʃɑːntɪŋ] *adj* enchanteur, -eresse

encircle [ɪn'sɜːkəl] *vt* entourer; *(of army, police)* encercler

encl *(abbr* **enclosure(s))** PJ

enclose [ɪn'kləʊz] *vt (send with letter)* joindre **(in** *or* **with** à); *(fence off)* clôturer ■ **enclosed** *adj (receipt, document)* ci-joint; **please find e....** veuillez trouver ci-joint...

enclosure [ɪn'kləʊʒə(r)] *n (in letter)* pièce *f* jointe; *(place)* enceinte *f*

encompass [ɪn'kʌmpəs] *vt (include)* inclure

encore ['ɒŋkɔː(r)] *exclam & n* bis *(m)*

encounter [ɪn'kaʊntə(r)] **1** *n* rencontre *f* **2** *vt (person, resistance)* rencontrer

encourage [ɪn'kʌrɪdʒ] *vt* encourager **(to do** à faire) ■ **encouragement** *n* encouragement *m*

encroach [ɪn'krəʊtʃ] *vi* empiéter **(on** *or* **upon** sur)

encyclop(a)edia [ɪnsaɪklə'piːdɪə] *n* encyclopédie *f*

end [end] **1** *n (extremity)* bout *m*, extrémité *f*; *(of month, meeting, book)* fin *f*; *(purpose)* but *m*; **at an e.** *(discussion, war)* fini; *(period of time)* écoulé; **in**

the e. à la fin; **to come to an e.** prendre fin; **for days on e.** pendant des jours et des jours; **to stand sth on e.** mettre qch debout

2 *adj (row, house)* dernier, -ère

3 *vt* finir, terminer **(with** par); *(rumour, speculation)* mettre fin à

4 *vi* finir, se terminer; **to e. up doing sth** finir par faire qch; **he ended up in prison/a doctor** il a fini en prison/médecin

endanger [ɪn'deɪndʒə(r)] *vt* mettre en danger; **endangered species** espèce *f* menacée

endearing [ɪn'dɪərɪŋ] *adj (quality)* qui inspire la sympathie

endeavour [ɪn'devə(r)] *(Am* **endeavor)** **1** *n* effort *m* **(to do** pour faire) **2** *vi* s'efforcer **(to do** de faire)

ending ['endɪŋ] *n* fin *f*; *(of word)* terminaison *f*

endless ['endləs] *adj (speech, series, list)* interminable; *(countless)* innombrable

endorse [ɪn'dɔːs] *vt (cheque)* endosser; *(action, plan)* approuver ■ **endorsement** *n* Br *(on driving licence)* = contravention inscrite sur le permis de conduire

endow [ɪn'daʊ] *vt* **to be endowed with** *(of person)* être doté de ■ **endowment** *n* dotation *f*

endurance [ɪn'djʊərəns] *n* endurance *f*

endure [ɪn'djʊə(r)] **1** *vt (violence)* endurer; *(person, insult)* supporter **2** *vi (last)* survivre

enemy ['enəmɪ] **1** *(pl* **-ies)** *n* ennemi, -e *mf* **2** *adj (army, tank)* ennemi

energetic [enə'dʒetɪk] *adj* énergique

energy ['enədʒɪ] **1** *(pl* **-ies)** *n* énergie *f* **2** *adj (resources)* énergétique; **e. crisis** crise *f* de l'énergie

enforce [ɪn'fɔːs] *vt (law)* faire respecter; *(discipline)* imposer **(on** à)

engage [ɪn'ɡeɪdʒ] *vt (take on)* engager ■ **engaged** *adj* **(a)** *(occupied) (person, toilet, phone)* occupé **(b)** **e. (to be married)** fiancé; **to get e.** se fiancer

engagement [ɪn'ɡeɪdʒmənt] *n (to*

marry) fiançailles *fpl*; (*meeting*) rendez-vous *m inv*; **e. ring** bague *f* de fiançailles

engine ['endʒɪn] *n* (*of vehicle, aircraft*) moteur *m*; (*of train*) locomotive *f*; (*of ship*) machine *f*

engineer [endʒɪ'nɪə(r)] **1** *n* ingénieur *m*; *Br* (*repairer*) dépanneur *m*; **civil e.** ingénieur *m* des travaux publics **2** *vt* (*arrange secretly*) manigancer ◼ **engineering** *n* ingénierie *f*; (**civil**) **e.** génie *m* civil

England ['ɪŋglənd] *n* l'Angleterre *f*

English ['ɪŋglɪʃ] **1** *adj* anglais; **E. teacher** professeur *m* d'anglais; **the E. Channel** la Manche **2** *n* (*language*) anglais *m*; **the E.** (*people*) les Anglais *mpl* ◼ **Englishman** (*pl* **-men**) *n* Anglais *m* ◼ **English-speaking** *adj* anglophone ◼ **Englishwoman** (*pl* **-women**) *n* Anglaise *f*

engraving [ɪn'greɪvɪŋ] *n* gravure *f*

engrossed [ɪn'grəʊst] *adj* **e. in one's work/book** absorbé par son travail/ dans sa lecture

engulf [ɪn'gʌlf] *vt* engloutir

enhance [ɪn'hɑːns] *vt* (*beauty, prestige*) rehausser; (*value*) augmenter

enigma [ɪ'nɪgmə] *n* énigme *f*

enjoy [ɪn'dʒɔɪ] *vt* (*like*) aimer (**doing** faire); (*meal*) savourer; (*benefit from*) jouir de; **to e. oneself** s'amuser ◼ **enjoyable** *adj* agréable; (*meal*) excellent ◼ **enjoyment** *n* plaisir *m*

enlarge [ɪn'lɑːdʒ] **1** *vt* agrandir **2** *vi* to **e. (up)on sth** s'étendre sur qch ◼ **enlargement** *n* (*increase*) & *Phot* agrandissement *m*

enlighten [ɪn'laɪtən] *vt* éclairer (**sb on** *or* **about sth** qn sur qch) ◼ **enlightening** *adj* instructif, -ive

enlist [ɪn'lɪst] **1** *vt* (*recruit*) engager; (*supporter*) recruter; (*support*) s'assurer **2** *vi* (*in the army*) s'engager

enormous [ɪ'nɔːməs] *adj* énorme; (*explosion, blow*) terrible; (*patience, gratitude, success*) immense ◼ **enormously** *adv* (*very much*) énormément; (*very*) extrêmement

enough [ɪ'nʌf] **1** *adj* assez de; **e. time/cups** assez de temps/de tasses **2** *pron* assez; **to have e. to live on** avoir de quoi vivre; **to have had e. of sb/sth** en avoir assez de qn/qch; **that's e.** ça suffit **3** *adv* (*work, sleep*) assez; **big/good e.** assez grand/bon (**to** pour)

enquire [ɪn'kwaɪə(r)] *vti* = **inquire**

enquiry [ɪn'kwaɪərɪ] *n* = **inquiry**

enrage [ɪn'reɪdʒ] *vt* mettre en rage

enrich [ɪn'rɪtʃ] *vt* enrichir; (*soil*) fertiliser

enrol [ɪn'rəʊl] (*Am* **enroll**) (*pt & pp* **-ll-**) **1** *vt* inscrire **2** *vi* s'inscrire (**on** *or* **for** à) ◼ **enrolment** (*Am* **enrollment**) *n* inscription *f*

ensemble [ɒn'sɒmbəl] *n* (*musicians, clothes*) ensemble *m*

ensue [ɪn'sjuː] *vi* s'ensuivre ◼ **ensuing** *adj* (*in the past*) qui a suivi; (*in the future*) qui suivra

ensure [ɪn'ʃʊə(r)] *vt* assurer; **to e. that…** s'assurer que…

entail [ɪn'teɪl] *vt* (*involve*) occasionner; **what does the job e.?** en quoi le travail consiste-t-il?

entangle [ɪn'tæŋgəl] *vt* **to get entangled in sth** (*of person, animal*) s'empêtrer dans qch

enter ['entə(r)] **1** *vt* (*room, army*) entrer dans; (*race, competition*) participer à; (*write down*) (*on list*) inscrire (**in** dans; **on** sur); (*in accounts book*) porter (**in** sur); *Comptr* (*data*) entrer; **it didn't e. my head** *or* **mind** ça ne m'est pas venu à l'esprit (**that** que) **2** *vi* entrer; **to e. for** (*exam*) se présenter à; (*race*) se faire inscrire à; **to e. into** (*relations*) entrer en; (*negotiations*) entamer; (*agreement*) conclure; (*contract*) passer (**with** avec)

enterprise ['entəpraɪz] *n* (*undertaking, firm*) entreprise *f*; (*spirit, initiative*) initiative *f* ◼ **enterprising** *adj* (*person*) entreprenant

entertain [entə'teɪn] **1** *vt* amuser, distraire; (*guest*) recevoir; (*idea, possibility*) envisager **2** *vi* (*receive guests*) recevoir ■ **entertainer** n (comedian) comique mf; (singer, dancer) artiste mf de music-hall ■ **entertainment** n amusement m; (show) spectacle m

enthusiasm [ɪnˈθjuːzɪæzəm] n enthousiasme m ■ **enthusiast** n enthousiaste mf; **jazz e.** passionné, -e mf de jazz

enthusiastic [ɪnθjuːzɪˈæstɪk] adj enthousiaste; (golfer, photographer) passionné; **to get e.** s'emballer (**about** pour)

entice [ɪnˈtaɪs] vt attirer (**into** dans); **to e. sb to do sth** inciter qn à faire qch ■ **enticing** adj séduisant

entire [ɪnˈtaɪə(r)] adj entier, -ère ■ **entirely** adv entièrement

entirety [ɪnˈtaɪərətɪ] n intégralité f; **in its e.** dans son intégralité

entitle [ɪnˈtaɪtəl] vt **to e. sb to sth/to do sth** donner à qn le droit à qch/de faire qch ■ **entitled** adj **to be e. to do sth** avoir le droit de faire qch; **to be e. to sth** avoir droit à qch

entrance [ˈentrəns] n entrée f (**to** de); (to university, school) admission f (**to** à); **e. fee** droit m d'entrée

entrant [ˈentrənt] n (in race) concurrent, -e mf; (for exam) candidat, -e mf

entrée [ˈɒntreɪ] n Culin (course before main dish) entrée f; Am (main dish) plat m principal

entrepreneur [ɒntrəprəˈnɜː(r)] n entrepreneur m

entrust [ɪnˈtrʌst] vt confier (**to** à); **to e. sb with sth** confier qch à qn

entry [ˈentrɪ] n entrée f; (in race) concurrent, -e mf; (to be judged in competition) objet m/œuvre f/projet m soumis au jury; **e. form** feuille f d'inscription; **'no e.'** (on door) 'entrée interdite'; (road sign) 'sens interdit'

envelope [ˈenvələʊp] n enveloppe f

enviable [ˈenvɪəbəl] adj enviable

envious [ˈenvɪəs] adj envieux, -euse (**of** de); **to be e. of sb** envier qn

environment [ɪnˈvaɪərənmənt] n (social, moral) milieu m; **the e.** (natural) l'environnement m ■ **environmental** [-ˈmentəl] adj (policy) de l'environnement; **e. disaster** catastrophe f écologique ■ **environmentally** adv **e. friendly product** produit m qui ne nuit pas à l'environnement

envisage [ɪnˈvɪzɪdʒ] (Am **envision** [ɪnˈvɪʒən]) vt (imagine) envisager; (foresee) prévoir; **to e. doing sth** envisager de faire qch

envoy [ˈenvɔɪ] n (messenger) envoyé, -e mf; (diplomat) ministre m plénipotentiaire

envy [ˈenvɪ] **1** n envie f (pt & pp **-ied**) vt envier; **to e. sb sth** envier qch à qn

ephemeral [ɪˈfemərəl] adj éphémère

epic [ˈepɪk] **1** adj épique **2** n (poem, novel) épopée f; (film) film m à grand spectacle

epidemic [epɪˈdemɪk] n épidémie f

epileptic [epɪˈleptɪk] adj & n épileptique (mf)

epilogue [ˈepɪlɒg] n épilogue m

episode [ˈepɪsəʊd] n (part of story) épisode m; (incident) incident m

epitaph [ˈepɪtɑːf] n épitaphe f

epitome [ɪˈpɪtəmɪ] n **to be the e. of sth** être l'exemple même de qch ■ **epitomize** vt incarner

epoch [ˈiːpɒk] n époque f

equal [ˈiːkwəl] **1** adj égal (**to** à); **to be e. to sth** (in quantity) égaler qch; (good enough) être à la hauteur de qch **2** n (person) égal, -e mf **3** (Br **-ll-**, Am **-l-**) vt égaler (**in** en)

equality [ɪˈkwɒlətɪ] n égalité f

equalize [ˈiːkwəlaɪz] vi (in sport) égaliser

equally [ˈiːkwəlɪ] adv (to an equal degree, also) également; (divide) en parts égales

equals [ˈiːkwəlz] n **e. sign** signe m d'égalité

equation [ɪˈkweɪʒən] n Math équation f

equator [ɪˈkweɪtə(r)] n équateur m; **at** or **on the e.** sous l'équateur

equilibrium [iːkwɪˈlɪbrɪəm] n équilibre m

equip [ɪ'kwɪp] (*pt & pp* **-pp-**) *vt* (*provide with equipment*) équiper (**with** de); (*prepare*) préparer (**for** pour); **to be (well-)equipped to do sth** être compétent pour faire qch ■ **equipment** *n* équipement *m*; (*in factory*) matériel *m*

equivalent [ɪ'kwɪvələnt] *adj & n* équivalent (*m*)

era [*Br* 'ɪərə, *Am* 'erə] *n* époque *f*; (*historical, geological*) ère *f*

eradicate [ɪ'rædɪkeɪt] *vt* éradiquer

erase [*Br* ɪ'reɪz, *Am* ɪ'reɪs] *vt* effacer; (*with eraser*) gommer ■ **eraser** *n* gomme *f*

erect [ɪ'rekt] **1** *adj* (*upright*) droit **2** *vt* (*building*) construire; (*statue, monument*) ériger; (*scaffolding*) monter; (*tent*) dresser

erode [ɪ'rəʊd] *vt* (*of sea*) éroder; *Fig* (*confidence*) miner ■ **erosion** [-ʒən] *n* érosion *f*

erotic [ɪ'rɒtɪk] *adj* érotique

errand ['erənd] *n* commission *f*, course *f*; **to run errands for sb** faire des courses pour qn

erratic [ɪ'rætɪk] *adj* (*unpredictable*) (*behaviour*) imprévisible; (*service, machine*) fantaisiste; (*person*) lunatique; (*irregular*) (*performance, results*) irrégulier, -ère

error ['erə(r)] *n* (*mistake*) erreur *f*; **typing/printing e.** faute *f* de frappe/d'impression

erupt [ɪ'rʌpt] *vi* (*of volcano*) entrer en éruption; (*of war, violence*) éclater ■ **eruption** *n* (*of volcano*) éruption *f*; (*of violence*) flambée *f*

escalate ['eskəleɪt] *vi* (*of war, violence*) s'intensifier; (*of prices*) monter en flèche

escalator ['eskəleɪtə(r)] *n* escalier *m* roulant

escapade ['eskəpeɪd] *n* frasque *f*

escape [ɪ'skeɪp] **1** *n* (*of gas, liquid*) fuite *f*; (*of person*) évasion *f*; **he had a lucky** *or* **narrow e.** il l'a échappé belle **2** *vt* (*death, punishment*) échapper à **3** *vi* (*of gas, animal*) s'échapper (**from** de); (*of prisoner*) s'évader (**from** de)

escort 1 ['eskɔːt] *n* (*for convoy*) escorte *f*, (*of woman*) cavalier *m* **2** [ɪ'skɔːt] *vt* escorter; (*prisoner*) conduire sous escorte

Eskimo ['eskɪməʊ] (*pl* **-os**) *n* Esquimau, -aude *mf*

especially [ɪs'peʃəlɪ] *adv* (*in particular*) surtout; (*more than normally*) particulièrement; (*for a purpose*) (tout) spécialement; **e. as** d'autant plus que

espresso [e'spresəʊ] (*pl* **-os**) *n* express *m*

Esq (*abbr* **Esquire**) *Br* John Smith Esq = Monsieur John Smith

essay ['eseɪ] *n* (*at school*) rédaction *f*; (*at university*) dissertation *f* (**on** sur)

essence ['esəns] *n* (*distinctive quality*) essence *f*; *Culin* (*extract*) extrait *m*; **the e. of sth** (*main point*) l'essentiel *m* de qch; **in e.** essentiellement

essential [ɪ'senʃəl] **1** *adj* (*principal*) essentiel, -elle; (*necessary*) indispensable, essentiel, -elle; **it's e. that...** il est indispensable que... (+ *subjunctive*) **2** *npl* **the essentials** l'essentiel *m* (**of** de)

establish [ɪ'stæblɪʃ] *vt* établir; (*state, society, company*) fonder; (*post*) créer ■ **established** *adj* (**well-**)**e.** (*company*) solide; (*fact*) reconnu; (*reputation*) établi ■ **establishment** *n* (*institution, company*) établissement *m*; **the E.** (*dominant group*) les classes *fpl* dirigeantes

estate [ɪ'steɪt] *n* (*land*) terres *fpl*, propriété *f*; (*possessions*) biens *mpl*; (*property after death*) succession *f*; *Br* **e. agent** agent *m* immobilier; *Br* **e. car** break *m*

esteem [ɪ'stiːm] **1** *n* estime *f*; **to hold sb in high e.** avoir qn en haute estime **2** *vt* estimer

esthetic [es'θetɪk] *adj Am* esthétique

estimate 1 ['estɪmət] *n* évaluation *f*; *Com* devis *m* **2** ['estɪmeɪt] *vt* (*value*) estimer, évaluer; (*consider*) estimer (**that** que)

estranged [ɪ'streɪndʒd] *adj* **her e.**

husband son mari, dont elle vit séparée

estuary ['estjʊərɪ] (*pl* **-ies**) *n* estuaire *m*

etc [et'setərə] (*abbr* **et cetera**) *adv* etc

etching ['etʃɪŋ] *n* (*picture*) eau-forte *f*

eternal [ɪ'tɜːnəl] *adj* éternel, -elle ■ **eternity** *n* éternité *f*

ethical ['eθɪkəl] *adj* moral, éthique

ethics ['eθɪks] *n* éthique *f*, morale *f*; (*of profession*) déontologie *f*

ethnic ['eθnɪk] *adj* ethnique

etiquette ['etɪket] *n* étiquette *f*

etymology [etɪ'mɒlədʒɪ] *n* étymologie *f*

EU [iː'juː] (*abbr* **European Union**) *n* UE *f*

euphemism ['juːfəmɪzəm] *n* euphémisme *m*

euphoria [juː'fɔːrɪə] *n* euphorie *f*

euro ['jʊərəʊ] (*pl* **-os**) *n* (*currency*) euro *m*

Euro- ['jʊərəʊ] *pref* euro-; **E.-MP** député *m* européen

Europe ['jʊərəp] *n* l'Europe *f* ■ **European** [-'piːən] **1** *adj* européen, -enne; **E. Union** Union *f* européenne **2** *n* Européen, -enne *mf*

evacuate [ɪ'vækjʊeɪt] *vt* évacuer

evade [ɪ'veɪd] *vt* éviter, esquiver; (*pursuer*) échapper à; (*law, question*) éluder; **to e. tax** frauder le fisc

evaluate [ɪ'væljʊeɪt] *vt* évaluer (**at** à)

evangelical [iːvæn'dʒelɪkəl] *adj* évangélique

evaporate [ɪ'væpəreɪt] *vi* (*of liquid*) s'évaporer; **evaporated milk** lait *m* condensé

evasion [ɪ'veɪʒən] *n* (*of pursuer, responsibility, question*) dérobade *f* (*of devant*); **tax e.** évasion *f* fiscale

evasive [ɪ'veɪsɪv] *adj* évasif, -ive

eve [iːv] *n* on the **e. of** à la veille de

even ['iːvən] **1** *adj* (*equal, flat*) égal; (*smooth*) uni; (*regular*) régulier, -ère; (*temperature*) constant; (*number*) pair; *Fig* **to get e. with sb** prendre sa revanche sur qn; **to break e.** (*financially*) s'y retrouver

2 *adv* même; **e. better/more** encore

mieux/plus; **e. if** *or* **though...** bien que... (*+ subjunctive*); **e. so** quand même

3 *vt* **to e. sth (out** *or* **up)** égaliser qch ■ **evenly** *adv* (*equally*) de manière égale; (*regularly*) régulièrement

evening ['iːvnɪŋ] *n* soir *m*; (*referring to duration, event*) soirée *f*; **tomorrow/yesterday e.** demain/hier soir; **in the e.,** *Am* **evenings** le soir; **at seven in the e.** à sept heures du soir; **every Tuesday e.** tous les mardis soir; **e. meal/paper** repas *m*/journal *m* du soir; **e. class** cours *m* du soir; **e. dress** (*of man*) tenue *f* de soirée; (*of woman*) robe *f* du soir

event [ɪ'vent] *n* événement *m*; (*in sport*) épreuve *f* ■ **eventful** *adj* (*day, journey, life*) mouvementé; (*occasion*) mémorable

eventual [ɪ'ventʃʊəl] *adj* (*final*) final, définitif, -ive ■ **eventuality** [-tjʊ'ælɪtɪ] (*pl* **-ies**) *n* éventualité *f* ■ **eventually** *adv* finalement; (*some day*) par la suite

ever ['evə(r)] *adv* jamais; **have you e. been to Spain?** es-tu déjà allé en Espagne?; **the first e.** le tout premier; **e. since (1990)** depuis (1990); **for e.** pour toujours; **e. so sorry** vraiment désolé; **she's e. so nice** elle est tellement gentille; **all she e. does is criticize** elle ne fait que critiquer

evergreen ['evəgriːn] *n* arbre *m* à feuilles persistantes

everlasting [evə'lɑːstɪŋ] *adj* éternel, -elle

every ['evrɪ] *adj* chaque; **e. time** chaque fois (**that** que); **e. one** chacun; **e. second** *or* **other day** tous les deux jours; **e. so often, e. now and then** de temps en temps

everybody ['evrɪbɒdɪ] *pron* tout le monde ■ **everyday** *adj* (*happening, life*) de tous les jours; (*ordinary*) banal (*mpl* **-als**); **in e. use** d'usage courant ■ **everyone** *pron* = **everybody** ■ **everyplace** *adv Am* = **everywhere** ■ **everything** *pron* tout; **e. (that) I**

have tout ce que j'ai ■ **everywhere** *adv* partout; **e. she goes** où qu'elle aille

evict [ɪ'vɪkt] *vt* expulser (**from** de)

evidence ['evɪdəns] *n (proof)* preuve(s) *f(pl); (testimony)* témoignage *m*; **to give e.** témoigner (**against** contre)

evident ['evɪdənt] *adj* évident (**that** que); **it is e. from...** il apparaît de... (**that** que) ■ **evidently** *adv (clearly)* manifestement; *(apparently)* apparemment

evil ['iːvəl] **1** *adj (spell, influence, person)* malfaisant; *(deed, system)* mauvais **2** *n* mal *m*

evoke [ɪ'vəʊk] *vt (conjure up)* évoquer ■ **evocative** [ɪ'vɒkətɪv] *adj* évocateur, -trice (**of** de)

evolution [iːvə'luːʃən] *n* évolution *f*

evolve [ɪ'vɒlv] **1** *vt (system)* mettre au point **2** *vi (of society, idea)* évoluer; *(of plan)* se développer

ewe [juː] *n* brebis *f*

ex [eks] *n Fam (former spouse)* ex *mf*

ex- [eks] *pref* ex-; **ex-minister** ancien ministre *m*

exact [ɪg'zækt] **1** *adj* exact **2** *vt (demand)* exiger (**from** de); *(money, promise)* extorquer (**from** à) ■ **exactly** *adv* exactement

exaggerate [ɪg'zædʒəreɪt] *vti* exagérer

exam [ɪg'zæm] *(abbr* **examination)** *n* examen *m*

examine [ɪg'zæmɪn] *vt (evidence, patient, question)* examiner; *(accounts, luggage)* vérifier; *(passport)* contrôler; *(student)* interroger ■ **examination** *n* examen *m*; *(of accounts)* vérification *f*; *(of passport)* contrôle *m*

example [ɪg'zɑːmpəl] *n* exemple *m*; **for e.** par exemple; **to set an e.** *or* **a good e.** donner l'exemple (**to** à); **to set a bad e.** donner le mauvais exemple (**to** à)

exasperate [ɪg'zɑːspəreɪt] *vt* exaspérer

excavate ['ekskəveɪt] *vt (dig)* creuser;

(archaeological site) faire des fouilles dans ■ **excavation** [-'veɪʃən] *n (archaeological)* fouilles *fpl*

exceed [ɪk'siːd] *vt* dépasser; *(one's powers)* excéder

exceedingly [ɪk'siːdɪŋlɪ] *adv* extrêmement

excel [ɪk'sel] *(pt & pp* **-ll-)** **1** *vt (be better than)* surpasser **2** *vi* **to e. in** *or* **at sth** exceller en qch

excellent ['eksələnt] *adj* excellent

except [ɪk'sept] **1** *prep* sauf, excepté; **e. for** à part; **e. that...** sauf que... **2** *vt* excepter (**from** de)

exception [ɪk'sepʃən] *n* exception *f*; **with the e. of...** à l'exception de...

exceptional [ɪk'sepʃənəl] *adj* exceptionnel, -elle

excerpt ['eksɜːpt] *n (from film, book)* extrait *m*

excess ['ekses] *n* excès *m*; *(surplus)* excédent *m*; **a sum in e. of...** une somme qui dépasse...; **e. luggage** excédent *m* de bagages

excessive [ɪk'sesɪv] *adj* excessif, -ive ■ **excessively** *adv (too much)* excessivement; *(very)* extrêmement

exchange [ɪks'tʃeɪndʒ] **1** *n* échange *m*; *Fin (of currency)* change *m*; **(telephone) e. central** *m* téléphonique; **in e.** en échange (**for** de); **e. rate** taux *m* de change **2** *vt* échanger (**for** contre)

Exchequer [ɪks'tʃekə(r)] *n Br* **Chancellor of the E.** ≃ ministre *m* des Finances

excitable [ɪk'saɪtəbəl] *adj* nerveux, -euse

excite [ɪk'saɪt] *vt (get worked up)* surexciter; *(enthuse)* passionner; *(provoke, stimulate)* exciter ■ **excited** *adj (happy)* surexcité; *(nervous)* énervé; *(enthusiastic)* enthousiaste; **to get e. (about)** s'exciter (pour); *(angry)* s'énerver (contre) ■ **exciting** *adj (book, adventure)* passionnant

excitement [ɪk'saɪtmənt] *n* agitation *f*; *(enthusiasm)* enthousiasme *m*

exclaim [ɪk'skleɪm] *vti* s'écrier (**that** que) ■ **exclamation** *n* exclamation *f*;

Br **e. mark,** *Am* **e. point** point *m* d'exclamation

exclude [ɪk'sklu:d] *vt* exclure (**from** de); **excluding…** à l'exclusion de…

exclusive [ɪk'sklu:sɪv] *adj (right, interview, design)* exclusif, -ive; *(club, group)* fermé ◾ **exclusively** *adv* exclusivement

excruciating [ɪk'skru:ʃɪeɪtɪŋ] *adj* atroce

excursion [ɪk'skɜ:ʃən] *n* excursion *f*

excuse 1 [ɪk'skju:s] *n* excuse *f*; **to make an e., to make excuses** se trouver une excuse **2** [ɪk'skju:z] *vt (forgive, justify)* excuser; *(exempt)* dispenser (**from** de); **e. me!** excusez-moi!, pardon!

ex-directory [eksdaɪ'rektərɪ] *adj Br* **to be e.** être sur la liste rouge

execute ['eksɪkju:t] *vt (prisoner, order)* exécuter; *(plan)* mettre à exécution

execution [eksɪ'kju:ʃən] *n* exécution *f*

executive [ɪg'zekjʊtɪv] **1** *adj (job)* de cadre; *(car)* de luxe **2** *n (person)* cadre *m*

exemplary [ɪg'zemplərɪ] *adj* exemplaire

exemplify [ɪg'zemplɪfaɪ] *(pt & pp -ied)* *vt* illustrer

exempt [ɪg'zempt] **1** *adj (person)* dispensé (**from** de) **2** *vt* dispenser (**from** de; **from doing** de faire)

exemption [ɪg'zem(p)ʃən] *n* dispense *f* (**from** de)

exercise ['eksəsaɪz] **1** *n* exercice *m*; **e. book** cahier *m* **2** *vt* exercer; *(dog, horse)* promener; *(caution, restraint)* user de **3** *vi* faire de l'exercice

exert [ɪg'zɜ:t] *vt* exercer; *(force)* employer; **to e. oneself** se donner du mal ◾ **exertion** *n* effort *m*

exhale [eks'heɪl] *vi* expirer

exhaust [ɪg'zɔ:st] **1** *n* **e. (fumes)** gaz *mpl* d'échappement; **e. (pipe)** tuyau *m* d'échappement **2** *vt (person, resources)* épuiser ◾ **exhausted** *adj (person, resources)* épuisé ◾ **exhausting** *adj* épuisant

exhaustive [ɪg'zɔ:stɪv] *adj (list)* exhaustif, -ive; *(analysis)* détaillé; *(inquiry)* approfondi

exhibit [ɪg'zɪbɪt] **1** *n* objet *m* exposé; *(in court)* pièce *f* à conviction **2** *vt (put on display)* exposer ◾ **exhibition** [eksɪ'bɪʃən] *n* exposition *f*

exhilarating [ɪg'zɪləreɪtɪŋ] *adj (experience)* grisant

exile ['egzaɪl] **1** *n (banishment)* exil *m*; *(person)* exilé, -e *mf* **2** *vt* exiler

exist [ɪg'zɪst] *vi* exister; *(live)* survivre (**on** avec) ◾ **existing** *adj (situation, circumstances)* actuel, -elle; *(law)* existant

existence [ɪg'zɪstəns] *n* existence *f*; **to come into e.** être créé; **to be in e.** exister

exit ['eksɪt, 'egzɪt] **1** *n* sortie *f* **2** *vi (leave) & Comptr* sortir

exodus ['eksədəs] *n inv* exode *m*

exorbitant [ɪg'zɔ:bɪtənt] *adj* exorbitant

exotic [ɪg'zɒtɪk] *adj* exotique

expand [ɪk'spænd] **1** *vt (production, influence)* accroître; *(knowledge)* étendre; *(trade, range, idea)* développer **2** *vi (of knowledge)* s'étendre; *(of trade)* se développer; *(of production)* augmenter; *(of gas)* se dilater; **to e. on** développer

expanse [ɪk'spæns] *n* étendue *f*

expatriate [*Br* eks'pætrɪət, *Am* eks'peɪtrɪət] *adj & n* expatrié, -e *(mf)*

expect [ɪk'spekt] *vt (anticipate)* s'attendre à; *(think)* penser (**that** que); *(await)* attendre; **to e. to do sth** compter faire qch; **to e. that…** *(anticipate)* s'attendre à ce que… (+ *subjunctive)*; **to be expecting a baby** attendre un enfant; **as expected** comme prévu

expectation [ekspek'teɪʃən] *n* **to come up to expectations** se montrer à la hauteur

expedient [ɪks'pi:dɪənt] **1** *adj* opportun **2** *n* expédient *m*

expedition [ekspɪ'dɪʃən] *n* expédition *f*

expel [ɪkˈspel] (*pt & pp* **-ll-**) *vt* expulser (**from** de); *(from school)* renvoyer

expend [ɪkˈspend] *vt (energy, money)* dépenser ▪ **expendable** *adj (person)* qui n'est pas irremplaçable

expenditure [ɪkˈspendɪtʃə(r)] *n (of money, energy)* dépense *f*

expense [ɪkˈspens] *n* frais *mpl*, dépense *f*; Com **expenses** frais *mpl*; **at the e. of sb/sth** aux dépens de qn/qch

expensive [ɪkˈspensɪv] *adj (goods, hotel, shop)* cher (*f* chère) ▪ **expensively** *adv* **e. dressed/furnished** habillé/meublé luxueusement

experience [ɪkˈspɪəriəns] **1** *n* expérience *f*; **from** *or* **by e.** par expérience **2** *vt (emotion)* ressentir; *(hunger, success)* connaître; *(difficulty)* éprouver ▪ **experienced** *adj (person)* expérimenté; **to be e. in sth** s'y connaître en qch

experiment 1 [ɪkˈsperɪmənt] *n* expérience *f* **2** [ɪkˈsperɪment] *vi* expérimenter (**on** sur); **to e. with sth** *(technique, drugs)* essayer qch

expert [ˈekspɜːt] **1** *n* expert *m* (**on** *or* **in** en) **2** *adj* expert (**in sth** en qch; **in** *or* **at doing** à faire) ▪ **expertise** [-tiːz] *n* compétence *f* (**in** en)

expiration [ekspəˈreɪʃən] *n Am* = **expiry**

expire [ɪkˈspaɪə(r)] *vi* expirer ▪ **expired** *adj (ticket, passport)* périmé

expiry [ɪkˈspaɪəri] *(Am* **expiration** [ekspəˈreɪʃən]) *n* expiration *f*; **e. date** *(on ticket)* date *f* d'expiration; *(on product)* date *f* limite d'utilisation

explain [ɪkˈspleɪn] *vt* expliquer (**to** à; **that** que); *(reasons)* exposer; *(mystery)* éclaircir

explanation [ekspləˈneɪʃən] *n* explication *f*

explanatory [ɪkˈsplænətəri] *adj* explicatif, -ive

expletive [ɪkˈspliːtɪv] *n* juron *m*

explicit [ɪkˈsplɪsɪt] *adj* explicite ▪ **explicitly** *adv* explicitement

explode [ɪkˈspləʊd] **1** *vt (bomb)* faire

exploser **2** *vi (of bomb)* exploser

exploit 1 [ˈeksplɔɪt] *n* exploit *m* **2** [ɪkˈsplɔɪt] *vt (person, land)* exploiter ▪ **exploitation** [eksplɔɪˈteɪʃən] *n* exploitation *f*

exploratory [ɪkˈsplɒrətəri] *adj (talks, surgery)* exploratoire

explore [ɪkˈsplɔː(r)] *vt* explorer; *(causes, possibilities)* examiner

explosion [ɪkˈspləʊʒən] *n* explosion *f*

explosive [ɪkˈspləʊsɪv] **1** *adj (weapon, situation)* explosif, -ive **2** *n* explosif *m*

export 1 [ˈekspɔːt] *n (activity, product)* exportation *f* **2** [ɪkˈspɔːt] *vt* exporter (**to** vers; **from** de) ▪ **exporter** *n* exportateur, -trice *mf*; *(country)* pays *m* exportateur

expose [ɪkˈspəʊz] *vt (to air, cold, danger)* & Phot exposer (**to** à); *(plot, scandal)* révéler; *(criminal)* démasquer

exposure [ɪkˈspəʊʒə(r)] *n* exposition *f* (**to** à); Phot pose *f*; **to get a lot of e.** *(in the media)* faire l'objet d'une importante couverture médiatique

express¹ [ɪkˈspres] *vt* exprimer; **to e. oneself** s'exprimer

express² [ɪkˈspres] **1** *adj (letter, delivery)* exprès *inv*; *(train)* rapide, express *inv* **2** *adv (send)* en exprès **3** *n (train)* rapide *m*, express *m inv*

expression [ɪkˈspreʃən] *n* expression *f*

expressive [ɪkˈspresɪv] *adj* expressif, -ive

expressly [ɪksˈpreslɪ] *adv (forbid)* expressément

expressway [ɪkˈspresweɪ] *n Am* autoroute *f*

expulsion [ɪkˈspʌlʃən] *n* expulsion *f*; *(from school)* renvoi *m*

exquisite [ɪkˈskwɪzɪt] *adj* exquis

extend [ɪkˈstend] **1** *vt (in space)* étendre; *(in time)* prolonger (**by** de); *(hand)* tendre (**to sb** à qn); *(house)* agrandir; *(knowledge)* accroître; *(thanks)* offrir (**to** à) **2** *vi (in space)* s'étendre (**to** jusqu'à); *(in time)* se prolonger

extension [ɪk'stenʃən] *n (for table)* rallonge *f; (to building)* annexe *f; (for telephone)* poste *m; (for essay)* délai *m* supplémentaire

extensive [ɪk'stensɪv] *adj (powers, forests)* vaste; *(repairs, damage)* important ■ **extensively** *adv (very much)* énormément

extent [ɪk'stent] *n (scope)* étendue *f; (size)* importance *f;* **to a large** or **great e.** dans une large mesure; **to some e.** or **a certain e.** dans une certaine mesure; **to such an e. that...** à tel point que...

exterior [ɪk'stɪərɪə(r)] *adj & n* extérieur *(m)*

exterminate [ɪk'stɜːmɪneɪt] *vt* exterminer

external [ɪk'stɜːnəl] *adj (trade, event)* extérieur; *(wall)* externe

extinct [ɪk'stɪŋkt] *adj (volcano)* éteint; *(species, animal)* disparu

extinguish [ɪk'stɪŋgwɪʃ] *vt* éteindre ■ **extinguisher** *n* **(fire) e.** extincteur *m*

extortionate [ɪk'stɔːʃənət] *adj* exorbitant

extra ['ekstrə] **1** *adj (additional)* supplémentaire; **to be e.** *(spare)* être en trop; *(cost more)* être en supplément; **e. charge** supplément *m;* **e. time** *(in sport)* prolongation *f* **2** *adv (more than usual)* extrêmement; **to pay e.** payer un supplément; **wine costs** or **is £10 e.** il y a un supplément de 10 livres pour le vin **3** *n (perk)* à-côté *m; (actor in film)* figurant, -e *mf; (on bill)* supplément *m*

extra- ['ekstrə] *pref* extra-

extract 1 ['ekstrækt] *n* extrait *m* **2** [ɪk'strækt] *vt* extraire (**from** de); *(information, money)* soutirer (**from** à)

extra-curricular [ekstrəkə'rɪkjʊlə(r)] *adj Sch* extrascolaire

extraordinary [ɪk'strɔːdənərɪ] *adj* extraordinaire

extravagant [ɪk'strævəgənt] *adj (behaviour, idea)* extravagant; *(wasteful)* dépensier, -ère; *(tastes)* dispendieux, -euse ■ **extravagance** *n (of behaviour)* extravagance *f; (wastefulness)* gaspillage *m; (thing bought)* folie *f*

extreme [ɪk'striːm] **1** *adj* extrême **2** *n* extrême *m;* **to carry** or **take sth to extremes** pousser qch à l'extrême ■ **extremely** *adv* extrêmement

extremist [ɪk'striːmɪst] *adj & n* extrémiste *(mf)*

extremity [ɪk'stremətɪ] *(pl* **-ies)** *n* extrémité *f*

extrovert ['ekstrəvɜːt] *n* extraverti, -e *mf*

exuberant [ɪg'zjuːbərənt] *adj* exubérant

exude [ɪg'zjuːd] *vt (health, honesty)* respirer

eye [aɪ] **1** *n* œil *m (pl* yeux); **to have one's e. on sth** avoir qch en vue; **to keep an e. on sb/sth** surveiller qn/qch; *Am* **e. doctor** opticien, -enne *mf* **2** *vt* regarder ■ **eyebrow** *n* sourcil *m* ■ **eyelash** *n* cil *m* ■ **eyelid** *n* paupière *f* ■ **eyeliner** *n* eye-liner *m* ■ **eyeshadow** *n* fard *m* à paupières ■ **eyesight** *n* vue *f* ■ **eyesore** *n* horreur *f* ■ **eyewitness** *n* témoin *m* oculaire

▶ **eye up** *vt sep* reluquer

Ff

F, f [ef] *n (letter)* F, f *m inv*

fable ['feɪbəl] *n* fable *f*

fabric ['fæbrɪk] *n (cloth)* tissu *m*, étoffe *f*

fabricate ['fæbrɪkeɪt] *vt* fabriquer

fabulous ['fæbjʊləs] *adj (legendary, incredible)* fabuleux, -euse

face [feɪs] **1** *n (of person)* visage *m*, figure *f; (expression)* mine *f; (of clock)* cadran *m; (of building)* façade *f; (of cube)* face *f; (of cliff)* paroi *f;* **f. down (wards)** *(person)* face contre terre; *(thing)* à l'envers; **f. to f.** face à face; **to save/lose f.** sauver/perdre la face; *Br* **f. cloth** gant *m* de toilette

2 *vt (danger, enemy, problem)* faire face à; **to f., to be facing** *(be opposite)* être en face de; *(of window, door, room)* donner sur; **faced with** *(prospect, problem)* confronté à; *(defeat)* menacé par

3 *vi* **to f. north** *(of building)* être orienté au nord; **to f. up to** *(danger, problem)* faire face à; *(fact)* accepter

faceless ['feɪsləs] *adj* anonyme

face-lift ['feɪslɪft] *n (by surgeon)* lifting *m; (of building)* ravalement *m*

facetious [fə'siːʃəs] *adj (person)* facétieux, -euse

facial ['feɪʃəl] **1** *adj (expression)* du visage **2** *n* soin *m* du visage

facilitate [fə'sɪlɪteɪt] *vt* faciliter ■ **facilities** *npl (for sports, cooking)* équipements *mpl; (in harbour, airport)* installations *fpl*

fact [fækt] *n* fait *m;* **as a matter of f., in f.** en fait

faction ['fækʃən] *n* faction *f*

factor ['fæktə(r)] *n* facteur *m*

factory ['fæktərɪ] *(pl* **-ies)** *n (large)* usine *f; (small)* fabrique *f*

factual ['fæktʃʊəl] *adj* basé sur les faits

faculty ['fækəltɪ] *(pl* **-ies)** *n (of mind, in university)* faculté *f*

fad [fæd] *n (fashion)* mode *f* **(for** de); *(personal habit)* marotte *f*

fade [feɪd] *vi (of flower, material, colour)* se faner; *(of light)* baisser; **to f. (away)** *(of memory, smile)* s'effacer; *(of sound)* s'affaiblir; *(of person)* dépérir

fag [fæg] *n Br Fam (cigarette)* clope *m* ou *f*

fail [feɪl] **1** *n* **without f.** sans faute **2** *vt (exam)* échouer à; *(candidate)* recaler; **to f. to do** *(forget)* manquer de faire; *(not be able)* ne pas arriver à faire **3** *vi (of person, plan)* échouer; *(of business)* faire faillite; *(of health, sight)* baisser; *(of memory, strength)* défaillir; *(of brakes)* lâcher ■ **failed** *adj (attempt, poet)* raté ■ **failing 1** *n (fault)* défaut *m* **2** *prep* à défaut de; **f. this, f. that** à défaut

failure ['feɪljə(r)] *n* échec *m; (of business)* faillite *f; (person)* raté, -e *mf*

faint [feɪnt] **1 (-er, -est)** *adj (weak) (voice, trace, breeze, hope)* faible; *(colour)* pâle; **to feel f.** se sentir mal **2** *vi* s'évanouir **(with** *or* **from** de)

fair¹ [feə(r)] *n (trade fair)* foire *f; Br (funfair)* fête *f* foraine ■ **fairground** *n* parc *m* d'attractions

fair² [feə(r)] **1 (-er, -est)** *adj* **(a)** *(just)* juste; *(game, fight)* loyal; **f. play** fairplay *m inv* **(b)** *(rather good)* assez bon (f bonne); (price) raisonnable; **a f. amount (of)** (a lot) pas mal (de) (c) (wind) favorable; (weather) beau (f belle) **2** adv (fight) loyalement; **to play f.** jouer franc jeu ■ **fairly** adv (a) (treat) équitablement; (act, fight, get) loyalement (b) (rather) assez

fair³ [feə(r)] adj (hair, person) blond; (complexion, skin) clair ■ **fair-haired** adj blond

fairy ['feərɪ] (pl -ies) n fée f ■ **fairytale** n conte m de fées

faith [feɪθ] n foi f; **to have f. in sb** avoir foi en qn; **in good/bad f.** (act) de bonne/mauvaise foi

faithful ['feɪθfəl] adj fidèle ■ **faithfully** adv fidèlement; **Br yours f.** (in letter) veuillez agréer l'expression de mes sentiments distingués

fake [feɪk] **1** adj faux (f fausse) **2** n (object) faux m; (person) imposteur m **3** vt (signature) contrefaire **4** vi (pretend) faire semblant

fall [fɔːl] **1** n (of person, snow, city) chute f; (in price, demand) baisse f; Am (season) automne m **2** (pt fell, pp fallen) vi tomber; (of price, temperature) baisser; **the dollar is falling** le dollar est en baisse; **to f. into** (hole, trap) tomber dans; (habit) prendre; **to f. off a bicycle/ladder** tomber d'une bicyclette/échelle; **to f. out of a window** tomber d'une fenêtre; **to f. over sth** tomber en butant contre qch; **to f. asleep** s'endormir; **to f. ill** tomber malade

▸ **fall apart** vi (of book, machine) tomber en morceaux; (of person) s'effondrer

▸ **fall back on** vt insep (resort to) se rabattre sur

▸ **fall behind** vi (in work, payments) prendre du retard

▸ **fall down** vi tomber; (of building) s'effondrer

▸ **fall for** vt insep (person) tomber amoureux, -euse de; (trick) se laisser prendre à

▸ **fall in** vi (collapse) s'écrouler

▸ **fall off** vi (come off) tomber; (of numbers) diminuer

▸ **fall out** vi (quarrel) se brouiller (**with** avec)

▸ **fall over** vi tomber; (of table, vase) se renverser

▸ **fall through** vi (of plan) tomber à l'eau, échouer

fallacy ['fæləsɪ] (pl -ies) n erreur f

fallen ['fɔːlən] **1** pp of fall **2** adj tombé; **f. leaves** feuilles fpl mortes

fallible ['fæləbəl] adj faillible

false [fɔːls] adj faux (f fausse); **f. teeth** dentier m

falsify ['fɔːlsɪfaɪ] (pt & pp -ied) vt (forge) falsifier

falter ['fɔːltə(r)] vi (of voice, speaker) hésiter

fame [feɪm] n renommée f ■ **famed** adj renommé (**for** pour)

familiar [fə'mɪljə(r)] adj (well-known) familier, -ère (**to** à); **to be familiar with sb/ sth** bien connaître qn/qch; **he looks f.** je l'ai déjà vu (quelque part)

familiarize [fə'mɪljəraɪz] vt **to f. oneself with sth** se familiariser avec qch

family ['fæmɪlɪ] **1** (pl -ies) n famille f **2** adj (name, doctor, jewels) de famille; (planning, problems, business) familial; **f. man** homme m attaché à sa famille

famine ['fæmɪn] n famine f

famished ['fæmɪʃt] adj affamé

famous ['feɪməs] adj célèbre (**for** pour)

fan¹ [fæn] n (held in hand) éventail m (pl -ails); (mechanical) ventilateur m **2** (pt & pp -nn-) vt (person) éventer

fan² [fæn] n (of person) fan mf; (of team) supporter m; **to be a jazz/sports f.** être passionné de jazz/de sport

fanatic [fə'nætɪk] n fanatique mf ■ **fanatical** adj fanatique

fanciful ['fænsɪfəl] adj fantaisiste

fancy ['fænsɪ] **1** n **I took a f. to it, I took my f.** j'en ai eu envie **2** adj (jewels, hat, button) fantaisie inv; (car) de luxe; (house, restaurant) chic inv; Br **f. dress** déguisement m; Br **f. dress**

party soirée f déguisée **3** (pt & pp **-ied**) vt (**a**) Br Fam (want) avoir envie de; **he fancies her** elle lui plaît (**b**) to f. **that…** (imagine) se figurer que…; (think) croire que…

fanfare [ˈfænfeə(r)] n fanfare f

fantastic [fænˈtæstɪk] adj fantastique; (wealth, size) prodigieux, -euse; Fam (excellent) formidable

fantasy [ˈfæntəsɪ] (pl -ies) n (imagination) fantaisie f; (dream) chimère f; (fanciful, sexual) fantasme m ▪ **fantasize** vi fantasmer (**about** sur)

FAR [fɑː(r)] **1** (**farther** or **further**, **farthest** or **furthest**) adj the f. side/ end l'autre côté/bout; the F. East l'Extrême-Orient m; Pol the f. left/ right l'extrême gauche f/droite f **2** adv (**a**) (in distance) loin (**from** de); how f. is it to Toulouse? combien y a-t-il d'ici à Toulouse?; is it f. to…? sommes-nous/suis-je/etc loin de…?; how f. has he got with his work? où en est-il dans son travail?; as f. as jusqu'à; as f. or so f. as I know autant que je sache; as f. or so f. as I'm con-cerned en ce qui me concerne; f. from doing sth loin de faire qch; f. away or off au loin; to be f. away être loin (**from** de)
(**b**) (in time) as f. back as 1820 dès 1820; so f. jusqu'ici
(**c**) (much) f. bigger/more expensive beaucoup plus grand/plus cher (f chère) (than que); f. more/better beaucoup plus/mieux (than que); by f. de loin ▪ **far-away** adj (country) lointain; (look) perdu dans le vague ▪ **far-fetched** adj tiré par les cheveux ▪ **far-reaching** adj de grande portée ▪ **far-sighted** adj clairvoyant

farce [fɑːs] n farce f ▪ **farcical** adj gro-tesque

fare [feə(r)] **1** n (for journey) (in train, bus) prix m du billet; (in taxi) prix m de la course **2** vi (manage) se dé-brouiller

farewell [feəˈwel] **1** n & exclam adieu

(m) **2** adj (party, speech) d'adieu

farm [fɑːm] **1** n ferme f **2** adj (worker, produce) agricole **3** vt cultiver **4** vi être agriculteur, -trice ▪ **farmer** n fer-mier, -ère mf, agriculteur, -trice mf ▪ **farmhouse** n ferme f ▪ **farming** n agriculture f; (breeding) élevage m ▪ **farmyard** n ferme f

fart [fɑːt] Fam **1** n pet m **2** vi péter

farther [ˈfɑːðə(r)] **1** comparative of **far 2** adj plus avancé; **to get f. away** s'éloigner ▪ **farthest 1** superlative of **far 2** adj le plus éloigné **3** adv le plus loin

fascinate [ˈfæsɪneɪt] vt fasciner ▪ **fascinating** adj fascinant

fascist [ˈfæʃɪst] adj & n fasciste (mf)

fashion [ˈfæʃən] **1** n (**a**) (in clothes) mode f; **in f.** à la mode; **out of f.** dé-modé; f. **show** défilé m de mode (**b**) (manner) façon f; **after a f.** tant bien que mal **2** vt (form) façonner; (make) confectionner ▪ **fashionable** adj à la mode ▪ **fashionably** adv (dressed) à la mode

fast¹ [fɑːst] **1** (-er, -est) adj rapide; **to be f.** (of clock) avancer (**by** de); f. **food** restauration f rapide; f. **food restau-rant** fast-food m **2** adv (**a**) (quickly) vite; **how f.?** à quelle vitesse? (**b**) f. **asleep** profondément endormi

fast² [fɑːst] **1** n jeûne m **2** vi jeûner

fasten [ˈfɑːsən] **1** vt attacher (**to** à); (door, window) fermer; **to f. sth down** attacher qch **2** vi (of dress) s'attacher; (of door, window) se fermer ▪ **fasten-er, fastening** n (clip) attache f; (hook) agrafe f; (press stud) bouton-pression m; (of bag) fermoir m

fat [fæt] **1** (**fatter, fattest**) adj gras (f grasse); (cheeks, salary, book) gros (f grosse); **to get f.** grossir **2** n graisse f; (on meat) gras m

fatal [ˈfeɪtəl] adj mortel, -elle ▪ **fatally** adv f. **wounded** mortellement blessé

fatality [fəˈtælɪtɪ] (pl -ies) n (person) victime f

fate [feɪt] n destin m, sort m ▪ **fateful** adj (words, day) fatidique

father ['fɑːðə(r)] **1** n père m; **F. Christmas** le père Noël **2** vt (child) engendrer ■ **father-in-law** (pl **fathers-in-law**) n beau-père m

fatherhood ['fɑːðəhʊd] n paternité f

fatherly ['fɑːðəlɪ] adj paternel, -elle

fatigue [fəˈtiːg] n (tiredness) fatigue f

fatten ['fætən] vt to f. (up) engraisser ■ **fattening** adj (food) qui fait grossir

fatty ['fætɪ] (-ier, -iest) adj (food) gras (f grasse)

faucet ['fɔːsɪt] n Am (tap) robinet m

fault [fɔːlt] **1** n (blame) faute f; (defect, failing) défaut m; Geol faille f; to find f. (with) trouver à redire (à); it's your f. c'est (de) ta faute **2** vt to f. sb/sth trouver des défauts chez qn/qch

faultless ['fɔːltləs] adj irréprochable

faulty ['fɔːltɪ] (-ier, -iest) adj défectueux, -euse

favour ['feɪvə(r)] (Am **favor**) **1** n (act of kindness) service m; (approval) faveur f; to do sb a f. rendre service à qn; in f. (with sb) bien vu (de qn); to be in f. of sth être partisan de qch **2** vt (encourage) favoriser; (support) être partisan de ■ **favourable** (Am **favorable**) adj favorable (to à)

favourite ['feɪvərɪt] (Am **favorite**) **1** adj favori, -ite, préféré **2** n favori, -ite mf ■ **favouritism** (Am **favoritism**) n favoritisme m

fawn [fɔːn] **1** n (deer) faon m **2** adj & n (colour) fauve m

fax [fæks] **1** n (message) télécopie f, fax m; **f. (machine)** télécopieur m, fax m **2** vt (message) faxer; to f. sb envoyer un fax à qn

fear [fɪə(r)] **1** n peur f; (worry) crainte f; for f. of doing sth de peur de faire qch; for f. that... de peur que... (+ ne + subjunctive) **2** vt craindre; I f. that he might leave je crains qu'il ne parte **3** vi to f. for one's life craindre pour sa vie ■ **fearful** adj (person) apeuré; (noise, pain, consequence) épouvantable ■ **fearless** adj intrépide

feasible ['fiːzəbəl] adj faisable

feast [fiːst] **1** n festin m; (religious) fête

f **2** vi to f. on sth se régaler de qch

feat [fiːt] n exploit m

feather ['feðə(r)] n plume f

feature ['fiːtʃə(r)] **1** n (of face, person) trait m; (of thing, place, machine) caractéristique f; **f. (article)** article m de fond; **f. (film)** long métrage m **2** vt (of newspaper, exhibition, film) (present) présenter; (portray) représenter; **a film featuring Nicole Kidman** un film ayant pour vedette Nicole Kidman **3** vi (appear) figurer (in dans)

February ['febrʊərɪ] n février m

fed [fed] **1** pt & pp of **feed 2** adj Fam to be f. up en avoir marre ou ras le bol (with de)

federal ['fedərəl] adj fédéral ■ **federation** [-'reɪʃən] n fédération f

fee [fiː] n fee(s) (of doctor, lawyer) honoraires mpl; (of artist) cachet m; (for registration, examination) droits mpl; (for membership) cotisation f; **school** or **tuition fees** frais mpl d'inscription

feeble ['fiːbəl] (-er, -est) adj faible; (excuse, smile) pauvre; (attempt) peu convaincant

feed [fiːd] **1** n (animal food) nourriture f; (for baby) (from breast) tétée f; (from bottle) biberon m **2** (pt & pp **fed**) vt donner à manger à; (baby) (from breast) donner la tétée à; (from bottle) donner son biberon à; to f. sb sth faire manger qch à qn **3** vi (eat) manger; to f. on sth se nourrir de qch

feedback ['fiːdbæk] n (response) réactions fpl

feel [fiːl] **1** n (touch) toucher m; to have a f. for sth avoir qch dans la peau

2 (pt & pp **felt**) vt (be aware of) sentir; (experience) éprouver, ressentir; (touch) tâter; to f. that... penser que...; to f. one's way avancer à tâtons **3** vi to f. (about) (grope) tâtonner; (in pocket) fouiller (for sth pour trouver qch); it feels hard c'est dur au toucher; to f. tired/old se sentir fatigué/vieux (f vieille); I f. hot/sleepy/hungry j'ai chaud/sommeil/faim; she

feels better elle va mieux; **to f. like sth** *(want)* avoir envie de qch; **it feels like cotton** on dirait du coton; **what do you f. about...?** que pensez-vous de...?; **I f. bad about it** ça m'ennuie

feeling ['fi:lɪŋ] *n (emotion, impression)* sentiment *m*; *(physical)* sensation *f*; **to have a f. for** *(music, painting)* être sensible à

feet [fi:t] *pl of* **foot**[1]

feign [feɪn] *vt* feindre

feline ['fi:laɪn] *adj* félin

fell [fel] **1** *pt of* **fall 2** *vt (tree)* abattre; *(opponent)* terrasser

fellow ['feləʊ] *n* (**a**) *(man, boy)* gars *m* (**b**) *(companion)* **f. countryman/f. countrywoman** compatriote *mf*; **f. worker** collègue *mf* (**c**) *(of society)* membre *m*

fellowship ['feləʊʃɪp] *n (scholarship)* bourse *f* de recherche

felt[1] [felt] *pt & pp of* **feel**

felt[2] [felt] *n* feutre *m* ■ **felt-tip** *n* **f. (pen)** crayon-feutre *m*

female ['fi:meɪl] **1** *adj (person, name, voice)* féminin; *(animal)* femelle **2** *n (woman)* femme *f*; *(girl)* fille *f*; *(animal, plant)* femelle *f*

feminine ['femɪnɪn] **1** *adj* féminin **2** *n (in grammar)* féminin *m* ■ **feminist** *adj & n* féministe *(mf)*

fence [fens] **1** *n (barrier)* clôture *f*; *(more solid)* barrière *f*; *(in race)* obstacle *m* **2** *vt* **to f. (in)** *(land)* clôturer **3** *vi (as sport)* faire de l'escrime ■ **fencing** *n (sport)* escrime *f*

fend [fend] **1** *vi* **to f. for oneself** se débrouiller **2** *vt* **to f. off** *(blow)* parer

fender ['fendə(r)] *n Am (of car)* aile *f*

ferment [fə'ment] *vi* fermenter

ferocious [fə'rəʊʃəs] *adj* féroce

ferret ['ferɪt] **1** *n (animal)* furet *m* **2** *vt* **to f. out** *(object, information)* dénicher

ferry ['ferɪ] **1** *n (pl -ies)* ferry-boat *m*; *(small, for river)* bac *m* **2** *vt (pt & pp -ied)* *vt* transporter

fertile [*Br* 'fɜ:taɪl, *Am* 'fɜ:rtəl] *adj (land, imagination)* fertile; *(person, animal)* fécond ■ **fertilizer** *n* engrais *m*

fervent ['fɜ:vənt] *adj* fervent

festival ['festɪvəl] *n (of music, film)* festival *m (pl* -als*)*; *(religious)* fête *f*

festive ['festɪv] *adj* de fête; *(mood)* festif, -ive; **the f. season** les fêtes *fpl* de fin d'année ■ **festivities** *npl* festivités *fpl*

fetch [fetʃ] *vt* (**a**) *(bring)* aller chercher (**b**) *(be sold for)* rapporter

fête [feɪt] **1** *n Br* fête *f* **2** *vt* fêter

fetus ['fi:təs] *n Am =* **foetus**

feud [fju:d] *n* querelle *f*

fever ['fi:və(r)] *n* fièvre *f*; **to have a f.** *(temperature)* avoir de la fièvre ■ **feverish** *adj (person, activity)* fiévreux, -euse

FEW [fju:] **1** *adj* (**a**) *(not many)* peu de; **f. towns** peu de villes; **every f. days** tous les trois ou quatre jours; **one of the f. books** l'un des rares livres; **f. and far between** rarissime (**b**) *(some)* **a f. towns** quelques villes; **a f. more books** encore quelques livres; **quite a f....,** **a good f....** bon nombre de...
2 *pron* peu; **f. came** peu sont venus; **f. of them** un petit nombre d'entre eux; **a f.** quelques-un(e)s (**of** de); **a f. of us** quelques-uns d'entre nous

fewer ['fju:ə(r)] **1** *adj* moins de; **f. houses** de maisons *(than* que*)*; **to be f.** *(than)* être moins nombreux *(que)* **2** *pron* moins ■ **fewest** **1** *adj* le moins de **2** *pron* le moins

fiancé [fɪ'ɒnseɪ] *n* fiancé *m*

fiancée [fɪ'ɒnseɪ] *n* fiancée *f*

fiasco [fɪ'æskəʊ] *(pl* -os, *Am* -oes*)* *n* fiasco *m*

fib [fɪb] *Fam* **1** *n* bobard *m* **2** *(pt & pp -bb-)* *vi* raconter des bobards

fibre ['faɪbə(r)] *(Am* **fiber**) *n* fibre *f*; *(in diet)* fibres *fpl*

fickle ['fɪkəl] *adj* inconstant

fiction ['fɪkʃən] *n (invention)* fiction *f*; **(works of) f.** livres *mpl* de fiction ■ **fictional** *adj (character)* fictif, -ive

fictitious [fɪk'tɪʃəs] *adj* fictif, -ive

fiddle ['fɪdəl] *n* **1** (**a**) *(violin)* violon *m*

(**b**) *Br Fam* (*dishonest act*) combine *f* **2**
vt Br Fam (*accounts*) truquer **3** *vi* **to f.**
about (*waste time*) traînailler; **to f.**
(**about**) **with sth** tripoter qch

fiddly ['fɪdlɪ] (**-ier, -iest**) *adj Fam*
(*task*) minutieux, -euse

fidget ['fɪdʒɪt] **1** *n* **to be a f.** ne pas
tenir en place **2** *vi* **to f.** (**about**) gigoter ▪ **fidgety** *adj* agité

field [fiːld] *n* champ *m*; (*for sports*) terrain *m*; (*sphere*) domaine *m*

fierce [fɪəs] (**-er, -est**) *adj* (*animal,
warrior, tone*) féroce; (*attack, wind*)
violent

fiery ['faɪərɪ] (**-ier, -iest**) *adj* (*person,
speech*) fougueux, -euse

fifteen [fɪf'tiːn] *adj & n* quinze (*m*)
▪ **fifteenth** *adj & n* quinzième (*mf*)

fifth [fɪfθ] *adj & n* cinquième (*mf*); **a f.**
(*fraction*) un cinquième

fifty ['fɪftɪ] *adj & n* cinquante (*m*)
▪ **fifty-fifty** *adj & adv* **a f. chance** une
chance sur deux; **to split the profits
f.** partager les bénéfices moitié-moi-
tié ▪ **fiftieth** *adj & n* cinquantième
(*mf*)

fig [fɪg] *n* figue *f*

fight [faɪt] **1** *n* (*between people*) bagarre *f*; (*between boxers, soldiers*)
combat *m*; (*struggle*) lutte *f* (**against/
for** contre/pour); (*quarrel*) dispute *f*
2 (*pt & pp* **fought**) *vt* (*person*) se battre contre; (*decision, enemy*) combat-
tre; (*fire, temptation*) lutter contre; **to
f. a battle** livrer bataille; *Pol* **to f. an
election** se présenter à une élection;
to f. off (*attacker, attack*) repousser
3 *vi* se battre (**against** contre); (*of soldiers*) combattre; (*struggle*) lutter
(**against/for** contre/pour); (*quarrel*)
se disputer; **to f. back** (*retaliate*) se défendre; **to f. over sth** se disputer qch

fighter ['faɪtə(r)] *n* (*determined person*) battant, -e *mf*; (*in brawl, battle*)
combattant, -e *mf*; (*boxer*) boxeur *m*;
(*aircraft*) avion *m* de chasse

fighting ['faɪtɪŋ] *n* (*brawling*) bagar-
res *fpl*; *Mil* combat *m*

figment ['fɪgmənt] *n* **it's a f. of your**

imagination c'est le fruit de ton imagination

figurative ['fɪgjʊrətɪv] *adj* (*meaning*)
figuré; (*art*) figuratif, -ive

figure¹ [*Br* 'fɪgə(r), *Am* 'fɪgjə(r)] *n* (**a**)
(*numeral*) chiffre *m* (**b**) (*shape*) forme
f; (*outline*) silhouette *f*; **she has a nice
f.** elle est bien faite (**c**) (*diagram*) figure *f*; **f. skating** patinage *m* artistique (**d**) (*expression, word*) **a f. of
speech** une figure de rhétorique (**e**)
(*important person*) personnage *m*

figure² [*Br* 'fɪgə(r), *Am* 'fɪgjə(r)] **1** *vt* **to
f. that…** (*think*) penser que…; (*esti-
mate*) supposer que…; **to f. out** (*person, motive*) arriver à comprendre;
(*answer*) trouver; (*amount*) calculer **2**
vi (*appear*) figurer (**on** sur); **to f. on
doing sth** compter faire qch

file¹ [faɪl] **1** *n* (*tool*) lime *f* **2** *vt* **to f.**
(**down**) limer

file² [faɪl] **1** *n* (*folder*) chemise *f*; (*documents*) dossier *m* (**on** sur); *Comptr* fichier *m*; **to be on f.** figurer au dossier
2 *vt* (*document*) classer; (*complaint,
claim*) déposer

file³ [faɪl] **1** *n* (*line*) file *f*; **in single f.** en
file indienne **2** *vi* **to f. in/out** entrer/
sortir à la queue leu leu; **to f. past
sb/sth** défiler devant qn/qch ▪ **filing**
adj **f. cabinet** classeur *m* (*meuble*)

fill [fɪl] **1** *n* **to eat one's f.** manger à sa
faim
2 *vt* remplir (**with** de); (*tooth*) plomber; (*time*) occuper; **to f. in** (*form*)
remplir; (*hole*) combler; **to f. sb in on
sth** mettre qn au courant de qch; **to f.
out** (*form*) remplir; **to f. up** (*container*)
remplir
3 *vi* **to f.** (**up**) se remplir (**with** de); **to
f. in for sb** remplacer qn; **to f. up** (*with
petrol*) faire le plein

fillet [*Br* 'fɪlɪt, *Am* fɪ'leɪ] **1** *n* (*of fish,
meat*) filet *m* **2** (*Am pt & pp* [fɪ'leɪd]) *vt*
(*fish*) découper en filets; (*meat*) désosser

filling ['fɪlɪŋ] **1** *adj* (*meal*) nourrissant
2 *n* (*in tooth*) plombage *m*; (*in food*)
garniture *f*; **f. station** station-service *f*

film [fɪlm] **1** n film m; (for camera, layer) pellicule f; (for food) film m plastique **2** adj (studio, technician, critic) de cinéma; **f. star** vedette f de cinéma **3** vt filmer **4** vi (of film maker, actor) tourner

Filofax® ['faɪləfæks] n organiseur m

filter ['fɪltə(r)] **1** n filtre m; Br (traffic sign) flèche f de dégagement; **f. coffee** café m filtre **2** vt filtrer **3** vi to **f. through** filtrer ■ **filter-tipped** adj (cigarette) bout filtre inv

filth [fɪlθ] n saleté f; Fig (obscenities) saletés fpl ■ **filthy** (**-ier, -iest**) adj (hands, shoes) sale; (language) obscène; (habit) dégoûtant

fin [fɪn] n (of fish) nageoire f; (of shark) aileron m

final ['faɪnəl] **1** adj (last) dernier, -ère; (definite) définitif, -ive **2** n (in sport) finale f; Univ **finals** examens mpl de dernière année ■ **finalist** n finaliste mf ■ **finalize** vt (plan) mettre au point; (date) fixer définitivement; (deal) conclure ■ **finally** adv (lastly) enfin; (eventually) finalement; (irrevocably) définitivement

finale [fɪ'nɑ:lɪ] n (musical) finale m

finance ['faɪnæns] **1** n finance f; **finances** (of person) finances fpl; (of company) situation f financière **2** vt financer

financial [faɪ'nænʃəl] adj financier, -ère; Br **f. year** exercice m comptable

financier [faɪ'nænsɪə(r)] n financier m

find [faɪnd] **1** n (discovery) découverte f **2** (pt & pp **found**) vt trouver; **I f. that...** je trouve que…
▶ **find out 1** vt (secret, information) découvrir; (person) prendre en défaut **2** vi (inquire) se renseigner (**about** sur); **to f. out about sth** (discover) apprendre qch

findings ['faɪndɪŋz] npl conclusions fpl

fine[1] [faɪn] **1** n (money) amende f; (for driving offence) contravention f **2** vt **to**

f. sb £100 infliger une amende de 100 livres à qn

fine[2] [faɪn] **1** (**-er, -est**) adj (**a**) (thin, not coarse) (hair, needle) fin; (gold, metal) pur; (distinction) subtil (**b**) (very good) excellent; (beautiful) (weather, statue) beau (f belle); **it's f.** (weather) il fait beau; **he's f.** (healthy) il va bien **2** adv (very well) très bien ■ **finely** adv (dressed) magnifiquement; (embroidered, ground) finement; **f. chopped** haché menu

finger ['fɪŋgə(r)] **1** n doigt m; **little f.** petit doigt m, auriculaire m **2** vt tâter ■ **fingernail** n ongle m ■ **fingertip** n bout m du doigt

finish ['fɪnɪʃ] **1** n (end) fin f; (of race) arrivée f; (of article, car) finition f **2** vt **to f. sth** (off or up) finir qch; **to f. doing sth** finir de faire qch **3** vi (of meeting, event) finir, se terminer; (of person) finir, terminer; **to have finished with** (object) ne plus avoir besoin de; (activity, person) en avoir fini avec; **to f. off** (of person) finir, terminer ■ **finishing** adj **f. line** (of race) ligne f d'arrivée; **to put the f. touches to sth** mettre la dernière main à qch ■ **finished** adj (ended, complete, ruined) fini

finite ['faɪnaɪt] adj fini

Finland ['fɪnlənd] n la Finlande ■ **Finn** n Finlandais, -e mf, Finnois, -e mf ■ **Finnish 1** adj finlandais, finnois **2** n (language) finnois m

fir [fɜ:(r)] n sapin m

fire ['faɪə(r)] **1** n feu m; (accidental) incendie m; Br (electric heater) radiateur m; **to light** or **make a f.** faire du feu; **to set f. to sth** mettre le feu à qch; **on f.** en feu; **f.!** (alarm) au feu!; **to open f.** ouvrir le feu; **f. alarm** sirène f d'incendie; Am **f. department** Br **f. brigade** pompiers mpl; **f. engine** voiture f des pompiers; **f. escape** escalier m de secours; **f. station** caserne f des pompiers **2** vt (cannon) tirer; (pottery) cuire; **to f. a gun** tirer un coup de fusil/de pistolet; **to f. questions at sb** bombarder qn de questions; **to f. sb** (*dismiss*) renvoyer qn

3 *vi* tirer (**at** sur); **f.!** feu! ■ **firearm** *n* arme *f* à feu ■ **fireguard** *n* garde-feu *m inv* ■ **fireman** (*pl* **-men**) *n* sapeur-pompier *m* ■ **fireplace** *n* cheminée *f* ■ **fireproof** *adj* (*door*) ignifugé ■ **fireside** *n* **by the f.** au coin du feu ■ **firewood** *n* bois *m* de chauffage ■ **firework** *n* fusée *f*; (*firecracker*) pétard *m*; **fireworks**, *Br* **f. display** feu *m* d'artifice

firm¹ [fɜːm] *n* (*company*) entreprise *f*, firme *f*

firm² [fɜːm] 1 (**-er, -est**) *adj* (*earth, decision*) ferme; (*foundations*) solide 2 *adv* **to stand f.** tenir bon *ou* ferme ■ **firmly** *adv* (*believe*) fermement; (*shut*) bien

first [fɜːst] 1 *adj* premier, -ère; **f. aid** premiers secours *mpl*

2 *adv* d'abord; (*for the first time*) pour la première fois; **f. of all, f. and foremost** tout d'abord; **at f.** d'abord; **to come f.** (*in race*) arriver premier; (*in exam*) être reçu premier

3 *n* (*person, thing*) premier, -ère *mf*; **f.** (**gear**) (*of vehicle*) première *f* ■ **first-class** 1 *adj* excellent; (*ticket*) de première classe; (*mail*) ordinaire 2 *adv* (*travel*) en première ■ **firsthand** *adj* **to have** (**had**) **f. experience of sth** avoir fait l'expérience personnelle de qch ■ **first-rate** *adj* excellent

firstly [ˈfɜːstlɪ] *adv* premièrement

fish [fɪʃ] 1 (*pl inv or* **-es** [-ɪz]) *n* poisson *m*; **f. bone** arête *f*; *Br* **f. fingers**, *Am* **f. sticks** bâtonnets *mpl* de poisson; **f. shop** poissonnerie *f*; **f. tank** aquarium *m*

2 *vt* **f. sth out** (*from water*) repêcher qch

3 *vi* pêcher ■ **fish-and-chip** *adj Br* **f. shop** = magasin où on vend du poisson frit et des frites ■ **fishing** *n* pêche *f*; **to go f.** aller à la pêche. **f. boat** bateau *m* de pêche; **f. net** filet *m* (de pêche); **f. rod** canne à pêche

fisherman [ˈfɪʃəmən] (*pl* **-men**) *n* pêcheur *m*

fishmonger [ˈfɪʃmʌŋgə(r)] *n* poissonnier, -ère *mf*

fishy [ˈfɪʃɪ] (**-ier, -iest**) *adj* (*smell, taste*) de poisson; *Fig* (*suspicious*) louche

fist [fɪst] *n* poing *m* ■ **fistful** *n* poignée *f* (**of** de)

fit¹ [fɪt] 1 (**fitter, fittest**) *adj* (**a**) (*healthy*) en forme; **to keep f.** se maintenir en forme

(**b**) (*suitable*) propre (**for** à; **to do** à faire); (*worthy*) digne (**for** de; **to do** de faire); (*able*) apte (**for** à; **to do** à faire)

2 *n* **a good f.** (*clothes*) à la bonne taille; **a tight f.** (*clothes*) ajusté

3 (*pt & pp* **-tt-**) *vt* (*be the right size for*) aller bien à; (*match*) correspondre à; (*put in*) poser; (*go in*) aller dans; (*go on*) aller sur; **to f. sth (on) to sth** (*put*) poser qch sur qch; (*adjust*) adapter qch à qch; (*fix*) fixer qch à qch; **to f. sth in** (*install*) poser qch; (*insert*) faire entrer qch

4 *vi* (*of clothes, lid, key, plug*) aller; **this shirt fits** (*me*) cette chemise me va; **to f. (in)** (*go in*) aller; (*of facts, plans*) cadrer (**with** avec); **he doesn't f. in** il n'est pas à sa place

fit² [fɪt] *n* (*seizure*) attaque *f*; **a f. of coughing** une quinte de toux; **in fits and starts** par à-coups

fitness [ˈfɪtnɪs] *n* (*health*) santé *f*; (*for job*) aptitude *f* (**for** à)

fitted [ˈfɪtɪd] *adj Br* (*cupboard*) encastré; (*garment*) ajusté; **f. carpet** moquette *f*; **f. kitchen** cuisine *f* intégrée

fitting [ˈfɪtɪŋ] 1 *adj* (*suitable*) approprié (**to** à) 2 *n* **f. room** cabine *f* d'essayage; **fittings** (*in house*) installations *fpl*

five [faɪv] *adj & n* cinq (*m*) ■ **fiver** *n Br Fam* billet *m* de cinq livres

fix [fɪks] 1 *vt* (*make firm, decide*) fixer (**to** à); (*mend*) réparer; (*deal with*) arranger; (*prepare*) préparer; *Fam* (*election*) truquer; **to f. sth on** (*lid*) mettre qch en place; **to f. sth up** *(trip, meeting)* arranger qch **2** *n Fam* **in a f.** dans le pétrin

fixed [fɪkst] *adj (price)* fixe; *(idea)* bien arrêté

fixture ['fɪkstʃə(r)] *n* (**a**) *(in sport)* rencontre *f* (**b**) **fixtures** *(in house)* installations *fpl*

fizz [fɪz] *vi (of champagne)* pétiller ▪ **fizzy** (**-ier, -iest**) *adj* gazeux, -euse ▶ **fizzle out** ['fɪzəl] *vi (of firework)* rater; *Fam (of plan)* tomber à l'eau

flabbergasted ['flæbəgɑːstɪd] *adj Fam* sidéré

flabby ['flæbɪ] (**-ier, -iest**) *adj (person)* bouffi; *(skin)* mou *(f* molle)

flag [flæg] **1** *n* drapeau *m*; *Naut* pavillon *m*; *(for charity)* insigne *m* **2** *(pt & pp* **-gg-**) *vt* marquer; **to f. down a taxi** héler un taxi **3** *vi (of person, conversation)* faiblir ▪ **flagpole** *n* mât *m*

flagrant ['fleɪgrənt] *adj* flagrant

flagstone ['flægstəʊn] *n* dalle *f*

flair [fleə(r)] *n (intuition)* don *m* **(for** pour); **to have a f. for business** avoir le sens des affaires

flake [fleɪk] **1** *n (of snow)* flocon *m*; *(of paint)* écaille *f*; *(of soap)* paillette *f* **2** *vi* **to f. (off)** *(of paint)* s'écailler ▪ **flaky** *adj Br* **f. pastry** pâte *f* feuilletée

flamboyant [flæm'bɔɪənt] *adj (person)* extraverti

flame [fleɪm] *n* flamme *f*; **to go up in flames** prendre feu

flamingo [flə'mɪŋgəʊ] *(pl* **-os** *or* **-oes)** *n* flamant *m*

flammable ['flæməbəl] *adj* inflammable

flan [flæn] *n* tarte *f*

flank [flæŋk] **1** *n* flanc *m* **2** *vt* flanquer **(with** *or* **by** de)

flannel ['flænəl] *n Br (face cloth)* gant *m* de toilette

flap [flæp] **1** *n (of pocket, envelope)* rabat *m*; *(of table)* abattant *m* **2** *(pt & pp* **-pp-**) *vt* **to f. its wings** *(of bird)* battre des ailes **3** *vi (of wings, sail, shutter)* battre

flare [fleə(r)] **1** *n* (**a**) *(rocket)* fusée *f* éclairante; (**b**) **(pair of) flares** *(trousers)* pantalon *m* pattes d'éléphant **2** *vi* **to f. up** *(of fire)* s'embraser; *(of violence, trouble)* éclater

flared [fleəd] *adj (skirt)* évasé; *(trousers)* (à) pattes d'éléphant

flash [flæʃ] **1** *n (of light)* éclair *m*; *(for camera)* flash *m*; **f. of lightning** éclair *m* **2** *vt (light)* projeter; *(aim)* diriger **(on** *or* **at** sur); *(show)* montrer rapidement; **to f. one's headlights** faire un appel de phares **3** *vi (shine)* briller; *(on and off)* clignoter; **to f. past** *or* **by** *(rush)* passer comme un éclair ▪ **flashback** *n* retour *m* en arrière ▪ **flashlight** *n Am (torch)* lampe *f* électrique; *(for camera)* flash *m*

flashy ['flæʃɪ] (**-ier, -iest**) *adj Fam (clothes, car)* tape-à-l'œil *inv*

flask [flɑːsk] *n (Thermos®)* Thermos® *f inv*; *(for alcohol)* flasque *f*

flat¹ [flæt] **1** (**flatter, flattest**) *adj* plat; *(tyre, battery)* à plat; *(drink)* éventé; *(refusal)* net *(f* nette); **f. rate** tarif *m* unique; **to put** *or* **lay sth (down)** mettre qch à plat **2** *n (puncture)* crevaison *f*; *(of hand)* plat *m*; *(in music)* bémol *m* **3** *adv* **to sing f.** chanter trop bas; **to fall f. on one's face** tomber à plat ventre; **to fall f.** *(of joke, play)* tomber à plat; **f. out** *(work)* d'arrache-pied; *(run)* à toute vitesse ▪ **flatly** *adv (deny, refuse)* catégoriquement

flat² [flæt] *n Br (in building)* appartement *m*

flatmate ['flætmeɪt] *n Br* colocataire *mf*

flatten ['flætən] *vt* aplatir; *(crops)* coucher; *(town, buildings)* raser

flatter ['flætə(r)] *vt* flatter ▪ **flattering** *adj (remark, words)* flatteur, -euse

flattery ['flætərɪ] *n* flatterie *f*

flaunt [flɔːnt] *vt (show off)* faire étalage de

flavour ['fleɪvə(r)] *(Am* **flavor**) **1** *n (taste)* goût *m*; *(of ice cream)* parfum *m* **2** *vt (food)* relever **(with** de); **lemon-flavoured** *(parfumé)* au citron

■ **flavouring** (*Am* **flavoring**) *n* (*seasoning*) assaisonnement *m*; (*in cake, ice cream*) parfum *m*

flaw [flɔː] *n* défaut *m* ■ **flawed** *adj* qui a un défaut/des défauts ■ **flawless** *adj* parfait

flea [fliː] *n* puce *f*; **f. market** marché *m* aux puces

fleck [flek] *n* (*mark*) petite tache *f*

fled [fled] *pt & pp of* **flee**

flee [fliː] **1** (*pt & pp* **fled**) *vt* (*place*) s'enfuir de; (*danger*) fuir **2** *vi* s'enfuir, fuir

fleece [fliːs] **1** *n* (*of sheep*) toison *f*; (*garment*) fourrure *f* polaire **2** *vt Fam* (*overcharge*) écorcher ■ **fleecy** (**-ier, -iest**) *adj* (*gloves*) molletonné

fleet [fliːt] *n* (*of ships*) flotte *f*; (*of taxis, buses*) parc *m* ■ **fleeting** *adj* (*visit, moment*) bref (*f* brève)

Flemish ['flemɪʃ] **1** *adj* flamand **2** *n* (*language*) flamand *m*

flesh [fleʃ] *n* chair *f*; **in the f.** en chair et en os

flew [fluː] *pt of* **fly**[2]

flex [fleks] **1** *n* (*wire*) fil *m*; (*for telephone*) cordon *m* **2** *vt* (*limb*) fléchir; (*muscle*) faire jouer

flexible ['fleksɪbəl] *adj* flexible

flexitime ['fleksɪtaɪm] *n* horaires *mpl* flexibles *ou* à la carte

flick [flɪk] **1** *n* (*with finger*) chiquenaude *f*; *Br* **f. knife** couteau *m* à cran d'arrêt **2** *vt* (*with finger*) donner une chiquenaude à; **to f. sth off** (*remove*) enlever qch d'une chiquenaude; **to f. a switch** pousser un bouton **3** *vi* **to f. through** (*book, magazine*) feuilleter

flicker ['flɪkə(r)] *vi* (*of flame, light*) vaciller

flier ['flaɪə(r)] *n* (*leaflet*) prospectus *m*

flies [flaɪz] *npl* (*of trousers*) braguette *f*

flight [flaɪt] *n* (**a**) (*of bird, aircraft*) vol *m*; **f. attendant** (*man*) steward *m*; (*woman*) hôtesse *f* de l'air (**b**) (*floor*) étage *m*; **f. of stairs** escalier *m* (**c**) (*escape*) fuite *f* (**from** de); **to take f.** prendre la fuite

flimsy ['flɪmzɪ] (**-ier, -iest**) *adj* (*cloth, structure*) (*light*) (*trop*) léger, -ère;

(*thin*) (*trop*) mince; (*excuse*) piètre

flinch [flɪntʃ] *vi* (*with pain*) tressaillir

fling [flɪŋ] **1** (*affair*) aventure *f* **2** (*pt & pp* **flung**) *vt* jeter

flint [flɪnt] *n* (*of lighter*) pierre *f*

flip [flɪp] **1** (*pt & pp* **-pp-**) *vt* (*with finger*) donner une chiquenaude à; **to f. a coin** jouer à pile ou face; **to f. sth over** retourner qch **2** *vi* **to f. through a book** feuilleter un livre

flip-flops ['flɪpflɒps] *npl* tongs *fpl*

flippant ['flɪpənt] *adj* désinvolte

flipper ['flɪpə(r)] *n* (*of swimmer*) palme *f*; (*of animal*) nageoire *f*

flirt [flɜːt] **1** *n* charmeur, -euse *mf* **2** *vi* flirter (**with** avec)

flit [flɪt] (*pt & pp* **-tt-**) *vi* (*fly*) voltiger; *Fig* **to f. in and out** (*of person*) entrer et sortir rapidement

float [fləʊt] **1** *n* (*for fishing line*) bouchon *m*; (*for swimming*) flotteur *m*; (*in procession*) char *m* **2** *vt* (*idea*) lancer; (*company*) introduire en Bourse **3** *vi* flotter (**on** sur); **to f. down the river** descendre la rivière ■ **floating** *adj* (*wood*) flottant; **f. voters** électeurs *mpl* indécis

flock [flɒk] **1** *n* (*of sheep*) troupeau *m*; (*of birds*) volée *f*; (*of people*) foule *f* **2** *vi* **people are flocking to the exhibition** les gens vont en foule voir l'exposition

flood [flʌd] **1** *n* inondation *f* **2** *vt* (*land, bathroom, market*) inonder (**with** de); **to f. (out)** (*house*) inonder **3** *vi* (*of river*) déborder; **to f. in** (*of people, money*) affluer ■ **flooding** *n* inondation(s) *f(pl)*

floodlight ['flʌdlaɪt] *n* projecteur *m* **2** (*pt & pp* **-lit**) *vt* illuminer

floor [flɔː(r)] **1** *n* (*of room*) sol *m*; (*wooden*) plancher *m*; (*storey*) étage *m*; **on the f.** par terre; **on the first f.** *Br* au premier étage; *Am* (*ground floor*) au rez-de-chaussée **2** *vt* (*knock down*) envoyer au tapis; (*puzzle*) stupéfier

floorboard ['flɔːbɔːd] *n* latte *f* (*de plancher*)

flop [flɒp] *Fam* **1** *n* fiasco *m*; (*play*) four *m* **2** (*pt & pp* **-pp-**) *vi* (*fail*) (*of business*)

échouer; *(of play, film)* faire un four;
to f. down s'effondrer

floppy ['flɒpɪ] *(-ier, -iest) adj (soft)*
mou *(f* molle); *(clothes)* (trop) large;
Comptr **f. disk** disquette *f*

floral ['flɔːrəl] *adj (material, pattern)* à
fleurs

florist ['flɒrɪst] *n* fleuriste *mf*

floss [flɒs] *n (dental)* **f.** fil *m* dentaire

flour ['flaʊə(r)] *n* farine *f*

flourish ['flʌrɪʃ] **1** *n (gesture)* grand
geste *m; (decoration)* fioriture *f* **2** *vt
(wave)* brandir **3** *vi (of person, plant)*
prospérer; *(of arts, business)* être florissant ■ **flourishing** *adj (plant)* qui
prospère; *(business)* florissant

flow [fləʊ] **1** *n (of river)* courant *m; (of
tide)* flux *m; (of current, information,
blood)* circulation *f; (of liquid)* écoulement *m;* **f. of traffic** circulation *f;* **f.
chart** organigramme *m* **2** *vi* couler;
(of electric current) circuler; *(of hair,
clothes)* flotter; *(of traffic)* s'écouler;
to f. in *(of money)* affluer ■ **flowing**
adj (movement, style) fluide; *(hair,
beard)* flottant

flower ['flaʊə(r)] **1** *n* fleur *f;* **in f.** en
fleur(s); **f. bed** parterre *m;* **f. pot** pot
m de fleurs; **f. shop** fleuriste *mf* **2** *vi*
fleurir ■ **flowering** *adj (in bloom)* en
fleurs; *(producing flowers) (shrub)* à
fleurs

flowery ['flaʊərɪ] *adj (style)* fleuri;
(material) à fleurs

flown [fləʊn] *pp of* **fly²**

flu [fluː] *n (influenza)* grippe *f*

fluctuate ['flʌktʃʊeɪt] *vi* varier ■ **fluc-
tuation** [-'eɪʃən] *n* variation *f* (**in** de)

fluent ['fluːənt] *adj* **he's f. in Russian,
his Russian is f.** il parle couramment
le russe; **to be a f. speaker** s'exprimer
avec facilité ■ **fluently** *adv (write, express oneself)* avec facilité; *(speak language)* couramment

fluff [flʌf] *n* peluche *f* ■ **fluffy (-ier,
-iest)** *adj (toy)* en peluche

fluid ['fluːɪd] **1** *adj* fluide; *(plans)* mal
défini; **f. ounce** = 0,03 l **2** *n* fluide *m,*
liquide *m*

fluke [fluːk] *n Fam* coup *m* de chance;
by a f. par hasard

flung [flʌŋ] *pt & pp of* **fling**

flunk [flʌŋk] *Am Fam* **1** *vt (exam)* être
collé à; *(pupil)* coller **2** *vi (in exam)*
être collé

fluorescent [flʊə'resənt] *adj* fluorescent

fluoride ['flʊəraɪd] *n* fluorure *m;* **f.
toothpaste** dentifrice *m* au fluor

flurry ['flʌrɪ] *(pl -ies) n (of snow)*
bourrasque *f;* **a f. of activity** une soudaine activité

flush [flʌʃ] **1** *adj (level)* de niveau
(**with** de) **2** *n* (**a**) *(blush)* rougeur *f*
(**b**) *(in toilet)* chasse *f* d'eau **3** *vt* **to f.
sth (out)** *(clean)* nettoyer qch à
grande eau; **to f. the toilet** tirer la
chasse d'eau **4** *vi (blush)* rougir (**with**
de)

fluster ['flʌstə(r)] *vt* démonter; **to get
flustered** se démonter

flute [fluːt] *n* flûte *f*

flutter ['flʌtə(r)] **1** *vt* **to f. its wings** *(of
bird)* battre des ailes **2** *vi (of bird, butterfly)* voleter; *(of flag)* flotter

fly¹ [flaɪ] *(pl -ies) n (insect)* mouche *f*

fly² [flaɪ] *(pt flew, pp flown) vt (aircraft)* piloter; *(passengers)* transporter; *(flag)* arborer; *(kite)* faire voler;
to f. the Atlantic traverser l'Atlantique en avion
2 *vi (of bird, aircraft)* voler; *(of passenger)* aller en avion; *(of time)* passer
vite; *(of flag)* flotter; **to f. away** *or* **off**
s'envoler; **to f. across** *or* **over** *(country,
city)* survoler; **I must f.!** il faut que je
file! ■ **flyer** *n =* **flier** ■ **flying 1** *n (as
passenger)* voyage *m* en avion **2** *adj*
to pass with f. colours réussir haut la
main; **to get off to a f. start** prendre
un très bon départ; **f. saucer** soucoupe *f* volante; **f. visit** visite *f* éclair
inv ■ **flyover** *n Br (bridge)* pont-route
m

fly³ [flaɪ] *n Br (on trousers)* braguette *f*

foal [fəʊl] *n* poulain *m*

foam [fəʊm] **1** *n (on sea, mouth)*
écume *f; (on beer)* mousse *f;* **f. bath**

bain *m* moussant; **f. rubber** caout-chouc *m* Mousse® 2 *vi (of beer, soap)* mousser

focal ['fəʊkəl] *adj* focal

focus ['fəʊkəs] **1** *(pl* **focuses** ['fəʊkəsəz] *or* **foci** ['fəʊkaɪ]) *n (of attention, interest)* centre *m; (optical)* foyer *m;* **the photo is in f./out of f.** la photo est nette/floue

2 *vt (image, camera)* mettre au point; *(attention, efforts)* concentrer *(on* sur) **3** *vi* **to f. on sb/sth** *(with camera)* faire la mise au point sur qn/qch **4** *vti* **to f. (one's eyes) on sb/sth** fixer les yeux sur qn/qch; **to f. (one's attention) on sb/sth** se tourner vers qn/qch

fodder ['fɒdə(r)] *n* fourrage *m*

foe [fəʊ] *n* ennemi, -e *mf*

foetus ['fiːtəs] *n* (Am **fetus**) *n* fœtus *m*

fog [fɒg] *n* brouillard *m* ▪ **foglamp, foglight** *n (on vehicle)* phare *m* antibrouillard

fogey ['fəʊgɪ] *n* = **fogy**

foggy ['fɒgɪ] (**-ier, -iest**) *adj* brumeux, -euse; **it's f.** il y a du brouillard; *Fam* **I haven't got the foggiest (idea)** je n'en ai pas la moindre idée

fogy ['fəʊgɪ] *n* old **f.** vieux schnock *m*

foil [fɔɪl] **1** *n* (**a**) *(for cooking)* papier *m* alu (**b**) *(sword)* fleuret *m* **2** *vt (plans)* contrecarrer

fold [fəʊld] **1** *n (in paper, cloth)* pli *m* **2** *vt* plier; **to f. away** *or* **down** *or* **up** *(chair)* plier; **to f. back** *or* **over** *(blanket)* replier; **to f. one's arms** croiser les bras **3** *vi Fam (of business)* fermer ses portes; **to f. (away** *or* **down** *or* **up)** *(of chair)* se plier ▪ **folding** *adj (chair, bed)* pliant

-fold [fəʊld] *suff* **1** *adj* **tenfold** par dix **2** *adv* **tenfold** dix fois

folder ['fəʊldə(r)] *n (file holder)* chemise *f; Comptr* répertoire *m*

foliage ['fəʊlɪɪdʒ] *n* feuillage *m*

folk [fəʊk] **1** *n* (*Am* **folks**) *npl* gens *mpl; Fam* **my folks** *(parents)* mes parents *mpl* **2** *adj (dance, costume)* folklorique; **f. music** *(contemporary)* folk *m*

follow ['fɒləʊ] **1** *vt* suivre; *(career)* poursuivre; **to f. through** *(plan, idea)* mener à son terme; **to f. up** *(idea, story)* creuser; *(clue, case)* suivre; *(letter)* donner suite à; *(remark)* faire suivre (**with** de); *(advantage)* exploiter **2** *vi (of person, event)* suivre; **it follows that…** il s'ensuit que…; **to f. on** *(come after)* suivre

follower ['fɒləʊə(r)] *n (of ideas, politician)* partisan *m*

following ['fɒləʊɪŋ] **1** *adj* suivant **2** *(of politician)* partisans *mpl* **3** *prep* à la suite de

folly ['fɒlɪ] (*pl* **-ies**) *n* folie *f*

fond [fɒnd] (**-er, -est**) *adj (loving)* affectueux, -euse; *(memory, thought)* doux *(f* douce); **to be (very) f. of sb/sth** aimer beaucoup qn/qch ▪ **fondly** *adv* tendrement

fondle ['fɒndəl] *vt* caresser

font [fɒnt] *n* (**a**) *Rel* fonts *mpl* baptismaux (**b**) *Typ & Comptr* police *f* de caractères

food [fuːd] **1** *n* nourriture *f; (particular substance)* aliment *m; (cooking)* cuisine *f; (for cats, dogs, pigs)* pâtée *f; (for plants)* engrais *m* **2** *adj (industry)* alimentaire; **f. poisoning** intoxication *f* alimentaire

foodstuffs ['fuːdstʌfs] *npl* denrées *fpl* alimentaires

fool [fuːl] **1** *n* imbécile *mf;* **to make a f. of sb** *(ridicule)* ridiculiser qn; *(trick)* rouler qn; **to make a f. of oneself** se couvrir de ridicule **2** *vt (trick)* duper **3** *vi* **to f. about** *or* **around** faire l'imbécile; *(waste time)* perdre son temps

foolish ['fuːlɪʃ] *adj* bête ▪ **foolishly** *adv* bêtement

foolproof ['fuːlpruːf] *adj (scheme)* infaillible

foot[1] [fʊt] (*pl* **feet**) *n* pied *m; (of animal)* patte *f; (unit of measurement)* = 30,48 cm, pied *m;* **at the f.** *(of page, stairs)* au bas de; **on f.** à pied ▪ **football** *n (soccer)* football *m; (American game)* football *m* américain; *(ball)* ballon *m* ▪ **footballer** *n Br* joueur,

-euse *mf* de football ■ **footbridge** *n* passerelle *f* ■ **foothold** *n* prise *f* (de pied); *Fig* position *f*; **to gain a f.** (of person) prendre pied (**in** dans) ■ **footnote** *n* note *f* de bas de page; *Fig* (extra comment) post-scriptum *m inv* ■ **footpath** *n* sentier *m* ■ **footstep** *n* pas *m*; **to follow in sb's footsteps** suivre les traces de qn ■ **footstool** *n* petit tabouret *m* ■ **footwear** *n* chaussures *fpl*

foot² [fʊt] *vt* (bill) payer

footage ['fʊtɪdʒ] *n Cin* séquences *fpl*

footing ['fʊtɪŋ] *n* (**a**) (balance) **to lose one's f.** perdre l'équilibre (**b**) (level) **to be on an equal f.** être sur un pied d'égalité (**with** avec)

FOR [fɔː(r), *unstressed* fə(r)] **1** *prep* pour; (for a distance or period of) pendant; (in spite of) malgré; **what's it f.?** ça sert à quoi?; **I did it f. love/pleasure** je l'ai fait par amour/par plaisir; **to swim/rush f.** (towards) nager/se précipiter vers; **a train f. ...** un train à destination de; **the road f. London** la route de Londres; **it's time f. breakfast** c'est l'heure du petit déjeuner; **to come f. dinner** venir dîner; **to sell sth f. 7 dollars** vendre qch 7 dollars; **what's the French f. 'book'?** comment dit-on f. en français?; **she walked f. a kilometre** elle a marché pendant un kilomètre; **he was away f. a month** il a été absent pendant un mois; **he's been here f. a month** il est ici depuis un mois; **I haven't seen him f. ten years** ça fait dix ans que je ne l'ai pas vu, je ne l'ai pas vu depuis dix ans; **it's easy f. her to do it** il lui est facile de le faire; **it that to be done** pour que ça soit fait **2** *conj* (because) car

forbad [fə'bæd] *pt of* **forbid**

forbade [fə'bæd, fə'beɪd] *pt of* **forbid**

forbid [fə'bɪd] (*pt* **forbad(e)**, *pp* **forbidden** [fə'bɪdən], *pres p* **forbidding**) *vt* interdire, défendre (**sb to do** à qn de faire); **to f. sb sth** interdire qch à qn; **she is f. to leave** il lui est interdit

de partir ■ **forbidden 1** *pp of* **forbid 2** *adj* (fruit, region) défendu

force [fɔːs] **1** *n* force *f*; **the (armed) forces** les forces *fpl* armées; **by f.** de force; **in f.** (rule) en vigueur; (in great numbers) en force **2** *vt* forcer (**to do** à faire); (impose) imposer (**on** à); (door, lock) forcer; (confession) arracher (**from** à); **to f. sth into sth** faire entrer qch de force dans qch ■ **forced** *adj* **f. to do** obligé *ou* forcé de faire; **a f. smile** un sourire forcé

forceful ['fɔːsfəl] *adj* énergique

ford [fɔːd] **1** *n* gué *m* **2** *vt* (river) passer à gué

fore [fɔː(r)] *n* **to come to the f.** (of issue) passer au premier plan

forearm ['fɔːrɑːm] *n* avant-bras *m inv*

foreboding [fɔː'bəʊdɪŋ] *n* (feeling) pressentiment *m*

forecast ['fɔːkɑːst] **1** *n* (of weather) prévisions *fpl*; (in racing) pronostic *m* **2** (*pt & pp* **forecast(ed)**) *vt* prévoir; (in racing) pronostiquer

forecourt ['fɔːkɔːt] *n* (of hotel) avant-cour *f*; (of petrol station) devant *m*

forefinger ['fɔːfɪŋgə(r)] *n* index *m*

forefront ['fɔːfrʌnt] *n* **in the f. of** au premier plan de

forego [fɔː'gəʊ] (*pp* **-gone**) *vt* renoncer à

foreground ['fɔːgraʊnd] *n* premier plan *m*

forehead ['fɒrɪd, 'fɔːhed] *n* front *m*

foreign ['fɒrɪn] *adj* (language, person, country) étranger, -ère; (trade) extérieur; (travel, correspondent) à l'étranger; **F. Minister**, *Br* **F. Secretary** ministre *m* des Affaires étrangères; *Br* **F. Office** ministère *m* des Affaires étrangères ■ **foreigner** *n* étranger, -ère *mf*

foreman ['fɔːmən] (*pl* **-men**) *n* (worker) contremaître *m*

foremost ['fɔːməʊst] *adj* principal

forerunner ['fɔːrʌnə(r)] *n* (person) précurseur *m*

foresee [fɔː'siː] (*pt* **-saw**, *pp* **-seen**) *vt* prévoir

foreshadow [fɔːˈʃædəʊ] vt annoncer
foresight [ˈfɔːsaɪt] n prévoyance f
forest [ˈfɒrɪst] n forêt f
forestall [fɔːˈstɔːl] vt devancer
foretell [fɔːˈtel] (pt & pp -**told**) vt prédire
forever [fəˈrevə(r)] adv (for always) pour toujours; (continually) sans cesse
foreword [ˈfɔːwɜːd] n avant-propos m inv
forfeit [ˈfɔːfɪt] **1** n (in game) gage m **2** vt (lose) perdre
forge [fɔːdʒ] **1** vt (signature, money) contrefaire; **to f. a passport** faire un faux passeport **2** vi **to f. ahead** (progress) aller de l'avant ■ **forged** adj faux (f fausse)
forgery [ˈfɔːdʒərɪ] (pl -**ies**) n contrefaçon f
forget [fəˈget] **1** (pt **forgot**, pp **forgotten**, pres p **forgetting**) vt oublier (**to do** de faire); Fam **f. it!** (when thanked) pas de quoi!; (it doesn't matter) laisse tomber! **2** vi oublier; **to f. about sth** oublier qn/qch ■ **forgetful** adj **to be f.** avoir une mauvaise mémoire
forgive [fəˈgɪv] (pt -**gave**, pp -**given**) vt pardonner (**sb sth** qch à qn) ■ **forgiveness** n pardon m
forgo [fɔːˈgəʊ] (pp -**gone**) vt renoncer à
forgot [fəˈgɒt] pt of **forget**
forgotten [fəˈgɒtən] pp of **forget**
fork [fɔːk] **1** n (for eating) fourchette f; (for gardening, in road) fourche f **2** vt Fam **to f. out** (money) allonger **3** vi (of road) bifurquer; Fam **to f. out** (pay) casquer (**for** or **on** pour) ■ **forklift** n **f. (truck)** chariot m élévateur
forlorn [fəˈlɔːn] adj (forsaken) abandonné; (unhappy) triste
form [fɔːm] **1** n (shape, type, style) forme f; (document) formulaire m; Br Sch classe f; **in the f. of** sous forme de; **on f., in good** or **top f.** en (pleine) forme **2** vt (group, basis, character) former; (clay) façonner; (habit) contracter; (obstacle) constituer; **to f. part of**

sth faire partie de qch **vi** (appear) se former
formal [ˈfɔːməl] adj (person, tone) cérémonieux, -euse; (announcement, dinner, invitation) officiel, -elle; (agreement) en bonne et due forme; (language) soutenu; **f. dress** tenue f de soirée ■ **formality** [-ˈmælɪtɪ] (pl -**ies**) n (procedure) formalité f ■ **formally** adv (declare) officiellement; **f. dressed** en tenue de soirée
format [ˈfɔːmæt] **1** n format m **2** (pt & pp -**tt**-) vt Comptr formater
formation [fɔːˈmeɪʃən] n formation f
former [ˈfɔːmə(r)] **1** adj (previous) (president, teacher, job, house) ancien, -enne (before noun) **2** pron **the f.** celui-là, celle-là ■ **formerly** adv autrefois
formidable [ˈfɔːmɪdəbəl] adj effroyable
formula [ˈfɔːmjʊlə] n (**a**) (pl -**as** or -**ae** [-iː]) (rule, symbols) formule f (**b**) (pl -**as**) (baby food) lait m en poudre ■ **formulate** [-leɪt] vt formuler
fort [fɔːt] n Mil fort m
forth [fɔːθ] adv en avant; **and so f.** et ainsi de suite
forthcoming [fɔːθˈkʌmɪŋ] adj (**a**) (event) à venir (**b**) (available) disponible (**c**) (informative) expansif, -ive (**about** sur)
forthright [ˈfɔːθraɪt] adj franc (f franche)
fortieth [ˈfɔːtɪəθ] adj & n quarantième (mf)
fortify [ˈfɔːtɪfaɪ] (pt & pp -**ied**) vt (strengthen) fortifier; **to f. sb** (of food, drink) réconforter qn, remonter qn ■ **fortification** [-fɪˈkeɪʃən] n fortification f
fortnight [ˈfɔːtnaɪt] n Br quinzaine f de jours
fortress [ˈfɔːtrɪs] n forteresse f
fortunate [ˈfɔːtʃənət] adj heureux, -euse; **to be f.** (of person) avoir de la chance; **it's f. (for her) that...** c'est heureux (pour elle) que... (+ subjunctive) ■ **fortunately** adv heureusement

fortune ['fɔːtʃuːn] n (wealth) fortune f; (luck) chance f ■ **fortune-teller** n diseur, -euse mf de bonne aventure

forty ['fɔːtɪ] adj & n quarante (m)

forum ['fɔːrəm] n forum m

forward ['fɔːwəd] **1** adj (position) avant inv; (movement) en avant; Fig (impudent) effronté **2** n (in sport) avant m **3** adv en avant; **to go f.** avancer **4** vt (letter) faire suivre; (goods) expédier

forwards ['fɔːwədz] adv = **forward**

fossil ['fɒsəl] n fossile m

foster ['fɒstə(r)] adj **f. child** = enfant placé dans une famille d'accueil; **f. parents** parents mpl nourriciers

fought [fɔːt] pt & pp of **fight**

foul [faʊl] **1** (-er, -est) adj (a) (smell, taste, weather, person) infect; (breath) fétide; (language) grossier, -ère; (place) immonde (b) **f. play** (in sport) jeu m irrégulier; (in law) acte m criminel **2** n (in sport) faute f **3** vt Fam **f. up** (ruin) gâcher

found¹ [faʊnd] pt & pp of **find**

found² [faʊnd] vt (town, party) fonder; (opinion, suspicions) fonder, baser (**on** sur) ■ **founder** n fondateur, -trice mf

foundation [faʊn'deɪʃən] n (basis) fondement m; **the foundations** (of building) les fondations fpl

fountain ['faʊntɪn] n fontaine f; **f. pen** stylo-plume m

four [fɔː(r)] adj & n quatre (m); **on all fours** à quatre pattes ■ **fourth** adj & n quatrième (mf) ■ **four-letter** adj **f. word** gros mot m

foursome ['fɔːsəm] n groupe m de quatre personnes

fourteen [fɔː'tiːn] adj & n quatorze (m) ■ **fourteenth** adj & n quatorzième (mf)

fowl [faʊl] n inv volaille f

fox [fɒks] **1** n renard m **2** vt (puzzle) laisser perplexe; (deceive) duper

foyer ['fɔɪeɪ] n (in theatre) foyer m; (in hotel) hall m

fraction ['frækʃən] n fraction f

fracture ['fræktʃə(r)] **1** n fracture f **2** vt

fracturer; **to f. one's leg** se fracturer la jambe

fragile [Br 'frædʒaɪl, Am 'frædʒəl] adj fragile

fragment ['frægmənt] n fragment m

fragrant ['freɪgrənt] adj parfumé ■ **fragrance** n parfum m

frail [freɪl] (-er, -est) adj (person) frêle; (health) fragile

frame [freɪm] **1** n (of picture, bicycle) cadre m; (of door, window) encadrement m; (of spectacles) monture f; **f. of mind** état m d'esprit **2** vt (picture) encadrer; Fig (proposals, ideas) formuler ■ **framework** n structure f; **(with)in the f. of** (context) dans le cadre de

franc [fræŋk] n franc m

France [frɑːns] n la France

franchise ['fræntʃaɪz] n (right to vote) droit m de vote; (right to sell product) franchise f

Franco- ['fræŋkəʊ] pref franco-

frank¹ [fræŋk] (-er, -est) adj (honest) franc (f franche) ■ **frankly** adv franchement

frank² [fræŋk] vt (letter) affranchir

frantic ['fræntɪk] adj (activity, shouts, pace) frénétique; (attempt, efforts) désespéré ■ **frantically** adv frénétiquement; (run, search) comme un fou/une folle; (work) avec frénésie

fraternize ['frætənaɪz] vi fraterniser (**with** avec)

fraud [frɔːd] n (a) (crime) fraude f (b) (person) imposteur m ■ **fraudulent** adj frauduleux, -euse

fraught [frɔːt] adj (situation) tendu; **f. with** plein de

fray [freɪ] vi (of garment) s'effilocher; (of rope) s'user ■ **frayed** adj (garment) élimé

freak [friːk] **1** n (person) monstre m; Fam **jazz f.** fana mf de jazz **2** adj (result, weather) anormal

▶ **freak out** Fam **1** vt sep (shock, scare) faire flipper **2** vi (panic) paniquer; (get angry) piquer une crise

freckle ['frekəl] n tache f de rousseur

■ **freckled** adj couvert de taches de rousseur

free [fri:] **1** (**freer, freest**) adj (at liberty, not occupied) libre; (without cost) gratuit; (lavish) généreux, -euse (**with** de); **to get f.** se libérer; **to be f. to do sth** être libre de faire qch; **f. of charge** gratuit; **f. gift** cadeau m; **f. kick** (in football) coup m franc; **f. trade** libre-échange m

2 adv **f. (of charge)** gratuitement

3 pt & pp **freed**) vt (prisoner, country) libérer; (trapped person) dégager; (untie) détacher ■ **Freefone®** n Br (phone number) ≃ numéro m vert ■ **freelance 1** adj indépendant **2** n travailleur, -euse mf indépendant(e) **3** adv **to work f.** travailler en indépendant ■ **Freepost®** n Br ≃ correspondance-réponse f ■ **free-range** adj Br **f. egg** œuf m de ferme ■ **freestyle** n (in swimming) nage f libre ■ **freeway** n Am autoroute f

freedom ['fri:dəm] n liberté f

freely ['fri:lɪ] adv (speak, act, circulate) librement; (give) sans compter

freeze [fri:z] **1** n (in weather) gel m; (of prices, salaries) blocage m **2** (pt **froze**, pp **frozen**) vt (food) congeler; (credits, river) geler; (prices, wages) bloquer; **frozen food** surgelés mpl **3** vi geler; **to f. to death** mourir de froid; **to f. up** or **over** (of lake) geler ■ **freezer** n (deep-freeze) congélateur m; (ice-box) freezer m ■ **freezing 1** adj (weather) glacial; (hands, feet) gelée; **it's f.** il gèle **2** n **it's 5 degrees below f.** il fait 5 degrés au-dessous de zéro **3** adv **f. cold** très froid

freight [freɪt] n Com (goods) cargaison f; **f. train** train m de marchandises ■ **freighter** n (ship) cargo m

French [frentʃ] **1** adj français; (teacher) de français; (embassy) de France; **F. fries** frites fpl **2** n (language) français m; **the F.** (people) les Français mpl ■ **Frenchman** (pl **-men**) n Français m ■ **French-speaking** adj francophone ■ **Frenchwoman** (pl **-women**) n Française f

frenzy ['frenzɪ] (pl **-ies**) n frénésie f ■ **frenzied** adj (activity) frénétique; (attack) violent

frequency ['fri:kwənsɪ] (pl **-ies**) n fréquence f

frequent 1 ['fri:kwənt] adj fréquent **2** [frɪ'kwent] vt fréquenter ■ **frequently** adv fréquemment

fresh [freʃ] **1** (**-er, -est**) adj frais (f fraîche); (new) nouveau (f nouvelle); Am Fam (cheeky) insolent; **to get some f. air** prendre l'air **2** adv **to be f. from** (school, university) sortir tout juste de ■ **freshly** adv (arrived, picked) fraîchement

► **freshen up** ['freʃən] **1** vi (have a wash) faire un brin de toilette **2** vt sep (house) retaper

fret [fret] (pt & pp **-tt-**) vi (worry) se faire du souci

friction ['frɪkʃən] n friction f

Friday ['fraɪdeɪ] n vendredi m; **Good F.** le vendredi saint

fridge [frɪdʒ] n frigo m

fried [fraɪd] **1** pt & pp of **fry 2** adj frit; **f. egg** œuf m sur le plat

friend [frend] n ami, -e mf ■ **friendly 1** (**-ier, -iest**) adj amical **2** n (match) match m amical ■ **friendship** n amitié f

fright [fraɪt] n peur f; **to give sb a f.** faire peur à qn

frighten ['fraɪtən] vt effrayer, faire peur à; **to f. sb away** or **off** faire fuir qn ■ **frightened** adj effrayé; **to be f.** avoir peur (**of** de) ■ **frightening** adj effrayant

frightful ['fraɪtfəl] adj affreux, -euse

frill [frɪl] n volant m

fringe [frɪndʒ] n (**a**) (of hair, on clothes) frange f (**b**) (margin) **on the fringes of society** en marge de la société

frisk [frɪsk] vt (search) fouiller

frisky ['frɪskɪ] (**-ier, -iest**) adj (lively) vif (f vive)

fritter ['frɪtə(r)] **1** n Culin beignet m **2** vt **to f. away** gaspiller

frivolous ['frɪvələs] *adj* frivole

frizzy ['frɪzɪ] *adj* crépu

fro [frəʊ] *adv* **to go to and f.** aller et venir

frock [frɒk] *n (dress)* robe *f*

frog [frɒg] *n* grenouille *f*

frolic ['frɒlɪk] *(pt & pp* **-ck-)** *vi* **to f. (about)** gambader

FROM [frɒm, *unstressed* frəm] *prep*
(**a**) *(expressing origin)* de; **a letter f. sb** une lettre de qn; **to suffer f. sth** souffrir de qch; **where are you f.?** d'où êtes-vous?; **a train f. Paris** un train en provenance de Paris; **to be 10 m (away) f. the house** être à 10 m de la maison
(**b**) *(expressing time)* à partir de; **f. today (on), as f. today** à partir d'aujourd'hui; **f. the beginning** dès le début
(**c**) *(expressing range)* **f.... to...** de... à...; **f. morning till night** du matin au soir; **they take children f. the age of five** ils acceptent les enfants à partir de cinq ans
(**d**) *(expressing source)* de; **to take/ borrow sth f. sb** prendre/emprunter qch à qn; **to drink f. a cup** boire dans une tasse
(**e**) *(expressing removal)* de; **to take sth f. sb** prendre qch à qn; **to take sth f. a box/f. the table** prendre qch dans une boîte/sur la table
(**f**) *(according to)* d'après; **f. what I saw...** d'après ce que j'ai vu...
(**g**) *(on behalf of)* de la part de; **tell her f. me** dis-lui de ma part

front [frʌnt] **1** *n* devant *m*; *(of boat, car)* avant *m*; *(of building)* façade *f*; *(of crowd)* premier rang *m*; *Mil, Pol & Met* front *m*; **in f. of sb/sth** devant qn/qch; **in f.** devant; *(further ahead)* en avant; *(in race)* en tête **2** *adj (tooth, garden)* de devant; *(car seat)* avant *inv*; *(row, page)* premier, -ère; **f. door** porte *f* d'entrée **3** *vt (organization)* être à la tête de; *(TV programme)* présenter
■ **frontrunner** *n Fig* favori, -ite *mf*

■ **front-wheel** *adj Aut* **f. drive** traction *f* avant

frontier ['frʌntɪə(r)] *n* frontière *f*

frost [frɒst] **1** *n* gel *m* **2** *vi* **to f. up** *(of window)* se couvrir de givre

frostbite ['frɒstbaɪt] *n* gelure *f*
■ **frostbitten** *adj* gelé

frosting ['frɒstɪŋ] *n Am (on cake)* glaçage *m*

frosty ['frɒstɪ] **(-ier, -iest)** *adj (air, night)* glacé; *Fig (welcome)* glacial; **it's f.** il gèle

froth [frɒθ] **1** *n (on beer)* mousse *f*; *(on waves)* écume *f* **2** *vi (liquid)* mousser
■ **frothy (-ier, -iest)** *adj (beer)* mousseux, -euse

frown [fraʊn] **1** *n* froncement *m* de sourcils **2** *vi* froncer les sourcils; *Fig* **to f. (up)on** désapprouver

froze [frəʊz] *pt of* **freeze**

frozen ['frəʊzən] *pp of* **freeze**

frugal ['fru:gəl] *adj* frugal

fruit [fru:t] *n* fruit *m*; **some f.** *(one item)* un fruit; *(more than one)* des fruits; **f. juice** jus *m* de fruits; **f. salad** salade *f* de fruits; *Br* **f. machine** *(for gambling)* machine *f* à sous ■ **fruitcake** *n* cake *m*

fruitful ['fru:tfəl] *adj (meeting, discussion)* fructueux, -euse ■ **fruitless** *adj (attempt, search)* vain, -euse

frustrate [frʌ'streɪt] *vt (person)* frustrer; *(plans)* contrarier ■ **frustrating** *adj* frustrant ■ **frustration** *n* frustration *f*

fry [fraɪ] *(pt & pp* **fried)** **1** *vt* faire frire **2** *vi* frire ■ **frying** *n* **f. pan** poêle *f* (à frire)

ft *(abbr* **foot, feet)** pied(s) *m(pl)*

fudge [fʌdʒ] **1** *n (sweet)* caramel *m* mou **2** *vt* **to f. the issue** éluder une question

fuel [fjʊəl] *n* combustible *m*; *(for engine)* carburant *m*; **f. oil** mazout *m*; **f. tank** *(in vehicle)* réservoir *m*

fugitive ['fju:dʒɪtɪv] *n* fugitif, -ive *mf*

fulfil [fʊl'fɪl] *(Am* **fulfill)** *(pt & pp* **-ll-)** *vt (ambition, dream)* réaliser; *(condition, duty)* remplir; *(desire, need)* satisfaire ■ **fulfilling** *adj* satisfaisant
■ **fulfilment** *(Am* **fulfillment)** *n (of*

ambition) réalisation *f* (**of** de); *(satisfaction)* épanouissement *m*

full [fʊl] **1** (**-er, -est**) *adj* plein (**of** de); *(bus, theatre, hotel, examination)* complet, -ète; *(amount)* intégral; *(day, programme)* chargé; *(skirt)* bouffant; **to be f. (up)** *(of person)* n'avoir plus faim; *(of hotel)* être complet; **at f. speed** à toute vitesse; **f. name** nom et prénom; *Br* **f. stop** point *m*

2 *n* **in f.** *(pay)* intégralement; *(write)* en toutes lettres

3 *adv* **to know f. well** savoir fort bien ■ **full-length** *adj (portrait)* en pied; *(dress)* long (f longue) ■ **f. film** long métrage *m* ■ **full-scale** *adj (model)* grandeur nature *inv*; *(operation)* de grande envergure ■ **full-time** *adj & adv (work)* à plein temps

fully [ˈfʊlɪ] *adv (completely)* entièrement; *(understand)* parfaitement; *(at least)* au moins ■ **fully-fledged** *(Am* **full-fledged)** *adj (engineer, teacher)* diplômé; *(member)* à part entière ■ **fully-grown** *adj* adulte

fumble [ˈfʌmbəl] *vi* **to f. (about)** *(grope)* tâtonner; *(search)* fouiller (**for** pour trouver)

fume [fjuːm] *vi* **to be fuming** *(of person)* rager ■ **fumes** *npl* émanations *fpl*; *(from car)* gaz *mpl* d'échappement

fun [fʌn] *n* plaisir *m*; **for f., for the f. of it** pour le plaisir; **to be (good** or **great) f.** être (très) amusant; **to have (some) f.** s'amuser; **to make f. of sb/ sth** se moquer de qn/qch

function [ˈfʌŋkʃən] **1** *n (role, duty) & Comptr* fonction *f*; *(party)* réception *f* **2** *vi* fonctionner; **to f. as** faire fonction de ■ **functional** *adj* fonctionnel, -elle

fund [fʌnd] **1** *n (of money)* fonds *m*; **funds** fonds *mpl* **2** *vt* financer

fundamental [fʌndəˈmentəl] *adj* fondamental

funeral [ˈfjuːnərəl] *n* enterrement *m*; *(grandiose)* funérailles *fpl*; **f. service** service *m* funèbre; *Br* **f. parlour,** *Am* **f. home** entreprise *f* de pompes funèbres

funfair [ˈfʌnfeə(r)] *n Br* fête *f* foraine

fungus [ˈfʌŋɡəs] *(pl* **-gi** [-ɡaɪ]) *n (plant)* champignon *m*; *(on walls)* moisissure *f*

funnel [ˈfʌnəl] *n* (**a**) *(of ship)* cheminée *f* (**b**) *(for filling)* entonnoir *m*

funny [ˈfʌnɪ] (**-ier, -iest**) *adj (amusing)* drôle; *(strange)* bizarre; **a f. idea** une drôle d'idée ■ **funnily** *adv* **f. enough, I was just about to…** bizarrement, j'étais sur le point de…

fur [fɜː(r)] **1** *n (of animal, for wearing)* fourrure *f*; *(of dog, cat)* poil *m*; **f. coat** manteau *m* de fourrure **2** *vi Br* **to f. (up)** *(of kettle)* s'entartrer

furious [ˈfjʊərɪəs] *adj (violent, angry)* furieux, -euse (**with** or **at** contre); *(efforts, struggle)* violent

furnace [ˈfɜːnɪs] *n (forge)* fourneau *m*

furnish [ˈfɜːnɪʃ] *vt* (**a**) *(room, house)* meubler (**b**) *(supply)* fournir (**sb with sth** qch à qn) ■ **furnishings** *npl* ameublement *m*

furniture [ˈfɜːnɪtʃə(r)] *n* meubles *mpl*; **a piece of f.** un meuble

furrow [ˈfʌrəʊ] *n (in earth, on brow)* sillon *m*

furry [ˈfɜːrɪ] *adj (animal)* à poil; *(toy)* en peluche

further [ˈfɜːðə(r)] **1** *adv & adj* = **farther 2** *adj (additional)* supplémentaire; *Br* **f. education** = enseignement supérieur dispensé par un établissement autre qu'une université **3** *adv (more)* davantage **4** *vt (cause, research, career)* promouvoir ■ **furthermore** *adv* en outre ■ **furthest** *adj & adv* = **farthest**

furtive [ˈfɜːtɪv] *adj* sournois

fury [ˈfjʊərɪ] *n (violence, anger)* fureur *f*

fuse [fjuːz] **1** *n (wire)* fusible *m*; *(of bomb)* amorce *f* **2** *vt (join)* fusionner; *Br* **to f. the lights** faire sauter les plombs **3** *vi Br* **the lights have fused** les plombs ont sauté

fusion [ˈfjuːʒən] *n* fusion *f*

fuss [fʌs] **1** *n* histoires *fpl*; **to kick up** or **make a f.** faire des histoires; **to make**

a f. of sb être aux petits soins pour qn **2** *vi* faire des histoires; **to f. over sb** être aux petits soins pour qn ■ **fussy** (**-ier, -iest**) *adj* exigeant (**about** sur); **I'm not f.** *(I don't mind)* ça m'est égal
futile [*Br* 'fjuːtaɪl, *Am* 'fjuːtəl] *adj (remark)* futile; *(attempt)* vain
futon ['fuːtɒn] *n* futon *m*

future ['fjuːtʃə(r)] **1** *n* avenir *m*; *(in grammar)* futur *m*; **in (the) f.** à l'avenir **2** *adj* futur; **my f. wife** ma future épouse; **the f. tense** le futur
fuze [fjuːz] *n & vti Am* = **fuse**
fuzzy ['fʌzɪ] (**-ier, -iest**) *adj* (**a**) *(unclear) (picture, idea)* flou (**b**) *(hair)* crépu

Gg

G, g [dʒiː] *n (letter)* G, g *m inv*
gabble ['gæbəl] *vi (chatter)* jacasser; *(indistinctly)* bredouiller
gable ['geɪbəl] *n* pignon *m*
gadget ['gædʒɪt] *n* gadget *m*
gaffe [gæf] *n (blunder)* gaffe *f*
gag [gæg] **1** *n* (**a**) *(on mouth)* bâillon *m* (**b**) *Fam (joke)* blague *f* **2** *(pt & pp* **-gg-**) *vt (person)* bâillonner; *Fig (press)* museler **3** *vi (choke)* s'étouffer (**on** avec)
gaily ['geɪlɪ] *adv* gaiement
gain [geɪn] **1** *n (increase)* augmentation *f* (**in** de); *(profit)* gain *m; Fig (advantage)* avantage *m* **2** *vt (obtain, win)* gagner; *(experience, reputation)* acquérir; **to g. speed/weight** prendre de la vitesse/du poids **3** *vi (of clock)* avancer; **to g. on sb** gagner du terrain sur qn; **to g. by sth** bénéficier de qch
gala [*Br* 'gɑːlə, *Am* 'geɪlə] *n* gala *m; Br* **swimming g.** concours *m* de natation
galaxy ['gæləksɪ] *(pl* **-ies)** *n* galaxie *f*
gale [geɪl] *n* grand vent *m*
gallant ['gælənt] *adj (brave)* brave; *(polite)* galant
gallery ['gælərɪ] *(pl* **-ies)** *n (room)* galerie *f; (museum)* musée *m; (for public, press)* tribune *f*
Gallic ['gælɪk] *adj (French)* français
gallon ['gælən] *n* gallon *m (Br* = 4,5 *l, Am* = 3,8 *l)*
gallop ['gæləp] **1** *n* galop *m* **2** *vi* galoper
gamble ['gæmbəl] **1** *n (risk)* coup *m* risqué **2** *vt (bet)* parier, jouer **3** *vi* jouer (**on** sur; **with** avec); **to g. on sth** *(count on)* miser sur qch ■ **gambler** *n*

joueur, -euse *mf* ■ **gambling** *n* jeu *m*
game¹ [geɪm] *n* (**a**) *(activity)* jeu *m; (of football, cricket)* match *m; (of tennis, chess, cards)* partie *f*; **to have a g. of football/tennis** faire un match de football/une partie de tennis; *Br* **games** *(in school)* le sport; **g. show** *(on television)* jeu *m* télévisé; *(on radio)* jeu *m* radiophonique (**b**) *(animals, birds)* gibier *m*
game² [geɪm] *adj (brave)* courageux, -euse; **to be g. (to do sth)** être partant (pour faire qch)
gammon ['gæmən] *n Br* jambon *m*
gang [gæŋ] **1** *n (of children, friends)* bande *f; (of workers)* équipe *f; (of criminals)* gang *m* **2** *vi* **to g. up on** *or* **against** se mettre à plusieurs contre
gangster ['gæŋstə(r)] *n* gangster *m*
gangway ['gæŋweɪ] *n Br* passage *m; (in train, plane)* couloir *m; (on ship)* passerelle *f; (in bus, cinema, theatre)* allée *f*
gaol [dʒeɪl] *n & vt Br* = **jail**
gap [gæp] *n (space)* espace *m (between* entre); *(in wall, fence)* trou *m; (in time)* intervalle *m; (in knowledge)* lacune *f*
gape [geɪp] *vi (stare)* rester bouche bée; **to g. at sb/sth** regarder qn/qch bouche bée ■ **gaping** *adj* béant
garage [*Br* 'gærɑːdʒ, 'gærɪdʒ, *Am* gə'rɑːʒ] *n* garage *m*
garbage ['gɑːbɪdʒ] *n Am* ordures *fpl;* **g. can** poubelle *f;* **g. man** *or* **collector** éboueur *m*
garbled ['gɑːbəld] *adj* confus
garden ['gɑːdən] **1** *n* jardin *m;* **gardens**

(park) parc *m*; **g. centre** jardinerie *f*; **g. party** garden-party *f* **2** *vi* jardiner, faire du jardinage ■ **gardener** *n* jardinier, -ère *mf* ■ **gardening** *n* jardinage *m*

gargle ['gɑːgəl] *vi* se gargariser

garish [*Br* 'geərɪʃ, *Am* 'gærɪʃ] *adj (clothes)* voyant; *(colour)* criard; *(light)* cru

garland ['gɑːlənd] *n* guirlande *f*

garlic ['gɑːlɪk] *n* ail *m*; **g. bread** = pain chaud au beurre d'ail

garment ['gɑːmənt] *n* vêtement *m*

garnish ['gɑːnɪʃ] **1** *n* garniture *f* **2** *vt* garnir (**with** de)

garter ['gɑːtə(r)] *n (round leg)* jarretière *f*; *(for socks)* fixe-chaussette *m*; *Am (attached to belt)* jarretelle *f*

gas [gæs] **1** *n* gaz *m inv*; *Am (gasoline)* essence *f*; *Br* **g. cooker** cuisinière *f* à gaz; *Br* **g. heater, g. fire** radiateur *m* à gaz; *Am* **g. station** station-service *f*; **g. stove** *(large)* cuisinière *f* à gaz; *(portable)* réchaud *m* à gaz; *Am* **g. tank** réservoir *m* à essence **2** *(pt & pp* **-ss-***) vt (person)* asphyxier; *(deliberately)* gazer

gash [gæʃ] **1** *n* entaille *f* **2** *vt* **to g. one's knee** se faire une blessure profonde au genou

gasoline ['gæsəliːn] *n Am* essence *f*

gasp [gɑːsp] **1** *n* halètement *m*; *(of surprise)* sursaut *m* **2** *vi* avoir le souffle coupé (**with** *or* **in** de); **to g. for breath** haleter

gassy ['gæsɪ] *(-ier, -iest) adj* gazeux, -euse

gastric ['gæstrɪk] *adj* gastrique

gate [geɪt] *n (in garden, field)* barrière *f*; *(made of metal)* grille *f*; *(of castle, at airport)* porte *f*; *(at stadium)* entrée *f*

gâteau ['gætəʊ] *(pl* **-eaux** [-əʊz]) *n Br (cake)* gros gâteau *m* à la crème

gatecrash ['geɪtkræʃ] *vt* **to g. a party** s'inviter à une réception

gateway ['geɪtweɪ] *n* entrée *f*

gather ['gæðə(r)] **1** *vt* (**a**) *(people, objects)* rassembler; *(pick up)* ramasser; *(flowers, fruit)* cueillir; *(information)*

recueillir; **to g. speed** prendre de la vitesse; **to g. in** *(crops, harvest)* rentrer; **to g. one's strength** rassembler ses forces (**b**) *(understand)* **I g. that...** je crois comprendre que... (**c**) *(sew pleats in)* froncer

2 *vi (of people)* se rassembler; *(of clouds)* se former; *(of dust)* s'accumuler; **to g. round** *(come closer)* s'approcher; **to g. round sb** entourer qn

gathering ['gæðərɪŋ] *n (group)* rassemblement *m*

gauge [geɪdʒ] **1** *n (instrument)* jauge *f*; *Fig* **to be a g. of sth** permettre de juger qch **2** *vt* évaluer

gaunt [gɔːnt] *adj* décharné

gauze [gɔːz] *n* gaze *f*

gave [geɪv] *pt of* **give**

gawk [gɔːk], **gawp** [gɔːp] *vi* **to g. at sb/sth** regarder qn/qch bouche bée

gay [geɪ] *(***-er, -est***)* **1** *adj (***a***) (homosexual)* homosexuel, -elle (**b**) *Old-fashioned (cheerful)* gai **2** *n* homosexuel, -elle *mf*

gaze [geɪz] **1** *n* regard *m* **2** *vi* **to g. at sb/sth** regarder fixement qn/qch

GB [dʒiː'biː] *(abbr* **Great Britain***) n* GB

GCSE [dʒiːsiːes'iː] *(abbr* **General Certificate of Secondary Education***) n Br* = diplôme de fin de premier cycle de l'enseignement secondaire, sanctionnant une matière déterminée

gear [gɪə(r)] **1** *n* (**a**) *Fam (equipment)* attirail *m*; *(belongings)* affaires *fpl*; *(clothes)* fringues *fpl* (**b**) *(on car, bicycle)* vitesse *f*; **in g.** *(engaged)* en prise; *Br* **g. lever**, *Am* **g. shift** levier *m* de (changement de) vitesse **2** *vt* **to g. sth to sth** adapter qch à qch; **to be geared up to do sth** être prêt à faire qch ■ **gearbox** *n* boîte *f* de vitesses

geese [giːs] *pl of* **goose**

gel [dʒel] *n* gel *m*

gelatin(e) [*Br* 'dʒelətiːn, *Am* -tən] *n* gélatine *f*

gem [dʒem] *n (stone)* pierre *f* précieuse; *Fig (person)* perle *f*; *Fig (thing)* bijou *m (pl* -oux)

gen [dʒen] *Br Fam* **1** *n (information)*

tuyaux *mpl* **2** *(pt & pp* **-nn-)** *vi* **to g. up on sb/sth** se rancarder sur qn/qch

gender ['dʒendə(r)] *n (in grammar)* genre *m; (of person)* sexe *m*

gene [dʒiːn] *n Biol* gène *m*

general ['dʒenərəl] **1** *adj* général; **in g.** en général; **the g. public** le grand public; *Am* **g. delivery** poste *f* restante **2** *n Mil* général *m*

generalize ['dʒenərəlaız] *vi* généraliser ■ **generalization** [-'zeıʃən] *n* généralisation *f*

generally ['dʒenərəlı] *adv* généralement; **g. speaking** de manière générale

generate ['dʒenəreıt] *vt (fear, hope, unemployment)* engendrer; *(heat, electricity)* produire; *(interest, ideas)* faire naître; *(jobs)* créer

generation [dʒenə'reıʃən] *n (of people, products)* génération *f; (of electricity)* production *f;* **g. gap** conflit *m* des générations

generator ['dʒenəreıtə(r)] *n* générateur *m*

generosity [dʒenə'rɒsıtı] *n* générosité *f*

generously ['dʒenərəslı] *adv* généreusement

genesis ['dʒenəsıs] *n* genèse *f*

genetic [dʒı'netık] *adj* génétique; **g. engineering** génie *m* génétique ■ **genetically** *adv* **g. modified** génétiquement modifié ■ **genetics** *n* génétique *f*

Geneva [dʒı'niːvə] *n* Genève *m ou f*

genitals ['dʒenıtəlz] *npl* organes *mpl* génitaux

genius ['dʒiːnıəs] *n (ability, person)* génie *m*

gent [dʒent] *n Br Fam* monsieur *m;* **gents' shoes** chaussures *fpl* pour hommes; **the gents** *(toilet)* les toilettes *fpl* des hommes

gentle ['dʒentəl] *(-er, -est) adj (person, sound, slope)* doux (*f* douce); *(hint)* discret, -ète; *(exercise, speed)* modéré ■ **gently** *adv* doucement; *(land)* en douceur

gentleman ['dʒentəlmən] *(pl* **-men)** *n* monsieur *m; (well-bred)* gentleman *m*

genuine ['dʒenjuın] *adj (leather, diamond)* véritable; *(signature, work of art)* authentique; *(sincere)* sincère ■ **genuinely** *adv (sincerely)* sincèrement

geography [dʒı'ɒgrəfı] *n* géographie *f* ■ **geographical** [dʒıə'græfıkəl] *adj* géographique

geology [dʒı'ɒlədʒı] *n* géologie *f* ■ **geological** [dʒıə'lɒdʒıkəl] *adj* géologique

geometry [dʒı'ɒmıtrı] *n* géométrie *f* ■ **geometric(al)** [dʒıə'metrık(əl)] *adj* géométrique

geriatric [dʒerı'ætrık] *adj (hospital)* gériatrique

germ [dʒɜːm] *n (causing disease)* microbe *m*

German ['dʒɜːmən] **1** *adj* allemand; **G. teacher** professeur *m* d'allemand; **G. measles** rubéole *f* **2** *n (person)* Allemand, -e *mf; (language)* allemand *m*

Germany ['dʒɜːmənı] *n* l'Allemagne *f*

germinate ['dʒɜːmıneıt] *vi (of seed, idea)* germer

gesticulate [dʒe'stıkjuleıt] *vi* gesticuler

gesture ['dʒestʃə(r)] **1** *n* geste *m* **2** *vi* to **g. to sb to do sth** faire signe à qn de faire qch

GET [get] *(pt & pp* **got,** *Am pp* **gotten,** *pres p* **getting) 1** *vt (obtain)* obtenir, avoir; *(find)* trouver; *(buy)* acheter; *(receive)* recevoir; *(catch)* attraper; *(bus, train)* prendre; *(seize)* prendre, saisir; *(fetch)* aller chercher; *(put)* mettre; *(derive)* tirer *(from* de); *(prepare)* préparer; *(lead)* mener; *(hit with fist, stick)* atteindre; *(reputation)* se faire; *Fam (understand)* piger; *Fam (annoy)* énerver; **to g. sb to do sth** faire faire qch à qn; **to g. sth done** faire faire qch; **to g. sth clean/dirty** nettoyer/salir qch; **to g. sth to sb** *(send)* faire parvenir qch à qn; **to g. sb to the station** amener qn à la gare,

can I g. you anything? je te rapporte quelque chose?

  2 *vi* (*go*) aller (**to** à); (*arrive*) arriver (**to** à); (*become*) devenir; **to g. old** vieillir; **to g. caught/run over** se faire prendre/écraser; **to g. dressed/ washed** s'habiller/se laver; **to g. paid** être payé; **where have you got** *or Am* **gotten to?** où en es-tu?; **you've got to stay** (*must*) tu dois rester; **to g. to do sth** (*succeed in doing*) parvenir à faire qch; **to g. going** (*leave*) se mettre en route; (*start working*) se mettre au travail ■ **getaway** *n* (*escape*) fuite *f* ■ **get-together** *n Fam* réunion *f* ■ **get-up** *n Fam* (*clothes*) accoutrement *m*

▸ **get about** *vi* se déplacer; (*of news*) circuler

▸ **get across 1** *vt sep* (*message*) faire passer **2** *vi* (*succeed in crossing*) traverser; **to g. across to sb that...** faire comprendre à qn que...

▸ **get along** *vi* (*manage*) se débrouiller; (*progress*) avancer; (*be on good terms*) s'entendre (**with** avec); (*leave*) s'en aller

▸ **get around** *vi* = **get about**

▸ **get at** *vt insep* (*reach*) atteindre; **what is he getting at?** où veut-il en venir?

▸ **get away** *vi* (*leave*) s'en aller; (*escape*) se sauver; **to g. away with a fine** s'en tirer avec une amende; **he got away with that crime** il n'a pas été inquiété pour ce crime

▸ **get back 1** *vt sep* (*recover*) récupérer; **to g. one's own back on sb** se venger de qn **2** *vi* (*return*) revenir; **to g. back at sb** se venger de qn

▸ **get by** *vi* (*manage*) se débrouiller

▸ **get down 1** *vi* (*go down*) descendre (**from** de); **to g. down to** (*work*) se mettre à **2** *vt sep* (*bring down*) descendre (**from** de); *Fam* **to g. sb down** (*depress*) déprimer qn **3** *vt insep* **to g. down the stairs/a ladder** descendre l'escalier/d'une échelle

▸ **get in 1** *vt sep* (*stock up with*) faire provision de; **to g. sb in** (*call for*)

venir qn **2** *vi* (*enter*) entrer; (*come home*) rentrer; (*enter vehicle or train*) monter; (*arrive*) arriver; (*be elected*) être élu

▸ **get into** *vt insep* entrer dans; (*vehicle, train*) monter dans; (*habit*) prendre; **to g. into bed/a rage** se mettre au lit/en colère

▸ **get off 1** *vt sep* (*remove*) enlever; (*send*) expédier; (*in court*) faire acquitter **2** *vt insep* **to g. off doing sth** se dispenser de faire qch **3** *vi* (*leave*) partir; (*from vehicle or train*) descendre (**from** de); (*escape punishment*) s'en tirer

▸ **get on 1** *vt sep* (*shoes, clothes*) mettre **2** *vt insep* (*bus, train*) monter dans **3** *vi* (*enter bus or train*) monter; (*manage*) se débrouiller; (*succeed*) réussir; (*be on good terms*) s'entendre (**with** avec); **how are you getting on?** comment ça va?; **how did you g. on?** (*in exam*) comment ça s'est passé?; **to be getting on (in years)** se faire vieux (*f* vieille); **to g. onto sb** (*on phone*) contacter qn; **to g. on with** (*task*) continuer

▸ **get out 1** *vt sep* (*remove*) enlever; (*bring out*) sortir **2** *vi* sortir; (*from vehicle or train*) descendre (**of** *or* **from** de); **to g. out of** (*obligation*) échapper à; (*danger*) se tirer de; (*habit*) perdre

▸ **get over 1** *vt sep* (*ideas*) faire passer; **let's g. it over with** finissons-en **2** *vt insep* (*illness*) se remettre de; (*shock*) revenir de

▸ **get round 1** *vt insep* (*obstacle*) contourner **2** *vi* (*visit*) passer; **to g. round to doing sth** trouver le temps de faire qch

▸ **get through 1** *vt sep* (*communicate*) **to g. sth through to sb** faire comprendre qch à qn **2** *vt insep* (*hole*) passer par; (*task*) venir à bout de; (*exam, interview*) survivre à; (*food*) consommer **3** *vi* (*pass*) passer; (*pass exam*) être reçu; **to g. through to sb** *(communicate with)* se faire comprendre de qn; *(on the phone)* obtenir la communication avec qn

▶ **get together** *vi (of people)* se réunir

▶ **get up 1** *vt sep* to g. sb up *(out of bed)* faire lever qn; to g. sth up *(bring up)* monter qch **2** *vt insep (ladder, stairs)* monter **3** *vi (rise, stand up)* se lever (**from** de); to g. up to something *or* to mischief faire des bêtises; where have you got up to? *(in book)* où en es-tu?

ghastly [ˈgɑːstlɪ] (**-ier, -iest**) *adj (horrible)* épouvantable

gherkin [ˈgɜːkɪn] *n* cornichon *m*

ghetto [ˈgetəʊ] (*pl* **-oes** *or* **-os**) *n* ghetto *m*; *Fam* **g. blaster** radiocassette *f*

ghost [gəʊst] *n* fantôme *m*; **g. story** histoire *f* de fantômes ■ **ghostly** *adj* spectral

giant [ˈdʒaɪənt] **1** *adj (tree, packet)* géant **2** *n* géant *m*

gibe [dʒaɪb] **1** *n* moquerie *f* **2** *vi* to g. at sb se moquer de qn

giddy [ˈgɪdɪ] (**-ier, -iest**) *adj* to be *or* feel g. avoir le vertige; to make sb g. donner le vertige à qn

gift [gɪft] *n* cadeau *m*; *(talent, donation)* don *m*; *Br* **g. voucher** *or* **token** chèque-cadeau *m* ■ **gifted** *adj* doué (**with** de; **for** pour)

gift-wrapped [ˈgɪftræpt] *adj* sous paquet-cadeau

gig [gɪg] *n Fam (pop concert)* concert *m*

gigantic [dʒaɪˈgæntɪk] *adj* gigantesque

giggle [ˈgɪgəl] **1** *n* petit rire *m* bête **2** *vi* rire *(bêtement)*

gilt [gɪlt] **1** *adj* doré **2** *n* dorure *f*

gimmick [ˈgɪmɪk] *n (trick, object)* truc *m*

gin [dʒɪn] *n (drink)* gin *m*

ginger [ˈdʒɪndʒə(r)] **1** *adj (hair)* roux (*f* rousse) **2** *n (spice)* gingembre *m*; **g. beer** limonade *f* au gingembre ■ **gingerbread** *n* pain *m* d'épice

gipsy [ˈdʒɪpsɪ] (*pl* **-ies**) *n* bohémien,

-enne *mf*; *(Eastern European)* tsigane *mf*; *(Spanish)* gitan, -e *mf*

giraffe [dʒɪˈrɑːf, *Br* dʒɪˈrɑːf] *n* girafe *f*

girl [gɜːl] *n (child)* (petite) fille *f*, fillette *f*; *(young woman)* jeune fille *f*; **English g.** jeune Anglaise *f*; **G. Guide** éclaireuse *f* ■ **girlfriend** *n (of girl)* amie *f*; *(of boy)* petite amie *f* ■ **girlish** *adj* de jeune fille

giro [ˈdʒaɪrəʊ] (*pl* **-os**) *n Br* bank g. virement *m* bancaire; **g. account** compte *m* courant postal, CCP *m*

gist [dʒɪst] *n* to get the g. of sth saisir l'essentiel de qch

GIVE [gɪv] **1** *n (of fabric)* élasticité *f* **2** (*pt* **gave**, *pp* **given**) *vt* donner; *(as present)* offrir; *(support)* apporter; *(smile, gesture, pleasure)* faire; *(sigh)* pousser; *(look)* jeter; *(blow)* porter; to g. sth to sb, to g. sb sth donner *ou* offrir qch à qn; to g. way *(of branch, person)* céder; *(of roof)* s'effondrer; *(in vehicle)* céder la priorité (to à)

3 *vi* (**a**) *(donate)* donner (**b**) *(of shoes)* se faire; *(of support)* céder

▶ **give away** *vt sep (prize)* distribuer; *(money)* donner; *(betray)* trahir

▶ **give back** *vt sep (return)* rendre

▶ **give in 1** *vt sep (hand in)* remettre **2** *vi (surrender)* céder (**to** à)

▶ **give off** *vt sep (smell, heat)* dégager

▶ **give out** *vt sep (hand out)* distribuer; *(make known)* annoncer

▶ **give over** *vi Br Fam* g. over! arrête!

▶ **give up 1** *vt sep (possessions)* abandonner; *(activity)* renoncer à; *(seat)* céder (**to** à); to g. up smoking cesser de fumer **2** *vi* abandonner

given [ˈgɪvən] **1** *pp* of **give 2** *adj (fixed)* donné **3** *conj (considering)* étant donné; **g. that...** étant donné que...

glacier [*Br* ˈglæsɪə(r), *Am* ˈgleɪʃər] *n* glacier *m*

glad [glæd] *adj (person)* content (**of/about** de; **that** que + *subjunctive*) ■ **gladly** *adv* volontiers

glamorous [ˈglæmərəs] *adj (person,*

dress) élégant; (job) prestigieux, -euse

glance [glɑːns] 1 n coup m d'œil 2 vi to g. at sb/sth jeter un coup d'œil à qn/qch

gland [glænd] n glande f

glare [gleə(r)] 1 n (look) regard m furieux 2 vi to g. at sb foudroyer qn (du regard) ■ **glaring** adj (light) éblouissant; (eyes) furieux, -euse; a g. mistake une faute grossière

glass [glɑːs] 1 n verre m 2 adj (bottle) de verre; g. door porte f vitrée ■ **glassful** n (plein) verre m

glasses ['glɑːsɪz] npl (spectacles) lunettes f pl

glaze [gleɪz] 1 n (on pottery) vernis m 2 vt (window) vitrer; (pottery) vernisser

gleam [gliːm] 1 n lueur f 2 vi luire

glean [gliːn] vt (information) glaner

glee [gliː] n joie f

glen [glen] n Scot vallon m

glide [glaɪd] vi glisser; (of aircraft, bird) planer ■ **glider** n (aircraft) planeur m ■ **gliding** n (sport) vol m à voile

glimmer ['glɪmə(r)] 1 n (light, of hope) faible lueur f 2 vi luire (faiblement)

glimpse [glɪmps] 1 n aperçu m; to catch or get a g. of sth entrevoir qch 2 vt entrevoir

glint [glɪnt] vi (of light, eye) briller

glisten ['glɪsən] vi (of wet surface) briller; (of water) miroiter

glitter ['glɪtə(r)] vi scintiller

gloat [gləʊt] vi jubiler (over à l'idée de)

global ['gləʊbəl] adj (universal) mondial; (comprehensive) global; g. warming réchauffement m de la planète ■ **globalization** n Econ mondialisation f

globe [gləʊb] n globe m

gloom [gluːm] n (sadness) morosité f; (darkness) obscurité f ■ **gloomy** (-ier, -iest) adj (sad) morose; (dark, dismal) sombre

glorious ['glɔːrɪəs] adj (splendid) magnifique; (full of glory) glorieux, -euse

glory ['glɔːrɪ] 1 n gloire f; (great

beauty) splendeur f 2 vi to g. in sth se glorifier de qch

gloss [glɒs] 1 n (shine) lustre m; g. paint peinture f brillante 2 vt to g. over sth glisser sur qch ■ **glossy** (-ier, -iest) adj brillant; (photo) glacé; (magazine) de luxe

glossary ['glɒsərɪ] (pl -ies) n glossaire m

glove [glʌv] n gant m; g. compartment (in car) boîte f à gants

glow [gləʊ] 1 n (light) lueur f 2 vi (of sky, fire) rougeoyer; Fig (of cheeks, person) rayonner (with de) ■ **glowing** adj (account, terms, reference) enthousiaste

glue [gluː] 1 n colle f 2 vt coller (to/on à)

glum [glʌm] (glummer, glummest) adj triste

glutton ['glʌtən] n goinfre mf

GM [dʒiː'em] (abbr genetically modified) adj génétiquement modifié

GMT [dʒiːem'tiː] (abbr Greenwich MeanTime) n GMT m

gnat [næt] n moucheron m

gnaw [nɔː] vti to g. (at) sth ronger qch

gnome [nəʊm] n gnome m

GO [gəʊ] 1 (pl goes) n (turn) tour m; (energy) dynamisme m; to have a go at (doing) sth essayer (de faire) qch; at or in one go d'un seul coup; on the go en mouvement; to make a go of sth réussir qch

2 (3rd person sing present tense goes; pt went; pp gone; pres p going) vi (make sound) faire; to go it alone lancer en solo

3 vi aller (to à; from de); (depart) partir, s'en aller; (disappear) disparaître; (be sold) se vendre; (function) marcher; (progress) aller; (become) devenir; (of time) passer; (of hearing, strength) baisser; (of fuse) sauter; (of light bulb) griller; to go well/badly (of event) se passer bien/mal; she's going to do sth (is about to, intends to) elle va faire qch; it's going to rain il va pleuvoir; it's all gone

(finished) il n'y en a plus; **to go and get sb/sth** *(fetch)* aller chercher qn/qch; **to go and see** aller voir; **to go riding/on a trip** faire du cheval/un voyage; **to go to a doctor/lawyer** aller voir un médecin/un avocat; **is there any beer going?** y a-t-il de la bière?; **two hours to go** encore deux heures

▶ **go about 1** *vi (of person)* se promener; *(of rumour)* se répandre **2** *(get on with)* s'occuper de; *(set about)* se mettre à; **how do you go about it?** comment est-ce qu'on procède?

▶ **go across 1** *vt insep* traverser **2** *vi (cross)* traverser; *(go)* aller (**to** à); **to go across to sb('s)** faire un saut chez qn

▶ **go after** *vt insep (chase)* poursuivre; *(job)* essayer d'obtenir

▶ **go against** *vt insep (contradict)* aller à l'encontre de; *(be unfavourable to)* être défavorable à

▶ **go ahead** *vi (take place)* avoir lieu; *(go in front)* passer devant; **to go ahead with sth** entreprendre qch; **go ahead!** allez-y!

▶ **go along** *vi (proceed)* se dérouler; **to go along with sb/sth** être d'accord avec qn/qch; **we'll see as we go along** nous verrons au fur et à mesure

▶ **go around** *vi* = **go about**

▶ **go away** *vi* partir, s'en aller

▶ **go back** *vi (return)* revenir; *(step back, retreat)* reculer; **to go back to sleep** se rendormir; **to go back to doing sth** se remettre à faire qch; **to go back to** *(in time)* remonter à; **to go back on one's promise** *or* **word** revenir sur sa promesse

▶ **go by 1** *vt insep (act according to)* se fonder sur; *(judge from)* juger d'après; **to go by the name of...** être connu sous le nom de... **2** *vi* passer

▶ **go down 1** *vt insep (stairs, street)* descendre **2** *vi* descendre; *(fall down)* tomber; *(of ship)* sombrer; *(of sun)* se coucher; *(of temperature, price)* baisser; *(of tyre, balloon)* se dégonfler; **to**

go down well/badly être bien/mal reçu

▶ **go for** *vt insep (fetch)* aller chercher; *(attack)* attaquer; **the same goes for you** ça vaut aussi pour toi

▶ **go forward(s)** *vi* avancer

▶ **go in** *vi* (r)entrer; *(of sun)* se cacher; *Br* **to go in for** *(exam)* s'inscrire à; **she doesn't go in for cooking** elle n'est pas très portée sur la cuisine

▶ **go into** *vt insep (enter)* entrer dans; *(examine)* examiner

▶ **go off 1** *vt insep (lose liking for)* se lasser de **2** *vi (leave)* partir; *(go bad)* se gâter; *(of alarm)* se déclencher; *(of bomb)* exploser

▶ **go on** *vi* continuer (**doing** à faire); *(travel)* poursuivre sa route; *(happen)* se passer; *(last)* durer; **to go on with** passer à qch; *Fam* **to go on at sb** *(nag)* s'en prendre à qn; *Fam* **to go on about sb/sth** parler sans cesse de qn/qch

▶ **go out** *vi* sortir; *(of light, fire)* s'éteindre; *(of tide)* descendre; *(depart)* partir; *(date)* sortir ensemble; **to go out for a meal** aller au restaurant; **to go out with sb** sortir avec qn; **to go out to work** travailler (hors de chez soi)

▶ **go over 1** *vt insep* (**a**) *(cross over)* traverser; **the ball went over the wall** la balle est passée par-dessus le mur (**b**) *(examine)* passer en revue; *(speech)* revoir **2** *vi* (**a**) aller (**to** à); *(to enemy)* passer (**to** à); **to go over to sb** aller vers qn; **to go over to sb's** *(visit)* faire un saut chez qn

▶ **go round 1** *vt insep* **to go round a corner** tourner au coin; **to go round the shops** faire les magasins; **to go round the world** faire le tour du monde **2** *vi (turn)* tourner; *(make a detour)* faire le tour; *(of rumour)* circuler; **to go round to sb's** faire un saut chez qn; **there is enough to go round** il y en a assez pour tout le monde

▶ **go through 1** *vt insep (suffer, undergo)* subir; *(examine)* passer en revue; *(search)* fouiller; *(spend)* dépenser; *(wear out)* user; *(perform)* accomplir

to go through with sth aller jusqu'au bout de qch **2** *vi* passer; *(of deal)* être conclu

▸ **go under** *vi (of ship)* couler; *Fig (of firm)* faire faillite

▸ **go up 1** *vt insep* monter **2** *vi* monter; *(explode)* sauter; **to go up to sth** *(approach)* se diriger vers qch; *(reach)* aller jusqu'à qch

▸ **go with** *vt insep* aller de pair avec; **the company car goes with the job** le poste donne droit à une voiture de fonction

▸ **go without** *vt insep* se passer de

goad [gəʊd] *vt* **to g. sb (on)** aiguillonner qn

go-ahead ['gəʊəhed] **1** *adj* dynamique **2** *n* **to get the g.** avoir le feu vert; **to give sb the g.** donner le feu vert à qn

goal [gəʊl] *n* but *m* ■ **goalkeeper** *n* gardien *m* de but, goal *m* ■ **goalpost** *n* poteau *m* de but

goat [gəʊt] *n* chèvre *f*

gobble ['gɒbəl] *vt* **to g. (up** *or* **down)** *(food)* engloutir

go-between ['gəʊbɪtwiːn] *n* intermédiaire *mf*

goblet ['gɒblɪt] *n* verre *m* à pied

god [gɒd] *n* dieu *m*; **G.** Dieu; *Fam* **oh G.!, my G.!** mon Dieu! ■ **goddaughter** *n* filleule *f* ■ **godfather** *n* parrain *m* ■ **godforsaken** *adj (place)* perdu ■ **godmother** *n* marraine *f* ■ **godson** *n* filleul *m*

goddam(n) ['gɒdæm] *adj Am Fam* foutu

goddess ['gɒdɪs] *n* déesse *f*

godsend ['gɒdsend] *n* **to be a g.** être un don du ciel

goes [gəʊz] *3rd person sing present tense & npl of* **go**

goggles ['gɒgəlz] *npl* lunettes *fpl (de protection, de plongée)*

going ['gəʊɪŋ] **1** *n* **it's hard** *or* **heavy g.** c'est difficile **2** *adj* **the g. rate** le tarif en vigueur; **a g. concern** une affaire qui tourne ■ **goings-on** *npl Pej* activités *fpl*

go-kart ['gəʊkɑːt] *n (for racing)* kart *m*

gold [gəʊld] **1** *n or m* **2** *adj (watch)* en or; *(coin, dust)* d'or; **g. medal** *(in sport)* médaille *f* d'or ■ **golden** *adj (of gold colour)* doré; **g. rule** règle *f* d'or ■ **goldmine** *n* mine *f* d'or ■ **gold-plated** *adj* plaqué or ■ **goldsmith** *n* orfèvre *m*

goldfish ['gəʊldfɪʃ] *n* poisson *m* rouge

golf [gɒlf] *n* golf *m*; **g. club** *(stick, association)* club *m* de golf; **g. course** parcours *m* de golf ■ **golfer** *n* golfeur, -euse *mf*

gone [gɒn] **1** *pp of* **go 2** *adj Br Fam* **it's g. two** il est plus de deux heures

gong [gɒŋ] *n* gong *m*

GOOD [gʊd] **1** (**better, best**) *adj* bon *(f* bonne); *(kind)* gentil, -ille; *(well-behaved)* sage; **my g. friend** mon cher ami; **g.!** bon!, bien!; **very g.!** *(all right)* très bien!; **that isn't g. enough** *(bad)* ça ne va pas; *(not sufficient)* ça ne suffit pas; **that's g. of you** c'est gentil de ta part; **to taste g.** avoir bon goût; **to feel g.** se sentir bien; **to have g. weather** avoir beau temps; **to be g. at French** être bon en français; **to be g. at swimming/telling jokes** savoir bien nager/raconter des blagues; **to be g. with children** savoir s'y prendre avec les enfants; **a g. many, a g. deal (of)** beaucoup (de); **as g. as** *(almost)* pratiquement; **g. afternoon, g. morning** bonjour; *(on leaving someone)* au revoir; **g. evening** bonsoir; **g. night** bonsoir; *(before going to bed)* bonne nuit

2 *n (advantage, virtue)* bien *m*; **for her (own) g.** pour son bien; **for the g. of your family/career** pour ta famille/carrière; **it will do you (some) g.** ça te fera du bien; **it's no g. crying/shouting** ça ne sert à rien de pleurer/crier; **that's no g.** *(worthless)* ça ne vaut rien; *(bad)* ça ne va pas; **for g.** *(leave, give up)* pour de bon ■ **good-for-nothing** *n* propre-à-rien *mf* ■ **good-looking** *adj* beau *(f* belle)

goodbye [gʊd'baɪ] *exclam & n* au revoir *(m inv)*

goodness ['gʊdnɪs] *n* bonté *f*; **my g.!** mon Dieu!

goods [gʊdz] *npl* marchandises *fpl*; **g. train** train *m* de marchandises

goodwill [gʊd'wɪl] *n (willingness)* bonne volonté *f*; *(benevolence)* bienveillance *f*

goose [guːs] *(pl geese) n* oie *f*; *Br* **pimples** *or Am* **bumps** chair *f* de poule ■ **gooseflesh** *n* chair *f* de poule

gooseberry ['gʊzbərɪ] *(pl -ies) n* groseille *f* à maquereau

gorge [gɔːdʒ] **1** *n (ravine)* gorge *f* **2** *vt* **to g. oneself** se gaver **(on** de)

gorgeous ['gɔːdʒəs] *adj* magnifique

gorilla [gəˈrɪlə] *n* gorille *m*

gormless ['gɔːmləs] *adj Br Fam* balourd

gory ['gɔːrɪ] *(-ier, -iest) adj (bloody)* sanglant

gosh [gɒʃ] *exclam Fam* mince (alors)!

go-slow [gəʊ'sləʊ] *n Br (strike)* grève *f* du zèle

gospel ['gɒspəl] *n* évangile *m*

gossip ['gɒsɪp] **1** *n (talk)* bavardages *mpl*; *(malicious)* cancans *mpl*; *(person)* commère *f*; **g. column** *(in newspaper)* échos *mpl* **2** *vi* bavarder; *(maliciously)* colporter des commérages

got [gɒt] *pt & Br pp of* **get**

Gothic ['gɒθɪk] *adj & n* gothique *(m)*

gotten ['gɒtən] *Am pp of* **get**

gourmet ['gʊəmeɪ] *n* gourmet *m*

govern ['gʌvən] **1** *vt (rule)* gouverner; *(city, province)* administrer; *(influence)* déterminer **2** *vi (rule)* gouverner

government ['gʌvənmənt] **1** *n* gouvernement *m*; **local g.** administration *f* locale **2** *adj (decision, policy)* gouvernemental

governor ['gʌvənə(r)] *n* gouverneur *m*; *(of school)* administrateur, -trice *mf*; *(of prison)* directeur, -trice *mf*

gown [gaʊn] *n (of woman)* robe *f*; *Br (of judge, lecturer)* toge *f*

GP [dʒiː'piː] *n (abbr* general practitioner*) n* généraliste *mf*

grab [græb] *(pt & pp -bb-) vt* **to g. (hold of)** sb/sth saisir qn/qch; **to g. sth from sb** arracher qch à qn

grace [greɪs] **1** *n (charm, goodwill, religious mercy)* grâce *f*; *Rel* **to say g.** dire le bénédicité; **ten days' g.** dix jours de grâce **2** *vt (adorn)* orner; *(honour)* honorer **(with** de) ■ **graceful** *adj (movement, person)* gracieux, -euse

gracious ['greɪʃəs] *adj (kind)* aimable **(to** envers); *Fam* **good g.!** bonté divine!

grade [greɪd] **1** *n* **(a)** *(rank)* grade *m*; *(in profession)* échelon *m*; *(quality)* qualité *f*; *Am* **g. crossing** passage *m* à niveau **(b)** *Am Sch (mark)* note *f*; *(year)* classe *f*; **g. school** école *f* primaire **2** *vt (classify)* classer; *Am (exam)* noter

gradient ['greɪdɪənt] *n (slope)* dénivellation *f*

gradual ['grædʒʊəl] *adj* progressif, -ive; *(slope)* doux *(f* douce) ■ **gradually** *adv* progressivement

graduate 1 ['grædʒʊət] *n Br (from university)* ≃ licencié, -e *mf*; *Am (from high school)* ≃ bachelier, -ère *mf* **2** ['grædʒʊeɪt] *vi Br (from university)* ≃ obtenir sa licence; *Am (from high school)* ≃ obtenir son baccalauréat; **to g. from sth to sth** passer de qch à qch ■ **graduation** *n Univ* remise *f* des diplômes

graffiti [grəˈfiːtiː] *npl* graffiti *mpl*

grain [greɪn] *n* **(a)** *(seed, particle)* grain *m*; *(cereals)* céréales *fpl* **(b)** *(in wood, leather)* grain *m*

gram [græm] *n* gramme *m*

grammar ['græmə(r)] *n* grammaire *f*; *Br* **g. school** ≃ lycée *m* ■ **grammatical** *adj* grammatical

gramme [græm] *n* gramme *m*

grand [grænd] **1** *(-er, -est) adj (splendid)* grandiose; *Fam (excellent)* excellent; **g. piano** piano *m* à queue; **g. total** somme *f* totale **2** *n inv Br Fam* mille livres *fpl*; *Am Fam* mille dollars *mpl* ■ **grandchild** *(pl -children) n* petit-fils *m*, petite-fille *f*; **grandchildren** petits-enfants *mpl* ■ **grand(d)ad**

Fam papi *m* ■ **granddaughter** *n* petite-fille *f* ■ **grandfather** *n* grand-père *m* ■ **grandma** *n Fam* mamie *f* ■ **grandmother** *n* grand-mère *f* ■ **grandpa** *n Fam* papi *m* ■ **grandparents** *npl* grands-parents *mpl* ■ **grandson** *n* petit-fils *m*

grandstand ['grændstænd] *n* tribune *f*

granite ['grænɪt] *n* granit *m*

granny ['grænɪ] (*pl* **-ies**) *n Fam* mamie *f*

grant [grɑːnt] **1** *n* subvention *f*; *(for student)* bourse *f* **2** *vt* accorder (**to** à); *(request)* accéder à; *(prayer, wish)* exaucer; *(admit)* admettre (**that** que); **to take sth for granted** considérer qch comme allant de soi; **to take sb for granted** ne pas avoir d'égard pour qn

granule ['grænjuːl] *n* granule *m*

grape [greɪp] *n* grain *m* de raisin; **some grapes** du raisin; **g. juice** jus *m* de raisin

grapefruit ['greɪpfruːt] *n* pamplemousse *m*

graph [græf, grɑːf] *n* graphique *m*; **g. paper** papier *m* millimétré

graphic ['græfɪk] *adj (description)* très détaillé; **g. artist** graphiste *mf* ■ **graphics** *npl* (**computer**) g. graphiques *mpl*

grapple ['græpəl] *vi* **to g. with** *(problem)* se débattre avec

grasp [grɑːsp] **1** *n* (*hold*) prise *f*; (*understanding*) compréhension *f*; **within sb's g.** à la portée de qn **2** *vt* (*seize, understand*) saisir ■ **grasping** *adj (mean)* avide

grass [grɑːs] *n* herbe *f*; *(lawn)* gazon *m* ■ **grasshopper** *n* sauterelle *f* ■ **grassy** *adj* herbeux, -euse

grate [greɪt] **1** *n (for fireplace)* grille *f* **2** *vt (cheese, carrot)* râper **3** *vi (of sound)* grincer ■ **grater** *n* râpe *f* ■ **grating** **1** *adj (sound)* grinçant **2** *n (bars)* grille *f*

grateful ['greɪtfəl] *adj* reconnaissant (**to** à; **for** de); *(words, letter)* de remerciement ■ **gratefully** *adv* avec reconnaissance

gratified ['grætɪfaɪd] *adj (pleased)* satisfait (**by** *or* **with** de; **to do** de faire) ■ **gratifying** *adj* très satisfaisant

gratis ['grætɪs, 'greɪtɪs] *adv* gratis

gratitude ['grætɪtjuːd] *n* gratitude *f* (**for** de)

gratuitous [grə'tjuːɪtəs] *adj (act)* gratuit

grave¹ [greɪv] *n* tombe *f* ■ **gravestone** *n* pierre *f* tombale ■ **graveyard** *n* cimetière *m*

grave² [greɪv] (**-er, -est**) *adj (serious)* grave; *(manner, voice)* solennel, -elle

gravel ['grævəl] *n* gravier *m*; **g. path** allée *f* de gravier

gravitate ['grævɪteɪt] *vi* **to g. towards sth** *(be drawn to)* être attiré par qch; *(move towards)* se diriger vers qch

gravity ['grævɪtɪ] *n* (**a**) *Phys (force)* pesanteur *f* (**b**) *(seriousness)* gravité *f*

gravy ['greɪvɪ] *n* = sauce à base de jus de viande

gray [greɪ] *adj, n & vi Am* = **grey**

graze¹ [greɪz] **1** *n (wound)* écorchure *f* **2** *vt (scrape)* écorcher

graze² [greɪz] *vi (of cattle)* paître

grease [griːs] **1** *n* graisse *f* **2** *vt* graisser ■ **greasy** (**-ier, -iest**) *adj* graisseux, -euse; *(hair, skin, food)* gras (*f* grasse)

great [greɪt] (**-er, -est**) *adj* grand; *(effort, heat)* gros (*f* grosse), grand; *Fam (very good)* génial; *Fam* **to be g. at tennis** être très doué pour le tennis; **a g. deal** *or* **number (of)**, **a g. many** beaucoup (de); **G. Britain** la Grande-Bretagne; **Greater London** le grand Londres ■ **great-grandfather** *n* arrière-grand-père *m* ■ **great-grandmother** *n* arrière-grand-mère *f*

greatly ['greɪtlɪ] *adv* très; *(much)* beaucoup

Greece [griːs] *n* la Grèce

greed [griːd] *n* avidité *f* (**for** de); *(for food)* gourmandise *f* ■ **greedy** (**-ier, -iest**) *adj* avide (**for** de); *(for food)* gourmand

Greek [griːk] **1** *adj* grec (*f* grecque) **2** *n (person)* Grec *m*, Grecque *f*; *(language)* grec *m*

green [griːn] **1** (**-er, -est**) *adj* vert; *Fig (immature)* inexpérimenté; *Pol* écologiste; **to turn** or **go g.** *(of traffic lights)* passer au vert; *(of person, garden, tree)* verdir; *Am* **g. card** ≃ permis de travail **2** *(colour)* vert *m*; *(grassy area)* pelouse *f*; **greens** *(vegetables)* légumes *mpl* vert; *Pol* **the Greens** les Verts *mpl* ■ **greenery** *n* verdure *f* ■ **greengrocer** *n Br* marchand, -e *mf* de fruits et légumes ■ **greenhouse** *n* serre *f*; **the g. effect** l'effet *m* de serre

greet [griːt] *vt (say hello to)* saluer; *(welcome)* accueillir ■ **greeting** *n* accueil *m*; **greetings** *(for birthday, festival)* vœux *mpl*

gregarious [grɪˈgeərɪəs] *adj* sociable

grenade [grəˈneɪd] *n (bomb)* grenade *f*

grew [gruː] *pt of* **grow**

grey [greɪ] **1** *adj* (**-er, -est**) gris; **to be going g.** grisonner **2** *n* gris *m* **3** *vi (of hair)* grisonner ■ **grey-haired** *adj* aux cheveux gris ■ **greyhound** *n* lévrier *m*

grid [grɪd] *n (bars)* grille *f*; *(on map)* quadrillage *m*

griddle [ˈgrɪdəl] *n (for cooking)* tôle *f*

gridlock [ˈgrɪdlɒk] *n (traffic jam)* embouteillage *m*

grief [griːf] *n* chagrin *m*; **to come to g.** échouer

grievance [ˈgriːvəns] *n* grief *m*; **grievances** *(complaints)* doléances *fpl*

grieve [griːv] **1** *vt* affliger **2** *vi* **to g. for sb/over sth** pleurer qn/qch

grill [grɪl] **1** *n (utensil)* gril *m*; *(dish)* grillade *f* **2** *vt* griller

grille [grɪl] *n (bars)* grille *f*

grim [grɪm] *adj* (**grimmer, grimmest**) *(stern)* sinistre; *Fam (bad)* lamentable

grimace [ˈgrɪməs] **1** *n* grimace *f* **2** *vi* grimacer

grime [graɪm] *n* crasse *f* ■ **grimy** (**-ier, -iest**) *adj* crasseux, -euse

grin [grɪn] **1** *n* large sourire *m* **2** *(pt & pp* **-nn-***) vi* avoir un large sourire

grind [graɪnd] **1** *n Fam (work)* corvée *f* **2** *(pt & pp* **ground***) vt (coffee, pepper)* moudre; *Am (meat)* hacher **3** *vi* **to**

to a halt s'immobiliser ■ **grinder** *n* **coffee g.** moulin *m* à café

grip [grɪp] **1** *n (hold)* prise *f*; *(handle)* poignée *f*; *Fig* **to get to grips with sth** s'attaquer à qch **2** *(pt & pp* **-pp-***) vt (seize)* saisir; *(hold)* empoigner; **the audience was gripped by the play** la pièce a captivé les spectateurs ■ **gripping** *adj* passionnant

grisly [ˈgrɪzlɪ] *adj (gruesome)* horrible

gristle [ˈgrɪsəl] *n (in meat)* nerfs *mpl*

grit [grɪt] **1** *n (sand)* sable *m*; *(gravel)* gravillons *mpl* **2** *(pt & pp* **-tt-***) vt* (**a**) *(road)* sabler (**b**) **to g. one's teeth** serrer les dents

groan [grəʊn] **1** *n (of pain)* gémissement *m*; *(of dissatisfaction)* grognement *m* **2** *vi (with pain)* gémir; *(complain)* grogner

grocer [ˈgrəʊsə(r)] *n* épicier, -ère *mf*; **g.'s (shop)** épicerie *f* ■ **groceries** *npl (food)* provisions *fpl* ■ **grocery** (*pl* **-ies**) *n Am (shop)* épicerie *f*

groin [grɔɪn] *n* aine *f*

groom [gruːm] **1** *n* (**a**) *(bridegroom)* marié *m* (**b**) *(for horses)* lad *m* **2** *vt (horse)* panser; **to g. sb for sth** préparer qn pour qch

groove [gruːv] *n (in wood, metal)* rainure *f*; *(in record)* sillon *m*

grope [grəʊp] *vi* **to g. (about) for sth** chercher qch à tâtons

gross [grəʊs] **1** *adj* (**a**) *(total) (weight, income, profit)* brut (**b**) (**-er, -est**) *(coarse)* grossier, -ère; *(injustice)* flagrant **2** *n inv* grosse *f* **3** *vt* gagner brut ■ **grossly** *adv (negligent)* extrêmement; *(exaggerated)* grossièrement; *(unfair)* vraiment

grotesque [grəʊˈtesk] *adj* grotesque

grotto [ˈgrɒtəʊ] (*pl* **-oes** or **-os**) *n* grotte *f*

grotty [ˈgrɒtɪ] (**-ier, -iest**) *adj Br Fam* minable

ground¹ [graʊnd] **1** *n (earth)* terre *f*, sol *m*; *(land)* terrain *m*; *(estate)* terres *fpl*; **grounds** *(gardens)* parc *m*; *Fig (reasons)* motifs *mpl*; **on the g.** *(lying, sitting)* par terre; **to gain/lose g.**

gagner/perdre du terrain; *Br* **g. floor** rez-de-chaussée *m inv*
2 *vt (aircraft)* interdire de vol ■ **grounding** *n (basic knowledge)* bases *fpl* (**in** de) ■ **groundless** *adj* sans fondement ■ **groundsheet** *n* tapis *m* de sol ■ **groundwork** *n* travail *m* préparatoire

ground² [graʊnd] **1** *pt & pp of* **grind 2** *adj (coffee)* moulu; *Am* **g. meat** viande *f* hachée **3** *npl (coffee)* **grounds** marc *m* (de café)

group [gruːp] **1** *n* groupe *m* **2** *vt* **to g. (together)** grouper **3** *vi* se grouper ■ **grouping** *n (group)* groupe *m*

grovel ['grɒvəl] (*Br* -ll-, *Am* -l-) *vi (be humble)* ramper, s'aplatir (**to** devant)

grow [grəʊ] **1** (*pt* grew, *pp* grown) *vt (vegetables)* cultiver; **to g. a beard** se laisser pousser la barbe **2** *vi (of person)* grandir; *(of plant, hair)* pousser; *(of economy, feeling)* croître; *(of firm, town)* se développer; *(of gap, family)* s'agrandir; **to g. to like sth** finir par aimer qch; **when I g. up** quand je serai grand; **it'll g. on you** *(of music, book)* tu finiras par t'y intéresser ■ **grower** *n (person)* cultivateur, -trice *mf* (**of** de) ■ **growing** *adj (child)* en pleine croissance; *(number, discontent)* grandissant

growl [graʊl] **1** *n* grognement *m* **2** *vi* grogner (**at** contre)

grown [grəʊn] **1** *pp of* **grow 2** *adj (man, woman)* adulte

grown-up ['grəʊnʌp] **1** *n* grande personne *f* **2** *adj (ideas, behaviour)* d'adulte

growth [grəʊθ] *n* croissance *f*; *(increase)* augmentation *f* (**in** de); *(lump)* grosseur *f* (**on** à)

grub [grʌb] *n* **(a)** *Fam (food)* bouffe *f* **(b)** *(insect)* larve *f*

grubby ['grʌbɪ] (-ier, -iest) *adj* sale

grudge [grʌdʒ] **1** *n* rancune *f*; **to have a g. against sb** garder rancune à qn **2** *vt* **to g. sb sth** *(give)* donner qch à qn à contrecœur ■ **grudgingly** *adv* à contrecœur

gruelling ['grʊəlɪŋ] (*Am* **grueling**) *adj (journey, experience)* épuisant

gruesome ['gruːsəm] *adj* horrible

gruff [grʌf] (-er, -est) *adj* bourru

grumble ['grʌmbəl] *vi (complain)* grommeler; **to g. about sth** rouspéter contre qch

grumpy ['grʌmpɪ] (-ier, -iest) *adj* grincheux, -euse

grunt [grʌnt] **1** *n* grognement *m* **2** *vti*

guarantee [gærən'tiː] **1** *n* garantie *f* **2** *vt* garantir (**against** contre); *(vouch for)* se porter garant de; **to g. sb that…** garantir à qn que…

guard [gɑːd] **1** *n (supervision)* garde *f*; *(sentry)* garde *m*; *(on train)* chef *m* de train; **under g.** sous surveillance; **on one's g.** sur ses gardes; **on g. (duty)** de garde; **to catch sb off (his/her) g.** prendre qn au dépourvu **2** *vt (protect)* garder **3** *vt insep* **to g. against** *(protect oneself)* se prémunir contre; *(prevent)* empêcher; **to g. against doing sth** se garder de faire qch

guardian ['gɑːdɪən] *n (of child)* tuteur, -trice *mf*; *(protector)* gardien, -enne *mf*

guerilla, guerrilla [gə'rɪlə] *n (person)* guérillero *m*

guess [ges] **1** *n (estimate)* estimation *f*; **to make** *or* **take a g.** deviner; **at a g.** à vue de nez **2** *vt* deviner (**that** que); *(suppose)* supposer, croire **3** *vi* deviner; **I g. (so)** je crois ■ **guesswork** *n* conjecture *f*; **by g.** au jugé

guest [gest] *n* invité, -e *mf*; *(in hotel)* client, -e *mf*; *(at meal)* convive *mf*; **g. room** chambre *f* d'amis; **g. speaker** conférencier, -ère *mf* ■ **guesthouse** *n* pension *f* de famille

guidance ['gaɪdəns] *n (advice)* conseils *mpl*

guide [gaɪd] **1** *n (person)* guide *m*; *(indication)* indication *f*; **g. (book)** guide *m*; *Br* **(Girl) G.** éclaireuse *f*; **g. dog** chien *m* d'aveugle **2** *vt (lead)* guider ■ **guided** *adj (missile)* guidé; **g. tour** visite *f* guidée ■ **guidelines** *npl* directives *fpl*

guild [gɪld] *n* association *f*

guilt [gɪlt] *n* culpabilité *f* ■ **guilty** (**-ier, -iest**) *adj* coupable; **to find sb g./not g.** déclarer qn coupable/non coupable

guinea [ˈgɪnɪ] *n* g. **pig** *(animal) & Fig* cobaye *m*

guise [gaɪz] *n* **under the g. of** sous l'apparence de

guitar [gɪˈtɑː(r)] *n* guitare *f* ■ **guitarist** *n* guitariste *mf*

gulf [gʌlf] *n (in sea)* golfe *m*; *(chasm)* gouffre *m* (**between** entre)

gull [gʌl] *n* mouette *f*

gullible [ˈgʌlɪbəl] *adj* crédule

gulp [gʌlp] **1** *n (of drink)* gorgée *f*; **in or at one go.** d'un coup **2** *vt* **to g. (down)** engloutir **3** *vi (with surprise)* avoir la gorge serrée

gum¹ [gʌm] *n (in mouth)* gencive *f*

gum² [gʌm] **1** *n* (**a**) *(glue)* colle *f* (**b**) *(for chewing)* chewing-gum *m* **2** *(pt & pp* **-mm-)** *vt* coller

gun [gʌn] **1** *n* pistolet *m*; *(rifle)* fusil *m*; *(firing shells)* canon *m* **2** *(pt & pp* **-nn-)** *vt sep* **to g. down** abattre ■ **gunfire** *n* coups *mpl* de feu; *(in battle)* tir *m* d'ar-

tillerie ■ **gunpowder** *n* poudre *f* à canon ■ **gunshot** *n* coup *m* de feu

gurgle [ˈgɜːgəl] *vi (of water)* gargouiller; *(of baby)* gazouiller

gush [gʌʃ] *vi* **to g. (out)** jaillir (**of** de)

gust [gʌst] **1** *n (of wind)* rafale *f* **2** *vi (of wind)* souffler par rafales

gusto [ˈgʌstəʊ] *n* **with g.** avec entrain

gut [gʌt] **1** *n (inside body)* intestin *m*; *Fam* **guts** *(insides)* entrailles *fpl*; *(courage)* cran *m* **2** *(pt & pp* **-tt-)** *vt (of fire)* ravager

gutter [ˈgʌtə(r)] *n (on roof)* gouttière *f*; *(in street)* caniveau *m* ■ **guttering** *n* gouttières *fpl*

guy [gaɪ] *n Fam (man)* type *m*

guzzle [ˈgʌzəl] *vt (eat)* engloutir; *(drink)* siffler

gym [dʒɪm] *n (activity)* gym *f*; *(gymnasium)* gymnase *m*; **g. shoes** chaussures *fpl* de gym ■ **gymnasium** [-ˈneɪzɪəm] *n* gymnase *m* ■ **gymnastics** *n* gymnastique *f*

gynaecologist [gaɪnɪˈkɒlədʒɪst] *(Am* **gynecologist**) *n* gynécologue *mf*

gypsy [ˈdʒɪpsɪ] *n* = **gipsy**

gyrate [dʒaɪˈreɪt] *vi* tournoyer

Hh

H, h [eɪtʃ] *n (letter)* H, h *m inv;* **H bomb** bombe *f* H

habit ['hæbɪt] *n* (**a**) *(custom, practice)* habitude *f;* **to be in/get into the h. of doing sth** avoir/prendre l'habitude de faire qch; **to make a h. of doing sth** avoir pour habitude de faire qch (**b**) *Fam (addiction)* accoutumance *f* (**c**) *(of monk, nun)* habit *m*

habitat ['hæbɪtæt] *n (of animal, plant)* habitat *m*

habitual [hə'bɪtʃʊəl] *adj* habituel, -elle; *(smoker, drunk)* invétéré

hack [hæk] *vt (cut)* tailler

hacker ['hækə(r)] *n Comptr* pirate *m* informatique

hackneyed ['hæknɪd] *adj (saying)* rebattu

had [hæd] *pt & pp of* have

haemorrhage ['hemərɪdʒ] *(Am* **hemorrhage)** *n* hémorragie *f*

haemorrhoids ['hemərɔɪdz] *(Am* **hemorrhoids)** *npl Med* hémorroïdes *fpl*

hag [hæg] *n Pej* **(old) h.** vieille taupe *f*

haggard ['hægəd] *adj* hâve

haggle ['hægəl] *vi* marchander; **to h. over the price of sth** chicaner sur le prix de qch ▪ **haggling** *n* marchandage *m*

Hague [heɪg] *n* **The H.** La Haye

hail¹ [heɪl] **1** *n* grêle *f* **2** *vi* **it's hailing** il grêle

hail² [heɪl] **1** *vt (greet)* saluer *(as* comme); *(taxi)* héler **2** *vt insep* **to h. from** *(of person)* être originaire de

hair [heə(r)] *n (on head)* cheveux *mpl;* *(on body, of animal)* poils *mpl;* **a h.** *(on*

head)* un cheveu; *(on body, of animal)* un poil; **by a h.'s breadth** de justesse ▪ **hairbrush** *n* brosse *f* à cheveux ▪ **haircut** *n* coupe *f* de cheveux; **to have a h.** se faire couper les cheveux ▪ **hairdo** *(pl* **-dos)** *n Fam* coiffure *f* ▪ **hairdresser** *n* coiffeur, -euse *mf* ▪ **hairdryer** *n* sèche-cheveux *m inv* ▪ **hairgrip** *n* pince *f* à cheveux ▪ **hairnet** *n* résille *f* ▪ **hairpin** *n* épingle *f* à cheveux; **h. bend** *(in road)* virage *m* en épingle à cheveux ▪ **hairspray** *n* laque *f* ▪ **hairstyle** *n* coiffure *f*

-haired [heəd] *suff* **long-/red-h.** aux cheveux longs/roux

hairy ['heərɪ] **(-ier, -iest)** *adj (person, animal, body)* poilu

half [hɑːf] **1** *(pl* **halves)** *n* moitié *f;* *(of match)* mi-temps *f; Br (half fare)* demi-tarif *m; Br (beer)* demi *m;* **h. (of) the apple** la moitié de la pomme; **h. past one** une heure et demie; **ten and a h.** dix et demi; **a dozen and a h.** une demi-douzaine; **to cut in h.** couper en deux

2 *adj* demi; **h. board** demi-pension *f;* **h. fare** demi-tarif *m;* **at h. price** à moitié prix

3 *adv (dressed, full, asleep)* à moitié; **h. as much as** moitié moins que ▪ **half-caste** *n* métis, -isse *mf* ▪ **halfday** *n* demi-journée *f* ▪ **half-hearted** *adj (person, manner)* peu enthousiaste ▪ **half-hour** *n* demi-heure *f* ▪ **half-light** *n* demi-jour *m* ▪ **halfopen** *adj* entrouvert ▪ **half-price** *adj & adv* à moitié prix ▪ **half-term** *n Br Sch* congé *m* de milieu de trimestre

■ **half-time** *n (in game)* mi-temps *f*
■ **halfway** *adv (between places)* à mi-chemin *(between* entre)

hall [hɔːl] *n (room)* salle *f; (entrance room)* entrée *f; (of hotel)* hall *m; (mansion)* manoir *m; BrUniv* **h. of residence** résidence *f* universitaire

hallelujah [hælɪˈluːjə] *n & exclam* alléluia *(m)*

hallo [həˈləʊ] *exclam* = **hello**

Hallowe'en [hæləʊˈiːn] *n* = veille de la Toussaint durant laquelle les enfants se déguisent en fantôme ou en sorcière

hallucination [həluːsɪˈneɪʃən] *n* hallucination *f*

hallway [ˈhɔːlweɪ] *n* entrée *f*

halo [ˈheɪləʊ] *(pl* -oes *or* -os) *n* auréole *f*

halt [hɔːlt] **1** *n* halte *f;* **to come to a h.** s'arrêter **2** *exclam* halte! **3** *vt* arrêter **4** *vi (of soldiers)* faire halte; *(of production)* s'arrêter

halve [hɑːv] *vt (reduce by half)* réduire de moitié; *(divide in two)* diviser en deux

ham [hæm] *n (meat)* jambon *m;* **h. and eggs** œufs *mpl* au jambon

hamburger [ˈhæmbɜːɡə(r)] *n* hamburger *m*

hammer [ˈhæmə(r)] **1** *n* marteau *m* **2** *vt (nail)* enfoncer **(into** dans); *(metal)* marteler; *Fam (defeat)* écraser; **to h. sth out** *(agreement, plan)* mettre au point qch

hammock [ˈhæmək] *n* hamac *m*

hamper [ˈhæmpə(r)] **1** *n Br (for food)* panier *m; Am (laundry basket)* panier *m* à linge **2** *vt (hinder)* gêner

hamster [ˈhæmstə(r)] *n* hamster *m*

hand[1] [hænd] **1** *n* **(a)** *(part of the body)* main *f;* **to hold sth in one's h.** tenir qch à la main; **to hold hands** se tenir par la main; **by h.** *(make, sew)* à la main; **on the one h....** d'une part...; **on the other h....** d'autre part...; **to lend sb a (helping) h.** donner un coup de main à qn; **to get out of h.** *(of child)* devenir impossible; *(of situation)*

devenir incontrôlable; **h. in h.** la main dans la main **(b)** *(of clock)* aiguille *f; (in card game)* jeu *m; (style of writing)* écriture *f*

2 *adj (luggage, grenade)* à main; *(cream, lotion)* pour les mains ■ **handbag** *n* sac *m* à main ■ **handball** *n* handball *m* ■ **handbook** *n (manual)* manuel *m; (guide)* guide *m* ■ **handbrake** *n* frein *m* à main ■ **handmade** *adj* fait à la main ■ **handshake** *n* poignée *f* de main ■ **hands-on** *adj (experience)* pratique ■ **handwriting** *n* écriture *f* ■ **handwritten** *adj* écrit à la main

hand[2] [hænd] *vt (give)* donner **(to** à); **to h. sth in** remettre qch; **to h. sth out** distribuer qch; **to h. sth over** remettre qch; **to h. sth round** faire circuler qch

handful [ˈhændfʊl] *n (bunch, group)* poignée *f*

handicap [ˈhændɪkæp] **1** *n (disadvantage, in sport)* handicap *m* **2** *(pt & pp* -pp-) *vt* handicaper ■ **handicapped** *adj (disabled)* handicapé

handicraft [ˈhændɪkrɑːft] *n (skill)* artisanat *m*

handkerchief [ˈhæŋkətʃɪf] *(pl* -chiefs) *n* mouchoir *m*

handle [ˈhændəl] **1** *n (of door)* poignée *f; (of knife)* manche *m; (of cup)* anse *f; (of saucepan)* queue *f* **2** *vt (manipulate)* manier; *(touch)* toucher à; *(deal with)* s'occuper de; *(vehicle)* manœuvrer; *(difficult child)* s'y prendre avec

handout [ˈhændaʊt] *n (leaflet)* prospectus *m; (money)* aumône *f*

handsome [ˈhænsəm] *adj (person, building)* beau *(f* belle); *(profit, sum)* considérable ■ **handsomely** *adv (generously)* généreusement

handy [ˈhændɪ] *(-ier, -iest) adj (convenient)* commode; *(useful)* pratique; *(skilful)* habile **(at** doing à faire); **to come in h.** être utile; **the flat is h. for the shops** l'appartement est près des commerces ■ **handyman** *(pl* -men) *n* homme *m* à tout faire

hang¹ [hæŋ] **1** *n Fam* **to get the h. of sth** piger qch **2** (*pt & pp* **hung**) *vt* suspendre (**on/from** à); (*on hook*) accrocher (**on** *or* **from** à); (*wallpaper*) poser **3** *vi* (*dangle*) pendre ■ **hanging** *adj* suspendu (**from** à); **h. on the wall** accroché au mur ■ **hang-up** *n Fam* complexe *m*
▸ **hang about, hang around** *vi* (*loiter*) traîner; *Fam* (*wait*) poireauter
▸ **hang down** *vi* (*dangle*) pendre
▸ **hang on** *vi* (*hold out*) tenir le coup; *Fam* (*wait*) patienter; **to h. on to sth** garder qch
▸ **hang out 1** *vt sep* (*washing*) étendre **2** *vi* (*from pocket, box*) dépasser; *Fam* (*spend time*) traîner
▸ **hang together** *vi* (*of facts*) se tenir
▸ **hang up 1** *vt sep* (*picture*) accrocher **2** *vi* (*on phone*) raccrocher
hang² [hæŋ] (*pt & pp* **hanged**) *vt* (*criminal*) pendre (**for** pour)
hanger ['hæŋə(r)] *n* (*coat*) **h.** cintre *m*
hang-glider ['hæŋglaɪdə(r)] *n* Deltaplane *m* ■ **hang-gliding** *n* vol *m* libre
hangover ['hæŋəʊvə(r)] *n Fam* gueule *f* de bois
hankie, hanky ['hæŋkɪ] (*pl* **-ies**) *n* Fam mouchoir *m*
haphazard [hæp'hæzəd] *adj* (*choice, decision*) pris au hasard
happen ['hæpən] *vi* arriver, se produire; **to h. to sb** arriver à qn; **do you h. to have…?** est-ce que par hasard vous avez…?
happily ['hæpɪlɪ] *adv* joyeusement; (*contentedly*) tranquillement; (*fortunately*) heureusement
happiness ['hæpɪnəs] *n* bonheur *m*
happy ['hæpɪ] (**-ier, -iest**) *adj* heureux, -euse (**to do** de faire; **about** de); **H. New Year!** bonne année!; **H. Christmas!** joyeux Noël!; **h. birthday!** joyeux anniversaire! ■ **happy-go-lucky** *adj* insouciant
harass [Br 'hærəs, Am hə'ræs] *vt* harceler ■ **harassment** *n* harcèlement *m*
harbour ['hɑːbə(r)] (Am **harbor**) **1** *n*

port *m* **2** *vt* (*fugitive*) cacher; (*hope, suspicion*) nourrir
hard [hɑːd] (**-er, -est**) **1** *adj* (*not soft, severe*) dur; (*difficult*) difficile, dur; (*water*) calcaire; **to be h. on sb** être dur avec qn; **to be h. of hearing** être dur d'oreille; *Fam* **h. up** (*broke*) fauché; *Comptr* **h. disk** disque *m* dur; **h. drugs** drogues *fpl* dures; **h. shoulder** (*on motorway*) bande *f* d'arrêt d'urgence
2 *adv* (*work*) dur; (*pull, push, hit*) fort; (*study*) assidûment; (*rain*) à verse; **to think h.** réfléchir bien; **to try h.** faire de son mieux; **h. at work** en plein travail ■ **hardback** *n* livre *m* relié ■ **hardboard** *n* aggloméré *m* ■ **hard-boiled** *adj* (*egg*) dur ■ **hard-earned** *adj* (*money*) durement gagné; (*rest*) bien mérité ■ **hard-wearing** *adj* résistant ■ **hard-working** *adj* travailleur, -euse
harden ['hɑːdən] **1** *vt* endurcir; **to become hardened to sth** s'endurcir à qch **2** *vi* (*of substance, attitude*) durcir
hardly ['hɑːdlɪ] *adv* à peine; **I had h. arrived when…** j'étais à peine arrivé que…; **h. anyone/anything** presque personne/rien; **h. ever** presque jamais
hardware ['hɑːdweə(r)] *n inv* quincaillerie *f*; Comptr & Mil matériel *m*
hardy ['hɑːdɪ] (**-ier, -iest**) *adj* résistant
hare [heə(r)] *n* lièvre *m*
harm [hɑːm] **1** *n* (*hurt*) mal *m*; (*wrong*) tort *m*; **to do sb h.** faire du mal à qn **2** *vt* (*physically*) faire du mal à; (*health, interests, cause*) nuire à; (*object*) abîmer ■ **harmful** *adj* (*influence*) néfaste; (*substance*) nocif, -ive ■ **harmless** *adj* (*person*) inoffensif, -ive; (*hobby, joke*) innocent
harmonica [hɑː'mɒnɪkə] *n* harmonica *m*
harmonious [hɑː'məʊnɪəs] *adj* harmonieux, -euse
harmonize ['hɑːmənaɪz] **1** *vt* harmoniser **2** *vi* s'harmoniser
harmony ['hɑːmənɪ] (*pl* **-ies**) *n* harmonie *f*

harness ['haːnɪs] **1** *n* (for horse, baby) harnais *m* **2** *vt* (of horse) harnacher; *Fig* (resources) exploiter

harp [haːp] **1** *n* harpe *f* **2** *vi Fam* **to h. on about** sth revenir sans arrêt sur qch

harrowing ['hærəʊɪŋ] *adj* (story) poignant; (experience) très éprouvant

harsh [haːʃ] *adj* (-er, -est) (person, treatment) dur; (winter, climate) rude; (sound, voice) strident; (light) cru; **to be h. with sb** être dur envers qn

harvest ['haːvɪst] **1** *n* moisson *f*; (of fruit) récolte *f* **2** *vt* moissonner; (fruit) récolter

has [hæz] *see* **have**

has-been ['hæzbiːn] *n Fam Pej* has been *mf inv*

hashish ['hæʃiːʃ] *n* haschisch *m*

hassle ['hæsəl] *n Fam* embêtements *mpl*

haste [heɪst] *n* hâte *f*; **in h.** à la hâte; **to make h.** se hâter

hasten ['heɪsən] **1** *vt* hâter **2** *vi* se hâter (**to do** de faire)

hasty ['heɪstɪ] *adj* (-ier, -iest) (departure) précipité; (visit) rapide; (decision) hâtif, -ive ∎ **hastily** *adv* (write, prepare) hâtivement; (say) précipitamment

hat [hæt] *n* chapeau *m*; (of child) bonnet *m*

hatch [hætʃ] **1** *n Br* (in kitchen) passeplat *m* **2** *vt* faire éclore; *Fig* (plot) tramer **3** *vi* (of chick, egg) éclore

hatchback ['hætʃbæk] *n* (car) (threedoor) trois-portes *f inv*; (five-door) cinq-portes *f inv*

hate [heɪt] **1** *n* haine *f* **2** *vt* haïr, détester; **to h. doing** *or* **to do sth** détester faire qch ∎ **hateful** *adj* odieux, -euse

hatred ['heɪtrɪd] *n* haine *f*

haughty ['hɔːtɪ] *adj* (-ier, -iest) hautain

haul [hɔːl] **1** *n* (fish caught) prise *f*; (of thief) butin *m*; **a long h.** (trip) un long voyage *m* **2** *vt* (pull) tirer

haunt [hɔːnt] **1** *n* (place) lieu *m* de rendez-vous; (of criminal) repaire *m* **2** *vt* hanter ∎ **haunted** *adj* (house) hanté

HAVE [hæv] **1** (3rd person sing present tense **has**, pt & pp **had**, pres p **having**) *vt* avoir; (meal, bath, lesson) prendre; **he has (got) a big house** il a une grande maison; **she doesn't h.** *or* **hasn't got a car** elle n'a pas de voiture; **to h. a drink** prendre un verre; **to h. a walk/dream** faire une promenade/un rêve; **to h. a wash** se laver; **to h. a pleasant holiday** passer d'agréables vacances; **to h. flu** avoir la grippe; **will you h. some tea?** est-ce que tu veux du thé?; **to let sb h. sth** donner qch à qn; *Fam* **you've had it!** tu es fichu!; *Fam* **I've been had** (cheated) je me suis fait avoir; **to h. gloves/a dress on** porter des gants/ une robe; **to h. sb over** *or* **round** inviter qn chez soi

2 *v aux* avoir; (with **entrer, monter, sortir** etc & pronominal verbs) être; **to h. decided** avoir décidé; **to h. gone** être allé; **she has been punished** elle a été punie, on l'a punie; **I've got to go, I h. to go** je dois partir, il faut que je parte; **I don't h. to go** je ne suis pas obligé de partir; **to h. sb do sth** faire faire qch à qn; **to h. one's hair cut** se faire couper les cheveux; **he's had his suitcase brought up** il a fait monter sa valise; **I've had my car stolen** on m'a volé mon auto; **I've been doing it for months** je le fais depuis des mois; **you h. told him, haven't you?** tu le lui as dit, n'est-ce pas?; **you've seen this film before – no I haven't!** tu as déjà vu ce film – mais non!; **you haven't done the dishes – yes I h.!** tu n'as pas fait la vaisselle – mais si, je l'ai faite!; **after he had eaten** *or* **after having eaten, he left** après avoir mangé, il partit

▸ **have on** *vt sep* (**a**) (be wearing) porter (**b**) *Br Fam* (fool) **to h. sb on** faire marcher qn (**c**) (have arranged) **to h. a lot on** avoir beaucoup à faire; **to h. nothing on** n'avoir rien de prévu

▸ **have out** *vt sep* (**a**) (have removed) **to h. a tooth out** se faire arracher une dent (**b**) (*resolve*) **to h. it out with sb** s'expliquer avec qn

haven ['heɪvən] *n* refuge *m*

haven't ['hævnt] = **have not**

havoc ['hævək] *n* ravages *mpl*; **to wreak** *or* **cause h.** faire des ravages

hawk [hɔːk] *n* faucon *m*

hay [heɪ] *n* foin *m* ■ **hayfever** *n* rhume *m* des foins ■ **haystack** *n* meule *f* de foin

haywire ['heɪwaɪə(r)] *adj* **to go h.** (*of machine*) se détraquer; (*of plan*) mal tourner

hazard ['hæzəd] **1** *n* risque *m*; *Br Aut* **h. (warning) lights** feux *mpl* de détresse **2** *vt* (*remark*) risquer ■ **hazardous** *adj* dangereux, -euse

haze [heɪz] *n* brume *f*

hazelnut ['heɪzəlnʌt] *n* noisette *f*

hazy ['heɪzɪ] (**-ier, -iest**) *adj* (*weather*) brumeux, -euse; (*photo, idea*) flou

he [hiː] **1** *pron* il; (*stressed*) lui; **he's a happy man** c'est un homme heureux; **he and I** lui et moi **2** *n Fam* **it's a he** (*baby*) c'est un garçon

head [hed] **1** *n* (*of person, hammer*) tête *f*; (*leader*) chef *m*; *Br* (*of school*) directeur, -trice *mf*; (*of bed*) chevet *m*, tête *f*; **h. of hair** chevelure *f*; **h. of state** chef *m* d'État; **h. first** la tête la première; **at the h. of** (*in charge of*) à la tête de; **it didn't enter my h.** ça ne m'est pas venu à l'esprit (**that** que); **heads or tails?** pile ou face?; **per h., a h.** (*each*) par personne

2 *adj* **h. office** siège *m* social; **h. waiter** maître *m* d'hôtel

3 *vt* (*group, firm*) être à la tête de; (*list, poll*) être en tête de; **to h. sb off** détourner qn de son chemin; **to h. sth off** éviter qch

4 *vi* **to h. for, to be heading for** (*place*) se diriger vers ■ **headache** *n* mal *m* de tête; *Fig* (*problem*) casse-tête *m inv*; **to have a h.** avoir mal à la tête ■ **headlamp, headlight** *n* (*of vehicle*) phare *m* ■ **headline** *n* (*of newspaper, TV news*) titre *m* ■ **headlong** *adv* (*fall*) la tête la première; (*rush*) tête

baissée ■ **headmaster** *n Br* (*of school*) directeur *m* ■ **headmistress** *n Br* (*of school*) directrice *f* ■ **head-on** *adv & adj* de front ■ **headphones** *npl* écouteurs *mpl* ■ **headquarters** *npl* (*of company, political party*) siège *m* (social); (*of army, police*) quartier *m* général, QG *m* ■ **headrest** *n* appuie-tête *m inv* ■ **headscarf** (*pl* -scarves) *n* foulard *m* ■ **headstrong** *adj* têtu

headed ['hedɪd] *adj Br* **h. (note)paper** papier *m* à en-tête

header ['hedə(r)] *n* (*in football*) (*coup m* de) tête *f*

heading ['hedɪŋ] *n* (*of chapter, page*) titre *m*; (*of subject*) rubrique *f*; (*printed on letter*) en-tête *m*

heady ['hedɪ] (**-ier, -iest**) *adj* (*wine, perfume*) capiteux, -euse; (*atmosphere*) enivrant

heal [hiːl] **1** *vt* (*wound*) cicatriser **2** *vi* **to h. (up)** (*of wound*) cicatriser

health [helθ] *n* santé *f*; **in good/bad h.** en bonne/mauvaise santé; **h. food shop** *or Am* **store** magasin *m* de produits biologiques; **h. resort** station *f* climatique; *Br* **the (National) H. Service** ≃ la Sécurité sociale

healthy ['helθɪ] (**-ier, -iest**) *adj* (*person*) en bonne santé; (*food, attitude*) sain; (*appetite*) robuste

heap [hiːp] **1** *n* tas *m*; *Fam* **heaps of** (*money, people*) des tas de **2** *vt* entasser; **to h. sth on sb** (*praise, gifts*) couvrir qn de qch; (*insults, work*) accabler qn de qch

hear [hɪə(r)] (*pt & pp* heard [hɜːd]) **1** *vt* entendre; (*listen to*) écouter; (*learn*) apprendre (**that** que); **I heard him come** *or* **coming** je l'ai entendu venir; **have you heard the news?** connais-tu la nouvelle?; **h., h.!** bravo!

2 *vi* entendre; **to h. from sb** avoir des nouvelles de qn; **I've heard of him** j'ai entendu parler de lui

hearing ['hɪərɪŋ] *n* (**a**) (*sense*) ouïe *f*; **h. aid** audiophone *m* (**b**) (*of committee*) séance *f*; (*inquiry*) audition *f*

hearse [hɜːs] *n* corbillard *m*

heart [hɑːt] n cœur m; **hearts** (in card games) cœur mpl; **(off) by h.** par cœur; **at h.** au fond; **h. attack** crise f cardiaque ■ **heartache** n chagrin m ■ **heartbeat** n battement m de cœur ■ **heartbreaking** adj navrant ■ **heartbroken** adj inconsolable

heartening ['hɑːtənɪŋ] adj encourageant

hearth [hɑːθ] n foyer m

hearty ['hɑːtɪ] (**-ier, -iest**) adj (appetite, meal) gros (f grosse)

heat [hiːt] **1** n (**a**) chaleur f; (heating) chauffage m; (of oven) température f; **on a low h.** (cook) à feu doux; **h. wave** vague f de chaleur (**b**) (in competition) éliminatoire f **2** vti **to h. (up)** chauffer ■ **heated** adj (swimming pool) chauffé; (argument) animé ■ **heating** n chauffage m

heater ['hiːtə(r)] n radiateur m

heath [hiːθ] n (land) lande f

heather ['heðə(r)] n bruyère f

heave [hiːv] vt (lift) soulever avec effort; (pull) tirer fort; Fam (throw) balancer

heaven ['hevən] n paradis m, ciel m; Fam **good heavens!** mon Dieu!

heavily ['hevɪlɪ] adv (walk, tax) lourdement; (breathe) bruyamment; (smoke, drink) beaucoup; **h. in debt** lourdement endetté; **to rain h.** pleuvoir à verse; **to be h. defeated** subir une lourde défaite

heavy ['hevɪ] (**-ier, -iest**) adj lourd; (work, cold) gros (f grosse); (blow) violent; (rain) fort; (traffic) dense; (timetable, schedule) chargé; **to be a h. drinker/smoker** boire/fumer beaucoup ■ **heavyweight** n (in boxing) poids m lourd; Fig personnage m important

Hebrew ['hiːbruː] n (language) hébreu m

heck [hek] n Fam zut!; **a h. of a lot** des masses (**of** de)

heckle ['hekəl] vt interpeller ■ **heckling** n chahut m

hectic ['hektɪk] adj (busy) agité;

(eventful) mouvementé

he'd [hiːd] = he had, he would

hedge [hedʒ] **1** n (in garden, field) haie f **2** vi (answer evasively) ne pas se mouiller

hedgehog ['hedʒhɒg] n hérisson m

hedgerow ['hedʒrəʊ] n Br haie f

heed [hiːd] **1** n to pay h. to sth, **to take h. of sth** tenir compte de qch **2** vt tenir compte de

heel [hiːl] n (of foot, shoe) talon m

hefty ['heftɪ] (**-ier, -iest**) adj (large, heavy) gros (f grosse); (person) costaud

height [haɪt] n hauteur f; (of person) taille f; (of mountain, aircraft) altitude f; **the h. of** (success, fame, glory) l'apogée m de; (folly) le comble de; **at the h. of** (summer, storm) au cœur de

heighten ['haɪtən] vt (tension, interest) augmenter

heir [eə(r)] n héritier m; **to be h. to sth** être l'héritier de qch ■ **heiress** n héritière f ■ **heirloom** n a family h. un objet de famille

held [held] pt & pp of hold

helicopter ['helɪkɒptə(r)] n hélicoptère m ■ **heliport** n héliport m

hell [hel] n enfer m; Fam **a h. of a lot (of)** énormément (de); Fam **what the h. are you doing?** qu'est-ce que tu fous?

he'll [hiːl] = he will

hello [hə'ləʊ] exclam bonjour!; (answering phone) allô!

helm [helm] n (of ship) barre f

helmet ['helmɪt] n casque m

help [help] **1** n aide f; Br (cleaning woman) femme f de ménage; (office or shop workers) employés, -es mfpl; **with the h. of sth** à l'aide de qch; **h.!** au secours!

2 vt aider; **to h. sb do** or **to do sth** aider qn à faire qch; **to h. oneself (to sth)** se servir (de qch); **to h. sb out** aider qn; **I can't h. laughing** je ne peux pas m'empêcher de rire

3 vi aider ■ **helper** n assistant, -e m ■ **helping** n (serving) portion f

helpful ['helpfəl] *adj (person)* serviable; *(useful)* utile

helpless ['helpləs] *adj (powerless)* impuissant

helpline ['helplaɪn] *n* service *m* d'assistance téléphonique

hem [hem] **1** *n* ourlet *m* **2** *(pt & pp -mm-) vt (garment)* ourler; **to be hemmed in** *(surrounded)* être cerné **(by** de)

hemisphere ['hemɪsfɪə(r)] *n* hémisphère *m*

hemorrhage ['hemərɪdʒ] *n Am* = **haemorrhage**

hemorrhoids ['hemərɔɪdz] *npl Am* = **haemorrhoids**

hen [hen] *n* poule *f*

hence [hens] *adv* (a) *(thus)* d'où (b) *(from now)* **ten years h.** d'ici dix ans

her [hɜː(r)] **1** *pron* la, l'; *(after prep,'than', 'it is')* elle; **(to) h.** *(indirect)* lui; **I saw h.** je l'ai vue; **I gave it (to) h.** je le lui ai donné **2** *possessive adj* son, sa, *pl* ses

herb [*Br* hɜːb, *Am* ɜːb] *n* herbe *f* aromatique ▪ **herbal** *adj* **h. tea** tisane *f*

herd [hɜːd] **1** *n* troupeau *m* **2** *vt (cattle, people)* rassembler

here [hɪə(r)] **1** *adv* ici; **h. it/he is** le voici; **h. she comes!** la voilà!; **h. is a good example** voici un bon exemple; **I won't be h. tomorrow** je ne serai pas là demain; **h. and there** çà et là; **h. you are!** *(take this)* tenez! **2** *exclam* **h.!** *(giving sb sth)* tenez! ▪ **hereabouts** *adv* par ici

hereditary [hɪˈredɪtərɪ] *adj* héréditaire

heritage ['herɪtɪdʒ] *n* patrimoine *m*

hero ['hɪərəʊ] *(pl* **-oes)** *n* héros *m* ▪ **heroic** *adj* héroïque ▪ **heroine** *n* héroïne *f*

heroin ['herəʊɪn] *n (drug)* héroïne *f*

heron ['herən] *n* héron *m*

herring ['herɪŋ] *n* hareng *m*

hers [hɜːz] *possessive pron* le sien, la sienne, *pl* les sien(ne)s; **this hat is h.** ce chapeau est à elle *ou* est le sien; **a friend of h.** un ami à elle

herself [hɜːˈself] *pron* elle-même; *(reflexive)* se, s'; *(after prep)* elle; **she cut h.** elle s'est coupée

hesitant ['hezɪtənt] *adj* hésitant

hesitate ['hezɪteɪt] **1** *vt* **to h. to do sth** hésiter à faire qch **2** *vi* hésiter **(over** *or* **about** sur) ▪ **hesitation** *n* hésitation *f*

heterosexual [hetərəˈseksjʊəl] *adj & n* hétérosexuel, -elle *(mf)*

hexagon ['heksəgən] *n* hexagone *m*

hey [heɪ] *exclam (calling sb)* hé!, ohé!; *(expressing surprise, annoyance)* ho!

hi [haɪ] *exclam Fam* salut!

hibernate ['haɪbəneɪt] *vi* hiberner

hiccup, hiccough ['hɪkʌp] **1** *n* hoquet *m*; *Fig (in plan)* accroc *m*; **to have (the) hiccups** *or* **(the) hiccoughs** avoir le hoquet **2** *vi* hoqueter

hide¹ [haɪd] *(pt* **hid** [hɪd], *pp* **hidden** [hɪdən]) **1** *vt* cacher **(from** à) **2** *vi* **to h. (away** *or* **out)** se cacher **(from** de)

hide² [haɪd] *n (skin)* peau *f* ▪ **hide-and-seek** *n* **to play h.** jouer à cache-cache

hideaway ['haɪdəweɪ] *n* cachette *f*

hideous ['hɪdɪəs] *adj (ugly)* hideux, -euse; *(horrific)* horrible

hide-out ['haɪdaʊt] *n* cachette *f*

hiding¹ ['haɪdɪŋ] *n* **to go into h.** se cacher; **h. place** cachette *f*

hiding² ['haɪdɪŋ] *n Fam* **a good h.** *(thrashing)* une bonne raclée

hierarchy ['haɪərɑːkɪ] *(pl* **-ies)** *n* hiérarchie *f*

hi-fi ['haɪfaɪ] **1** *n (system, equipment)* chaîne *f* hi-fi **2** *adj* hi-fi *inv*

high [haɪ] **1** *(-er, -est) adj haut; (speed)* grand; *(price, standards)* élevé; *(number, ideal)* grand, élevé; *(voice, tone)* aigu *(faiguë)*; *Fam (on drugs)* défoncé; **to be 5 metres h.** avoir 5 mètres de haut; **it is h. time that you went** il est grand temps que tu y ailles; **h. jump** *(sporting event)* saut *m* en hauteur; **h. school** ≃ lycée *m*; *Br* **h. street** grand-rue *f*; **h. tide** marée *f* haute

2 *adv* **h. (up)** *(fly, throw, aim)* haut **3** *n* **a new h., an all-time h.** *(peak)* un nouveau record ▪ **highchair** *n* chaise *f* haute ▪ **high-class** *adj (service)* de premier ordre; *(person)* raffiné ■ **high-powered** *adj (engine, car)* très puissant; *(job)* à hautes responsabilités ■ **high-profile** *adj (person)* très en vue; *(campaign)* de grande envergure ■ **high-rise** *adj Br* **h. building** tour *f* ■ **high-speed** *adj* ultrarapide; **h. train** train *m* à grande vitesse ■ **high-tech** *adj (appliance)* perfectionné; *(industry)* de pointe

highbrow ['haɪbraʊ] *adj & n* intellectuel, -elle *(mf)*

higher ['haɪə(r)] **1** *adj (number, speed, quality)* supérieur (**than** à); **h. education** enseignement *m* supérieur **2** *adv (fly, aim)* plus haut (**than** que)

highlands ['haɪləndz] *npl* régions *fpl* montagneuses

highlight ['haɪlaɪt] **1** *n (of visit, day)* point *m* culminant; *(of show)* clou *m*; *(in hair)* reflet *m* **2** *vt* souligner; *(with marker)* surligner

highly ['haɪlɪ] *adv (very)* très; *(recommend)* chaudement; **h. paid** très bien payé; **to speak h. of sb** dire beaucoup de bien de qn; *Br* **h. strung** hypersensible

Highness ['haɪnɪs] *n* **His/Her Royal H.** Son Altesse *f*

highway ['haɪweɪ] *n Am (motorway)* autoroute *f*; *Br* **H. Code** code *m* de la route

hijack ['haɪdʒæk] **1** *n* détournement *m* **2** *vt (plane)* détourner ■ **hijacker** *n (of plane)* pirate *m* de l'air

hike [haɪk] **1** *n (walk)* randonnée *f* **2** *vi* faire de la randonnée ■ **hiker** *n* randonneur, -euse *mf*

hilarious [hɪ'leərɪəs] *adj* hilarant

hill [hɪl] *n* colline *f*; *(slope)* pente *f* ■ **hillside** *n* **on the h.** à flanc de coteau ■ **hilly** (**-ier, -iest**) *adj* vallonné

him [hɪm] *pron* le, l'; *(after prep, 'than', 'as') 'it is'*) lui; **(to) h.** *(indirect)* lui; **I saw h.** je l'ai vu; **I gave it (to) h.** je le lui ai donné

himself [hɪm'self] *pron* lui-même; *(reflexive)* se, s'; *(after prep)* lui; **he cut h.** il s'est coupé

hind [haɪnd] *adj* **h. legs** pattes *fpl* de derrière

hinder ['hɪndə(r)] *vt (obstruct)* gêner; *(delay)* retarder; **to h. sb from doing sth** empêcher qn de faire qch ■ **hindrance** *n* obstacle *m*

hindsight ['haɪndsaɪt] *n* **with h.** avec le recul

Hindu ['hɪnduː] **1** *adj* hindou **2** *n* Hindou, -e *mf*

hinge [hɪndʒ] **1** *n* gond *m*, charnière *f* **2** *vt insep* **to h. on** *(depend on)* dépendre de

hint [hɪnt] **1** *n (insinuation)* allusion *f*; *(sign)* signe *m*; *(clue)* indice *m* **2** *vt* laisser entendre *(that* que) **3** *vt insep* **to h. at sb/sth** faire allusion à qn/qch

hip [hɪp] *n* hanche *f*

hippie ['hɪpɪ] *n* hippie *mf*

hippopotamus [hɪpə'pɒtəməs] *n* hippopotame *m*

hire ['haɪə(r)] **1** *n* location *f*; **for h.** à louer; *Br (sign on taxi)* 'libre'; **on h.** en location; *Br* **on h. purchase** à crédit **2** *vt (vehicle)* louer; *(worker)* engager; **to h. sth out** louer qch

his [hɪz] **1** *possessive pron* le sien, la sienne, *pl* les sien(ne)s; **this hat is h.** ce chapeau est à lui *ou* est le sien; **a friend of h.** un ami à lui **2** *possessive adj* son, sa, *pl* ses

Hispanic [hɪ'spænɪk] *Am* **1** *adj* hispano-américain **2** *n* Hispano-Américain, -e *mf*

hiss [hɪs] **1** *n* sifflement *m*; **hisses** *(booing)* sifflets *mpl* **2** *vti* siffler

history ['hɪstərɪ] *(pl* **-ies***) n (study, events)* histoire *f*; **medical h.** antécédents *mpl* médicaux ■ **historian** *n* historien, -enne *mf* ■ **historic(al)** [hɪ'stɒrɪk(əl)] *adj* historique

hit [hɪt] **1** *n (blow)* coup *m*; *(in shooting)* tir *m* réussi; *(success)* succès *m*; *Comptr (visit to website)* hit *m*, contact *m*; **h. (song)** hit *m* **2** *(pt & pp* **hit***, pres p* **hitting***) vt (beat)* frapper; *(bump into)* heurter; *(reach)* atteindre; *(affect)* toucher; *(problem, difficulty)* rencontrer; *Fam* **to h. it off**

s'entendre bien (**with sb** avec qn)
3 *vi* frapper; **to h. back** riposter (**at** à); **to h. out at sb** (*physically*) frapper qn; (*verbally*) s'en prendre à qn; **to h. (up)on sth** (*solution, idea*) trouver qch ■ **hit-and-run** *n* h. driver chauffard *m* (qui prend la fuite) ■ **hit-or-miss** *adj* (*chancy, random*) aléatoire

hitch [hɪtʃ] **1** *n* (*difficulty*) problème *m* **2** *vt* (*fasten*) accrocher (**to** à)
3 *vti* **to h. (a ride)**, *Br* **to h. a lift** faire du stop (**to** jusqu'à) ■ **hitchhike** *vi* faire du stop (**to** jusqu'à) ■ **hitchhiker** *n* auto-stoppeur, -euse *mf* ■ **hitchhiking** *n* auto-stop *m*

HIV [eɪtʃaɪˈviː] *n* (*abbr* **human immunodeficiency virus**) *n* (*virus*) VIH *m*; **HIV positive** séropositif, -ive; **HIV negative** séronégatif, -ive

hive [haɪv] **1** *n* ruche *f* **2** *vt* **to h. off** (*separate*) séparer

hoard [hɔːd] **1** *n* réserve *f*; (*of money*) trésor *m* **2** *vt* amasser

hoarding ['hɔːdɪŋ] *n Br* (*for advertising*) panneau *m* d'affichage

hoarse [hɔːs] (**-er, -est**) *adj* enroué

hoax [həʊks] *n* canular *m*

hob [hɒb] *n* (*on stove*) plaque *f* chauffante

hobby ['hɒbɪ] (*pl* **-ies**) *n* passe-temps *m inv*

hockey ['hɒkɪ] *n* hockey *m*; *Br* (*field hockey*) hockey *m* sur gazon; *Am* (*ice hockey*) hockey *m* sur glace; **h. stick** crosse *f* de hockey

hog [hɒg] **1** *n* (*pig*) porc *m* châtré **2** (*pt & pp* **-gg-**) *vt Fam* monopoliser

hoist [hɔɪst] **1** *n* (*machine*) palan *m* **2** *vt* hisser

HOLD [həʊld] **1** *n* (*grip*) prise *f*; (*of ship*) cale *f*; (*of plane*) soute *f*; **to get h. of** (*grab*) saisir; (*contact*) joindre; (*find*) trouver; **to be on h.** (*of project*) être en suspens; **to put sb on h.** (*on phone*) mettre qn en attente
2 (*pt & pp* **held**) *vt* tenir; (*heat, attention*) retenir; (*post*) occuper; (*record*) détenir; (*title, opinion*) avoir; (*party, exhibition*) organiser; (*ceremony*)

célébrer; (*contain*) contenir; (*keep*) garder; **to h. sb prisoner** retenir qn prisonnier; **to h. one's breath** retenir son souffle; **h. the line!** (*on phone*) ne quittez pas!; **h. it!** (*stay still*) ne bouge pas!; **to be held** (*of event*) avoir lieu
3 *vi* (*of nail, rope*) tenir; (*of weather*) se maintenir ■ **hold-up** *n* (*attack*) hold-up *m inv*; *Br* (*traffic jam*) ralentissement *m*; (*delay*) retard *m*

► **hold back** *vt sep* (*restrain*) retenir; (*hide*) cacher (**from sb** à qn)

► **hold down** *vt sep* (*person on ground*) maintenir au sol; **to h. down a job** (*keep*) garder un emploi; (*occupy*) avoir un emploi

► **hold forth** *vi Pej* (*talk*) disserter

► **hold off 1** *vt sep* (*enemy*) tenir à distance **2** *vi* **if the rain holds off** s'il ne pleut pas

► **hold on 1** *vt sep* (*keep in place*) tenir en place **2** *vi* (*wait*) patienter; (*stand firm*) tenir bon; **h. on!** (*on phone*) ne quittez pas!; **h. on (tight)!** tenez bon!

► **hold on to** *vt insep* (*cling to*) tenir bien; (*keep*) garder

► **hold out 1** *vt sep* (*offer*) offrir; (*hand*) tendre **2** *vi* (*resist*) résister; (*last*) durer

► **hold over** *vt sep* (*postpone*) remettre

► **hold together** *vt sep* (*nation, group*) assurer l'union de

► **hold up** *vt sep* (*raise*) lever; (*support*) soutenir; (*delay*) retarder; (*rob*) attaquer

holdall ['həʊldɔːl] *n Br* fourre-tout *m inv*

holder ['həʊldə(r)] *n* (**a**) (*of passport, degree, post*) titulaire *mf*; (*of record, card, ticket*) détenteur, -trice *mf* (**b**) (*container*) support *m*

hole [həʊl] *n* trou *m*

holiday ['hɒlɪdeɪ] **1** *n Br* **holiday(s)** (*from work, school*) vacances *fpl*; **a h.** (*day off*) un congé; **a** (*public or bank*) **h.**, *Am* **a legal h.** un jour férié; **to be/go on h.** être/partir en vacances **2** *adj* (*camp, clothes*) de vacances ■ **holidaymaker** *n Br* vacancier, -ère *mf*

Holland ['hɒlənd] *n* la Hollande
hollow ['hɒləʊ] **1** *adj* creux (*f* creuse); *(promise)* vain **2** *n* creux *m* **3** *vt* **to h. sth out** évider qch
holly ['hɒlɪ] *n* houx *m*
holy ['həʊlɪ] (**-ier, -iest**) *adj* saint; *(bread, water)* bénit; *(ground)* sacré
homage ['hɒmɪdʒ] *n* hommage *m*; **to pay h. to sb** rendre hommage à qn
home¹ [həʊm] **1** *n* maison *f*; *(country)* patrie *f*; **at h.** à la maison, chez soi; **to feel at h.** se sentir chez soi; **make yourself at h.** faites comme chez vous **2** *adv* à la maison, chez soi; **to go or come (back) h.** rentrer chez soi **3** *adj (cooking)* familial; *(visit, match)* à domicile; **h. address** adresse *f* personnelle; *Br* **h. help** aide *f* ménagère; *Br* **H. Office** ≃ ministère *m* de l'Intérieur; **h. owner** propriétaire *m*; *Comptr* **h. page** page *f* d'accueil; *Br* **H. Secretary** ≃ ministre *m* de l'Intérieur; **h. team** équipe *f* qui reçoit; **h. town** ville *f* natale ▪ **homegrown** *adj (fruit, vegetables)* du jardin; *(not grown abroad)* du pays ▪ **homeland** *n* patrie *f* ▪ **homemade** *adj* (fait) maison *inv* ▪ **homesick** *adj* **to be h.** avoir le mal du pays
home² [həʊm] *vi* **to h. in on sth** se diriger automatiquement sur qch
homeless ['həʊmlɪs] **1** *adj* sans abri **2** *npl* **the h.** les sans-abri *mpl*
homely ['həʊmlɪ] (**-ier, -iest**) *adj (comfortable)* agréable et sans prétention; *Am (ugly)* sans charme
homeward ['həʊmwəd] **1** *adj (trip)* de retour **2** *adv* **h. bound** sur le chemin de retour
homework ['həʊmwɜːk] *n Sch* devoirs *mpl*
homicide ['hɒmɪsaɪd] *n* homicide *m*
homosexual [həʊmə'sekʃʊəl] *adj & n* homosexuel, -elle *(mf)*
honest ['ɒnɪst] *adj* honnête (**with** avec) ▪ **honestly** *adv* honnêtement ▪ **honesty** *n* honnêteté *f*
honey ['hʌnɪ] *n* miel *m* ▪ **honeymoon** *n* voyage *m* de noces

honk [hɒŋk] *vi (of driver)* klaxonner
honorary ['ɒnərərɪ] *adj (member)* honoraire; *(title)* honorifique
honour ['ɒnə(r)] *(Am* **honor) 1** *n* honneur *m*; **in h. of** en l'honneur de; *Br Univ* **honours degree** diplôme *m* universitaire **2** *vt* honorer (**with** de)
honourable ['ɒnərəbəl] *(Am* **honorable)** *adj* honorable
hood [hʊd] *n (of coat)* capuche *f*; *(with eye-holes)* cagoule *f*; *Br (of car, pram)* capote *f*; *Am (car bonnet)* capot *m*
hoof [huːf] *(pl* **hoofs** [huːfs] or **hooves** [huːvz]) *n* sabot *m*
hook [hʊk] **1** *n* crochet *m*; *(on clothes)* agrafe *f*; *(for fishing)* hameçon *m*; **off the h.** *(phone)* décroché **2** *vt* **to h.** (**on** or **up**) accrocher (**to** à) ▪ **hooked** *adj (nose)* crochu; *Fam* **to be h. on sth** être accro à qch
hook(e)y ['hʊkɪ] *n Am Fam* **to play h.** sécher (les cours)
hooligan ['huːlɪgən] *n* hooligan *m*
hoot [huːt] *vi Br (of vehicle)* klaxonner; *(of owl)* hululer ▪ **hooter** *n Br (of vehicle)* Klaxon® *m*
hoover® ['huːvə(r)] *Br* **1** *n* aspirateur *m* **2** *vt (room)* passer l'aspirateur dans; *(carpet)* passer l'aspirateur sur; **to h. sth up** *(dust, crumbs)* enlever qch à l'aspirateur
hop [hɒp] **1** *n (leap)* saut *m* **2** *(pt & pp* **-pp-**) *vi (jump)* sautiller; *(on one leg)* sauter à cloche-pied **3** *vt Fam* **h. it!** fiche le camp!
hope [həʊp] **1** *n* espoir *m* **2** *vt* **to h. to do sth** espérer faire qch; **to h. that...** espérer que... **3** *vi* espérer; **to h. for sth** espérer qch; **I h. so/not** j'espère que oui/non ▪ **hopeful** *adj (person)* optimiste; *(situation)* encourageant; **to be h. that...** avoir bon espoir que... ▪ **hopefully** *adv (with luck)* avec un peu de chance ▪ **hopeless** ['həʊplɪs] *adj* désespéré; *Fam (useless, bad)* nul *(f* nulle) ▪ **hopelessly** *adv (lost)* complètement; *(in love)* éperdument
horde [hɔːd] *n* horde *f*

horizon [hə'raɪzən] n horizon m; **on the h.** à l'horizon ■ **horizontal** adj horizontal

hormone ['hɔːməʊn] n hormone f

horn [hɔːn] n (of animal) corne f; (on vehicle) Klaxon® m; (musical instrument) cor m

hornet ['hɔːnɪt] n frelon m

horoscope ['hɒrəskəʊp] n horoscope m

horrendous [hɒ'rendəs] adj horrible

horrible ['hɒrəbəl] adj horrible

horrid ['hɒrɪd] adj (unpleasant) affreux, -euse; (unkind) méchant

horrific [hə'rɪfɪk] adj horrible

horrify ['hɒrɪfaɪ] (pt & pp -ied) vt horrifier

horror ['hɒrə(r)] n horreur f; **h. film** film m d'horreur; **h. story** histoire f épouvantable

hors d'œuvre [ɔː'dɜːv] (pl inv or **hors d'œuvres**) n hors-d'œuvre m inv

horse [hɔːs] n (a) (animal) cheval m; **to go h. riding** faire du cheval; **h. racing** courses fpl (b) (fruit) marron m ■ **horseback** n **on h.** à cheval; Am **to go h. riding** faire du cheval ■ **horsepower** n (unit) cheval-vapeur m ■ **horseradish** n raifort m

horticulture ['hɔːtɪkʌltʃə(r)] n horticulture f

hose [həʊz] 1 n (pipe) tuyau m 2 vt arroser (au jet d'eau); **to h. sth down** (car) laver qch au jet ■ **hosepipe** n Br tuyau m d'arrosage

hospitable [hɒ'spɪtəbəl] adj hospitalier, -ère (**to** envers) ■ **hospitality** [-'tælɪtɪ] n hospitalité f

hospital ['hɒspɪtəl] n hôpital m; **in h.**, Am **in the h.** à l'hôpital; **h. bed** lit m d'hôpital; **h. staff** personnel m hospitalier ■ **hospitalize** vt hospitaliser

host¹ [həʊst] 1 n (of guests) hôte m; (on TV or radio show) présentateur, -trice mf; **h. country** pays m d'accueil 2 vt (programme) présenter

host² [həʊst] n **a h. of** (many) une foule de

host³ [həʊst] n Rel hostie f

hostage ['hɒstɪdʒ] n otage m; **to take sb h.** prendre qn en otage; **to be held h.** être retenu en otage

hostel ['hɒstəl] n foyer m; (youth) h. auberge f de jeunesse

hostess ['həʊstɪs] n (in house, nightclub) hôtesse f; (air) h. hôtesse f (de l'air)

hostile [Br 'hɒstaɪl, Am 'hɒstəl] adj hostile (**to** or **towards** à)

hostility [hɒs'tɪlɪtɪ] n hostilité f (**to** or **towards** envers); **hostilities** (in battle) hostilités fpl

hot¹ [hɒt] (**hotter, hottest**) adj chaud; (spice) fort; **to be** or **feel h.** avoir chaud; **it's h.** il fait chaud ■ **hotdog** n hot dog m ■ **hotheaded** adj exalté ■ **hotly** adv passionnément ■ **hotplate** n chauffe-plat m; (on stove) plaque f chauffante ■ **hot-water bottle** bouillotte f

hot² [hɒt] (pt & pp -tt-) vi Fam **to h. up** (increase) s'intensifier; (become dangerous or excited) s'envenimer

hotchpotch ['hɒtʃpɒtʃ] n Fam fatras m

hotel [həʊ'tel] n hôtel m; **h. room/bed** chambre f/lit m d'hôtel

hound [haʊnd] 1 n (dog) chien m de chasse 2 vt (pursue) traquer; (bother, worry) harceler

hour ['aʊə(r)] n heure f; **half an h.** une demi-heure; **a quarter of an h.** un quart d'heure; **paid £10 an h.** payé 10 livres (de) l'heure; **10 miles an h.** 10 miles à l'heure; **h. hand** (of watch, clock) petite aiguille f

hourly ['aʊəlɪ] 1 adj (rate, pay) horaire 2 adv toutes les heures; **h. paid, paid h.** payé à l'heure

house 1 [haʊs] (pl -ses [-zɪz]) n maison f; Pol **the H. of Commons/Lords** la Chambre des communes/lords; **the Houses of Parliament** le Parlement; **the H. of Representatives** la Chambre des représentants; **at/to my h.** chez moi; **on the h.** (free of charge) aux frais de la maison; **h. plant** plante f d'intérieur; **h. prices**

prix *mpl* de l'immobilier; **h. wine** vin *m* maison

2 [hauz] *vt* loger; *(of building)* abriter ■ **houseboat** *n* péniche *f* aménagée ■ **housebound** *adj* confiné chez soi ■ **household** *n* ménage *m*; **h. chores** tâches *fpl* ménagères ■ **householder** *n (owner)* propriétaire *mf* ■ **housekeeper** *n (employee)* gouvernante *f* ■ **housekeeping** *n* ménage *m* ■ **houseproud** *adj* qui s'occupe méticuleusement de sa maison ■ **housetrained** *adj Br (dog)* propre ■ **housewarming** *n & adj* **to have a h. (party)** pendre la crémaillère ■ **housewife** *(pl -wives)* *n* ménagère *f* ■ **housework** *n* ménage *m*

housing [ˈhauzɪŋ] *n* logement *m*; *(houses)* logements *mpl*; *Br* **h. estate** lotissement *m*; *(council-owned)* cité *f*

hovel [ˈhɒvəl] *n* taudis *m*

hover [ˈhɒvə(r)] *vi (of bird, aircraft)* planer; **to h. (around)** *(of person)* rôder

hovercraft [ˈhɒvəkrɑːft] *n* aéroglisseur *m*

how [hau] *adv* comment; **h. kind!** comme c'est gentil!; **h. long/high is…?** quelle est la longueur/hauteur de…?; **h. much?, h. many?** combien?; **h. much time?** combien de temps?; **h. many apples?** combien de pommes?; **h. about some coffee?** (si on prenait) du café?; **h. do you do?** *(greeting)* enchanté; *Fam* **h.'s that?, h. so?, h. come?** comment ça?

however [hauˈevə(r)] **1** *adv* **h. big he may be** si grand soit-il; **h. she may do it, h. she does it** de quelque manière qu'elle le fasse; **h. did she find out?** comment a-t-elle bien pu l'apprendre? **2** *conj* cependant

howl [haul] **1** *n* hurlement *m*; **h. of laughter** éclat *m* de rire **2** *vi* hurler; *(of wind)* mugir

HP [eɪtʃˈpiː] *n (abbr* hire purchase*)* *n Br* achat *m* à crédit

hp *(abbr* horsepower*)* CV

HQ [eɪtʃˈkjuː] *(abbr* headquarters*)* *n* QG *m*

hub [hʌb] *n (of wheel)* moyeu *m*; *Fig* centre *m* ■ **hubcap** *n (of wheel)* enjoliveur *m*

huddle [ˈhʌdəl] *vi* **to h. (together)** se blottir (les uns contre les autres)

huff [hʌf] *n Fam* **in a h.** *(offended)* fâché

hug [hʌg] **1** *n* **to give sb a h.** serrer qn (dans ses bras) **2** *(pt & pp -gg-)* *vt (person)* serrer dans ses bras

huge [hjuːdʒ] *adj* énorme

hull [hʌl] *n (of ship)* coque *f*

hullo [hʌˈləu] *exclam Br* bonjour!; *(answering phone)* allô!

hum [hʌm] **1** *n (of insect)* bourdonnement *m* **2** *(pt & pp -mm-)* *vi (of tune)* fredonner **3** *vi (of insect)* bourdonner; *(of person)* fredonner; *(of engine)* ronronner

human [ˈhjuːmən] **1** *adj* humain; **h. being** être *m* humain; **h. rights** droits *mpl* de l'homme **2** *n* être *m* humain

humane [hjuːˈmeɪn] *adj (kind)* humain

humanity [hjuːˈmænɪtɪ] *n (human beings, kindness)* humanité *f*

humble [ˈhʌmbəl] **1** *adj* humble **2** *vt* humilier

humid [ˈhjuːmɪd] *adj* humide ■ **humidity** *n* humidité *f*

humiliate [hjuːˈmɪlɪeɪt] *vt* humilier ■ **humiliation** [-ˈeɪʃən] *n* humiliation *f*

humility [hjuːˈmɪlɪtɪ] *n* humilité *f*

humorous [ˈhjuːmərəs] *adj (book, writer)* humoristique; *(person, situation)* drôle

humour [ˈhjuːmə(r)] *(Am* **humor***)* **1** *n (fun)* humour *m* **2** *vt* **to h. sb** faire plaisir à qn

hump [hʌmp] *n (lump, mound in road)* bosse *f*

hunch [hʌntʃ] **1** *n Fam (intuition)* intuition *f* **2** *vt* **to h. one's shoulders** rentrer les épaules ■ **hunchback** *n* bossu, -e *mf*

hundred [ˈhʌndrəd] *adj & n* cent *(m)*; **a h. pages** cent pages; **two h. pages** deux cents pages; **hundreds of** des centaines de ■ **hundredth** *adj & n* centième *(mf)* ■ **hundredweight** *n Br* = 50,8 kg, 112 livres; *Am* = 45,3 kg, 100 livres

hung [hʌŋ] *pt & pp of* **hang¹**

Hungary ['hʌŋgərɪ] *n* la Hongrie ■ **Hungarian** [-'geərɪən] **1** *adj* hongrois **2** *n (person)* Hongrois, -e *mf*; *(language)* hongrois *m*

hunger ['hʌŋgə(r)] *n* faim *f* ■ **hungry** (**-ier, -iest**) *adj* **to be** *or* **feel h.** avoir faim; **h. for sth** avide de qch

hunk [hʌŋk] *n (piece)* gros morceau *m*

hunt [hʌnt] **1** *n (search)* recherche *f* (**for** de); *(for animals)* chasse *f* **2** *vt (animals)* chasser; *(pursue)* poursuivre; **to h. down** *(animal, fugitive)* traquer **3** *vi (kill animals)* chasser; **to h. for sth** rechercher qch ■ **hunter** *n* chasseur *m* ■ **hunting** *n* chasse *f*

hurdle ['hɜːdəl] *n (fence in race)* haie *f*; *Fig (problem)* obstacle *m*

hurl [hɜːl] *vt (throw)* jeter, lancer (**at** à); **to h. insults** *or* **abuse at sb** lancer des insultes à qn

hurray [hʊ'reɪ] *exclam* hourra!

hurricane [*Br* 'hʌrɪkən, *Am* 'hʌrɪkeɪn] *n* ouragan *m*

hurried ['hʌrɪd] *adj (decision)* précipité; *(work)* fait à la hâte; *(visit)* éclair *inv*

hurry ['hʌrɪ] **1** *n* hâte *f*; **in a h.** à la hâte; **to be in a h.** être pressé; **to be in a h. to do sth** avoir hâte de faire qch; **there's no h.** rien ne presse **2** *(pt & pp* **-ied**) *vt (person)* presser; *(work)* hâter **3** *vi* se dépêcher, se presser (**to do** de faire); **to h. up** se dépêcher; **to h. out** sortir à la hâte; **to h. towards sb/sth** se précipiter vers qn/qch

hurt [hɜːt] **1** *adj (wounded, offended)* blessé **2** *n (emotional)* blessure *f* **3** *(pt & pp* **hurt**) *vt (physically)* faire du mal à; *(causing a wound)* blesser; *(emotionally)* faire de la peine à; *(reputation, chances)* nuire à; **to h. sb's feelings** blesser qn **4** *vi* faire mal; **his**

arm **hurts** son bras lui fait mal ■ **hurtful** *adj (remark)* blessant

hurtle ['hɜːtəl] *vi* **to h. along** aller à toute vitesse

husband ['hʌzbənd] *n* mari *m*

hush [hʌʃ] **1** *n* silence *m* **2** *exclam* chut! **3** *vt (person)* faire taire; *(baby)* calmer; **to h. up** *(scandal)* étouffer ■ **hushed** *adj (voice)* étouffé; *(silence)* profond

husky ['hʌskɪ] (**-ier, -iest**) *adj (voice)* rauque

hustle ['hʌsəl] **1** *n* **h. and bustle** effervescence *f* **2** *vt (shove, push)* **to h. sb away** emmener qn de force

hut [hʌt] *n* cabane *f*; *(dwelling)* hutte *f*

hybrid ['haɪbrɪd] *adj & n* hybride *(m)*

hydrogen ['haɪdrədʒən] *n Chem* hydrogène *m*

hygiene ['haɪdʒiːn] *n* hygiène *f* ■ **hygienic** *adj* hygiénique

hymn [hɪm] *n* cantique *m*

hype [haɪp] *n Fam (publicity)* battage *m* publicitaire

hyper- ['haɪpə(r)] *pref* hyper-

hypermarket ['haɪpəmɑːkɪt] *n* hypermarché *m*

hyphen ['haɪfən] *n* trait *m* d'union ■ **hyphenated** *adj (word)* à trait d'union

hypnotize ['hɪpnətaɪz] *vt* hypnotiser

hypochondriac [haɪpə'kɒndrɪæk] *n* hypocondriaque *mf*

hypocrisy [hɪ'pɒkrɪsɪ] *n* hypocrisie *f* ■ **hypocrite** ['hɪpəkrɪt] *n* hypocrite *mf* ■ **hypocritical** [hɪpə'krɪtɪkəl] *adj* hypocrite

hypothesis [haɪ'pɒθɪsɪs] *(pl* **-theses** [-θɪsiːz]*) n* hypothèse *f* ■ **hypothetical** [haɪpə'θetɪkəl] *adj* hypothétique

hysterical [hɪs'terɪkəl] *adj (very upset)* qui a une crise de nerfs; *Fam (funny)* tordant ■ **hysterics** *npl (tears)* crise *f* de nerfs; *(with laughter)* crise *f* de nerfs; **to be in h.** avoir une crise de nerfs; *(with laughter)* être écroulé de rire

Ii

I¹, i [aɪ] *n (letter)* I, i *m inv*

I² [aɪ] *pron* je, j'; *(stressed)* moi

ice¹ [aɪs] **1** *n* glace *f*; *(on road)* verglas *m*; **i. cream** glace *f*; **i. cube** glaçon *m*; **i. hockey** hockey *m* sur glace **2** *vi* **to i. over** *or* **up** *(of lake)* geler; *(of window)* se givrer ■ **iceberg** *n* iceberg *m* ■ **icebox** *n Am (fridge)* réfrigérateur *m*; *Br (in fridge)* freezer *m* ■ **iced** *adj (tea, coffee)* glacé ■ **ice-skating** *n* patinage *m* (sur glace)

ice² [aɪs] *vt Br (cake)* glacer ■ **icing** *n Br (on cake)* glaçage *m*

Iceland [ˈaɪslənd] *n* l'Islande *f* ■ **Icelandic** [-ˈlændɪk] *adj* islandais

icicle [ˈaɪsɪkəl] *n* glaçon *m (de gouttière etc)*

icon [ˈaɪkɒn] *n* icône *f*

icy [ˈaɪsɪ] **(-ier, -iest)** *adj (road)* verglacé; *(water, hands)* glacé

ID [aɪˈdiː] *n* pièce *f* d'identité

I'd [aɪd] = **I had, I would**

idea [aɪˈdɪə] *n* idée *f*; **I have an i. that…** j'ai l'impression que…

ideal [aɪˈdɪəl] *adj & n* idéal *(m)*

idealistic [aɪdɪəˈlɪstɪk] *adj* idéaliste

ideally [aɪˈdɪəlɪ] *adv* idéalement; **i., we should stay** l'idéal, ce serait que nous restions

identical [aɪˈdentɪkəl] *adj* identique (**to** *or* **with** à)

identify [aɪˈdentɪfaɪ] *(pt & pp* **-ied)** *vt* identifier; **to i. (oneself) with** s'identifier avec ■ **identification** [-fɪˈkeɪʃən] *n* identification *f*; **to have (some) i.** *(document)* avoir une pièce d'identité

identity [aɪˈdentɪtɪ] *(pl* **-ies)** *n* identité *f*; **i. card** carte *f* d'identité

ideology [aɪdɪˈɒlədʒɪ] *(pl* **-ies)** *n* idéologie *f*

idiom [ˈɪdɪəm] *n (phrase)* expression *f* idiomatique

idiosyncrasy [ɪdɪəˈsɪŋkrəsɪ] *(pl* **-ies)** *n* particularité *f*

idiot [ˈɪdɪət] *n* idiot, -e *mf* ■ **idiotic** [-ˈɒtɪk] *adj* idiot, bête

idle [ˈaɪdəl] **1** *adj (unoccupied)* désœuvré; *(lazy)* oisif, -ive; *(rumour)* sans fondement; **to lie i.** *(of machine)* être au repos **2** *vt* **to i. away** *the or* **one's time** passer son temps à ne rien faire **3** *vi (of engine, machine)* tourner au ralenti

idol [ˈaɪdəl] *n* idole *f* ■ **idolize** *vt (adore)* idolâtrer

idyllic [aɪˈdɪlɪk] *adj* idyllique

i.e. [aɪˈiː] *(abbr* **id est**) c'est-à-dire

if [ɪf] *conj* si; **if he comes** s'il vient; **if so** si c'est le cas; **if not** sinon; **as if** comme si; **if necessary** s'il le faut

ignite [ɪgˈnaɪt] **1** *vt* mettre le feu à **2** *vi* prendre feu ■ **ignition** [-ˈnɪʃən] *n (in vehicle)* allumage *m*; **to switch on/off the i.** mettre/couper le contact; **i. key** clef *f* de contact

ignorance [ˈɪgnərəns] *n* ignorance *f* (**of** de) ■ **ignorant** *adj* ignorant (**of** de)

ignore [ɪgˈnɔː(r)] *vt* ignorer

I'll [aɪl] = **I will, I shall**

ill [ɪl] **1** *adj (sick)* malade; *(bad)* mauvais; **i. will** malveillance *f* **2** *npl* **ills** maux *mpl* **3** *adv* mal ■ **ill-advised** *adj (person)* malavisé ■ **ill-informed** *adj* mal renseigné ■ **ill-mannered** *adj* mal élevé

illegal [ɪˈliːgəl] *adj* illégal

illegible [ɪˈledʒəbəl] *adj* illisible

illegitimate [ɪlɪˈdʒɪtɪmət] *adj* illégitime

illicit [ɪˈlɪsɪt] *adj* illicite

illiterate [ɪˈlɪtərət] *adj & n* analphabète *(mf)*

illness [ˈɪlnɪs] *n* maladie *f*

illogical [ɪˈlɒdʒɪkəl] *adj* illogique

illuminate [ɪˈluːmɪneɪt] *vt (monument)* illuminer; *(street, question)* éclairer

illusion [ɪˈluːʒən] *n* illusion *f* (**about** sur)

illustrate [ˈɪləstreɪt] *vt (with pictures, examples)* illustrer (**with** de) ▪ **illustration** *n* illustration *f*

image [ˈɪmɪdʒ] *n* image *f*; **(public) i.** *(of company)* image *f* de marque; **he's the (living** or **spitting** or **very) i. of his brother** c'est tout le portrait de son frère ▪ **imagery** *n* imagerie *f*

imaginary [ɪˈmædʒɪnərɪ] *adj* imaginaire

imagination [ɪmædʒɪˈneɪʃən] *n* imagination *f*

imaginative [ɪˈmædʒɪnətɪv] *adj (plan, novel)* original; *(person)* imaginatif, -ive

imagine [ɪˈmædʒɪn] *vt* imaginer (**that** que) ▪ **imaginable** *adj* imaginable

imitate [ˈɪmɪteɪt] *vt* imiter ▪ **imitation** *n* imitation *f*; *Br* **i. jewellery,** *Am* **i. jewelry** faux bijoux *mpl*

immaculate [ɪˈmækjʊlət] *adj* impeccable

immaterial [ɪməˈtɪərɪəl] *adj* sans importance (**to** pour)

immature [ɪməˈtʃʊə(r)] *adj (person)* immature

immediate [ɪˈmiːdɪət] *adj* immédiat ▪ **immediately 1** *adv (at once)* tout de suite, immédiatement; **it's i. above/below** c'est juste au-dessus/en dessous **2** *conj Br (as soon as)* dès que

immense [ɪˈmens] *adj* immense ▪ **immensely** *adv (rich)* immensément; **to enjoy oneself i.** s'amuser énormément

immerse [ɪˈmɜːs] *vt (in liquid)* plonger; *Fig* **to i. oneself in sth** se plonger dans qch ▪ **immersion** *n Br* **i. heater** chauffe-eau *m inv* électrique

immigrate [ˈɪmɪgreɪt] *vi* immigrer ▪ **immigrant** *adj & n* immigré, -e *(mf)* ▪ **immigration** *n* immigration *f*

imminent [ˈɪmɪnənt] *adj* imminent

immobile [*Br* ɪˈməʊbaɪl, *Am* ɪˈməʊbəl] *adj* immobile ▪ **immobilize** *vt* immobiliser

immoral [ɪˈmɒrəl] *adj* immoral

immortal [ɪˈmɔːtəl] *adj* immortel, -elle

immune [ɪˈmjuːn] *adj Med (to disease)* immunisé (**to** contre); *Fig* **i. to criticism** imperméable à la critique ▪ **immunize** [ˈɪmjʊnaɪz] *vt* immuniser (**against** contre)

impact [ˈɪmpækt] *n* impact *m*; **to make an i. on sb/sth** avoir un impact sur qn/qch

impair [ɪmˈpeə(r)] *vt (sight, hearing)* diminuer, affaiblir

impartial [ɪmˈpɑːʃəl] *adj* impartial

impassable [ɪmˈpɑːsəbəl] *adj (road)* impraticable; *(river)* infranchissable

impasse [*Br* æmˈpɑːs, *Am* ˈɪmpæs] *n (situation)* impasse *f*

impassive [ɪmˈpæsɪv] *adj* impassible

impatient [ɪmˈpeɪʃənt] *adj* impatient (**to do** de faire); **to get i. (with sb)** s'impatienter (contre qn)

impeccable [ɪmˈpekəbəl] *adj (manners, person)* impeccable

impede [ɪmˈpiːd] *vt* gêner; **to i. sb from doing** *(prevent)* empêcher qn de faire

impediment [ɪmˈpedɪmənt] *n* obstacle *m*; **speech i.** défaut *m* d'élocution

impending [ɪmˈpendɪŋ] *adj* imminent

impenetrable [ɪmˈpenɪtrəbəl] *adj (forest, mystery)* impénétrable

imperative [ɪmˈperətɪv] **1** *adj* **it is i. that he should come** il faut impérativement qu'il vienne **2** *n (in grammar)* impératif *m*

imperceptible [ɪmpəˈseptəbəl] *adj* imperceptible (**to** à)

imperfect [ɪmˈpɜːfɪkt] **1** *adj* imparfait; *(goods)* défectueux, -euse **2** *adj & n* **i.** *(tense) (in grammar)* imparfait *(m)* ■ **imperfection** [-pəˈfekʃən] *n* imperfection *f*

imperial [ɪmˈpɪərɪəl] *adj* impérial; *Br* **i. measure** = système de mesure anglo-saxon utilisant les miles, les pints etc

impersonal [ɪmˈpɜːsənəl] *adj* impersonnel, -elle

impersonate [ɪmˈpɜːsəneɪt] *vt (pretend to be)* se faire passer pour; *(imitate)* imiter

impertinent [ɪmˈpɜːtɪnənt] *adj* impertinent *(to* envers)

impervious [ɪmˈpɜːvɪəs] *adj also Fig* imperméable *(to* à)

impetuous [ɪmˈpetjʊəs] *adj* impétueux, -euse

impetus [ˈɪmpɪtəs] *n* impulsion *f*

impinge [ɪmˈpɪndʒ] *vi* **to i. on sth** *(affect)* affecter qch; *(encroach on)* empiéter sur qch

implant 1 [ˈɪmplɑːnt] *n Med* implant *m* **2** [ɪmˈplɑːnt] *vt Med* implanter *(in* dans); *(ideas)* inculquer *(in* dans)

implement¹ [ˈɪmplɪmənt] *n (tool)* instrument *m*; *(utensil)* ustensile *m*

implement² [ˈɪmplɪment] *vt (carry out)* mettre en œuvre

implicate [ˈɪmplɪkeɪt] *vt* impliquer *(in* dans) ■ **implication** *n (consequence)* conséquence *f*; *(innuendo)* insinuation *f*; *(impact)* portée *f*; **by i.** implicitement

implicit [ɪmˈplɪsɪt] *adj (implied)* implicite; *(absolute)* absolu

implore [ɪmˈplɔː(r)] *vt* implorer *(sb to do* qn de faire)

imply [ɪmˈplaɪ] *(pt & pp* **-ied)** *vt (insinuate)* insinuer *(that* que); *(presuppose)* supposer *(that* que); *(involve)* impliquer *(that* que) ■ **implied** *adj* implicite

impolite [ɪmpəˈlaɪt] *adj* impoli

import 1 [ˈɪmpɔːt] *n (item, activity)* importation *f* **2** [ɪmˈpɔːt] *vt (goods) & Comptr* importer *(from* de)

■ **importer** *n* importateur, -trice *mf*

importance [ɪmˈpɔːtəns] *n* importance *f*; **to be of i.** avoir de l'importance

important [ɪmˈpɔːtənt] *adj* important **(to/for** pour); **it's i. that...** il est important que... *(+ subjunctive)*

impose [ɪmˈpəʊz] **1** *vt (conditions, silence)* imposer **(on** à); *(fine, punishment)* infliger **(on sb** à qn); *(take advantage)* s'imposer; **to i. on sb** abuser de la gentillesse de qn ■ **imposition** [-pəˈzɪʃən] *n (inconvenience)* dérangement *m*

imposing [ɪmˈpəʊzɪŋ] *adj* imposant

impossible [ɪmˈpɒsəbəl] **1** *adj* impossible **(to do** à faire); **it is i. (for us) to do it** il (nous) est impossible de le faire **2** *n* **to do the i.** faire l'impossible ■ **impossibility** *(pl* **-ies)** *n* impossibilité *f*

impostor [ɪmˈpɒstə(r)] *n* imposteur *m*

impotent [ˈɪmpətənt] *adj* impuissant

impound [ɪmˈpaʊnd] *vt (of police)* saisir; *(vehicle)* mettre à la fourrière

impoverished [ɪmˈpɒvərɪʃd] *adj* appauvri

impractical [ɪmˈpræktɪkəl] *adj* peu réaliste

imprecise [ɪmprɪˈsaɪs] *adj* imprécis

impregnate [ˈɪmpregneɪt] *vt (soak)* imprégner **(with** de)

impress [ɪmˈpres] *vt (person)* impressionner; **to be impressed with** *or* **by sb/sth** être impressionné par qn/qch

impression [ɪmˈpreʃən] *n* impression *f*; **to be under** *or* **have the i. that...** avoir l'impression que...; **to make a good/bad i. on sb** faire une bonne/mauvaise impression à qn ■ **impressionable** *adj (person)* impressionnable

impressionist [ɪmˈpreʃənɪst] *n (mimic)* imitateur, -trice *mf*

impressive [ɪmˈpresɪv] *adj* impressionnant

imprint 1 [ˈɪmprɪnt] *n* empreinte *f* **2** [ɪmˈprɪnt] *vt* imprimer

imprison [ɪmˈprɪzən] *vt* emprisonner

■ **imprisonment** *n* emprisonnement *m*; **life i.** la prison à vie

improbable [ɪmˈprɒbəbəl] *adj (unlikely)* improbable; *(unbelievable)* invraisemblable

impromptu [ɪmˈprɒmptjuː] *adj (speech, party)* improvisé

improper [ɪmˈprɒpə(r)] *adj* (a) *(indecent)* indécent (b) *(use, purpose)* mauvais; *(behaviour)* déplacé

improve [ɪmˈpruːv] **1** *vt* améliorer; *(technique, invention)* perfectionner; **to i. one's English** se perfectionner en anglais **2** *vi* s'améliorer; *(of business)* reprendre ■ **improvement** *n* amélioration *f* (**in** de); *(progress)* progrès *mpl*; **to be an i. on sth** *(be better than)* être meilleur que qch

improvise [ˈɪmprəvaɪz] *vti* improviser ■ **improvisation** *n* improvisation *f*

impudent [ˈɪmpjʊdənt] *adj* impudent

impulse [ˈɪmpʌls] *n* impulsion *f*; **on i.** sur un coup de tête ■ **impulsive** *adj (person)* impulsif, -ive

impunity [ɪmˈpjuːnɪtɪ] *n* **with i.** impunément

impurity [ɪmˈpjʊərətɪ] *(pl -ies)* *n* impureté *f*

IN [ɪn] **1** *prep* (a) dans; **in the box/the school** dans la boîte/l'école; **in an hour's (time)** dans une heure; **in so far as** dans la mesure où

(b) à; **in school** à l'école; **in Paris** à Paris; **in the USA** aux USA; **in pencil** au crayon; **in spring** au printemps; **the woman in the red dress** la femme à la robe rouge

(c) en; **in summer/French** en été/français; **in Spain** en Espagne; **in May** en mai; **in 2001** en 2001; **in an hour** *(during an hour)* en une heure; **in doing sth** en faisant qch; **dressed in black** habillé en noir

(d) de; **in a soft voice** d'une voix douce; **the best in the class** le meilleur/la meilleure de la classe; **an increase in salary** une augmentation de salaire; **at six in the evening** à six heures du soir

(e) chez; **in children/animals** chez les enfants/les animaux; **in Shakespeare** chez Shakespeare

(f) **in the morning** le matin; **he hasn't done it in months** ça fait des mois qu'il ne l'a pas fait; **one in ten** un sur dix; **in tens** dix par dix; **in hundreds/thousands** par centaines/milliers; **in here** ici; **in there** là-dedans

2 *adv* **to be in** *(home)* être là; *(of train)* être arrivé; *(in fashion)* être en vogue; *(in power)* être au pouvoir; **day in, day out** jour après jour; **in on a secret** au courant d'un secret; **we're in for some rain/trouble** on va avoir de la pluie/des ennuis

3 *npl* **the ins and outs of** les moindres détails de

in- [ɪn] *pref* in-

inability [ɪnəˈbɪlɪtɪ] *(pl -ies)* *n* incapacité *f* (**to do** de faire)

inaccessible [ɪnəkˈsesəbəl] *adj* inaccessible

inaccurate [ɪnˈækjʊrət] *adj* inexact

inadequate [ɪnˈædɪkwət] *adj (quantity)* insuffisant; *(person)* pas à la hauteur; *(work)* médiocre

inadmissible [ɪnədˈmɪsəbəl] *adj* inadmissible

inadvertently [ɪnədˈvɜːtəntlɪ] *adv* par inadvertance

inadvisable [ɪnədˈvaɪzəbəl] *adj* **it is i. to go out alone** il est déconseillé de sortir seul

inanimate [ɪnˈænɪmət] *adj* inanimé

inappropriate [ɪnəˈprəʊprɪət] *adj (unsuitable) (place, clothes)* peu approprié; *(remark, moment)* inopportun

inarticulate [ɪnɑːˈtɪkjʊlət] *adj (person)* incapable de s'exprimer

inasmuch as [ɪnəzˈmʌtʃəz] *conj (because)* dans la mesure où; *(to the extent that)* en ce sens que

inattentive [ɪnəˈtentɪv] *adj* inattentif, -ive (**to** à)

inaudible [ɪnˈɔːdɪbəl] *adj* inaudible

inauguration [ɪnɔːgjʊˈreɪʃən] *n* inauguration *f*; *(of official)* investiture *f*

inborn [ɪnˈbɔːn] *adj* inné

Inc (*abbr* **Incorporated**) *Am Com* ≃ SARL

incalculable [ɪnˈkælkjʊləbəl] *adj* incalculable

incapable [ɪnˈkeɪpəbəl] *adj* incapable (**of doing** de faire)

incapacitate [ɪnkəˈpæsɪteɪt] *vt* rendre infirme

incense¹ [ˈɪnsens] *n* (*substance*) encens *m*

incense² [ɪnˈsens] *vt* rendre furieux, -euse

incentive [ɪnˈsentɪv] *n* motivation *f*; (*payment*) prime *f*; **to give sb an i. to work** encourager qn à travailler

incessant [ɪnˈsesənt] *adj* incessant

incestuous [ɪnˈsestjʊəs] *adj* incestueux, -euse

inch [ɪntʃ] **1** *n* pouce *m* (*2,54 cm*); **i. by i.** petit à petit **2** *vti* **to i. (one's way) forward** avancer tout doucement

incident [ˈɪnsɪdənt] *n* incident *m*; (*in book, film*) épisode *m*

incidental [ɪnsɪˈdentəl] *adj* (*additional*) accessoire; **i. music** (*in film*) musique *f* ■ **incidentally** *adv* (*by the way*) au fait

incinerator [ɪnˈsɪnəreɪtə(r)] *n* incinérateur *m*

incision [ɪnˈsɪʒən] *n* incision *f*

incisive [ɪnˈsaɪsɪv] *adj* incisif, -ive

incite [ɪnˈsaɪt] *vt* inciter (**to do** à faire)

inclination [ɪnklɪˈneɪʃən] *n* (*liking*) inclination *f*; (*desire*) envie *f* (**to do** de faire)

incline 1 [ˈɪnklaɪn] *n* (*slope*) pente *f* **2** [ɪnˈklaɪn] *vt* (*bend, tilt*) incliner; **to be inclined to do sth** (*feel desire to*) avoir bien envie de faire qch; (*tend to*) avoir tendance à faire qch **3** [ɪnˈklaɪn] *vi* **to i. to** or **towards sth** pencher pour qch

include [ɪnˈkluːd] *vt* (*contain*) comprendre, inclure; (*in letter*) joindre; **to be included** être compris; (*on list*) être inclus ■ **including** *prep* y compris; **not i.** sans compter; **i. service** service compris

inclusive [ɪnˈkluːsɪv] *adj* inclus; **from the fourth to the tenth of May i.** du quatre au dix mai inclus; **to be i. of**

comprendre; **i. of tax** toutes taxes comprises

incoherent [ɪnkəʊˈhɪərənt] *adj* incohérent

income [ˈɪnkʌm] *n* revenu *m* (**from** de); **private i.** rentes *fpl*; **i. tax** impôt *m* sur le revenu

incoming [ˈɪnkʌmɪŋ] *adj* (*president*) nouveau (*f* nouvelle); **i. calls** (*on telephone*) appels *mpl* de l'extérieur; **i. tide** marée *f* montante

incomparable [ɪnˈkɒmpərəbəl] *adj* incomparable

incompatible [ɪnkəmˈpætəbəl] *adj* incompatible (**with** avec)

incompetent [ɪnˈkɒmpɪtənt] *adj* incompétent

incomplete [ɪnkəmˈpliːt] *adj* incomplet, -ète

incomprehensible [ɪnkɒmprɪˈhensəbəl] *adj* incompréhensible

inconceivable [ɪnkənˈsiːvəbəl] *adj* inconcevable

inconclusive [ɪnkənˈkluːsɪv] *adj* peu concluant

inconsiderate [ɪnkənˈsɪdərət] *adj* (*action, remark*) inconsidéré; (*person*) sans égards pour les autres

inconsistent [ɪnkənˈsɪstənt] *adj* (*person*) incohérent; (*uneven*) irrégulier, -ère

inconspicuous [ɪnkənˈspɪkjʊəs] *adj* qui passe inaperçu

inconvenient [ɪnkənˈviːnɪənt] *adj* (*moment*) mauvais; (*arrangement*) peu commode; **it's i. (for me) to...** ça me dérange de... ■ **inconvenience 1** *n* (*bother*) dérangement *m*; (*disadvantage*) inconvénient *m* **2** *vt* déranger

incorporate [ɪnˈkɔːpəreɪt] *vt* (*contain*) contenir; (*introduce*) incorporer (**into** dans)

incorrect [ɪnkəˈrekt] *adj* incorrect

increase [ɪnˈkriːs] [ˈɪnkriːs] *n* augmentation *f* (**in** or **of** de); **on the i.** en hausse **2** *vt* augmenter **3** *vi* augmenter; **to i. in price** augmenter ■ **increasing** *adj* croissant ■ **increasingly** *adv* de plus en plus

incredible [ɪn'kredəbəl] *adj* incroyable

incredulous [ɪn'kredjʊləs] *adj* incrédule

increment ['ɪŋkrəmənt] *n* augmentation *f*

incriminate [ɪn'krɪmɪneɪt] *vt* incriminer ■ **incriminating** *adj* compromettant

incubate ['ɪŋkjʊbeɪt] *vt (eggs)* couver ■ **incubator** *n (for baby)* couveuse *f*

incur [ɪn'kɜː(r)] *(pt & pp* **-rr-***) vt (expenses)* encourir; *(debt)* contracter; *(criticism, anger)* s'attirer

incurable [ɪn'kjʊərəbəl] *adj* incurable

indebted [ɪn'detɪd] *adj* **i. to sb/for sth/for doing sth** redevable à qn de qch/d'avoir fait qch

indecent [ɪn'diːsənt] *adj (obscene)* indécent

indecisive [ɪndɪ'saɪsɪv] *adj (person)* indécis

indeed [ɪn'diːd] *adv* en effet; **very good i.** vraiment très bon; **thank you very much i.!** merci infiniment!

indefensible [ɪndɪ'fensəbəl] *adj* indéfendable

indefinite [ɪn'defɪnət] *adj (duration, number)* indéterminé; *(plan)* mal défini ■ **indefinitely** *adv* indéfiniment

indented [ɪn'dentɪd] *adj (edge, coastline)* découpé

independence [ɪndɪ'pendəns] *n* indépendance *f*

independent [ɪndɪ'pendənt] *adj* indépendant (**of** de); *(opinions, reports)* de sources différentes ■ **independently** *adv* de façon indépendante; **i. of** indépendamment de

indescribable [ɪndɪ'skraɪbəbəl] *adj* indescriptible

indestructible [ɪndɪ'strʌktəbəl] *adj* indestructible

indeterminate [ɪndɪ'tɜːmɪnət] *adj* indéterminé

index ['ɪndeks] **1** *n (in book)* index *m*; *(in library)* fichier *m*; *(number, sign)* indice *m*; **i. card** fiche *f*, **i. finger** index *m* **2** *vt (classify)* classer

India ['ɪndɪə] *n* l'Inde *f* ■ **Indian 1** *adj* indien, -enne **2** *n* Indien, -enne *mf*

indicate ['ɪndɪkeɪt] *vt* indiquer (**that** que); **I was indicating right** *(in vehicle)* j'avais mis mon clignotant droit ■ **indication** *n (sign)* signe *m*; *(information)* indication *f*

indicative [ɪn'dɪkətɪv] *adj* **to be i. of** *(symptomatic)* être symptomatique de

indicator ['ɪndɪkeɪtə(r)] *n (sign)* indication *f* (**of** de); *Br (in vehicle)* clignotant *m*

indifferent [ɪn'dɪfərənt] *adj* indifférent (**to** à); *(mediocre)* médiocre

indigestion [ɪndɪ'dʒestʃən] *n* troubles *mpl* digestifs; **(an attack of) i.** une indigestion

indignant [ɪn'dɪgnənt] *adj* indigné *(at or* **about** de)

indirect [ɪndaɪ'rekt] *adj* indirect

indiscreet [ɪndɪ'skriːt] *adj* indiscret, -ète

indiscriminately [ɪndɪ'skrɪmɪnətlɪ] *adv (at random)* au hasard; *(without discrimination)* sans discernement

indispensable [ɪndɪ'spensəbəl] *adj* indispensable (**to** à)

indisputable [ɪndɪ'spjuːtəbəl] *adj* incontestable

indistinct [ɪndɪ'stɪŋkt] *adj* indistinct

indistinguishable [ɪndɪ'stɪŋgwɪʃəbəl] *adj* indifférenciable (**from** de)

individual [ɪndɪ'vɪdʒʊəl] **1** *adj (specific, personal)* individuel, -elle; *(specific)* particulier, -ère **2** *n (person)* individu *m* ■ **individually** *adv (separately)* individuellement

indivisible [ɪndɪ'vɪzəbəl] *adj* indivisible

indoctrinate [ɪn'dɒktrɪneɪt] *vt* endoctriner

Indonesia [ɪndəʊ'niːzɪə] *n* l'Indonésie *f*

indoor ['ɪndɔː(r)] *adj (games, shoes)* d'intérieur; *(swimming pool)* couvert ■ **indoors** *adv* à l'intérieur; **to go/come in** rentrer

induce [ɪn'djuːs] *vt (persuade)* persuader (**to do** de faire); *(cause)* provoquer

indulge [ɪn'dʌldʒ] **1** *vt (sb's wishes)* satisfaire; *(child)* gâter **2** *vi* **to i. in sth** *(ice cream, cigar)* s'offrir qch; *(hobby, vice)* s'adonner à qch **▪ indulgent** *adj* indulgent **(to** envers)

industrial [ɪn'dʌstrɪəl] *adj* industriel, -elle; *Br* **to take i. action** se mettre en grève; *Br* **i. estate,** *Am* **i. park** zone f industrielle **▪ industrialist** *n* industriel *m* **▪ industrialized** *adj* industrialisé

industrious [ɪn'dʌstrɪəs] *adj* travailleur, -euse

industry ['ɪndəstrɪ] *(pl* **-ies)** *n (economic sector)* industrie f; *(hard work)* application f

inedible [ɪn'edəbəl] *adj* immangeable

ineffective [ɪnɪ'fektɪv] *adj (measure)* inefficace; *(person)* incapable

ineffectual [ɪnɪ'fektʃəl] *adj (measure)* inefficace; *(person)* incompétent

inefficient [ɪnɪ'fɪʃənt] *adj (person, measure)* inefficace; *(machine)* peu performant

ineligible [ɪn'elɪdʒəbəl] *adj (candidate)* inéligible; **to be i. for sth** *(scholarship)* ne pas avoir droit à qch

inept [ɪ'nept] *adj (incompetent)* incompétent; *(foolish)* inepte

inequality [ɪnɪ'kwɒlətɪ] *(pl* **-ies)** *n* inégalité f

inert [ɪ'nɜːt] *adj* inerte

inescapable [ɪnɪ'skeɪpəbəl] *adj (outcome)* inéluctable; *(conclusion)* incontournable

inevitable [ɪn'evɪtəbəl] *adj* inévitable

inexcusable [ɪnɪk'skjuːzəbəl] *adj* inexcusable

inexpensive [ɪnɪk'spensɪv] *adj* bon marché *inv*

inexperienced [ɪnɪks'pɪərɪənst] *adj* inexpérimenté

inexplicable [ɪnɪk'splɪkəbəl] *adj* inexplicable

infallible [ɪn'fæləbəl] *adj* infaillible

infamous ['ɪnfəməs] *adj (well-known)*

tristement célèbre; *(crime)* infâme

infant ['ɪnfənt] *n* bébé *m*; *Br* **i. school** = école primaire pour enfants de cinq à sept ans

infantry ['ɪnfəntrɪ] *n* infanterie f

infatuated [ɪn'fætʃʊeɪtɪd] *adj* entiché **(with** de)

infect [ɪn'fekt] *vt (wound, person)* infecter; *(water, food)* contaminer; **to get** *or* **become infected** s'infecter **▪ infection** *n* infection f **▪ infectious** [-ʃəs] *adj (disease)* infectieux, -euse

infer [ɪn'fɜː(r)] *(pt & pp* **-rr-)** *vt* déduire **(from** de; **that** que)

inferior [ɪn'fɪərɪə(r)] **1** *adj* inférieur **(to** à); *(goods, work)* de qualité inférieure **2** *n (person)* inférieur, -e *mf* **▪ inferiority** [-rɪ'ɒrɪtɪ] *n* infériorité f

infernal [ɪn'fɜːnəl] *adj* infernal

inferno [ɪn'fɜːnəʊ] *(pl* **-os)** *n (blaze)* brasier *m*

infertile [*Br* ɪn'fɜːtaɪl, *Am* ɪn'fɜːrtəl] *adj (person, land)* stérile

infest [ɪn'fest] *vt* infester **(with** de)

infidelity [ɪnfɪ'delɪtɪ] *(pl* **-ies)** *n* infidélité f

infiltrate ['ɪnfɪltreɪt] **1** *vt* infiltrer **2** *vi* s'infiltrer **(into** dans)

infinite ['ɪnfɪnɪt] *adj* infini **▪ infinitely** *adv* infiniment

infinitive [ɪn'fɪnɪtɪv] *n (in grammar)* infinitif *m*

infinity [ɪn'fɪnɪtɪ] *n Math & Phot* infini *m*

infirmary [ɪn'fɜːmərɪ] *(pl* **-ies)** *n (hospital)* hôpital *m*

inflamed [ɪn'fleɪmd] *adj (throat, wound)* enflammé; **to become i.** s'enflammer

inflammable [ɪn'flæməbəl] *adj* inflammable **▪ inflammation** [-flə'meɪʃən] *n* inflammation f

inflate [ɪn'fleɪt] *vt (balloon, prices)* gonfler **▪ inflatable** *adj* gonflable

inflation [ɪn'fleɪʃən] *n Écon* inflation f

inflexible [ɪn'fleksəbəl] *adj* inflexible

inflict [ɪn'flɪkt] *vt (punishment, defeat)*

infliger (**on** à); (*wound, damage*) occasionner (**on** à)

influence ['ɪnflʊəns] **1** n influence f (**on** sur) **2** vt influencer ■ **influential** [-'enʃəl] adj influent

influenza [ɪnflʊ'enzə] n grippe f

influx ['ɪnflʌks] n afflux m (**of** de)

info ['ɪnfəʊ] n Fam renseignements mpl (**on** sur)

inform [ɪn'fɔːm] **1** vt informer (**of** or about: de; **that** que) **2** vt to i. **on** sb dénoncer qn ■ **informed** adj to keep sb i. **of** sth tenir qn au courant de qch

informal [ɪn'fɔːməl] adj (*unaffected*) simple; (*casual*) décontracté; (*tone, language*) familier, -ère; (*unofficial*) officieux, -euse ■ **informally** adv (*unaffectedly*) avec simplicité; (*casually*) avec décontraction; (*meet, discuss*) officieusement

information [ɪnfə'meɪʃən] n (*facts, news*) renseignements mpl (**about** or **on** sur); Comptr information f; **a piece of i.** un renseignement, une information; **to get some i.** se renseigner; **i. technology** informatique f

informative [ɪn'fɔːmətɪv] adj instructif, -ive

infrequent [ɪn'friːkwənt] adj peu fréquent

infringe [ɪn'frɪndʒ] **1** vt (*rule, law*) enfreindre à **2** vt insep **to i. upon** sth empiéter sur qch

infuriating [ɪn'fjʊərɪeɪtɪŋ] adj exaspérant

infusion [ɪn'fjuːʒən] n (*drink*) infusion f

ingenious [ɪn'dʒiːnɪəs] adj ingénieux, -euse

ingrained [ɪn'greɪnd] adj (*prejudice, attitude*) enraciné; **i. dirt** crasse f

ingredient [ɪn'griːdɪənt] n ingrédient m

inhabit [ɪn'hæbɪt] vt habiter ■ **inhabitant** n habitant, -e mf

inhale [ɪn'heɪl] vt (*gas, fumes*) inhaler; (*cigarette smoke*) avaler

inherent [ɪn'hɪərənt] adj inhérent (**in** à)

inherit [ɪn'herɪt] vt hériter (**from** de); (*title*) accéder à ■ **inheritance** n (*legacy*) héritage m

inhibit [ɪn'hɪbɪt] vt (*progress, growth*) entraver; (*of person*) inhiber; **to i. sb from doing** sth empêcher qn de faire qch ■ **inhibited** adj (*person*) inhibé ■ **inhibition** n inhibition f

inhospitable [ɪnhɒ'spɪtəbəl] adj inhospitalier, -ère

inhuman [ɪn'hjuːmən] adj inhumain ■ **inhumane** [-'meɪn] adj inhumain

initial [ɪ'nɪʃəl] **1** adj initial **2** npl **initials** (*letters*) initiales fpl; (*signature*) paraphe m **3** (Br -ll-, Am -l-) vt parapher ■ **initially** adv au début, initialement

initiate [ɪ'nɪʃɪeɪt] vt (*reform, negotiations*) amorcer; (*attack, rumour, project*) lancer

initiative [ɪ'nɪʃətɪv] n initiative f

inject [ɪn'dʒekt] vt injecter (**into** dans); **to i.** sth **into** sb, **to i.** sb **with** sth faire une piqûre de qch à qn ■ **injection** n injection f, piqûre f; **to give** sb **an i.** faire une piqûre à qn

injure ['ɪndʒə(r)] vt (*physically*) blesser; (*reputation*) nuire à; **to i. one's foot** se blesser au pied ■ **injured 1** adj blessé **2** npl **the i.** les blessés mpl

injury ['ɪndʒərɪ] (pl -ies) n (*physical*) blessure f; **i. time** (*in sport*) arrêts mpl de jeu

injustice [ɪn'dʒʌstɪs] n injustice f

ink [ɪŋk] n encre f

inlaid [ɪn'leɪd] adj (*with jewels*) incrusté (**with** de); (*with wood*) marqueté

inland 1 ['ɪnlənd, 'ɪnlænd] adj intérieur; Br **the I. Revenue** ≃ le fisc **2** [ɪn'lænd] adv (*travel*) vers l'intérieur

in-laws ['ɪnlɔːz] npl belle-famille f

inlet ['ɪnlet] n (*of sea*) crique f

inmate ['ɪnmeɪt] n (*of prison*) détenu, -e mf; (*of asylum*) interné, -e mf

inn [ɪn] n auberge f

innate [ɪ'neɪt] adj inné

inner ['ɪnə(r)] adj intérieur; (*feelings*) intime; **i. circle** (*of society*) initiés mpl; **i. city** quartiers mpl déshérités du centre-ville; **i. tube** chambre *f* à air ■ **innermost** *adj* le plus profond (*f* la plus profonde); *(thoughts)* le plus secret (*f.*la plus secrète)

inning ['ɪnɪŋ] *n (in baseball)* tour *m* de batte ■ **innings** *n inv (in cricket)* tour *m* de batte

innocent ['ɪnəsənt] *adj* innocent

innovation [ɪnə'veɪʃən] *n* innovation *f*

innumerable [ɪ'njuːmərəbəl] *adj* innombrable

inoculate [ɪ'nɒkjʊleɪt] *vt* vacciner (**against** contre) ■ **inoculation** *n* inoculation *f*

inoffensive [ɪnə'fensɪv] *adj* inoffensif, -ive

inopportune [ɪn'ɒpətjuːn] *adj* inopportun

in-patient ['ɪnpeɪʃənt] *n Br* malade *mf* hospitalisé(e)

input ['ɪnpʊt] **1** *n (contribution)* contribution *f*; *Comptr (operation)* entrée *f*; *(data)* données *fpl* **2** *(pt & pp* -put) *vt Comptr (data)* entrer

inquest ['ɪnkwest] *n (legal investigation)* enquête *f*

inquire [ɪn'kwaɪə(r)] **1** *vt* demander; **to i. how to get to...** demander le chemin de... **2** *vi* se renseigner (**about** sur); **to i. after sb** demander des nouvelles de qn; **to i. into sth** faire des recherches sur qch

inquiry [ɪn'kwaɪərɪ] *(pl* -ies) *n (request for information)* demande *f (request for information)* demande *f (official investigation)* enquête *f*; **to make inquiries** demander des renseignements; *(of police)* enquêter

inquisitive [ɪn'kwɪzɪtɪv] *adj* curieux, -euse

insane [ɪn'seɪn] *adj* dément, fou (*f* folle); **to go i.** perdre la raison

insatiable [ɪn'seɪʃəbəl] *adj* insatiable

inscribe [ɪn'skraɪb] *vt* inscrire; *(book)* dédicacer (**to** à) ■ **inscription** [-'skrɪpʃən] *n* inscription *f*; *(in book)* dédicace *f*

insect ['ɪnsekt] *n* insecte *m*; **i. repellent** anti-moustiques *m inv*

insecure [ɪnsɪ'kjʊə(r)] *adj (unsafe)* peu sûr; *(job, future)* précaire; *(person)* angoissé

insemination [ɪnsemɪ'neɪʃən] *n* **artificial i.** insémination *f* artificielle

insensitive [ɪn'sensɪtɪv] *adj (person)* insensible (**to** à); *(remark)* indélicat

inseparable [ɪn'sepərəbəl] *adj* inséparable (**from** de)

insert [ɪn'sɜːt] *vt* insérer (**in** *or* **into** dans) ■ **insertion** *n* insertion *f*

inside 1 ['ɪnsaɪd] *adj* intérieur; *(information)* obtenu à la source; *Aut* **the i. lane** *Br* la voie de gauche, *Am* la voie de droite

2 ['ɪnsaɪd] *n* intérieur *m*; *Fam* **insides** *(stomach)* entrailles *fpl*; **on the i.** à l'intérieur (**of** de); **i. out** *(clothes)* à l'envers; *(know, study)* à fond

3 [ɪn'saɪd] *adv* à l'intérieur

4 [ɪn'saɪd] *prep* à l'intérieur de, dans; *(time)* en moins de

insider [ɪn'saɪdə(r)] *n* initié, -e *mf*

insidious [ɪn'sɪdɪəs] *adj* insidieux, -euse

insight ['ɪnsaɪt] *n* perspicacité *f*; *(into question)* aperçu *m*

insignificant [ɪnsɪg'nɪfɪkənt] *adj* insignifiant

insincere [ɪnsɪn'sɪə(r)] *adj* peu sincère

insinuate [ɪn'sɪnjʊeɪt] *vt (suggest)* insinuer (**that** que)

insipid [ɪn'sɪpɪd] *adj* insipide

insist [ɪn'sɪst] **1** *vt (maintain)* soutenir (**that** que); **I i. that you come** *or* **on your coming** *(I demand it)* j'insiste pour que tu viennes **2** *vi* insister; **to i. on sth** *(demand)* exiger qch; *(assert)* affirmer qch; **to i. on doing sth** tenir à faire qch

insistence [ɪn'sɪstəns] *n* insistance *f* ■ **insistent** *adj (person)* pressant; **to be i. (that)** insister (pour que + *subjunctive*)

insolent ['ɪnsələnt] *adj* insolent

insoluble [ɪn'sɒljʊbəl] *adj* insoluble

insolvent [ɪn'sɒlvənt] *adj (financially)* insolvable

insomnia [ɪn'sɒmnɪə] *n* insomnie *f*

insomuch as [ɪnsəʊ'mʌtʃəz] *adv* = **inasmuch as**

inspect [ɪn'spekt] *vt* inspecter; *(tickets)* contrôler; *(troops)* passer en revue ▪ **inspector** *n* inspecteur, -trice *mf*; *(on train)* contrôleur, -euse *mf*

inspire [ɪn'spaɪə(r)] *vt* inspirer; **to i. sb to do sth** pousser qn à faire qch ▪ **inspiration** [-spə'reɪʃən] *n* inspiration *f*; *(person)* source *f* d'inspiration

instability [ɪnstə'bɪlɪtɪ] *n* instabilité *f*

install [ɪn'stɔːl] *(Am* **instal)** *vt* installer

instalment [ɪn'stɔːlmənt] *(Am* **installment)** *n (part payment)* versement *m*; *(of serial, story)* épisode *m*; *(of publication)* fascicule *m*; **to pay by instalments** payer par versements échelonnés; *Am* **to buy on the i. plan** acheter à crédit

instance [ɪnstəns] *n (example)* exemple *m*; *(case)* cas *m*; **for i.** par exemple; **in this i.** dans le cas présent

instant [ɪnstənt] **1** *adj* immédiat; **i. coffee** café *m* instantané **2** *n (moment)* instant *m*; **this (very) i.** *(at once)* à l'instant; **the i. that I saw her** dès que je l'ai vue ▪ **instantly** *adv* immédiatement

instantaneous [ɪnstən'teɪnɪəs] *adj* instantané

instead [ɪn'sted] *adv (in place of sth)* à la place; *(in place of sb)* à ma/ta/*etc* place; **i. of sth** au lieu de qch; **i. of doing sth** au lieu de faire qch; **i. of him/her** à sa place

instigate [ɪnstɪgeɪt] *vt* provoquer ▪ **instigator** *n* instigateur, -trice *mf*

instil [ɪn'stɪl] *(Am* **instill)** *(pt & pp -ll-)* *vt (idea)* inculquer *(into* à); *(doubt)* instiller *(in* à)

instinct [ɪnstɪŋkt] *n* instinct *m*; **by i.** d'instinct ▪ **instinctive** *adj* instinctif, -ive

institute [ɪnstɪtjuːt] **1** *n* institut *m* **2** *vt (rule, practice)* instituer; *(legal inquiry)* ordonner

institution [ɪnstɪ'tjuːʃən] *n (organization, custom)* institution *f*; *(public, financial, religious, psychiatric)* établissement *m*

instruct [ɪn'strʌkt] *vt (teach)* enseigner *(sb in sth* qch à qn); **to i. sb about sth** *(inform)* instruire qn de qch; **to i. sb to do** *(order)* charger qn de faire ▪ **instruction** [-ʃən] *n (teaching, order)* instruction *f*; **instructions (for use)** mode *m* d'emploi ▪ **instructor** *n (for judo, dance)* professeur *m*; *(for skiing, swimming)* moniteur, -trice *mf*; **driving i.** moniteur, -trice *mf* d'auto-école

instrument [ɪnstrəmənt] *n* instrument *m*

instrumental [ɪnstrə'mentəl] *adj (music)* instrumental; **to be i. in sth/in doing sth** contribuer à qch/à faire qch

insubordinate [ɪnsə'bɔːdɪnət] *adj* insubordonné

insufferable [ɪn'sʌfərəbəl] *adj* intolérable

insufficient [ɪnsə'fɪʃənt] *adj* insuffisant ▪ **insufficiently** *adv* insuffisamment

insulate [ɪnsjʊleɪt] *vt (against cold)* & *El* isoler; *(against sound)* insonoriser ▪ **insulation** *n (against cold)* isolation *f*; *(against sound)* insonorisation *f*; *(material)* isolant *m*

insulin [ɪnsjʊlɪn] *n* insuline *f*

insult 1 [ɪnsʌlt] *n* insulte *f* *(to* à) **2** [ɪn'sʌlt] *vt* insulter

insure [ɪn'ʃʊə(r)] *vt* **(a)** *(house, car, goods)* assurer *(against* contre) **(b)** *Am* = **ensure** ▪ **insurance** *n* assurance *f*; **i. policy** police *f* d'assurance

insurmountable [ɪnsə'maʊntəbəl] *adj* insurmontable

intact [ɪn'tækt] *adj* intact

intake [ɪnteɪk] *n (of food)* consommation *f*; *(of students, schoolchildren)* admissions *fpl*

intangible [ɪn'tændʒəbəl] *adj* intangible

integral [ɪntɪgrəl] *adj* intégral; **to be**

an i. part of sth faire partie intégrante de qch

integrate [ˈɪntɪgreɪt] **1** *vt* intégrer (**into** dans) **2** *vi* s'intégrer (**into** dans) ■ **integration** *n* intégration *f*; **(racial)** i. déségrégation *f* raciale

integrity [ɪnˈtegrɪtɪ] *n* intégrité *f*

intellect [ˈɪntɪlekt] *n* intelligence *f*, intellect *m* ■ **intellectual** *adj & n* intellectuel, -elle *(mf)*

intelligence [ɪnˈtelɪdʒəns] *n* intelligence *f*

intelligent [ɪnˈtelɪdʒənt] *adj* intelligent

intelligible [ɪnˈtelɪdʒəbəl] *adj* intelligible

intend [ɪnˈtend] *vt (gift, remark)* destiner (**for** à); **to be intended to do sth** être destiné à faire qch; **to i. to do sth** avoir l'intention de faire qch ■ **intended** *adj (deliberate)* voulu; *(planned)* prévu

intense [ɪnˈtens] *adj* intense; *(interest)* vif *(f* vive); *(person)* passionné ■ **intensely** *adv (look at)* intensément; *Fig (very)* extrêmement

intensify [ɪnˈtensɪfaɪ] *(pt & pp -ied)* **1** *vt* intensifier **2** *vi* s'intensifier

intensity [ɪnˈtensətɪ] *n* intensité *f*

intensive [ɪnˈtensɪv] *adj* intensif, -ive; **in i. care** en réanimation

intent [ɪnˈtent] **1** *adj (look)* intense; **to be i. on doing** être résolu à faire **2** *n* intention *f*; **to all intents and purposes** quasiment

intention [ɪnˈtenʃən] *n* intention *f* **(of doing** de faire)

intentional [ɪnˈtenʃənəl] *adj* intentionnel, -elle; **it wasn't i.** ce n'était pas fait exprès ■ **intentionally** *adv* intentionnellement, exprès

inter [ɪnˈtɜ:(r)] *(pt & pp -rr-)* *vt* enterrer

inter- [ˈɪntə(r)] *pref* inter-

interact [ɪntərˈækt] *vi (of person)* communiquer (**with** avec); *(of several people)* communiquer entre eux/ elles; *(of chemicals)* réagir (**with** avec)

interactive [ɪntəˈræktɪv] *adj Comptr* interactif, -ive

intercept [ɪntəˈsept] *vt* intercepter

interchange [ˈɪntətʃeɪndʒ] *n Br (on road)* échangeur *m*

interchangeable [ɪntəˈtʃeɪndʒəbəl] *adj* interchangeable

inter-city [ɪntəˈsɪtɪ] *adj Br* **i. train** train *m* de grandes lignes

intercom [ˈɪntəkɒm] *n* Interphone® *m*

interconnected [ɪntəkəˈnektɪd] *adj (facts)* lié(e)s

intercourse [ˈɪntəkɔ:s] *n (sexual)* rapports *mpl* sexuels

interdependent [ɪntədɪˈpendənt] *adj* interdépendant; *(parts of machine)* solidaire

interest [ˈɪntərest, ˈɪntrɪst] **1** *n* intérêt *m*; *(hobby)* centre *m* d'intérêt; *(money)* intérêts *mpl*; **to take an i. in sth/ sb** s'intéresser à qn/qch; **to lose i. in sb/ sth** se désintéresser de qn/qch; **to be of i. to sb** intéresser qn **2** *vt* intéresser ■ **interested** *adj* intéressé; **to be i. in sb/sth** s'intéresser à qn/qch; **are you i.?** ça vous intéresse? ■ **interest-free** *adj (loan)* sans intérêts; *(credit)* gratuit ■ **interesting** *adj* intéressant

interfere [ɪntəˈfɪə(r)] *vi (meddle)* se mêler (**in** de); **to i. with sth** *(hinder)* gêner qch; *(touch)* toucher à qch

interference [ɪntəˈfɪərəns] *n* ingérence *f*; *(on television, radio)* parasites *mpl*

interim [ˈɪntərɪm] **1** *n* **in the i.** entre-temps **2** *adj (measure)* provisoire

interior [ɪnˈtɪərɪə(r)] *adj & n* intérieur *(m)*

interlock [ɪntəˈlɒk] *vi (of machine parts)* s'emboîter

interlude [ˈɪntəlu:d] *n (on TV)* interlude *m*; *(in theatre)* intermède *m*; *(period of time)* intervalle *m*

intermediary [ɪntəˈmi:dɪərɪ] *(pl -ies)* *n* intermédiaire *mf*

intermediate [ɪntəˈmi:dɪət] *adj* intermédiaire; *(course, student)* de niveau moyen

intermission [ɪntəˈmɪʃən] *n* entracte *m*

intermittent [ɪntə'mɪtənt] *adj* intermittent

intern 1 [ˈɪntɜːn] *n Am Med* interne *mf* **2** [ɪn'tɜːn] *vt (imprison)* interner

internal [ɪn'tɜːnəl] *adj* interne; *(flight, policy)* intérieur; *Am* **the I. Revenue Service** ≃ le fisc ■ **internally** *adv* intérieurement

international [ɪntə'næʃənəl] **1** *adj* international **2** *n (match)* rencontre *f* internationale; *(player)* international *m*

Internet [ˈɪntənet] *n Comptr* **the I.** l'Internet *m*; **I. access** accès *m* (à l')Internet; **I. service provider** fournisseur *m* d'accès Internet

interpret [ɪn'tɜːprɪt] **1** *vt* interpréter **2** *vi (translate for people)* faire l'interprète ■ **interpretation** *n* interprétation *f* ■ **interpreter** *n* interprète *mf*

interrelated [ɪntərɪ'leɪtɪd] *adj* lié

interrogate [ɪn'terəgeɪt] *vt* interroger ■ **interrogation** [-'geɪʃən] *n* interrogation *f*; *(by police)* interrogatoire *m*

interrupt [ɪntə'rʌpt] **1** *vt* interrompre **2** *vi* **I'm sorry to i.** je vous suis désolé de vous interrompre ■ **interruption** *n* interruption *f*

intersect [ɪntə'sekt] **1** *vt* couper **2** *vi* se couper ■ **intersection** *n* intersection *f*; *(of roads)* croisement *m*

interval [ˈɪntəvəl] *n* intervalle *m*; *Br (in theatre, cinema)* entracte *m*; **at intervals** *(in time)* de temps à autre; *(in space)* par intervalles; **at five-minute intervals** toutes les cinq minutes

intervene [ɪntə'viːn] *vi (of person)* intervenir *(in* dans); *(of event)* survenir ■ **intervention** [-'venʃən] *n* intervention *f*

interview [ˈɪntəvjuː] **1** *n* entretien *m* **(with** avec); *TV & Journ* interview *m* ou *f* **2** *vt (for job)* faire passer un entretien à; *TV & Journ* interviewer ■ **interviewer** *n TV* intervieweur, -euse *mf*; *(for research, in canvassing)* enquêteur, -euse *mf*

intestine [ɪn'testɪn] *n* intestin *m*

intimate [ˈɪntɪmət] *adj* intime; *(friendship)* profond; *(knowledge)* approfondi ■ **intimately** *adv* intimement

intimidate [ɪn'tɪmɪdeɪt] *vt* intimider

into [ˈɪntuː, *unstressed* ˈɪntə] *prep* **(a)** dans; **to put sth i. sth** mettre qch dans qch; **to go i. a room** entrer dans une pièce

(b) en; **to translate i. French** traduire en français; **to change sb i. sth** changer qn en qch; **to break sth i. pieces** briser qch en morceaux; **to go i. town** aller en ville

(c) *Math* **three i. six goes two** six divisé par trois fait deux

(d) *Fam* **to be i. jazz** être branché jazz

intolerable [ɪn'tɒlərəbəl] *adj* intolérable **(that** que + *subjunctive)*

intolerance [ɪn'tɒlərəns] *n* intolérance *f* ■ **intolerant** *adj* intolérant

intonation [ɪntə'neɪʃən] *n* intonation *f*

intoxicated [ɪn'tɒksɪkeɪtɪd] *adj* ivre

intransigent [ɪn'trænsɪdʒənt] *adj* intransigeant

intransitive [ɪn'trænsɪtɪv] *adj (in grammar)* intransitif, -ive

intricate [ˈɪntrɪkət] *adj* compliqué

intrigue 1 [ˈɪntriːg] *n (plot)* intrigue *f* **2** [ɪn'triːg] *vt (interest)* intriguer ■ **intriguing** *adj (news, attitude)* curieux, -euse

introduce [ɪntrə'djuːs] *vt (bring in, insert)* introduire **(into** dans); *(programme, subject)* présenter; **to i. sb (to sb)** présenter qn (à qn)

introduction [ɪntrə'dʌkʃən] *n* introduction *f*; *(of person to person)* présentation *f* ■ **introductory** *adj (words, speech)* d'introduction; *(course)* d'initiation

introvert [ˈɪntrəvɜːt] *n* introverti, -e *mf*

intrude [ɪn'truːd] *vi (of person)* déranger **(on sb** qn) ■ **intruder** *n* intrus, -e *mf* ■ **intrusion** *n (bother)* dérangement *m*; *(interference)* intrusion *f* **(into** dans)

intuition [ɪntjuː'ɪʃən] *n* intuition *f*

inundate ['ɪnʌndeɪt] vt inonder (with de); **inundated with work/letters** submergé de travail/lettres

invade [ɪn'veɪd] vt envahir ■ **invader** n envahisseur, -euse mf

invalid[1] ['ɪnvəlɪd] adj & n malade (mf); (disabled person) infirme (mf)

invalid[2] [ɪn'vælɪd] adj (ticket, passport) non valable ■ **invalidate** vt (ticket) annuler; (election, law) invalider; (theory) infirmer

invaluable [ɪn'væljʊəbəl] adj inestimable

invariably [ɪn'veərɪəblɪ] adv invariablement

invasion [ɪn'veɪʒən] n invasion f

invent [ɪn'vent] vt inventer ■ **invention** n invention f ■ **inventor** n inventeur, -trice mf

inventory ['ɪnvəntrɪ] (pl -ies) n inventaire m

invert [ɪn'vɜːt] vt (order) intervertir; (turn upside down) renverser; Br **inverted commas** guillemets mpl

invest [ɪn'vest] 1 vt (money) investir (in dans); (time, effort) consacrer (in à) 2 vi to i. in (company) investir dans; Fig (car) se payer ■ **investment** n investissement m ■ **investor** n (in shares) investisseur m

investigate [ɪn'vestɪgeɪt] vt (examine) examiner; (crime) enquêter sur ■ **investigation** n examen m, étude f; (inquiry by journalist, police) enquête f (of or into sur) ■ **investigator** n (detective) enquêteur, -euse mf; (private) détective m

invigilator [ɪn'vɪdʒɪleɪtə(r)] n Br surveillant, -e mf (à un examen)

invigorating [ɪn'vɪgəreɪtɪŋ] adj vivifiant

invincible [ɪn'vɪnsəbəl] adj invincible

invisible [ɪn'vɪzəbəl] adj invisible

invite 1 [ɪn'vaɪt] vt inviter (**to do** à faire); (ask for) demander; **to i. sb out** inviter qn (à sortir) 2 ['ɪnvaɪt] n Fam invit' f ■ **invitation** [-vɪ'teɪʃən] n invitation f

invoice ['ɪnvɔɪs] 1 n facture f 2 vt (goods) facturer; (person) envoyer la facture à

invoke [ɪn'vəʊk] vt invoquer

involuntary [ɪn'vɒləntərɪ] adj involontaire

involve [ɪn'vɒlv] vt (entail) entraîner; **to i. sb in sth** impliquer qn dans qch; (in project) associer qn à qch; **the job involves going abroad** le poste nécessite des déplacements à l'étranger ■ **involved** adj (**a**) **to be i. in an accident** avoir un accident; **fifty people were i. in the project** cinquante personnes ont pris part au projet; **to be i. with sb** (emotionally) avoir une liaison avec qn; **the factors i.** (at stake) les facteurs en jeu; **the person i.** (concerned) la personne en question (**b**) (complicated) compliqué ■ **involvement** [ɪn'vɒlvmənt] n participation f (**in** à); (commitment) engagement m (**in** dans)

invulnerable [ɪn'vʌlnərəbəl] adj invulnérable

inward ['ɪnwəd] 1 adj & adv (movement, move) vers l'intérieur 2 adj (inner) (happiness) intérieur; (thoughts) intime ■ **inwardly** adv (laugh, curse) intérieurement ■ **inwards** adv vers l'intérieur

iodine [Br 'aɪədiːn, Am 'aɪədaɪn] n (antiseptic) teinture f d'iode

IOU [aɪəʊ'juː] (abbr **I owe you**) n reconnaissance f de dette

IQ [aɪ'kjuː] (abbr **intelligence quotient**) n QI m inv

Iran [ɪ'rɑːn, ɪ'ræn] n l'Iran m ■ **Iranian** [ɪ'reɪnɪən, Am ɪ'rɑːnɪən] 1 adj iranien, -enne 2 n Iranien, -enne mf

Iraq [ɪ'rɑːk] n l'Irak m ■ **Iraqi** 1 adj irakien, -enne 2 n Irakien, -enne mf

irate [aɪ'reɪt] adj furieux, -euse

Ireland ['aɪələnd] n l'Irlande f ■ **Irish** ['aɪrɪʃ] 1 adj irlandais 2 n (language) irlandais m; **the I.** (people) les Irlandais mpl ■ **Irishman** (pl -men) n Irlandais m ■ **Irishwoman** (pl -women) n Irlandaise f

iris ['aɪərɪs] *n (plant, of eye)* iris *m*

iron ['aɪən] **1** *n* fer *m*; *(for clothes)* fer *m* à repasser **2** *vt (clothes)* repasser; *Fig* **to i. out difficulties** aplanir les difficultés ▪ **ironing** *n* repassage *m*; **i. board** planche *f* à repasser

ironmonger ['aɪənmʌŋɡə(r)] *n* quincaillier, -ère *mf*; **i.'s (shop)** quincaillerie *f*

irony ['aɪərənɪ] *n* ironie *f* ▪ **ironic(al)** [aɪ'rɒnɪk(əl)] *adj* ironique

irrational [ɪ'ræʃənəl] *adj* irrationnel, -elle

irrefutable [ɪrɪ'fjuːtəbəl] *adj (evidence)* irréfutable

irregular [ɪ'reɡjʊlə(r)] *adj* irrégulier, -ère ▪ **irregularity** [-'lærɪtɪ] *(pl* **-ies)** *n* irrégularité *f*

irrelevant [ɪ'reləvənt] *adj* sans rapport (**to** avec); *(remark)* hors de propos; **that's i.** ça n'a rien à voir (avec la question)

irreparable [ɪ'repərəbəl] *adj (harm, loss)* irréparable

irreplaceable [ɪrɪ'pleɪsəbəl] *adj* irremplaçable

irresistible [ɪrɪ'zɪstəbəl] *adj (person, charm)* irrésistible

irrespective [ɪrɪ'spektɪv] *prep* **i. of** indépendamment de

irresponsible [ɪrɪ'spɒnsəbəl] *adj (act)* irréfléchi; *(person)* irresponsable

irreverent [ɪ'revərənt] *adj* irrévérencieux, -euse

irreversible [ɪrɪ'vɜːsəbəl] *adj (process)* irréversible; *(decision)* irrévocable

irrigate ['ɪrɪɡeɪt] *vt* irriguer

irritable ['ɪrɪtəbəl] *adj (easily annoyed)* irritable

irritant ['ɪrɪtənt] *n (to eyes, skin)* irritant *m*

irritate ['ɪrɪteɪt] *vt (annoy, inflame)* irriter ▪ **irritating** *adj* irritant

is [ɪz] *see* be

Islam ['ɪzlɑːm] *n* l'Islam *m* ▪ **Islamic** [ɪz'læmɪk] *adj* islamique

island ['aɪlənd] *n* île *f*; **(traffic) i.** refuge *m* (pour piétons) ▪ **islander** *n* insulaire *mf*

isle [aɪl] *n* île *f*

isn't ['ɪzənt] = **is not**

isolate ['aɪsəleɪt] *vt* isoler (**from** de) ▪ **isolated** *adj (remote, unique)* isolé ▪ **isolation** *n* isolement *m*; **in i.** isolément

ISP [aɪes'piː] *(abbr* **Internet Service Provider)** *n Comptr* fournisseur *m* d'accès Internet

Israel ['ɪzreɪl] *n* Israël *m* ▪ **Israeli 1** *adj* israélien, -enne **2** *n* Israélien, -enne *mf*

issue ['ɪʃuː] **1** *n (of newspaper, magazine)* numéro *m*; *(matter)* question *f*; **at i.** *(at stake)* en cause; **to make an i.** *or* **a big i. of sth** faire toute une affaire de qch **2** *vt (book)* publier; *(tickets)* distribuer; *(passport)* délivrer; *(order)* donner; *(warning)* lancer; *(stamps, banknotes)* émettre; *(supply)* fournir (**with** de; **to** à); **to i. a statement** faire une déclaration

IT [ɪt] *pron* (**a**) *(subject)* il, elle; *(object)* le, la, l'; **(to) it** *(indirect object)* lui; **it bites** *(dog)* il mord; **I've done it** je l'ai fait

(**b**) *(impersonal)* il; **it's snowing** il neige; **it's hot** il fait chaud

(**c**) *(non-specific)* ce, cela, ça; **it's good** c'est bon; **who is it?** qui est-ce?; **to consider it wise to do sth** juger prudent de faire qch; **it was Paul who...** c'est Paul qui... **to have it in for sb** en vouloir à qn

(**d**) *of it, from it, about it* en; **in it, to it, at it** y; **on it** dessus; **under it** dessous

italics [ɪ'tælɪks] *npl* italique *m*; **in i.** en italique

Italy ['ɪtəlɪ] *n* l'Italie *f* ▪ **Italian** [ɪ'tæljən] **1** *adj* italien, -enne **2** *n (person)* Italien, -enne *mf*; *(language)* italien *m*

itch [ɪtʃ] **1** *n* démangeaison *f* **2** *vi (of person)* avoir des démangeaisons; **his arm itches** son bras le *ou* lui démange; *Fig* **to be itching to do sth** brûler d'envie de faire qch

item ['aɪtəm] *n (in collection, on list, in newspaper)* article *m*; *(matter)* question *f*; **i. of clothing** vêtement *m*; **news i.** information *f* ■ **itemize** *vt (invoice)* détailler
itinerary [aɪ'tɪnərərɪ] *(pl* **-ies)** *n* itinéraire *m*

its [ɪts] *possessive adj* son, sa, *pl* ses ■ **itself** *pron* lui-même, elle-même; *(reflexive)* se, s'; **by i.** tout seul
I've [aɪv] = **I have**
ivory ['aɪvərɪ] *n* ivoire *m*
ivy ['aɪvɪ] *n* lierre *m*

Jj

J, j [dʒeɪ] *n (letter)* J, j *m inv*

jab [dʒæb] **1** *n* coup *m*; *Br Fam (injection)* piqûre *f* **2** *(pt & pp -bb-) vt (knife, stick)* enfoncer (**into** dans); *(prick)* piquer (**with** du bout de)

jack [dʒæk] **1** *n* (**a**) *(for vehicle)* cric *m* (**b**) *(card)* valet *m* **2** *vt* **to j. up** *(vehicle)* soulever *(avec un cric)*

jacket ['dʒækɪt] *n (coat)* veste *f*; *(of book)* jaquette *f*; *Br* **j. potato** pomme *f* de terre en robe des champs

jackknife ['dʒæknaɪf] **1** *(pl -knives) n* couteau *m* de poche **2** *vi Br (of truck)* se mettre en travers de la route

jackpot ['dʒækpɒt] *n* gros lot *m*

Jacuzzi® [dʒə'kuːzɪ] *n* Jacuzzi® *m*

jagged ['dʒæɡɪd] *adj* déchiqueté

jail [dʒeɪl] **1** *n* prison *f* **2** *vt* emprisonner (**for** pour)

jam¹ [dʒæm] *n (preserve)* confiture *f*; **strawberry j.** confiture *f* de fraises ■ **jamjar** *n* pot *m* à confiture

jam² [dʒæm] **1** *n (traffic)* j. embouteillage *m* **2** *(pt & pp -mm-) vt (squeeze, make stuck)* coincer; *(street, corridor)* encombrer; **to j. sth into sth** entasser qch dans qch; **to j. on the brakes** écraser la pédale de frein **3** *vi (get stuck)* se coincer ■ **jammed** *adj (machine)* coincé; *(street)* encombré ■ **jam-packed** *adj (hall, train)* bourré

Jamaica [dʒə'meɪkə] *n* la Jamaïque

jangle ['dʒæŋɡəl] *vi* cliqueter

janitor ['dʒænɪtə(r)] *n Am & Scot (caretaker)* concierge *m*

January ['dʒænjʊərɪ] *n* janvier *m*

Japan [dʒə'pæn] *n* le Japon ■ **Japanese** [dʒæpə'niːz] **1** *adj* japonais **2** *n (person)* Japonais, -e *mf*; *(language)* japonais *m*

jar¹ [dʒɑː(r)] *n (container)* pot *m*; *(large, glass)* bocal *m*

jar² [dʒɑː(r)] **1** *n (jolt)* choc *m* **2** *(pt & pp -rr-) vt (shake)* ébranler **3** *vi (of noise)* grincer; *(of colours, words)* jurer (**with** avec) ■ **jarring** *adj (noise, voice)* discordant

jargon ['dʒɑːɡən] *n* jargon *m*

jaunt [dʒɔːnt] *n (journey)* balade *f*

javelin ['dʒævlɪn] *n* javelot *m*

jaw [dʒɔː] *n Anat* mâchoire *f*

jazz [dʒæz] **1** *n* jazz *m* **2** *vt Fam* **to j. sth up** *(clothes, room, style)* égayer qch; *(music)* jazzifier qch

jealous ['dʒeləs] *adj* jaloux, -ouse (**of** de) ■ **jealousy** *n* jalousie *f*

jeans [dʒiːnz] *npl (pair of)* j. jean *m*

Jeep® [dʒiːp] *n* Jeep® *f*

jeer [dʒɪə(r)] **1** *n* jeers *(boos)* huées *fpl* **2** *vt (boo)* huer; *(mock)* se moquer de **3** *vi* **to j. at sb/sth** *(boo)* huer qn/qch; *(mock)* se moquer de qn/qch ■ **jeering 1** *adj* railleur, -euse **2** *n (mocking)* railleries *fpl*; *(of crowd)* huées *fpl*

jell [dʒel] *vi Fam (of ideas)* prendre tournure

jello® ['dʒeləʊ] *n Am (dessert)* gelée *f*

jelly ['dʒelɪ] *(pl -ies) n (preserve, dessert)* gelée *f* ■ **jellyfish** *n* méduse *f*

jeopardy ['dʒepədɪ] *n* **in j.** en péril ■ **jeopardize** *vt* mettre en danger

jerk [dʒɜːk] **1** *n* secousse *f* **2** *vt (pull)* tirer brusquement

jerky ['dʒɜːkɪ] *(-ier, -iest) adj (movement, voice)* saccadé

Jersey ['dʒɜːzɪ] *n* Jersey *m ou f*

jersey ['dʒɜːzɪ] (pl **-eys**) n (garment) tricot m; (of footballer) maillot m

jest [dʒest] 1 n plaisanterie f; **in j.** pour rire 2 vi plaisanter

Jesus ['dʒiːzəs] n Jésus m; **J. Christ** Jésus-Christ m

jet [dʒet] 1 n (a) (plane) avion m à réaction; **j. engine** réacteur m, moteur m à réaction; **j. lag** fatigue f due au décalage horaire (b) (steam, liquid) jet m 2 vi Fam **to j. off** s'envoler (**to** pour)

jet-black [dʒet'blæk] adj (noir) de jais

jetfoil ['dʒetfɔɪl] n hydroglisseur m

jet-lagged ['dʒetlægd] adj qui souffre du décalage horaire

jetty ['dʒetɪ] (pl **-ies**) f jetée f; (landing place) embarcadère m

Jew [dʒuː] n (man) Juif m; (woman) Juive f ■ **Jewish** adj juif (f juive)

jewel ['dʒuːəl] n bijou m (pl -oux); (in watch) rubis m ■ **jeweller** (Am **jeweler**) n bijoutier, -ère mf ■ **jewellery** (Am **jewelry**) n bijoux mpl

jibe [dʒaɪb] n & vi = **gibe**

Jiffy ['dʒɪfɪ] n **J. bag**® enveloppe f matelassée

jiffy ['dʒɪfɪ] n Fam instant m

jig [dʒɪg] n (dance, music) gigue f

jigsaw ['dʒɪgsɔː] n **j. (puzzle)** puzzle m

jilt [dʒɪlt] vt (lover) laisser tomber

jingle ['dʒɪŋgəl] 1 vt faire tinter 2 vi (of keys, bell) tinter

jinx [dʒɪŋks] n (spell, curse) mauvais sort m

jittery ['dʒɪtərɪ] adj Fam **to be j.** être à cran

job [dʒɒb] n (employment, post) travail m, emploi m; (task) tâche f; **to have a (hard) j. doing** or **to do sth** avoir du mal à faire qch; **j. offer** offre f d'emploi

Jobcentre ['dʒɒbsentə(r)] n Br ≃ agence f nationale pour l'emploi

jobless ['dʒɒbləs] adj au chômage

jockey ['dʒɒkɪ] (pl **-eys**) n jockey m

jocular ['dʒɒkjʊlə(r)] adj jovial

jog [dʒɒg] (pt & pp **-gg-**) 1 vt (shake) secouer; (push) pousser; Fig (memory) rafraîchir 2 vi (for fitness) faire du

jogging ■ **jogging** n (for fitness) jogging m; **to go jogging** aller faire un jogging

john [dʒɒn] n Am Fam **the j.** (lavatory) le petit coin

join [dʒɔɪn] 1 n raccord m

2 vt (a) (put together) joindre; (wires, pipes) raccorder; (words, towns) relier; **to j. two things together** relier une chose à une autre; **to j. sb** (catch up with, meet) rejoindre qn; (associate oneself with, go with) se joindre à qn (**in doing** pour faire)

(b) (become a member of) s'inscrire à; (army, police, company) entrer dans; **to j. the queue** or Am **line** prendre la queue

3 vi (a) (of roads, rivers) se rejoindre; **to j. (together** or **up)** (of objects) se joindre (**with** à); **to j. in sth** prendre part à qch

(b) (become a member) devenir membre; Mil **to j. up** s'engager

joiner ['dʒɔɪnə(r)] n Br menuisier m

joint [dʒɔɪnt] 1 n (a) (in body) articulation f; Br (meat) rôti m; Tech joint m; (in carpentry) assemblage m (b) Fam (nightclub) boîte f (c) Fam (cannabis cigarette) joint m 2 adj (decision) commun; **j. account** compte m joint; **j. efforts** efforts mpl conjugués ■ **jointly** adv conjointement

joke [dʒəʊk] 1 n plaisanterie f; (trick) tour m 2 vi plaisanter (**about** sur) ■ **joker** n plaisantin m; (card) joker m ■ **jokingly** adv (say) en plaisantant

jolly ['dʒɒlɪ] (**-ier, -iest**) adj (happy) gai

jolt [dʒəʊlt] 1 n secousse f 2 vt (shake) secouer

jostle ['dʒɒsəl] 1 vt (push) bousculer 2 vi (push each other) se bousculer (**for** sth pour obtenir qch)

jot [dʒɒt] (pt & pp **-tt-**) vt **to j. sth down** noter qch ■ **jotter** n (notepad) bloc-notes m

journal ['dʒɜːnəl] n (periodical) revue f

journalism ['dʒɜːnəlɪzəm] n journalisme m ■ **journalist** n journaliste mf

journey ['dʒɜːnɪ] 1 (pl **-eys**) n (trip)

voyage *m*; *(distance)* trajet *m*; **to go on a j.** partir en voyage **2** *vi* voyager

jovial ['dʒəʊvɪəl] *adj* jovial

joy [dʒɔɪ] *n* joie *f*; **the joys of** *(countryside, motherhood)* les plaisirs *mpl* de ■ **joyful** *adj* joyeux, -euse

joyrider ['dʒɔɪraɪdə(r)] *n* = chauffard qui conduit une voiture volée

joystick ['dʒɔɪstɪk] *n (of aircraft, computer)* manche *m* à balai

jubilant ['dʒuːbɪlənt] *adj* **to be j.** jubiler

jubilee ['dʒuːbɪliː] *n* **(golden) j.** jubilé *m*

judder ['dʒʌdə(r)] **1** *n* vibration *f* **2** *vi (shake)* vibrer

judge [dʒʌdʒ] **1** *n* juge *m* **2** *vti* juger; **to j. sb by** *or* **on sth** juger qn sur *ou* d'après qch; **judging by...** à en juger par... ■ **judg(e)ment** *n* jugement *m*

judicial [dʒuːˈdɪʃəl] *adj* judiciaire

judo ['dʒuːdəʊ] *n* judo *m*

jug [dʒʌg] *n* cruche *f*; *(for milk)* pot *m*

juggle ['dʒʌgəl] **1** *vt* jongler avec **2** *vi* jongler **(with** avec**)** ■ **juggler** *n* jongleur, -euse *mf*

juice [dʒuːs] *n* jus *m* ■ **juicy (-ier, -iest)** *adj (fruit)* juteux, -euse; *(meat)* succulent; *Fig (story)* savoureux, -euse

jukebox ['dʒuːkbɒks] *n* juke-box *m*

July [dʒuːˈlaɪ] *n* juillet *m*

jumble ['dʒʌmbəl] **1** *n (disorder)* fouillis *m*; *Br (unwanted articles)* bric-à-brac *m inv*; *Br* **j. sale** vente *f* de charité *(articles d'occasion uniquement)* **2** *vt* **to j. (up)** *(objects, facts)* mélanger

jumbo ['dʒʌmbəʊ] **1** *adj (packet)* géant **2** *(pl* **-os)** *adj & n* **j. (jet)** jumbo-jet *(m)*

jump [dʒʌmp] **1** *n (leap)* saut *m*; *(start)* sursaut *m*; *(increase)* hausse *f* soudaine; *Am* **j. rope** corde *f* à sauter **2** *vt (ditch)* sauter; *Br* **to j. the queue** passer avant son tour, resquiller **3** *vi* sauter **(at** sur**)**; *(start)* sursauter; *(of price)* faire un bond; **to j. across sth** traverser qch d'un bond; **to j. in** *or* **on** *(train, vehicle, bus)* sauter dans; **to j. off** *or* **out** sauter; *(from bus)* descendre; **to j. off sth, to j. out of sth** sauter

de qch; **to j. out of the window** sauter par la fenêtre; **to j. up** se lever d'un bond ■ **jumpy (-ier, -iest)** *adj* nerveux, -euse

jumper ['dʒʌmpə(r)] *n Br* pull(-over) *m*; *Am (dress)* robe *f* chasuble

junction ['dʒʌŋkʃən] *n (crossroads)* carrefour *m*; *Br* **j. 23** *(on motorway) (exit)* la sortie 23; *(entrance)* l'entrée *f* 23

June [dʒuːn] *n* juin *m*

jungle ['dʒʌŋgəl] *n* jungle *f*

junior ['dʒuːnɪə(r)] **1** *adj (younger)* plus jeune; *(in rank, status)* subalterne; *(teacher, doctor)* jeune; **to be sb's j.** être plus jeune que qn; *(in rank, status)* être au-dessous de qn; *Br* **j. school** école *f* primaire *(entre 7 et 11 ans)*; *Am* **j. high school** ≃ collège *m* d'enseignement secondaire **2** *n* cadet, -ette *mf*; *(in school)* petit, -e *mf*; *(in sports)* junior *mf*, cadet, -ette *mf*

junk [dʒʌŋk] **1** *n (unwanted objects)* bric-à-brac *m inv*; *(inferior goods)* camelote *f*; *(bad film, book)* navet *m*; **j. food** cochonneries *fpl*; **j. mail** prospectus *mpl*; **j. shop** boutique *f* de brocanteur **2** *vt Fam (get rid of)* balancer

junkie ['dʒʌŋkɪ] *n Fam* drogué, -e *mf*

jury ['dʒʊərɪ] *(pl* **-ies)** *n (in competition, court)* jury *m*

just [dʒʌst] **1** *adv (exactly, slightly)* juste; *(only)* juste, seulement; *(simply)* (tout) simplement; **it's j. as I thought** c'est donc ce que je pensais; **she has/ had j. left** elle vient/venait de partir; **he j. missed it** il l'a manqué de peu; **j. as big/light** tout aussi grand/léger **(as** que**)**; **j. a moment!** un instant!; **j. one** un(e) seul(e) **(of** de**)**; **j. about** *(approximately)* à peu près; *(almost)* presque; **to be j. about to do sth** être sur le point de faire qch **2** *adj (fair)* juste **(to** envers**)**

justice ['dʒʌstɪs] *n* justice *f*; **it doesn't do you j.** *(hat, photo)* cela ne vous avantage pas

justify ['dʒʌstɪfaɪ] *(pt & pp* **-ied)** *vt*

justifier; **to be justified in doing sth** *(have reason)* être fondé à faire qch ■ **justifiable** *adj* justifiable ■ **justification** [-fɪˈkeɪʃən] *n* justification *f*

jut [dʒʌt] *(pt & pp* **-tt-***) vi* **to j. out** faire saillie

juvenile [ˈdʒuːvənaɪl, *Am* -ənəl] **1** *n (in law)* mineur, -e *mf* **2** *adj (court)* pour enfants; *Pej (behaviour)* puéril; **j. delinquent** jeune délinquant, -e *mf*

juxtapose [dʒʌkstəˈpəʊz] *vt* juxtaposer

Kk

K, k [keɪ] *n (letter)* K, k *m inv*

kangaroo [kæŋgə'ru:] *n* kangourou *m*

karate [kə'rɑːtɪ] *n* karaté *m*

kebab [kə'bæb] *n* brochette *f*

keel [kiːl] **1** *n (of boat)* quille *f* **2** *vi* **to k. over** *(of boat)* chavirer

keen [kiːn] *adj* **(a)** *Br (eager, enthusiastic)* plein d'enthousiasme; **to be k. on sth** *(music, sport)* être passionné de qch; **he is k. on her/the idea** elle/l'idée lui plaît beaucoup **(b)** *(edge, appetite)* aiguisé; *(interest)* vif *(f* vive); *(mind)* pénétrant; *(wind)* glacial

KEEP [kiːp] **1** *(pt & pp* **kept)** *vt* garder; *(shop, car)* avoir; *(diary, promise)* tenir; *(family)* entretenir; *(rule)* respecter; *(delay, detain)* retenir; *(put)* mettre; **to k. doing sth** continuer à faire qch; **to k. sth clean** garder qch propre; **to k. sth from sb** dissimuler qch à qn; **to k. sb from doing sth** empêcher qn de faire qch; **to k. sb waiting/working** faire attendre/travailler qn; **to k. an appointment** se rendre à un rendez-vous

2 *vi (remain)* rester; *(continue)* continuer; *(of food)* se conserver; **how is he keeping?** comment va-t-il?; **to k. still** rester immobile; **to k. left** tenir sa gauche; **to k. going** continuer; **to k. at it** *(keep doing it)* persévérer

3 *n (food)* subsistance *f*; *Fam* **for keeps** pour toujours

▸ **keep away 1** *vt (person)* éloigner **(from** à) **2** *vi* ne pas s'approcher **(from** de)

▸ **keep back 1** *vt sep (crowd)* contenir; *(delay, withhold)* retarder; *(hide)* cacher **(from** à) **2** *vi* ne pas s'approcher **(from** de)

▸ **keep down** *vt sep (restrict)* limiter; *(price, costs)* maintenir bas

▸ **keep in** *vt sep (not allow out)* empêcher de sortir; *(as punishment in school)* garder en retenue

▸ **keep off 1** *vt sep (person)* éloigner; **k. your hands off!** n'y touche pas! **2** *vt insep* **'k. off the grass'** 'défense de marcher sur les pelouses' **3** *vi (not go near)* ne pas s'approcher

▸ **keep on 1** *vt sep (hat, employee)* garder; **to k. on doing sth** continuer à faire qch **2** *vi* **to k. on at sb** harceler qn

▸ **keep out 1** *vt sep* empêcher d'entrer **2** *vi* rester en dehors **(of** de)

▸ **keep to 1** *vt insep (subject, path)* ne pas s'écarter de; *(room)* garder **2** *vi* **to k. to the left** tenir la gauche; **to k. to oneself** rester à l'écart

▸ **keep up 1** *vt sep (continue, maintain)* continuer; *(keep awake)* empêcher de dormir; **to k. up appearances** sauver les apparences **2** *vi (continue)* continuer; *(follow)* suivre; **to k. up with sb** *(follow)* aller à la même allure que qn; *(in quality of work)* se maintenir à la hauteur de qn

keeper ['kiːpə(r)] *n (in park, in zoo, goalkeeper)* gardien, -enne *mf*

keeping ['kiːpɪŋ] *n* **in k. with** conformément à

kennel ['kenəl] *n Br* niche *f*

Kenya ['kiːnjə, 'kenjə] *n* le Kenya

kept [kept] **1** *pt & pp* of **keep 2** *adj* **well** or **nicely k.** *(house)* bien tenu

kerb [kɜːb] n Br bord m du trottoir

kernel ['kɜːnəl] n (of nut) amande f

kerosene ['kerəsiːn] n Am (paraffin) pétrole m (lampant)

ketchup ['ketʃəp] n ketchup m

kettle ['ketəl] n bouilloire f; **the k. is boiling** l'eau bout; **to put the k. on** mettre l'eau à chauffer

key [kiː] **1** n clef f, clé f; (of piano, typewriter, computer) touche f **2** adj (industry, post) clef, clé **3** vt **to k. in** (data) saisir ■ **keyboard** n (of piano, computer) clavier m ■ **keyhole** n trou m de serrure ■ **keynote** n (of speech) point m essentiel ■ **keyring** n porte-clefs m inv

keyed [kiːd] adj **to be k. up** être surexcité

khaki ['kɑːkɪ] adj & n kaki (m) inv

kick [kɪk] **1** n coup m de pied; (of horse) ruade f **2** vt donner un coup de pied/des coups de pied à; (of horse) lancer une ruade à **3** vi donner des coups de pied; (of horse) ruer ■ **kick-off** n (in football) coup m d'envoi

▸ **kick down, kick in** vt sep (door) démolir à coups de pied

▸ **kick off** vi (of footballer) donner le coup d'envoi; Fam (start) démarrer

▸ **kick out** vt sep Fam (throw out) flanquer dehors

▸ **kick up** vt sep Br Fam **to k. up a fuss** faire des histoires

kid [kɪd] **1** n (a) Fam (child) gosse mf; Am Fam **my k. brother** mon petit frère (b) (goat) chevreau m **2** (pt & pp -dd-) vti Fam (joke, tease) faire marcher; **to be kidding** plaisanter; **no kidding!** sans blague!

kidnap ['kɪdnæp] (pt & pp -pp-) vt kidnapper ■ **kidnapper** n ravisseur, -euse mf ■ **kidnapping** n enlèvement m

kidney ['kɪdnɪ] n (pl -eys) n rein m; (as food) rognon m; **k. bean** haricot m rouge

kill [kɪl] **1** vt (person, animal, plant) tuer; **to k. oneself** se tuer; Fam **my feet are killing me** j'ai les pieds en

compote; **to k. time** tuer le temps **2** vi tuer ■ **killer** n tueur, -euse mf ■ **killing** n (of person) meurtre m; (of group) massacre m; (of animal) mise f à mort

killjoy ['kɪldʒɔɪ] n rabat-joie mf inv

kilo ['kiːləʊ] (pl -os) n kilo m ■ **kilogram(me)** ['kɪləgræm] n kilogramme m

kilobyte ['kɪləbaɪt] n Comptr kilo-octet m

kilometre [kɪ'lɒmɪtə(r)] (Am **kilometer**) n kilomètre m

kilt [kɪlt] n kilt m

kin [kɪn] n **one's next of k.** son plus proche parent

kind¹ [kaɪnd] n (sort, type) genre m, espèce f (of de); **what k. of drink is it?** qu'est-ce que c'est comme boisson?; Fam **k. of worried/sad** plutôt inquiet/triste

kind² [kaɪnd] (-er, -est) adj (helpful, pleasant) gentil, -ille (to avec); **that's k. of you** c'est gentil de votre part

kindergarten ['kɪndəgɑːtən] n jardin m d'enfants

kindly ['kaɪndlɪ] **1** adv gentiment; **k. wait** ayez la bonté d'attendre **2** adj (person) bienveillant

kindness ['kaɪndnɪs] n gentillesse f

king [kɪŋ] n roi m ■ **kingdom** n royaume m; **animal/plant k.** règne m animal/végétal ■ **king-size(d)** adj géant

kiosk ['kiːɒsk] n kiosque m; Br (telephone) **k.** cabine f téléphonique

kip [kɪp] (pt & pp -pp-) vi Br Fam (sleep) roupiller

kipper ['kɪpə(r)] n hareng m salé et fumé

kiss [kɪs] **1** n baiser m; **the k. of life** (in first aid) le bouche-à-bouche **2** vt (person) embrasser **3** vi s'embrasser

kit [kɪt] **1** n équipement m, matériel m; (set of articles) trousse f; Br (belongings) affaires fpl; Br (sports clothes) tenue f; **first-aid k.** trousse f de pharmacie; **(do-it-yourself) k.** kit m **2** (pt & pp -tt-) vt Br **to k. sb out** équiper qn (with de)

kitchen ['kɪtʃɪn] n cuisine f; **k. sink**

évier m; **k. units** éléments mpl de cuisine ∎ **kitchenette** n coin-cuisine m

kite [kaɪt] n (toy) cerf-volant m

kitten ['kɪtən] n chaton m

kitty ['kɪtɪ] (pl **-ies**) n (fund) cagnotte f

kiwi ['kiːwiː] n (bird, fruit) kiwi m

km (abbr **kilometre(s)**) km

knack [næk] n (skill) talent m; **to have the k. of doing sth** avoir le don de faire qch

knackered ['nækəd] adj Br Fam (tired) vanné

knapsack ['næpsæk] n sac m à dos

knead [niːd] vt (dough) pétrir

knee [niː] n genou m; **to go down on one's knees** s'agenouiller ∎ **kneecap** n rotule f

kneel [niːl] (pt & pp **knelt** or **kneeled**) vi **to k. (down)** s'agenouiller (**before** devant); **to be kneeling (down)** être à genoux

knelt [nelt] pt & pp of **kneel**

knew [njuː] pt of **know**

knickers ['nɪkəz] npl Br (underwear) culotte f

knick-knack ['nɪknæk] n Fam babiole f

knife [naɪf] **1** (pl **knives**) n couteau m; (penknife) canif m **2** vt poignarder

knight [naɪt] **1** n chevalier m; (chess piece) cavalier m **2** vt Br **to be knighted** être fait chevalier ∎ **knighthood** n Br titre m de chevalier

knit [nɪt] (pt & pp **-tt-**) **1** vt tricoter **2** vi tricoter; **to k. (together)** (of bones) se ressouder ∎ **knitting** n (activity, material) tricot m; **k. needle** aiguille f à tricoter

knob [nɒb] n (on door) poignée f; (on radio) bouton m

knock [nɒk] **1** n (blow) coup m; **there's a k. at the door** on frappe à la porte **2** vt (strike) frapper; (collide with) heurter; **to k. one's head on sth** se cogner la tête contre qch **3** vi (strike) frapper; **to k. against** or **into sth** heurter qch ∎ **knocker** n (for door) marteau m ∎ **knockout** n (in boxing) knock-out m inv

▶ **knock about** vt sep (ill-treat) malmener

▶ **knock back** vt sep Br Fam (drink, glass) s'envoyer (derrière la cravate)

▶ **knock down** vt sep (object, pedestrian) renverser; (house, tree, wall) abattre; (price) baisser

▶ **knock in** vt sep (nail) enfoncer

▶ **knock off 1** vt sep (person, object) faire tomber (**from** de); Fam (do quickly) expédier; **to k. £5 off (the price)** baisser le prix de 5 livres **2** vi Fam (stop work) s'arrêter de travailler

▶ **knock out** vt sep (make unconscious) assommer; (boxer) mettre K.-O.; (beat in competition) éliminer

▶ **knock over** vt sep (pedestrian, object) renverser

knot [nɒt] **1** n (a) (in rope) nœud m; Fig **to tie the k.** se marier (b) Naut (unit of speed) nœud m **2** (pt & pp **-tt-**) vt nouer

KNOW [nəʊ] **1** n Fam **to be in the k.** être au courant **2** (pt **knew**, pp **known**) vt (facts, language) savoir; (person, place) connaître; (recognize) reconnaître (**by** à); **to k. that...** savoir que...; **to k. how to do sth** savoir faire qch; **for all I k.** que je sache; **I'll let you k.** je vous le ferai savoir; **to k. (a lot) about cars/sewing** s'y connaître en voitures/couture; **to get to k. sb** apprendre à connaître qn **3** vi savoir; **I k.** je (le) sais; **I wouldn't k., I k. nothing about it** je n'en sais rien; **to k. about sth** être au courant de qch; **do you k. of a good dentist?** connais-tu un bon dentiste? ∎ **know-all** n Fam Pej je-sais-tout m ∎ **know-how** n Fam savoir-faire m inv ∎ **knowingly** adv (consciously) sciemment ∎ **know-it-all** n Fam Pej je-sais-tout mf

knowledge ['nɒlɪdʒ] n (of fact) connaissance f; (learning) connaissances fpl, savoir m; **general k.** culture f générale ∎ **knowledgeable** adj savant; **to be k. about sth** bien s'y connaître en qch

known [nəʊn] **1** *pp of* **know 2** *adj* connu; **she is k. to be...** on sait qu'elle est...

knuckle ['nʌkəl] *n* articulation *f* (du doigt)

▸ **knuckle down** *vi Fam* se mettre au boulot; **to k. down to sth** se mettre à qch

Koran [kə'rɑːn] *n* **the K.** le Coran

Korea [kə'rɪə] *n* la Corée

kosher ['kəʊʃə(r)] *adj Rel (food)* kasher *inv*

kudos ['kjuːdɒs] *n (glory)* gloire *f*; *(prestige)* prestige *m*

Kuwait [kʊ'weɪt] *n* le Koweït

Ll

L, l [el] *n (letter)* L, l *m inv*

lab [læb] *n Fam* labo *m* ■ **laboratory** [ləˈbɒrətrɪ, *Am* ˈlæbrətɔːrɪ] *n* laboratoire *m*

label [ˈleɪbəl] **1** *n* étiquette *f; (of record company)* label *m* **2** *(Br* -**ll**-, *Am* -**l**-) *vt* étiqueter; *Fig* **to l. sb (as) a liar** qualifier qn de menteur

laborious [ləˈbɔːrɪəs] *adj* laborieux, -euse

labour [ˈleɪbə(r)] *(Am* **labor**) **1** *n (work)* travail *m; (workers)* main-d'œuvre *f; Br* **L.** *(political party)* le parti travailliste; **in l.** *(woman)* en train d'accoucher **2** *adj (market)* du travail; **l. force** effectifs *mpl; Am* **l. union** syndicat *m* **3** *vi (toil)* peiner **(over** sur) ■ **labourer** *(Am* **laborer)** *n (on roads)* manœuvre *m; (on farm)* ouvrier *m* agricole

labyrinth [ˈlæbərɪnθ] *n* labyrinthe *m*

lace [leɪs] **1** *n* **(a)** *(cloth)* dentelle *f* **(b)** *(of shoe)* lacet *m* **2** *vt* **to l. (up)** *(tie up)* lacer

lack [læk] **1** *n* manque *m* (of de); **for l. of sth** à défaut de qch **2** *vt* manquer de **3** *vi* **to be lacking** manquer **(in** de)

lad [læd] *n Fam (young man)* jeune gars *m; (child)* garçon *m*

ladder [ˈlædə(r)] **1** *n* échelle *f; Br (in tights)* maille *f* filée **2** *vti Br* filer

laden [ˈleɪdən] *adj* chargé **(with** de)

lady [ˈleɪdɪ] *(pl* -**ies**) *n* dame *f;* **a young l.** une jeune fille; *(married)* une jeune dame; **Ladies and Gentlemen!** Mesdames, Mesdemoiselles, Messieurs!; **the ladies' room,** *Br* **the ladies** les toilettes *fpl* pour dames

ladybird [ˈleɪdɪbɜːd] *(Am* **ladybug** [ˈleɪdɪbʌg]) *n* coccinelle *f*

lag [læg] **1** *n* **time l.** *(between events)* décalage *m; (between countries)* décalage *m* horaire **2** *(pt & pp* -**gg**-) *vt (pipe)* isoler **3** *vi* **to l. behind** *(in progress, work)* avoir du retard; *(dawdle)* être à la traîne

lager [ˈlɑːgə(r)] *n Br* bière *f* blonde

lagoon [ləˈguːn] *n* lagune *f; (of atoll)* lagon *m*

laid [leɪd] *pt & pp of* **lay³** ■ **laid-back** *adj Fam* cool *inv*

lain [leɪn] *pp of* **lie²**

lair [leə(r)] *n* tanière *f*

lake [leɪk] *n* lac *m*

lamb [læm] *n* agneau *m*

lame [leɪm] *(-er, -est) adj (person, argument)* boiteux, -euse; *(excuse)* piètre; **to be l.** *(of person)* boiter

lament [ləˈment] *vt* **to l. (over)** se lamenter sur

laminated [ˈlæmɪneɪtɪd] *adj (glass)* feuilleté; *(wood, plastic)* stratifié

lamp [læmp] *n* lampe *f* ■ **lamppost** *n* réverbère *m* ■ **lampshade** *n* abat-jour *m inv*

lance [lɑːns] **1** *n (weapon)* lance *f* **2** *vt (abscess)* inciser

land [lænd] **1** *n* terre *f; (country)* pays *m;* **(plot of)** l. terrain *m*

2 *adj (reform)* agraire

3 *vt (passengers, cargo)* débarquer; *(aircraft)* poser; *(blow)* flanquer **(on** à); *Fam (job, prize)* décrocher

4 *vi (of aircraft)* atterrir; *(of passengers)* débarquer; *(of bomb, missile)* tomber; **to l. up in a ditch/in jail** se

retrouver dans un fossé/en prison
■ **landing** n (**a**) (of aircraft) atterrissage m; (of cargo, troops) débarquement m (**b**) (of staircase) palier m
■ **landlady** (pl **-ies**) n propriétaire f; (of pub) patronne f ■ **landlord** n propriétaire m; (of pub) patron m
■ **landmark** n point m de repère
■ **landowner** n propriétaire m foncier
■ **landslide** n (falling rocks) glissement m de terrain; (election victory) raz de marée m inv électoral

landscape ['lændskeɪp] n paysage m

lane [leɪn] n (in country) chemin m; (in town) ruelle f; (division of road) voie f; (line of traffic) file f; (for shipping, swimming) couloir m

language ['læŋgwɪdʒ] **1** n (of a people) langue f; (faculty, style) langage m **2** adj (laboratory) de langues; (teacher, studies) de langue(s)

languish ['læŋgwɪʃ] vi languir (**for** or **after** après)

lanky ['læŋkɪ] (**-ier, -iest**) adj dégingandé

lantern ['læntən] n lanterne f

lap [læp] **1** n (**a**) (of person) genoux mpl (**b**) (in race) tour m de piste **2** (pt & pp **-pp-**) vt to **l. up** (drink) laper **3** vi (of waves) clapoter

lapel [lə'pel] n revers m

lapse [læps] **1** n (**a**) (in concentration, standards) baisse f; **a l. of memory** un trou de mémoire (**b**) (interval) laps m de temps; **a l. of time** un intervalle (**between** entre) **2** vi (**a**) (of concentration, standards) baisser (**b**) (expire) (of subscription) expirer

laptop ['læptɒp] adj & n **l.** (computer) ordinateur m portable

lard [lɑːd] n saindoux m

larder ['lɑːdə(r)] n garde-manger m inv

large [lɑːdʒ] (**-er, -est**) adj (big) grand; (fat, bulky) gros (f grosse); (quantity) grand, important; **to become** or **grow** or **get l.** s'agrandir; (of person) grossir; **at l.** (of prisoner, animal) en liberté; (as a whole) en général ■ **large-scale** adj

(operation, reform) de grande envergure

largely ['lɑːdʒlɪ] adv en grande partie

lark¹ [lɑːk] n (bird) alouette f

lark² [lɑːk] Fam **1** n (joke) rigolade f **2** vi Br to **l. about** faire le fou/la folle

larva ['lɑːvə] (pl **-vae** [-viː]) n larve f

laryngitis [lærɪn'dʒaɪtɪs] n Med laryngite f

lasagne, lasagna [lə'zænjə] n lasagnes fpl

laser ['leɪzə(r)] n laser m; **l. beam/printer** rayon m/imprimante f laser

lash¹ [læʃ] **1** n (with whip) coup m de fouet **2** vt (strike) fouetter; (tie) attacher (**to** à) **3** vi to **l. out at sb** (hit) donner des coups à qn; (criticize) fustiger qn

lash² [læʃ] n (eyelash) cil m

lass [læs] n Br jeune fille f

last¹ [lɑːst] **1** adj dernier, -ère; **the l. ten lines** les dix dernières lignes; **l. night** (evening) hier soir; (night) la nuit dernière; **l. name** nom m de famille
2 adv (lastly) en dernier lieu; (on last occasion) (pour) la dernière fois; **to leave l.** sortir le dernier
3 n (person, object) dernier, -ère mf; **l. but one** avant-dernier m (f avant-dernière); **at (long) l.** enfin ■ **last-minute** adj (decision) de dernière minute

last² [lɑːst] vi durer; to **l. (out)** (endure, resist) tenir (le coup); (of money, supplies) suffire; **it lasted me ten years** ça m'a fait dix ans

lasting ['lɑːstɪŋ] adj (impression, peace) durable

lastly ['lɑːstlɪ] adv en dernier lieu

latch [lætʃ] **1** n loquet m; **the door is on the l.** la porte n'est pas fermée à clef **2** vt insep Fam to **l. onto** (understand) piger; (adopt) adopter

late¹ [leɪt] **1** (**-er, -est**) adj (meal, season, hour) tardif, -ive; (stage) avancé; (edition) dernier, -ère; **to be l. (for sth)** être en retard (pour qch); **he's an hour l.** il a une heure de retard; **it's l.** il est tard; **in the l. nineties** à la fin des années 90; **to be in one's l. for-ties** approcher de la cinquantaine; **at a later date** à une date ultérieure; **at the latest** au plus tard

2 *adv (in the day, season)* tard; *(not on time)* en retard; **it's getting l.** il se fait tard; **later (on)** plus tard; **of l.** récemment

late² [leɪt] *adj* **the l. Mr Smith** feu Monsieur Smith

latecomer ['leɪtkʌmə(r)] *n* retardataire *mf*

lately ['leɪtlɪ] *adv* dernièrement

latent ['leɪtənt] *adj (disease, tendency)* latent

lateral ['lætərəl] *adj* latéral

lather ['lɑːðə(r)] **1** *n* mousse *f* **2** *vt* savonner

Latin ['lætɪn] **1** *adj* latin; **L. America** l'Amérique *f* latine ■ **L. American 1** *adj* d'Amérique latine **2** *n* Latino-Américain, -e *mf* **2** *n (language)* latin *m*

latitude ['lætɪtjuːd] *n (on map, freedom)* latitude *f*

latter ['lætə(r)] **1** *adj (later, last-named)* dernier, -ère; *(second)* deuxième **2** *n* **the l.** le dernier (*f* la dernière); *(of two)* le second (*f* la seconde)

lattice ['lætɪs] *n* treillis *m*

laudable ['lɔːdəbəl] *adj* louable

laugh [lɑːf] **1** *n* rire *m*; **to have a good l.** bien rire **2** *vt* **to l. sth off** tourner qch en plaisanterie **3** *vi* rire (**at/about** de) ■ **laughing** *adj* riant; **it's no l. matter** il n'y a pas de quoi rire; **to be the l. stock of** être la risée de

laughable ['lɑːfəbəl] *adj* ridicule

laughter ['lɑːftə(r)] *n* rire(s) *m(pl)*

launch [lɔːntʃ] **1** *n* (**a**) *(motorboat)* vedette *f*; *(pleasure boat)* bateau *m* de plaisance (**b**) *(of ship, rocket, product)* lancement *m* **2** *vt (ship, rocket, product)* lancer **3** *vi* **to l. (out) into** *(begin)* se lancer dans

launder ['lɔːndə(r)] *vt (clothes, money)* blanchir

launderette [lɔːndə'ret] (*Am* **Laundromat®** ['lɔːndrəmæt]) *n* laverie *f* automatique

laundry ['lɔːndrɪ] *n (place)* blanchisserie *f*; *(clothes)* linge *m*; **to do the l.** faire la lessive

lava ['lɑːvə] *n* lave *f*

lavatory ['lævətərɪ] (*pl* **-ies**) *n* toilettes *fpl*

lavender ['lævɪndə(r)] *n* lavande *f*

lavish ['lævɪʃ] **1** *adj* prodigue (**with** de); *(meal, décor, gift)* somptueux, -euse; *(expenditure)* excessif, -ive **2** *vt* **to l. sth on sb** couvrir qn de qch

law [lɔː] *n (rule, rules)* loi *f*; *(study, profession, system)* droit *m*; **against the l.** illégal; **court of l.** cour *f* de justice; **l. and order** l'ordre *m* public

lawful ['lɔːfəl] *adj (action)* légal; *(claim)* légitime

lawless ['lɔːləs] *adj (country)* anarchique

lawn [lɔːn] *n* pelouse *f*, gazon *m*; **l. mower** tondeuse *f* à gazon

lawsuit ['lɔːsuːt] *n* procès *m*

lawyer ['lɔːjə(r)] *n (in court)* avocat, -e *mf*; *(for wills, sales)* notaire *m*; *(legal expert)* juriste *mf*

lax [læks] *adj (person)* laxiste; *(discipline, behaviour)* relâché

laxative ['læksətɪv] *n* laxatif *m*

lay¹ [leɪ] *pt of* **lie²**

lay² [leɪ] *adj (non-religious)* laïque; **l. person** profane *mf* ■ **layman** (*pl* **-men**) *n (nonspecialist)* profane *mf*

lay³ [leɪ] (*pt & pp* **laid**) **1** *vt (put down, place)* poser; *(blanket)* étendre (**over** sur); *(trap)* tendre; *(egg)* pondre; *Br* **to l. the table** mettre la table **2** *vi (of bird)* pondre ■ **layabout** *n Fam* fainéant, -e *mf* ■ **lay-by** (*pl* **-bys**) *n Br (for vehicles)* aire *f* de stationnement ■ **layout** *n* disposition *f*; *(of text)* mise *f* en page

▸ **lay down** *vt sep (put down)* poser; *(arms)* déposer; *(principle, condition)* établir; **to l. down the law** dicter sa loi (**to** à)

▸ **lay into** *vt insep Fam (physically)* rosser; *(verbally)* voler dans les plumes à

▸ **lay off** *vt sep* **to l. sb off** *(worker)* licencier qn

▶ **lay on** *vt sep Br (install)* installer; *(supply)* fournir

▶ **lay out** *vt sep (garden)* dessiner; *(house)* concevoir; *(display)* disposer; *Fam (money)* mettre (**on** dans)

layer ['leɪə(r)] *n* couche *f*

laze [leɪz] *vi* **to l. (about** *or* **around)** paresser

lazy ['leɪzɪ] (**-ier, -iest**) *adj (person)* paresseux, -euse ◼ **lazybones** *n Fam* flemmard, -e *mf*

lb *(abbr libra)* **3lb** 3 livres *(unité de poids)*

lead¹ [led] *n (metal)* plomb *m*; *(of pencil)* mine *f* ◼ **leaded** *adj (petrol)* au plomb ◼ **lead-free** *adj (paint)* sans plomb

lead² [li:d] **1** *n (distance or time ahead)* avance *f* (**over** sur); *(example)* exemple *m*; *(clue)* indice *m*; *(in film)* rôle *m* principal; *Br (for dog)* laisse *f*; *(electric wire)* fil *m* électrique; **to take the l.** *(in race)* prendre la tête; **to be in the l.** *(in race)* être en tête; *(in match)* mener (à la marque)

2 *(pt & pp* **led)** *vt (guide, conduct, take)* mener, conduire (**to** à); *(team, government)* diriger; *(expedition, attack)* commander; *(procession)* être en tête de; **to l. a happy life** mener une vie heureuse; **to l. sb in/out** faire entrer/ sortir qn; **to l. sb to do sth** *(cause, induce)* amener qn à faire qch

3 *vi (of street, door)* mener, conduire (**to** à); *(in race)* être en tête; *(in match)* mener (à la marque); *(go ahead)* aller devant; **to l. to sth** *(result in)* aboutir à qch; *(cause)* mener à; **to l. up to** *(precede)* précéder

▶ **lead away** *vt sep* emmener

▶ **lead off** *vt sep* emmener

▶ **lead on** *vt sep (deceive)* tromper, duper

leader ['li:də(r)] *n* (**a**) *(person)* chef *m*; *(of country, party)* dirigeant, -e *mf*; *(of strike, riot)* meneur, -euse *mf*; *(guide)* guide *m*; **to be the l.** *(in race)* être en tête (**b**) *Br (newspaper article)* éditorial *m* ◼ **leadership** *n* direction *f*; *(qualities)*

qualités *fpl* de chef; *(leaders) (of country, party)* dirigeants *mpl*

leading ['li:dɪŋ] *adj (best, most important)* principal; **a l. figure, a l. light** un personnage marquant

leaf [li:f] **1** *(pl* **leaves)** *n* feuille *f*; *(of book)* feuillet *m*; *(of table)* rallonge *f* **2** *vi* **to l. through** *(book)* feuilleter

leaflet ['li:flɪt] *n* prospectus *m*; *(containing instructions)* notice *f*

league [li:g] *n (alliance)* ligue *f*; *(in sport)* championnat *m*; *Pej* **in l. with** de connivence avec

leak [li:k] **1** *n (in pipe, information)* fuite *f*; *(in boat)* voie *f* d'eau **2** *vt Fig (information)* divulguer; **the pipe was leaking gas** du gaz fuyait du tuyau **3** *vi (of liquid, pipe, tap)* fuir; *(of ship)* faire eau; *Fig* **to l. out** *(of information)* être divulgué ◼ **leaky** ['li:kɪ] (**-ier, -iest**) *adj (kettle, pipe, tap)* qui fuit; *(roof)* qui a une fuite

lean¹ [li:n] (**-er, -est**) *adj (meat)* maigre; *(person)* mince

lean² [li:n] *(pt & pp* **leaned** *or* **leant** [lent]) **1** *vt* **to l. sth on/against sth** appuyer qch sur/contre qch **2** *vi (of object)* pencher; *(of person)* se pencher; **to l. against/on sth** *(of person)* s'appuyer contre/sur qch; **to l. forward** *(of person)* se pencher (en avant); **to l. over** *(of person)* se pencher; *(of object)* pencher ◼ **leaning** *adj* penché; **l. against** *(resting)* appuyé contre ◼ **leanings** *npl* tendances *fpl* (**towards** à)

leap [li:p] **1** *n (jump)* bond *m*, saut *m*; *Fig (change, increase)* bond *m*; **l. year** année *f* bissextile **2** *(pt & pp* **leaped** *or* **leapt)** *vi* bondir, sauter; **to l. to one's feet, to l. up** se lever d'un bond

leapt [lept] *pt & pp of* **leap**

learn [lɜːn] *(pt & pp* **learned** *or* **learnt** [lɜːnt]) **1** *vt* apprendre (**that** que); **to l. (how) to do sth** apprendre à faire qch **2** *vi* apprendre; **to l. about sth** *(study)* étudier qch; *(hear about)* apprendre qch ◼ **learned** [-ɪd] *adj* savant ◼ **learner** *n (beginner)* débutant,

-e *mf*; (*student*) étudiant, -e *mf* ■ **learning** *n* (*of language*) apprentissage *m* (**of** de); (*knowledge*) savoir *m*

lease [li:s] **1** *n* bail *m* (*pl* baux) **2** *vt* (*house*) louer à bail (**from/to** à)

leash [li:ʃ] *n* (*of dog*) laisse *f*; **on a l.** en laisse

least [li:st] **1** *adj* **the l.** (*smallest amount of*) le moins de; **he has (the) l. talent** il a le moins de talent (**of all** de tous); **the l. effort/noise** le moindre effort/bruit **2** *n* **the l.** le moins; **at l.** du moins; (*with quantity*) au moins; **not in the l.** pas du tout **3** *adv* **the l.** le moins; **the l. difficult** le/la moins difficile; **l. of all** (*especially not*) surtout pas

leather ['leðə(r)] *n* cuir *m*

leave [li:v] **1** *n* (*holiday*) congé *m*; (*of soldier, permission*) permission *f*; **to be on l.** être en congé; (*of soldier*) être en permission; **to take (one's) l. of sb** prendre congé de qn

  2 (*pt & pp* left) *vt* (*allow to remain, forget*) laisser; (*depart from*) quitter; **to l. sth with sb** (*entrust, give*) laisser qch à qn; **to be left (over)** rester; **there's no bread left** il ne reste plus de pain; **I'll l. it (up) to you** je m'en remets à toi

  3 *vi* (*go away*) partir (**from** de; **for** pour)

▶ **leave behind** *vt sep* **to l. sth behind** (*on purpose*) laisser qch; (*accidentally*) oublier qch; **to l. sb behind** (*not take*) partir sans qn; (*surpass*) dépasser qn; (*in race, at school*) distancer qn

▶ **leave off** *vt sep* (*lid*) ne pas remettre; *Fam* **to l. off doing sth** (*stop*) arrêter de faire qch

▶ **leave on** *vt sep* (*clothes*) garder

▶ **leave out** *vt sep* (*forget to put*) oublier de mettre; (*deliberately omit*) décider de ne pas include; (*when reading*) (*word, line*) sauter; (*exclude*) exclure

Lebanon ['lebənən] *n* le Liban

lecherous ['letʃərəs] *adj* lubrique

lecture ['lektʃə(r)] **1** *n* (*public speech*) conférence *f*; (*as part of series at*

university) cours *m* magistral; (*scolding*) sermon *m*; **l. hall** amphithéâtre *m* **2** *vt Fam* (*scold*) faire la morale à **3** *vi* faire une conférence/un cours ■ **lecturer** *n* conférencier, -ère *mf*; (*at university*) enseignant, -e *mf*

led [led] *pt & pp of* **lead²**

ledge [ledʒ] *n* (*on wall, window*) rebord *m*

ledger ['ledʒə(r)] *n* grand livre *m*

leek [li:k] *n* poireau *m*

leer [lɪə(r)] *vi* **to l. at sb** (*lustfully*) regarder qn d'un air lubrique

leeway ['li:weɪ] *n* marge *f* (de manœuvre)

left¹ [left] *pt & pp of* **leave** ■ **left-luggage** *n Br* **l. office** consigne *f*

left² [left] **1** *adj* (*side, hand*) gauche **2** *n* gauche *f*; **on** *or* **to the l.** à gauche (**of** de) **3** *adv* à gauche ■ **left-hand** *adj* de gauche; **on the l. side** à gauche (**of** de); **l. drive** conduite *f* à gauche ■ **left-handed** *adj* (*person*) gaucher, -ère ■ **left-wing** *adj* (*views, government*) de gauche

leftovers ['leftəʊvəz] *npl* restes *mpl*

leg [leg] *n* jambe *f*; (*of dog, bird*) patte *f*; (*of table*) pied *m*; (*of journey*) étape *f*; **l. of chicken, chicken l.** cuisse *f* de poulet; **to pull sb's l.** (*make fun of*) mettre qn en boîte

legacy ['legəsɪ] (*pl* -**ies**) *n* (*in a will*) & *Fig* legs *m*

legal ['li:gəl] *adj* (*lawful*) légal; (*affairs, adviser*) juridique ■ **legalize** *vt* légaliser ■ **legally** *adv* légalement

legend ['ledʒənd] *n* (*story, inscription*) légende *f* ■ **legendary** *adj* légendaire

leggings ['legɪŋz] *npl* (*of woman*) caleçon *m*

legible ['ledʒɪbəl] *adj* lisible

legislation [ledʒɪs'leɪʃən] *n* (*laws*) législation *f*; (**piece of**) **l.** loi *f*

legislative ['ledʒɪslətɪv] *adj* législatif, -ive

legitimate [lɪ'dʒɪtɪmət] *adj* légitime

legroom ['legru:m] *n* place *f* pour les jambes

leisure [*Br* 'leʒə(r), *Am* 'li:ʒər] *n* **l.**

(time) loisirs *mpl*; **l. centre** *or* **complex** centre *m* de loisirs; **at (one's) l.** à tête reposée ■ **leisurely** [*Br* 'leʒəlɪ, *Am* 'liːʒərlɪ] *adj* (*walk, occupation*) peu fatigant; (*meal, life*) tranquille; **at a l. pace, in a l. way** sans se presser

lemon ['lemən] *n* citron *m*; *Br* **l. drink, l. squash** citronnade *f*; **l. tea** thé *m* au citron ■ **lemonade** *n* (*still*) citronnade *f*; *Br* (*fizzy*) limonade *f*

lend [lend] (*pt & pp* **lent**) *vt* prêter (**to** à); (*support*) apporter (**to** à); *Fig* (*charm, colour*) donner (**to** à) ■ **lender** *n* prêteur, -euse *mf*

length [leŋθ] *n* (*in space*) longueur *f*; (*section of road, string*) tronçon *m*; (*of cloth*) métrage *m*; (*duration*) durée *f*; **at l.** (*at last*) enfin; **at (great) l.** (*in detail*) dans le détail; **to go to great lengths** se donner beaucoup de mal (**to do** pour faire)

lengthen ['leŋθən] *vt* (*garment*) allonger; (*holiday, visit*) prolonger ■ **lengthwise** *adv* dans le sens de la longueur ■ **lengthy** (**-ier, -iest**) *adj* long (*f* longue)

lenient ['liːnɪənt] *adj* indulgent (**to** envers) ■ **leniently** *adv* avec indulgence

lens [lenz] (*pl* **lenses** [-zəz]) *n* lentille *f*; (*in spectacles*) verre *m*; (*of camera*) objectif *m*

Lent [lent] *n Rel* carême *m*

lent [lent] *pt & pp of* **lend**

lentil ['lentəl] *n* lentille *f*

leopard ['lepəd] *n* léopard *m*

leotard ['liːətɑːd] *n* justaucorps *m*

lesbian ['lezbɪən] **1** *adj* lesbien, -enne **2** *n* lesbienne *f*

less [les] **1** *adj & pron* moins (de) (**than** que); **l. time** moins de temps; **she has l. (than you)** elle en a moins (que toi); **l. than a kilo** moins d'un kilo **2** *adv* moins (**than** que); **l. (often)** moins souvent; **one l.** un(e) de moins **3** *prep* moins

-less [ləs] *suff* sans; **childless** sans enfants

lessen ['lesən] *vti* diminuer

lesser ['lesə(r)] **1** *adj* moindre **2** *n* **the l. of** le/la moindre de

lesson ['lesən] *n* leçon *f*; **an English l.** une leçon d'anglais; *Fig* **he has learnt his l.** ça lui a servi de leçon

lest [lest] *conj* de peur que... (**+ ne + subjunctive**)

LET¹ [let] **1** (*pt & pp* **let**, *pres p* **letting**) *vt* (*allow*) **to l. sb do sth** laisser qn faire qch; **to l. sb have sth** donner qch à qn; **to l. go of sb/sth** lâcher qn/qch **2** *v aux* **l.'s eat/go** mangeons/partons; **l.'s go for a stroll** allons nous promener; **l. him come** qu'il vienne ■ **letdown** *n* déception *f*

▶ **let down** *vt sep* (*lower*) baisser; (*hair*) dénouer; (*tyre*) dégonfler; **to l. sb down** (*disappoint*) décevoir qn; **don't l. me down** je compte sur toi

▶ **let in** *vt sep* (*person, dog*) faire entrer; (*light*) laisser entrer; **to l. sb in on sth** mettre qn au courant de qch; **to l. oneself in for trouble** s'attirer des ennuis

▶ **let off** *vt sep* (*firework*) tirer; (*bomb*) faire exploser; (*gun*) faire partir; **to l. sb off** (*allow to leave*) laisser partir qn; (*not punish*) ne pas punir qn; **to be l. off with a fine** s'en tirer avec une amende; **to l. sb off doing sth** dispenser qn de faire qch

▶ **let on** *vi Fam* **to l. on that...** (*reveal*) dire que...

▶ **let out** *vt sep* (*allow to leave*) laisser sortir; (*prisoner*) relâcher; (*cry, secret*) laisser échapper; (*skirt*) élargir

▶ **let up** *vi* (*of rain, person*) s'arrêter

let² [let] (*pt & pp* **let**, *pres p* **letting**) *vt* (*to* l. (out)) (*house, room*) louer

lethal ['liːθəl] *adj* (*blow, dose*) mortel, -elle; (*weapon*) meurtrier, -ère

lethargic [lɪ'θɑːdʒɪk] *adj* léthargique

letter ['letə(r)] *n* (*message, part of word*) lettre *f*; **l. opener** coupe-papier *m inv* ■ **letterbox** *n Br* boîte *f* aux lettres ■ **letterheaded** *adj* **l. paper** papier *m* à en-tête ■ **lettering** *n* (*letters*) lettres *fpl*

lettuce ['letɪs] n laitue f
letup ['letʌp] n répit m
level ['levəl] **1** n niveau m; **at eye l.** à hauteur des yeux **2** adj (surface) plat; (equal in score) à égalité (**with** avec); (in height) à la même hauteur (**with** que); Br **l. crossing** (for train) passage m à niveau **3** (Br **-ll-**, Am **-l-**) vt (surface, differences) aplanir; (building) raser; (gun) braquer (**at** sur); (accusation) lancer (**at** contre) **4** vi **to l. off** or **out** (of prices) se stabiliser ■ **level-headed** adj équilibré
lever [Br 'li:və(r), Am 'levər] n levier m
levy ['levɪ] **1** (pl **-ies**) n (tax) impôt m (**on** sur) **2** (pt & pp **-ied**) vt (tax) lever
lewd [lu:d] (**-er, -est**) adj obscène
liability [laɪə'bɪlətɪ] n (legal responsibility) responsabilité f (**for** de); (disadvantage) handicap m; Fin **liabilities** (debts) passif m
liable ['laɪəbəl] adj **l. to** (dizziness) sujet, -ette à; (fine, tax) passible de; **to be l. to do sth** risquer de faire qch; **l. for sth** (responsible) responsable de qch
liaise [li:'eɪz] vi travailler en liaison (**with** avec) ■ **liaison** [li:'eɪzɒn] n (contact, love affair) liaison f
liar ['laɪə(r)] n menteur, -euse mf
libel ['laɪbəl] **1** n (in law) diffamation f **2** (Br **-ll-**, Am **-l-**) vt diffamer (par écrit)
liberal ['lɪbərəl] **1** adj (open-minded) & Pol libéral; (generous) généreux, -euse (**with** de) **2** n Pol libéral, -e mf
liberate ['lɪbəreɪt] vt libérer ■ **liberation** n libération f
liberty ['lɪbətɪ] (pl **-ies**) n liberté f; **to be at l. to do sth** être libre de faire qch; **to take liberties with sb/sth** prendre des libertés avec qn/qch
library ['laɪbrərɪ] (pl **-ies**) n bibliothèque f ■ **librarian** [-'breərɪən] n bibliothécaire mf
libretto [lɪ'bretəʊ] (pl **-os**) n Mus livret m
Libya ['lɪbɪə] n la Libye
lice [laɪs] pl of **louse**
licence ['laɪsəns] (Am **license**) n

(permit) permis m; (for trading) licence f; (**TV**) **l.** redevance f; **l. plate/number** (of vehicle) plaque f/numéro m d'immatriculation
license ['laɪsəns] **1** n Am = **licence 2** vt accorder un permis/une licence à
lick [lɪk] vt lécher
licorice ['lɪkərɪʃ, 'lɪkərɪs] n réglisse f
lid [lɪd] n (of box, pan) couvercle m
lie¹ [laɪ] **1** n mensonge m **2** (pt & pp **lied**, pres p **lying**) vi (tell lies) mentir
lie² [laɪ] (pt **lay**, pp **lain**, pres p **lying**) vi (**a**) (of person, animal) (be in a flat position) être allongé; (get down) s'allonger; **to be lying on the grass** être allongé sur l'herbe; **he lay asleep** il dormait; **here lies…** (on tomb) ci-gît… (**b**) (of object) être, se trouver; **the problem lies in the fact that…** le problème réside dans le fait que… ■ **lie-down** n Br **to have a l.** faire une sieste ■ **lie-in** n Br **to have a l.** faire la grasse matinée
▶ **lie about, lie around** vi (of objects, person) traîner
▶ **lie down** vi s'allonger; **to be lying down** être allongé
▶ **lie in** vi Br faire la grasse matinée
lieu [lu:] n **in l. of sth** au lieu de qch
lieutenant [lu:'tenənt, Br lef'tenənt] n lieutenant m
life [laɪf] (pl **lives**) n vie f; (of battery, machine) durée f de vie; **to come to l.** (of party, street) s'animer; **to take one's (own) l.** se donner la mort; **l. expectancy** espérance f de vie; **l. insurance** assurance-vie f; **l. jacket** gilet m de sauvetage ■ **lifebelt** n ceinture f de sauvetage ■ **lifeboat** n canot m de sauvetage ■ **lifebuoy** n bouée f de sauvetage ■ **lifeguard** n maître nageur m ■ **lifeless** adj sans vie ■ **lifelike** adj très ressemblant ■ **lifelong** adj de toute sa vie; (friend) de toujours ■ **lifesize(d)** adj grandeur nature inv ■ **lifestyle** n style m de vie ■ **lifetime** n vie f; Fig éternité f
lift [lɪft] **1** n Br (elevator) ascenseur m; **to give sb a l.** emmener qn en voiture

(to à) 2 *vt* lever; *(heavy object)* soulever; *Fig (ban)* lever; *Fig (steal)* piquer **(from à) 3** *vi (of fog)* se lever ■ **lift-off** *n (of space vehicle)* décollage *m*

▶ **lift down** *vt sep (take down)* descendre **(from** de**)**

▶ **lift off 1** *vt sep (take down)* descendre **(from** de**) 2** *vi (of spacecraft)* décoller

▶ **lift out** *vt sep (take out)* sortir

▶ **lift up** *vt sep (arm, object, eyes)* lever; *(heavy object)* soulever

ligament ['lɪgəmənt] *n* ligament *m*

light¹ [laɪt] **1** *n* lumière *f*, *(on vehicle)* feu *m*; *(vehicle headlight)* phare *m*; **by the l. of sth** à la clarté de qch; **in the l. of...** *(considering)* à la lumière de...; **to bring sth to l.** mettre qch en lumière; **to come to l.** être découvert; **do you have a l.?** *(for cigarette)* est-ce que vous avez du feu?; **to set l. to sth** mettre le feu à qch; **turn right at the lights** tournez à droite après le feux; **l. bulb** ampoule *f*; **l. switch** interrupteur *m*

2 *adj* **it will soon be l.** il fera bientôt jour

3 *(pt & pp* lit *or* lighted*) vt (fire, candle, gas)* allumer; *(match)* allumer, gratter; **to l. (up)** *(room)* éclairer; *(cigarette)* allumer

4 *vi* **to l. up** *(of smoker)* allumer une cigarette/un cigare/sa pipe ■ **lighting** *n (act, system)* éclairage *m*

light² [laɪt] *adj (bright, not dark)* clair; **a l. green jacket** une veste vert clair

light³ [laɪt] *adj (in weight, quantity, strength)* léger, -ère; *(task)* facile; **l. rain** pluie *f* fine; **to travel l.** voyager avec peu de bagages ■ **light-hearted** *adj* enjoué

lighten ['laɪtən] *vt (make less heavy)* alléger

lighter ['laɪtə(r)] *n* briquet *m*; *(for cooker)* allume-gaz *m inv*

lighthouse ['laɪthaʊs] *n* phare *m*

lightly ['laɪtlɪ] *adv* légèrement; **to get off l.** s'en tirer à bon compte

lightning ['laɪtnɪŋ] **1** *n* éclairs *mpl*;

(flash of) l. éclair *m* **2** *adj (speed)* foudroyant; *(visit)* éclair *inv*

lightweight ['laɪtweɪt] **1** *adj (shoes, fabric)* léger, -ère; *Fig & Pej (person)* pas sérieux, -euse **2** *n (in boxing)* poids *m* léger

like¹ [laɪk] **1** *prep* comme; **l. this** comme ça; **what's he l.?** comment est-il?; **to be** *or* **look l. sb/sth** ressembler à qn/qch; **what was the book l.?** comment as-tu trouvé le livre?

2 *adv* **nothing l. as big** loin d'être aussi grand

3 *conj Fam (as)* comme; **do l. I do** fais comme moi

4 *n* **...and the l.** ...et ainsi de suite; **the likes of you** des gens de ton acabit

like² [laɪk] **1** *vt* aimer (bien) **(to do** *or* **doing** faire**); I l. him** je l'aime bien; **I'd l. to come** j'aimerais bien venir; **I'd l. a kilo of apples** je voudrais un kilo de pommes; **would you l. an apple?** voulez-vous une pomme?; **if you l.** si vous voulez

2 *npl* **one's likes and dislikes** nos préférences *fpl* ■ **liking** *n* **a l. for** *(person)* de la sympathie pour; *(thing)* du goût pour; **to my l.** à mon goût

likeable ['laɪkəbəl] *adj* sympathique

likely ['laɪklɪ] **1** *(-ier, -iest) adj (result, event)* probable; *(excuse)* vraisemblable; **it's l. (that) she'll come** il est probable qu'elle viendra **2** *adv* **very l.** très probablement ■ **likelihood** *n* probabilité *f*; **there isn't much l. that...** il y a peu de chances que... *(+ subjunctive)*

liken ['laɪkən] *vt* comparer **(to** à**)**

likeness ['laɪknɪs] *n (similarity)* ressemblance *f*; **it's a good l.** c'est très ressemblant

likewise ['laɪkwaɪz] *adv (similarly)* de même

lilac ['laɪlək] **1** *n* lilas *m* **2** *adj (colour)* lilas *inv*

Lilo® ['laɪləʊ] *(pl* -os*) n Br* matelas *m* pneumatique

lily ['lɪlɪ] *(pl* -ies*) n* lis *m*

limb [lɪm] n (of body) membre m

limber ['lɪmbə(r)] vi **to l. up** s'échauffer

lime [laɪm] n (fruit) citron m vert

limelight ['laɪmlaɪt] n **to be in the l.** occuper le devant de la scène

limit ['lɪmɪt] **1** n limite f; (restriction) limitation f (on de); Fam **that's the l.!** c'est le comble!; **within limits** jusqu'à un certain point **2** vt limiter (**to** à); **to l. oneself to sth/doing sth** se borner à qch/faire qch ■ **limitation** n limitation f

limited ['lɪmɪtɪd] adj (restricted) limité; (edition) à tirage limité; Br **l. company** société f à responsabilité limitée; Br **(public) l. company** (with shareholders) société f anonyme

limousine [lɪmə'ziːn] n (car) limousine f

limp¹ [lɪmp] **1** n **to have a l.** boiter **2** vi (of person) boiter

limp² [lɪmp] (**-er, -est**) adj (soft) mou (f molle); (flabby) (skin) flasque; (person, hat) avachi

line¹ [laɪn] **1** n ligne f; (stroke) trait m; (of poem) vers m; (wrinkle) ride f; (track) voie f; (rope) corde f; (row) rangée f; (of vehicles) file f; (queue of people) file f, queue f; (of goods) ligne f (de produits); **to learn one's lines** (of actor) apprendre son texte; **to be on the l.** (at other end of phone line) être au bout du fil; (at risk) (of job) être menacé; Am **to stand in l.** faire la queue; **in l. with sth** conforme à qch; **along the same lines** (work, think, act) de la même façon; Fam **to drop sb a l.** (send a letter) envoyer un mot à qn; **l. dancing** = danse de style country effectuée en rangs

2 vt **to l. the street** (of trees) border la rue; (of people) s'aligner le long du trottoir; **to l. up** (children, objects) aligner; (arrange) organiser; **lined paper** papier m réglé

3 vi **to l. up** s'aligner; Am (queue up) faire la queue ■ **line-up** n (row of people) file f; TV (of guests) plateau m

line² [laɪn] vt (clothes) doubler

linen ['lɪnɪn] n (sheets) linge m; (material) (toile f de) lin m

liner ['laɪnə(r)] n (**a**) (ocean) **l.** paquebot m (**b**) (dust)bin **l.**, Am **garbage can l.** sac-poubelle m

linesman ['laɪnzmən] (pl **-men**) n (in football) juge m de touche

linger ['lɪŋgə(r)] vi **to l. (on)** (of person) s'attarder; (of smell, memory) persister; (of doubt) subsister

linguist ['lɪŋgwɪst] n (specialist) linguiste mf ■ **linguistic** adj linguistique ■ **linguistics** n linguistique f

lining ['laɪnɪŋ] n (of clothes) doublure f

link [lɪŋk] **1** n (connection) & Comptr lien m; (of chain) maillon m; (by road, rail) liaison f **2** vt (connect) relier (**to** à); (relate, associate) lier (**to** à); **to l. up** relier; (computer) connecter **3** vi **to l. up** (of companies, countries) s'associer; (of roads) se rejoindre

lino ['laɪnəʊ] (pl **-os**) n Br lino m

lint [lɪnt] n (bandage) tissu m ouaté; (fluff) peluches fpl

lion ['laɪən] n lion m; **l. cub** lionceau m

lip [lɪp] n (of person) lèvre f; (of cup) bord m ■ **lip-read** (pt & pp **-read** [-red]) vi lire sur les lèvres ■ **lipstick** n rouge m à lèvres

liqueur [Br lɪ'kjʊə(r), Am lɪ'kɜːr] n liqueur f

liquid ['lɪkwɪd] n & adj liquide (m)

liquidate ['lɪkwɪdeɪt] vt (debt) & Fam (kill) liquider

liquidizer ['lɪkwɪdaɪzə(r)] n Br (for fruit juices, purées) mixeur m ■ **liquidize** vt Br passer au mixeur

liquor ['lɪkə(r)] n Am alcool m; **l. store** magasin m de vins et de spiritueux

liquorice ['lɪkərɪʃ, 'lɪkərɪs] n Br réglisse f

lira ['lɪərə] (pl **lire** ['lɪəreɪ]) n lire f

lisp [lɪsp] **1** n **to have a l.** zézayer **2** vi zézayer

list [lɪst] **1** n liste f **2** vt (things) faire la liste de; (names) mettre sur la liste; (name one by one) énumérer; Br **listed**

building monument *m* classé

listen ['lɪsən] *vi* écouter; **to l. to sb/ sth** écouter qn/qch; **to l. (out) for** *(telephone, person)* guetter ■ **listener** *n* *(to radio)* auditeur, -trice *mf*

listless ['lɪstləs] *adj* apathique

lit [lɪt] *pt & pp of* **light¹**

liter ['liːtə(r)] *n Am* litre *m*

literal ['lɪtərəl] *adj* littéral; *(not exaggerated)* réel (*f* réelle)

literally ['lɪtərəlɪ] *adv* littéralement; *(really)* réellement ■ **literary** *adj* littéraire

literate ['lɪtərət] *adj* qui sait lire et écrire

literature ['lɪtərətʃə(r)] *n* littérature *f*; *(pamphlets)* documentation *f*

lithe [laɪð] *adj* agile

litigation [lɪtɪ'geɪʃən] *n* litige *m*

litre ['liːtə(r)] *(Am* **liter)** *n* litre *m*

litter ['lɪtə(r)] **1** *n* (**a**) *(rubbish)* détritus *mpl*; *(papers)* papiers *mpl* (**b**) *Br* **l. bin** boîte *f* à ordures; *(young animals)* portée *f*; *(for cat)* litière *f* **2** *vt Br* **to be littered with sth** être jonché de qch

LITTLE ['lɪtəl] **1** *n* peu *m*; **I've l. left** il m'en reste peu; **she eats l.** elle mange peu; **I have a l.** j'en ai un peu
2 *adj* (**a**) *(small)* petit; **a l. bit** un (petit) peu (**b**) *(not much)* peu de; **l. time/money** peu de temps/d'argent; **a l. time/money** un peu de temps/ d'argent
3 *adv* *(somewhat, rather)* peu; **l. by l.** peu à peu; **as l. as possible** le moins possible; **a l. heavy/better** un peu lourd/mieux; **to work a l.** travailler un peu

live¹ [laɪv] **1** *adj* (**a**) *(electric wire)* sous tension; *(plugged in) (appliance)* branché; *(ammunition)* réel (*f* réelle), de combat (**b**) *(alive)* vivant **2** *adj & adv* *(on radio, television)* en direct; **a l. broadcast** une émission en direct; **a l. recording** un enregistrement public

live² [lɪv] **1** *vt (life)* mener, vivre **2** *vi* vivre; **where do you l.?** où habitezvous?; **to l. in Paris** habiter (à) Paris

▸ **live down** *vt sep* faire oublier

▸ **live off** *vt insep (eat)* vivre de; *(sponge off)* vivre aux crochets de

▸ **live on 1** *vt sep* = **live off 2** *vi (of memory)* survivre

▸ **live through** *vt insep (experience)* vivre

▸ **live up to** *vt insep (sb's expectations)* se montrer à la hauteur de

livelihood ['laɪvlɪhʊd] *n* **my l.** mon gagne-pain; **to earn one's** *or* **a l.** gagner sa vie

lively ['laɪvlɪ] **(-ier, -iest)** *adj (person, style)* plein de vie; *(story)* vivant; *(mind)* vif (*f* vive); *(discussion, conversation)* animé

▸ **liven up** ['laɪvən] **1** *vt sep (person)* égayer; *(party)* animer **2** *vi (of person, party)* s'animer

liver ['lɪvə(r)] *n* foie *m*

livestock ['laɪvstɒk] *n* bétail *m*

livid ['lɪvɪd] *adj (angry)* furieux, -euse

living ['lɪvɪŋ] **1** *adj (alive)* vivant; **within l. memory** de mémoire d'homme; **the l.** les vivants *mpl* **2** *n (livelihood)* vie *f*; **to make** *or* **earn a** *or* **one's l.** gagner sa vie; **l. room** salle *f* de séjour

lizard ['lɪzəd] *n* lézard *m*

load [ləʊd] **1** *n (object carried, burden)* charge *f*; *(freight)* chargement *m*; *(strain, weight)* poids *m*; *Fam* **a l. of,** **loads of** *(people, money)* un tas de **2** *vt (truck, gun)* charger (**with** de); **to l. up** *(car, ship)* charger (**with** de) **3** *vi* **to l. (up)** prendre un chargement

loaded ['ləʊdɪd] *adj (gun, vehicle)* chargé; *Fam (rich)* plein aux as

loaf [ləʊf] **1** *(pl* **loaves)** *n* pain *m* **2** *vi* **to l. (about)** fainéanter

loan [ləʊn] **1** *n (money lent)* prêt *m*; *(money borrowed)* emprunt *m*; **on l. from** prêté par **2** *vt (lend)* prêter (**to** à)

loathe [ləʊð] *vt* détester (**doing** faire)

lobby ['lɒbɪ] **1** *(pl* **-ies)** *n (of hotel)* hall *m*; *(of theatre)* foyer *m* (**b**) *(in politics)* groupe *m* de pression **2** *(pt & pp* **-ied)** *vt* faire pression sur **3** *vi* **to l. for sth** faire pression pour obtenir qch

lobster ['lɒbstə(r)] n homard m; *(spiny)* langouste f

local ['ləʊkəl] **1** adj local; *(regional)* régional; *(of the neighbourhood)* du quartier; **a l. phone call** *(within town)* une communication urbaine **2** n Br Fam *(pub)* bistrot m du coin; **the locals** *(people)* les gens mpl du coin

locality [ləʊ'kælɪtɪ] (pl -ies) n *(neighbourhood)* environs mpl

locally ['ləʊkəlɪ] adv dans le quartier

locate [ləʊ'keɪt] vt *(find)* repérer; *(pain, noise, leak)* localiser; *(situate)* situer; **to be located in Paris** être situé à Paris ■ **location** n *(site)* emplacement m; **on l.** *(shoot a film)* en extérieur

lock¹ [lɒk] n *(of hair)* mèche f

lock² [lɒk] **1** n **(a)** *(on door, chest)* serrure f; *(anti-theft)* **l.** *(on vehicle)* antivol m **(b)** *(on canal)* écluse f **2** vt *(door, car)* fermer à clef **3** vi fermer à clef

► **lock away** vt sep *(prisoner)* enfermer; *(jewels)* mettre sous clef

► **lock in** vt sep *(person)* enfermer; **to l. sb in sth** enfermer qn dans qch

► **lock out** vt sep *(person)* enfermer dehors

► **lock up 1** vt sep *(house, car)* fermer à clef; *(prisoner)* enfermer; *(jewels)* mettre sous clef, enfermer **2** vi fermer à clef

locker ['lɒkə(r)] n *(in school)* casier m; *(for luggage)* *(at station, airport)* casier m de consigne automatique; *(for clothes)* vestiaire m (métallique); Am Sport **l. room** vestiaire m

locket ['lɒkɪt] n médaillon m

locksmith ['lɒksmɪθ] n serrurier m

locomotive [ləʊkə'məʊtɪv] n locomotive f

locust ['ləʊkəst] n sauterelle f

lodge [lɒdʒ] **1** n *(house)* pavillon m; *(of porter)* loge f **2** vt *(person)* loger **3** vi *(of bullet)* se loger *(in dans)*

lodger ['lɒdʒə(r)] n *(room and meals)* pensionnaire mf; *(room only)* locataire mf

lodgings ['lɒdʒɪŋz] n *(flat)* logement m; *(room)* chambre f; **in l.** en meublé

loft [lɒft] n grenier m

lofty ['lɒftɪ] (-ier, -iest) adj *(high, noble)* élevé

log [lɒg] **1** n *(tree trunk)* tronc m d'arbre; *(for fire)* bûche f; **l. cabin** hutte f en rondins; **l. fire** feu m de bois **2** *(pt & pp -gg-)* vt *(facts)* noter **3** vi Comptr **l. in/out** entrer/sortir ■ **logbook** n *(on ship)* journal m de bord; *(on plane)* carnet m de vol

logic ['lɒdʒɪk] n logique f ■ **logical** adj logique ■ **logically** adv logiquement

logistics [lə'dʒɪstɪks] n logistique f

logo ['ləʊgəʊ] (pl -os) n logo m

loiter ['lɔɪtə(r)] vi traîner

loll [lɒl] vi *(in armchair)* se prélasser

lollipop ['lɒlɪpɒp] n sucette f; Br **l. man/lady** = contractuel ou contractuelle qui aide les écoliers à traverser la rue ■ **lolly** (pl -ies) n Fam *(lollipop)* sucette f; *(ice)* **l.** glace f à l'eau

London ['lʌndən] **1** n Londres m ou f **2** adj londonien, -enne

lone [ləʊn] adj solitaire

loneliness ['ləʊnlɪnəs] n solitude f ■ **lonely** (-ier, -iest) adj *(road, house, life)* solitaire; *(person)* seul

loner ['ləʊnə(r)] n solitaire mf

LONG¹ [lɒŋ] **1** (-er, -est) adj long (f longue); **to be 10 metres l.** avoir 10 mètres de long; **to be six weeks l.** durer six semaines; **how l. is...?** quelle est la longueur de...?; *(time)* quelle est la durée de...?; **l. time** longtemps; **l. jump** *(sport)* saut m en longueur

2 adv *(a long time)* longtemps; **has he been here l.?** il y a longtemps qu'il est ici?; **how l.?** *(in time)* combien de temps?; **not l.** peu de temps; **before l.** sous peu; **no longer** ne... plus; **a bit longer** *(wait)* encore un peu; **I won't be l.** je n'en ai pas pour longtemps; **don't be l.** dépêche-toi; **all summer/winter l.** tout l'été/l'hiver; **l. live the queen!** vive la reine!; **as l. as, so l. as**

(provided that) pourvu que *(+ subjunctive)*; **as l. as l live** tant que je vivrai ■ **long-distance** *adj (race)* de fond; *(phone call)* interurbain ■ **longhaired** *adj* aux cheveux longs ■ **longlife** *adj (battery)* longue durée *inv*; *(milk)* longue conservation *inv* ■ **long-range** *adj (forecast)* à long terme ■ **longsighted** *adj (person)* presbyte ■ **longstanding** *adj* de longue date ■ **long-term** *adj* à long terme ■ **long-winded** *adj (speech, speaker)* verbeux, -euse

long² [lɒŋ] *vi* **to l. for sth** avoir très envie de qch; **to l. to do sth** avoir très envie de faire qch ■ **longing** *n* désir *m*

longitude ['lɒndʒɪtju:d] *n* longitude *f*

loo [lu:] *(pl loos) n Br Fam* **the l.** le petit coin

look [lʊk] **1** *n (glance)* regard *m*; *(appearance)* air *m*, allure *f*; **to have a l. (at sth)** jeter un coup d'œil (à qch); **to have a l. (for sth)** chercher (qch); **to have a l. (a)round** regarder; *(walk)* faire un tour; **let me have a l.** fais voir

2 *vi* **to l. sb in the face** regarder qn dans les yeux

3 *vi* regarder; **to l. tired/happy** *(seem)* avoir l'air fatigué/heureux; **to l. pretty/ugly** être joli/laid; **you l. like** *or* **as if** *or* **as though you're tired** tu as l'air fatigué; **to l. like an apple** avoir l'air d'une pomme; **you l. like my brother** tu ressembles à mon frère; **it looks like rain** on dirait qu'il va pleuvoir; **what does he l. like?** comment est-il?; **to l. well** *or* **good** *(of person)* avoir bonne mine; **you l. good in that hat** ce chapeau te va très bien; **that looks bad** *(action)* ça fait mauvais effet

▸ **look after** *vt insep (take care of)* s'occuper de; *(keep safely)* garder *(for sb pour qn)*; **to l. after oneself** *(keep healthy)* faire bien attention à soi; *(manage, cope)* se débrouiller

▸ **look around 1** *vt insep (town, shops)* faire un tour dans **2** *vi (have a look)* regarder; *(walk round)* faire un tour

▸ **look at** *vt insep* regarder; *(consider)* considérer

▸ **look away** *vi* détourner les yeux

▸ **look back** *vi* regarder derrière soi; *(in time)* regarder en arrière

▸ **look down** *vi* baisser les yeux; *(from a height)* regarder en bas; **to l. down on** *(consider scornfully)* regarder de haut

▸ **look for** *vt insep (seek)* chercher

▸ **look forward to** *vt insep (event)* attendre avec impatience; **to l. forward to doing sth** avoir hâte de faire qch

▸ **look in** *vi* regarder à l'intérieur; **to l. in on sb** passer voir qn

▸ **look into** *vt insep (examine)* examiner; *(find out about)* se renseigner sur

▸ **look on 1** *vt insep (consider)* considérer *(as comme)* **2** *vi (watch)* regarder; **to l. on to** *(of window, house)* donner sur

▸ **look out** *vi (be careful)* faire attention; **to l. out for sb/sth** *(seek)* chercher qn/qch; *(watch)* guetter qn/qch; **to l. out on to** *(of window, house)* donner sur

▸ **look over** *vt insep (examine fully)* examiner; *(briefly)* parcourir; *(region, town)* parcourir, visiter

▸ **look round 1** *vt insep (visit)* visiter **2** *vi (have a look)* regarder; *(walk round)* faire un tour; *(look back)* se retourner; **to l. round for sb/sth** *(seek)* chercher qn/qch

▸ **look through** *vt insep (inspect)* passer en revue

▸ **look up 1** *vt sep (word)* chercher; **to l. sb up** *(visit)* passer voir qn **2** *vi (of person)* lever les yeux; *(into the air or sky)* regarder en l'air; *(improve)* *(of situation)* s'améliorer; *Fig* **to l. up to sb** respecter qn

-looking ['lʊkɪŋ] *suff* **pleasant-/tired-l.** à l'air agréable/fatigué

lookout ['lʊkaʊt] *n (soldier)* guetteur *m*; **l. (post)** observatoire *m*; **to be on the l. for sb/sth** guetter qn/qch

loom [lu:m] **1** *n (weaving machine)* métier *m* à tisser **2** *vi* **to l. (up)** *(of* *mountain)* apparaître indistinctement; *(of event)* paraître imminent

loony ['luːnɪ] *(pl* **-ies)** *n & adj Fam* dingue *(mf)*

loop [luːp] *n* boucle *f*

loophole ['luːphəʊl] *n (in law)* vide *m* juridique

loose [luːs] **1** **(-er, -est)** *adj (screw, belt, knot)* desserré; *(tooth, stone)* qui bouge; *(page)* détaché; *(clothes)* flottant; *(hair)* dénoué; *(translation)* vague; *(articles for sale)* en vrac; *Br (cheese, tea)* au poids; **there's an animal/prisoner l.** *(having escaped)* il y a un animal échappé/un prisonnier évadé; **l. change** petite monnaie *f*; **to come l.** *(of knot, screw)* se desserrer; *(of page)* se détacher; *(of tooth)* se mettre à bouger; **to get l.** *(of dog)* se détacher; **to set** *or* **turn l.** *(dog)* lâcher **2** *n* **on the l.** *(prisoner)* en cavale; *(animal)* en liberté

loosely ['luːslɪ] *adv (hang)* lâchement; *(hold, tie)* sans serrer; *(translate)* de façon approximative

loosen ['luːsən] *vt (knot, belt, screw)* desserrer; *(rope)* détendre; **to l. one's grip** relâcher son étreinte

loot [luːt] **1** *n* butin *m*; *Fam (money)* fric *m* **2** *vt* piller ■ **looting** *n* pillage *m*

lop [lɒp] *(pt & pp* **-pp-)** *vt* **to l. (off)** couper

lop-sided [lɒp'saɪdɪd] *adj (crooked)* de travers

lord [lɔːd] *n* seigneur *m*; *(British title)* lord *m*; **the L.** *(God)* le Seigneur; *Fam* **good L.!** bon sang!

lorry ['lɒrɪ] *(pl* **-ies)** *n Br* camion *m*; *(heavy)* poids *m* lourd; **l. driver** camionneur *m*; **(long-distance) l. driver** routier *m*

lose [luːz] *(pt & pp* **lost) 1** *vt* perdre; **to l. one's life** trouver la mort **(in** dans); **to l. one's way, to get lost** *(of person)* se perdre; *Fam* **get lost!** va te faire camper!; **that lost us the war/our jobs** cela nous a coûté la guerre/notre travail; **the clock loses six minutes a day** la pendule retarde de six minutes par jour

2 *vi* perdre; **to l. out** être perdant; **to l. to sb** *(in contest)* être battu par qn ■ **loser** *n (in contest)* perdant, -e *mf*; *Fam (failure in life)* minable *mf* ■ **losing** *adj (number, team, horse)* perdant

loss [lɒs] *n* perte *f*; **to sell sth at a l.** vendre qch à perte; **to make a l.** *(financially)* perdre de l'argent

lost [lɒst] **1** *pt & pp of* **lose 2** *adj* perdu; *Br* **l. property,** *Am* **l. and found** objets *mpl* trouvés

lot¹ [lɒt] *n (destiny)* sort *m*; *(batch)* lot *m*; **to draw lots** tirer au sort

lot² [lɒt] *n* **the l.** *(everything)* (le) tout; **the l. of you** vous tous; **a l. of, lots of** beaucoup de; **l.** beaucoup; **quite a l.** pas mal **(of** de)

lotion ['ləʊʃən] *n* lotion *f*

lottery ['lɒtərɪ] *(pl* **-ies)** *n* loterie *f*; **l. ticket** billet *m* de loterie

loud [laʊd] **1** **(-er, -est)** *adj (voice, music)* fort; *(noise, cry)* grand; *(laugh)* gros *(f* grosse); *(gaudy)* voyant **2** *adv (shout)* fort; **out l.** tout haut ■ **loudly** *adv (speak, laugh, shout)* fort ■ **loudspeaker** *n* haut-parleur *m*; *(for speaking to crowd)* porte-voix *m inv*; *(of stereo system)* enceinte *f*

lounge [laʊndʒ] **1** *n (in house, hotel)* salon *m*; **airport l.** salle *f* d'aéroport **2** *vi (loll in armchair)* se prélasser; **to l. about** *(idle)* paresser

louse [laʊs] *(pl* **lice)** *n (insect)* pou *m*

lousy ['laʊzɪ] **(-ier, -iest)** *adj Fam (bad)* nul *(f* nulle); *(food, weather)* dégueulasse; **to feel l.** être mal fichu

lout [laʊt] *n* voyou *m*

love [lʌv] **1** *n* **(a)** *(feeling)* amour *m*; **in l.** amoureux, -euse **(with** de); **they're in l.** ils s'aiment; **give him/her my l.** *(greeting)* dis-lui bien des choses de ma part; **l. affair** liaison *f* **(b)** *(in tennis)* rien *m*; **15 l.** 15 à rien **2** *vt (person)* aimer; *(thing, activity)* adorer **(to do** *or* **doing** faire) ■ **loving** *adj* affectueux, -euse

lovely ['lʌvlɪ] **(-ier, -iest)** *adj (idea, smell)* très bon *(f* bonne); *(pretty)* joli;

(charming) charmant; *(kind)* gentil, -ille; **the weather's l., it's l.** il fait beau; **(it's) l. to see you!** je suis ravi de te voir!

lover ['lʌvə(r)] *n* (man) amant *m*; (woman) maîtresse *f*; **a l. of music/art** un amateur de musique/d'art

low¹ [ləʊ] **1** (-er, -est) *adj* bas (*f* basse); *(speed, income, intelligence)* faible; *(opinion, quality)* mauvais; **she's l. on** *(money)* elle n'a plus beaucoup de; **to feel l.** *(depressed)* être déprimé; **lower** inférieur; *Am* **l. beams** *(of vehicle)* codes *mpl*

2 (-er, -est) *adv* bas; **to turn (down) l.** mettre plus bas; **to run l.** *(of supplies)* s'épuiser

3 *n* **to reach a new l.** *or* **an all-time l.** *(of prices)* atteindre leur niveau le plus bas ■ **low-cut** *adj* décolleté ■ **lowdown** *n Fam (facts)* tuyaux *mpl* ■ **lowfat** *adj (milk)* écrémé; *(cheese)* allégé ■ **low-key** *adj (discreet)* discret, -ète ■ **low-paid** *adj* mal payé

low² [ləʊ] *vi (of cattle)* meugler

lower ['ləʊə(r)] *vt* baisser; **to l. sb/sth** *(by rope)* descendre qn/qch; *Fig* **to l. oneself** s'abaisser

lowly ['ləʊlɪ] (-ier, -iest) *adj* humble

loyal ['lɔɪəl] *adj* loyal (**to** envers) ■ **loyalty** *n* loyauté *f*

lozenge ['lɒzɪndʒ] *n (tablet)* pastille *f*; *(shape)* losange *m*

LP [el'piː] *(abbr* **long-playing record)** *n* 33 tours *m inv*

L-plate ['elpleɪt] *n Br* = plaque apposée sur une voiture pour signaler que le conducteur est en conduite accompagnée

Ltd *(abbr* **Limited)** *Br Com* ≃ SARL

lubricate ['luːbrɪkeɪt] *vt* lubrifier; *(machine, car wheels)* graisser

lucid ['luːsɪd] *adj* lucide

luck [lʌk] *n (chance)* chance *f*; *(good fortune)* (bonne) chance *f*, bonheur *m*; **to be in l.** avoir de la chance; **to be out of l.** ne pas avoir de chance; **to wish sb l.** souhaiter bonne chance à qn; **bad l.** malchance *f*; **hard l.!**,

tough l.! pas de chance!

luckily ['lʌkɪlɪ] *adv* heureusement

lucky ['lʌkɪ] (-ier, -iest) *adj (person)* chanceux, -euse; **to be l.** *(of person)* avoir de la chance; **it's l. that...** c'est une chance que... *(+ subjunctive)*; **l. number** chiffre *m* porte-bonheur

lucrative ['luːkrətɪv] *adj* lucratif, -ive

ludicrous ['luːdɪkrəs] *adj* ridicule

luggage ['lʌgɪdʒ] *n* bagages *mpl*; **a piece of l.** un bagage; **hand l.** bagages *mpl* à main; **l. compartment** compartiment *m* à bagages

lukewarm ['luːkwɔːm] *adj (water, soup)* tiède

lull [lʌl] **1** *n* arrêt *m*; *(in storm)* accalmie *f* **2** *vt* **to l. sb to sleep** endormir qn en le/la berçant

lullaby ['lʌləbaɪ] *(pl* **-ies)** *n* berceuse *f*

lumber¹ ['lʌmbə(r)] *n (timber)* bois *m* de charpente; *Br (junk)* bric-à-brac *m inv*

lumber² ['lʌmbə(r)] *vt Br Fam* **to l. sb with sb/sth** coller qn/qch à qn

luminous ['luːmɪnəs] *adj (colour, paper, ink)* fluorescent; *(dial, clock)* lumineux, -euse

lump [lʌmp] **1** *n* morceau *m*; *(in soup)* grumeau *m*; *(bump)* bosse *f*; *(swelling)* grosseur *f*; **l. sum** somme *f* forfaitaire **2** *vt* **to l. together** réunir; *Fig & Pej* mettre dans le même sac ■ **lumpy** (-ier, -iest) *adj (soup)* grumeleux, -euse; *(surface)* bosselé

lunar ['luːnə(r)] *adj* lunaire; **l. eclipse** éclipse *f* de lune

lunatic ['luːnətɪk] *n* fou *m*, folle *f*

lunch [lʌntʃ] **1** *n* déjeuner *m*; **to have l.** déjeuner; **l. break, l. hour, l. time** heure *f* du déjeuner **2** *vi* déjeuner **(on** *or* **off** de) ■ **lunchbox** *n* = boîte dans laquelle on transporte son déjeuner

luncheon ['lʌnʃən] *n* déjeuner *m*; *Br* **l. voucher** Chèque-Restaurant *m*

lung [lʌŋ] *n* poumon *m*

lunge [lʌndʒ] *vi* **to l. at sb** se ruer sur qn

lurch [lɜːtʃ] **1** *n Fam* **to leave sb in the l.**

laisser qn dans le pétrin **2** *vi (of person)* tituber

lure [lʊə(r)] **1** *n (attraction)* attrait *m* **2** *vt* attirer (par la ruse) (**into** dans)

lurid ['lʊərɪd] *adj (story, description)* cru; *(gaudy)* voyant

lurk [lɜːk] *vi (hide)* être tapi (**in** dans); *(prowl)* rôder

luscious ['lʌʃəs] *adj (food)* appétissant

lush [lʌʃ] *adj (vegetation)* luxuriant; *(wealthy) (surroundings)* luxueux, -euse

lust [lʌst] **1** *n (for person)* désir *m*; *(for object)* convoitise *f* (**for** de); *(for power, knowledge)* soif *f* (**for** de) **2** *vi*

to l. after *(object, person)* convoiter; *(power, knowledge)* avoir soif de

lustre ['lʌstə(r)] *(Am* **luster***)* *n (gloss)* lustre *m*

Luxembourg ['lʌksəmbɜːg] *n* le Luxembourg

luxury ['lʌkʃərɪ] **1** *n* luxe *m* **2** *adj (goods, car, home)* de luxe ■ **luxurious** [lʌg'ʒʊərɪəs] *adj* luxueux, -euse

lying ['laɪɪŋ] **1** *pres p of* **lie**[1,2] **2** *n* mensonges *mpl* **3** *adj (person)* menteur, -euse

lynch [lɪntʃ] *vt* lyncher

lyric ['lɪrɪk] *adj* lyrique ■ **lyrics** *npl (of song)* paroles *fpl*

Mm

M, m [em] *n (letter)* M, m *m inv*

m (**a**) *(abbr metre)* mètre *m* (**b**) *(abbr mile)* mile *m*

MA *(abbr Master of Arts)* n Univ **to have an MA in French** ≃ avoir une maîtrise de français

mac [mæk] *n Br Fam (raincoat)* imper *m*

macabre [mə'kɑ:brə] *adj* macabre

machine [mə'ʃi:n] *n (apparatus, car, system)* machine *f*; **m. gun** mitrailleuse *f*

machinery [mə'ʃi:nərɪ] *n (machines)* machines *fpl*; *(works)* mécanisme *m*

mackerel ['mækrəl] *n* maquereau *m*

mackintosh ['mækɪntɒʃ] *n Br* imperméable *m*

macro ['mækrəʊ] *(pl -os)* n Comptr macrocommande *f*

mad [mæd] (**madder, maddest**) *adj* fou (*f* folle); **to be m. at sb** être furieux, -euse contre qn ■ **madly** *adv (insanely, desperately)* comme un fou/une folle ■ **madman** *(pl -men)* n fou *m* ■ **madness** n folie *f*

madam ['mædəm] *n* **yes, m.** oui, madame

made [meɪd] *pt & pp of* **make** ■ **made-to-measure** *adj Br (garment)* (fait) sur mesure

magazine [mægə'zi:n] *n* (**a**) *(periodical, TV or radio broadcast)* magazine *m* (**b**) *(of gun, slide projector)* magasin *m*

magic ['mædʒɪk] **1** *adj* magique **2** *n* magie *f* ■ **magician** [mə'dʒɪʃən] *n* magicien, -enne *mf*

magistrate ['mædʒɪstreɪt] *n* magistrat *m*

magnet ['mægnɪt] *n* aimant *m* ■ **magnetic** [-'netɪk] *adj* magnétique

magnificent [mæg'nɪfɪsənt] *adj* magnifique

magnify ['mægnɪfaɪ] *(pt & pp -ied) vt (image)* grossir; **magnifying glass** loupe *f*

mahogany [mə'hɒgənɪ] *n* acajou *m*

maid [meɪd] *n (servant)* bonne *f*

maiden ['meɪdən] *adj (flight, voyage)* inaugural; **m. name** nom *m* de jeune fille

mail [meɪl] **1** *n (system)* poste *f*; *(letters)* courrier *m*; *(e-mails)* méls *mpl*, courrier *m* électronique **2** *adj (bag, train)* postal; **m. order** vente *f* par correspondance **3** *vt* poster; **mailing list** liste *f* d'adresses ■ **mailbox** *n Am & Comptr* boîte *f* aux lettres

maim [meɪm] *vt* mutiler

main¹ [meɪn] *adj* principal; **m. course** plat *m* de résistance; **m. road** grande route *f*

main² [meɪn] *n* **water/gas m.** conduite *f* d'eau/de gaz; **the mains** *(electricity)* le secteur ■ **mainland** *n* ■ **mainly** *adv* principalement; **they were m. Spanish** la plupart étaient espagnols

mainstay ['meɪnsteɪ] *n (of organization, policy)* pilier *m*

maintain [meɪn'teɪn] *vt (continue)* maintenir; *(machine, road)* entretenir; **to m. that...** affirmer que... ■ **maintenance** ['meɪntənəns] *n (of vehicle, road)* entretien *m*; *(alimony)* pension *f* alimentaire

maize [meɪz] *n Br* maïs *m*

majesty ['mædʒəstɪ] n majesté f; **Your M.** Votre Majesté ■ **majestic** [mə'dʒes-tɪk] adj majestueux, -euse

major ['meɪdʒə(r)] **1** adj (main, great) & Mus majeur **2** n (**a**) (officer) commandant m (**b**) Am Univ (subject) dominante f **3** vi Am Univ **to m. in** se spécialiser en

Majorca [mə'jɔːkə] n Majorque f

majority [mə'dʒɒrətɪ] (pl -ies) n majorité f (**of de**); **the m. of people** la plupart des gens

MAKE [meɪk] **1** (pt & pp made) vt faire; (tool, vehicle) fabriquer; **to m. a decision** prendre une décision; **to m. sb happy/sad** rendre qn heureux/triste; **to m. sb do sth** faire faire qch à qn; Fam **to m. it** (succeed) réussir; **sorry I can't m. it to the meeting** désolé, je ne pourrai pas assister à la réunion; **what time do you m. it?** quelle heure avez-vous?; **what do you m. of it?** qu'en penses-tu?; **he made 10 pounds on it** ça lui a rapporté 10 livres; **to be made of wood** être en bois; **made in France** fabriqué en France

2 vi **to m. do** (manage) se débrouiller (**with avec**); **to m. do with sb/sth** (be satisfied with) se contenter de qn/qch; **to m. believe that one is…** faire semblant d'être…

3 n (brand) marque f; **of French m.** de fabrication française ■ **make-up** n (for face) maquillage m; (of team, group) constitution f

▸ **make for** vt insep (go towards) aller vers

▸ **make off** vi Fam (leave) filer

▸ **make out 1** vt sep (see, hear) distinguer; (understand) comprendre; (decipher) déchiffrer; (cheque, list) faire; Fam **to m. out that…** (claim) prétendre que… **2** vi Fam (manage) se débrouiller

▸ **make over** vt sep (transfer) céder (**to à**); (change, convert) transformer (**into en**)

▸ **make up 1** vt sep (story) inventer;

(put together) (list, collection, bed) faire; (prepare) préparer; (form) former, composer; (loss) compenser; (quantity) compléter; (quarrel) régler; **to m. oneself up** se maquiller

2 vi (of friends) se réconcilier; **to m. up for** (loss, damage, fault) compenser; (lost time, mistake) rattraper

makeshift ['meɪkʃɪft] adj (arrangement, building) de fortune

malaria [mə'leərɪə] n Med paludisme m

male [meɪl] **1** adj (child, animal) mâle; (sex) masculin; **m. nurse** infirmier m **2** n (person) homme m; (animal) mâle m

malfunction [mæl'fʌŋkʃən] vi fonctionner mal

malice ['mælɪs] n méchanceté f ■ **malicious** [mə'lɪʃəs] adj malveillant

malignant [mə'lɪgnənt] adj **m. tumour or growth** tumeur f maligne

mall [mɔːl] n Am (**shopping**) **m.** centre m commercial

malnutrition [mælnjuː'trɪʃən] n malnutrition f

malt [mɔːlt] n malt m

Malta ['mɔːltə] n Malte f

mammal ['mæməl] n mammifère m

man [mæn] **1** (pl **men**) n (adult male) homme m; (player in sports team) joueur m; (humanity) l'homme m; (chess piece) pièce f; Fam **my old m.** (father) mon père; (husband) mon homme

2 (pt & pp -nn-) vt (be on duty at) être de service à; (machine) assurer le fonctionnement de; (plane, ship) être membre de l'équipage de

manage ['mænɪdʒ] **1** vt (company, project) diriger; (shop, hotel) être le gérant de; (economy, money, time, situation) gérer; **to m. to do sth** (succeed) réussir ou arriver à faire qch; (by being smart) se débrouiller pour faire qch

2 vi (succeed) y arriver; (make do) se débrouiller (**with avec**); **to m. without sb/sth** se passer de qn/qch; **managing director** directeur, -trice mf général, -e ■ **management** n (running, *managers*) direction f; *(of property, economy)* gestion f; *(executive staff)* cadres mpl

manager ['mænɪdʒə(r)] n *(of company)* directeur, -trice mf; *(of shop, café)* gérant, -e mf; **(business) m.** *(of singer, boxer)* manager m ■ **manageress** n directrice f; *(of shop, café)* gérante f

mandate ['mændeɪt] n mandat m

mane [meɪn] n crinière f

maneuver [mə'nu:və(r)] n & vti Am = **manoeuvre**

mangle ['mæŋgəl] vt *(body)* mutiler

mango ['mæŋgəʊ] *(pl* -oes *or* -os) n mangue f

manhunt ['mænhʌnt] n chasse f à l'homme

mania ['meɪnɪə] n *(liking)* passion f; *(psychological)* manie f

maniac ['meɪnɪæk] n fou m, folle f

manicure ['mænɪkjʊə(r)] n manucure f

manifesto [mænɪ'festəʊ] *(pl* -os *or* -oes) n Pol manifeste m

manipulate [mə'nɪpjʊleɪt] vt manipuler

mankind [mæn'kaɪnd] n l'humanité f

man-made ['mænmeɪd] adj *(lake)* artificiel, -elle; *(fibre)* synthétique

manner ['mænə(r)] n *(way)* manière f; *(behaviour)* comportement m; **manners** *(social habits)* manières fpl; **in this m.** *(like this)* de cette manière; **to have good/bad manners** être bien/mal élevé

mannerism ['mænərɪzəm] n Pej tic m

manoeuvre [mə'nu:və(r)] *(Am* **maneuver**) **1** n manœuvre f **2** vti manœuvrer

manpower ['mænpaʊə(r)] n *(labour)* main-d'œuvre f

mansion ['mænʃən] n *(in town)* hôtel m particulier; *(in country)* manoir m

manslaughter ['mænslɔ:tə(r)] n *(in law)* homicide m involontaire

mantelpiece ['mæntəlpi:s] n dessus m de cheminée; **on the m.** sur la cheminée

manual ['mænjʊəl] **1** adj *(work, worker)* manuel, -elle **2** n *(book)* manuel m

manufacture [mænjʊ'fæktʃə(r)] **1** n fabrication f; *(of cars)* construction f **2** vt fabriquer; *(cars)* construire ■ **manufacturer** n fabricant, -e mf; *(of cars)* constructeur m

manure [mə'njʊə(r)] n fumier m

manuscript ['mænjʊskrɪpt] n manuscrit m

many ['menɪ] **1** adj beaucoup de; **(a good** *or* **great) m. of** un (très) grand nombre de; **how m.?** combien (de)?; **too m.** trop de **2** pron beaucoup; **too m.** trop; **m. of them** beaucoup d'entre eux; **as m. as fifty** *(up to)* jusqu'à cinquante

map [mæp] **1** n carte f; *(plan of town, underground)* plan m **2** *(pt & pp* -pp-) vt **to m. out** *(plan, programme)* élaborer

maple ['meɪpəl] n *(tree, wood)* érable m; **m. syrup** sirop m d'érable

marathon ['mærəθən] n marathon m

marble ['mɑ:bəl] n *(substance)* marbre m; *(toy ball)* bille f

March [mɑ:tʃ] n mars m

march [mɑ:tʃ] **1** n marche f **2** vi *(of soldiers, demonstrators)* défiler; *(walk in step)* marcher au pas

mare [meə(r)] n jument f

margarine [mɑ:dʒə'ri:n] n margarine f

margin ['mɑ:dʒɪn] n *(on page)* marge f; **to win by a narrow m.** gagner de justesse ■ **marginally** adv très légèrement

marijuana [mærɪ'wɑ:nə] n marijuana f

marinate ['mærɪneɪt] vti Culin (faire) mariner

marine [mə'ri:n] **1** adj *(life, flora)* marin **2** n *(soldier)* fusilier m marin; *Am* marine m

marital ['mærɪtəl] adj conjugal; **m. status** situation f de famille

maritime ['mærɪtaɪm] adj maritime

mark [mɑ:k] **1** n *(symbol)* marque f; *(stain, trace)* tache f, marque f; *(token, sign)* signe m; *(in test, exam)* note f **2** vt marquer; *(exam)* noter; **to m. sth off** *(separate)* délimiter qch; *(on list)* cocher qch; **to m. sb out** distinguer qn

marked [mɑːkt] *adj (noticeable)* marqué

market ['mɑːkɪt] **1** *n* marché *m*; **to put sth on the m.** mettre qch en vente; **on the black m.** au marché noir; **m. price** prix *m* courant

  2 *vt* commercialiser ▪ **marketing** *n* marketing *m*, mercatique *f* ▪ **marketplace** *n (in village, town)* place *f* du marché

markings ['mɑːkɪŋz] *npl (on animal)* taches *fpl*; *(on road)* signalisation *f* horizontale

marmalade ['mɑːməleɪd] *n* confiture *f* d'oranges

marooned [mə'ruːnd] *adj* abandonné

marriage ['mærɪdʒ] *n* mariage *m*; **m. certificate** extrait *m* d'acte de mariage

marrow ['mærəʊ] *n Br (vegetable)* courge *f*

marry ['mærɪ] **1** *(pt & pp -ied)* vt épouser, se marier avec; *(of priest)* marier **2** *vi* se marier ▪ **married** *adj* marié; **m. life** vie *f* maritale; **m. name** nom *m* de femme mariée; **to get m.** se marier

marsh [mɑːʃ] *n* marais *m*, marécage *m*

martial ['mɑːʃəl] *adj* martial

martyr ['mɑːtə(r)] *n* martyr, -e *mf*

marvel ['mɑːvəl] **1** *n (wonder)* merveille *f* **2** *(Br -ll-, Am -l-)* vi s'émerveiller (**at** de)

marvellous ['mɑːvələs] *(Am* **marvelous)** *adj* merveilleux, -euse

Marxist ['mɑːksɪst] *adj & n* marxiste *(mf)*

marzipan ['mɑːzɪpæn] *n* pâte *f* d'amandes

mascara [mæ'skɑːrə] *n* mascara *m*

masculine ['mæskjʊlɪn] *adj* masculin

mash [mæʃ] **1** *n Br (potatoes)* purée *f* (de pommes de terre) **2** *vt* **to m. (up)** *(vegetables)* écraser *(en* purée); **mashed potatoes** purée *f* de pommes de terre

mask [mɑːsk] **1** *n* masque *m* **2** *vt (cover, hide)* masquer (**from** à)

masochist ['mæsəkɪst] *n* masochiste *mf*

mason ['meɪsən] *n (stonemason, Freemason)* maçon *m* ▪ **masonry** *n* maçonnerie *f*

mass[1] [mæs] **1** *n Phys & (shapeless substance)* masse *f*; **a m. of** *(many)* une multitude de; *Pol* **the masses** le peuple

  2 *adj (demonstration, culture)* de masse; *(protests)* en masse; *(unemployment, destruction)* massif, -ive; **m. media** mass media *mpl*; **m. production** production *f* en série

  3 *vi (of troops, people)* se masser ▪ **mass-produce** *vt* fabriquer en série

mass[2] [mæs] *n (in church service)* messe *f*

massacre ['mæsəkə(r)] **1** *n* massacre *m* **2** *vt* massacrer

massage ['mæsɑːʒ] **1** *n* massage *m* **2** *vt* masser

massive ['mæsɪv] *adj (increase, dose, vote)* massif, -ive; *(amount, building)* énorme

mast [mɑːst] *n (of ship)* mât *m*; *(for TV, radio)* pylône *m*

master ['mɑːstə(r)] **1** *n* maître *m*; *Br (teacher)* professeur *m*; **M. of Arts/ Science** *(qualification)* ≃ maîtrise *f* ès lettres/sciences; *(person)* ≃ maître *mf* ès lettres/sciences; **m. of ceremonies** *(presenter)* animateur, -trice *mf*; **m. copy** original *m*; **m. key** passe-partout *m inv*; **m. plan** *m* d'action **2** *vt* maîtriser; *(subject, situation)* dominer

mastermind ['mɑːstəmaɪnd] **1** *n (person)* cerveau *m* **2** *vt* organiser

masterpiece ['mɑːstəpiːs] *n* chef-d'œuvre *m*

mastery ['mɑːstərɪ] *n* maîtrise *f* (**of** de)

masturbate ['mæstəbeɪt] *vi* se masturber

mat [mæt] *n* tapis *m*; *(of straw)* natte *f*; *(at door)* paillasson *m*; **(table) m.** *(for plates)* set *m* de table; *(for dishes)* dessous-de-plat *m inv*

match[1] [mætʃ] *n (for lighting fire, cigarette)* allumette *f* ▪ **matchbox** *n* boîte *f* d'allumettes ∎ **matchstick** *n* allumette *f*

match² [mætʃ] *n* (*in sport*) match *m*

match³ [mætʃ] **1** *n* (*equal*) égal, -e *mf*; (*marriage*) mariage *m*; **to be a good m.** (*of colours, people*) aller bien ensemble; **to meet one's m.** trouver son maître **2** *vt* (*of clothes, colour*) être assorti à; (*coordinate*) assortir; (*equal*) égaler; **to m. up** (*colours, clothes, plates*) assortir **3** *vi* (*of colours, clothes*) être assortis, -es ∎ **matching** *adj* assorti

mate¹ [meɪt] **1** *n* (*of animal*) (*male*) mâle *m*; (*female*) femelle *f*; *Br* (*friend*) copain *m*, copine *f* **2** *vi* (*of animals*) s'accoupler (**with** avec)

mate² [meɪt] **1** *n* (*in chess*) mat *m* **2** *vt* mettre mat

material [məˈtɪərɪəl] **1** *adj* (*needs, world*) matériel, -elle; (*important*) essentiel, -elle **2** *n* (*substance*) matière *f*; (*cloth*) tissu *m*; (*for book*) matériaux *mpl*; **material(s)** (*equipment*) matériel *m* ∎ **materialistic** *adj* matérialiste

materialize [məˈtɪərɪəlaɪz] *vi* se matérialiser; (*of hope, threat*) se réaliser

maternal [məˈtɜːnəl] *adj* maternel, -elle

maternity [məˈtɜːnɪtɪ] *n* **m. dress** robe *f* de grossesse; **m. hospital, m. unit** maternité *f*; **m. leave** congé *m* de maternité

mathematical [mæθəˈmætɪkəl] *adj* mathématique

mathematics [mæθəˈmætɪks] *n* (*subject*) mathématiques *fpl* ∎ **maths** (*Am* **math**) *n Fam* maths *fpl*

matinée [ˈmætɪneɪ] *n* (*of play, film*) matinée *f*

matrimony [ˈmætrɪmənɪ] *n* mariage *m*

matt [mæt] *adj* (*paint, paper*) mat

matter [ˈmætə(r)] **1** *n* (*substance*) matière *f*; (*issue, affair*) question *f*; **as a m. of fact** en fait; **no m. what she does** quoi qu'elle fasse; **no m. who you are** qui que vous soyez; **what's**

the m.? qu'est-ce qu'il y a?; **there's something the m. with my leg** j'ai quelque chose à la jambe **2** *vi* (*be important*) importer (**to** à); **it doesn't m. if/when/who…** peu importe si/quand/qui…; **it doesn't m. ça ne fait rien

matter-of-fact [mætərəvˈfækt] *adj* (*person, manner*) terre à terre *inv*

mattress [ˈmætrəs] *n* matelas *m*

mature [məˈtʃʊə(r)] **1** *adj* (*person*) mûr; (*cheese*) fort **2** *vi* (*person*) mûrir

maul [mɔːl] *vt* (*of animal*) mutiler

maximize [ˈmæksɪmaɪz] *vt* maximaliser

maximum [ˈmæksɪməm] **1** (*pl* **-ima** [-ɪmə] *or* **-imums**) *n* maximum *m* **2** *adj* maximal

May [meɪ] *n* mai *m*

MAY [meɪ] (*pt* **might** [maɪt])

May et *m* might peuvent s'utiliser indifféremment ou presque dans les expressions de la catégorie (**a**).

v aux (**a**) (*expressing possibility*) **he m. come** il se peut qu'il vienne; **I m.** *or* **might be wrong** je me trompe peut-être; **he m.** *or* **might have lost it** il se peut qu'il l'ait perdu; **we m.** *or* **might as well go** autant y aller; **she's afraid I m.** *or* **might get lost** elle a peur que je ne me perde

(**b**) *Formal* (*for asking permission*) **m. I stay?** puis-je rester?; **you m. go** tu peux partir

(**c**) *Formal* (*expressing wish*) **m. you be happy** sois heureux; **m. the best man win!** que le meilleur gagne!

maybe [ˈmeɪbiː] *adv* peut-être

mayhem [ˈmeɪhem] *n* (*chaos*) pagaille *f*

mayonnaise [meɪəˈneɪz] *n* mayonnaise *f*

mayor [meə(r)] *n* maire *m*

maze [meɪz] *n* labyrinthe *m*

me [miː] *pron* me, m'; (*after prep, 'than', 'it is'*) moi; (**to) me** (*indirect*) me, m'; **he helps me** il m'aide; **he gave it to me** il me l'a donné

meadow ['medəʊ] n pré m, prairie f

meagre ['miːɡə(r)] (Am **meager**) adj maigre

meal [miːl] n (food) repas m

mean¹ [miːn] (pt & pp **meant**) vt (of word, event) signifier; (of person) vouloir dire; (result in) entraîner; (represent) représenter; **to m. to do sth** avoir l'intention de faire qch; **it means a lot to me** c'est très important pour moi; **I didn't m. to!** je ne l'ai pas fait exprès!

mean² [miːn] (-er, -est) adj (miserly) avare; (nasty) méchant

mean³ [miːn] **1** adj (average) moyen, -enne **2** n Math (average, mid-point) moyenne f

meaning ['miːnɪŋ] n sens m, signification f ■ **meaningful** adj significatif, -ive ■ **meaningless** adj vide de sens

means [miːnz] **1** n (method) moyen m (**to do** or **of doing** de faire); **by m. of...** au moyen de...; **by no m.** nullement **2** npl (wealth) moyens mpl

meant [ment] pt & pp of **mean¹**

meantime ['miːntaɪm] adv & n (**in the) m.** (at the same time) pendant ce temps; (between two events) entretemps

meanwhile ['miːnwaɪl] adv (at the same time) pendant ce temps; (between two events) entre-temps

measles ['miːzəlz] n Med rougeole f

measure ['meʒə(r)] **1** n mesure f; (ruler) règle f **2** vt mesurer; **to m. sth out** (ingredient) mesurer qch **3** vi **to m. up to** (task) être à la hauteur de

measurement ['meʒəmənt] n mesure f; **hip/waist measurement(s)** tour m de hanches/de taille

meat [miːt] n viande f; (of crab, lobster) chair f; Fig substance f

mechanic [mɪ'kænɪk] n mécanicien, -enne mf ■ **mechanical** adj mécanique ■ **mechanics** n (science) mécanique f; **the m.** (working parts) le mécanisme

mechanism ['mekənɪzəm] n mécanisme m

medal ['medəl] n médaille f

medallion [mə'dæljən] n médaillon m

meddle ['medəl] vi (interfere) se mêler (**in** de); (tamper) toucher (**with** à)

media ['miːdɪə] npl **1 the m.** les médias mpl **2** pl of **medium**

mediaeval [medɪ'iːvəl] adj médiéval

mediate ['miːdɪeɪt] vi servir d'intermédiaire (**between** entre) ■ **mediator** n médiateur, -trice mf

medical ['medɪkəl] **1** adj médical; (school, studies) de médecine; (student) en médecine; **m. insurance** assurance f maladie

   2 n (in school, army) visite f médicale; (private) examen m médical

medication [medɪ'keɪʃən] n médicaments mpl; **to be on m.** être en traitement

medicine ['medəsən] n (substance) médicament m; (science) médecine f; **m. cabinet, m. chest** (armoire f à) pharmacie f

medieval [medɪ'iːvəl] adj médiéval

mediocre [miːdɪ'əʊkə(r)] adj médiocre

meditate ['medɪteɪt] vi méditer (**on** sur) ■ **meditation** n méditation f

Mediterranean [medɪtə'reɪnɪən] **1** adj méditerranéen, -enne **2** n **the M.** la Méditerranée

medium ['miːdɪəm] **1** adj (average, middle) moyen, -enne **2** n (a) (pl **media** ['miːdɪə]) (for conveying data or publicity) support m (b) (pl **mediums**) (person) médium m ■ **medium-sized** adj de taille moyenne

medley ['medlɪ] (pl **-eys**) n mélange m; (of songs, tunes) pot-pourri m

meet [miːt] **1** vt (pt & pp **met**) (person, team) rencontrer; (by arrangement) retrouver; (pass in street, road) croiser; (fetch) aller chercher; (wait for) attendre; (debt, enemy, danger) faire face à; (need) combler; **have you met my husband?** connaissez-vous mon mari?

   2 vi (of people, teams) se rencontrer; (by arrangement) se retrouver; (of club,

society) se réunir; *(of rivers)* se rejoindre **3** *n Am Sport* réunion *f*
▶ **meet up** *vi (by arrangement)* se retrouver; **to m. up with sb** retrouver qn
▶ **meet with** *vt insep (problem, refusal)* se heurter à; *(accident)* avoir; *Am* **to m. with sb** rencontrer qn; *(as arranged)* retrouver qn

meeting ['mi:tɪŋ] *n (for business)* réunion *f*, *(large)* assemblée *f*, *(by accident)* rencontre *f*, *(by arrangement)* rendez-vous *m inv*; **to be in a m.** être en réunion; **m. place** lieu *m* de rendez-vous

megaphone ['megəfəʊn] *n* porte-voix *m inv*

mellow ['meləʊ] **(-er, -est)** *adj (wine)* moelleux, -euse; *(flavour)* suave; *(colour, voice)* chaud

melodic [mɪ'lɒdɪk] *adj* mélodique

melodrama ['melədrɑːmə] *n* mélodrame *m* ■ **melodramatic** [-drə'mætɪk] *adj* mélodramatique

melody ['melədɪ] **(pl -ies)** *n* mélodie *f*

melon ['melən] *n* melon *m*

melt [melt] **1** *vt* faire fondre; **to m. down** *(metal object)* fondre **2** *vi* fondre

member ['membə(r)] *n* membre *m*; *Br* **M. of Parliament,** *Am* **M. of Congress** ≃ député *m* ■ **membership** *n (state)* adhésion *f* (**of** à); *(members)* membres *mpl*; **m. card** carte *f* de membre; **m. fee** cotisation *f*

memento [mə'mentəʊ] **(pl -os** *or* **-oes)** *n* souvenir *m*

memo ['meməʊ] **(pl -os)** *n* note *f* de service

memoirs ['memwɑːz] *npl (autobiography)* mémoires *mpl*

memorable ['memərəbəl] *adj* mémorable

memorial [mə'mɔːrɪəl] **1** *adj* commémoratif, -ive; **m. service** commémoration *f* **2** *n* mémorial *m*

memorize ['meməraɪz] *vt* mémoriser

memory ['memərɪ] **(pl -ies)** *n (faculty* & *Comptr)* mémoire *f*, *(recollection)* souvenir *m*; **to the** *or* **in m. of...** à la mémoire de...

men [men] *npl see* **man; the men's room** les toilettes *fpl* pour hommes

menace ['menɪs] **1** *n (danger)* danger *m*; *(threat)* menace *f* **2** *vt* menacer

mend [mend] *vt (repair)* réparer; *(clothes)* raccommoder

menial ['mi:nɪəl] *adj (work)* subalterne

meningitis [menɪn'dʒaɪtɪs] *n Med* méningite *f*

menopause ['menəpɔːz] *n* ménopause *f*

menstruation [menstrʊ'eɪʃən] *n* menstruation *f*

menswear ['menzweə(r)] *n* vêtements *mpl* pour hommes

mental ['mentəl] *adj* mental; **m. block** blocage *m*

mentality [men'tælətɪ] **(pl -ies)** *n* mentalité *f* ■ **mentally** *adv* mentalement; **he's m. handicapped** c'est un handicapé mental; **she's m. ill** c'est une malade mentale

mention ['menʃən] **1** *n* mention *f* **2** *vt* mentionner; **not to m....** sans parler de...; **don't m. it!** il n'y a pas de quoi!

menu ['menju:] *n (in restaurant) (for set meal)* menu *m*; *(list)* carte *f*; *Comptr* menu

MEP [emi:'pi:] *n (abbr* **Member of the European Parliament)** *n* député *m* du Parlement européen

merchandise ['mɜːtʃəndaɪz] *n* marchandises *fpl*

merchant ['mɜːtʃənt] *n (trader)* négociant, -e *mf*; *(retailer)* commerçant, -e *mf*

merciless ['mɜːsɪləs] *adj* impitoyable

mercury ['mɜːkjʊrɪ] *n (metal)* mercure *m*

mercy ['mɜːsɪ] **(pl -ies)** *n* pitié *f*, *(of God)* miséricorde *f*; **at the m. of** à la merci de

mere [mɪə(r)] *adj* simple; **she's a m. child** ce n'est qu'une enfant ■ **merely** *adv* simplement

merge [mɜːdʒ] **1** *vt (companies)* & *Comptr* fusionner **2** *vi (blend)* se mêler (**with** à); *(of roads)* se rejoindre; *(of* *companies, banks)* fusionner ■ **merger** n Com fusion f

merit ['merɪt] **1** n mérite m **2** vt mériter

merry ['merɪ] (**-ier, -iest**) adj (happy, drunk) gai ■ **merry-go-round** n manège m

mesh [meʃ] n (of net, sieve) mailles fpl

mesmerize ['mezməraɪz] vt hypnotiser

mess [mes] **1** n (confusion) désordre m; (muddle) gâchis m; (dirt) saletés fpl; **in a m.** en désordre; (in trouble) dans le pétrin; **to make a m. of sth** (do badly, get dirty) saloper qch

2 vt Br Fam **to m. sb about** (bother, treat badly) embêter qn; **to m. sth up** (plans) traîner; (hair, room, papers) mettre qch en désordre

3 vi **to m. about** or **around** (waste time) traîner; (play the fool) faire l'imbécile; **to m. about** or **around with sth** (fiddle with) tripoter avec qch

message ['mesɪdʒ] n message m

messenger ['mesɪndʒə(r)] n messager, -ère mf; (in office, hotel) coursier, -ère mf

messy ['mesɪ] (**-ier, -iest**) adj (untidy) en désordre; (dirty) sale; (job) salissant

met [met] pt & pp of **meet**

metal ['metəl] n métal m; **m. ladder** échelle f métallique ■ **metallic** [mɪ'tælɪk] adj (sound) métallique; (paint) métallisé ■ **metalwork** n (study, craft) travail m des métaux; (objects) ferronnerie f

metaphor ['metəfə(r)] n métaphore f ■ **metaphorical** [-'fɒrɪkəl] adj métaphorique

meteor ['miːtɪə(r)] n météore m

meteorological [miːtɪərə'lɒdʒɪkəl] adj météorologique

meter¹ ['miːtə(r)] n (device) compteur m; (parking) **m.** parcmètre m

meter² ['miːtə(r)] n Am (measurement) mètre m

method ['meθəd] n méthode f ■ **methodical** [mɪ'θɒdɪkəl] adj méthodique

meticulous [mɪ'tɪkjʊləs] adj méticuleux, -euse

metre ['miːtə(r)] (Am **meter**) n mètre m ■ **metric** ['metrɪk] adj métrique

metropolitan [metrə'pɒlɪtən] adj métropolitain

Mexico ['meksɪkəʊ] n le Mexique ■ **Mexican 1** adj mexicain **2** n Mexicain, -e mf

miaow [miː'aʊ] **1** exclam miaou! **2** vi miauler

mice [maɪs] pl of **mouse**

mickey ['mɪkɪ] n Br Fam **to take the m. out of sb** charrier qn

microchip ['maɪkrəʊtʃɪp] n Comptr microprocesseur m

microfilm ['maɪkrəʊfɪlm] n microfilm m

microphone ['maɪkrəfəʊn] n micro m

microscope ['maɪkrəskəʊp] n microscope m

microwave ['maɪkrəʊweɪv] n **m. (oven)** (four m à) micro-ondes m inv

mid [mɪd] adj **(in) m. June** (à) la mi-juin; **in m. air** en plein ciel; **to be in one's m.-twenties** avoir environ vingt-cinq ans

midday [mɪd'deɪ] **1** n at m. à midi **2** adj (sun, meal) de midi

middle ['mɪdəl] **1** n milieu m; Fam (waist) taille f; **(right) in the m. of sth** au (beau) milieu de qch

2 adj (central) du milieu; **the M. Ages** le Moyen Âge; **the M. East** le Moyen-Orient; **the m. class(es)** les classes moyennes; **m. name** deuxième prénom m ■ **middle-aged** adj d'âge mûr ■ **middle-class** adj bourgeois ■ **middle-of-the-road** adj (politics, views) modéré; (music) grand public inv

midge [mɪdʒ] n moucheron m

midget ['mɪdʒɪt] n (small person) nain, -e mf

midnight ['mɪdnaɪt] n minuit m

midst [mɪdst] n **in the m. of** (middle) au milieu de

midway [mɪd'weɪ] adj & adv à mi-chemin

midweek [mɪd'wi:k] *adv* en milieu de semaine

midwife ['mɪdwaɪf] (*pl* **-wives**) *n* sage-femme *f*

might¹ [maɪt] *v aux see* **may**

La forme **mightn't** s'écrit **might not** dans un style plus soutenu.

might² [maɪt] *n* (*strength*) force *f* ■ **mighty** (**-ier, -iest**) **1** *adj* puissant; *Fam* (*very great*) sacré **2** *adv Am Fam* (*very*) rudement

migraine ['mi:greɪn, 'maɪgreɪn] *n* migraine *f*

migrate [maɪ'greɪt] *vi* (*of people*) émigrer; (*of birds*) migrer ■ **migrant** ['maɪgrənt] *adj & n* **m.** (**worker**) (travailleur, -euse *mf*) immigré, -e

mike [maɪk] (*abbr* **microphone**) *n Fam* micro *m*

mild [maɪld] (**-er, -est**) *adj* (*weather, cheese, soap, person*) doux (*f* douce); (*punishment*) léger, -ère; (*curry*) peu épicé

mile [maɪl] *n* mile *m*; **he lives miles away** il habite très loin d'ici ■ **mileage** *n* (*distance*) ≃ kilométrage *m*; (*rate of fuel consumption*) consommation *f* ■ **mileometer** *n Br* ≃ compteur *m* kilométrique ■ **milestone** *n* (*in history, career*) étape *f* importante

militant ['mɪlɪtənt] *adj & n* militant, -e (*mf*)

military ['mɪlɪtərɪ] **1** *adj* militaire **2** *n* **the m.** les militaires *mpl*

milk [mɪlk] **1** *n* lait *m*; **m. chocolate** chocolat *m* au lait; **m. shake** milkshake *m* **2** *vt* (*cow*) traire; *Fig* (*exploit*) exploiter ■ **milky** (**-ier, -iest**) *adj* (*coffee, tea*) au lait

mill [mɪl] **1** *n* (*for flour*) moulin *m*; (*textile factory*) filature *f* **2** *vi* **to m. around** (*of crowd*) grouiller

millennium [mɪ'lenɪəm] (*pl* **-nia** [-nɪə]) *n* millénaire *m*

milligram(me) ['mɪlɪgræm] *n* milligramme *m*

millimetre ['mɪlɪmi:tə(r)] (*Am* **millimeter**) *n* millimètre *m*

million ['mɪljən] *n* million *m*; **a m.**

men un million d'hommes; **two m.** deux millions ■ **millionaire** *n* millionnaire *mf*

milometer [maɪ'lɒmɪtə(r)] *n Br* ≃ compteur *m* kilométrique

mime [maɪm] **1** *n* (*art*) mime *m* **2** *vti* mimer; (*of singer*) chanter en playback

mimic ['mɪmɪk] **1** *n* imitateur, -trice *mf* **2** (*pt & pp* **-ck-**) *vt* imiter

mince [mɪns] **1** *n* (*meat*) viande *f* hachée; **m. pie** (*containing fruit*) = tartelette fourrée aux fruits secs et aux épices **2** *vt* hacher ■ **mincemeat** *n* (*dried fruit*) = mélange de fruits secs et d'épices utilisé en pâtisserie ■ **mincer** *n* (*machine*) hachoir *m*

MIND¹ [maɪnd] *n* esprit *m*; (*sanity*) raison *f*; *Br* **to my m.** à mon avis; **to change one's m.** changer d'avis; **to speak one's m.** dire ce que l'on pense; *Br* **to be in two minds** (*undecided*) hésiter; **to bear** *or* **keep sth in m.** garder qch à l'esprit; **to have sb/sth in m.** avoir qn/qch en vue; **to make up one's m.** se décider; *Fam* **to be out of one's m.** avoir perdu la tête; **it's on my m.** cela me préoccupe; *Br* **to have a good m. to do sth** avoir bien envie de faire qch

MIND² [maɪnd] **1** *vt Br* (*pay attention to*) faire attention à; (*look after*) garder; *Br* **m. you don't fall** fais attention à ne pas tomber; **I don't m. the cold/noise** le froid/bruit ne me gêne pas; **if you don't m. my asking...** si je peux me permettre...; **never m. the car** peu importe la voiture; *Br* **m. you...** remarquez...; **m. your own business!** occupe-toi de tes affaires!

2 *vi* **I don't m.** ça m'est égal; **do you m. if I smoke?** ça vous gêne si je fume?; **never m.!** ça ne fait rien!, tant pis!; *Br* **m. (out)!** (*watch out*) attention!

mind-boggling ['maɪndbɒglɪŋ] *adj* stupéfiant

minder ['maɪndə(r)] *n Fam (bodyguard)* gorille *m*

mindless ['maɪndləs] *adj (job, destruction)* stupide

mine¹ [maɪn] *possessive pron* le mien, la mienne, *pl* les mien(ne)s; **this hat is m.** ce chapeau est à moi *ou* est le mien; **a friend of m.** un ami à moi, un de mes amis

mine² [maɪn] **1** *n* (**a**) *(for coal, gold)* & *Fig* mine *f* (**b**) *(explosive)* mine *f* **2** *vt (coal, gold)* extraire ■ **mining** *n* exploitation *f* minière

mineral ['mɪnərəl] *adj* & *n* minéral (*m*); **m. water** eau *f* minérale

mingle ['mɪŋgəl] *vi (of things)* se mêler (**with** à); *(of people)* parler un peu à tout le monde

miniature ['mɪnɪtʃə(r)] **1** *adj (train, model)* miniature *inv* **2** *n* miniature *f*; **in m.** en miniature

minicab ['mɪnɪkæb] *n Br* radio-taxi *m*

minimal ['mɪnɪməl] *adj* minimal

minimize ['mɪnɪmaɪz] *vt* minimiser

minimum ['mɪnɪməm] **1** *(pl* **-ima** *ou* **-imums)** *n* minimum *m* **2** *adj* minimal; **m. wage** salaire *m* minimum

miniskirt ['mɪnɪskɜːt] *n* minijupe *f*

minister ['mɪnɪstə(r)] *n Br (politician)* ministre *m*; *(of religion)* pasteur *m* ■ **ministry** *(pl* **-ies)** *n Br* Pol ministère *m*

minor ['maɪnə(r)] **1** *adj (unimportant)* & *Mus* mineur; *Med (operation)* bénin, -igne; *(road)* secondaire **2** *n (in age)* mineur, -e *mf*

minority [maɪ'nɒrɪtɪ] **1** *(pl* **-ies)** *n* minorité *f*; **to be in the** *ou* **a m.** être minoritaire **2** *adj* minoritaire

mint¹ [mɪnt] **1** *n* **the (Royal) M.** ≃ l'hôtel *m* de la Monnaie **2** *vt (coins)* frapper

mint² [mɪnt] *n (herb)* menthe *f*; *(sweet)* bonbon *m* à la menthe

minus ['maɪnəs] **1** *adj* & *n* **m. (sign)** (signe *m*) moins *m* **2** *prep (with numbers)* moins; *Fam (without)* sans; **it's m. 10 (degrees)** il fait moins 10

minute¹ ['mɪnɪt] *n (of time)* minute *f*; **this (very) m.** *(now)* tout de suite; **any**

m. (now) d'une minute à l'autre ■ **minutes** *npl (of meeting)* procès-verbal *m*

minute² [maɪ'njuːt] *adj (tiny)* minuscule

miracle ['mɪrəkəl] *n* miracle *m* ■ **miraculous** [mɪ'rækjələs] *adj* miraculeux, -euse

mirror ['mɪrə(r)] *n* miroir *m*, glace *f*; **(rearview) m.** *(of vehicle)* rétroviseur *m*

misbehave [mɪsbɪ'heɪv] *vi* se conduire mal

miscalculate [mɪs'kælkjʊleɪt] *vi* faire une erreur de calcul; *Fig* faire un mauvais calcul

miscarriage [mɪs'kærɪdʒ] *n Med* **to have a m.** faire une fausse couche; **m. of justice** erreur *f* judiciaire

miscellaneous [mɪsə'leɪnɪəs] *adj* divers

mischief ['mɪstʃɪf] *n* espièglerie *f*; **to get into m.** faire des bêtises ■ **mischievous** *adj (naughty)* espiègle; *(malicious)* méchant

misconduct [mɪs'kɒndʌkt] *n (bad behaviour)* inconduite *f*

misdemeanor [mɪsdɪ'miːnə(r)] *n Am (crime)* délit *m*

miser ['maɪzə(r)] *n* avare *mf* ■ **miserly** *adj* avare

miserable ['mɪzərəbəl] *adj (wretched)* misérable; *(unhappy)* malheureux, -euse; *(awful)* affreux, -euse

misery ['mɪzərɪ] *(pl* **-ies)** *n (suffering)* malheur *m*; *(sadness)* détresse *f*

misfire [mɪs'faɪə(r)] *vi (of plan)* rater

misfit ['mɪsfɪt] *n Pej* inadapté, -e *mf*

misfortune [mɪs'fɔːtʃuːn] *n* malheur *m*

misgivings [mɪs'gɪvɪŋz] *npl (doubts)* doutes *mpl* (**about** sur); *(fears)* craintes *fpl* (**about** à propos de)

misguided [mɪs'gaɪdɪd] *adj (attempt)* malencontreux, -euse

mishandle [mɪs'hændəl] *vt (situation)* mal gérer; *(person)* malmener

mishap ['mɪshæp] *n* incident *m*

misinform [mɪsɪn'fɔːm] *vt* mal renseigner

misinterpret [misin'tɜ:prit] *vt* mal interpréter

mislay [mis'lei] (*pt & pp* **-laid**) *vt* égarer

mislead [mis'li:d] (*pt & pp* **-led**) *vt* tromper ▪ **misleading** *adj* trompeur, -euse

mismanage [mis'mænidʒ] *vt* mal gérer

misplace [mis'pleis] *vt (lose)* égarer

misprint ['misprint] *n* faute *f* d'impression, coquille *f*

mispronounce [misprə'naʊns] *vt* mal prononcer

misrepresent [misrepri'zent] *vt (theory)* dénaturer; *(person)* présenter sous un faux jour

Miss [mis] *n* Mademoiselle *f*

miss [mis] **1** *n* coup *m* raté; **that was** *or* **we had a near m.** on l'a échappé belle; *Fam* **I'll give it a m.** *(not go)* je n'y irai pas

2 *vt (train, target, opportunity)* manquer, rater; *(not see)* ne pas voir; *(not understand)* ne pas comprendre; *(feel the lack of)* regretter; **to m. sth out** *(accidentally)* oublier qch; *(intentionally)* omettre qch

3 *vi* manquer *ou* rater son coup; **m. out on sth** rater qch

missile [Br 'misail, Am 'misəl] *n (rocket)* missile *m*; *(object thrown)* projectile *m*

missing ['misin] *adj (absent)* absent; *(in war, after disaster)* disparu; *(object)* manquant; **there are two cups/students m.** il manque deux tasses/étudiants; **to go m.** disparaître

mission ['miʃən] *n* mission *f*

missionary ['miʃənəri] (*pl* **-ies**) *n Rel* missionnaire *m*

misspell [mis'spel] (*pt & pp* **-ed** *or* **-spelt**) *vt* mal écrire

mist [mist] **1** *n (fog)* brume *f*; *(on glass)* buée *f* **2** *vi* **m. over** *or* **up** s'embuer

mistake [mi'steik] **1** *n* erreur *f*, faute *f*; **to make a m.** faire une erreur; **by m.** par erreur **2** (*pt* **-took**, *pp* **-taken**) *vt (meaning, intention)* se tromper sur;

to m. sb for prendre qn pour ▪ **mistaken** *adj (belief, impression)* erroné; **to be m.** *(of person)* se tromper *(about sur)* ▪ **mistakenly** *adv* par erreur

Mister ['mistə(r)] *n* Monsieur *m*

mistreat [mis'tri:t] *vt* maltraiter

mistress ['mistris] *n* maîtresse *f*; *Br (in secondary school)* professeur *m*

mistrust [mis'trʌst] **1** *n* méfiance *f* **2** *vt* se méfier de

misty ['misti] (**-ier, -iest**) *adj (foggy)* brumeux, -euse

misunderstand [misʌndə'stænd] (*pt & pp* **-stood**) *vti* mal comprendre ▪ **misunderstanding** *n (disagreement)* mésentente *f*; *(misconception)* malentendu *m*

misuse 1 [mis'ju:s] *n (of equipment, resources)* mauvais emploi *m*; *(of power)* abus *m* **2** [mis'ju:z] *vt (equipment, resources)* mal employer; *(power)* abuser de

mitt(en) [mit, 'mitən] *n (glove)* moufle *f*

mix [miks] **1** *n (mixture)* mélange *m* **2** *vt* mélanger; *(cement, drink, cake)* préparer; **to m. up** *(papers)* mélanger; *(mistake)* confondre *(with* avec); **to be mixed up in sth** être mêlé à qch **3** *vi (blend)* se mélanger; **to m. with sb** *(socially)* fréquenter qn

mixed [mikst] *adj (school, marriage)* mixte; *(nuts, chocolates)* assortis; **to be (all) m. up** *(of person)* être désorienté; *(of facts, account)* être confus

mixer ['miksə(r)] *n (for cooking)* mixeur *m*

mixture ['mikstʃə(r)] *n* mélange *m*

mix-up ['miksʌp] *n* confusion *f*

mm *(abbr* millimetre(s)) mm

moan [məʊn] **1** *n (sound)* gémissement *m* **2** *vi (make sound)* gémir; *(complain)* se plaindre (**to** à; **about** de; **that** que)

mob [mob] **1** *n (crowd)* foule *f* **2** (*pt & pp* **-bb-**) *vt* prendre d'assaut

mobile [Br 'məʊbail, Am 'məʊbəl] **1** *adj* mobile; **m. home** mobile home *m*; *Br*

m. phone téléphone *m* portable **2** *n Br (phone)* portable *m*

mobilize ['məʊbɪlaɪz] *vti* mobiliser

mock [mɒk] **1** *adj (false)* simulé; *Br Sch* **m. exam** examen *m* blanc **2** *vt* se moquer de; *(mimic)* singer ■ **mockery** *n (act)* moqueries *fpl*; *(farce, parody)* parodie *f*; **to make a m. of sth** tourner qch en ridicule

mode [məʊd] *n (manner, way) & Comptr* mode *m*

model ['mɒdəl] **1** *n (example, person)* modèle *m*; *(small version)* maquette *f*; *(in fashion show, magazine* mannequin *m*; **(scale) m.** modèle *m* réduit **2** *adj (behaviour, student)* modèle; *(car, plane)* modèle réduit *inv* **3** *(Br* **-ll-**, *Am* **-l-)** *vt (clay)* modeler; *(hats, dresses)* présenter; **to m. sth on** modeler qch sur **4** *vi (for fashion)* être mannequin; *(pose for artist)* poser

modem ['məʊdəm] *n Comptr* modem *m*

moderate ['mɒdərət] **1** *adj* modéré **2** *n Pol* modéré, -e *mf* ■ **moderately** *adv (in moderation)* modérément; *(averagely)* moyennement

moderation [mɒdə'reɪʃən] *n* modération *f*; **in m.** avec modération

modern ['mɒdən] *adj (recent, new)*; **m. languages** langues *fpl* vivantes

modernize ['mɒdənaɪz] *vt* moderniser

modest ['mɒdɪst] *adj (unassuming, moderate)* modeste

modify ['mɒdɪfaɪ] *(pt & pp* **-ied)** *vt* modifier ■ **modification** *n* modification *f* **(to** à)

module ['mɒdjuːl] *n* module *m*

moist [mɔɪst] **(-er, -est)** *adj* humide; *(skin, hand)* moite ■ **moisten** ['mɔɪsən] *vt* humecter

moisture ['mɔɪstʃə(r)] *n* humidité *f*; *(on glass)* buée *f* ■ **moisturizer** *n* crème *f* hydratante

mold [məʊld] *n & vt Am* = **mould**

mole [məʊl] *n* **(a)** *(on skin)* grain *m* de beauté **(b)** *(animal, spy)* taupe *f*

molecule ['mɒlɪkjuːl] *n* molécule *f*

molest [mə'lest] *vt (child, woman)* agresser (sexuellement)

molt [məʊlt] *vi Am* = **moult**

mom [mɒm] *n Am Fam* maman *f*

moment ['məʊmənt] *n* moment *m*, instant *m*; **at the m.** en ce moment; **for the m.** pour le moment; **in a m.** dans un instant; **any m. (now)** d'un instant à l'autre

momentary ['məʊməntərɪ] *adj* momentané ■ **momentarily** [*Br* 'məʊməntərɪlɪ, *Am* məʊmən'terɪlɪ] *adv (temporarily)* momentanément; *Am (soon)* tout de suite

momentum [məʊ'mentəm] *n (speed)* élan *m*; **to gather** or **gain m.** *(of campaign)* prendre de l'ampleur

mommy ['mɒmɪ] *n Am Fam* maman *f*

monarch ['mɒnək] *n* monarque *m* ■ **monarchy** *(pl* **-ies)** *n* monarchie *f*

monastery ['mɒnəstərɪ] *(pl* **-ies)** *n* monastère *m*

Monday ['mʌndeɪ] *n* lundi *m*

monetary ['mʌnɪtərɪ] *adj* monétaire

money ['mʌnɪ] *n* argent *m*; **to make m.** *(of person)* gagner de l'argent; *(of business)* rapporter de l'argent ■ **moneybox** *n* tirelire *f* ■ **moneylender** *n* prêteur, -euse *mf*

mongrel ['mʌŋgrəl] *n* bâtard *m*

monitor ['mɒnɪtə(r)] **1** *n Comptr, TV & Tech (screen, device)* moniteur *m* **2** *vt (check)* surveiller

monk [mʌŋk] *n* moine *m*

monkey ['mʌŋkɪ] *(pl* **-eys)** *n* singe *m*

monologue ['mɒnəlɒg] *n* monologue *m*

monopoly [mə'nɒpəlɪ] *n* monopole *m* ■ **monopolize** *vt* monopoliser

monotonous [mə'nɒtənəs] *adj* monotone

monster ['mɒnstə(r)] *n* monstre *m*

monstrosity [mɒn'strɒsətɪ] *(pl* **-ies)** *n* monstruosité *f*

monstrous ['mɒnstrəs] *adj* monstrueux, -euse

month [mʌnθ] *n* mois *m* ■ **monthly** **1** *adj* mensuel, -elle; **m. payment**

mensualité *f* 2 (*pl* **-ies**) *n* (*periodical*)

mensuel *m* 3 *adv* tous les mois

Montreal [mɒntrɪˈɔːl] *n* Montréal *m*
ou f

monument [ˈmɒnjʊmənt] *n* monument *m*

moo [muː] (*pt & pp* **mooed**) *vi* meugler

mood [muːd] *n* (*of person*) humeur *f*;
(*in grammar*) mode *m*; **in a good/bad
m.** de bonne/mauvaise humeur; **to
be in the m. to do** *or* **for doing sth**
être d'humeur à faire qch

moody [ˈmuːdɪ] (**-ier, -iest**) *adj* (*bad-
tempered*) maussade; (*changeable*) lunatique

moon [muːn] *n* lune *f* ■ **moonlight** *n*
by m. au clair de lune

moor [mʊə(r)] **1** *n* (*heath*) lande *f* 2 *vt*
(*ship*) amarrer 3 *vi* (*of ship*) mouiller

moose [muːs] *n inv* (*animal*) élan *m*

mop [mɒp] **1** *n* (*for floor*) balai *m* à
franges; (*with sponge*) balai-éponge
m 2 (*pt & pp* **-pp-**) *vt* **to m. sth up** (*liquid*) éponger qch

mope [məʊp] *vi* **to m. about** broyer du
noir

moped [ˈməʊped] *n* Mobylette® *f*

moral [ˈmɒrəl] **1** *adj* moral 2 *n* (*of
story*) morale *f*; **morals** (*principles*) moralité *f* ■ **morale** [mɒˈrɑːl] *n* moral *m*
■ **morality** [məˈrælətɪ] *n* moralité *f*

morbid [ˈmɔːbɪd] *adj* morbide

MORE [mɔː(r)] **1** *adj* plus de; **m. cars**
plus de voitures; **he has m. books
than you** il a plus de livres que toi; **a
few m. months** quelques mois de
plus; (**some**) **m.** tea encore du thé;
(**some**) **m. details** d'autres détails; **m.
than a kilo** plus d'un kilo/de dix

2 *adv* (*to form comparative of ad-
jectives and adverbs*) plus (**than** que);
m. and m. de plus en plus; **m. or less**
plus ou moins

3 *pron* plus; **have some m.** reprenez-
en; **she doesn't have any m.** elle n'en a
plus; **the m. he shouts, the m. hoarse
he gets** plus il crie, plus il s'enroue;
what's m. qui plus est

moreover [mɔːˈrəʊvə(r)] *adv* de plus

morning [ˈmɔːnɪŋ] **1** *n* matin *m*; (*referring to duration*) matinée *f*; **in the m.** le
matin; (*during the course of the morning*) pendant la matinée; (*tomorrow*)
demain matin; **every Tuesday m.** tous
les mardis matin **2** *adj* (*newspaper*) du
matin ■ **mornings** *adv Am* le matin

Morocco [məˈrɒkəʊ] *n* le Maroc
■ **Moroccan 1** *adj* marocain **2** *n* Marocain, -e *mf*

moron [ˈmɔːrɒn] *n* crétin, -e *mf*

mortal [ˈmɔːtəl] *adj & n* mortel, -elle
(*mf*)

mortgage [ˈmɔːgɪdʒ] *n* (*money lent*)
prêt *m* immobilier; (*money borrowed*)
emprunt *m* immobilier

mortuary [ˈmɔːtʃʊərɪ] (*pl* **-ies**) *n* morgue *f*

mosaic [məʊˈzeɪɪk] *n* mosaïque *f*

Moscow [*Br* ˈmɒskəʊ, *Am* ˈmɒskaʊ] *n*
Moscou *m ou f*

Moslem [ˈmɒzlɪm] *adj & n* musulman,
-e (*mf*)

mosque [mɒsk] *n* mosquée *f*

mosquito [mɒˈskiːtəʊ] (*pl* **-oes** *or* **-os**)
n moustique *m*

moss [mɒs] *n* mousse *f*

MOST [məʊst] **1** *adj* (**a**) (*the majority
of*) la plupart de; **m. women** la plupart
des femmes

(**b**) (*greatest amount of*) **the m.** le plus
de; **I have the m. books** j'ai le plus de
livres

2 *adv* (**a**) (*to form superlative of ad-
jectives and adverbs*) plus; **the m.
beautiful** le plus beau (*f* la plus belle)
(**in/of** de); **to talk (the) m.** parler le
plus; **m. of all** (*especially*) surtout

(**b**) (*very*) extrêmement

3 *pron* (**a**) (*the majority*) la plupart; **m.
of the people/the time** la plupart des
gens/du temps; **m. of the cake** la plus
grande partie du gâteau; **m. of them**
la plupart d'entre eux

(**b**) (*greatest amount*) le plus; **he
earns the m.** c'est lui qui gagne le
plus; **to make the m. of sth** (*situation,
talent*) tirer le meilleur parti de qch

(holiday) profiter au maximum de qch; **at (the very) m.** tout au plus ■ **mostly** *adv (in the main)* surtout; *(most often)* le plus souvent

MOT [eməʊˈtiː] *(abbr* **Ministry of Transport)** *n Br* = contrôle obligatoire des véhicules de plus de trois ans

motel [məʊˈtel] *n* motel *m*

moth [mɒθ] *n* papillon *m* de nuit; *(in clothes)* mite *f*

mother [ˈmʌðə(r)] *n* mère *f*; **M.'s Day** la fête des Mères ■ **motherhood** *n* maternité *f* ■ **mother-in-law** *(pl* **mothers-in-law)** *n* belle-mère *f* ■ **mother-to-be** *(pl* **mothers-to-be)** *n* future mère *f*

motion [ˈməʊʃən] **1** *n (of arm)* mouvement *m*; *(in meeting)* motion *f*; **to set sth in m.** mettre qch en mouvement; **m. picture** film *m* **2** *vti* **to m. (to) sb to do sth** faire signe à qn de faire qch ■ **motionless** *adj* immobile

motivate [ˈməʊtɪveɪt] *vt (person, decision)* motiver ■ **motivation** *n* motivation *f*

motive [ˈməʊtɪv] *n* motif *m* **(for** de**)**

motor [ˈməʊtə(r)] **1** *n (engine)* moteur *m*; *Br Fam (car)* auto *f* **2** *adj (industry, insurance)* automobile; **m. racing** courses *fpl* automobiles ■ **motorbike** *n* moto *f* ■ **motorboat** *n* canot *m* à moteur ■ **motorcycle** *n* moto *f*, motocyclette *f* ■ **motorcyclist** *n* motocycliste *mf* ■ **motorist** *n Br* automobiliste *mf* ■ **motorway** *n Br* autoroute *f*

motto [ˈmɒtəʊ] *(pl* **-oes** *or* **-os)** *n* devise *f*

mould¹ [məʊld] *(Am* **mold) 1** *n (shape)* moule *m* **2** *vt (clay, person's character)* modeler

mould² [məʊld] *(Am* **mold)** *n (fungus)* moisissure *f*

mouldy [ˈməʊldɪ] *(Am* **moldy)** **(** **-ier,** **-iest)** *adj* moisi; **to go m.** moisir

moult [məʊlt] *(Am* **molt)** *vi* muer

mound [maʊnd] *n (of earth)* tertre *m*; *Fig (untidy pile)* tas *m*

mount [maʊnt] **1** *n (frame for photo or slide)* cadre *m* **2** *vt (horse, jewel, photo,*

demonstration) monter; *(ladder)* monter à **3** *vi* **(a)** *(on horse)* se mettre en selle **(b)** *(increase, rise)* monter; **to m. up** *(add up)* monter, augmenter; *(accumulate)* *(of debts, bills)* s'accumuler

mountain [ˈmaʊntɪn] *n* montagne *f*; **m. bike** vélo *m* tout-terrain, VTT *m* ■ **mountaineer** *n* alpiniste *mf* ■ **mountaineering** *n* alpinisme *m* ■ **mountainous** *adj* montagneux, -euse

mourn [mɔːn] *vti* **to m. (for) sb** pleurer qn ■ **mourner** *n* = personne assistant aux obsèques ■ **mourning** *n* deuil *m*; **in m.** en deuil

mouse [maʊs] *(pl* **mice** [maɪs]) *n (animal)* & *Comptr* souris *f*

mousse [muːs] *n* mousse *f*

moustache [*Br* məˈstɑːʃ, *Am* ˈmʌstæʃ] *n* moustache *f*

mouth [maʊθ] *(pl* **-s** [maʊðz]) *n (of person, horse)* bouche *f*; *(of other animals)* gueule *f*; *(of river)* embouchure *f*; *(of cave, harbour)* entrée *f* ■ **mouthful** [ˈmaʊθfʊl] *n (of food)* bouchée *f*; *(of liquid)* gorgée *f* ■ **mouth-organ** *n* harmonica *m* ■ **mouthpiece** *n (of musical instrument)* embouchure *f*; *(spokesperson)* porte-parole *m inv* ■ **mouthwash** *n* bain *m* de bouche ■ **mouthwatering** *adj* appétissant

movable [ˈmuːvəbəl] *adj* mobile

move [muːv] **1** *n* mouvement *m*; *(change of house)* déménagement *m*; *(change of job)* changement *m* d'emploi; *(in game)* coup *m*; **to make a m.** *(leave)* se préparer à partir; *(act)* passer à l'action; **it's your m.** *(turn)* c'est à toi de jouer; *Fam* **to get a m. on** se grouiller

2 *vt* déplacer; *(arm, leg)* remuer; *(employee)* muter; *(piece in game)* jouer; **to m. sb** *(emotionally)* émouvoir qn; **to m. house** déménager

3 *vi* bouger; *(change position)* se déplacer *(to* à**)**; *(leave)* partir; *(act)* agir; *(play)* jouer; *(change house)* déménager; **to m. to Paris** aller habiter Paris

► **move about** *vi* se déplacer; *(fidget)* remuer

▸ **move along** *vi* avancer
▸ **move around** *vi* = **move about**
▸ **move away** *vi (go away)* s'éloigner; *(move house)* déménager
▸ **move back 1** *vt sep (chair)* reculer; *(to its original position)* remettre en place* **2** *vi (withdraw)* reculer; *(return)* retourner *(to* à)
▸ **move down** *vt sep (take down)* descendre
▸ **move forward** *vt sep & vi* avancer
▸ **move in** *vi (into house)* emménager
▸ **move off** *vi (go away)* s'éloigner; *(of vehicle)* démarrer
▸ **move out** *vi (out of house)* déménager
▸ **move over 1** *vt sep* pousser **2** *vi (make room)* se pousser
▸ **move up** *vi (on seats)* se pousser
movement ['mu:vmənt] *n* mouvement *m*
movie ['mu:vɪ] *n* film *m*; **the movies** *(cinema)* le cinéma; **m. star** vedette *f* de cinéma; *Am* **m. theater** cinéma *m*
moving ['mu:vɪŋ] *adj* en mouvement; *(vehicle)* en marche; *(touching)* émouvant
mow [məʊ] *(pp* **mown** [məʊn] *or* **mowed)** *vt* to m. the lawn tondre le gazon ■ **mower** *n* **(lawn) m.** tondeuse *f* (à gazon)
MP [em'pi:] *(abbr* **Member of Parliament)** *n* député *m*
mph [empi:'eɪtʃ] *(abbr* **miles per hour)** ≃ km/h
Mr ['mɪstə(r)] *n* **Mr Brown** M. Brown
Mrs ['mɪsɪz] *n* **Mrs Brown** Mme Brown
MS [em'es] *(abbr* **Master of Science)** *n Am Univ* **to have an MS in chemistry** avoir une maîtrise de chimie
Ms [mɪz] *n* **Ms Brown** ≃ Mme Brown *(ne renseigne pas sur le statut de famille)*
MSc [emes'si:] *(abbr* **Master of Science)** *n Univ* **to have an M. in chemistry** avoir une maîtrise de chimie

MUCH [mʌtʃ] **1** *adj*

Hormis dans la langue soutenue et dans certaines expressions, ne s'utilise que dans des structures négatives ou interrogatives.

beaucoup de; **not m. time/money** pas beaucoup de temps/d'argent; **how m. sugar do you want?** combien de sucre voulez-vous?; **twice as m.** traffic deux fois plus de circulation; **too m. work** trop de travail
 2 *adv* beaucoup; **very m.** beaucoup; **m. better** bien meilleur; **I love him so m.** je l'aime tellement; **she doesn't say very m.** elle ne dit pas grand-chose
 3 *pron* beaucoup; **there isn't m. left** il n'en reste pas beaucoup; **it's not m. of a garden** ce n'est pas terrible comme jardin; **twice as m.** deux fois plus; **as m. as you like** autant que tu veux; *Fam* **that's a bit m.!** c'est un peu fort!

muck [mʌk] **1** *n (manure)* fumier *m; Fig (filth)* saleté *f* **2** *vt Br Fam* **to m. sth up** *(task)* bâcler qch; *(plans)* chambouler qch **3** *vi Br Fam* **to m. about** *or* **around** *(waste time)* traîner; *(play the fool)* faire l'imbécile ■ **mucky** **(-ier, -iest)** *adj Fam* sale
mud [mʌd] *n* boue *f* ■ **muddy** **(-ier, -iest)** *adj (water, road)* boueux, -euse; *(hands)* couvert de boue ■ **mudguard** *n* garde-boue *m inv*
muddle ['mʌdəl] **1** *n* confusion *f*; **to be in a m.** *(person)* ne plus s'y retrouver; *(of things)* être en désordre **2** *vt (facts)* mélanger; **to get muddled** *(of person)* s'embrouiller
muesli ['mju:zlɪ, 'mu:zlɪ] *n* muesli *m*
muffin ['mʌfɪn] *n (cake)* muffin *m*
muffled ['mʌfəld] *adj (noise)* sourd
muffler ['mʌflə(r)] *n Am (on vehicle)* silencieux *m*
mug¹ [mʌg] *n* **(a)** *(for tea, coffee)* grande tasse *f*; **(beer) m.** chope *f* **(b)** *Br Fam (face)* poire *f*
mug² [mʌg] *(pt & pp* **-gg-)** *vt (attack in street)* agresser ■ **mugger** *n* agresseur *m*
mule [mju:l] *n (male)* mulet *m*; *(female)* mule *f*
multicoloured ['mʌltɪkʌləd] *adj* multicolore

multimedia [mʌltɪ'miːdɪə] adj multimédia

multimillionaire [mʌltɪmɪljə'neə(r)] n multimillionnaire mf

multiple ['mʌltɪpəl] **1** adj multiple **2** n Math multiple m

multiple-choice [mʌltɪpəl'tʃɔɪs] adj à choix multiple

multiplication [mʌltɪplɪ'keɪʃən] n multiplication f

multiply ['mʌltɪplaɪ] (pt & pp -ied) **1** vt multiplier **2** vi (of animals, insects) se multiplier

multiracial [mʌltɪ'reɪʃəl] adj multiracial

multistorey [mʌltɪ'stɔːrɪ] (Am **multistoried**) adj (car park) à plusieurs niveaux

multitude ['mʌltɪtjuːd] n multitude f

mum [mʌm] n Br Fam maman f

mumble ['mʌmbəl] vti marmotter

mummy¹ ['mʌmɪ] (pl -ies) n Br Fam (mother) maman f

mummy² ['mʌmɪ] (pl -ies) n (embalmed body) momie f

mumps [mʌmps] n Med oreillons mpl

munch [mʌntʃ] vti (chew) mâcher

municipal [mjuː'nɪsɪpəl] adj municipal

mural ['mjʊərəl] n peinture f murale

murder ['mɜːdə(r)] **1** n meurtre m **2** vt (kill) assassiner ■ **murderer** n meurtrier, -ère mf, assassin m

murky ['mɜːkɪ] (-ier, -iest) adj (water, business, past) trouble

murmur ['mɜːmə(r)] **1** n murmure m **2** vti murmurer

muscle ['mʌsəl] n muscle m ■ **muscular** ['mʌskjʊlə(r)] adj (person, arm) musclé

museum [mjuː'zɪəm] n musée m

mush [mʌʃ] n (pulp) bouillie f ■ **mushy** (-ier, -iest) adj (food) en bouillie

mushroom ['mʌʃrʊm] n champignon m

music ['mjuːzɪk] n musique f ■ **musical 1** adj musical; **m. instrument** instrument m de musique **2** n (film, play)

comédie f musicale ■ **musician** [-'zɪʃən] n musicien, -enne mf

Muslim ['mʊzlɪm] adj & n musulman, -e (mf)

mussel ['mʌsəl] n moule f

MUST [mʌst] **1** n this is a m. c'est indispensable; this film is a m. il faut absolument voir ce film

2 v aux (a) (expressing necessity) you m. obey tu dois obéir, il faut que tu obéisses (b) (expressing probability) she m. be clever elle doit être intelligente; I m. have seen it j'ai dû le voir

mustache ['mʌstæʃ] n Am moustache f

mustard ['mʌstəd] n moutarde f

muster ['mʌstə(r)] vt (gather) rassembler

mustn't ['mʌsənt] = must not

musty ['mʌstɪ] (-ier, -iest) adj (smell, taste) de moisi

mute [mjuːt] adj (silent) & Ling muet (f muette)

mutiny ['mjuːtɪnɪ] **1** (pl -ies) n mutinerie f **2** (pt & pp -ied) vi se mutiner

mutter ['mʌtə(r)] vti marmonner

mutton ['mʌtən] n (meat) mouton m

mutual ['mjuːtʃʊəl] adj (help, love) mutuel, -elle; (friend) commun ■ **mutually** adv mutuellement

muzzle ['mʌzəl] **1** n (device for dog) muselière f; (snout) museau m **2** vt (animal, the press) museler

my [maɪ] possessive adj mon, ma, pl mes

myself [maɪ'self] pron moi-même; (reflexive) me, m'; (after prep) moi; I wash m. je me lave

mystery ['mɪstərɪ] (pl -ies) n mystère m ■ **mysterious** [mɪs'tɪərɪəs] adj mystérieux, -euse

mystical ['mɪstɪkəl] adj mystique

mystify ['mɪstɪfaɪ] (pt & pp -ied) vt (bewilder) déconcerter

myth [mɪθ] n mythe m ■ **mythology** (pl -ies) n mythologie f

Nn

N, n [en] *n (letter)* N, n *m inv*

nab [næb] *(pt & pp -bb-) vt Fam (catch, arrest)* coffrer

nag [næg] *(pt & pp -gg-) vti* **to n. (at)** sb *(of person)* être sur le dos de qn

nail [neɪl] **1** *n* **(a)** *(of finger, toe)* ongle *m*; **n. file** lime *f* à ongles; **n. polish,** *Br* **n. varnish** vernis *m* à ongles **(b)** *(metal)* clou *m*
2 *vt* clouer; **to n. sth down** *(lid)* clouer qch

naïve [naɪˈiːv] *adj* naïf *(f* naïve)

naked [ˈneɪkɪd] *adj (person, flame)* nu

name [neɪm] **1** *n (of person)* nom *m; (reputation)* réputation *f*; **my n. is…** je m'appelle…; **in the n. of** au nom de; **first n.,** given n. prénom *m* **2** *vt* nommer; *(ship, street)* baptiser; *(date, price)* fixer

namely [ˈneɪmlɪ] *adv* à savoir

nanny [ˈnænɪ] *(pl -ies) n* nurse *f; Fam (grandmother)* mamie *f*

nap [næp] **1** *n (sleep)* **to have** *or* **take a n.** faire un petit somme **2** *(pt & pp -pp-) vi* faire un somme

napkin [ˈnæpkɪn] *n (at table)* serviette *f*

nappy [ˈnæpɪ] *(pl -ies) n Br (for baby)* couche *f*

narcotic [nɑːˈkɒtɪk] *adj & n* narcotique *(m)*

narrate [nəˈreɪt] *vt* raconter ■ **narrative** [ˈnærətɪv] *n* récit *m* ■ **narrator** *n* narrateur, -trice *mf*

narrow [ˈnærəʊ] **1** *(-er, -est) adj* étroit **2** *vt* **to n. (down)** *(choice, meaning)* limiter **3** *vi (of path)* se rétrécir ■ **narrowly** *adv (only just)* de peu; **he n. escaped being killed** il a bien failli être tué

narrow-minded [nærəʊˈmaɪndɪd] *adj* borné

nasty [ˈnɑːstɪ] *(-ier, -iest) adj (bad)* mauvais; *(spiteful)* méchant **(to** *or* **towards** avec)

nation [ˈneɪʃən] *n* nation *f*

national [ˈnæʃənəl] **1** *adj* national; **n. anthem** hymne *m* national; *Br* **N. Health Service** ≃ Sécurité *f* sociale; *Br* **n. insurance** contributions *fpl* sociales **2** *n (citizen)* ressortissant, -e *mf*

nationalist [ˈnæʃənəlɪst] *n* nationaliste *mf*

nationality [næʃəˈnælətɪ] *(pl -ies) n* nationalité *f*

nationalize [ˈnæʃənəlaɪz] *vt* nationaliser

nationwide [ˈneɪʃənwaɪd] *adj & adv* dans tout le pays

native [ˈneɪtɪv] **1** *adj (country)* natal *(mpl -als); (tribe, plant)* indigène; **to be an English n. speaker** avoir l'anglais comme langue maternelle **2** *n (person)* indigène *mf*; **to be a n. of** être originaire de

NATO [ˈneɪtəʊ] *(abbr* **North Atlantic Treaty Organization)** *n Mil* OTAN *f*

natter [ˈnætə(r)] *vi Br Fam* bavarder

natural [ˈnætʃərəl] *adj* naturel, -elle; *(talent)* inné ■ **naturally** *adv (unaffectedly, of course)* naturellement; *(by nature)* de nature

nature [ˈneɪtʃə(r)] *n (world, character)* nature *f*; **by n.** de nature; **n. reserve** réserve *f* naturelle

naughty [ˈnɔːtɪ] *(-ier, -iest) adj (child)* vilain

nausea ['nɔːzɪə] n nausée f ■ **nauseate** ['nɔːzɪeɪt] vt écœurer ■ **nauseous** ['nɔːʃəs] adj Am **to feel n.** (sick) avoir envie de vomir

nautical ['nɔːtɪkəl] adj nautique

naval ['neɪvəl] adj naval (mpl -als); (power) maritime; (officer) de marine

nave [neɪv] n (of church) nef f

navel ['neɪvəl] n nombril m

navigate ['nævɪgeɪt] **1** vt (boat) piloter; (river) naviguer sur **2** vi naviguer

navy ['neɪvɪ] **1** (pl -ies) n marine f **2** adj n. **(blue)** bleu marine inv

Nazi ['nɑːtsɪ] adj & n Pol & Hist nazi, -e (mf)

NB [en'biː] (abbr **nota bene**) NB

near [nɪə(r)] **1** (-er, -est) prep n. (to) près de; n. **(to) the end** vers la fin

2 (-er, -est) adv près; n. **to sth** près de qch; n. **enough** (more or less) plus ou moins

3 (-er, -est) adj proche; **in the n. future** dans un avenir proche; **to the nearest euro** (calculate) à un euro près; Aut **n. side** Br côté m gauche, Am côté m droit

4 vt (approach) approcher de

nearby 1 [nɪə'baɪ] adv tout près **2** ['nɪəbaɪ] adj proche

nearly ['nɪəlɪ] adv presque; **she (very) n. fell** elle a failli tomber

neat [niːt] (-er, -est) adj (clothes, work) soigné; (room) bien rangé; Am Fam (good) super inv ■ **neatly** adv (carefully) avec soin; (skilfully) habilement

necessary ['nesɪsərɪ] adj nécessaire ■ **necessarily** [-'serəlɪ] adv **not** n. pas forcément

necessity [nɪ'sesɪtɪ] (pl -ies) n (obligation, need) nécessité f; **to be a n.** être indispensable ■ **necessitate** vt nécessiter

neck [nek] n cou m; (of dress) encolure f; (of bottle) goulot m

necklace ['neklɪs] n collier m ■ **necktie** n cravate f

nectarine ['nektəriːn] n (fruit) nectarine f, brugnon m

need [niːd] **1** n besoin m; **to be in n. of**

sth avoir besoin de qch; **there's no n. (for you) to do that** tu n'as pas besoin de faire cela

2 vt avoir besoin de; **you n. it** tu en as besoin; **her hair needs cutting** il faut qu'elle se fasse couper les cheveux

3 v aux I **needn't have rushed** ce n'était pas la peine de me presser; **you needn't worry** inutile de t'inquiéter

needle ['niːdəl] n aiguille f; (of record player) saphir m ■ **needlework** n couture f; (object) ouvrage m

needlessly ['niːdlɪslɪ] adv inutilement

needy ['niːdɪ] (-ier, -iest) adj nécessiteux, -euse

negative ['negətɪv] **1** adj négatif, -ive **2** n (of photo) négatif m

neglect [nɪ'glekt] **1** n (of person) négligence f **2** vt (person, health, work) négliger; (garden, car) ne pas s'occuper de; (duty) manquer à; **to n. to do sth** négliger de faire qch ■ **neglected** adj (appearance) négligé; (garden, house) mal tenu; **to feel n.** se sentir abandonné

negligent ['neglɪdʒənt] adj négligent

negligible ['neglɪdʒəbəl] adj négligeable

negotiate [nɪ'gəʊʃɪeɪt] vti (discuss) négocier ■ **negotiation** n négociation f

neigh [neɪ] vi hennir

neighbour ['neɪbə(r)] (Am **neighbor**) n voisin, -e mf

neighbourhood ['neɪbəhʊd] (Am **neighborhood**) n (district) quartier m, voisinage m; (neighbours) voisinage m; **in the n. of $10/10 kilos** dans les 10 dollars/10 kilos

neighbouring ['neɪbərɪŋ] (Am **neighboring**) adj voisin

neither [Br 'naɪðə(r), Am 'niːðə(r)] **1** conj n.... nor... ni... ni...; **he n. sings nor dances** il ne chante ni ne danse

2 adv n. **do I/n. can I** (ni) moi non plus

3 adj n. **boy came** aucun des deux garçons n'est venu

4 *pron* n. **(of them)** aucun(e) (des deux)

neon ['niːɒn] *adj* n. **sign** enseigne *f* au néon

nephew ['nefjuː] *n* neveu *m*

nerve [nɜːv] *n* nerf *m*; *(courage)* courage *m*; *Fam (impudence)* culot *m*; *Fam* **he gets on my nerves** il me tape sur les nerfs ■ **nerve-racking** *adj* éprouvant

nervous ['nɜːvəs] *adj (apprehensive)* nerveux, -euse; **to be n. about sth/ doing sth** être nerveux à l'idée de qch/de faire qch

nest [nest] **1** *n* nid *m*; *Fig* n. **egg** pécule *m* **2** *vi (of bird)* nicher

nestle ['nesəl] *vi* se pelotonner (**up to** contre)

Net [net] *n Comptr* **the N.** le Net

net[1] [net] *n* filet *m*

net[2] [net] **1** *adj (profit, weight)* net (*f* nette) **2** *(pt & pp* **-tt-**) *vt (of person, company)* gagner net

Netherlands ['neðələndz] *npl* **the N.** les Pays-Bas *mpl*

nettle ['netəl] *n* ortie *f*

network ['netwɜːk] *n* réseau *m*

neurotic [njʊ'rɒtɪk] *adj & n* névrosé, -e (*mf*)

neuter ['njuːtə(r)] **1** *adj & n Gram* neutre (*m*) **2** *vt (cat)* châtrer

neutral ['njuːtrəl] **1** *adj* neutre; *(policy)* de neutralité **2** *n* in n. **(gear)** *(vehicle)* au point mort ■ **neutralize** *vt* neutraliser

never ['nevə(r)] *adv (not ever)* (ne...) jamais; **she n. lies** elle ne ment jamais; **n. again** plus jamais ■ **never-ending** *adj* interminable

nevertheless [nevəðə'les] *adv* néanmoins

new [njuː] *adj* **(a)** (**-er, -est**) nouveau (*f* nouvelle); *(brand-new)* neuf (*f* neuve); **to be n. to** *(job)* être nouveau dans; *(city)* être un nouveau-venu (*f* une nouvelle-venue) dans **(b)** *(different)* **a n. glass/pen** un autre verre/ stylo ■ **newborn** *adj* **a n. baby** un nouveau-né, une nouveau-née

■ **newcomer** [-kʌmə(r)] *n* nouveau-venu *m*, nouvelle-venue *f* (**to** dans) ■ **newly** *adv* nouvellement ■ **newlyweds** *n* jeunes mariés *mpl*

news [njuːz] *n* nouvelles *fpl*; *(in the media)* informations *fpl*; **a piece of n.** une nouvelle; **sports n.** *(newspaper column)* rubrique *f* sportive ■ **newsagent** *n Br* marchand, -e *mf* de journaux ■ **newsdealer** *n Am* marchand, -e *mf* de journaux ■ **newsflash** *n* flash *m* d'informations ■ **newsletter** *n (of club, group)* bulletin *m* ■ **newspaper** *n* journal *m* ■ **newsreader** *n Br* présentateur, -trice *mf* de journal

New Zealand [njuː'ziːlənd] *n* la Nouvelle-Zélande

next [nekst] **1** *adj* prochain; *(room, house)* d'à côté; *(following)* suivant; **n. month** *(in the future)* le mois prochain; **the n. day** le lendemain; **within the n. ten days** d'ici dix jours; **you're n.** c'est ton tour; **the n. size up** la taille au-dessus; **to live n. door** habiter à côté (**to** de)

2 *n (in series)* suivant, -e *mf*

3 *adv (afterwards)* ensuite, après; *(now)* maintenant; **when you come n.** la prochaine fois que tu viendras; **n. to** *(beside)* à côté de

next-door ['nekstdɔː(r)] *adj* n. **neighbour/room** voisin *m*/pièce *f* d'à côté

NHS [eneɪtʃ'es] *(abbr* **National Health Service)** *n Br* ≃ Sécurité *f* sociale

nibble ['nɪbəl] *vti* grignoter

nice [naɪs] (**-er, -est**) *adj (pleasant)* agréable; *(tasty)* bon (*f* bonne); *(physically attractive)* beau (*f* belle); *(kind)* gentil, -ille (**to** avec); **n. and warm** bien chaud; **have a n. day!** bonne journée! ■ **nicely** *adv (well)* bien

niche [niːʃ, nɪtʃ] *n (recess)* niche *f*; *(market)* n. créneau *m*

nick [nɪk] **1** *n (on skin, wood)* entaille *f*; *(in blade, crockery)* brèche *f*; **in the n. of time** juste à temps **2** *vt Br Fam (steal)* piquer

nickel ['nɪkəl] *n Am (coin)* pièce *f* de cinq cents

nickname ['nɪkneɪm] **1** *n (informal)* surnom *m* **2** *vt* surnommer

niece [niːs] *n* nièce *f*

night [naɪt] **1** *n* nuit *f*; *(evening)* soir *m*; **at n.** la nuit; **last n.** *(evening)* hier soir; *(night)* cette nuit; **to have an early/a late n.** se coucher tôt/tard
2 *adj (work, flight)* de nuit; **n. shift** *(job)* poste *m* de nuit; *(workers)* équipe *f* de nuit ◾ **nightcap** *n (drink)* = boisson alcoolisée ou chaude prise avant de se coucher ◾ **nightclub** *n* boîte *f* de nuit ◾ **nightdress** ['naɪtdres], **nightgown** ['naɪtgaʊn], *Fam* **nightie** ['naɪtɪ] *n* chemise *f* de nuit ◾ **nightfall** *n* **at n.** à la tombée de la nuit ◾ **nightlife** *n* vie *f* nocturne ◾ **night-time** *n* nuit *f*

nightingale ['naɪtɪŋgeɪl] *n* rossignol *m*

nightly ['naɪtlɪ] **1** *adv* chaque nuit; *(every evening)* chaque soir **2** *adj* de chaque nuit/soir

nightmare ['naɪtmeə(r)] *n* cauchemar *m*

nil [nɪl] *n (nothing)* & *Br (score)* zéro *m*; **two n.** deux à zéro

Nile [naɪl] *n* **the N.** le Nil

nimble ['nɪmbəl] **(-er, -est)** *adj (person)* souple

nine [naɪn] *adj* & *n* neuf *(m)*

nineteen [naɪn'tiːn] *adj* & *n* dix-neuf *(m)*

ninety ['naɪntɪ] *adj* & *n* quatre-vingt-dix *(m)*

ninth ['naɪnθ] *adj* & *n* neuvième *(mf)*; **a n.** *(fraction)* un neuvième

nip [nɪp] **1** *(pt & pp* **-pp-)** *vt (pinch)* pincer **2** *vi Br Fam* **to n. round to sb's house** faire un saut chez qn; **to n. out** sortir un instant

nipple ['nɪpəl] *n* mamelon *m*; *Am (on baby's bottle)* tétine *f*

nitrogen ['naɪtrədʒən] *n* azote *m*

NO [nəʊ] **1** *(pl* **noes** *or* **nos)** *n* non *m inv*
2 *adj (not any)* pas de; **there's no bread** il n'y a pas de pain; **I have no idea** je n'ai aucune idée; **no child**
came aucun enfant n'est venu; **of no importance** sans importance
3 *adv (interjection)* non; **no more time** plus de temps; **no more/ fewer than ten** pas plus/moins de dix

noble ['nəʊbəl] **(-er, -est)** *adj* noble ◾ **nobility** *n* noblesse *f*

nobody ['nəʊbɒdɪ] *pron* (**no**…) personne; **n. came** personne n'est venu; **he knows n.** il ne connaît personne **2** *n* **a nullité**

nod [nɒd] **1** *n* signe *m* de tête **2** *(pt & pp* **-dd-)** *vti* **to n. (one's head)** faire un signe de tête **3** *vi Fam* **to n. off** s'assoupir

noise [nɔɪz] *n* bruit *m*; **to make a n.** faire du bruit

noisy ['nɔɪzɪ] **(-ier, -iest)** *adj (person, street)* bruyant ◾ **noisily** *adv* bruyamment

nominal ['nɒmɪnəl] *adj* nominal; *(rent, salary)* symbolique

nominate ['nɒmɪneɪt] *vt (appoint)* nommer; *(propose)* proposer (**for** comme candidat à) ◾ **nomination** *n (appointment)* nomination *f*; *(proposal)* candidature *f*

nondescript ['nɒndɪskrɪpt] *adj* très ordinaire

NONE [nʌn] **1** *pron* aucun, -e *mf*; *(in filling out a form)* néant; **n. of them** aucun d'eux; **she has n. (at all)** elle n'en a pas (du tout); **n. came** pas un(e) seul(e) n'est venu(e)
2 *adv* **n. too hot** pas très chaud; **he's n. the wiser (for it)** il n'est pas plus avancé ◾ **nonetheless** *adv* néanmoins

nonentity [nɒ'nentɪtɪ] *(pl* **-ies)** *n (person)* nullité *f*

nonexistent [nɒnɪg'zɪstənt] *adj* inexistant

non-fiction [nɒn'fɪkʃən] *n* ouvrages *mpl* généraux

nonsense ['nɒnsəns] *n* bêtises *fpl*; **that's n.** c'est absurde

non-smoker [nɒn'sməʊkə(r)] *n*

(person) non-fumeur, -euse *mf*; *(compartment on train)* compartiment *m* non-fumeurs

non-stop [nɒn'stɒp] **1** *adj* sans arrêt; *(train, flight)* sans escale **2** *adv* *(work)* sans arrêt; *(fly)* sans escale

noodles ['nu:dəlz] *npl* nouilles *fpl*; *(in soup)* vermicelles *mpl*

noon [nu:n] *n* midi *m*

no-one ['nəʊwʌn] *pron* = **nobody**

noose [nu:s] *n* nœud *m* coulant

nor [nɔ:(r)] *conj* ni; **neither you n. me** ni toi ni moi; **she neither drinks n. smokes** elle ne fume ni ne boit; **n. do I/can I***etc* (ni) moi non plus

norm [nɔ:m] *n* norme *f*

normal ['nɔ:məl] **1** *adj* normal **2** *n* **above/below n.** au-dessus/au-dessous de la normale ■ **normally** *adv* normalement

north [nɔ:θ] **1** *n* nord *m*; **(to the) n. of** au nord de

2 *adj (coast)* nord *inv*; *(wind)* du nord; **N. America/Africa** Amérique *f*/ Afrique *f* du Nord; **N. American** *adj* nord-américain; *n* Nord-Américain, -e *mf*

3 *adv* au nord; *(travel)* vers le nord ■ **northbound** *adj (traffic)* en direction du nord; *Br (carriageway)* nord *inv* ■ **north-east** *n & adj* nord-est *m* ■ **northerly** ['nɔ:ðəlɪ] *adj (direction)* du nord ■ **northern** ['nɔ:ðən] *adj (coast)* nord *inv*; *(town)* du nord; **N. France** le nord de la France; **N. Ireland** l'Irlande *f* du Nord ■ **northerner** ['nɔ:ðənə(r)] *n* habitant, -e *mf* du Nord ■ **northward(s)** *adj & adv* vers le nord ■ **north-west** *n & adj* nord-ouest *m*

Norway ['nɔ:weɪ] *n* la Norvège ■ **Norwegian 1** *adj* norvégien, -enne **2** *n (person)* Norvégien, -enne *mf*; *(language)* norvégien *m*

nose [nəʊz] *n* nez *m*; **her n. is bleeding** elle saigne du nez ■ **nosebleed** *n* saignement *m* de nez

nosey ['nəʊzɪ] **(-ier, -iest)** *adj Fam* indiscret, -ète

no-smoking [nəʊ'sməʊkɪŋ] *adj*

(carriage, area) non-fumeurs

nostalgic [nɒs'tældʒɪk] *adj* nostalgique

nostril ['nɒstrəl] *n (of person)* narine *f*

nosy ['nəʊzɪ] *adj* = **nosey**

NOT [nɒt]

À l'oral, et à l'écrit dans un style familier, on utilise généralement **not** à la forme contractée lors qu'il suit un modal ou un auxiliaire (**don't go!**; **she wasn't there**; **he couldn't see me**).

adv **(a)** (ne…) pas; **he's n. there, he isn't there** il n'est pas là; **n. yet** pas encore; **n. at all** pas du tout; *(after 'thank you')* je vous en prie

(b) non; **I think/hope n.** je pense/ j'espère que non; **n. guilty** non coupable; **isn't she?/don't you?***etc* non?

notable ['nəʊtəbəl] *adj* notable ■ **notably** *adv (noticeably)* notablement; *(particularly)* notamment

notch [nɒtʃ] **1** *n (in wood)* encoche *f*; *(in belt, wheel)* cran *m* **2** *vt* **to n. up** *(points)* marquer; *(victory)* remporter

note [nəʊt] **1** *n (information, reminder) & Mus* note *f*; *Br (banknote)* billet *m*; *(letter)* mot *m*; **to take (a) n. of sth, to make a n. of sth** prendre note de qch **2** *vt (notice)* remarquer, noter; **to n. sth down** *(word, remark)* noter qch ■ **notebook** *n* carnet *m*; *(for school)* cahier *m* ■ **notepad** *n* bloc-notes *m* ■ **notepaper** *n* papier *m* à lettres

noted ['nəʊtɪd] *adj* éminent

nothing ['nʌθɪŋ] **1** *pron* (ne…) rien; **he knows n.** il ne sait rien; **n. at all** rien du tout; **n. much** pas grand-chose; **I've got n. to do with it** je n'y suis pour rien; **for n.** *(in vain, free of charge)* pour rien

2 *adv* **to look n. like sb** ne ressembler nullement à qn

3 *n* **to come to n.** être anéanti

notice ['nəʊtɪs] **1** *n (notification)* avis *m*; *(sign)* pancarte *f*, écriteau *m*; *(poster)* affiche *f*; **to give sb (advance) n.** *(inform)* avertir qn *(of* de*)*; **n. (to quit), n. of dismissal** congé *m*; **to give in** *or*

hand in one's n. (*resign*) donner sa démission; **to take n.** faire attention (**of à**); **until further n.** jusqu'à nouvel ordre; **at short n.** au dernier moment **2** *vt* remarquer (**that que**) ■ **noticeboard** *n Br* tableau *m* d'affichage

noticeable ['nəʊtɪsəbəl] *adj* perceptible

notify ['nəʊtɪfaɪ] (*pt & pp* -**ied**) *vt* (*inform*) avertir (**sb of sth** qn de qch); (*announce*) notifier (**to à**) ■ **notification** [-fɪ'keɪʃən] *n* avis *m*

notion ['nəʊʃən] *n* notion *f*

notorious [nəʊ'tɔːrɪəs] *adj* tristement célèbre; (*criminal*) notoire

nought [nɔːt] *n Br Math* zéro *m*

noun [naʊn] *n* nom *m*

nourish ['nʌrɪʃ] *vt* nourrir ■ **nourishment** *n* nourriture *f*

novel ['nɒvəl] **1** *n* roman *m* **2** *adj* (*new*) nouveau (*f* nouvelle), original ■ **novelist** *n* romancier, -ère *mf* ■ **novelty** *n* nouveauté *f*

November [nəʊ'vembə(r)] *n* novembre *m*

novice ['nɒvɪs] *n* (*beginner*) débutant, -e *mf* (**at** en)

now [naʊ] **1** *adv* maintenant; **for n.** pour le moment; **from n. on** désormais; **until n., up to n.** jusqu'ici, jusqu'à maintenant; **n. and then** de temps à autre; **she ought to be here by n.** elle devrait déjà être ici **2** *conj* **n. (that)...** maintenant que...

nowadays ['naʊədeɪz] *adv* de nos jours

nowhere ['nəʊweə(r)] *adv* nulle part; **n. else** nulle part ailleurs; **n. near enough** loin d'être assez

nozzle ['nɒzəl] *n* embout *m*; (*of hose*) jet *m*

nuance ['njuːɑːns] *n* nuance *f*

nuclear ['njuːklɪə(r)] *adj* nucléaire

nucleus ['njuːklɪəs] (*pl* -**clei** [-klɪaɪ]) *n* noyau *m* (*pl* -aux)

nude [njuːd] **1** *adj* nu **2** *n* nu *m*; **in the n.** tout nu (*f* toute nue)

nudge [nʌdʒ] **1** *n* coup *m* de coude **2** *vt* pousser du coude

nudist ['njuːdɪst] **1** *n* nudiste *mf* **2** *adj* (*camp*) de nudistes

nuisance ['njuːsəns] *n* **to be a n.** être embêtant

null [nʌl] *adj* **n. (and void)** nul (et non avenu) (*f* nulle (et non avenue))

numb [nʌm] *adj* (*stiff*) (*hand*) engourdi

number ['nʌmbə(r)] **1** *n* nombre *m*; (*of page, house, telephone*) numéro *m*; (*song*) chanson *f*; **a/any n. of** un certain/grand nombre de **2** *vt* (*assign number to*) numéroter ■ **numberplate** *n Br* plaque *f* d'immatriculation

numeral ['njuːmərəl] *n* chiffre *m*

numerical [njuː'merɪkəl] *adj* numérique

numerous ['njuːmərəs] *adj* nombreux, -euse

nun [nʌn] *n* religieuse *f*

nurse [nɜːs] **1** *n* infirmière *f*; (*for children*) nurse *f* **2** *vt* (*look after*) soigner; (*suckle*) allaiter ■ **nursing** *n* (*care*) soins *mpl*; (*job*) profession *f* d'infirmière; *Br* **n. home** (*for old people*) maison *f* de retraite

nursery ['nɜːsərɪ] (*pl* -**ies**) *n* (*children's room*) chambre *f* d'enfants; (*for plants, trees*) pépinière *f*; **(day) n.** (*school*) garderie *f*; **n. rhyme** comptine *f*; **n. school** école *f* maternelle

nut¹ [nʌt] *n* (*fruit*) = noix, noisette ou autre fruit sec de cette nature; **Brazil n.** noix *f* du Brésil ■ **nutcrackers** *npl* casse-noix *m inv* ■ **nutshell** *n Fig* **in a n.** en un mot

nut² [nʌt] *n* (*for bolt*) écrou *m*

nut³ [nʌt] *n Fam* (*crazy person*) cinglé, -e *mf* ■ **nutcase** *n Fam* cinglé, -e *mf*

nutmeg ['nʌtmeg] *n* muscade *f*

nutritious [njuː'trɪʃəs] *adj* nutritif, -ive ■ **nutrition** [-ʃən] *n* nutrition *f*

nuts [nʌts] *adj Fam* (*crazy*) cinglé

nylon ['naɪlɒn] *n* Nylon® *m*; **n. shirt** chemise *f* en Nylon®

Oo

O, o [əʊ] *n (letter)* O, o *m inv*

oaf [əʊf] *n* balourd *m*

oak [əʊk] *n (tree, wood)* chêne *m*

OAP [əʊeɪ'piː] *(abbr* **old-age pensioner)** *n Br* retraité, -e *mf*

oar [ɔː(r)] *n* aviron *m*, rame *f*

oasis [əʊ'eɪsɪs] *(pl* **oases** [əʊ'eɪsiːz]) *n* oasis *f*

oath [əʊθ] *(pl* **-s** [əʊðz]) *n (promise)* serment *m*; *(profanity)* juron *m*

oats [əʊts] *npl* avoine *f*; **(porridge) o.** flocons *mpl* d'avoine

obedient [ə'biːdɪənt] *adj* obéissant ▪ **obedience** *n* obéissance *f* (**to** à)

obese [əʊ'biːs] *adj* obèse

obey [ə'beɪ] **1** *vt* obéir à **2** *vi* obéir

obituary [ə'bɪtʃʊərɪ] *(pl* **-ies**) *n* nécrologie *f*

object¹ ['ɒbdʒɪkt] *n (thing)* objet *m*; *(aim)* but *m*, objet; *(in grammar)* complément *m* d'objet

object² [əb'dʒekt] **1** *vt* **to o. that...** objecter que... **2** *vi* émettre une objection; **to o. to sth/to doing sth** ne pas être d'accord avec qch/pour faire qch

objection [əb'dʒekʃən] *n* objection *f*

objective [əb'dʒektɪv] **1** *adj (impartial)* objectif, -ive **2** *n (aim, target)* objectif *m*

obligation [ɒblɪ'geɪʃən] *n* obligation *f*; **to be under an o. to do sth** être dans l'obligation de faire qch

obligatory [ə'blɪgətərɪ] *adj* obligatoire

oblige [ə'blaɪdʒ] *vt* **(a)** *(compel)* **to o. sb to do sth** obliger qn à faire qch **(b)** *(help)* rendre service à; **to be obliged to sb** être reconnaissant à qn (**for** de)

▪ **obliging** *adj* serviable

oblique [ə'bliːk] *adj (line, angle)* oblique; *(reference)* indirect

oblivion [ə'blɪvɪən] *n* oubli *m* ▪ **oblivious** *adj* inconscient (**to** or **of** de)

oblong ['ɒblɒŋ] **1** *adj (rectangular)* rectangulaire **2** *n* rectangle *m*

obnoxious [əb'nɒkʃəs] *adj (person, behaviour)* odieux, -euse

oboe ['əʊbəʊ] *n* hautbois *m*

obscene [əb'siːn] *adj* obscène ▪ **obscenity** [əb'senətɪ] *(pl* **-ies**) *n* obscénité *f*

obscure [əb'skjʊə(r)] **1** *adj* obscur **2** *vt (hide)* cacher; *(confuse)* obscurcir

observant [əb'zɜːvənt] *adj* observateur, -trice

observation [ɒbzə'veɪʃən] *n (observing, remark)* observation *f*; **under o.** *(hospital patient)* en observation

observe [əb'zɜːv] *vt* observer; **to o. the speed limit** respecter la limitation de vitesse ▪ **observer** *n* observateur, -trice *mf*

obsess [əb'ses] *vt* obséder ▪ **obsession** *n* obsession *f* ▪ **obsessive** *adj (idea)* obsédant; *(person)* obsessionnel, -elle; **to be o. about sth** être obsédé par qch

obsolete ['ɒbsəliːt] *adj* obsolète; *(design, model)* dépassé

obstacle ['ɒbstəkəl] *n* obstacle *m*

obstinate ['ɒbstɪnət] *adj* obstiné

obstruct [əb'strʌkt] *vt (block)* **(road, pipe)** obstruer; *(view)* cacher; *(hinder)* gêner ▪ **obstruction** *n (action, in sport), Med & Pol* obstruction *f*; *(obstacle)* obstacle *m*; *(in pipe)* bouchon *m*

obtain [əb'teɪn] *vt* obtenir

obvious ['ɒbvɪəs] *adj* évident (**that** que) ▪ **obviously** *adv (of course)* évidemment; *(conspicuously)* manifestement

occasion [ə'keɪʒən] *n (time, opportunity)* occasion *f; (event)* événement *m;* **on the o.** ... à l'occasion de...; **on several occasions** à plusieurs reprises

occasional [ə'keɪʒənəl] *adj* occasionnel, -elle; **she drinks the o. whisky** elle boit un whisky de temps en temps ▪ **occasionally** *adv* de temps en temps

occupant ['ɒkjʊpənt] *n (of house, car)* occupant, -e *mf*

occupation [ɒkjʊ'peɪʃən] *n* (**a**) *(pastime)* occupation *f; (profession)* métier *m* (**b**) *(of house, land)* occupation *f*

occupier ['ɒkjʊpaɪə(r)] *n (of house)* occupant, -e *mf; (of country)* occupant *m*

occupy ['ɒkjʊpaɪ] *(pt & pp* **-ied)** *vt (space, time, attention)* occuper; **to keep oneself occupied** s'occuper (**doing** à faire)

occur [ə'kɜ:(r)] *(pt & pp* **-rr-)** *vi (happen)* avoir lieu; *(of opportunity)* se présenter; *(be found)* se trouver; **it occurs to me that...** il me vient à l'esprit que...

occurrence [ə'kʌrəns] *n (event)* événement *m*

ocean ['əʊʃən] *n* océan *m*

o'clock [ə'klɒk] *adv* (**it's**) **three o.** (il est) trois heures

octagonal [ɒk'tægənəl] *adj* octogonal

October [ɒk'təʊbə(r)] *n* octobre *m*

octopus ['ɒktəpəs] *n* pieuvre *f*

odd [ɒd] *adj* (**a**) *(strange)* bizarre, curieux, -euse
(**b**) *(number)* impair
(**c**) *(left over)* **sixty o.** soixante et quelques; **an o. glove/sock** un gant/une chaussette dépareillé(e)
(**d**) *(occasional)* **I smoke the o. cigarette** je fume une cigarette de temps en temps; **o. jobs** petits travaux *mpl* ▪ **oddly** *adv* bizarrement; **o. enough,**

he was elected chose curieuse, il a été élu

odds [ɒdz] *npl* (**a**) *(in betting)* cote *f; (chances)* chances *fpl; Fam* **it makes no o.** ça n'a pas d'importance (**b**) *(expressions)* **to be at o. (with sb)** être en désaccord (avec qn); *Fam* **o. and ends** des bricoles *fpl*

odious ['əʊdɪəs] *adj* odieux, -euse

odometer [əʊ'dɒmɪtə(r)] *n Am* compteur *m* kilométrique

odour ['əʊdə(r)] *(Am* **odor)** *n* odeur *f*

OF [əv, *stressed* ɒv] *prep* de, d'; **of the boy** du garçon; **of the boys** des garçons; **of wood/paper** de *ou* en bois/papier; **she has a lot of it/of them** elle en a beaucoup; **there are ten of us** nous sommes dix; **a friend of his** un ami à lui, un de ses amis; **that's nice of you** c'est gentil de ta part; **of no value/interest** sans valeur/intérêt; *Br* **the fifth of June** le cinq juin

OFF [ɒf] **1** *adj (light, gas, radio)* éteint; *(tap)* fermé; *(switched off at mains)* coupé; *(removed)* enlevé; *(cancelled)* annulé; *(not fit to eat or drink)* mauvais; *(milk, meat)* tourné; **I'm o. today** j'ai congé aujourd'hui

2 *adv* **to be o.** *(leave)* partir; **a day o.** *(holiday)* un jour de congé; **I have today o.** j'ai congé aujourd'hui; **five percent o.** une réduction de cinq pour cent; **on and o., o. and on** *(sometimes)* de temps à autre

3 *prep (from)* de; *(distant)* éloigné de; **to fall o. the wall/ladder** tomber du mur/de l'échelle; **to take sth o. the table** prendre qch sur la table; **she's o. her food** elle ne mange plus rien ▪ **off-chance** *n* **on the o.** à tout hasard ▪ **off-colour** *(Am* **off-color)** *adj Br (ill)* patraque; *(indecent)* d'un goût douteux ▪ **offhand 1** *adj* désinvolte **2** *adv (immediately)* au pied levé ▪ **off-licence** *n Br* ≃ magasin *m* de vins et de spiritueux ▪ **off-line** *adj (computer)* autonome ▪ **off-peak** *adj (rate, price)* heures creuses *inv* ▪ **off-putting** *adj*

■ **oilcan** *n* burette *f* ■ **oilfield** *n* gisement *m* de pétrole ■ **oily** (**-ier, -iest**) *adj* (*hands, rag*) graisseux, -euse; (*skin, hair*) gras (*f* grasse)

ointment ['ɔɪntmənt] *n* pommade *f*

OK, okay ['əʊ'keɪ] **1** *adj & adv see* **all right 2** (*pt & pp* OKed, okayed, *pres p* OKing, okaying) *vt* donner le feu vert à

old [əʊld] **1** (**-er, -est**) *adj* vieux (*f* vieille); (*former*) ancien, -enne; **how o. is he?** quel âge a-t-il?; **he's ten years o.** il a dix ans; **he's older than me** il est plus âgé que moi; **the oldest son** le fils aîné; **to get** *or* **grow old(er)** vieillir; **o. age** vieillesse *f*; **o. man** vieillard *m*, vieil homme *m*; **o. people** les personnes *fpl* âgées; **o. people's home** maison *f* de retraite; *Fam* **any o. how** n'importe comment
2 *npl* **the o.** les personnes *fpl* âgées

old-fashioned [əʊld'fæʃənd] *adj* (*out-of-date*) démodé; (*person*) vieux jeu *inv*; (*traditional*) d'autrefois

olive ['ɒlɪv] *n* (*fruit*) olive *f*; **o. oil** huile *f* d'olive

Olympic [ə'lɪmpɪk] *adj* **the O. Games** les jeux *mpl* Olympiques

omelet(te) ['ɒmlɪt] *n* omelette *f*; **cheese o.** omelette *f* au fromage

omen ['əʊmən] *n* augure *m*

ominous ['ɒmɪnəs] *adj* inquiétant; (*event*) de mauvais augure

omit [əʊ'mɪt] (*pt & pp* **-tt-**) *vt* omettre (**to do** de faire) ■ **omission** *n* omission *f*

ON [ɒn] **1** *prep* (**a**) (*expressing position*) sur; **on page 4** à la page 4; **on the right/left** à droite/gauche (**b**) (*about*) sur (**c**) (*expressing manner or means*) **on the train/plane** dans le train/l'avion; **to be on** (*a course*) suivre; (*project*) travailler à; (*salary*) toucher; (*team, committee*) faire partie de; *Fam* **it's on me!** (*I'll pay*) c'est pour moi! (**d**) (*with time*) **on Monday** lundi; **on Mondays** le lundi; **(on the evening of) May 3rd** le 3 mai (au soir); **on my arrival** à mon arrivée

---

Br Fam peu engageant ■ **offside** *adj* **to be o.** (*of footballer*) être hors jeu ■ **offspring** *n* progéniture *f* ■ **off-the-peg** (*Am* **off-the-rack**) *adj* (*clothes*) de confection

offence [ə'fens] (*Am* **offense**) *n* (*against the law*) infraction *f*; (*more serious*) délit *m*; **to take o.** s'offenser (**at** de); **to give o.** offenser

offend [ə'fend] *vt* offenser; **to be offended** s'offenser (**at** de) ■ **offender** *n* (*criminal*) délinquant, -e *mf*

offense [ə'fens] *n Am* = **offence**

offensive [ə'fensɪv] **1** *adj* choquant **2** *n* offensive *f*; **to be on the o.** être passé à l'offensive

offer ['ɒfə(r)] **1** *n* offre *f*; **to make sb an o.** faire une offre à qn; **on (special) o.** en promotion **2** *vt* offrir; (*explanation*) donner; (*apologies*) présenter; **to o. sb sth, to o. sth to sb** offrir qch à qn; **to o. to do sth** proposer *ou* offrir de faire qch ■ **offering** *n* (*gift*) offrande *f*

office ['ɒfɪs] *n* (**a**) (*room*) bureau *m*; *Am* (*of doctor*) cabinet *m*; **o. hours** heures *fpl* de bureau; **o. worker** employé, -e *mf* de bureau (**b**) (*position*) fonctions *fpl*; **to be in o.** être au pouvoir

officer ['ɒfɪsə(r)] *n* (*in the army, navy*) officier *m*; (**police**) **o.** agent *m* de police

official [ə'fɪʃəl] **1** *adj* officiel, -elle **2** *n* responsable *mf*; (*civil servant*) fonctionnaire *mf* ■ **officially** *adv* officiellement

offset ['ɒfset, ɒf'set] (*pt & pp* offset, *pres p* offsetting) *vt* (*compensate for*) compenser

often ['ɒf(t)ən] *adv* souvent; **how o.?** combien de fois?; **every so o.** de temps en temps

oh [əʊ] *exclam* oh!, ah!; (*in pain*) aïe!; **oh yes!** mais oui!

oil [ɔɪl] **1** *n* (*for machine, cooking*) huile *f*; (*petroleum*) pétrole *m*; (*fuel*) mazout *m* **2** *adj* (*industry*) pétrolier, -ère; (*painting, paint*) à l'huile; **o. lamp** lampe *f* à pétrole **3** *vt* (*machine*) huiler (**e**) (+ *present participle*) en; **on learning that…** en apprenant que…

2 *adv* (*ahead*) en avant; (*in progress*) en cours; (*lid, brake*) mis; (*light, radio*) allumé; (*gas, tap*) ouvert; (*machine*) en marche; **she has her hat on** elle a mis son chapeau; **I've got something on** (*I'm busy*) je suis pris; **the strike is on** la grève aura lieu; **what's on?** (*on TV*) qu'est-ce qu'il y a à la télé?; (*in theatre, cinema*) qu'est-ce qu'on joue?; **he went on and on about it** il n'en finissait pas; *Fam* **that's just not on!** c'est inadmissible!; **I've been on to him** (*on phone*) je l'ai eu au bout du fil ▪ **ongoing** *adj* (*project, discussion*) en cours ▪ **on-line** *adj* (*computer*) en ligne

once [wʌns] **1** *adv* (*on one occasion*) une fois; (*formerly*) autrefois; **o. a month** une fois par mois; **o. more** encore une fois; **at o.** (*immediately*) tout de suite; **all at o.** (*suddenly*) tout à coup; (*at the same time*) à la fois **2** *conj* une fois que

ONE [wʌn] **1** *adj* (**a**) un, une; **page o.** la page un; **twenty-o.** vingt et un

(**b**) (*only*) seul

(**c**) (*same*) le même (*f* la même); **in the o. bus** dans le même bus

2 *pron* (**a**) un, une; **do you want o.?** en veux-tu (un)?; **o. of them** l'un d'eux, l'une d'elles; **a big/small o.** un grand/petit; **this o.** celui-ci, celle-ci; **that o.** celui-là, celle-là; **the o. who/ which…** celui/celle qui…; **another o.** un(e) autre; **I for o.** pour ma part

(**b**) (*impersonal*) on; **o. knows** on sait; **it helps o.** ça vous aide; **o.'s family** sa famille ▪ **one-off, one-of-a-kind** *adj Fam* unique ▪ **one-sided** *adj* (*biased*) partial; (*contest*) inégal ▪ **one-time** *adj* (*former*) ancien, -enne ▪ **one-to-one** *adj* (*discussion*) en tête à tête ▪ **one-way** *adj* (*street*) à sens unique; **o. ticket** billet *m* simple

oneself [wʌn'self] *pron* soi-même; (*reflexive*) se, s'; **to cut o.** se couper

onion ['ʌnjən] *n* oignon *m*

onlooker ['ɒnlʊkə(r)] *n* spectateur, -trice *mf*

only ['əʊnlɪ] **1** *adj* seul; **the o. one** le seul, la seule; **an o. son** un fils unique **2** *adv* seulement, ne… que; **I o. have ten** je n'en ai que dix, j'en ai dix seulement; **if o.** si seulement; **I have o. just seen it** je viens tout juste de le voir; **o. he knows** lui seul le sait **3** *conj Fam* (*but*) mais

onset ['ɒnset] *n* (*of disease, winter*) début *m*

onto ['ɒntuː, *unstressed* 'ɒntə] *prep* = **on to**

onward(s) ['ɒnwəd(z)] *adv* en avant; **from that day o.** à partir de ce jour-là

opaque [əʊ'peɪk] *adj* opaque

open ['əʊpən] **1** *adj* ouvert; (*view, road*) dégagé; (*post, job*) vacant; (*airline ticket*) open *inv*; **in the o. air** au grand air; **o. to** (*criticism, attack*) exposé à; (*ideas, suggestions*) ouvert à; **to leave sth o.** (*date*) ne pas préciser qch

2 *n* (*out*) **in the o.** (*outside*) dehors; **to sleep (out) in the o.** dormir à la belle étoile

3 *vt* ouvrir; (*arms, legs*) écarter; **to o. sth out** (*paper, map*) ouvrir qch; **to o. sth up** (*bag, shop*) ouvrir qch

4 *vi* (*of flower, door, eyes*) s'ouvrir; (*of shop, office*) ouvrir; (*of play*) débuter; **to o. on to sth** (*of window*) donner sur qch; **to o. out** (*widen*) s'élargir; **to o. up** (*of flower, person*) s'ouvrir; (*of shopkeeper*) ouvrir ▪ **open-air** *adj* (*pool*) en plein air ▪ **open-minded** *adj* à l'esprit ouvert ▪ **open-plan** *adj* (*office*) paysager, -ère

opening ['əʊpənɪŋ] **1** *n* ouverture *f*; (*job, trade outlet*) débouché *m*; (*opportunity*) occasion *f* favorable; **late-night o.** (*of shops*) nocturne *f*

2 *adj* (*time, hours, speech*) d'ouverture; **o. night** (*of play, musical*) première *f*

openly ['əʊpənlɪ] *adv* ouvertement

opera ['ɒprə] *n* opéra *m*

operate ['ɒpəreɪt] **1** vt (machine) faire fonctionner; (service) assurer **2** vi (**a**) **to o. on sb (for sth)** (of surgeon) opérer qn (de qch) (**b**) (of machine) fonctionner; (of company) opérer ■ **operating** adj Br **o. theatre**, Am **o. room** salle f d'opération; Comptr **o. system** système m d'exploitation

operation [ɒpə'reɪʃən] n Med, Mil & Math opération f; (of machine) fonctionnement m; **in o.** (machine) en service; (plan) en vigueur; **to have an o.** se faire opérer

operator ['ɒpəreɪtə(r)] n (on phone, machine) opérateur, -trice mf

opinion [ə'pɪnjən] n opinion f; **in my o.** à mon avis

opponent [ə'pəʊnənt] n adversaire mf

opportune ['ɒpətjuːn] adj opportun

opportunity [ɒpə'tjuːnətɪ] (pl **-ies**) f occasion f (**to do** or **of doing** de faire); **opportunities** (prospects) perspectives fpl; **to take the o. to do sth** profiter de l'occasion pour faire qch

oppose [ə'pəʊz] vt s'opposer à ■ **opposed** adj opposé (**to** à); **as o. to…** par opposition à… ■ **opposing** adj (viewpoints) opposé; (team) adverse

opposite ['ɒpəzɪt] **1** adj (side) opposé; (house, page) d'en face; **in the o. direction** en sens inverse **2** adv en face; **the house o.** la maison d'en face **3** prep **o. (to)** en face de **4** n **the o.** le contraire

opposition [ɒpə'zɪʃən] n opposition f (**to** à); **the o.** (rival camp) l'adversaire m; (in business) la concurrence

oppress [ə'pres] vt (treat cruelly) opprimer ■ **oppression** n oppression f ■ **oppressive** adj (heat) accablant, étouffant; (ruler, regime) oppressif, -ive

opt [ɒpt] vi **to o. for sth** opter pour qch; **to o. to do sth** choisir de faire qch; **to o. out** se désengager (**of** de)

optical ['ɒptɪkəl] adj optique; (instrument, illusion) d'optique

optician [ɒp'tɪʃən] n (dispensing) opticien, -enne mf

optimism ['ɒptɪmɪzəm] n optimisme m ■ **optimistic** adj optimiste (**about** quant à)

optimum ['ɒptɪməm] adj & n optimum (m)

option ['ɒpʃən] n (choice) choix m; (school subject) matière f à option; **she has no o.** elle n'a pas le choix ■ **optional** adj facultatif, -ive

or [ɔː(r)] conj ou; **he doesn't drink or smoke** il ne boit ni ne fume; **ten or so** environ dix

oral ['ɔːrəl] **1** adj oral **2** n (exam) oral m

orange ['ɒrɪndʒ] **1** n (fruit) orange f; **o. juice** jus m d'orange **2** adj & n (colour) orange (m) inv

orbit ['ɔːbɪt] **1** n (of planet) orbite f **2** vt être en orbite autour de

orchard ['ɔːtʃəd] n verger m

orchestra ['ɔːkɪstrə] n orchestre m; Am **the o.** (in theatre) l'orchestre m

orchid ['ɔːkɪd] n orchidée f

ordeal [ɔː'diːl] n épreuve f

order ['ɔːdə(r)] **1** n (instruction, arrangement) & Rel ordre m; (purchase) commande f; **in o.** (passport) en règle; **in o. of age** par ordre d'âge; **in o. to do sth** afin de faire qch; **in o. that…** afin que… (+ subjunctive); **out of o.** (machine) en panne; (telephone) en dérangement; **o. form** bon m de commande **2** vt (meal, goods) commander; (taxi) appeler; **to o. sb to do sth** ordonner à qn de faire qch **3** vi (in café) commander

orderly ['ɔːdəlɪ] adj (room, life) ordonné; (crowd) discipliné

ordinary ['ɔːdənrɪ] adj ordinaire; **it's out of the o.** ça sort de l'ordinaire; **she was just an o. tourist** c'était une touriste comme une autre

organ ['ɔːgən] n (**a**) (part of body) organe m (**b**) (musical instrument) orgue m

organic [ɔː'gænɪk] adj organique; (vegetables, farming) biologique

organism ['ɔːgənɪzəm] n organisme m

organization [ɔːgənaɪ'zeɪʃən] n organisation f

organize [ˈɔːgənaɪz] *vt* organiser
■ **organizer** *n (person)* organisateur,
-trice *mf*; **(personal) o.** *(diary)* agenda
m

orgasm [ˈɔːgæzəm] *n* orgasme *m*

oriental [ɔːrɪˈentəl] *adj* oriental

orientate [ˈɔːrɪənteɪt] *(Am* **orient**
[ˈɔːrɪənt]*) vt* orienter

origin [ˈɒrɪdʒɪn] *n* origine *f*

original [əˈrɪdʒɪnəl] **1** *adj (novel, innovative)* original; *(first)* d'origine **2** *n
(document, painting)* original *m* ■ **originally** *adv (at first)* à l'origine

originate [əˈrɪdʒɪneɪt] **1** *vt* être à l'origine de **2** *vi (begin)* prendre naissance (**in** dans); **to o. from** *(of idea)*
émaner de

ornament [ˈɔːnəmənt] *n* ornement *m*
■ **ornamental** [-ˈmentəl] *adj* ornemental

ornate [ɔːˈneɪt] *adj* très orné

orphan [ˈɔːfən] *n* orphelin, -e *mf*

orthodox [ˈɔːθədɒks] *adj* orthodoxe

Oscar [ˈɒskə(r)] *n Cin* oscar *m*

ostentatious [ɒstenˈteɪʃəs] *adj* prétentieux, -euse

ostrich [ˈɒstrɪtʃ] *n* autruche *f*

other [ˈʌðə(r)] **1** *adj* autre; **o. doctors**
d'autres médecins; **the o. one** l'autre
mf
2 *pron* **the o.** l'autre *mf*; **(some)
others** d'autres; **none o. than, no o.
than** nul autre que
3 *adv* **o. than** autrement que
■ **otherwise** *adv & conj* autrement

ouch [aʊtʃ] *exclam* aïe!

ought [ɔːt]

La forme négative **ought not** s'écrit
oughtn't en forme contractée.

v aux (**a**) *(expressing obligation, desir-
ability)* **you o. to leave** tu devrais
partir; **I o. to have done it** j'aurais
dû le faire (**b**) *(expressing probability)*
it o. to be ready ça devrait être
prêt

ounce [aʊns] *n (unit of weight)* = 28,35
g, once *f*

our [aʊə(r)] *possessive adj* notre, *pl* nos

ours [aʊəz] *possessive pron* le nôtre, la

nôtre, *pl* les nôtres; **this book is o.** ce
livre est à nous *ou* est le nôtre; **a
friend of o.** un de nos amis

ourselves [aʊəˈselvz] *pron* nous-
mêmes; *(reflexive and after prep)* nous;
we wash o. nous nous lavons

oust [aʊst] *vt* évincer (**from** de)

OUT [aʊt] **1** *adv (outside)* dehors; *(not
at home)* sorti; *(light, fire)* éteint;
(flower) ouvert; *(book)* publié; **to have
a day o.** sortir pour la journée; **the
sun's o.** il fait soleil; **the tide's o.** la
marée est basse; **you're o.** *(wrong)* tu
t'es trompé; *(in game)* tu es éliminé
(**of** de); **I was £10 o.** *(under)* il me
manquait 10 livres; **before the week
is o.** avant la fin de la semaine; **the
journey o.** l'aller *m*; **o. here** ici; **o.
there** là-bas
2 *prep* **o. of** *(outside)* hors de; **to be o.
of the country** être à l'étranger; **she's
o. of town** elle n'est pas en ville; **to
look/jump o. of the window** re-
garder/sauter par la fenêtre; **to
drink/take/copy sth o. of sth** boire/
prendre/copier qch dans qch; **made
o. of wood** fait en bois; **o. of pity/love**
par pitié/amour; **four o. of five**
quatre sur cinq ■ **out-of-date** *adj (expired)* périmé; *(old-fashioned)* démodé ■ **out-of-doors** *adv* dehors
■ **out-of-the-way** *adj (place)* isolé

outbreak [ˈaʊtbreɪk] *n (of war, epidemic)* début *m*; *(of violence)* flambée
f; *(of hostilities)* déclenchement *m*

outburst [ˈaʊtbɜːst] *n (of anger, joy)*
explosion *f*; *(of violence)* flambée *f*

outcast [ˈaʊtkɑːst] *n* **(social) o.** paria *m*

outcome [ˈaʊtkʌm] *n* résultat *m*, issue
f

outcry [ˈaʊtkraɪ] *(pl* **-ies)** *n* tollé *m*

outdated [aʊtˈdeɪtɪd] *adj* démodé

outdo [aʊtˈduː] *(pt* **-did,** *pp* **-done)** *vt*
surpasser (**in** en)

outdoor [ˈaʊtdɔː(r)] *adj (pool, market)*
découvert ■ **outdoors** *adv* dehors

outer [ˈaʊtə(r)] *adj* extérieur; **o. space**
l'espace *m* intersidéral

outfit ['aʊtfɪt] n (clothes) ensemble m; **sports/ski o.** tenue f de sport/de ski

outgoing ['aʊtgəʊɪŋ] adj (**a**) (minister) sortant; (mail) en partance; **o. calls** (on phone) appels mpl vers l'extérieur (**b**) (sociable) liant ■ **outgoings** npl (expenses) dépenses fpl

outgrow [aʊt'grəʊ] (pt -**grew**, pp -**grown**) vt (habit) passer l'âge de; **she's outgrown her jacket** sa veste est devenue trop petite pour elle

outing ['aʊtɪŋ] n (excursion) sortie f

outlast [aʊt'lɑːst] vt (object) durer plus longtemps que; (person) survivre à

outlaw ['aʊtlɔː] **1** n hors-la-loi m inv **2** vt (ban) proscrire

outlay ['aʊtleɪ] n (expense) dépenses fpl

outlet ['aʊtlet] n (shop) point m de vente; (market for goods) débouché m; (for liquid) sortie f; (for feelings, energy) exutoire m

outline ['aʊtlaɪn] **1** n (shape) contour m; (of play, novel) résumé m; **rough o.** (of article, plan) esquisse f; **the broad** or **general** or **main o.** (of plan, policy) les grandes lignes **2** vt (plan, situation) esquisser

outlive [aʊt'lɪv] vt survivre à

outlook ['aʊtlʊk] n (for future) perspectives fpl; (point of view) façon f de voir les choses; (of weather) prévisions fpl

outmoded [aʊt'məʊdɪd] adj démodé

outnumber [aʊt'nʌmbə(r)] vt l'emporter en nombre sur

outpatient ['aʊtpeɪʃənt] n Br malade mf en consultation externe

output ['aʊtpʊt] n (of goods) production f, (computer data) données fpl de sortie

outrage ['aʊtreɪdʒ] **1** n (scandal) scandale m; (anger) indignation f (**at** face à); (crime) atrocité f **2** vt (make indignant) scandaliser

outrageous [aʊt'reɪdʒəs] adj (shocking) scandaleux, -euse; (atrocious) atroce

outright 1 [aʊt'raɪt] adv (refuse) catégoriquement; (be killed) sur le coup **2** ['aʊtraɪt] adj (failure) total; (refusal) catégorique; (winner) incontesté

outset ['aʊtset] n **at the o.** au début; **from the o.** dès le départ

outside 1 [aʊt'saɪd] adv dehors, à l'extérieur; **to go o.** sortir

2 [aʊt'saɪd] prep à l'extérieur de, en dehors de; (in front of) devant; (apart from) en dehors de

3 [aʊt'saɪd] n extérieur m

4 ['aʊtsaɪd] adj extérieur m; **the o. lane** (on road) Br la voie de droite, Am la voie de gauche; **an o. chance** une petite chance

outsider [aʊt'saɪdə(r)] n (stranger) étranger, -ère mf; (horse in race) outsider m

outskirts ['aʊtskɜːts] npl banlieue f

outspoken [aʊt'spəʊkən] adj (frank) franc (f franche)

outstanding [aʊt'stændɪŋ] adj exceptionnel, -elle; (problem, business) en suspens; (debt) impayé

outstay [aʊt'steɪ] vt **to o. one's welcome** abuser de l'hospitalité de son hôte

outstretched [aʊt'stretʃt] adj (arm) tendu

outward ['aʊtwəd] adj (sign, appearance) extérieur; **o. journey** or **trip** aller m ■ **outward(s)** adv vers l'extérieur

oval ['əʊvəl] adj & n ovale (m)

ovary ['əʊvəri] (pl -**ies**) n Anat ovaire m

ovation [əʊ'veɪʃən] n ovation f; **to give sb a standing o.** se lever pour applaudir qn

oven ['ʌvən] n four m

OVER ['əʊvə(r)] **1** prep (on) sur; (above) au-dessus de; (on the other side of) par-dessus; **the bridge o. the river** le pont qui traverse le fleuve; **to jump/look o. sth** sauter/regarder par-dessus qch; **o. it** (on) dessus; (above) au-dessus; **to fight o. sth** se battre pour qch; **o. the phone** au téléphone; Br **o. the holidays** pendant les vacances; **o. ten days** *(more than)* plus de dix jours; **men o. sixty** les hommes de plus de soixante ans; **o. and above** en plus de; **he's o. his flu** il est remis de sa grippe

2 *adv (above)* par-dessus; **o. here** ici; **o. there** là-bas; **he's o. in Italy** il est en Italie; **she's from Paris** elle est venue de Paris; **to ask sb o.** inviter qn; **to be (all) o.** être terminé; **to start all o. (again)** recommencer à zéro; **a kilo or o.** *(more)* un kilo ou plus; **I have ten o.** *(left)* il m'en reste dix; **o. and o. (again)** *(often)* à plusieurs reprises; **children of five and o.** les enfants de cinq ans et plus

overall 1 [ˈəʊvərɔːl] *adj (measurement, length)* total; *(result)* global

2 [əʊvərˈɔːl] *adv* dans l'ensemble

3 [ˈəʊvərɔːl] *n (protective coat)* blouse *f*; *Am (boiler suit)* bleu *m* de travail

■ **overalls** *npl Br (boiler suit)* bleu *m* de travail; *Am (dungarees)* salopette *f*

overbearing [əʊvəˈbeərɪŋ] *adj* autoritaire

overboard [ˈəʊvəbɔːd] *adv* par-dessus bord

overcast [ˈəʊvəkɑːst] *adj* nuageux, -euse

overcharge [əʊvəˈtʃɑːdʒ] *vt* **to o. sb for sth** faire payer qch trop cher à qn

overcoat [ˈəʊvəkəʊt] *n* pardessus *m*

overcome [əʊvəˈkʌm] *(pt -came, pp -come)* *vt (problem, disgust)* surmonter; *(shyness, fear, enemy)* vaincre; **to be o. by grief** être accablé de chagrin

overcook [əʊvəˈkʊk] *vt* faire cuire trop

overcrowded [əʊvəˈkraʊdɪd] *adj (house, country)* surpeuplé; *(bus, train)* bondé

overdo [əʊvəˈduː] *(pt-did, pp-done)* *vt* exagérer; *(overcook)* faire cuire trop; **to o. it** se surmener

overdose [ˈəʊvədəʊs] *n* overdose *f*

overdraft [ˈəʊvədrɑːft] *n Fin* découvert *m*

overdrawn [əʊvəˈdrɔːn] *adj Fin (account)* à découvert

overdue [əʊvəˈdjuː] *adj (train, bus)* en retard; *(bill)* impayé; *(book)* qui n'a pas été rendu

overestimate [əʊvərˈestɪmeɪt] *vt* surestimer

overexcited [əʊvərɪkˈsaɪtɪd] *adj* surexcité

overflow 1 [ˈəʊvəfləʊ] *n (outlet)* trop-plein *m* **2** [əʊvəˈfləʊ] *vi (of river, bath)* déborder; **to be overflowing with sth** *(of town, shop, house)* regorger de qch

overgrown [əʊvəˈgrəʊn] *adj (garden, path)* envahi par la végétation

overhaul 1 [ˈəʊvəhɔːl] *n* révision *f* **2** [əʊvəˈhɔːl] *vt (vehicle, schedule, text)* réviser

overhead 1 [əʊvəˈhed] *adv* au-dessus **2** [ˈəʊvəhed] *adj (cable)* aérien, -enne **3** [ˈəʊvəhed] *n Am =* **overheads** ■ **overheads** *npl Br (expenses)* frais *mpl* généraux

overhear [əʊvəˈhɪə(r)] *(pt & pp -heard)* *vt (conversation)* surprendre; *(person)* entendre

overheat [əʊvəˈhiːt] *vi (of engine)* chauffer

overjoyed [əʊvəˈdʒɔɪd] *adj* fou *(f* folle) de joie

overland [ˈəʊvəlænd] *adj & adv* par voie de terre

overlap [əʊvəˈlæp] **1** *(pt & pp -pp-)* *vt* chevaucher **2** *vi* se chevaucher

overleaf [əʊvəˈliːf] *adv* au verso

overload [əʊvəˈləʊd] *vt* surcharger

overlook [əʊvəˈlʊk] *vt* (**a**) *(not notice)* ne pas remarquer; *(forget)* oublier; *(disregard)* fermer les yeux sur (**b**) *(of window, house)* donner sur

overnight 1 [əʊvəˈnaɪt] *adv (during the night)* pendant la nuit; *Fig (suddenly)* du jour au lendemain; **to stay o.** passer la nuit **2** [ˈəʊvənaɪt] *adj (train, flight)* de nuit; *(stay)* d'une nuit; **o. bag** (petit) sac *m* de voyage

overpopulated [əʊvəˈpɒpjʊleɪtɪd] *adj* surpeuplé

overpower [əʊvəˈpaʊə(r)] *vt* maîtriser ■ **overpowering** *adj (heat, smell)* suffocant

overpriced [əʊvə'praɪst] *adj* trop cher (*f* trop chère)

overrated [əʊvə'reɪtɪd] *adj* surfait

overreach [əʊvə'riːtʃ] *vt* to o. oneself trop présumer de ses forces

overreact [əʊvəri'ækt] *vi* réagir excessivement

override [əʊvə'raɪd] (*pt* -rode, *pp* -ridden) *vt* (*be more important than*) l'emporter sur; (*invalidate*) annuler; (*take no notice of*) passer outre à ■ **overriding** *adj* (*importance*) capital; (*factor*) prédominant

overrule [əʊvə'ruːl] *vt* (*decision*) annuler; (*objection*) rejeter

overrun [əʊvə'rʌn] (*pt* -ran, *pp* -run, *pres p* -running) *vt* (*invade*) envahir; (*go beyond*) dépasser

overseas 1 ['əʊvəsiːz] *adj* d'outre-mer; (*trade*) extérieur **2** [əʊvə'siːz] *adv* à l'étranger

oversee [əʊvə'siː] (*pt* -saw, *pp* -seen) *vt* (*work*) superviser

overshadow [əʊvə'ʃædəʊ] *vt* (*make less important*) éclipser; (*make gloomy*) assombrir

oversight ['əʊvəsaɪt] *n* oubli *m*, omission *f*

oversleep [əʊvə'sliːp] (*pt & pp* -slept) *vi* ne pas se réveiller à temps

overspend [əʊvə'spend] (*pt & pp* -spent) *vi* dépenser trop

overstate [əʊvə'steɪt] *vt* exagérer

overstay [əʊvə'steɪ] *vt* to o. one's welcome abuser de l'hospitalité de son hôte

overstep [əʊvə'step] (*pt & pp* -pp-) *vt* outrepasser; *Fig* to o. the mark dépasser les bornes

overt ['əʊvɜːt] *adj* manifeste

overtake [əʊvə'teɪk] (*pt* -took, *pp* -taken) **1** *vt* dépasser **2** *vi* (*in vehicle*) doubler, dépasser

overthrow [əʊvə'θrəʊ] (*pt* -threw, *pp* -thrown) *vt* renverser

overtime ['əʊvətaɪm] **1** *n* heures *fpl*

supplémentaires **2** *adv* to work o. faire des heures supplémentaires

overturn [əʊvə'tɜːn] **1** *vt* (*chair, table, car*) renverser; (*boat*) faire chavirer; *Fig* (*decision*) annuler **2** *vi* (*of car*) capoter; (*of boat*) chavirer

overweight [əʊvə'weɪt] *adj* trop gros (*f* trop grosse)

overwhelm [əʊvə'welm] *vt* (*of feelings, heat*) accabler; (*enemy, opponent*) écraser; (*amaze*) bouleverser ■ **overwhelmed** *adj* o. with (*work, offers*) submergé de; **o. by** (*kindness, gift*) vivement touché par ■ **overwhelming** *adj* (*heat, grief*) accablant; (*majority, defeat*) écrasant; (*desire*) irrésistible

overwork [əʊvə'wɜːk] **1** *n* surmenage *m* **2** *vt* (*person*) surcharger de travail **3** *vi* se surmener

owe [əʊ] *vt* devoir; to o. sb sth, to o. sth to sb devoir qch à qn ■ **owing 1** *adj* the money o. to me l'argent que l'on me doit **2** *prep* o. to à cause de

owl [aʊl] *n* hibou *m* (*pl* -oux)

own [əʊn] **1** *adj* propre
2 *pron* my o. le mien, la mienne; **a house of his o.** sa propre maison, sa maison à lui; **to do sth on one's o.** faire qch tout seul; **to be (all) on one's o.** être tout seul; **to get one's o. back (on sb)** se venger (de qn)
3 *vt* (*possess*) posséder; **who owns this ball?** à qui appartient cette balle?
4 *vi* to o. up (to sth) (*confess*) avouer (qch)

owner ['əʊnə(r)] *n* propriétaire *mf* ■ **ownership** *n* possession *f*

ox [ɒks] (*pl* oxen ['ɒksən]) *n* bœuf *m*

oxygen ['ɒksɪdʒən] *n* oxygène *m*; o. mask masque *m* à oxygène

oyster ['ɔɪstə(r)] *n* huître *f*

oz (*abbr* ounce) once *f*

ozone ['əʊzəʊn] *n Chem* ozone *m*; o. layer couche *f* d'ozone

Pp

P, p¹ [piː] *n (letter)* P, p *m inv*

p² [piː] *n (abbr* **penny, pence)** *Br* penny *m*/pence *mpl*

pa [pɑː] *n Fam (father)* papa *m*

pace [peɪs] **1** *n (speed)* allure *f; (step, measure)* pas *m;* **to keep p. with sb** *(follow)* suivre qn; *(in quality of work)* se maintenir à la hauteur de qn **2** *vi* **to p. up and down** faire les cent pas

pacemaker [ˈpeɪsmeɪkə(r)] *n (for heart)* stimulateur *m* cardiaque

Pacific [pəˈsɪfɪk] *adj* **the P. (Ocean)** le Pacifique, l'océan *m* Pacifique

pacifier [ˈpæsɪfaɪə(r)] *n Am (of baby)* tétine *f*

pacifist [ˈpæsɪfɪst] *n* pacifiste *mf*

pacify [ˈpæsɪfaɪ] *(pt & pp* -**ied)** *vt (crowd, person)* calmer

pack [pæk] **1** *n* **(a)** *(of cigarettes, washing powder)* paquet *m; (of beer)* pack *m; (of cards)* jeu *m; (of hounds, wolves)* meute *f;* **a p. of lies** un tissu de mensonges

(b) *(rucksack)* sac *m* à dos

2 *vt (fill)* remplir **(with** de); *(object into box, suitcase)* mettre; *(make into package)* empaqueter; *(crush, compress)* tasser; **to p. one's bags** faire ses valises

3 *vi (fill one's bags)* faire sa valise/ses valises

▶ **pack in** *vt sep Br Fam (stop)* arrêter; *(give up)* laisser tomber

▶ **pack into 1** *vt sep (cram)* entasser dans; *(put)* mettre dans **2** *vt insep (crowd into)* s'entasser dans

▶ **pack off** *vt sep Fam (person)* expédier

▶ **pack up 1** *vt sep (put into box)* emballer; *Fam (give up)* laisser tomber **2** *vi Fam (of machine, vehicle)* tomber en panne

package [ˈpækɪdʒ] **1** *n* paquet *m; (contract)* contrat *m* global; *Br* **p. deal** *or* **holiday** forfait *m (comprenant au moins transport et logement)* **2** *vt* emballer ■ **packaging** *n (material, action)* emballage *m*

packed [pækt] *adj (bus, room)* bondé

packet [ˈpækɪt] *n* paquet *m; Fam* **to cost a p.** coûter les yeux de la tête

packing [ˈpækɪŋ] *n (material, action)* emballage *m;* **to do one's p.** faire sa valise/ses valises

pact [pækt] *n* pacte *m*

pad [pæd] **1** *n (of cotton wool)* tampon *m; (for writing)* bloc *m;* **ink(ing) p.** tampon encreur **2** *(pt & pp* -**dd-)** *vt* **to p. out** *(speech, essay)* étoffer ■ **padded** *adj (jacket)* matelassé ■ **padding** *n (material)* rembourrage *m; (in speech, essay)* remplissage *m*

paddle [ˈpædl] **1** *n (for canoe)* pagaie *f;* **to have a p.** patauger **2** *vt* **to p. a canoe** pagayer **3** *vi (walk in water)* patauger

paddling [ˈpædlɪŋ] *n Br* **p. pool** *(inflatable)* piscine *f* gonflable; *(in park)* pataugeoire *f*

padlock [ˈpædlɒk] **1** *n* cadenas *m* **2** *vt* cadenasser

paediatrician [piːdɪəˈtrɪʃən] *(Am* **pediatrician)** *n* pédiatre *mf*

page¹ [peɪdʒ] *n (of book)* page *f;* **on p. 6** à la page 6

page² [peɪdʒ] **1** *n* **p. (boy)** *(in hotel)*

groom *m* **2** *vt* **to p. sb** faire appeler qn; *(by electronic device)* biper qn ▪ **pager** *n* récepteur *m* d'appel

paid [peɪd] **1** *pt & pp of* **pay 2** *adj (person, work)* rémunéré

pain [peɪn] *n (physical)* douleur *f*; *(emotional)* peine *f*; **to have a p. in one's arm** avoir une douleur au bras; **to go to** *or* **take (great) pains to do sth** se donner du mal pour faire qch; *Fam* **to be a p. (in the neck)** être casse-pieds ▪ **painful** *adj (physically)* douloureux, -euse; *(emotionally)* pénible ▪ **painless** *adj (not painful)* indolore

painkiller ['peɪnkɪlə(r)] *n* calmant *m*

painstaking ['peɪnzteɪkɪŋ] *adj* minutieux, -euse

paint [peɪnt] **1** *n* peinture *f* **2** *vt* peindre; **to p. sth blue** peindre qch en bleu **3** *vi* peindre ▪ **painter** *n* peintre *m*; *Br* **p. and decorator,** *Am* **(house) p.** peintre-tapissier *m* ▪ **painting** *n (activity)* la peinture; *(picture)* tableau *m*, peinture *f*

paintbrush ['peɪntbrʌʃ] *n* pinceau *m*
paintwork ['peɪntwɜ:k] *n (of building, vehicle)* peinture *f*

pair [peə(r)] *n* paire *f*; **a p. of shorts/trousers** un short/pantalon

pajamas [pə'dʒɑ:məz] *npl Am* = **pyjamas**

Pakistan [pɑ:kɪ'stɑ:n] *n* le Pakistan ▪ **Pakistani** **1** *adj* pakistanais **2** *n* Pakistanais, -e *mf*

pal [pæl] *n Fam* copain *m*, copine *f*
palace ['pælɪs] *n* palais *m*
pale [peɪl] **1** (**-er, -est**) *adj* pâle **2** *vi* pâlir

Palestine ['pælɪstaɪn] *n* la Palestine ▪ **Palestinian** [-'stɪnɪən] **1** *adj* palestinien, -enne **2** *n* Palestinien, -enne *mf*

palette ['pælɪt] *n (of artist)* palette *f*
palm¹ [pɑ:m] *n (of hand)* paume *f*
palm² [pɑ:m] *n* **p. (tree)** palmier *m*
pamper ['pæmpə(r)] *vt* dorloter
pamphlet ['pæmflɪt] *n* brochure *f*
pan [pæn] *n (saucepan)* casserole *f*; *(for frying)* poêle *f*

Panama ['pænəmɑ:] *n* **the P. Canal** le canal de Panama

pancake ['pænkeɪk] *n* crêpe *f*; **P. Day** mardi *m* gras

panda ['pændə] *n* panda *m*
pandemonium [pændɪ'məʊnɪəm] *n (confusion)* chaos *m*; *(uproar)* vacarme *m*

pander ['pændə(r)] *vi* **to p. to sb/sth** flatter qn/qch

pane [peɪn] *n* vitre *f*
panel ['pænəl] *n* (**a**) *(of door)* panneau *m*; **(instrument) p.** *(in aircraft, vehicle)* tableau *m* de bord (**b**) *(of judges)* jury *m*; *(of experts)* comité *m*; *(of TV or radio guests)* invités *mpl*

panic ['pænɪk] **1** *n* panique *f* **2** (*pt & pp* **-ck-**) *vi* paniquer

panorama [pænə'rɑ:mə] *n* panorama *m*

pansy ['pænzɪ] (*pl* **-ies**) *n (flower)* pensée *f*

pant [pænt] *vi* haleter
pantomime ['pæntəmaɪm] *n Br (show)* = spectacle de Noël

pantry ['pæntrɪ] (*pl* **-ies**) *n (larder)* garde-manger *m inv*

pants [pænts] *npl (underwear)* slip *m*; *Am (trousers)* pantalon *m*

pantyhose ['pæntɪhəʊz] *n Am (tights)* collant *m*

paper ['peɪpə(r)] **1** *n* papier *m*; *(newspaper)* journal *m*; *(wallpaper)* papier *m* peint; *(exam)* épreuve *f* écrite; *(student's exercise)* copie *f*; *(scholarly study, report)* article *m*; **a piece of p.** un bout de papier; **to put sth down on p.** mettre qch par écrit; **papers** *(documents)* papiers

2 *adj (bag)* en papier; *(cup, plate)* en carton; *Br* **p. shop** marchand *m* de journaux; **p. towel** essuie-tout *m inv*

3 *vt (room, wall)* tapisser ▪ **paperback** *n* livre *m* de poche ▪ **paperclip** *n* trombone *m* ▪ **paperweight** *n* presse-papiers *m inv* ▪ **paperwork** *n (in office)* écritures *fpl*; *Pej (red tape)* paperasserie *f*

par [pɑ:(r)] *n (in golf)* par *m*; **on a p.** au

même niveau (**with** que)

paracetamol [pærə'si:təmɒl] n paracétamol m

parachute ['pærəʃu:t] n parachute m; **p. jump** saut m en parachute

parade [pə'reɪd] 1 n (**a**) (procession) défilé m (**b**) Br (street) avenue f 2 vt Fig (wealth, knowledge) faire étalage de 3 vi (of troops) défiler; **to p. about** (of person) se pavaner

paradise ['pærədaɪs] n paradis m

paradoxically [pærə'dɒksɪklɪ] adv paradoxalement

paraffin ['pærəfɪn] n Br pétrole m lampant; Br **p. lamp** lampe f à pétrole

paragliding ['pærəglaɪdɪŋ] n parapente m; **to go p.** faire du parapente

paragraph ['pærəgrɑ:f] n paragraphe m

parallel ['pærəlel] 1 adj Math parallèle (**with** or **to** à); Fig (comparable) semblable (**with** or **to** à) 2 n Math (line) parallèle f; Fig (comparison) & Geog parallèle m

paralysis [pə'ræləsɪs] (pl -yses [-əsi:z]) n paralysie f ■ **paralyse** ['pærəlaɪz] (Am **paralyze**) vt paralyser

paramedic [pærə'medɪk] n auxiliaire mf médical(e)

paranoid ['pærənɔɪd] adj paranoïaque

paraphrase ['pærəfreɪz] vt paraphraser

parasite ['pærəsaɪt] n (person, organism) parasite m

parasol ['pærəsɒl] n (over table, on beach) parasol m; (lady's) ombrelle f

parcel ['pɑ:səl] 1 n colis m, paquet m 2 (Br -ll-, Am -l-) vt **to p. sth up** empaqueter

parched [pɑ:tʃt] adj **to be p.** (of person) être assoiffé

pardon ['pɑ:dən] 1 n (forgiveness) pardon m; (in law) grâce f; **I beg your p.** (apologizing) je vous prie de m'excuser; **I beg your p.?** (not hearing) pardon? 2 vt (in law) gracier; **to p. sb** (**for sth**) pardonner (qch) à qn; **p. (me)!** (sorry) pardon!

parent ['peərənt] n (father) père m; (mother) mère f; **parents** parents mpl

Paris ['pærɪs] n Paris m ou f ■ **Parisian** [pə'rɪzɪən, Am pə'ri:ʒən] 1 adj parisien, -enne 2 n Parisien, -enne mf

parish ['pærɪʃ] n (religious) paroisse f; (civil) ≃ commune f

park¹ [pɑ:k] n (garden) parc m

park² [pɑ:k] 1 vt (vehicle) garer 2 vi (of vehicle) se garer; (remain parked) stationner ■ **parking** n stationnement m; 'no p.' 'défense de stationner'; Am **p. lot** parking m; **p. meter** parcmètre m; **p. place** or **space** place f de parking; **p. ticket** contravention f

parliament ['pɑ:ləmənt] n parlement m

parody ['pærədɪ] 1 (pl -ies) n parodie f 2 (pt & pp -ied) vt parodier

parole [pə'rəʊl] n **to be (out) on p.** être en liberté conditionnelle

parrot ['pærət] n perroquet m

parsley ['pɑ:slɪ] n persil m

parsnip ['pɑ:snɪp] n panais m

parson ['pɑ:sən] n pasteur m

part¹ [pɑ:t] 1 n partie f; (quantity in mixture) mesure f; (of machine) pièce f; (of serial) épisode m; (role in play, film) rôle m; Am (in hair) raie f; **to take p.** participer (**in** à); **to be a p. of sth** faire partie de qch; **for the most p.** dans l'ensemble; **on the p. of...** de la part de...; **for my p.** pour ma part 2 adv (partly) en partie; **p. silk, p. cotton** soie et coton

part² [pɑ:t] 1 vt (separate) séparer; **to p. one's hair** se faire une raie 2 vi (of friends) se quitter; (of married couple) se séparer; **to p. with sth** se défaire de qch

partial ['pɑ:ʃəl] adj (not total) partiel, -elle; (biased) partial (**towards** envers); **to be p. to sth** avoir un faible pour qch

participate [pɑ:'tɪsɪpeɪt] vi participer (**in** à) ■ **participant** n participant, -e mf ■ **participation** n participation f

particular [pə'tɪkjʊlə(r)] 1 adj (specific, special) particulier, -ère; (exacting) méticuleux, -euse; **this p. book** ce livre en particulier; **to be p. about sth** faire très attention à qch **2** *n* in p. en particulier ■ **particularly** *adv* particulièrement ■ **particulars** *npl (details)* détails *mpl*; **to take down sb's p.** noter les coordonnées de qn

parting ['pɑ:tɪŋ] *n Br (in hair)* raie *f*

partition [pɑ:'tɪʃən] **1** *n (of room)* cloison *f* **2** *vt* **to p. sth off** cloisonner qch

partly ['pɑ:tlɪ] *adv* en partie; **p. English, p. French** moitié anglais, moitié français

partner ['pɑ:tnə(r)] *n (in game)* partenaire *mf*; *(in business)* associé, -e *mf*; *(in relationship)* compagnon *m*, compagne *f*; *(dancing)* cavalier, -ère *mf* ■ **partnership** *n* association *f*; **in p. with** en association avec

partridge ['pɑ:trɪdʒ] *n* perdrix *f*

part-time ['pɑ:t'taɪm] *adj & adv* à temps partiel

party ['pɑ:tɪ] *(pl* **-ies***) n (a) (gathering)* fête *f*; **to have** *or* **throw a p.** donner une fête **(b)** *(group)* groupe *m*; *(political)* parti *m*; *(in contract, lawsuit)* partie *f*

pass¹ [pɑ:s] *n (over mountains)* col *m*

pass² [pɑ:s] *n (entry permit)* laissez-passer *m inv*; *(for travel)* carte *f* d'abonnement; *(in sport)* passe *f*; **p. mark** *(in exam)* moyenne *f*

pass³ [pɑ:s] **1** *vt (move, give)* passer **(to** à**)**; *(go past)* passer devant; *(vehicle, runner)* dépasser; *(exam)* être reçu à; *(law)* voter; **to p. sb** *(in street)* croiser qn; **to p. the time** passer le temps; **to p. sentence** *(of judge)* prononcer le verdict
2 *vi (go past, go away)* passer **(to** à; **through** par**)**; *(in exam)* avoir la moyenne; *(of time)* passer

▸ **pass away** *vi* décéder

▸ **pass by 1** *vt insep (building)* passer devant; **to p. by sb** *(in street)* croiser qn **2** *vi* passer à côté

▸ **pass off** *vt sep* **to p. oneself off as sb** se faire passer pour qn

▸ **pass on** *vt sep (message, illness)* transmettre **(to** à**)**

▸ **pass out 1** *vt sep (hand out)* distribuer **2** *vi (faint)* s'évanouir

▸ **pass over** *vt insep (ignore)* passer sur

▸ **pass round** *vt sep (cakes, document)* faire passer; *(hand out)* distribuer

▸ **pass through** *vi* passer

▸ **pass up** *vt sep (opportunity)* laisser passer

passable ['pɑ:səbəl] *adj (not bad)* passable

passage ['pæsɪdʒ] *n* **(a)** *(way through)* passage *m*; *(corridor)* couloir *m*; **with the p. of time** avec le temps **(b)** *(of text)* passage *m*

passbook ['pɑ:sbʊk] *n* livret *m* de caisse d'épargne

passenger ['pæsɪndʒə(r)] *n* passager, -ère *mf*; *(on train)* voyageur, -euse *mf*

passer-by [pɑ:sə'baɪ] *(pl* passers-by*) n* passant, -e *mf*

passing ['pɑ:sɪŋ] **1** *adj (vehicle)* qui passe **2** *n (of time)* écoulement *m*; **in p.** en passant

passion ['pæʃən] *n* passion *f*; **to have a p. for sth** adorer qch ■ **passionate** *adj* passionné

passive ['pæsɪv] **1** *adj* passif, -ive **2** *n (in grammar)* passif *m*; **in the p.** au passif

passport ['pɑ:spɔ:t] *n* passeport *m*; **p. photo** photo *f* d'identité

password ['pɑ:swɜ:d] *n* mot *m* de passe

past [pɑ:st] **1** *n* passé *m*; **in the p.** autrefois
2 *adj (gone by)* passé; *(former)* ancien, -enne; **these p. months** ces derniers mois; **in the p. tense** au passé
3 *prep (in front of)* devant; *(after)* après; *(beyond)* au-delà de; **it's p. four o'clock** il est quatre heures passées
4 *adv* devant; **to go p.** passer

pasta ['pæstə] *n* pâtes *fpl*

paste [peɪst] **1** *n* **(a)** *(mixture)* pâte *f*; *(of meat)* pâté *m* **(b)** *(glue)* colle *f* **2** *vt* coller; **to p. sth up** coller qch

pastel [Br ˈpæstəl, Am pæˈstel] n pastel m

pasteurized [ˈpæstʃəraɪzd] adj **p. milk** lait m pasteurisé

pastille [Br ˈpæstɪl, Am pæˈstiːl] n pastille f

pastime [ˈpɑːstaɪm] n passe-temps m inv

pastor [ˈpɑːstə(r)] n Rel pasteur m

pastry [ˈpeɪstrɪ] (pl -ies) n (dough) pâte f; (cake) pâtisserie f

pasture [ˈpɑːstʃə(r)] n pré m, pâture f

pasty [ˈpæstɪ] (pl -ies) n (pie) feuilleté m

pat [pæt] (pt & pp -tt-) vt (tap) tapoter; (animal) caresser

patch [pætʃ] 1 n (for clothes) pièce f; (over eye) bandeau m; (of colour) tache f; (of ice) plaque f; Fig **to be going through a bad p.** traverser une mauvaise passe 2 vt **to p. (up)** (clothing) rapiécer; **to p. things up** (after argument) se raccommoder

patchwork [ˈpætʃwɜːk] n patchwork m

patchy [ˈpætʃɪ] (-ier, -iest) adj inégal

patent [ˈpeɪtənt, ˈpætənt] 1 n brevet m d'invention 2 vt (faire) breveter ▪ **patently** adv manifestement

paternal [pəˈtɜːnəl] adj paternel, -elle

path [pɑːθ] (pl -s [pɑːðz]) n chemin m; (narrow) sentier m; (in park) allée f; (of river) cours m; (of bullet) trajectoire f

pathetic [pəˈθetɪk] adj pitoyable

pathway [ˈpɑːθweɪ] n sentier m

patience [ˈpeɪʃəns] n (a) (quality) patience f; **to lose p.** perdre patience (**with sb** avec qn) (b) Br (card game) **to play p.** faire une réussite

patient [ˈpeɪʃənt] 1 adj patient 2 n patient, -e mf ▪ **patiently** adv patiemment

patio [ˈpætɪəʊ] (pl -os) n patio m

patriot [ˈpætrɪət, ˈpeɪtrɪət] n patriote mf ▪ **patriotic** [-rɪˈɒtɪk, peɪtrɪˈɒtɪk] adj (views, speech) patriotique; (person) patriote

patrol [pəˈtrəʊl] 1 n patrouille f; **to be on p.** être de patrouille; **p. car** voiture f de police 2 (pt & pp -ll-) vt patrouiller dans 3 vi patrouiller ▪ **patrolman** (pl -men) n Am (policeman) agent m de police

patron [ˈpeɪtrən] n (of arts) protecteur, -trice mf; (of charity) patron, -onne mf; (customer) client, -e mf; Rel **p. saint** patron, -onne mf

patronize [Br ˈpætrənaɪz, Am ˈpeɪtrənaɪz] vt (be condescending towards) traiter avec condescendance ▪ **patronizing** adj condescendant

patter [ˈpætə(r)] n (of footsteps) petit bruit m; (of rain) crépitement m

pattern [ˈpætən] n (design) dessin m, motif m; (in sewing) patron m; (in knitting) modèle m; Fig (norm) modèle m; (tendency) tendance f

paunch [pɔːntʃ] n ventre m

pause [pɔːz] 1 n pause f; (in conversation) silence m 2 vi (stop) faire une pause; (hesitate) hésiter

pave [peɪv] vt (road) paver (**with** de); Fig **to p. the way for sth** ouvrir la voie à qch ▪ **paving n p. stone** pavé m

pavement [ˈpeɪvmənt] n Br (beside road) trottoir m; Am (roadway) chaussée f

pavilion [pəˈvɪljən] n pavillon m

paw [pɔː] n patte f

pawn[1] [pɔːn] n (chess piece) pion m

pawn[2] [pɔːn] vt mettre en gage ▪ **pawnbroker** n prêteur, -euse mf sur gages ▪ **pawnshop** n mont-de-piété m

pay [peɪ] 1 n paie f, salaire m; (of soldier) solde f; **p. rise** augmentation f de salaire; Br **p. slip,** Am **p. stub** fiche f de paie

2 (pt & pp paid) vt (person, money, bill) payer; (sum, deposit) verser; (yield) (of investment) rapporter; **I paid £5 for it** je l'ai payé 5 livres; **to p. sb to do sth** or **for doing sth** payer qn pour qu'il fasse qch; **to p. sb for sth** payer qch à qn

3 vi payer ▪ **payable** adj (due) payable; **to make a cheque p. to sb** libeller un chèque à l'ordre de qn

■ **payment** n paiement m; (of deposit) versement 20 m; **on p. of 20 euros** moyennant 20 euros ■ **payphone** n téléphone m public

▶ **pay back** vt sep (person, loan) rembourser; Fig **I'll p. you back for this!** tu me le paieras!

▶ **pay for** vt insep payer

▶ **pay in** vt sep (cheque, money) verser sur un compte

▶ **pay off 1** vt sep (debt) rembourser; (in instalments) rembourser par acomptes **2** vi (of work, effort) porter ses fruits

▶ **pay out** vt sep (spend) dépenser

▶ **pay up** vi payer

PC [pi:'si:] (a) (abbr **personal computer**) PC m, micro m (b) (abbr **politically correct**) politiquement correct

PE [pi:'i:] (abbr **physical education**) n EPS f

pea [pi:] n pois m; **peas**, Br **garden** or **green peas** petits pois mpl

peace [pi:s] n paix f; **p. of mind** tranquillité f d'esprit; **at p.** en paix (**with** avec); **I'd like some p. and quiet** j'aimerais un peu de silence

peaceful ['pi:sfəl] adj (calm) paisible; (non-violent) pacifique

peach [pi:tʃ] n (fruit) pêche f

peacock ['pi:kɒk] n paon m

peak [pi:k] **1** n (mountain top) sommet m; (mountain) pic m; (of cap) visière f; Fig (of fame, success) apogée m **2** adj (hours, period) de pointe

peal [pi:l] **1** n (of bells) sonnerie f; **peals of laughter** éclats mpl de rire **2** vi **to p. (out)** (of bells) sonner à toute volée

peanut ['pi:nʌt] n cacah(o)uète f; **p. butter** beurre m de cacah(o)uètes

pear [peə(r)] n poire f

pearl [pɜ:l] n perle f; **p. necklace** collier m de perles

peasant ['pezənt] n & adj paysan, -anne (mf)

peat [pi:t] n tourbe f

pebble ['pebəl] n (stone) caillou m (pl -oux); (on beach) galet m

pecan ['pi:kən] n (nut) noix f de pécan

peck [pek] vti **to p. (at)** (grain) picorer; (person) donner un coup de bec à

peckish ['pekɪʃ] adj Br **to be p.** avoir un petit creux

peculiar [pɪ'kju:lɪə(r)] adj (strange) bizarre; (special, characteristic) particulier, -ère (**to** à)

pedal ['pedəl] **1** n pédale f; **p. bin** poubelle f à pédale **2** (Br -ll-, Am -l-) vt **to p. a bicycle** être à bicyclette **3** vi pédaler

pedantic [pɪ'dæntɪk] adj pédant

peddle ['pedəl] vt (goods, ideas) colporter; (drugs) faire du trafic de ■ **peddler** n (door-to-door) colporteur, -euse mf; (in street) camelot m; (drug) **p.** trafiquant, -e mf de drogue

pedestal ['pedɪstəl] n piédestal m

pedestrian [pə'destrɪən] n piéton m; Br **p. crossing** passage m pour piétons; Br **p. precinct** zone f piétonnière

pediatrician [pi:dɪə'trɪʃən] n Am = **paediatrician**

pedigree ['pedɪgri:] **1** n (of animal) pedigree m; (of person) ascendance f **2** adj (animal) de race

pedlar ['pedlə(r)] n (door-to-door) colporteur, -euse mf; (in street) camelot m

pee [pi:] Fam **1** n **to go for a p.** faire pipi **2** vi faire pipi

peek [pi:k] vi jeter un coup d'œil furtif (**at** à)

peel [pi:l] **1** n (of vegetable, fruit) peau f; (of orange, lemon) écorce f **2** vt (vegetable) éplucher; (fruit) peler; **to p. sth off** (label) décoller qch **3** vi (of skin, person) peler; (of paint) s'écailler ■ **peeler** n **(potato) p.** épluche-légumes m inv ■ **peelings** npl épluchures fpl

peep [pi:p] vi jeter un coup d'œil furtif (**at** à); **to p. out** se montrer

peer [pɪə(r)] **1** n (equal) & Br (nobleman) pair m **2** vi **to p. at sb/sth** scruter qn/qch du regard

peeved [pi:vd] adj en rogne

peevish ['pi:vɪʃ] adj irritable

peg [peg] n (for coat, hat) patère f; (for drying clothes) pince f à linge; (for tent) piquet m; (wooden pin) cheville f; Br **to buy sth off the p.** acheter qch en prêt-à-porter

pejorative [pɪˈdʒɒrətɪv] adj péjoratif, -ive

pelican [ˈpelɪkən] n pélican m; Br **p. crossing** feux mpl à commande manuelle

pelt [pelt] **1** vt bombarder (**with** de) **2** vi Fam **it's pelting down** il pleut à verse

pelvis [ˈpelvɪs] n Anat pelvis m

pen¹ [pen] n (for writing) stylo m; **p. friend** or **pal** correspondant, -e mf

pen² [pen] n (for sheep, cattle) parc m

penal [ˈpiːnəl] adj (code, law) pénal ▪ **penalize** vt pénaliser

penalty [ˈpenltɪ] (pl **-ies**) n (prison sentence) peine f; (fine) amende f; (in football) penalty m; (in rugby) pénalité f

pence [pens] pl of **penny**

pencil [ˈpensəl] **1** n crayon m; **in p.** au crayon; **p. sharpener** taille-crayon m **2** (Br **-ll-**, Am **-l-**) vt Fig **to p. sth in** fixer qch provisoirement

pendant [ˈpendənt] n (around neck) pendentif m

pending [ˈpendɪŋ] **1** adj (matter, business) en attente **2** prep (until) en attendant

pendulum [ˈpendjʊləm] n pendule m

penetrate [ˈpenɪtreɪt] **1** vt (substance) pénétrer; (mystery) percer **2** vi **to p. (into)** (forest) pénétrer dans; (group) s'infiltrer dans ▪ **penetrating** adj (mind, cold) pénétrant

penguin [ˈpeŋgwɪn] n manchot m

penicillin [penɪˈsɪlɪn] n pénicilline f

peninsula [pɪˈnɪnsjʊlə] n presqu'île f; (larger) péninsule f

penis [ˈpiːnɪs] n pénis m

penitentiary [penɪˈtenʃərɪ] (pl **-ies**) n Am prison f centrale

penknife [ˈpennaɪf] (pl **-knives**) n canif m

penniless [ˈpenɪləs] adj sans le sou

penny [ˈpenɪ] n (a) (pl **-ies**) Br (coin) penny m; Am & Can (cent) cent m; Fig

I don't have a p. je n'ai pas un sou (**b**) (pl **pence**) Br (value, currency) penny m

pension [ˈpenʃən] **1** n pension f; (retirement) **p.** retraite f; Br old age **p.** pension f de vieillesse **2** vt **to p. sb off** mettre qn à la retraite ▪ **pensioner** n retraité, -e mf; Br old age **p.** retraité, -e mf

pent-up [ˈpentˈʌp] adj (feelings) refoulé

penultimate [pɪˈnʌltɪmət] adj avant-dernier, -ère

people [ˈpiːpəl] **1** n (nation) peuple m **2** npl (as group) gens mpl; (as individuals) personnes fpl; **the p.** (citizens) le peuple; **two p.** deux personnes; **English p.** les Anglais mpl; **p. think that…** les gens pensent que…

pepper [ˈpepə(r)] n (spice) poivre m; (vegetable) poivron m; **p. mill** moulin m à poivre

peppermint [ˈpepəmɪnt] n (flavour) menthe f; (sweet) bonbon m à la menthe

per [pɜː(r)] prep par; **p. annum** par an; **50 pence p. kilo** 50 pence le kilo; **40 km p. hour** 40 km à l'heure

perceive [pəˈsiːv] vt (see, hear) percevoir; (notice) remarquer (**that** que)

percentage [pəˈsentɪdʒ] n pourcentage m ▪ **percent** adv pour cent

perception [pəˈsepʃən] n perception f (**of** de)

perceptive [pəˈseptɪv] adj (person) perspicace; (study, remark) pertinent

perch [pɜːtʃ] **1** n (for bird) perchoir m **2** vi se percher

percolator [ˈpɜːkəleɪtə(r)] n cafetière f à pression; (in café, restaurant) percolateur m

perennial [pəˈrenɪəl] **1** adj (plant) vivace; (worry) perpétuel, -elle **2** n plante f vivace

perfect 1 [ˈpɜːfɪkt] adj parfait; Gram **p. tense** parfait m **2** [ˈpɜːfɪkt] n Gram parfait m **3** [pəˈfekt] vt parfaire; **to p. one's French** parfaire ses connaissances en français

perfection [pə'fekʃən] *n (quality)* perfection *f* ■ **perfectly** *adv* parfaitement

perforate ['pɜːfəreɪt] *vt* perforer ■ **perforation** *n* perforation *f*

perform [pə'fɔːm] **1** *vt (task, miracle)* accomplir; *(duty, function)* remplir; *(play, piece of music)* jouer **2** *vi (act, play)* jouer; *(sing)* chanter; *(dance)* danser; **to p. well/badly** *(in job)* bien/mal s'en tirer ■ **performance** *n* (**a**) *(of play)* représentation *f* (**b**) *(of actor, musician)* interprétation *f*; *(of athlete)* performance *f*; *(of company)* résultats *mpl*

performer [pə'fɔːmə(r)] *n (entertainer)* artiste *mf*; *(in play, of music)* interprète *mf* (**of** de)

perfume ['pɜːfjuːm] *n* parfum *m*

perhaps [pə'hæps] *adv* peut-être; **p. not/so** peut-être que non/que oui; **p. she'll come** peut-être qu'elle viendra, elle viendra peut-être

peril ['perɪl] *n* péril *m*, danger *m*

period ['pɪərɪəd] **1** *n* (**a**) *(stretch of time)* période *f*; *(historical)* époque *f*; *(school lesson)* heure *f* de cours; **(monthly) period(s)** *(of woman)* règles *fpl* (**b**) *Am (full stop)* point *m*; **I refuse, p.!** je refuse, un point c'est tout! **2** *adj (furniture, costume)* d'époque ■ **periodical** [-rɪ'ɒdɪkəl] *n (magazine)* périodique *m* ■ **periodically** [-rɪ'ɒdɪklɪ] *adv* périodiquement

peripheral [pə'rɪfərəl] *n Comptr* périphérique *m*

perish ['perɪʃ] *vi (of person)* périr

perishable ['perɪʃəbəl] *adj (food)* périssable

perjury ['pɜːdʒərɪ] *n* faux témoignage *m*

perk [pɜːk] **1** *n Br Fam (in job)* avantage *m* **2** *vt* **to p. sb up** *(revive)* ragaillardir qn; *(cheer up)* remonter le moral à qn **3** *vi* **to p. up** reprendre du poil de la bête

perm [pɜːm] **1** *n* permanente *f* **2** *vt* **to have one's hair permed** se faire faire une permanente

permanent ['pɜːmənənt] *adj* permanent; *(address)* fixe ■ **permanently** *adv* à titre permanent

permissible [pə'mɪsəbəl] *adj* permis

permission [pə'mɪʃən] *n* permission *f*, autorisation *f* (**to do** de faire); **to give sb p. (to do sth)** donner la permission à qn (de faire qch)

permissive [pə'mɪsɪv] *adj* permissif, -ive

permit 1 ['pɜːmɪt] *n* permis *m* **2** [pə'mɪt] *(pt & pp* **-tt-)** *vt* permettre (**sb to do** à qn de faire)

perpendicular [pɜːpən'dɪkjələ(r)] *adj & n* perpendiculaire (*f*)

perpetrate ['pɜːpɪtreɪt] *vt (crime)* perpétrer ■ **perpetrator** *n* auteur *m*

perpetual [pə'petʃʊəl] *adj* perpétuel, -elle ■ **perpetuate** [-eɪt] *vt* perpétuer

perplexed [pə'plekst] *adj* perplexe

persecute ['pɜːsɪkjuːt] *vt* persécuter ■ **persecution** *n* persécution *f*

persevere [pɜːsɪ'vɪə(r)] *vi* persévérer (**with** dans) ■ **perseverance** *n* persévérance *f*

Persian ['pɜːʃən, 'pɜːʒən] **1** *adj (carpet, cat)* persan; **the P. Gulf** le golfe Persique **2** *n (language)* persan *m*

persist [pə'sɪst] *vi* persister (**in doing** à faire; **in sth** dans qch) ■ **persistent** *adj (person)* tenace; *(smell, rumours)* persistant; *(attempts)* continuel, -elle

person ['pɜːsən] *n* personne *f*; **in p.** en personne

personal ['pɜːsənəl] *adj* personnel, -elle; *(friend)* intime; *(life)* privé; *(indiscreet)* indiscret, -ète; **p. computer** ordinateur *m* individuel; **p. organizer** agenda *m* électronique; **p. stereo** baladeur *m*

personality [pɜːsə'nælɪtɪ] *(pl* **-ies)** *n (character, famous person)* personnalité *f*

personally ['pɜːsənəlɪ] *adv* personnellement; *(in person)* en personne

personify [pə'sɒnɪfaɪ] *(pt & pp* **-ied)** *vt* personnifier

personnel [pɜːsə'nel] *n (staff)* personnel *m*

perspective [pə'spektɪv] *n* perspective *f*; *Fig* **in p.** sous son vrai jour

perspire [pə'spaɪə(r)] *vi* transpirer

persuade [pə'sweɪd] *vt* persuader (**sb to do qn de faire**) ■ **persuasion** *n* persuasion *f*; *(creed)* religion *f* ■ **persuasive** *adj (person, argument)* persuasif, -ive

pertain [pə'teɪn] *vi Formal* **to p. to** *(relate)* se rapporter à

pertinent ['pɜːtɪnənt] *adj* pertinent

perturb [pə'tɜːb] *vt* troubler

Peru [pə'ruː] *n* le Pérou

peruse [pə'ruːz] *vt Formal (read carefully)* lire attentivement; *(skim through)* parcourir

pervade [pə'veɪd] *vt* imprégner ■ **pervasive** *adj (feeling)* général; *(influence)* omniprésent

perverse [pə'vɜːs] *adj (awkward)* contrariant ■ **perversion** [-ʃən, *Am* -ʒən] *n (sexual)* perversion *f*

pervert 1 ['pɜːvɜːt] *n (sexual deviant)* pervers, -e *mf* **2** [pə'vɜːt] *vt* pervertir; *(mind)* corrompre

pessimism ['pesɪmɪzəm] *n* pessimisme *m* ■ **pessimistic** *adj* pessimiste

pest [pest] *n (animal)* animal *m* nuisible; *(insect)* insecte *m* nuisible; *Fam (person)* plaie *f*

pester ['pestə(r)] *vt* tourmenter; **to p. sb to do sth** harceler qn pour qu'il fasse qch

pesticide ['pestɪsaɪd] *n* pesticide *m*

pet [pet] **1** *n* animal *m* domestique; *(favourite person)* chouchou, -oute *mf*; *(term of address)* petit chou *m* **2** *adj (dog, cat)* domestique; *(favourite)* favori, -ite; **p. shop** animalerie *f* **3** *(pt & pp* **-tt-)** *vt (fondle)* caresser **4** *vi Fam* se peloter

petal ['petəl] *n* pétale *m*

peter ['piːtə(r)] *vi* **to p. out** *(of conversation)* tarir; *(of scheme)* n'aboutir à rien; *(of path, stream)* disparaître

petition [pə'tɪʃən] *n (signatures)* pétition *f*; *(request to court of law)* requête *f*

petrify ['petrɪfaɪ] *(pt & pp* **-ied)** *vt* pétrifier

petrol ['petrəl] *n Br* essence *f*; **p. station** station-service *f*; **p. tank** réservoir *m* d'essence

petticoat ['petɪkəʊt] *n* jupon *m*

petty ['petɪ] **(-ier, -iest)** *adj (trivial)* insignifiant; *(mean)* mesquin; **p. cash** petite caisse *f*

pew [pjuː] *n* banc *m* d'église

phantom ['fæntəm] *n* fantôme *m*

pharmacy ['faːməsɪ] *(pl* **-ies)** *n* pharmacie *f* ■ **pharmacist** *n* pharmacien, -enne *mf*

phase [feɪz] **1** *n* phase *f* **2** *vt* **to p. sth in/out** introduire/supprimer qch progressivement

PhD [piːeɪtʃ'diː] *(abbr* **Doctor of Philosophy)** *n (degree)* doctorat *m* (**in** de); *(person)* docteur *m*

phenomenon [fɪ'nɒmɪnən] *(pl* **-ena** [-ɪnə]) *n* phénomène *m* ■ **phenomenal** *adj* phénoménal

Philippines ['fɪlɪpiːnz] *npl* **the P.** les Philippines *fpl*

philistine ['fɪlɪstaɪn] *n* béotien, -enne *mf*, philistin *m*

philosopher [fɪ'lɒsəfə(r)] *n* philosophe *mf*

philosophical [fɪlə'sɒfɪkəl] *adj* philosophique; *Fig (stoical, resigned)* philosophe

philosophy [fɪ'lɒsəfɪ] *(pl* **-ies)** *n* philosophie *f*

phlegm [flem] *n (in throat)* glaires *fpl*

phobia ['fəʊbɪə] *n* phobie *f*

phone [fəʊn] **1** *n* téléphone *m*; **to be on the p.** *(be talking)* être au téléphone; *(have a telephone)* avoir le téléphone; **p. call** coup *m* de téléphone; **to make a p. call** téléphoner (**to** à); **p. book** annuaire *m*; **p. box**, *Br* **p. booth** cabine *f* téléphonique; **p. number** numéro *m* de téléphone

2 *vt* téléphoner (**to** à); **to p. sb (up)** téléphoner à qn; **to p. sb back** rappeler qn

3 *vi* **to p. (up)** téléphoner; **to p. back** rappeler ■ **phonecard** *n Br* carte *f* de téléphone

phonetic [fə'netɪk] *adj* phonétique

phoney ['fəʊnɪ] *Fam* **1** (**-ier, -iest**) *adj* (*company, excuse*) bidon *inv* **2** *n* (*impostor*) imposteur *m*; (*insincere person*) faux jeton *m*

photo ['fəʊtəʊ] (*pl* **-os**) *n* photo *f*; **to take sb's p.** prendre qn en photo; **to have one's p. taken** se faire prendre en photo; **p. album** album *m* de photos

photocopy ['fəʊtəʊkɒpɪ] **1** (*pl* **-ies**) *n* photocopie *f* **2** (*pt & pp* **-ied**) *vt* photocopier ■ **photocopier** *n* photocopieuse *f*

photograph ['fəʊtəgrɑːf] **1** *n* photographie *f* **2** *vt* photographier ■ **photographer** [fə'tɒɡrəfə(r)] *n* photographe *mf* ■ **photography** [fə'tɒɡrəfɪ] *n* (*activity*) photographie *f*

phrase [freɪz] **1** *n* (*saying*) expression *f*; (*idiom, in grammar*) locution *f*; **p. book** manuel *m* de conversation **2** *vt* (*verbally*) exprimer; (*in writing*) rédiger

physical ['fɪzɪkəl] *adj* physique; **p. education** éducation *f* physique; **p. examination** visite *f* médicale

physician [fɪ'zɪʃən] *n* médecin *m*

physics ['fɪzɪks] *n* (*science*) physique *f*

physiology [fɪzɪ'ɒlədʒɪ] *n* physiologie *f*

physiotherapy [fɪzɪəʊ'θerəpɪ] *n* kinésithérapie *f*

physique [fɪ'ziːk] *n* physique *m*

piano [pɪ'ænəʊ] (*pl* **-os**) *n* piano *m* ■ **pianist** ['pɪənɪst] *n* pianiste *mf*

pick¹ [pɪk] **1** *n* (*choice*) choix *m*; **to take one's p.** choisir **2** *vt* (*choose*) choisir; (*flower, fruit*) cueillir; (*hole*) faire (*in* dans); (*lock*) crocheter; **to p. a fight** chercher la bagarre (**with** avec)

▸ **pick at** *vt insep* **to p. at one's food** picorer

▸ **pick off** *vt sep* (*remove*) enlever

▸ **pick on** *vt insep* (*nag, blame*) s'en prendre à

▸ **pick out** *vt sep* (*choose*) choisir; (*identify*) repérer

▸ **pick up** *vt sep* (*lift up*) ramasser;

(*person into air, weight*) soulever; (*baby*) prendre dans ses bras; (*cold*) attraper; (*habit, accent, speed*) prendre; (*fetch, collect*) passer prendre; (*radio programme*) capter; (*arrest*) arrêter; (*learn*) apprendre; **to p. up the phone** décrocher le téléphone

2 *vi* (*improve*) s'améliorer; (*of business*) reprendre; **let's p. up where we left off** reprenons (là où nous en étions restés)

pick² [pɪk] *n* (*tool*) pic *m*; **ice p.** pic *m* à glace

pickaxe ['pɪkæks] (*Am* **pickax**) *n* pioche *f*

picket ['pɪkɪt] *n* (*in strike*) **p. (line)** piquet *m* de grève

pickle ['pɪkəl] **1** *n* **pickles** (*vegetables*) *Br* conserves *fpl* (au vinaigre); *Am* concombres *mpl*, cornichons *mpl*; *Fam* **to be in a p.** être dans le pétrin **2** *vt* conserver dans du vinaigre; **pickled onion** oignon *m* au vinaigre

pickpocket ['pɪkpɒkɪt] *n* pickpocket *m*

pick-up ['pɪkʌp] *n* **p. (truck)** pick-up *m inv* (*petite camionnette à plateau*); **p. point** (*for goods, passengers*) point *m* de ramassage

picky ['pɪkɪ] (**-ier, -iest**) *adj Fam* (*choosy*) difficile (**about** sur)

picnic ['pɪknɪk] **1** *n* pique-nique *m* **2** (*pt & pp* **-ck-**) *vi* pique-niquer

picture ['pɪktʃə(r)] *n* image *f*; (*painting*) tableau *m*; (*drawing*) dessin *m*; (*photo*) photo *f*; *Fig* (*situation*) situation *f*; *Br Fam* (*film*) film *m*; *Br Fam* **the pictures** le cinéma; **p. frame** cadre *m* **2** *vt* **to p. sth (to oneself)** s'imaginer qch

picturesque [pɪktʃə'resk] *adj* pittoresque

pie [paɪ] *n* (*open*) tarte *f*; (*with pastry on top*) tourte *f*; **p. chart** camembert *m*

piece [piːs] **1** *n* morceau *m*; (*smaller*) bout *m*; (*in chess, puzzle*) pièce *f*; **to take sth to pieces** démonter qch; **a p. of news/advice/luck** une nouvelle/

un conseil/une chance; **in one p.** *(object)* intact **2** *vt* **to p. together** *(facts)* reconstituer

pier [pɪə(r)] *n (for walking, with entertainments)* jetée *f*

pierce [pɪəs] *vt* percer; *(of cold, bullet, sword)* transpercer; **to have one's ears pierced** se faire percer les oreilles ∎ **piercing** *adj (voice, look)* perçant; *(wind)* vif *(f* vive)

pig [pɪg] *n (animal)* cochon *m,* porc *m; Fam (greedy person)* goinfre *m*

pigeon ['pɪdʒɪn] *n* pigeon *m*

pigeonhole ['pɪdʒɪnhəʊl] **1** *n* casier *m* **2** *vt (classify, label)* classer; *(person)* étiqueter

piggy ['pɪgɪ] *n* **p. bank** tirelire *f (en forme de cochon)*

piggyback ['pɪgɪbæk] *n* **to give sb a p.** porter qn sur son dos

pigment ['pɪgmənt] *n* pigment *m*

pigtail ['pɪgteɪl] *n (in hair)* natte *f*

pilchard ['pɪltʃəd] *n* pilchard *m*

pile [paɪl] **1** *n (heap)* tas *m; (neat stack)* pile *f; Fam* **to have piles of** or **a p. of things to do** avoir un tas de choses à faire **2** *vt* entasser; *(stack)* empiler

▸ **pile up 1** *vt sep* entasser; *(stack)* empiler **2** *vi (accumulate)* s'accumuler

piles [paɪlz] *npl (illness)* hémorroïdes *fpl*

pile-up ['paɪlʌp] *n Fam (on road)* carambolage *m*

pilgrim ['pɪlgrɪm] *n* pèlerin *m* ∎ **pilgrimage** *n* pèlerinage *m*

pill [pɪl] *n* pilule *f;* **to be on the p.** *(of woman)* prendre la pilule

pillage ['pɪlɪdʒ] **1** *n* pillage *m* **2** *vti* piller

pillar ['pɪlə(r)] *n* pilier *m; Br* **p. box** boîte *f* aux lettres

pillow ['pɪləʊ] *n* oreiller *m* ∎ **pillowcase** *n* taie *f* d'oreiller

pilot ['paɪlət] **1** *n (of plane, ship)* pilote *m* **2** *adj* **p. light** veilleuse *f;* **p. scheme** projet *m* pilote **3** *vt (plane, ship)* piloter

pimple ['pɪmpəl] *n* bouton *m*

PIN [pɪn] *(abbr* **personal identification**

number) *n Br* **P. (number)** code *m* confidentiel

pin [pɪn] **1** *n* épingle *f; Br (drawing pin)* punaise *f; (in machine)* goupille *f* **2** *(pt & pp* **-nn-)** *vt (attach)* épingler (**to** à); *(to wall)* punaiser (**to** or **on** à); **to p. down** *(immobilize)* immobiliser; *(fix)* fixer; **to p. sth up** *(notice)* fixer qch au mur

pinball ['pɪnbɔːl] *n* flipper *m;* **p. machine** flipper *m*

pincers ['pɪnsəz] *npl (tool)* tenailles *fpl*

pinch [pɪntʃ] **1** *n (of salt)* pincée *f;* **to give sb a p.** pincer qn; *Br* **at a p.,** *Am* **in a p.** à la rigueur **2** *vt (person); Br Fam (steal)* piquer (**from** à) **3** *vi (of shoes)* serrer

pine [paɪn] **1** *n (tree, wood)* pin *m;* **p. forest** pinède *f* **2** *vi* **to p. for sb/sth** se languir de qn/qch

pineapple ['paɪnæpəl] *n* ananas *m*

pink [pɪŋk] *adj & n (colour)* rose *(m)*

pinnacle ['pɪnəkəl] *n Fig (of fame, career)* apogée *m*

pinpoint ['pɪnpɔɪnt] *vt (locate)* repérer; *(identify)* identifier

pint [paɪnt] *n* pinte *f (Br = 0,57 l, Am = 0,47 l);* **a p. of beer** ≃ un demi

pioneer [paɪə'nɪə(r)] **1** *n* pionnier, -ère *mf* **2** *vt* **to p. sth** être le premier/ la première à mettre au point qch

pious ['paɪəs] *adj (person, deed)* pieux *(f* pieuse)

pip [pɪp] *n Br (of fruit)* pépin *m*

pipe [paɪp] **1** *n* tuyau *m; (for smoking)* pipe *f; (musical instrument)* pipeau *m;* **to smoke a p.** fumer la pipe **2** *vi Fam* **to p. down** *(shut up)* se taire ∎ **piping** *adv* **p. hot** très chaud

pipeline ['paɪplaɪn] *n (for oil)* pipeline *m; Fig* **to be in the p.** être en préparation

pirate ['paɪərət] *n* pirate *m* ∎ **pirated** *adj (book, record, CD)* pirate

pissed [pɪst] *adj very Fam (drunk)* bourré; *Am (angry)* en rogne

pistachio [pɪ'stæʃɪəʊ] *(pl* **-os)** *n (nut, flavour)* pistache *f*

pistol ['pɪstəl] *n* pistolet *m*

pit¹ [pɪt] n (hole) fosse f; (mine) mine f
pit² [pɪt] n Am (stone of fruit) noyau m (pl -aux); (smaller) pépin m
pit³ [pɪt] (pt & pp -tt-) vt to p. oneself against sb se mesurer à qn
pitch¹ [pɪtʃ] 1 n (a) (for football) terrain m (b) (of voice) hauteur f; (musical) ton m 2 vt (tent) dresser; (ball) lancer 3 vi Fam to p. in (cooperate) mettre du sien ■ pitch-black, pitch-dark adj noir comme dans un four
pitcher ['pɪtʃə(r)] n cruche f
pitfall ['pɪtfɔːl] n (trap) piège m
pith [pɪθ] n (of orange) peau f blanche
pitiful ['pɪtɪfəl] adj pitoyable ■ pitiless adj impitoyable
pittance ['pɪtəns] n (income) salaire m de misère
pity ['pɪtɪ] 1 n pitié f; to take or have p. on sb avoir pitié de qn; what a p.! quel dommage!; it's a p. that... c'est dommage que... (+ subjunctive) 2 (pt & pp -ied) vt plaindre
pivot ['pɪvət] 1 n pivot m 2 vi pivoter (on sur)
pizza ['piːtsə] n pizza f
placard ['plækɑːd] n (on wall) affiche f; (hand-held) pancarte f
place [pleɪs] 1 n endroit m, lieu m; (seat, position, rank) place f; Fam my p. chez moi; to lose one's p. (in queue) perdre sa place; (in book) perdre sa page; to take the p. of sb/sth remplacer qn/qch; to take p. (happen) avoir lieu; Br to set or lay three places (at the table) mettre trois couverts; Am some p. (somewhere) quelque part; Am no p. (nowhere) nulle part; all over the p. un peu partout; in the first p. (firstly) en premier lieu; in p. of à la place de; out of p. (remark) déplacé; (object) pas à sa place; p. of work lieu m de travail
    2 vt (put, situate, invest, in sport) placer; to be placed third se classer troisième; to p. an order with sb passer une commande à qn
placement ['pleɪsmənt] n stage m
placid ['plæsɪd] adj placide

plague [pleɪg] 1 n (disease) peste f 2 vt (of person) harceler (with de)
plaice [pleɪs] n (fish) carrelet m
plain¹ [pleɪn] 1 (-er, -est) adj (clear, obvious) clair; (simple) simple; (without a pattern) uni; (not beautiful) quelconque; in p. clothes en civil; to make it p. to sb that... faire comprendre à qn que...; p. chocolate chocolat m noir; p. flour farine f (sans levure) 2 adv Fam (utterly) complètement ■ plainly adv (clearly) clairement; (frankly) franchement
plain² [pleɪn] n (land) plaine f
plait [plæt] 1 n tresse f, natte f 2 vt tresser, natter
plan [plæn] 1 n (proposal, intention) projet m; (of building, town, essay) plan m; to go according to p. se passer comme prévu 2 (pt & pp -nn-) vt (arrange) projeter; (crime) comploter; (building, town) faire le plan de; to p. to do or on doing sth (intend) projeter de faire qch; as planned comme prévu 3 vi faire des projets
plane¹ [pleɪn] n (aircraft) avion m
plane² [pleɪn] n (tool) rabot m 2 vt raboter
plane³ [pleɪn] n (level, surface) & Fig plan m
planet ['plænɪt] n planète f
plank [plæŋk] n planche f
planning ['plænɪŋ] n conception f; family p. planning m familial
plant [plɑːnt] 1 n (a) (living thing) plante f (b) (factory) usine f; (machinery) matériel m 2 vt (tree, flower) planter; (crops, seeds) semer; (field) ensemencer (with en); Fig (bomb) poser
plantation [plæn'teɪʃən] n (trees, land) plantation f
plaque [plæk] n (sign) plaque f; (on teeth) plaque f dentaire
plaster ['plɑːstə(r)] 1 n (a) (on wall) plâtre m; to put sb's leg in p. mettre la jambe de qn dans le plâtre; p. cast (for broken bone) plâtre m (b) Br (sticking) p. pansement m adhésif 2 vt

(wall) plâtrer; **to p. sth with** *(cover)* couvrir qch de

plastic ['plæstɪk] **1** *adj (object)* en plastique; **p. bag** sac *m* en plastique; **p. surgery** *(cosmetic)* chirurgie *f* esthétique **2** *n* plastique *m*

plate [pleɪt] *n (dish)* assiette *f*; *(metal sheet)* plaque *f*; *(book illustration)* gravure *f*

plateau ['plætəʊ] *(pl* **-eaus** [-əʊz] *or* **-eaux)** *n (flat land)* plateau *m*

platform ['plætfɔːm] *n (raised surface)* plate-forme *f*; *(in train station)* quai *m*; *(for speaker)* estrade *f*

platinum ['plætɪnəm] *n (metal)* platine *m*

plausible ['plɔːzəbəl] *adj (argument, excuse)* plausible

play [pleɪ] **1** *n (drama)* pièce *f* (de théâtre); *(amusement)* jeu *m*; **to come into p.** entrer en jeu; **a p. on words** un jeu de mots

2 *vt (part, tune, card)* jouer; *(game)* jouer à; *(instrument)* jouer de; *(match)* disputer (**with** avec); *(team, opponent)* jouer contre; *(record, compact disc)* passer; *(radio, tape recorder)* faire marcher; *Fig* **to p. a part in doing/in sth** contribuer à faire/à qch **3** *vi* jouer (**with** avec; **at** à); *(of record player, tape recorder)* marcher; **Fam what are you playing at?** à quoi tu joues? ■ **playboy** *n* play-boy *m* ■ **playground** *n Br (in school)* cour *f* de récréation; *(in park)* terrain *m* de jeux ■ **playgroup** *n* garderie *f* ■ **playmate** *n* camarade *mf* de jeu ■ **playschool** *n* garderie *f* ■ **playtime** *n (in school)* récréation *f* ■ **playwright** *n* dramaturge *mf*

▸ **play about, play around** *vi* jouer, s'amuser

▸ **play back** *vt sep (tape)* réécouter

▸ **play down** *vt sep* minimiser

▸ **play on** *vt insep (feelings, fears)* jouer sur

▸ **play out** *vt sep (scene, fantasy)* jouer

▸ **play up** *vi Fam (of child, machine)* faire des siennes

player ['pleɪə(r)] *n (in game, of instrument)* joueur *m*, joueuse *f*; **clarinet p.** joueur *m*/joueuse *f* de clarinette

playful ['pleɪfəl] *adj (mood, tone)* enjoué; *(child, animal)* joueur (*f* joueuse)

playing ['pleɪɪŋ] *n* jeu *m*; **p. card** carte *f* à jouer; **p. field** terrain *m* de jeux

plc [piːel'siː] *n (abbr* **public limited company)** *n Br Com* ≃ SA *f*

plea [pliː] *n (request)* appel *m*

plead [pliːd] **1** *vt (argue)* plaider; *(as excuse)* alléguer **2** *vi* **to p. with sb (to do sth)** implorer qn (de faire qch); **p. guilty** plaider coupable

pleasant ['plezənt] *adj* agréable (**to** avec)

please [pliːz] **1** *adv* s'il te/vous plaît; **p. sit down** asseyez-vous, je vous prie; **p. do!** bien sûr!, je vous en prie!

2 *vt* **to p. sb** faire plaisir à qn; *(satisfy)* contenter qn

3 *vi* plaire; **do as you p.** fais comme tu veux ■ **pleased** *adj* content (**with** de); **p. to meet you!** enchanté! ■ **pleasing** *adj* agréable, plaisant

pleasure ['pleʒə(r)] *n* plaisir *m*

pleat [pliːt] *n* pli *m* ■ **pleated** *adj* plissé

pledge [pledʒ] **1** *n (promise)* promesse *f* (**to do** de faire) **2** *vt* promettre (**to do** de faire)

plenty ['plentɪ] *n* **p. of** beaucoup de; **that's p.** *(of food)* merci, j'en ai assez ■ **plentiful** *adj* abondant

pliers ['plaɪəz] *npl* pince *f*

plight [plaɪt] *n (crisis)* situation *f* critique

plimsolls ['plɪmsəʊlz] *npl Br* tennis *mpl*

plod [plɒd] *(pt & pp* **-dd-)** *vi* **to p. (along)** *(walk)* avancer laborieusement; *(work)* travailler laborieusement

plonk¹ [plɒŋk] *vt Fam* **to p. sth (down)** *(drop)* poser qch

plonk² [plɒŋk] *n Br Fam (wine)* pinard *m*

plot [plɒt] **1** *n (conspiracy)* complot *m*; *(of novel, film)* intrigue *f*; **p. (of land)** parcelle *f* de terrain **2** *(pt & pp* **-tt-)** *vti*

plough comploter (**to do** de faire) **3** vt **to p. (out)** (route) déterminer; (graph) tracer

plough [plaʊ] (Am **plow**) **1** n charrue f **2** vt (field) labourer **3** vi labourer ∎ **ploughman** (pl -**men**) n Br **p.'s lunch** = assiette de fromage ou jambon avec de la salade et des condiments

pluck [plʌk] **1** n courage m **2** vt (hair, feathers) arracher; (flower) cueillir; (fowl) plumer; (eyebrows) épiler; (string of guitar) pincer; **to p. up the courage to do sth** trouver le courage de faire qch ∎ **plucky** (-**ier**, -**iest**) adj courageux, -euse

plug [plʌg] **1** n (a) (of cotton wool, wood) tampon m; (for sink, bath) bonde f (b) (electrical) (on device) fiche f; (socket) prise f (de courant); Aut (spark) bougie f **2** (pt & pp -**gg**-) vt (a) **to p. (up)** (gap, hole) boucher; **to p. sth in** (appliance) brancher qch (b) Fam (promote) faire de la pub pour ∎ **plughole** n trou m d'écoulement

plum [plʌm] n prune f

plumb [plʌm] adv Am Fam (crazy) complètement
▸ **plumb in** vt sep (washing machine) brancher

plumber ['plʌmə(r)] n plombier m ∎ **plumbing** n (job, system) plomberie f

plummet ['plʌmɪt] vi (of prices) s'effondrer; (of aircraft) plonger

plump [plʌmp] **1** (-**er**, -**est**) adj (person, arm) potelé; (chicken) dodu; (cheek) rebondi **2** vi Fam **to p. for sth** se décider pour qch

plunder ['plʌndə(r)] **1** n (goods) butin m **2** vt piller

plunge [plʌndʒ] **1** n (dive) plongeon m; Fig (decrease) chute f; Fam **to take the p.** (take on difficult task) se jeter à l'eau; (get married) se marier **2** vt (thrust) plonger (**into** dans) **3** vi (dive) plonger (**into** dans); Fig (decrease) chuter

plural ['plʊərəl] **1** adj (noun) au pluriel **2** n pluriel m; **in the p.** au pluriel

plus [plʌs] **1** prep plus; (as well as) en plus de **2** adj (factor) & El positif, -ive; **twenty p.** plus de vingt **3** (pl **plusses** ['plʌsɪz]) n **p. (sign)** (signe m) plus m; **that's a p.** c'est un plus

ply [plaɪ] (pt & pp plied) **1** vt (trade) exercer; **to p. sb with questions** bombarder qn de questions **2** vi **to p. between** (travel) faire la navette entre

p.m. [pi:'em] adv (afternoon) de l'après-midi; (evening) du soir

pneumonia [njuː'məʊnɪə] n pneumonie f

poach [pəʊtʃ] **1** vt (egg) pocher; (employee) débaucher **2** vi (hunt) braconner

PO Box [pi:'əʊbɒks] (abbr **Post Office Box**) n boîte f postale, BP f

pocket ['pɒkɪt] **1** n poche f; **to be out of p.** en être de sa poche; **p. calculator** calculette f; **p. money** argent m de poche **2** vt (put in pocket) empocher; Fam (steal) rafler ∎ **pocketbook** n Am (handbag) sac m à main ∎ **pocketful** n **a p. of** une pleine poche de

podium ['pəʊdɪəm] n podium m

poem ['pəʊɪm] n poème m ∎ **poet** n poète m ∎ **poetic** [pəʊ'etɪk] adj poétique ∎ **poetry** n poésie f

poignant ['pɔɪnjənt] adj poignant

point [pɔɪnt] **1** n (a) (of knife, needle) pointe f; Br **points** (for train) aiguillage m (b) (dot, score, degree, argument) point m; (location) endroit m; (importance) intérêt m; **to make a p. of doing sth** mettre un point d'honneur à faire qch; **you have a p.** tu as raison; **there's no p. (in) staying** ça ne sert à rien de rester; **to get to the p.** en arriver au fait; **at this p. in time** en ce moment; **to be on the p. of doing sth** être sur le point de faire qch; **his good points** ses qualités fpl; **p. of view** point m de vue (c) Math **three p. five** trois virgule cinq
2 vt (aim) diriger; (camera, gun) braquer (**at** sur); **to p. one's finger at sb**

montrer qn du doigt; **to p. sth out** *(show)* montrer qch; *(error, fact)* signaler qch

3 *vi* **to p. at** *or* **to sb/sth** *(with finger)* montrer qn/qch du doigt; **to p. north** *(of arrow, compass)* indiquer le nord

point-blank [pɔɪnt'blæŋk] **1** *adj (refusal)* catégorique; **at p. range** à bout portant **2** *adv (refuse)* (tout) net

pointed ['pɔɪntɪd] *adj* pointu; *(beard)* en pointe; *Fig (remark, criticism)* pertinent

pointer ['pɔɪntə(r)] *n (on dial)* aiguille *f*; *(stick)* baguette *f*; *(clue)* indice *m*

pointless ['pɔɪntləs] *adj* inutile

poise [pɔɪz] *n (composure)* assurance *f*; *(grace)* grâce *f* ■ **poised** *adj (composed)* calme; *(hanging)* suspendu; *(balanced)* en équilibre; **to be p. to do sth** *(ready)* être prêt à faire qch

poison ['pɔɪzən] **1** *n* poison *m*; *(of snake)* venin *m* **2** *vt* empoisonner ■ **poisonous** *adj (fumes, substance)* toxique; *(snake)* venimeux, -euse; *(plant)* vénéneux, -euse

poke [pəʊk] **1** *vt (person)* donner un coup à; *(object)* tâter; *(fire)* attiser; **to p. sth into sth** enfoncer qch dans qch; **to p. one's finger at sb** pointer son doigt vers qn; *Fig* **to p. one's nose into sth** mettre son nez dans qch **2** *vi* **to p. at sth** *(with finger, stick)* tâter qch

poker[1] ['pəʊkə(r)] *n (for fire)* tisonnier *m*

poker[2] ['pəʊkə(r)] *n (card game)* poker *m*

Poland ['pəʊlənd] *n* la Pologne ■ **Pole** *n* Polonais, -e *mf* ■ **Polish** ['pəʊlɪʃ] **1** *adj* polonais **2** *n (language)* polonais *m*

polar ['pəʊlə(r)] *adj* polaire; **p. bear** ours *m* blanc

Polaroid® ['pəʊlərɔɪd] *n (camera, photo)* Polaroid® *m*

pole[1] [pəʊl] *n (rod)* perche *f*; *(fixed)* poteau *m*; *(for flag)* hampe *f*; **p. vault** *or* **vaulting** saut *m* à la perche

pole[2] [pəʊl] *n Geog* pôle *m*; **North/ South P.** pôle *m* Nord/Sud

police [pə'li:s] **1** *n* police *f* **2** *adj (inquiry, dog)* policier, -ère; **p. car** voiture *f* de police; **p. station** poste *m* de police **3** *vt (city, area)* maintenir l'ordre dans ■ **policeman** *(pl* **-men)** *n* agent *m* de police ■ **policewoman** *(pl* **-women)** *n* agent *m* de police

policy ['pɒlɪsɪ] *(pl* **-ies)** *n* **(a)** *(of government, organization)* politique *f* **(b)** **(insurance) p.** police *f* (d'assurance)

polio ['pəʊlɪəʊ] *n* polio *f*

polish ['pɒlɪʃ] **1** *n (for shoes)* cirage *m*; *(for floor, furniture)* cire *f*; *(for nails)* vernis *m*; *Fig* raffinement *m*; **to give sth a p.** faire briller qch

2 *vt (floor, table, shoes)* cirer; *(metal)* astiquer; *(style)* polir; *Fam* **to p. off** *(food)* avaler; *(drink)* descendre; *(work)* expédier; **to p. up one's French** travailler son français

polite [pə'laɪt] (-**er**, -**est**) *adj* poli (**to** *or* **with** avec) ■ **politely** *adv* poliment

political [pə'lɪtɪkəl] *adj* politique ■ **politically** *adv* **p. correct** politiquement correct

politician [pɒlɪ'tɪʃən] *n* homme *m*/ femme *f* politique

politics ['pɒlɪtɪks] *n* politique *f*

poll [pəʊl] **1** *n (voting)* scrutin *m*; **to go to the polls** aller aux urnes; **(opinion) p.** sondage *m* (d'opinion) **2** *vt (votes)* obtenir; *(people)* sonder

pollen ['pɒlən] *n* pollen *m*

polling ['pəʊlɪŋ] *n (election)* élections *fpl*; *Br* **p. station**, *Am* **p. place** bureau *m* de vote

pollute [pə'lu:t] *vt* polluer ■ **pollution** *n* pollution *f*

polo ['pəʊləʊ] *n (sport)* polo *m*; **p. neck** *(sweater, neckline)* col *m* roulé

polyester [pɒlɪ'estə(r)] *n* polyester *m*; **p. shirt** chemise *f* en polyester

polythene ['pɒlɪθi:n] *n Br* polyéthylène *m*; **p. bag** sac *m* en plastique

pompous ['pɒmpəs] *adj* pompeux, -euse

pond [pɒnd] *n* étang *m*; *(smaller)* mare *f*; *(artificial)* bassin *m*

ponder ['pɒndə(r)] **1** *vt* réfléchir à **2** *vi*

to p. (over sth) réfléchir (à qch)

pong [pɒŋ] *Br Fam* **1** *n (smell)* puanteur *f* **2** *vi* puer

pony ['pəʊnɪ] *(pl* **-ies)** *n* poney *m* ■ **ponytail** *n* queue *f* de cheval

poodle ['puːdəl] *n* caniche *m*

pool¹ [puːl] *n (puddle)* flaque *f*; *(of blood)* mare *f*; *(for swimming)* piscine *f*

pool² [puːl] *n* **1** *(of money, helpers)* réserve *f*; *(of typists)* pool *m*; *Br* **the (football) pools** = concours de pronostics des matchs de football **2** *vt (share)* mettre en commun

pool³ [puːl] *n (game)* billard *m* américain

poor [pʊə(r)] **1** (**-er, -est**) *adj (not rich)* pauvre; *(bad)* mauvais; *(chances)* maigre; *(harvest, reward)* faible; **to be in p. health** ne pas bien se porter **2** *npl* **the p.** les pauvres *mpl* ■ **poorly 1** *adv* mal; *(clothed, furnished)* pauvrement **2** *adj Br Fam* malade

pop¹ [pɒp] **1** *exclam* pan! **2** *n (noise)* bruit *m* sec; **to go p.** faire pan **3** *(pt & pp* **-pp-)** *vt* (**a**) *(balloon)* crever; *(cork)* faire sauter (**b**) *Fam (put)* mettre **4** *vi* (**a**) *(burst)* éclater; *(of cork)* sauter (**b**) *Br Fam* **to p. in** passer; **to p. out** sortir (un instant); **to p. up** surgir

pop² [pɒp] **1** *n (music)* pop *f* **2** *adj (concert, singer, group)* pop *inv*

pop³ [pɒp] *n Am Fam (father)* papa *m*

pop⁴ [pɒp] *n Am (soda)* **p.** *(drink)* soda *m*

popcorn ['pɒpkɔːn] *n* pop-corn *m inv*

pope [pəʊp] *n* pape *m*

poplar ['pɒplə(r)] *n (tree, wood)* peuplier *m*

poppy ['pɒpɪ] *(pl* **-ies)** *n (red, wild)* coquelicot *m*; *(cultivated)* pavot *m*

Popsicle® ['pɒpsɪkəl] *n Am (ice lolly)* ≃ Esquimau® *m*

popular ['pɒpjʊlə(r)] *adj* populaire; *(fashionable)* à la mode; *(restaurant)* qui a beaucoup de succès ■ **popularity** [-'lærətɪ] *n* popularité *f* (**with** auprès de)

populated ['pɒpjʊleɪtɪd] *adj* **densely/sparsely populated** très/peu peuplé

population [pɒpjʊ'leɪʃən] *n* population *f*

porcelain ['pɔːsəlɪn] *n* porcelaine *f*

porch [pɔːtʃ] *n* porche *m*; *Am (veranda)* véranda *f*

pore [pɔː(r)] **1** *n (of skin)* pore *m* **2** *vi* **to p. over sth** *(book, question)* étudier qch de près

pork [pɔːk] *n (meat)* porc *m*; **p. pie** ≃ pâté *m* en croûte

pornography [pɔː'nɒɡrəfɪ] *n* pornographie *f*

porridge ['pɒrɪdʒ] *n* porridge *m*

port¹ [pɔːt] *n (harbour)* port *m*; **p. of call** escale *f*

port² [pɔːt] *n Naut (left-hand side)* bâbord *m*

port³ [pɔːt] *n (wine)* porto *m*

portable ['pɔːtəbəl] *adj* portable

porter ['pɔːtə(r)] *n (for luggage)* porteur *m*; *(door attendant)* chasseur *m*

portfolio [pɔːt'fəʊlɪəʊ] *(pl* **-os)** *n (for documents)* porte-documents *m inv*; *(of shares, government minister)* portefeuille *m*

porthole ['pɔːthəʊl] *n* hublot *m*

portion ['pɔːʃən] *n* partie *f*; *(share, helping)* portion *f*

portrait ['pɔːtreɪt, 'pɔːtrɪt] *n* portrait *m*

portray [pɔː'treɪ] *vt (describe)* dépeindre ■ **portrayal** *n (description)* tableau *m*

Portugal ['pɔːtjʊɡəl] *n* le Portugal ■ **Portuguese** [-'ɡiːz] **1** *adj* portugais **2** *n (person)* Portugais, -e *mf*; *(language)* portugais *m*; **the P.** *(people)* les Portugais

pose [pəʊz] **1** *n (position)* pose *f* **2** *vt (question)* poser; *(threat)* représenter **3** *vi* poser (**for** pour); **to p. as a lawyer** se faire passer pour un avocat

posh [pɒʃ] *adj Fam (smart)* chic *inv*

position [pə'zɪʃən] *n* **1** *n (place, posture, opinion)* position *f*; *(of building, town)* emplacement *m*; *(job, circumstances)* situation *f*; **in a p. to do sth** en mesure de faire qch; **in p.** en place **2** *vt (put)* placer; *(troops)* poster

positive ['pɒzɪtɪv] *adj (person, answer, test)* positif, -ive; *(progress, change)* réel *(f* réelle)*; *certain* (**of** de; **that** que) ■ **positively** *adv (identify)* formellement; *(think, react)* de façon positive; *(for emphasis)* véritablement

possess [pə'zes] *vt* posséder ■ **possession** *n (ownership)* possession *f; (thing possessed)* bien *m;* **to be in p. of sth** être en possession de qch

possessive [pə'zesɪv] **1** *adj* possessif, -ive **2** *adj & n (in grammar)* possessif *(m)*

possibility [pɒsə'bɪlətɪ] *(pl* **-ies)** *n* possibilité *f*

possible ['pɒsəbəl] *adj* possible; **it is p. (for us) to do it** il (nous) est possible de le faire; **it is p. that...** il est possible que... (*+ subjunctive);* **as soon as p.** dès que possible

possibly ['pɒsəblɪ] *adv* (**a**) *(perhaps)* peut-être (**b**) *(for emphasis)* **to do all one p. can** faire tout son possible (**to do** pour faire); **he cannot p. stay** il ne peut absolument pas rester

post- [pəʊst] *pref* post-; **post-1800** après 1800

post¹ [pəʊst] **1** *n Br (postal system)* poste *f; (letters)* courrier *m;* **by p.** par la poste; **p. office** *(bureau m* de) poste *f* **2** *vt (letter)* poster; **to keep sb posted** tenir qn au courant ■ **postbox** *n Br* boîte *f* aux lettres ■ **postcard** *n* carte *f* postale ■ **postcode** *n Br* code *m* postal ■ **postdate** *vt* postdater ■ **postman** *(pl* **-men)** *n Br* facteur *m* ■ **postmark** *n* cachet *m* de la poste

post² [pəʊst] **1** *n (job, place)* poste *m* **2** *vt (sentry, guard)* poster; *Br (employee)* affecter (**to** à)

post³ [pəʊst] *n (pole)* poteau *m; (of door, bed)* montant *m; (finishing or winning p.* (in race) poteau *m* d'arrivée

postage ['pəʊstɪdʒ] *n* affranchissement *m* (**to** pour); **p. paid** port *m* payé; **p. stamp** timbre-poste *m*

postal ['pəʊstəl] *adj (services)* postal; *(vote)* par correspondance; *Br* **p. order** mandat *m* postal

poster ['pəʊstə(r)] *n* affiche *f; (for decoration)* poster *m*

postgraduate [pəʊst'grædjʊət] **1** *adj* de troisième cycle **2** *n* étudiant, -e *mf* de troisième cycle

posthumous ['pɒstjʊməs] *adj* posthume

postmortem [pəʊst'mɔːtəm] *adj & n* **p. (examination)** autopsie *f* (**on** de)

postpone [pəʊs'pəʊn] *vt* reporter

posture ['pɒstʃə(r)] *n (of body)* posture *f; Fig* attitude *f*

postwar ['pəʊstwɔː(r)] *adj* d'après-guerre

posy ['pəʊzɪ] *(pl* **-ies)** *n* petit bouquet *m*

pot¹ [pɒt] *n* pot *m; (for cooking)* casserole *f; Fam* **to go to p.** aller à la ruine

pot² [pɒt] *n Fam (drug)* hasch *m*

potato [pə'teɪtəʊ] *(pl* **-oes)** *n* pomme *f* de terre; *Br* **p. crisps,** *Am* **p. chips** chips *fpl*

potent ['pəʊtənt] *adj* puissant; *(drink)* fort

potential [pə'tenʃəl] **1** *adj* potentiel, -elle **2** *n* potentiel *m;* **to have p.** avoir du potentiel

pothole ['pɒthəʊl] *n (in road)* nid-de-poule *m; (cave)* caverne *f*

potion ['pəʊʃən] *n* potion *f*

potter ['pɒtə(r)] **1** *n (person)* potier, -ère *mf* **2** *vi Br* **to p. about** *(do odd jobs)* bricoler ■ **pottery** *n (art)* poterie *f; (objects)* poteries *fpl;* **a piece of p.** une poterie

potty¹ ['pɒtɪ] *n (for baby)* pot *m*

potty² ['pɒtɪ] **(-ier, -iest)** *adj Br Fam (mad)* dingue

pouch [paʊtʃ] *n* bourse *f; (for tobacco)* blague *f*

poultry ['pəʊltrɪ] *n* volaille *f*

pounce [paʊns] *vi (of animal)* bondir (**on** sur); *(of person)* se précipiter (**on** sur)

pound¹ [paʊnd] *n* (**a**) *(weight)* livre *f* (= 453,6 *g*) (**b**) **p. (sterling)** livre *f* (sterling)

pound² [paʊnd] *n (for cars, dogs)* fourrière *f*

pound³ [paʊnd] 1 *vt Mil (town)* pilonner 2 *vi (of heart)* battre à tout rompre

pour [pɔː(r)] 1 *vt* verser; **to p. sb a drink** verser à boire à qn 2 *vi* **it's pouring** il pleut à verse

▸ **pour down** *vi* **it's pouring down** il pleut à verse

▸ **pour in** 1 *vt sep (liquid)* verser 2 *vi (of water, sunshine)* entrer à flots; *Fig (of people, money)* affluer

▸ **pour off** *vt sep (liquid)* vider

▸ **pour out** 1 *vt sep (liquid)* verser; *Fig (anger, grief)* déverser 2 *vi (of liquid)* se déverser; *Fig (of people)* sortir en masse (**from** de)

pout [paʊt] *vi* faire la moue

poverty ['pɒvətɪ] *n* pauvreté *f*

powder ['paʊdə(r)] 1 *n* poudre *f*; **p. puff** houppette *f*; **p. room** toilettes *fpl* pour dames 2 *vt (body, skin)* poudrer; **to p. one's face** *or* **nose** se poudrer ■ **powdered** *adj (milk, eggs)* en poudre

power ['paʊə(r)] 1 *n (ability, authority)* pouvoir *m*; *(strength, nation)* puissance *f*; *(energy)* énergie *f*; *(electric current)* courant *m*; **to be in p.** être au pouvoir; **to have sb in one's p.** tenir qn à sa merci; *Br* **p. failure** *or* **cut** coupure *f* de courant; *Br* **p. station**, *Am* **p. plant** centrale *f* électrique; *Aut* **p. steering** direction *f* assistée

2 *vt (provide with power)* actionner

powerful ['paʊəfəl] *adj* puissant; *(drug)* fort ■ **powerless** *adj* impuissant (**to do** à faire)

PR [piː'ɑː(r)] *(abbr* public relations*) n* RP *fpl*

practical ['præktɪkəl] *adj (tool, knowledge, solution)* pratique; **to be p.** *(of person)* avoir l'esprit pratique; **p. joke** farce *f*

practically ['præktɪkəlɪ] *adv (almost)* pratiquement

practice ['præktɪs] 1 *n (action, exercise, custom)* pratique *f*; *(in sport)* entraînement *m*; *(surgery)* centre *m* médical; **in p.** *(in reality)* dans la *ou* en pratique; **to put sth into p.** mettre qch en pratique; **to be out of p.** avoir perdu l'habitude 2 *vti Am* = **practise**

practise ['præktɪs] *(Am* **practice***)* 1 *vt (sport, language, art, religion)* pratiquer; *(medicine, law)* exercer; *(musical instrument)* travailler

2 *vi (of musician)* s'exercer; *(of sportsperson)* s'entraîner; *(of doctor, lawyer)* exercer ■ **practising** *adj (doctor, lawyer)* en exercice; *Rel* pratiquant

practitioner [præk'tɪʃənə(r)] *n* **general p.** (médecin *m*) généraliste *m*

pragmatic [præg'mætɪk] *adj* pragmatique

Prairie ['preərɪ] *n* **the P.** *(in USA)* la (Grande) Prairie; *(in Canada)* les Prairies *fpl*

praise [preɪz] 1 *n* éloges *mpl* 2 *vt* faire l'éloge de; *(God)* louer; **to p. sb for doing** *or* **having done sth** louer qn d'avoir fait qch

pram [præm] *n Br* landau *m (pl* -aus*)*

prank [præŋk] *n* farce *f*

prawn [prɔːn] *n* crevette *f* rose

pray [preɪ] 1 *vt* **to p. that…** prier pour que… (+ *subjunctive*) 2 *vi* prier; *Fig* **to p. for good weather** prier pour qu'il fasse beau

prayer [preə(r)] *n* prière *f*

pre- [priː-] *pref* **pre-1800** avant 1800

preach [priːtʃ] *vti* prêcher; **to p. to sb** prêcher qn; *Fig* faire la morale à qn ■ **preacher** *n* prédicateur, -trice *mf*

prearrange [priːə'reɪndʒ] *vt* arranger à l'avance

precarious [prɪ'keərɪəs] *adj* précaire

precaution [prɪ'kɔːʃən] *n* précaution *f*; **as a p.** par précaution

precede [prɪ'siːd] *vti* précéder

precedence ['presɪdəns] *n* **to take p. over sb** avoir la préséance sur qn; **to take p. over sth** passer avant qch

precedent ['presɪdənt] *n* précédent *m*

precinct ['priːsɪŋkt] *n Br (for shopping)* zone *f* commerçante piétonnière; *Am (electoral district)* circonscription *f*; *Am (police district)* secteur *m*

precious [ˈpreʃəs] **1** *adj* précieux, -euse **2** *adv* **p. little** très peu (de)

precipice [ˈpresɪpɪs] *n* précipice *m*

precipitate [prɪˈsɪpɪteɪt] *vt* (*hasten, throw*) & *Chem* précipiter

precise [prɪˈsaɪs] *adj* (*exact*) précis; (*meticulous*) méticuleux, -euse **= precisely** *adv* précisément; **at three o'clock p.** à trois heures précises **= precision** [-ˈsɪʒən] *n* précision *f*

preclude [prɪˈkluːd] *vt* (*prevent*) empêcher (**from doing** de faire); (*possibility*) exclure

precocious [prɪˈkəʊʃəs] *adj* précoce

preconception [priːkənˈsepʃən] *n* idée *f* préconçue

precondition [priːkənˈdɪʃən] *n* condition *f* préalable

predator [ˈpredətə(r)] *n* prédateur *m*

predecessor [ˈpriːdɪsesə(r)] *n* prédécesseur *m*

predicament [prɪˈdɪkəmənt] *n* situation *f* difficile

predict [prɪˈdɪkt] *vt* prédire **= predictable** *adj* prévisible **= prediction** *n* prédiction *f*

predispose [priːdɪsˈpəʊz] *vt* prédisposer (**to do** à faire)

predominant [prɪˈdɒmɪnənt] *adj* prédominant **= predominate** *vi* prédominer (**over** sur)

pre-empt [priːˈempt] *vt* devancer

preface [ˈprefɪs] *n* (*of book*) préface *f*

prefect [ˈpriːfekt] *n Br Sch* = élève chargé de la surveillance

prefer [prɪˈfɜː(r)] (*pt* & *pp* -**rr**-) *vt* préférer (**to** à); **to p. to do sth** préférer faire qch **= preferable** [ˈprefərəbəl] *adj* préférable (**to** à)

preference [ˈprefərəns] *n* préférence *f* (**for** pour); **in p. to** plutôt que

prefix [ˈpriːfɪks] *n* (*before word*) préfixe *m*

pregnant [ˈpregnənt] *adj* (*woman*) enceinte; (*animal*) pleine; **five months p.** enceinte de cinq mois **= pregnancy** (*pl* -**ies**) *n* grossesse *f*; **p. test** test *m* de grossesse

prehistoric [priːhɪˈstɒrɪk] *adj* préhistorique

prejudge [priːˈdʒʌdʒ] *vt* (*question*) préjuger de; (*person*) juger sans connaître

prejudice [ˈpredʒədɪs] **1** *n* (*bias*) préjugé *m* **2** *vt* (*bias*) prévenir (**against/in favour of** contre/en faveur de); (*harm*) nuire à **= prejudiced** *adj* **to be p.** avoir des préjugés (**against/in favour of** contre/en faveur de)

preliminary [prɪˈlɪmɪnərɪ] *adj* préliminaire **= preliminaries** *npl* préliminaires *mpl*

prelude [ˈpreljuːd] *n* prélude *m* (**to** à)

premature [*Br* ˈprematʃʊə(r), *Am* priːməˈtʃʊər] *adj* prématuré

premeditate [priːˈmedɪteɪt] *vt* préméditer

premier [*Br* ˈpremɪə(r), *Am* prɪˈmɪər] *n* Premier ministre *m*

première [*Br* ˈpremɪeə(r), *Am* prɪˈmɪər] *n* (*of play, film*) première *f*

premises [ˈpremɪsɪz] *npl* locaux *mpl*; **on the p.** sur place

premium [ˈpriːmɪəm] *n Fin* (*for insurance*) prime *f*; (*additional sum*) supplément *m*

premonition [*Br* preməˈnɪʃən, *Am* priːməˈnɪʃən] *n* prémonition *f*

prenatal [priːˈneɪtəl] *adj Am* prénatal

preoccupy [priːˈɒkjʊpaɪ] (*pt* & *pp* -**ied**) *vt* préoccuper au plus haut point; **to be preoccupied** être préoccupé (**with** par) **= preoccupation** *n* préoccupation *f* (**with** pour)

prep [prep] *adj* **p. school** *Br* école *f* primaire privée; *Am* école *f* secondaire privée

pre-packed [priːˈpækt] *adj* (*meat, vegetables*) préemballé

prepaid [priːˈpeɪd] *adj* prépayé

preparation [prepəˈreɪʃən] *n* préparation *f*; **preparations** préparatifs *mpl* (**for** de)

preparatory [prəˈpærətərɪ] *adj* préparatoire; **p. school** *Br* école *f* primaire privée; *Am* école *f* secondaire privée

prepare [prɪ'peə(r)] **1** *vt* préparer (**sth for** qch pour; **sb for** qn à) **2** *vi* se préparer pour; **to p. to do sth** se préparer à faire qch ■ **prepared** *adj (ready)* prêt (**to do** à faire); **to be p. for sth** s'attendre à qch

preposition [prepə'zɪʃən] *n* préposition *f*

preposterous [prɪ'pɒstərəs] *adj* ridicule

prerecorded [priːrɪ'kɔːdɪd] *adj* préenregistré

prerequisite [priː'rekwɪzɪt] *n* (condition *f*) préalable *m*

prerogative [prɪ'rɒgətɪv] *n* prérogative *f*

preschool ['priːskuːl] *adj* préscolaire

prescribe [prɪ'skraɪb] *vt (of doctor)* prescrire ■ **prescribed** *adj (textbook)* (inscrit) au programme ■ **prescription** *n (for medicine)* ordonnance *f*; **on p.** sur ordonnance

presence ['prezəns] *n* présence *f*; **in the p. of** en présence de; **p. of mind** présence *f* d'esprit

present¹ ['prezənt] **1** *adj* (**a**) *(in attendance)* présent (**at** à; **in** dans) (**b**) *(current)* actuel, -elle; **the p. tense** le présent **2** *n* **the p.** *(time, tense)* le présent; **for the p.** pour l'instant; **at p.** en ce moment ■ **present-day** *adj* actuel, -elle ■ **presently** *adv (soon)* bientôt; *Am (now)* actuellement

present²1 ['prezənt] *n (gift)* cadeau *m* **2** [prɪ'zent] *vt (show, introduce)* présenter (**to** à); *(concert, film)* donner; **to p. sb with** *(gift)* offrir à qn; *(prize)* remettre à qn ■ **presentable** [prɪ'zentəbəl] *adj (person, appearance)* présentable ■ **presenter** [prɪ'zentə(r)] *n* présentateur, -trice *mf*

presentation [prezən'teɪʃən] *n* présentation *f*; *(of prize)* remise *f*

preservation [prezə'veɪʃən] *n (of building)* conservation *f*; *(of species)* protection *f*

preservative [prɪ'zɜːvətɪv] *n* conservateur *m*

preserve [prɪ'zɜːv] **1** *n (jam)* confiture

f **2** *vt (keep, maintain)* conserver; *(fruit)* mettre en conserve

preside [prɪ'zaɪd] *vi* présider; **to p. over** *or* **at a meeting** présider une réunion

presidency ['prezɪdənsɪ] *(pl* **-ies)** *n* présidence *f*

president ['prezɪdənt] *n (of country)* président, -e *mf* ■ **presidential** [-'denʃəl] *adj* présidentiel, -elle

press¹ [pres] *n* (**a**) **the p.** *(newspapers)* la presse; **p. conference** conférence *f* de presse; **p. release** communiqué *m* de presse (**b**) *(machine)* presse *f*; *(for making wine)* pressoir *m*; *(printing)* **p.** presse *f*

press² [pres] **1** *n* **to give sth a p.** *(clothes)* repasser qch; **p. stud** bouton-pression *m* **2** *vt (button, doorbell)* appuyer sur; *(hand)* serrer; *(clothes)* repasser; **to p. sb to do sth** presser qn de faire qch **3** *vi (push)* appuyer (**on** sur); *(of weight)* faire pression (**on** sur) ■ **press-up** *n (exercise)* pompe *f*

▸ **press down** *vt insep (button)* appuyer sur

▸ **press for** *vt sep (demand)* exiger

▸ **press on** *vi (carry on)* continuer

pressed [prest] *adj* **to be hard p.** *(in difficulties)* être en difficulté; **to be p. for time** être pressé par le temps

pressing ['presɪŋ] *adj (urgent)* pressant

pressure ['preʃə(r)] **1** *n* pression *f*; **to be under p.** être stressé; **to put p. on sb (to do sth)** faire pression sur qn (pour qu'il fasse qch) **2** *vt* **to p. sb to do sth** *or* **into doing sth** faire pression sur qn pour qu'il fasse qch

pressurize ['preʃəraɪz] *vt* **to p. sb (into doing sth)** faire pression sur qn (pour qu'il fasse qch)

prestige [pre'stiːʒ] *n* prestige *m* ■ **prestigious** [pres'tɪdʒəs, *Am* pre'stiːdʒəs] *adj* prestigieux, -euse

presume [prɪ'zjuːm] *vt (suppose)* présumer (**that** que) ■ **presumably** *adv* sans doute ■ **presumption** [-'zʌmp-ʃən] n présomption f

presumptuous [prɪ'zʌmptʃʊəs] adj présomptueux, -euse

pretence [prɪ'tens] (Am **pretense**) n (sham) simulation f; (claim, affectation) prétention f; **to make a p. of doing sth** feindre de faire qch; **under false pretences** sous des prétextes fallacieux

pretend [prɪ'tend] 1 vt (make believe) faire semblant (**to do** de faire); (claim, maintain) prétendre (**to do** faire; **that** que) 2 vi faire semblant

pretense [prɪ'tens] n Am = **pretence**

pretentious [prɪ'tenʃəs] adj prétentieux, -euse

pretext [ˈpriːtekst] n prétexte m; **on the p. of/that** sous prétexte de/que

pretty [ˈprɪtɪ] 1 (-ier, -iest) adj joli 2 adv Fam (rather, quite) assez; **p. well, p. much** (almost) pratiquement

prevail [prɪ'veɪl] vi (predominate) prédominer; (be successful) l'emporter (**over** sur); **to p. (up)on sb to do sth** persuader qn de faire qch ■ **prevailing** adj prédominant; (wind) dominant

prevalent [ˈprevələnt] adj très répandu

prevent [prɪ'vent] vt empêcher (**from doing** de faire) ■ **prevention** n prévention f

preview [ˈpriːvjuː] n (of film, play) avant-première f

previous [ˈpriːvɪəs] 1 adj précédent; **to have p. experience** avoir une expérience préalable 2 adv **p. to** avant ■ **previously** adv auparavant

prewar [ˈpriːˈwɔː(r)] adj d'avant-guerre

prey [preɪ] 1 n proie f; Fig **to be (a) p. to** être en proie à 2 vi **to p. on** (person) prendre pour cible; (fears, doubts) exploiter; **to p. on sb's mind** tourmenter qn

price [praɪs] 1 n prix m; **he wouldn't do it at any p.** il ne le ferait à aucun prix 2 adj (control, rise) des prix; **p. list**

tarif m 3 vt **it's priced at £5** ça coûte 5 livres ■ **priceless** adj (invaluable) qui n'a pas de prix

pricey [ˈpraɪsɪ] (-ier, -iest) adj Fam cher (f chère)

prick [prɪk] 1 n (of needle) piqûre f 2 vt (jab) piquer (**with** avec); (burst) crever ■ **prickly** (-ier, -iest) adj (plant) à épines; (animal) couvert de piquants; (beard) piquant

pride [praɪd] 1 n (satisfaction) fierté f; (self-esteem) amour-propre m; Pej (vanity) orgueil m; **to take p. in sth** mettre toute sa fierté dans qch 2 vt **to p. oneself on sth/on doing sth** s'enorgueillir de qch/de faire qch

priest [priːst] n prêtre m

prim [prɪm] (**primmer, primmest**) adj **p. (and proper)** (person) collet monté inv; (manner) guindé

primarily [Br ˈpraɪmərəlɪ, Am praɪ-ˈmerəlɪ] adv essentiellement

primary [ˈpraɪmərɪ] 1 adj (main) principal; Br **p. school** école f primaire 2 (pl -ies) n Am (election) primaire f

prime [praɪm] 1 adj (principal) principal; (importance) capital; (excellent) excellent; **P. Minister** Premier ministre m; Math **p. number** nombre m premier

2 n **in the p. of life** dans la fleur de l'âge

3 vt (surface) apprêter ■ **primer** n (a) (book) manuel m élémentaire (b) (paint) apprêt m

primitive [ˈprɪmɪtɪv] adj (original) primitif, -ive; (basic) de base

prince [prɪns] n prince m ■ **princess** n princesse f

principal [ˈprɪnsɪpəl] 1 adj (main) principal 2 n (of school) proviseur m; (of university) ≃ président, -e mf

principle [ˈprɪnsɪpəl] n principe m; **in p.** en principe; **on p.** par principe

print [prɪnt] 1 n (of finger, foot) empreinte f; (letters) caractères mpl; (engraving) estampe f; (photo) épreuve f; (fabric) imprimé m; **out of p.** (book) épuisé

2 vt (book, newspaper) imprimer; (photo) tirer; (write) écrire en script; Comptr **to p. out** imprimer ■ **printed** adj imprimé; **p. matter** imprimés mpl ■ **printing** n (technique, industry) imprimerie f; (action) tirage m ■ **p. error** faute f d'impression ■ **printout** n Comptr sortie f papier

printer ['prɪntə(r)] n (machine) imprimante f

prior ['praɪə(r)] **1** adj antérieur; (experience) préalable **2** adv **p. to sth** avant qch

priority [praɪ'ɒrɪtɪ] (pl -ies) n priorité f (**over** sur)

prison ['prɪzən] **1** n prison f; **in p.** en prison **2** adj (life, system) pénitentiaire; (camp) de prisonniers; **p. officer** gardien, -enne mf de prison ■ **prisoner** n prisonnier, -ère mf; **to take sb p.** faire qn prisonnier; **p. of war** prisonnier m de guerre

privacy ['praɪvəsɪ, Br 'prɪvəsɪ] n intimité f

private ['praɪvɪt] **1** adj privé; (lesson) particulier, -ère; (letter) confidentiel, -elle; (personal) personnel, -elle; (dinner, wedding) intime; **p. detective, p. investigator**, Fam **p. eye** détective m privé

2 n (**a**) **in p.** (not publicly) en privé; (have dinner, get married) dans l'intimité (**b**) (soldier) simple soldat m

privately ['praɪvɪtlɪ] adv (in private) en privé; (in one's heart of hearts) en son for intérieur; (personally) à titre personnel; **p. owned** (company) privé

privatize ['praɪvətaɪz] vt privatiser

privilege ['prɪvɪlɪdʒ] n privilège m ■ **privileged** adj privilégié; **to be p. to do sth** avoir le privilège de faire qch

prize¹ [praɪz] n prix m; (in lottery) lot m ■ **prizegiving** n distribution f des prix ■ **prizewinner** n (in contest) lauréat, -e mf; (in lottery) gagnant, -e mf

prize² [praɪz] vt (value) attacher de la valeur à

prize³ [praɪz] vt Br = **prise**

pro [prəʊ] (pl **pros**) n Fam (professional) pro mf

probable ['prɒbəbəl] adj probable (**that** que) ■ **probability** (pl -ies) n probabilité f; **in all p.** selon toute probabilité ■ **probably** adv probablement

probation [prə'beɪʃən] n **on p.** (criminal) en liberté surveillée; (in job) en période d'essai

probe [prəʊb] **1** n (device) sonde f; (inquiry) enquête f (**into** dans) **2** vt (prod) sonder; (inquire into) enquêter sur **3** vi **to p. into sth** (past, private life) fouiller dans qch ■ **probing** adj (question) perspicace

problem ['prɒbləm] n problème m; Fam **no p.!** pas de problème! ■ **problematic** adj problématique

procedure [prə'si:dʒə(r)] n procédure f

proceed [prə'si:d] vi (go on) se poursuivre; **to p. with sth** poursuivre qch; **to p. to do sth** se mettre à faire qch

proceedings [prə'si:dɪŋz] npl (events) opérations fpl; **to take (legal) p.** intenter un procès ■ **proceeds** ['prəʊsi:dz] npl recette f

process ['prəʊses] **1** n processus m; (method) procédé m; **in the p. of doing sth** en train de faire qch **2** vt (food, data) traiter; (film) développer; **processed food** aliments mpl conditionnés

procession [prə'seʃən] n défilé m

processor ['prəʊsesə(r)] n Comptr processeur m; **food p.** robot m de cuisine

proclaim [prə'kleɪm] vt proclamer (**that** que); **to p. sb king** proclamer qn roi

prod [prɒd] (pt & pp **-dd-**) vt (poke) donner un petit coup dans

prodigy ['prɒdɪdʒɪ] (pl -ies) n prodige m; **child p.** enfant mf prodige

produce¹ [prə'dju:s] vt (create) produire; (machine) fabriquer; (passport, ticket) présenter; (documents) fournir; (from bag, pocket) sortir; (film, play, *programme)* produire ■ **producer** *n* producteur, -trice *mf*

produce² ['prɒdjuːs] *n (products)* produits *mpl*

product ['prɒdʌkt] *n (article, creation)* & *Math* produit *m*

production [prə'dʌkʃən] *n* production *f; (of play)* mise *f* en scène; **to work on a p. line** travailler à la chaîne

productive [prə'dʌktɪv] *adj* productif, -ive ■ **productivity** [prɒdʌk'tɪvɪtɪ] *n* productivité *f*

profession [prə'feʃən] *n* profession *f*; **by p.** de profession ■ **professional 1** *adj* professionnel, -elle; *(man, woman)* qui exerce une profession libérale; *(army)* de métier; *(piece of work)* de professionnel **2** *n* professionnel, -elle *mf*

professor [prə'fesə(r)] *n Br* ≃ professeur *m* d'université; *Am* = enseignant d'université

proficient [prə'fɪʃənt] *adj* compétent (**in** en)

profile ['prəʊfaɪl] *n (of person, object)* profil *m; (description)* portrait *m*; **in p.** de profil; *Fig* **to keep a low p.** garder un profil bas

profit ['prɒfɪt] **1** *n* profit *m*, bénéfice *m*; **to sell at a p.** vendre à profit **2** *vi* **to p. by** *or* **from sth** tirer profit de qch ■ **profit-making** *adj (aiming to make profit)* à but lucratif; *(profitable)* rentable

profitable ['prɒfɪtəbəl] *adj (commercially)* rentable; *Fig (worthwhile)* profitable

profound [prə'faʊnd] *adj* profond ■ **profoundly** *adv* profondément

profusely [prə'fjuːslɪ] *adv (bleed)* abondamment; *(thank)* avec effusion; **to apologize p.** se confondre en excuses

programme ['prəʊɡræm] *(Am* **program) 1** *n (for play, political party, computer)* programme *m; (on TV, radio)* émission *f* **2** *(pt & pp* **-mm-***) vt (machine)* programmer ■ **programmer (computer) p.** programmer,

-euse *mf* ■ **programming** *n (computer)* p. programmation *f*

progress 1 ['prəʊɡres] *n* progrès *m*; **to make (good) p.** faire des progrès; **in p.** en cours **2** [prə'ɡres] *vi (advance, improve)* progresser; *(of story, meeting)* se dérouler

progressive [prə'ɡresɪv] *adj (gradual)* progressif, -ive; *(company, ideas, political party)* progressiste

prohibit [prə'hɪbɪt] *vt* interdire (**sb from doing** à qn de faire)

prohibitive [prə'hɪbɪtɪv] *adj* prohibitif, -ive

project 1 ['prɒdʒekt] *n (plan, undertaking)* projet *m; (at school)* dossier *m; Am (housing)* cité *f* HLM **2** [prə'dʒekt] *vt (propel, show)* projeter **3** [prə'dʒekt] *vi (protrude)* dépasser

projector [prə'dʒektə(r)] *n* projecteur *m*

proliferate [prə'lɪfəreɪt] *vi* proliférer

prolific [prə'lɪfɪk] *adj* prolifique

prologue ['prəʊlɒɡ] *n* prologue *m* (**to** de)

prolong [prə'lɒŋ] *vt* prolonger

prom [prɒm] *(abbr* **promenade)** *n* (**a**) *Br (at seaside)* front *m* de mer (**b**) *Am (dance)* bal *m* d'étudiants

promenade [prɒmə'nɑːd] *n Br (at seaside)* front *m* de mer

prominent ['prɒmɪnənt] *adj (important)* important; *(nose, chin)* proéminent ■ **prominently** *adv* bien en vue

promiscuous [prə'mɪskjʊəs] *adj (person)* qui a de multiples partenaires

promise ['prɒmɪs] **1** *n* promesse *f*; **to show p.** promettre **2** *vt* promettre (**to do sth** de faire); **to p. sth to sb, to p. sb sth** promettre qch à qn **3** *vi* **I p.!** je te le promets! ■ **promising** *adj* prometteur, -euse

promote [prə'məʊt] *vt (raise in rank, encourage)* promouvoir; *(advertise)* faire la promotion de ■ **promotion** *n* promotion *f*

prompt¹ [prɒmpt] **1** *adj (speedy)* rapide; *(punctual)* ponctuel, -elle **2** *adv* **at eight o'clock p.** à huit heures précises ■ **promptly** adv (rapidly) rapidement; (punctually) ponctuellement; (immediately) immédiatement

prompt² [prɒmpt] vt (a) (cause) provoquer; **to p. sb to do sth** pousser qn à faire qch (**b**) (actor) souffler à

prone [prəʊn] adj **to be p. to sth** être sujet, -ette à qch; **to be p. to do sth** avoir tendance à faire qch

pronoun ['prəʊnaʊn] n pronom m

pronounce [prə'naʊns] vt (say, articulate) prononcer ■ **pronunciation** [-nʌnsɪ'eɪʃən] n prononciation f

proof [pruːf] n (evidence) preuve f; (of book, photo) épreuve f; **p. of identity** pièce f d'identité ■ **proofreader** n correcteur, -trice mf

prop [prɒp] **1** n (physical support) support m; (in a play) accessoire m **2** (pt & pp **-pp-**) vt **to p. sth (up) against sth** appuyer qch contre qch; **to p. sth up** (building, tunnel) étayer qch; Fig (economy, regime) soutenir qch

propaganda [prɒpə'gændə] n propagande f

propel [prə'pel] (pt & pp **-ll-**) vt propulser ■ **propeller** n hélice f

proper ['prɒpə(r)] adj (**a**) (correct) vrai; (word) correct; **the village p.** le village proprement dit (**b**) (appropriate) bon (f bonne); (equipment) adéquat; (behaviour) convenable (**c**) Br (downright) véritable ■ **properly** adv (suitably) convenablement; (correctly) correctement

property ['prɒpətɪ] **1** (pl **-ies**) n (**a**) (land, house) propriété f; (possessions) biens mpl (**b**) (quality) propriété f **2** (market) immobilier; **p. developer** promoteur m immobilier

prophecy ['prɒfɪsɪ] (pl **-ies**) n prophétie f

prophet ['prɒfɪt] n prophète m

proportion [prə'pɔːʃən] n (ratio, part) proportion f; **proportions** (size) proportions fpl; **in p.** proportionné (**to** avec); **out of p.** disproportionné (**to** par rapport à) ■ **proportional, proportionate** adj proportionnel, -elle (**to** à)

proposal [prə'pəʊzəl] n proposition f; (plan) projet m; (for marriage) demande f en mariage ■ **proposition** [prɒpə'zɪʃən] n proposition f

propose [prə'pəʊz] **1** vt proposer; **to p. to do sth, to p. doing sth** (suggest) proposer de faire qch; (intend) se proposer de faire qch **2** vi **to p., to sb** demander qn en mariage

proprietor [prə'praɪətə(r)] n propriétaire mf

pros [prəʊz] npl **the p. and cons** le pour et le contre

prose [prəʊz] n prose f; Br (translation) thème m

prosecute ['prɒsɪkjuːt] vt (in law court) poursuivre (en justice) ■ **prosecution** n (in law court) poursuites fpl judiciaires; **the p.** (lawyers) ≃ le ministère public

prospect¹ ['prɒspekt] n (expectation, thought) perspective f; (chance, likelihood) perspectives fpl; (future) **prospects** perspectives fpl d'avenir ■ **prospective** [prə'spektɪv] adj (potential) potentiel, -elle; (future) futur

prospect² [prə'spekt] vi **to p. for gold** chercher de l'or

prospectus [prə'spektəs] n (publicity leaflet) prospectus m; Br (for university) guide m (de l'étudiant)

prosper ['prɒspə(r)] vi prospérer ■ **prosperity** [-'sperɪtɪ] n prospérité f ■ **prosperous** adj prospère

prostitute ['prɒstɪtjuːt] n (woman) prostituée f; **male p.** prostitué m ■ **prostitution** n prostitution f

prostrate ['prɒstreɪt] adj (lying flat) sur le ventre

protagonist [prəʊ'tægənɪst] n protagoniste mf

protect [prə'tekt] vt protéger (**from** or **against** de) ■ **protection** n protection f ■ **protective** adj (clothes, screen) de protection; (person, attitude) protecteur, -trice (**to** or **towards** envers)

protein ['prəʊtiːn] n protéine f

protest [prə'test] **1** ['prəʊtest] n protestation f (**against** contre); **in p.** en signe de protestation (**at** contre) **2** vt protester contre; (*one's innocence*) protester de; **to p. that...** protester en disant que... **3** vi protester (**against** contre) ■ **protester** n contestataire mf

Protestant ['prɒtɪstənt] adj & n protestant, -e (mf)

protracted [prə'træktɪd] adj prolongé

protrude [prə'truːd] vi dépasser (**from** de); (*of tooth*) avancer ■ **protruding** adj (chin, veins, eyes) saillant

proud [praʊd] (**-er, -est**) adj (person) fier (f fière) (**of** de) ■ **proudly** adv fièrement

prove [pruːv] **1** vt prouver (**that** que); **to p. sb wrong** prouver que qn a tort **2** vi **to p. (to be) difficult** s'avérer difficile ■ **proven** adj (method) éprouvé

proverb ['prɒvɜːb] n proverbe m

provide [prə'vaɪd] **1** vt (supply) fournir; (service) offrir (**to** à); **to p. sb with sth** fournir qch à qn **2** vi **to p. for sb** (sb's needs) pourvoir aux besoins de qn; (sb's future) assurer l'avenir de qn; **to p. for sth** (make allowance for) prévoir qch ■ **provided, providing** conj **p. (that)...** pourvu que... (+ subjunctive)

province ['prɒvɪns] n province f; **in the provinces** en province ■ **provincial** [prə'vɪnʃəl] adj & n provincial, -e (mf)

provision [prə'vɪʒən] n (clause) disposition f; **provisions** (supplies) provisions fpl

provisional [prə'vɪʒənəl] adj provisoire

provocation [prɒvə'keɪʃən] n provocation f

provocative [prə'vɒkətɪv] adj provocateur, -trice

provoke [prə'vəʊk] vt provoquer; **to p. sb into doing sth** pousser qn à faire qch

prowl [praʊl] **1** n **to be on the p.** rôder **2** vi **to p. (around)** rôder

proxy ['prɒksɪ] (pl **-ies**) n **by p.** par procuration

prudent ['pruːdənt] adj prudent

prudish ['pruːdɪʃ] adj pudibond

prune[1] [pruːn] n (dried plum) pruneau m

prune[2] [pruːn] vt (tree, bush) tailler

pry [praɪ] **1** (pt & pp **pried**) vt Am **to p. open** forcer (avec un levier) **2** vi être indiscret, -ète; **to p. into sth** (meddle) mettre son nez dans qch; (sb's reasons) chercher à découvrir qch

PS [piː'es] (abbr **postscript**) n PS m

psalm [sɑːm] n psaume m

pseudonym ['sjuːdənɪm] n pseudonyme m

psychiatry [saɪ'kaɪətrɪ] n psychiatrie f ■ **psychiatric** [-kɪ'ætrɪk] adj psychiatrique ■ **psychiatrist** n psychiatre mf

psychic ['saɪkɪk] adj (paranormal) paranormal

psycho- ['saɪkəʊ] pref psycho- ■ **psychoanalyst** n psychanalyste mf

psychology [saɪ'kɒlədʒɪ] n psychologie f ■ **psychological** [-kə'lɒdʒɪkəl] adj psychologique ■ **psychologist** n psychologue mf

psychopath ['saɪkəʊpæθ] n psychopathe mf

PTO (abbr **please turn over**) TSVP

pub [pʌb] n Br pub m

puberty ['pjuːbətɪ] n puberté f

public ['pʌblɪk] **1** adj public, -ique; (library, swimming pool) municipal; **p. holiday** jour m férié; **p. school** Br école f privée; Am école f publique; **p. transport** transports mpl en commun **2** n public m; **in p.** en public

publication [pʌblɪ'keɪʃən] n publication f

publicity [pʌ'blɪsɪtɪ] n publicité f

publicize ['pʌblɪsaɪz] vt faire connaître au public

publicly ['pʌblɪklɪ] adv publiquement; **p. owned** à capitaux publics

publish ['pʌblɪʃ] vt publier ■ **publisher** n (person) éditeur, -trice mf; (company) maison f d'édition

pudding ['pʊdɪŋ] n (dish) pudding m; Br (dessert) dessert m

puddle ['pʌdəl] n flaque f (d'eau)

puff [pʌf] **1** n (of smoke) bouffée f; (of wind, air) souffle m; **p. pastry**, Am **p. paste** pâte f feuilletée **2** vt to **p. sth out** (cheeks, chest) gonfler qch **3** vi (of person) souffler; **to p. at a cigar** tirer sur un cigare

puke [pjuːk] vi Fam dégueuler

pull [pʊl] **1** n (attraction) attraction f; **to give sth a p.** tirer qch **2** vt (draw, tug) tirer; (tooth) arracher; (trigger) appuyer sur; (muscle) se froisser; Fig to **p. sth apart** or **to bits** or **to pieces** démolir qch **3** vi (tug) tirer (**on** sur)

▸ **pull along** vt sep (drag) traîner (**to** jusqu'à)

▸ **pull away 1** vt sep (move) éloigner; (snatch) arracher (**from** à) **2** vi (in vehicle) démarrer

▸ **pull back 1** vt sep retirer; (curtains) ouvrir **2** vi (withdraw) se retirer

▸ **pull down** vt sep (lower) baisser; (knock down) faire tomber; (demolish) démolir

▸ **pull in 1** vt sep (drag into room) faire entrer (de force); (rope) ramener; (stomach) rentrer **2** vi (arrive) arriver; (stop in vehicle) s'arrêter

▸ **pull off** vt sep (remove) enlever; Fig (plan, deal) réaliser

▸ **pull on** vt sep (boots, clothes) mettre

▸ **pull out 1** vt sep (tooth, hair) arracher; (cork, pin) enlever (**from** de); (from pocket, bag) sortir (**from** de) **2** vi (of car) déboîter; (of train) partir; (withdraw) se retirer (**of** de)

▸ **pull over 1** vt sep (drag) traîner (**to** jusqu'à); (knock down) faire tomber **2** vi (in vehicle) s'arrêter

▸ **pull through** vi (recover) s'en tirer

▸ **pull together** vt sep to **p. oneself together** se ressaisir

▸ **pull up 1** vt sep (socks, blinds) remonter; (haul up) hisser; (plant, tree) arracher; (stop) arrêter **2** vi (of car) s'arrêter

pullover ['pʊləʊvə(r)] n pull-over m

pulp [pʌlp] n (of fruit) pulpe f

pulse [pʌls] n Med pouls m

pump¹ [pʌmp] **1** n (machine) pompe f;

Br **petrol p.**, Am **gas p.** pompe f à essence **2** vt pomper; **to p. sth up** (mattress) gonfler qch

pump² [pʌmp] n (flat shoe) escarpin m; (for sports) tennis f

pumpkin ['pʌmpkɪn] n potiron m

pun [pʌn] n jeu m de mots

punch¹ [pʌntʃ] **1** n (blow) coup m de poing; **p. line** (of joke, story) chute f **2** vt (person) donner un coup de poing à; (sb's nose) donner un coup de poing sur ■ **punch-up** n Br Fam bagarre f

punch² [pʌntʃ] **1** n (for paper) perforeuse f; (for tickets) poinçonneuse f **2** vt (ticket) poinçonner; (with date) composter; (paper, card) perforer; **to p. a hole in sth** faire un trou dans qch

punch³ [pʌntʃ] n (drink) punch m

punctual ['pʌŋktʃʊəl] adj ponctuel, -elle ■ **punctually** adv à l'heure

punctuation [pʌŋktjʊ'eɪʃən] n ponctuation f; **p. mark** signe m de ponctuation

puncture ['pʌŋktʃə(r)] **1** n (in tyre) crevaison f; **to have a p.** crever **2** vt (tyre) crever **3** vi (of tyre) crever

pungent ['pʌndʒənt] adj âcre

punish ['pʌnɪʃ] vt punir (**for** de); **to p. sb for doing sth** punir qn pour avoir fait qch

punishment ['pʌnɪʃmənt] n punition f; (in law) peine f

punk [pʌŋk] n punk mf; **p. (rock)** le punk

punter ['pʌntə(r)] n Br (gambler) parieur, -euse mf; Fam (customer) client, -e m

puny ['pjuːnɪ] (**-ier, -iest**) adj chétif, -ive

pupil¹ ['pjuːpəl] n (student) élève mf

pupil² ['pjuːpəl] n (of eye) pupille f

puppet ['pʌpɪt] n marionnette f; **p. show** spectacle m de marionnettes

puppy ['pʌpɪ] (pl -ies) n (dog) chiot m

purchase ['pɜːtʃɪs] **1** n (action, thing bought) achat m **2** vt acheter (**from** à) ■ **purchaser** n acheteur, -euse mf

pure [pjʊə(r)] (**-er, -est**) adj pur

purée ['pjʊəreɪ] n purée f

purely ['pjʊəlɪ] adv purement

purge [pɜːdʒ] **1** n purge f **2** vt purger (of de)

purify ['pjʊərɪfaɪ] (pt & pp -ied) vt purifier

puritanical [pjʊərɪ'tænɪkəl] adj puritain

purity ['pjʊərətɪ] n pureté f

purple ['pɜːpəl] **1** adj violet, -ette **2** n violet m

purpose ['pɜːpəs] n (**a**) (aim) but m; on p. exprès; **for the purposes of** pour les besoins de (**b**) (determination) résolution f

purposely ['pɜːpəslɪ] adv exprès

purr [pɜː(r)] vi ronronner

purse [pɜːs] **1** n (for coins) porte-monnaie m inv; Am (handbag) sac m à main **2** vt to p. one's lips pincer les lèvres

pursue [pə'sjuː] vt poursuivre; (fame, pleasure) rechercher ■ **pursuit** n (of person) poursuite f; (of pleasure, glory) quête f; (of pleasure) occupation f

push [pʊʃ] **1** n (act of pushing, attack) poussée f; **to give sb/sth a p.** pousser qn/qch; **at a p.** à la rigueur
2 vt pousser (**to** or **as far as** jusqu'à); (button) appuyer sur; (lever) abaisser; (product) faire la promotion de; Fam (drugs) vendre; **to p. sth into/between** enfoncer qch dans/entre; Fig **to p. sb into doing sth** pousser qn à faire qch; **to p. sth off the table** faire tomber qch de la table (en le poussant)
3 vi pousser; (on button) appuyer (**on** sur)

▸ **push about, push around** vt sep Fam **to p. sb about** or **around** faire de qn ce que l'on veut

▸ **push aside** vt sep écarter

▸ **push down** vt sep (button) appuyer sur; (lever) abaisser

▸ **push in** vi Br (in queue) resquiller

▸ **push off** vi Fam ficher le camp

▸ **push on** vi (go on) continuer; **to p. on with sth** continuer qch

▸ **push over** vt sep faire tomber

▸ **push up** vt sep (lever, collar) relever; (sleeves) remonter; (increase) augmenter ■ **push-button** n bouton m; (of phone) touche f; **p. phone** téléphone m à touches ■ **pushchair** n Br poussette f ■ **push-up** n Am (exercise) pompe f

pushed [pʊʃt] adj **to be p. for time** être très pressé

pushy ['pʊʃɪ] (**-ier, -iest**) adj Fam batailleur, -euse

puss, pussy ['pʊs, 'pʊsɪ] (pl **-ies**) n Fam (cat) minou m

PUT [pʊt] (pt & pp **put**, pres p **putting**) vt mettre; (on flat surface) poser; (problem, argument) présenter (**to** à); (question) poser (**to** à); (say) dire; (estimate) évaluer (**at** à); **to p. money on a horse** parier sur un cheval; **to p. a lot of work into sth** beaucoup travailler à qch; **to p. it bluntly** pour parler franc

▸ **put across** vt sep (message, idea) faire comprendre (**to** à)

▸ **put aside** vt sep (money, object) mettre de côté

▸ **put away** vt sep (tidy away) ranger; **to p. sb away** (criminal) mettre qn en prison

▸ **put back** vt sep (replace, postpone) remettre; (telephone receiver) raccrocher; (clock) retarder

▸ **put by** vt sep (money) mettre de côté

▸ **put down** vt sep (on floor, table) poser; (a deposit) verser; (revolt) réprimer; (write down) inscrire; (attribute) attribuer (**to** à); (kill) faire piquer; **to p. oneself down** se rabaisser

▸ **put forward** vt sep (clock, meeting, argument) avancer; (candidate) proposer (**for** à)

▸ **put in 1** vt sep (into box) mettre dedans; (insert) introduire; (add) ajouter; (install) installer; (claim, application) soumettre; (time) passer (**doing** à faire) **2** vi **to p. in for sth** (new job, transfer) faire une demande de qch

▸ **put off** vt sep (postpone) remettre (à

plus tard); *(dismay)* déconcerter; **to p. off doing sth** retarder le moment de faire qch; **to p. sb off sth** dégoûter qn de qch

▸ **put on** *vt sep (clothes, shoe, record)* mettre; *(accent)* prendre; *(play, show)* monter; *(gas, radio)* allumer; *(clock)* avancer; **to p. on weight** prendre du poids; **she p. me on to you** elle m'a donné votre adresse; **p. me on to him!** *(on phone)* passez-le-moi!

▸ **put out** *vt sep (take outside)* sortir; *(arm, leg, hand)* tendre; *(gas, light)* éteindre; *(inconvenience)* déranger; *(upset)* vexer; *(report, statement)* publier; **to p. one's shoulder out** se démettre l'épaule

▸ **put through** *vt sep* **to p. sb through (to sb)** *(on phone)* passer qn (à qn)

▸ **put together** *vt sep (assemble)* assembler; *(meal, team)* composer; *(file, report)* préparer; *(collection)* rassembler

▸ **put up** *vt sep (lift)* lever; *(tent, fence)* monter; *(statue, ladder)* dresser; *(flag)* hisser; *(building)* construire; *(umbrella)* ouvrir; *(picture, poster)* mettre; *(price, numbers)* augmenter; *(resistance)* offrir; *(candidate)* présenter (**for** à); *(guest)* loger; **to p. sth up for sale** mettre qch en vente

▸ **put up with** *vt insep* supporter

putting ['pʌtɪŋ] *n (in golf)* putting *m*; **p. green** green *m*

puzzle ['pʌzəl] **1** *n (jigsaw)* puzzle *m*; *(game)* casse-tête *m inv*; *(mystery)* mystère *m* **2** *vt* laisser perplexe **3** *vi* **to p. over sth** essayer de comprendre qch ∎ **puzzled** *adj* perplexe

PVC [piːviːˈsiː] *n* PVC *m*

pyjamas [pəˈdʒɑːməz] *npl Br* pyjama *m*; **a pair of p.** un pyjama

pylon ['paɪlən] *n* pylône *m*

pyramid ['pɪrəmɪd] *n* pyramide *f*

Pyrex® ['paɪreks] *n* Pyrex® *m*; **P. dish** plat *m* en Pyrex®

Qq

Q, q [kjuː] n (letter) Q, q m inv

quack [kwæk] n (of duck) coin-coin m inv

quadruple [kwɒˈdruːpəl] vti quadrupler

quaint [kweɪnt] (-er, -est) adj (picturesque) pittoresque; (old-fashioned) vieillot, -otte; (odd) bizarre

quake [kweɪk] 1 n Fam tremblement m de terre 2 vi trembler (**with** de)

Quaker [ˈkweɪkə(r)] n Rel quaker, -eresse mf

qualification [kwɒlɪfɪˈkeɪʃən] n (diploma) diplôme m; (skill) compétence f; (modification) précision f

qualify [ˈkwɒlɪfaɪ] (pt & pp -ied) 1 vt (a) (make competent, in sport) qualifier (**for sth** pour qch) (b) (modify) nuancer 2 vi (of sportsperson) se qualifier (**for** pour); **to q. as a doctor** obtenir son diplôme de médecin; **to q. for sth** (be eligible) avoir droit à qch **■ qualified** adj (competent) compétent; (having diploma) diplômé; (support) mitigé

quality [ˈkwɒlətɪ] (pl -ies) n qualité f

quantity [ˈkwɒntɪtɪ] (pl -ies) n quantité f

quarantine [ˈkwɒrəntiːn] n quarantaine f

quarrel [ˈkwɒrəl] 1 n dispute f, querelle f 2 (Br -ll-, Am -l-) vi se disputer (**with** avec); **to q. with sth** ne pas être d'accord avec qch

quarry [ˈkwɒrɪ] (pl -ies) n (for stone) carrière f

quart [kwɔːt] n (liquid measurement) Br = 1,14 l, Am = 0,95 l

quarter¹ [ˈkwɔːtə(r)] n quart m; (of fruit, moon) quartier m; (division of year) trimestre m; Am & Can (money) pièce f de 25 cents; **q. (of a) pound** quart m de livre; Br **a q. past nine**, Am **a q. after nine** neuf heures et quart; **a q. to nine** neuf heures moins le quart

quarter² [ˈkwɔːtə(r)] n (district) quartier m; (living) **quarters** logements mpl; (of soldier) quartiers mpl

quarterfinal [kwɔːtəˈfaɪnəl] n quart m de finale

quarterly [ˈkwɔːtəlɪ] 1 adj (magazine, payment) trimestriel, -elle 2 adv tous les trimestres

quartet(te) [kwɔːˈtet] n (music, players) quatuor m; (jazz) **q.** quartette m

quartz [kwɔːts] 1 n quartz m 2 adj (watch) à quartz

quash [kwɒʃ] vt (rebellion) réprimer; (sentence) annuler

quasi- [ˈkweɪzaɪ] pref quasi-

quay [kiː] n quai m

queasy [ˈkwiːzɪ] (-ier, -iest) adj **to feel** or **be q.** avoir mal au cœur

Quebec [kwɪˈbek] n le Québec

queen [kwiːn] n reine f

queer [ˈkwɪə(r)] (-er, -est) adj (strange) bizarre

quench [kwentʃ] vt (thirst) étancher

query [ˈkwɪərɪ] 1 (pl -ies) n question f 2 (pt & pp -ied) vt mettre en question

quest [kwest] n quête f (**for** de)

question [ˈkwestʃən] 1 n question f; **there's no q. of it, it's out of the q.** c'est hors de question; **the matter/ person in q.** l'affaire/la personne en question; **q. mark** point *m* d'interrogation **2** *vt* interroger (**about** sur); *(doubt)* mettre en question

questionable ['kwestʃənəbəl] *adj* discutable

questionnaire [kwestʃə'neə(r)] *n* questionnaire *m*

queue [kjuː] *Br* **1** *n (of people)* queue *f; (of cars)* file *f;* **to form a q., to stand in a q.** faire la queue **2** *vi* **to q. (up)** faire la queue

quiche [kiːʃ] *n* quiche *f*

quick [kwɪk] **1** (**-er, -est**) *adj (rapid)* rapide; *(clever)* vif *(f* vive); **be q.!** fais vite!; **to have a q. shower/meal** se doucher/manger en vitesse **2** (**-er, -est**) *adv Fam* vite

quicken ['kwɪkən] **1** *vt* accélérer **2** *vi* s'accélérer

quickly ['kwɪklɪ] *adv* vite

quid [kwɪd] *n inv Br Fam (pound)* livre *f*

quiet ['kwaɪət] **1** (**-er, -est**) *adj (silent, still, peaceful)* tranquille, calme; *(machine, vehicle)* silencieux, -euse; *(person, voice, music)* doux *(f* douce); **to be** *or* **keep q.** *(say nothing)* se taire; *(make no noise)* ne pas faire de bruit; **to keep q. about sth, to keep sth q.** ne rien dire au sujet de qch; **q.!** silence! **2** *n Fam* **on the q.** *(secretly)* en cachette

quieten ['kwaɪətən] *Br* **1** *vt* **to q. (down)** calmer **2** *vi* **to q. down** se calmer

quietly ['kwaɪətlɪ] *adv* tranquillement; *(gently, not loudly)* doucement; *(silently)* silencieusement; *(secretly)*

en cachette; *(discreetly)* discrètement

quilt [kwɪlt] *n* édredon *m; Br* (**continental**) **q.** *(duvet)* couette *f*

quip [kwɪp] **1** *n* boutade *f* **2** *(pt & pp* **-pp-**) *vti* plaisanter

quirk [kwɜːk] *n (of character)* particularité *f* ■ **quirky** (**-ier, -iest**) *adj* bizarre

quit [kwɪt] *(pt & pp* **quit** *or* **quitted**, *pres p* **quitting**) **1** *vt (leave)* quitter; *Comptr* sortir de; **to q. doing sth** arrêter de faire qch **2** *vi (give up)* abandonner; *(resign)* démissionner; *Comptr* sortir

quite [kwaɪt] *adv (entirely)* tout à fait; *(really)* vraiment; *(fairly)* assez; **q. good** *(not bad)* pas mal du tout; **q. (so)!** exactement!; **q. a lot** pas mal *(of* de)

quits [kwɪts] *adj* quitte (**with** envers); **to call it q.** en rester là

quiver ['kwɪvə(r)] *vi (of voice)* trembler

quiz [kwɪz] **1** (*pl* **-zz-**) *n (on radio)* jeu *m* radiophonique; *(on TV)* jeu *m* télévisé; *(in magazine)* questionnaire *m* **2** *(pt & pp* **-zz-**) *vt* interroger

quota ['kwəʊtə] *n* quota *m*

quotation [kwəʊ'teɪʃən] *n (from author)* citation *f; (estimate)* devis *m;* **in q. marks** entre guillemets

quote [kwəʊt] **1** *n (from author)* citation *f; (estimate)* devis *m;* **in quotes** entre guillemets **2** *vt (author, passage)* citer; *(reference number)* rappeler; *(price)* indiquer **3** *vi* **to q. from** *(author, book)* citer

Rr

R, r [ɑ:(r)] *n* (*lettre*) R, r *m inv*
rabbi ['ræbaɪ] *n* rabbin *m*
rabbit ['ræbɪt] *n* lapin *m*
rabies ['reɪbi:z] *n* rage *f*
raccoon [rə'ku:n] *n* raton *m* laveur
race¹ [reɪs] **1** *n* (*contest*) course *f*
 2 *vt* **to r. (against** *or* **with)** sb faire
une course avec qn
 3 *vi* (*run*) courir ■ **racecourse** *n*
champ *m* de courses ■ **racehorse** *n*
cheval *m* de course ■ **racetrack** *n Am*
(*for horses*) champ *m* de courses; *Br*
(*for cars, bicycles*) piste *f* ■ **racing**
n courses *fpl*; **r. car** voiture *f* de course;
r. driver coureur *m* automobile
race² [reɪs] *n* (*group*) race *f*; **r. relations**
relations *fpl* interraciales ■ **racial**
['reɪʃəl] *adj* racial ■ **racism** *n* racisme
m ■ **racist** *adj & n* raciste (*mf*)
rack [ræk] **1** *n* (*for bottles, letters, records*) casier *m*; (*for plates*) égouttoir
m; (**luggage**) **r.** porte-bagages *m inv*;
(**roof**) **r.** (*of car*) galerie *f* **2** *vt* **to r. one's
brains** se creuser la cervelle
racket¹ ['rækɪt] *n* (*for tennis*) raquette *f*
racket² ['rækɪt] *n Fam* (**a**) (*din*) vacarme *m* (**b**) (*criminal activity*) racket *m*
radar ['reɪdɑ:(r)] *n* radar *m*
radiant ['reɪdɪənt] *adj* (*person, face*)
resplendissant (**with** de)
radiate ['reɪdɪeɪt] **1** *vt* (*heat, light*) dégager; *Fig* (*joy, health*) être rayonnant
de **2** *vi* rayonner (**from** de) ■ **radiation** *n* (*radioactivity*) radiation *f*
radiator ['reɪdɪeɪtə(r)] *n* (*heater*) radiateur *m*
radical ['rædɪkəl] *adj & n* radical, -e
(*mf*)

radio ['reɪdɪəʊ] **1** (*pl* **-os**) *n* radio *f*; **on
the r.** à la radio; **r. cassette (player)**
radiocassette *f* **2** (*pt & pp* **-oed**) *vt*
(*message*) transmettre par radio (**to**
à); **to r.** sb contacter qn par radio
■ **radio-controlled** *adj* radioguidé
radioactivity [reɪdɪəʊæk'tɪvətɪ] *n* radioactivité *f*
radish ['rædɪʃ] *n* radis *m*
radius ['reɪdɪəs] (*pl* **-dii**) *n* rayon *m*;
within a r. of 10 km dans un rayon
de 10 km
RAF [ɑ:reɪ'ef] (*abbr* **Royal Air Force**) *n*
= armée de l'air britannique
raffle ['ræfəl] *n* tombola *f*
raft [rɑ:ft] *n* radeau *m*
rag [ræg] *n* (**a**) (*piece of old clothing*)
chiffon *m*; **in rags** (*clothes*) en loques;
(*person*) en haillons (**b**) *Fam Pej*
(*newspaper*) torchon *m*
rage [reɪdʒ] **1** *n* (*of person*) rage *f*; **to fly
into a r.** entrer dans une rage folle;
Fam **to be all the r.** (*of fashion*) faire
fureur **2** *vi* (*be angry*) être furieux,
-euse; (*of storm, battle*) faire rage ■ **raging** *adj* (*storm, fever, fire*) violent
ragged ['rægɪd] *adj* (*clothes*) en loques; (*person*) en haillons; (*edge*) irrégulier, -ère
raid [reɪd] **1** *n* (*military*) raid *m*; (*by police*) descente *f*; (*by thieves*) hold-up
m inv; **air r.** raid *m* aérien **2** *vt* faire
un raid/une descente/un hold-up
dans
rail [reɪl] **1** *n* (**a**) (*for train*) rail *m*; **by r.**
par le train (**b**) (*rod on balcony*) balustrade *f*; (*on stairs*) rampe *f*; (*curtain
rod*) tringle *f* **2** *adj* (*ticket*) de chemin

de fer; (strike) des cheminots ∎ **railcard** n carte f d'abonnement de train

railings ['reɪlɪŋz] npl grille f

railroad ['reɪlrəʊd] n Am (system) chemin m de fer; (track) voie f ferrée

railway ['reɪlweɪ] Br **1** n (system) chemin m de fer; (track) voie f ferrée **2** adj (ticket) de chemin de fer; (timetable) des chemins de fer; (network, company) ferroviaire; **r. line** ligne f de chemin de fer; **r. station** gare f

rain [reɪn] **1** n pluie f; **in the r.** sous la pluie **2** vi pleuvoir; **it's raining** il pleut ∎ **rainbow** n arc-en-ciel m ∎ **raincoat** n imperméable m ∎ **rainfall** n (amount) précipitations fpl ∎ **rainforest** n forêt f tropicale humide ∎ **rainwater** n eau f de pluie ∎ **rainy** (**-ier, -iest**) adj pluvieux, -euse; (day) de pluie; **the r. season** la saison des pluies

raise [reɪz] **1** vt (lift) lever; (child, family, voice) élever; (salary, price) augmenter; (temperature) faire monter; (question, protest) soulever; (taxes) lever; **to r. money** réunir des fonds; **to r. the alarm** donner l'alarme **2** n Am (pay rise) augmentation f (de salaire)

raisin ['reɪzən] n raisin m sec

rake [reɪk] **1** n râteau m **2** vt (soil) ratisser; **to r. (up)** (leaves) ratisser

rally ['rælɪ] **1** (pl **-ies**) n (political) rassemblement m; (car race) rallye m **2** (pt & pp **-ied**) vt (unite, win over) rallier (**to** à) **3** vi se rallier (**to** à); (recover) reprendre ses forces; **to r. round sb** venir en aide à qn

RAM [ræm] (abbr **random access memory**) n Comptr mémoire f vive

ram [ræm] **1** n (animal) bélier m **2** (pt & pp **-mm-**) vt (vehicle) emboutir; (ship) aborder; **to r. sth into sth** enfoncer qch dans qch

ramble ['ræmbəl] **1** n (hike) randonnée f **2** vi (hike) faire une randonnée; **to r. on** (talk) divaguer ∎ **rambler** n randonneur, -euse mf

rambling ['ræmblɪŋ] adj (**a**) (house) plein de coins et de recoins; (spread

out) vaste (**b**) (speech) décousu

ramp [ræmp] n (for wheelchair) rampe f d'accès; (in garage) pont m (de graissage); (on road) petit dos m d'âne

rampant ['ræmpənt] adj endémique

ran [ræn] pt of **run**

ranch [rɑːntʃ] n ranch m

rancid ['rænsɪd] adj rance

random ['rændəm] **1** n **at r.** au hasard **2** adj (choice) (fait) au hasard; (sample) prélevé au hasard

rang [ræŋ] pt of **ring²**

range [reɪndʒ] **1** n (**a**) (of gun, voice) portée f; (of singer's voice) registre m; (of aircraft, ship) rayon m d'action; (of colours, prices, products) gamme f; (of sizes) choix m (**b**) (of mountains) chaîne f (**c**) (stove) fourneau m (**d**) (**shooting**) **r.** champ m de tir **2** vi (vary) varier (**from** de; **to** à); (extend) s'étendre

ranger ['reɪndʒə(r)] n (forest) **r.** garde m forestier

rank¹ [ræŋk] **1** n (position, class) rang m; (military grade) grade m; (row) rangée f; (for taxis) station f **2** vt placer (**among** parmi) **3** vi compter (**among** parmi)

rank² [ræŋk] (**-er, -est**) adj (smell) fétide

ransack ['rænsæk] vt (house) mettre sens dessus dessous; (shop, town) piller

ransom ['rænsəm] **1** n rançon f; **to hold sb to r.** rançonner qn **2** vt rançonner

rant [rænt] vi Fam **to r. and rave** tempêter (**at** contre)

rap [ræp] **1** n (**a**) (blow) coup m sec (**b**) **r. (music)** rap m **2** vi (hit) frapper (**on** à)

rape [reɪp] **1** n viol m **2** vt violer ∎ **rapist** n violeur m

rapid ['ræpɪd] adj rapide ∎ **rapidly** adv rapidement

rapids ['ræpɪdz] npl (of river) rapides mpl

rare [reə(r)] adj (**a**) (**-er, -est**) (uncommon) rare (**b**) (meat) saignant

■ **rarely** adv rarement ■ **rarity** (pl -ies) n (quality, object) rareté f

raring [ˈreərɪŋ] adj **r. to do sth** impatient de faire qch

rascal [ˈrɑːskəl] n coquin, -e mf

rash[1] [ræʃ] n (on skin) (red patches) rougeurs fpl; (spots) (éruption f de) boutons mpl

rash[2] [ræʃ] (-er, -est) adj (imprudent) irréfléchi ■ **rashly** adv sans réfléchir

rasher [ˈræʃə(r)] n Br tranche f (de bacon)

raspberry [ˈrɑːzbərɪ] (pl -ies) n (fruit) framboise f

rat [ræt] n rat m; Fig **r. race** foire f d'empoigne

rate [reɪt] 1 n (level, percentage) taux m; (speed) rythme m; (price) tarif m; **interest r.** taux m d'intérêt; **at the r. of** au rythme de; (amount) à raison de; **at this r.** (slow speed) à ce train-là; **at any r.** en tout cas 2 vt (regard) considérer (as comme); (deserve) mériter; **to r. sb/sth highly** tenir qn/qch en haute estime

rather [ˈrɑːðə(r)] adv (preferably, quite) plutôt; **I'd r. stay** j'aimerais mieux rester (**than** que); **I r. liked it** j'ai bien aimé

ratify [ˈrætɪfaɪ] (pt & pp -ied) vt ratifier

rating [ˈreɪtɪŋ] n (classification) classement m

ratio [ˈreɪʃɪəʊ] (pl -os) n rapport m

ration [ˈræʃən] 1 n ration f; rations (food) vivres mpl 2 vt rationner ■ **rationing** n rationnement m

rational [ˈræʃənəl] adj (sensible) raisonnable, (sane) rationnel, -elle ■ **rationalize** vt (organize) rationaliser; (explain) justifier ■ **rationally** adv (behave) raisonnablement

rattle [ˈrætəl] 1 n (for baby) hochet m 2 vt (window) faire vibrer; (keys, chains) faire cliqueter; Fam **to r. sth off** (speech, list) débiter qch 3 vi (of window) vibrer

raucous [ˈrɔːkəs] adj (noisy, rowdy) bruyant

rave [reɪv] 1 n (party) rave f 2 vi (talk nonsense) délirer; **to r. about sb/sth** (enthuse) ne pas tarir d'éloges sur qn/qch ■ **raving** adj **to be r. mad** être complètement fou (f folle)

raven [ˈreɪvən] n corbeau m

ravenous [ˈrævənəs] adj **I'm r.** j'ai une faim de loup

ravine [rəˈviːn] n ravin m

ravioli [rævɪˈəʊlɪ] n ravioli(s) mpl

raw [rɔː] (-er, -est) adj (vegetable) cru; (data) brut; **r. material** matière f première

ray [reɪ] n (of light, sun) rayon m; Fig (of hope) lueur f

rayon [ˈreɪɒn] n rayonne f

razor [ˈreɪzə(r)] n rasoir m; **r. blade** lame f de rasoir

Rd (abbr road) rue

re [riː] prep Com en référence à; **re your letter** suite à votre lettre

reach [riːtʃ] 1 n portée f; **within r. of** à portée de; (near) à proximité de; **within (easy) r.** (object) à portée de main; (shops) tout proche
2 vt (place, aim, distant object) atteindre, arriver à; (decision) prendre; (agreement) aboutir à; (contact) joindre; **to r. a conclusion** arriver à une conclusion; **to r. out one's arm** tendre le bras
3 vi (extend) s'étendre (**to** jusqu'à); **to r. (out) for sth** tendre le bras pour prendre qch

react [rɪˈækt] vi réagir (**against** contre; **to** à) ■ **reaction** n réaction f

reactionary [rɪˈækʃənərɪ] (pl -ies) adj & n réactionnaire (mf)

reactor [rɪˈæktə(r)] n réacteur m

read [riːd] 1 (pt & pp read [red]) vt lire; (meter) relever; (of instrument) indiquer; Br Univ (study) étudier 2 vi (of person) lire (**about** sur); **to r. to sb** faire la lecture à qn 3 **n to be a good r.** être agréable à lire ■ **readable** adj (handwriting) lisible; (book) facile à lire

▸ **read back** vt sep relire
▸ **read out** vt sep lire (à haute voix)
▸ **read over** vt sep relire

▶ **read through** vt sep (skim) parcourir

▶ **read up (on)** vt insep (study) étudier

reader ['riːdə(r)] n lecteur, -trice mf; (book) livre m de lecture

readily ['redɪlɪ] adv (willingly) volontiers; (easily) facilement

reading ['riːdɪŋ] n lecture f; (of meter) relevé m; **r. glasses** lunettes fpl de lecture; **r. lamp** (on desk) lampe f de bureau; (at bedside) lampe f de chevet; **r. matter** de quoi lire

readjust [riːə'dʒʌst] 1 vt (instrument) régler 2 vi (of person) se réadapter (**to** à)

ready ['redɪ] 1 (-ier, -iest) adj prêt (**to do** à faire; **for sth** pour qch); **to get sb/sth r.** préparer qn/qch; **to get r.** se préparer (**for sth** pour qch; **to do** à faire); **r. cash, r. money** argent m liquide
  2 n **to be at the r.** être tout prêt (f toute prête) ■ **ready-made** adj (food) tout prêt (f toute prête); **r. clothes** le prêt-à-porter ■ **ready-to-wear** adj **r. clothes** le prêt-à-porter

real [rɪəl] 1 adj vrai; (leather) véritable; (world, danger) réel (f réelle); **in r. life** dans la réalité; Am **r. estate** immobilier m 2 adv Fam vraiment 3 n Fam **for r.** pour de vrai

realistic [rɪə'lɪstɪk] adj réaliste

reality [rɪ'ælətɪ] (pl -ies) n réalité f; **in r.** en réalité

realization [rɪəlaɪ'zeɪʃən] n (awareness) prise f de conscience

realize ['rɪəlaɪz] vt (a) (become aware of) se rendre compte de; **to r. that...** se rendre compte que... (b) (carry out) réaliser

really ['rɪəlɪ] adv vraiment

ream [riːm] n (of paper) rame f

reap [riːp] vt (crop) moissonner; Fig (profits) récolter

reappear [riːə'pɪə(r)] vi réapparaître

rear¹ [rɪə(r)] 1 (back part) arrière m; **in** or **at the r.** à l'arrière (**of** de) 2 adj (entrance, legs) de derrière; (lights, window) arrière inv

rear² [rɪə(r)] 1 vt (child, animals) élever; (one's head) relever 2 vi **to r. (up)** (of horse) se cabrer

rearrange [riːə'reɪndʒ] vt (hair, room) réarranger; (plans) changer

rearview ['rɪəvjuː] n **r. mirror** rétroviseur m

reason ['riːzən] 1 n (cause, sense) raison f; **the r. for/why** la raison de/pour laquelle; **for no r.** sans raison; **it stands to r.** cela va de soi; **within r.** dans des limites raisonnables
  2 vt **to r. that...** estimer que...
  3 vi raisonner (**about** sur); **to r. with sb** raisonner qn ■ **reasoning** n raisonnement m

reasonable ['riːzənəbəl] adj (fair) raisonnable; (quite good) passable ■ **reasonably** adv (behave, act) raisonnablement; (quite) plutôt

reassure [riːə'ʃʊə(r)] vt rassurer ■ **reassuring** adj rassurant

rebate ['riːbeɪt] n (discount) rabais m; (refund) remboursement m

rebel 1 ['rebəl] n rebelle mf 2 ['rebəl] adj (camp, chief, attack) des rebelles 3 [rɪ'bel] (pt & pp -ll-) vi se rebeller (**against** contre) ■ **rebellion** [rɪ'beljən] n rébellion f

rebound 1 ['riːbaʊnd] n (of ball) rebond m 2 [rɪ'baʊnd] vi (of ball) rebondir; Fig (of lies, action) se retourner (**on** contre)

rebuild [riː'bɪld] (pt & pp -built) vt reconstruire

rebuke [rɪ'bjuːk] 1 n réprimande f 2 vt réprimander

recall [rɪ'kɔːl] 1 n (calling back) rappel m 2 vt (remember) se rappeler (**that** que; **doing** avoir fait); (call back) rappeler; **to r. sth to sb** rappeler qch à qn

recap ['riːkæp] 1 n récapitulation f 2 (pt & pp -pp-) vti récapituler

recapitulate [riːkə'pɪtjʊleɪt] vti récapituler

recede [rɪ'siːd] vi (into the distance) s'éloigner; (of floods) baisser ■ **receding** adj **his hairline is r., he has a r. hairline** son front se dégarnit

receipt [rɪ'siːt] n (for payment, object) reçu m (**for** de); (for letter, parcel) récépissé m; **receipts** (at box office) recette f; **on r. of sth** dès réception de qch

receive [rɪ'siːv] vt recevoir; (stolen goods) receler

receiver [rɪ'siːvə(r)] n (of phone) combiné m; (radio) récepteur m; **to pick up** or **lift the r.** (of phone) décrocher

recent ['riːsənt] adj récent; (development) dernier, -ère; **in r. months** au cours des derniers mois ■ **recently** adv récemment

reception [rɪ'sepʃən] n (party, of radio) réception f; (welcome) accueil m; **r. (desk)** réception f ■ **receptionist** n réceptionniste mf

receptive [rɪ'septɪv] adj réceptif, -ive (**to** à)

recess [Br 'riːses, Am 'riːses] n (a) (holiday) vacances fpl; Am (between classes) récréation f (b) (in wall) renfoncement m; (smaller) recoin m

recession [rɪ'seʃən] n Econ récession f

recharge [riː'tʃɑːdʒ] vt (battery, mobile phone) recharger ■ **rechargeable** adj (battery) rechargeable

recipe ['resɪpɪ] n (for food) & Fig recette f (**for sth** de qch)

recipient [rɪ'sɪpɪənt] n (of gift, letter) destinataire mf; (of award) lauréat, -e mf

reciprocal [rɪ'sɪprəkəl] adj réciproque ■ **reciprocate 1** vt retourner **2** vi rendre la pareille

recital [rɪ'saɪtəl] n (of music) récital m (pl -als)

recite [rɪ'saɪt] vt (poem) réciter; (list) énumérer

reckless ['reklɪs] adj (rash) imprudent

reckon ['rekən] **1** vt (calculate) calculer; (consider) considérer; Fam (think) penser (**that** que) **2** vi calculer, compter; **to r. with** (take into account) compter avec; (deal with) avoir affaire à; **to r. on sb/sth** (rely on) compter sur

qn/qch ■ **reckoning** n (calculation) calcul m

reclaim [rɪ'kleɪm] vt (lost property, luggage) récupérer; (expenses) se faire rembourser

recline [rɪ'klaɪn] vi (be stretched out) être allongé ■ **reclining** adj **r. seat** siège m à dossier inclinable

recluse [rɪ'kluːs] n reclus, -e mf

recognition [rekəg'nɪʃən] n reconnaissance f; **to gain r.** être reconnu

recognize ['rekəgnaɪz] vt reconnaître ■ **recognizable** adj reconnaissable

recoil [rɪ'kɔɪl] vi (of person) avoir un mouvement de recul

recollect [rekə'lekt] vt se souvenir de ■ **recollection** n souvenir m

recommend [rekə'mend] vt (praise, support, advise) recommander (**to** à; **for** pour); **to r. sb to do sth** recommander à qn de faire qch ■ **recommendation** n recommandation f

recompense ['rekəmpens] **1** n récompense f **2** vt (reward) récompenser

reconcile ['rekənsaɪl] vt (person) réconcilier (**with** or **to** avec); (opinions, facts) concilier; **to r. oneself to sth** se résigner à qch

reconditioned [riːkən'dɪʃənd] adj (engine, machine) remis à neuf

reconsider [riːkən'sɪdə(r)] **1** vt réexaminer **2** vi réfléchir

reconstruct [riːkən'strʌkt] vt (crime) reconstituer

record 1 ['rekɔːd] n (**a**) (disc) disque m; **r. player** électrophone m

(**b**) (best sporting performance) record m

(**c**) (report) rapport m; (background) antécédents mpl; (file) dossier m; **to make** or **keep a r. of sth** garder une trace écrite de qch; **on r.** (fact, event) attesté; **(police) r.** casier m judiciaire; **(public) records** archives fpl

2 ['rekɔːd] adj record inv; **to be at a r. high/low** être à son taux le plus haut/bas

3 [rɪ'kɔːd] vt (on tape, in register) enregistrer; (in diary) noter

4 [rɪˈkɔːd] *vi (on tape, of tape recorder)* enregistrer

recorded [rɪˈkɔːdɪd] *adj* enregistré; *(fact)* attesté; *(TV broadcast)* en différé; *Br* **to send sth (by) r. delivery** ≃ envoyer qch en recommandé avec accusé de réception

recorder [rɪˈkɔːdə(r)] *n (musical instrument)* flûte *f* à bec

recording [rɪˈkɔːdɪŋ] *n* enregistrement *m*

recount [rɪˈkaʊnt] *vt (relate)* raconter

recoup [rɪˈkuːp] *vt* récupérer

recourse [rɪˈkɔːs] *n* recours *m*; **to have r. to** avoir recours à

recover [rɪˈkʌvə(r)] **1** *vt (get back)* récupérer; *(one's appetite, balance)* retrouver **2** *vi (from illness, shock, surprise)* se remettre (**from** de); *(of economy, country)* se redresser; *(of sales)* reprendre ■ **recovery** *(pl -ies)* *n* (**a**) *(from illness)* rétablissement *m*; *(of economy)* redressement *m* (**b**) *Br* **r. vehicle** dépanneuse *f*

re-create [riːkrɪˈeɪt] *vt* recréer

recreation [rekrɪˈeɪʃən] *n Sch (break)* récréation *f*

recrimination [rɪkrɪmɪˈneɪʃən] *n* récrimination *f*

recruit [rɪˈkruːt] **1** *n* recrue *f* **2** *vt* recruter

rectangle [ˈrektæŋɡəl] *n* rectangle *m* ■ **rectangular** *adj* rectangulaire

rectify [ˈrektɪfaɪ] *(pt & pp -ied)* *vt* rectifier

rector [ˈrektə(r)] *n (priest)* pasteur *m* anglican

recuperate [rɪˈkuːpəreɪt] *vi (from illness)* récupérer

recur [rɪˈkɜː(r)] *(pt & pp -rr-)* *vi (of event, problem)* se reproduire; *(of illness)* réapparaître; *(of theme)* revenir

recycle [riːˈsaɪkəl] *vt* recycler

red [red] **1** *(redder, reddest)* *adj* rouge; *(hair)* roux (*f* rousse); **to turn** *or* **go r.** rougir; **the R. Cross** la Croix-Rouge; **r. light** *(traffic light)* feu *m* rouge; *Fig* **r. tape** paperasserie *f* **2** *(colour)* rouge *m*; **in the r.** *(in debt)*

dans le rouge ■ **red-handed** *adv* **to be caught r. handed** être pris la main dans le sac ■ **redhead** *n* roux *m*, rousse *f* ■ **red-hot** *adj* brûlant

redcurrant [red'kʌrənt] *n* groseille *f*

redecorate [riːˈdekəreɪt] *vt (repaint)* refaire la peinture de

redeem [rɪˈdiːm] *vt (restore to favour, buy back, free)* racheter; *(gift token, coupon)* échanger; **his one redeeming feature is…** la seule chose qui le rachète, c'est…

redirect [riːdaɪˈrekt] *vt (mail)* faire suivre

redo [riːˈduː] *(pt -did, pp -done)* *vt* refaire

reduce [rɪˈdjuːs] *vt* réduire (**to** à; **by** de); *(temperature, price)* baisser; **at a reduced price** à prix réduit; **to be reduced to doing sth** en être réduit à faire qch ■ **reduction** [-ˈdʌkʃən] *n (of temperature, price)* baisse *f*; *(discount)* réduction *f* (**in/on** de/sur)

redundant [rɪˈdʌndənt] *adj (not needed)* superflu; *Br* **to make sb r.** licencier qn ■ **redundancy** *(pl -ies)* *n Br (of worker)* licenciement *m*; **r. pay** *or* **payment** *or* **money** prime *f* de licenciement

reed [riːd] *n (plant)* roseau *m*

reef [riːf] *n* récif *m*

reek [riːk] *vi* **to r. (of sth)** puer (qch)

reel [riːl] **1** *n (of thread, film)* bobine *f*; *(for fishing line)* moulinet *m* **2** *vt sep* **to r. off** *(names, statistics)* débiter

re-elect [riːɪˈlekt] *vt* réélire

re-establish [riːɪˈstæblɪʃ] *vt* rétablir

ref [ref] *(abbr* referee) *n Fam* arbitre *m*

refectory [rɪˈfektərɪ] *(pl -ies)* *n* réfectoire *m*

refer [rɪˈfɜː(r)] *(pt & pp -rr-)* **1** *vt* **to r. sth to sb** *(submit)* soumettre qch à qn; **to r. sb to a specialist** envoyer qn voir un spécialiste **2** *vi insep* **to r. to** *(allude to)* faire allusion à; *(mention)* parler de; *(apply to)* s'appliquer à; *(consult)* consulter

referee [refəˈriː] **1** *n (in sport)* arbitre *m*; **to give the names of two referees**

(for job) fournir deux références **2** *vti* arbitrer

reference ['refərəns] *n (source, consultation)* référence *f; (allusion)* allusion *f* (**to** à); *(mention)* mention *f* (**to** de); *(for employer)* lettre *f* de référence; **with** *or* **in r. to** concernant; **r. book** ouvrage *m* de référence

referendum [refə'rendəm] *n* référendum *m*

refill 1 ['ri:fɪl] *n (for pen)* cartouche *f; (for lighter)* recharge *f;* **would you like a r.?** *(of drink)* je te ressers? **2** [ri:'fɪl] *vt (glass)* remplir à nouveau; *(lighter, pen)* recharger

refine [rɪ'faɪn] *vt (oil, sugar, manners)* raffiner; *(technique, machine)* perfectionner ■ **refined** *adj (person, manners)* raffiné ■ **refinement** *n (of person, manners)* raffinement *m;* **refinements** *(technical improvements)* améliorations *fpl*

reflect [rɪ'flekt] **1** *vt* (**a**) *(light, image)* refléter, réfléchir; *Fig (portray)* refléter; **to be reflected (in)** *(of light)* se refléter (**dans**) (**b**) **to r. that…** se dire que… **2** *vi* (**a**) **to r. on sb** *(of prestige, honour)* rejaillir sur qn; **to r. badly on sb** faire du tort à qn (**b**) *(think)* réfléchir (**on** à)

reflection [rɪ'flekʃən] *n* (**a**) *(image) & Fig* reflet *m* (**b**) *(thought, criticism)* réflexion *f;* **on r.** tout bien réfléchi

reflector [rɪ'flektə(r)] *n (on bicycle, vehicle)* catadioptre *m*

reflex ['ri:fleks] *n & adj* réflexe *(m);* **r. action** réflexe *m*

reflexive [rɪ'fleksɪv] *adj (verb)* réfléchi

reform [rɪ'fɔːm] **1** *n* réforme *f* **2** *vt* réformer; *(person, conduct)* corriger **3** *vi (of person)* se réformer

refrain [rɪ'freɪn] **1** *n (of song) & Fig* refrain *m* **2** *vi* s'abstenir (**from sth de** qch; **from doing de** faire)

refresh [rɪ'freʃ] *vt (of drink)* rafraîchir; *(of bath)* revigorer; *(of sleep, rest)* reposer; **to r. one's memory** se rafraîchir la mémoire ■ **refreshing** *adj*

(drink) rafraîchissant; *(bath)* revigorant; *(original)* nouveau *(f* nouvelle)

refreshments [rɪ'freʃmənts] *npl* rafraîchissements *mpl*

refrigerate [rɪ'frɪdʒəreɪt] *vt* réfrigérer ■ **refrigerator** *n (domestic)* réfrigérateur *m*

refuel [riː'fjʊəl] **1** *(Br* -ll-, *Am* -l-*) vt (aircraft)* ravitailler en carburant **2** *vi (of aircraft)* se ravitailler en carburant

refuge ['refjuːdʒ] *n* refuge *m;* **to take r.** se réfugier (**in** dans)

refugee [refjʊ'dʒiː] *n* réfugié, -e *mf*

refund 1 [rɪ'fʌnd] *n* remboursement *m* **2** [rɪ'fʌnd] *vt* rembourser

refurbish [riː'fɜːbɪʃ] *vt* rénover

refusal [rɪ'fjuːzəl] *n* refus *m*

refuse¹ [rɪ'fjuːz] **1** *vt* refuser; **to r. to do sth** refuser de faire qch; **to r. sb sth** refuser qch à qn **2** *vi* refuser

refuse² ['refjuːs] *n Br (rubbish)* ordures *fpl,* **r. collection** ramassage *m* des ordures

refute [rɪ'fjuːt] *vt* réfuter

regain [rɪ'geɪn] *vt (lost ground, favour)* regagner; *(health, sight)* retrouver; **to r. consciousness** reprendre connaissance

regal ['riːgəl] *adj* royal

regard [rɪ'gɑːd] **1** *n (admiration)* respect *m; (consideration)* égard *m;* **to hold sb in high r.** tenir qn en haute estime; **with r. to** en ce qui concerne; **to give** *or* **send one's regards to sb** transmettre son meilleur souvenir à qn **2** *vt (admire, respect)* estimer; **to r. sb/sth as…** considérer qn/qch comme… ■ **regarding** *prep* en ce qui concerne

regardless [rɪ'gɑːdləs] **1** *adj* **r. of…** *(without considering)* sans tenir compte de… **2** *adv (all the same)* quand même

regenerate [rɪ'dʒenəreɪt] *vt* régénérer

reggae ['regeɪ] *n (music)* reggae *m*

régime [reɪ'ʒiːm] *n* régime *m*

regiment ['redʒɪmənt] *n* régiment *m*

region ['riːdʒən] *n* région *f; Fig* **in the r.**

of (about) environ ■ **regional** adj régional

register ['redʒɪstə(r)] **1** n registre m; (in school) cahier m d'appel; **electoral r.** liste f électorale; **to take the r.** (of teacher) faire l'appel

2 vt (birth, death) déclarer; (record, note) enregistrer; (vehicle) immatriculer; (complaint) déposer

3 vi (enrol) s'inscrire (**for** à); (at hotel) signer le registre; (of voter) s'inscrire sur les listes électorales; ■ **registered** adj (member) inscrit; (letter, package) recommandé; **to send sth by r. post** or Am **mail** envoyer qch en recommandé

registration [redʒɪ'streɪʃən] n (enrolment) inscription f; Br **r. (number)** (of vehicle) numéro m d'immatriculation; Br **r. document** (of vehicle) ≃ carte f grise

registry ['redʒɪstrɪ] adj & n Br **r.** (office) bureau m de l'état civil; **to get married in a r. office** se marier à la mairie

regret [rɪ'gret] **1** n regret m **2** (pt & pp -tt-) vt regretter (**to do** de faire; **that** que + subjunctive); **to r. doing sth** regretter d'avoir fait qch

regrettable [rɪ'gretəbəl] adj regrettable (**that** que + subjunctive)

regroup [riː'gruːp] vi se regrouper

regular ['regjʊlə(r)] **1** adj (steady, even, in grammar) régulier, -ère; (error) habituel, -elle; (price) normal; (size) moyen, -enne; (listener, reader) fidèle; Am Fam **a r. guy** un chic type **2** n (in bar) habitué, -e mf ■ **regularly** adv régulièrement

regulate ['regjʊleɪt] vt (adjust) régler; (control) réglementer ■ **regulations** npl (rules) règlement m

rehabilitate [riːhə'bɪlɪteɪt] vt réhabiliter

rehearse [rɪ'hɜːs] vti répéter ■ **rehearsal** n répétition f

reign [reɪn] **1** n règne m; **in** or during **the r. of** sous le règne de **2** vi régner (**over** sur)

reimburse [riːɪm'bɜːs] vt rembourser (**for** de)

reindeer ['reɪndɪə(r)] n inv renne m

reinforce [riːɪn'fɔːs] vt renforcer (**with** de); **reinforced concrete** béton m armé ■ **reinforcements** npl (troops) renforts mpl

reinstate [riːɪn'steɪt] vt réintégrer

reiterate [riː'ɪtəreɪt] vt réitérer

reject 1 ['riːdʒekt] n (object) rebus m **2** [rɪ'dʒekt] vt rejeter; (candidate, goods, offer) refuser ■ **rejection** [rɪ'dʒekʃən] n rejet m; (of candidate, goods, offer) refus m

rejoice [rɪ'dʒɔɪs] vi se réjouir (**over** or **at** de) ■ **rejoicing** n réjouissance f

rejoin [rɪ'dʒɔɪn] vt (join up with) rejoindre

rejuvenate [rɪ'dʒuːvəneɪt] vt rajeunir

relapse ['riːlæps] n rechute f

relate [rɪ'leɪt] **1** vt (a) (narrate) raconter (**that** que); (report) rapporter (**that** que) (b) (connect) mettre en rapport (**to** avec)

2 vi **to r. to** (apply to) avoir rapport à; (person) avoir des affinités avec ■ **related** adj (linked) lié (**to** à); (languages, styles) apparenté; **to be r. to sb** (by family) être parent de qn

relation [rɪ'leɪʃən] n (a) (relative) parent, -e mf (b) (relationship) rapport m; **international relations** relations fpl internationales

relationship [rɪ'leɪʃənʃɪp] n (within family) lien m de parenté; (between people) relation f; (between countries) relations fpl; (connection) rapport m

relative ['relətɪv] **1** n parent, -e mf **2** adj (comparative) relatif, -ive; (respective) respectif, -ive; **r. to** (compared to) relativement à ■ **relatively** adv relativement

relax [rɪ'læks] **1** vt (person, mind) détendre; (grip, pressure) relâcher; (law, control) assouplir **2** vi (of person) se détendre; **r.!** (calm down) du calme! ■ **relaxed** adj (person, atmosphere) détendu ■ **relaxing** adj délassant

relaxation [riːlæk'seɪʃən] *n (of person)* détente *f*

relay 1 ['riːleɪ] *n* **r. (race)** (course *f* de) relais *m* 2 [riː'leɪ] *vt (information)* transmettre (**to** à)

release [riː'liːs] 1 *n (of prisoner)* libération *f; (of film)* sortie *f* (**of** de); *(film)* nouveau film *m; (record)* nouveau disque *m* 2 *vt (prisoner)* libérer (**from** de); *(brake)* desserrer; *(film, record)* sortir; *(news)* communiquer; **to r. sb's hand** lâcher la main de qn

relegate ['relɪgeɪt] *vt* reléguer (**to** à); *Br* **to be relegated** *(of team)* descendre en division inférieure

relent [rɪ'lent] *vi (of person)* céder

relentless [rɪ'lentləs] *adj* implacable

relevant ['reləvənt] *adj* (a) *(apt)* pertinent; **to be r. to sth** avoir rapport à qch; **that's not r.** ça n'a rien à voir (b) *(appropriate) (chapter)* correspondant; *(authorities)* compétent; *(qualifications)* requis (c) *(topical)* d'actualité ■ **relevance** *n* pertinence *f* (**to** à); *(connection)* rapport *m* (**to** avec)

reliable [rɪ'laɪəbəl] *adj (person, machine)* fiable; *(information)* sûr ■ **reliability** *n (of person)* sérieux *m; (of machine)* fiabilité *f*

relic ['relɪk] *n* relique *f; Fig* **relics** vestiges *mpl*

relief [rɪ'liːf] 1 *n (comfort)* soulagement *m; (help)* secours *m; (in art)* relief *m* 2 *adj (train, bus)* supplémentaire; *(work)* de secours; **r. map** carte *f* en relief; *Br* **r. road** route *f* de délestage

relieve [rɪ'liːv] *vt (alleviate)* soulager; *(boredom)* tromper; *(replace)* remplacer; *(free)* libérer; **to r. sb of sth** débarrasser qn de qch; *Hum* **to r. oneself** se soulager

religion [rɪ'lɪdʒən] *n* religion *f* ■ **religious** *adj* religieux, -euse

relinquish [rɪ'lɪŋkwɪʃ] *vt (hope, habit, thought)* abandonner; *(share, claim)* renoncer à

relish ['relɪʃ] 1 *n (pickle)* condiments *mpl; (pleasure)* goût *m* (**for** pour); **to do sth with r.** faire qch avec délectation 2 *vt* savourer

reload [riː'ləʊd] *vt (gun, camera)* recharger

relocate [*Br* riːləʊ'keɪt, *Am* riː'ləʊkeɪt] *vi (of company)* être transféré; *(of person)* se déplacer

reluctant [rɪ'lʌktənt] *adj (greeting, promise)* accordé à contrecœur; **to be r. (to do sth)** être réticent (à faire qch) ■ **reluctantly** *adv* à contrecœur

rely [rɪ'laɪ] *(pt & pp -ied)* vi **to r. (up)on** *(count on)* compter sur; *(be dependent on)* dépendre de

remain [rɪ'meɪn] *vi (stay behind, continue to be)* rester; *(be left)* subsister ■ **remaining** *adj* restant ■ **remains** *npl* restes *mpl*

remainder [rɪ'meɪndə(r)] *n* reste *m; (book)* invendu *m* soldé

remark [rɪ'mɑːk] 1 *n* remarque *f* 2 *vt* faire remarquer 3 *vi* **to r. on sth** *(comment)* faire un commentaire sur qch ■ **remarkable** *adj* remarquable ■ **remarkably** *adv* remarquablement

remarry [riː'mærɪ] *(pt & pp -ied)* vi se remarier

remedy ['remɪdɪ] 1 *(pl -ies)* n remède *m* 2 *(pt & pp -ied)* vt remédier à

remember [rɪ'membə(r)] 1 *vt* se souvenir de, se rappeler; *(commemorate)* commémorer; **to r. that/doing** se rappeler que/d'avoir fait; **to r. to do sth** penser à faire qch; **to r. sb to sb** rappeler qn au bon souvenir de qn 2 *vi* se souvenir, se rappeler

remind [rɪ'maɪnd] *vt* **to r. sb of sth** rappeler qch à qn; **to r. sb to do sth** rappeler à qn de faire qch ■ **reminder** *n (letter, of event)* rappel *m*

reminisce [remɪ'nɪs] *vi* évoquer des souvenirs; **to r. about sth** évoquer qch ■ **reminiscence** *n* souvenir *m*

reminiscent [remɪ'nɪsənt] *adj* **r. of** qui rappelle

remittance [rɪ'mɪtəns] *n (sum)* paiement *m*

remorse [rɪ'mɔːs] *n* remords *m;* **to feel r.** avoir du *ou* des remords

■ **remorseless** *adj* impitoyable

remote [rɪ'məʊt] (**-er, -est**) *adj* (**a**) *(far-off)* éloigné (**from** de); **r. control** télécommande *f* (**b**) *(slight)* vague ■ **remotely** *adv (slightly)* vaguement

removable [rɪ'muːvəbəl] *adj (lining)* amovible

removal [rɪ'muːvəl] *n* (**a**) *(of control, threat)* suppression *f*; *(of politician)* renvoi *m* (**b**) *Br* **r. van** camion *m* de déménagement

remove [rɪ'muːv] *vt (clothes, stain, object)* enlever (**from sb** à qn; **from sth** de qch); *(obstacle, threat, word)* supprimer; *(fear, doubt)* dissiper; *(politician)* renvoyer

remover [rɪ'muːvə(r)] *n (for nail polish)* dissolvant *m*; *(for paint)* décapant *m*; *(for stains)* détachant *m*

remunerate [rɪ'mjuːnəreɪt] *vt* rémunérer

rename [riː'neɪm] *vt* rebaptiser; *Comptr (file)* renommer

rendezvous ['rɒndɪvuː, *pl* -vuːz] *n inv* rendez-vous *m inv*

renew [rɪ'njuː] *vt* renouveler; *(resume)* reprendre; *(library book)* renouveler le prêt de ■ **renewed** *adj (efforts)* renouvelé; *(attempt)* nouveau *(f* nouvelle)

renounce [rɪ'naʊns] *vt (give up)* renoncer à; *(disown)* renier

renovate ['renəveɪt] *vt (house)* rénover; *(painting)* restaurer

renowned [rɪ'naʊnd] *adj* renommé (**for** pour)

rent [rent] **1** *n (for house, flat)* loyer *m* **2** *vt* louer; **to r. out** louer; **rented car** voiture *f* de location

rental ['rentəl] *n (of television, car)* location *f*; *(of telephone)* abonnement *m*

reopen [riː'əʊpən] *vti* rouvrir

reorganize [riː'ɔːgənaɪz] *vt* réorganiser

rep [rep] *(abbr* **representative)** *n Fam* VRP *m*

repair [rɪ'peə(r)] **1** *n* réparation *f*; **under r.** en travaux **2** *vt* réparer

repay [riː'peɪ] *(pt & pp* **-paid)** *vt (pay back)* rembourser; *(reward)* remercier (**for** de) ■ **repayment** *n* remboursement *m*

repeal [rɪ'piːl] *vt* abroger

repeat [rɪ'piːt] **1** *n (of event)* répétition *f*; *(on TV, radio)* rediffusion *f*

2 *vt* répéter (**that** que); *(promise, threat)* réitérer; *(class)* redoubler; *(TV programme)* rediffuser; **to r. oneself** se répéter

3 *vi* répéter ■ **repeated** *adj (attempts)* répété; *(efforts)* renouvelé ■ **repeatedly** *adv* à maintes reprises

repel [rɪ'pel] *(pt & pp* **-ll-)** *vt* repousser ■ **repellent 1** *adj (disgusting)* repoussant **2** *n* **insect r.** anti-moustiques *m inv*

repent [rɪ'pent] *vi* se repentir (**of** de) ■ **repentant** *adj* repentant

repercussions [riːpə'kʌʃənz] *npl* répercussions *fpl* (**on** sur)

repertoire ['repətwɑː(r)] *n Theatre & Fig* répertoire *m* ■ **repertory** [-tərɪ] *(pl* **-ies)** *n Theatre & Fig* répertoire *m*; **r. theatre** théâtre *m* de répertoire

repetition [repɪ'tɪʃən] *n* répétition *f* ■ **repetitious, repetitive** [repə'tɪʃəs, rɪ'petɪtɪv] *adj* répétitif, -ive

rephrase [riː'freɪz] *vt* reformuler

replace [rɪ'pleɪs] *vt (take the place of)* remplacer (**by** *or* **with** par); *(put back)* remettre (à sa place); **to r. the receiver** *(on phone)* raccrocher ■ **replacement** *n (substitution)* remplacement *m* (**of** de); *(person)* remplaçant, -e *mf*; *(machine part)* pièce *f* de rechange

replay 1 ['riːpleɪ] *n (match)* nouvelle rencontre *f*; **(instant** *or* **action) r.** *(on TV)* = répétition d'une séquence précédente **2** [riː'pleɪ] *vt (match)* rejouer

replica ['replɪkə] *n* réplique *f*

reply [rɪ'plaɪ] **1** *(pl* **-ies)** *n* réponse *f*; **in r.** en réponse (**to** à) **2** *(pt & pp* **-ied)** *vti* répondre (**to** à; **that** que)

report [rɪ'pɔːt] **1** *n (analysis)* rapport *m*; *(account)* compte rendu *m*; *(in media)* reportage *m*; *Br* **(school) r.**, *Am* **r. card** bulletin *m* scolaire

2 vt (information) rapporter; (accident, theft) signaler (**to** à); **to r. sb to the police** dénoncer qn à la police
3 vi (give account) faire un rapport (**on** sur); (of journalist) faire un reportage (**on** sur); (go) se présenter (**to** à) ■ **reported** adj **r. speech** (in grammar) discours m indirect; **it is r. that...** on dit que...; **to be r. missing** être porté disparu ■ **reporter** n reporter m

repossess [ri:pə'zes] vt saisir
represent [repri'zent] vt représenter ■ **representation** n représentation f
representative [repri'zentətiv] **1** adj représentatif, -ive (**of** de) **2** n représentant, -e mf; Am Pol ≃ député m
repress [ri'pres] vt réprimer; (memory, feeling) refouler; **to be repressed** (of person) être un(e) refoulé(e) ■ **repressive** adj (régime) répressif, -ive; (measures) de répression
reprieve [ri'pri:v] n (cancellation of sentence) commutation f de la peine capitale; (temporary) & Fig sursis m
reprimand ['reprimɑ:nd] **1** n réprimande f **2** vt réprimander
reprint 1 ['ri:print] n réimpression f **2** [ri:'print] vt réimprimer
reprisal [ri'praizəl] n représailles fpl; **as a r. for, in r. for** en représailles de
reproach [ri'prəʊtʃ] **1** n (blame) reproche m **2** vt faire des reproches à; **to r. sb with sth** reprocher qch à qn
reproduce [ri:prə'dju:s] **1** vt reproduire **2** vi se reproduire ■ **reproduction** [-'dʌkʃən] n reproduction f
reptile ['reptail] n reptile m
republic [ri'pʌblik] n république f ■ **republican** adj & n républicain, -e (mf)
repugnant [ri'pʌɡnənt] adj répugnant
repulsive [ri'pʌlsiv] adj repoussant
reputable ['repjʊtəbəl] adj de bonne réputation ■ **reputed** adj **she's r. to be wealthy** on la dit riche
reputation [repjʊ'teiʃən] n réputation f
request [ri'kwest] **1** n demande f (**for**

de); **on r.** sur demande; **at sb's r.** à la demande de qn; Br **r. stop** (for bus) arrêt m facultatif **2** vt demander; **to r. sb to do sth** prier qn de faire qch
require [ri'kwaiə(r)] vt (of task, problem, situation) requérir; (of person) avoir besoin de; **to be required to do sth** être tenu de faire qch; **the required qualities** les qualités fpl requises ■ **requirement** n (need) exigence f; (condition) condition f (requise)
requisite ['rekwizit] adj requis
reschedule [Br ri:'ʃedju:l, Am ri:-'skedʒʊəl] vt changer la date/l'heure de
rescue ['reskju:] **1** n (action) sauvetage m (of de); **to go/come to sb's r.** aller/venir au secours de qn **2** adj (team, operation, attempt) de sauvetage **3** vt (save) sauver; (set free) délivrer (**from** de)
research [ri'sɜ:tʃ] **1** n recherches fpl (**on** or **into** sur) **2** vi faire des recherches (**on** or **into** sur) ■ **researcher** n chercheur, -euse mf
resemble [ri'zembəl] vt ressembler à ■ **resemblance** n ressemblance f (**to** avec)
resent [ri'zent] vt ne pas aimer ■ **resentment** n ressentiment m
reservation [rezə'veiʃən] n (**a**) (booking) réservation f; **to make a r.** réserver (**b**) (doubt) réserve f (**c**) (land for Indians, animals) réserve f
reserve [ri'zɜ:v] **1** n (**a**) (reticence) réserve f (**b**) (stock, land) réserve f; **r.** (**player**) (in team) remplaçant, -e mf; Mil **the reserves** les réservistes mpl; **in r.** en réserve; **r. tank** (of vehicle, aircraft) réservoir m de secours
2 vt (room, decision) réserver; (right) se réserver ■ **reserved** adj (person, room) réservé
reservoir ['rezəvwɑ:(r)] n (of water) réservoir m
reset [ri:'set] vt (counter) remettre à zéro
reshuffle [ri:'ʃʌfəl] n (cabinet) **r.** remaniement m (ministériel)

reside [rɪ'zaɪd] *vi* résider

residence ['rezɪdəns] *n (home)* résidence *f; (of students)* foyer *m; Br* **r. permit** permis *m* de séjour

resident ['rezɪdənt] **1** *n (of country, street)* habitant, -e *mf; (of hotel)* pensionnaire *mf; (foreigner)* résident, -e *mf* **2** *adj* **to be r. in London** résider à Londres

residential [rezɪ'denʃəl] *adj (neighbourhood)* résidentiel, -elle

resign [rɪ'zaɪn] **1** *vt (job)* démissionner de; **to r. oneself to sth/to doing sth** se résigner à qch/à faire qch **2** *vi* démissionner (**from** de) ■ **resigned** *adj* résigné

resignation [rezɪg'neɪʃən] *n (from job)* démission *f; (attitude)* résignation *f*

resilient [rɪ'zɪlɪənt] *adj* élastique; *Fig (person)* résistant

resist [rɪ'zɪst] **1** *vt* résister à; **to r. doing sth** s'empêcher de faire qch **2** *vi* résister ■ **resistance** *n* résistance *f* (**to** à) ■ **resistant** *adj* résistant (**to** à)

resit [ri:'sɪt] *(pt & pp* **-sat,** *pres p* **-sitting)** *vt Br (exam)* repasser

resolute ['rezəlu:t] *adj* résolu ■ **resolution** *n* résolution *f*

resolve [rɪ'zɒlv] **1** *n* résolution *f* **2** *vt (problem)* résoudre; **to r. to do sth** *(of person)* se résoudre à faire qch

resort [rɪ'zɔ:t] **1** *n* **(a)** *(holiday place)* lieu *m* de villégiature; *Am* **beach r. station** *f* balnéaire **(b)** *(recourse)* **as a last r., in the last r.** en dernier ressort **2** *vi* **to r. to sth** avoir recours à qch; **to r. to doing sth** finir par faire qch

resounding [rɪ'zaʊndɪŋ] *adj (failure)* retentissant; *(success)* éclatant

resource [rɪ'sɔ:s, rɪ'zɔ:s] *n* ressource *f* ■ **resourceful** *adj* ingénieux, -euse

respect [rɪ'spekt] **1** *n* respect *m* (**for** pour); *(aspect)* égard *m;* **in many respects** à bien des égards; **with r. to, in r. of** en ce qui concerne **2** *vt* respecter

respectable [rɪ'spektəbəl] *adj (decent, fairly large)* respectable; *(fairly good)* honorable

respective [rɪ'spektɪv] *adj* respectif, -ive ■ **respectively** *adv* respectivement

respond [rɪ'spɒnd] *vi (answer)* répondre (**to** à); *(react)* réagir (**to** à); **to r. to treatment** bien réagir (au traitement) ■ **response** *n (answer)* réponse *f; (reaction)* réaction *f;* **in r. to** en réponse à

responsible [rɪ'spɒnsəbəl] *adj* responsable (**for** de); *(job)* à responsabilités ■ **responsibility** *(pl* **-ies)** *n* responsabilité *f* (**for** de) ■ **responsibly** *adv* de façon responsable

responsive [rɪ'spɒnsɪv] *adj (reacting)* qui réagit bien; *(alert)* éveillé; **r. to** *(suggestion)* réceptif, -ive à

rest¹ [rest] **1** *n (relaxation)* repos *m; (support)* support *m;* **to have** *or* **take a r.** se reposer; **to set** *or* **put sb's mind at r.** tranquilliser qn; *Am* **r. room** toilettes *fpl* **2** *vt (lean)* poser (**on** sur); *(horse)* laisser reposer **3** *vi (relax)* se reposer; *(lean)* être posé (**on** sur); **to r. on** *(of argument, roof)* reposer sur; **a resting place** un lieu de repos

rest² [rest] **1** *n (remainder)* reste *m* (**of** de); **the r.** *(others)* les autres *mfpl* **2** *vi* **to r. with sb** *(of decision, responsibility)* incomber à qn

restaurant ['restərɒnt] *n* restaurant *m; Br* **r. car** *(on train)* wagon-restaurant *m*

restful ['restfəl] *adj* reposant

restless ['restləs] *adj* agité

restore [rɪ'stɔ:(r)] *vt (give back)* rendre (**to** à); *(order, peace, rights)* rétablir; *(building, painting, monarchy)* restaurer

restrain [rɪ'streɪn] *vt (person, dog)* maîtriser; *(crowd, anger)* contenir; **to r. sb from doing sth** retenir qn pour qu'il ne fasse pas qch ■ **restrained** *adj (manner)* réservé ■ **restraint** *n (moderation)* mesure *f; (restriction)* restriction *f*

restrict [rɪˈstrɪkt] *vt* restreindre; **to r. oneself to sth/doing sth** se limiter à qch/à faire qch ▪ **restricted** *adj* restreint ▪ **restriction** *n* restriction *f* (**on** à)

result [rɪˈzʌlt] **1** *n (outcome, success)* résultat *m*; **as a r.** en conséquence; **as a r. of** à la suite de **2** *vi* résulter (**from** de); **to r. in sth** aboutir à qch

resume [rɪˈzjuːm] *vti* reprendre; **to r. doing sth** se remettre à faire qch ▪ **resumption** [-ˈzʌmpʃən] *n* reprise *f*

résumé [ˈrezjʊmeɪ] *n (summary)* résumé *m*; *Am (CV)* curriculum vitae *m inv*

resurgence [rɪˈsɜːdʒəns] *n* réapparition *f*

resurrect [rezəˈrekt] *vt Fig (fashion)* remettre au goût du jour ▪ **resurrection** *n Rel* résurrection *f*

resuscitate [rɪˈsʌsɪteɪt] *vt Med* ranimer

retail [ˈriːteɪl] **1** *n (vente f au)* détail *m* **2** *adj (price)* de détail **3** *vi* se vendre (au détail) (**at** à) ▪ **retailer** *n* détaillant *m*

retain [rɪˈteɪn] *vt (keep)* conserver; *(hold in place)* retenir

retaliate [rɪˈtælɪeɪt] *vi* riposter ▪ **retaliation** *n* représailles *fpl*; **in r. for** en représailles à

retch [retʃ] *vi* avoir des haut-le-cœur

rethink [riːˈθɪŋk] *(pt & pp* -**thought**) *vt* repenser

reticent [ˈretɪsənt] *adj* peu communicatif, -ive

retire [rɪˈtaɪə(r)] *vi* (**a**) *(from work)* prendre sa retraite (**b**) *(withdraw)* se retirer (**from** de; **to** à); *(go to bed)* aller se coucher ▪ **retired** *adj (no longer working)* retraité

retirement [rɪˈtaɪəmənt] *n* retraite *f*; **r. age** l'âge *m* de la retraite

retrace [rɪˈtreɪs] *vt* **to r. one's steps** revenir sur ses pas

retract [rɪˈtrækt] **1** *vt* (**a**) *(statement)* revenir sur (**b**) *(claws)* rentrer **2** *vi (of person)* se rétracter

retrain [riːˈtreɪn] **1** *vt* recycler **2** *vi* se recycler ▪ **retraining** *n* recyclage *m*

retreat [rɪˈtriːt] **1** *n (withdrawal)* retraite *f*; *(place)* refuge *m* **2** *vi* se réfugier; *(of troops)* battre en retraite

retribution [retrɪˈbjuːʃən] *n* châtiment *m*

retrieve [rɪˈtriːv] *vt (recover)* récupérer

retrospect [ˈretrəspekt] *n* **in r.** rétrospectivement

retrospective [retrəˈspektɪv] *adj* rétrospectif, -ive; *(law)* à effet rétroactif

return [rɪˈtɜːn] **1** *n* retour *m*; *Fin (on investment)* rapport *m*; **returns** *(profits)* bénéfices *mpl*; *Br* **r. (ticket)** (billet *m*) aller et retour *m*; **many happy returns!** bon anniversaire!; **in r.** en échange (**for** de); **by r. of post** par retour du courrier

2 *adj (trip, flight)* (de) retour; **r. match** match *m* retour

3 *vt (give back)* rendre; *(put back)* remettre; *(bring back)* rapporter; *(send back)* renvoyer; **to r. sb's call** *(on phone)* rappeler qn

4 *vi (come back)* revenir; *(go back)* retourner; *(go back home)* rentrer; **to r. to** *(subject)* revenir à

reunion [riːˈjuːnjən] *n* réunion *f* ▪ **reunite** *vt* réconcilier; **to be reunited with sb** retrouver qn

reuse [riːˈjuːz] *vt* réutiliser

reveal [rɪˈviːl] *vt (make known)* révéler (**that** que); *(make visible)* laisser voir ▪ **revealing** *adj (sign, comment)* révélateur, -trice

revel [ˈrevəl] *(Br* -**ll**-, *Am* -**l**-) *vi* faire la fête; **to r. in sth** savourer qch

revelation [revəˈleɪʃən] *n* révélation *f*

revenge [rɪˈvendʒ] **1** *n* vengeance *f*; **to have** *or* **get one's r. (on sb)** se venger (de qn); **in r.** pour se venger **2** *vt* venger

revenue [ˈrevənjuː] *n (income)* revenu *m*; *(from sales)* recettes *fpl*

reverence [ˈrevərəns] *n* révérence *f*

reversal [rɪˈvɜːsəl] *n (of situation, roles)* renversement *m*; *(of policy, opinion)* revirement *m*; **r. (of fortune)** revers *m* (de fortune)

reverse [rɪ'vɜːs] **1** *adj (opposite)* contraire; *(image)* inverse; **in r. order** dans l'ordre inverse

2 *n* contraire *m*; *(of coin)* revers *m*; *(of fabric)* envers *m*; *(of paper)* verso *m*; **in r. (gear)** *(when driving)* en marche arrière

3 *vt (situation)* renverser; *(order, policy)* inverser; *(decision)* revenir sur; **to r. the car** faire marche arrière; **Br to r. the charges** *(when phoning)* téléphoner en PCV

4 *vi Br (in car)* faire marche arrière; **to r. in/out** rentrer/sortir en marche arrière

revert [rɪ'vɜːt] *vi* **to r. to** revenir à

review [rɪ'vjuː] **1** *n* (**a**) *(of book, film)* critique *f*; **to be under r.** faire l'objet d'une révision (**b**) *(magazine)* revue *f* **2** *vt (book, film)* faire la critique de; *(troops)* passer en revue; *(situation)* faire le point sur; *(salary)* réviser ■ **reviewer** *n* critique *m*

revise [rɪ'vaɪz] **1** *vt (opinion, notes, text)* réviser **2** *vi (for exam)* réviser (**for** pour) ■ **revision** *n* révision *f*

revival [rɪ'vaɪvəl] *n (of custom, business, play)* reprise *f*; *(of fashion)* renouveau *m*

revive [rɪ'vaɪv] **1** *vt (person)* ranimer; *(custom, industry)* faire renaître; *(fashion)* relancer **2** *vi (of person)* reprendre connaissance; *(of industry)* connaître un renouveau; *(of interest)* renaître

revolt [rɪ'vəʊlt] **1** *n* révolte *f* **2** *vt (disgust)* révolter **3** *vi (rebel)* se révolter (**against** contre) ■ **revolting** *adj* dégoûtant

revolution [revə'luːʃən] *n* révolution *f* ■ **revolutionary** *(pl* **-ies)** *adj & n* révolutionnaire *(mf)*

revolve [rɪ'vɒlv] *vi* tourner (**around** autour de) ■ **revolving** *adj* **r. door(s)** porte *f* à tambour

revolver [rɪ'vɒlvə(r)] *n* revolver *m*

revulsion [rɪ'vʌlʃən] *n (disgust)* dégoût *m*

reward [rɪ'wɔːd] **1** *n* récompense *f*

(**for** de) **2** *vt* récompenser (**for** de *ou* pour) ■ **rewarding** *adj* intéressant

rewind [riː'waɪnd] *(pt & pp* **-wound)** *vt (tape, film)* rembobiner

rewrite [riː'raɪt] *(pt* **-wrote,** *pp* **-written)** *vt* réécrire

rhetoric ['retərɪk] *n* rhétorique *f* ■ **rhetorical** [rɪ'tɒrɪkəl] *adj* **r. question** question *f* de pure forme

rheumatism ['ruːmətɪzəm] *n* rhumatisme *m*; **to have r.** avoir des rhumatismes

rhinoceros [raɪ'nɒsərəs] *n* rhinocéros *m*

rhubarb ['ruːbɑːb] *n* rhubarbe *f*

rhyme [raɪm] **1** *n* rime *f*; *(poem)* vers *mpl* **2** *vi* rimer (**with** avec)

rhythm ['rɪðəm] *n* rythme *m* ■ **rhythmic(al)** ['rɪðmɪk(əl)] *adj* rythmé

rib [rɪb] *n (bone)* côte *f*

ribbon ['rɪbən] *n* ruban *m*

rice [raɪs] *n* riz *m*; **r. pudding** riz *m* au lait

rich [rɪtʃ] **1** (**-er, -est**) *adj (person, food)* riche; **to be r. in sth** être riche en qch **2** *npl* **the r.** les riches *mpl* ■ **riches** *npl* richesses *fpl*

rid [rɪd] *(pt & pp* **rid,** *pres p* **ridding)** *vt* débarrasser (**of** de); **to get r. of, to r. oneself of** se débarrasser de ■ **riddance** ['rɪdəns] *n Fam* **good r.!** bon débarras!

ridden ['rɪdən] *pp of* **ride**

riddle ['rɪdəl] **1** *n (puzzle)* devinette *f*; *(mystery)* énigme *f* **2** *vt* cribler (**with** de); **riddled with mistakes** truffé de fautes

ride [raɪd] **1** *n (on horse)* promenade *f*; *(on bicycle, in car)* tour *m*; *(in taxi)* course *f*; **to go for a r.** aller faire un tour; **to give sb a r.** *(in car)* emmener qn en voiture; *Fam* **to take sb for a r.** mener qn en bateau

2 *(pt* **rode,** *pp* **ridden)** *vt (horse, bicycle)* monter à; *(a particular horse)* monter; **to know how to r. a bicycle** savoir faire de la bicyclette

3 *vi (on horse)* faire du cheval; *(on bicycle)* faire de la bicyclette; **to go**

riding *(on horse)* faire du cheval; **I ride to work** *(on bicycle)* je vais travailler à bicyclette

rider ['raɪdə(r)] *n (on horse)* cavalier, -ère *mf*; *(cyclist)* cycliste *mf*

ridge [rɪdʒ] *n (of mountain)* crête *f*

ridicule ['rɪdɪkjuːl] **1** *n* ridicule *m*; **to hold sb/sth up to r.** tourner qn/qch en ridicule **2** *vt* tourner en ridicule, ridiculiser

ridiculous [rɪ'dɪkjələs] *adj* ridicule

riding ['raɪdɪŋ] *n (horse)* **r.** équitation *f*

rife [raɪf] *adj (widespread)* répandu

riffraff ['rɪfræf] *n* racaille *f*

rifle ['raɪfəl] *n* fusil *m*

rift [rɪft] *n (in political party)* scission *f*; *(disagreement)* désaccord *m*

rig [rɪg] **1** *n (oil)* **r.** derrick *m*; *(at sea)* plate-forme *f* pétrolière **2** *(pt & pp -gg-) vt Fam (result, election)* truquer; **to r. up** *(equipment)* installer

right¹ [raɪt] **1** *adj* **(a)** *(correct)* bon (*f* bonne), exact; *(word)* juste; **to be r.** *(of person)* avoir raison (**to do** de faire); **to have (the) r. time** c'est l'heure exacte; **that's r.** c'est ça; **r.!** bon!

(b) *(appropriate)* bon (*f* bonne); **he's the r. man** c'est l'homme qu'il faut

(c) *(morally good)* bien *inv*; **to do the r. thing** faire ce qu'il faut

(d) *Fam (for emphasis)* véritable; **I felt a r. fool** je me suis vraiment senti stupide

(e) *Math* **r. angle** angle *m* droit

2 *adv (straight)* (tout) droit; *(completely)* tout à fait; *(correctly)* correctement; **to put sth r.** *(rectify)* corriger qch; *(fix)* arranger qch; **to put sb r.** détromper qn; **r. round** tout autour (**sth de** qch); **r. behind** juste derrière; **r. here** ici même; **r. away, r. now** tout de suite

3 *n* **to be in the r.** avoir raison; **r. and wrong** le bien et le mal

4 *vt (error, wrong, boat, car)* redresser

right² [raɪt] **1** *adj (not left) (hand, side)* droit **2** *adv* à droite **3** *n* droite *f*; **on or to the r.** à droite (**of** de) ◾ **right-hand** *adj* de droite; **on the r. side** à droite (**of** de) ◾ **right-handed** *adj (person)* droitier, -ère ◾ **right-wing** *adj Pol* de droite

right³ [raɪt] *n (entitlement)* droit *m* (**to do** faire); **to have a r. to sth** avoir droit à qch; **to have (the) r. of way** *(on road)* avoir la priorité

rightful ['raɪtfəl] *adj* légitime

rightly ['raɪtlɪ] *adv (correctly)* bien; *(justifiably)* à juste titre

rigid ['rɪdʒɪd] *adj* rigide

rigorous ['rɪgərəs] *adj* rigoureux, -euse

rim [rɪm] *n (of cup)* bord *m*; *(of wheel)* jante *f*

rind [raɪnd] *n (of cheese)* croûte *f*; *(of bacon)* couenne *f*

ring¹ [rɪŋ] *n (for finger, curtain)* anneau *m*; *(for finger, with stone)* bague *f*; *(on stove)* brûleur *m*; *(of people, chairs)* cercle *m*; *(of criminals)* bande *f*; *(at circus)* piste *f*; *(for boxing)* ring *m*; **to have rings under one's eyes** avoir les yeux cernés; *Br* **r. road** périphérique *m*

ring² [rɪŋ] **1** *n (sound)* **there's a r. at the door** on sonne à la porte; *Fam* **to give sb a r.** passer un coup de fil à qn

2 *(pt rang, pp rung) vt (bell)* sonner; *(alarm)* déclencher; **to r. sb** *(on phone)* téléphoner à qn; **to r. the doorbell** sonner à la porte; *Fam* **that rings a bell** ça me dit quelque chose

3 *vi (of bell, phone, person)* sonner; *(of sound, words)* retentir; *(of ears)* bourdonner; *(make a phone call)* téléphoner ◾ **ringing** *adj Br* **r. tone** *(on phone)* sonnerie *f*

▸ **ring back 1** *vt sep* **to r. sb back** rappeler qn **2** *vi* rappeler

▸ **ring off** *vi (on phone)* raccrocher

▸ **ring out** *vi (of bell)* sonner; *(of voice, shout)* retentir

▸ **ring up 1** *vt sep* **to r. sb up** téléphoner à qn **2** *vi* téléphoner

ringleader ['rɪŋliːdə(r)] *n Pej (of rebellion, strike)* meneur, -euse *mf*

rink [rɪŋk] n (for ice-skating) patinoire f; (for roller-skating) piste f

rinse [rɪns] **1** n rinçage m; **to give sth a r.** rincer qch **2** vt rincer; **to r. one's hands** se rincer les mains; **to r. out** rincer

riot ['raɪət] **1** n (uprising) émeute f; **to run r.** se déchaîner **2** vi (rise up) faire une émeute; (of prisoners) se mutiner ■ **rioter** n émeutier, -ère mf; (vandal) casseur m ■ **rioting** n émeutes fpl

rip [rɪp] **1** n déchirure f **2** (pt & pp **-pp-**) vt déchirer; **to r. sth off** arracher qch (**from** de); Fam (steal) faucher qch; Fam **to r. sb off** (deceive) rouler qn; **to r. sth up** déchirer qch **3** vi (of fabric) se déchirer ■ **rip-off** n Fam arnaque f

ripe [raɪp] **(-er, -est)** adj (fruit) mûr; (cheese) fait ■ **ripen** vti mûrir

rise [raɪz] **1** n (in price, pressure) hausse f (**in** de); (slope in ground) montée f; (of leader, party) ascension f; Br (pay) r. augmentation f (de salaire); **to give r. to sth** donner lieu à qch

2 (pt **rose**, pp **risen** ['rɪzən]) vi (of temperature, balloon, price) monter; (in society) s'élever; (of sun, theatre curtain) se lever; (of dough) lever; (get up from chair or bed) se lever; **to r. (up)** (rebel) se soulever (**against** contre)

rising ['raɪzɪŋ] adj (sun) levant; (number) croissant; (prices) en hausse

risk [rɪsk] **1** n risque m; **at r.** (person) en danger; (job) menacé; **to run the r. of doing sth** courir le risque de faire qch **2** vt (life, reputation) risquer; **I can't r. going** je ne peux pas prendre le risque d'y aller ■ **risky (-ier, -iest)** adj risqué

rite [raɪt] n rite m; Rel **the last rites** les derniers sacrements mpl ■ **ritual** ['rɪtjʊəl] **1** adj rituel, -elle **2** n rituel m

rival ['raɪvəl] **1** adj rival **2** n rival, -e mf **3** (Br **-ll-**, Am **-l-**) vt (equal) égaler (**in** en) ■ **rivalry** (pl **-ies**) n rivalité f (**between** entre)

river ['rɪvə(r)] **1** n (small) rivière f; (flowing into sea) fleuve m **2** adj r.

bank rive f ■ **riverside 1** n bord m de l'eau **2** adj au bord de l'eau

riveting ['rɪvɪtɪŋ] adj Fig fascinant

Riviera [rɪvɪ'eərə] n **the (French) R.** la Côte d'Azur

road [rəʊd] **1** n route f; (small) chemin m; (in town) rue f; (roadway) chaussée f; **the Paris r.** la route de Paris; **by r.** par la route; **to live across** or **over the r.** habiter en face

2 adj (map, safety) routier, -ère; (accident) de la route; (sign) panneau m de signalisation; Br **r. works**, Am **r. work** travaux mpl de voirie ■ **roadblock** n barrage m routier ■ **roadside** n bord m de la route

roam [rəʊm] **1** vt parcourir; **to r. the streets** traîner dans les rues **2** vi errer

roar [rɔː(r)] **1** n (of lion) rugissement m; (of person) hurlement m **2** vt **to r. sth (out)** hurler qch **3** vi (of lion, wind, engine) rugir; (of person, crowd) hurler; **to r. with laughter** hurler de rire ■ **roaring** adj **a r. fire** une belle flambée; **to do a r. trade** faire des affaires en or

roast [rəʊst] **1** n (meat) rôti m **2** adj rôti; **r. beef** rosbif m **3** vt (meat, potatoes) faire rôtir **4** vi (of meat) rôtir

rob [rɒb] (pt & pp **-bb-**) vt (person) voler; (shop, bank) dévaliser; **to r. sb of sth** voler qch à qn; Fig (deprive) priver qn de qch ■ **robber** n voleur, -euse mf ■ **robbery** (pl **-ies**) n vol m; **it's daylight r.!** c'est du vol pur et simple!

robe [rəʊb] n (of priest, judge) robe f

robin ['rɒbɪn] n (bird) rouge-gorge m

robot ['rəʊbɒt] n robot m

robust [rəʊ'bʌst] adj robuste

rock[1] [rɒk] **1** n (music) rock m **2** vt (boat) balancer; (building) secouer **3** vi (sway) se balancer; (of building, ground) trembler ■ **rocking** adj **r. chair** fauteuil m à bascule

rock[2] [rɒk] **1** n (substance) roche f; (boulder, rock face) rocher m; Am (stone) pierre f; Br (sweet) = sucrerie en forme de bâton parfumée à la menthe; **on the rocks** (whisky) avec des glaçons; *(marriage)* en pleine débâcle; **r. climbing** varappe *f*; **r. face** paroi *f* rocheuse

rocket ['rɒkɪt] **1** *n* fusée *f* **2** *vi (of prices, unemployment)* monter en flèche

rocky ['rɒkɪ] **(-ier, -iest)** *adj (road)* rocailleux, -euse; *Fig (relationship)* instable

rod [rɒd] *n (wooden)* baguette *f*; *(metal)* tige *f*; *(of curtain)* tringle *f*; *(for fishing)* canne *f* à pêche

rode [rəʊd] *pt of* **ride**

rodent ['rəʊdənt] *n* rongeur *m*

rodeo [*Br* 'rəʊdɪəʊ, *Am* rəʊ'deɪəʊ] *(pl -os)* *n Am* rodéo *m*

rogue [rəʊg] *n (dishonest)* crapule *f*; *(mischievous)* coquin, -e *mf*

role [rəʊl] *n* rôle *m*; **r. model** modèle *m*

roll [rəʊl] **1** *n (of paper)* rouleau *m*; *(of drum, thunder)* roulement *m*; *(of bread)* petit pain *m*; *(list)* liste *f*; **r. of film** pellicule *f*; **to have a r. call** faire l'appel; **r. neck** col *m* roulé
   2 *vt (cigarette)* rouler; *(ball)* faire rouler
   3 *vi (of ball)* rouler; *(of camera)* tourner ▪ **rolling** *adj (hills)* ondulant; **r. pin** rouleau *m* à pâtisserie
▸ **roll down** *vt sep (car window)* baisser; *(sleeves)* redescendre
▸ **roll in** *vi Fam (flow in)* affluer; *(of person)* s'amener
▸ **roll on** *vi Fam* **r. on tonight!** vivement ce soir!
▸ **roll out** *vt sep (dough)* étaler
▸ **roll over 1** *vt sep* retourner **2** *vi (many times)* se rouler; *(once)* se retourner
▸ **roll up 1** *vt sep (map, cloth)* rouler; *(sleeve)* retrousser **2** *vi Fam (arrive)* s'amener

roller ['rəʊlə(r)] *n (for hair, painting)* rouleau *m*; **r. coaster** montagnes *fpl* russes; **r. skate** patin *m* à roulettes ▪ **roller-skate** *vi* faire du patin à roulettes

rollerblades ['rəʊləbleɪdz] *npl* patins *mpl* en ligne

ROM [rɒm] *n (abbr* **read only memory)**

n Comptr mémoire *f* morte

Roman ['rəʊmən] **1** *adj* romain **2** *n* Romain, -e *mf* **3** *adj & n* **R. Catholic** catholique *(mf)*

romance [rəʊ'mæns] *n (love)* amour *m*; *(affair)* aventure *f* amoureuse; *(story)* histoire *f* d'amour; *(charm)* poésie *f*

Romania [rəʊ'meɪnɪə] *n* la Roumanie ▪ **Romanian 1** *adj* roumain **2** *n (person)* Roumain, -e *mf*; *(language)* roumain *m*

romantic [rəʊ'mæntɪk] **1** *adj (of love, tenderness)* romantique; *(fanciful, imaginary)* romanesque **2** *n* romantique *mf*

romp [rɒmp] *vi* s'ébattre

rompers ['rɒmpəz] *npl (for baby)* barboteuse *f*

roof [ruːf] *n (of building, vehicle)* toit *m*; *(of tunnel, cave)* plafond *m*; **r. rack** *(of car)* galerie *f* ▪ **rooftop** *n* toit *m*

room [ruːm, rʊm] *n* **(a)** *(in house)* pièce *f*; *(bedroom)* chambre *f*; *(large, public)* salle *f* **(b)** *(space)* place *f*; **to make r.** faire de la place **(for** pour) ▪ **roommate** *n* camarade *mf* de chambre ▪ **roomy (-ier, -iest)** *adj* spacieux, -euse

roost [ruːst] *vi* se percher

rooster ['ruːstə(r)] *n* coq *m*

root [ruːt] **1** *n (of plant, tooth, hair) & Math* racine *f*; *Fig (origin)* origine *f*; *(cause)* cause *f*; **to take r.** *(of plant, person)* prendre racine **2** *vt* **to r. sth out** supprimer qch

rooted ['ruːtɪd] *adj* **deeply r.** bien enraciné **(in** dans); **r. to the spot** *(immobile)* cloué sur place

rope [rəʊp] **1** *n* corde *f*; *(on ship)* cordage *m*; *Fam* **to know the ropes** connaître son affaire **2** *vt Fam* **to r. sb in** recruter qn

rop(e)y ['rəʊpɪ] **(-ier, -iest)** *adj Br Fam (thing)* minable; *(person)* patraque

rosary ['rəʊzərɪ] *(pl -ies)* *n Rel* chapelet *m*

rose¹ [rəʊz] *n (flower)* rose *f*

rose² [rəʊz] *pt of* **rise**

rosette [rəʊˈzet] n rosette f

roster [ˈrɒstə(r)] n (duty) r. liste f de service

rostrum [ˈrɒstrəm] n tribune f; (for prizewinner) podium m

rosy [ˈrəʊzɪ] (-ier, -iest) adj (pink) rose; Fig (future) prometteur, -euse

rot [rɒt] 1 n pourriture f; Br Fam (nonsense) inepties fpl 2 (pt & pp -tt-) vti pourrir

rota [ˈrəʊtə] n roulement m

rotary [ˈrəʊtərɪ] 1 adj rotatif, -ive 2 (pl -ies) n Am (for traffic) rond-point m

rotate [rəʊˈteɪt] 1 vt faire tourner 2 vi tourner

rotation [rəʊˈteɪʃən] n in r. à tour de rôle

rotten [ˈrɒtən] adj (fruit, egg, wood) pourri; Fam (bad) nul (f nulle); Fam (weather) pourri; Fam to feel r. (ill) être mal fichu

rough¹ [rʌf] 1 (-er, -est) adj (surface) rugueux, -euse; (ground) accidenté; (life) rude; (wine) âpre; (neighbourhood) dur; (sea) agité; (brutal) brutal 2 adv Br to sleep/live r. coucher/vivre à la dure 3 vt Fam to r. it vivre à la dure

rough² [rʌf] 1 (-er, -est) adj (approximate) approximatif, -ive; r. guess, r. estimate approximation f; r. copy, r. draft brouillon m; r. paper papier m brouillon 2 vt to r. sth out (plan) ébaucher

rough-and-ready [rʌfənˈredɪ] adj (solution) rudimentaire; (accommodation) sommaire

roughen [ˈrʌfən] vt rendre rugueux, -euse

roughly¹ [ˈrʌflɪ] adv (brutally) brutalement

roughly² [ˈrʌflɪ] adv (approximately) à peu près

round [raʊnd] 1 (-er, -est) adj rond; Am r. trip aller et retour m

2 adv autour; all r., right r. tout autour; all year r. toute l'année; the wrong way r. à l'envers

3 prep autour de; r. here par ici; r. about (approximately) environ

4 n Br (slice) tranche f; (in competition) manche f; (of golf) partie f; (in boxing) round m; (of talks) série f; (of drinks) tournée f

5 vt to r. sth off (meal, speech) terminer qch (with par); to r. up (gather) rassembler; (price) arrondir au chiffre supérieur

roundabout [ˈraʊndəbaʊt] 1 adj (method, route) indirect 2 n Br (at funfair) manège m; (road junction) rond-point m

rounders [ˈraʊndəz] npl = jeu similaire au base-ball

rouse [raʊz] vt (awaken) éveiller; roused (to anger) en colère

rousing [ˈraʊzɪŋ] adj (speech) vibrant

route [ruːt] n itinéraire m; (of aircraft, ship) route f; bus r. ligne f d'autobus

routine [ruːˈtiːn] 1 n (habit) routine f; the daily r. le train-train quotidien 2 adj (inquiry, work) de routine; Pej routinier, -ère

row¹ [rəʊ] n (line) rangée f; two days in a r. deux jours d'affilée

row² [rəʊ] 1 n Am r. boat bateau m à rames 2 vt (boat) faire aller à la rame; (person) transporter en canot 3 vi (in boat) ramer

row³ [raʊ] 1 n (noise) vacarme m; (quarrel) dispute f 2 vi se disputer (with avec)

rowdy [ˈraʊdɪ] (-ier, -iest) adj chahuteur, -euse

rowing [ˈrəʊɪŋ] n (as sport) aviron m; Br r. boat bateau m à rames

royal [ˈrɔɪəl] adj royal; the R. Air Force = l'armée de l'air britannique

royalty [ˈrɔɪəltɪ] 1 n (rank, position) royauté f 2 npl royalties (from book) droits mpl d'auteur

rub [rʌb] 1 n (massage) friction f; to give sth a r. frotter qch 2 (pt & pp -bb-) vti frotter

▶ **rub down** vt sep (person) frictionner; (wood, with sandpaper) poncer

▶ **rub in** vt sep (cream) faire pénétrer (en massant); Fam to r. it in retourner le couteau dans la plaie

▶ **rub off** vt sep (mark) effacer
▶ **rub out** vt sep (mark, writing) effacer

rubber ['rʌbə(r)] n (substance) caoutchouc m; Br (eraser) gomme f; Am Fam (contraceptive) capote f; **r. band** élastique m; **r. stamp** tampon m

rubbish ['rʌbɪʃ] n Br (waste) ordures fpl; Fig (nonsense) idioties fpl; Fam that's r. (absurd) c'est absurde; (worthless) ça ne vaut rien; **r. bin** poubelle f

rubbishy ['rʌbɪʃɪ] adj (book, film) nul (f nulle); (goods) de mauvaise qualité

rubble ['rʌbəl] n décombres mpl

ruby ['ru:bɪ] (pl -ies) n (gem) rubis m

rucksack ['rʌksæk] n sac m à dos

rudder ['rʌdə(r)] n gouvernail m

ruddy ['rʌdɪ] (-ier, -iest) adj (complexion) rose; Br Fam (bloody) fichu

rude [ru:d] (-er, -est) adj (impolite) impoli (**to** envers); (indecent) obscène

rudiments ['ru:dɪmənts] npl rudiments mpl

ruffian ['rʌfɪən] n voyou m (pl -ous)

rug [rʌg] n tapis m; (over legs) plaid m

rugby ['rʌgbɪ] n **r. (football)** rugby m

rugged ['rʌgɪd] adj (terrain, coast) accidenté; (features) rude

ruin ['ru:ɪn] **1** n (destruction, rubble, building) ruine f; **in ruins** (building) en ruine **2** vt (health, country, person) ruiner; (clothes) abîmer; (effect, meal, party) gâcher ▪ **ruined** adj (person, country) ruiné; (building) en ruine

rule [ru:l] **1** n (**a**) (principle) règle f; (regulation) règle m; (government) autorité f; Br **against the rules** or Am **r.** contraire au règlement; **as a r.** en règle générale
(**b**) (for measuring) règle f
2 vt (country) gouverner; (decide) (of judge, referee) décider (**that** que); **to r. sth out** (exclude) exclure qch
3 vi (of king) régner (**over** sur); (of judge) statuer (**against** contre; **on** sur) ▪ **ruling 1** adj Pol **the r. party** le parti au pouvoir **2** n (of judge, referee) décision f

ruler ['ru:lə(r)] n (**a**) (for measuring)

règle f (**b**) (king, queen) souverain, -e mf; (political leader) dirigeant, -e mf

rum [rʌm] n rhum m

Rumania [ru:'meɪnɪə] see **Romania**

rumble ['rʌmbəl] vi (of train, thunder) gronder; (of stomach) gargouiller

rummage ['rʌmɪdʒ] vi **to r. (about)** farfouiller; Am **r. sale** vente f de charité (articles d'occasion uniquement)

rumour ['ru:mə(r)] (Am **rumor**) n rumeur f ▪ **rumoured** (Am **rumored**) adj **it is r. that...** on dit que...

rump [rʌmp] n (of horse) croupe f; **r. steak** romsteck m

RUN [rʌn] **1** n (series) série f; (running) course f; (outing) tour m; (for skiing) piste f; (in cricket, baseball) point m; (in stocking) maille f filée; **to go for a r.** aller courir; **on the r.** (prisoner) en fuite; **in the long/short r.** à long/court terme
2 (pt ran, pp run, pres p running) vt (distance, race) courir; (machine) faire fonctionner; (business, country) diriger; (courses, events) organiser; Comptr (program) exécuter; (bath) faire couler; **to r. one's hand over** passer la main sur; **to r. sb to the airport** conduire qn à l'aéroport
3 vi (flee) courir; (of river, nose, tap) couler; (of colour in washing) déteindre; (of ink) baver; (function) (of machine) marcher; (idle) (of engine) tourner; **to r. down/in/out** descendre/entrer/sortir en courant; **to go running** faire du jogging; **to r. for president** être candidat à la présidence; **it runs in the family** c'est de famille
▶ **run about** vi courir çà et là
▶ **run across** vt insep (meet) tomber sur
▶ **run along** vi **r. along!** filez!
▶ **run around** vi = **run about**
▶ **run away** vi (flee) s'enfuir (**from** de)
▶ **run down** vt sep (pedestrian) renverser; (knock over and kill) écraser; Fig (belittle) dénigrer; (restrict) limiter peu à peu

▸ **run into** vt insep (meet) tomber sur; (crash into) (of vehicle) percuter

▸ **run off** 1 vt sep (print) tirer 2 vi (flee) s'enfuir (**with** avec)

▸ **run out** vi (of stocks) s'épuiser; (of lease) expirer; (of time) manquer; **to r. out of time/money** manquer de temps/d'argent; **we've r. out of coffee** on n'a plus de café; **I ran out of petrol** or Am **gas** je suis tombé en panne d'essence

▸ **run over** 1 vt sep (kill) écraser; (knock down) renverser 2 vt insep (notes, text) revoir 3 vi (of liquid) déborder

▸ **run round** vt insep (surround) entourer

▸ **run through** vt insep (recap) revoir

▸ **run up** vt sep (debts, bill) laisser s'accumuler

runaway ['rʌnəweɪ] 1 n fugitif, -ive mf 2 adj (car, horse) fou (f folle); (inflation) galopant

run-down [rʌn'daʊn] adj (weak, tired) fatigué; (district) délabré

rung[1] [rʌŋ] n (of ladder) barreau m

rung[2] [rʌŋ] pp of **ring**[1]

runner ['rʌnə(r)] n (athlete) coureur m; Br **r. bean** haricot m d'Espagne

runner-up [rʌnər'ʌp] n (in race) second, -e mf

running ['rʌnɪŋ] 1 n course f; (of business, country) gestion f; **to be in/out of the r.** être/ne plus être dans la course 2 adj **six days r.** six jours de suite; **r. water** eau f courante; **r. costs** (of factory) frais mpl d'exploitation; (of car) dépenses fpl courantes

runny ['rʌnɪ] (**-ier, -iest**) adj (cream, sauce) liquide; (nose) qui coule

run-up ['rʌnʌp] n **in the r. to** (elections, Christmas) dans la période qui précède

runway ['rʌnweɪ] n (for aircraft) piste f (d'envol)

rupture ['rʌptʃə(r)] 1 n (hernia) hernie f 2 vt rompre

rural ['rʊərəl] adj rural

ruse [ruːz] n ruse f

rush[1] [rʌʃ] 1 n (demand) ruée f (for vers; on sur); (confusion) bousculade f; **to be in a r.** être pressé (**to do de** faire); **r. hour** heures fpl de pointe
2 vt **to r. sb** (hurry) bousculer qn; **to r. sb to hospital** or Am **the hospital** transporter qn d'urgence à l'hôpital; **to r. sth** (job) faire qch en vitesse; (decision) prendre qch à la hâte 3 vi (move fast, throw oneself) se ruer (**at** sur; **towards** vers); (hurry) se dépêcher (**to do** de faire); (of vehicle) foncer; **to r. out** sortir précipitamment

rush[2] [rʌʃ] n (plant) jonc m

rusk [rʌsk] n Br biscotte f

Russia ['rʌʃə] n la Russie ▪ **Russian 1** adj russe 2 n (person) Russe mf; (language) russe m

rust [rʌst] 1 n rouille f 2 vi rouiller

rustic ['rʌstɪk] adj rustique

rustle ['rʌsəl] 1 vt Fam **to r. sth up** (meal, snack) improviser qch 2 vi (of leaves) bruire

rustproof ['rʌstpruːf] adj inoxydable

rusty ['rʌstɪ] (**-ier, -iest**) adj rouillé

rut [rʌt] n ornière f; Fig **to be in a r.** être encroûté

ruthless ['ruːθləs] adj impitoyable

rye [raɪ] n seigle m; **r. bread** pain m de seigle

Ss

S, s [es] *n (letter)* S, s *m inv*

sabotage ['sæbətɑːʒ] **1** *n* sabotage *m*
2 *vt* saboter

sachet ['sæʃeɪ] *n* sachet *m*

sack [sæk] **1** *n (bag)* sac *m; Fam* **to get
the s.** se faire virer **2** *vt Fam (dismiss)*
virer

sacred ['seɪkrɪd] *adj* sacré

sacrifice ['sækrɪfaɪs] **1** *n* sacrifice *m* **2**
vt sacrifier (**to** à)

sad [sæd] (**sadder, saddest**) *adj* triste
■ **sadden** *vt* attrister ■ **sadly** *adv (un-
happily)* tristement; *(unfortunately)*
malheureusement ■ **sadness** *n* tristesse *f*

saddle ['sædəl] **1** *n* selle *f* **2** *vt (horse)*
seller

sadistic [sə'dɪstɪk] *adj* sadique

sae [eseɪ'iː] *(abbr Br* **stamped addressed envelope,** *Am* **self-addressed
envelope)** *n* enveloppe *f* timbrée

safari [sə'fɑːrɪ] *n* safari *m*

safe [seɪf] **1** (**-er, -est**) *adj (person)* en
sécurité; *(equipment, animal)* sans
danger; *(place, investment, method)*
sûr; **s. (and sound)** sain et sauf *(f
saine et sauve)* **2** *n (for money)* coffre-fort *m* ■ **safely** *adv (without risk)*
en toute sécurité; *(drive)* prudemment; *(with certainty)* avec certitude

safeguard ['seɪfgɑːd] **1** *n* garantie *f*
(**against** contre) **2** *vt* sauvegarder

safety ['seɪftɪ] **1** *n* sécurité *f* **2** *adj
(belt, device, margin)* de sécurité;
(pin, chain, valve) de sûreté

sag [sæg] *(pt & pp* -**gg**-) *vi (of roof, bed)*
s'affaisser

saga ['sɑːgə] *n* saga *f*

Sahara [sə'hɑːrə] *n* **the S. (desert)** le
Sahara

said [sed] *pt & pp of* **say**

sail [seɪl] **1** *n (on boat)* voile *f;* **to set s.**
prendre la mer **2** *vt (boat)* comman-
der **3** *vi (of person, ship)* naviguer;
(leave) prendre la mer ■ **sailing** *n
(sport)* voile *f;* **to go s.** faire de la voile;
Br **s. boat** voilier *m* ■ **sailboat** *n Am*
voilier *m*

sailor ['seɪlə(r)] *n* marin *m*

saint [seɪnt] *n* saint *m,* sainte *f*

sake [seɪk] *n* **for my/your/his s.** pour
moi/toi/lui; **for heaven's** *or* **God's s.!**
pour l'amour de Dieu!; **(just) for
the s. of eating** simplement pour
manger

salad ['sæləd] *n* salade *f; Br* **s. cream** =
sorte de mayonnaise; **s. dressing** =
sauce pour salade

salami [sə'lɑːmɪ] *n* salami *m*

salary ['sælərɪ] *(pl* -**ies**) *n* salaire *m*

sale [seɪl] *n (action, event)* vente *f; (at
reduced price)* solde *m;* **on s.** en vente;
in the sales en solde; **(up) for s.** à vendre; *Am* **sales check** *or* **slip** reçu *m*
■ **salesclerk** *n Am* vendeur, -euse *mf*
■ **salesman** *(pl* -**men**) *n (in shop)* vendeur *m; (for company)* représentant
m ■ **saleswoman** *(pl* -**women**) *n (in
shop)* vendeuse *f; (for company)* repré-
sentante *f*

salmon ['sæmən] *n inv* saumon *m*

salon ['sælɒn] *n* **beauty s.** institut *m* de
beauté; **hairdressing s.** salon *m* de
coiffure

saloon [sə'luːn] *n Am (bar)* bar *m; Br* **s.
car** berline *f*

salt [sɔːlt] **1** n sel m **2** vt saler ▪ **salt-cellar** n Br salière f ▪ **salt-shaker** n Am salière f ▪ **saltwater** adj (lake) salé; (fish) de mer ▪ **salty** (-ier, -iest) adj salé

salute [sə'luːt] **1** n salut m **2** vt (greet) & Mil saluer **3** vi faire un salut

salvage ['sælvɪdʒ] vt (ship) sauver; (waste material) récupérer

salvation [sæl'veɪʃən] n salut m

SAME [seɪm] **1** adj même; **the (very) s. house as...** (exactement) la même maison que...
2 pron **the s.** le même, la même, pl les mêmes; **I would have done the s.** j'aurais fait la même chose; **it's all the s. to me** ça m'est égal
3 adv **to look the s.** (of two things) sembler pareils; **all the s.** (nevertheless) tout de même

sample ['sɑːmpəl] **1** n échantillon m; (of blood) prélèvement m **2** vt (wine, cheese) goûter

sanction ['sæŋkʃən] n (penalty) sanction f

sanctuary [Br 'sæŋktʃʊərɪ, Am -erɪ] (pl -ies) n (for fugitive, refugee) refuge m; (for wildlife) réserve f

sand [sænd] **1** n sable m; **s. castle** château m de sable **2** vt **to s. (down)** (wood) poncer

sandal ['sændəl] n sandale f

sandwich ['sænwɪdʒ] **1** n sandwich m; **cheese s.** sandwich m au fromage **2** vt **to be sandwiched between** (of person, building) être coincé entre

sandy ['sændɪ] (-ier, -iest) adj (**a**) (beach) de sable; (ground) sablonneux, -euse (**b**) (hair) blond roux inv

sane [seɪn] (-er, -est) adj (person) sain d'esprit

sang [sæŋ] pt of **sing**

sanitary [Br 'sænɪtərɪ, Am -erɪ] adj (fittings) sanitaire; Br **s. towel**, Am **s. napkin** serviette f hygiénique

sanitation [sænɪ'teɪʃən] n hygiène f publique; (plumbing) installations fpl sanitaires

sanity ['sænɪtɪ] n santé f mentale

sank [sæŋk] pt of **sink²**

Santa Claus ['sæntəklɔːz] n le Père Noël

sap [sæp] **1** n (of tree, plant) sève f **2** (pt & pp -pp-) vt (weaken) saper

sapphire ['sæfaɪə(r)] n saphir m

sarcastic [sɑː'kæstɪk] adj sarcastique

sardine [sɑː'diːn] n sardine f

Sardinia [sɑː'dɪnɪə] n la Sardaigne

sat [sæt] pt & pp of **sit**

Satan ['seɪtən] n Satan m

satchel ['sætʃəl] n cartable m

satellite ['sætəlaɪt] n satellite m; **s. dish** antenne f parabolique; **s. television** télévision f par satellite

satin ['sætɪn] n satin m

satire ['sætaɪə(r)] n satire f (**on** contre) ▪ **satirical** adj satirique

satisfaction [sætɪs'fækʃən] n satisfaction f ▪ **satisfactory** adj satisfaisant

satisfy ['sætɪsfaɪ] (pt & pp -ied) vt satisfaire; (convince) persuader (**that** que); (condition) remplir; **to be satisfied (with)** être satisfait (de) ▪ **satisfying** adj satisfaisant; (meal, food) substantiel, -elle

satsuma [sæt'suːmə] n Br mandarine f

saturate ['sætʃəreɪt] vt saturer (**with** de)

Saturday ['sætədeɪ] n samedi m

sauce [sɔːs] n sauce f; **mint s.** sauce à la menthe

saucepan ['sɔːspən] n casserole f

saucer ['sɔːsə(r)] n soucoupe f

Saudi Arabia [saʊdɪə'reɪbɪə] n l'Arabie f saoudite

sauna ['sɔːnə] n sauna m

saunter ['sɔːntə(r)] vi flâner

sausage ['sɒsɪdʒ] n saucisse f; Br **s. roll** feuilleté m à la viande

savage ['sævɪdʒ] **1** adj (animal, person) féroce; (attack, criticism) violent **2** vt (physically) attaquer

save¹ [seɪv] **1** vt (rescue) sauver (**from** de); (keep) garder; (money) économiser; (time) gagner; Comptr sauvegarder; **to s. sb's life** sauver la vie de qn; **to s. sb from doing sth** empêcher qn de faire qch **2** *vi* **to s. (up)** faire des économies (**for/on** pour/sur) **3** *n* (*by goalkeeper*) arrêt *m*

save² [seɪv] *prep Formal (except)* hormis

saving ['seɪvɪŋ] *n (of time, money)* économie *f*; **savings** *(money saved)* économies *fpl*; **savings account** compte *m* d'épargne

saviour ['seɪvjə(r)] *(Am* **savior**) *n* sauveur *m*

savour ['seɪvə(r)] *(Am* **savor**) *vt* savourer ■ **savoury** *(Am* **savory**) *adj (not sweet)* salé

saw¹ [sɔː] **1** *n* scie *f* **2** *(pt* **sawed**, *pp* **sawn** *or* **sawed**) *vt* scier; **to s. sth off** scier qch ■ **sawdust** *n* sciure *f*

saw² [sɔː] *pt of* **see¹**

sawn [sɔːn] *pp of* **saw¹**

saxophone ['sæksəfəʊn] *n* saxophone *m*

say [seɪ] **1** *(pt & pp* **said**) *vt* dire (**to** à; **that** que); (*of dial, watch*) indiquer; **to s. again** répéter; **that is to s.** c'est-à-dire

2 *vi* dire; *Am Fam* **s.!** dis donc!; **that goes without saying** ça va sans dire **3** *n* **to have one's s.** avoir son mot à dire; **to have no s.** ne pas avoir voix au chapitre (**in** concernant)

saying ['seɪɪŋ] *n* maxime *f*

scab [skæb] *n (of wound)* croûte *f*

scaffolding ['skæfəldɪŋ] *n* échafaudage *m*

scald [skɔːld] *vt* ébouillanter

scale¹ [skeɪl] **1** *n (of instrument, map)* échelle *f*; (*of salaries*) barème *m*; *Fig (of problem)* étendue *f*; **on a small/large s.** sur une petite/grande échelle **2** *vt* **to s. sth down** revoir qch à la baisse

scale² [skeɪl] *n (on fish)* écaille *f*; (*in kettle*) dépôt *m* calcaire

scales [skeɪlz] *npl (for weighing)* balance *f*; (**bathroom**) **s.** pèse-personne *m*

scalp [skælp] *n* cuir *m* chevelu

scamper ['skæmpə(r)] *vi* **to s. off** *or* **away** détaler

scampi ['skæmpɪ] *n* scampi *mpl*

scan [skæn] **1** *n* **to have a s.** passer une échographie **2** *(pt & pp* **-nn-**) *vt (look at briefly)* parcourir; (*scrutinize*) scruter; *Comptr* passer au scanner

scandal ['skændəl] *n (outrage)* scandale *m*; (*gossip*) ragots *mpl* ■ **scandalous** *adj* scandaleux, -euse

Scandinavia [skændɪ'neɪvɪə] *n* la Scandinavie ■ **Scandinavian 1** *adj* scandinave **2** *n* Scandinave *mf*

scanner ['skænə(r)] *n Med & Comptr* scanner *m*

scant [skænt] *adj* insuffisant ■ **scanty** (**-ier, -iest**) *adj* insuffisant; (*bikini*) minuscule

scapegoat ['skeɪpgəʊt] *n* bouc *m* émissaire

scar [skɑː] **1** *n* cicatrice *f* **2** *(pt & pp* **-rr-**) *vt* marquer d'une cicatrice; *Fig (of experience)* marquer

scarce [skeəs] (**-er, -est**) *adj* rare ■ **scarcely** *adv* à peine; **s. anything** presque rien

scare [skeə(r)] **1** *n* to give sb a s. faire peur à qn **2** *vt* faire peur à; **to s. sb off** faire fuir qn ■ **scared** *adj* effrayé; **to be s. of sb/sth** avoir peur de qn/qch

scarf [skɑːf] *(pl* **scarves**) *n (long)* écharpe *f*; (*square*) foulard *m*

scarlet ['skɑːlət] *adj* écarlate; **s. fever** scarlatine *f*

scary ['skeərɪ] (**-ier, -iest**) *adj Fam* effrayant

scathing ['skeɪðɪŋ] *adj (remark)* acerbe; **to be s. about sb/sth** faire des remarques acerbes sur qn/qch

scatter ['skætə(r)] **1** *vt (demonstrators)* disperser; (*corn, seed*) jeter à la volée; (*papers*) laisser traîner **2** *vi (of crowd)* se disperser

scavenge ['skævɪndʒ] *vi* **to s. for sth** fouiller pour trouver qch

scenario [sɪ'nɑːrɪəʊ] *(pl* **-os**) *n (of film)* scénario *m*

scene [siːn] *n (in book, film, play)* scène *f*; (*of event, crime, accident*) lieu *m*; *also Fig* **behind the scenes** dans les coulisses; **on the s.** sur les lieux; **to**

make a s. faire un scandale

scenery ['si:nərɪ] (pl **-ies**) n (landscape) paysage m; (in play, film) décors mpl

scenic ['si:nɪk] adj pittoresque; **s. route** route f touristique

scent [sent] n (smell) odeur f; (perfume) parfum m; (in hunting) fumet m

sceptical ['skeptɪkəl] (Am **skeptical**) adj sceptique

schedule [Br 'ʃedju:l, Am 'skedʒʊl] **1** n (plan) programme m; (for trains, buses) horaire m; (list) liste f; **according to s.** comme prévu **2** vt prévoir; (event) fixer la date/l'heure de ▪ **scheduled** [Br 'ʃedju:ld, Am 'skedʒʊld] adj (planned) prévu; (service, flight, train) régulier, -ère

scheme [ski:m] **1** n (plan) plan m (**to do** pour faire); (plot) complot m; (arrangement) arrangement m **2** vi Pej comploter ▪ **scheming** Pej **1** adj intrigant **2** n machinations fpl

schizophrenic [skɪtsəʊ'frenɪk] adj & n schizophrène (mf)

scholar ['skɒlə(r)] n érudit, -e mf ▪ **scholarly** adj érudit ▪ **scholarship** n (learning) érudition f; (grant) bourse f d'études

school [sku:l] **1** n école f; (within university) département m; Am Fam (college) université f; Br **secondary s.,** Am **high s.** établissement m d'enseignement secondaire

2 adj (year, book, equipment) scolaire; **s. bag** cartable m; **s. fees** frais mpl de scolarité; **s. yard** cour f de récréation ▪ **schoolboy** n écolier m ▪ **schoolchildren** npl écoliers mpl ▪ **schoolfriend** n camarade mf de classe ▪ **schoolgirl** n écolière f ▪ **schoolteacher** n (primary) instituteur, -trice mf; (secondary) professeur m

science ['saɪəns] n science f; **to study s.** étudier les sciences; **s. fiction** science-fiction f ▪ **scientific** adj scientifique ▪ **scientist** n scientifique mf

scissors ['sɪzəz] npl ciseaux mpl

scoff [skɒf] **1** vt **to s. at** sb/sth se moquer de qn/qch **2** vti Br Fam (eat) bouffer

scold [skəʊld] vt gronder (**for doing** pour avoir fait)

scone [skəʊn, skɒn] n Br scone m

scoop [sku:p] n (for flour, sugar) pelle f; (for ice cream) cuillère f; (amount) (of ice cream) boule f **2** vt **to s. sth out** (hollow out) évider qch; **to s. sth up** ramasser qch

scooter ['sku:tə(r)] n (for child) trottinette f; (motorcycle) scooter m

scope [skəʊp] n (range) étendue f; (of action) possibilité f

scorch [skɔ:tʃ] **1** n **s. (mark)** brûlure f **2** vt roussir ▪ **scorching** adj (day) torride; (sun, sand) brûlant

score[1] [skɔ:(r)] **1** n (in sport) score m; (in music) partition f; (of film) musique f **2** vt (point, goal) marquer; (exam mark) avoir; (piece of music) adapter (**for** pour) **3** vi (score a goal) marquer; (count points) marquer les points ▪ **scoreboard** n tableau m d'affichage ▪ **scorer** n marqueur m

score[2] [skɔ:(r)] n a s. (twenty) vingt; Fam **scores of** des tas de

scorn [skɔ:n] **1** n mépris m **2** vt mépriser ▪ **scornful** adj méprisant

scorpion ['skɔ:pɪən] n scorpion m

Scot [skɒt] n Écossais, -e mf ▪ **Scotland** n l'Écosse f ▪ **Scotsman** (pl **-men**) n Écossais m ▪ **Scotswoman** (pl **-women**) n Écossaise f ▪ **Scottish** adj écossais

Scotch [skɒtʃ] **1** n (whisky) scotch **2** adj Am **S. tape**® Scotch® m

scoundrel ['skaʊndrəl] n crapule f

scour ['skaʊə(r)] vt (pan) récurer; Fig (streets, house) ratisser (**for** à la recherche de) ▪ **scourer** n tampon m à récurer

scout [skaʊt] n (boy) s. scout m, éclaireur m; Am (girl) s. éclaireuse f

scowl [skaʊl] vi lancer des regards noirs (**at** à)

scram [skræm] (pt & pp **-mm-**) vi Fam se tirer

scramble ['skræmbəl] 1 vt **scrambled eggs** œufs mpl brouillés 2 vi **to s. up a hill** gravir une colline en s'aidant des mains

scrap [skræp] 1 n (a) (piece) bout m (of de); (of information) bribe f; **scraps** (food) restes mpl; **s. paper** papier m brouillon

(b) **s. (metal)** ferraille f; **s. heap** tas m de ferraille; **s. dealer, s. merchant** ferrailleur m; **s. yard** casse f

2 (pt & pp **-pp-**) vt (get rid of) se débarrasser de; (car) envoyer à la casse; Fig (plan, idea) abandonner ■ **scrapbook** n album m (de coupures de presse etc)

scrape [skreɪp] 1 vt gratter; (skin) érafler; **to s. a living** arriver tout juste à vivre 2 vi **to s. against sth** frotter contre qch

► **scrape away, scrape off** vt sep racler

► **scrape through** vt insep & vi **to s. through (an exam)** passer de justesse (à un examen)

► **scrape together** vt sep (money, people) parvenir à rassembler

scratch [skrætʃ] 1 n (mark, injury) éraflure f; (on glass, wood) rayure f; Fam **to start from s.** repartir de zéro; **it isn't up to s.** ce n'est pas au niveau

2 vt (to relieve itching) gratter; (by accident) érafler; (glass) rayer; (with claw) griffer; (write, draw) griffonner (on sur)

3 vi (of person) se gratter; (of pen, new clothes) gratter ■ **scratchcard** n (lottery card) carte f à gratter

scrawl [skrɔːl] 1 n gribouillis m 2 vt gribouiller

scream [skriːm] 1 n hurlement m 2 vt hurler 3 vi hurler; **to s. at sb** crier après qn

screech [skriːtʃ] vti hurler

screen [skriːn] 1 n (of TV set, computer, cinema) écran m; Comptr **s. saver** économiseur m d'écran

2 vt (hide) cacher (**from sb** à qn); (protect) protéger (**from** de); (film) projeter; (visitors, calls) filtrer; (for

disease) faire subir un test de dépistage à ■ **screening** n (of film) projection f; (selection) tri m; (for disease) dépistage m ■ **screenplay** n (of film) scénario m

screw [skruː] 1 n vis f 2 vt visser (**to** à); **to s. sth down** or **on** visser qch; **to s. sth off** dévisser qch; **to s. sth up** (paper) chiffonner qch ■ **screwdriver** n tournevis m

scribble ['skrɪbəl] 1 n griffonnage m 2 vti griffonner

script [skrɪpt] n (a) (of film) script m; (of play) texte m; (in exam) copie f (b) (handwriting) script m

Scripture(s) ['skrɪptʃə(z)] n(pl) Rel les saintes Écritures fpl

scroll [skrəʊl] 1 n rouleau m; (manuscript) manuscrit m 2 vi Comptr défiler; **to s. down/up** défiler vers le bas/haut

scrounge [skraʊndʒ] vt Fam (meal) se faire payer (**off** or **from sb** par qn); (steal) taper (**off** or **from sb** à qn); **to s. money off** or **from sb** taper qn ■ **scrounger** n Fam parasite m

scrub [skrʌb] 1 n (a) **to give sth a s.** bien frotter qch; Am **s. brush** brosse f dure (b) (land) broussailles fpl 2 (pt & pp **-bb-**) vt (surface) frotter; (pan) récurer; **to s. sth off** (remove) enlever qch (à la brosse ou en frottant)

scrubbing ['skrʌbɪŋ] n **s. brush** brosse f dure

scruff [skrʌf] n **by the s. of the neck** par la peau du cou

scruffy ['skrʌfɪ] (**-ier, -iest**) adj (person) peu soigné

scrum [skrʌm] n (in rugby) mêlée f

scrupulous ['skruːpjʊləs] adj scrupuleux, -euse

scrutinize ['skruːtɪnaɪz] vt (document) éplucher

scuba ['skuːbə] n **s. diving** la plongée sous-marine

scuff [skʌf] vt **to s. sth (up)** (shoe) érafler qch

scuffle ['skʌfəl] n bagarre f

sculpt [skʌlpt] vti sculpter ■ **sculptor**

n sculpteur *m* ▪ **sculpture** *n* (*art, object*) sculpture *f*

scum [skʌm] *n* (**a**) (*froth*) écume *f* (**b**) *Fam Pej* (*people*) racaille *f*; (*person*) ordure *f*

scurry ['skʌrɪ] *vi* (*rush*) courir; **to s. off** se sauver

sea [siː] **1** *n* mer *f*; (*out*) **at s.** en mer; **by s.** par mer; **by** *or* **beside the s.** au bord de la mer

2 *adj* (*level, breeze*) de la mer; (*water, fish, salt*) de mer; (*air*) marin; (*battle*) naval (*mpl* -als); (*route*) maritime; **s. bed, s. floor** fond *m* de la mer ▪ **seafood** *n* fruits *mpl* de mer ▪ **seafront** *n Br* front *m* de mer ▪ **seagull** *n* mouette *f* ▪ **seashell** *n* coquillage *m* ▪ **seaside** *n Br* bord *m* de mer; **s. resort** station *f* balnéaire ▪ **seashore** *n* rivage *m* ▪ **seasick** *adj* **to be s.** avoir le mal de mer ▪ **seaweed** *n* algues *fpl*

seal¹ [siːl] *n* (*animal*) phoque *m*

seal² [siːl] **1** *n* (*stamp*) sceau *m*; (*device for sealing*) joint *m* d'étanchéité **2** *vt* (*document, container*) sceller; (*stick down*) cacheter; (*make airtight*) fermer hermétiquement; **to s. off an area** boucler un quartier

seam [siːm] *n* (*in cloth*) couture *f*

search [sɜːtʃ] **1** *n* recherches *fpl* (**for** de); (*of place*) fouille *f*; **in s. of** à la recherche de; *Comptr* **to do a s. for sth** rechercher qch; *Comptr* **s. engine** moteur *m* de recherche **2** *vt* (*person, place*) fouiller (**for** pour trouver) **3** *vi* chercher; **to s. for sth** chercher qch ▪ **searchlight** *n* projecteur *m*

season¹ ['siːzən] *n* saison *f*; (*of films*) cycle *m*; **in the peak s., in high s.** en haute saison; **in the low** or **off s.** en basse saison; **s. ticket** abonnement *m*

season² ['siːzən] *vt* (*food*) assaisonner ▪ **seasoning** *n Culin* assaisonnement *m*

seasonal ['siːzənəl] *adj* (*work, change*) saisonnier, -ère

seat [siːt] **1** *n* siège *m*; (*of trousers*) fond *m*; **to take** or **have a s.** s'asseoir; **s. belt**

ceinture *f* de sécurité **2** *vt* (*at table*) placer; (*on one's lap*) asseoir ▪ **seated** *adj* (*sitting*) assis ▪ **seating** *n* (*seats*) places *fpl* assises

-seater ['siːtə(r)] *suff* **two-s. (car)** voiture *f* à deux places

secluded [sɪ'kluːdɪd] *adj* (*remote*) isolé ▪ **seclusion** *n* solitude *f*

second¹ ['sekənd] **1** *adj* deuxième, second; **every s. week** une semaine sur deux; *Aut* **in s. (gear)** en seconde

2 *adv* (*say*) deuxièmement; **to come s.** (*in competition*) se classer deuxième; **the s. biggest** le deuxième en ordre de grandeur

3 *n* (*in series*) deuxième *mf*, second, -e *mf*; (*in month*) deux *m*; **Louis the S.** Louis Deux; **seconds** (*goods*) articles *mpl* défectueux

4 *vt* (*motion, proposal*) appuyer ▪ **second-class** *adj* (*ticket on train*) de seconde (*classe*); (*mail*) non urgent; (*product*) de qualité inférieure ▪ **secondly** *adv* deuxièmement ▪ **second-rate** *adj* médiocre

second² ['sekənd] *n* (*part of minute*) seconde *f*; **s. hand** (*of clock, watch*) trotteuse *f*

secondary ['sekəndərɪ] *adj* secondaire; *Br* **s. school** établissement *m* secondaire

second-hand [sekənd'hænd] **1** *adj* & *adv* (*not new*) d'occasion **2** *adj* (*report, news*) de seconde main

secrecy ['siːkrəsɪ] *n* (*discretion, silence*) secret *m*

secret ['siːkrɪt] **1** *adj* secret, -ète **2** *n* secret *m*; **in s.** en secret ▪ **secretly** *adv* secrètement

secretary [*Br* 'sekrətərɪ, *Am* -erɪ] (*pl* -ies) *n* secrétaire *mf*; *Br* **Foreign S.,** *Am* **S. of State** ≃ ministre *m* des Affaires étrangères ▪ **secretarial** [-'teərɪəl] *adj* (*work*) administratif, -ive; (*job, course*) de secrétariat

secretive ['siːkrətɪv] *adj* (*person*) secret, -ète; **to be s. about sth** faire des cachotteries à propos de qch

sect [sekt] *n* secte *f*

section ['sekʃən] *n* partie *f*; *(of road)* tronçon *m*; *(of machine)* élément *m*; *(of organization)* département *m*; **the sports s.** *(of newspaper)* la page des sports

sector ['sektə(r)] *n* secteur *m*

secular ['sekjʊlə(r)] *adj* (music, art) profane

secure [sɪ'kjʊə(r)] **1** *adj* (person) en sécurité; (investment, place) sûr; (door, window) bien fermé **2** *vt* (fasten) attacher; (window, door) bien fermer; (position, future) assurer; (support, promise) procurer; **to s. sth (for oneself)** se procurer qch ■ **securely** *adv* (firmly) solidement; (safely) en sûreté

security [sɪ'kjʊərɪtɪ] (*pl* -**ies**) *n* sécurité *f*; Fin (for loan, bail) garantie *f*; **securities** (stocks, bonds) titres *mpl*

sedan [sɪ'dæn] *n Am* (saloon) berline *f*

sedate [sɪ'deɪt] **1** *adj* calme **2** *vt* mettre sous calmants

sedative ['sedətɪv] *n* calmant *m*

seduce [sɪ'dju:s] *vt* séduire ■ **seductive** [-'dʌktɪv] *adj* (person, offer) séduisant

SEE [si:] (*pt* saw, *pp* seen) *vti* voir; **we'll s.** on verra; **I can s. a hill** je vois une colline; **I saw him run(ning)** je l'ai vu courir; **to s. reason** entendre raison; **s. you (later)!** à tout à l'heure!; **to s. that...** (make sure that) faire en sorte que... (+ subjunctive); (check) s'assurer que... (+ indicative); **to s. sb to the door** accompagner qn jusqu'à la porte

▶ **see about** *vt insep* (deal with) s'occuper de; (consider) songer à

▶ **see off** *vt sep* (say goodbye to) dire au revoir à

▶ **see out** *vt sep* accompagner jusqu'à la porte

▶ **see through 1** *vt sep* (task) mener à bien **2** *vt insep* **to s. through sb** percer qn à jour

▶ **see to** *vt insep* (deal with) s'occuper de; (mend) réparer; **to s. to it that...** (make sure that) faire en sorte que...

(+ subjunctive); (check) s'assurer que... (+ indicative)

seed [si:d] *n* graine *f*; (of fruit) pépin *m*; Fig (source) germe *m*

seedy ['si:dɪ] (-**ier**, -**iest**) *adj* miteux, -euse

seeing ['si:ɪŋ] *conj* **s. (that)** vu que

seek [si:k] (*pt & pp* sought) *vt* chercher (**to do** à faire); (ask for) demander (**from** à); **to s. sb out** dénicher qn

seem [si:m] *vi* sembler (**to do** faire); **it seems that...** (impression) il semble que... (+ subjunctive); **it seems to me that...** il me semble que... (+ indicative)

seemingly ['si:mɪŋlɪ] *adv* apparemment

seemly ['si:mlɪ] *adj Formal* bienséant

seen [si:n] *pp of* **see**

seep [si:p] *vi* suinter; **to s. into sth** s'infiltrer dans qch

seesaw ['si:sɔ:] *n* balançoire *f* à bascule

see-through ['si:θru:] *adj* transparent

segment ['segmənt] *n* segment *m*; (of orange) quartier *m*

segregate ['segrɪgeɪt] *vt* séparer (**from** de) ■ **segregation** *n* ségrégation *f*

seize [si:z] **1** *vt* saisir; (power, land) s'emparer de **2** *vi* **to s. (up)on** (offer) sauter sur; **to s. up** (of engine) se bloquer

seizure ['si:ʒə(r)] *n* (of goods, property) saisie *f*; Med crise *f*

seldom ['seldəm] *adv* rarement

select [sɪ'lekt] **1** *vt* sélectionner **2** *adj* (exclusive) sélect ■ **selection** *n* sélection *f*

selective [sɪ'lektɪv] *adj* sélectif, -ive

self [self] (*pl* selves [selvz]) *n* **he's back to his old s.** il est redevenu comme avant ■ **self-addressed** *n* **s. envelope** enveloppe *f* libellée à ses nom et adresse ■ **self-assured** *adj* sûr de soi ■ **self-catering** *adj Br* (holiday) en appartement meublé; (accommodation) meublé ■ **self-centred** (*Am* -**centered**) *adj* égocentrique ■ **self-confidence** *n* confiance *f* en soi ■ **self-confident** *adj* sûr de soi ■ **self-conscious** *adj* gêné ■ **self-contained** *adj (flat)* indépendant ■ **self-control** *n* maîtrise *f* de soi ■ **self-defence** *(Am* -defense*) n (in law)* légitime défense *f;* **in s.** en état de légitime défense ■ **self-discipline** *n* autodiscipline *f* ■ **self-employed** *adj* indépendant ■ **self-esteem** *n* confiance *f* en soi ■ **self-evident** *adj* évident ■ **self-important** *adj* suffisant ■ **self-indulgent** *adj* complaisant ■ **self-interest** *n* intérêt *m* personnel ■ **self-pity** *n* **to be full of s.** s'apitoyer sur son propre sort ■ **self-portrait** *n* autoportrait *m* ■ **self-raising** *(Am* -rising*) n* **s. flour** = farine contenant de la levure chimique ■ **self-respect** *n* amour-propre *m* ■ **self-righteous** *adj* suffisant ■ **self-sacrifice** *n* abnégation *f* ■ **self-satisfied** *adj* content de soi ■ **self-service** *n & adj* libre-service *(m inv)* ■ **self-sufficient** *adj* indépendant ■ **self-taught** *adj* autodidacte

selfish ['selfɪʃ] *adj* égoïste; *(motive)* intéressé ■ **selfishness** *n* égoïsme *m* ■ **selfless** *adj* désintéressé

sell [sel] **1** *(pt & pp* sold*) vt* vendre; *Fig (idea)* faire accepter; **to s. sb sth, to s. sth to sb** vendre qch à qn; **she sold it to me for £20** elle me l'a vendu 20 livres **2** *vi (of product)* se vendre; *(of person)* vendre ■ **sell-by** *adj* **s. date** date *f* limite de vente

▸ **sell off** *vt sep* liquider

▸ **sell out** *vt insep* **to have** *or* **be sold out of sth** n'avoir plus de qch; **to be sold out** *(of book, item)* être épuisé; *(of show, concert)* afficher complet

▸ **sell up** *vi (sell home, business)* tout vendre

seller ['selə(r)] *n* vendeur, -euse *mf*

Sellotape® ['seləteɪp] *n Br* Scotch® *m*

semblance ['sembləns] *n* semblant *m*

semen ['siːmən] *n* sperme *m*

semester [sɪ'mestə(r)] *n* semestre *m*

semi- ['semɪ] *pref* semi-, demi-

■ **semi-circle** *n* demi-cercle *m* ■ **semi-colon** *n* point-virgule *m* ■ **semi-detached** *adj Br* **s. house** maison *f* jumelée ■ **semi-final** *n* demi-finale *f* ■ **semi-skimmed** *adj (milk)* demi-écrémé

seminar ['semɪnɑː(r)] *n* séminaire *m*

semolina [seməˈliːnə] *n* semoule *f*

senate ['senɪt] *n* **the S.** le Sénat ■ **senator** [-ɪtə(r)] *n* sénateur *m*

send [send] *(pt & pp* sent*) vt* envoyer (**to** à); **to s. sth to sb, to s. sb sth** envoyer qch à qn; **to s. sb home** renvoyer qn chez soi; *Fam* **to s. sb packing** envoyer promener qn ■ **sender** *n* expéditeur, -trice *mf*

▸ **send away 1** *vt sep (person)* renvoyer **2** *vi* **to s. away for sth** se faire envoyer qch

▸ **send back** *vt sep* renvoyer

▸ **send for** *vt insep* envoyer chercher; *(doctor)* faire venir; *(send away for)* se faire envoyer

▸ **send in** *vt sep (form, invoice, troops)* envoyer; *(person)* faire entrer

▸ **send off 1** *vt sep (letter)* envoyer (**to** à); *(player)* expulser **2** *vi* **to s. off for sth** se faire envoyer qch

▸ **send on** *vt sep (letter)* faire suivre

▸ **send out 1** *vt sep* envoyer **2** *vi* **to s. out for sth** envoyer chercher qch

▸ **send up** *vt sep Br Fam (parody)* se moquer de

senile ['siːnaɪl] *adj* sénile

senior ['siːnɪə(r)] **1** *adj (in age)* aîné; *(in position, rank)* supérieur; **to be sb's s., to be s. to sb** être l'aîné de qn; *(in rank, status)* être le supérieur de qn; **Brown s.** Brown père; **s. citizen** personne *f* âgée; *Am* **s. year** *(in school, college)* dernière année *f* **2** *n* aîné, -e *mf; Am (in last year of school or college)* étudiant, -e *mf* de dernière année; *(in sport)* senior *mf*

sensation [sen'seɪʃən] *n* sensation *f* ■ **sensational** *adj* sensationnel, -elle

sense [sens] **1** *n (faculty, awareness, meaning)* sens *m;* **s. of smell** odorat *m;* **a s. of shame** un sentiment de honte; **s. of direction** sens de l'orientation; **to have a s. of humour** avoir le sens de l'humour; **to have the s. to do sth** avoir l'intelligence de faire qch; **to bring sb to his/her senses** ramener qn à la raison; **to make s.** être logique; **to make s. of sth** comprendre qch **2** vt sentir (**that** que)

senseless ['sensləs] adj (pointless) absurde

sensibility [sensɪ'bɪlətɪ] n sensibilité f

sensible ['sensəbəl] adj (wise) sensé; (clothes, shoes) pratique

sensitive ['sensɪtɪv] adj (person) sensible (**to** à); (skin, question) délicat; (information) confidentiel, -elle ■ **sensitivity** n sensibilité f; (touchiness) susceptibilité f

sensor ['sensə(r)] n détecteur m

sensual ['senfʊəl] adj sensuel, -elle ■ **sensuous** adj sensuel, -elle

sent [sent] pt & pp of **send**

sentence ['sentəns] **1** n (**a**) (words) phrase f (**b**) (in prison) peine f **2** vt (criminal) condamner; **to s. sb to three years (in prison)/to death** condamner qn à trois ans de prison/à mort

sentiment ['sentɪmənt] n sentiment m ■ **sentimental** [-'mentəl] adj sentimental

separate 1 ['sepərət] adj (distinct) séparé; (organization) indépendant; (occasion, entrance) différent; (room) à part **2** ['sepəreɪt] vt séparer (**from** de) **3** ['sepəreɪt] vi se séparer (**from** de) ■ **separately** ['sepərətlɪ] adv séparément ■ **separation** n séparation f

September [sep'tembə(r)] n septembre m

septic ['septɪk] adj (wound) infecté; **to go** or **turn s.** s'infecter

sequel ['si:kwəl] n (book, film) suite f

sequence ['si:kwəns] n (order) ordre m; (series) succession f; (in film & Comptr, Mus & Cards) séquence f; **in s.** dans l'ordre

sequin ['si:kwɪn] n paillette f

Serbia ['sɜːbɪə] n la Serbie

serenade [serə'neɪd] **1** n sérénade f **2** vt chanter la sérénade à

serene [sə'riːn] adj serein

sergeant ['sɑːdʒənt] n Mil sergent m; (in police) brigadier m

serial ['sɪərɪəl] n (story, film) feuilleton m; **s. killer** tueur m en série; **s. number** numéro m de série ■ **serialize** vt (in newspaper) publier en feuilleton; (on television or radio) adapter en feuilleton

series ['sɪəriːz] n inv série f

serious ['sɪərɪəs] adj (person) sérieux, -euse; (illness, mistake, tone) grave; (damage) important; **to be s. about doing sth** envisager sérieusement de faire qch ■ **seriously** adv sérieusement; (ill, damaged) gravement; **to take sb/sth s.** prendre qn/qch au sérieux

sermon ['sɜːmən] n sermon m

servant ['sɜːvənt] n domestique mf

serve [sɜːv] **1** n (in tennis) service m
2 vt (country, cause, meal, customer) servir; (prison sentence) purger; (apprenticeship) faire; Fam (**it**) **serves you right!** ça t'apprendra!
3 vi servir (**as** de); **to s. on** (committee, jury) être membre de ■ **server** n (in tennis) serveur, -euse mf; Comptr serveur m

service ['sɜːvɪs] **1** n (with army, firm, in restaurant, in tennis) & Rel service m; (of machine) entretien m; (of car) révision f; **to be at sb's s.** être au service de qn; **the (armed) services** les forces fpl armées; **s. charge** service m; Br **s. area** (on motorway) aire f de service; Comptr **s. provider** fournisseur m d'accès Internet; **s. station** station-service f
2 vt (machine) entretenir; (car) réviser

serviceman ['sɜːvɪsmən] (pl -**men**) n militaire m

serviette [sɜːvɪ'et] n Br serviette f de table

servile ['sɜːvaɪl] adj servile

serving ['sɜːvɪŋ] n (of food) portion f; **s. dish** plat m

session ['seʃən] n (meeting, period) séance f; (university term) trimestre m; (university year) année f universitaire

set [set] **1** n (of keys, tools) jeu m; (of stamps, numbers) série f; (of people) groupe m; (of facts, laws) & Math ensemble m; (of books) collection f; (of dishes) service m; (kit) trousse f; (in theatre) décor m; (for film) plateau m; (in tennis) set m; **chess s.** jeu d'échecs; **tea s.** service m à thé; **television s., TV s.** téléviseur m

2 adj (time, price) fixe; (lunch) à prix fixe; (school book) au programme; (ideas, purpose) déterminé; **to be s. on doing sth** être résolu à faire qch; **to be dead s. against sth** être formellement opposé à qch; **to be all s.** être prêt (**to do** pour faire); **s. menu** menu m; **s. phrase** expression f figée

3 (pt & pp set, pres p setting) vt (put) mettre, poser; (date, limit, task) fixer; (homework) donner (**for sb à** qn); (jewel) sertir; (watch) régler; (alarm clock) mettre (**for** pour); (bone fracture) réduire; (trap) tendre (**for** à); **to s. a record** établir un record; **to s. a precedent** créer un précédent; **to s. sb free** libérer qn

4 vi (of sun) se coucher; (of jelly) prendre; (of bone) se ressouder

▶ **set about** vt insep (begin) se mettre à; **to s. about doing sth** se mettre à faire qch

▶ **set back** vt sep (in time) retarder; Fam (cost) coûter à

▶ **set down** vt sep (object) poser

▶ **set off 1** vt sep (bomb) faire exploser; (mechanism) déclencher; Fig (beauty) rehausser; **to s. sb off (crying)** faire pleurer qn **2** vi (leave) partir

▶ **set out 1** vt sep (display, explain) exposer; (arrange) disposer **2** vi (leave) partir; **to s. out to do sth** avoir l'intention de faire qch

▶ **set up 1** vt sep (tent, statue) dresser;

(roadblock) mettre en place; (company) créer; (meeting) organiser; (inquiry) ouvrir **2** vi **to s. up in business** s'installer (**as** comme)

setback ['setbæk] n revers m

settee [se'tiː] n canapé m

setting ['setɪŋ] n (surroundings) cadre m; (of sun) coucher m; (on machine) réglage m

settle ['setəl] **1** vt (put in place) installer; (decide, arrange, pay) régler; (date) fixer; (nerves) calmer; (land) coloniser; **that settles it!** c'est décidé! **2** vi (of person, family) s'installer; (of dust) se déposer; (of bird) se poser ▶ **settled** adj (weather, period) stable; (life) rangé

▶ **settle down** vi (in chair, house) s'installer; (become quieter) s'assagir; (of situation) se calmer; **to s. down with sb** mener une vie stable avec qn; **to s. down to work** se mettre au travail

▶ **settle for** vt insep se contenter de

▶ **settle in** vi (in new home) s'installer

▶ **settle up** vi (pay) régler; **to s. up with sb** régler qn

settlement ['setəlmənt] n (agreement) accord m; (payment) règlement m; (colony) colonie f

settler ['setlə(r)] n colon m

setup ['setʌp] n Fam (arrangement) système m

seven ['sevən] adj & n sept (m) ■ **seventh** adj & n septième (mf)

seventeen [sevən'tiːn] adj & n dix-sept (m) ■ **seventeenth** adj & n dix-septième (mf)

seventy ['sevəntɪ] adj & n soixante-dix (m); **s.-one** soixante et onze ■ **seventieth** adj & n soixante-dixième (mf)

sever ['sevə(r)] vt couper; Fig (relations) rompre

several ['sevərəl] adj & pron plusieurs (**of** d'entre)

severe [sə'vɪə(r)] adj (person, punishment, tone) sévère; (winter) rigoureux, -euse; (illness, injury) grave; (blow, pain) violent; (cold, frost) intense

■ **severely** *adv (criticize, punish)* sévèrement; *(damaged, wounded)* gravement

sew [səʊ] *(pt* **sewed**, *pp* **sewn** *or* **sewed)** *vt* coudre; **to s. a button on a shirt** coudre un bouton à une chemise; **to s. sth up** recoudre qch ■ **sewing** *n* couture *f*; **s. machine** machine *f* à coudre

sewage ['suːɪdʒ] *n* eaux *fpl* d'égout ■ **sewer** *n* égout *m*.

sewn [səʊn] *pp of* **sew**

sex [seks] **1** *n* sexe *m*; **to have s. with sb** coucher avec qn **2** *adj (education, life, act)* sexuel, -elle ■ **sexist** *adj & n* sexiste *(mf)*

sexual ['sekʃʊəl] *adj* sexuel, -elle ■ **sexuality** [seksjʊ'ælətɪ] *n* sexualité *f* ■ **sexy** ['seksɪ] *(-ier, -iest) adj Fam* sexy *inv*

sh [ʃ] *exclam* chut!

shabby ['ʃæbɪ] *(-ier, -iest) adj* miteux, -euse; *(behaviour, treatment)* mesquin

shack [ʃæk] *n* cabane *f*

shade [ʃeɪd] **1** *n* ombre *f*; *(of colour, meaning, opinion)* nuance *f*; *(for lamp)* abat-jour *m inv*; **in the s.** à l'ombre; **a s. faster/taller** un rien plus vite/plus grand **2** *vt (of tree)* ombrager ■ **shady** *(-ier, -iest) adj (place)* ombragé; *Fig (person, business)* louche

shadow ['ʃædəʊ] **1** *n* ombre *f* **2** *adj Br Pol* **s. cabinet** cabinet *m* fantôme **3** *vt* **to s. sb** *(follow)* filer qn

shaft [ʃɑːft] *n (a) (of tool)* manche *m*; **s. of light** rayon *m* de lumière *(b) (of mine)* puits *m*; *(of lift)* cage *f*

shaggy ['ʃægɪ] *(-ier, -iest) adj (hairy)* hirsute

shake [ʃeɪk] **1** *n* secousse *f*; **to give sth a s.** secouer qch

2 *(pt* **shook**, *pp* **shaken)** *vt (move up and down)* secouer; *(bottle, fist)* agiter; *(building)* faire trembler; *Fig (belief, resolution)* ébranler; **to s. one's head** faire non de la tête; **to s. hands with sb** serrer la main à qn; **to s. off** *(dust)* secouer; *Fig (illness, pursuer)* se débarrasser de; **to s. up** *(reorganize)*

réorganiser de fond en comble

3 *vi (of person, windows, voice)* trembler **(with** de)

shaken ['ʃeɪkən] *pp of* **shake**

shaky ['ʃeɪkɪ] *(-ier, -iest) adj (voice)* tremblant; *(table, chair)* branlant; *(handwriting)* tremblé; *(health)* précaire

On trouve généralement **I/you/he/** etc **shall** sous leurs formes contractées **I'll/you'll/he'll/**etc. La forme négative correspondante est **shan't**, que l'on écrira **shall not** dans des contextes formels.

v aux (a) (expressing future tense) **I s. come, I'll come** je viendrai; **we s. not come, we shan't come** nous ne viendrons pas

(b) (making suggestion) **s. I leave?** veux-tu que je parte?; **let's go in, s. we?** entrons, tu veux bien?

(c) Formal (expressing order) **he s. do it if I order it** il le fera si je l'ordonne

shallow ['ʃæləʊ] *(-er, -est) adj (water, river)* peu profond; *Fig & Pej (argument, person)* superficiel, -elle

sham [ʃæm] **1** *n (pretence)* comédie *f* **2** *adj (false)* faux *(f* fausse); *(illness, emotion)* feint **3** *(pt & pp* **-mm-)** *vt* feindre **4** *vi* faire semblant

shambles ['ʃæmbəlz] *n* pagaille *f*

shame [ʃeɪm] **1** *n (guilt, disgrace)* honte *f*; **it's a s.** c'est dommage **(to do** de faire); **it's a s. (that)...** c'est dommage que... *(+ subjunctive)*; **what a s.!** quel dommage! **2** *vt (make ashamed)* faire honte à

shameful ['ʃeɪmfəl] *adj* honteux, -euse

shameless ['ʃeɪmləs] *adj* impudique

shampoo [ʃæm'puː] **1** *n* shampooing *m* **2** *vt (carpet)* shampouiner

shandy ['ʃændɪ] *n Br* panaché *m*

shan't [ʃɑːnt] = **shall not**

shape [ʃeɪp] **1** *n* forme *f*; **what s. is it?** quelle forme cela a-t-il?; **to take s.** *(of plan)* prendre forme; **to be in good/**

bad s. (*of person*) être en bonne/mauvaise forme; (*of business*) marcher bien/mal; **to keep in s.** garder la forme

2 vt (*clay*) modeler; (*wood*) façonner (**into** en); *Fig* (*events, future*) influencer

3 vi **to s. up** (*of person*) progresser; (*of teams, plans*) prendre forme ■ **-shaped** suff pear-s. en forme de poire ■ **shapeless** adj informe ■ **shapely** (**-ier, -iest**) adj bien fait

share [ʃeə(r)] **1** n part f (**of** or **in** de); *Fin* (*in company*) action f; **to do one's (fair) s.** mettre la main à la pâte **2** vt partager; (*characteristic*) avoir en commun; **to s. sth out** partager qch **3** vi partager; **to s. in sth** avoir sa part de qch ■ **shareholder** n *Fin* actionnaire mf

shark [ʃɑːk] n (*fish, crook*) requin m

sharp [ʃɑːp] **1** (**-er, -est**) adj (*knife*) bien aiguisé; (*pencil*) bien taillé; (*point*) aigu (f aiguë); (*claws*) acéré; (*rise, fall*) brusque; (*focus*) net (f nette); (*contrast*) marqué; (*eyesight*) perçant; (*taste*) acide; (*intelligent*) vif (f vive)

2 adv **five o'clock s.** cinq heures pile; **to turn s. right/left** tourner tout de suite à droite/à gauche

3 n *Mus* dièse m

sharpen ['ʃɑːpən] vt (*knife*) aiguiser; (*pencil*) tailler

sharply ['ʃɑːplɪ] adv (*rise, fall*) brusquement; (*contrast*) nettement

shatter ['ʃætə(r)] **1** vt (*glass*) faire voler en éclats; (*health, hopes*) briser **2** vi (*of glass*) voler en éclats ■ **shattered** adj *Fam* (*exhausted*) crevé ■ **shattering** adj (*news, experience*) bouleversant

shave [ʃeɪv] **1** n **to have a s.** se raser **2** vt (*person, head*) raser **3** vi se raser ■ **shaver** n rasoir m électrique ■ **shaving** n (*strip of wood*) copeau m; **s. cream, s. foam** mousse f à raser

shawl [ʃɔːl] n châle m

she [ʃiː] **1** pron elle; **she's a happy woman** c'est une femme heureuse **2** n

Fam **it's a s.** (*of baby*) c'est une fille

sheaf [ʃiːf] (pl **sheaves** [ʃiːvz]) n (*of corn*) gerbe f; (*of paper*) liasse f

shear [ʃɪə(r)] **1** vt tondre **2** npl **shears** cisaille f

sheath [ʃiːθ] (pl -**s** [ʃiːðz]) n (*for sword*) fourreau m; (*contraceptive*) préservatif m

she'd [ʃiːd] = she had, she would

shed¹ [ʃed] n (*in garden*) abri m

shed² [ʃed] (pt & pp shed, pres p shedding) vt (*leaves*) perdre; (*tears, blood*) verser; *Fig* **to s. light on sth** éclairer qch

sheep [ʃiːp] n inv mouton m ■ **sheepdog** n chien m de berger ■ **sheepskin** n peau f de mouton

sheepish ['ʃiːpɪʃ] adj penaud

sheer [ʃɪə(r)] adj (*pure*) pur; (*stockings*) très fin; (*cliff*) à pic; **by s. chance** tout à fait par hasard

sheet [ʃiːt] n (*on bed*) drap m; (*of paper*) feuille f; (*of glass, ice*) plaque f

shelf [ʃelf] (pl **shelves** [ʃelvz]) n étagère f; (*in shop*) rayon m

shell [ʃel] **1** n (**a**) (*of egg, snail, nut*) coquille f; (*of tortoise, lobster*) carapace f; (*on beach*) coquillage m; (*of peas*) cosse f (**b**) (*explosive*) obus m **2** vt (**a**) (*peas*) écosser; (*nut*) décortiquer (**b**) (*town*) bombarder

she'll [ʃiːl] = she will, she shall

shellfish ['ʃelfɪʃ] npl fruits mpl de mer

shelter ['ʃeltə(r)] **1** n (*place, protection*) abri m; **to take s.** se mettre à l'abri (**from** de) **2** vt abriter (**from** de); (*criminal*) accueillir **3** vi s'abriter (**from** de) ■ **sheltered** adj (*place*) abrité

shelve [ʃelv] vt (*postpone*) mettre au placard

shelving ['ʃelvɪŋ] n rayonnages mpl

shepherd ['ʃepəd] n berger m; *Br* **s.'s pie** ≃ hachis m Parmentier

sherbet ['ʃɜːbət] n *Br* (*powder*) poudre f acidulée; *Am* (*sorbet*) sorbet m

sheriff ['ʃerɪf] n *Am* shérif m

sherry ['ʃerɪ] n sherry m, xérès m

shield [ʃiːld] **1** n (*of warrior*) bouclier m **2** vt protéger (**from** de)

shift [ʃɪft] **1** n (change) changement m (of or in de); (period of work) poste m; (workers) équipe f; **s. key** (on computer, typewriter) touche f des majuscules

2 vt (move) déplacer; (stain) enlever; Am **to s. gear(s)** (in vehicle) changer de vitesse

3 vi (move) bouger ▪ **shiftwork** n travail m posté

shifty [ˈʃɪftɪ] (**-ier, -iest**) adj (person) louche

shimmer [ˈʃɪmə(r)] vi (of silk) chatoyer; (of water) miroiter

shin [ʃɪn] n tibia m; **s. pad** (of hockey player) jambière f

shine [ʃaɪn] **1** n brillant m; (on metal) éclat m **2** (pt & pp **shone**) vt (polish) faire briller; (light, torch) braquer **3** vi briller

shiny [ˈʃaɪnɪ] (**-ier, -iest**) adj brillant

ship [ʃɪp] **1** n navire m **2** (pt & pp **-pp-**) vt (send) expédier; (transport) transporter ▪ **shipment** n cargaison f ▪ **shipping** n (traffic) navigation f; (ships) navires mpl ▪ **shipwreck** n naufrage m ▪ **shipwrecked** adj naufragé; **to be s.** faire naufrage ▪ **shipyard** n chantier m naval

shirk [ʃɜːk] **1** vt (duty) se dérober à; (work) éviter de faire **2** vi tirer au flanc

shirt [ʃɜːt] n chemise f; (of woman) chemisier m; (of sportsman) maillot m

shiver [ˈʃɪvə(r)] **1** n frisson m **2** vi frissonner (**with** de)

shoal [ʃəʊl] n (of fish) banc m

shock [ʃɒk] **1** n (impact, emotional blow) choc m; (**electric**) **s.** décharge f (électrique) **2** adj (wave, tactics, troops) de choc; Aut **s. absorber** amortisseur m **3** vt (offend) choquer; (surprise) stupéfier ▪ **shocking** adj (outrageous) choquant; (very bad) atroce

shoddy [ˈʃɒdɪ] (**-ier, -iest**) adj (goods) de mauvaise qualité

shoe [ʃuː] n chaussure f; (for horse) fer m à cheval; **s. polish** cirage m; **s. shop** magasin m de chaussures ▪ **shoelace** n lacet m

shone [Br ʃɒn, Am ʃəʊn] pt & pp of **shine**

shoo [ʃuː] **1** (pt & pp **shooed**) vt **to s.** (**away**) chasser **2** exclam ouste!

shook [ʃʊk] pt of **shake**¹

shoot [ʃuːt] **1** n (of plant) pousse f **2** (pt & pp **shot**) vt (bullet) tirer; (arrow) lancer; (film, scene) tourner; **to s. sb** (kill) tuer qn par balle; (wound) blesser qn par balle; (execute) fusiller qn **3** vi (with gun) tirer (**at** sur); (of footballer) shooter ▪ **shooting** n (shots) coups mpl de feu; (incident) fusillade f; (film, scene) tournage m

▸ **shoot down** vt sep (plane) abattre

▸ **shoot off** vi (leave quickly) filer

▸ **shoot up** vi (of price) monter en flèche; (of plant, child) pousser vite; (of rocket) s'élever

shop [ʃɒp] **1** n magasin m; (small) boutique f; (workshop) atelier m; **at the baker's s.** à la boulangerie, chez le boulanger; Br **s. assistant** vendeur, -euse mf; **s. window** vitrine f

2 (pt & pp **-pp-**) vi faire ses courses (**at** chez); **to s. around** comparer les prix ▪ **shopkeeper** n commerçant, -e mf ▪ **shoplifter** n voleur, -euse mf à l'étalage ▪ **shopper** n (customer) client, -e mf ▪ **shopping** n (goods) achats mpl; **to go s.** faire des courses; **to do one's s.** faire ses courses **2** adj (street, district) commerçant; **s. bag** sac m à provisions; **s. centre** centre m commercial; **s. list** liste f des commissions

shore [ʃɔː(r)] n (of sea) rivage m; (of lake) bord m; **on s.** à terre

short [ʃɔːt] **1** (**-er, -est**) adj court; (person, distance) petit; (impatient, curt) brusque; **to be s. of sth** être à court de qch; **money/time is s.** l'argent/le temps manque; **a s. time** or **while ago** il y a peu de temps; **Tony is s. for Anthony** Tony est le diminutif d'Anthony; **in s.** bref; **s. cut** raccourci m; **s. story** nouvelle f

2 adv **to cut s.** (hair) couper court; (visit) abréger; (person) couper la parole à; **to stop s. of doing sth** se retenir tout juste de faire qch; **to be running s. of sth** n'avoir presque plus de qch ■ **shortbread** n sablé m ■ **short-circuit 1** n court-circuit m **2** vt court-circuiter **3** vi se mettre en court-circuit ■ **shortcoming** n défaut m ■ **shorthand** n sténo f; **s. typist** sténodactylo m ■ **short-lived** adj de courte durée ■ **short-sighted** adj myope; Fig (in one's judgement) imprévoyant ■ **short-sleeved** adj à manches courtes ■ **short-staffed** adj à court de personnel ■ **short-term** adj à court terme

shortage ['ʃɔːtɪdʒ] n pénurie f

shorten ['ʃɔːtən] vt raccourcir

shortly ['ʃɔːtlɪ] adv (soon) bientôt; **s. before/after** peu avant/après

shorts [ʃɔːts] npl **(pair of) s.** short m; boxer s. caleçon m

shot [ʃɒt] **1** pt & pp of **shoot 2** n (from gun) coup m; (with camera) prise f de vue; (in football) coup m de pied; Fam (injection) piqûre f; **to fire a s.** tirer; **to be a good s.** (of person) être bon tireur; **to have a s. at sth/doing sth** essayer qch/de faire qch ■ **shotgun** n fusil m de chasse

SHOULD [ʃʊd, unstressed ʃəd]

La forme négative **should not** s'écrit **shouldn't** en forme contractée.

v aux **(a)** (expressing obligation) **you s. do it** vous devriez le faire; **I s. have stayed** j'aurais dû rester

(b) (expressing possibility) **the weather s. improve** le temps devrait s'améliorer; **she s. have arrived by now** elle devrait être arrivée à l'heure qu'il est

(c) (expressing preferences) **I s. like to stay** j'aimerais bien rester; **I s. like to** j'aimerais bien; **I s. hope so** j'espère bien

(d) (in subordinate clauses) **it's strange (that) she s. say no** il est étrange qu'elle dise non; **he insisted that she s. meet her parents** il a insisté pour qu'elle rencontre ses parents

(e) (in conditional clauses) **if he s. come, s. he come** s'il vient

(f) (in rhetorical questions) **why s. you suspect me?** pourquoi me soupçonnez-vous?; **who s. I meet but Martin!** et qui a-t-il fallu que je rencontre? Martin!

shoulder ['ʃəʊldə(r)] **1** n épaule f; **s. bag** sac m besace; **s. pad** épaulette f; **s. strap** (of garment) bretelle f **2** vt (responsibility) endosser

shout [ʃaʊt] **1** n cri m; **to give sb a s.** appeler qn **2** vt **to s. sth (out)** crier qch **3** vi **to s. (out)** crier; **to s. to sb to do sth** crier à qn de faire qch; **to s. at sb** crier après qn ■ **shouting** n (shouts) cris mpl

shove [ʃʌv] **1** n poussée f; **to give sb/ sth a s.** pousser qn/qch **2** vt pousser; Fam **to s. sth into sth** fourrer qch dans qch **3** vi pousser; Fam **to s. over** (move over) se pousser

shovel ['ʃʌvəl] **1** n pelle f **2** (Br -ll-, Am -l-) vt pelleter; **to s. leaves up** ramasser des feuilles à la pelle

show [ʃəʊ] **1** n (concert, play) spectacle m; (on TV) émission f; (exhibition) exposition f; (of force, friendship) démonstration f; (pretence) semblant m (of de); **to be on s.** être exposé; **to put sth on s.** exposer qch; **s. business** le monde du spectacle; **s. jumping** jumping m

2 (pt showed, pp shown) vt montrer (**to** à; **that** que); (in exhibition) exposer; (film) passer; (indicate) indiquer; **to s. sb sth, to s. sth to sb** montrer qch à qn; **to s. sb to the door** reconduire qn à la porte

3 vi (be visible) se voir; (of film) passer ■ **showdown** n confrontation f ■ **show-off** n Pej crâneur, -euse mf ■ **showroom** n magasin m d'exposition

▸ **show around** vt sep **to s. sb around the town/the house** faire visiter la ville/la maison à qn

▶ **show in** *vt sep (visitor)* faire entrer

▶ **show off** 1 *vt sep Pej (display)* étaler; *(highlight)* faire valoir 2 *vi Pej* crâner

▶ **show out** *vt sep (visitor)* reconduire

▶ **show round** *vt sep* = **show around**

▶ **show up** 1 *vt sep (embarrass)* faire honte à; *(reveal)* faire ressortir 2 *vi (stand out)* ressortir (**against** contre); *Fam (of person)* se présenter

shower ['ʃaʊə(r)] 1 *n (bathing, device)* douche *f; (of rain)* averse *f;* **to have** or **take a s.** prendre une douche; **s. gel** gel *m* de douche 2 *vt* **to s. sb with** *(gifts, abuse)* couvrir qn de ▪ **showery** *adj* pluvieux, -euse

shown [ʃəʊn] *pp of* **show**

showy ['ʃəʊɪ] (**-ier, -iest**) *adj* voyant

shrank [ʃræŋk] *pt of* **shrink**

shred [ʃred] 1 *n* lambeau *m;* **to tear sth to shreds** mettre qch en lambeaux; *Fig* **not a s. of truth** pas une once de vérité 2 *(pt & pp* **-dd-**) *vt* mettre en lambeaux; *(documents)* déchiqueter; *(food)* couper grossièrement

shrewd [ʃruːd] (**-er, -est**) *adj (person, plan)* astucieux, -euse

shriek [ʃriːk] 1 *n* cri *m* strident 2 *vi* pousser un cri strident; **to s. with pain/laughter** hurler de douleur/de rire

shrill [ʃrɪl] (**-er, -est**) *adj* aigu *(f* aiguë)

shrimp [ʃrɪmp] *n* crevette *f*

shrine [ʃraɪn] *n (place of worship)* lieu *m* saint; *(tomb)* tombeau *m*

shrink [ʃrɪŋk] 1 *(pt* **shrank** *or Am* **shrunk,** *pp* **shrunk** *or* **shrunken**) *vt (of clothes)* faire rétrécir 2 *vi* rétrécir

shrivel ['ʃrɪvəl] *(Br* **-ll-,** *Am* **-l-**) *vt* **to s. (up)** dessécher 2 *vi* **to s. (up)** se dessécher

shroud [ʃraʊd] 1 *n* linceul *m* 2 *vt* **to be shrouded in sth** être enveloppé de qch

Shrove [ʃrəʊv] *adj* **S. Tuesday** mardi *m* gras

shrub [ʃrʌb] *n* arbuste *m*

shrug [ʃrʌg] 1 *n* haussement *m* d'épaules 2 *(pt & pp* **-gg-**) *vt* **to s. one's**

shoulders hausser les épaules; **to s. sth off** dédaigner qch

shrunk(en) ['ʃrʌŋk(ən)] *pp of* **shrink**

shudder ['ʃʌdə(r)] *vi (of person)* frémir (**with** de); *(of machine)* vibrer

shuffle ['ʃʌfəl] 1 *vt (cards)* battre 2 *vti* **to s. (one's feet)** traîner les pieds

shun [ʃʌn] *(pt & pp* **-nn-**) *vt* fuir, éviter

shush [ʃʊʃ] *exclam* chut!

shut [ʃʌt] 1 *(pt & pp* **shut,** *pres p* **shutting**) *vt* fermer 2 *vi (of door)* se fermer; *(of shop, museum)* fermer

▶ **shut away** *vt sep (lock away)* enfermer

▶ **shut down** 1 *vt sep* fermer (définitivement) 2 *vi* fermer (définitivement)

▶ **shut in** *vt sep (lock in)* enfermer

▶ **shut off** *vt sep (gas, electricity)* couper; *(engine)* arrêter; *(road)* fermer; *(isolate)* isoler

▶ **shut out** *vt sep (keep outside)* empêcher d'entrer; *(exclude)* exclure *(of* or *from* de); **to s. sb out** enfermer qn dehors

▶ **shut up** 1 *vt sep (close)* fermer; *(confine)* enfermer; *Fam (silence)* faire taire 2 *vi Fam (be quiet)* se taire

shutter ['ʃʌtə(r)] *n (on window)* volet *m; (of shop)* store *m; (of camera)* obturateur *m*

shuttle ['ʃʌtəl] 1 *n (bus, train, plane)* navette *f;* **s. service** navette *f* 2 *vi* faire la navette

shy [ʃaɪ] 1 (**-er, -est**) *adj* timide 2 *vi* **to s. away from doing sth** éviter de faire qch

sibling ['sɪblɪŋ] *n (brother)* frère *m; (sister)* sœur *f*

Sicily ['sɪsɪlɪ] *n* la Sicile

sick [sɪk] 1 (**-er, -est**) *adj (ill)* malade; **to be s.** *(be ill)* être malade; *(vomit)* vomir; **to feel s.** avoir mal au cœur; **to be off s.,** **to be on s. leave** être en congé de maladie; **to be s. of sb/sth** en avoir assez de qn/qch; *Fig* **he makes me s.** il m'écœure 2 *n Br Fam (vomit)* vomi *m* 3 *npl Fig* **the s.** *(sick people)* les malades *mpl*

sicken ['sɪkən] 1 *vt* écœurer 2 *vi Br* **to**

be sickening for something couver quelque chose ■ **sickening** *adj* écœurant

sickly ['sɪklɪ] (**-ier, -iest**) *adj* maladif, -ive; *(pale, faint)* pâle; *(taste)* écœurant

sickness ['sɪknɪs] *n (illness)* maladie *f*

side [saɪd] **1** *n* côté *m*; *(of hill, animal)* flanc *m*; *(of road, river)* bord *m*; *(of question, character)* aspect *m*; *(team)* équipe *f*; **at** *or* **by the s.** *(of (nearby))* à côté de; **at** *or* **by my s.** à côté de moi, à mes côtés; **s. by s.** l'un à côté de l'autre; **to move to one s.** s'écarter; **on this s. of** de ce côté; **to take sides with sb** se ranger du côté de qn; **she's on our s.** elle est de notre côté

2 *adj (lateral)* latéral; *(view, glance)* de côté; *(street)* transversal; *(effect, issue)* secondaire

3 *vi* **to s. with sb** se ranger du côté de qn ■ **sideboard** *n* buffet *m* ■ **sideburns** *npl (hair)* pattes *fpl* ■ **-sided** *suff* **ten-sided** à dix côtés ■ **sidelight** *n Br (on vehicle)* feu *m* de position ■ **sideline** *n (activity)* activité *f* secondaire; *(around playing field)* ligne *f* de touche ■ **sidestep** *(pt & pp* **-pp-)** *vt* éviter ■ **sidetrack** *vt* distraire; **to get sidetracked** s'écarter du sujet ■ **sidewalk** *n Am* trottoir *m* ■ **sideways** *adv (look, walk)* de côté

siege [siːdʒ] *n (by soldiers, police)* siège *m*; **under s.** assiégé

siesta [sɪ'estə] *n* sieste *f*; **to take** *or* **have a s.** faire la sieste

sieve [sɪv] *n* tamis *m*; *(for liquids)* passoire *f*

sift [sɪft] **1** *vt (flour)* tamiser **2** *vi* **to s. through** *(papers)* examiner (à la loupe)

sigh [saɪ] **1** *n* soupir *m* **2** *vti* soupirer

sight [saɪt] **1** *n (faculty)* vue *f*; *(thing seen)* spectacle *m*; *(on gun)* viseur *m*; **to lose s. of sb/sth** perdre qn/qch de vue; **to catch s. of sb/sth** apercevoir qn/qch; **at first s.** à première vue; **by s.** de vue; **in s.** *(target, end, date)* en vue; **out of s.** *(hidden)* caché; *(no longer visible)* disparu; **he hates the s. of me** il ne peut pas me voir; **the (tourist) sights** les attractions *fpl* touristiques; **to set one's sights on** *(job)* viser **2** *vt (land)* apercevoir

sightseer ['saɪtsiːə(r)] *n* touriste *mf* ■ **sightseeing** *n* **to go s., to do some s.** faire du tourisme

sign [saɪn] **1** *n* signe *m*; *(notice)* panneau *m*; *(over shop, pub)* enseigne *f*; **no s. of** aucune trace de **2** *vt (put signature to)* signer; **to s. on** *or* **up** *(worker, soldier)* engager **3** *vi* signer; **to s. for** *(letter)* signer le reçu de; **Br to s. on** *(on the dole)* s'inscrire au chômage; **to s. on** *or* **up** *(of soldier, worker)* s'engager; *(for course)* s'inscrire

signal ['sɪɡnəl] **1** *n* signal *m*; *Rail Br* **s. box**, *Am* **s. tower** poste *m* d'aiguillage **2** *(Br* **-ll-,** *Am* **-l-)** *vt (be a sign of)* indiquer; *(make gesture to)* faire signe à **3** *vi (make gesture)* faire signe (**to** à); *(of driver)* mettre son clignotant; **to s. (to) sb to do sth** faire signe à qn de faire qch

signature ['sɪɡnətʃə(r)] *n* signature *f*; **s. tune** indicatif *m*

significance [sɪɡ'nɪfɪkəns] *n (meaning)* signification *f*; *(importance)* importance *f*

significant [sɪɡ'nɪfɪkənt] *adj (important, large)* important; *(meaningful)* significatif, -ive ■ **significantly** *adv (appreciably)* sensiblement

signify ['sɪɡnɪfaɪ] *(pt & pp* **-ied)** *vt (mean, make known)* signifier (**that** que)

signpost ['saɪnpəʊst] **1** *n* poteau *m* indicateur **2** *vt* signaliser

silence ['saɪləns] **1** *n* silence *m*; **in s.** en silence **2** *vt* faire taire

silent ['saɪlənt] *adj* silencieux, -euse; *(film, anger)* muet *(f* muette); **to keep** *or* **be s.** garder le silence (**about** sur) ■ **silently** *adv* silencieusement

silhouette [sɪluː'et] *n* silhouette *f*

silicon ['sɪlɪkən] *n* silicium *m*; **s. chip** puce *f* électronique

silk [sɪlk] *n* soie *f* ■ **silky** (**-ier, -iest**) *adj* soyeux, -euse

sill [sɪl] n (of window) rebord m

silly ['sɪlɪ] (**-ier, -iest**) adj bête, idiot; **to do something s.** faire une bêtise; **to look s.** avoir l'air ridicule

silver ['sɪlvə(r)] **1** n argent m; (plates) argenterie f **2** adj (spoon) en argent, d'argent; (colour) argenté; **s. jubilee** vingt-cinquième anniversaire m; Br **s. paper** papier m d'argent ■ **silver-plated** adj plaqué argent

similar ['sɪmɪlə(r)] adj semblable (**to** à) ■ **similarity** [-'lærətɪ] (pl **-ies**) n ressemblance f (**between** entre; **to** avec) ■ **similarly** adv de la même façon; (likewise) de même

simile ['sɪmɪlɪ] n comparaison f

simmer ['sɪmə(r)] **1** vt (vegetables) mijoter **2** vi (of vegetables) mijoter; (of water) frémir; Fig (of revolt, hatred) couver

simple ['sɪmpəl] (**-er, -est**) adj (easy) simple ■ **simple-minded** adj simple d'esprit ■ **simplicity** n simplicité f

simplify ['sɪmplɪfaɪ] (pt & pp **-ied**) vt simplifier

simply ['sɪmplɪ] adv (plainly, merely) simplement; (absolutely) absolument

simulate ['sɪmjʊleɪt] vt simuler

simultaneous [Br sɪməl'teɪnɪəs, Am saɪməl'teɪnɪəs] adj simultané ■ **simultaneously** [Br sɪməl'teɪnɪəslɪ, Am saɪməl'teɪnɪəslɪ] adv simultanément

sin [sɪn] **1** n péché m **2** (pt & pp **-nn-**) vi pécher

since [sɪns] **1** prep (in time) depuis; **s. then** depuis **2** conj (in time) depuis que; (because) puisque; **it's a year s. I saw him** ça fait un an que je ne l'ai pas vu **3** adv (ever) **s.** depuis

sincere [sɪn'sɪə(r)] adj sincère ■ **sincerely** adv sincèrement; Br **yours s.,** Am **s.** (in letter) veuillez agréer, Madame/Monsieur, mes salutations distinguées ■ **sincerity** [-'serətɪ] n sincérité f

sinful ['sɪnfəl] adj (act) coupable; (waste) scandaleux, -euse

sing [sɪŋ] (pt **sang**, pp **sung**) vti chanter ■ **singer** n chanteur, -euse mf

■ **singing 1** n (of bird, musical technique) chant m **2** adj **s. lesson/teacher** leçon f/professeur m de chant

singe [sɪndʒ] vt (cloth) roussir; (hair) brûler

single ['sɪŋgəl] **1** adj (only one) seul; (room, bed) pour une personne; (unmarried) célibataire; **not a s. book** pas un seul livre; **every s. day** tous les jours sans exception; Br **s. ticket** aller m simple; **s. parent** père m/mère f célibataire

2 n Br (ticket) aller m simple; (record) single m; **singles** (in tennis) simples mpl

3 vt **to s. sb out** sélectionner qn ■ **single-handedly** adv tout seul (f toute seule) ■ **single-minded** adj (person) résolu; (determination) farouche ■ **single-sex** adj Br **s. school** école f non mixte

singly ['sɪŋglɪ] adv (one by one) un à un

singular ['sɪŋgjʊlə(r)] **1** adj (in grammar) singulier, -ère; (remarkable) remarquable **2** n singulier m; **in the s.** au singulier

sinister ['sɪnɪstə(r)] adj sinistre

sink[1] [sɪŋk] n (in kitchen) évier m; (in bathroom) lavabo m

sink[2] [sɪŋk] (pt **sank**, pp **sunk**) **1** vt (ship) couler **2** vi (of ship, person) couler; (of water level, sun, price) baisser; (collapse) s'affaisser; **my heart sank** j'ai eu un pincement de cœur; **to s. (down) into** (mud) s'enfoncer dans; (armchair) s'affaler dans; Fam **it hasn't sunk in yet** je n'ai/il n'a/etc pas encore digéré la nouvelle

sinner ['sɪnə(r)] n pécheur(eresse) mf

sinus ['saɪnəs] n Anat sinus m

sip [sɪp] **1** n petite gorgée f **2** (pt & pp **-pp-**) vt siroter

siphon ['saɪfən] **1** n siphon m **2** vt **to s. sth off** (liquid) siphonner qch; (money) détourner qch

sir [sɜː(r)] n monsieur m; **S. Walter Raleigh** (title) sir Walter Raleigh

siren ['saɪərən] n sirène f

sister ['sɪstə(r)] n sœur f; *(nurse)* infirmière-chef f ■ **sister-in-law** *(pl sisters-in-law)* n belle-sœur f

sit [sɪt] *(pt & pp sat, pres p sitting)* **1** *vt (child on chair)* asseoir; *Br (exam)* se présenter à **2** *vi (of person)* s'asseoir; *(for artist)* poser *(for pour); (of assembly)* siéger; **to be sitting** *(of person, cat)* être assis; **she was sitting reading, she sat reading** elle était assise à lire

▸ **sit around** *vi* rester assis à ne rien faire

▸ **sit back** *vi (in chair)* se caler; *(rest)* se détendre; *(do nothing)* ne rien faire

▸ **sit down 1** *vt* to s. sb down asseoir qn **2** *vi* s'asseoir; **to be sitting down** être assis

▸ **sit for** *vt insep Br (exam)* se présenter à

▸ **sit in on** *vt insep (lecture)* assister à

▸ **sit on** *vt insep (jury)* être membre de

▸ **sit out** *vt sep (dance)* ne pas prendre part à

▸ **sit through** *vt insep (film)* rester jusqu'au bout de

▸ **sit up** *vi* to s. up *(straight)* s'asseoir (bien droit); **to s. up waiting for sb** veiller jusqu'au retour de qn

sitcom ['sɪtkɒm] n sitcom m

site [saɪt] n *(position)* emplacement m; *(archaeological, on Internet)* site m; **(building) s.** chantier m (de construction)

sitting ['sɪtɪŋ] n séance f; *(in restaurant)* service m; **s. room** salon m

situate ['sɪtʃʊeɪt] vt situer; **to be situated** être situé ■ **situation** n situation f

six [sɪks] adj & n six (m) ■ **sixth** adj & n sixième (mf); **a s.** *(fraction)* un sixième; *Br Sch* **(lower) s. form** ≃ classe f de première; *Br Sch* **(upper) s. form** ≃ classe f terminale

sixteen [sɪk'stiːn] adj & n seize (m) ■ **sixteenth** adj & n seizième (mf)

sixty ['sɪkstɪ] adj & n soixante (m) ■ **sixtieth** adj & n soixantième (mf)

size [saɪz] **1** n *(of person, animal,*

clothes) taille f; *(of shoes, gloves)* pointure f; *(of shirt)* encolure f; *(measurements)* dimensions fpl; *(of packet)* grosseur f; *(of town, damage, problem)* étendue f; *(of sum)* montant m; **hip/chest s.** tour m de hanches/de poitrine **2** *vt* to s. up *(person)* jauger; *(situation)* évaluer ■ **sizeable** adj non négligeable

sizzle ['sɪzəl] vi grésiller

skate [skeɪt] **1** n *(on foot)* patin m **2** vi *(on ice-skates)* faire du patin à glace; *(on roller-skates)* faire du roller ■ **skateboard** n planche f à roulettes ■ **skater** n patineur, -euse mf ■ **skating** n patinage m; **to go s.** faire du patinage

skeleton ['skelɪtən] n squelette m; **s. staff** personnel m minimum

skeptical ['skeptɪkəl] adj Am sceptique

sketch [sketʃ] **1** n *(drawing)* croquis m; *(comic play)* sketch m **2** vt to s. (out) *(idea, view)* exposer brièvement **3** vi faire un/des croquis ■ **sketchy** (-ier, -iest) adj vague

skewer ['skjuːə(r)] n *(for meat)* broche f; *(for kebab)* brochette f

ski [skiː] **1** *(pl skis)* n ski m; **s. boot** chaussure f de ski; **s. lift** remonte-pente m; **s. mask** cagoule f, passe-montagne m; **s. pants** fuseau m; **s. resort** station f de ski; **s. run** *or* **slope** piste f de ski

2 *(pt skied* [skiːd]*, pres p skiing)* vi skier, faire du ski ■ **skier** n skieur, -euse mf ■ **skiing 1** n *(sport)* ski m **2** adj *(clothes)* de ski

skid [skɪd] **1** n dérapage m **2** *(pt & pp -dd-)* vi déraper; **to s. into sth** déraper et heurter qch

skill [skɪl] n *(ability)* qualités fpl; *(technique)* compétence f ■ **skilful** (Am **skillful**) adj habile *(at doing* à faire; **at sth** en qch) ■ **skilled** adj habile (**at doing** à faire; **at sth** en qch); *(worker)* qualifié; *(work)* de spécialiste

skim [skɪm] *(pt & pp -mm-)* **1** vt *(milk)* écrémer; *(soup)* écumer; **to s. (over) sth** *(surface)* effleurer qch; **skimmed**

milk lait *m* écrémé **2** *vt insep* **to s. through** *(book)* parcourir

skimp [skɪmp] *vi (on food, fabric)* lésiner (**on** sur) ■ **skimpy** (**-ier, -iest**) *adj (clothes)* étriqué; *(meal)* maigre

skin [skɪn] **1** *n* peau *f*; **s. diving** plongée *f* sous-marine **2** *(pt & pp* **-nn-)** *vt (fruit)* peler; *(animal)* écorcher ■ **skin-tight** *adj* moulant

skinflint [ˈskɪnflɪnt] *n* avare *mf*

skinhead [ˈskɪnhed] *n Br* skinhead *mf*

skinny [ˈskɪnɪ] (**-ier, -iest**) *adj* maigre

skint [skɪnt] *adj Br Fam (penniless)* fauché

skip¹ [skɪp] **1** *(pt & pp* **-pp-)** *vt (miss, omit)* sauter; **to s. classes** sécher les cours **2** *vi (hop about)* sautiller; *Br (with rope)* sauter à la corde; *Br* **skipping rope** corde *f* à sauter

skip² [skɪp] *n Br (for rubbish)* benne *f*

skipper [ˈskɪpə(r)] *n (of ship, team)* capitaine *m*

skirt [skɜːt] *n* jupe *f*

skittle [ˈskɪtəl] *n Br* quille *f*; **to play skittles** jouer aux quilles

skulk [skʌlk] *vi* rôder

skull [skʌl] *n* crâne *m*

skunk [skʌŋk] *n (animal)* mouffette *f*

sky [skaɪ] *n* ciel *m* ■ **skydiving** *n* parachutisme *m* en chute libre ■ **skylight** *n* lucarne *f* ■ **skyline** *n (horizon)* horizon *m* ■ **skyscraper** *n* gratte-ciel *m inv*

slack [slæk] **1** (**-er, -est**) *adj (not tight)* mou *(f* molle*)*; *(careless)* négligent; **to be s.** *(of rope)* avoir du mou; **business is s.** les affaires vont mal **2** *vi* **to s. off** *(in effort)* se relâcher

slacken [ˈslækən] **1** *vt* **to s. (off)** *(rope)* relâcher; *(pace, effort)* ralentir **2** *vi* **to s. (off)** *(in effort)* se relâcher; *(of production, demand, speed, enthusiasm)* diminuer

slam [slæm] **1** *(pt & pp* **-mm-)** *vt (door, lid)* claquer; *(hit)* frapper violemment; **to s. sth (down)** *(put down)* poser qch violemment; **to s. on the brakes** écraser la pédale de frein **2** *vi (of door)* claquer

slander [ˈslɑːndə(r)] **1** *n* calomnie *f* **2** *vt* calomnier

slang [slæŋ] **1** *n* argot *m* **2** *adj (word)* d'argot, argotique

slant [slɑːnt] **1** *n* pente *f*; *Fig (point of view)* perspective *f*; *Fig (bias)* parti pris **2** *vi (of roof, handwriting)* être incliné ■ **slanted, slanting** *adj* penché; *(roof)* en pente

slap [slæp] **1** *n (with hand)* claque *f*; **a s. in the face** une gifle **2** *(pt & pp* **-pp-)** *vt (person)* donner une claque à; **to s. sb's face** gifler qn; **to s. sb's bottom** donner une fessée à qn

slapdash [ˈslæpdæʃ] *adj (person)* négligent; *(work)* fait à la va-vite

slapstick [ˈslæpstɪk] *adj & n* **s. (comedy)** grosse farce *f*

slash [slæʃ] **1** *n* entaille *f* **2** *vt (cut)* taillader; *(reduce)* réduire considérablement

slat [slæt] *n* latte *f*

slate [sleɪt] *n* ardoise *f*

slaughter [ˈslɔːtə(r)] **1** *n (of people)* massacre *m*; *(of animal)* abattage *m* **2** *vt (people)* massacrer; *(animal)* abattre; *Fam (defeat)* massacrer

slave [sleɪv] **1** *n* esclave *mf* **2** *vi* **to s. (away)** trimer ■ **slavery** *n* esclavage *m*

sleazy [ˈsliːzɪ] (**-ier, -iest**) *adj Fam* sordide

sledge [sledʒ] *(Am* **sled** [sled]*)* *n Br* luge *f*

sledgehammer [ˈsledʒhæmə(r)] *n* masse *f*

sleek [sliːk] (**-er, -est**) *adj (smooth)* lisse et brillant; *Pej (manner)* mielleux, -euse

sleep [sliːp] **1** *n* sommeil *m*; **to have a s., to get some s.** dormir; **to go to s.** *(of person)* s'endormir; *Fig* **to put an animal to s.** *(kill)* faire piquer un animal **2** *(pt & pp* **slept**) *vi* dormir; *Euph* **to s. with sb** coucher avec qn **3** *vt* **this flat sleeps six** on peut dormir à six dans cet appartement ■ **sleeping** *adj (asleep)* endormi; **s. bag** sac *m* de couchage; **s. car**

wagon-lit *m*; **s. pill** somnifère *m*

sleeper ['sli:pə(r)] *n* (**a**) **to be a light/ sound s.** avoir le sommeil léger/lourd (**b**) *Br Rail (on track)* traverse *f*; *(bed in train)* couchette *f*; *(train)* train-couchettes *m* ∎ **sleepless** *adj (night)* d'insomnie

sleepy ['sli:pɪ] (**-ier, -iest**) *adj (town, voice)* endormi; **to be s.** *(of person)* avoir sommeil

sleet [sli:t] **1** *n* neige *f* fondue **2** *vi* **it's sleeting** il tombe de la neige fondue

sleeve [sli:v] *n (of shirt, jacket)* manche *f*; *(of record)* pochette *f*; **long-/ short-sleeved** à manches longues/ courtes

sleigh [sleɪ] *n* traîneau *m*

slender ['slendə(r)] *adj (person)* svelte; *(neck, hand, waist)* fin; *Fig (small, feeble)* faible

slept [slept] *pt & pp of* **sleep**

slice [slaɪs] **1** *n* tranche *f*; *Fig (portion)* part *f* **2** *vt* **to s. sth (up)** couper qch en tranches; **to s. sth off** couper qch

slick [slɪk] **1** (**-er, -est**) *adj (campaign)* bien mené; *(reply, person)* habile **2** *n (on beach)* marée *f* noire

slide [slaɪd] **1** *n (in playground)* toboggan *m*; *(for hair)* barrette *f*; *Phot* diapositive *f*; *(in prices, popularity)* baisse *f* **2** *(pt & pp* **slid** [slɪd]) *vt* glisser (**into** dans); *(table, chair)* faire glisser **3** *vi* glisser ∎ **sliding** *adj (door, panel)* coulissant

slight [slaɪt] **1** (**-er, -est**) *adj (small, unimportant)* léger, -ère; *(chance)* faible; **the slightest thing** la moindre chose; **not in the slightest** pas le moins du monde **2** *n* affront *m* (**on** à) **3** *vt (offend)* offenser; *(ignore)* bouder

slightly ['slaɪtlɪ] *adv* légèrement

slim [slɪm] **1** (**slimmer, slimmest**) *adj* mince **2** *(pt & pp* **-mm-**) *vi Br* suivre un régime

slime [slaɪm] *n* vase *f*; *(of snail)* bave *f* ∎ **slimy** (**-ier, -iest**) *adj (muddy)* boueux *(f* boueuse); *Fig (sticky, smarmy)* visqueux, -euse

sling [slɪŋ] **1** *n (weapon)* fronde *f*; *(for injured arm)* écharpe *f*; **in a s.** en écharpe **2** *(pt & pp* **slung**) *vt (throw)* lancer

slip [slɪp] **1** *n (mistake)* erreur *f*; *(garment)* combinaison *f*; *(fall)* chute *f*; **a s. of paper** un bout de papier; *(printed)* un bordereau; **a s. of the tongue** un lapsus; *Br* **s. road** bretelle *f* **2** *(pt & pp* **-pp-**) *vt (slide)* glisser (**to** à; **into** dans); **it slipped my mind** ça m'est sorti de l'esprit **3** *vi* glisser; *Br (of popularity, ratings)* baisser; **to let sth s.** *(chance, secret)* laisser échapper qch

► **slip away** *vi (escape)* s'éclipser

► **slip into** *vt insep (room)* se glisser dans; *(bathrobe)* passer

► **slip off** *vt sep (coat)* enlever

► **slip on** *vt sep (coat)* mettre

► **slip out** *vi (leave)* sortir furtivement; *(for a moment)* sortir (un instant); *(of secret)* s'éventer

► **slip up** *vi Fam* se planter

slipper ['slɪpə(r)] *n* pantoufle *f*

slippery ['slɪpərɪ] *adj* glissant

slit [slɪt] **1** *n* fente *f* **2** *(pt & pp* **slit**, *pres p* **slitting**) *vt (cut)* couper; **to s. open** *(sack)* éventrer

slither ['slɪðə(r)] *vi* glisser; *(of snake)* se couler

slob [slɒb] *n Fam (lazy person)* gros fainéant *m*; *(dirty person)* porc *m*

slobber ['slɒbə(r)] *vi (of dog, baby)* baver

slog [slɒg] *Br Fam* **1** *n* **a (hard) s.** *(effort)* un gros effort **2** *(pt & pp* **-gg-**) *vi* **to s. (away)** trimer

slogan ['sləʊgən] *n* slogan *m*

slop [slɒp] **1** *(pt & pp* **-pp-**) *vt* renverser **2** *vi* **to s. (over)** se renverser

slope [sləʊp] **1** *n* pente *f*; *(of mountain)* versant *m*; *(for skiing)* piste *f* **2** *vi (of ground, roof)* être en pente ∎ **sloping** *adj (roof)* en pente

sloppy ['slɒpɪ] (**-ier, -iest**) *adj (work, appearance)* négligé; *(person)* négligent; *(sentimental)* sentimental

slot [slɒt] **1** *n (slit)* fente *f*; *(in schedule,*

list) créneau *m*; **s. machine** (*for vending*) distributeur *m* automatique; (*for gambling*) machine *f* à sous **2** (*pt & pp* **-tt-**) *vt* (*insert*) insérer (**into** dans) **3** *vi* s'insérer (**into** dans)

slouch [slaʊtʃ] *vi* ne pas se tenir droit; (*in chair*) être avachi

slovenly ['slʌvənlɪ] *adj* négligé

slow [sləʊ] **1** (**-er, -est**) *adj* lent; **in s. motion** au ralenti; **to be s.** (*of clock, watch*) retarder; **business is s.** les affaires tournent au ralenti **2** *adv* lentement **3** *vt* **to s. sth down** *or* **up** ralentir qch; (*delay*) retarder qch **4** *vi* **to s. down** *or* **up** ralentir ■ **slowcoach** *n Br Fam* lambin, -e *mf* ■ **slowly** *adv* lentement; (*bit by bit*) peu à peu

sludge [slʌdʒ] *n* gadoue *f*

slug [slʌg] **1** *n* (**a**) (*mollusc*) limace *f* (**b**) *Am Fam* (*bullet*) pruneau *m* **2** (*pt & pp* **-gg-**) *vt Am Fam* (*hit*) frapper

sluggish ['slʌgɪʃ] *adj* (*person*) amorphe; **business is s.** les affaires ne marchent pas très bien

slum [slʌm] *n* (*house*) taudis *m*; **the slums** les quartiers *mpl* délabrés

slump [slʌmp] **1** *n* baisse *f* soudaine (**in** de); (*in prices*) effondrement *m*; (*economic depression*) crise *f* **2** *vi* (*of person, prices*) s'effondrer

slung [slʌŋ] *pt & pp of* **sling**

slur [slɜː(r)] **1** *n* (*insult*) insulte *f* **2** (*pt & pp* **-rr-**) *vt* mal articuler ■ **slurred** *adj* (*speech*) indistinct

slush [slʌʃ] *n* (*snow*) neige *f* fondue

slut [slʌt] *n Pej* (*promiscuous woman*) salope *f*; (*untidy woman*) souillon *f*

sly [slaɪ] **1** (**-er, -est**) *adj* (*deceitful*) sournois; (*cunning, crafty*) rusé **2** *n* **on the s.** en douce

smack [smæk] **1** *n* (*blow*) claque *f*; (*on bottom*) fessée *f* **2** *vt* (*person*) donner une claque à; **to s. sb's face** gifler qn; **to s. sb('s bottom)** donner une fessée à qn **3** *vi* **to s. of** (*be suggestive of*) avoir des relents de

small [smɔːl] **1** (**-er, -est**) *adj* petit; **s. change** petite monnaie *f*; **s. talk** banalités *fpl* **2** *adv* (*cut, chop*) menu; (*write*)

petit **3** *n* **the s. of the back** la chute des reins ■ **small-minded** *adj* à l'esprit étroit ■ **small-scale** *adj* (*model*) réduit; (*research*) à petite échelle

smallpox ['smɔːlpɒks] *n* variole *f*

smarmy ['smɑːmɪ] (**-ier, -iest**) *adj Fam Pej* obséquieux, -euse

smart[1] [smɑːt] (**-er, -est**) *adj* (*in appearance*) élégant; (*clever*) intelligent; (*astute*) astucieux, -euse; (*quick*) rapide; **s. card** carte *f* à puce

smart[2] [smɑːt] *vi* (*sting*) brûler

smarten ['smɑːtən] **1** *vt* **to s. sth up** égayer qch **2** *vti* **to s. (oneself) up** se faire beau (*f* belle)

smartly ['smɑːtlɪ] *adv* (*dressed*) avec élégance

smash [smæʃ] **1** *n* (*accident*) collision *f*; (*in tennis*) smash *m* **2** *vt* (*break*) briser; (*shatter*) fracasser; (*record*) pulvériser **3** *vi* **to s. into sth** (*of vehicle*) entrer dans qch; **to s. into pieces** éclater en mille morceaux ■ **smash-up** *n* collision *f*

▶ **smash down, smash in** *vt sep* (*door*) enfoncer

▶ **smash up** *vt sep* (*vehicle*) esquinter

smashing ['smæʃɪŋ] *adj Br Fam* (*wonderful*) génial

smattering ['smætərɪŋ] *n* **a s. of French** quelques notions *fpl* de français

smear [smɪə(r)] **1** *n* (*mark*) trace *f* **2** *vt* (*coat*) enduire (**with** de); (*stain*) tacher (**with** de); (*smudge*) faire une trace sur; **to s. sb** calomnier qn

smell [smel] **1** *n* odeur *f*; (**sense of**) **s.** odorat *m* **2** (*pt & pp* **smelled** *or* **smelt**) *vt* sentir; (*of animal*) flairer **3** *vi* (*stink*) sentir mauvais; (*have a smell*) sentir; **to s. of smoke** sentir la fumée ■ **smelly** (**-ier, -iest**) *adj* **to be s.** sentir mauvais

smelt [smelt] *pt & pp of* **smell**

smile [smaɪl] **1** *n* sourire *m* **2** *vi* sourire (**at sb** à qn; **at sth** de qch)

smirk [smɜːk] *n* (*smug*) sourire *m* suffisant; (*scornful*) sourire *m* goguenard

smog [smɒg] *n* smog *m*

smoke [sməʊk] **1** n fumée f; **to have a s.** fumer; **s. detector** or **alarm** détecteur m de fumée **2** vt (cigarette) fumer; **smoked salmon** saumon m fumé **3** vi fumer; **'no smoking'** 'défense de fumer'; **smoking compartment** (on train) compartiment m fumeurs ■ **smoker** n fumeur, -euse mf ■ **smoky** (-ier, -iest) adj (room, air) enfumé

smooth [smuːð] **1** (-er, -est) adj (surface, skin) lisse; (cream, sauce) onctueux, -euse; (sea, flight) calme; Pej (person, manners) doucereux, -euse; **the s. running of** (machine, service, business) la bonne marche de **2** vt **to s. sth down** (hair, sheet, paper) lisser qch; **to s. sth out** (paper, sheet, dress) lisser qch; (crease) faire disparaître qch ■ **smoothly** adv (without problems) sans problèmes

smother ['smʌðə(r)] vt (stifle) étouffer; **to s. sth in sth** recouvrir qch de qch

smoulder ['sməʊldə(r)] (Am **smolder**) vi (of fire, passion) couver

smudge [smʌdʒ] **1** n tache f **2** vt (paper) faire des taches sur; (ink) étaler

smug [smʌg] (**smugger, smuggest**) adj (person) content de soi

smuggle ['smʌgəl] vt passer en fraude; **smuggled goods** contrebande f ■ **smuggler** n contrebandier, -ère mf; (of drugs) trafiquant, -e mf ■ **smuggling** n contrebande f

smut [smʌt] n inv (obscenity) cochonneries fpl ■ **smutty** (-ier, -iest) adj (joke) cochon, -onne

snack [snæk] n (meal) casse-croûte m inv; **s. bar** snack-bar m

snag [snæg] n (hitch) problème m

snail [sneɪl] n escargot m

snake [sneɪk] n serpent m

snap [snæp] **1** n Fam (photo) photo f; **s. fastener** pression f; **cold s.** coup m de froid **2** adj (judgement, decision) hâtif, -ive **3** (pt & pp **-pp-**) vt (break) casser net; (fingers) faire claquer; **to s. up a bargain** sauter sur une occasion **4** vi se casser net; Fig (of person) parler sèchement (at à); **to s. off** se casser net; Fam **s. out of it!** secoue-toi!

snare [sneə(r)] n piège m

snarl [snɑːl] vi grogner (en montrant les dents)

snatch [snætʃ] vt (grab) saisir; (steal) arracher; **to s. sth from sb** arracher qch à qn

sneak [sniːk] **1** n Br Fam (telltale) mouchard, -e mf **2** (pt & pp **sneaked** or Am **snuck**) vi Br Fam (tell tales) rapporter; **to s. in/out** entrer/sortir furtivement; **to s. off** s'esquiver

sneaker ['sniːkə(r)] n Am (shoe) chaussure f de sport

sneer [snɪə(r)] vi ricaner; **to s. at sb/sth** se moquer de qn/qch

sneeze [sniːz] vi éternuer

snicker ['snɪkə(r)] vi Am = **snigger**

snide [snaɪd] adj méprisant

sniff [snɪf] **1** vt renifler; **to s. glue** sniffer de la colle **2** vi renifler

sniffle ['snɪfəl] **1** n Fam **to have the sniffles** avoir un petit rhume **2** vi renifler

snigger ['snɪgə(r)] vi ricaner

snip [snɪp] **1** n (cut) petite entaille f; Br Fam (bargain) bonne affaire f **2** (pt & pp **-pp-**) vt **to s. sth (off)** couper qch

snivel ['snɪvəl] (Br **-ll-**, Am **-l-**) vi pleurnicher

snob [snɒb] n snob mf ■ **snobbish** adj snob inv

snooker ['snuːkə(r)] n (game) = billard qui se joue avec vingt-deux billes

snoop [snuːp] vi fouiner; **to s. on sb** espionner qn

snooze [snuːz] **1** n petit somme m; **to have a s.** faire un petit somme **2** vi faire un petit somme

snore [snɔː(r)] vi ronfler ■ **snoring** n ronflements mpl

snorkel ['snɔːkəl] **1** n tuba m **2** (Br **-ll-**, Am **-l-**) vi nager sous l'eau avec un tuba

snort [snɔːt] vi (of person) grogner; (of horse) s'ébrouer

snot [snɒt] n Fam morve f

snout [snaʊt] n museau m

snow [snəʊ] **1** *n* neige *f* **2** *vi* it's snowing il neige **3** *vt* to be snowed in être bloqué par la neige; *Fig* to be snowed under with work être submergé de travail ■ snowball **1** *n* boule *f* de neige **2** *vi* (*increase*) faire boule de neige ■ snowdrop *n* (*flower*) perce-neige *m ou f inv* ■ snowflake *n* flocon *m* de neige ■ snowman (*pl* -men) *n* bonhomme *m* de neige ■ snowplough (*Am* snowplow) *n* chasse-neige *m inv* ■ snowshoe *n* raquette *f* ■ snowstorm *n* tempête *f* de neige

snub [snʌb] **1** *n* rebuffade *f* **2** (*pt & pp* -bb-) *vt* (*offer*) rejeter; to s. sb snober qn **3** *adj* s. nose nez *m* retroussé

snuck [snʌk] *Am pt & pp of* **sneak**

snuff [snʌf] **1** *n* tabac *m* à priser **2** *vt* to s. (out) (*candle*) moucher

snug [snʌg] (**snugger, snuggest**) *adj* (*house*) douillet, -ette; (*garment*) bien ajusté

snuggle ['snʌgəl] *vi* to s. up to sb se blottir contre qn

so [səʊ] **1** *adv* (*to such a degree*) si, tellement (**that** que); (*thus*) ainsi, comme ça; to work/drink so much that... travailler/boire tellement que...; so much courage tellement de courage (**that** que); so many books tant de livres (**that** que); and so on et ainsi de suite; I think so je crois que oui; is that so? c'est vrai?; so am I moi aussi; I told you so je vous l'avais bien dit; *Fam* so long! au revoir!

2 *conj* (*therefore*) donc; (*in that case*) alors; so what? et alors?; so that... pour que... (+ *subjunctive*); so as to do sth pour faire qch ■ So-and-so *n* Mr S. Monsieur Untel ■ so-called *adj* soi-disant *inv* ■ so-so *adj & adv Fam* comme ci comme ça

soak [səʊk] **1** *vt* (*drench*) tremper; (*washing, food*) faire tremper; to be soaked (through *or* to the skin) être trempé (jusqu'aux os); to s. sth up absorber qch **2** *vi* (*of washing*) tremper ■ soaking *adj & adv* s. (wet) trempé

soap [səʊp] *n* savon *m*; s. opera feuilleton *m* populaire; s. powder lessive *f* ■ soapsuds *npl* mousse *f* de savon

soar [sɔː(r)] *vi* (*of bird*) s'élever; (*of price*) monter en flèche

sob [sɒb] **1** *n* sanglot *m* **2** (*pt & pp* -bb-) *vi* sangloter

sober ['səʊbə(r)] **1** *adj* (*sensible*) sobre; he's s. (*not drunk*) il n'est pas ivre **2** *vti* to s. up dessoûler

soccer ['sɒkə(r)] *n* football *m*

sociable ['səʊʃəbəl] *adj* (*person*) sociable; (*evening*) amical

social ['səʊʃəl] *adj* social; to have a good s. life sortir beaucoup; S. Security ≃ la Sécurité sociale; *Am* (*retirement pension*) pension *f* de retraite; the s. services les services *mpl* sociaux; s. worker assistant, -e *mf* social(e)

socialist ['səʊʃəlɪst] *adj & n* socialiste (*mf*)

socialize ['səʊʃəlaɪz] *vi* fréquenter des gens; to s. with sb fréquenter qn

socially ['səʊʃəlɪ] *adv* socialement; (*meet*) en société

society [sə'saɪətɪ] (*pl* -ies) *n* (*community, club, companionship*) société *f*; (*school/university club*) club *m*; (**high**) s. haute société *f*

sociology [səʊsɪ'ɒlədʒɪ] *n* sociologie *f*

sock [sɒk] *n* chaussette *f*

socket ['sɒkɪt] *n Br* (*of electric plug*) prise *f* de courant; *Br* (*of lamp*) douille *f*

soda ['səʊdə] *n Am* s. (pop) boisson *f* gazeuse; s. (water) eau *f* de Seltz

sofa ['səʊfə] *n* canapé *m*; s. bed canapé-lit *m*

soft [sɒft] (-er, -est) *adj* (*gentle, not stiff*) doux (*f* douce); (*butter, ground, paste, snow*) mou (*f* molle); (*wood, heart, colour*) tendre; (*indulgent*) indulgent; s. drink boisson *f* non alcoolisée; s. drugs drogues *fpl* douces; s. toy peluche *f* ■ soft-boiled *adj* (*egg*) à la coque

soften ['sɒfən] **1** *vt* (*object*) ramollir;

(colour, light, voice, skin) adoucir **2** *vi* ramollir ■ **softener** *n* adoucissant *m*

softly ['sɒftlɪ] *adv* doucement

software ['sɒftweə(r)] *n inv* Comptr logiciel *m*; **s. package** progiciel *m*

soggy ['sɒgɪ] (**-ier, -iest**) *adj* trempé

soil [sɔɪl] **1** *n* (*earth*) terre *f* **2** *vt* (*dirty*) salir

solar ['səʊlə(r)] *adj* solaire

sold [səʊld] *pt & pp of* **sell**

soldier ['səʊldʒə(r)] *n* soldat *m*

sole¹ [səʊl] **1** *n* (*of shoe*) semelle *f*; (*of foot*) plante *f* **2** *vt* (*shoe*) ressemeler

sole² [səʊl] *adj* (*only*) unique; (*rights, representative, responsibility*) exclusif, -ive ■ **solely** *adv* uniquement

solemn ['sɒləm] *adj* solennel, -elle

solicit [sə'lɪsɪt] **1** *vt* (*seek*) solliciter **2** *vi* (*of prostitute*) racoler

solicitor [sə'lɪsɪtə(r)] *n Br* (*for wills*) notaire *m*

solid ['sɒlɪd] **1** *adj* (*not liquid*) solide; (*not hollow*) plein; (*gold, silver*) massif, -ive **2** *adj* **frozen s.** complètement gelé; **ten days s.** dix jours d'affilée **3** *n* solide *m*; **solids** (*food*) aliments *mpl* solides ■ **solidly** *adv* (*built*) solidement; (*work*) sans interruption

solidarity [sɒlɪ'dærətɪ] *n* solidarité *f* (**with** avec)

solitary ['sɒlɪtərɪ] *adj* (*lonely, alone*) solitaire; (*only*) seul ■ **solitude** *n* solitude *f*

solo ['səʊləʊ] **1** (*pl* **-os**) *n Mus* solo *m* **2** *adj* (*guitar, violin*) solo *inv* **3** *adv* (*play, sing*) en solo; (*fly*) en solitaire ■ **soloist** *n Mus* soliste *mf*

soluble ['sɒljʊbəl] *adj* (*substance, problem*) soluble

solution [sə'luːʃən] *n* (**a**) (*to problem*) solution *f* (**to** de) (**b**) (*liquid*) solution *f*

solve [sɒlv] *vt* (*problem*) résoudre

solvent ['sɒlvənt] **1** *adj* (*financially*) solvable **2** *n Chem* solvant *m*

sombre ['sɒmbə(r)] (*Am* **somber**) *adj* sombre

SOME [sʌm] **1** *adj* (**a**) (*a quantity of*) du, de la, des; **s. wine** du vin; **s. water**

de l'eau; **s. dogs** des chiens; **s. pretty flowers** de jolies fleurs

(**b**) (*unspecified*) un, une; **s. man (or other)** un homme (quelconque); **for s. reason or other** pour une raison ou pour une autre; **I have been waiting s. time** ça fait un moment que j'attends

(**c**) (*a few*) quelques; (*in contrast to others*) certains; **s. days ago** il y a quelques jours; **s. people think that...** certains pensent que...

2 *pron* (**a**) (*a certain quantity*) en; **I want s.** j'en veux; **s. of my wine** un peu de mon vin; **s. of the time** une partie du temps

(**b**) (*as opposed to others*) certain(e)s; **some say...** certains disent...; **s. of the guests** certains invités

3 *adv* (*about*) environ; **s. ten years** environ dix ans ■ **somebody** *pron* quelqu'un; **s. small** quelqu'un de petit ■ **someday** *adv* un jour ■ **somehow** *adv* (*in some way*) d'une manière ou d'une autre; (*for some reason*) on ne sait pourquoi ■ **someone** *pron* quelqu'un; **s. small** quelqu'un de petit ■ **someplace** *adv Am* quelque part ■ **something 1** *pron* quelque chose; **s. awful** quelque chose d'affreux **2** *adv* **she plays s. like...** elle joue un peu comme... ■ **sometime** *adv* un jour; **s. in May** au mois de mai ■ **sometimes** *adv* quelquefois, parfois ■ **somewhat** *adv* quelque peu, assez ■ **somewhere** *adv* quelque part; **s. about fifteen** (*approximately*) environ quinze

somersault ['sʌməsɔːlt] *n* (*on ground*) roulade *f*; (*in air*) saut *m* périlleux

son [sʌn] *n* fils *m* ■ **son-in-law** (*pl* **sons-in-law**) *n* gendre *m*

sonata [sə'nɑːtə] *n* sonate *f*

song [sɒŋ] *n* chanson *f*; (*of bird*) chant *m*

soon [suːn] (**-er, -est**) *adv* (*in a short time*) bientôt; (*quickly*) vite; (*early*) tôt; **s. after** peu après; **as s. as...** aussitôt que...; **no sooner had he spoken than...** à peine avait-il parlé que...;

I'd **sooner leave** je préférerais partir; **sooner or later** tôt ou tard

soot [sʊt] n suie f

soothe [suːð] vt calmer

sophisticated [səˈfɪstɪkeɪtɪd] adj (person, taste) raffiné; (machine, method) sophistiqué

sophomore ['sɒfəmɔː(r)] n Am étudiant, -e mf de deuxième année

sopping ['sɒpɪŋ] adj & adv **s. (wet)** trempé

soppy ['sɒpɪ] (**-ier, -iest**) adj Br Fam (sentimental) sentimental

soprano [səˈprɑːnəʊ] (pl **-os**) n (singer) soprano mf

sordid ['sɔːdɪd] adj sordide

sore [sɔː(r)] **1** (**-er, -est**) adj (painful) douloureux, -euse; Am (angry) fâché (**at** contre); **to have a s. throat** avoir mal à la gorge **2** n (wound) plaie f

sorrow ['sɒrəʊ] n chagrin m

sorry ['sɒrɪ] (**-ier, -iest**) adj (sight, state) triste; **to be s. (about sth)** (regret) être désolé (de qch); **to feel or be s. for sb** plaindre qn; **I'm s. she can't come** je regrette qu'elle ne puisse pas venir; **s.!** pardon!; **to say s.** demander pardon (**to** à)

sort¹ [sɔːt] n sorte f; **a s. of** une sorte de; **all sorts of** toutes sortes de; **what s. of drink is it?** qu'est-ce que c'est comme boisson?; **s. of sad** (somewhat) plutôt triste

sort² [sɔːt] **1** vt (papers) trier; **to s. out** (classify, select) trier; (separate) séparer (**from** de); (organize) ranger; (problem) résoudre **2** vi **to s. through letters/magazines** trier des lettres/magazines

sought [sɔːt] pt & pp of **seek**

soul [səʊl] n âme f

sound¹ [saʊnd] **1** n son m; (noise) bruit m; **s. effects** bruitage m **2** vt (bell, alarm) sonner; (bugle) sonner de; **to s. one's horn** (in vehicle) klaxonner **3** vi (seem) sembler; **to s. like** sembler être; (resemble) ressembler à; **it sounds like** or **as if…** il semble que… (+ subjunctive or indicative)

sound² [saʊnd] **1** (**-er, -est**) adj (healthy) sain; (in good condition) en bon état; (basis) solide; (argument) valable; (advice) bon (f bonne); (investment) sûr **2** adv **s. asleep** profondément endormi ■ **soundly** adv (asleep, sleep) profondément

sound³ [saʊnd] vt (test, measure) sonder; **to s. sb out** sonder qn (**about** sur)

soundproof ['saʊndpruːf] **1** adj insonorisé **2** vt insonoriser

soundtrack ['saʊndtræk] n (of film) bande f sonore

soup [suːp] n soupe f; **s. dish** or **plate** assiette f creuse

sour ['saʊə(r)] (**-er, -est**) adj aigre; (milk) tourné; **to turn s.** (of milk) tourner; (of friendship) se détériorer

source [sɔːs] n (origin) source f

south [saʊθ] **1** n sud m; (**to the**) **s. of** au sud de **2** adj (coast) sud inv; (wind) du sud; **S. America/Africa** l'Amérique f/l'Afrique f du sud; **S. American** adj sud-américain; n Sud-Américain, -e mf; **S. African** adj sudafricain; n Sud-Africain, -e mf **3** adv au sud; (travel) vers le sud ■ **southbound** adj (traffic) en direction du sud; Br (carriageway) sud inv ■ **south-east** n & adj sud-est (m) ■ **southerly** adj (direction) du sud ■ **southern** ['sʌðən] adj (town) du sud; (coast) sud inv; **S. Italy** le sud de l'Italie ■ **southerner** ['sʌðənə(r)] n habitant, -e mf du sud ■ **southward(s)** adj & adv vers le sud ■ **south-west** n & adj sud-ouest (m)

souvenir [suːvəˈnɪə(r)] n souvenir m

sovereign ['sɒvrɪn] n (monarch) souverain, -e mf ■ **sovereignty** [-rəntɪ] n souveraineté f

sow¹ [saʊ] n (pig) truie f

sow² [səʊ] (pt **sowed**, pp **sowed** or **sown** [səʊn]) vt (seeds, doubt) semer; (land) ensemencer (**with** de)

soya ['sɔɪə] n Br soja m; **s. bean** graine

spa [spɑː] *n (town)* station *f* thermale

space [speɪs] **1** *n (gap, emptiness, atmosphere)* espace *m*; *(for parking)* place *f*; **to take up s.** prendre de la place; **blank s.** espace *m*, blanc *m*; **s. bar** *(on keyboard)* barre *f* d'espacement **2** *adj (voyage, capsule)* spatial **3** *vt* **to s. out** espacer ■ **spaceship** *n* vaisseau *m* spatial ■ **spacing** *n Typ* **in double/single s.** à double/simple interligne

spacious ['speɪʃəs] *adj* spacieux, -euse

spade [speɪd] *n* (**a**) *(for garden)* bêche *f* (**b**) *Cards* **spade(s)** pique *m*

spaghetti [spə'getɪ] *n* spaghettis *mpl*

Spain [speɪn] *n* l'Espagne *f*

span [spæn] *(pt & pp* **-nn-)** *vt (of bridge)* enjamber; *Fig (in time)* couvrir

Spaniard ['spænjəd] *n* Espagnol, -e *mf* ■ **Spanish 1** *adj* espagnol **2** *n (language)* espagnol *m*

spank [spæŋk] *vt* donner une tape sur les fesses à ■ **spanking** *n* fessée *f*

spanner ['spænə(r)] *n Br (tool)* clef *f*

spare [speə(r)] **1** *adj (extra, surplus)* de ou en trop; *(reserve)* de rechange; *(wheel)* de secours; *(available)* disponible; **s. room** chambre *f* d'ami; **s. time** loisirs *mpl*
2 *n* **s. (part)** *(for vehicle, machine)* pièce *f* détachée
3 *vt (do without)* se passer de; *(efforts, sb's feelings)* ménager; **to s. sb sth** *(grief, details)* épargner qch à qn; **I can't s. the time** je n'ai pas le temps; **with five minutes to s.** avec cinq minutes d'avance

sparingly ['speərɪŋlɪ] *adv* en petite quantité

spark [spɑːk] **1** *n* étincelle *f*; *Aut* **s. plug** bougie *f* **2** *vt* **to s. off** *(cause)* provoquer

sparkle ['spɑːkəl] *vi* briller; *(of diamond, star)* scintiller ■ **sparkling** *adj (wine, water)* pétillant

sparrow ['spærəʊ] *n* moineau *m*

sparse [spɑːs] *adj* clairsemé ■ **sparsely** *adv (populated)* peu; **s. furnished** à peine meublé

spasm ['spæzəm] *n (of muscle)* spasme *m*

spat [spæt] *pt & pp* of **spit**

spate [speɪt] *n* **a s. of sth** *(of letters, calls)* une avalanche de qch; *(of crimes)* une vague de qch

spatter ['spætə(r)] *vt (clothes, person)* éclabousser (**with** de)

speak [spiːk] **1** *(pt* **spoke***, pp* **spoken***) vt (language)* parler; *(say)* dire; **to s.one's mind** dire ce que l'on pense
2 *vi* parler (**about** or **of** de); *(formally, in assembly)* prendre la parole; **so to s.** pour ainsi dire; **that speaks for itself** c'est évident; **Jayne speaking!** *(on the telephone)* Jayne à l'appareil!; **to s. out** or **up** *(boldly)* parler (franchement); **to s. up** *(more loudly)* parler plus fort

speaker ['spiːkə(r)] *n (at meeting)* intervenant, -e *mf*; *(at conference)* conférencier, -ère *mf*; *(loudspeaker)* enceinte *f*; **to be a Spanish s.** parler espagnol

spear [spɪə(r)] *n* lance *f*

spearmint ['spɪəmɪnt] *adj (sweet)* à la menthe; *(chewing gum)* mentholé

spec [spek] *n Br Fam* **on s.** à tout hasard

special ['speʃəl] **1** *adj* spécial; *(care, attention)* particulier, -ère; *Br* **by s. delivery** en exprès; **s. effects** effets *mpl* spéciaux **2** *n* **today's s.** *(in restaurant)* le plat du jour

specialist ['speʃəlɪst] **1** *n* spécialiste *mf* (**in** de) **2** *adj (dictionary, knowledge)* spécialisé; *(equipment)* de spécialiste ■ **speciality** [-ʃɪ'ælɪtɪ] *(pl* **-ies***) n Br* spécialité *f*

specialize ['speʃəlaɪz] *vi* se spécialiser (**in** dans)

specially ['speʃəlɪ] *adv (specifically)* spécialement; *(particularly)* particulièrement

specialty ['speʃəltɪ] *(pl* **-ies***) n Am* spécialité *f*

species ['spiːʃiːz] *n inv* espèce *f*

specific [spə'sıfık] *adj* précis ■ **specifically** *adv* (*explicitly*) expressément; (*exactly*) précisément; (*specially*) spécialement

specify ['spesıfaı] (*pt & pp* **-ied**) *vt* (*state exactly*) préciser; (*stipulate*) stipuler ■ **specification** [-fı'keıʃən] *n* spécification *f*

specimen ['spesımın] *n* (*individual example*) spécimen *m*; (*of urine, blood*) échantillon *m*

speck [spek] *n* (*stain*) petite tache *f*; (*of dust*) grain *m*; (*dot*) point *m*

speckled ['spekəld] *adj* tacheté

specs [speks] *npl Fam* lunettes *fpl*

spectacle ['spektəkəl] *n* (*sight*) spectacle *m* ■ **spectacles** *npl* (*glasses*) lunettes *fpl*

spectacular [spek'tækjʊlə(r)] *adj* spectaculaire

spectator [spek'teıtə(r)] *n* spectateur, -trice *mf*

spectre ['spektə(r)] *n* spectre *m* (**of** de)

spectrum ['spektrəm] (*pl* **-tra** [-trə]) *n* spectre *m*; *Fig* (*range*) gamme *f*

speculate ['spekjʊleıt] **1** *vt* **to s. that...** (*guess*) conjecturer que... **2** *vi Fin* spéculer; **to s. about** (*make guesses*) faire des suppositions sur ■ **speculation** *n* suppositions *fpl*; *Fin* spéculation *f*

sped [sped] *pt & pp of* **speed**

speech [spi:tʃ] *n* (*talk, lecture*) discours *m* (**on** *or* **about** sur); (*faculty*) parole *f*; (*diction*) élocution *f*; **to make a s.** faire un discours ■ **speechless** *adj* muet (*f* muette) (**with** de)

speed [spi:d] **1** *n* (*rapidity, gear*) vitesse *f*; **at top** *or* **full s.** à toute vitesse; **s. limit** (*on road*) limitation *f* de vitesse **2** (*pt & pp* **sped**) *vt* **to s. sth up** accélérer qch **3** *vi* (**a**) **to s. up** (*of person*) aller plus vite; **to s. past sth** passer à toute vitesse devant qch (**b**) (*pt & pp* **speeded**) (*exceed speed limit*) faire un excès de vitesse ■ **speedboat** *n* vedette *f* ■ **speeding** *n* (*in vehicle*) excès *m* de vitesse

■ **speedometer** *n Br* (*in vehicle*) compteur *m* de vitesse

speedy ['spi:dı] (**-ier, -iest**) *adj* rapide

spell[1] [spel] *n* (*magic words*) formule *f* magique; **to cast a s. on sb** jeter un sort à qn ■ **spellbound** *adj* fasciné

spell[2] [spel] *n* (*period*) période *f*; **cold s.** vague *f* de froid

spell[3] [spel] (*pt & pp* **spelled** *or* **spelt** [spelt]) *vt* (*write*) écrire; (*say aloud*) épeler; (*of letters*) former; *Fig* (*mean*) signifier; **how do you s. it?** comment ça s'écrit?; **to s. sth out** (*word*) épeler qch; *Fig* (*explain*) expliquer clairement qch ■ **spell-checker** *n Comptr* correcteur *m* d'orthographe ■ **spelling** *n* orthographe *f*; **s. mistake** faute *f* d'orthographe

spend [spend] (*pt & pp* **spent**) *vt* (*money*) dépenser (**on** pour/en); (*time*) passer (**on sth** sur qch; **doing** à faire); (*energy*) consacrer (**on sth** à qch; **doing** à faire) ■ **spending** *n* dépenses *fpl*; **s. money** argent *m* de poche ■ **spendthrift** *n* **to be a s.** être dépensier, -ère

spent [spent] *pt & pp of* **spend**

sperm [spɜ:m] *n* sperme *m*

spew [spju:] *vt* vomir

sphere [sfıə(r)] *n* (*of influence, action*), *Math & Pol* sphère *f* ■ **spherical** ['sferıkəl] *adj* sphérique

spice [spaıs] **1** *n* épice *f*; *Fig* (*interest*) piquant *m* **2** *vt* (*food*) épicer; **to s. sth (up)** (*add interest to*) ajouter du piquant à qch ■ **spicy** (**-ier, -iest**) *adj* épicé

spider ['spaıdə(r)] *n* araignée *f*

spike [spaık] *n* (*of metal*) pointe *f* ■ **spiky** (**-ier, -iest**) *adj* (*hair*) tout hérissé

spill [spıl] (*pt & pp* **spilled** *or* **spilt** [spılt]) **1** *vt* (*liquid*) renverser **2** *vi* se répandre

▸ **spill out** *vt sep* (*empty*) vider

▸ **spill over** *vi* (*of liquid*) déborder

spin [spın] **1** *n* (*motion*) tournoiement *m*; (*on ball*) effet *m*; *Fam* **to go for a s.** (*in car*) aller faire un tour

2 (*pt & pp* **spun**, *pres p* **spinning**) *vt* (*wool, cotton*) filer; (*wheel, top*) faire tourner; (*spin-dry*) essorer; **to s. sth out** (*speech*) faire durer qch

3 *vi* tourner; **to s. round** (*of dancer, wheel, top, planet*) tourner; **my head's spinning** j'ai la tête qui tourne

spinach ['spɪnɪdʒ] *n* épinards *mpl*

spin-dry ['spɪndraɪ] *vt* essorer ▪ **spin-dryer** *n* essoreuse *f*

spine [spaɪn] *n* (*backbone*) colonne *f* vertébrale; (*of book*) dos *m*

spinster ['spɪnstə(r)] *n* vieille fille *f*

spiral ['spaɪərəl] **1** *n* spirale *f* **2** *adj* en spirale; (*staircase*) en colimaçon **3** (*Br* **-ll-**, *Am* **-l-**) *vi* (*of prices*) s'envoler

spire [spaɪə(r)] *n* (*of church*) flèche *f*

spirit ['spɪrɪt] **1** *n* (*soul, ghost, mood*) esprit *m*; *Fig* (*determination*) courage *m*; **spirits** (*drink*) spiritueux *mpl*; **in good spirits** de bonne humeur **2** *adj* (*lamp*) à alcool; **s. level** niveau *m* (à bulle) ▪ **spirited** *adj* (*campaign, attack*) vigoureux, -euse; (*person, remark*) énergique

spiritual ['spɪrɪtʃʊəl] *adj* spirituel, -elle

spit[1] [spɪt] **1** *n* (*on ground*) crachat *m*; (*in mouth*) salive *f* **2** (*pt & pp* **spat** *or* **spit**, *pres p* **spitting**) *vt* cracher; **to s. sth out** cracher qch; **to be the spitting image of sb** être le portrait (tout craché) de qn **3** *vi* cracher

spit[2] [spɪt] *n* (*for meat*) broche *f*

spite [spaɪt] **1** *n* (*dislike*) dépit *m*; **in s. of sb/sth** malgré qn/qch; **in s. of the fact that...** bien que... (*+ subjunctive*) **2** *vt* vexer ▪ **spiteful** *adj* vexant

splash [splæʃ] **1** *n* (*of liquid*) éclaboussure *f*; *Fig* (*of colour*) tache *f* **2** *vt* (*spatter*) éclabousser (**with** de) **3** *vi* (*of mud*) faire des éclaboussures; (*of waves*) clapoter; **to s. (about)** (*in river, mud*) patauger; (*in bath*) barboter; *Fam* **to s. out** (*spend money*) claquer des ronds

splendid ['splendɪd] *adj* splendide ▪ **splendour** (*Am* **splendor**) *n* splendeur *f*

splint [splɪnt] *n* attelle *f*

splinter ['splɪntə(r)] *n* (*of wood, glass*) éclat *m*; (*in finger*) écharde *f*

split [splɪt] **1** *n* fente *f*; (*tear*) déchirure *f*; (*in political party*) scission *f* **2** *adj* **in a s. second** en une fraction de seconde **3** (*pt & pp* **split**, *pres p* **splitting**) *vt* (*break apart*) fendre; (*tear*) déchirer; **to s. (up)** (*group*) diviser; (*money, work*) partager (**between** entre) **4** *vi* se fendre; (*tear*) se déchirer; **to s. (up)** (*of group*) se diviser (**into** en); **to s. up** (*because of disagreement*) (*of couple, friends*) se séparer; (*of group*) se disperser; **to s. up with sb** rompre avec qn

spoil [spɔɪl] (*pt & pp* **spoilt** *or* **spoiled**) *vt* (*ruin*) gâcher; (*indulge*) gâter ▪ **spoilsport** *n* rabat-joie *mf inv*

spoilt [spɔɪlt] *pt & pp of* **spoil**

spoke[1] [spəʊk] *n* (*of wheel*) rayon *m*

spoke[2] [spəʊk] *pt of* **speak** ▪ **spoken 1** *pp of* **speak 2** *adj* (*language*) parlé ▪ **spokesman** (*pl* -**men**) *n* ▪ **spokesperson, spokeswoman** (*pl* -**women**) *n* porte-parole *mf inv* (**for** *or* of de)

sponge [spʌndʒ] **1** *n* éponge *f*; *Br* **s. bag** trousse *f* de toilette; **s. cake** génoise *f* **2** *vt* **to s. sth down/off** laver/enlever qch avec une éponge **3** *vi* *Fam* **to s. off** *or* **on sb** vivre aux crochets de qn ▪ **sponger** *n* *Fam* parasite *m*

sponsor ['spɒnsə(r)] **1** *n* sponsor *m* **2** *vt* sponsoriser ▪ **sponsorship** *n* sponsoring *m*

spontaneous [spɒn'teɪnɪəs] *adj* spontané

spooky ['spu:kɪ] (**-ier, -iest**) *adj* *Fam* qui donne le frisson

spoon [spu:n] *n* cuillère *f* ▪ **spoonful** *n* cuillerée *f*

sporadic [spə'rædɪk] *adj* sporadique

sport[1] [spɔːt] *n* sport *m*; **to play** *Br* **s.** *or* *Am* **sports** faire du sport; **sports club** club *m* de sport; **sports car/ground** voiture *f*/terrain *m* de sport ▪ **sporting** *adj* (*attitude, person*) sportif, -ive ▪ **sportsman** (*pl* -**men**) *n* sportif *m*

■ **sportswoman** (*pl* -**women**) *n* sportive *f* ■ **sporty** (-**ier**, -**iest**) *adj* sportif, -ive

sport² [spɔːt] *vt* (*wear*) arborer

spot¹ [spɒt] *n* (*stain*, *mark*) tache *f*; (*dot*) point *m*; (*polka dot*) pois *m*; (*drop*) goutte *f*; (*pimple*) bouton *m*; (*place*) endroit *m*; **on the s.** sur place; (*at once*) sur le coup; **to be in a tight s.** (*difficulty*) être dans le pétrin

spot² [spɒt] (*pt & pp* -**tt**-) *vt* (*notice*) apercevoir

spotless ['spɒtləs] *adj* (*clean*) impeccable

spotlight ['spɒtlaɪt] *n* projecteur *m*; (*for photography*) spot *m*

spotty ['spɒtɪ] (-**ier**, -**iest**) *adj* (*face*, *person*) boutonneux, -euse

spouse [spaʊs, spaʊz] *n* époux *m*, épouse *f*

spout [spaʊt] **1** *n* (*of teapot*, *jug*) bec *m* **2** *vt Pej* (*say*) débiter

sprain [spreɪn] **1** *n* entorse *f* **2** *vt* **to s. one's ankle/wrist** se fouler la cheville/le poignet

sprang [spræŋ] *pt of* **spring¹**

spray [spreɪ] **1** *n* (*can*, *device*) vaporisateur *m*; (*water drops*) gouttelettes *fpl*; (*from sea*) embruns *mpl* **2** *vt* (*liquid*, *surface*) vaporiser; (*plant*, *crops*) pulvériser; (*car*) peindre à la bombe

spread [spred] **1** *n* (*of idea*, *religion*, *language*) diffusion *f*; (*of disease*) propagation *f*; *Fam* (*meal*) festin *m*; **cheese s.** fromage *m* à tartiner **2** (*pt & pp* **spread**) *vt* (*stretch*, *open out*) étendre; (*legs*, *fingers*) écarter; (*paint*, *payment*, *visits*, *cards*) étaler; (*sand*, *fear*) répandre; (*news*, *illness*) propager; **to s. out** (*map*, *payments*, *visits*) étaler; (*fingers*) écarter **3** *vi* (*of fog*) s'étendre; (*of fire*, *epidemic*) se propager; (*of news*, *fear*) se répandre; **to s. out** (*of people*) se disperser ■ **spreadsheet** *n* Comptr tableur *m*

spree [spriː] *n* **to go on a spending s.** faire des folies dans les magasins

sprightly ['spraɪtlɪ] (-**ier**, -**iest**) *adj* alerte

spring¹ [sprɪŋ] **1** *n* (*device*) ressort *m*; (*leap*) bond *m* **2** (*pt* **sprang**, *pp* **sprung**) *vi* (*surprise*) faire (**on** à) **3** *vi* (*leap*) bondir; **to s. to mind** venir à l'esprit; **to s. from** (*stem from*) provenir de; **to s. up** (*appear*) surgir ■ **springboard** *n* tremplin *m*

spring² [sprɪŋ] *n* (*season*) printemps *m*; **in (the) s.** au printemps; *Br* **s. onion** petit oignon *m* ■ **spring-cleaning** *n* nettoyage *m* de printemps ■ **spring- time** *n* printemps *m*

spring³ [sprɪŋ] *n* (*of water*) source *f*; **s. water** eau *f* de source

sprinkle ['sprɪŋkəl] *vt* (*sand*) répandre (**on** *or* **over** sur); **to s. sth with water**, **to s. water on sth** arroser qch; **to s. sth with sth** (*sugar*, *salt*, *flour*) saupoudrer qch de qch

sprint [sprɪnt] *vi* (*run*) sprinter

sprout [spraʊt] **1** *n* (**Brussels**) **s.** chou *m* de Bruxelles **2** *vt* (*leaves*) pousser **3** *vi* (*of seed*, *bulb*) pousser

spruce [spruːs] **1** (-**er**, -**est**) *adj* (*neat*) impeccable **2** *vt* **to s. oneself up** se faire beau (*f* belle)

sprung [sprʌŋ] *pp of* **spring¹**

spud [spʌd] *n Fam* (*potato*) patate *f*

spun [spʌn] *pt & pp of* **spin**

spur [spɜː(r)] **1** *n* (*of horse rider*) éperon *m*; *Fig* (*stimulus*) aiguillon *m*; **to do sth on the s. of the moment** faire qch sur un coup de tête **2** (*pt & pp* -**rr**-) *vt* **to s. sb on** (*urge on*) aiguillonner qn

spurn [spɜːn] *vt* rejeter

spurt [spɜːt] **1** *n* (*of energy*) regain *m*; **to put on a s.** foncer **2** *vi* **to s. (out)** (*of liquid*) gicler

spy [spaɪ] **1** (*pl* -**ies**) *n* espion, -onne *mf* **2** *adj* (*story*, *film*) d'espionnage **3** (*pt & pp* -**ied**) *vt* (*notice*) repérer **4** *vi* espionner; **to s. on sb** espionner qn ■ **spying** *n* espionnage *m*

squabble ['skwɒbəl] **1** *n* querelle *f* **2** *vi* se quereller (**over** à propos de)

squad [skwɒd] *n* (*of workmen*, *footballers*) équipe *f*; (*of soldiers*) section *f*; (*of police*) brigade *f*

squalid ['skwɒlɪd] *adj* sordide

■ **squalor** *n (poverty)* misère *f*

squander ['skwɒndə(r)] *vt (money, resources)* gaspiller; *(time)* perdre

square ['skweə(r)] **1** *n* carré *m*; *(on chessboard, map)* case *f*; *(in town)* place *f* **2** *adj* carré; *Math* **s. root** racine *f* carrée **3** *vt (settle)* régler; *Math (number)* élever au carré **4** *vi (tally)* cadrer (**with** avec)

squash [skwɒʃ] **1** *n (game)* squash *m*; *(vegetable)* courge *f*; *Br* **lemon/orange s.** ≃ sirop *m* de citron/d'orange **2** *vt* écraser

squat [skwɒt] **1** *adj (person, object, building)* trapu **2** *(pt & pp* -**tt**-*) vi* squatter; **to s. (down)** s'accroupir; **to be squatting (down)** être accroupi

squawk [skwɔːk] *vi* pousser un cri rauque

squeak [skwiːk] *vi (of person)* pousser un cri aigu; *(of door)* grincer

squeal [skwiːl] *vi* pousser un cri perçant

squeamish ['skwiːmɪʃ] *adj* de nature délicate

squeeze [skwiːz] **1** *n* **to give sth a s.** presser qch; **to give sb's hand/arm a s.** serrer la main/le bras à qn **2** *vt (press)* presser; **to s. sb's hand** serrer la main à qn; **to s. sth into sth** faire rentrer qch dans qch; **to s. the juice (out)** faire sortir le jus (**of** de) **3** *vi* **to s. through/into sth** *(force oneself)* se glisser par/dans qch; **to s. in** trouver de la place; **to s. up** se serrer (**against** contre)

squelch [skweltʃ] *vi* patauger

squid [skwɪd] *n inv* calmar *m*

squint [skwɪnt] **1** *n* **to have a s.** loucher **2** *vi* loucher; *(in the sunlight)* plisser les yeux

squirm [skwɜːm] *vi (wriggle)* se tortiller

squirrel [*Br* 'skwɪrəl, *Am* 'skwɜːrəl] *n* écureuil *m*

squirt [skwɜːt] **1** *vt (liquid)* faire gicler **2** *vi (of liquid)* gicler

St (a) *(abbr* **Street)** rue **(b)** *(abbr* **Saint)** St, Ste

stab [stæb] **1** *n* **s. (wound)** coup *m* de couteau **2** *(pt & pp* -**bb**-*) vt (with knife)* poignarder

stability [stə'bɪlɪtɪ] *n* stabilité *f*

stabilize ['steɪbəlaɪz] **1** *vt* stabiliser **2** *vi* se stabiliser

stable¹ ['steɪbəl] **(-er, -est)** *adj* stable

stable² ['steɪbəl] *n* écurie *f*

stack [stæk] **1** *n (heap)* tas *m*; *Fam* **stacks of** *(lots of)* des tas de **2** *vt* **to s. (up)** entasser

stadium ['steɪdɪəm] *n* stade *m*

staff [stɑːf] *n* personnel *m*; *(of school, university)* professeurs *mpl*; *Br* **s. room** *(in school)* salle *f* des professeurs

stag [stæg] *n* cerf *m*; **s. night** *or* **party** enterrement *m* de la vie de garçon

stage¹ [steɪdʒ] **1** *n (platform)* scène *f*; **on s.** sur scène **2** *vt (play)* monter; *Fig* organiser

stage² [steɪdʒ] *n (phase)* stade *m*

stagger ['stægə(r)] **1** *vt (holidays)* échelonner; *(astound)* stupéfier **2** *vi (reel)* chanceler ■ **staggering** *adj* stupéfiant

stagnant ['stægnənt] *adj* stagnant
■ **stagnate** *vi* stagner

staid [steɪd] *adj* collet monté *inv*

stain [steɪn] **1** *n (mark)* tache *f* **2** *vt (mark)* tacher (**with** de); *(dye)* teinter
■ **stained-glass** *adj* **s. window** vitrail *m (pl* -aux*)* ■ **stainless** *n* **s. steel** acier *m* inoxydable, Inox®*m*

stair [steə(r)] *n* **a s.** *(step)* une marche; **the stairs** *(staircase)* l'escalier *m* ■ **staircase, stairway** *n* escalier *m*

stake [steɪk] **1** *n* **(a)** *(post)* pieu *m*; *(for plant)* tuteur *m* **(b)** *(in betting)* enjeu *m*; **to have a s. in sth** *(share)* avoir des intérêts dans qch; **at s.** en jeu **2** *vt (bet)* jouer (**on** sur)

stale [steɪl] **(-er, -est)** *adj (bread)* rassis; *(air)* vicié; *(joke)* éculé

stalemate ['steɪlmeɪt] *n (in chess)* pat *m*; *Fig* impasse *f*

stalk [stɔːk] **1** *n (of plant)* tige *f*; *(of fruit)* queue *f* **2** *vt (animal, criminal)* traquer; *(celebrity)* harceler **3** *vi* **to s. out** *(walk* *angrily*) sortir d'un air furieux mais digne

stall [stɔːl] **1** *n* (*in market*) étal *m*; *Br* (*for newspapers, flowers*) kiosque *m*; (*in stable*) stalle *f*; *Br* **the stalls** (*in cinema, theatre*) l'orchestre *m* **2** *vt* (*engine, car*) caler **3** *vi* (*of car*) caler; **to s. (for time)** chercher à gagner du temps

stamina ['stæmɪnə] *n* résistance *f* physique

stammer ['stæmə(r)] **1** *n* **to have a s.** être bègue **2** *vi* bégayer

stamp [stæmp] **1** *n* (*for letter*) timbre *m*; (*mark*) cachet *m*; (*device*) tampon *m*; **s. collector** philatéliste *mf* **2** *vt* (*document*) tamponner; (*letter*) timbrer; (*metal*) estamper; **to s. one's foot** taper du pied; *Br* **stamped addressed envelope**, *Am* **stamped self-addressed envelope** enveloppe *f* timbrée libellée à ses noms et adresse **3** *vi* **to s. on sth** écraser qch

stampede [stæm'piːd] **1** *n* débandade *f* **2** *vi* se ruer

stance [stɑːns] *n* position *f*

STAND [stænd] **1** *n* (*opinion*) position *f*; (*support*) support *m*; (*stall*) étal *m*; (*at exhibition*) stand *m*; (*at sports ground*) tribune *f*; **to take a s.** prendre position

2 (*pt & pp* **stood**) *vt* (*pain, journey*) supporter; (*put straight*) mettre debout; **to s. a chance** avoir des chances; **I can't s. him** je ne peux pas le supporter

3 *vi* (*be upright*) se tenir debout; (*get up*) se mettre debout; (*remain*) rester debout; (*of building*) se trouver; (*of object*) être

▸ **stand about, stand around** *vi* (*in street*) traîner

▸ **stand aside** *vi* s'écarter

▸ **stand back** *vi* reculer

▸ **stand by 1** *vt insep* (*opinion*) s'en tenir à; (*person*) soutenir **2** *vi* (*do nothing*) rester sans rien faire; (*be ready*) être prêt

▸ **stand down** *vi* (*withdraw*) se retirer

▸ **stand for** *vt insep* (*mean*) signifier;

(*represent*) représenter; *Br* (*be candidate for*) être candidat à; (*tolerate*) supporter

▸ **stand in for** *vt insep* (*replace*) remplacer

▸ **stand out** *vi* (*be visible*) ressortir (**against** sur)

▸ **stand over** *vt insep* (*watch closely*) surveiller

▸ **stand up 1** *vt sep* mettre debout; *Fam* **to s. sb up** poser un lapin à qn **2** *vi* (*get up*) se lever

▸ **stand up for** *vt insep* (*defend*) défendre

▸ **stand up to** *vt insep* (*resist*) résister à; (*defend oneself against*) tenir tête à

standard ['stændəd] **1** *n* (*norm*) norme *f*; (*level*) niveau *m*; **standards** (*principles*) principes *mpl* moraux; **s. of living, living standards** niveau *m* de vie **2** *adj* (*average*) ordinaire; (*model, size*) standard *inv* ∎ **standardize** *vt* standardiser

stand-by ['stændbaɪ] **1** (*pl* **-bys**) *n* **on s.** (*troops, emergency services*) prêt à intervenir **2** *adj* (*plane ticket*) en stand-by

stand-in ['stændɪn] *n* remplaçant, -e *mf* (**for** de); (*actor*) doublure *f* (**for** de)

standing ['stændɪŋ] **1** *adj* (*upright*) debout; (*permanent*) permanent; *Br* **s. order** virement *m* automatique **2** *n* (*reputation*) réputation *f*; (*social, professional*) rang *m*; **of long s.** de longue date

stand-offish [stænd'ɒfɪʃ] *adj* distant

standpoint ['stændpɔɪnt] *n* point *m* de vue

standstill ['stændstɪl] *n* **to bring sth to a s.** immobiliser qch; **to come to a s.** s'immobiliser; **at a s.** immobile; (*negotiations, industry*) paralysé

stank [stæŋk] *pt of* **stink**

stanza ['stænzə] *n* strophe *f*

staple¹ ['steɪpəl] *adj* (*basic*) de base; **s. food** *or* **diet** nourriture *f* de base

staple² ['steɪpəl] **1** *n* (*for paper*) agrafe *f* **2** *vt* agrafer ∎ **stapler** *n* (*for paper*) agrafeuse *f*

star [stɑ:(r)] **1** n étoile f; (famous person) star f; Br **four-s. (petrol)** du super **2** (pt & pp **-rr-**) vt (of film) avoir pour vedette **3** vi (of actor, actress) être la vedette (**in** de)

starboard ['stɑ:bəd] n Naut tribord m

starch [stɑ:tʃ] n amidon m

stare [steə(r)] **1** n regard m fixe **2** vi to **s. at sb/sth** fixer qn/qch (du regard)

stark [stɑ:k] **1** (**-er, -est**) adj (place) désolé; (fact, reality) brutal; **to be in s. contrast** to contraster nettement avec **2** adv **s. naked** complètement nu

start¹ [stɑ:t] **1** n début m; (of race) départ m; **for a s.** pour commencer; **from the s.** dès le début; **to make a s.** commencer

2 vt commencer; (packet, conversation) entamer; (fashion, campaign, offensive) lancer; (engine, vehicle) mettre en marche; (business, family) fonder; **to s. doing** or **to do sth** commencer à faire qch

3 vi commencer (**with sth** par qch); **by doing** par faire; (of vehicle) démarrer; (leave) partir (**for** pour); (in job) débuter; **to s. with** (firstly) pour commencer; **starting from now/10 euros** à partir de maintenant/10 euros ■ **starting** adj (point, line, salary) de départ; **s. post** (in race) ligne f de départ

▶ **start off** vi (leave) partir (**for** pour); (in job) débuter

▶ **start out** vi (begin) débuter; (on journey) se mettre en route

▶ **start up 1** vt sep (engine, vehicle) mettre en marche; (business) fonder **2** vi (of engine, vehicle) démarrer

start² [stɑ:t] **1** n (movement) sursaut m; **to give sb a s.** faire sursauter qn **2** vi sursauter

starter ['stɑ:tə(r)] n (in vehicle) démarreur m; (in meal) entrée f; (runner) partant, -e mf; Fam **for starters** (firstly) pour commencer

startle ['stɑ:təl] vt faire sursauter

starvation [stɑ:'veɪʃən] **1** n faim f **2** adj (wage, ration) de misère

starve [stɑ:v] **1** vt (make suffer) faire souffrir de la faim; Fig (deprive) priver (**of** de) **2** vi (suffer) souffrir de la faim; **to s. to death** mourir de faim; Fam **I'm starving!** je meurs de faim!

state¹ [steɪt] **1** n (**a**) (condition) état m; (situation) situation f; **not in a (fit) s. to...**, **in no (fit) s. to...** hors d'état de; **to s. that** déclarer (**that** que); (opinion) formuler; (problem) exposer

statement ['steɪtmənt] n déclaration f; (in court) déposition f; (bank) **s.** relevé m de compte

statesman ['steɪtsmən] (pl **-men**) n homme m d'État

static ['stætɪk] adj statique

station ['steɪʃən] **1** n (for trains) gare f; (underground) station f; (social) rang m; **bus s.** gare f routière; **radio s.** station f de radio; Am **s. wagon** break m **2** vt (position) placer; **to be stationed at/in** (of troops) être en garnison à/en

stationary ['steɪʃənərɪ] adj (vehicle) à l'arrêt

stationer ['steɪʃənə(r)] n papetier, -ère mf; **s.'s (shop)** papeterie f ■ **stationery** n (articles) articles mpl de bureau; (paper) papier m

statistic [stə'tɪstɪk] n (fact) statistique f; **statistics** (science) la statistique

statue ['stætʃuː] n statue f

stature ['stætʃə(r)] n (importance) envergure f

status ['steɪtəs] n (position) situation f; (legal, official) statut m; (prestige) prestige m; **s. symbol** marque f de prestige

staunch [stɔ:ntʃ] (**-er, -est**) adj (resolute) convaincu; (supporter) ardent

stave [steɪv] vt **to s. off sth** (disaster, danger) conjurer qch; **to s. off hunger** tromper la faim

stay [steɪ] **1** n (visit) séjour m **2** vi (remain) rester; (reside) loger; (visit) séjourner; **to s. put** ne pas bouger

▸ **stay away** *vi* ne pas s'approcher (**from** de); **to s. away from school** ne pas aller à l'école

▸ **stay behind** *vi* rester en arrière

▸ **stay in** *vi* (*at home*) rester à la maison; (*of nail, screw, tooth*) tenir

▸ **stay out** *vi* (*outside*) rester dehors; (*not come home*) ne pas rentrer; **to s. out of sth** (*not interfere in*) ne pas se mêler de qch; (*avoid*) éviter qch

▸ **stay up** *vi* (*at night*) ne pas se coucher; (*of fence*) tenir; **to s. up late** se coucher tard

stead [sted] *n* **to stand sb in good s.** être bien utile à qn; **in sb's s.** à la place de qn

steadfast ['stedfɑ:st] *adj* dévoué; (*opponent*) constant

steady ['stedɪ] **1** (**-ier, -iest**) *adj* (*firm, stable*) stable; (*hand, voice*) assuré; (*progress, speed, demand*) constant; **to be s. on one's feet** être solide sur ses jambes **2** *vt* faire tenir; **to s. one's nerves** se calmer; **to s. oneself** retrouver son équilibre ▪ **steadily** *adv* (*gradually*) progressivement; (*regularly*) régulièrement; (*continuously*) sans arrêt; (*walk*) d'un pas assuré

steak [steɪk] *n* (*beef*) steak *m*

steal[1] [sti:l] (*pt* **stole**, *pp* **stolen**) *vti* voler (**from sb** à qn)

steal[2] [sti:l] (*pt* **stole**, *pp* **stolen**) *vi* **to s. in/out** entrer/sortir furtivement

stealthy ['stelθɪ] (**-ier, -iest**) *adj* furtif, -ive

steam [sti:m] **1** *n* vapeur *f*; (*on glass*) buée *f*; *Fam* **to let off s.** se défouler; **s. engine/iron** locomotive *f*/fer *m* à vapeur **2** *vt* (*food*) cuire à la vapeur; **to get steamed up** (*of glass*) se couvrir de buée **3** *vi* **to s. up** (*of glass*) s'embuer ▪ **steamer** *n* bateau *m* à vapeur; (*for food*) panier *m* pour cuisson à la vapeur

steel [sti:l] **1** *n* acier *m* **2** *vt* **to s. oneself** s'armer de courage

steep [sti:p] **1** (**-er, -est**) *adj* (*stairs, slope*) raide; (*hill, path*) escarpé; *Fig* (*price*) excessif, -ive **2** *vt* (*soak*) tremper (**in** dans) ▪ **steeply** *adv* (*rise*) en pente raide; *Fig* (*of prices*) excessivement

steeple ['sti:pəl] *n* clocher *m*

steer [stɪə(r)] **1** *vt* diriger **2** *vi* (*of person*) conduire; (*of ship*) se diriger (**for** vers); **to s. clear of sb/sth** éviter qn/qch ▪ **steering** *n* (*in vehicle*) direction *f*; **s. wheel** volant *m*

stem [stem] **1** *n* (*of plant*) tige *f*; (*of glass*) pied *m* **2** (*pt & pp* **-mm-**) *vt* (*stop*) arrêter **3** *vi* **to s. from sth** provenir de qch

stench [stentʃ] *n* puanteur *f*

step [step] **1** *n* (*movement, sound*) pas *m*; (*of stairs*) marche *f*; (*on train, bus*) marchepied *m*; (*doorstep*) pas de la porte; *Fig* (*action*) mesure *f*; **(flight of) steps** (*indoors*) escalier *m*; (*outdoors*) perron *m*; *Br* **(pair of) steps** (*ladder*) escabeau *m*; **s. by s.** pas à pas **2** (*pt & pp* **-pp-**) *vi* (*walk*) marcher (**on** sur) ▪ **stepdaughter** *n* belle-fille *f* ▪ **stepfather** *n* beau-père *m* ▪ **stepladder** *n* escabeau *m* ▪ **stepmother** *n* belle-mère *f* ▪ **stepson** *n* beau-fils *m*

▸ **step aside** *vi* s'écarter

▸ **step back** *vi* reculer

▸ **step down** *vi* descendre (**from** de); *Fig* (*withdraw*) se retirer

▸ **step forward** *vi* faire un pas en avant

▸ **step in** *vi* (*intervene*) intervenir

▸ **step off** *vt insep* (*chair*) descendre de

▸ **step over** *vt insep* (*obstacle*) enjamber

▸ **step up** *vt sep* (*increase*) augmenter; (*speed up*) accélérer

stereo ['sterɪəʊ] **1** (*pl* **-os**) *n* (*hi-fi, record player*) chaîne *f* stéréo; **in s.** en stéréo **2** *adj* (*record*) stéréo *inv*; (*broadcast*) en stéréo

stereotype ['sterɪətaɪp] *n* stéréotype *m*

sterile [*Br* 'steraɪl, *Am* 'sterəl] *adj* stérile

sterilize ['sterəlaɪz] *vt* stériliser

sterling ['stɜːlɪŋ] *n Br (currency)* livre *f* sterling

stern¹ [stɜːn] **(-er, -est)** *adj* sévère

stern² [stɜːn] *n (of ship)* arrière *m*

steroid ['stɪərɔɪd] *n* stéroïde *m*

stethoscope ['steθəskəʊp] *n* stéthoscope *m*

stew [stjuː] **1** *n* ragoût *m* **2** *vt (meat)* faire cuire en ragoût; *(fruit)* faire de la compote de; **stewed fruit** compote *f* **3** *vi* cuire

steward ['stjuːəd] *n (on plane, ship)* steward *m* ■ **stewardess** *n (on plane)* hôtesse *f*

stick¹ [stɪk] *n (piece of wood, chalk, dynamite)* bâton *m*; *(for walking)* canne *f*

stick² [stɪk] **1** *(pt & pp stuck) vt (glue)* coller; *Fam (put)* fourrer; *Fam (tolerate)* supporter; **to s. sth into sth** fourrer qch dans qch **2** *vi* coller (**to** à); *(of food in pan)* attacher (**to** dans); *(of drawer)* se coincer

▸ **stick by** *vt insep* rester fidèle à

▸ **stick down** *vt sep (envelope, stamp)* coller

▸ **stick on** *vt sep (stamp, label)* coller

▸ **stick out 1** *vt sep (tongue)* tirer; *Fam (head or arm from window)* sortir **2** *vi (of shirt)* dépasser; *(of tooth)* avancer

▸ **stick up** *vt sep (notice)* coller; *Fam (hand)* lever

▸ **stick up for** *vt insep* défendre

sticker ['stɪkə(r)] *n* autocollant *m*

sticky ['stɪkɪ] **(-ier, -iest)** *adj* collant; *(label)* adhésif, -ive

stiff [stɪf] **(-er, -est)** *adj* raide; *(joint)* ankylosé; *(brush, paste)* dur; *Fig (person)* guindé; **to have a s. neck** avoir un torticolis; *Fam* **to be bored s.** s'ennuyer à mourir; *Fam* **frozen s.** complètement gelé

stiffen ['stɪfən] **1** *vt* raidir **2** *vi* se raidir

stifle ['staɪfəl] **1** *vt (feeling, person)* étouffer **2** *vi* **it's stifling** on étouffe

stigma ['stɪgmə] *n (moral stain)* flétrissure *f*

stiletto [stɪ'letəʊ] *adj Br* **s. heels** talons *mpl* aiguille

still¹ [stɪl] *adv* encore, toujours; *(even)* encore; *(nevertheless)* tout de même; **better s., s. better** encore mieux

still² [stɪl] **(-er, -est)** *adj (not moving)* immobile; *(calm)* calme; *Br (drink)* non gazeux, -euse; **to stand s.** rester immobile; **s. life** nature *f* morte

stilted ['stɪltɪd] *adj (speech, person)* guindé

stimulate ['stɪmjʊleɪt] *vt* stimuler ■ **stimulant** *n* stimulant *m* ■ **stimulus** (*pl* **-li** [-laɪ]) *n (encouragement)* stimulant *m*; *(physiological)* stimulus *m inv*

sting [stɪŋ] **1** *n* piqûre *f* **2** *(pt & pp stung) vt (of insect, ointment, wind)* piquer **3** *vi* piquer

stingy ['stɪndʒɪ] **(-ier, -iest)** *adj* avare

stink [stɪŋk] **1** *n* puanteur *f* **2** *(pt & pp stank or stunk, pp stunk) vi* puer; *Fam (of book, film)* être infect **3** *vt* **to s. out** *(room)* empester

stint [stɪnt] **1** *n (period)* période *f* de travail; *(share)* part *f* de travail **2** *vi* **to s. on sth** lésiner sur qch

stipulate ['stɪpjʊleɪt] *vt* stipuler (**that** que) ■ **stipulation** *n* stipulation *f*

stir [stɜː(r)] **1** *n* **to give sth a s.** remuer qch; *Fig* **to cause a s.** faire du bruit **2** *(pt & pp* **-rr-)** *vt (coffee, leaves)* remuer; *Fig (excite)* exciter; *(incite)* inciter (**sb to do** qn à faire); **to s. up trouble** semer la zizanie; **to s. things up** envenimer les choses **3** *vi (move)* remuer, bouger ■ **stirring** *adj (speech)* émouvant

stirrup ['stɪrəp] *n* étrier *m*

stitch [stɪtʃ] **1** *n* point *m*; *(in knitting)* maille *f*, *(in wound)* point *m* de suture; *(sharp pain)* point *m* de côté; *Fam* **to be in stitches** être plié (de rire) **2** *vt* **to s. (up)** *(sew up)* coudre; *Med* recoudre

stock [stɒk] **1** *n (supply)* provisions *fpl*; *Com* stock *m*; *Fin* valeurs *fpl*; *(soup)* bouillon *m*; *Fin* **stocks and shares** valeurs *fpl* mobilières; **in s.** *(goods)* en stock; **out of s.** *(goods)* épuisé; *Fig* **to take s.** faire le point (**of** de); **the S. Exchange** *or* **Market** la Bourse

2 vt (sell) vendre; (keep in store) stocker; **to s. (up)** (shop) approvisionner; (fridge, cupboard) remplir

3 vi **to s. up** s'approvisionner (**with** en) ■ **stockbroker** n agent m de change ■ **stockpile** vt faire des réserves de ■ **stocktaking** n Br Com inventaire m

stocky ['stɒkɪ] (**-ier, -iest**) adj trapu

stodgy ['stɒdʒɪ] (**-ier, -iest**) adj Fam (food) bourratif, -ive; Fig (book) indigeste

stole[1] [stəʊl] n (shawl) étole f

stole[2] [stəʊl] pt of **steal**[1,2]

stolen ['stəʊlən] pp of **steal**[1,2]

stomach ['stʌmək] **1** n ventre m; (organ) estomac m **2** vt (put up with) supporter ■ **stomachache** n mal m de ventre; **to have (a) s.** avoir mal au ventre

stone [stəʊn] n pierre f; (pebble) caillou m; (in fruit) noyau m; Br (unit of weight) = 6,348 kg ■ **stone-cold** adj glacé ■ **stone-deaf** adj sourd comme un pot

stoned [stəʊnd] adj Fam (on drugs) défoncé (**on** à)

stony ['stəʊnɪ] (**-ier, -iest**) adj (path) caillouteux, -euse; Br Fam **s. broke** (penniless) fauché

stood [stʊd] pt & pp of **stand**

stool [stuːl] n tabouret m

stoop [stuːp] vi se baisser; Fig **to s. to doing sth** s'abaisser à faire qch

stop [stɒp] **1** n (place, halt) arrêt m; (for plane, ship) escale f; **to put a s. to sth** mettre fin à qch; **to come to a s.** s'arrêter; **s. sign** (on road) stop

2 (pt & pp **-pp-**) vt arrêter; (end) mettre fin à; (cheque) faire opposition à; **to s. sb/sth from doing sth** empêcher qn/qch de faire qch

3 vi s'arrêter; (of pain, bleeding) cesser; (stay) rester; **to s. snowing** cesser de neiger ■ **stopgap** n bouche-trou m ■ **stopoff** n halte f; (in plane journey) escale f ■ **stopover** n arrêt m; (in plane journey) escale f ■ **stopwatch** n chronomètre m

▶ **stop by** vi (visit) passer (**sb's** chez qn)

▶ **stop off, stop over** vi (on journey) s'arrêter

▶ **stop up** vt sep (sink, pipe, leak) boucher

stoppage ['stɒpɪdʒ] n (strike) débrayage m; Br (in pay) retenue f; **s. time** (in sport) arrêts mpl de jeu

stopper ['stɒpə(r)] n bouchon m

store [stɔː(r)] **1** n (supply) provision f; Fig (of knowledge) fonds m; (warehouse) entrepôt m; (shop) Br grand magasin m, Am magasin m; **to have sth in s. for sb** réserver qch à qn

2 vt (in warehouse) stocker; (furniture) entreposer; (food) ranger; Comptr (in memory) mettre en mémoire ■ **storage** n emmagasinage m; **s. space** espace m de rangement; Comptr **s. capacity** capacité f de mémoire

▶ **store away** vt sep (put away, file away) ranger; (furniture) entreposer

▶ **store up** vt sep accumuler

storekeeper ['stɔːkiːpə(r)] n Am (shopkeeper) commerçant, -e mf

storeroom ['stɔːruːm] n (in house) débarras m; (in office, shop) réserve f

storey ['stɔːrɪ] (pl **-eys**) n Br (of building) étage m

stork [stɔːk] n cigogne f

storm [stɔːm] **1** n (bad weather) tempête f; (thunderstorm) orage m **2** vt (of soldiers, police) prendre d'assaut **3** vi **to s. out** (angrily) sortir comme une furie ■ **stormy** (**-ier, -iest**) adj (weather, meeting) orageux, -euse

story[1] ['stɔːrɪ] (pl **-ies**) n histoire f; (newspaper article) article m

story[2] ['stɔːrɪ] (pl **-ies**) n Am (of building) étage m

stout [staʊt] **1** (**-er, -est**) adj (person) corpulent; (shoes) solide **2** n Br (beer) bière f brune

stove [stəʊv] n (for cooking) cuisinière f; (for heating) poêle m

stow [stəʊ] **1** vt (cargo) arrimer; **to s. sth away** (put away) ranger qch **2** vi

to s. away *(on ship)* voyager clandestinement ■ **stowaway** *n (on ship)* passager, -ère *mf* clandestin(e)

straddle ['strædəl] *vt (chair, fence)* se mettre à califourchon sur; *(step over, span)* enjamber

straggle ['strægəl] *vi (lag behind)* être à la traîne ■ **straggler** *n* retardataire *mf*

straight [streɪt] **1** *(-er, -est) adj* droit; *(hair)* raide; *(honest)* honnête; *(answer)* clair; *(consecutive)* consécutif, -ive; *(conventional)* conformiste; *Fam (heterosexual)* hétéro

2 *adv (in straight line)* droit; *(directly)* directement; *(immediately)* tout de suite; *(at once)* tout de suite; *Br* **s. ahead** *or* **on** *(walk)* tout droit; **to look s. ahead** regarder droit devant soi

straightaway [streɪtə'weɪ] *adv* tout de suite

straighten ['streɪtən] *vt* **to s. (out)** *(wire)* redresser; **to s. (up)** *(tie, hair, room)* arranger

straightforward [streɪt'fɔːwəd] *adj (easy, clear)* simple; *(frank)* franc (*f* franche)

strain [streɪn] **1** *n* tension *f*; *(mental stress)* stress *m*

2 *vt* (**a**) *(rope, wire)* tendre excessivement; *(muscle)* se froisser; *(ankle, wrist)* se fouler; *(eyes)* fatiguer; *(voice)* forcer; *Fig (patience, friendship)* mettre à l'épreuve; **to s. oneself** *(hurt oneself)* se faire mal; *(tire oneself)* se fatiguer (**b**) *(soup)* passer; *(vegetables)* égoutter

3 *vi* faire un effort (**to do** pour faire)

strained [streɪnd] *adj (muscle)* froissé; *(ankle, wrist)* foulé; *(relations)* tendu

strainer ['streɪnə(r)] *n* passoire *f*

strait [streɪt] *n Geog* **strait(s)** détroit *m*; **in financial straits** dans l'embarras

strand [strænd] *n (of wool)* brin *m*; *(of hair)* mèche *f*; *Fig (of story)* fil *m*

stranded ['strændɪd] *adj (person, vehicle)* en rade

strange [streɪndʒ] *(-er, -est) adj (odd)* bizarre; *(unknown)* inconnu ■ **strangely** *adv* étrangement; **s. (enough), she…** chose étrange, elle…

stranger ['streɪndʒə(r)] *n (unknown)* inconnu, -e *mf*; *(outsider)* étranger, -ère *mf*

strangle ['stræŋgəl] *vt* étrangler

strap [stræp] **1** *n* sangle *f*; *(on dress)* bretelle *f*; *(on watch)* bracelet *m*; *(on sandal)* lanière *f* **2** *(pt & pp* **-pp-***) vt* **to s. (down** *or* **in)** attacher *(avec une sangle);* **to s. sb in** attacher qn avec une ceinture de sécurité

strapping ['stræpɪŋ] *adj* robuste

strategy ['strætədʒɪ] *n (pl* **-ies***)* stratégie *f* ■ **strategic** [strə'tiːdʒɪk] *adj* stratégique

straw [strɔː] *n (from wheat, for drinking)* paille *f*

strawberry ['strɔːbərɪ] **1** *(pl* **-ies***) n* fraise *f* **2** *adj (flavour, ice cream)* à la fraise; *(jam)* de fraises; *(tart)* aux fraises

stray [streɪ] **1** *adj (animal, bullet)* perdu; **a few s. cars** quelques rares voitures **2** *n (dog)* chien *m* errant; *(cat)* chat *m* égaré **3** *vi* s'égarer; **to s. from** *(subject, path)* s'écarter de

streak [striːk] *n (of paint, dirt)* traînée *f*; *(of light)* rai *m*; *(in hair)* mèche *f* ■ **streaked** *adj (marked)* strié; *(stained)* taché *(with* de*)*

stream [striːm] **1** *n (brook)* ruisseau *m*; *(of light, blood)* jet *m*; *(of people)* flot *m* **2** *vi* ruisseler *(with* de*)*; **to s. in** *(of sunlight, people)* entrer à flots

streamer ['striːmə(r)] *n (banner)* banderole *f*

streamline ['striːmlaɪn] *vt (work, method)* rationaliser ■ **streamlined** *adj (shape)* aérodynamique; *(industry, production)* rationalisé

street [striːt] *n* rue *f*; **s. lamp, s. light** lampadaire *m*; **s. map** plan *m* des rues ■ **streetcar** *n Am (tram)* tramway *m*

strength [streŋθ] *n* force *f* ■ **strengthen** *vt (building, position)* renforcer; *(body, limb)* fortifier

strenuous ['strenjʊəs] *adj* (effort) vigoureux, -euse; (work) fatigant

stress [stres] **1** *n* (physical) tension *f*; (mental) stress *m*; (emphasis, in grammar) accent *m*; **under s.** (person) stressé, sous pression; (relationship) tendu **2** *vt* insister sur; (word) accentuer; **to s. that…** souligner que… ■ **stressful** *adj* stressant

stretch [stretʃ] **1** *n* (area) étendue *f*; (period of time) période *f*; (of road) tronçon *m*

2 *vt* (rope, neck) tendre; (shoe, rubber) étirer; (income, supplies) faire durer; **to s. (out)** (arm, leg) tendre; **to s. one's legs** se dégourdir les jambes; *Fig* **to s. sb** pousser qn à son maximum

3 *vi* (of person, elastic) s'étirer; (of influence) s'étendre; **to s. (out)** (of rope, plain) s'étendre

stretcher ['stretʃə(r)] *n* brancard *m*

strew [struː] (*pt* strewed, *pp* strewed *or* strewn [struːn]) *vt* (scatter) éparpiller; **strewn with** (covered) jonché de

stricken ['strɪkən] *adj* (town, region) sinistré

strict [strɪkt] (-er, -est) *adj* (severe, absolute) strict ■ **strictly** *adv* strictement; **s. forbidden** formellement interdit

stride [straɪd] **1** *n* pas *m*; *Fig* **to make great strides** faire de grands progrès **2** (*pt* strode) *vi* **to s. across** *or* **over** (fields) traverser à grandes enjambées; **to s. along/out** avancer/sortir à grands pas

strike [straɪk] **1** *n* (of workers) grève *f*; *Mil* raid *m*; **to go on s.** se mettre en grève **2** (*pt & pp* struck) *vt* (hit, impress) frapper; (collide with) heurter; (gold, oil) trouver; (match) craquer; **it strikes me that…** il me semble que… (+ indicative) **3** *vi* (of workers) faire grève; (attack) attaquer

▸ **strike at** *vt insep* (attack) attaquer

▸ **strike back** *vi* (retaliate) riposter

▸ **strike down** *vt sep* (of illness) terrasser

▸ **strike off** *vt sep* (from list) rayer; **to be struck off** (of doctor) être radié

▸ **strike out** *vi* **to s. out at sb** essayer de frapper qn

▸ **strike up** *vt sep* **to s. up a friendship** se lier amitié (**with sb** avec qn)

striker ['straɪkə(r)] *n* (worker) gréviste *mf*; (footballer) buteur *m*

striking ['straɪkɪŋ] *adj* (impressive) frappant

string [strɪŋ] **1** *n* ficelle *f*; (of apron) cordon *m*; (of violin, racket) corde *f*; (of questions) série *f*; *Fig* **to pull strings** faire jouer ses relations **2** *adj* (instrument, quartet) à cordes **3** (*pt & pp* strung) *vt* (beads) enfiler ■ **stringed** *adj* (instrument) à cordes

stringent ['strɪndʒənt] *adj* rigoureux, -euse

strip [strɪp] **1** *n* (piece) bande *f*; (of metal) lame *f*; (of sports team) tenue *f*; **s. cartoon** bande *f* dessinée **2** (*pt & pp* -pp-) *vt* (undress) déshabiller; (deprive) dépouiller (**of** de); **to s.** (remove) enlever **3** *vi* **to s. (off)** (get undressed) se déshabiller ■ **stripper** *n* (woman) strip-teaseuse *f*; (paint) **s.** (substance) décapant *m* ■ **striptease** *n* strip-tease *m*

stripe [straɪp] *n* rayure *f*; (indicating rank) galon *m* ■ **striped** *adj* rayé (**with** de)

strive [straɪv] (*pt* strove, *pp* striven ['strɪvən]) *vi* s'efforcer (**to do** de faire; **for** d'obtenir)

strode [strəʊd] *pt of* stride

stroke [strəʊk] **1** *n* (movement) coup *m*; (of pen) trait *m*; (of brush) touche *f*; (caress) caresse *f*; *Med* (illness) attaque *f*; **at a s.** d'un coup; **s. of luck** coup *m* de chance **2** *vt* (caress) caresser

stroll [strəʊl] **1** *n* promenade *f* **2** *vi* se promener; **to s. in** entrer sans se presser

stroller ['strəʊlə(r)] *n Am* (for baby) poussette *f*

strong [strɒŋ] **1** (-er, -est) *adj* fort;

(shoes, chair, nerves) solide; (interest) vif (f vive); (measures) énergique; (supporter) ardent **2** adv **to be going s.** aller toujours bien ■ **strong-box** n coffre-fort m ■ **stronghold** n bastion m ■ **strongly** adv (protest, defend) énergiquement; (advise, remind, desire) fortement

strove [strəʊv] pt of **strive**

struck [strʌk] pt & pp of **strike**

structure ['strʌktʃə(r)] n structure f; (building) édifice m ■ **structural** adj structural; (building defect) de construction

struggle ['strʌgəl] **1** n (fight) lutte f (**to do** pour faire); **to have a s. doing** or **to do sth** avoir du mal à faire qch **2** vi (fight) lutter (**with** avec); **to be struggling** (financially) avoir du mal; **to s. to do sth** s'efforcer de faire qch

strung [strʌŋ] pt & pp of **string**

strut[1] [strʌt] (pt & pp -**tt**-) vi **to s. (about** or **around)** se pavaner

strut[2] [strʌt] n (for frame) étai m

stub [stʌb] **1** n (of pencil, cigarette) bout m; (of cheque) talon m **2** (pt & pp -**bb**-) vt **to s. one's toe** se cogner l'orteil (**on** or **against** contre); **to s. out** (cigarette) écraser

stubble ['stʌbəl] n (on face) barbe f de plusieurs jours

stubborn ['stʌbən] adj (person) têtu

stuck [stʌk] **1** pt & pp of **stick**[2] **2** adj (caught, trapped) coincé; **s. in bed/indoors** cloué au lit/chez soi; **to get s.** être coincé; **to be s. with sb/sth** se farcir qn/qch

stuck-up [stʌ'kʌp] adj Fam snob

stud[1] [stʌd] n (on football boot) crampon m; (earring) clou m d'oreille ■ **studded** adj **s. with** (covered) constellé de

stud[2] [stʌd] n (farm) haras m; (stallion) étalon m

student ['stjuːdənt] **1** n (at university) étudiant, -e mf; (at school) élève mf; **music s.** étudiant, -e mf en musique **2** adj (life, protest) étudiant; (restaurant, residence, grant) universitaire

studio ['stjuːdɪəʊ] (pl -**os**) n studio m; (of artist) atelier m; Br **s. flat**, Am **s. apartment** studio m

studious ['stjuːdɪəs] adj (person) studieux, -euse

study ['stʌdɪ] **1** (pl -**ies**) n étude f; (office) bureau m **2** (pp & pp -**ied**) vt (learn, observe) étudier **3** vi étudier; **to s. to be a doctor** faire des études de médecine; **to s. for an exam** préparer un examen

stuff [stʌf] **1** n (possessions) affaires fpl; Fam **some s.** (substance) un truc; (things) des trucs; Fam **this s.'s good, it's good s.** c'est bien

2 vt (pocket) remplir (**with** de); (cushion) rembourrer (**with** avec); (animal) empailler; (chicken, tomatoes) farcir; **to s. sth into sth** fourrer qch dans qch ■ **stuffing** n (padding) bourre f; (for chicken, tomatoes) farce f

stuffy ['stʌfɪ] (-**ier**, -**iest**) adj (room) qui sent le renfermé; (person) vieux jeu inv

stumble ['stʌmbəl] vi trébucher; **to s. across** or **on** (find) tomber sur

stump [stʌmp] n (of tree) souche f; (of limb) moignon m; (in cricket) piquet m

stun [stʌn] (pt & pp -**nn**-) vt (make unconscious) assommer; Fig (amaze) stupéfier ■ **stunned** adj (amazed) stupéfait (**by** par) ■ **stunning** adj Fam (excellent) excellent; Fam (beautiful) superbe

stung [stʌŋ] pt & pp of **sting**

stunk [stʌŋk] pt & pp of **stink**

stunt[1] [stʌnt] n (in film) cascade f; (for publicity) coup m de pub; **s. man** cascadeur m

stunt[2] [stʌnt] vt (growth) retarder ■ **stunted** adj (person) rabougri

stupid ['stjuːpɪd] adj stupide; **to do/say a s. thing** faire/dire une stupidité ■ **stupidity** n stupidité f ■ **stupidly** adv bêtement

sturdy ['stɜːdɪ] (-**ier**, -**iest**) adj (person, shoe) robuste

stutter ['stʌtə(r)] **1** n **to have a s.** être bègue **2** vi bégayer

sty¹ [staɪ] n (for pigs) porcherie f

sty², **stye** [staɪ] n (on eye) orgelet m

style [staɪl] 1 n style m; (sophistication) classe f 2 vt (design) créer; **to s. sb's hair** coiffer qn

stylish [ˈstaɪlɪʃ] adj chic inv

stylist [ˈstaɪlɪst] n **(hair) s.** coiffeur, -euse mf

sub- [sʌb] pref sous-, sub-

subconscious [sʌbˈkɒnʃəs] adj & n subconscient (m) ▪ **subconsciously** adv inconsciemment

subcontract [sʌbkənˈtrækt] vt sous-traiter

subdivide [sʌbdɪˈvaɪd] vt subdiviser (into en)

subdue [səbˈdjuː] vt (country, people) soumettre; (feelings) maîtriser ▪ **subdued** adj (light) tamisé; (voice, tone) bas (f basse); (person) inhabituellement calme

subject¹ [ˈsʌbdʒɪkt] n (a) (matter, in grammar) sujet m; (at school, university) matière f; **s. matter** (topic) sujet m; (content) contenu m (b) (of monarch) sujet, -ette mf

subject² 1 [ˈsʌbdʒɪkt] adj **to be s. to depression/jealousy** avoir tendance à la dépression/à la jalousie; **it's s. to my agreement** c'est sous réserve de mon accord 2 [səbˈdʒɛkt] vt soumettre (**to** à)

subjective [səbˈdʒɛktɪv] adj subjectif, -ive ▪ **subjectively** adv subjectivement

subjunctive [səbˈdʒʌŋktɪv] n subjonctif m

sublet [sʌbˈlet] (pt & pp -let, pres p -letting) vt sous-louer

sublime [səˈblaɪm] adj sublime; (utter) suprême

submarine [ˈsʌbməriːn] n sous-marin m

submerge [səbˈmɜːdʒ] vt (flood, overwhelm) submerger; (immerse) immerger (in dans)

submit [səbˈmɪt] 1 (pt & pp -tt-) vt soumettre (**to** à) 2 vi se soumettre (**to** à) ▪ **submissive** adj (person) soumis; (attitude) de soumission

subordinate [səˈbɔːdɪnət] 1 adj subalterne; **s. to** subordonné à 2 n subordonné, -e mf

subscribe [səbˈskraɪb] vi (pay money) cotiser (**to** à); **to s. to a newspaper** s'abonner à un journal ▪ **subscriber** n (to newspaper, telephone) abonné, -e mf ▪ **subscription** [sʌbˈskrɪpʃən] n (to newspaper) abonnement m; (to club) cotisation f

subsequent [ˈsʌbsɪkwənt] adj ultérieur (**to** à); **our s. problems** les problèmes que nous avons eus par la suite ▪ **subsequently** adv par la suite

subside [səbˈsaɪd] vi (of ground, building) s'affaisser; (of wind, flood, fever) baisser ▪ **subsidence** n (of ground) affaissement m

subsidiary [Br səbˈsɪdɪərɪ, Am -dɪerɪ] 1 adj subsidiaire 2 (pl -ies) n (company) filiale f

subsidize [ˈsʌbsɪdaɪz] vt subventionner ▪ **subsidy** (pl -ies) n subvention f

substance [ˈsʌbstəns] n substance f; (solidity, worth) fondement m

substantial [səbˈstænʃəl] adj important; (meal) substantiel, -elle ▪ **substantially** adv considérablement

substitute [ˈsʌbstɪtjuːt] 1 n (thing) produit m de remplacement; (person) remplaçant, -e mf (**for** de) 2 vt **to s. sb/sth for** substituer qn/qch à 3 vi **to s. for sb** remplacer qn ▪ **substitution** n substitution f

subtitle [ˈsʌbtaɪtəl] 1 n (of film) sous-titre m 2 vt (film) sous-titrer

subtle [ˈsʌtəl] (-er, -est) adj subtil

subtotal [ˈsʌbtəʊtəl] n sous-total m

subtract [səbˈtrækt] vt soustraire (**from** de) ▪ **subtraction** n soustraction f

suburb [ˈsʌbɜːb] n banlieue f; **the suburbs** la banlieue ▪ **suburban** [səˈbɜːbən] adj (train, house) de banlieue ▪ **suburbia** [səˈbɜːbɪə] n la banlieue; **in s.** en banlieue

subversive [səbˈvɜːsɪv] adj subversif, -ive

subway [ˈsʌbweɪ] n Br (under road)

passage *m* souterrain; *Am* (railroad) métro *m*

succeed [sək'si:d] **1** *vt* to s. sb succéder à qn **2** *vi* réussir (**in doing** à faire; **in sth** dans qch); **to s. to the throne** monter sur le trône ▪ **succeeding** *adj* (in past) suivant; (in future) futur; (consecutive) consécutif, -ive

success [sək'ses] *n* succès *m*, réussite *f*; **he was a s.** il a eu du succès; **it was a s.** c'était réussi

successful [sək'sesfəl] *adj* (effort, venture) couronné de succès; (outcome) heureux, -euse; (company, businessman) prospère; (candidate in exam) admis, reçu; (candidate in election) élu; (writer, film) à succès; **to be s.** réussir; **to be s. in doing sth** réussir à faire qch ▪ **successfully** *adv* avec succès

succession [sək'seʃən] *n* succession *f*; **ten days in s.** dix jours consécutifs ▪ **successive** *adj* successif, -ive; **ten days in s.** dix jours consécutifs ▪ **successor** *n* successeur *m* (**to** de)

succinct [sək'sɪŋkt] *adj* succinct

succumb [sə'kʌm] *vi* succomber (**to** à)

such [sʌtʃ] **1** *adj* (of this or that kind) tel (*f* telle); **s. a car** une telle voiture; **s. happiness/noise** tant de bonheur/ bruit; **there's no s. thing** ça n'existe pas; **s. as** comme, tel que **2** *adv* (so very) si; (in comparisons) aussi; **s. long trips** de si longs voyages **3** *pron* happiness **as s.** le bonheur en tant que tel ▪ **suchlike** *pron* & *adj* **...and s.** ...et autres

suck [sʌk] **1** *vt* sucer; (of baby) téter; **to s. (up)** (with straw, pump) aspirer; **to s. up** or **in** (absorb) absorber **2** *vi* (of baby) téter

suckle ['sʌkəl] **1** *vt* (of woman) allaiter **2** *vi* (of baby) téter

suction ['sʌkʃən] *n* succion *f*

sudden ['sʌdən] *adj* soudain; **all of a s.** tout à coup ▪ **suddenly** *adv* tout à coup, soudain; (die) subitement

suds [sʌdz] *npl* mousse *f* de savon

sue [su:] **1** *vt* poursuivre (en justice) **2** *vi* engager des poursuites judiciaires

suede [sweɪd] *n* daim *m*

suffer ['sʌfə(r)] **1** *vt* (loss, damage, defeat) subir; (pain) ressentir; (tolerate) supporter **2** *vi* souffrir (**from** de); **your work will s.** ton travail s'en ressentira ▪ **sufferer** *n* (from misfortune) victime *f*; **AIDS s.** malade *mf* du SIDA ▪ **suffering** *n* souffrance *f*

suffice [sə'faɪs] *vi* suffire

sufficient [sə'fɪʃənt] *adj* suffisant; **s. money** (enough) suffisamment d'argent; **to be s.** suffire ▪ **sufficiently** *adv* suffisamment

suffix ['sʌfɪks] *n* suffixe *m*

suffocate ['sʌfəkeɪt] **1** *vt* étouffer **2** *vi* suffoquer

sugar ['ʃʊgə(r)] **1** *n* sucre *m*; **s. bowl** sucrier *m*; **s. lump** morceau *m* de sucre **2** *vt* (tea) sucrer

suggest [sə'dʒest] *vt* (propose) suggérer; (imply) indiquer ▪ **suggestion** *n* suggestion *f* ▪ **suggestive** *adj* suggestif, -ive; **to be s. of** évoquer

suicide ['su:ɪsaɪd] *n* suicide *m*; **to commit s.** se suicider

suit¹ [su:t] *n* (**a**) (man's) costume *m*; (woman's) tailleur *m*; **flying/diving/ ski s.** combinaison *f* de vol/plongée/ ski (**b**) (in card games) couleur *f*, *Fig* **to follow s.** faire de même (**c**) (lawsuit) procès *m*

suit² [su:t] *vt* (please, be acceptable to) convenir à; (of dress, colour) aller (bien) à; (adapt) adapter (**to** à); **suited to** (job, activity) fait pour; (appropriate to) qui convient à; **to be well suited** (of couple) être bien assorti

suitable ['su:təbəl] *adj* convenable (**for** à); (candidate, date) adéquat; (example) approprié; **this film is not s. for children** ce film n'est pas pour les enfants

suitcase ['su:tkeɪs] *n* valise *f*

suite [swi:t] *n* (rooms) suite *f*

sulk [sʌlk] *vi* bouder

sullen ['sʌlən] *adj* maussade

sultana [sʌl'tɑ:nə] *n* (raisin) raisin *m* de Smyrne

sum [sʌm] **1** *n (amount of money)* somme *f*; *(mathematical problem)* problème *m*; **s. total** somme *f* totale **2** *(pt & pp* **-mm-**) *vt* **to s. up** *(summarize)* résumer; *(assess)* évaluer **3** *vi* **to s. up** résumer

summarize ['sʌməraɪz] *vt* résumer ■ **summary** *(pl* **-ies***) n* résumé *m*

summer ['sʌmə(r)] **1** *n* été *m*; **in (the) s.** en été **2** *adj* d'été; *Am* **s. camp** colonie *f* de vacances; *Br* **s. holidays,** *Am* **s. vacation** grandes vacances *fpl* ■ **summertime** *n* été *m*; **in (the) s.** en été

summit ['sʌmɪt] *n* sommet *m*

summon ['sʌmən] *vt (call)* appeler; *(meeting, person)* convoquer *(to* à); **to s. up one's courage/strength** rassembler son courage/ses forces

summons ['sʌmənz] **1** *n (in law)* assignation *f* à comparaître **2** *vt* assigner à comparaître

sumptuous ['sʌmptʃʊəs] *adj* somptueux, -euse

sun [sʌn] **1** *n* soleil *m*; **in the s.** au soleil; **the s. is shining** il fait soleil **2** *(pt & pp* **-nn-***) vt* **to s. oneself** prendre le soleil ■ **sunbathe** *vi* prendre un bain de soleil ■ **sunbed** *n* lit *m* à ultraviolets ■ **sunblock** *n (cream)* écran *m* total ■ **sunburn** *n* coup *m* de soleil ■ **sunburnt** *adj* brûlé par le soleil ■ **sundial** *n* cadran *m* solaire ■ **sunflower** *n* tournesol *m* ■ **sunglasses** *npl* lunettes *fpl* de soleil ■ **sunhat** *n* chapeau *m* de soleil ■ **sunlamp** *n* lampe *f* à bronzer ■ **sunlight** *n* lumière *f* du soleil ■ **sunrise** *n* lever *m* du soleil ■ **sunroof** *n (in car)* toit *m* ouvrant ■ **sunset** *n* coucher *m* du soleil ■ **sunshade** *n (on table)* parasol *m*; *(portable)* ombrelle *f* ■ **sunshine** *n* soleil *m* ■ **sunstroke** *n* insolation *f* ■ **suntan** *n* bronzage *m*; **s. lotion/oil** crème *f*/huile *f* solaire ■ **suntanned** *adj* bronzé

Sunday ['sʌndeɪ] *n* dimanche *m*; **S. school** ≃ catéchisme *m*

sundry ['sʌndrɪ] **1** *adj* divers **2** *n* **all and s.** tout le monde

sung [sʌŋ] *pp of* **sing**

sunk [sʌŋk] *pp of* **sink²** ■ **sunken** *adj (rock, treasure)* submergé

sunny ['sʌnɪ] *(-ier, -iest) adj (day)* ensoleillé; **it's s.** il fait soleil; **s. periods** *or* **intervals** éclaircies *fpl*

super ['suːpə(r)] *adj Fam* super *inv*

super- ['suːpə(r)] *pref* super-

superb [suːˈpɜːb] *adj* superbe

superficial [suːpəˈfɪʃəl] *adj* superficiel, -elle

superfluous [suːˈpɜːflʊəs] *adj* superflu

superglue ['suːpəgluː] *n* colle *f* extraforte

superior [suːˈpɪərɪə(r)] **1** *adj* supérieur *(to* à**) 2** *n (person)* supérieur, -eure *mf* ■ **superiority** [-rɪˈɒrətɪ] *n* supériorité *f*

superlative [suːˈpɜːlətɪv] **1** *adj* sans pareil **2** *adj & n Gram* superlatif *(m)*

supermarket ['suːpəmɑːkɪt] *n* supermarché *m*

supernatural [suːpəˈnætʃərəl] *adj & n* surnaturel, -elle *(m)*

superpower ['suːpəpaʊə(r)] *n Pol* superpuissance *f*

supersede [suːpəˈsiːd] *vt* supplanter

supersonic [suːpəˈsɒnɪk] *adj* supersonique

superstition [suːpəˈstɪʃən] *n* superstition *f* ■ **superstitious** *adj* superstitieux, -euse

superstore ['suːpəstɔːr] *n* hypermarché *m*

supervise ['suːpəvaɪz] *vt (person, work)* surveiller; *(research)* superviser ■ **supervisor** *n* surveillant, -e *mf*; *(in office)* chef *m* de service; *(in store)* chef *m* de rayon

supper ['sʌpə(r)] *n (meal)* dîner *m*; *(snack)* = casse-croûte pris avant d'aller se coucher

supple ['sʌpəl] *adj* souple

supplement 1 ['sʌplɪmənt] *n* supplément *m (to* à**) 2** ['sʌplɪment] *vt* compléter; **to s. one's income** arrondir ses fins de mois ■ **supplementary** [-ˈmentərɪ] *adj* supplémentaire

supplier [sə'plaɪə(r)] n Com fournisseur m

supply [sə'plaɪ] 1 (pl -ies) n (stock) provision f; **s. and demand** l'offre f et la demande; Br **s. teacher** suppléant, -e mf 2 (pt & pp -ied) vt (provide) fournir; (with gas, electricity, water) alimenter (**with** en); (equip) équiper (**with** de); **to s. sb with sth, to s. sth to sb** fournir qch à qn

support [sə'pɔːt] 1 n (backing, person supporting) soutien m; (thing supporting) support m; **in s. of** (person) en faveur de; (evidence, theory) à l'appui de 2 vt (bear weight of) supporter; (help, encourage) soutenir; (theory, idea) appuyer; (family, wife, husband) subvenir aux besoins de

supporter [sə'pɔːtə(r)] n partisan m; (of football team) supporter m

supportive [sə'pɔːtɪv] adj **to be s. of sb** être d'un grand soutien à qn

suppose [sə'pəʊz] vti supposer (**that** que); **I'm supposed to be working** je suis censé travailler; **he's supposed to be rich** on le dit riche; **I s. (so)** je pense; **s. or supposing (that) you're right** supposons que tu aies raison

suppress [sə'pres] vt (revolt, feelings, smile) réprimer; (fact, evidence) faire disparaître

supreme [suː'priːm] adj suprême

surcharge ['sɜːtʃɑːdʒ] n (extra charge) supplément m

sure [ʃʊə(r)] (-er, -est) adj sûr (**of** de; **that** que); **she's s. to accept** c'est sûr qu'elle acceptera; **to make s. of sth** s'assurer de qch; **for s.** à coup sûr; Fam **s.!, s. thing!** bien sûr! ■ **surely** adv (certainly) sûrement; **s. he didn't refuse?** il n'a quand même pas refusé?

surf [sɜːf] 1 n (waves) ressac m 2 vt Comptr **to s. the Net** naviguer sur l'Internet ■ **surfboard** n planche f de surf ■ **surfing** n (sport) surf m; **to go s.** faire du surf

surface ['sɜːfɪs] 1 n surface f; **s. area** superficie f; **on the s.** (of water) à la surface; Fig (to all appearances) en

apparence 2 vi (of swimmer) remonter à la surface; Fam (of person, thing) réapparaître

surge ['sɜːdʒ] 1 n (of enthusiasm) vague f; (of anger, pride) bouffée f 2 vi (of crowd) déferler; (of prices) monter (soudainement); **to s. forward** (of person) se lancer en avant

surgeon ['sɜːdʒən] n chirurgien m ■ **surgery** ['sɜːdʒərɪ] n Br (doctor's office) cabinet m; (period, sitting) consultation f; (science) chirurgie f; **to have heart s.** se faire opérer du cœur ■ **surgical** adj chirurgical

surly ['sɜːlɪ] (-ier, -iest) adj revêche

surmount [sə'maʊnt] vt surmonter

surname ['sɜːneɪm] n nom m de famille

surpass [sə'pɑːs] vt surpasser (**in** en)

surplus ['sɜːpləs] 1 n surplus m 2 adj (goods) en surplus

surprise [sə'praɪz] 1 n surprise f; **to give sb a s.** faire une surprise à qn; **s. visit/result** visite f/résultat m inattendu(e) 2 vt étonner, surprendre ■ **surprised** adj surpris (**that** que + subjunctive; **at sth** de qch; **at seeing** de voir) ■ **surprising** adj surprenant

surrender [sə'rendə(r)] 1 n (of soldiers) reddition f 2 vt (town) livrer; (right, claim) renoncer à 3 vi (give oneself up) se rendre (**to** à)

surrogate ['sʌrəgət] n substitut m; **s. mother** mère f porteuse

surround [sə'raʊnd] vt entourer (**with** de); (of army, police) cerner; **surrounded by** entouré de ■ **surrounding** adj environnant ■ **surroundings** npl (of town) environs mpl; (setting) cadre m

surveillance [sɜː'veɪləns] n surveillance f

survey 1 ['sɜːveɪ] n (investigation) enquête f; (of opinion) sondage m; (of house) inspection f
2 [sə'veɪ] vt (look at) regarder; (review) passer en revue; (house) inspecter; (land) faire un relevé de

■ **surveyor** n (of land) géomètre m; (of house) expert m

survive [sə'vaɪv] **1** vt survivre à **2** vi survivre ■ **survival** n (act) survie f; (relic) vestige m ■ **survivor** n survivant, -e mf

susceptible [sə'septəbəl] adj (sensitive) sensible (**to** à)

suspect 1 ['sʌspekt] n & adj suspect, -ecte (mf) **2** [sə'spekt] vt soupçonner (**sb of** qn de qch; **sb of doing** qn d'avoir fait); (have intuition of) se douter de

suspend [sə'spend] vt (**a**) (hang) suspendre (**from** à) (**b**) (service, employee, player) suspendre; (pupil) renvoyer temporairement

suspense [sə'spens] n (uncertainty) incertitude f; (in film, book) suspense m; **to keep sb in s.** tenir qn en haleine

suspicion [sə'spɪʃən] n soupçon m; **to be under s.** être soupçonné

suspicious [sə'spɪʃəs] adj (person) soupçonneux, -euse; (behaviour) suspect; **to be s. of** or **about sth** se méfier de qch

sustain [sə'steɪn] vt (effort, theory) soutenir; (weight) supporter; (life) maintenir; (damage, loss, attack) subir; **to s. an injury** être blessé

swagger ['swægə(r)] vi (walk) se pavaner

swallow¹ ['swɒləʊ] **1** vt avaler; **to s. sth down** avaler qch **2** vi avaler

swallow² ['swɒləʊ] n (bird) hirondelle f

swam [swæm] pt of **swim**

swamp [swɒmp] **1** n marais m **2** vt (flood, overwhelm) submerger (**with** de)

swan [swɒn] n cygne m

swap [swɒp] **1** n échange m **2** (pt & pp -pp-) vt échanger (**for** contre); **to s. seats** or **places** changer de place **3** vi échanger

swarm [swɔːm] **1** n (of bees, people) essaim m **2** vi (of streets, insects, people) fourmiller (**with** de)

swat [swɒt] (pt & pp -tt-) vt écraser

sway [sweɪ] **1** vt balancer; Fig (person, public opinion) influencer **2** vi se balancer

swear [sweə(r)] **1** (pt **swore**, pp **sworn**) vt (promise) jurer (**to do** de faire; **that** que); **to s. an oath** prêter serment **2** vi (take an oath) jurer (**to sth** de qch); **to s. at sb** injurier qn ■ **swearword** n juron m

sweat [swet] **1** n sueur f **2** vi suer ■ **sweatshirt** n sweat-shirt m

sweater ['swetə(r)] n pull m

sweaty ['swetɪ] (**-ier, -iest**) adj (shirt) plein de sueur; (hand) moite; (person) en sueur

Swede [swiːd] n Suédois, -e mf ■ **Sweden** n la Suède ■ **Swedish 1** adj suédois **2** n (language) suédois m

sweep [swiːp] **1** (pt & pp **swept**) vt (with broom) balayer; (chimney) ramoner **2** vi balayer

▶ **sweep aside** vt sep (opposition, criticism) écarter

▶ **sweep away** vt sep (leaves) balayer; (carry off) emporter

▶ **sweep out** vt sep (room) balayer

▶ **sweep through** vt insep (of fear) saisir; (of disease) ravager

▶ **sweep up** vt sep & vi balayer

sweeping ['swiːpɪŋ] adj (gesture) large; (change) radical; (statement) trop général

sweet [swiːt] **1** (**-er, -est**) adj doux (f douce); (tea, coffee, cake) sucré; (pretty, kind) adorable; **to have a s. tooth** aimer les sucreries

2 n Br (piece of confectionery) bonbon m; Br (dessert) dessert m; Br **s. shop** confiserie f ■ **sweetcorn** n Br maïs m

sweeten ['swiːtən] vt (food) sucrer; Fig (person) amadouer

sweetheart ['swiːthɑːt] n petit, -e ami, -e mf

swell¹ [swel] **1** (pt **swelled**, pp **swollen** or **swelled**) vt (river, numbers) grossir **2** vi (of hand, leg) enfler; (of wood) gonfler; (of river, numbers) grossir; **to s. up** (of body part) enfler ■ **swelling** n (on body) enflure f

swell² [swel] *adj Am Fam (excellent)* super *inv*

swelter ['sweltə(r)] *vi* étouffer ■ **sweltering** *adj* étouffant; **it's s.** on étouffe

swept [swept] *pt & pp of* **sweep**

swerve [swɜːv] *vi (of vehicle)* faire une embardée; *(of player)* faire un écart

swift [swift] 1 (**-er, -est**) *adj* rapide 2 *n (bird)* martinet *m* ■ **swiftly** *adv* rapidement

swill [swil] *vt Fam (drink)* écluser; **to s. (out or down)** rincer à grande eau

swim [swim] 1 *n* **to go for a s.** aller nager

2 *(pt* **swam**, *pp* **swum**, *pres p* **swimming**) *vt (river)* traverser à la nage; *(length, crawl)* nager

3 *vi* nager; *(as sport)* faire de la natation; **to go swimming** aller nager; **to s. away** s'éloigner à la nage ■ **swimmer** *n* nageur, -euse *mf* ■ **swimming** *n* natation *f*; **s. cap** bonnet *m* de bain; *Br* **s. costume** maillot *m* de bain; *Br* **s. pool** piscine *f*; **s. trunks** slip *m* de bain

swindle ['swindəl] 1 *n* escroquerie *f* 2 *vt* escroquer ■ **swindler** *n* escroc *m*

swine [swain] *n inv Pej (person)* salaud *m*

swing [swiŋ] 1 *n (in playground)* balançoire *f*; *(movement)* balancement *m*; *(in opinion)* revirement *m*; *(of golfer)* swing *m*

2 *(pt & pp* **swung**) *vt (arms, legs)* balancer; *(axe)* brandir

3 *vi (sway)* se balancer; *(turn)* virer; **to s. round** *(turn suddenly)* se retourner

swipe [swaip] *vt (card)* passer dans un lecteur de cartes; *Fam* **to s. sth** *(steal)* faucher qch (**from sb** à qn)

swirl [swɜːl] *vi* tourbillonner

Swiss [swis] 1 *adj* suisse; *Br* **S. roll** roulé *m* 2 *n inv* Suisse *m*, Suissesse *f*; **the S.** les Suisses *mpl*

switch [switʃ] 1 *n (electrical)* interrupteur *m*; *(change)* changement *m* (**in** de); *(reversal)* revirement *m* (**in** de) 2 *vt (money, employee)* transférer (**to** à);

(support, affection) reporter (**to** sur); *(exchange)* échanger (**for** contre) 3 *vi* **to s.** *(change to)* passer à ■ **switchboard** *n Tel* standard *m*; **s. operator** standardiste *mf*

▶ **switch off** 1 *vt sep (lamp, gas, radio)* éteindre; *(engine)* arrêter; *(electricity)* couper 2 *vi (of appliance)* s'éteindre

▶ **switch on** 1 *vt sep (lamp, gas, radio)* allumer; *(engine)* mettre en marche 2 *vi (of appliance)* s'allumer

▶ **switch over** *vi (change TV channels)* changer de chaîne; **to s. over to** *(change to)* passer à

Switzerland ['switsələnd] *n* la Suisse

swivel ['swivəl] 1 (*Br* **-ll-**, *Am* **-l-**) *vi* **to s. (round)** *(of chair)* pivoter 2 *adj* **s. chair** chaise *f* pivotante

swollen ['swəʊlən] 1 *pp of* **swell¹** 2 *adj (leg)* enflé; *(stomach)* gonflé

swoop [swuːp] 1 *vi* faire une descente (**on** dans); **to s. (down) on** *(of bird)* fondre sur

swop [swɒp] *n & vti* = **swap**

sword [sɔːd] *n* épée *f*

swore [swɔː(r)] *pt of* **swear**

sworn [swɔːn] *pp of* **swear**

swot [swɒt] *Br Fam Pej* 1 *n* bûcheur, -euse *mf* 2 *(pt & pp* **-tt-**) *vti* **to s. (up)** bûcher; **to s. up on sth** bûcher qch

swum [swʌm] *pp of* **swim**

swung [swʌŋ] *pt & pp of* **swing**

sycamore ['sikəmɔː(r)] *n (maple)* sycomore *m*; *Am (plane tree)* platane *m*

syllable ['siləbəl] *n* syllabe *f*

syllabus ['siləbəs] *n* programme *m*

symbol ['simbəl] *n* symbole *m* ■ **symbolic** [-'bɒlɪk] *adj* symbolique ■ **symbolize** *vt* symboliser

symmetrical [si'metrikəl] *adj* symétrique

sympathetic [simpə'θetik] *adj (showing pity)* compatissant; *(understanding)* compréhensif, -ive; **s. to sb/sth** *(favourable)* bien disposé à l'égard de qn/qch

sympathize ['simpəθaiz] *vi* **I s. with you** *(pity)* je suis désolé (pour vous); *(understanding)* je vous comprends

sympathy ['sɪmpəθɪ] n (pity) compassion f; (understanding) compréhension f; **to have s. for sb** éprouver de la compassion pour qn

symphony ['sɪmfənɪ] **1** (pl -ies) n symphonie f **2** adj (orchestra, concert) symphonique

symptom ['sɪmptəm] n Med & Fig symptôme m

synagogue ['sɪnəgɒg] n synagogue f

synchronize ['sɪŋkrənaɪz] vt synchroniser

syndicate ['sɪndɪkət] n syndicat m

syndrome ['sɪndrəʊm] n Med & Fig syndrome m

synonym ['sɪnənɪm] n synonyme m

■ **synonymous** [-'nɒnɪməs] adj synonyme (**with** de)

synopsis [sɪ'nɒpsɪs] (pl -opses [-ɒpsi:z]) n résumé m; (of film) synopsis m

synthetic [sɪn'θetɪk] adj synthétique

syphon ['saɪfən] n & vt = **siphon**

syringe [sə'rɪndʒ] n seringue f

syrup ['sɪrəp] n sirop m; Br (**golden**) **s.** mélasse f raffinée

system ['sɪstəm] n (structure) & Comptr système m; (human body) organisme m; (method) méthode f; **the digestive s.** l'appareil m digestif; Comptr **systems analyst** analyste m programmeur

systematic [sɪstə'mætɪk] adj systématique

Tt

T, t [tiː] *n (letter)* T, t *m inv*
ta [tɑː] *exclam Br Fam* merci!
tab [tæb] *n* (a) *(label)* étiquette *f* (b) *Am Fam (bill)* addition *f* (c) *(on computer, typewriter)* tabulateur *m*; **t. key** touche *f* de tabulation
table¹ ['teɪbəl] *n* (a) *(furniture)* table *f*; *Br* **to set** *or* **lay/clear the t.** mettre/débarrasser la table; **(sitting) at the t.** à table; **t. tennis** tennis *m* de table; **t. wine** vin *m* de table (b) *(list)* table *f*; **t. of contents** table *f* des matières ■ **tablecloth** *n* nappe *f* ■ **tablespoon** *n* ≃ cuillère *f* à soupe ■ **tablespoonful** *n* ≃ cuillerée *f* à soupe
table² ['teɪbəl] *vt Br (motion)* présenter; *Am (postpone)* ajourner
tablet ['tæblɪt] *n (pill)* comprimé *m*
tabloid ['tæblɔɪd] *n (newspaper)* tabloïd *m*
taboo [təˈbuː] *(pl -oos) adj & n* tabou *(m)*
tack [tæk] **1** *n (nail)* clou *m*; *Am (thumbtack)* punaise *f* **2** *vt* **to t. (down)** clouer
tackle ['tækəl] **1** *n (gear)* matériel *m*; *(in rugby)* plaquage *m*; *(in football)* tacle *m* **2** *vt (task, problem)* s'attaquer à; *(subject)* aborder; *(rugby player)* plaquer; *(football player)* tacler
tacky ['tækɪ] *(-ier, -iest) adj (sticky)* collant; *Fam (shoddy)* minable, moche
tact [tækt] *n* tact *m* ■ **tactful** *adj (remark)* diplomatique; **to be t.** *(of person)* avoir du tact ■ **tactless** *adj (person, remark)* qui manque de tact
tactic ['tæktɪk] *n* **a t.** une tactique; **tactics** la tactique ■ **tactical** *adj* tactique
tag [tæg] **1** *n (label)* étiquette *f* **2** *vi* **to t.**

along with sb venir avec qn
tail [teɪl] **1** *n (of animal)* queue *f*; **tails, t. coat** queue-de-pie *f*; **the t. end** la fin **(of** de) **2** *vt Fam (follow)* filer **3** *vi* **to t. off** *(lessen)* diminuer ■ **tailback** *n Br (of traffic)* bouchon *m* ■ **taillight** *n Am (of vehicle)* feu *m* arrière *inv*
tailor ['teɪlə(r)] **1** *n (person)* tailleur *m* **2** *vt (garment)* faire; *Fig (adjust)* adapter **(to** à)
tainted ['teɪntɪd] *adj (air)* pollué; *(food)* gâté; *Fig (reputation, system)* souillé

TAKE [teɪk] *(pt* **took,** *pp* **taken)** *vt* prendre; *(bring)* amener **(to** à); *(by car)* conduire **(to** à); *(escort)* accompagner **(to** à); *(lead away)* emmener **(to** à); *(exam)* passer; *(credit card)* accepter; *(contain)* avoir une capacité de; *(tolerate)* supporter; *Math (subtract)* soustraire **(from** de); **to t. sth to sb** apporter qch à qn; **to t. sth with one** emporter qch; **it takes an army/courage** il faut une armée/ du courage **(to do** pour faire); **I took an hour to do it** j'ai mis une heure à le faire; **I t. it that...** je présume que...
■ **takeaway** *Br* **1** *adj (meal)* à emporter **2** *n (shop)* restaurant *m* qui fait des plats à emporter; *(meal)* plat *m* à emporter ■ **takeoff** *n (of plane)* décollage *m* ■ **take-out** *adj & n Am* ≃ **takeaway** ■ **takeover** *n (of company)* rachat *m*
► **take after** *vt insep* **to t. after sb** ressembler à qn
► **take along** *vt sep (object)* emporter; *(person)* emmener

► **take apart** *vt sep* *(machine)* démonter

► **take away** *vt sep* *(thing)* emporter; *(person)* emmener; *(remove)* enlever (**from** à); *Math (subtract)* soustraire (**from** de)

► **take back** *vt sep* reprendre; *(return)* rapporter; *(statement)* retirer; *(accompany)* ramener (**to** à)

► **take down** *vt sep* *(object)* descendre; *(notes)* prendre

► **take in** *vt sep* *(chair, car)* rentrer; *(skirt)* reprendre; *(include)* inclure; *(understand)* saisir; *Fam (deceive)* rouler

► **take off 1** *vt sep* *(remove)* enlever; *(lead away)* emmener; *(mimic)* imiter; *Math (deduct)* déduire (**from** de) **2** *vi* *(of aircraft)* décoller

► **take on** *vt sep* *(work, staff, passenger, shape)* prendre

► **take out** *vt sep* *(from pocket)* sortir; *(tooth)* arracher; *(insurance policy, patent)* prendre; *Fam* **to t. it out on sb** passer sa colère sur qn

► **take over 1** *vt sep* *(become responsible for)* reprendre; *(buy out)* racheter; *(overrun)* envahir; *Fig (book, play)* remplacer qn **2** *vi* *(relieve)* prendre la relève (**from** de); *(succeed)* prendre la succession (**from** de)

► **take round** *vt sep* *(bring)* apporter (**to** à); *(distribute)* distribuer; *(visitor)* faire visiter

► **take to** *vt insep* **to t. to doing sth** se mettre à faire qch; **I didn't t. to him/it** il/ça ne m'a pas plu

► **take up 1** *vt sep* *(carry up)* monter; *(continue)* reprendre; *(space, time)* prendre; *(offer)* accepter; *(hobby)* se mettre à **2** *vi* **to t. up with sb** se lier avec qn

---

taken ['teɪkən] *adj* *(seat)* pris; *(impressed)* impressionné (**with** *or* **by** par); **to be t. ill** tomber malade

takings ['teɪkɪŋz] *npl* *(money)* recette *f*

talc [tælk], **talcum powder** ['tælkəmpaʊdə(r)] *n* talc *m*

tale [teɪl] *n* *(story)* histoire *f*; *(lie)*

salades *fpl*; **to tell tales** rapporter (**on sb** sur qn)

talent ['tælənt] *n* talent *m* ■ **talented** *adj* talentueux, -euse

talk [tɔːk] **1** *n* *(conversation)* conversation *f* (**about** à propos de); *(lecture)* exposé *m* (**on** sur); **talks** *(negotiations)* pourparlers *mpl*; **to have a t. with sb** parler avec qn

2 *vt* *(nonsense)* dire; **to t. politics** parler politique; **to t. sb into doing/out of doing sth** persuader qn de faire/de ne pas faire qch; **to t. sth over** discuter (de) qch

3 *vi* parler (**to/about** à/de); *(gossip)* jaser

talkative ['tɔːkətɪv] *adj* bavard

tall [tɔːl] (**-er, -est**) *adj* *(person)* grand; *(tree, house)* haut; *Fig* **a t. story** une histoire invraisemblable

tally ['tælɪ] (*pt & pp* **-ied**) *vi* correspondre (**with** à)

tambourine [tæmbə'riːn] *n* tambourin *m*

tame [teɪm] **1** (**-er, -est**) *adj* *(animal)* apprivoisé; *Fig (book, play)* fade **2** *vt* *(animal)* apprivoiser

tamper ['tæmpə(r)] *vt insep* **to t. with** *(lock, car)* essayer de forcer; *(machine)* toucher à; *(documents)* trafiquer

tampon ['tæmpɒn] *n* tampon *m* (hygiénique)

tan [tæn] **1** *n* *(suntan)* bronzage *m* **2** *adj* *(colour)* marron clair *inv* **3** (*pt & pp* **-nn-**) *vt* *(skin)* hâler; *(leather)* tanner **4** *vi* *(of person, skin)* bronzer

tangerine [tændʒə'riːn] *n* mandarine *f*

tangible ['tændʒəbəl] *adj* tangible

tangle ['tæŋgəl] *n* **to get into a t.** *(of rope)* s'enchevêtrer; *(of hair)* s'emmêler; *Fig (of person)* s'embrouiller ■ **tangled** *adj* enchevêtré; *(hair)* emmêlé

tango ['tæŋgəʊ] (*pl* **-os**) *n* tango *m*

tangy ['tæŋɪ] (**-ier, -iest**) *adj* acidulé

tank [tæŋk] *n* *(container)* réservoir *m*; *(military vehicle)* tank *m*; **(fish) t.** aquarium *m*

tanker ['tæŋkə(r)] n (lorry) camion-citerne m; (oil) t. (ship) pétrolier m

Tannoy® ['tænɔɪ] n Br **over the T.** au haut-parleur

tantalizing ['tæntəlaɪzɪŋ] adj alléchant

tantrum ['tæntrəm] n caprice m

tap¹ [tæp] **1** n Br (for water) robinet m; **t. water** eau f du robinet **2** (pt & pp -pp-) vt (resources) puiser dans; (phone) placer sur écoute

tap² [tæp] **1** n (blow) petit coup m; **t. dancing** claquettes fpl **2** (pt & pp -pp-) vt (hit) tapoter

tape [teɪp] **1** n (a) (ribbon) ruban m; (sticky or adhesive) t. ruban m adhésif; **t. measure** mètre m (à) ruban (b) (for recording) bande f; (cassette) cassette f; **t. deck** platine f cassette; **t. recorder** magnétophone m **2** vt (a) (stick) scotcher (b) (record) enregistrer

taper ['teɪpə(r)] **1** n (candle) bougie f filée **2** vi s'effiler; Fig **to t. off** diminuer

tapestry ['tæpəstrɪ] n tapisserie f

tar [tɑː(r)] n goudron m

target ['tɑːgɪt] **1** n cible f; (objective) objectif m **2** vt (campaign, product) destiner (**at** à); (age group) viser

tariff ['tærɪf] n (tax) tarif m douanier; Br (price list) tarif m

tarmac ['tɑːmæk] n Br (on road) macadam m; (runway) piste f

tarnish ['tɑːnɪʃ] vt ternir

tart [tɑːt] **1** (-er, -est) adj (sour) aigre **2** n (pie) (large) tarte f; (small) tartelette f

tartan ['tɑːtən] **1** n tartan m **2** adj (skirt, tie) écossais

task [tɑːsk] n tâche f

tassel ['tæsəl] n gland m

taste [teɪst] **1** n goût m; **in good/bad t.** de bon/mauvais goût; **to have a t. of sth** goûter à qch **2** vt (detect flavour of) sentir; (sample) goûter; Fig (experience) goûter à **3** vi **to t. of** or **like sth** avoir un goût de qch; **to t. good** être bon (f bonne)

tasteful ['teɪstfəl] adj de bon goût

■ **tasteless** adj (food) insipide; Fig (joke) de mauvais goût ■ **tasty** (-ier, -iest) adj savoureux, -euse

tatters ['tætəz] npl **in t.** (clothes) en lambeaux

tattoo [tæ'tuː] **1** (pl -oos) n (design) tatouage m **2** (pt & pp -ooed) vt tatouer

tatty ['tætɪ] (-ier, -iest) adj Br Fam minable

taught [tɔːt] pt & pp of **teach**

taunt [tɔːnt] **1** n raillerie f **2** vt railler

taut [tɔːt] adj tendu

tax¹ [tæks] **1** n (on goods) taxe f, impôt m; (on income) impôts mpl; Br **road t.** ≃ vignette f automobile

2 adj fiscal; **t. collector** percepteur m; Br (**road**) **t. disc** ≃ vignette f automobile

3 vt (person) imposer; (goods) taxer ■ **taxable** adj imposable ■ **taxation** n (taxes) impôts mpl; (act) imposition f ■ **tax-free** adj exempt d'impôts ■ **taxpayer** n contribuable mf

tax² [tæks] vt (put under strain) mettre à l'épreuve

taxi ['tæksɪ] n taxi m; Br **t. rank**, Am **t. stand** station f de taxis

tea [tiː] n (plant, drink) thé m; Br (snack) goûter m; Br **high t.** dîner m (pris tôt dans la soirée); Br **t. break** ≃ pause-café f; **t. leaves** feuilles fpl de thé; **t. set** service m à thé; Br **t. towel** torchon m ■ **teabag** n sachet m de thé ■ **teacup** n tasse f à thé ■ **teapot** n théière f ■ **tearoom** n salon m de thé ■ **teaspoon** n petite cuillère f ■ **teaspoonful** n cuillerée f à café ■ **teatime** n l'heure f du thé

teach [tiːtʃ] **1** (pt & pp taught) vt apprendre (**sb sth** qch à qn), (**sb that**) (que); (in school, at university) enseigner (**sb sth** qch à qn); **to t. sb (how) to do sth** apprendre à qn à faire qch **2** vi enseigner ■ **teaching 1** n enseignement m **2** adj (staff) enseignant; (method, material) pédagogique

teacher ['tiːtʃə(r)] n professeur m; (in primary school) instituteur, -trice mf

team [tiːm] **1** n équipe f; (of horses,

oxen) attelage *m*; **t. mate** coéquipier, -ère *mf* **2** *vi* **to t. up** faire équipe (**with sb** avec qn) ■ **teamwork** *n* travail *m* d'équipe

tear¹ [teə(r)] **1** *n* déchirure *f* **2** (*pt* **tore**, *pp* **torn**) *vt* (*rip*) déchirer; (*snatch*) arracher; (**from**à); **to t. off** *or* **out** arracher; **to t. up** déchirer **3** *vi* **to t. along/past** aller/passer à toute vitesse

tear² [tɪə(r)] *n* larme *f*; **in tears** en larmes

tease [tiːz] **1** *n* (*person*) taquin, -e *mf* **2** *vt* taquiner

technical ['teknɪkəl] *adj* technique

technician ['teknɪʃən] *n* technicien, -enne *mf*

technique [tek'niːk] *n* technique *f*

technology [tek'nɒlədʒɪ] (*pl* **-ies**) *n* technologie *f* ■ **technological** [-nə'lɒdʒɪkəl] *adj* technologique

tedious ['tiːdɪəs] *adj* fastidieux, -euse

teem [tiːm] *vi* (*swarm*) grouiller (**with** de); **to t. (with rain)** pleuvoir à torrents

teenage ['tiːneɪdʒ] *adj* (*boy, girl, behaviour*) adolescent; (*fashion, magazine*) pour adolescents ■ **teenager** *n* adolescent, -e *mf* ■ **teens** *npl* **to be in one's t.** être adolescent

tee-shirt ['tiːʃɜːt] *n* tee-shirt *m*

teeth [tiːθ] *pl of* **tooth**

teethe [tiːð] *vi* faire ses dents

teetotaller [tiː'təʊtələ(r)] (*Am* **teetotaler**) *n* = personne qui ne boit jamais d'alcool

telecommunications [telɪkəmjuːnɪ'keɪʃənz] *npl* télécommunications *fpl*

telegram ['telɪgræm] *n* télégramme *m*

telegraph ['telɪgrɑːf] *adj* **t. pole/wire** poteau *m*/fil *m* télégraphique

telephone ['telɪfəʊn] **1** *n* téléphone *m*; **to be on the t.** (*speaking*) être au téléphone **2** *adj* (*call, line, message*) téléphonique; *Br* **t. booth**, **t. box** cabine *f* téléphonique; **t. directory** annuaire *m* du téléphone; **t. number** numéro *m* de téléphone

3 *vt* (*message*) téléphoner (**to** à); **to t. sb** téléphoner à qn **4** *vi* téléphoner ■ **telephonist** *n Br* téléphoniste *mf*

telescope ['telɪskəʊp] *n* télescope *m*

teletext ['telɪtekst] *n* télétexte *m*

televise ['telɪvaɪz] *vt* téléviser

television [telɪ'vɪʒən] **1** *n* télévision *f*; **on (the) t.** à la télévision **2** *adj* (*programme, screen*) de télévision; (*interview, report*) télévisé

telex ['teleks] **1** *n* (*service, message*) télex *m* **2** *vt* (*message*) télexer

tell [tel] **1** (*pt & pp* **told**) *vt* dire (**sb sth** qch à qn; **that** que); (*story*) raconter; (*distinguish*) distinguer (**from** de); **to t. sb to do sth** dire à qn de faire qch; **to t. the difference** voir la différence (**between** entre); **I could t. she was lying** je savais qu'elle mentait; *Fam* **to t. sb off** disputer qn **2** *vi* dire; (*have an effect*) se faire sentir; **to t. of** *or* **about sth/sb** parler de qn/qch; **you can never t.** on ne sait jamais; *Fam* **to t. on sb** dénoncer qn

telltale ['telteɪl] **1** *adj* révélateur, -trice **2** *n* rapporteur, -euse *mf*

telly ['telɪ] *n Br Fam* télé *f*; **on the t.** à la télé

temp [temp] *Br Fam* **1** *n* intérimaire *mf* **2** *vi* faire de l'intérim

temper ['tempə(r)] **1** *n* (*mood, nature*) humeur *f*; (*bad mood*) mauvaise humeur *f*; **in a bad t.** de mauvaise humeur; **to lose one's t.** se mettre en colère **2** *vt* (*moderate*) tempérer

temperament ['temprəmənt] *n* tempérament *m* ■ **temperamental** [-'mentəl] *adj* (*person, machine*) capricieux, -euse

temperate ['tempərət] *adj* (*climate*) tempéré

temperature ['temprətʃə(r)] *n* température *f*

template ['templət, -pleɪt] *n* gabarit *m*; *Comptr* modèle *m*

temple¹ ['tempəl] *n* (*religious building*) temple *m*

temple² ['tempəl] *n Anat* tempe *f*

tempo ['tempəʊ] (pl -os) n (of life, work) rythme m; Mus tempo m

temporary [Br 'tempərərɪ, Am -erɪ] adj temporaire; (secretary) intérimaire ■ **temporarily** [Br tempə'reərəlɪ, Am tempə'reərəlɪ] adv temporairement

tempt [tempt] vt tenter; **tempted to do sth** tenté de faire qch ■ **temptation** n tentation f ■ **tempting** adj tentant

ten [ten] adj & n dix (m)

tenable ['tenəbəl] adj (argument, position) défendable

tenacious [tə'neɪʃəs] adj tenace

tenant ['tenənt] n locataire mf ■ **tenancy** n (lease) location f; (period) occupation f

tend[1] [tend] vi to t. to do sth avoir tendance à faire qch; to t. towards incliner vers ■ **tendency** (pl -ies) n tendance f (to do à faire)

tend[2] [tend] vt (look after) s'occuper de

tender[1] ['tendə(r)] adj (soft, delicate, loving) tendre; (painful) sensible

tender[2] ['tendə(r)] 1 n to be legal t. (of money) avoir cours 2 vt (offer) offrir

tenement ['tenəmənt] n immeuble m

tenner ['tenə(r)] n Br Fam billet m de 10 livres

tennis ['tenɪs] n tennis m; t. court court m de tennis

tenor ['tenə(r)] n Mus ténor m

tenpin ['tenpɪn] adj Br t. bowling bowling m

tense[1] [tens] 1 (-er, -est) adj (person, muscle, situation) tendu 2 vt tendre; (muscle) contracter 3 vi to t. (up) (of person, face) se crisper ■ **tension** n tension f

tense[2] [tens] n (in grammar) temps m

tent [tent] n tente f; Br t. peg piquet m de tente; Br t. pole, Am t. stake mât m de tente

tentative ['tentətɪv] adj (not definite) provisoire; (hesitant) timide

tenth [tenθ] adj & n dixième (mf); a t. (fraction) un dixième

tenuous ['tenjʊəs] adj (link) ténu

tepid ['tepɪd] adj (liquid) & Fig tiède

term [tɜːm] 1 n (word) terme m; (period) période f; Br (of school or university year) trimestre m; Am (semester) semestre m; **terms** (conditions) conditions fpl; (of contract) termes mpl; to be on good/bad terms être en bons/mauvais termes (with sb avec qn); in terms of (speaking of) sur le plan de; to come to terms with sth se résigner à qch; in the long/short/medium t. à long/court/moyen terme 2 vt appeler

terminal ['tɜːmɪnəl] 1 n (electronic) & Comptr terminal m; (of battery) borne f 2 adj (patient, illness) en phase terminale

terminate ['tɜːmɪneɪt] 1 vt mettre fin à; (contract) résilier; (pregnancy) interrompre 2 vi se terminer

terminus ['tɜːmɪnəs] n terminus m

terrace ['terɪs] n (next to house, on hill) terrasse f; Br (houses) = rangée de maisons attenantes; Br the terraces (at football ground) les gradins mpl ■ **terraced** n Br t. house = maison située dans une rangée d'habitations attenantes

terrain [tə'reɪn] n Mil & Geol terrain m

terrestrial [tə'restrɪəl] adj terrestre

terrible ['terəbəl] adj terrible ■ **terribly** adv Fam (extremely) terriblement; (badly) affreusement mal

terrier ['terɪə(r)] n (dog) terrier m

terrific [tə'rɪfɪk] adj Fam (excellent) super inv ■ **terrifically** adv Fam (extremely) terriblement; (extremely well) terriblement bien

terrify ['terɪfaɪ] (pt & pp -ied) vt terrifier; to be terrified of sb/sth avoir une peur bleue de qn/qch ■ **terrifying** adj terrifiant

territory ['terɪtərɪ] (pl -ies) n territoire m

terror ['terə(r)] n terreur f ■ **terrorism** n terrorisme m ■ **terrorist** n & adj terroriste (mf) ■ **terrorize** vt terroriser

test [test] 1 n (trial) essai m; (of product) test m; Sch & Univ interrogation f; (by doctor) examen m; (of blood) analyse f

2 *adj* t. **drive** essai *m* sur route; t. **tube** éprouvette f; t. **tube baby** bébé-éprouvette *m*

3 *vt (try)* essayer; *(product, machine)* tester; *(pupil)* interroger; *(of doctor)* examiner; *(blood)* analyser; *Fig (try out)* mettre à l'épreuve; **to t. sb for AIDS** faire subir à qn un test de dépistage du SIDA

4 *vi* **to t. positive** *(for drugs)* être positif, -ive

testament ['testəmənt] *n (will)* testament *m*; *(tribute)* preuve f; *Rel* the **Old/New T.** l'Ancien/le Nouveau Testament

testicle ['testɪkəl] *n Anat* testicule *m*

testify ['testɪfaɪ] *(pt & pp -ied)* **1** *vt* to **t. that…** témoigner que… **2** *vi (in law)* témoigner (**against** contre); **to t. to sth** *(be the proof of)* témoigner de qch ▪ **testimony** ['testɪmənɪ] *(pl -ies)* *n* témoignage *m*

tetanus ['tetənəs] *n Med* tétanos *m*

tether ['teðə(r)] *n* **at the end of one's t.** à bout

text [tekst] *n* texte *m*; t. **message** message *m* texte, mini-message *m* ▪ **textbook** *n* manuel *m*

textile ['tekstaɪl] *adj & n* textile *(m)*

texture ['tekstʃə(r)] *n (of fabric, cake)* texture f; *(of paper, wood)* grain *m*

Thames [temz] *n* the **(River) T.** la Tamise

than [ðən, *stressed* ðæn] *conj* que; **happier t. me** plus heureux que moi; **he has more/less t. you** il en a plus/moins que toi; **more t. six** plus de six

thank [θæŋk] *vt* remercier (**for sth** de qch; **for doing** d'avoir fait); t. **you** merci; **no, t. you** (non) merci; t. **God!, t. heavens!, t. goodness!** Dieu merci! ▪ **thanks** *npl* remerciements *mpl*; **(many) t.!** merci (beaucoup)!; **t. to** *(because of)* grâce à

thankful ['θæŋkfəl] *adj* reconnaissant (**for** de); **to be t. that…** être heureux, -euse que… (+ *subjunctive*) ▪ **thankless** *adj* ingrat

Thanksgiving [θæŋks'gɪvɪŋ] *n Am* T.

(Day) = quatrième jeudi de novembre, commémorant la première action de grâce des colons anglais

THAT [ðət, *stressed* ðæt] **1** *conj (so-vent omise)* que; **she said t. she would come** elle a dit qu'elle viendrait **2** *relative pron*

On peut omettre le pronom relatif that sauf s'il est en position sujet.

(subject) qui; *(object)* que; *(with preposition)* lequel, laquelle, *pl* lesquel(le)s; **the boy t. left** le garçon qui est parti; **the book t. I read** le livre que j'ai lu; **the house t. she told me about** la maison dont elle m'a parlé; **the day/morning t. she arrived** le jour/matin où elle est arrivée

3 *(pl those)* *demonstrative adj* ce, cet *(before vowel or mute h)*, cette; *(opposed to 'this')* ce…-là *(f* cette…-là*)*; t. **woman** cette femme(-là); t. **day** ce jour-là; t. **one** celui-là *m*, celle-là *f*

4 *(pl those)* *demonstrative pron* cela, *Fam* ça; **give me t.** donne-moi ça; **t.'s right** c'est exact; **who's t.?** qui est-ce?; **t.'s the house** voilà la maison; **what do you mean by t.?** qu'entends-tu par là?; **t. is (to say)…** c'est-à-dire…

5 *adv Fam (so)* si; **not t. good** pas si bon que ça; **it cost t. much** ça a coûté tant que ça

thatched [θætʃt] *adj (roof)* de chaume; t. **cottage** chaumière f

thaw [θɔː] **1** *n* dégel *m* **2** *vt (snow, ice)* faire fondre; t. **(out)** *(food)* décongeler **3** *vi* dégeler; *(of snow, ice)* fondre; *(of food)* décongeler

the [ðə, *before vowel* ðɪ, *stressed* ðiː] *definite article* l', le, la, *pl* les; **of t., from t.** du, de l', de la, *pl* des; **to t., at t.** au, à l', à la, *pl* aux; **Elizabeth t. Second** Élisabeth Deux

theatre ['θɪətə(r)] *(Am* **theater**) *n (place, art)* théâtre *m*; *Br* **(operating) t.** *(in hospital)* salle f d'opération ▪ **theatrical** [θɪ'ætrɪkəl] *adj also Fig* théâtral

theft [θeft] *n* vol *m*

their [ðeə(r)] *possessive adj* leur, *pl* leurs ∎ **theirs** *possessive pron* le leur, la leur, *pl* les leurs; **this book is t.** ce livre est à eux *ou* est le leur; **a friend of t.** un ami à eux

them [ðəm, *stressed* ðem] *pron* les; *(after prep, 'than', 'it is')* eux *mpl*, elles *fpl*; **(to) t.** *(indirect)* leur; **I see t.** je les vois; **I gave it (to) t.** je le leur ai donné; **ten of t.** dix d'entre eux/elles; **all of t. came** tous sont venus, toutes sont venues; **I like all of t.** je les aime tous/toutes

theme [θiːm] *n* thème *m*; **t. tune** *(of TV, radio programme)* indicatif *m*; **t. park** parc *m* à thème

themselves [ðəm'selvz, *stressed* ðem-'selvz] *pron* eux-mêmes *mpl*, elles-mêmes *fpl*; *(reflexive)* se, s'; *(after prep)* eux *mpl*, elles *fpl*; **they cut t.** ils/elles se sont coupé(e)s

then [ðen] **1** *adv (at that time)* à cette époque-là, alors; *(just a moment ago)* à ce moment-là; *(next)* ensuite, puis; *(therefore)* donc, alors; **from t. on** dès lors; **before t.** avant cela; **until t.** jusque-là, alors **2** *adj* **the t. mayor** le maire d'alors

theory ['θɪərɪ] *(pl -ies) n* théorie *f*; **in t.** en théorie ∎ **theoretical** *adj* théorique

therapy ['θerəpɪ] *(pl -ies) n* thérapeutique *f* ∎ **therapeutic** [-'pjuːtɪk] *adj* thérapeutique

there [ðeə(r)] *adv* là; **(down/over) t.** là-bas; **on t.** là-dessus; **she'll be t.** elle y sera; **t. is, t. are** il y a; *(pointing)* voilà; **t. he is** le voilà; **that man t.** cet homme-là; **t. (you are)!** *(take this)* tenez! ∎ **thereabouts** *adv* dans les environs; *(in amount)* à peu près ∎ **thereby** *adv Formal* ainsi ∎ **therefore** *adv* donc

thermometer [θə'mɒmɪtə(r)] *n* thermomètre *m*

Thermos® ['θɜːməs] *(pl -moses* [-mə-səz]*) n* **T. (flask)** Thermos® *f*

thermostat ['θɜːməstæt] *n* thermostat *m*

these [ðiːz] *(sing* **this) 1** *demonstrative adj* ces; *(opposed to 'those')* ces…-ci; **t. men** ces hommes(-ci); **t. ones** ceux-ci *mpl*, celles-ci *fpl* **2** *demonstrative pron* ceux-ci *mpl*, celles-ci *fpl*; **t. are my friends** ce sont mes amis

thesis ['θiːsɪs] *(pl* theses ['θiːsiːz]*) n* thèse *f*

they [ðeɪ] *pron* (**a**) *(subject)* ils *mpl*, elles *fpl*; *(stressed)* eux *mpl*, elles *fpl*; **t. are doctors** ce sont des médecins (**b**) *(people in general)* on ∎ **they'd** = **they had, they would** ∎ **they'll** = **they will**

thick [θɪk] **1** (**-er, -est**) *adj* épais (*f* épaisse); *Fam (stupid)* lourd **2** *adv* *(spread)* en couche épaisse ∎ **thickly** *adv* (spread) en couche épaisse

thicken ['θɪkən] **1** *vt* épaissir **2** *vi (of fog)* s'épaissir; *(of cream, sauce)* épaissir ∎ **thickness** *n* épaisseur *f*

thick-skinned [θɪk'skɪnd] *adj (person)* peu susceptible

thief [θiːf] *(pl* thieves*) n* voleur, -euse *mf* ∎ **thieving 1** *adj* voleur, -euse **2** *n* vol *m*

thigh [θaɪ] *n* cuisse *f*

thimble ['θɪmbəl] *n* dé *m* à coudre

thin [θɪn] **1** (**thinner, thinnest**) *adj (person, slice, paper)* mince; *(soup)* peu épais (*f* peu épaisse); *(crowd, hair)* clairsemé **2** *adv (spread)* en couche mince; *(cut)* en tranches minces **3** (*pt & pp* **-nn-**) *vt* **to t. (down)** *(paint)* diluer **4** *vi* **to t. out** *(of crowd, mist)* s'éclaircir ∎ **thinly** *adv (spread)* en couche mince; *(cut)* en tranches minces

thing [θɪŋ] *n* chose *f*; **things** *(belongings, clothes)* affaires *fpl*; **poor little t.!** pauvre petit!; **how are things?**, *Fam* **how's things?** comment ça va?; **for one t.… and for another t.…** d'abord… et ensuite…

think [θɪŋk] **1** (*pt & pp* **thought**) *vt* penser (**that** que); **I t. so** je pense *ou* crois que oui; **what do you t. of him?** que penses-tu de lui?; **to t. out** *(plan,* *method)* élaborer; *(reply)* réfléchir sérieusement à; **to t. sth over** réfléchir à qch; **to t. sth up** *(invent)* inventer qch

2 *vi* penser *(about/of* à); **to t.** *(carefully)* réfléchir *(about/of* à); **to t. of doing sth** penser à faire qch; **to t. highly of sb** penser beaucoup de bien de qn

3 *n Fam* **to have a t.** réfléchir *(about* à)

third [θɜːd] **1** *adj* troisième; **the T. World** le tiers-monde **2** *n* troisième *mf*; **a t.** *(fraction)* un tiers **3** *adv* **to come t.** *(in race)* se classer troisième ■ **thirdly** *adv* troisièmement

third-party [θɜːd'pɑːtɪ] *adj* **t. insurance** assurance *f* au tiers

third-rate [θɜːd'reɪt] *adj* très inférieur

thirst [θɜːst] *n* soif *f* *(for* de) ■ **thirsty** *(-ier, -iest) adj* **to be** *or* **feel t.** avoir soif; **to make sb t.** donner soif à qn

thirteen [θɜː'tiːn] *adj & n* treize *(m)* ■ **thirteenth** *adj & n* treizième *(mf)*

thirty ['θɜːtɪ] *adj & n* trente *(m)* ■ **thirtieth** *adj & n* trentième *(mf)*

this [ðɪs] **1** *(pl* **these)** *demonstrative adj* ce, cet *(before vowel or mute h),* cette; *(opposed to 'that')* ce...-ci; **t. man** cet homme(-ci); **t. one** celui-ci *m,* celle-ci *f*

2 *(pl* **these)** *demonstrative pron (subject)* ce, ceci; *(object)* ceci; **I prefer t.** je préfère celui-ci; **who's t.?** qui est-ce; **it is Paul** c'est Paul; *(pointing)* voici Paul

3 *adv (so)* **t. high** *(pointing)* haut comme ceci; **t. far** *(until now)* jusqu'ici

thistle ['θɪsəl] *n* chardon *m*

thorn [θɔːn] *n* épine *f*

thorough ['θʌrə] *adj (search, cleaning, preparation)* minutieux, -euse; *(knowledge, examination)* approfondi ■ **thoroughly** *adv (completely)* tout à fait; *(carefully)* avec minutie; *(know, clean, wash)* à fond

thoroughfare ['θʌrəfeə(r)] *n Br* **'no t.'** 'passage interdit'

those [ðəʊz] **1** *demonstrative adj* ces; *(opposed to 'these')* ces...-là; **t. men** ces hommes(-là); **t. ones** ceux-là *mpl,* celles-là *fpl*

2 *(sing* **that)** *demonstrative pron* ceux-là *mpl,* celles-là *fpl;* **t. are my friends** ce sont mes amis

though [ðəʊ] **1** *conj* bien que *(+ subjunctive);* **(even) t.** même si; **as t.** comme si; **strange t. it may seem** si étrange que cela puisse paraître **2** *adv (however)* pourtant

thought [θɔːt] **1** *pt & pp of* **think 2** *n* pensée *f;* **(careful) t.** réflexion *f;* **to have second thoughts** changer d'avis; *Br* **on second thoughts,** *Am* **on second t.** à la réflexion

thoughtful ['θɔːtfəl] *adj (considerate, kind)* attentionné; *(pensive)* pensif, -ive

thoughtless ['θɔːtləs] *adj* irréfléchi

thousand ['θaʊzənd] *adj & n* mille *(m) inv;* **a t. pages** mille pages; **two t. pages** deux mille pages; **thousands of** des milliers de

thrash [θræʃ] **1** *vt* **to t. sb** donner une correction à qn; *(defeat)* écraser qn **2** *vi* **to t. around** *or* **about** *(struggle)* se débattre ■ **thrashing** *n (beating)* correction *f*

thread [θred] **1** *n (yarn)* & *Fig* fil *m;* *(of screw)* filetage *m* **2** *vt (needle, beads)* enfiler

threat [θret] *n* menace *f* ■ **threaten 1** *vt* menacer **(to do sth** de qch; **with sth** de qch) **2** *vi* menacer ■ **threatening** *adj* menaçant

three [θriː] *adj & n* trois *(m)* ■ **three-dimensional** *adj* à trois dimensions ■ **threefold 1** *adj* triple **2** *adv* **to increase t.** tripler ■ **three-piece** *adj Br* **t. suite** canapé *m* et deux fauteuils assortis ■ **three-quarters 1** *n* **t. (of)** les trois quarts *mpl* (de) **2** *adv* **it's t. full** c'est aux trois quarts plein

threshold ['θreʃhəʊld] *n* seuil *m*

threw [θruː] *pt of* **throw**

thrifty ['θrɪftɪ] (-ier, -iest) *adj* économe

thrill [θrɪl] **1** *n* frisson *m*; **to get a t. out of doing sth** prendre plaisir à faire qch **2** *vt* (*delight*) réjouir; (*excite*) faire frissonner ■ **thrilled** *adj* ravi (**with sth** de qch; **to do** de faire) ■ **thriller** *n* thriller *m* ■ **thrilling** *adj* passionnant

thrive [θraɪv] *vi* (*of business, person, plant*) prospérer; **to t. on sth** avoir besoin de qch pour s'épanouir ■ **thriving** *adj* (*business*) prospère

throat [θrəʊt] *n* gorge *f*

throb [θrɒb] (*pt & pp* -bb-) *vi* (*of heart*) palpiter; **my head is throbbing** j'ai une douleur lancinante dans la tête

throes [θrəʊz] *npl* **in the t. of** au milieu de; (*illness, crisis*) en proie à; **in the t. of doing sth** en train de faire qch

throne [θrəʊn] *n* trône *m*

throttle ['θrɒtəl] **1** *n* (*accelerator*) manette *f* des gaz **2** *vt* (*strangle*) étrangler

through [θru:] **1** *prep* (*place*) à travers; (*by means of*) par; (*because of*) à cause de; **t. the window/door** par la fenêtre/porte; **t. ignorance** par ignorance; *Am***Tuesday t. Saturday** de mardi à samedi

2 *adv* à travers; **to go t.** (*of bullet, nail*) traverser; **to let sb t.** laisser passer qn; **to be t. with sb/sth** (*finished*) en avoir fini avec qn/qch; **t. to** *or* **till** jusqu'à; **I'll put you t. (to him)** (*on telephone*) je vous le passe

3 *adj* (*train, ticket*) direct; *Br* **'no t. road'** (*no exit*) 'voie sans issue'

throughout [θru:'aʊt] **1** *prep* **t. the neighbourhood** dans tout le quartier; **t. the day** pendant toute la journée **2** *adv* (*everywhere*) partout; (*all the time*) tout le temps

throw [θrəʊ] **1** *n* (*in sport*) lancer *m*; (*of dice*) coup *m* **2** (*pt* **threw**, *pp* **thrown**) *vt* jeter (**to/at** à); (*javelin, discus*) lancer; (*image, shadow*) projeter; (*of horse*) désarçonner; (*party*) donner; *Fam* (*baffle*) déconcerter

▶ **throw away** *vt sep* (*discard*) jeter; *Fig* (*life, chance*) gâcher

▶ **throw back** *vt sep* (*ball*) renvoyer (**to** à); (*one's head*) rejeter en arrière

▶ **throw in** *vt sep Fam* (*include as extra*) donner en prime

▶ **throw out** *vt sep* (*unwanted object*) jeter; (*suggestion*) repousser; (*expel*) mettre à la porte

▶ **throw up** *vi Fam* (*vomit*) vomir

thrown [θrəʊn] *pp of* **throw**

thrush [θrʌʃ] *n* (*bird*) grive *f*

thrust [θrʌst] **1** *n* (*movement*) mouvement *m* en avant; (*of argument*) idée *f* principale **2** (*pt & pp* **thrust**) *vt* **to t. sth into sth** enfoncer qch dans qch; **to t. sb/sth aside** écarter qn/qch

thud [θʌd] *n* bruit *m* sourd

thug [θʌg] *n* voyou *m* (*pl* -ous)

thumb [θʌm] **1** *n* pouce *m* **2** *vt Fam* **to t. a lift** *or* **a ride** faire du stop **3** *vi* **to t. through a book** feuilleter un livre

thump [θʌmp] **1** *n* (*blow*) coup *m*; (*noise*) bruit *m* sourd **2** *vt* (*hit*) frapper; **to t. one's head** se cogner la tête (**on** contre) **3** *vi* frapper, cogner (**on** sur); (*of heart*) battre la chamade

thunder ['θʌndə(r)] **1** *n* tonnerre *m* **2** *vi* tonner; **to t. past** (*of train, truck*) passer dans un bruit de tonnerre ■ **thunderstorm** *n* orage *m*

Thursday ['θɜ:zdeɪ] *n* jeudi *m*

thus [ðʌs] *adv* ainsi

thyme [taɪm] *n* thym *m*

tic [tɪk] *n* tic *m*

tick [tɪk] **1** *n* (*of clock*) tic-tac *m inv*; (*mark*) ≃ croix *f*; *Fam* (*moment*) instant *m* **2** *vt* **to t. sth (off)** (*on list*) cocher qch **3** *vi* faire tic-tac; *Br* **to t. over** (*of engine, factory*) tourner au ralenti ■ **ticking** *n* (*of clock*) tic-tac *m inv*

tickle ['tɪkəl] *vt* chatouiller; *Fig* (*amuse*) amuser ■ **ticklish** *adj* (*person*) chatouilleux, -euse

ticket ['tɪkɪt] *n* billet *m*; (*for bus, metro*) ticket *m*; *Fam* (*for parking, speeding*) contravention *f*; (**price**) **t.** étiquette *f*; **t. collector** contrôleur, -euse *mf*; **t. office** guichet *m*

tidbit ['tɪdbɪt] n Am (food) bon morceau m

tide [taɪd] **1** n marée f **2** vt **to t. sb over** dépanner qn

tidy ['taɪdɪ] **1** (-ier, -iest) adj (place, toys) bien rangé; (clothes, hair) soigné; (person) (methodical) ordonné; (in appearance) soigné **2** vt **to t. sth (up** or **away)** ranger qch; **to t. sth out** mettre de l'ordre dans qch; **to t. oneself up** s'arranger **3** vi **to t. up** ranger ■ **tidily** adv (put away) soigneusement, avec soin

tie [taɪ] **1** n (garment) cravate f; (link) lien m; (draw) égalité f; (drawn match) match m nul **2** vt (fasten) attacher (**to** à); (knot) faire (**in** à); (shoe) lacer **3** vi (draw) être à égalité; (at end of match) faire match nul; (in race) être ex aequo

▸ **tie down** vt sep attacher

▸ **tie in** vi (of facts) concorder

▸ **tie up** vt sep (animal) attacher; (parcel) ficeler; (money) immobiliser; Fig **to be tied up** (busy) être occupé

tier [tɪə(r)] n (of seats) gradin m; (of cake) étage m

tiger ['taɪɡə(r)] n tigre m

tight [taɪt] **1** (-er, -est) adj (clothes, knot, race, bend) serré; (control) strict; Fam (mean) radin **2** adv (hold, shut) bien; (squeeze) fort; **to sit t.** ne pas bouger ■ **tight-fitting** adj (garment) ajusté ■ **tightly** adv (hold) bien; (squeeze) fort ■ **tightrope** n corde f raide

tighten ['taɪtən] vt **to t. (up)** (bolt) serrer; (rope) tendre; Fig (security) renforcer

tights [taɪts] npl Br (garment) collant m

tile [taɪl] **1** n (on roof) tuile f; (on wall, floor) carreau m **2** vt (wall, floor) carreler ■ **tiled** adj (roof) de tuiles; (wall, floor) carrelé

till[1] [tɪl] prep & conj = **until**

till[2] [tɪl] n Br (for money) caisse f enregistreuse

tilt [tɪlt] **1** n inclinaison f **2** vti pencher

timber ['tɪmbə(r)] n Br (wood) bois m (de construction)

time [taɪm] **1** n temps m; (period, moment) moment m; (age) époque f; (on clock) heure f; (occasion) fois f; Mus mesure f; **in t., with t.** avec le temps; **it's t. to do sth** il est temps de faire qch; **some of the t.** (not always) une partie du temps; **all (of) the t.** tout le temps; **in a year's t.** dans un an; **a long t.** longtemps; **a short t.** peu de temps; **to have a good** or **a nice t.** s'amuser (bien); **to have t. off** avoir du temps libre; **in no t. (at all)** en un rien de temps; **(just) in t.** (arrive) à temps (**for sth** pour qch; **to do** pour faire); **from t. to t.** de temps en temps; **what t. is it?** quelle heure est-il?; **the right** or **exact t.** l'heure f exacte; **on t.** à l'heure; **at the same t.** en même temps (**as** que); (simultaneously) à la fois; **for the t. being** pour le moment; **at the** or **that t.** à ce moment-là; **at times** parfois; **(the) next t. you come** la prochaine fois que tu viendras; **(the) last t.** la dernière fois; **one at a t.** un à un; **ten times ten** fois dix; **t. difference** décalage m horaire; **t. limit** délai m; **t. zone** fuseau m horaire

2 vt (sportsman, worker) chronométrer; (activity, programme) minuter; (choose the moment of) choisir le moment de; (plan) prévoir ■ **time-consuming** adj qui prend du temps

timely ['taɪmlɪ] adj à propos

timer ['taɪmə(r)] n (device) minuteur m; (sand-filled) sablier m; (built into appliance) programmateur m; (plugged into socket) prise f programmable

timetable ['taɪmteɪbəl] n horaire m; (in school) emploi m du temps

timid ['tɪmɪd] adj timide

timing ['taɪmɪŋ] n (of election) moment m choisi; (of musician) sens m du rythme

tin [tɪn] n (metal) étain m; Br (can)

boîte *f*; **cake t.** moule *m* à gâteaux; **t. opener** ouvre-boîtes *m inv* ■ **tinfoil** *n* papier *m* aluminium

tinge [tɪndʒ] *n* pointe *f* ■ **tinged** *adj* **t. with sth** teinté de qch

tingle [tɪŋgəl] *vi* picoter

tinker [tɪŋkə(r)] *vi* **to t. (about** or **around) with sth** bricoler qch

tinkle [tɪŋkəl] *vi* tinter

tinned [tɪnd] *adj Br* **t. pears/salmon** poires *fpl*/saumon *m* en boîte; **t. food** conserves *fpl*

tinsel [tɪnsəl] *n* guirlandes *fpl* de Noël

tint [tɪnt] *n* teinte *f*; (for hair) rinçage *m* ■ **tinted** *adj* (paper, glass) teinté

tiny [taɪnɪ] (**-ier, -iest**) *adj* minuscule

tip¹ [tɪp] *n* (end) bout *m*; (pointed) pointe *f*

tip² [tɪp] **1** *n Br* (rubbish dump) décharge *f* **2** (*pt & pp* **-pp-**) *vt* (pour) déverser; **to t. sth up** or **over** renverser qch; **to t. sth out** (liquid, load) déverser qch (**into** dans) **3** *vi* **to t. (up** or **over)** (tilt) se renverser; (overturn) basculer

tip³ [tɪp] **1** *n* (money) pourboire *m*; (advice) conseil *m*; (information) tuyau *m* **2** (*pt & pp* **-pp-**) *vt* (waiter) donner un pourboire à; **to t. off** (police) prévenir

tipsy [tɪpsɪ] (**-ier, -iest**) *adj* (drunk) éméché, gai

tiptoe [tɪptəʊ] **1** *n* **on t.** sur la pointe des pieds **2** *vi* marcher sur la pointe des pieds; **to t. into/out of a room** entrer dans une pièce/sortir d'une pièce sur la pointe des pieds

tire¹ [taɪə(r)] **1** *vt* fatiguer; **to t. sb out** épuiser qn **2** *vi* se fatiguer ■ **tired** *adj* fatigué; **to be t. of sth/doing sth** en avoir assez de qch/de faire qch ■ **tiredness** *n* fatigue *f* ■ **tireless** *adj* infatigable ■ **tiresome** *adj* ennuyeux, -euse ■ **tiring** *adj* fatigant

tire² [taɪə(r)] *n Am* pneu *m* (*pl* pneus)

tissue [tɪʃuː] *n* (handkerchief) mouchoir *m* en papier; *Biol* tissu *m*; **t. paper** papier *m* de soie

titbit [tɪtbɪt] *n Br* (food) bon morceau *m*

titillate [tɪtɪleɪt] *vt* exciter

title [taɪtəl] **1** *n* (name, claim, in sport) titre *m*; **t. role** (in film, play) rôle-titre *m* **2** *vt* intituler

titter [tɪtə(r)] *vi* rire bêtement

TO [tə, *stressed* tuː] **1** *prep* (**a**) (towards) à; (until) jusqu'à; **give it to him/her** donne-le-lui; **to go to town** aller en ville; **to go to France/Portugal** aller en France/au Portugal; **to go to the butcher's** aller chez le boucher; **the road to London** la route de Londres; **the train to Paris** le train pour Paris; **kind/cruel to sb** gentil/cruel envers qn; **to my surprise** à ma grande surprise; **it's ten (minutes) to one** il est une heure moins dix; **ten to one** (proportion) dix contre un; **one person to a room** une personne par chambre

(**b**) (with infinitive) **to say/jump** dire/sauter; (in order) **to do sth** pour faire qch; **she tried to** elle a essayé

(**c**) (with adjective) **I'd be happy to do it** je serais heureux de le faire; **it's easy to do** c'est facile à faire

2 *adv* **to push the door to** fermer la porte; **to go** or **walk to and fro** aller et venir

toad [təʊd] *n* crapaud *m*

toadstool [təʊdstuːl] *n* champignon *m* vénéneux

toast¹ [təʊst] **1** *n* (bread) pain *m* grillé **2** *vt* (bread) faire griller ■ **toaster** *n* grille-pain *m inv*

toast² [təʊst] **1** *n* (drink) toast *m* **2** *vt* (person) porter un toast à; (success, event) arroser

tobacco [təbækəʊ] (*pl* **-os**) *n* tabac *m*; *Am* **t. store** (bureau *m* de) tabac ■ **tobacconist** [-kənɪst] *n* buraliste *mf*; *Br* **t.'s (shop)** (bureau *m* de) tabac

toboggan [təbɒgən] *n* luge *f*

today [tədeɪ] *adv* aujourd'hui

toddler [tɒdlə(r)] *n* enfant *mf* (en bas âge)

toe [təʊ] **1** *n* orteil *m* **2** *vt* **to t. the line** bien se tenir

toffee ['tɒfɪ] *n Br* caramel *m* (dur); **t. apple** pomme *f* d'amour

together [tə'geðə(r)] *adv* ensemble; *(at the same time)* en même temps

toil [tɔɪl] **1** *n* labeur *m* **2** *vi* travailler dur

toilet ['tɔɪlɪt] *n Br (room)* toilettes *fpl*; *(bowl, seat)* cuvette *f* des toilettes; *Br* **to go to the t.** aller aux toilettes; **t. paper** papier *m* hygiénique; **t. roll** rouleau *m* de papier hygiénique; *(paper)* papier *m* hygiénique ■ **toiletries** *npl* articles *mpl* de toilette

token ['təʊkən] **1** *n (for vending machine)* jeton *m*; *(symbol)* signe *m*; *Br* **book t.** chèque-livre *m* **2** *adj* symbolique

told [təʊld] **1** *pt & pp of* **tell 2** *adv* **all t.** *(taken together)* en tout

tolerable ['tɒlərəbəl] *adj (bearable)* tolérable; *(fairly good)* acceptable

tolerant ['tɒlərənt] *adj* tolérant (**of** à l'égard de) ■ **tolerance** *n* tolérance *f*

tolerate ['tɒləreɪt] *vt* tolérer

toll [təʊl] **1** *n* (**a**) *(fee)* péage *m*; **t. road/bridge** route *f*/pont *m* à péage (**b**) **the death t.** le nombre de morts; *Fig* **to take its t.** faire des dégâts **2** *vi (of bell)* sonner ■ **toll-free** *Am* **1** *adj* **t. number** ≃ numéro *m* vert **2** *adv (call)* gratuitement

tomato [*Br* tə'mɑːtəʊ, *Am* tə'meɪtəʊ] *(pl* **-oes**) *n* tomate *f*; **t. sauce** sauce *f* tomate

tomb [tuːm] *n* tombeau *m* ■ **tombstone** *n* pierre *f* tombale

tomorrow [tə'mɒrəʊ] *adv & n* demain *(m)*; **t. morning/evening** demain matin/soir; **the day after t.** après-demain

ton [tʌn] *n* tonne *f*; *Fam* **tons of** *(lots of)* des tonnes de

tone [təʊn] **1** *n* ton *m*; *(of telephone, radio)* tonalité *f*; *(of answering machine)* signal *m* sonore; *Br* **the engaged t.** *(on telephone)* la sonnerie 'occupé' **2** *vt* **to t. sth down** atténuer qch; **to t. up** *(muscles, skin)* tonifier

tongs [tɒŋz] *npl* pinces *fpl*; **sugar t.**

pince *f* à sucre; **curling t.** fer *m* à friser

tongue [tʌŋ] *n (in mouth, language)* langue *f*

tonic ['tɒnɪk] *n (medicine)* fortifiant *m*; **t. (water)** Schweppes® *m*; **gin and t.** gin-tonic *m*

tonight [tə'naɪt] *adv & n (this evening)* ce soir *(m)*; *(during the night)* cette nuit *(f)*

tonne [tʌn] *n (metric)* tonne *f*

tonsil ['tɒnsəl] *n* amygdale *f* ■ **tonsillitis** [-'laɪtɪs] *n* **to have t.** avoir une angine

too [tuː] *adv* (**a**) *(excessively)* trop; **t. tired to play** trop fatigué pour jouer; **t. much, t. many** trop; **t. much salt** trop de sel; **t. many people** trop de gens; **one t. many** un de trop (**b**) *(also)* aussi; *(moreover)* en plus

took [tʊk] *pt of* **take**

tool [tuːl] *n* outil *m*; **t. bag, t. kit** trousse *f* à outils

tooth [tuːθ] *(pl* **teeth**) *n* dent *f*; **t. decay** carie *f* dentaire ■ **toothache** *n* mal *m* de dents; **to have t.** avoir mal aux dents ■ **toothbrush** *n* brosse *f* à dents ■ **toothpaste** *n* dentifrice *m*

top¹ [tɒp] *n (of mountain, tower, tree)* sommet *m*; *(of wall, ladder, page)* haut *m*; *(of table, box, surface)* dessus *m*; *(of list)* tête *f*; *(of bottle, tube)* bouchon *m*; *(crown cap)* capsule *f*; *(of pen)* capuchon *m*; *(garment)* haut *m*; **(at the) t. of the class** le premier/la première de la classe; **on t.** dessus; *(in bus)* en haut; **on t. of** sur; *Fig (in addition to)* en plus de; **from t. to bottom** de fond en comble; *Fam* **over the t.** *(excessive)* exagéré

2 *adj (drawer, shelf)* du haut; *(step, layer)* dernier, -ère; *(upper)* supérieur; *(in rank, exam)* premier, -ère; *(chief)* principal; *(best)* meilleur; **on the t. floor** au dernier étage; **at t. speed** à toute vitesse; **t. hat** haut-de-forme *m* ■ **top-secret** *adj* top secret *inv* ■ **topsy-turvy** *adj & adv* sens dessus dessous [sɑːdsydsu]

top² [tɒp] (*pt & pp* **-pp-**) *vt* (*exceed*) dépasser; *Br* **to t. up** (*glass*) remplir (de nouveau); **topped with cream** nappé de crème ■ **topping** *n* (*of pizza*) garniture *f*

top³ [tɒp] *n* (*spinning*) **t.** toupie *f*

topic ['tɒpɪk] *n* sujet *m* ■ **topical** *adj* d'actualité

topple ['tɒpəl] *vi* **to t. (over)** tomber

torch [tɔːtʃ] *n Br* (*electric*) lampe *f* de poche; (*flame*) torche *f*

tore [tɔː(r)] *pt of* **tear¹**

torment 1 ['tɔːment] *n* supplice *m* **2** [tɔː'ment] *vt* tourmenter

torn [tɔːn] *pp of* **tear¹**

tornado [tɔː'neɪdəʊ] (*pl* **-oes**) *n* tornade *f*

torpedo [tɔː'piːdəʊ] **1** (*pl* **-oes**) *n* torpille *f* **2** *vt* torpiller

torrent ['tɒrənt] *n* torrent *m* ■ **torrential** [tə'renʃəl] *adj* **t. rain** pluie *f* torrentielle

tortoise ['tɔːtəs] *n* tortue *f*

tortuous ['tɔːtʃʊəs] *adj* tortueux, -euse

torture ['tɔːtʃə(r)] **1** *n* torture *f*; *Fig* **it's (sheer) t.!** quel supplice! **2** *vt* torturer

Tory ['tɔːrɪ] *Pol* **1** *n* tory *m* **2** *adj* tory *inv*

toss [tɒs] **1** *vt* (*throw*) lancer (**to** à); (*pancake*) faire sauter; **to t. sb (about)** (*of boat, vehicle*) ballotter qn; **to t. a coin** jouer à pile ou face **2** *vi* **to t. (about), to t. and turn** (*in bed*) se tourner et se retourner; **let's t. up, let's t. (up) for it** jouons-le à pile ou face

tot [tɒt] **1** *n* (*tiny*) **t.** tout-petit *m* **2** (*pt & pp* **-tt-**) *vt Fam* **to t. up** (*total*) additionner

total ['təʊtəl] **1** *adj* total; **the t. sales** le total des ventes **2** *n* total *m*; **in t.** au total **3** (*Br* **-ll-**, *Am* **-l-**) *vt* (*of sum*) s'élever à; **to t. (up)** (*find the total of*) totaliser; **that totals $9** ça fait 9 dollars en tout ■ **totally** *adv* totalement

totter ['tɒtə(r)] *vi* chanceler

touch [tʌtʃ] **1** *n* (*contact*) contact *m*; (*sense*) toucher *m*; (*of painter*) touche *f*; **a t. of** (*small amount*) une pointe de; **to have a t. of flu** être un peu

grippé; **to be/get in t. with sb** être/se mettre en contact avec qn

2 *vt* toucher; (*interfere with, eat*) toucher à

3 *vi* (*of lines, hands, ends*) se toucher; **don't t.!** ne touche pas! ■ **touchdown** *n* (*of aircraft*) atterrissage *m*; (*in American football*) but *m* ■ **touched** *adj* (*emotionally*) touché (**by** de) ■ **touching** *adj* (*moving*) touchant ■ **touchline** *n* ligne *f* de touche

► **touch down** *vi* (*of plane*) atterrir

► **touch on** *vt insep* aborder

► **touch up** *vt sep* (*photo*) retoucher

touchy ['tʌtʃɪ] (**-ier, -iest**) *adj* (*sensitive*) susceptible (**about** à propos de)

tough [tʌf] (**-er, -est**) *adj* (*strict, hard*) dur; (*sturdy*) solide ■ **toughen** *vt* (*body, person*) endurcir

toupee ['tuːpeɪ] *n* postiche *m*

tour [tʊə(r)] **1** *n* (*journey*) voyage *m*; (*visit*) visite *f*; (*by artiste, team*) tournée *f*; (*on bicycle, on foot*) randonnée *f*; **to go on t.** (*of artiste, team*) être en tournée; (**package**) **t.** voyage *m* organisé; **t. guide** guide *mf*; **t. operator** voyagiste *m* **2** *vt* visiter; (*of artiste, team*) être en tournée en/dans

tourism ['tʊərɪzəm] *n* tourisme *m* ■ **tourist 1** *n* touriste *mf* **2** *adj* (*region*) touristique; **t. office** syndicat *m* d'initiative

tournament ['tʊənəmənt] *n* (*in sport*) & *Hist* tournoi *m*

tout [taʊt] **1** *n* racoleur, -euse *mf* **2** *vi* **to t. for trade** racoler des clients

tow [təʊ] *vt* remorquer; **to t. a car away** (*of police*) mettre une voiture à la fourrière

toward(s) [tə'wɔːd(z)] *prep* vers; (*of feelings*) envers; **cruel t. sb** cruel envers qn

towel ['taʊəl] *n* serviette *f* (de toilette); (**kitchen**) **t.** (*paper*) essuie-tout *m inv*

tower ['taʊə(r)] **1** *n* tour *f*; *Br* **t. block** tour **2** *vi* **to t. over sb/sth** dominer qn/qch

town [taʊn] *n* ville *f*; **to go into t.** aller en ville; **t. centre** centre-ville *m*; *Br* **t.**

council conseil *m* municipal; *Br* **t. hall** mairie *f*; *Br* **t. planning** urbanisme *m*

toxic ['tɒksɪk] *adj* toxique

toy [tɔɪ] **1** *n* jouet *m*; **t. shop** magasin *m* de jouets **2** *adj* (*gun*) d'enfant; (*car, train*) miniature **3** *vi* **to t. with an idea** caresser une idée

trace [treɪs] **1** *n* trace *f*; **without t.** sans laisser de traces **2** *vt* (*diagram, picture*) tracer; (*person*) retrouver la trace de; **to t. sth back to…** faire remonter qch à… ■ **tracing** *n* (*drawing*) calque *m*; **t. paper** papier-calque *m*

track [træk] **1** *n* (*mark*) trace *f*; (*trail*) piste *f*; (*path*) chemin *m*, piste *f*; (*for trains*) voie *f*; (*of record, CD, tape*) morceau *m*; *Am* (*racetrack*) champ *m* de courses; **to keep t. of sth** surveiller qch; **to lose t. of** (*friend*) perdre de vue; **to be on the right t.** être sur la bonne voie; **t. event** (*in athletics*) épreuve *f* sur piste; *Fig* **t. record** passé *m*

2 *vt* **to t. (down)** (*find*) retrouver ■ **tracksuit** *n* survêtement *m*

tractor ['træktə(r)] *n* tracteur *m*

trade [treɪd] **1** *n* commerce *m*; (*job*) métier *m*; (*exchange*) échange *m*

2 *adj* (*fair, balance, route*) commercial; (*price*) de (demi-)gros; (*secret*) de fabrication; (*barrier*) douanier, -ère; *Br* **t. union** syndicat *m*

3 *vt* (*exchange*) échanger (**for** contre); **to t. sth in** (*old article*) faire reprendre qch

4 *vi* faire du commerce (**with** avec); **to t. in** (*sugar*) faire le commerce de ■ **trademark** *n* marque *f* de fabrique ■ **trader** *n* *Br* (*shopkeeper*) commerçant, -e *mf*; (*on Stock Exchange*) opérateur, -trice *mf*; *Br* **street t.** vendeur, -euse *mf* de rue ■ **tradesman** (*pl* -men) *n* *Br* commerçant *m*

trading ['treɪdɪŋ] **1** *n* commerce *m* **2** *adj* (*port, debts, activity*) commercial

tradition [trə'dɪʃən] *n* tradition *f* ■ **traditional** *adj* traditionnel, -elle

traffic ['træfɪk] **1** *n* (**a**) (*on road*) circulation *f*; (*air, sea, rail*) trafic *m*; *Am* **t.**

circle rond-point *m*; **t. island** refuge *m* (pour piétons); **t. jam** embouteillage *m* (**b**) *Pej* (*trade*) trafic *m* (**in** de) **2** (*pt & pp* -**ck**-) *vi* trafiquer (**in** de) ■ **trafficker** *n* *Pej* trafiquant, -e *mf*

tragedy ['trædʒədɪ] (*pl* -**ies**) *n* tragédie *f* ■ **tragic** *adj* tragique

trail [treɪl] **1** *n* (*of smoke, blood, powder*) traînée *f*; (*path*) piste *f*, sentier *m*

2 *vt* (*drag*) traîner; (*follow*) suivre

3 *vi* (*drag*) traîner; (*of plant*) ramper; (*move slowly*) se traîner; **to be trailing (behind)** (*in sporting contest*) être mené ■ **trailer** *n* (**a**) (*for car*) remorque *f*; *Am* (*caravan*) caravane *f*; *Am* (*camper*) camping-car *m* (**b**) (*advertisement for film*) bande-annonce *f*

train [treɪn] **1** *n* (**a**) (*engine, transport*) train *m*; (*underground*) rame *f*; **t. set** (*toy*) petit train *m* (**b**) (*procession*) file *f*; (*of events*) suite *f*; (*of dress*) traîne *f*; **my t. of thought** le fil de ma pensée

2 *vt* (*person*) former (**to do** à faire); (*sportsman*) entraîner (*animal*) dresser (**to do** à faire); **to t. oneself to do sth** s'entraîner à faire qch; **to t. sth on sb/sth** (*aim*) braquer qch sur qn/qch

3 *vi* (*of sportsman*) s'entraîner; **to t. as a nurse** faire une formation d'infirmière ■ **trained** *adj* (*skilled*) qualifié; (*nurse, engineer*) diplômé ■ **training** *n* formation *f*; (*in sport*) entraînement *m*; (*of animal*) dressage *m*; **to be in t.** (*of sportsman*) s'entraîner

trainee [treɪ'niː] *n & adj* stagiaire (*mf*)

trainer ['treɪnə(r)] *n* (*of athlete, racehorse*) entraîneur *m*; (*of animals*) dresseur *m*; *Br* **trainers** (*shoes*) chaussures *fpl* de sport

traipse [treɪps] *vi* *Fam* **to t. around** (*tiredly*) traîner les pieds; (*wander*) se balader

trait [treɪt] *n* trait *m* (**de** caractère)

traitor ['treɪtə(r)] *n* traître *m*, traîtresse *f*

tram [træm] *n* tram(way) *m*

tramp [træmp] **1** n Br (vagrant) clochard, -e mf **2** vi marcher d'un pas lourd

trample ['træmpəl] vti to t. sth (underfoot), to t. on sth piétiner qch

trampoline [træmpə'li:n] n trampoline m

trance [trɑ:ns] n to be in a t. être en transe

tranquillizer ['træŋkwɪlaɪzə(r)] (Am **tranquilizer**) n tranquillisant m

transaction [træn'zækʃən] n opération f, transaction f

transatlantic [trænzət'læntɪk] adj transatlantique

transcend [træn'send] vt transcender

transfer 1 ['trænsfɜ:(r)] n transfert m (to à); (of political power) passation f; Br (picture, design) décalcomanie f; **credit t.** virement m bancaire

2 [træns'fɜ:(r)] (pt & pp -rr-) vt transférer (to à); (political power) faire passer (to à)

3 [træns'fɜ:(r)] vi être transféré (to à)

transform [træns'fɔ:m] vt transformer (into en) ■ **transformation** [-fə'meɪʃən] n transformation f ■ **transformer** n El transformateur m

transfusion [træns'fju:ʒən] n (blood) t. transfusion f (sanguine)

transit ['trænzɪt] n **in t.** en transit

transition [træn'zɪʃən] n transition f

transitional [træn'zɪʃənəl] adj de transition

transitive ['trænsɪtɪv] adj (verb) transitif

translate [trænz'leɪt] vt traduire (from de; into en) ■ **translation** n traduction f ■ **translator** n traducteur, -trice mf

transmit [trænz'mɪt] **1** (pt & pp -tt-) vt transmettre **2** vti (broadcast) émettre ■ **transmission** n transmission f; (broadcast) émission f ■ **transmitter** n (for radio, TV) émetteur m

transparent [træn'spærənt] adj transparent

transpire [træn'spaɪə(r)] vi Fam (happen) arriver; **it transpired that…** il s'est avéré que…

transplant 1 ['trænsplɑ:nt] n (surgical) greffe f, transplantation f **2** [træns-'plɑ:nt] vt transplanter

transport 1 ['trænspɔ:t] n transport m (of de); Br t. **café** routier m (restaurant) **2** [træn'spɔ:t] vt transporter

transpose [træn'spəʊz] vt transposer

transvestite [trænz'vestaɪt] n travesti m

trap [træp] **1** n piège m **2** (pt & pp -pp-) vt prendre au piège; **to t. one's finger** se coincer le doigt (in dans) ■ **trapdoor** n trappe f

trappings ['træpɪŋz] npl signes mpl extérieurs

trash [træʃ] n (nonsense) bêtises fpl; (junk) bric-à-brac m inv; Am (waste) ordures fpl; (riffraff) racaille f; Am **t. can** poubelle f ■ **trashy** (-ier, -iest) adj Fam à la noix

trauma ['trɔ:mə] n traumatisme m ■ **traumatic** [-'mætɪk] adj traumatisant ■ **traumatize** vt traumatiser

travel ['trævəl] **1** n voyage m; **t. agent** agent m de voyages; **t. insurance** assurance f voyage; **t. sickness** (in car) mal m de la route; (in aircraft) mal m de l'air

2 (Br -ll-, Am -l-) vt (country, distance, road) parcourir

3 vi (of person) voyager; (of vehicle, light, sound) se déplacer ■ **travelling** (Am **traveling**) **1** n voyages mpl **2** adj (bag, clothes) de voyage; (expenses) de déplacement; (musician, circus) ambulant

traveller ['trævələ(r)] (Am **traveler**) n voyageur, -euse mf; **t.'s cheque** chèque m de voyage

travesty ['trævəstɪ] (pl -ies) n parodie f; **a t. of justice** un simulacre de justice

tray [treɪ] n plateau m; (in office) corbeille f; **baking t.** plaque f de four

treacherous ['tretʃərəs] adj (road, conditions) très dangereux, -euse; (person, action) traître ■ **treachery** (pl -ies) n traîtrise f

treacle ['tri:kəl] n Br mélasse f

tread [tred] **1** n (footstep) pas m; (step of stairs) marche f; (of tyre) chape f **2** (pt trod, pp **trodden**) vt **to t. sth into a carpet** étaler qch sur un tapis (avec ses chaussures) **3** vi (walk) marcher (on sur)

treason ['tri:zən] n trahison f

treasure ['treʒə(r)] **1** n trésor m; **t. hunt** chasse f au trésor **2** vt (value) tenir beaucoup à ■ **treasurer** n trésorier, -ère mf

treat [tri:t] **1** n (pleasure) plaisir m; (gift) cadeau m; **it's my t.** c'est moi qui régale **2** vt (person, illness, product) traiter; **to t. sb to sth** offrir qch à qn

treatment ['tri:tmənt] n traitement m

treaty ['tri:ti] (pl -ies) n (international) traité m

treble ['trebəl] **1** adj triple **2** n le triple; **it's t. the price** c'est le triple du prix **3** vti tripler

tree [tri:] n arbre m; **t. trunk** tronc m d'arbre

trek [trek] **1** n (long walk) randonnée f **2** (pt & pp -kk-) vi faire de la randonnée

tremble ['trembəl] vi trembler (**with** de)

tremendous [trə'mendəs] adj (huge) énorme; (dreadful) terrible; (wonderful) formidable

trench [trentʃ] n tranchée f

trend [trend] n tendance f (**towards** à); (fashion) mode f ■ **trendy** (**-ier, -iest**) adj Br Fam branché

trespass ['trespəs] vi = s'introduire illégalement dans une propriété privée; **'no trespassing'** 'entrée interdite'

trial ['traɪəl] **1** n (in law) procès m; (test) essai m; (ordeal) épreuve f; **to go** or **be on t., to stand t.** passer en jugement; **by t. and error** par tâtonnements **2** adj (period, flight, offer) d'essai

triangle ['traɪæŋgəl] n triangle m ■ **triangular** [-'æŋgjʊlə(r)] adj triangulaire

tribe [traɪb] n tribu f

tribunal [traɪ'bju:nəl] n tribunal m

tribute ['trɪbju:t] n hommage m; **to pay t. to** rendre hommage à

trick [trɪk] **1** n (joke, deception, of conjurer) tour m; (clever method) astuce f; (in card game) pli m; **to play a t. on sb** jouer un tour à qn **2** vt (deceive) duper; **to t. sb into doing sth** amener qn à faire qch par la ruse ■ **trickery** n ruse f

trickle ['trɪkəl] **1** n (of liquid) filet m **2** vi (of liquid) couler goutte à goutte; Fig **to t. in** (of letters, people) arriver en petit nombre

tricky ['trɪki] (**-ier, -iest**) adj (problem) délicat

tricycle ['traɪsɪkəl] n tricycle m

trifle ['traɪfəl] **1** n (insignificant thing) bagatelle f; Br (dessert) = dessert où alternent génoise, fruits en gelée et crème anglaise **2** adv **a t. wide** un tantinet trop large **3** vi **to t. with** plaisanter avec ■ **trifling** adj insignifiant

trigger ['trɪgə(r)] **1** n (of gun) détente f **2** vt **to t. sth (off)** déclencher qch

trilogy ['trɪlədʒi] (pl -ies) n trilogie f

trim [trɪm] **1** (**trimmer, trimmest**) adj (neat) soigné; (slim) svelte **2** n **to give sb's hair a t.** faire une coupe d'entretien à qn **3** (pt & pp -mm-) vt couper (un peu); **to t. sth with sth** orner qch de qch ■ **trimmings** npl (on clothes) garniture f; (of meal) accompagnements mpl traditionnels

trinket ['trɪŋkɪt] n babiole f

trio ['tri:əʊ] (pl -os) n trio m

trip [trɪp] **1** n (journey) voyage m; (outing) excursion f **2** (pt & pp -pp-) vt **to t. sb up** faire trébucher qn **3** vi **to t.** (**over** or **up**) trébucher; **to t. over sth** trébucher sur qch

triple ['trɪpəl] **1** adj triple **2** vti tripler ■ **triplets** npl (children) triplés, -es mfpl

triplicate ['trɪplɪkət] n **in t.** en trois exemplaires

tripod ['traɪpɒd] n trépied m

triumph ['traɪəmf] **1** n triomphe m (**over** sur) **2** vi triompher (**over** de) ■ **triumphant** [traɪ'ʌmfənt] adj triomphant; (success, welcome, return) triomphal

trivial ['trɪvɪəl] *adj (unimportant)* insignifiant; *(trite)* banal *(mpl* -als)

trod [trɒd] *pt of* **tread**

trodden ['trɒdən] *pp of* **tread**

trolley ['trɒlɪ] *(pl* -eys*) n Br* chariot *m*; *Br* **(tea) t.** table *f* roulante; *Am* **t. (car)** tramway *m*

trombone [trɒm'bəʊn] *n* trombone *m*

troop [tru:p] **1** *n* bande *f; (of soldiers)* troupe *f;* **the troops** *(soldiers)* les troupes *fpl* **2** *vi* **to t. in/out** entrer/sortir en groupe

trophy ['trəʊfɪ] *(pl* -ies*) n* trophée *m*

tropics ['trɒpɪks] *n* **in the tropics** sous les tropiques ■ **tropical** *adj* tropical

trot [trɒt] **1** *n* trot *m; Fam* **on the t.** *(consecutively)* de suite **2** *(pt & pp* -tt-*) vt Fam* **to t. sth out** débiter qch **3** *vi (of horse)* trotter

trouble ['trʌbəl] **1** *n (difficulty)* ennui *m; (inconvenience)* problème *m; (social unrest, illness)* trouble *m;* **to be in t.** avoir des ennuis; **to get into t.** s'attirer des ennuis; **to have t. doing sth** avoir du mal à faire qch; **to go to the t. of doing sth** se donner la peine de faire qch; **it's no t.** pas de problème **2** *vt (inconvenience)* déranger; *(worry)* inquiéter

troublemaker ['trʌbəlmeɪkə(r)] *n (in school)* élément *m* perturbateur; *(political)* fauteur *m* de troubles

troublesome ['trʌbəlsəm] *adj* pénible

trough [trɒf] *n (for drinking)* abreuvoir *m; (for feeding)* auge *f*

troupe [tru:p] *n (of actors)* troupe *f*

trousers ['traʊzəz] *npl Br* pantalon *m;* **a pair of t., some t.** un pantalon; **short t.** culottes *fpl* courtes

trout [traʊt] *n inv* truite *f*

trowel ['traʊəl] *n (for cement or plaster)* truelle *f; (for plants)* déplantoir *m*

truant ['tru:ənt] *n* **to play t.** faire l'école buissonnière

truce [tru:s] *n* Mil trêve *f*

truck [trʌk] *n (lorry)* camion *m;* **t. driver** camionneur *m; Am* **t. stop** *(restaurant)* routier *m* ■ **trucker** *n Am* camionneur *m*

trudge [trʌdʒ] *vi* marcher péniblement

true [tru:] *(-er, -est) adj* vrai; *(genuine)* véritable; *(accurate)* exact; *(faithful)* fidèle **(to** à**)** ■ **truly** *adv* vraiment; **well and t.** bel et bien

trump [trʌmp] *n* atout *m*

trumpet ['trʌmpɪt] *n* trompette *f*

truncheon ['trʌntʃən] *n Br* matraque *f*

trundle ['trʌndəl] *vti* **to t. along** rouler bruyamment

trunk [trʌŋk] *n (of tree, body)* tronc *m; (of elephant)* trompe *f; (case)* malle *f; Am (of vehicle)* coffre *m;* **trunks** *(for swimming)* slip *m* de bain

trust [trʌst] **1** *n (faith)* confiance *f* **(in** en**) 2** *vt (believe in)* faire confiance à; **to t. sb with sth, to t. sth to sb** confier qch à qn; **I t. that...** j'espère que... **3** *vi* **to t. in sb** faire confiance à qn ■ **trusted** *adj (method)* éprouvé

trustworthy ['trʌstwɜ:ðɪ] *adj* digne de confiance

truth [tru:θ] *(pl* -s [tru:ðz]*) n* vérité *f;* **there's some t. in...** il y a du vrai dans... ■ **truthful** *adj (story)* véridique; *(person)* sincère

try [traɪ] **1** *(pl* -ies*) n (attempt, in rugby)* essai *m;* **to have a t. at doing sth** essayer de faire qch; **it's worth a t.** ça vaut la peine d'essayer

2 *(pt & pp* -ied*) vt (attempt, sample)* essayer; *(food, drink)* goûter à; *(in law court)* juger **(for** pour**); to t. doing** *or* **to do sth** essayer de faire qch

3 *vi* essayer ■ **trying** *adj* difficile

▸ **try on** *vt sep (clothes, shoes)* essayer

▸ **try out** *vt sep (car, method, recipe)* essayer; *(person)* mettre à l'essai

T-shirt ['ti:ʃɜ:t] *n* tee-shirt *m*

tub [tʌb] *n (basin)* baquet *m; (bath)* baignoire *f; Br (for ice cream)* pot *m; Br (for flower, bush)* bac *m*

tuba ['tju:bə] *n Mus* tuba *m*

tube [tju:b] *n* tube *m; (of tyre)* chambre *f* à air; *Br Fam* **the t.** *(underground railway)* le métro

tuberculosis [tju:bɜ:kjʊ'ləʊsɪs] *n Med* tuberculose *f*

tuck [tʌk] **1** *vt (put)* mettre; **to t. sth away** *(put)* ranger qch; *(hide)* cacher qch; **to t. in** *(shirt, blanket)* rentrer; *(child)* border **2** *vi Br Fam* **to t. in** *(start eating)* attaquer

Tuesday ['tju:zdeɪ] *n* mardi *m*

tuft [tʌft] *n* touffe *f*

tug [tʌg] **1** *n* **to give sth a t.** tirer sur qch **2** *(pt & pp* **-gg-***) vt (pull)* tirer sur **3** *vi* tirer (**at** *or* **on** sur)

tuition [tju:'ɪʃən] *n (lessons)* cours *mpl; (fee)* frais *mpl* de scolarité

tulip ['tju:lɪp] *n* tulipe *f*

tumble ['tʌmbəl] **1** *n (fall)* chute *f; Br* **t. dryer** *or* **drier** sèche-linge *m inv* **2** *vi (of person)* faire une chute; *Fig (of prices)* chuter

tumbler ['tʌmblə(r)] *n (glass)* verre *m* droit

tummy ['tʌmɪ] *n Fam* ventre *m*

tumour ['tju:mə(r)] *(Am* **tumor***) n* tumeur *f*

tuna ['tju:nə] *n* **t. (fish)** thon *m*

tune [tju:n] **1** *n (melody)* air *m;* **in t.** *(instrument)* accordé; **out of t.** *(instrument)* désaccordé; **to be** *or* **sing in t./out of t.** chanter juste/faux; *Fig* **to be in t. with sb/sth** être en harmonie avec qn/qch

    2 *vt* **to t. (up)** *(instrument)* accorder; *(engine)* régler

    3 *vi* **to t. in** brancher son poste (**to** sur)

tuner ['tju:nə(r)] *n (on TV, radio)* tuner *m*

tunic ['tju:nɪk] *n* tunique *f*

Tunisia [tju:'nɪzɪə] *n* la Tunisie

tunnel ['tʌnəl] **1** *n* tunnel *m* **2** *(Br* **-ll-***, Am* **-l-***) vi* creuser un tunnel (**into** dans)

turban ['tɜ:bən] *n* turban *m*

turbulence ['tɜ:bjʊləns] *n* turbulence *f*

turf [tɜ:f] *n (grass)* gazon *m*

Turkey ['tɜ:kɪ] *n* la Turquie ■ **Turk** *n* Turc *m,* Turque *f* ■ **Turkish** *adj* turc *(f* turque); **T. delight** des loukoums *mpl* **2** *n (language)* turc *m*

turkey ['tɜ:kɪ] *n (pl* **-eys***) n (bird)* dinde *f*

turmoil ['tɜ:mɔɪl] *n* **to be in t.** *(of person)* être dans tous ses états; *(of country)* être en ébullition

turn [tɜ:n] **1** *n (of wheel, in game, queue)* tour *m; (in road)* tournant *m; (of events)* tournure *f; Br Fam (fit)* crise *f;* **to take turns** se relayer; **in t.** à tour de rôle; **it's your t. (to play)** c'est à toi (de jouer); **the t. of the century** le tournant du siècle; **t. of phrase** tournure de phrase

    2 *vt* tourner; *(mechanically)* faire tourner; *(mattress, pancake)* retourner; **to t. sth into sth** changer qn/qch en qn/qch; **to t. sth red/black** rougir/noircir qch; **to t. sth on sb** *(aim)* braquer qch sur qn; **she has turned twenty** elle a vingt ans passés

    3 *vi (of wheel, driver)* tourner; *(of person)* se retourner; **to t. red/black** rougir/noircir; **to t. nasty** *(of person)* devenir méchant; *(of situation)* mal tourner; **to t. to sb** se tourner vers qn; **to t. into sb/sth** devenir qn/qch; **to t. against sb** se retourner contre qn ■ **turn-off** *n (on road)* sortie *f* ■ **turnout** *n (people)* assistance *f; (at polls)* participation *f* ■ **turnover** *n Com (sales)* chiffre *m* d'affaires; *(of stock)* rotation *f; (of staff)* renouvellement *m* ■ **turnup** *n Br (on trousers)* revers *m*

▸ **turn around** *vi (of person)* se retourner

▸ **turn away 1** *vt sep (eyes)* détourner (**from** de); *(person)* refuser **2** *vi* se détourner

▸ **turn back 1** *vt sep (sheets)* rabattre; *(clock)* retarder **2** *vi (return)* faire demi-tour

▸ **turn down** *vt sep (gas, radio)* baisser; *(fold down)* rabattre; *(refuse)* rejeter

▸ **turn in 1** *vt sep (person)* livrer à la police **2** *vi Fam (go to bed)* aller au pieu

▸ **turn off 1** *vt sep (light, radio)* éteindre; *(tap)* fermer; *(machine)* arrêter; *Fam* **to t. sb off** dégoûter qn **2** *vi*

(leave road) sortir
▶ **turn on 1** *vt sep (light, radio)* allumer; *(tap)* ouvrir; *(machine)* mettre en marche; *Fam* **to t. sb on** *(sexually)* exciter qn **2** *vi* **to t. on sb** *(attack)* attaquer qn
▶ **turn out 1** *vt sep (light)* éteindre; *(pocket, box)* vider; *(produce)* produire **2** *vi (appear, attend)* se déplacer; **it turns out that...** il s'avère que...; **she turned out to be...** elle s'est révélée être...
▶ **turn over 1** *vt sep (page)* tourner **2** *vi (of person)* se retourner; *(of car)* faire un tonneau
▶ **turn round 1** *vt sep (head)* tourner; *(object)* retourner; *(situation)* renverser **2** *vi (of person)* se retourner; *(in vehicle)* faire demi-tour
▶ **turn up 1** *vt sep (radio, heat)* mettre plus fort; *(collar)* remonter **2** *vi (arrive)* arriver; *(be found)* être retrouvé

turning ['tɜːnɪŋ] *n Br (street)* petite rue *f*; *(bend in road)* tournant *m*; *Fig* **t. point** tournant *m*
turnip ['tɜːnɪp] *n* navet *m*
turnpike ['tɜːnpaɪk] *n Am* autoroute *f* à péage
turnstile ['tɜːnstaɪl] *n* tourniquet *m*
turntable ['tɜːnteɪbəl] *n* platine *f*
turquoise ['tɜːkwɔɪz] *adj* turquoise *inv*
turret ['tʌrɪt] *n* tourelle *f*
turtle ['tɜːtəl] *n Br* tortue *f* de mer; *Am* tortue *f*
tusk [tʌsk] *n* défense *f* (dent)
tussle ['tʌsəl] *n* bagarre *f*
tutor ['tjuːtə(r)] **1** *n* professeur *m* particulier; *(in British university)* directeur, -trice *mf* d'études **2** *vt* donner des cours particuliers à ■ **tutorial** [-'tɔːrɪəl] *n Univ* ≃ travaux *mpl* dirigés
tuxedo [tʌk'siːdəʊ] *(pl* **-os)** *n Am* smoking *m*
TV [tiː'viː] *n* télé *f*; **on TV** à la télé
tweed [twiːd] *n* tweed *m*; **t. jacket** veste *f* en tweed
tweezers ['twiːzəz] *npl* pince *f* à épiler
twelve [twelv] *adj & n* douze *(m)*

■ **twelfth** *adj & n* douzième *(mf)*
twenty ['twentɪ] *adj & n* vingt *(m)*
■ **twentieth** *adj & n* vingtième *(mf)*
twice [twaɪs] *adv* deux fois; **t. as heavy (as)** deux fois plus lourd (que); **t. a month, t. monthly** deux fois par mois
twiddle ['twɪdəl] *vti* **to t. (with) sth** tripoter qch; **to t. one's thumbs** se tourner les pouces
twig[1] [twɪg] *n (of branch)* brindille *f*
twig[2] [twɪg] *(pt & pp* **-gg-)** *vti Br Fam* piger
twilight ['twaɪlaɪt] *n* crépuscule *m*
twin [twɪn] **1** *n* jumeau *m*, jumelle *f*; **t. brother** frère *m* jumeau; **t. sister** sœur *f* jumelle; **t. beds** lits *mpl* jumeaux; **t. town** ville *f* jumelée **2** *(pt & pp* **-nn-)** *vt (town)* jumeler
twine [twaɪn] **1** *n (string)* ficelle *f* **2** *vi (twist)* s'enrouler (**round** autour de)
twinge [twɪndʒ] *n* **a t. (of pain)** un élancement; **a t. of remorse** un peu de remords
twinkle ['twɪŋkəl] *vi (of star)* scintiller; *(of eye)* pétiller
twirl [twɜːl] **1** *vt* faire tournoyer; *(moustache)* tortiller **2** *vi* tournoyer
twist [twɪst] **1** *n (action)* tour *m*; *(bend)* tortillement *m*; *Fig (in story)* tour *m* inattendu
2 *vt (wire, arm)* tordre; *(roll)* enrouler (**round** autour de); **to t. one's ankle** se tordre la cheville; *Fig* **to t. sb's arm** forcer la main à qn; **to t. sth off** *(lid)* dévisser qch
3 *vi (wind)* s'entortiller (**round sth** autour de qch); *(of road, river)* serpenter ■ **twisted** *adj (person, mind, logic)* tordu
twit [twɪt] *n Br Fam* andouille *f*
twitch [twɪtʃ] **1** *n (nervous)* tic *m* **2** *vi (of person)* avoir un tic; *(of muscle)* se contracter nerveusement
twitter ['twɪtə(r)] *vi (of bird)* pépier
two [tuː] *adj & n* deux *(m)* ■ **two-dimensional** *adj* à deux dimensions ■ **two-faced** *adj Fig* hypocrite ■ **two-piece** *adj (suit, swimsuit)* deux-pièces ■ **two-seater** *n (car)* voiture *f* à deux

places

twofold ['tu:fəʊld] **1** *adj* double **2** *adv* **to increase t.** doubler

twosome ['tu:səm] *n* couple *m*

tycoon [taɪ'ku:n] *n* magnat *m*

type¹ [taɪp] *n* (**a**) *(sort)* genre *m*, type *m* (**b**) *(print)* caractères *mpl*; **in large t.** en gros caractères

type² [taɪp] **1** *vti (write)* taper (à la machine) **2** *vt* **to t. sth in** *(on computer)* entrer qch au clavier; **to t. sth out** *(letter)* taper qch ■ **typewriter** *n* machine *f* à écrire ■ **typewritten** *adj* dactylographié ■ **typing** *n* dactylographie *f*; **t. error** faute *f* de frappe ■ **typist** *n* dactylo *mf*

typhoid ['taɪfɔɪd] *n Med* typhoïde *f*

typhoon [taɪ'fu:n] *n* typhon *m*

typical ['tɪpɪkəl] *adj* typique (**of** de)

tyrant ['taɪrənt] *n* tyran *m*

tyre ['taɪə(r)] *n Br* pneu *m* (*pl* pneus)

Uu

U, u [ju:] *n (letter)* U, u *m inv*

ugh [ʌx] *exclam* berk!

ugly [ˈʌglɪ] (**-ier, -iest**) *adj* laid

UK [juːˈkeɪ] *(abbr* United Kingdom) *n* **the UK** le Royaume-Uni

ulcer [ˈʌlsə(r)] *n* ulcère *m*

ulterior [ʌlˈtɪərɪə(r)] *adj* **u. motive** arrière-pensée *f*

ultimate [ˈʌltɪmət] *adj (last)* final; *(supreme, best)* absolu ▪ **ultimately** *adv (finally)* finalement; *(basically)* en fin de compte

ultimatum [ʌltɪˈmeɪtəm] *n* ultimatum *m*

ultra- [ˈʌltrə] *pref* ultra-

ultraviolet [ʌltrəˈvaɪələt] *adj* ultraviolet, -ette

umbrella [ʌmˈbrelə] *n* parapluie *m*

umpire [ˈʌmpaɪə(r)] *n* arbitre *m*

umpteen [ʌmpˈtiːn] *adj Fam* **u. times** je ne sais combien de fois ▪ **umpteenth** *adj Fam* énième

UN [juːˈen] *(abbr* United Nations) *n* **the UN** les Nations *fpl* unies

unable [ʌnˈeɪbəl] *adj* **to be u. to do sth** être incapable de faire qch

unabridged [ʌnəˈbrɪdʒd] *adj* intégral

unacceptable [ʌnəkˈseptəbəl] *adj* inacceptable

unaccompanied [ʌnəˈkʌmpənɪd] *adj (person)* non accompagné; *(singing)* sans accompagnement

unaccustomed [ʌnəˈkʌstəmd] *adj* inaccoutumé; **to be u. to sth/to doing sth** ne pas être habitué à qch/à faire qch

unaided [ʌnˈeɪdɪd] *adv* sans aide

unanimous [juːˈnænɪməs] *adj* unanime ▪ **unanimously** *adv* à l'unanimité

unappetizing [ʌnˈæpɪtaɪzɪŋ] *adj* peu appétissant

unarmed [ʌnˈɑːmd] *adj* non armé

unashamedly [ʌnəˈʃeɪmədlɪ] *adv* sans aucune honte

unassuming [ʌnəˈsjuːmɪŋ] *adj* sans prétention

unattached [ʌnəˈtætʃt] *adj (without partner)* sans attaches

unattainable [ʌnəˈteɪnəbəl] *adj* inaccessible

unattended [ʌnəˈtendɪd] *adj* **to leave sb/sth u.** laisser qn/qch sans surveillance

unattractive [ʌnəˈtræktɪv] *adj* peu attrayant

unauthorized [ʌnˈɔːθəraɪzd] *adj* non autorisé

unavailable [ʌnəˈveɪləbəl] *adj* **to be u.** ne pas être disponible

unavoidable [ʌnəˈvɔɪdəbəl] *adj* inévitable

unaware [ʌnəˈweə(r)] *adj* **to be u. of sth** ignorer qch; **to be u. that…** ignorer que… ▪ **unawares** *adv* **to catch sb u.** prendre qn au dépourvu

unbalanced [ʌnˈbælənst] *adj (mind, person)* instable

unbearable [ʌnˈbeərəbəl] *adj* insupportable

unbeatable [ʌnˈbiːtəbəl] *adj* imbattable

unbeaten [ʌnˈbiːtən] *adj (player)* invaincu; *(record)* jamais battu

unbelievable [ʌnbɪˈliːvəbəl] *adj* incroyable

unbias(s)ed [ʌnˈbaɪəst] *adj* impartial

unblock [ʌnˈblɒk] *vt (sink, pipe)* déboucher

unbolt [ʌnˈbəʊlt] *vt (door)* déverrouiller

unborn [ʌnˈbɔːn] *adj* u. child enfant *mf* à naître

unbreakable [ʌnˈbreɪkəbəl] *adj* incassable ■ **unbroken** *adj (intact)* intact; *(continuous)* continu; *(record)* jamais battu

unbutton [ʌnˈbʌtən] *vt* déboutonner

uncalled-for [ʌnˈkɔːldfɔː(r)] *adj* déplacé

uncanny [ʌnˈkænɪ] (-ier, -iest) *adj* étrange

uncertain [ʌnˈsɜːtən] *adj* incertain; **to be u. about sth** ne pas être certain de qch; **it's u. whether** *or* **that...** il n'est pas certain que... (+ *subjunctive*) ■ **uncertainty** *(pl* -ies) *n* incertitude *f*

unchanged [ʌnˈtʃeɪndʒd] *adj* inchangé ■ **unchanging** *adj* immuable

unclaimed [ʌnˈkleɪmd] *adj (luggage)* non réclamé

uncle [ˈʌŋkəl] *n* oncle *m*

unclear [ʌnˈklɪə(r)] *adj* vague; *(result)* incertain; **it's u. whether...** on ne sait pas très bien si...

uncomfortable [ʌnˈkʌmftəbəl] *adj* inconfortable; *(heat, experience)* désagréable; **to feel u.** *(physically)* ne pas être à l'aise; *(ill at ease)* être mal à l'aise

uncommon [ʌnˈkɒmən] *adj* peu commun

uncompromising [ʌnˈkɒmprəmaɪzɪŋ] *adj* intransigeant

unconditional [ʌnkənˈdɪʃənəl] *adj* sans condition

unconfirmed [ʌnkənˈfɜːmd] *adj* non confirmé

unconnected [ʌnkəˈnektɪd] *adj* sans lien

unconscious [ʌnˈkɒnʃəs] **1** *adj (person)* sans connaissance; *(desire)* inconscient; **to be u. of sth** ne pas avoir conscience de qch **2** *n* **the u.**

l'inconscient *m* ■ **unconsciously** *adv* inconsciemment

uncontrollable [ʌnkənˈtrəʊləbəl] *adj* incontrôlable

unconventional [ʌnkənˈvenʃənəl] *adj* non conformiste

unconvinced [ʌnkənˈvɪnst] *adj* **to be** *or* **remain u.** ne pas être convaincu (**of** de) ■ **unconvincing** *adj* peu convaincant

uncooked [ʌnˈkʊkt] *adj* cru

uncooperative [ʌnkəʊˈɒpərətɪv] *adj* peu coopératif, -ive

uncouth [ʌnˈkuːθ] *adj* fruste

uncover [ʌnˈkʌvə(r)] *vt* découvrir

undaunted [ʌnˈdɔːntɪd] *adj* nullement impressionné

undecided [ʌndɪˈsaɪdɪd] *adj (person)* indécis (**about** sur); **I'm u. whether to do it or not** je n'ai pas décidé si je le ferai ou non

undeniable [ʌndɪˈnaɪəbəl] *adj* indéniable

under [ˈʌndə(r)] **1** *prep* sous; *(less than)* moins de; **children u. nine** les enfants de moins de neuf ans; **u. it** dessous; **u. (the command of) sb** sous les ordres de qn; **u. the circumstances** dans ces circonstances; **to be u. discussion/repair** être en discussion/réparation; **to be u. way** *(in progress)* être en cours; *(on the way)* être en route; **to get u. way** *(of campaign)* démarrer **2** *adv* au-dessous

undercharge [ʌndəˈtʃɑːdʒ] *vt* **I undercharged him (for it)** je ne (le) lui ai pas fait payer assez

underclothes [ˈʌndəkləʊðz] *npl* sous-vêtements *mpl*

undercooked [ʌndəˈkʊkt] *adj* pas assez cuit

undercover [ˈʌndəkʌvə(r)] *adj* secret, -ète

undercut [ʌndəˈkʌt] *(pt & pp* -cut, *pres p* -cutting) *vt* vendre moins cher que

underdeveloped [ʌndədɪˈveləpt] *adj (country, region)* sous-développé

underdog [ˈʌndədɒg] n (politically, socially) opprimé, -e mf; (likely loser) outsider m

underdone [ʌndəˈdʌn] adj (food) pas assez cuit; (steak) saignant

underestimate [ʌndərˈestɪmeɪt] vt sous-estimer

underfoot [ʌndəˈfʊt] adv sous les pieds

undergo [ʌndəˈgəʊ] (pt -went, pp -gone) vt subir; **to u. surgery** être opéré

undergraduate [ʌndəˈgrædʒʊət] n étudiant, -e mf de licence

underground 1 [ˈʌndəgraʊnd] adj (subterranean) souterrain **2** [ˈʌndəgraʊnd] n Br (railway) métro m **3** [ʌndəˈgraʊnd] adv sous terre; Fig **to go u.** (of fugitive) passer dans la clandestinité

undergrowth [ˈʌndəgrəʊθ] n broussailles fpl

underhand [ʌndəˈhænd] adj sournois

underline [ʌndəˈlaɪn] vt souligner

underlying [ʌndəˈlaɪɪŋ] adj sous-jacent

undermine [ʌndəˈmaɪn] vt (weaken) saper

underneath [ʌndəˈniːθ] **1** prep sous **2** adv (en) dessous; **the book u.** le livre d'en dessous **3** n **the u. (of)** le dessous (de)

underpaid [ʌndəˈpeɪd] adj sous-payé

underpants [ˈʌndəpænts] npl (male underwear) slip m

underpass [ˈʌndəpɑːs] n (for pedestrians) passage m souterrain; (for vehicles) passage m inférieur

underprivileged [ʌndəˈprɪvɪlɪdʒd] adj défavorisé

underrate [ʌndəˈreɪt] vt sous-estimer

underside [ˈʌndəsaɪd] n **the u. (of)** le dessous (de)

understaffed [ʌndəˈstɑːft] adj **to be u.** manquer de personnel

understand [ʌndəˈstænd] (pt & pp -stood) vti comprendre; **I u. that...** je crois comprendre que... ■ **understanding 1** n (act, faculty) compréhension f; (agreement) accord m, entente f; (sympathy) entente f; **on the u. that...** à condition que... (+ subjunctive) **2** adj (person) compréhensif, -ive ■ **understood** adj (agreed) entendu; (implied) sous-entendu

understandable [ʌndəˈstændəbəl] adj compréhensible

understatement [ˈʌndəsteɪtmənt] n euphémisme m

undertake [ʌndəˈteɪk] (pt -took, pp -taken) vt (task) entreprendre; **to u. to do sth** entreprendre de faire qch

undertaker [ˈʌndəteɪkə(r)] n entrepreneur m de pompes funèbres

undertaking [ʌndəˈteɪkɪŋ] n (task) entreprise f; (promise) promesse f

undertone [ˈʌndətəʊn] n **in an u.** à mi-voix

underwater [ʌndəˈwɔːtə(r)] adv sous l'eau

underwear [ˈʌndəweə(r)] n sous-vêtements mpl

undesirable [ʌndɪˈzaɪərəbəl] adj & n indésirable (mf)

undignified [ʌnˈdɪgnɪfaɪd] adj indigne

undisciplined [ʌnˈdɪsɪplɪnd] adj indiscipliné

undiscovered [ʌndɪˈskʌvəd] adj **to remain u.** (of crime, body) ne pas être découvert

undisputed [ʌndɪˈspjuːtɪd] adj incontesté

undistinguished [ʌndɪˈstɪŋgwɪʃt] adj médiocre

undo [ʌnˈduː] (pt -did, pp -done) vt défaire; (bound person) détacher; (parcel) ouvrir; (mistake, damage) réparer; Comptr (command) annuler ■ **undoing** n ruine f ■ **undone** adj **to come u.** (of knot) se défaire; **to leave sth u.** (work) ne pas faire qch

undoubtedly [ʌnˈdaʊtɪdlɪ] adv indubitablement

undress [ʌnˈdres] **1** vt déshabiller; **to get undressed** se déshabiller **2** vi se déshabiller

undrinkable [ʌnˈdrɪŋkəbəl] adj imbuvable

undue [ʌnˈdjuː] adj excessif, -ive ■ **unduly** adv excessivement

unearth [ʌnˈɜːθ] vt (from ground) déterrer; Fig (discover) mettre à jour

unearthly [ʌnˈɜːθlɪ] adj Fam **at an u. hour** à une heure impossible

uneasy [ʌnˈiːzɪ] adj (person) mal à l'aise; (silence) gêné

uneconomic(al) [ʌniːkəˈnɒmɪk(əl)] adj peu économique

uneducated [ʌnˈedjʊkeɪtɪd] adj (person) sans éducation

unemployed [ʌnɪmˈplɔɪd] 1 adj au chômage 2 npl **the u.** les chômeurs mpl ■ **unemployment** n chômage m; Br **u. benefit** allocation f chômage

unenthusiastic [ʌnɪnθjuːzɪˈæstɪk] adj peu enthousiaste

unenviable [ʌnˈenvɪəbəl] adj peu enviable

unequal [ʌnˈiːkwəl] adj inégal

unequivocal [ʌnɪˈkwɪvəkəl] adj sans équivoque

uneven [ʌnˈiːvən] adj inégal

uneventful [ʌnɪˈventfəl] adj sans histoires

unexpected [ʌnɪkˈspektɪd] adj inattendu ■ **unexpectedly** adv (arrive) à l'improviste; (fail, succeed) contre toute attente

unexplained [ʌnɪkˈspleɪnd] adj inexpliqué

unfailing [ʌnˈfeɪlɪŋ] adj (optimism, courage) à toute épreuve

unfair [ʌnˈfeə(r)] adj injuste (**to sb** envers qn); (competition) déloyal ■ **unfairly** adv injustement

unfaithful [ʌnˈfeɪθfəl] adj infidèle (**to** à)

unfamiliar [ʌnfəˈmɪlɪə(r)] adj inconnu; **to be u. with sth** ne pas connaître qch

unfashionable [ʌnˈfæʃənəbəl] adj démodé

unfasten [ʌnˈfɑːsən] vt défaire

unfavourable [ʌnˈfeɪvərəbəl] (Am **unfavorable**) adj défavorable

unfinished [ʌnˈfɪnɪʃt] adj inachevé

unfit [ʌnˈfɪt] adj (unsuitable) inapte; (in bad shape) pas en forme; **to be u. to do sth** être incapable de faire qch

unflattering [ʌnˈflætərɪŋ] adj peu flatteur, -euse

unfold [ʌnˈfəʊld] 1 vt déplier; (wings) déployer 2 vi (of story) se dérouler

unforeseeable [ʌnfɔːˈsiːəbəl] adj imprévisible ■ **unforeseen** adj imprévu

unforgettable [ʌnfəˈgetəbəl] adj inoubliable

unforgivable [ʌnfəˈgɪvəbəl] adj impardonnable

unfortunate [ʌnˈfɔːtʃənət] adj malchanceux, -euse; (event) fâcheux, -euse; **you were u.** tu n'as pas eu de chance ■ **unfortunately** adv malheureusement

unfounded [ʌnˈfaʊndɪd] adj (rumour) sans fondement

unfriendly [ʌnˈfrendlɪ] adj peu aimable (**to** avec)

unfulfilled [ʌnfʊlˈfɪld] adj (plan, dream) non réalisé

unfurnished [ʌnˈfɜːnɪʃt] adj non meublé

ungainly [ʌnˈgeɪnlɪ] adj (clumsy) gauche

ungrateful [ʌnˈgreɪtfəl] adj ingrat

unhappy [ʌnˈhæpɪ] (**-ier, -iest**) adj (sad, unfortunate) malheureux, -euse; (not pleased) mécontent; **to be u. about doing sth** ne pas vouloir faire qch

unharmed [ʌnˈhɑːmd] adj indemne

unhealthy [ʌnˈhelθɪ] (**-ier, -iest**) adj (person) maladif, -ive; (climate, place, job) malsain

unheard-of [ʌnˈhɜːdɒv] adj (unprecedented) inouï

unhelpful [ʌnˈhelpfəl] adj (person) peu serviable; (advice) peu utile

unhurt [ʌnˈhɜːt] adj indemne

unhygienic [ʌnhaɪˈdʒiːnɪk] adj contraire à l'hygiène

uniform [ˈjuːnɪfɔːm] 1 n uniforme m 2 adj (regular) uniforme; (temperature) constant

unify [ˈjuːnɪfaɪ] (pt & pp **-ied**) vt unifier

unilateral [juːnɪˈlætərəl] *adj* unilatéral

unimaginable [ˌʌnɪˈmædʒɪnəbəl] *adj* inimaginable ■ **unimaginative** *adj (person, plan)* qui manque d'imagination

unimportant [ˌʌnɪmˈpɔːtənt] *adj* sans importance

uninhabitable [ˌʌnɪnˈhæbɪtəbəl] *adj* inhabitable ■ **uninhabited** *adj* inhabité

uninhibited [ˌʌnɪnˈhɪbɪtɪd] *adj (person)* sans complexes

uninjured [ʌnˈɪndʒəd] *adj* indemne

uninspiring [ˌʌnɪnˈspaɪərɪŋ] *adj (subject)* pas très inspirant

unintelligible [ˌʌnɪnˈtelɪdʒəbəl] *adj* inintelligible

unintentional [ˌʌnɪnˈtenʃənəl] *adj* involontaire

uninterested [ʌnˈɪntrɪstɪd] *adj* indifférent (**in** à) ■ **uninteresting** *adj* inintéressant

uninterrupted [ˌʌnɪntəˈrʌptɪd] *adj* ininterrompu

uninvited [ˌʌnɪnˈvaɪtɪd] *adv (arrive)* sans invitation ■ **uninviting** *adj* peu attrayant

union [ˈjuːnɪən] **1** *n* union *f*; *(trade union)* syndicat *m* **2** *adj* syndical; **the U. Jack** = le drapeau britannique

unique [juːˈniːk] *adj* unique

unisex [ˈjuːnɪseks] *adj (clothes)* unisexe

unison [ˈjuːnɪsən] *n* **in u.** à l'unisson (**with** de)

unit [ˈjuːnɪt] *n* unité *f*; *(of furniture)* élément *m*; *(system)* bloc *m*; *(group, team)* groupe *m*; **psychiatric/heart u.** *(of hospital)* service *m* de psychiatrie/cardiologie

unite [juːˈnaɪt] **1** *vt* unir; *(country, party)* unifier; **the United Kingdom** le Royaume-Uni; **the United Nations** les Nations *fpl* unies; **the United States (of America)** les États-Unis *mpl* (d'Amérique) **2** *vi* s'unir

unity [ˈjuːnətɪ] *n (cohesion)* unité *f*; *Fig (harmony)* harmonie *f*

universal [ˌjuːnɪˈvɜːsəl] *adj* universel, -elle

universe [ˈjuːnɪvɜːs] *n* univers *m*

university [ˌjuːnɪˈvɜːsətɪ] **1** (*pl* -**ies**) *n* université *f*; **to go to u.** aller à l'université; *Br* **at u.** à l'université **2** *adj (teaching, town, restaurant)* universitaire; *(student, teacher)* d'université

unjust [ʌnˈdʒʌst] *adj* injuste

unjustified [ʌnˈdʒʌstɪfaɪd] *adj* injustifié

unkind [ʌnˈkaɪnd] *adj* pas gentil (*f* pas gentille) (**to sb** avec qn)

unknowingly [ʌnˈnəʊɪŋlɪ] *adv* inconsciemment

unknown [ʌnˈnəʊn] **1** *adj* inconnu **2** *n (person)* inconnu, -e *mf*; *Math & Fig* **u. (quantity)** inconnue *f*

unlawful [ʌnˈlɔːfəl] *adj* illégal

unleaded [ʌnˈledɪd] *adj* sans plomb

unleash [ʌnˈliːʃ] *vt (emotion)* susciter

unless [ʌnˈles] *conj* à moins que (+ *subjunctive*); **u. she comes** à moins qu'elle ne vienne; **u. you work harder, you'll fail** à moins de travailler plus dur, vous échouerez

unlike [ʌnˈlaɪk] *prep* **to be u. sb/sth** ne pas être comme qn/qch; **u. her brother, she…** à la différence de son frère, elle…; **it's very u. him to…** ça ne lui ressemble pas du tout de…

unlikely [ʌnˈlaɪklɪ] *adj* improbable; *(unbelievable)* invraisemblable; **she's u. to win** il est peu probable qu'elle gagne

unlimited [ʌnˈlɪmɪtɪd] *adj* illimité

unlisted [ʌnˈlɪstɪd] *adj Am (phone number)* sur liste rouge

unload [ʌnˈləʊd] *vti* décharger

unlock [ʌnˈlɒk] *vt* ouvrir

unlucky [ʌnˈlʌkɪ] (-**ier**, -**iest**) *adj (person)* malchanceux, -euse; *(number, colour)* qui porte malheur ■ **unluckily** *adv* malheureusement

unmade [ʌnˈmeɪd] *adj (bed)* défait

unmanageable [ʌnˈmænɪdʒəbəl] *adj (child)* difficile; *(hair)* difficile à coiffer

unmarried [ʌnˈmærɪd] *adj* non marié

unmistakable [ˌʌnmɪˈsteɪkəbəl] *adj*

(obvious) indubitable; (face, voice) caractéristique

unmoved [ʌnˈmuːvd] adj **to be u. by sth** rester insensible à qch

unnatural [ʌnˈnætʃərəl] adj (abnormal) anormal; (affected) affecté

unnecessary [ʌnˈnesəsərɪ] adj inutile; (superfluous) superflu

unnerve [ʌnˈnɜːv] vt troubler

unnoticed [ʌnˈnəʊtɪst] adv **to go u.** passer inaperçu

unobtainable [ʌnəbˈteɪnəbəl] adj impossible à obtenir

unoccupied [ʌnˈɒkjʊpaɪd] adj (house) inoccupé; (seat) libre

unofficial [ʌnəˈfɪʃəl] adj officieux, -euse; (visit) privé; (strike) sauvage

unorthodox [ʌnˈɔːθədɒks] adj peu orthodoxe

unpack [ʌnˈpæk] **1** vt (suitcase) défaire; (contents) déballer **2** vi défaire sa valise

unpaid [ʌnˈpeɪd] adj (bill, sum) impayé; (work, worker) bénévole; (leave) non payé

unparalleled [ʌnˈpærəleld] adj sans égal

unplanned [ʌnˈplænd] adj imprévu

unpleasant [ʌnˈplezənt] adj désagréable (**to sb** avec qn)

unplug [ʌnˈplʌg] (pt & pp **-gg-**) vt (appliance) débrancher

unpopular [ʌnˈpɒpjʊlə(r)] adj impopulaire; **to be u. with sb** ne pas plaire à qn

unprecedented [ʌnˈpresɪdentɪd] adj sans précédent

unpredictable [ʌnprɪˈdɪktəbəl] adj imprévisible; (weather) indécis

unprepared [ʌnprɪˈpeəd] adj **to be u. for sth** (not expect) ne pas s'attendre à qch

unprofessional [ʌnprəˈfeʃənəl] adj (person, behaviour) pas très professionnel, -elle

unprovoked [ʌnprəˈvəʊkt] adj gratuit

unpublished [ʌnˈpʌblɪʃt] adj (text, writer) inédit

unqualified [ʌnˈkwɒlɪfaɪd] adj (teacher) non diplômé; (support) sans réserve; (success) parfait; **to be u. to do sth** ne pas être qualifié pour faire qch

unquestionable [ʌnˈkwestʃənəbəl] adj incontestable

unravel [ʌnˈrævəl] (Br **-ll-**, Am **-l-**) vt (threads) démêler; Fig (mystery) éclaircir

unreal [ʌnˈrɪəl] adj irréel, -elle

unrealistic [ʌnrɪəˈlɪstɪk] adj irréaliste

unreasonable [ʌnˈriːzənəbəl] adj (person, attitude) déraisonnable

unrecognizable [ʌnˈrekəgnaɪzəbəl] adj méconnaissable

unrelated [ʌnrɪˈleɪtɪd] adj (facts) sans rapport (**to** avec); **we're u.** il n'y a aucun lien de parenté entre nous

unrelenting [ʌnrɪˈlentɪŋ] adj incessant; (person) tenace

unreliable [ʌnrɪˈlaɪəbəl] adj peu fiable

unremarkable [ʌnrɪˈmɑːkəbəl] adj quelconque

unrepentant [ʌnrɪˈpentənt] adj impénitent

unreservedly [ʌnrɪˈzɜːvɪdlɪ] adv sans réserve

unrest [ʌnˈrest] n agitation f, troubles mpl

unrestricted [ʌnrɪˈstrɪktɪd] adj illimité

unrewarding [ʌnrɪˈwɔːdɪŋ] adj ingrat; (financially) peu rémunérateur, -trice

unrivalled [ʌnˈraɪvəld] (Am **unrivaled**) adj hors pair inv

unroll [ʌnˈrəʊl] **1** vt dérouler **2** vi se dérouler

unruly [ʌnˈruːlɪ] (**-ier, -iest**) adj indiscipliné

unsafe [ʌnˈseɪf] adj (place, machine) dangereux, -euse

unsaid [ʌnˈsed] adj **to leave sth u.** passer qch sous silence

unsatisfactory [ʌnsætɪsˈfæktərɪ] adj peu satisfaisant ■ **unsatisfied** adj insatisfait; **u. with sb/sth** peu satisfait de qn/qch

unscheduled [*Br* ʌnˈʃedjuːld, *Am* ʌnˈskedʒuːld] *adj* imprévu

unscrew [ʌnˈskruː] *vt* dévisser

unscrupulous [ʌnˈskruːpjʊləs] *adj (person)* peu scrupuleux, -euse

unseemly [ʌnˈsiːmlɪ] *adj* inconvenant

unseen [ʌnˈsiːn] *adv* to do sth u. faire qch sans qu'on vous voie

unselfish [ʌnˈselfɪʃ] *adj (person, motive)* désintéressé

unsettle [ʌnˈsetəl] *vt (person)* troubler ∎ **unsettled** *adj (weather, situation)* instable

unshak(e)able [ʌnˈʃeɪkəbəl] *adj* inébranlable

unshaven [ʌnˈʃeɪvən] *adj* pas rasé

unsightly [ʌnˈsaɪtlɪ] *adj* laid

unskilled [ʌnˈskɪld] *adj* non qualifié

unsociable [ʌnˈsəʊʃəbəl] *adj* peu sociable

unsolved [ʌnˈsɒlvd] *adj (mystery)* inexpliqué; *(crime)* dont l'auteur n'est pas connu

unsophisticated [ʌnsəˈfɪstɪkeɪtɪd] *adj* simple

unsound [ʌnˈsaʊnd] *adj (construction)* peu solide; *(method)* peu sûr; *(decision)* peu judicieux, -euse

unspeakable [ʌnˈspiːkəbəl] *adj* indescriptible

unspecified [ʌnˈspesɪfaɪd] *adj* non spécifié

unsporting [ʌnˈspɔːtɪŋ] *adj* qui n'est pas fair-play

unstable [ʌnˈsteɪbəl] *adj* instable

unsteady [ʌnˈstedɪ] *adj (hand, voice, step)* mal assuré; *(table, ladder)* bancal *(mpl* -als) ∎ **unsteadily** *adv (walk)* d'un pas mal assuré

unstuck [ʌnˈstʌk] *adj* to come u. *(of stamp)* se décoller; *Br Fam (of person, plan)* se casser la figure

unsuccessful [ʌnsəkˈsesfəl] *adj (attempt)* infructueux, -euse; *(outcome, candidate)* malheureux, -euse; *(application)* non retenu; to be u. ne pas réussir (**in doing** à faire); *(of book, film, artist)* ne pas avoir de succès

∎ **unsuccessfully** *adv* en vain, sans succès

unsuitable [ʌnˈsuːtəbəl] *adj* qui ne convient pas (**for** à); *(manners, clothes)* peu convenable; to be u. for sth ne pas convenir à qch ∎ **unsuited** *adj* to be u. to sth ne pas être fait pour qch; they're u. (to each other) ils ne sont pas compatibles

unsupervised [ʌnˈsuːpəvaɪzd] *adv (play)* sans surveillance

unsure [ʌnˈʃʊə(r)] *adj* incertain (**of** or **about** de)

unsympathetic [ʌnsɪmpəˈθetɪk] *adj* peu compatissant (**to** à); u. to a cause/request insensible à une cause/requête

untangle [ʌnˈtæŋgəl] *vt (rope, hair)* démêler

unthinkable [ʌnˈθɪŋkəbəl] *adj* impensable, inconcevable

untidy [ʌnˈtaɪdɪ] (**-ier, -iest**) *adj (clothes, hair)* peu soigné; *(room)* en désordre; *(person)* désordonné

untie [ʌnˈtaɪ] *vt (person, hands)* détacher; *(knot, parcel)* défaire

until [ʌnˈtɪl] **1** *prep* jusqu'à; u. now jusqu'à présent; u. then jusque-là; not u. tomorrow pas avant demain; I didn't see her u. Monday c'est seulement lundi que je l'ai vue
2 *conj* jusqu'à ce que (+ *subjunctive*); u. she comes jusqu'à ce qu'elle vienne; do nothing u. I come ne fais rien avant que j'arrive

untimely [ʌnˈtaɪmlɪ] *adj (remark, question)* inopportun; *(death)* prématuré

untold [ʌnˈtəʊld] *adj (wealth, quantity)* incalculable

untoward [ʌntəˈwɔːd] *adj* fâcheux, -euse

untrue [ʌnˈtruː] *adj* faux *(f* fausse) ∎ **untruthful** *adj (person)* menteur, -euse; *(statement)* mensonger, -ère

unusable [ʌnˈjuːzəbəl] *adj* inutilisable

unused[1] [ʌnˈjuːzd] *adj (new)* neuf *(f* neuve); *(not in use)* inutilisé

unused² [ʌnˈjuːzd] *adj* u. to sth/to doing sth peu habitué à qch/à faire qch

unusual [ʌnˈjuːʒʊəl] *adj (not common)* inhabituel, -elle; *(strange)* étrange ▪ **unusually** *adv* exceptionnellement

unveil [ʌnˈveɪl] *vt* dévoiler

unwanted [ʌnˈwɒntɪd] *adj* non désiré

unwarranted [ʌnˈwɒrəntɪd] *adj* injustifié

unwelcome [ʌnˈwelkəm] *adj (news)* fâcheux, -euse; *(gift, visit)* inopportun; *(person)* importun

unwell [ʌnˈwel] *adj* souffrant

unwieldy [ʌnˈwiːldɪ] *adj (package)* encombrant; *(system)* lourd

unwilling [ʌnˈwɪlɪŋ] *adj* to be u. to do sth être réticent à faire qch ▪ **unwillingly** *adv* à contrecœur

unwind [ʌnˈwaɪnd] *(pt & pp* **-wound)** **1** *vt (thread)* dérouler **2** *vi* se dérouler; *Fam (relax)* décompresser

unwise [ʌnˈwaɪz] *adj* imprudent

unwittingly [ʌnˈwɪtɪŋlɪ] *adv* involontairement

unworthy [ʌnˈwɜːðɪ] *adj* indigne (**of** de)

unwrap [ʌnˈræp] *(pt & pp* **-pp-)** *vt* déballer

unwritten [ʌnˈrɪtən] *adj (agreement)* verbal

unzip [ʌnˈzɪp] *(pt & pp* **-pp-)** *vt* ouvrir (la fermeture Éclair® de)

UP [ʌp] **1** *adv* en haut; **to come/go up** monter; **to walk up and down** marcher de long en large; **up there** là-haut; **up above** au-dessus; **further** or **higher up** plus haut; **up to** *(as far as)* jusqu'à; **to be up to doing sth** *(capable of)* être de taille à faire qch; **to feel up to doing sth** *(well enough)* être assez bien pour faire qch; **it's up to you to do it** c'est à toi de le faire; **it's up to you** *(you decide)* c'est à toi de décider; **where are you up to?** *(in book)* où en es-tu?; *Fam* **what are you up to?** que fais-tu?; *Fam* **to be well up in** *(versed in)* s'y connaître en

2 *prep* **up a hill** en haut d'une colline;

up a tree dans un arbre; **up a ladder** sur une échelle; **to live up the street** habiter plus loin dans la rue

3 *adj (out of bed)* levé; **we were up all night** nous sommes restés debout toute la nuit; **the two weeks were up** les deux semaines étaient terminées; *Fam* **what's up?** qu'est-ce qu'il y a?

4 *npl* **ups and downs** des hauts et des bas *mpl*

5 *(pt & pp* **-pp-)** *vt Fam (price, offer)* augmenter ▪ **up-and-coming** *adj* qui monte ▪ **upbeat** *adj Fam* optimiste ▪ **upbringing** *n* éducation *f* ▪ **update** *vt* mettre à jour ▪ **upgrade** *vt (job)* revaloriser; *(person)* promouvoir; *Comptr (hardware)* augmenter la puissance de ▪ **uphill 1** [ʌpˈhɪl] *adv* **to go u.** monter **2** [ˈʌphɪl] *adj Fig (struggle, task)* pénible ▪ **uphold** *(pt & pp* **-held)** *vt (decision)* maintenir ▪ **upkeep** *n* entretien *m* ▪ **up-market** *adj Br (car, product)* haut de gamme *inv; (area, place)* chic *inv* ▪ **upright 1** *(straight)* droit **2** *adj (vertical, honest)* droit ▪ **uprising** *n* insurrection *f* ▪ **uproot** *vt (plant, person)* déraciner ▪ **upside** *adv* **u. down** à l'envers; **to turn sth u. down** retourner qch; *Fig* mettre qch sens dessus dessous ▪ **upstairs 1** [ʌpˈsteəz] *adv* en haut; **to go u.** monter **2** [ˈʌpsteəz] *adj (people, room)* du dessus ▪ **upstream** *adv* en amont ▪ **uptight** *adj Fam (tense)* crispé; *(inhibited)* coincé ▪ **up-to-date** *adj* moderne; *(information)* à jour; *(well-informed)* au courant (**on** de) ▪ **upturn** *n (improvement)* amélioration *f* (**in** de) ▪ **upward** *adj (movement)* ascendant; *(path)* qui monte; *(trend)* à la hausse ▪ **upwards** *adv* vers le haut; **from 5 euros u.** à partir de 5 euros; **u. of fifty** cinquante et plus

upheaval [ʌpˈhiːvəl] *n* bouleversement *m*

upholstery [ʌpˈhəʊlstərɪ] *n (padding)* rembourrage *m; (covering)* revêtement *m; (in car)* sièges *mpl*

upon [əˈpɒn] *prep* sur

upper ['ʌpə(r)] **1** adj supérieur; **u. class** aristocratie f; **to have/get the u. hand** avoir/prendre le dessus **2** n (of shoe) empeigne f ■ **upper-class** adj aristocratique ■ **uppermost** adj le plus haut (f la plus haute)

uproar ['ʌprɔ:(r)] n tumulte m

upset 1 [ʌp'set] (pt & pp **-set**, pres p **-setting**) vt (knock over, spill) renverser; (person, plans, schedule) bouleverser

2 [ʌp'set] adj (unhappy) bouleversé (**about** par); **to have an u. stomach** avoir l'estomac dérangé

3 ['ʌpset] n (disturbance) bouleversement m; (surprise) défaite f; **to have a stomach u.** avoir l'estomac dérangé ■ **upsetting** adj bouleversant

upshot ['ʌpʃɒt] n résultat m

urban ['ɜ:bən] adj urbain

urge [ɜ:dʒ] **1** n forte envie f; **to have an u. to do sth** avoir très envie de faire qch **2** vt **to u. sb to do sth** presser qn de faire qch

urgency ['ɜ:dʒənsɪ] n urgence f; **it's a matter of u.** il y a urgence

urgent ['ɜ:dʒənt] adj urgent ■ **urgently** adv d'urgence

urine ['jʊərɪn] n urine f ■ **urinate** vi uriner

urn [ɜ:n] n urne f; (for coffee or tea) fontaine f

US [ju:'es] (abbr **United States**) n the **US** les USA mpl

us [əs, stressed ʌs] pron nous; **(to) us** (indirect) nous; **she saw us** elle nous a vus; **he gave it (to) us** il nous l'a donné

USA [ju:es'eɪ] (abbr **United States of America**) n the **U.** les USA mpl

usage ['ju:sɪdʒ] n usage m

use 1 [ju:s] n (utilization) emploi m, usage m; (ability, permission to use) emploi m; **to have the u. of sth** avoir l'usage de qch; **to make (good) u. of sth** faire (bon) usage de qch; **to be of u. to sb** être utile à qn; **in u.** en usage; **not in u., out of u.** hors d'usage; **it's no u. crying** ça ne sert à rien de

pleurer; **what's the u. of worrying?** à quoi bon s'inquiéter?

2 [ju:z] vt (utilize) utiliser, se servir de; (force, diplomacy) avoir recours à; (electricity) consommer; **it's used to do** or **for doing sth** ça sert à faire qch; **it's used as...** ça sert de...; **to u. sth up** (food, fuel) finir; (money) dépenser ■ **use-by date** ['ju:zbaɪ] adj **u. date** date f limite de consommation

used 1 adj (a) [ju:zd] (second-hand) d'occasion; (stamp) oblitéré (b) [ju:st] **to be u. to sth/to doing sth** être habitué à qch/à faire qch; **to get u. to sb/ sth** s'habituer à qn/qch

2 [ju:st] v aux **I u. to sing** avant, je chantais; **she u. to jog every Sunday** elle faisait du jogging tous les dimanches

useful ['ju:sfəl] adj utile (**to** à); **to come in u.** être utile; **to make oneself u.** se rendre utile ■ **useless** adj inutile; (person) nul (f nulle) (**at** en)

user ['ju:zə(r)] n (of train, telephone) usager m; (of road, machine) utilisateur, -trice mf ■ **user-friendly** adj convivial

usher ['ʌʃə(r)] **1** n (in church, theatre) ouvreur m **2** vt **to u. sb in** faire entrer qn ■ **usherette** n ouvreuse f

usual ['ju:ʒʊəl] **1** adj habituel, -elle; **as u.** comme d'habitude **2** n Fam the **u.** (food, excuse) la même chose que d'habitude ■ **usually** adv d'habitude

usurp [ju:'zɜ:p] vt usurper

utensil [ju:'tensəl] n ustensile m

utility [ju:'tɪlɪtɪ] n (public) **u.** service m public

utilize ['ju:tɪlaɪz] vt utiliser

utmost ['ʌtməʊst] **1** adj **the u. ease** (greatest) la plus grande facilité; **it is of the u. importance that...** il est de la plus haute importance que... (+ subjunctive)

2 n **to do one's u.** faire de son mieux (**to do** pour faire)

utter[1] ['ʌtə(r)] *adj* total; *(folly, lie)* pur; **it's u. nonsense** c'est complètement absurde ■ **utterly** *adv* complètement

utter[2] ['ʌtə(r)] *vt (cry, sigh)* pousser; *(word)* prononcer; *(threat)* proférer

U-turn ['juːtɜːn] *n (in vehicle)* demi-tour *m*; *Fig (change of policy)* virage *m* à 180°

Vv

V, v [viː] *n (letter)* V, v *m inv*

vacant ['veɪkənt] *adj (room, seat)* libre; *(post)* vacant ■ **vacancy** *(pl -ies)* *n (post)* poste *m* vacant; *(room)* chambre *f* libre

vacate [*Br* vəˈkeɪt, *Am* ˈveɪkeɪt] *vt* quitter

vacation [veɪˈkeɪʃən] *n Am* vacances *fpl*; **to take a v.** prendre des vacances

vaccinate ['væksɪneɪt] *vt* vacciner ■ **vaccination** *n* vaccination *f* ■ **vaccine** [-'siːn] *n* vaccin *m*

vacuum ['vækjʊəm] **1** *n* vide *m*; **v. cleaner** aspirateur *m*; *Br* **v. flask** Thermos® *f* **2** *vt (room)* passer l'aspirateur dans; *(carpet)* passer l'aspirateur sur

vagabond ['vægəbɒnd] *n* vagabond, -e *mf*

vagina [vəˈdʒaɪnə] *n Anat* vagin *m*

vague [veɪg] (**-er, -est**) *adj* vague; *(outline)* flou; **he was v. (about it)** il est resté vague ■ **vaguely** *adv* vaguement

vain [veɪn] (**-er, -est**) *adj* (**a**) *(attempt, hope)* vain; **in v.** en vain; **her efforts were in v.** ses efforts ont été inutiles (**b**) *(conceited)* vaniteux, -euse

valentine ['væləntaɪn] *n (card)* carte *f* de la Saint-Valentin; **(Saint) V.'s Day** la Saint-Valentin

valid ['vælɪd] *adj* valable ■ **validate** *vt* valider

valley ['vælɪ] *(pl -eys)* *n* vallée *f*

valuable ['væljʊəbəl] **1** *adj (object)* de valeur; *Fig (help, time)* précieux, -euse **2** *npl* **valuables** objets *mpl* de valeur

value ['væljuː] **1** *n* valeur *f*; **to be of v.** avoir de la valeur; **to be good v. (for money)** être d'un bon rapport qualité-prix **2** *vt (appreciate)* apprécier; *(assess)* évaluer ■ **valuation** [-jʊˈeɪʃən] *n (by expert)* expertise *f*

valve [vælv] *n (of machine, car)* soupape *f*; *(of pipe, tube)* valve *f*

van [væn] *n (vehicle)* camionnette *f*, fourgonnette *f*

vandal ['vændəl] *n* vandale *mf* ■ **vandalism** *n* vandalisme *m* ■ **vandalize** *vt* saccager

vanilla [vəˈnɪlə] **1** *n* vanille *f* **2** *adj (ice cream)* à la vanille

vanish ['vænɪʃ] *vi* disparaître

vanity ['vænɪtɪ] *n* vanité *f*

vapour ['veɪpə(r)] *(Am* **vapor***)* *n* vapeur *f*

variable ['veərɪəbəl] *adj & n* variable *(f)*

variant ['veərɪənt] *n* variante *f*

variation [veərɪˈeɪʃən] *n* variation *f*

varicose ['værɪkəʊs] *adj* **v. veins** varices *fpl*

varied ['veərɪd] *adj* varié

variety [vəˈraɪətɪ] *n* (**a**) *(diversity)* variété *f*; **a v. of** toutes sortes de (**b**) **v. show** spectacle *m* de variétés

various ['veərɪəs] *adj* divers

varnish ['vɑːnɪʃ] **1** *n* vernis *m* **2** *vt* vernir

vary ['veərɪ] *(pt & pp -ied)* *vti* varier (**in/with** en/selon) ■ **varying** *adj* variable

vase [*Br* vɑːz, *Am* veɪs] *n* vase *m*

vast [vɑːst] *adj* immense

VAT [viːeɪˈtiː, væt] *(abbr* **value added tax)** *n Br* TVA *f*

vat [væt] n cuve f

Vatican ['vætɪkən] n **the V.** le Vatican

vault¹ [vɔːlt] n (roof) voûte f; (tomb) caveau m; (cellar) cave f; (in bank) salle f des coffres

vault² [vɔːlt] vti (jump) sauter

VCR [viːsiːˈɑː(r)] n (abbr **video cassette recorder**) n magnétoscope m

VDU [viːdiːˈjuː] n (abbr **visual display unit**) n Comptr moniteur m

veal [viːl] n veau m

veer [vɪə(r)] vi (of car) virer; **to v. off the road** quitter la route

vegan ['viːgən] n végétalien, -enne mf

vegetable ['vedʒtəbəl] n légume m ■ **vegetarian** [vedʒɪ'teərɪən] adj & n végétarien, -enne (mf) ■ **vegetation** [vedʒɪ'teɪʃən] n végétation f

vehicle ['viːɪkəl] n véhicule m

veil [veɪl] n (covering) & Fig voile m ■ **veiled** adj voilé

vein [veɪn] n (in body) veine f

Velcro® ['velkrəʊ] n Velcro® m

velvet ['velvɪt] **1** n velours m **2** adj de velours

vending ['vendɪŋ] n **v. machine** distributeur m automatique

vendor ['vendə(r)] n vendeur, -euse mf

veneer [vəˈnɪə(r)] n (wood) placage m; Fig (appearance) vernis m

vengeance ['vendʒəns] n vengeance f; **to take v. on sb** se venger de qn; Fig **with a v.** de plus belle

venison ['venɪsən] n venaison f

venom ['venəm] n (poison) & Fig venin m

vent [vent] n conduit m

ventilate ['ventɪleɪt] vt ventiler, aérer ■ **ventilation** n ventilation f, aération f

ventriloquist [ven'trɪləkwɪst] n ventriloque mf

venture ['ventʃə(r)] **1** n entreprise f (hasardeuse) **2** vt risquer; **to v. to do sth** se risquer à faire qch **3** vi s'aventurer (**into** dans)

venue ['venjuː] n (for meeting, concert) salle f; (for football match) stade m

veranda(h) [vəˈrændə] n véranda f

verb [vɜːb] n verbe m ■ **verbal** adj verbal

verdict ['vɜːdɪkt] n verdict m

verge [vɜːdʒ] **1** n Br (of road) bord m; **on the v. of ruin/tears** au bord de la ruine/des larmes; **to be on the v. of doing sth** être sur le point de faire qch **2** vi **to v. on** friser; (of colour) tirer sur

verify ['verɪfaɪ] (pt & pp -ied) vt vérifier

vermin ['vɜːmɪn] n (animals) animaux mpl nuisibles; (insects, people) vermine f

versatile [Br 'vɜːsətaɪl, Am 'vɜːrsətəl] adj polyvalent

verse [vɜːs] n (poetry) vers mpl; (stanza) strophe f; (of Bible) verset m

versed [vɜːst] adj (well) v. **in sth** versé dans qch

version [Br 'vɜːʃən, Am 'vɜːrʒən] n version f

versus ['vɜːsəs] prep (in sport, law) contre; (compared to) comparé à

vertical ['vɜːtɪkəl] adj vertical

very ['verɪ] **1** adv très; **v. much** beaucoup; **the v. first** le tout premier (f la toute première); **the v. next day** le lendemain même; **at the v. least/most** tout au moins/plus; **at the v. latest** au plus tard

2 adj (emphatic use) **this v. house** cette maison même; **at the v. end** tout à la fin

vessel ['vesəl] n (ship) vaisseau m; (container) récipient m

vest [vest] n Br maillot m de corps; Am (waistcoat) gilet m

vested ['vestɪd] adj **to have a v. interest in sth** avoir un intérêt personnel dans qch

vestige ['vestɪdʒ] n vestige m

vet¹ [vet] n vétérinaire mf

vet² [vet] (pt & pp -tt-) vt Br faire une enquête sur

veteran ['vetərən] n Mil ancien combattant m; Fig vétéran m

veto ['viːtəʊ] **1** (pl -oes) n veto m inv **2** (pt & pp -oed) vt mettre son veto à

via ['vaɪə, 'vɪə] *prep* via, par

viable ['vaɪəbəl] *adj* viable

viaduct ['vaɪədʌkt] *n* viaduc *m*

vibrant ['vaɪbrənt] *adj (colour)* vif (*f* vive)

vibrate [vaɪ'breɪt] *vi* vibrer ■ **vibration** *n* vibration *f*

vicar ['vɪkə(r)] *n (in Church of England)* pasteur *m* ■ **vicarage** [-rɪdʒ] *n* presbytère *m*

vice [vaɪs] *n (depravity, fault)* vice *m*; *Br (tool)* étau *m*

vice- [vaɪs] *pref* vice-

vice versa [vaɪs(ɪ)'vɜːsə] *adv* vice versa

vicinity [və'sɪnətɪ] *n* environs *mpl*; **in the v. of** aux environs de

vicious ['vɪʃəs] *adj (malicious)* méchant; *(violent)* brutal; **v. circle** cercle *m* vicieux

victim ['vɪktɪm] *n* victime *f*; **to be the v. of** être victime de

victimize ['vɪktɪmaɪz] *vt* persécuter

Victorian [vɪk'tɔːrɪən] **1** *adj* victorien, -enne **2** *n* Victorien, -enne *mf*

victory ['vɪktərɪ] (*pl* **-ies**) *n* victoire *f* ■ **victorious** [-'tɔːrɪəs] *adj* victorieux, -euse

video ['vɪdɪəʊ] **1** (*pl* **-os**) *n (medium)* vidéo *f*; *(cassette)* cassette *f* vidéo; *(recorder)* magnétoscope *m*; **on v.** sur cassette vidéo
2 *adj (camera, cassette, game)* vidéo *inv*; **v. recorder** magnétoscope *m*
3 (*pt* & *pp* **-oed**) *vt (on camcorder)* filmer en vidéo; *(on video recorder)* enregistrer (sur magnétoscope) ■ **videotape** *n* bande *f* vidéo

vie [vaɪ] (*pres p* **vying**) *vi* **to v. with sb (for sth/to do sth)** rivaliser avec qn (pour qch/pour faire qch)

Vietnam [*Br* vjet'næm, *Am* -'nɑːm] *n* le Viêt Nam

view [vjuː] **1** *n* vue *f*; *(opinion)* opinion *f*; **in my v.** *(opinion)* à mon avis; **in v. of** *(considering)* étant donné; **on v.** *(exhibit)* exposé; **with a v. to doing sth** dans l'intention de faire qch
2 *vt (regard)* considérer; *(look at)* voir; *(house)* visiter ■ **viewer** *n* (**a**) TV téléspectateur, -trice *mf* (**b**) *(for slides)* visionneuse *f* ■ **viewfinder** *n (in camera)* viseur *m* ■ **viewpoint** *n* point *m* de vue

vigilant ['vɪdʒɪlənt] *adj* vigilant

vigorous ['vɪgərəs] *adj* vigoureux, -euse

vile [vaɪl] (**-er, -est**) *adj (unpleasant)* abominable; *(food, drink)* infect

villa ['vɪlə] *n* villa *f*

village ['vɪlɪdʒ] *n* village *m* ■ **villager** *n* villageois, -e *mf*

villain ['vɪlən] *n (scoundrel)* scélérat *m*; *(in story, play)* méchant *m*

vindicate ['vɪndɪkeɪt] *vt* justifier

vindictive [vɪn'dɪktɪv] *adj* vindicatif, -ive

vine [vaɪn] *n* vigne *f* ■ **vineyard** ['vɪnjəd] *n* vigne *f*

vinegar ['vɪnɪgə(r)] *n* vinaigre *m*

vintage ['vɪntɪdʒ] **1** *n (year)* année *f*; *(wine)* cru *m* **2** *adj (wine)* de cru; *(car)* de collection *(datant généralement des années 1920)*

vinyl ['vaɪnəl] *n* vinyle *m*

viola [vɪ'əʊlə] *n Mus* alto *m*

violate ['vaɪəleɪt] *vt (agreement)* violer

violence ['vaɪələns] *n* violence *f* ■ **violent** *adj* violent ■ **violently** *adv* violemment

violet ['vaɪələt] **1** *adj (colour)* violet, -ette **2** *n (colour)* violet *m*; *(plant)* violette *f*

violin [vaɪə'lɪn] *n* violon *m* ■ **violinist** *n* violoniste *mf*

VIP [viːaɪ'piː] *(abbr* **very important person**) *n* VIP *mf*

viper ['vaɪpə(r)] *n* vipère *f*

virgin ['vɜːdʒɪn] *n* vierge *f*

virile [*Br* 'vɪraɪl, *Am* 'vɪrəl] *adj* viril

virtual ['vɜːtʃʊəl] *adj* quasi; *Comptr* virtuel, -elle ■ **virtually** *adv (almost)* quasiment

virtue ['vɜːtʃuː] *n (goodness, chastity)* vertu *f*; *(advantage)* mérite *m* ■ **virtuous** [-tjʊəs] *adj* vertueux, -euse

virus ['vaɪərəs] *n Med* & *Comptr* virus *m*

Visa® ['viːzə] *n* **V. (card)** carte *f* Visa®
visa ['viːzə] *n* visa *m*
visible ['vɪzəbəl] *adj* visible ■ **visibility** *n* visibilité *f*
vision ['vɪʒən] *n* (*eyesight*) vue *f*; (*foresight*) clairvoyance *f*; (*apparition*) vision *f*
visit ['vɪzɪt] **1** *n* visite *f*; **to pay sb a v.** rendre visite à qn
  2 *vt* (*place*) visiter; (*person*) rendre visite à
  3 *vi* **to be visiting** être de passage; *Br* **v. hours/card** heures *fpl*/carte *f* de visite ■ **visitor** *n* visiteur, -euse *mf*; (*guest*) invité, -e *mf*
visor ['vaɪzə(r)] *n* visière *f*
visual ['vɪʒʊəl] *adj* visuel, -elle; **v. aid** support *m* visuel; **v. arts** arts *mpl* plastiques ■ **visualize** *vt* (*imagine*) visualiser; (*foresee*) envisager
vital ['vaɪtəl] *adj* vital; **it's v. that...** il est vital que... (+ *subjunctive*)
vitality [vaɪ'tælətɪ] *n* vitalité *f*
vitamin [*Br* 'vɪtəmɪn, *Am* 'vaɪtəmɪn] *n* vitamine *f*
vivacious [vɪ'veɪʃəs] *adj* enjoué
vivid ['vɪvɪd] *adj* vif (*f* vive); (*description*) vivant; (*memory*) clair
V-neck ['viːnek] *adj* à col en V
vocabulary [*Br* və'kæbjʊlərɪ, *Am* -erɪ] *n* vocabulaire *m*
vocal ['vəʊkəl] *adj* (*cords, music*) vocal; (*noisy, critical*) qui se fait entendre
vocation [vəʊ'keɪʃən] *n* vocation *f* ■ **vocational** *adj* professionnel, -elle
vociferous [və'sɪfərəs] *adj* bruyant
vodka ['vɒdkə] *n* vodka *f*
vogue [vəʊg] *n* vogue *f*; **in v.** en vogue
voice [vɔɪs] **1** *n* voix *f*; **at the top of one's v.** à tue-tête **2** *vt* (*opinion, feelings*) exprimer

void [vɔɪd] **1** *n* vide *m* **2** *adj* (*deed, contract*) nul (*f* nulle)
volatile [*Br* 'vɒlətaɪl, *Am* 'vɒlətəl] *adj* (*person*) inconstant; (*situation*) explosif, -ive
volcano [vɒl'keɪnəʊ] (*pl* -oes) *n* volcan *m*
volley ['vɒlɪ] *n* (*in tennis*) volée *f* ■ **volleyball** *n* volley(-ball) *m*
volt [vəʊlt] *n* volt *m* ■ **voltage** [-tɪdʒ] *n* voltage *m*
volume ['vɒljuːm] *n* (*book, capacity, loudness*) volume *m*
voluntary [*Br* 'vɒləntərɪ, *Am* -erɪ] *adj* volontaire; (*unpaid*) bénévole ■ **voluntarily** *adv* volontairement; (*on an unpaid basis*) bénévolement
volunteer [vɒlən'tɪə(r)] **1** *n* volontaire *mf*; (*for charity*) bénévole *mf* **2** *vt* (*information*) donner spontanément **3** *vi* se porter volontaire (**for sth** pour qch; **to do sth** pour faire)
vomit ['vɒmɪt] **1** *n* vomi *m* **2** *vti* vomir
vote [vəʊt] **1** *n* (*choice*) vote *m*; (*election*) scrutin *m*; (*paper*) voix *f*; **to take a v. on sth** voter sur qch; **to have the v.** avoir le droit de vote **2** *vt* (*funds, bill*) voter **3** *vi* voter; **to v. Labour** voter travailliste ■ **voter** *n* (*elector*) électeur, -trice *mf* ■ **voting** *n* (*polling*) scrutin *m*
vouch [vaʊtʃ] *vi* **to v. for sb/sth** répondre de qn/qch
voucher ['vaʊtʃə(r)] *n* coupon *m*, bon *m*; (*gift-*)v. chèque-cadeau *m*
vow [vaʊ] **1** *n* vœu *m* **2** *vt* jurer (**to** à); **to v. to do sth** jurer de faire qch
vowel ['vaʊəl] *n* voyelle *f*
voyage ['vɔɪɪdʒ] *n* voyage *m*
vulgar ['vʌlgə(r)] *adj* vulgaire
vulnerable ['vʌlnərəbəl] *adj* vulnérable
vulture ['vʌltʃə(r)] *n* vautour *m*

Ww

W, w [ˈdʌbəljuː] *n* (letter) W, w *m inv*

wacky [ˈwækɪ] (-ier, -iest) *adj Fam* farfelu

wad [wɒd] *n* (of papers, banknotes) liasse *f*; (of cotton wool) morceau *m*

waddle [ˈwɒdəl] *vi Fig* (of duck, person) se dandiner

wade [weɪd] *vi* to w. through (mud, water) patauger dans; *Fig* (book) venir péniblement à bout de

wafer [ˈweɪfə(r)] *n* (biscuit) gaufrette *f*; *Rel* hostie *f*

waffle¹ [ˈwɒfəl] *n* (cake) gaufre *f*

waffle² [ˈwɒfəl] *Br Fam* **1** *n* remplissage *m* **2** *vi* faire du remplissage

waft [wɒft] *vi* (of smell, sound) parvenir

wag [wæg] (pt & pp -gg-) *vt* remuer, agiter; to w. one's finger at sb menacer qn du doigt

wage [weɪdʒ] **1** *n* wage(s) salaire *m*, paie *f*; w. earner salarié, -e; *mf*; *Br* w. packet (money) paie **2** *vt* to w. war faire la guerre (on à)

wager [ˈweɪdʒə(r)] **1** *n* pari *m* **2** *vt* parier (that que)

waggle [ˈwægəl] *vti* remuer

wag(g)on [ˈwægən] *n Br* (of train) wagon *m* (découvert); (horse-drawn) charrette *f*

wail [weɪl] *vi* (of person) gémir; (of siren) hurler

waist [weɪst] *n* taille *f* ▪ **waistcoat** *n Br* gilet *m* ▪ **waistline** *n* taille *f*

wait [weɪt] **1** *n* attente *f*; to lie in w. for sb guetter qn

2 *vt* to w. one's turn attendre son tour

3 *vi* (a) attendre; to w. for sb/sth attendre qn/qch; to keep sb waiting faire attendre qn; w. till *ou* until I've gone, w. for me to go attends que je sois parti; I can't w. to see her j'ai vraiment hâte de la voir (b) to w. on sb servir qn ▪ waiting **1** *n* attente *f*; *Br* 'no w.' 'arrêt interdit' **2** *adj* w. list/room liste *f*/salle *f* d'attente

▸ **wait about, wait around** *vi* attendre

▸ **wait behind** *vi* rester

▸ **wait up** *vi* veiller; to w. up for sb attendre le retour de qn pour aller se coucher

waiter [ˈweɪtə(r)] *n* serveur *m* ▪ **waitress** *n* serveuse *f*

wake¹ [weɪk] (pt woke, pp woken) **1** *vt* to w. sb (up) réveiller qn **2** *vi* to w. (up) se réveiller; to w. up to sth prendre conscience de qch

wake² [weɪk] *n* (of ship) sillage *m*; *Fig* in the w. of sth à la suite de qch

Wales [weɪlz] *n* le pays de Galles

walk [wɔːk] **1** *n* (short) promenade *f*; (long) marche *f*; (gait) démarche *f*; (path) avenue *f*; to go for a w., to take a w. aller se promener; to take the dog for a w. promener le chien; five minutes' w. (away) à cinq minutes à pied

2 *vt* to w. the dog promener le chien; to w. sb home raccompagner qn; I walked 3 miles ≃ j'ai fait presque 5 km à pied

3 *vi* marcher; (as opposed to cycling, driving) aller à pied; (for exercise, pleasure) se promener; to w. home rentrer à pied ∎ **walker** *n* marcheur, -euse *mf*; *(for pleasure)* promeneur, -euse *mf* ∎ **walking** *n* marche *f* (à pied); **w. stick** canne *f* ∎ **walkway** *n* passage *m* couvert; **moving w.** trottoir *m* roulant

► **walk away** *vi* s'en aller (**from** de)

► **walk in** *vi* entrer

► **walk off** *vi* s'en aller; **to w. off with sth** *(steal)* partir avec qch

► **walk out** *vi (leave)* sortir; *Br (of workers)* se mettre en grève; **to w. out on sb** quitter qn

► **walk over** *vi* **to w. over to** *(go up to)* s'approcher de

Walkman® ['wɔ:kmən] *(pl* **-mans**) *n* baladeur *m*, Walkman® *m*

wall [wɔ:l] **1** *n* mur *m*; *(of cabin, tunnel, stomach)* paroi *f* **2** *adj (map, hanging)* mural ∎ **wallpaper 1** *n* papier *m* peint **2** *vt* tapisser ∎ **wall-to-wall** *adj* **w. carpet(ing)** moquette *f*

wallet ['wɒlɪt] *n* portefeuille *m*

wallow ['wɒləʊ] *vi* se vautrer

walnut ['wɔ:lnʌt] *n (nut)* noix *f*; *(tree, wood)* noyer *m*

walrus ['wɔ:lrəs] *(pl* **-ruses** [-rəsəz]) *n* morse *m*

waltz [Br wɔ:ls, Am wɒlts] **1** *n* valse *f* **2** *vi* valser

wand [wɒnd] *n (magic)* **w.** baguette *f* magique

wander ['wɒndə(r)] **1** *vt* **to w. the streets** errer dans les rues **2** *vi (of thoughts)* vagabonder; *(of person)* errer, vagabonder; **to w. from** *(path, subject)* s'écarter de

► **wander about, wander around** *vi (roam)* errer, vagabonder; *(stroll)* flâner

► **wander off** *vi (go away)* s'éloigner

wangle ['wæŋgəl] *vt Br Fam (obtain)* se débrouiller pour avoir

want [wɒnt] **1** *n (lack)* manque *m* (**of** de); **for w. of** par manque de; **for w. of money/time** faute d'argent/de temps

  2 *vt* vouloir (**to do** faire); **I w. him to go** je veux qu'il parte; **the lawn wants cutting** la pelouse a besoin d'être

tondue; **you're wanted on the phone** on vous demande au téléphone ∎ **wanted** *adj (criminal)* recherché par la police

wanton ['wɒntən] *adj (gratuitous)* gratuit

war [wɔ:(r)] **1** *n* guerre *f*; **at w.** en guerre (**with** avec); **to declare w.** déclarer la guerre (**on** à) **2** *adj (wound, crime)* de guerre; **w. memorial** monument *m* aux morts

ward¹ [wɔ:d] *n (in hospital)* salle *f*

ward² [wɔ:d] *vt* **to w. off** *(blow)* éviter; *(danger)* chasser

warden ['wɔ:dən] *n (of institution, hostel)* directeur, -trice *mf*

warder ['wɔ:də(r)] *n Br* gardien *m* (de prison)

wardrobe ['wɔ:drəʊb] *n (cupboard)* penderie *f*; *(clothes)* garde-robe *f*

warehouse ['weəhaʊs] *(pl* **-ses** [-zɪz]) *n* entrepôt *m*

wares [weəz] *npl* marchandises *fpl*

warfare ['wɔ:feə(r)] *n* guerre *f*

warm [wɔ:m] **1** (**-er, -est**) *adj* chaud; *Fig (welcome)* chaleureux, -euse; **to be or feel w.** avoir chaud; **to get w.** *(of person, room)* se réchauffer; **it's w.** *(of weather)* il fait chaud

  2 *vt* **to w. (up)** *(person, food)* réchauffer

  3 *vi* **to w. up** *(of person, room)* se réchauffer; *(of athlete)* s'échauffer ∎ **warmly** *adv (dress)* chaudement; *Fig (welcome, thank)* chaleureusement ∎ **warmth** *n* chaleur *f*

warn [wɔ:n] *vt* avertir, prévenir (**that** que); **to w. sb against or of sth** mettre qn en garde contre qch ∎ **warning** *n (caution)* avertissement *m*; *(advance notice)* avis *m*; **without w.** sans prévenir; **w. light** *(on appliance)* voyant *m* lumineux; *Br (hazard)* **w. lights** feux *mpl* de détresse

warp [wɔ:p] **1** *vt (wood)* gauchir; *Fig (judgement, person)* pervertir **2** *vi (of door)* gauchir

warrant ['wɒrənt] *n (in law)* mandat *m* ∎ **warranty** *(pl* **-ies**) *n Com* garantie *f*

warren ['wɒrən] *n* (rabbit) w. garenne *f*

warrior ['wɒrɪə(r)] *n* guerrier, -ère *mf*

wart [wɔːt] *n* verrue *f*

wartime ['wɔːtaɪm] *n* in w. en temps de guerre

wary ['weərɪ] (-ier, -iest) *adj* prudent; **to be w. of sb/sth** se méfier de qn/qch; **to be w. of doing sth** hésiter beaucoup à faire qch

was [wəz, *stressed* wɒz] *pt of* **be**

wash [wɒʃ] **1** *n* **to have a w.** se laver; **to give sth a w.** laver qch
2 *vt* laver; **to w. one's hands** se laver les mains (**of** sth de qch)
3 *vi* (have a wash) se laver ■ **washbasin** *n Br* lavabo *m* ■ **washcloth** *n Am* gant *m* de toilette ■ **washing-up** *n Br* vaisselle *f*; **to do the w.** faire la vaisselle; **w. liquid** liquide *m* vaisselle ■ **washroom** *n Am* toilettes *fpl*

► **wash down** *vt sep* (car, deck) laver à grande eau; (food) arroser (**with** de)

► **wash off** **1** *vt sep* enlever **2** *vi* partir

► **wash out** **1** *vt sep* (bowl, cup) rincer; (stain) faire partir (en lavant) **2** *vi* (of stain) partir (au lavage)

► **wash up** **1** *vt sep Br* (dishes, forks) laver **2** *vi Br* (do the dishes) faire la vaisselle; *Am* (have a wash) se débarbouiller

washable ['wɒʃəbəl] *adj* lavable

washer ['wɒʃə(r)] *n* (ring) joint *m*

washing ['wɒʃɪŋ] *n* (action) lavage *m*; (clothes) linge *m*; **to do the w.** faire la lessive; **w. machine** machine *f* à laver; *Br* **w. powder** lessive *f*

wasp [wɒsp] *n* guêpe *f*

waste [weɪst] **1** *n* gaspillage *m*; (of time) perte *f*; (rubbish) déchets *mpl*; **w. material** *or* **products** déchets *mpl*; *Br* **w. ground** (in town) terrain *m* vague; **w. land** (uncultivated) terres *fpl* incultes; (in town) terrain *m* vague; **w. pipe** tuyau *m* d'évacuation
2 *vt* (money, food) gaspiller; (time) perdre; (opportunity) gâcher; **to w. no time doing sth** ne pas perdre de temps pour faire qch

3 *vi* **to w. away** dépérir ■ **wasted** *adj* (effort) inutile

wastebin ['weɪstbɪn] *n* (in kitchen) poubelle *f*

wasteful ['weɪstfəl] *adj* (person) gaspilleur, -euse; (process) peu économique

watch [wɒtʃ] **1** *n* (a) (timepiece) montre *f* (b) **to keep a close w. on sb/sth** surveiller qn/qch de près
2 *vt* regarder; (observe) observer; (suspect, baby, luggage) surveiller; (be careful of) faire attention à; **w. it!** attention!
3 *vi* regarder; **to w. out for sb/sth** guetter qn/qch; **to w. out** (take care) faire attention (**for** à); **w. out!** attention!; **to w. over** surveiller ■ **watchdog** *n* chien *m* de garde ■ **watchstrap** *n* bracelet *m* de montre

watchful ['wɒtʃfəl] *adj* vigilant

water ['wɔːtə(r)] **1** *n* eau *f*; **under w.** (road, field) inondé; (swim) sous l'eau; **w. heater** chauffe-eau *m inv*; **w. pistol** pistolet *m* à eau; **w. polo** water-polo *m*; **w. skiing** ski *m* nautique; **w. wings** brassards *mpl* de natation
2 *vt* (plant) arroser; **to w. sth down** (wine) diluer qch; (text) édulcorer qch
3 *vi* (of eyes) larmoyer; **it makes my mouth w.** ça me met l'eau à la bouche ■ **watercolour** (*Am* **-color**) *n* aquarelle *f* ■ **watercress** *n* cresson *m* (de fontaine) ■ **waterfall** *n* cascade *f* ■ **watering** *n* **w. can** arrosoir *m* ■ **watermark** *n* filigrane *m* ■ **watermelon** *n* pastèque *f* ■ **waterproof** *adj* imperméable; (watch) étanche ■ **watertight** *adj* (container) étanche

watery ['wɔːtərɪ] *adj* (soup) trop liquide; (coffee, tea) insipide; (colour) délavé

watt [wɒt] *n* watt *m*

wave [weɪv] **1** *n* (of water, crime) vague *f*; (in hair) ondulation *f*; *Phys* onde *f* **2** *vt* (arm, flag) agiter; (stick) brandir **3** *vi* (of person) faire signe (de la main); **to w. to sb** (signal) faire signe de la main à qn; (greet) saluer qn de la main

■ **waveband** n bande f de fréquences

■ **wavelength** n longueur f d'onde; Fig **on the same w.** sur la même longueur d'onde

waver ['weɪvə(r)] vi (of person, flame) vaciller

wavy ['weɪvɪ] (**-ier, -iest**) adj (line) qui ondule; (hair) ondulé

wax [wæks] 1 n cire f, (for ski) fart m 2 adj (candle, doll) de cire; Am **w. paper** (for wrapping) papier m paraffiné 3 vt cirer; (ski) farter; (car) lustrer

WAY [weɪ] 1 n (a) (path, road) chemin m (**to** de); (direction) sens m, direction f; **the w. in** l'entrée f; **the w. out** la sortie; **the w. to the station** le chemin pour aller à la gare; **to ask sb the w.** demander son chemin à qn; **to show sb the w.** montrer le chemin à qn; **to lose one's w.** se perdre; **I'm on my w.** (coming) j'arrive; (going) je pars; **to make w. for sb** faire de la place à qn; **out of the w.** (isolated) isolé; **to get out of the w.** s'écarter; **to go all the w.** aller jusqu'au bout; **to give w.** céder; Br (in vehicle) céder le passage (**to** à); **it's a long w. away** or **off** c'est très loin; **it's the wrong w. up** c'est dans le mauvais sens; **this w.** par ici; **that w.** par là; **which w.?** par où? (**b**) (manner) manière f; **in this w.** de cette manière; **by w. of** (via) par; Fig (as) comme; Fig **by the w.** à propos; Fam **no w.!** (certainly not) pas question!; **w. of life** mode m de vie 2 adv Fam **w. behind** très en arrière; **w. ahead** très en avance (**of** sur)

wayward ['weɪwəd] adj difficile

WC [dʌblju:'si:] n W.-C. mpl

we [wi:] pron nous; (indefinite) on; **we teachers** nous autres professeurs; **we all make mistakes** tout le monde peut se tromper

weak [wi:k] (**-er, -est**) adj faible; (tea, coffee) léger, -ère; **to have a w. heart** avoir le cœur fragile ■ **weakling** n (in body) mauviette f, (in character) faible mf ■ **weakness** n faiblesse f, (fault)

point m faible; **to have a w. for sb/ sth** avoir un faible pour qch/qn

weaken ['wi:kən] 1 vt affaiblir 2 vi s'affaiblir

wealth [welθ] n richesse f; Fig **a w. of sth** une abondance de qch ■ **wealthy** 1 (**-ier, -iest**) adj riche 2 npl **the w.** les riches mpl

weapon ['wepən] n arme f

wear [weə(r)] 1 n (**a**) men's **w.** vêtements mpl pour hommes; **evening w.** tenue f de soirée (**b**) (use) **w. and tear** usure f naturelle 2 (pt **wore**, pp **worn**) vt (garment, glasses) porter; **to w. black** porter du noir 3 vi **to w. thin** (of clothing) s'user; **to w. well** (of clothing) bien vieillir

▶ **wear down** 1 vt sep user; **to w. sb down** avoir qn à l'usure 2 vi s'user

▶ **wear off** vi (of colour, pain) disparaître

▶ **wear out** 1 vt sep (clothes) user; **to w. sb out** épuiser qn 2 vi (of clothes) s'user; Fig (of patience) s'épuiser

weary ['wɪərɪ] 1 (**-ier, -iest**) adj las (f lasse) (**of doing** de faire) 2 vi se lasser (**of** de)

weather ['weðə(r)] 1 n temps m; **what's the w. like?** quel temps fait-il?; **in hot w.** par temps chaud; **under the w.** (ill) patraque 2 adj **w. forecast** prévisions fpl météorologiques; **w. report** (bulletin m) météo f 3 vt (storm) essuyer; Fig (crisis) surmonter ■ **weatherman** (pl **-men**) n (on TV, radio) présentateur m météo

weave [wi:v] 1 (pt **wove**, pp **woven**) vt (cloth, plot) tisser; (basket, garland) tresser 2 vi tisser; Fig **to w. in and out of** (crowd, cars) se faufiler entre

web [web] n (of spider) toile f, Fig (of lies) tissu m; Comptr **the W.** le Web; **w. page** page f Web; **w. site** site m Web

wed [wed] (pt & pp **-dd-**) 1 vt (marry) épouser 2 vi se marier

we'd [wi:d] = **we had, we would**

wedding ['wedɪŋ] 1 n mariage m; **golden/silver w.** noces fpl d'or/d'argent 2 adj (anniversary, present, cake) de mariage; *(dress)* de mariée; **his/ her w. day** le jour de son mariage; *Br* **w. ring,** *Am* **w. band** alliance *f*

wedge [wedʒ] **1** *n (of wheel, table)* cale *f* **2** *vt (wheel, table)* caler; *(push)* enfoncer **(into** dans); **to w. a door open** maintenir une porte ouverte avec une cale; **wedged (in) between** coincé entre

Wednesday ['wenzdeɪ] *n* mercredi *m*

wee[1] [wiː] *adj Scot Fam (tiny)* tout petit *(f* toute petite)

wee[2] [wiː] *vi Br Fam* faire pipi

weed [wiːd] **1** *n (plant)* mauvaise herbe *f* **2** *vti* désherber; *Fig* **to w. sth out** éliminer qch **(from** de) ■ **weedkiller** *n* désherbant *m* ■ **weedy** (**-ier, -iest**) *adj Fam (person)* malingre

week [wiːk] *n* semaine *f*; **tomorrow w., a w. tomorrow** demain en huit ■ **weekday** *n* jour *m* de semaine

weekend [wiːk'end] *n* week-end *m*; **at** *or* **on** *or* **over the w.** ce week-end; *(every weekend)* le week-end

weekly ['wiːklɪ] **1** *adj* hebdomadaire **2** *adv* toutes les semaines **3** *n (magazine)* hebdomadaire *m*

weep [wiːp] *(pt & pp* **wept)** *vi* pleurer

weigh [weɪ] **1** *vt* peser; **to w. sb/sth down** *(with load)* surcharger qn/qch **(with** de); **to w. up** *(chances)* peser **2** *vi* peser; **it's weighing on my mind** ça me tracasse ■ **weighing-machine** *n* balance *f*

weight [weɪt] **1** *n* poids *m*; **to put on w.** grossir; **to lose w.** maigrir; *Fig* **to carry w.** *(of argument)* avoir du poids **2** *vt* **to w. sth (down)** *(hold down)* faire tenir qch avec un poids ■ **weightlifter** *n* haltérophile *mf* ■ **weightlifting** *n* haltérophilie *f*

weighty ['weɪtɪ] (**-ier, -iest**) *adj (serious, important)* grave

weir [wɪə(r)] *n* barrage *m*

weird [wɪəd] (**-er, -est**) *adj* bizarre

welcome ['welkəm] **1** *adj (person, news, change)* bienvenu; **to make sb w.** faire un bon accueil à qn; **w.!** bienvenue!; **you're w.!** *(after 'thank you')* il

n'y a pas de quoi!; **you're w. to use my bike** mon vélo est à ta disposition **2** *n* accueil *m*; **to give sb a warm w.** faire un accueil chaleureux à qn **3** *vt (person)* souhaiter la bienvenue à; *(news, change)* accueillir favorablement ■ **welcoming** *adj* accueillant; *(speech, words)* de bienvenue

welfare ['welfeə(r)] *n (wellbeing)* bien-être *m*; *Am Fam* **to be on w.** recevoir l'aide sociale; *Br* **the W. State** l'État *m* providence

we'll [wiːl] = **we will, we shall**

well[1] [wel] *n (for water, oil)* puits *m*

well[2] [wel] **1** *(better, best) adj* bien; **to be w.** aller bien; **to get w.** se remettre; **it's just as w....** heureusement que...

2 *adv* bien; **you'd do w. to refuse** tu ferais bien de refuser; **she might (just) as w. have stayed at home** elle aurait mieux fait de rester chez elle; **as w.** *(also)* aussi; **as w. as** aussi bien que; **as w. as two cats, he has...** en plus de deux chats, il a...

3 *exclam* eh bien!; **w., w.!** *(surprise)* tiens, tiens!; **huge, w. quite big** énorme, enfin, assez grand ■ **well-behaved** *adj* sage ■ **well-being** *n* bien-être *m* ■ **well-built** *adj (person, car)* solide ■ **well-dressed** *adj* bien habillé ■ **well-informed** *adj* bien informé ■ **well-known** *adj* (bien) connu ■ **well-meaning** *adj* bien intentionné ■ **well-off** *adj* riche ■ **well-paid** *adj* bien payé ■ **well-read** *adj* instruit ■ **well-timed** *adj* opportun ■ **well-to-do** *adj* aisé ■ **wellwisher** *n* sympathisant, -e *mf* ■ **well-worn** *adj (clothes, carpet)* très usé

wellington ['welɪŋtən] *(Fam* **welly** [welɪ], *pl* **-ies)** *n Br* **w. (boot)** botte *f* de caoutchouc

Welsh [welʃ] **1** *adj* gallois **2** *n (language)* gallois *m*; **the W.** *(people)* les Gallois *mpl* ■ **Welshman** *(pl* **-men)** *n* Gallois *m* ■ **Welshwoman** *(pl* **-women)** *n* Galloise *f*

went [went] *pt of* **go**

wept [wept] *pt & pp of* **weep**
were [wə(r), *stressed* wɜː(r)] *pt of* **be**
we're [wɪə(r)] = **we are**
west [west] **1** *n* ouest *m*; **(to the) w. of** à l'ouest de; *Pol* **the W.** l'Occident *m*
2 *adj* (*coast*) ouest *inv*; (*wind*) d'ouest; **W. Africa** l'Afrique *f* occidentale; **W. Indian** *adj* antillais; *n* Antillais, -e *mf*; **the W. Indies** les Antilles *fpl*
3 *adv* à l'ouest; (*travel*) vers l'ouest
■ **westbound** *adj* (*traffic*) en direction de l'ouest; *Br* (*carriageway*) ouest *inv*
■ **westerly** *adj* (*direction*) de l'ouest
■ **western 1** *adj* (*coast*) ouest *inv*; *Pol* (*culture*) occidental; **W. Europe** l'Europe *f* de l'Ouest **2** *n* (*film*) western *m*
■ **westerner** *n Pol* occidental, -e *mf*
■ **westward** *adj & adv* vers l'ouest
■ **westwards** *adv* vers l'ouest

wet [wet] **1** (*wetter, wettest*) *adj* mouillé; (*weather*) pluvieux, -euse; (*day*) de pluie; **to get w.** se mouiller; **to be w. through** être trempé; **it's w.** (*raining*) il pleut; **'w. paint'** 'peinture fraîche'; **w. suit** combinaison *f* de plongée **2** *n* **the w.** (*rain*) la pluie; (*damp*) l'humidité *f* **3** (*pt & pp* -**tt**-) *vt* mouiller
we've [wiːv] = **we have**
whack [wæk] *vt Fam* donner un grand coup à
whale [weɪl] *n* baleine *f*

WHAT [wɒt] **1** *adj* quel, quelle, *pl* quel(le)s; **w. book?** quel livre?; **w. a fool!** quel idiot!; **w. little she has** le peu qu'elle a
2 *pron* (**a**) (*in questions*) (*subject*) qu'est-ce qui; (*object*) (qu'est-ce) que; (*after prep*) quoi; **w.'s happening?** qu'est-ce qui se passe?; **w. does he do?** qu'est-ce qu'il fait?, que fait-il?; **w. is it?** qu'est-ce que c'est?; **w.'s that book?** c'est quoi, ce livre?; **w.!** (*surprise*) quoi!, comment!; **w.'s it called?** comment ça s'appelle?; **w. for?** pourquoi?; **w. about going out for lunch?** si on allait déjeuner?
(**b**) (*in relative construction*) (*subject*)

ce qui; (*object*) ce que; **I know w. will happen/w. she'll do** je sais ce qui arrivera/ce qu'elle fera; **w. I need...** ce dont j'ai besoin...

whatever [wɒt'evə(r)] **1** *adj* **w. (the) mistake** quelle que soit l'erreur; **of w. size** de n'importe quelle taille; **no chance w.** pas la moindre chance; **nothing w.** rien du tout **2** *pron* (*no matter what*) quoi que (+ *subjunctive*); **w. you do** quoi que tu fasses; **do w. you want** fais tout ce que tu veux
whatsit ['wɒtsɪt] *n Fam* machin *m*
whatsoever [wɒtsəʊ'evə(r)] *adj* **for no reason w.** sans aucune raison; **none w.** aucun
wheat [wiːt] *n* blé *m*
wheedle ['wiːdəl] *vt* **to w. sb** enjôler qn (**into doing** pour qu'il/elle fasse); **to w. sth out of sb** obtenir qch de qn par la flatterie
wheel [wiːl] **1** *n* roue *f*; **to be at the w.** être au volant **2** *vt* (*push*) pousser
■ **wheelbarrow** *n* brouette *f* ■ **wheelchair** *n* fauteuil *m* roulant ■ **wheelclamp** *n* sabot *m* de Denver
wheeze [wiːz] *vi* respirer bruyamment ■ **wheezy** (-**ier**, -**iest**) *adj* poussif, -ive
when [wen] **1** *adv* quand **2** *conj* (*with time*) quand, lorsque; **w. I finish, w. I've finished** quand j'aurai fini; **the day/moment w.** le jour/moment où
whenever [wen'evə(r)] *conj* (*at whatever time*) quand; (*each time that*) chaque fois que
where [weə(r)] **1** *adv* où; **w. are you from?** d'où êtes-vous?
2 *conj* où; **I found it w.** she'd left it je l'ai trouvé là où elle l'avait laissé; **the place/house w.** I live l'endroit/la maison où j'habite; ■ **whereabouts 1** *adv* où **2** ['weərəbaʊts] *n* **his w.** l'endroit *m* où il est ■ **whereas** *conj* alors que ■ **whereby** *adv Formal* par quoi
wherever [weər'evə(r)] *conj* **w. you go** (*everywhere*) partout où tu iras, où que tu ailles; **I'll go w. you like** j'irai (là) où vous voudrez

whet [wet] (*pt & pp* -**tt**-) *vt* (*appetite, desire*) aiguiser

whether ['weðə(r)] *conj* si; **I don't know w. to leave** je ne sais pas si je dois partir; **w. she does it or not** qu'elle le fasse ou non; **it's doubtful w....** il est douteux que… (+ *subjunctive*)

WHICH [wɪtʃ] **1** *adj* (*in questions*) quel, quelle, *pl* quel(le)s; **w. book?** quel livre?; **w. one?** lequel/laquelle?; **in w. case** auquel cas

2 *relative pron* (*subject*) qui; (*object*) que; (*after prep*) lequel, laquelle, *pl* lesquel(le)s; (*referring to a whole clause*) (*subject*) ce qui; (*object*) ce que; **the house, w. is old…** la maison, qui est vieille…; **the book w. I like…** le livre que j'aime…; **the table w. I put it on…** la table sur laquelle je l'ai mis…; **the film of w. she was speaking** le film dont *ou* duquel elle parlait; **she's ill, w. is sad** elle est malade, ce qui est triste; **he lies, w. I don't like** il ment, ce que je n'aime pas; **after w.** (*whereupon*) après quoi

3 *interrogative pron* (*in questions*) lequel, laquelle, *pl* lesquel(le)s; **w. of us?** lequel/laquelle d'entre nous?; **w. are the best of the books?** quels sont les meilleurs de ces livres?

4 *pron* **w. (one)** (*the one that*) (*subject*) celui qui, celle qui, *pl* ceux qui, celles qui; (*object*) celui que, celle que, *pl* ceux que, celles que; **I know w. (ones) you want** je sais ceux/celles que vous désirez

whichever [wɪtʃ'evə(r)] **1** *adj* (*no matter which*) **take w. books interest you** prenez les livres qui vous intéressent; **take w. one you like** prends celui/celle que tu veux **2** *pron* (*no matter which*) quel que soit celui qui (*f* quelle que soit celle qui); **w. you choose…** quel que soit celui que tu choisiras…; **take w. you want** prends celui/celle que tu veux

while [waɪl] **1** *conj* (*when*) pendant que; (*although*) bien que (+ *subjunctive*); (*as long as*) tant que; (*whereas*) tandis que; **w. eating** en mangeant **2** *n* **a w.** un moment; **all the w.** tout le temps **3** *vt* **to w. away the time** passer le temps (**doing sth** à faire qch) ■ **whilst** *conj Br* = **while**

whim [wɪm] *n* caprice *m*; **on a w.** sur un coup de tête

whimper ['wɪmpə(r)] *vi* gémir

whine [waɪn] *vi* gémir

whip [wɪp] **1** *n* fouet *m* **2** (*pt & pp* -**pp**-) *vt* fouetter; **whipped cream** crème *f* fouettée

▶ **whip off** *vt sep Fam* (*clothes*) enlever rapidement

▶ **whip out** *vt sep Fam* sortir brusquement (**from** de)

▶ **whip up** *vt sep* (*interest*) susciter; *Fam* (*meal*) préparer rapidement

whirl [wɜːl] **1** *vt* **to w. sb/sth (round)** faire tourbillonner qn/qch **2** *vi* **to w. (round)** tourbillonner ■ **whirlpool** *n* tourbillon *m* ■ **whirlwind** *n* tourbillon *m*

whirr [wɜː(r)] *vi* ronfler

whisk [wɪsk] **1** *n* (*for eggs*) fouet *m* **2** *vt* battre; **to w. away** *or* **off** (*object*) enlever rapidement; (*person*) emmener rapidement

whiskers ['wɪskəz] *npl* (*of cat*) moustaches *fpl*; (*of man*) favoris *mpl*

whisky ['wɪskɪ] (*Am* **whiskey**) *n* whisky *m*

whisper ['wɪspə(r)] **1** *n* chuchotement *m* **2** *vti* chuchoter; **to w. sth to sb** chuchoter qch à l'oreille de qn

whistle ['wɪsəl] **1** *n* sifflement *m*; (*object*) sifflet *m* **2** *vti* siffler

white [waɪt] **1** (-**er, -est**) *adj* blanc (*f* blanche); **to go** *or* **turn w.** blanchir; *Br* **w. coffee** café *m* au lait; **w. lie** pieux mensonge *m*; **w. man** Blanc *m*; **w. woman** Blanche *f* **2** *n* (*colour, of egg, eye*) blanc *m* ■ **whitewash 1** *n* (*paint*) badigeon *m* à la chaux **2** *vt* (*paint*) badigeonner à la chaux; *Fig* (*person*) blanchir

Whitsun ['wɪtsən] *n Br* la Pentecôte

whizz [wɪz] **1** *vi (rush)* aller à toute vitesse; **to w. past** *or* **by** passer à toute vitesse **2** *adj Fam* **w. kid** petit prodige *m*

who [huː] *pron* qui; **w. did it?** qui (est-ce qui) a fait ça?; **the woman w. came** la femme qui est venue; **w. were you talking to?** à qui est-ce que tu parlais?

whodun(n)it [huːˈdʌnɪt] *n Fam* polar *m*

whoever [huːˈevə(r)] *pron (no matter who) (subject)* qui que ce soit qui; *(object)* qui que ce soit que; **w. has seen this** *(anyone who)* quiconque a vu cela; **w. you are** qui que vous soyez; **this man, w. he is** cet homme, quel qu'il soit

whole [həʊl] **1** *adj* entier, -ère; **the w. time** tout le temps; **the w. apple** toute la pomme, la pomme tout entière; **the w. world** le monde entier

2 *n* totalité *f*; **the w. of the village** le village tout entier, tout le village; **on the w., as a w.** dans l'ensemble ■ **wholefood** *n* aliment *m* complet ■ **whole-hearted** *adj* sans réserve ■ **wholemeal** *(Am* **wholewheat)** *adj (bread)* complet, -ète ■ **wholesome** *adj (food, climate)* sain

wholesale [ˈhəʊlseɪl] **1** *adj (price)* de gros; **w. business** *or* **trade** commerce *m* de gros **2** *adv (buy, sell)* au prix de gros

wholly [ˈhəʊlɪ] *adv* entièrement

whom [huːm] *pron Formal (object)* que; *(in questions and after prep)* qui; **w. did she see?** qui a-t-elle vu?; **the man w. you know** l'homme que tu connais; **the man of w. we were speaking** l'homme dont nous parlions

whooping [ˈhuːpɪŋ] *adj* **w. cough** coqueluche *f*

whoops [wʊps] *exclam* houp-là!

whopping [ˈwɒpɪŋ] *adj Fam (big)* énorme

whore [hɔː(r)] *n Fam* putain *f*

whose [huːz] *possessive pron & adj* à qui, de qui; **w. book is this?, w. is this book?** à qui est ce livre?; **w. daughter are you?** de qui es-tu la fille?; **the woman w. book I have** la femme dont j'ai le livre; **the man w. mother I spoke to** l'homme à la mère de qui j'ai parlé

why [waɪ] **1** *adv* pourquoi; **w. not?** pourquoi pas? **2** *conj* **the reason w. they...** la raison pour laquelle ils... **3** *exclam (surprise)* tiens!

wick [wɪk] *n (of candle, lighter, oil lamp)* mèche *f*

wicked [ˈwɪkɪd] *adj (evil)* méchant

wicker [ˈwɪkə(r)] *n* osier *m*

wicket [ˈwɪkɪt] *n (cricket stumps)* guichet *m*

wide [waɪd] **1** (-er, -est) *adj* large; *(choice, variety, knowledge)* grand; **to be 3 metres w.** avoir 3 mètres de large **2** *adv (fall, shoot)* loin du but; **w. open** *(eyes, mouth, door)* grand ouvert; **w. awake** complètement réveillé ■ **widely** *adv (travel)* beaucoup; *(spread)* largement; **it's w. thought that...** on pense généralement que... ■ **widen 1** *vt* élargir **2** *vi* s'élargir

widespread [ˈwaɪdspred] *adj* répandu

widow [ˈwɪdəʊ] *n* veuve *f* ■ **widower** *n* veuf *m*

width [wɪdθ] *n* largeur *f*

wield [wiːld] *vt (brandish)* brandir; *Fig* **to w. power** exercer le pouvoir

wife [waɪf] *(pl* **wives)** *n* femme *f*, épouse *f*

wig [wɪg] *n* perruque *f*

wiggle [ˈwɪgəl] **1** *vt* remuer **2** *vi (of worm)* se tortiller; *(of tail)* remuer

wild [waɪld] **1** (-er, -est) *adj (animal, flower, region)* sauvage; *(idea)* fou (*f* folle); **w. with joy/anger** fou de joie/colère; **to be w.** *(of person)* mener une vie agitée; *Fam* **I'm not w. about it** ça ne m'emballe pas; **the W. West** le Far West

2 *adv* **to grow w.** *(of plant)* pousser à l'état sauvage; **to run w.** *(of animals)* courir en liberté; *(of crowd)* se déchaîner

3 *n* **in the w.** à l'état sauvage; **in the wilds** en pleine brousse ▪ **wildlife** *n* nature *f*

wilderness ['wɪldənəs] *n* région *f* sauvage

wildly ['waɪldlɪ] *adv* (*cheer*) frénétiquement; (*guess*) au hasard

wilful ['wɪlfəl] (*Am* **willful**) *adj* (*intentional, obstinate*) volontaire

WILL¹ [wɪl]

On trouve généralement **I/you/he/** etc **will** sous leurs formes contractées **I'll/you'll/he'll/**etc. La forme négative correspondante est **won't**, que l'on écrira **will not** dans des contextes formels.

v aux (*expressing future tense*) **he w. come, he'll come** il viendra; **you w. not come, you won't come** tu ne viendras pas; **w. you have some tea?** veux-tu du thé?; **w. you be quiet!** veux-tu te taire!; **it won't open** ça ne s'ouvre pas

will² [wɪl] *n* (*resolve, determination*) volonté *f*; (*legal document*) testament *m*; **free w.** libre arbitre *m*; **against one's w.** à contrecœur; **at w.** à volonté; (*cry*) à la demande

willing ['wɪlɪŋ] *adj* (*helper, worker*) plein de bonne volonté; **to be w. to do sth** bien vouloir faire qch ▪ **willingly** *adv* (*with pleasure*) volontiers; (*voluntarily*) de son plein gré ▪ **willingness** *n* bonne volonté *f*; **her w. to do sth** (*enthusiasm*) son empressement à faire qch

willpower ['wɪlpaʊə(r)] *n* volonté *f*

wilt [wɪlt] *vi* (*of plant*) dépérir

wily ['waɪlɪ] (**-ier, -iest**) *adj* rusé

wimp [wɪmp] *n* Fam (*weakling*) mauviette *f*

win [wɪn] **1** *n* (*victory*) victoire *f* **2** (*pt & pp* **won**, *pres p* **winning**) *vt* (*money, race, prize*) gagner; (*victory*) remporter; (*fame*) acquérir; (*friends*) se faire; *Br* **to w. sb over** *or* **round** gagner qn (**to** à) **3** *vi* gagner ▪ **winning 1** *adj* (*number, horse*) gagnant; (*team*) victorieux,

-euse; (*goal*) décisif, -ive **2** *npl* **winnings** gains *mpl*

wince [wɪns] *vi* faire une grimace

winch [wɪntʃ] **1** *n* treuil *m* **2** *vt* **to w. (up)** hisser

wind¹ [wɪnd] **1** *n* vent *m*; (*breath*) souffle *m*; **to have w.** (*in stomach*) avoir des gaz; **to get w. of sth** avoir vent de qch; *Mus* **w. instrument** instrument *m* à vent

2 *vt* **to w. sb** (*of blow*) couper le souffle à qn ▪ **windcheater** (*Am* **windbreaker**) *n* coupe-vent *m inv* ▪ **windfall** *n* (*unexpected money*) aubaine *f* ▪ **windmill** *n* moulin *m* à vent ▪ **windscreen** (*Am* **windshield**) *n* (*of vehicle*) pare-brise *m inv*; **w. wiper** essuie-glace *m* ▪ **windsurfer** *n* (*person*) véliplanchiste *mf* ▪ **windsurfing** *n* **to go w.** faire de la planche à voile ▪ **windy** (**-ier, -iest**) *adj* **it's w.** (*of weather*) il y a du vent; **w. day** jour *m* de grand vent

wind² [waɪnd] **1** (*pt & pp* **wound**) *vt* (*roll*) enrouler (**round** autour de); (*clock*) remonter; **to w. a cassette back** rembobiner une cassette **2** *vi* (*of river, road*) serpenter ▪ **winding** *adj* (*road*) sinueux, -euse; (*staircase*) en colimaçon

▸ **wind down 1** *vt sep* (*car window*) baisser **2** *vi* Fam (*relax*) se détendre

▸ **wind up 1** *vt sep* (*clock*) remonter; (*meeting, speech*) terminer; *Br* Fam **to w. sb up** faire marcher qn **2** *vi* (*end up*) finir (**doing sth** par faire qch); **to w. up with sb/sth** se retrouver avec qn/qch

window ['wɪndəʊ] *n* fenêtre *f*; (*pane*) vitre *f*; (*of shop*) vitrine *f*; (*counter*) guichet *m*; *Br* **French w.** porte-fenêtre *f*; **w. box** jardinière *f*; *Br* **w. cleaner**, *Am* **w. washer** laveur, -euse *mf* de vitres; *Br* **w. ledge** rebord *m* de fenêtre ▪ **windowpane** *n* vitre *f*, carreau *m* ▪ **window-shopping** *n* **to go w.** faire du lèche-vitrines ▪ **windowsill** *n* rebord *m* de fenêtre

wine [waɪn] *n* vin *m*; **w. bar/bottle** bar *m*/bouteille *f* à vin; **w. cellar** cave *f* à vin; **w. list** carte *f* des vins; **w. tasting** dégustation *f*; **w. waiter** sommelier *m* ▪ **wineglass** *n* verre *m* à vin

wing [wɪŋ] *n* aile *f*; **the wings** *(in theatre)* les coulisses *fpl*

wink [wɪŋk] *vi* faire un clin d'œil (**at** à)

winner ['wɪnə(r)] *n* gagnant, -e *mf*

winter ['wɪntə(r)] **1** *n* hiver *m*; **in (the) w.** en hiver **2** *adj* d'hiver ▪ **wintertime** *n* hiver *m* ▪ **wintry** *adj* hivernal; **w. day** jour *m* d'hiver

wipe [waɪp] **1** *n* to give sth a w. essuyer qch **2** *vt* essuyer; **to w. one's feet/hands** s'essuyer les pieds/les mains; **to w. sth away** *or* **off** *or* **up** *(liquid)* essuyer qch; **to w. sth out** *(clean)* essuyer qch; *(destroy)* anéantir qch ▪ **wiper** *n* essuie-glace *m*

wire ['waɪə(r)] **1** *n* fil *m*; **w. mesh** *or* **netting** toile *f* métallique **2** *vt* **to w. (up)** *(house)* faire l'installation électrique de; **to w. sth (up) to** *(connect electrically)* relier qch à qch ▪ **wiring** *n* *(system)* installation *f* électrique

wisdom ['wɪzdəm] *n* sagesse *f*

wise [waɪz] (**-er, -est**) *adj (in knowledge)* sage; *(advisable)* prudent; **to be none the wiser** ne pas être plus avancé ▪ **wisely** *adv* sagement

-wise [waɪz] *suff (with regard to)* money-**w.** question argent

wish [wɪʃ] **1** *n (specific)* souhait *m*, vœu *m*; *(general)* désir *m*; **to do sth against sb's wishes** faire qch contre le souhait de qn; **best wishes, all good wishes** *(in letter)* amitiés *fpl*; **send him my best wishes** fais-lui mes amitiés

2 *vt* souhaiter (**to do** faire); **I w. (that) you could help me** je voudrais que vous m'aidiez; **I w. she could come** j'aurais bien aimé qu'elle vienne; **I w. you (a) happy birthday/ (good) luck** je vous souhaite bon anniversaire/bonne chance; **I w. I could** si seulement je pouvais

3 *vi* **to w. for sth** souhaiter qch; **as**

you w. comme vous voudrez ▪ **wishful** *adj* it's. w. thinking (on your part) tu prends tes désirs pour des réalités

wisp [wɪsp] *n (of smoke)* traînée *f*; *(of hair)* mèche *f*

wistful ['wɪstfəl] *adj* nostalgique

wit [wɪt] *n (humour)* esprit *m*; *(person)* homme *m*/femme *f* d'esprit; **wits** *(intelligence)* intelligence *f*; **to be at one's wits'** *or* **w.'s end** ne plus savoir que faire

witch [wɪtʃ] *n* sorcière *f*

WITH [wɪð] *prep* (**a**) *(expressing accompaniment)* avec; **come w. me** viens avec moi; **w. no hat/gloves** sans chapeau/gants; **I'll be right w. you** je suis à vous dans une seconde; *Fam* **I'm w. you** *(I understand)* je te suis; *Fam* **to be w. it** *(up-to-date)* être dans le vent

(**b**) *(at the house, flat of)* chez; **she's staying w. me** elle loge chez moi

(**c**) *(expressing cause)* de; **to tremble w. fear** trembler de peur; **to be ill w. measles** être malade de la rougeole

(**d**) *(expressing instrument, means)* **to write w. a pen** écrire avec un stylo; **to fill w. sth** remplir de qch; **satisfied w. sb/sth** satisfait de qn/qch; **w. my own eyes** de mes propres yeux

(**e**) *(in description)* à; **a woman w. blue eyes** une femme aux yeux bleus

(**f**) *(despite)* malgré; **w. all his faults** malgré tous ses défauts

withdraw [wɪð'drɔː] **1** *(pt* **-drew,** *pp* **-drawn)** *vt* retirer (**from** de) **2** *vi* se retirer (**from** de) ▪ **withdrawal** *n* retrait *m* ▪ **withdrawn** *adj (person)* renfermé

withhold [wɪð'həʊld] *(pt & pp* **-held)** *vt (permission, help)* refuser (**from** à); *(decision)* différer; *(money)* retenir (**from** de); *(information)* cacher (**from** à)

within [wɪð'ɪn] **1** *prep (inside)* à l'intérieur de; **w. 10 km (of)** *(less than)* à moins de 10 km de; *(inside an area of)* dans un rayon de 10 km (de); **w. a month** *(return)* avant un mois; *(finish)* en moins d'un mois; **w. sight** en vue 2 *adv* à l'intérieur

without [wɪð'aʊt] **1** *prep* sans; **w. a tie** sans cravate; **w. doing sth** faire sans faire qch; **to do w. sb/sth** se passer de qn/qch **2** *adv* **to do w.** se priver

withstand [wɪð'stænd] (*pt & pp* **-stood**) *vt* résister à

witness ['wɪtnɪs] **1** *n* (*person*) témoin *m* **2** *vt* (*accident*) être témoin de; (*document*) signer (pour attester l'authenticité de)

witty ['wɪtɪ] (**-ier, -iest**) *adj* spirituel, -elle

wives [waɪvz] *pl of* **wife**

wizard ['wɪzəd] *n* magicien *m*; *Fig* (*genius*) as *m*

wobble ['wɒbəl] *vi* (*of chair*) branler; (*of jelly, leg*) trembler; (*of wheel*) tourner de façon irrégulière; (*of person*) chanceler ■ **wobbly** *adj* (*table, chair*) branlant

woe [wəʊ] *n* malheur *m*

wok [wɒk] *n* poêle *f* chinoise

woke [wəʊk] *pt of* **wake**[1]

woken ['wəʊkən] *pp of* **wake**[1]

wolf [wʊlf] **1** (*pl* **wolves**) *n* loup *m* **2** *vt* **to w. (down)** (*food*) engloutir

woman ['wʊmən] (*pl* **women**) *n* femme *f*; **women's** (*clothes, attitudes, magazine*) féminin; **women's rights** droits *mpl* des femmes

womb [wu:m] *n Anat* utérus *m*

women ['wɪmɪn] *pl of* **woman**

won [wʌn] *pt & pp of* **win**

wonder ['wʌndə(r)] **1** *n* (*marvel*) merveille *f*; (*feeling*) émerveillement *m*; **it's no w.** ce n'est pas étonnant (**that** que + *subjunctive*); **it's a w. she wasn't killed** c'est un miracle qu'elle n'ait pas été tuée

2 *vt* (*ask oneself*) se demander (**if** si; **why** pourquoi)

3 *vi* (*ask oneself questions*) s'interroger (**about** au sujet de *ou* sur); **I was just wondering** je réfléchissais

wonderful ['wʌndəfəl] *adj* merveilleux, -euse

wonky ['wɒŋkɪ] (**-ier, -iest**) *adj Br Fam*

(*table*) déglingué; (*hat, picture*) de travers

won't [wəʊnt] = **will not**

woo [wu:] (*pt & pp* **wooed**) *vt* (*voters*) chercher à plaire à

wood [wʊd] *n* (*material, forest*) bois *m* ■ **wooded** *adj* boisé ■ **wooden** *adj* en bois; *Fig* (*manner, dancer, actor*) raide ■ **woodland** *n* région *f* boisée ■ **woodwind** *n* **the w.** (*musical instruments*) les bois *mpl* ■ **woodwork** *n* (*school subject*) menuiserie *f* ■ **woodworm** *n* **it has w.** c'est vermoulu

wool [wʊl] *n* laine *f* ■ **woollen** (*Am* **woolen**) **1** *adj* (*dress*) en laine **2** *npl* **woollens** (*Am* **woolens**) (*garments*) lainages *mpl* ■ **woolly** (**-ier, -iest**) **1** *adj* en laine; *Fig* (*unclear*) nébuleux, -euse **2** *n Br Fam* (*garment*) lainage *m*

word [wɜ:d] **1** *n* mot *m*; (*promise*) parole *f*; **words** (*of song*) paroles *fpl*; **to have a w. with sb** parler à qn; **to keep one's w.** tenir sa promesse; **in other words** autrement dit; **w. for w.** (*report*) mot pour mot; (*translate*) mot à mot; **w. processing** traitement *m* de texte; **w. processor** machine *f* à traitement de texte

2 *vt* (*express*) formuler ■ **wording** *n* termes *mpl* ■ **wordy** (**-ier, -iest**) *adj* prolixe

wore [wɔ:(r)] *pt of* **wear**

work [wɜ:k] **1** *n* travail *m*; (*literary, artistic*) œuvre *f*; **works** (*construction*) travaux *mpl*; **to be at w.** travailler; **it's hard w. (doing that)** ça demande beaucoup de travail (de faire ça); **to be out of w.** être sans travail; **a day off w.** un jour de congé; **w. permit** permis *m* de travail; **w. station** poste *m* de travail; **w. of art** œuvre *f* d'art

2 *vt* (*person*) faire travailler; (*machine*) faire marcher; (*metal, wood*) travailler

3 *vi* (*of person*) travailler; (*of machine*) marcher, fonctionner; (*of drug*) agir; **to w. loose** (*of knot, screw*) se desserrer; **to w. towards** (*result, agreement, aim*) travailler à ■ **workaholic** [-ə'hɒlɪk] *n*

Fam bourreau *m* de travail ■ **work-force** *n* main-d'œuvre *f* ■ **workload** *n* charge *f* de travail ■ **workman** (*pl* **-men**) *n* ouvrier *m* ■ **workmanship** *n* travail *m* ■ **workmate** *n Br* camarade *mf* de travail ■ **workout** *n* (*sports training*) séance *f* d'entraînement ■ **work-shop** *n* (*place, study course*) atelier *m*

▸ **work at** *vt insep* (*improve*) travailler

▸ **work off** *vt sep* (*debt*) payer en travaillant; (*excess fat*) se débarrasser de (par l'exercice)

▸ **work on** *vt insep* (*book, problem*) travailler à; (*French*) travailler

▸ **work out 1** *vt sep* (*calculate*) calculer; (*problem*) résoudre; (*plan*) préparer; (*understand*) comprendre **2** *vi* (*succeed*) marcher; (*do exercises*) s'entraîner; **it works out at 50 euros** ça fait 50 euros

▸ **work up 1** *vt sep* to w. up enthusiasm s'enthousiasmer (**for** pour); **I worked up an appetite** ça m'a ouvert l'appétit; **to get worked up** s'énerver **2** *vi* **to w. up to sth** se préparer à qch

worker ['wɜːkə(r)] *n* travailleur, -euse *mf*; (*manual*) ouvrier, -ère *mf*; (*office*) w. employé, -e *mf* (de bureau)

working ['wɜːkɪŋ] **1** *adj* (*day, clothes*) de travail; **in w. order** en état de marche; **w. class** classe *f* ouvrière; **w. conditions** conditions *fpl* de travail **2** *npl* **the workings of** (*clock*) le mécanisme de ■ **working-class** *adj* ouvrier, -ère

world [wɜːld] **1** *n* monde *m*; **all over the w.** dans le monde entier **2** *adj* (*war, production*) mondial; (*champion, record*) du monde; **the W. Cup** (*in football*) la Coupe du Monde ■ **worldly** *adj* (*person*) qui a l'expérience du monde ■ **worldwide 1** *adj* mondial **2** *adv* dans le monde entier

worm [wɜːm] **1** *n* ver *m* **2** *vt* **to w. one's way into** s'insinuer dans; **to w. sth out of sb** soutirer qch à qn

worn [wɔːn] **1** *pp of* **wear 2** *adj* (*clothes, tyre*) usé ■ **worn-out** *adj* (*object*) complètement usé; (*person*) épuisé

worry ['wʌrɪ] **1** (*pl* **-ies**) *n* souci *m*; **it's a w.** ça me cause du souci

2 (*pt & pp* **-ied**) *vt* inquiéter

3 *vi* s'inquiéter (**about sth** de qch; **about sb** pour qn) ■ **worried** *adj* inquiet, -ète (**about** au sujet de) ■ **worrying** *adj* inquiétant

worse [wɜːs] **1** *adj* (*than* que); **to get w.** se détériorer; **he's getting w.** (*in health*) il va de plus en plus mal; (*in behaviour*) il se conduit de plus en plus mal

2 *adv* plus mal (*than* que); **I could do w.** j'aurais pu tomber plus mal; **she's w. off (than before)** sa situation est pire (qu'avant); (*financially*) elle est encore plus pauvre (qu'avant)

3 *n* there's w. to come le pire reste à venir; **a change for the w.** une détérioration

worsen ['wɜːsən] **1** *vt* aggraver **2** *vi* empirer

worship ['wɜːʃɪp] **1** *n* culte *m* **2** (*pt & pp* **-pp-**) *vt* (*person, god*) adorer; *Pej* (*money*) avoir le culte de

worst [wɜːst] **1** *adj* pire; **the w. book I've ever read** le plus mauvais livre que j'aie jamais lu **2** *adv* (**the**) w. le plus mal **3** *n* **the w. (one)** (*object, person*) le/la pire, le/la plus mauvais(e); **the w. (thing) is that…** le pire, c'est que…; **at (the) w.** au pire

worth [wɜːθ] **1** *adj* **to be w. sth** valoir qch; **how much** *or* **what is it w.?** ça vaut combien?; **the film's (well) w. seeing** le film vaut la peine d'être vu **2** *n* valeur *f*; **to buy 50 pence w. of chocolates** acheter pour 50 pence de chocolats; **to get one's money's w.** en avoir pour son argent ■ **worthless** *adj* qui ne vaut rien

worthwhile ['wɜːθ'waɪl] *adj* (*book, film*) qui vaut la peine d'être lu/vu; (*activity*) qui vaut la peine; (*plan, contribution*) valable; (*cause*) louable; (*satisfying*) qui donne des satisfactions

worthy ['wɜːðɪ] (**-ier, -iest**) *adj* (*person*) digne; (*cause, act*) louable; **to be w. of sb/sth** être digne de qn/qch

WOULD [wʊd, *unstressed* wəd]

On trouve généralement **I/you/he** etc **would** sous leurs formes contractées **I'd/you'd/he'd** etc. La forme négative correspondante est **wouldn't**, que l'on écrira **would not** dans des contextes formels.

v aux (**a**) *(expressing conditional tense)* **I w.** stay if I could je resterais si je le pouvais; **he w.** have done it il l'aurait fait; **I said she'd come** j'ai dit qu'elle viendrait

(**b**) *(willingness, ability)* **w. you help me, please?** veux-tu bien m'aider?; **she wouldn't help me** elle n'a pas voulu m'aider; **w. you like some tea?** prendrez-vous du thé?; **the car wouldn't start** la voiture ne démarrait pas

(**c**) *(expressing past habit)* **I w.** see her every day je la voyais chaque jour

wound[1] [wuːnd] **1** *n* blessure *f* **2** *vt (hurt)* blesser; **the wounded** les blessés *mpl*

wound[2] [waʊnd] *pt & pp of* **wind**[2]

wove [wəʊv] *pt of* **weave**

woven ['wəʊvən] *pp of* **weave**

wow [waʊ] *exclam Fam* oh là là!

wrap [ræp] **1** *n Am* plastic **w.** film *m* plastique

2 (*pt & pp* **-pp-**) *vt* **to w. (up)** envelopper; *(parcel)* emballer; *Fig* **wrapped up in** *(engrossed)* absorbé par

3 *vti* **to w. (oneself) up** *(dress warmly)* s'emmitoufler ■ **wrapper** *n (of sweet)* papier *m* ■ **wrapping** *n (action, material)* emballage *m*; **w. paper** papier *m* d'emballage

wreath [riːθ] (*pl* **-s** [riːðz]) *n* couronne *f*

wreck [rek] **1** *n (ship)* épave *f*; *(train)* train *m* accidenté; *(person)* épave *f* (humaine); **to be a nervous w.** être à bout de nerfs **2** *vt (break, destroy)* détruire; *Fig (spoil)* gâcher; *(career, hopes)* briser ■ **wreckage** [-ɪdʒ] *n (of plane, train)* débris *mpl*

wrench [rentʃ] **1** *n Am (tool)* clef *f* (à

écrous) **2** *vt* **to w. sth from sb** arracher qch à qn

wrestle ['resəl] *vi* lutter (**with sb** avec qn); *Fig* **to w. with a problem** se débattre avec un problème ■ **wrestler** *n* lutteur, -euse *mf*; *(in all-in wrestling)* catcheur, -euse *mf* ■ **wrestling** *n* lutte *f*; **(all-in) w.** *(with relaxed rules)* catch *m*

wretch [retʃ] *n (unfortunate person)* malheureux, -euse *mf*; *(rascal)* misérable *mf* ■ **wretched** [-ɪd] *adj (poor, pitiful)* misérable; *(dreadful)* affreux, -euse; *Fam (annoying)* maudit

wriggle ['rɪgəl] **1** *vt (toes, fingers)* tortiller **2** *vi* **to w. (about)** se tortiller; *(of fish)* frétiller; **to w. out of sth** couper à qch

wring [rɪŋ] (*pt & pp* **wrung**) *vt* **to w. (out)** *(clothes)* essorer; **to w. one's hands** se tordre les mains

wrinkle ['rɪŋkəl] **1** *n (on skin)* ride *f*; *(in cloth, paper)* pli *m* **2** *vi (of skin)* se rider; *(of cloth)* faire des plis ■ **wrinkled** *adj (skin)* ridé; *(cloth)* froissé

wrist [rɪst] *n* poignet *m* ■ **wristwatch** *n* montre-bracelet *f*

write [raɪt] (*pt* **wrote**, *pp* **written**) *vti* écrire; **to w. to sb** écrire à qn ■ **write-off** *n Br* **to be a (complete) w.** *(of vehicle)* être bon pour la casse

▶ **write away for** *vt insep (details)* écrire pour demander

▶ **write back** *vi* répondre

▶ **write down** *vt sep* noter

▶ **write in 1** *vt sep (insert)* inscrire **2** *vi (send letter)* écrire

▶ **write off** *vt sep (debt)* annuler

▶ **write out** *vt sep (list, recipe)* noter; *(cheque)* faire

▶ **write up** *vt sep (notes)* rédiger

writer ['raɪtə(r)] *n* auteur *m* (**of** de); *(literary)* écrivain *m*

writing ['raɪtɪŋ] *n (handwriting, action, profession)* écriture *f*; **to put sth (down) in w.** mettre qch par écrit; **w. pad** bloc-notes *m*; **w. paper** papier *m* à lettres

written ['rɪtən] *pp of* **write**

wrong [rɒŋ] **1** *adj (sum, idea)* faux (*f* fausse); *(direction, time)* mauvais; *(unfair)* injuste; **to be w.** *(of person)* avoir tort (**to do** de faire); **it's the w. road** ce n'est pas la bonne route; **the clock's w.** la pendule n'est pas à l'heure; **to get the w. number** *(on phone)* se tromper de numéro; **something's w. with the phone** le téléphone ne marche pas bien; **something's w. with her leg** elle a quelque chose à la jambe; **what's w. with you?** qu'est-ce que tu as?; **the w. way round** *or* **up** à l'envers

2 *adv* mal; **to go w.** *(of plan)* mal tourner; *(of vehicle, machine)* tomber en panne; *(of person)* se tromper

3 *n (injustice)* injustice *f*; **to be in the w.** être dans son tort; **right and w.** le bien et le mal

4 *vt* faire du tort à ■ **wrongful** *adj* **w. arrest** arrestation *f* arbitraire ■ **wrongly** *adv (inform, translate)* mal; *(accuse, condemn, claim)* à tort

wrote [rəʊt] *pt of* **write**

wrung [rʌŋ] *pt & pp of* **wring**

wry [raɪ] (**wryer, wryest**) *adj* ironique

Xx

X, x [eks] *n (letter)* X, x *m inv*
xenophobia [*Br* zenə'fəʊbɪə, *Am* ziːnəʊ-] *n* xénophobie *f*
Xerox® ['zɪərɒks] **1** *n (copy)* photocopie *f* **2** *vt* photocopier
Xmas ['krɪsməs] *n Fam* Noël *m*

X-ray ['eksreɪ] **1** *n (picture)* radio *f*; **to have an X.** passer une radio **2** *vt* radiographier
xylophone ['zaɪləfəʊn] *n* xylophone *m*

Yy

Y, y [waɪ] n (letter) Y, y m inv

yacht [jɒt] n (sailing boat) voilier m; (large private boat) yacht m ■ **yachting** n voile f

yap [jæp] (pt & pp **-pp-**) vi (of dog) japper

yard¹ [jɑːd] n (of house, farm, school, prison) cour f; (for working) chantier m; (for storage) dépôt m de marchandises; Am (garden) jardin m

yard² [jɑːd] n (measure) yard m (= 91,44 cm)

yarn [jɑːn] n (thread) fil m; Fam (tale) histoire f à dormir debout

yawn [jɔːn] vi bâiller

year [jɪə(r)] n an m, année f; (of wine) année f; **school/tax y.** année f scolaire/fiscale; **in the y. 2004** en (l'an) 2004; **he's ten years old** il a dix ans; **New Y.** Nouvel An m; **New Y.'s Day** le jour de l'An; **New Y.'s Eve** la Saint-Sylvestre ■ **yearly 1** adj annuel, -elle **2** adv annuellement; **twice y.** deux fois par an

yearn [jɜːn] vi **to y. for sb** languir après qn; **to y. for sth** désirer ardemment qch; **to y. to do sth** brûler de faire qch

yeast [jiːst] n levure f

yell [jel] vti **to y. (out)** hurler; **to y. at sb** (scold) crier après qn

yellow ['jeləʊ] **1** adj (in colour) jaune; **y. card** (in football) carton m jaune **2** n jaune m

yes [jes] **1** adv oui; (after negative question) si **2** n oui m inv

yesterday ['jestədeɪ] **1** adv hier **2** n hier m; **y. morning/evening** hier

matin/soir; **the day before y.** avant-hier

yet [jet] **1** adv (a) (still) encore; (already) déjà; **she hasn't arrived (as) y.** elle n'est pas encore arrivée; **the best y.** le meilleur jusqu'ici; **y. another mistake** encore une erreur; **not (just) y.** pas pour l'instant (b) (in questions) **has he come y.?** est-il arrivé? **2** conj (nevertheless) pourtant

yew [juː] n (tree, wood) if m

yield [jiːld] **1** n (of field, shares) rendement m **2** vt (result) donner; (interest) rapporter; (territory, right) céder; **to y. a profit** rapporter **3** vi (surrender) se rendre; Am **'y.'** (road sign) 'cédez le passage'

yob [jɒb], **yobbo** ['jɒbəʊ] (pl yob(-bo)s) n Br Fam loubard m

yoga ['jəʊgə] n yoga m

yog(h)urt [Br 'jɒgət, Am 'jəʊgərt] n yaourt m

yolk [jəʊk] n jaune m (d'œuf)

you [juː] pron (a) (subject) (pl, polite form sing) vous; (familiar form sing) tu; (object) vous, te, t', pl vous; (after prep, 'than', 'it is') vous, toi, pl vous; **(to) y.** (indirect) vous, te, t', pl vous; **I gave it (to) y.** je vous/te l'ai donné; **y. teachers** vous autres professeurs; **y. idiot!** espèce d'imbécile!

(b) (indefinite) on; (object) vous, te, t', pl vous; **y. never know** on ne sait jamais ■ **you'd** = you had, you would ■ **you'll** = you will

young [jʌŋ] **1** (-er, -est) adj jeune; **she's two years younger than me** elle a deux ans de moins que moi; **my**

young(er) brother mon (frère) cadet; **my youngest sister** la cadette de mes sœurs; **y. people** les jeunes *mpl* **2** *n (of animals)* petits *mpl*; **the y.** *(people)* les jeunes *mpl*; **she's my youngest** *(daughter)* c'est ma petite dernière ▪ **youngster** *n* jeune *mf*

your [jɔː(r)] *possessive adj (polite form sing, polite and familiar form pl)* votre, *pl* vos; *(familiar form sing)* ton, ta, *pl* tes; *(one's)* son, sa, *pl* ses

yours [jɔːz] *possessive pron* le vôtre, la vôtre, *pl* les vôtres; *(familiar form sing)* le tien, la tienne, *pl* les tien(ne)s; **this book is y.** ce livre est à vous *ou* est le vôtre/ce livre est à toi *ou* est le tien; **a friend of y.** un ami à vous/toi

yourself [jɔːˈself] *pron (polite form)* vous-même; *(familiar form)* toi-même; *(reflexive)* vous, te, t'; *(after prep)* vous, toi; **you wash y.** vous vous lavez/tu te laves ▪ **yourselves** *pron pl* vous-mêmes; *(reflexive and after prep)* vous; **did you cut y.?** est-ce que vous vous êtes coupés?

youth [juːθ] *(pl* **-s** [juːðz]) *n (age)* jeunesse *f*; *(young man)* jeune *m*; **y. club** centre *m* de loisirs pour les jeunes; **y. hostel** auberge *f* de jeunesse ▪ **youthful** *adj (person)* jeune

you've [juːv] = **you have**

yo-yo [ˈjəʊjəʊ] *(pl* **yo-yos)** *n* Yo-Yo® *m inv*

yuppie [ˈjʌpɪ] *n* yuppie *mf*

Zz

Z, z [*Br* zed, *Am* zi:] *n* (letter) Z, z *m inv*

zany ['zeɪnɪ] (**-ier, -iest**) *adj* loufoque

zap [zæp] (*pt & pp* **-pp-**) *vt Fam Comptr* effacer

zeal [zi:l] *n* zèle *m* ▪ **zealous** ['zeləs] *adj* zélé

zebra ['zi:brə, *Br* 'zebrə] *n* zèbre *m*; *Br* **z. crossing** passage *m* pour piétons

zero ['zɪərəʊ] (*pl* **-os**) *n* zéro *m*

zest [zest] *n* (*enthusiasm*) enthousiasme *m*; (*of lemon, orange*) zeste *m*

zigzag ['zɪgzæg] **1** *n* zigzag *m* **2** *adj & adv* en zigzag **3** (*pt & pp* **-gg-**) *vi* zigzaguer

zinc [zɪŋk] *n* zinc *m*

zip [zɪp] **1** *n Br* **z. (fastener)** fermeture *f* Éclair® **2** *adj Am* **z. code** code *m* postal **3** (*pt & pp* **-pp-**) *vt* **to z. sth (up)** remonter la fermeture Éclair® de qch **4** *vi* **to z. past** (*of car*) passer en trombe ▪ **zipper** *n Am* fermeture *f* Éclair®

zit [zɪt] *n Fam* (*pimple*) bouton *m*

zodiac ['zəʊdɪæk] *n* zodiaque *m*

zone [zəʊn] *n* zone *f*

zoo [zu:] (*pl* **zoos**) *n* zoo *m*

zoom [zu:m] **1** *n* **z. lens** zoom *m* **2** *vi* **to z. in** (*of camera*) faire un zoom avant (**on** sur); *Fam* **to z. past** passer comme une flèche

zucchini [zu:'ki:nɪ] (*pl* **-ni** *or* **-nis**) *n Am* courgette *f*

French Verb Conjugations

Regular Verbs

	-ER verbs	-IR verbs	-RE verbs
Infinitive	*donn/er*	*fin/ir*	*vend/re*
1 Present	je donne	je finis	je vends
	tu donnes	tu finis	tu vends
	il donne	il finit	il vend
	nous donnons	nous finissons	nous vendons
	vous donnez	vous finissez	vous vendez
	ils donnent	ils finissent	ils vendent
2 Imperfect	je donnais	je finissais	je vendais
	tu donnais	tu finissais	tu vendais
	il donnait	il finissait	il vendait
	nous donnions	nous finissions	nous vendions
	vous donniez	vous finissiez	vous vendiez
	ils donnaient	ils finissaient	ils vendaient
3 Past historic	je donnai	je finis	je vendis
	tu donnas	tu finis	tu vendis
	il donna	il finit	il vendit
	nous donnâmes	nous finîmes	nous vendîmes
	vous donnâtes	vous finîtes	vous vendîtes
	ils donnèrent	ils finirent	ils vendirent
4 Future	je donnerai	je finirai	je vendrai
	tu donneras	tu finiras	tu vendras
	il donnera	il finira	il vendra
	nous donnerons	nous finirons	nous vendrons
	vous donnerez	vous finirez	vous vendrez
	ils donneront	ils finiront	ils vendront
5 Subjunctive	je donne	je finisse	je vende
	tu donnes	tu finisses	tu vendes
	il donne	il finisse	il vende
	nous donnions	nous finissions	nous vendions
	vous donniez	vous finissiez	vous vendiez
	ils donnent	ils finissent	ils vendent
6 Imperative	donne	finis	vends
	donnons	finissons	vendons
	donnez	finissez	vendez
7 Present participle	donnant	finissant	vendant
8 Past participle	donné	fini	vendu

Note The conditional is formed by adding the following endings to the infinitive: **-ais, -ais, -ait, -ions, -iez, -aient**. The final **e** is dropped in infinitives ending **-re**.

Irregular French Verbs

Listed below are those verbs considered to be the most useful. Forms and tenses not given are fully derivable, such as the third person singular of the **present tense** which is normally formed by substituting 't' for the final 's' of the first person singular, eg 'crois' becomes 'croit', 'dis' becomes 'dit'. Note that the endings of the **past historic** fall into three categories, the 'a' and 'i' categories shown at donner, and at finir and vendre, and the 'u' category which has the following endings: -us, -ut, -ûmes, -ûtes, -urent. Most of the verbs listed below form their past historic with 'u'.

The **imperfect** may usually be formed by adding -ais, -ait, -ions, -iez, -aient to the stem of the first person plural of the present tense, eg 'je buvais' etc may be derived from 'nous buvons' (stem 'buv-' and ending '-ons'); similarly, the **present participle** may generally be formed by substituting -ant for -ons (eg buvant). The **future** may usually be formed by adding -ai, -as, -a, -ons, -ez, -ont to the infinitive or to an infinitive without final 'e' where the ending is -re (eg conduire). The **imperative** usually has the same forms as the second persons singular and plural and first person plural of the present tense.

1 = Present	2 = Imperfect	3 = Past historic	4 = Future
5 = Subjunctive	6 = Imperative	7 = Present participle	8 = Past participle
n = nous	v = vous	*verbs conjugated with **être** only	

abattre	like	**battre**
absoudre	1 j'absous, n absolvons 2 j'absolvais	
	3 j'absolus *(rarely used)* 5 j'absolve 7 absolvant	
	8 absous, absoute	
s'abstenir	like	**tenir**
abstraire	1 j'abstrais, n abstrayons 2 j'abstrayais 3 *none* 5 j'abstraie	
	7 abstrayant 8 abstrait	
accourir	like	**courir**
accroître	like	**croître** *except* 8 accru
accueillir	like	**cueillir**
acquérir	1 j'acquiers, n acquérons 2 j'acquérais 3 j'acquis	
	4 j'acquerrai 5 j'acquière 7 acquérant 8 acquis	
adjoindre	like	**joindre**
admettre	like	**mettre**
advenir	like	**venir** *(third person only)*
***aller**	1 je vais, tu vas, il va, n allons, v allez, ils vont 4 j'irai	
	5 j'aille, n allions, ils aillent 6 va, allons, allez (*but note* vas-y)	
apercevoir	like	**recevoir**
apparaître	like	**connaître**
appartenir	like	**tenir**

(2)

apprendre	*like*	**prendre**
asseoir		1 j'assieds, il assied, n asseyons, ils asseyent 2 j'asseyais
		3 j'assis 4 j'assiérai 5 j'asseye 7 asseyant 8 assis
astreindre	*like*	**atteindre**
atteindre		1 j'atteins, n atteignons, ils atteignent 2 j'atteignais
		3 j'atteignis 4 j'atteindrai 5 j'atteigne 7 atteignant 8 atteint
avoir		1 j'ai, tu as, il a, n avons, v avez, ils ont 2 j'avais 3 j'eus
		4 j'aurai 5 j'aie, il ait, n ayons, ils aient 6 aie, ayons, ayez
		7 ayant 8 eu
battre		1 je bats, il bat, n battons 5 je batte
boire		1 je bois, n buvons, ils boivent 2 je buvais 3 je bus
		5 je boive, n buvions 7 buvant 8 bu
bouillir		1 je bous, n bouillons, ils bouillent 2 je bouillais
		3 je bouillis 5 je bouille 7 bouillant
braire		(*defective*) 1 il brait, ils braient 4 il braira, ils brairont
circonscrire	*like*	**écrire**
circonvenir	*like*	**tenir**
clore	*like*	**éclore**
combattre	*like*	**battre**
commettre	*like*	**mettre**
comparaître	*like*	**connaître**
complaire	*like*	**plaire**
comprendre	*like*	**prendre**
compromettre	*like*	**mettre**
concevoir	*like*	**recevoir**
conclure		1 je conclus, n concluons, ils concluent 5 je conclue
concourir	*like*	**courir**
conduire		1 je conduis, n conduisons 3 je conduisis 5 je conduise
		8 conduit
confire	*like*	**suffire**
connaître		1 je connais, il connaît, n connaissons 3 je connus
		5 je connaisse 7 connaissant 8 connu
conquérir	*like*	**acquérir**
consentir	*like*	**mentir**
construire	*like*	**conduire**
contenir	*like*	**tenir**
contraindre	*like*	**craindre**
contredire	*like*	**dire** *except* 1 v contredisez
convaincre	*like*	**vaincre**
convenir	*like*	**tenir**
corrompre	*like*	**rompre**
coudre		1 je couds, il coud, n cousons, ils cousent 3 je cousis
		5 je couse 7 cousant 8 cousu
courir		1 je cours, n courons 3 je courus 4 je courrai 5 je coure
		8 couru
couvrir		1 je couvre, n couvrons 2 je couvrais 5 je couvre 8 couvert
craindre		1 je crains, n craignons, ils craignent 2 je craignais

	3 je craignis 4 je craindrai 5 je craigne 7 craignant	
	8 craint	
croire	1 je crois, n croyons, ils croient 2 je croyais 3 je crus	
	5 je croie, n croyions 7 croyant 8 cru	
croître	1 je crois, il croît, n croissons 2 je croissais 3 je crûs	
	5 je croisse 7 croissant 8 crû, crue	
cueillir	1 je cueille, n cueillons 2 je cueillais 4 je cueillerai	
	5 je cueille 7 cueillant	
cuire	1 je cuis, n cuisons 2 je cuisais 3 je cuisis 5 je cuise	
	7 cuisant 8 cuit	
débattre	*like*	**battre**
décevoir	*like*	**recevoir**
déchoir	(*defective*) 1 je déchois, 2 *none* 3 je déchus 4 je déchoirai	
	6 *none* 7 *none* 8 déchu	
découdre	*like*	**coudre**
découvrir	*like*	**couvrir**
décrire	*like*	**écrire**
décroître	*like*	**croître** *except* 8 décru
se dédire	*like*	**dire**
déduire	*like*	**conduire**
défaillir	1 je défaille, n défaillons 2 je défaillais 3 je défaillis	
	5 je défaille 7 défaillant 8 défailli	
défaire	*like*	**faire**
démentir	*like*	**mentir**
démettre	*like*	**mettre**
se départir	*like*	**mentir**
dépeindre	*like*	**atteindre**
déplaire	*like*	**plaire**
déteindre	*like*	**atteindre**
détenir	*like*	**tenir**
détruire	*like*	**conduire**
*devenir	*like*	**tenir**
se dévêtir	*like*	**vêtir**
devoir	1 je dois, n devons, ils doivent 2 je devais 3 je dus	
	4 je devrai 5 je doive, n devions 6 *not used* 7 devant	
	8 dû, due, *pl* dus, dues	
dire	1 je dis, n disons, v dites 2 je disais 3 je dis 5 je dise	
	7 disant 8 dit	
disconvenir	*like*	**tenir**
disjoindre	*like*	**joindre**
disparaître	*like*	**connaître**
dissoudre	*like*	**absoudre**
distraire	*like*	**abstraire**
dormir	*like*	**mentir**
échoir	(*defective*) 1 il échoit 2 *none* 3 il échut, ils échurent	
	4 il échoira 6 *none* 7 échéant 8 échu	
éclore	1 il éclôt, ils éclosent 8 éclos	

éconduire	*like*	**conduire**
écrire	1 j'écris, n écrivons 2 j'écrivais 3 j'écrivis 5 j'écrive 7 écrivant 8 écrit	
élire	*like*	**lire**
émettre	*like*	**mettre**
émouvoir	*like*	**mouvoir** *except* 8 ému
enclore	*like*	**éclore**
encourir	*like*	**courir**
endormir	*like*	**mentir**
enduire	*like*	**conduire**
enfreindre	*like*	**atteindre**
***s'enfuir**	*like*	**fuir**
enjoindre	*like*	**joindre**
s'enquérir	*like*	**acquérir**
s'ensuivre	*like*	**suivre** *(third person only)*
entreprendre	*like*	**prendre**
entretenir	*like*	**tenir**
entrevoir	*like*	**voir**
entrouvrir	*like*	**couvrir**
envoyer	4 j'enverrai	
***s'éprendre**	*like*	**prendre**
équivaloir	*like*	**valoir**
éteindre	*like*	**atteindre**
être	1 je suis, tu es, il est, n sommes, v êtes, ils sont 2 j'étais 3 je fus 4 je serai 5 je sois, n soyons, ils soient 6 sois, soyons, soyez 7 étant 8 été	
étreindre	*like*	**atteindre**
exclure	*like*	**conclure**
extraire	*like*	**abstraire**
faillir	*(defective)* 3 je faillis 4 je faillirai 8 failli	
faire	1 je fais, n faisons, v faites, ils font 2 je faisais 3 je fis 4 je ferai 5 je fasse 7 faisant 8 fait	
falloir	*(impersonal)* 1 il faut 2 il fallait 3 il fallut 4 il faudra 5 il faille 6 *none* 7 *none* 8 fallu	
feindre	*like*	**atteindre**
foutre	1 je fous, n foutons 2 je foutais 3 *none* 5 je foute 7 foutant 8 foutu	
frire	*(defective)* 1 je fris, tu fris, il frit 4 je frirai 6 fris 8 frit *(for other persons and tenses use* faire frire*)*	
fuir	1 je fuis, n fuyons, ils fuient 2 je fuyais 3 je fuis 5 je fuie 7 fuyant 8 fui	
geindre	*like*	**atteindre**
haïr	1 je hais, il hait, n haïssons	
inclure	*like*	**conclure**
induire	*like*	**conduire**
inscrire	*like*	**écrire**
instruire	*like*	**conduire**

(5)

interdire	*like*	**dire** *except* 1 v interdisez
interrompre	*like*	**rompre**
intervenir	*like*	**tenir**
introduire	*like*	**conduire**
joindre		1 je joins, n joignons, ils joignent 2 je joignais 3 je joignis 4 je joindrai 5 je joigne 7 joignant 8 joint
lire		1 je lis, n lisons 2 je lisais 3 je lus 5 je lise 7 lisant 8 lu
luire	*like*	**nuire**
maintenir	*like*	**tenir**
maudire		1 je maudis, n maudissons 2 je maudissais 3 je maudis 4 je maudirai 5 je maudisse 7 maudissant 8 maudit
méconnaître	*like*	**connaître**
médire	*like*	**dire** *except* 1 v médisez
mentir		1 je mens, n mentons 2 je mentais 5 je mente 7 mentant
mettre		1 je mets, n mettons 2 je mettais 3 je mis 5 je mette 7 mettant 8 mis
moudre		1 je mouds, il moud, n moulons 2 je moulais 3 je moulus 5 je moule 7 moulant 8 moulu
***mourir**		1 je meurs, n mourons, ils meurent 2 je mourais 3 je mourus 4 je mourrai 5 je meure, n mourions 7 mourant 8 mort
mouvoir		1 je meus, n mouvons, ils meuvent 2 je mouvais 3 je mus 4 je mouvrai 5 je meuve, n mouvions 8 mû, mue, *pl* mus, mues
***naître**		1 je nais, il naît, n naissons 2 je naissais 3 je naquis 4 je naîtrai 5 je naisse 7 naissant 8 né
nuire		1 je nuis, n nuisons 2 je nuisais 3 je nuisis 5 je nuise 7 nuisant 8 nui
obtenir	*like*	**tenir**
offrir	*like*	**couvrir**
omettre	*like*	**mettre**
ouvrir	*like*	**couvrir**
paître		(*defective*) 1 il paît 2 ils paissait 3 *none* 4 il paîtra 5 il paisse 7 paissant 8 *none*
paraître	*like*	**connaître**
parcourir	*like*	**courir**
parfaire	*like*	**faire** (*present tense, infinitive and past participle only*)
***partir**	*like*	**mentir**
***parvenir**	*like*	**tenir**
peindre	*like*	**atteindre**
percevoir	*like*	**recevoir**
permettre	*like*	**mettre**
plaindre	*like*	**craindre**
plaire		1 je plais, il plaît, n plaisons 2 je plaisais 3 je plus 5 je plaise 7 plaisant 8 plu
pleuvoir		(*impersonal*) 1 il pleut 2 il pleuvait 3 il plut 4 il pleuvra 5 il pleuve 6 *none* 7 pleuvant 8 plu

(6)

poindre	(*defective*)	1 il point 4 il poindra 8 point
poursuivre	*like*	**suivre**
pourvoir	*like*	**voir** *except* 3 je pourvus *and* 4 je pourvoirai
pouvoir		1 je peux *or* je puis, tu peux, il peut, n pouvons, ils peuvent
		2 je pouvais 3 je pus 4 je pourrai 5 je puisse 6 *not used*
		7 pouvant 8 pu
prédire	*like*	**dire** *except* v prédisez
prendre		1 je prends, il prend, n prenons, ils prennent 2 je prenais 3 je pris
		5 je prenne 7 prenant 8 pris
prescrire	*like*	**écrire**
pressentir	*like*	**mentir**
prévaloir	*like*	**valoir** *except* 5 je prévale
prévenir	*like*	**tenir**
prévoir	*like*	**voir** *except* 4 je prévoirai
produire	*like*	**conduire**
promettre	*like*	**mettre**
promouvoir	*like*	**mouvoir** *except* 8 promu
proscrire	*like*	**écrire**
***provenir**	*like*	**tenir**
rabattre	*like*	**battre**
rasseoir	*like*	**asseoir**
réapparaître	*like*	**connaître**
recevoir		1 je reçois, n recevons, ils reçoivent 2 je recevais 3 je reçus
		4 je recevrai 5 je reçoive, n recevions, ils reçoivent 7 recevant
		8 reçu
reconduire	*like*	**conduire**
reconnaître	*like*	**connaître**
reconquérir	*like*	**acquérir**
reconstruire	*like*	**conduire**
recoudre	*like*	**coudre**
recourir	*like*	**courir**
recouvrir	*like*	**couvrir**
récrire	*like*	**écrire**
recueillir	*like*	**cueillir**
redevenir	*like*	**tenir**
redire	*like*	**dire**
réduire	*like*	**conduire**
réécrire	*like*	**écrire**
réélire	*like*	**lire**
refaire	*like*	**faire**
rejoindre	*like*	**joindre**
relire	*like*	**lire**
reluire	*like*	**nuire**
remettre	*like*	**mettre**
***renaître**	*like*	**naître**
rendormir	*like*	**mentir**

renvoyer	*like*	**envoyer**
se repaître	*like*	**paître**
reparaître	*like*	**connaître**
***repartir**	*like*	**mentir**
repeindre	*like*	**atteindre**
repentir	*like*	**mentir**
reprendre	*like*	**prendre**
reproduire	*like*	**conduire**
résoudre	1 je résous, n résolvons 2 je résolvais 3 je résolus 5 je résolve 7 résolvant 8 résolu	
ressentir	*like*	**mentir**
resservir	*like*	**mentir**
ressortir	*like*	**mentir**
restreindre	*like*	**atteindre**
retenir	*like*	**tenir**
retransmettre	*like*	**mettre**
***revenir**	*like*	**tenir**
revêtir	*like*	**vêtir**
revivre	*like*	**vivre**
revoir	*like*	**voir**
rire	1 je ris, n rions 2 je riais 3 je ris 5 je rie, n riions 7 riant 8 ri	
rompre	*regular except* 1 il rompt	
rouvrir	*like*	**couvrir**
satisfaire	*like*	**faire**
savoir	1 je sais, n savons, il savent 2 je savais 3 je sus 4 je saurai 5 je sache 6 sache, sachons, sachez 7 sachant 8 su	
séduire	*like*	**conduire**
sentir	*like*	**mentir**
servir	*like*	**mentir**
sortir	*like*	**mentir**
souffrir	*like*	**couvrir**
soumettre	*like*	**mettre**
sourire	*like*	**rire**
souscrire	*like*	**écrire**
soustraire	*like*	**abstraire**
soutenir	*like*	**tenir**
***se souvenir**	*like*	**tenir**
subvenir	*like*	**tenir**
suffire	1 je suffis, n suffisons 2 je suffisais 3 je suffis 5 je suffise 7 suffisant 8 suffi	
suivre	1 je suis, n suivons 2 je suivais 3 je suivis 5 je suive 7 suivant 8 suivi	
surprendre	*like*	**prendre**
***survenir**	*like*	**tenir**
survivre	*like*	**vivre**
taire	1 je tais, n taisons 2 je taisais 3 je tus 5 je taise 7 taisant 8 tu	

teindre	*like*	**atteindre**
tenir	1 je tiens, ne tenons, ils tiennent 2 je tenais	
	3 je tins, tu tins, il tint, n tînmes, v tîntes, ils tinrent	
	4 je tiendrai 5 je tienne 7 tenant 8 tenu	
traduire	*like*	**conduire**
traire	*like*	**abstraire**
transcrire	*like*	**écrire**
transmettre	*like*	**mettre**
transparaître	*like*	**connaître**
tressaillir	*like*	**défaillir**
vaincre	1 je vaincs, il vainc, n vainquons 2 je vainquais 3 je vainquis	
	5 je vainque 7 vainquant 8 vaincu	
valoir	1 je vaux, il vaut, n valons 2 je valais 3 je valus 4 je vaudrai	
	5 je vaille 6 *not used* 7 valant 8 valu	
*venir	*like*	**tenir**
vêtir	1 je vêts, n vêtons 2 je vêtais 5 je vête 7 vêtant 8 vêtu	
vivre	1 je vis, n vivons 2 je vivais 3 je vécus 5 je vive 7 vivant	
	8 vécu	
voir	1 je vois, n voyons 2 je voyais 3 je vis 4 je verrai	
	5 je voie, n voyions 7 voyant 8 vu	
vouloir	1 je veux, il veut, n voulons, ils veulent 2 je voulais	
	3 je voulus 4 je voudrai 5 je veuille	
	6 veuille, veuillons, veuillez 7 voulant 8 voulu	

Verbes anglais irréguliers

Infinitif	Prétérit	Participe passé
arise	arose	arisen
awake	awoke	awoken
awaken	awoke, awakened	awakened, awoken
be	were/was	been
bear	bore	borne
beat	beat	beaten
become	became	become
begin	began	begun
bend	bent	bent
beseech	besought, beseeched	besought, beseeched
bet	bet, betted	bet, betted
bid	bade, bid	bidden, bid
bind	bound	bound
bite	bit	bitten
bleed	bled	bled
blow	blew	blown
break	broke	broken
breed	bred	bred
bring	brought	brought
build	built	built
burn	burnt, burned	burnt, burned
burst	burst	burst
bust	bust, busted	bust, busted
buy	bought	bought
cast	cast	cast
catch	caught	caught
chide	chided, chid	chided, chidden
choose	chose	chosen
cleave	cleaved, cleft, clove	cleaved, cleft, cloven
cling	clung	clung
clothe	clad, clothed	clad, clothed
come	came	come
cost	cost	cost
creep	crept	crept
crow	crowed, crew	crowed
cut	cut	cut
deal	dealt	dealt
dig	dug	dug
dive	dived, *Am* dove	dived
do	did	done
draw	drew	drawn
dream	dreamt, dreamed	dreamt, dreamed
drink	drank	drunk
drive	drove	driven
dwell	dwelt	dwelt
eat	ate	eaten

Infinitif	Prétérit	Participe passé
fall	fell	fallen
feed	fed	fed
feel	felt	felt
fight	fought	fought
find	found	found
flee	fled	fled
fling	flung	flung
fly	flew	flown
forget	forgot	forgotten
forgive	forgave	forgiven
forsake	forsook	forsaken
freeze	froze	frozen
get	got	got, *Am* gotten
gild	gilded, gilt	gilded, gilt
gird	girded, girt	girded, girt
give	gave	given
go	went	gone
grind	ground	ground
grow	grew	grown
hang	hung/hanged	hung/hanged
have	had	had
hear	heard	heard
hew	hewed	hewn, hewed
hide	hid	hidden
hit	hit	hit
hold	held	held
hurt	hurt	hurt
keep	kept	kept
kneel	knelt	knelt
knit	knitted, knit	knitted, knit
know	knew	known
lay	laid	laid
lead	led	led
lean	leant, leaned	leant, leaned
leap	leapt, leaped	leapt, leaped
learn	learnt, learned	learnt, learned
leave	left	left
lend	lent	lent
let	let	let
lie	lay	lain
light	lit	lit
lose	lost	lost
make	made	made
mean	meant	meant
meet	met	met
mow	mowed	mown
pay	paid	paid
plead	pleaded, *Am* pled	pleaded, *Am* pled
prove	proved	proved, proven
put	put	put
quit	quit	quit
read	read	read

Infinitif	Prétérit	Participe passé
rend	rent	rent
rid	rid	rid
ride	rode	ridden
ring	rang	rung
rise	rose	risen
run	ran	run
saw	sawed	sawn, sawed
say	said	said
see	saw	seen
seek	sought	sought
sell	sold	sold
send	sent	sent
set	set	set
sew	sewed	sewn
shake	shook	shaken
shear	sheared	shorn, sheared
shed	shed	shed
shine	shone	shone
shoe	shod	shod
shoot	shot	shot
show	showed	shown
shrink	shrank	shrunk
shut	shut	shut
sing	sang	sung
sink	sank	sunk
sit	sat	sat
slay	slew	slain
sleep	slept	slept
slide	slid	slid
sling	slung	slung
slink	slunk	slunk
slit	slit	slit
smell	smelled, smelt	smelled, smelt
smite	smote	smitten
sow	sowed	sown, sowed
speak	spoke	spoken
speed	sped, speeded	sped, speeded
spell	spelt, spelled	spelt, spelled
spend	spent	spent
spill	spilt, spilled	spilt, spilled
spin	span	spun
spit	spat, *Am* spit	spat, *Am* spit
split	split	split
spoil	spoilt, spoiled	spoilt, spoiled
spread	spread	spread
spring	sprang	sprung
stand	stood	stood
stave in	staved in, stove in	staved in, stove in
steal	stole	stolen
stick	stuck	stuck
sting	stung	stung
stink	stank, stunk	stunk

Infinitif	Prétérit	Participe passé
strew	strewed	strewed, strewn
stride	strode	stridden
strike	struck	struck
string	strung	strung
strive	strove	striven
swear	swore	sworn
sweep	swept	swept
swell	swelled	swollen, swelled
swim	swam	swum
swing	swung	swung
take	took	taken
teach	taught	taught
tear	tore	torn
tell	told	told
think	thought	thought
thrive	thrived, throve	thrived
throw	threw	thrown
thrust	thrust	thrust
tread	trod	trodden
wake	woke	woken
wear	wore	worn
weave	wove, weaved	woven, weaved
weep	wept	wept
wet	wet, wetted	wet, wetted
win	won	won
wind	wound	wound
wring	wrung	wrung
write	wrote	written

Verbes modaux anglais

Formes

Les modaux sont : **can, could, may, might, will, would, shall, should, must, need, ought to**. Ils ont toujours la même forme et sont suivis d'un infinitif sans **to** (sauf la construction **ought to**).

Les formes contractées sont très courantes :

affirmatives : **'ll** (**will**), **'d** (**would**)

négatives : **can't, couldn't, won't** (**will not**), **wouldn't, shan't** (**shall not**), **shouldn't, mustn't, needn't**.

Les formes de remplacement **be able to, be allowed to** et **have to** se conjuguent normalement.

Différents degrés de certitude

* Certitude

you must be joking!	vous voulez rire !
we must have met before	on a dû déjà se rencontrer
you can't miss it, it's just opposite the station	vous ne pouvez pas le rater, c'est juste en face de la gare

* Probabilité et possibilité

you may change your mind when you see it!	tu changera peut-être d'avis quand tu le verras !
I might join you later	je vous rejoindrai peut-être plus tard
they might have forgotten altogether	ils ont peut-être carrément oublié
they should have arrived by now	ils devraient être arrivés maintenant

* Fait généralement ou parfois vrai

the roads can get dangerous in the winter	les routes peuvent être dangereuses en hiver

* Certitude liée à certaines conditions

if I had the time, I would take Chinese lessons	si j'avais le temps, je prendrais des cours de chinois

Obligation ou nécessité

I must/have to/'ve got to be in London by Monday	je dois être à Londres pour lundi
do I have to stay?	dois-je rester ?

Interdiction

children must not run near the swimming pool	les enfants ne doivent pas courir au bord de la piscine
drinks may not be taken into the cinema	les boissons sont interdites dans la salle de cinéma
I'm afraid you can't smoke in here	j'ai bien peur que vous ne puissiez pas fumer ici
dogs are not allowed in the shop	les chiens ne sont pas autorisés dans le magasin

Absence d'obligation ou de nécessité

you needn't worry so much	ce n'est pas la peine de te faire autant de souci
you don't have to come if you don't want to	tu n'es pas obligé de venir si tu n'en as pas envie

Permission

Could est plus poli, et **may** plus formel.

can I borrow your pen, please?	est-ce que je peux emprunter ton stylo ?
candidates may/are allowed to leave after one hour	les candidats sont autorisés à partir au bout d'une heure

Suggestion

* Conseil

you really ought to/should see a doctor	tu devrais aller voir un docteur
shall I open the window?	voulez-vous que j'ouvre la fenêtre ?

* Invitation

Should est moins insistant et **ought to** plus formel.

you must come and see me some time	viens me voir un jour

Notez ici l'emploi de **must** : il s'agit bien d'une invitation et non d'un ordre.

I'll give you a lift if you want	je peux te déposer si tu veux
can I get you a drink?	je t'offre quelque chose à boire ?

* Proposition

would you like anything to drink?	est-ce que tu voudrais quelque chose à boire ?
will you pass me the salt, please?	veux-tu me passer le sel, s'il te plaît ?
shall we go to the cinema instead?	et si on allait au cinéma à la place ?

Capacité

he can be very irritating	il peut être vraiment agaçant quelquefois
you could have warned me!	tu aurais pu me prévenir !
it's great being able to send files by e-mail	c'est génial de pouvoir envoyer des fichiers par e-mail

Numbers/Les Nombres

Cardinal numbers		Les nombres cardinaux
nought, zero	0	zéro
one	1	un
two	2	deux
three	3	trois
four	4	quatre
five	5	cinq
six	6	six
seven	7	sept
eight	8	huit
nine	9	neuf
ten	10	dix
eleven	11	onze
twelve	12	douze
thirteen	13	treize
fourteen	14	quatorze
fifteen	15	quinze
sixteen	16	seize
seventeen	17	dix-sept
eighteen	18	dix-huit
nineteen	19	dix-neuf
twenty	20	vingt
twenty-one	21	vingt et un
twenty-two	22	vingt-deux
thirty	30	trente
forty	40	quarante
fifty	50	cinquante
sixty	60	soixante
seventy	70	soixante-dix
eighty	80	quatre-vingts
eighty-one	81	quatre-vingt-un
ninety	90	quatre-vingt-dix
ninety-one	91	quatre-vingt-onze
a *or* one hundred	100	cent
a hundred and one	101	cent un
a hundred and two	102	cent deux
a hundred and fifty	150	cent cinquante
two hundred	200	deux cents
two hundred and one	201	deux cent un

two hundred and two	202		deux cent deux
a or one thousand	1,000 (1 000)		mille
a thousand and one	1,001 (1 001)		mille un
a thousand and two	1,002) (1 002)		mille deux
two thousand	2,000 (2 000)		deux mille
a or one million	1,000,000 (1 000 000)		un million

Ordinal numbers   Les nombres ordinaux

first	1st	1er	premier
second	2nd	2e	deuxième
third	3rd	3e	troisième
fourth	4th	4e	quatrième
fifth	5th	5e	cinquième
sixth	6th	6e	sixième
seventh	7th	7e	septième
eighth	8th	8e	huitième
ninth	9th	9e	neuvième
tenth	10th	10e	dixième
eleventh	11th	11e	onzième
twelfth	12th	12e	douzième
thirteenth	13th	13e	treizième
fourteenth	14th	14e	quatorzième
fifteenth	15th	15e	quinzième
twentieth	20th	20e	vingtième
twenty-first	21st	21e	vingt et unième
twenty-second	22nd	22e	vingt deuxième
thirtieth	30th	30e	trentième

Examples of usage   Exemples d'emplois

three (times) out of ten	trois (fois) sur dix
ten at a time, in or by tens, ten by ten	dix par dix, dix à dix
the ten of us/you, we ten/you ten	nous/vous dix
all ten of them or us or you	tous les dix, toutes les dix
there are ten of us/them	nous sommes/elles sont dix
(between) the ten of them	à eux dix, à elles dix
ten of them were living together/came	ils vivaient/sont venus à dix
page ten	page dix
Charles the Tenth	Charles Dix
to live at number ten	habiter au (numéro) dix
to be the tenth to arrive/to leave	arriver/partir le dixième
to come tenth, to be tenth (in a race)	arriver dixième, être dixième
it's the tenth (today)	nous sommes le dix (aujourd'hui)

the tenth of May, May the tenth, *Am* May tenth	le dix mai
to arrive/be paid on the tenth	arriver/être payé le dix
to arrive/be paid on the tenth of May *or* on May the tenth *orAm* on May tenth	arriver/être payé le dix mai
by the tenth, before the tenth	avant le dix, pour le dix
it's ten (o'clock)	il est dix heures
it's half past ten	il est dix heures et demie
ten past ten, *Am* ten after ten	dix heures dix
ten to ten	dix heures moins dix
by ten (o'clock), before ten (o'clock)	pour dix heures, avant dix heures
to be ten (years old)	avoir dix ans
a child of ten, a ten-year-old (child)	un enfant de dix ans

Days and Months/
Les Jours et les mois

Monday	lundi
Tuesday	mardi
Wednesday	mercredi
Thursday	jeudi
Friday	vendredi
Saturday	samedi
Sunday	dimanche
January	janvier
February	février
March	mars
April	avril
May	mai
June	juin
July	juillet
August	août
September	septembre
October	octobre
November	novembre
December	décembre

Examples of usage	**Exemples d'emplois**
he arrives on Monday	il arrive lundi
(on) Mondays	le lundi
see you on Monday!	à lundi
by Monday, before Monday	avant lundi, pour lundi
Monday morning/evening	lundi matin/soir
a week/two weeks on Monday, *Am* a week/two weeks from Monday	lundi en huit/en quinze
it's Monday (today)	nous sommes (aujourd'hui) lundi
Monday the tenth of May, Monday May the tenth, *Am* Monday May tenth	le lundi dix mai
tomorrow is Tuesday	demain c'est mardi
in May	en mai, au mois de mai
every May, each May	tous les ans en mai, chaque année en mai
by May, before May	avant mai, pour mai

Time/L'Heure

what time is it?, what's the time?   quelle heure est-il?

Hours	**Les heures**
it's one o'clock	il est une heure
it's 12 (noon)	il est midi
it's 12 (midnight)	il est minuit
at five o'clock	à cinq heures
at about ten o'clock	à dix heures environ
(at) around midday/midnight	vers midi/minuit
at exactly nine o'clock	à neuf heures précises, à neuf heures pile

Half-hours	**Les demi-heures**
it's half past nine, it's nine thirty, it's half nine (familier)	il est neuf heures et demie

Quarter-hours	**Les quarts d'heure**
it's a quarter to six	il est six heures moins le quart
it's a quarter past (*Br*)/after (*Am*) six	il est six heures et quart

Minutes	**Les minutes**
it's ten past seven, it's 7:10	il est sept heures dix
it's ten to seven, it's 6:50	il est sept heures moins dix
it's four minutes past two	il est deux heures quatre

a.m. and p.m.	**a.m. et p.m.**
a.m.	du matin
p.m.	de l'après-midi/du soir
it's 7 a.m., it's seven (o'clock) in the morning	il est sept heures du matin
it's 7 p.m., it's seven (o'clock) in the evening	il est sept heures du soir

L'heure sur 24 heures

Les expressions du type quinze heures, etc (à la place de trois heures, etc) ne s'emploient pas dans l'anglais de tous les jours. On les rencontre cependant parfois dans les horaires et surtout dans le langage militaire (souvent suivies du mot **hours**) :

| o five hundred hours | 5 heures du matin |
| fifteen hundred hours | quinze heures |

The 24-hour clock

In French the use of the 24-hour clock is not restricted to military contexts and timetables. It is therefore not uncommon to hear French people use **seize heures**, rather than **quatre heures**, to refer to four p.m.

Conversation guide

Meeting people

Hello, how are you?
Bonjour, comment ça va ?

Fine thanks, and you?
Ça va bien, merci, et vous/toi ?

What's your name?
Comment tu t'appelles ? /
Comment vous vous appelez ?

My name's...
Je m'appelle...

Nice to meet you!
Enchanté(e) !

This is my wife/my brother.
Voici ma femme/mon frère.

How old are you?
Quel âge as-tu? / Quel âge avez-vous ?

I'm 15/21/40.
J'ai quinze ans/vingt-et-un ans/quarante ans.

Where are you from ?
D'où viens-tu ? / D'où venez-vous ?

I'm from Edinburgh.
Je viens d'Édimbourg.

We're English.
Nous sommes anglais(es).

We live in the north of England
Nous habitons au nord de l'Angleterre..

What do you do?
Qu'est-ce que tu fais / Qu'est-ce que vous faites dans la vie ?

I'm a student.
Je suis étudiant(e).

I'm a teacher.
Je suis professeur.

I work in a bank.
Je travaille dans une banque.

I like football/going to the cinema.
J'aime bien le foot/aller au cinéma.

I don't like beer/cycling.
Je n'aime pas la bière/faire du vélo.

Can I have your address?
Je peux avoir ton/votre adresse ?

You must come and visit us one day!
Vous devez venir nous voir un jour !

Here's my e-mail address.
Voici mon adresse e-mail.

See you soon/later.
À bientôt/plus tard.

Understanding

Pardon?
Pardon ?

Could you repeat that, please?
Vous pouvez répéter ?

I don't understand.
Je ne comprends pas.

Do you speak English?
Parlez-vous anglais ?

I don't speak much French.
Je parle à peine français.

I can understand a little.
Je comprends un peu.

What does that mean?
Qu'est-ce que ça veut dire ?

How do you say ... in French?
Comment dit-on ... en français ?

I'm learning French.
J'apprends le français.

Could you write it down for me?
Pourriez-vous me l'écrire ?

Your stay

We're on holiday.
Nous sommes en vacances.

I'm here on business.
Je suis ici pour mon travail.

I'm just here for the weekend.
Je ne suis ici que pour le weekend.

We're here for a week.
Nous sommes ici pour une semaine.

We have a house here.
Nous avons une maison ici.

I really like it here.
Je me plais beaucoup ici.

Have a good holiday!
Bonnes vacances !

Have fun!
Amuse-toi /Amusez-vous bien !

Asking for directions

Excuse me, can you tell me where the bus station is, please?
Excusez-moi, pourriez-vous me dire où se trouve la gare routière ?

How do I get to the beach?
Comment je fais pour aller à la plage ?

Which way is it to the market?
Le marché, c'est par où ?

I'm looking for...
Je cherche...

Is there a bakery round here?
Y a-t-il une boulangerie par ici ?

Could you show me on the map?
Pourriez-vous me montrer sur la carte ?

Is it far to the next town?
C'est loin jusqu'à la prochaine ville ?

You may hear...

Continuez tout droit.
Go straight on.

Tournez à gauche/à droite.
Turn left/right.

Continuez jusqu'à...
Carry on as far as...

Prenez la prochaine sortie.
Take the next exit.

Requests, thanks, opinions

Could I have a glass of water, please?
Est-ce que je pourrais avoir un verre d'eau ?

Would you be able to give me a lift?
Est-ce que vous pourriez m'emmener en voiture ?

Do you mind if I open the window?
Ça vous dérange si j'ouvre la fenêtre ?

Can you show me?
Vous pouvez me montrer ?

Is it ok if I smoke?
Je peux fumer ?

Thank you (very much)!
Merci (beaucoup) !

You're welcome!
De rien !

Merci, c'est très gentil.
Thanks, that's very kind of you.

Thanks a lot for your help.
Merci beaucoup pour votre aide.

I enjoyed it.
Je l'ai bien aimé.

I didn't enjoy it.
Ça ne m'a pas plu.

It's beautiful!
C'est très joli(e) !

It was boring.
C'était ennuyeux.

I agree/disagree.
Je suis d'accord/Je ne suis pas d'accord.

You're right.
Vous avez raison.

I think it's delicious!
Je le trouve délicieux !

It's not bad.
Ce n'est pas mal.

Really? That's interesting!
Ah bon ? C'est intéressant !

I think so/don't think so.
Je crois que oui/non.

I don't mind.
Ça m'est égal.

I don't know.
Je ne sais pas.

Travelling

I'd like a ticket to Lille, please.
Je voudrais un billet pour Lille, s'il vous plaît.

A single/return ticket.
Un aller simple/aller-retour.

When's the next train to Paris?
À quelle heure est le prochain train pour Paris ?

Which platform does it go from?
Il part de quel quai ?

Do I have to change?
Est-ce qu'il y a une correspondance ?

Is this seat free?
Est-ce que cette place est libre ?

Sorry, there's someone sitting there.
Désolé(e), il y a déjà quelqu'un.

Where's the Easyjet check-in ?
Où est l'enregistrement pour Easyjet ?

I'd like an aisle/window seat.
Je voudrais une place côté couloir/côté hublot.

What time do we board?   **I've missed my connection.**
À quelle heure embarque-t-on ? J'ai raté ma correspondance.

My luggage hasn't arrived.
Mes bagages ne sont pas arrivés.

Do you have a timetable/a map of the underground?
Avez-vous un dépliant avec les horaires/un plan du métro ?

Does this bus go to the station ?
Est-ce que ce bus va à la gare ?

Is this the stop for the market?
Est-ce que c'est l'arrêt pour le marché ?

Which line do I take?
Je prends quelle ligne ?

What time's the last bus/train?
À quelle heure part le dernier bus/train ?

I'd like to hire a car for a week.
Je voudrais louer une voiture pour une semaine.

Is there a petrol station near here ?
Ya-t-il une station-service près d'ici ?

We've run out of petrol.
On est en panne d'essence.

I've broken down.   **We've got a puncture.**
Je suis tombé en panne.   *Nous avons crevé.*

Is there a taxi rank near here?
Y a-t-il une station de taxis près d'ici ?

I'd like to go to the airport.
Je voudrais aller à l'aéroport.

How much will it be?
Ça va coûter combien ?

You can drop me off here, thanks.
Vous pouvez me déposer ici, merci.

You may hear...

Combien de bagages avez-vous ?
How many bags do you have ?

Votre passeport, s'il vous plaît.
Can I see your passport, please ?

Voici votre carte d'embarquement.
Here's your boarding card.

Embarquement immédiat à la porte numéro...
Immediate boarding at gate...

Vous avez une correspondance à Lyon.
You have to change in Lyon.

Le train à destination de...
The train to...

Prenez le bus numéro...
Take bus number...

Descendez au troisième arrêt.
Get off at the third stop.

Accommodation

Have you got a room available for tonight?
Avez-vous une chambre de libre pour ce soir ?
I'd like to book a double/single room for three nights.
Je voudrais réserver une chambre double/individuelle pour trois nuits.

I'd like an ensuite room.
Je voudrais une chambre avec salle de bains.

I have a reservation in the name of...
J'ai fait une réservation au nom de...

Do you have family rooms ?
Avez-vous des chambres familiales ?

Don't you have anything cheaper?
Vous n'avec rien de moins cher ?

Is breakfast included?
Est-ce que le petit déjeuner est compris ?

What time is breakfast?
À quelle heure est le petit déjeuner ?

What time do we have to check out?
À quelle heure doit-on libérer la chambre ?

There's a problem with the shower/the air conditioning.
Il y a un problème avec la douche/la climatisation.

It's broken.
C'est cassé.

It doesn't work.
Ça ne marche pas.

Can we pay, please?
Nous venons régler.

Can I leave my bags here?
Je peux laisser mes bagages ici ?

We'd like to rent a cottage in the country.
Nous voudrons louer une gîte rurale.

Are sheets and towels provided?
Les draps et serviettes sont-ils fournis ?

Is there a pool?
Est-ce qu'il y a une piscine ?

Is there a campsite nearby?
Est-ce qu'il y a un camping par ici ?

Can we pitch our tent here?
Pouvons-nous monter notre tente ici ?

You may hear...

C'ést à quel nom?
What's the name?

Désolé, on est complet.
Sorry, we're fully booked.

La chambre sera disponible à 14 heures.
The room will be ready at 2pm.

La chambre doit être libérée à midi.
Check-out is at midday.

Le petit déjeuner est servi de sept heures à dix heures.
Breakfast is from 7 to 10.

Eating and drinking

Can you recommend a good restaurant?
Pouvez-vous me recommander un bon restaurant ?

I'd like to book a table for two for tomorrow night.
Je voudrais réserver une table pour deux personnes pour demain soir.

Do you have a table for four ?
Avez-vous une table pour quatre ?

I've booked a table, the name's...
J'ai réservé une table au nom de...

We're ready to order now.
Nous avons choisi.

I'll have the salmon.
Je vais prendre le saumon.

I'm vegetarian.
Je suis végétarien(enne).

I'm allergic to shellfish.
Je suis allergique aux fruits de mer.

What's "bouillabaisse"?
C'est quoi, la bouillabaisse ?

What are today's specials?
Quels sont les plats du jour ?

A bottle of red/white wine.
Une bouteille de vin rouge/ blanc.

Two beers and a Coke®, please.
Deux bières et un Coca®, s'il vous plaît.

Could we have some more bread/water?
Est-ce qu'on pourrait avoir encore du pain/de l'eau ?

What desserts do you have?
Qu'est-ce que vous avez comme desserts ?

That was delicious.
C'était délicieux.

Excuse me!
S'il vous plaît !

Could we have the bill, please?
L'addition, s'il vous plaît.

Excuse me, where are the toilets?
Où sont les toilettes, s'il vous plaît ?

Vous avez réservé ?
Have you booked?

À quel nom ?
What's the name?

À quelle heure ?
For what time?

Désolé, on est complet.
Sorry, we're full.

Vous avez choisi ?
Are you ready to order?

Cette table-ci vous convient ?
Is this table here all right for you?

Pour combien de personnes ?
For how many people?

Qu'est-ce que vous voulez boire ?
What would you like to drink?

Bon appétit !
Enjoy your meal!

Vous voulez un dessert ?
Would you like a dessert?

Ça a été ?
Was everything ok?

Shopping

Do you sell stamps/milk?
Est-ce que vous vendez des timbres/du lait ?

I'd like some of that cheese.
Je voudrais un peu de ce fromage-là.

How much is it?
Ça coûte combien ?

Four apples, please.
Quatre pommes, s'il vous plaît.

A bit more/less.
Un peu plus/moins.

That's all, thanks.
Ce sera tout, merci.

Can I try it on?
Est-ce que je peux essayer ?

No thanks, I'm just looking.
Non merci, je regarde seulement.

I need a size 12.
Je fais du 40.

I'm a size 5. (in shoes)
Je chausse du 38.

Do you have it in a bigger/smaller size?
Est-ce que vous l'avez dans une plus grande/plus petite taille ?

That's fine, I'll take it.
C'est bon, je le/la prends.

No, I don't like it.
No, je ne l'aime pas.

Do you take credit cards?
Est-ce qu'on peut payer par carte ?

Can I have a plastic bag?
Je peux avoir un sac plastique ?

Health

Where can I find a doctor?
Où est-ce que je peux trouver un médecin ?

I need an ambulance!
J'ai besoin d'une ambulance !

I'd like to make an appointment.
Je voudrais prendre rendez-vous.

I have an appointment with Dr...
J'ai rendez-vous avec le Docteur...

As soon as possible.
Le plus tôt possible.

I don't feel well.
Je ne me sens pas bien.

I've got a headache/stomachache.
J'ai mal à la tête/au ventre.

I've got a sore throat/back.
J'ai mal à la gorge/au dos.

I feel sick.
J'ai envie de vomir.

I've got a temperature.
J'ai de la fièvre.

It hurts.
Ça fait mal.

I have asthma/diabetes.
J'ai de l'asthme/du diabète.

I'm four months pregnant.
Je suis enceinte de quatre mois.

I'm allergic to penicillin.
Je suis allergique à la pénicilline.

It's been three days.
Ça fait trois jours.

It's got worse.
Ça s'est aggravé.

Where's the nearest pharmacy?
Où est la pharmacie la plus proche ?

I need some plasters/aspirin.
J'ai besoin de pansements/d'aspirine.

Do you have anything for a cold/diarrhoea ?
Pouvez-vous me donner quelque chose contre le rhume/la diarrée ?

You may hear...

Prenez place dans la salle d'attente.
Take a seat in the waiting room.

Où est-ce que ça fait mal ?
Where does it hurt?

Respirez bien fort.
Take a deep breath.

Allongez-vous.
Lie down.

Ça devrait passer dans quelques jours.
It should clear up in a few days.

Je vais vous faire une ordonnance.
I'll write you a prescription.

Revenez me voir dans une semaine.
Come back and see me in a week.

Prenez-le trois fois par jour avant les repas.
Take it three times a day before meals.

Emergencies

| Help!
Au secours ! | Fire!
Au feu ! | Stop, thief!
Au voleur ! |

There's been an accident.
Il y a eu un accident.

It's an emergency!
C'est urgent !

Where's the nearest police station/hospital?
Où est le commissariat/l'hôpital le plus proche ?

Can you help me?
Est-ce que vous pouvez m'aider ?

My bag/passport's been stolen.
On m'a volé mon sac/mon passeport.

I've lost my car keys.
J'ai perdu mes clés de voiture.

My son/daughter is missing.
Mon fils/Ma fille a disparu.

There's someone following me.
Il y a quelqu'un qui me suit.

I want to report a theft.
Je voudrais faire une déclaration de vol.

What do I have to do?
Qu'est-ce que je dois faire ?

I need a document from the police for my insurance company.
J'ai besoin d'un certificat de police pour ma compagnie d'assurances.

You may hear...

Qu'est-ce qui s'est passé ?
What happened?

Quand cela est-il passé ?
When did it happen?

Pouvez-vous le/la décrire ?
Can you describe him/her ?

Qu'est-ce qu'il vous manque ?
What's missing?

Vous devez remplir ce formulaire.
You need to fill in this form.

Guide de conversation

Rencontres

Bonjour, comment ça va ?
Hello, how are you?

Ça va bien, merci, et vous / toi ?
Fine thanks, and you?

Comment tu t'appelles/vous vous appelez ?
What's your name?

Je m'appelle...
My name's...

Enchanté(e) !
Nice to meet you!

Voici mon mari/ma sœur.
This is my husband/my sister.

Quel âge as-tu/avez-vous ?
How old are you?

J'ai 15/21/40 ans.
I'm fifteen/twenty-one/forty.

D'où viens-tu/venez-vous ?
Where are you from ?

Je viens de Bordeaux.
I'm from Bordeaux.

Nous sommes français(es).
We're French.

Nous habitons dans le sud de la France.
We live in the south of France.

Qu'est-ce que tu fais/vous faites dans la vie ?
What do you do?

Je suis étudiant(e).
I'm a student.

Je suis professeur.
I'm a teacher.

Je travaille dans une banque.
I work in a bank.

J'aime bien le foot/aller au cinéma.
I like football/going to the cinema.

Je n'aime pas la bière/faire du vélo.
I don't like beer/cycling.

Je peux avoir ton/votre adresse ?
Can I have your address?

Vous devez venir nous voir un jour !
You must come and visit us one day!

Voici mon adresse e-mail.
Here's my e-mail address.

À bientôt/plus tard.
See you soon/later.

Comprendre

Pardon ?
Pardon?

Vous pouvez répéter ?
Could you repeat that, please?

Je ne comprends pas.
I don't understand.

Parlez-vous français ?
Do you speak French?

Je parle à peine anglais.
I don't speak much English.

Je comprends un peu.
I can understand a little.

Qu'est-ce que ça veut dire ?
What does that mean?

Comment dit-on ... en anglais ?
How do you say ... in English?

J'apprends l'anglais.
I'm learning English.

Pourriez-vous me l'écrire ?
Could you write it down for me?

Votre séjour

Nous sommes en vacances.
We're on holiday.

Je suis ici pour mon travail.
I'm here on business.

Je ne suis ici que pour le weekend.
I'm only here for the weekend.

Nous sommes ici pour une semaine.
We're here for a week.

Nous avons des amis/de la famille ici.
We have friends/family here.

Je me plais beaucoup ici.
I really like it here.

Bonnes vacances !
Have a good holiday!

Amuse-toi / Amusez-vous bien !
Have fun!

Demander son chemin

Excusez-moi, pourriez-vous me dire où se trouve la gare routière ?
Excuse me, can you tell me where the bus station is, please?

Comment je fais pour aller au zoo ?
How do I get to the zoo?

Le marché, c'est par où ?   **Je cherche...**
Which way is it to the market?   *I'm looking for...*

Y a-t-il une papeterie par ici ?
Is there a newsagent's round here?

Pourriez-vous me montrer sur la carte ?
Could you show me on the map?

C'est loin jusqu'à la prochaine ville ?
Is it far to the next town?

Vous entendrez peut-être...

Go straight on.   **Turn left/right.**
Continuez tout droit.   Tournez à gauche/à droite.

Carry on as far as...   **Take the next exit.**
Continuez jusqu'à...   Prenez la prochaine sortie.

Demandes, remerciements, opinions

Est-ce que pourrais avoir de l'eau?
Could I have some water, please?

Est-ce que vous pourriez m'emmener en voiture ?
Would you be able to give me a lift?

Vous pouvez me montrer ?   **Je peux fumer ?**
Can you show me?   *Is it ok if I smoke?*

(39)

Ça vous dérange si j'ouvre la fenêtre ?
Do you mind if I open the window?

Merci (beaucoup) !
Thank you (very much)!

De rien !
You're welcome!

Merci, c'est très gentil.
Thanks, that's very kind of you.

Merci beaucoup pour votre aide.
Thanks a lot for your help.

Je l'ai bien aimé.
I enjoyed it.

Ça ne m'a pas plu.
I didn't enjoy it.

C'est très joli(e) !
It's beautiful!

C'était ennuyeux.
It was boring.

Je suis/ne suis pas d'accord.
I agree/disagree.

Vous avez raison.
You're right.

Je le trouve délicieux !
I think it's delicious!

Ce n'est pas mal.
It's not bad.

Ah bon ? C'est intéressant !
Really? That's interesting!

Je crois que oui/non.
I think so/don't think so.

Ça m'est égal.
I don't mind.

Je ne sais pas.
I don't know.

Voyages

Un billet pour York, s'il vous plaît.
I'd like a ticket to York, please.

Un aller simple/aller-retour.
A single/return ticket.

À quelle heure est le prochain train pour Birmingham ?
When's the next train to Birmingham?

Il part de quel quai ?
Which platform does it go from?

Est-ce qu'il y a une correspondance ?
Do I have to change?

Est-ce que cette place est libre ?
Is this seat free?

Désolé(e), il y a déjà quelqu'un.
Sorry, there's someone sitting there.

Où est l'enregistrement pour Easyjet ?
Where's the Easyjet check-in ?

À quelle heure embarque-t-on ?
What time do we board?

Je voudrais une place côté couloir/côté hublot.
I'd like an aisle/window seat please.

J'ai raté ma correspondance.
I've missed my connection.

Mes bagages ne sont pas arrivés.
My luggage hasn't arrived.

Avez-vous un dépliant avec les horaires/un plan du métro ?
Do you have a timetable/a map of the underground?

Est-ce que ce bus va à la gare ? Je prends quelle ligne ?
Does this bus go to the station? Which line do I take?

Est-ce que c'est l'arrêt pour le musée ?
Is this the stop for the museum?

À quelle heure part le dernier bus/train ?
What time is the last bus/train?
Je voudrais louer une voiture pour une semaine.
I'd like to hire a car for a week.

Y a-t-il une station-service près d'ici ?
Is there a petrol station near here ?

On est en panne d'essence.
We've run out of petrol.

Je suis tombé en panne.   **Nous avons crevé.**
I've broken down.   *We've got a puncture.*

Y a-t-il une station de taxis près d'ici ?
Is there a taxi rank near here?

Je voudrais aller à l'aéroport.   **Ça va coûter combien ?**
I'd like to go to the airport.   *How much will it be?*

Vous pouvez me déposer ici, merci.
You can drop me off here, thanks.

Vous entendrez peut-être...

How many bags do you have ?
Combien de bagages avez-vous ?

Can I see your passport, please ?
Votre passeport, s'il vous plaît.

Here's your boarding card.   **Immediate boarding at gate...**
Voici votre carte   Embarquement immédiat à la
d'embarquement.   porte numéro...

You have to change at Peterborough.
Vous avez une correspondance à Peterborough.

The train to...
Le train à destination de...

Take bus number...   **Get off at the third stop.**
Prenez le bus numéro...   Descendez au troisième arrêt.

Logement

Avez-vous une chambre de libre pour ce soir ?
Have you got a room available for tonight?

Je voudrais réserver une chambre double/individuelle pour trois nuits.
I'd like to book a double/single room for three nights.

Je voudrais une chambre avec salle de bains.
I'd like an ensuite room.

J'ai fait une réservation au nom de...
I have a reservation in the name of...

Avez-vous des chambres familiales ?
Do you have family rooms ?

Vous n'avez rien de moins cher ?
Don't you have anything cheaper?

Est-ce que le petit déjeuner est compris ?
Is breakfast included?

À quelle heure est le petit déjeuner ?
What time is breakfast?

À quelle heure doit-on libérer la chambre ?
What time do we have to check out?

Je peux laisser mes bagages ici ?
Can I leave my bags here?

Il y a un problème avec la douche/la climatisation.
There's a problem with the shower/the air conditioning.

C'est cassé.
It's broken.

Ça ne marche pas.
It doesn't work.

Je viens régler.
I'd like to pay, please.

Il n'y a pas de papier toilette.
There's no toilet paper.

Nous voudrons louer une gîte rurale.
We'd like to rent a cottage in the country.

Les draps et serviettes sont-ils fournis ?
Are sheets and towels provided?

Est-ce qu'on a besoin d'une voiture ?
Do you need a car?

Est-ce qu'il y a un camping par ici ?
Is there a campsite nearby?

Pouvons-nous monter notre tente ici?
Can we pitch our tent here?

Manger et boire

Pouvez-vous me recommander un bon restaurant ?
Can you recommend a good restaurant?

Je voudrais réserver une table pour deux personnes pour demain soir.
I'd like to book a table for two for tomorrow night.

Avez-vous une table pour quatre ?
Do you have a table for four ?

J'ai réservé une table au nom de...
I've booked a table, the name's...

Nous avons choisi.	**Je vais prendre le saumon.**
We're ready to order now.	*I'll have the salmon.*

Je suis végétarien(enne).
I'm vegetarian.

Je suis allergique aux produits laitiers.
I'm allergic to dairy products.

C'est quoi, le « black pudding » ?
What's black pudding?

Quels sont les plats du jour ?
What are today's specials?

A bottle of red/white wine.
Une bouteille de vin rouge/blanc.

Two beers and a Coke®, please.
Deux bières et un Coca®, s'il vous plaît.

Est-ce qu'on pourrait avoir encore du pain/de l'eau ?
Could we have some more bread/water?

Vous avez quoi comme desserts ?
What desserts do you have?

C'était délicieux.
That was delicious.

S'il vous plaît !
Excuse me!

L'addition, s'il vous plaît.
Could we have the bill, please?

Où sont les toilettes, s'il vous plaît ?
Excuse me, where are the toilets?

Vous entendrez peut-être...

Do you have a reservation?
Vous avez réservé ?

What's the name?
À quel nom ?

For what time?
À quelle heure ?

For how many people?
Pour combien de personnes ?

Sorry, we're full.
Désolé, on est complet.

Are you ready to order?
Vous avez choisi ?

Is this table here all right for you?
Cette table-ci vous convient ?

What would you like to drink?
Qu'est-ce que vous voulez boire ?

Enjoy your meal!
Bon appétit !

Would you like a dessert?
Vous voulez un dessert ?

Was everything ok?
Ça a été ?

Achats

Est-ce que vous vendez des timbres/du lait ?
Do you sell stamps/milk?

Je voudrais un peu de ce fromage-là.
I'd like a bit of that cheese.

Ça coûte combien ?
How much is it?

Four apples, please.
Quatre pommes, s'il vous plaît.

Un peu plus/moins.
A bit more/less.

Ce sera tout, merci.
That's all, thanks.

Est-ce que je peux essayer ?
Can I try it on?
Non merci, je regarde seulement.
No thanks, I'm just looking.

Je fais du 40. (vêtements)
I'm a size 12.

Je chausse du 38.
I take a size 5.

Est-ce que vous l'avez dans une plus grande/plus petite taille?
Do you have it in a bigger/smaller size?

C'est bon, je le/la prends.
That's fine, I'll take it.

No, je ne l'aime pas.
No, I don't like it.

Est-ce qu'on peut payer par carte ?
Do you take credit cards?

Je peux avoir un sac plastique ?
Can I have a (plastic) bag?

Vous entendrez peut-être...

Can I help you?
Je peux vous aider ?

Will there be anything else?
Et avec ceci ?

Don't you have anything smaller?
Vous n'avez pas plus petit ?

Would you like a bag?
Voulez-vous un sac en plastique ?

Santé

J'ai besoin de voir un médecin.
I need to see a doctor.

J'ai besoin d'une ambulance !
I need an ambulance!

Je voudrais prendre rendez-vous.
I'd like to make an appointment.

J'ai rendez-vous avec le Docteur...
I have an appointment with Dr...

Le plus tôt possible.
As soon as possible.

Je ne me sens pas bien.
I don't feel well.

J'ai mal au ventre/à la tête.
I've got stomachache/a headache.

J'ai mal à la gorge/au dos.
I've got a sore throat/back.

J'ai envie de vomir.
I feel sick.

J'ai de la fièvre.
I've got a temperature.

Ça fait mal.
It hurts.

J'ai de l'asthme/du diabète.
I have asthma/diabetes.

Je suis enceinte de quatre mois.
I'm four months pregnant.

Je suis allergique à la pénicilline.
I'm allergic to penicillin.

Ça fait trois jours.
It's been three days.

Ça s'est aggravé.
It's got worse.

Où est la pharmacie la plus proche ?
Where's the nearest pharmacy?

J'ai besoin de pansements/d'aspirine.
I need some plasters/aspirin.

Pouvez-vous me donner quelque chose contre le rhume/la diarrée ?
Do you have anything for a cold/diarrhoea ?

Vous entendrez peut-être...

Take a seat in the waiting room.
Prenez place dans la salle d'attente.

Where does it hurt ?
Où est-ce que ça fait mal ?

Take a deep breath.
Respirez bien fort.

Lie down.
Allongez-vous.

It should clear up in a few days.
Ça devrait passer dans quelques jours.

I'll write you a prescription.
Je vais vous faire une ordonnance.

Come back and see me in a week.
Revenez me voir dans une semaine.

Take it three times a day before meals.
Prenez-le trois fois par jour avant les repas.

Urgences

Au secours !
Help!

Au feu !
Fire!

Au voleur !
Stop, thief!

Il y a eu un accident.
There's been an accident.

C'est urgent !
It's an emergency!

Où est le commissariat/l'hôpital le plus proche ?
Where's the nearest police station/hospital?

Est-ce que vous pouvez m'aider ?
Can you help me?

On m'a volé mon sac/mon passeport.
My bag/passport's been stolen.

J'ai perdu mes clés de voiture.
I've lost my car keys.

Mon fils/Ma fille a disparu.
My son/daughter is missing.

Il y a quelqu'un qui me suit.
There's someone following me.

Qu'est-ce que je dois faire ?
What do I have to do?

Je voudrais faire une déclaration de vol.
I want to report a theft.

J'ai besoin d'un certificat de police pour ma compagnie d'assurances.
I need a document from the police for my insurance company.

Conversion tables
•
Tables de conversion

Note that when writing numbers in French, commas are used instead of decimal points. For example, **2.5** would be written **2,5** in French and pronounced *deux virgule cinq*.

***

Notez que les chiffres en anglais s'écrivent avec un point là ou en français on utilise une virgule. Par exemple, **2,5** s'écrira **2.5** en anglais et se prononcera *two point five*.

Measurements *Mesures*
Length *Longueur*

1 cm ≈ 0.4 inches   1 inch (*pouce*) ≈ 2,5 cm
30 cm ≈ 1 foot (*pied*)

Lengths in France are always given in metres and centimetres.

***

Les Britanniques et les Américains se mesurent normalement en **feet** et en **inches**. On dira donc « he's 6 foot four » (6 pieds et 4 pouces, ou 1m90).

Distance *Distance*

> On French road signs, distances are always shown in kilometres.
>
> ***
>
> Sur les panneaux de route britanniques et américains, les distances sont toujours données en miles.

1 m ≈ 1 yard
1 km ≈ 0.6 miles   1 mile ≈ 1,6 km

To convert kilometers into miles, divide by 8 and then multiply by 5.
Pour convertir des kilomètres en miles, divisez par 8 puis multipliez par 5.

km	1	2	5	10	20	50	100
miles	0.6	1.25	3.1	6.25	12.5	31.25	62.5

To convert miles into kilometers, divide by 5 and then multiply by 8.
Pour convertir des miles en kilomètres, divisez par 5 puis multipliez par 8.

miles	1	2	5	10	20	50	100
km	1.6	3.2	8	16	32	80	160

Weight *Poids*

Weights in France are always in kilos (or grams for small amounts).

***

Les fruits et légumes se vendent par livres (**pounds**). Pour parler du poids d'une personne, les britanniques utilisent le plus souvent les **stones** (14 livres = 1 stone). On dira donc « I weigh nine stone ten » (neuf stones et dix livres, ou 61kg). Aux États-Unis, on emploie les pounds pour les personnes.

25 g ≈ 1 oz (ounce/*once*)
1 kg ≈ 2 lb (pound/*livre*)   1lb ≈ 0.5 kg
6 kg ≈ 1 stone

To convert kilos into pounds, divide by 5 and then multiply by 11.
Pour convertir des kilos en livres, divisez par 5 puis multipliez par 11.

kilos	1	2	10	20	60	80
pounds	2.2	4.4	2.2	44	132	176
kilos	10	20	50	60	75	90
stone	1.6	3.2	8	9.4	11.8	14

To convert pounds into kilos, divide by 11 and then multiply by 5.
Pour convertir des livres en kilos, divisez par 11 puis multipliez par 5.

pounds	1	2	10	20	60	80
kilos	0.45	0.9	4.5	9	27	36

stone	1	2	8	10	12	14
kilos	6.35	12.7	50.8	63.5	76	89

Liquids *Liquides*

1 litre ≈ 2 pints   1 pint ≈ 0.5 litres
1 gallon (*Br*) ≈ 4.54 litres, (*Am*) ≈ 3.78 litres

Temperatures *Températures*

To convert Celsius into Fahrenheit, divide by 5, multiply by 9 and then add 32.
Pour convertir des degrés Celsius en degrés Fahrenheit, divisez par 5, multipliez par 9 puis ajoutez 32.

To convert Fahrenheit into Celsius, subtract 32, multiply by 5 and then divide by 9.
Pour convertir des degrés Fahrenheit en degrés Celsius, soustrayez 32, multipliez par 5 puis divisez par 9.

°C	0	10	20	30	37	40	100
°F	32	50	68	104	98.6	80	212

Clothes sizes *Tailles de vêtements*

> Clothes in France may also be labelled with the English-language abbreviations XS, S, M, L and XL, or with the numbers 1 to 4 (increasing in size).
>
>   ***
>
> Vous connaissez sans doute déjà les abréviations XS (extra small), S (small), M (medium), L (large) et XL (extra large).

Women's clothes *Vêtements pour femmes*

UK	6	8	10	12	14	16
US	4	6	8	10	12	14
Europe	38	36	38	40	42	44

Bras *Soutiens-gorge*

UK/US	32	34	36	38	40
France	85	90	95	100	105
Europe	70	75	80	85	90

Cup sizes are the same.
La taille de bonnet est identique.

Men's clothes *Vêtements pour hommes*

UK/US	30	32	34	36	38	40
Europe	40	42	44	46	48	50

Men's shirts *Chemises pour hommes*

UK/US	14	15	16	17	18
Europe	36	38	41	43	48

Women's shoes *Chaussures de femmes*

UK	4	5	6	7	8
US	6	7	8	9	10
Europe	37	38	39	40	41

Men's shoes *Chaussures d'hommes*

UK	7	8	9	10	11
US	8	9	10	11	12
Europe	40	41	42	43	44

Currency *Monnaie*

£1 (pound) = 100 pence
$1 (dollar) = 100 cents
€1 (euro) = 100 cents

As exchange rates vary, we have left blanks in the following tables for you to fill in with the most up-to-date figures.

***

Comme les taux de change varient, nous avons laissé des blancs dans ces tableaux que vous pouvez remplir avec les chiffres les plus récentes.

£	1	5	10	25	50	100
$	1	5	10	25	50	100
€						

€	1	5	10	25	50	100
£						
$						

FRANÇAIS-ANGLAIS

Aa

A, a [ɑ] *nm inv* A, a; **A1** *(autoroute) Br* ≃ M1, *Am* ≃ I1

a [a] *voir* **avoir**

A [a]

à + **le** = **au** [o], à + **les** = **aux** [o]

prép (**a**) *(indique la direction)* to; **aller à Paris** to go to Paris; **partir au Venezuela** to leave for Venezuela; **de Paris à Lyon** from Paris to Lyons (**b**) *(indique la position)* at; **être au bureau/à la ferme/à Paris** to be at *or* in the office/on *or* at the farm/in Paris; **à la maison** at home (**c**) *(dans l'expression du temps)* **à 8 heures** at 8 o'clock; **du lundi au vendredi** from Monday to Friday, *Am* Monday through Friday; **au vingt-et-unième siècle** in the twenty-first century; **à mon arrivée** on (my) arrival; **à lundi!** see you (on) Monday! (**d**) *(dans les descriptions)* **l'homme à la barbe** the man with the beard; **verre à vin** wine glass (**e**) *(introduit le complément d'objet indirect)* **donner qch à qn** to give sth to sb, to give sb sth; **penser à qn/qch** to think about *or* of sb/sth (**f**) *(devant infinitif)* **apprendre à lire** to learn to read; **avoir du travail à faire** to have work to do; **maison à vendre** house for sale; **prêt à partir** ready to leave (**g**) *(indique l'appartenance)* **un ami à moi** a friend of mine; **c'est à lui** it's his; **c'est à vous de…** *(il vous incombe de)* it's up to you to…; *(c'est votre tour)* it's your turn to…

(**h**) *(indique le moyen, la manière)* **à bicyclette** by bicycle; **à pied** on foot; **à la main** by hand; **au crayon** in pencil; **deux à deux** two by two (**i**) *(prix)* **pain à 1 euro** loaf for 1 euro (**j**) *(poids)* **vendre au kilo** to sell by the kilo (**k**) *(vitesse)* **100 km à l'heure** 100 km an *or* per hour (**l**) *(pour appeler)* **au voleur!** (stop) thief!; **au feu!** (there's a) fire!

abaisser [abese] **1** *vt (levier, pont-levis)* to lower; *(store)* to pull down **2 s'abaisser** *upr* (**a**) *(barrière)* to lower (**b**) *(être en pente)* to slope down

abandon [abɑ̃dɔ̃] *nm (d'enfant, de projet)* abandonment; *(de lieu)* neglect; *(de sportif)* withdrawal; *Ordinat* abort ■ **abandonner 1** *vt (personne, animal, lieu)* to desert, to abandon; *(pouvoir, combat)* to give up; *(projet)* to abandon; **a. ses études** to drop out (of school) **2** *vi (renoncer)* to give up; *(sportif)* to withdraw

abasourdi, -e [abazurdi] *adj* stunned

abat-jour [abaʒur] *nm inv* lampshade

abats [aba] *nmpl* offal; *(de volaille)* giblets

abattement [abatmɑ̃] *nm (mental)* dejection; *(physique)* exhaustion; **a. fiscal** tax allowance

abattoir [abatwar] *nm* slaughterhouse

abattre* [abatr] **1** *vt (arbre)* to cut down; *(personne)* to kill; *(animal de boucherie)* to slaughter; *(animal blessé ou malade)* to destroy; *(avion)* to shoot down; *Fig (déprimer)* to demoralize **2**

s'abattre *vpr* (*tomber*) to crash down (**sur** on); (*pluie*) to pour down (**sur** on)

abattu, -e [abaty] *adj* (*mentalement*) dejected; (*physiquement*) exhausted

abbaye [abei] *nf* abbey

abcès [apsɛ] *nm* abscess

abdomen [abdɔmɛn] *nm* abdomen ■ **abdominal, -e, -aux, -ales** *adj* abdominal

abeille [abɛj] *nf* bee

aberrant, -e [aberã, -ãt] *adj* absurd

abîme [abim] *nm* abyss

abîmer [abime] **1** *vt* to spoil, to damage **2 s'abîmer** *vpr* (*object*) to get spoilt; (*fruit*) to go bad

abject, -e [abʒɛkt] *adj* despicable

abolir [abɔlir] *vt* to abolish ■ **abolition** *nf* abolition

abominable [abɔminabl] *adj* appalling

abondant, -e [abɔ̃dã, -ãt] *adj* plentiful, abundant ■ **abondance** *nf* abundance (**de** of) ■ **abonder** *vi* to be plentiful

abonné, -e [abɔne] *nmf* (*d'un journal, du téléphone*) subscriber; (*du gaz*) consumer ■ **abonnement** *nm* (*de journal*) subscription; (*de téléphone*) line rental ■ **s'abonner** *vpr* (*à un journal*) to subscribe (**à** to)

abord [abɔr] *nm* (**a**) (*accès*) **d'un a. facile** easy to approach; **abords** (*d'un bâtiment*) surroundings; (*d'une ville*) outskirts (**b**) (*expressions*) **au premier a., de prime a.** at first sight; **d'a., tout d'a.** (*pour commencer*) at first, to begin with; (*premièrement*) first (and foremost)

abordable [abɔrdabl] *adj* (*prix, marchandises*) affordable

aborder [abɔrde] **1** *vt* (*personne, lieu, virage*) to approach; (*problème*) to tackle **2** *vi* to land

aborigène [abɔriʒɛn] *nm* (*d'un pays*) native; **les Aborigènes d'Australie** the (Australian) Aborigines

aboutir [abutir] *vi* (*réussir*) to be successful; **a. à qch** (*avoir pour résultat*) to result in sth ■ **aboutissement** *nm*

(*succès*) success; (*résultat*) outcome

aboyer [abwaje] *vi* to bark

abréger [abreʒe] *vt* (*texte*) to shorten; (*visite*) to cut short; (*mot*) to abbreviate ■ **abrégé** *nm* (*d'un texte*) summary; (*livre*) abstract; **en a.** (*mot*) in abbreviated form

abréviation [abrevjasjɔ̃] *nf* abbreviation

abri [abri] *nm* shelter; **mettre qn/qch à l'a.** to shelter sb/sth; **se mettre à l'a.** to take shelter; **être à l'a. de qch** to be sheltered from sth; **sans a.** homeless ■ **abriter 1** *vt* (*protéger*) to shelter (**de** from); (*loger*) to house **2 s'abriter** *vpr* to (take) shelter (**de** from)

abricot [abriko] *nm* apricot

abroger [abrɔʒe] *vt* to repeal

abrupt, -e [abrypt] *adj* (*pente*) steep

abrutir [abrytir] *vt* (*hébéter*) to daze ■ **abrutissant, -e** *adj* mind-numbing

absence [apsɑ̃s] *nf* (*d'une personne*) absence; (*manque*) lack ■ **absent, -e 1** *adj* (*personne*) absent (**de** from); (*chose*) missing **2** *nmf* absentee ■ **s'absenter** *vpr* to go away

absolu, -e [apsɔly] *adj* absolute ■ **absolument** *adv* absolutely

absorber [apsɔrbe] *vt* (*liquid*) to absorb; (*nourriture*) to eat; (*boisson*) to drink; (*médicament*) to take ■ **absorbant, -e** *adj* (*papier*) absorbent; (*travail*) absorbing ■ **absorption** *nf* (*de liquide*) absorption; (*de nourriture*) eating; (*de boisson*) drinking; (*de médicament*) taking

abstenir* [apstənir] **s'abstenir** *vpr* (*ne pas voter*) to abstain; **s'a. de qch/de faire qch** to refrain from sth/from doing sth ■ **abstention** *nf* Pol abstention

abstrait, -e [apstrɛ, -ɛt] *adj* abstract ■ **abstraction** *nf* abstraction

absurde [apsyrd] *adj* absurd ■ **absurdité** *nf* absurdity; **dire des absurdités** to talk nonsense

abus [aby] *nm* (*excès*) overindulgence (**de** in); (*pratique*) abuse (**de** of); **a. de pouvoir** abuse of power; **a. d'alcool**

alcohol abuse; **a. de confiance** breach of trust ■ **abuser 1** *vi* to go too far; **a. de** (*situation, personne*) to take unfair advantage of; (*autorité*) to abuse; (*nourriture*) to overindulge in **2 s'abuser** *upr* **si je ne m'abuse** if I am not mistaken

abusif, -ive [abyzif, -iv] *adj* excessive; (*mère*) possessive

académie [akademi] *nf* academy; (*administration scolaire*) ≃ local education authority; **l'A. française** = learned society responsible for promoting the French language and imposing standards

acajou [akaʒu] *nm* mahogany

accabler [akable] *vt* to overwhelm (**de** with); **accablé de dettes** (over)-burdened with debt ■ **accablant, -e** *adj* (*chaleur*) oppressive; (*témoignage*) damning

accalmie [akalmi] *nf* lull

accaparer [akapare] *vt* (*personne*) to monopolize

accéder [aksede] *vi* **a. à** (*lieu*) to reach; (*rang*) to gain; (*requête*) to comply with; *Ordinat* (*programme*) to access; **a. au trône** to accede to the throne

accélérer [akselere] **1** *vt* (*allure, pas*) to quicken **2** *vi* (*en voiture*) to accelerate **3 s'accélérer** *upr* to speed up ■ **accélérateur** *nm* (*de voiture, d'ordinateur*) accelerator ■ **accélération** *nf* acceleration

accent [aksɑ̃] *nm* (*prononciation*) accent; (*sur une syllabe*) stress; *Fig* **mettre l'a. sur qch** to stress sth; **a. aigu/circonflexe/grave** acute/circumflex/grave (accent) ■ **accentuation** *nf* (*sur lettre*) accentuation; (*de phénomène*) intensification ■ **accentuer 1** *vt* (*syllabe*) to stress; (*lettre*) to put an accent on; *Fig* (*renforcer*) to emphasize **2 s'accentuer** *upr* to become more pronounced

accepter [aksepte] *vt* to accept; **a. de faire qch** to agree to do sth ■ **acceptable** *adj* (*recevable*) acceptable ■ **acceptation** *nf* acceptance

acception [aksɛpsjɔ̃] *nf* (*de mot*) meaning

accès [aksɛ] *nm* (**a**) (*approche*) & *Ordinat* access (**à** to); **avoir a. à qch** to have access to sth; **'a. interdit'** 'no entry'; **'a. aux quais'** 'to the trains (**b**) (*de folie, de colère*) fit; (*de fièvre*) bout ■ **accessible** *adj* (*lieu, livre*) accessible

accession [aksɛsjɔ̃] *nf* accession (**à** to); **a. à la propriété** home ownership

accessoire [akseswar] *adj* minor ■ **accessoires** *nmpl* (*de théâtre*) props; (*de mode, de voiture*) accessories; **a. de toilette** toilet accessories

accident [aksidɑ̃] *nm* accident; **a. de chemin de fer** train crash; **a. de la route** road accident; **a. du travail** industrial accident; **a. de parcours** hitch; **par a.** by accident, by chance ■ **accidenté, -e 1** *adj* (*terrain*) uneven; (*voiture*) damaged **2** *nmf* accident victim ■ **accidentel, -elle** *adj* accidental

acclamer [aklame] *vt* to cheer ■ **acclamations** *nfpl* cheers

acclimater [aklimate] **1** *vt Br* to acclimatize, *Am* to acclimate (**à** to) **2 s'acclimater** *upr* to become *Br* acclimatized *or Am* acclimated (**à** to) ■ **acclimatation** *nf Br* acclimatization, *Am* acclimation (**à** to)

accolade [akɔlad] *nf* (*embrassade*) embrace; (*signe*) curly bracket

accommoder [akɔmɔde] **1** *vt* (*nourriture*) to prepare; (*restes*) to use up **2** *vi* (*œil*) to focus **3 s'accommoder** *upr* **s'a. de qch** to put up with sth ■ **accommodant, -e** *adj* accommodating

accompagner [akɔ̃paɲe] *vt* (*personne*) to accompany; **a. qn à la gare** (*en voiture*) to take sb to the station ■ **accompagnateur, -trice** *nmf* (*musical*) accompanist; (*de touristes*) guide; (*d'enfants*) group leader ■ **accompagnement** *nm* (*de musique*) accompaniment

accomplir [akɔ̃plir] *vt* (*tache*) to carry out; (*formalités*) to go through ■ **accompli, -e** *adj* (*parfait*) accomplished

accord [akɔr] *nm* (*traité, entente*) &

Gram agreement; *(autorisation)* consent; *(musical)* chord; **être d'a.** to agree (**avec** with); **d'a.!** all right! ■ **accorder 1** *vt (instrument)* to tune; **a. qch à qn** *(faveur)* to grant sb sth; *(prêt)* to authorize sth to sb **2 s'accorder** *vpr (se mettre d'accord)* to agree (**avec/sur** with/on); *Gram (mots)* to agree (**avec** with); **s'a. qch** to allow oneself sth

accordéon [akɔrdeɔ̃] *nm* accordion

accoster [akɔste] **1** *vt (personne)* to approach **2** *vi Naut* to dock

accotement [akɔtmɑ̃] *nm (de route)* verge; *(de voie ferrée)* shoulder

accoucher [akuʃe] *vi* to give birth (**de** to) ■ **accouchement** *nm* delivery

accouder [akude] **s'accouder** *vpr* **s'a. à** *ou* **sur qch** to lean one's elbows on sth ■ **accoudoir** *nm* armrest

accoupler [akuple] **s'accoupler** *vpr (animaux)* to mate

accourir* [akurir] *vi* to run up

accoutrement [akutrəmɑ̃] *nm Péj* rigout

accoutumer [akutyme] **1** *vt* **a. qn à qch** to get sb accustomed to sth **2 s'accoutumer** *vpr* to get accustomed (**à** to) ■ **accoutumance** *nf (adaptation)* familiarization (**à** with); *Méd (dépendance)* addiction ■ **accoutumé, -e** *adj* usual; **comme à l'accoutumée** as usual

accroc [akro] *nm (déchirure)* tear; *(difficulté)* hitch; **sans a.** without a hitch

accrocher [akrɔʃe] **1** *vt (déchirer)* to catch; *(fixer)* to hook (**à** onto); *(suspendre)* to hang up (**à** on)

2 *vi (achopper)* to hit a stumbling block; *(se remarquer)* to grab one's attention

3 s'accrocher *vpr (se fixer)* to fasten; *Fam (persévérer)* to stick at it; **s'a. à qn/qch** *(s'agripper)* to cling to sb/sth ■ **accrochage** *nm (de véhicules)* minor accident ■ **accrocheur, -euse** *adj (personne)* tenacious; *(titre, slogan)* catchy

accroître* [akrwatr] **1** *vt* to increase **2**

s'accroître *vpr* to increase ■ **accroissement** *nm* increase (**de** in)

accroupir [akrupir] **s'accroupir** *vpr* to squat (down)

accueil [akœj] *nm (bureau)* reception; *(manière)* welcome; **faire un bon a. à qn** to give sb a warm welcome ■ **accueillant, -e** *adj* welcoming ■ **accueillir*** *vt (personne, proposition)* to greet; *(sujet: hôtel)* to accommodate

acculer [akyle] *vt* **a. qn à qch** to drive sb to sth

accumuler [akymyle] *vt*, **s'accumuler** *vpr* to accumulate ■ **accumulation** *nf* accumulation

accuser [akyze] *vt (dénoncer)* to accuse; *(accentuer)* to bring out; *(baisse)* to show; **a. qn de qch/de faire qch** to accuse sb of sth/of doing sth ■ **accusateur, -trice 1** *adj (regard)* accusing **2** *nmf* accuser ■ **accusation** *nf* accusation ■ **accusé, -e** *nmf* **1 l'a.** the accused; *(au tribunal)* the defendant

achalandé, -e [aʃalɑ̃de] *adj* **bien a.** *(magasin)* well-stocked

acharner [aʃarne] **s'acharner** *vpr* **s'a. sur** *ou* **contre qn** *(persécuter)* to persecute sb; **s'a. à faire qch** to try very hard to do sth ■ **acharné, -e** *adj (effort, travail)* relentless; *(combat)* fierce ■ **acharnement** *nm* relentlessness; *(dans un combat)* fury

achat [aʃa] *nm* purchase; **faire l'a. de qch** to buy sth; **achats** *(paquets)* shopping

acheter [aʃte] **1** *vt* to buy; **a. qch à qn** *(faire une transaction)* to buy sth from sb; *(faire un cadeau)* to buy sth for sb **2** *vi* to buy **3 s'acheter** *vpr* **je vais m'acheter une glace** I'm going to buy (myself) an ice cream ■ **acheteur, -euse** *nmf* buyer; *(dans un magasin)* shopper

achever [aʃəve] **1** *vt* (**a**) *(finir)* to end; *(travail)* to complete; **a. de faire qch** to finish doing sth (**b**) *(tuer)* *(animal malade)* to put out of its misery; **a. qn** to finish sb off **2 s'achever** *vpr* to end ■ **achèvement** *nm* completion

acide [asid] **1** adj acid(ic); (au goût) sour **2** nm acid ■ **acidité** nf acidity; (au goût) sourness

acier [asje] nm steel; **a. inoxydable** stainless steel ■ **aciérie** nf steelworks

acné [akne] nf acne

acompte [akɔ̃t] nm down payment; **verser un a.** to make a down payment

à-coup [aku] (pl à-coups) nm jolt; **sans à-coups** smoothly; **par à-coups** (avancer) in fits and starts

acoustique [akustik] nf (qualité) acoustics (pluriel)

acquérir* [akerir] vt (acheter) to purchase; (obtenir) to acquire; **a. de la valeur** to increase in value; **tenir qch pour acquis** to take sth for granted ■ **acquéreur** nm purchaser ■ **acquis** nm (expérience) experience; **les a. sociaux** social benefits ■ **acquisition** nf (action) acquisition; (bien acheté) purchase

acquitter [akite] **1** vt (accusé) to acquit; (dette) to pay **2 s'acquitter** vpr **s'a. d'un devoir** to fulfil a duty ■ **acquittement** nm (d'un accusé) acquittal; (d'une dette) payment

âcre [akr] adj (goût) bitter; (odeur) acrid

acrobate [akrɔbat] nmf acrobat ■ **acrobatie** nf acrobatics (sing); **acrobaties aériennes** aerobatics (sing)

acrylique [akrilik] nm acrylic

acte [akt] nm (action) & Théât act; **faire a. de candidature** to apply; **prendre a. de qch** to take note of sth; **a. terroriste** terrorist act; **a. unique européen** Single European Act; **a. de naissance** birth certificate

acteur [aktœr] nm actor

actif, -ive [aktif, -iv] **1** adj active **2** nm Gram active; Com (d'une entreprise) assets

action [aksjɔ̃] nf (acte) action; (en Bourse) share; **bonne a.** good deed; **passer à l'a.** to take action ■ **actionnaire** nmf shareholder ■ **actionner** vt (mettre en marche) to start up

activer [aktive] **1** vt (accélérer) to speed up; Ordinat (option) to select **2 s'activer** vpr (être actif) to be busy

activité [aktivite] nf activity; **en a.** (personne) working; (volcan) active

actrice [aktris] nf actress

actualisation [aktyalizasjɔ̃] nf (de texte) updating

actualité [aktyalite] nf (d'un problème) topicality; **l'a.** current affairs; **les actualités** (à la radio, à la télévision) the news; **d'a.** topical

actuel, -elle [aktyɛl] adj (présent) present; (d'actualité) topical ■ **actuellement** adv at present

acupuncture [akypɔ̃ktyr] nf acupuncture ■ **acupuncteur, -trice** nmf acupuncturist

adapter [adapte] **1** vt to adapt (à to) **2 s'adapter** vpr (s'acclimater) to adapt (à to); **s'a. à qn/qch** to get used to sb/sth ■ **adaptateur** nm adapter ■ **adaptation** nf adaptation; **faculté d'a.** adaptability

additif [aditif] nm (substance) additive

addition [adisjɔ̃] nf addition (à to); (de restaurant) Br bill, Am check ■ **additionner** vt to add (up) (à to)

adepte [adept] nmf follower

adéquat, -e [adekwa, -at] adj appropriate; (quantité) adequate

adhérer [adere] vi **a. à qch** (coller) to stick to sth; (s'inscrire) to join sth ■ **adhérent, -e** nmf member

adhésif, -ive [adezif, -iv] adj adhesive ■ **adhésion** nf (inscription) joining (à of)

adieu, -x [adjø] **1** exclam farewell **2** nm farewell; **faire ses adieux** to say one's goodbyes

adjacent, -e [adʒasɑ̃, -ɑ̃t] adj adjacent (à to)

adjectif [adʒɛktif] nm adjective

adjoint, -e [adʒwɛ̃, -ɛt] nmf assistant; **a. au maire** deputy mayor

adjuger [adʒyʒe] **1** vt **a. qch à qn** (prix, contrat) to award sth to sb; (aux enchères) to knock sth down to sb **2 s'adjuger** vpr **s'a. qch** to appropriate sth

admettre* [admetr] vt (accueillir,

reconnaître) to admit; (*autoriser*) to allow; **être admis à un examen** to pass an exam

administrer [administʀe] *vt* (*gérer*) to administer ■ **administrateur, -trice** *nmf* (*de société*) director ■ **administration** *nf* administration; **l'A.** (*service public*) ≃ the Civil Service; (*fonctionnaires*) civil servants

admirer [admiʀe] *vt* to admire ■ **admirable** *adj* admirable ■ **admirateur, -trice** *nmf* admirer ■ **admiratif, -ive** *adj* admiring ■ **admiration** *nf* admiration; **être en a. devant qn/qch** to be filled with admiration for sb/sth

admissible [admisibl] *adj* (*tolérable*) acceptable, admissible; *Scol & Univ* **candidats admissibles** = candidates who have qualified for the oral examination ■ **admission** *nf* admission (**à/dans** to)

adolescent, -e [adɔlesɑ̃, -ɑ̃t] *nmf* adolescent, teenager ■ **adolescence** *nf* adolescence

adonner [adɔne] **s'adonner** *vpr* **s'a. à qch** to devote oneself to sth; **s'a. à la boisson** to be an alcoholic

adopter [adɔpte] *vt* to adopt ■ **adoptif, -ive** *adj* (*enfant, patrie*) adopted; (*parents*) adoptive ■ **adoption** *nf* adoption

adorer [adɔʀe] **1** *vt* (*dieu*) to worship; (*chose, personne*) to adore; **a. faire qch** to adore doing sth **2 s'adorer** *vpr* **ils s'adorent** they adore each other ■ **adorable** *adj* adorable

adosser [adose] **s'adosser** *vpr* **s'a. à qch** to lean (back) against sth

adoucir [adusiʀ] **1** *vt* (*traits, peau*) to soften; (*caractère*) to take the edge off **2 s'adoucir** *vpr* (*temps*) to turn milder; (*voix*) to soften; (*caractère*) to mellow

adresse [adʀɛs] *nf* (**a**) (*domicile*) address; **a. électronique** e-mail address (**b**) (*habileté*) skill ■ **adresser 1** *vt* (*lettre, remarque*) to address (**à** to); **a. qch à qn** (*lettre*) to send sb sth; **a. la parole à qn** to speak to sb **2 s'adresser** *vpr*

s'a. à qn (*parler*) to speak to sb; (*aller trouver*) to go and see sb; (*être destiné à*) to be aimed at sb

Adriatique [adʀiatik] *nf* **l'A.** the Adriatic

adroit, -e [adʀwa, -at] *adj* (*habile*) skilful

adulte [adylt] **1** *adj* (*personne, animal*) adult **2** *nmf* adult

adultère [adyltɛʀ] *nm* adultery

advenir* [advəniʀ] (*aux être*) *v impersonnel* to happen; **a. de qn** (*devenir*) to become of sb

adverbe [advɛʀb] *nm* adverb

adversaire [advɛʀsɛʀ] *nmf* opponent ■ **adverse** *adj* opposing

aérer [aeʀe] **1** *vt* (*pièce, lit*) to air **2 s'aérer** *vpr* to get some fresh air ■ **aération** *nf* ventilation

aérien, -enne [aeʀjɛ̃, -ɛn] *adj* (*transport, attaque, défense*) air; (*photo*) aerial; (*câble*) overhead

aérobic [aeʀɔbik] *nm* aerobics (*sing*) ■ **aérodynamique** *adj* aerodynamic ■ **aérogare** *nf* air terminal ■ **aéroglisseur** *nm* hovercraft ■ **aérogramme** *nm* airmail letter ■ **aéroport** *nm* airport ■ **aérosol** *nm* aerosol

affable [afabl] *adj* affable

affaiblir [afeblir] *vt*, **s'affaiblir** *vpr* to weaken ■ **affaiblissement** *nm* weakening

affaire [afɛʀ] *nf* (*question*) matter, affair; (*marché*) deal; (*firme*) business; (*scandale*) affair; (*procès*) case; **affaires** (*commerce*) business (*sing*); (*effets personnels*) belongings; **les Affaires étrangères** *Br* ≃ the Foreign Office, *Am* ≃ the State Department; **avoir a. à qn/qch** to have to deal with sb/sth; **faire une bonne a.** to get a bargain; **c'est mon a.** that's my business; **ça fera l'a.** that will do nicely; **a. de cœur** love affair

affairer [afeʀe] **s'affairer** *vpr* to busy oneself ■ **affairé, -e** *adj* busy

affaisser [afese] **s'affaisser** *vpr* (*personne, bâtiment*) to collapse; (*sol*) to subside

affaler [afale] *s'affaler* *upr* to collapse; **affalé dans un fauteuil** slumped in an armchair

affamé, -e [afame] *adj* starving

affecter [afɛkte] *vt* (**a**) *(employé)* to appoint (**à** to); *(soldat)* to post (**à** to); *(fonds)* to assign (**à** to) (**b**) *(feindre, émouvoir)* to affect ▪ **affectation** *nf* *(d'employé)* appointment (**à** to); *(de soldat)* posting (**à** to); *(de fonds)* assignment (**à** to); *Péj (pose)* affectation ▪ **affecté, -e** *adj* *Péj (manières, personne)* affected

affection [afɛksjɔ̃] *nf* *(attachement)* affection; *(maladie)* ailment; **avoir de l'a. pour qn** to be fond of sb ▪ **affectionner** *vt* to be fond of ▪ **affectueux, -euse** *adj* affectionate

affiche [afiʃ] *nf* notice; *(publicitaire)* poster; **être à l'a.** *(spectacle)* to be on ▪ **afficher** *vt* *(avis)* to put up; *(prix, horaire, résultat)* & *Ordinat (message)* to display; *(sentiment)* to show; **a. complet** *(sujet: spectacle)* to be sold out ▪ **affichage** *nm* bill-posting; *Ordinat* display

affiliation [afiljasjɔ̃] *nf* affiliation ▪ **affilié, -e** *adj* affiliated

affiner [afine] *vt* *(métal, goût)* to refine **2** *s'affiner* *upr* *(goût)* to become more refined; *(visage)* to get thinner

affinité [afinite] *nf* affinity

affirmatif, -ive [afirmatif, -iv] *adj* *(réponse)* & *Gram* affirmative

affirmer [afirme] **1** *vt* *(manifester)* to assert; *(soutenir)* to maintain **2** *s'affirmer* *upr* *(personne)* to assert oneself; *(tendance)* to be confirmed ▪ **affirmation** *nf* assertion

affliger [afliʒe] *vt* *(peiner)* to distress; *(atteindre)* to afflict (**de** with)

affluence [aflyɑ̃s] *nf* *(de personnes)* crowd; *(de marchandises)* abundance

affluer [aflye] *vi* *(sang)* to rush (**à** to); *(gens)* to flock (**vers** to)

afflux [afly] *nm* *(de sang)* rush; *(de visiteurs)* flood; *(de capitaux)* influx

affoler [afɔle] **1** *vt* to throw into a

panic **2** *s'affoler* *upr* to panic ▪ **affolant, -e** *adj* terrifying ▪ **affolement** *nm* panic

affranchir [afrɑ̃ʃir] *vt* *(timbrer)* to put a stamp on; *(émanciper)* to free ▪ **affranchissement** *nm* *(timbrage)* postage; *(tarif)* postage

affreux, -euse [afrø, -øz] *adj* *(laid)* hideous; *(atroce)* dreadful

affront [afrɔ̃] *nm* insult; **faire un a. à qn** to insult sb

affronter [afrɔ̃te] **1** *vt* to confront; *(mauvais temps)* to brave **2** *s'affronter* *upr* *(ennemis, équipes)* to clash ▪ **affrontement** *nm* confrontation

affût [afy] *nm* *Fig* **à l'a. de** on the lookout for

affûter [afyte] *vt* to sharpen

Afghanistan [afganistɑ̃] *nm* l'A. Afghanistan ▪ **afghan, -e 1** *adj* Afghan **2**, **A., Afghane** Afghan

afin [afɛ̃] **1** *prep* **a. de faire qch** in order to do sth **2** *conj* **a. que...** (+ *subjunctive*) so that...

Afrique [afrik] *nf* l'A. Africa ▪ **africain, -e 1** *adj* African **2** *nmf* **A., Africaine** African

agacer [agase] *vt* *(personne)* to irritate ▪ **agaçant, -e** *adj* irritating

âge [aʒ] *nm* age; **quel â. as-tu?** how old are you?; **d'un certain â.** middle-aged ▪ **âgé, -e** *adj* old; **être â. de six ans** to be six years old; **un enfant â. de six ans** a six-year-old child

agence [aʒɑ̃s] *nf* agency; *(de banque)* branch; **a. de voyage** travel agent's; **a. immobilière** *Br* estate agent's, *Am* real estate office

agencer [aʒɑ̃se] *vt* to arrange; **bien agencé** *(maison)* well laid-out

agenda [aʒɛ̃da] *nm Br* diary, *Am* datebook

agenouiller [aʒənuje] *s'agenouiller* *upr* to kneel (down); **être agenouillé** to be kneeling (down)

agent [aʒɑ̃] *nm* *(employé, espion)* agent; **a. de police** police officer; **a. de change** stockbroker; **a. immobilier** *Br* estate agent, *Am* real estate agent; **a. secret** secret agent

agglomération [aglɔmerɑsjɔ̃] *nf* (*ville*) built-up area, town; **l'a. parisienne** Paris and its suburbs

aggraver [agrave] **1** *vt* (*situation, maladie*) to make worse; (*difficultés*) to increase **2 s'aggraver** *vpr* (*situation, maladie*) to get worse; (*état de santé*) to deteriorate; (*difficultés*) to increase ■ **aggravation** *nf* (*de maladie*) aggravation; (*de conflit*) worsening

agile [aʒil] *adj* agile, nimble ■ **agilité** *nf* agility, nimbleness

agir [aʒir] **1** *vi* to act **2 s'agir** *v impersonnel* **de quoi s'agit-il?** what is it about?; **il s'agit de se dépêcher** we have to hurry

agitateur, -trice [aʒitatœr, -tris] *nmf* agitator

agitation [aʒitasjɔ̃] *nf* (*fébrilité*) restlessness; (*troubles*) unrest

agiter [aʒite] **1** *vt* (*remuer*) to stir; (*secouer*) to shake; (*brandir*) to wave; (*troubler*) to agitate **2 s'agiter** *vpr* (*enfant*) to fidget ■ **agité, -e** *adj* (*mer*) rough; (*personne*) restless; (*enfant*) fidgety; (*period*) unsettled

agneau, -x [aɲo] *nm* lamb

agonie [agɔni] *nf* death throes; **être à l'a.** to be at death's door ■ **agoniser** *vi* to be dying

agrafe [agraf] *nf* (*pour vêtement*) hook; (*pour papiers*) staple ■ **agrafer** *vt* (*vêtement*) to fasten; (*papiers*) to staple ■ **agrafeuse** *nf* stapler

agrandir [agrɑ̃dir] **1** *vt* (*rendre plus grand*) to enlarge; (*grossir*) to magnify **2 s'agrandir** *vpr* (*entreprise*) to expand; (*ville*) to grow ■ **agrandissement** *nm* (*d'entreprise*) expansion; (*de ville*) growth; (*de maison*) extension; (*de photo*) enlargement

agréable [agreabl] *adj* pleasant

agréer [agree] *vt* (*fournisseur*) to approve; **veuillez a. l'expression de mes salutations distinguées** (*dans une lettre*) (*à quelqu'un dont on ne connaît pas le nom*) *Br* yours faithfully, *Am* sincerely; (*à quelqu'un dont on connaît le nom*) *Br* yours sincerely, *Am* sincerely

■ **agréé, -e** *adj* (*fournisseur, centre*) approved

agrémenter [agremɑ̃te] *vt* to adorn (**de** with)

agrès [agrɛ] *nmpl* (*de voilier*) tackle; *Gym Br* apparatus, *Am* equipment

agresser [agrese] *vt* to attack; **se faire a.** to be attacked; (*pour son argent*) to be mugged ■ **agresseur** *nm* attacker; (*dans un conflit*) aggressor ■ **agression** *nf* attack; (*pour de l'argent*) mugging; (*d'un État*) aggression; **être victime d'une a.** to be attacked; (*pour son argent*) to be mugged

agressif, -ive [agresif, -iv] *adj* aggressive ■ **agressivité** *nf* aggressiveness

agricole [agrikɔl] *adj* agricultural; (*ouvrier, machine*) farm; **travaux agricoles** farm work

agriculteur, -trice [agrikyltœr, -tris] *nmf* farmer ■ **agriculture** *nf* farming, agriculture

agripper [agripe] **s'agripper** *vpr* **s'a. à qn/qch** to cling on to sb/sth

agrume [agrym] *nm* citrus fruit

aguerri, -e [ageri] *adj* seasoned, hardened

aguets [agɛ] **aux aguets** *adv* on the lookout

aguichant, -e [agiʃɑ̃, -ɑ̃t] *adj* seductive

ahurir [ayrir] *vt* (*étonner*) to astound

ai [ɛ] *voir* **avoir**

aide [ɛd] **1** *nf* help, assistance; **à l'a. de qch** with the aid of sth; **appeler à l'a.** to call for help; **a. humanitaire** aid **2** *nmf* (*personne*) assistant; **a. de camp** aide-de-camp ■ **aide-mémoire** *nm inv* notes ■ **aide-soignante** (*pl* **aides-soignantes**) *nf Br* nursing auxiliary, *Am* nurse's aid

aider [ede] **1** *vt* to help; **a. qn à faire qch** to help sb to do sth **2 s'aider** *vpr* **s'a. de qch** to use sth

aïe [aj] *exclam* ouch!

aie(s), aient [ɛ] *voir* **avoir**

aigle [ɛgl] *nm* eagle

aigre [ɛgr] *adj* (*acide*) sour; (*parole*) cutting; **d'un ton a.** sharply ■ **aigreur**

nf (de goût) sourness; *(de ton)* sharpness; **aigreurs d'estomac** heartburn

aigri, -e [egri] *adj (personne)* embittered

aigu, -ë [egy] *adj (douleur, crise, accent)* acute; *(son)* high-pitched

aiguille [egɥij] *nf (à coudre)* needle; *(de montre)* hand; *(de balance)* pointer; **a. (rocheuse)** peak; **a. de pin** pine needle

aiguiller [egɥije] *vt (train) Br* to shunt, *Am* to switch; *Fig (personne)* to steer *(vers towards)* ■ **aiguillage** *nm (appareil) Br* points, *Am* switches ■ **aiguilleur** *nm (de trains)* signalman; **a. du ciel** air-traffic controller

aiguiser [egize] *vt (outil)* to sharpen; *Fig (appétit)* to whet

ail [aj] *nm* garlic

aile [ɛl] *nf* wing; *(de moulin)* sail; *(de voiture) Br* wing, *Am* fender ■ **ailé, -e** *adj* winged ■ **aileron** *nm (de requin)* fin; *(d'avion)* aileron ■ **ailier** *nm (au football)* winger; *(au rugby)* wing

aille, aillent [aj] *voir* **aller[1]**

ailleurs [ajœr] *adv* somewhere else, elsewhere; **d'a.** *(du reste)* besides, anyway; **par a.** *(en outre)* moreover; *(par d'autres côtés)* in other respects

aimable [ɛmabl] *adj (gentil)* kind

aimant[1] [ɛmã] *nm* magnet ■ **aimanter** *vt* to magnetize

aimant[2], -e [ɛmã, -ãt] *adj* loving

aimer [eme] **1** *vt* to love; **a. bien qn/qch** to like sb/sth; **a. faire qch** to like doing sth; **j'aimerais qu'il vienne** I would like him to come; **a. mieux qch** to prefer sth **2 s'aimer** *upr* **ils s'aiment** they're in love

aine [ɛn] *nf* groin

aîné, -e [ene] **1** *adj (de deux enfants)* elder; *(de plus de deux)* eldest **2** *nmf (de deux enfants)* elder; *(de plus de deux)* eldest

ainsi [ɛ̃si] *adv (de cette façon)* in this way; *(alors)* so; **a. que...** as well as...; **et a. de suite** and so on; **pour a. dire** so to speak; **a. soit-il!** amen!

air [ɛr] *nm* **(a)** *(gaz)* air; **prendre l'a.** to get some fresh air; **au grand a.** in the fresh air; **en plein a.** outside; **en l'a.** *(jeter)* (up) in the air; *(paroles, menaces)* empty; **regarder en l'a.** to look up

(b) *(expression)* look, appearance; **avoir l'a. content** to look happy; **avoir l'a. de s'ennuyer** to look bored; **a. de famille** family likeness

(c) *(mélodie)* tune

aire [ɛr] *nf (surface) & Math* area; *(d'oiseau)* eyrie; **a. de jeux** (children's) play area; **a. de lancement** launch pad; **a. de repos** *(sur autoroute)* rest area; **a. de stationnement** lay-by

aisance [ɛzãs] *nf (facilité)* ease; *(prospérité)* affluence

aise [ɛz] *nf* **à l'a.** *(dans un vêtement)* comfortable; *(dans une situation)* at ease; *(fortuné)* comfortably off; **mal à l'a.** uncomfortable, ill at ease ■ **aisé, -e** [ɛze] *adj (fortuné)* comfortably off; *(facile)* easy ■ **aisément** *adv* easily

aisselle [ɛsɛl] *nf* armpit

ait [ɛ] *voir* **avoir**

ajourner [aʒurne] *vt* to postpone; *(après le début de la séance)* to adjourn

ajout [aʒu] *nm* addition *(à* to) ■ **ajouter** *vti* to add *(à* to) **2 s'ajouter** *upr* **s'a. à qch** to add to sth

ajuster [aʒyste] *vt (appareil, outil)* to adjust; *(vêtement)* to alter

alarme [alarm] *nf* alarm; **donner l'a.** to raise the alarm; **a. antivol/d'incendie** burglar/fire alarm ■ **alarmer 1** *vt* to alarm **2 s'alarmer** *upr* **s'a. de qch** to become alarmed at sth

Albanie *nf* **l'A.** Albania ■ **albanais, -e 1** *adj* Albanian **2** *nmf* **A.,** **Albanaise** Albanian

album [albɔm] *nm* album; **a. de photos** photo album

alcool [alkɔl] *nm Chim* alcohol; *(spiritueux)* spirits; **a. à 90°** *Br* surgical spirit, *Am* rubbing alcohol; **a. à brûler** *Br* methylated spirits, *Am* wood alcohol ■ **alcoolique** *adj & nmf* alcoholic ■ **alcoolisée** *adj f* **boisson a.** alcoholic drink; **boisson non a.** soft drink ■ **alcoolisme** *nm* alcoholism ■ **Alcootest®**

nm (test) breath test; *(appareil)* Breathalyzer®

alcôve [alkov] *nf* alcove

aléas [alea] *nmpl* hazards ∎ **aléatoire** *adj (résultat)* uncertain; *(nombre)* & *Ordinat* random

alentour [alɑ̃tur] *adv* round about; **les villages a.** the surrounding villages ∎ **alentours** *nmpl* surroundings; **aux a. de la ville** in the vicinity of the town

alerte [alɛrt] **1** *adj (leste)* sprightly; *(éveillé)* alert **2** *nf* alarm; **en état d'a.** on the alert; **donner l'a.** to give the alarm; **a. à la bombe** bomb scare; **fausse a.** false alarm ∎ **alerter** *vt* to alert (**de** to)

alezan [alzɑ̃, -an] *adj & nmf (cheval)* chestnut

algèbre [alʒɛbr] *nf* algebra

Algérie [alʒeri] *nf* **l'A.** Algeria ∎ **algérien, -enne 1** *adj* Algerian **2** *nmf* **A., Algérienne** Algerian

algues [alg] *nfpl* seaweed

alias [aljas] *adv* alias

alibi [alibi] *nm* alibi

aliéner [aljene] **1** *vt* to alienate **2 s'aliéner** *vpr* **s'a. qn** to alienate sb

aligner [aliɲe] **1** *vt* to line up; *(politique)* to align (**sur** with) **2 s'aligner** *vpr (personnes)* to line up; *(pays)* to align oneself (**sur** with) ∎ **alignement** *nm* alignment

aliment [alimɑ̃] *nm* food ∎ **alimentaire** *adj (ration, industrie)* food; **produits alimentaires** foods ∎ **alimentation** *nf (action)* feeding; *(en eau, en électricité)* supply(ing); *(régime)* diet; *(nourriture)* food; **magasin d'a.** grocer's, grocery store ∎ **alimenter** *vt (nourrir)* to feed; *(fournir)* to supply (**en** with); *(débat, feu)* to fuel

alité, -e [alite] *adj* bedridden

allaiter [alete] *vt (femme)* to breastfeed

allécher [aleʃe] *vt* to tempt

allée [ale] *nf (de parc)* path; *(de ville)* avenue; *(de cinéma, de supermarché)* aisle; *(devant une maison)* driveway; **allées et venues** comings and goings

allégation [alegasjɔ̃] *nf* allegation

alléger [aleʒe] *vt (impôt)* to reduce; *(fardeau)* to lighten ∎ **allégé, -e** *adj (fromage)* low-fat

allégorie [alegɔri] *nf* allegory

allègre [alɛgr] *adj* lively, cheerful

allégresse [alegrɛs] *nf* joy

Allemagne [almaɲ] *nf* **l'A.** Germany ∎ **allemand, -ande 1** *adj* German **2** *nmf* **A., Allemande** German **3** *nm (langue)* German

ALLER[1] [ale] **1** *(aux* **être)** *vi* to go; **a. à Paris** to go to Paris; **a. à la pêche** to go fishing; **a. faire qch** to go and do sth; **a. à qn** *(convenir à)* to suit sb; **a. avec** *(vêtement)* to go with; **a. bien/mieux** *(personne)* to be well/better; **comment vas-tu?** *(personne)* ça va? how are you?; **ça va!** all right!, fine!; **allez-y** go ahead

2 *v aux (futur proche)* **a. faire qch** to be going to do sth; **il va venir** he'll come; **il va partir** he's about to leave

3 s'en aller [sɑ̃nale] *vpr (personne)* to go away; *(tache)* to come out

aller[2] [ale] *nm* outward journey; **a. (simple)** *Br* single (ticket), *Am* oneway (ticket); **a. (et) retour** *Br* return (ticket), *Am* round-trip (ticket)

allergie [alɛrʒi] *nf* allergy ∎ **allergique** *adj* allergic (**à** to)

alliage [aljaʒ] *nm* alloy

alliance [aljɑ̃s] *nf (anneau)* wedding ring; *(mariage)* marriage; *(de pays)* alliance

allier [alje] **1** *vt (associer)* to combine (**à** with); *(pays)* to ally (**à** with); *(famille)* to unite by marriage **2 s'allier** *vpr (couleurs)* to combine; *(pays)* to become allied (**à** with); **s'a. à contre qn/qch** to unite against sb/sth ∎ **allié, -e** *nmf/a* ally

allô [alo] *exclam* hello!

allocation [alɔkasjɔ̃] *nf (somme)* allowance; **a. (de) chômage** unemployment benefit; **a. (de) logement** housing benefit; **allocations familiales** child benefit

allocution [alɔkysjɔ̃] *nf* address

allonger [alɔ̃ʒe] **1** *vt* (*bras*) to stretch out; (*sauce*) to thin; **a. le pas** to quicken one's pace **2** *vi* (*jours*) to get longer **3 s'allonger** *vpr* (*jours*) to get longer; (*personne*) to lie down ■ **allongé, -e** *adj* (*étiré*) elongated; **être a.** (*personne*) to be lying down

allouer [alwe] *vt* **a. qch à qn** (*ration*) to allocate sb sth; (*indemnité*) to grant sb sth

allumer [alyme] **1** *vt* (*feu, pipe*) to light; (*électricité, radio*) to switch on; (*incendie*) to start **2 s'allumer** *vpr* (*lumière, lampe*) to come on ■ **allumage** *nm* (*de feu*) lighting; (*de moteur*) ignition

allumette [alymɛt] *nf* match

allure [alyr] *nf* (*vitesse*) speed; (*démarche*) gait, walk; (*maintien*) bearing; **à toute a.** at top speed; **avoir de l'a.** to look stylish

allusion [alyzjɔ̃] *nf* (*référence*) allusion (**à** to); (*voilée*) hint; **faire a. à qch** to allude to sth; (*en termes voilés*) to hint at sth

aloi [alwa] *nm* **de bon a.** (*plaisanterie*) in good taste

alors [alɔr] *adv* (*donc*) so; (*à ce moment-là*) then; (*dans ce cas*) in that case; **a. que...** (*lorsque*) when...; (*tandis que*) whereas...; **et a.?** so what?

alouette [alwɛt] *nf* lark

alourdir [alurdir] **1** *vt* (*chose*) to make heavier **2 s'alourdir** *vpr* to get heavy

alpage [alpaʒ] *nm* mountain pasture ■ **Alpes** *nfpl* **les A.** the Alps ■ **alpestre, alpin, -e** [alpɛ̃, -in] *adj* alpine

alphabet [alfabɛ] *nm* alphabet ■ **alphabétique** *adj* alphabetical

alphanumérique [alfanymerik] *adj* alphanumeric

alpinisme [alpinism] *nm* mountaineering; **faire de l'a.** to go mountaineering ■ **alpiniste** *nmf* mountaineer

altérer [altere] **1** *vt* (**a**) (*viande, vin*) to spoil (**b**) (*changer*) to affect **2 s'altérer** *vpr* (*relations*) to deteriorate

alternatif, -ive [alternatif, -iv] *adj*

(*successif*) alternating; (*de remplacement*) alternative ■ **alternative** *nf* alternative ■ **alternativement** *adv* alternately

alterner [alterne] **1** *vt* (*crops*) to rotate **2** *vi* (*se succéder*) to alternate (**avec** with); (*personnes*) to take turns (**avec** with) ■ **alternance** *nf* alternation; **en a.** alternately

Altesse [altɛs] *nf* **son A. royale** His/Her Royal Highness

altier, -ère [altje, -ɛr] *adj* haughty

altitude [altityd] *nf* altitude; **prendre de l'a.** to climb

aluminium [alyminjɔm] *nm* *Br* aluminium, *Am* aluminum; **papier (d')a.** tinfoil

amabilité [amabilite] *nf* kindness

amaigrir [amegrir] *vt* to make thin or thinner ■ **amaigri, -e** *adj* gaunt

amande [amãd] *nf* almond

amant [amã] *nm* lover

amarre [amar] *nf* (*mooring*) rope; **amarres** moorings

amas [ama] *nm* heap, pile ■ **amasser 1** *vt* to amass **2 s'amasser** *vpr* (*preuves, foule*) to build up; (*neige*) to pile up

amateur [amatœr] **1** *nm* (*non professionnel*) amateur; **a. de tennis** tennis enthusiast; **faire de la photo en a.** to be an amateur photographer **2** *adj* **une équipe a.** an amateur team

amazone [amazon] *nf* horsewoman; **monter en a.** to ride sidesaddle

ambages [ãbaʒ] **sans ambages** *adv* without beating about the bush

ambassade [ãbasad] *nf* embassy ■ **ambassadeur, -drice** *nmf* ambassador

ambiance [ãbjãs] *nf* atmosphere ■ **ambiant, -e** *adj* surrounding; **température a.** room temperature

ambidextre [ãbidɛkstr] *adj* ambidextrous

ambigu, -ë [ãbigy] *adj* ambiguous ■ **ambiguïté** *nf* ambiguity

ambitieux, -euse [ãbisjø, -øz] *adj* ambitious ■ **ambition** *nf* ambition ■ **ambitionner** *vt* to aspire to

ambre [ɑ̃br] nm (résine) amber

ambulance [ɑ̃bylɑ̃s] nf ambulance

ambulant, -e [ɑ̃bylɑ̃, -ɑ̃t] adj travelling, itinerant; **marchand a.** (street) hawker

âme [ɑm] nf soul; **rendre l'â.** to give up the ghost; **â. sœur** soul mate

améliorer [ameljɔre] vt, **s'améliorer** vpr to improve ▪ **amélioration** nf improvement

amen [amɛn] adv amen

aménager [amenaʒe] vt (changer) to adjust, (maison) to convert (**en** into) ▪ **aménagement** nm (changement) adjustment; (de pièce) conversion (**en** into); **a. du temps de travail** flexibility of working hours

amende [amɑ̃d] nf fine; **infliger une a. à qn** to impose a fine on sb

amender [amɑ̃de] vt (texte de loi) to amend

amener [amne] **1** vt (apporter) to bring; (causer) to bring about; (tirer à soi) to pull in; **a. qn à faire qch** (sujet: personne) to get sb to do sth; **ce qui nous amène à parler de…** which brings us to the issue of… **2 s'amener** vpr Fam to turn up

amenuiser [amənɥize] **s'amenuiser** vpr to dwindle; (écart) to get smaller

amer, -ère [amɛr] adj bitter

Amérique [amerik] nf l'A. America; **l'A. du Nord/du Sud** North/South America; **l'A. latine** Latin America ▪ **américain, -e** **1** adj American **2** nmf **A., Américaine** American

amertume [amɛrtym] nf bitterness

ameublement [amœbləmɑ̃] nm (meubles) furniture

ami, -e [ami] **1** nmf friend; **petit a.** boyfriend; **petite amie** girlfriend **2** adj friendly; **être a. avec qn** to be friends with sb

amiable [amjabl] **à l'amiable 1** adj amicable **2** adv amicably

amical, -e, -aux, -ales [amikal, -o] adj friendly ▪ **amicale** nf association

amincir [amɛ̃sir] vt to make thin or thinner; **cette robe t'amincit** that dress makes you look thinner

amiral, -aux [amiral, -o] nm admiral

amitié [amitje] nf friendship; **mes amitiés à votre mère** give my best wishes to your mother

amnésie [amnezi] nf amnesia

amnistie [amnisti] nf amnesty

amoindrir [amwɛ̃drir] vt, **s'amoindrir** vpr to diminish

amonceler [amɔ̃sle] vt, **s'amonceler** vpr to pile up ▪ **amoncellement** nm heap, pile

amont [amɔ̃] **en amont** adv upstream (**de** from)

amoral, -e, -aux, -ales [amɔral, -o] adj amoral

amorce [amɔrs] nf (début) start; (de pêcheur) bait; (détonateur) detonator; (de pistolet d'enfant) cap ▪ **amorcer 1** vt (commencer) to start; (hameçon) to bait; (bombe) to arm; Ordinat to boot up **2 s'amorcer** vpr to start

amortir [amɔrtir] vt (coup) to absorb; (bruit) to deaden; (chute) to break; (achat) to recoup the costs of; Fin (dette) to pay off ▪ **amortissement** nm (d'un emprunt) redemption ▪ **amortisseur** nm (de véhicule) shock absorber

amour [amur] nm (sentiment, liaison) love; **faire l'a. avec qn** to make love with or to sb; **pour l'a. du ciel!** for heaven's sake!; **mon a.** my darling, my love ▪ **amour-propre** nm self-respect ▪ **amoureux, -euse 1** adj être a. de qn in love with sb; **tomber a. de qn** to fall in love with sb **2** nm boyfriend; **un couple d'a.** a pair of lovers

amovible [amɔvibl] adj removable, detachable

amphétamine [ɑ̃fetamin] nf amphetamine

amphithéâtre [ɑ̃fiteɑtr] nm (romain) amphitheatre; (à l'université) lecture hall

ample [ɑ̃pl] adj (vêtement) full; (geste) sweeping; **de plus amples renseignements** more detailed information ▪ **amplement** adv amply, fully; **c'est a. suffisant** it is more than enough

■ **ampleur** *nf (de vêtement)* fullness; *(importance)* scale, extent; **prendre de l'a.** to grow in size

amplifier [ɑ̃plifje] **1** *vt (son)* to amplify; *(phénomène)* to intensify **2 s'amplifier** *vpr (son)* to increase; *(phénomène)* to intensify ■ **amplificateur** *nm* amplifier ■ **amplification** *nf (de son)* amplification; *(de phénomène)* intensification

amplitude [ɑ̃plityd] *nf (de désastre)* magnitude; *(variation)* range

ampoule [ɑ̃pul] *nf (électrique)* (light) bulb; *(sur la peau)* blister; *(de médicament)* phial

amputer [ɑ̃pyte] *vt (membre)* to amputate; **a. qn de la jambe** to amputate sb's leg ■ **amputation** *nf (de membre)* amputation

amuser [amyze] **1** *vt* to amuse **2 s'amuser** *vpr* to amuse oneself; **s'a. avec qn/qch** to play with sb/sth; **s'a. à faire qch** to amuse oneself doing sth; **bien s'a.** to have a good time ■ **amusant, -e** *adj* amusing ■ **amusement** *nm* amusement

amygdales [amidal] *nfpl* tonsils

an [ɑ̃] *nm* year; **il a dix ans** he's ten (years old); **par a.** per year; **en l'an 2005** in the year 2005; **bon a., mal a.** on average over the years

anachronisme [anakrɔnism] *nm* anachronism

anagramme [anagram] *nf* anagram

analogie [analɔʒi] *nf* analogy

analogue [analɔg] *adj* similar (**à** to)

analphabète [analfabɛt] *adj & nmf* illiterate

analyse [analiz] *nf* analysis; **a. de sang/d'urine** blood/urine test ■ **analyser** *vt* to analyse

ananas [anana(s)] *nm* pineapple

anarchie [anarʃi] *nf* anarchy ■ **anarchiste 1** *adj* anarchistic **2** *nmf* anarchist

anatomie [anatɔmi] *nf* anatomy ■ **anatomique** *adj* anatomical

ancestral, -e, -aux, -ales [ɑ̃sɛstral, -o] *adj* ancestral

ancêtre [ɑ̃sɛtr] *nm* ancestor

anchois [ɑ̃ʃwa] *nm* anchovy

ancien, -enne [ɑ̃sjɛ̃, -ɛn] **1** *adj (vieux)* old; *(meuble)* antique; *(qui n'est plus)* former, old; **dans l'a. temps** in the old days; **a. combattant** *Br* ex-serviceman, *Am* veteran **2** *nmf (par l'âge)* elder ■ **anciennement** *adv* formerly ■ **ancienneté** *nf (âge)* age; *(expérience)* seniority

ancre [ɑ̃kr] *nf* anchor ■ **ancrer** *vt (navire)* to anchor

Andorre [ɑ̃dɔr] *nf* Andorra

andouille [ɑ̃duj] *nf* (**a**) *(charcuterie)* = sausage made from pigs' intestines (**b**) *Fam (idiot)* twit

âne [ɑn] *nm (animal)* donkey

anéantir [aneɑ̃tir] *vt (ville)* to destroy; *(armée)* to crush; *(espoirs)* to shatter ■ **anéanti, -e** *adj (épuisé)* exhausted; *(accablé)* overwhelmed ■ **anéantissement** *nm (de ville)* destruction

anecdote [anɛkdɔt] *nf* anecdote ■ **anecdotique** *adj* anecdotal

anémie [anemi] *nf* an(a)emia ■ **anémique** *adj* an(a)emic

anémone [anemɔn] *nf* anemone

ânerie [ɑnri] *nf (parole)* stupid remark; *(action)* stupid act

anesthésie [anɛstezi] *nf* an(a)esthesia; **être sous a.** to be under ana(e)sthetic; **a. générale/locale** general/local an(a)esthetic ■ **anesthésier** *vt* to an(a)esthetize ■ **anesthésiste** *nmf* *Br* an(a)esthetist, *Am* anesthesiologist

ange [ɑ̃ʒ] *nm* angel; **être aux anges** to be in seventh heaven; **a. gardien** guardian angel ■ **angélique 1** *adj* angelic **2** *nf Culin* angelica

angine [ɑ̃ʒin] *nf* sore throat; **a. de poitrine** angina (pectoris)

anglais, -e [ɑ̃glɛ, -ɛz] **1** *adj* English **2** *nmf* **A., Anglaise** Englishman, Englishwoman; **les A.** the English **3** *nm (langue)* English **4** *nf Fam* **filer à l'anglaise** to slip away

angle [ɑ̃gl] *nm (point de vue) & Math* angle; *(coin de rue)* corner; **la maison**

qui fait l'a. the house on the corner; *Aut a.* **mort** blind spot

Angleterre [ɑ̃glətεr] *nf* l'A. England

anglican, -e [ɑ̃glikɑ̃, -an] *adj & nmf* Anglican

anglo-normand, -e [ɑ̃glonɔrmɑ̃, -ɑ̃d] *adj* **les îles anglo-normandes** the Channel Islands

anglophone [ɑ̃glɔfɔn] **1** *adj* English-speaking **2** *nmf* English speaker

anglo-saxon, -onne [ɑ̃glosaksɔ̃, -ɔn] *(mpl* **anglo-saxons,** *fpl* **anglo-saxonnes)** *adj & nmf* Anglo-Saxon

angoisse [ɑ̃gwas] *nf* anguish; **une crise d'a.** an anxiety attack ■ **angoissant, -e** *adj (nouvelle)* distressing; *(attente)* agonizing; *(livre)* frightening ■ **angoissé, -e** *adj (personne)* anxious; *(cri, regard)* anguished ■ **angoisser 1** *vt* **a. qn** to make sb anxious **2 s'angoisser** *vpr* to get anxious

angora [ɑ̃gɔra] *nm (laine)* angora; **pull en a.** angora sweater

anguille [ɑ̃gij] *nf* eel

anguleux, -euse [ɑ̃gylø, -øz] *adj (visage)* angular

anicroche [anikrɔʃ] *nf* hitch, snag

animal, -aux [animal, -o] **1** *nm* animal; **a. domestique** pet **2** *adj (règne, graisse)* animal

animateur, -trice [animatœr, -tris] *nmf (de télévision, de radio)* presenter; *(de club)* leader

animer [anime] **1** *vt (débat)* to lead; *(jeu télévisé)* to present; *(inspirer)* to prompt **2 s'animer** *vpr (rue)* to come to life; *(visage)* to light up; *(conversation)* to get more lively ■ **animation** *nf (vie)* life; *(divertissement)* event; *Cin* animation; **mettre de l'a. dans une soirée** to liven up a party ■ **animé, -e** *adj (personne, conversation)* lively; *(rue, quartier)* busy

animosité [animozite] *nf* animosity

anis [ani(s)] *nm* aniseed

ankylosé, -e [ɑ̃kiloze] *adj* stiff

annales [anal] *nfpl* annals

anneau, -x [ano] *nm (bague)* ring; *(de chaîne)* link; *Gym* **les anneaux** the rings

année [ane] *nf* year; **les années 90** the nineties

annexe [anεks] **1** *nf (bâtiment)* annexe; *(de lettre)* enclosure; *(de livre)* appendix; **document en a.** enclosed document **2** *adj (pièces)* enclosed; *(revenus)* supplementary; **bâtiment a.** annex(e) ■ **annexer** *vt (pays)* to annex; *(document)* to append

annihiler [aniile] *vt (ville, armée)* to annihilate

anniversaire [anivεrsεr] **1** *nm (d'événement)* anniversary; *(de naissance)* birthday **2** *adj* **date a.** anniversary

annonce [anɔ̃s] *nf (déclaration)* announcement; *(publicitaire)* advertisement; *(indice)* sign; **passer une a. dans un journal** to put an ad(vertisement) in a newspaper; **petites annonces** classified advertisements, *Br* small ads ■ **annoncer 1** *vt (déclarer)* to announce; *(dans la presse)* (soldes, exposition) to advertise; *(indiquer)* to herald; **a. qn** *(visiteur)* to show sb in **2 s'annoncer** *vpr* **ça s'annonce bien/mal** things aren't looking too bad/good ■ **annonceur** *nm (publicitaire)* advertiser

annuaire [anɥεr] *nm (d'organisme)* yearbook; *(liste d'adresses)* directory; **a. téléphonique** telephone directory; **a. électronique** = telephone directory available on Minitel®

annuel, -elle [anɥεl] *adj* annual, yearly

annuité [anɥite] *nf (d'emprunt)* annual repayment

annulaire [anɥlεr] *nm* ring finger

annuler [anɥle] **1** *vt (commande, rendez-vous)* to cancel; *(dette)* to write off; *(marriage)* to annul; *(jugement)* to quash **2 s'annuler** *vpr* to cancel each other out ■ **annulation** *nf (de commande, de rendez-vous)* cancellation; *(de dette)* writing off; *(de mariage)* annulment; *(de jugement)* quashing; *Ordinat* deletion

anodin, -e [anɔdɛ̃, -in] *adj (remarque)* harmless; *(personne)* insignificant

anomalie [anɔmali] *nf (bizarrerie)* anomaly

anonymat [anɔnima] *nm* anonymity; **garder l'a.** to remain anonymous ■ **anonyme** *adj & nmf* anonymous

anorak [anɔrak] *nm* anorak

anorexie [anɔreksi] *nf Méd* anorexia ■ **anorexique** *adj & nmf Méd* anorexic

anormal, -e, -aux, -ales [anɔrmal, -o] *adj (non conforme)* abnormal; *(mentalement)* educationally subnormal; *(injuste)* unfair

anse [ɑ̃s] *nf (de tasse, de panier)* handle

antagonisme [ɑ̃tagɔnism] *nm* antagonism

antan [ɑ̃tɑ̃] **d'antan** *adj Littéraire* of yesteryear

antarctique [ɑ̃tarktik] *nm* **l'A.** the Antarctic, Antarctica

antécédent [ɑ̃tesedɑ̃] *nm Gram* antecedent; **antécédents** *(de personne)* past record; **antécédents médicaux** medical history

antenne [ɑ̃tɛn] *nf (de radio, de satellite)* aerial, antenna; *(d'insecte)* antenna, feeler; *(société)* branch; **être à l'a.** to be on the air; **a. parabolique** satellite dish

antérieur, -e [ɑ̃terjœr] *adj (période)* former; *(année)* previous; *(date)* earlier; *(placé devant)* front; **a. à qch** prior to sth

anthologie [ɑ̃tɔlɔʒi] *nf* anthology

anthropologie [ɑ̃trɔpɔlɔʒi] *nf* anthropology

antiaérien, -enne [ɑ̃tiaerjɛ̃, -ɛn] *adj* **abri a.** air-raid shelter

antiatomique [ɑ̃tiatɔmik] *adj* **abri a.** fallout shelter

antibiotique [ɑ̃tibjɔtik] *nm* antibiotic

antibrouillard [ɑ̃tibrujar] *adj & nm* **(phare) a.** fog lamp

antichambre [ɑ̃tiʃɑ̃br] *nf* antechamber

antichoc [ɑ̃tiʃɔk] *adj inv* shock-proof

anticipation [ɑ̃tisipasjɔ̃] *nf* anticipation; **d'a.** *(roman, film)* futuristic ■ **anticipé, -e** *adj (retraite, retour)* early; *(paiement)* advance

anticommuniste [ɑ̃tikɔmynist] *adj* anti-communist

anticonformiste [ɑ̃tikɔ̃fɔrmist] *adj & nmf* nonconformist

anticonstitutionnel, -elle [ɑ̃tikɔ̃stitysjɔnɛl] *adj* unconstitutional

anticorps [ɑ̃tikɔr] *nm* antibody

anticyclone [ɑ̃tisiklon] *nm* anticyclone

antidépresseur [ɑ̃tidepresœr] *nm* antidepressant

antidérapant, -e [ɑ̃tiderapɑ̃, -ɑ̃t] *adj (surface, pneu)* non-skid; *(semelle)* non-slip

antidopage [ɑ̃tidɔpaʒ] *adj* **contrôle a.** drug detection test

antidote [ɑ̃tidɔt] *nm* antidote

antigel [ɑ̃tiʒɛl] *nm* antifreeze

antihistaminique [ɑ̃tiistaminik] *adj Méd* antihistamine

anti-inflamatoire [ɑ̃tiɛ̃flamatwar] *adj Méd* anti-inflammatory

Antilles [ɑ̃tij] *nfpl* **les A.** the West Indies ■ **antillais, -e 1** *adj* West Indian **2** *nmf* **A., Antillaise** West Indian

antilope [ɑ̃tilɔp] *nf* antelope

antimite [ɑ̃timit] *nm* **de l'a.** mothballs

antinucléaire [ɑ̃tinykleɛr] *adj* antinuclear

antipathique [ɑ̃tipatik] *adj* unpleasant; **elle m'est a.** I find her unpleasant

antipodes [ɑ̃tipɔd] *nmpl* antipodes; **être aux a. de** to be on the other side of the world from; *Fig* to be the exact opposite of

antique [ɑ̃tik] *adj (de l'Antiquité)* ancient ■ **antiquaire** *nmf* antique dealer ■ **antiquité** *nf (objet ancien)* antique; **l'a. grecque/romaine** ancient Greece/Rome; **antiquités** *(de musée)* antiquities

antirabique [ɑ̃tirabik] *adj Méd* anti-rabies

antireflet [ɑ̃tirəflɛ] *adj inv* non-reflecting

antiseptique [ɑ̃tisɛptik] *adj & nm* antiseptic

antisocial, -e, -aux, -ales [ɑ̃tisɔsjal, -o] *adj* antisocial

antitabac [ɑ̃titaba] *adj inv* lutte a. anti-smoking campaign

antiterroriste [ɑ̃titerɔrist] *adj* anti-terrorist

antithèse [ɑ̃titɛz] *nf* antithesis

antivol [ɑ̃tivɔl] *nm* anti-theft device

Anvers [ɑ̃ver(s)] *nm ou f* Antwerp

anxiété [ɑ̃ksjete] *nf* anxiety ■ **anxieux, -euse** *adj* anxious

août [u(t)] *nm* August

apaiser [apeze] **1** *vt (personne)* to calm (down); *(douleur)* to soothe; *(craintes)* to allay **2 s'apaiser** *upr (personne, colère)* to calm down; *(tempête, douleur)* to subside ■ **apaisant, -e** *adj* soothing

apanage [apanaʒ] *nm* prerogative

aparté [aparte] *nm Théât* aside; *(dans une réunion)* private exchange; **en a.** in private

apathique [apatik] *adj* apathetic

apercevoir* [apersəvwar] **1** *vt* to see; *(brièvement)* to catch a glimpse of **2 s'apercevoir** *upr* **s'a. de qch** to realize sth; **s'a. que...** to realize that... ■ **aperçu** *nm (idea)* general idea

apéritif [aperitif] *nm* aperitif; **prendre un a.** to have a drink before lunch/dinner

à-peu-près [apøprɛ] *nm inv* vague approximation

apeuré, -e [apœre] *adj* frightened, scared

aphone [afɔn] *adj* voiceless; **je suis complètement a.** I've lost my voice

aphrodisiaque [afrodizjak] *nm* aphrodisiac

aphte [aft] *nm* mouth ulcer

aphteuse [aftøz] *adj f* fièvre a. foot-and-mouth disease

apiculture [apikyltyr] *nf* beekeeping ■ **apiculteur, -trice** *nmf* beekeeper

apitoyer [apitwaje] **1** *vt* **a. qn** to move sb to pity **2 s'apitoyer** *upr* **s'a. sur qn** to feel sorry for sb; **s'a. sur son sort** to feel sorry for oneself

aplanir [aplanir] *vt (terrain)* to level; *(difficulté)* to iron out

aplatir [aplatir] **1** *vt* to flatten **2 s'aplatir** *upr (être plat)* to be flat; *(devenir plat)* to go flat; **s'a. contre qch** to flatten oneself against sth ■ **aplati, -e** *adj* flat

aplomb [aplɔ̃] *nm (assurance)* self-confidence; *Péj* cheek; **mettre qch d'a.** to stand sth up straight

apocalypse [apɔkalips] *nf* apocalypse; **d'a.** *(vision)* apocalyptic

apogée [apɔʒe] *nm (d'orbite)* apogee; *Fig* **être à l'a. de sa carrière** to be at the height of one's career

apostrophe [apɔstrɔf] *nf (signe)* apostrophe ■ **apostropher** *vt (pour attirer l'attention)* to shout at

apothéose [apɔteoz] *nf (consécration)* crowning glory

apparaître* [aparɛtr] *(aux être)* *vi (se montrer, sembler)* to appear; **il m'apparaît comme le seul capable d'y parvenir** he seems to me to be the only person capable of doing it

appareil [aparɛj] *nm (instrument, machine)* apparatus; *(téléphone)* telephone; *(avion)* aircraft; **qui est à l'a.?** *(au téléphone)* who's speaking?; **a. (dentaire)** *(correctif)* brace; **a. photo** camera; **appareils ménagers** household appliances

apparence [aparɑ̃s] *nf* appearance; **en a.** outwardly; **sauver les apparences** to keep up appearances ■ **apparemment** *adv* apparently ■ **apparent, -e** *adj* apparent

apparenter (s') [aparɑ̃te] *s'apparenter* *upr (ressembler)* to be akin (**à** to)

apparition [aparisjɔ̃] *nf (manifestation)* appearance; *(fantôme)* apparition; **faire son a.** *(personne)* to make one's appearance

appartement [apartəmɑ̃] *nm Br* flat, *Am* apartment

appartenance [apartənɑ̃s] *nf (de groupe)* belonging (**à** to); *(de parti)* membership (**à** of)

appartenir* [apartənir] **1** *vi* to belong (**à** to) **2** *v impersonnel* **il vous appartient de prendre la décision** it's up to you to decide

appât [apɑ] *nm (amorce)* bait; *Fig*

(attrait) lure ■ **appâter** *vt (hameçon)* to bait; *(animal)* to lure; *Fig (personne)* to entice

appauvrir [apovrir] **1** *vt* to impoverish **2 s'appauvrir** *vpr* to become impoverished ■ **appauvrissement** *nm* impoverishment

appel [apɛl] *nm (cri, attrait)* call; *(invitation)* & *Jur* appeal; *Mil (recrutement)* call-up; *(pour sauter)* take-off; **faire l'a.** *(à l'école)* to take the register; *Mil* to have a roll call; **faire a. à qn** to appeal to sb; *(plombier, médecin)* to send for sb; **a. au secours** call for help; **a. gratuit** *Br* freefone call, *Am* toll-free call; **a. téléphonique** telephone call ■ **appeler 1** *vt (personne, nom)* to call; *(en criant)* to call out to; *Mil (recruter)* to call up; *(nécessiter)* to call for; **a. qn à l'aide** to call to sb for help; **a. qn au téléphone** to call sb **2 s'appeler** *vpr* to be called; **comment vous appelez-vous?** what's your name?; **je m'appelle David** my name is David ■ **appellation** *nf (nom)* term; **a. contrôlée** *(de vin)* guaranteed vintage ■ **appelé** *nm Mil* conscript

appendice [apɛ̃dis] *nm (du corps, de livre)* appendix; *(d'animal)* appendage ■ **appendicite** *nf* appendicitis

appesantir [apəzɑ̃tir] **s'appesantir** *vpr* to become heavier; **s'a. sur** *(sujet)* to dwell upon

appétit [apeti] *nm* appetite (**de** for); **couper l'a. à qn** to spoil sb's appetite; **manger de bon a.** to tuck in; **bon a.!** enjoy your meal! ■ **appétissant, -e** *adj* appetizing

applaudir [aplodir] *vti* to applaud ■ **applaudissements** *nmpl* applause

applicable [aplikabl] *adj* applicable (**à** to) ■ **application** *nf (action, soin)* application; *(de loi)* enforcement; **entrer en a.** to come into force

applique [aplik] *nf* wall light

appliquer [aplike] **1** *vt* to apply (**à/sur** to); *(loi, décision)* to enforce **2 s'appliquer** *vpr (se concentrer)* to apply oneself (**à** to); **s'a. à faire qch** to take

pains to do sth; **cette décision s'applique à…** *(concerne)* this decision applies to… ■ **appliqué, -e** *adj (personne)* hard-working; *(écriture)* careful; *(sciences)* applied

appoint [apwɛ̃] *nm* (**a**) **faire l'a.** to give the exact money (**b**) **d'a.** extra

apport [apɔr] *nm* contribution (**à** to)

apporter [apɔrte] *vt* to bring (**à** to); *(preuve)* to provide; *(modification)* to bring about

apposer [apoze] *vt (sceau, signature)* to affix (**à** to); *(affiche)* to put up

apprécier [apresje] *vt (aimer, percevoir)* to appreciate; *(évaluer)* to estimate ■ **appréciable** *adj* appreciable ■ **appréciation** *nf (opinion de professeur)* comment (**sur** on); *(évaluation)* valuation; *(augmentation de valeur)* appreciation

appréhender [apreɑ̃de] *vt (craindre)* to dread (**de faire qch** doing sth); *(arrêter)* to arrest; *(comprendre)* to grasp ■ **appréhension** *nf (crainte)* apprehension (**de** about)

apprendre* [aprɑ̃dr] *vti (étudier)* to learn; *(nouvelle)* to hear; *(mariage, mort)* to hear of; **a. à faire qch** to learn to do sth; **a. qch à qn** *(enseigner)* to teach sb sth; *(informer)* to tell sb sth; **a. à qn à faire qch** to teach sb to do sth; **a. que…** to learn that…; *(être informé)* to hear that…

apprenti, -e [aprɑ̃ti] *nmf* apprentice ■ **apprentissage** *nm (professionnel)* training; *(chez un artisan)* apprenticeship; *(d'une langue)* learning (**de** of); **faire l'a. de qch** to learn about sth

apprivoiser [aprivwaze] **1** *vt* to tame **2 s'apprivoiser** *vpr* to become tame

approbation [aprɔbasjɔ̃] *nf* approval ■ **approbateur, -trice** *adj* approving

approche [aprɔʃ] *nf* approach; **approches** *(de ville)* outskirts

approcher [aprɔʃe] **1** *vt (objet)* to bring up; *(personne)* to approach, to get close to; **a. qch de qn** to bring sth near to sb **2** *vi* to approach, to get closer; **a. de qn/qch** to approach sb/sth

3 s'approcher *vpr* to approach, to get closer; **s'a. de qn/qch** to approach sb/sth; **il s'est approché de moi** he came up to me

approfondir [aprɔfɔ̃dir] *vt* (*question, idée*) to go thoroughly into ■ **approfondi, -e** *adj* (*étude, examen*) thorough

approprié, -e [aprɔprije] *adj* appropriate (**à** for)

approprier [aprɔprije] **s'approprier** *vpr* **s'a. qch** to appropriate sth

approuver [apruve] *vt* (*facture, contrat*) to approve; (*décision*) to approve of

approvisionner [aprɔvizjɔne] **1** *vt* (*ville, armée*) to supply (**en** with); (*magasin*) to stock (**en** with); (*compte bancaire*) to pay money into

2 s'approvisionner *vpr* to get supplies (**en** of) ■ **approvisionnement** *nm* (*d'une ville, d'une armée*) supplying (**en** with); (*d'un magasin*) stocking (**en** with)

approximatif, -ive [aprɔksimatif, -iv] *adj* approximate ■ **approximation** *nf* approximation

appui [apɥi] *nm* support; **prendre a. sur qch** to lean on sth; **à l'a. de qch** in support of sth; **a. de fenêtre** window sill ■ **appui-tête** (*pl* **appuis-tête**) *nm* headrest

appuyer [apɥije] **1** *vt* (*poser*) to lean, to rest; *Fig* (*proposition*) to second; **a. qch sur qch** (*poser*) to rest sth on sth; (*presser*) to press sth on sth **2** *vi* (*presser*) to press; **a. sur un bouton** to press a button **3 s'appuyer** *vpr* **s'a. sur qch** to lean on sth, to rest on sth; *Fig* (*être basé sur*) to be based on sth

âpre [apr] *adj* sour; *Fig* (*lutte*) fierce

après [aprɛ] **1** *prép* (*dans le temps*) after; (*dans l'espace*) beyond; **a. tout** after all; **a. avoir mangé** after eating; **a. qu'il t'a vu** after he saw you; **d'a.** (*selon*) according to

2 *adv* after(wards); **l'année d'a.** the following year; **et a.?** (*et ensuite*) and then what?; (*et alors*) so what? ■ **après-demain** *adv* the day after

tomorrow ■ **après-guerre** *nm* postwar period; **d'a.** post-war ■ **après-midi** *nm ou f inv* afternoon; **trois heures de l'a.** three o'clock in the afternoon ■ **après-rasage** (*pl* **après-rasages**) *nm* aftershave ■ **après-shampooing** *nm inv* conditioner ■ **après-ski** (*pl* **après-skis**) *nm* snowboot ■ **après-vente** *adj inv Com* **service a.** after-sales service

âpreté [aprəte] *nf* sourness; *Fig* (*lutte*) fierceness

à-propos [aprɔpo] *nm* aptness; **avoir l'esprit d'a.** to have presence of mind

apte [apt] *adj* **a. à qch/à faire qch** fit to sth/for doing sth ■ **aptitude** *nf* aptitude (**à** *ou* **pour** for); **avoir des aptitudes pour qch** to have an aptitude for sth

aquarelle [akwarɛl] *nf* watercolour

aquarium [akwarjɔm] *nm* aquarium

aquatique [akwatik] *adj* aquatic

arabe **1** *adj* (*peuple, litterature*) Arab; (*langue*) Arabic **2** *nmf* **A.** Arab **3** *nm* (*langue*) Arabic ■ **Arabie** *nf* **l'A.** Arabia; **l'A. Saoudite** Saudi Arabia

arable [arabl] *adj* arable

arachide [araʃid] *nf* peanut

araignée [arɛɲe] *nf* spider

arbitraire [arbitrɛr] *adj* arbitrary

arbitre [arbitr] *nm* (*de football*) referee; (*de tennis*) umpire ■ **arbitrage** *nm* (*de football*) refereeing; (*de tennis*) umpiring

arborer [arbɔre] *vt* (*insigne*) to sport

arbre [arbr] *nm* (*végétal*) tree; *Tech* shaft; **a. fruitier** fruit tree; **a. de transmission** transmission shaft ■ **arbuste** *nm* shrub

arc [ark] *nm* (*arme*) bow; (*voûte*) arch; (*de cercle*) arc ■ **arcade** *nf* archway; **arcades** (*de place*) arcade

arc-boutant [arkbutɑ̃] (*pl* **arcs-boutants**) *nm* flying buttress

arc-en-ciel [arkɑ̃sjɛl] (*pl* **arcs-en-ciel**) *nm* rainbow

archaïque [arkaik] *adj* archaic

arche [arʃ] *nf* (*voûte*) arch; **l'a. de Noé** Noah's ark

archéologie [arkeɔlɔʒi] *nf* archaeology ■ **archéologique** *adj* archaeological ■ **archéologue** *nmf* archaeologist

archet [arʃɛ] *nm (de violon)* bow

architecte [arʃitɛkt] *nm* architect ■ **architecture** *nf* architecture

archives [arʃiv] *nfpl* archives, records

arctique [arktik] **1** *adj* arctic **2** *nm* l'A. the Arctic

ardent, -e [ardã, -ãt] *adj (désir)* burning; *(soleil)* scorching ■ **ardeur** *nf (passion)* fervour, ardour; *(du soleil)* intense heat

ardoise [ardwaz] *nf* slate

ardu, -e [ardy] *adj* arduous

arène [arɛn] *nf (pour taureaux)* bullring; *(romaine)* arena; **arènes** bullring; *(romaines)* amphitheatre

arête [arɛt] *nf (de poisson)* bone; *(de cube)* edge; *(de montagne)* ridge

argent [arʒã] **1** *nm (métal)* silver; *(monnaie)* money; **a. liquide** cash; **a. de poche** pocket money **2** *adj (couleur)* silver ■ **argenté, -e** *adj (plaqué)* silver-plated; *(couleur)* silvery ■ **argenterie** *nf* silverware

Argentine [arʒãtin] *nf* l'A. Argentina ■ **argentin, -e 1** *adj* Argentinian **2** *nmf* A., Argentine Argentinian

argile [arʒil] *nf* clay

argot [argo] *nm* slang ■ **argotique** *adj (terme)* slang

argument [argymã] *nm* argument

argumenter [argymãte] *vi* to argue

aride [arid] *adj (terre)* arid, barren; *(sujet)* dry

aristocrate [aristɔkrat] *nmf* aristocrat ■ **aristocratie** [-asi] *nf* aristocracy ■ **aristocratique** *adj* aristocratic

arithmétique [aritmetik] *nf* arithmetic

armature [armatyr] *nf (charpente)* framework; *(de lunettes, de tente)* frame

arme [arm] *nf* weapon; **prendre les armes** to take up arms; *Fig* **à armes égales** on equal terms; **a. à feu** firearm; **a. blanche** knife ■ **armes** *nfpl (blason)* (coat of) arms

armée [arme] *nf* army; **être à l'a.** to be doing one's military service; **a. de l'air** air force; **a. de terre** army; **a. active/ de métier** regular/professional army

armer [arme] **1** *vt (personne)* to arm (**de** with); *(fusil)* to cock; *(appareil photo)* to set **2 s'armer** *vpr* to arm oneself (**de** with); **s'a. de patience** to summon up one's patience ■ **armements** *nmpl (armes)* armaments

armistice [armistis] *nm* armistice

armoire [armwar] *nf (penderie) Br* wardrobe, *Am* closet; **a. à pharmacie** medicine cabinet

armure [armyr] *nf* armour

aromate [arɔmat] *nm (herbe)* herb; *(épice)* spice

aromathérapie [arɔmaterapi] *nf* aromatherapy

aromatique [arɔmatik] *adj* aromatic

arôme [arom] *nm (goût)* flavour; *(odeur)* aroma

arpenter [arpãte] *vt (parcourir)* to pace up and down

arqué, -e [arke] *adj (jambes)* bandy

arraché [araʃe] *nm* **gagner à l'a.** to snatch victory

arrache-pied [araʃpje] **d'arrache-pied** *adv* relentlessly

arracher [araʃe] *vt (plante)* to uproot; *(clou, dent, mauvaise herbe)* to pull out; *(page)* to tear out; **a. qch à qn** *(objet)* to snatch sth from sb; *(promesse)* to force sth out of sb; **se faire a. une dent** to have a tooth out

arrangement [arãʒmã] *nm (disposition) & Mus* arrangement; *(accord)* agreement

arranger [arãʒe] **1** *vt (fleurs)* to arrange; *(col)* to straighten; *(réparer)* to repair; **ça m'arrange** that suits me (fine) **2 s'arranger** *vpr (se mettre d'accord)* to come to an agreement; *(finir bien)* to turn out fine; *(s'organiser)* to manage

arrestation [arɛstɑsjɔ̃] *nf* arrest

arrêt [arɛ] *nm (halte, endroit)* stop; *(action)* stopping; *Jur* judgement; **temps d'a.** pause; **à l'a.** stationary; **sans a.**

continuously; **a. du cœur** cardiac arrest; *Sport* **a. de jeu** stoppage; **a. de mort** death sentence; **a. de travail** (*congé*) sick leave

arrêté¹ [arete] *nm* (*décret*) order, decree

arrêté², -e [arete] *adj* (*idées*) fixed

arrêter [arete] **1** *vt* (*personne, animal, véhicule*) to stop; (*criminel*) to arrest; (*moteur*) to turn off; (*date*) to fix; (*études*) to give up **2** *vi* to stop; **a. de faire qch** to stop doing sth **3 s'arrêter** *vpr* to stop; **s'a. de faire qch** to stop doing sth

arriéré, -e [arjere] **1** *adj* (*pays, idées, enfant*) backward **2** *nm* (*dette*) arrears

arrière [arjer] **1** *nm* (*de maison*) back, rear; (*de bateau*) stern; (*au football*) full back; **à l'a.** in/at the back

2 *adj inv* (*siège*) back, rear; **feu a.** rear light

3 *adv* **en a.** (*marcher, tomber*) backwards; (*rester*) behind; (*regarder*) back, behind; **en a. de qn/qch** behind sb/sth ■ **arrière-goût** (*pl* **arrière-goûts**) *nm* aftertaste ■ **arrière-pays** *nm inv* hinterland ■ **arrière-pensée** (*pl* **arrière-pensées**) *nf* ulterior motive ■ **arrière-plan** *nm* background; **à l'a.** in the background ■ **arrière-saison** (*pl* **arrière-saisons**) *nf Br* late autumn, *Am* late fall

arriver [arive] **1** (*aux être*) *vi* (*venir*) to arrive; **a. à** (*lieu*) to reach; (*résultat*) to achieve; **a. à faire qch** to manage to do sth

2 *v impersonnel* (*survenir*) to happen; **a. à qn** to happen to sb; **qu'est-ce qu'il t'arrive?** what's wrong with you? ■ **arrivage** *nm* consignment ■ **arrivée** *nf* arrival; (*ligne, poteau*) winning post ■ **arriviste** *nmf Péj* social climber

arrogant, -e [arɔgã, -ãt] *adj* arrogant ■ **arrogance** *nf* arrogance

arroger [arɔʒe] **s'arroger** *vpr* (*droit*) to claim

arrondir [arɔ̃dir] *vt* (*chiffre, angle*) to round off; **a. qch** to make sth round; **a. à l'euro supérieur/inférieur** to

round up/down to the nearest euro; *Fam* **a. ses fins de mois** to supplement one's income ■ **arrondi, -e** *adj* round

arrondissement [arɔ̃dismã] *nm* = administrative subdivision of Paris, Lyons and Marseilles

arroser [aroze] *vt* (*plante*) to water; (*pelouse*) to sprinkle; *Fam* (*succès*) to drink to ■ **arrosage** *nm* (*de plante*) watering; (*de pelouse*) sprinkling ■ **arrosoir** *nm* watering can

arsenal, -aux [arsənal, -o] *nm Mil* arsenal

arsenic [arsənik] *nm* arsenic

art [ar] *nm* art; **critique d'a.** art critic; **arts martiaux** martial arts; **arts ménagers** home economics; **arts plastiques** fine arts

artère [arter] *nf* (*veine*) artery; (*rue*) main road

artichaut [artiʃo] *nm* artichoke; **fond d'a.** artichoke heart

article [artikl] *nm* (*de presse, de contrat*) & *Gram* article; *Com* item; **articles de toilette** toiletries; **articles de voyage** travel goods

articuler [artikyle] **1** *vt* (*mot*) to articulate **2 s'articuler** *vpr* (*membre*) to articulate; **s'a. autour de qch** (*théorie*) to centre on ■ **articulation** *nf* (*de membre*) joint; (*prononciation*) articulation

artifice [artifis] *nm* trick

artificiel, -elle [artifisjel] *adj* artificial

artillerie [artijri] *nf* artillery ■ **artilleur** *nm* artilleryman

artisan [artizã] *nm* craftsman, artisan ■ **artisanal, -e, -aux, -ales** *adj* **objet a.** object made by craftsmen; **bombe artisanale** homemade bomb ■ **artisanat** *nm* craft industry

artiste [artist] *nmf* artist; (*acteur, musicien*) performer, artiste ■ **artistique** *adj* artistic

as [as] *nm* (*carte, champion*) ace

ascendant [asãdã] **1** *adj* ascending; (*mouvement*) upward **2** *nm* (*influence*) influence; **ascendants** ancestors ■ **ascendance** *nf* (*ancêtres*) ancestry

ascenseur [asɑ̃sœr] *nm Br* lift, *Am* elevator

ascension [asɑ̃sjɔ̃] *nf (escalade)* ascent; *Rel* **l'A.** Ascension Day

Asie [azi] *nf* **l'A.** Asia ■ **asiatique 1** *adj* Asian **2** *nmf* **A.** Asian

asile [azil] *nm (abri)* refuge, shelter; *(pour vieillards)* home; *Péj* **a. (d'aliénés)** (lunatic) asylum; **a. politique** (political) asylum

aspect [aspɛ] *nm (air)* appearance; *(perspective)* aspect

asperger [aspɛrʒe] **1** *vt (par jeu ou accident)* to splash *(de* with); **se faire a.** to get splashed **2** *s'asperger vpr* **s'a. de parfum** to splash oneself with perfume

asperges [aspɛrʒ] *nfpl* asparagus

asphalte [asfalt] *nm* asphalt

asphyxie [asfiksi] *nf* asphyxiation ■ **asphyxier** *vt*, **s'asphyxier** *vpr* to suffocate

aspirateur [aspiratœr] *nm* vacuum cleaner, *Br* Hoover®; **passer l'a. dans la maison** to vacuum the house

aspirer [aspire] **1** *vt (liquide)* to suck up; *(air)* to breathe in, to inhale **2** *vi* **a. à qch** *(bonheur, gloire)* to aspire to sth ■ **aspiration** *nf (inhalation)* inhalation; *(ambition)* aspiration *(à* for)

aspirine [aspirin] *nf* aspirin

assaillir [asajir] *vt* to attack ■ **assaillant** *nm* attacker, assailant

assainir [asenir] *vt (purifier)* to clean up; *(marché, économie)* to stabilize

assaisonner [asɛzɔne] *vt* to season ■ **assaisonnement** *nm* seasoning

assassin [asasɛ̃] *nm* murderer; *(de politicien)* assassin ■ **assassinat** *nm* murder; *(de politicien)* assassination ■ **assassiner** *vt* to murder; *(politicien)* to assassinate

assaut [aso] *nm* attack, assault; *Mil* charge

assécher [asefe] **1** *vt* to drain **2** *s'assécher vpr* to dry up

assemblée [asɑ̃ble] *nf (personnes réunies)* gathering; *(réunion)* meeting; **a. générale** *(de compagnie)* annual

general meeting; **l'A. nationale** *Br* ≃ the House of Commons, *Am* ≃ the House of Representatives

assembler [asɑ̃ble] **1** *vt* to put together, to assemble **2** **s'assembler** *vpr* to gather ■ **assemblage** *nm (montage)* assembly; *(réunion d'objets)* collection

asséner [asene] *vt* **a. un coup à qn** to deliver a blow to sb

asseoir* [aswar] **1** *vt (personne)* to seat *(sur* on); *Fig (autorité)* to establish **2** *vi* **faire a. qn** to ask sb to sit down **3** **s'asseoir** *vpr* to sit (down)

assermenté, -e [asɛrmɑ̃te] *adj* sworn; *(témoin)* under oath

asservir [asɛrvir] *vt* to enslave

assez [ase] *adv* **(a)** *(suffisamment)* enough; **a. de pain/de gens** enough bread/people; **j'en ai a. (de)** I've had enough (of); **a. grand/intelligent (pour faire qch)** big/clever enough (to do sth) **(b)** *(plutôt)* quite, rather

assidu, -e [asidy] *adj (toujours présent)* regular; *(appliqué)* diligent; **a. auprès de qn** attentive to sb ■ **assiduité** *nf (d'élève)* regularity

assiéger [asjeʒe] *vt (ville, magasin)* to besiege

assiette [asjɛt] *nf (récipient)* plate; *Culin* **a. anglaise** *Br* (assorted) cold meats, *Am* cold cuts

assigner [asiɲe] *vt (attribuer)* to assign *(à* to); *(en justice)* to summon ■ **assignation** *nf Jur* summons

assimiler [asimile] *vt (aliments, savoir, immigrés)* to assimilate

assis, -e¹ [asi, -iz] *(pp de asseoir) adj* sitting (down), seated; **rester a.** to remain seated; **place assise** seat

assise² [asiz] *nf (base)* foundation; **assises** *(d'un parti)* congress; *Jur* **les assises** the assizes

assistance [asistɑ̃s] *nf* **(a)** *(public)* audience **(b)** *(aide)* assistance

assister [asiste] **1** *vt (aider)* to assist **2** *vi* **a. à** *(réunion, cours)* to attend; *(accident)* to witness ■ **assistant, -e** *nmf* assistant; **assistante sociale** social worker; **assistante maternelle** *Br* child minder, *Am* baby-sitter ■ **assisté, -e** *adj* **a. par ordinateur** computer-aided

association [asɔsjɑsjɔ̃] *nf* association; *Com* partnership; **a. de parents d'élèves** parent-teacher association; **a. sportive** sports club

associer [asɔsje] **1** *vt* to associate (à with); **a. qn à** *(travaux)* to involve sb in **2 s'associer** *upr* to join forces (à *ou* avec with); *Com* **s'a. avec qn** to enter into partnership with sb ■ **associé, -e** *nmf* partner, associate

assoiffé, -e [aswafe] *adj* thirsty (**de** for)

assombrir [asɔ̃brir] **1** *vt* (*obscurcir*) to darken; (*attrister*) to cast a shadow over **2 s'assombrir** *upr* (*ciel, visage*) to cloud over; (*personne*) to become gloomy

assommer [asɔme] *vt* **a. qn** to knock sb unconscious; *Fig* (*ennuyer*) to bore sb to death ■ **assommant, -e** *adj* very boring

Assomption [asɔ̃psjɔ̃] *nf Rel* **l'A.** the Assumption

assortir [asɔrtir] *vt* (*harmoniser*) to match ■ **assorti, -e** *adj* (*objet semblable*) matching; (*bonbons*) assorted; **a. de** accompanied by ■ **assortiment** *nm* assortment

assoupir [asupir] **s'assoupir** *upr* to doze off

assouplir [asuplir] **1** *vt* (*cuir, muscles*) to make supple; (*corps*) to limber up; *Fig* (*réglementation*) to relax **2 s'assouplir** *upr* (*personne, cuir*) to get supple ■ **assouplissement** *nm* **exercices d'a.** warm-up exercises

assourdissant, -e [asurdisɑ̃, -ɑ̃t] *adj* deafening

assouvir [asuvir] *vt* to satisfy

assujettir [asyʒetir] *vt* (*soumettre*) to subject (à to); (*peuple*) to subjugate; (*objet*) to fix (à to)

assumer [asyme] **1** *vt* (*tâche, rôle*) to assume, to take on; (*risque*) to take **2 s'assumer** *upr* to come to terms with oneself

assurance [asyrɑ̃s] *nf* (*confiance*) (self-)assurance; (*promesse*) assurance; (*contrat*) insurance; **prendre une a.** to take out insurance; **a. au tiers/tous risques** third-party/comprehensive insurance; **a. maladie/vie** health/life insurance

assurer [asyre] **1** *vt* (*garantir*) *Br* to ensure, *Am* to insure; (*par contrat*) to insure; **a. qn de qch, a. qch à qn** to assure sb of sth; **un service régulier est assuré** there is a regular service **2 s'assurer** *upr* (*par contrat*) to insure oneself; **s'a. de qch/que...** to make sure of sth/that... ■ **assuré, -e 1** *adj* (*succès*) guaranteed; (*air, personne*) confident **2** *nmf* policyholder ■ **assurément** *adv* certainly

asthme [asm] *nm* asthma ■ **asthmatique** *adj & nmf* asthmatic

asticot [astiko] *nm Br* maggot, *Am* worm

astiquer [astike] *vt* to polish

astre [astr] *nm* star

astreindre* [astrɛ̃dr] **1** *vt* **a. qn à faire qch** to compel sb to do sth **2 s'astreindre** *upr* **s'a. à faire qch** to force oneself to do sth ■ **astreignant, -e** *adj* exacting ■ **astreinte** *nf* constraint

astrologie [astrɔlɔʒi] *nf* astrology

astrologue [astrɔlɔg] *nm* astrologer

astronaute [astrɔnot] *nmf* astronaut ■ **astronautique** *nf* space travel

astronomie [astrɔnɔmi] *nf* astronomy ■ **astronome** *nm* astronomer

astuce [astys] *nf* (*truc*) trick; (*plaisanterie*) witticism ■ **astucieux, -euse** *adj* clever

atelier [atəlje] *nm* (*d'ouvrier*) workshop; (*de peintre*) studio; (*personnel*) workshop staff; **a. de montage** assembly shop; **a. de réparation** repair shop

athée [ate] **1** *adj* atheistic **2** *nmf* atheist

Athènes [atɛn] *nm ou f* Athens

athlète [atlɛt] *nmf* athlete ■ **athlétique** *adj* athletic ■ **athlétisme** *nm* athletics (*sing*)

atlantique [atlɑ̃tik] **1** *adj* Atlantic **2** *nm* l'A. the Atlantic

atlas [atlɑs] *nm* atlas

atmosphère [atmɔsfɛr] *nf* atmosphere ■ **atmosphérique** *adj* atmospheric

atome [atom] *nm* atom ■ **atomique** *adj* atomic

atomiser [atɔmize] *vt* (*liquide*) to spray; (*région*) to destroy with nuclear weapons ■ **atomiseur** *nm* spray

atout [atu] *nm* trump; *Fig* (*avantage*) asset

âtre [ɑtr] *nm* (*foyer*) hearth

atroce [atrɔs] *adj* atrocious; (*douleur*) excruciating ■ **atrocité** *nf* (*cruauté*) atrociousness; **les atrocités de la guerre** the atrocities committed in wartime

attabler [atable] **s'attabler** *vpr* to sit down at a/the table

attache [ataʃ] *nf* (*lien*) fastener

attaché, -e [ataʃe] **1** *adj* (*fixé*) fastened; (*chien*) chained up; **être a. à qn** to be attached to sb **2** *nmf* attaché; **a. de presse** press officer

attaché-case [ataʃekez] (*pl* attachés-cases) *nm* attaché case

attacher [ataʃe] **1** *vt* **a. qch à qch** to fasten sth to sth; (*avec de la ficelle*) to tie sth to sth; (*avec une chaîne*) to chain sth to sth; **a. de l'importance à qch** to attach great importance to sth **2** *vi* (*en cuisant*) to stick (to the pan) **3** **s'attacher** *vpr* (*se fixer*) to be fastened; **s'a. à qn** to get attached to sb ■ **attachant, -e** *adj* engaging ■ **attachement** *nm* (*affection*) attachment (à to)

attaque [atak] *nf* attack; **a. aérienne** air raid ■ **attaquer 1** *vt* (*physiquement, verbalement*) to attack **2** *vi* to attack **3** **s'attaquer** *vpr* **s'a. à** (*adversaire*) to attack; (*problème*) to tackle ■ **attaquant, -e** *nmf* attacker

attarder [atarde] **s'attarder** *vpr* to linger ■ **attardé, -e** *adj* (*enfant*) mentally retarded

atteindre* [atɛ̃dr] *vt* (*parvenir à*) to

reach; (*cible*) to hit; **être atteint d'une maladie** to be suffering from a disease

atteinte [atɛ̃t] *nf* attack (à on); **porter a. à** to undermine; **hors d'a.** (*objet, personne*) out of reach

atteler [atle] **1** *vt* (*bêtes*) to harness **2** **s'atteler** *vpr* **s'a. à une tâche** to apply oneself to a task

attenant, -e [atnɑ̃, -ɑ̃t] *adj* **a. (à)** adjoining

attendre [atɑ̃dr] **1** *vt* (*personne, train*) to wait for; **a. son tour** to wait one's turn; **elle attend un bébé** she's expecting a baby; **a. que qn fasse qch** to wait for sb to do sth; **a. qch de qn** to expect sth from sb **2** *vi* to wait; **faire a. qn** to keep sb waiting; **en attendant** meanwhile; **en attendant que...** (+ *subjunctive*) until... **3** **s'attendre** *vpr* **s'a. à qch** to expect sth; **s'a. à ce que qn fasse qch** to expect sb to do sth ■ **attendu, -e 1** *adj* (*prévu*) expected **2** *prép Formel* considering

attendrir [atɑ̃drir] **1** *vt* (*émouvoir*) to move **2** **s'attendrir** *vpr* to be moved (**sur** by) ■ **attendri, -e** *adj* compassionate ■ **attendrissant, -e** *adj* moving

attentat [atɑ̃ta] *nm* attack; **a. à la bombe** bombing; **a. à la pudeur** indecent assault

attente [atɑ̃t] *nf* (*fait d'attendre*) waiting; (*période*) wait; **en a.** (*au téléphone*) on hold; **contre toute a.** against all expectations

attentif, -ive [atɑ̃tif, -iv] *adj* attentive; **a. à qch** to pay attention to sth

attention [atɑ̃sjɔ̃] *nf* (*soin, amabilité*) attention; **faire a. à qch** to pay attention to sth; **faire a. (à ce) que...** (+ *subjunctive*) to be careful that...; **a.!** watch out!; **a. à la voiture!** watch out for the car!; **à l'a. de qn** (*sur lettre*) for the attention of sb ■ **attentionné, -e** *adj* considerate

atténuer [atenɥe] **1** *vt* (*effet, douleur*) to reduce **2** **s'atténuer** *vpr* (*douleur*) to ease

atterrir [aterir] *vi* to land; **a. en catastrophe** to make an emergency landing ■ **atterrissage** *nm* landing; **a. forcé** forced landing

attester [ateste] *vt* to testify to; **a. que…** to testify that… ■ **attestation** *nf (document)* certificate

attirail [atiraj] *nm* equipment; *Fam Péj* gear

attirance [atirãs] *nf* attraction (**pour** for)

attirer [atire] **1** *vt (sujet: aimant, personne)* to attract; *(sujet: matière, pays)* to appeal to; **a. l'attention de qn** to catch sb's attention; **a. qn dans un piège** to lure sb into a trap **2** **s'attirer** *vpr (mutuellement)* to be attracted to each other; **s'a. des ennuis** to get oneself into trouble ■ **attirant, -e** *adj* attractive

attitré, -e [atitre] *adj (représentant)* appointed

attitude [atityd] *nf (conduite, position)* attitude

attraction [atraksjɔ̃] *nf (force, centre d'intérêt)* attraction

attrait [atrɛ] *nm* attraction

attraper [atrape] *vt (ballon, maladie, voleur)* to catch; **a. froid** to catch cold

attrayant, -e [atrɛjɑ̃, -ɑ̃t] *adj* attractive

attribuer [atribɥe] *vt (allouer)* to assign (**à** to); *(prix, bourse)* to award (**à** to); *(œuvre)* to attribute (**à** to); **a. de l'importance à qch** to attach importance to sth ■ **attribution** *nf (allocation)* assigning (**à** to); *(de prix)* awarding (**à** to); *(d'une œuvre)* attribution (**à** to); **attributions** *(fonctions)* duties

attribut [atriby] *nm (caractéristique)* attribute

attrister [atriste] *vt* to sadden

attrouper [atrupe] **s'attrouper** *vpr* to gather ■ **attroupement** *nm* crowd

au [o] *voir* à

aube [ob] *nf* dawn; **dès l'a.** at the crack of dawn

auberge [obɛrʒ] *nf* inn; **a. de jeunesse** youth hostel

aubergine [obɛrʒin] *nf Br* aubergine, *Am* eggplant

aucun, -e [okœ̃, -yn] **1** *adj* no, not any; **il n'a a. talent** he has no talent; **a. professeur n'est venu** no teacher came **2** *pron* none; **il n'en a a.** he has none (at all); **a. d'entre nous** none of us; **a. des deux** neither of the two

audace [odas] *nf (courage)* daring, boldness; *(impudence)* audacity ■ **audacieux, -euse** *adj (courageux)* daring, bold

au-dehors [odəɔr] *adv* outside

au-delà [odəla] **1** *adv* beyond; **100 euros mais pas a.** 100 euros but no more **2** *prép* **a. de** beyond **3** *nm* **l'a.** the next world

au-dessous [odəsu] **1** *adv (à l'étage inférieur)* downstairs; *(moins, dessous)* below, under **2** *prép* **a. de** *(dans l'espace)* below, under, beneath; *(âge, prix)* under; *(température)* below

au-dessus [odəsy] **1** *adv* above; *(à l'étage supérieur)* upstairs **2** *prép* **a. de** above; *(âge, température, prix)* over; *(posé sur)* on top of

au-devant [odəvɑ̃] *prép* **aller a. de** *(personne)* to go to meet; *(danger)* to court; *(désirs de qn)* to anticipate

audible [odibl] *adj* audible

audience [odjɑ̃s] *nf (entretien)* audience; *(de tribunal)* hearing; *Jur* **l'a. est suspendue** the case is adjourned

audiovisuel, -elle [odjovizɥɛl] **1** *adj (méthodes)* audiovisual; *(de radio, de télévision)* radio and television **2** *nm* **l'a.** radio and television

auditeur, -trice [oditœr, -tris] *nmf (de radio)* listener ■ **audition** *nf (ouïe)* hearing; *(d'acteurs)* audition; **passer une a.** to have an audition ■ **auditionner** *vti* to audition ■ **auditoire** *nm* audience ■ **auditorium** *nm* concert hall

augmenter [ɔgmɑ̃te] **1** *vt* to increase (**de** by); **a. qn** to give sb a *Br* rise *or Am* raise **2** *vi* to increase (**de** by); *(prix,* *population)* to rise ■ **augmentation** *nf* increase (in, of); **a. de salaire** *Br* (pay) rise, *Am* raise; **être en a.** to be on the increase

augure [ɔgyr] *nm (présage)* omen; **être de bon/mauvais a.** to be a good/bad omen

aujourd'hui [oʒurdɥi] *adv* today; *(de nos jours)* nowadays, today; **a. en quinze** two weeks from today

auparavant [oparavɑ̃] *adv (avant)* before(-hand); *(d'abord)* first

auprès [oprɛ] **auprès de** *prép (près de)* by, next to; **se renseigner a. de qn** to ask sb

auquel [okɛl] *voir* **lequel**

aura, aurait [ora, orɛ] *voir* **avoir**

auréole [oreɔl] *nf (de saint)* halo; *(tache)* ring

auriculaire [ɔrikyler] *nm* little finger

aurore [ɔrɔr] *nf* dawn, daybreak; **à l'a.** at dawn

auspices [ospis] *nmpl* **sous les a. de** under the auspices of

aussi [osi] **1** *adv* **(a)** *(comparaison)* as; **a. lourd que…** as heavy as… **(b)** *(également)* too, as well; **moi a.** so do/can/am/*etc* I; **a. bien que…** as well as… **(c)** *(tellement)* so; **un repas a. délicieux** such a delicious meal **(d)** *(quelque)* **a. bizarre que cela paraisse** however odd this may seem **2** *conj (donc)* therefore

aussitôt [osito] *adv* immediately, straight away; **a. que…** as soon as…; **a. dit, a. fait** no sooner said than done

austère [ɔstɛr] *adj (vie, style)* austere; *(vêtement)* severe ■ **austérité** *nf (de vie, de style)* austerity; *(de vêtement)* severity; **mesure d'a.** austerity measures

austral, -e, -als, -ales [ɔstral] *adj* southern

Australie [ɔstrali] *nf* **l'A.** Australia ■ **australien, -enne 1** *adj* Australian **2** *nmf* A., Australienne Australian

AUTANT [otɑ̃] *adv* **(a)** **a. de… que** *(quantité)* as much… as; *(nombre)* as

many… as; **il a a. d'argent/de pommes que vous** he has as much money/as many apples as you **(b)** **a. de** *(tant de)* so much; *(nombre)* so many; **je n'ai jamais vu a. d'argent/de pommes** I've never seen so much money/so many apples; **pourquoi manges-tu a.?** why are you eating so much?

(c) **a. que** *(quantité)* as much as; *(nombre)* as many as; **il lit a. que vous/que possible** he reads as much as you/as possible; **il n'a jamais souffert a.** he's never suffered as *or* so much

(d) *(expressions)* **d'a. (plus) que…** all the more (so) since…; **en faire a.** to do the same; **j'aimerais a. aller au musée** I'd just as soon go to the museum

autel [otɛl] *nm* altar

auteur [otœr] *nm (de livre)* author, writer; *(de chanson)* composer

authenticité [otɑ̃tisite] *nf* authenticity ■ **authentique** *adj* genuine, authentic

autiste [otist] *adj* autistic

autobiographie [otobjɔgrafi] *nf* autobiography ■ **autobiographique** *adj* autobiographical

autobus [otobys] *nm* bus

autocar [otokar] *nm* bus, *Br* coach

autocollant, -e [otokɔlɑ̃, -ɑ̃t] **1** *adj* self-adhesive; *(enveloppe, timbre)* self-seal **2** *nm* sticker

autodéfense [otodefɑ̃s] *nf* self-defence

autodidacte [otodidakt] *nmf* self-taught person

autographe [otɔgraf] *nm* autograph

automation [ɔtɔmasjɔ̃] *nf* automation ■ **automatiser** *vt* to automate

automatique [ɔtɔmatik] *adj* automatic ■ **automatiquement** *adv* automatically

automatisation [ɔtɔmatizasjɔ̃] *nf* = **automation**

automne [otɔn] *nm* autumn, *Am* fall

automobile [otɔmɔbil] *nf* car, *Br* motorcar, *Am* automobile; **l'a.** *(industrie)* the car industry ■ **automobiliste** *nmf* motorist

autonettoyant, -e [otonetwajã, -ãt] *adj* **four a.** self-cleaning oven

autonome [otonɔm] *adj (région)* autonomous, self-governing; *(personne)* self-sufficient ■ **autonomie** *nf (de région)* autonomy; *(de personne)* self-sufficiency

autopsie [ɔtɔpsi] *nf* autopsy, postmortem

autoradio [otoradjo] *nm* car radio

autoriser [otorize] *vt* **a. qn à faire qch** to authorize *or* permit sb to do sth ■ **autorisation** *nf (permission)* permission, authorization; *(document)* authorization; **demander à qn l'a. de faire qch** to ask sb permission to do sth; **donner à qn l'a. de faire qch** to give sb permission to do sth ■ **autorisé, -e** *adj (qualifié)* authoritative; *(permis)* permitted, allowed

autorité [otorite] *nf (fermeté, domination)* authority; **faire qch d'a.** to do sth on one's own authority

autoroute [otorut] *nf Br* motorway, *Am* highway, *Am* freeway; **a. à péage** *Br* toll motorway, *Am* turnpike (road); *Ordinat* **a. de l'information** information superhighway ■ **autoritaire** *adj* authoritarian

auto-stop [otostɔp] *nm* hitchhiking; **faire de l'a.** to hitchhike ■ **auto-stoppeur, -euse** *nmf* hitchhiker

autour [otur] **1** *adv* around; **tout a.** all around **2** *prép* **a. de** around; round; *(environ)* around, round about

AUTRE [otr] *adj & pron* other; **un a. livre** another book; **un a.** another (one); **d'autres** others; **d'autres livres** other books; **quelqu'un d'a.** somebody else; **personne/rien d'a.** no one/ nothing else; **a. chose/part** something/somewhere else; **qui/quoi d'a.?** who/what else?; **l'un ou l'a.** either (of them); **ni l'un ni l'a.** neither (of them)

autrefois [otrəfwa] *adv* in the past, once

autrement [otrəmã] *adv (différemment)* differently; *(sinon)* otherwise; *(plus)* far more (**que** than)

Autriche [otriʃ] *nf* **l'A.** Austria ■ **autrichien, -enne 1** *adj* Austrian **2** *nmf* **A., Autrichienne** Austrian

autruche [otryʃ] *nf* ostrich

autrui [otrɥi] *pron* others, other people

auvent [ovã] *nm (toit)* porch roof; *(de tente, de magasin)* awning, canopy

aux [o] *voir* **à**

auxiliaire [ɔksiljɛr] **1** *adj (machine, troupes)* auxiliary **2** *nm (verbe)* auxiliary **3** *nmf (aide)* assistant; *(d'hôpital)* auxiliary; *(dans l'administration)* temporary worker

auxquels, -elles [okɛl] *voir* **lequel**

av. *(abrév avenue)* [ave] Ave

avait [avɛ] *voir* **avoir**

aval [aval] *nm* downstream section; **en a. (de)** downstream (from)

avalanche [avalãʃ] *nf* avalanche

avaler [avale] *vti* to swallow

avance [avãs] *nf (progression, acompte)* advance; *(avantage)* lead; **faire une a. à qn** *(donner de l'argent)* to give sb an advance; **avoir de l'a. sur qn** to be ahead of sb; **à l'a., d'a., par a.** in advance; **en a.** early; **avoir une heure d'a.** to be an hour early

avancé, -e [avãse] *adj* advanced; **à un âge/stade a.** at an advanced age/ stage

avancée [avãse] *nf (saillie)* projection; *(progression, découverte)* advance

avancement [avãsmã] *nm (de personne)* promotion; *(de travail)* progress

avancer [avãse] **1** *vt (dans le temps)* to bring forward; *(dans l'espace)* to move forward; *(pion, thèse)* to advance; *(montre)* to put forward; **a. de l'argent à qn** to lend sb money **2** *vi (aller de l'avant)* to move forward; *(armée)* to advance; *(faire des progrès)* to progress; *(faire saillie)* to jut out (sur over); **a. (de cinq minutes)** (montre) to be (five minutes) fast

3 s'avancer upr to move forward; **s'a. vers qch** to head towards sth

AVANT [avã] **1** prép before; **a. de faire qch** before doing sth; **je vous verrai a. de partir/que vous (ne) partiez** I'll see you before I/you leave; **a. tout** above all

2 adv (auparavant) before; (d'abord) beforehand; **a. j'avais les cheveux longs** I used to have long hair; **en a.** (mouvement) forward; (en tête) ahead; **en a. de** in front of; **la nuit d'a.** the night before

3 nm (de navire, de voiture) front; (joueur de football) forward; **à l'a.** in (the) front; **aller de l'a.** to get on with it

4 adj inv (pneu, roue) front ■ **avant-bras** nm inv forearm ■ **avant-centre** (pl **avants-centres**) nm (au football) centre-forward ■ **avant-dernier, -ère** (mpl **avant-derniers,** fpl **avant-dernières**) adj & nmf second last ■ **avant-hier** adv the day before yesterday ■ **avant-première** (pl **avant-premières**) nf preview ■ **avant-propos** nm inv foreword

avantage [avãtaʒ] nm advantage; **être/tourner à l'a. de qn** to be/turn to sb's advantage; **avantages sociaux** social security benefits ■ **avantager** vt **a. qn** (favoriser) to give sb an advantage over; (faire valoir) to show sb off to advantage ■ **avantageux, -euse** adj (offre) attractive; (prix) reasonable

avare [avar] **1** adj miserly **2** nmf miser ■ **avarice** nf miserliness, avarice

avaries [avari] nf damage; **subir une a.** to be damaged ■ **avarié, -e** adj (aliment) rotten

avec [avɛk] prép with; **méchant/aimable a. qn** nasty/kind to sb; **a. enthousiasme** with enthusiasm, enthusiastically; Fam **et a. ça?** (dans un magasin) anything else?

avenant, -e [avnã, -ãt] **1** adj

(personne, manières) pleasing **2** nm **à l'a. (de)** in keeping with

avènement [avɛnmã] nm (d'une ère) advent; (d'un roi) accession

avenir [avnir] nm future; **à l'a.** (désormais) in future; **d'a.** (métier) with good prospects

aventure [avãtyr] nf adventure; (en amour) affair; **dire la bonne a. à qn** to tell sb's fortune ■ **aventurer** vpr **s'aventurer** to venture (**dans** into) ■ **aventurier, -ère** nmf adventurer

avenue [avny] nf avenue

avérer [avere] vpr **s'avérer** (se révéler) to prove to be; **il s'avère que...** it turns out that... ■ **avéré, -e** adj (fait) established

averse [avers] nf shower

aversion [aversjɔ̃] nf aversion (**pour** to)

avertir [avertir] vt **a. qn de qch** (informer) to inform sb of sth; (danger) to warn sb of sth ■ **avertissement** nm warning; (de livre) foreword ■ **avertisseur** nm (klaxon®) horn

aveu, -x [avø] nm confession

aveugle [avœgl] **1** adj blind; **devenir a.** to go blind; **avoir une confiance a. en qn** to trust sb implicitly **2** nmf blind man, f blind woman; **les aveugles** the blind ■ **aveuglement** nm (moral, mental) blindness ■ **aveuglément** adv blindly ■ **aveugler** vt (éblouir) & Fig to blind; **aveuglé par la colère** blind with rage

aveuglette [avœglɛt] **à l'aveuglette** adv blindly; **chercher qch à l'a.** to grope for sth

aviateur, -trice [avjatœr, -tris] nmf aviator ■ **aviation** nf (secteur) aviation; (armée de l'air) air force; **l'a.** (activité) flying

avide [avid] adj (cupide) greedy; (passionné) eager (**de** for) ■ **avidité** nf (voracité, cupidité) greed; (passion) eagerness

avilir [avilir] vt to degrade

avion [avjɔ̃] nm plane, Br aeroplane, Am airplane; **par a.** (sur lettre) airmail;

en a., par a. (*voyager*) by plane, by air; a. à réaction jet; a. de tourisme private plane

aviron [avirɔ̃] *nm* oar; l'a. (*sport*) rowing; faire de l'a. to row

avis [avi] *nm* opinion; (*communiqué*) notice; (*conseil*) advice; à mon a. in my opinion, to my mind; être de l'a. de qn to be of the same opinion as sb; changer d'a. to change one's mind; sauf a. contraire unless I/you/*etc* hear to the contrary

aviser [avize] 1 *vt* a. qn de qch/que... to inform sb of sth/that... 2 s'aviser *vpr* s'a. de qch to become aware of sth; s'a. que... to notice that... ■ avisé, -e *adj* wise (de faire to do); bien/mal a. well-/ill-advised

avocat¹, -e [avɔka, -at] *nmf Jur* lawyer; *Fig* advocate

avocat² [avɔka] *nm* (*fruit*) avocado

avoine [avwan] *nf* oats

[AVOIR*] [avwar] 1 *v aux* to have; je l'ai vu I have *or* I've seen him
2 *vt* (*posséder*) to have; (*obtenir*) to get; (*porter*) to wear; *Fam* (*tromper*) to take for a ride; qu'est-ce que tu as? what's the matter with you?; j'ai à faire I have things to do; il n'a qu'à essayer he only has to try; a. faim/chaud to be *or* feel hungry/hot; a. cinq

ans to be five (years old); a. du diabète to be diabetic
3 *v impersonnel* il y a there is, *pl* there are; il y a six ans six years ago; il n'y a pas de quoi! (*en réponse à 'merci'*) don't mention it!; qu'est-ce qu'il y a? what's the matter?
4 *nm* assets, property; (*d'un compte*) credit

avoisiner [avwazine] *vt* (*dans l'espace*) to border on; (*en valeur*) to be close to ■ avoisinant, -e *adj* neighbouring, nearby

avorter [avɔrte] *vi* (*subir une IVG*) to have an abortion; *Fig* (*projet*) to fall through; se faire a. to have an abortion ■ avortement *nm* abortion

avouer [avwe] 1 *vt* (*crime*) to confess to; il faut a. que... it must be admitted that... 2 s'avouer *vpr* s'a. vaincu to acknowledge defeat

avril [avril] *nm* April

axe [aks] *nm* (*géométrique*) axis; (*essieu*) axle; les grands axes (*routes*) the main roads ■ axer *vt* to centre (sur on)

ayant [ɛjɑ̃], **ayez** [ɛje], **ayons** [ɛjɔ̃] *voir* avoir

azote [azɔt] *nm* nitrogen

Bb

B, b [be] *nm inv* B, b

babiller [babije] *vi (enfant)* to babble

babines [babin] *nfpl (lèvres)* chops

bâbord [babɔr] *nm* port (side); **à b.** to port

baby-foot [babifut] *nm inv* table football

baby-sitting [babisitiŋ] *nm* baby-sitting ■ **baby-sitter** (*pl* **baby-sitters**) *nmf* baby-sitter

bac¹ [bak] *nm (bateau)* ferry(boat); *(cuve)* tank; **b. à glace** ice tray

bac² [bak] *(abrév* **baccalauréat**) *nm Fam* = secondary school examination qualifying for entry to university, *Br* ≃ A-levels, *Am* ≃ high school diploma

baccalauréat [bakalɔrea] *nm* = secondary school examination qualifying for entry to university, *Br* ≃ A-levels, *Am* ≃ high school diploma

bâche [baʃ] *nf (de toile)* tarpaulin; *(de plastique)* plastic sheet ■ **bâcher** *vt* to cover *(with a tarpaulin or plastic sheet)*

bachelier, -ère [baʃəlje, -ɛr] *nmf* = student who has passed the "baccalauréat"

bâcler [bakle] *vt Fam* to botch (up)

bactérie [bakteri] *nf* bacterium

badaud, -aude [bado, -od] *nmf (promeneur)* stroller; *(curieux)* onlooker

badge [badʒ] *nm Br* badge, *Am* button

badigeonner [badiʒɔne] *vt (surface)* to daub *(de* with*)*; *(mur)* to whitewash; *Culin* to brush *(de* with*)*; *(plaie)* to paint *(de* with*)*

badinage [badinaʒ] *nm* banter

badine [badin] *nf* switch

badiner [badine] *vi* to jest

baffle [bafl] *nm* speaker

bafouer [bafwe] *vt (person)* to jeer at; *(autorité)* to flout

bafouiller [bafuje] *vti* to stammer

bagages [bagaʒ] *nmpl (valises)* luggage, baggage; **faire ses b.** to pack (one's bags)

bagarre [bagar] *nf* fight, brawl ■ **se bagarrer** to fight ■ **bagarreur, -euse** *adj (personne, caractère)* aggressive

bague [bag] *nf (anneau)* ring; *(de cigare)* band ■ **baguer** *vt (oiseau, arbre)* to ring

baguette [baget] *nf (canne)* stick; *(de chef d'orchestre)* baton; *(pain)* baguette; **baguettes** *(de tambour)* drumsticks; *(pour manger)* chopsticks

bahut [bay] *nm (buffet)* sideboard

baie¹ [be] *nf Géog* bay

baie² [be] *nf (fruit)* berry

baie³ [be] *nf* **b. vitrée** picture window

baignade [bɛɲad] *nf (activité)* swimming, *Br* bathing; **'b. interdite'** 'no swimming'

baigner [beɲe] **1** *vt (pied, blessure)* to bathe; *(enfant) Br* to bath, *Am* to bathe; *(sujet: mer)* to wash **2** *vi (tremper)* to soak *(dans* in*)* **3 se baigner** *vpr (nager)* to have a swim ■ **baigneur, -euse 1** *nmf* swimmer **2** *nm (poupée)* baby doll ■ **baignoire** *nf* bath (tub)

bail [baj] *(pl* **baux** [bo]*)* *nm* lease; *Fam* **ça fait un b. que je ne l'ai pas vu** I haven't seen him for ages ■ **bailleur** *nm* **b. de fonds** financial backer

bâiller [baje] *vi* to yawn; *(col)* to gape; *(porte)* to be ajar

bâillon [bajɔ̃] *nm* gag; **mettre un b. à qn** to gag sb ■ **bâillonner** *vt (victime, presse)* to gag

bain [bɛ̃] *nm* bath; **prendre un b.** to have *or* take a bath; **prendre un b. de soleil** to sunbathe; **petit/grand b.** *(de piscine)* small/large pool

baiser [beze] *nm* kiss

baisse [bes] *nf* fall, drop (**de** in); **en b.** *(température)* falling; *(popularité)* declining

baisser [bese] **1** *vt (rideau, vitre, prix)* to lower; *(radio, chauffage)* to turn down; **b. la tête** to lower one's head; **b. les yeux** to look down **2** *vi (prix, niveau, température)* to fall; *(vue, mémoire)* to fail; *(popularité, qualité)* to decline **3** **se baisser** *vpr* to bend down; *(pour éviter quelque chose)* to duck

baissier [besje] *adj m Fin* **marché b.** bear market

bal [bal] *(pl* **bals**) *nm (élégant)* ball; *(populaire)* dance; **b. costumé, b. masqué** fancy dress ball; **b. populaire** = dance, usually outdoors, open to the public

balade [balad] *nf Fam (à pied)* walk; *(en voiture)* drive; **faire une b.** *(à pied)* to go for a walk; *(en voiture)* to go for a drive ■ **balader** *Fam* **1** *vt* **envoyer qn b.** to send sb packing **2** **se balader** *vpr (à pied)* to go for a walk; *(en voiture)* to go for a drive ■ **baladeur** *nm* personal stereo

balafre [balafr] *nf (cicatrice)* scar; *(coupure)* gash ■ **balafrer** *vt* to gash

balai [bale] *nm* broom; **donner un coup de b.** to give the floor a sweep

balance [balɑ̃s] *nf* **(a)** *(instrument)* (pair of) scales (**b**) **la B.** *(signe)* Libra

balancer [balɑ̃se] **1** *vt (bras, jambe)* to swing **2** **se balancer** *vpr (arbre, bateau)* to sway; *(sur une balançoire)* to swing ■ **balancement** *nm* swaying

balancier [balɑ̃sje] *nm (d'horloge)* pendulum

balançoire [balɑ̃swar] *nf (suspendue)* swing; *(bascule)* see-saw

balayer [baleje] *vt (pièce)* to sweep; *(feuilles, saletés)* to sweep up ■ **balayage** *nm (nettoyage)* sweeping; *(coiffure)* highlighting

balayeur, -euse [balejœr, -øz] *nmf (personne)* road-sweeper

balbutier [balbysje] *vti* to stammer ■ **balbutiement** *nm* **balbutiement(s)** stammering

balcon [balkɔ̃] *nm* balcony; *(de théâtre)* circle, *Am* mezzanine; **premier/ deuxième b.** dress/upper circle

Baléares [balear] *nfpl* **les B.** the Balearic Islands

baleine [balɛn] *nf (animal)* whale; *(de corset)* whalebone; *(de parapluie)* rib

balèze [balɛz] *adj Fam (grand et fort)* hefty; *(intelligent)* brainy

balise [baliz] *nf Naut* beacon; *Aviat* light; *(de piste de ski)* marker; *Ordinat* tag ■ **balisage** *nm (signaux) Naut* beacons; *Aviat* lights ■ **baliser** *vt (chenal)* to beacon; *(aéroport)* to equip with lights; *(route)* to mark out with beacons; *(piste de ski)* to mark out; *Ordinat* to tag

balivernes [balivern] *nfpl* twaddle

Balkans [balkɑ̃] *nmpl* **les B.** the Balkans

ballant, -e [balɑ̃, -ɑ̃t] *adj (bras, jambes)* dangling

ballast [balast] *nm (de route, de voie ferrée)* ballast

balle [bal] *nf (pour jouer)* ball; *(d'arme)* bullet; **b. de tennis** tennis ball; **b. perdue** stray bullet

ballet [balɛ] *nm* ballet ■ **ballerine** *nf (danseuse)* ballerina; *(chaussure)* pumps

ballon [balɔ̃] *nm (balle, dirigeable)* balloon; *(verre)* round wine glass; **jouer au b.** to play with a ball; **b. de football** *Br* football, *Am* soccer ball

ballonné [balɔne] *adj m (ventre, personne)* bloated

ballottage [balɔtaʒ] *nm Pol* **il y a b.** there will be a second ballot

ballotter [balɔte] *vt (bateau)* to toss about; *(passagers)* to shake about

balluchon [balyʃɔ̃] *nm* bundle; **faire son b.** to pack one's bags

balnéaire [balneɛr] *adj* **station b.** *Br* seaside resort, *Am* beach resort

balourd, -e [balur, -urd] *adj* oafish

balte [balt] *adj* **les États baltes** the Baltic states

Baltique [baltik] *nf* **la (mer) B.** the Baltic (Sea)

baluchon [balyʃɔ̃] *nm* = **balluchon**

balustrade [balystrad] *nf (de pont)* railing; *(de balcon)* balustrade

bambou [bãbu] *nm* bamboo

ban [bã] *nm (applaudissements)* round of applause; **bans** *(de mariage)* banns

banal, -e, -als, -ales [banal] *adj (objet, gens)* ordinary; *(idée)* trite, banal; **pas b.** unusual ■ **banalité** *nf (d'objet, de gens)* ordinariness; *(d'idée)* triteness

banaliser [banalize] *vt (rendre commun)* to trivialize

banane [banan] *nf (fruit)* banana; *(coiffure)* quiff ■ **bananier** *nm (arbre)* banana tree

banc [bã] *nm (siège)* bench; *(établi)* (work-)bench; *(de poissons)* shoal; **b. des accusés** dock; **b. d'essai** *Ind* test bed; *Fig* testing ground; **b. de sable** sandbank

bancaire [bãkɛr] *adj (opération)* banking; *(chèque, compte)* bank

bancal, -e, -als, -ales [bãkal] *adj (meuble)* wobbly; *Fig (raisonnement)* unsound

bandage [bãdaʒ] *nm (pansement)* bandage

bande [bãd] *nf* (**a**) *(de tissu, de papier, de terre)* strip; *(pansement)* bandage; *(pellicule)* film; **b. magnétique** tape; *Aut* **b. d'arrêt d'urgence** *Br* hard shoulder, *Am* shoulder; **b. dessinée** comic strip; **b. sonore** soundtrack (**b**) *(de personnes)* band, group; *(de voleurs)* gang; *(de loups)* pack; **faire b. à part** *(agir seul)* to do one's own

thing ■ **bande-annonce** *(pl* **bandes-annonces**) *nf* trailer (**de** for) ■ **bande-son** *(pl* **bandes-son**) *nf* soundtrack

bandeau, -x [bãdo] *nm (pour cheveux)* headband; *(sur les yeux)* blindfold

bander [bãde] *vt (blessure, main)* to bandage; *(arc)* to bend; **b. les yeux à qn** to blindfold sb

banderole [bãdrɔl] *nf (de manifestants)* banner; *(publicitaire)* streamer

bandit [bãdi] *nm (escroc)* crook

bandoulière [bãduljɛr] *nf (de sac)* shoulder strap; **en b.** slung across the shoulder

banlieue [bãljø] *nf* suburbs; **la b. parisienne** the suburbs of Paris; **de b.** *(maison, magasin)* suburban; **train de b.** commuter train ■ **banlieusard, -e** *nmf (habitant)* suburbanite; *(voyageur)* commuter

bannière [banjɛr] *nf* banner; **la b. étoilée** the Star-spangled Banner

bannir [banir] *vt (personne, idée)* to banish (**de** from)

banque [bãk] *nf (établissement)* bank; **la b.** *(activité)* banking; **employé de b.** bank clerk; *Ordinat* **b. de données** data bank

banqueroute [bãkrut] *nf* bankruptcy; **faire b.** to go bankrupt

banquet [bãkɛ] *nm* banquet

banquette [bãkɛt] *nf (siège)* (bench) seat

banquier, -ère [bãkje, -ɛr] *nmf* banker

banquise [bãkiz] *nf* ice floe

baptême [batɛm] *nm* christening, baptism ■ **baptiser** *vt* to christen, to baptize

baquet [bakɛ] *nm (cuve)* tub

bar¹ [bar] *nm (café, comptoir)* bar

bar² [bar] *nm (poisson)* bass

baraque [barak] *nf (cabane)* hut, shack; *(de foire)* stall ■ **baraquement** *nm* shacks; *Mil* camp

baratin [baratɛ̃] *nm Fam (verbiage)* waffle; *(de séducteur)* sweet talk; *(de vendeur)* sales talk ■ **baratiner** *vt Fam* to chatter; *(sujet: séducteur)* *Br* to chat up, *Am* to hit on

barbare [barbar] **1** adj (cruel, sauvage) barbaric **2** nmf barbarian ■ **barbarie** nf (cruauté) barbarity

barbe [barb] nf beard; **b. à papa** Br candyfloss, Am cotton candy

barbecue [barbəkju] nm barbecue

barbelés [barbəle] nmpl barbed wire

barber [barbe] Fam **1** vt **b. qn** to bore sb stiff **2 se barber** vpr to be bored stiff

barbiche [barbiʃ] nf goatee

barbiturique [barbityrik] nm barbiturate

barboter [barbɔte] vi to splash about ■ **barboteuse** nf rompers

barbouiller [barbuje] vt (salir) to smear (**de** with)

barbu, -e [barby] **1** adj bearded **2** nm bearded man

barder¹ [barde] vt Culin to bard; Fig **bardé de décorations** covered with decorations

barder² [barde] v impersonnel Fam **ça va b.!** there's going to be trouble!

barème [barɛm] nm (de notes, de salaires, de prix) scale; (pour calculer) ready reckoner

baril [baril] nm (de pétrole, de vin) barrel; (de lessive) drum

bariolé, -e [barjɔle] adj multicoloured

barjo(t) [barʒo] adj inv Fam (fou) nutty

barman [barman] (pl **-men** [-men] ou **-mans**) nm Br barman, Am bartender

baromètre [barɔmɛtr] nm barometer

baron [barɔ̃] nm baron; Fig **b. de la finance** financial tycoon ■ **baronne** nf baroness

baroque [barɔk] **1** adj (édifice, style, musique) baroque **2** nm Archit & Mus **le b.** the baroque

baroudeur [barudœr] nm Fam (combattant) fighter; (voyageur) keen traveller

barque [bark] nf (small) boat ■ **barquette** nf (de fruit) punnet; (de plat cuisiné) container

barrage [baraʒ] nm (sur l'eau) dam; **b. de police** police roadblock; **b. routier** roadblock

barre [bar] nf (de fer, de bois) bar; (de danse) barre; (trait) line, stroke; Naut (volant) helm; **b. chocolatée** chocolate bar; Mus **b. de mesure** bar (line); Jur **b. des témoins** Br witness box, Am witness stand; **b. d'appui** (de fenêtre) rail; **b. d'espacement** (de clavier) space bar; Ordinat **b. d'outils** tool bar; Ordinat **b. de sélection** menu bar

barreau, -x [baro] nm (de fenêtre, de cage) bar; (d'échelle) rung; Jur **le b.** the bar; **être derrière les barreaux** (en prison) to be behind bars

barrer [bare] **1** vt (voie) to block off; (porte) to bar; (chèque) to cross; (mot) to cross out; Naut (bateau) to steer; **b. le passage** ou **la route à qn** to bar sb's way; 'route barrée' 'road closed' **2 se barrer** vpr Fam to beat it

barrette [barɛt] nf (pour cheveux) Br (hair)slide, Am barrette

barricade [barikad] nf barricade ■ **barricader 1** vt (rue, porte) to barricade **2 se barricader** vpr to barricade oneself (**dans** in)

barrière [barjɛr] nf (obstacle) barrier; (de passage à niveau) gate; (clôture) fence

barrique [barik] nf (large) barrel

barrir [barir] vi (éléphant) to trumpet

baryton [baritɔ̃] nm Mus baritone

BAS¹, BASSE¹ [bɑ, bɑs] **1** adj (dans l'espace, en quantité, en intensité) & Mus low; (origine) lowly; Péj (acte) mean, low; **à b. prix** cheaply; **enfant en b. âge** young child; **avoir la vue basse** to be short-sighted

2 adv (dans l'espace) low (down); (dans une hiérarchie) low; (parler) quietly; **plus b.** further or lower down; **voir plus b.** (sur document) see below; **en b.** at the bottom; **en b. de** at the bottom of; **à b. les dictateurs!** down with dictators!

3 nm (partie inférieure) bottom; **l'étagère du b.** the bottom shelf; **au b. de** at the bottom of; **de b. en haut** upwards

bas² [ba] *nm (chaussette)* stocking; *Fig* **b. de laine** *(économies)* nest egg

basané, -e [bazane] *adj (bronzé)* tanned

bas-côté [bakote] *(pl* **bas-côtés)** *nm (de route)* verge; *(d'église)* (side)aisle

bascule [baskyl] *nf (balançoire)* see-saw; *(balance)* weighing machine; **fauteuil à b.** rocking chair ■ **basculer** **1** *vt (chargement)* to tip over; *(benne)* to tip up **2** *vi (tomber)* to topple over; **faire b.** *(personne)* to knock over; *(chargement)* to tip over

base [baz] *nf (partie inférieure)* & *Chim, Math* & *Mil* base; *(de parti politique)* rank and file; *(principe)* basis; **avoir de bonnes bases en anglais** to have a good grounding in English; **de b.** basic; **salaire de b.** basic pay; *Ordinat* **b. de données** database ■ **baser 1** *vt* to base **(sur** on) **2 se baser** *vpr* **se b. sur qch** to base oneself on sth

bas-fond [bafɔ̃] *(pl* **bas-fonds)** *nm (de mer, de rivière)* shallow; *Péj* **les bas-fonds** *(de ville)* the rough areas

basic [bazik] *nm Ordinat* BASIC

basilic [bazilik] *nm (plante, aromate)* basil

basilique [bazilik] *nf* basilica

basket-ball [basketbol] *nm* basketball

baskets [basket] *nmpl ou nfpl (chaussures)* baseball boots

basque¹ [bask] **1** *adj* Basque **2** *nmf* B. Basque

basque² [bask] *nfpl (de veste)* tail; *Fig* **être toujours pendu aux basques de qn** to be always at sb's heels

basse² [bas] **1** *voir* **bas¹ 2** *nf Mus (contrebasse)* (double) bass; *(guitare)* bass (guitar)

basse-cour [baskur] *(pl* **basses-cours)** *nf Br* farmyard, *Am* barnyard

bassesse [bases] *nf (d'action)* lowness; *(action)* low act

bassin [basɛ̃] *nm* **(a)** *(pièce d'eau)* or-namental lake; *(de fontaine)* basin; *(récipient)* bowl, basin; **petit b.** *(de piscine)* children's pool; **grand b.** *(de piscine)* large pool **(b)** *(du corps)* pelvis

(c) *(région)* basin; **le b. parisien** the Paris Basin ■ **bassine** *nf* bowl

basson [basɔ̃] *nm (instrument)* bas-soon; *(musicien)* bassoonist

bastion [bastjɔ̃] *nm aussi Fig* bastion

bas-ventre [bavɑ̃tr] *nm* lower abdomen

bat [ba] *voir* **battre**

bataille [bataj] *nf (lutte)* battle; *(jeu de cartes)* ≃ beggar-my-neighbour ■ **batailleur, -euse** *adj* aggressive

bataillon [batajɔ̃] *nm Mil* battalion

bâtard, -e [batar, -ard] **1** *adj (enfant)* illegitimate; *(solution)* hybrid **2** *nmf (enfant)* illegitimate child; *Péj* bastard; *(chien)* mongrel; *(pain)* = small, thick baguette

bateau, -x [bato] **1** *nm (embarcation)* boat; *(grand)* ship; **faire du b.** to go boating; **b. à moteur** motorboat; **b. à voiles** *Br* sailing boat, *Am* sailboat; **b. de plaisance** pleasure boat **2** *adj inv Fam (sujet)* hackneyed; **col b.** boat neck ■ **bateau-mouche** *(pl* **bateaux-mouches)** *nm* river boat *(on the Seine)*

bâtiment [batimɑ̃] *nm (édifice)* building; *(navire)* vessel; **le b., l'industrie du b.** the building trade

bâtir [batir] *vt (construire)* to build; *Couture* to tack; **terrain à b.** building plot ■ **bâti, -e 1** *adj* **bien b.** *(personne)* well-built **2** *adj (charpente)* frame; *Couture* tacking ■ **bâtisse** *nf Péj* ugly building

bâton [batɔ̃] *nm (canne)* stick; *(de maréchal)* baton; *(d'agent de police) Br* truncheon, *Am* nightstick; *(trait)* vertical line; **donner des coups de b. à qn** to beat sb (with a stick); **b. de rouge** lipstick; **bâtons de ski** ski sticks ■ **bâtonnet** *nm* stick

battant¹ [batɑ̃] *nm* **(a)** *(de porte, de volet)* leaf; **porte à deux battants** double door **(b)** *(personne)* fighter

battant², -e [batɑ̃, -ɑ̃t] *adj* **pluie b.** driving rain; **porte b.** *Br* swing door, *Am* swinging door

battement [batmɑ̃] *nm* **(a)** *(de tambour)* beat(ing); *(de porte)* banging;

(de paupières) blink(ing); *(d'ailes)* flapping (**b**) *(délai)* gap

batterie [batri] *nf (d'orchestre)* drums; *(ensemble)* & *Mil, Él* battery; *(de questions)* series; **être à la b.** *(sujet: musicien)* to be on drums; **élevage en b.** battery farming; **b. de cuisine** kitchen utensils

batteur [batœr] *nm (musicien)* drummer; *(de cuisine)* mixer

battre* [batr] **1** *vt (frapper, vaincre)* to beat; *(œufs)* to whisk; *(beurre)* to churn; *(record)* to break; *(cartes)* to shuffle; *Mus* **b. la mesure** to beat time **2** *vi (cœur)* to beat; *(porte, volet)* to bang; **b. des mains** to clap one's hands; **b. des ailes** to flap its wings **3 se battre** *upr* to fight (**avec** with); **se b. au couteau** to fight with a knife

battu, -e¹ [baty] *adj (femme, enfant)* battered

battue² [baty] *nf (à la chasse)* beat; *(recherche)* search

baume [bom] *nm aussi Fig* balm

baux [bo] *voir* **bail**

bavard, -e [bavar, -ard] **1** *adj (qui parle beaucoup)* chatty **2** *nmf (qui parle beaucoup)* chatterbox ■ **bavardage** *nm (action)* chatting; *(commérage)* gossiping; **bavardages** *(paroles)* chats ■ **bavarder** *vi (parler)* to chat; *(commérer)* to gossip

bave [bav] *nf (de personne)* dribble; *(de chien)* slaver; *(de chien enragé)* froth ■ **baver** *vi (personne)* to dribble; *(chien)* to slaver; *(chien enragé)* to foam at the mouth; *(stylo)* to leak; *Fam* **en b.** to have a hard time of it

bavette [bavɛt] *nf (de bébé)* bib; *(de bœuf)* skirt (of beef)

baveux, -euse [bavø, -øz] *adj (omelette)* runny

bavoir [bavwar] *nm* bib

bavure [bavyr] *nf (tache)* smudge; *(erreur)* slip-up

bayer [baje] *vi* **b. aux corneilles** to stare into space

bazar [bazar] *nm (marché)* bazaar; *(magasin)* general store; *Fam (désordre)*

---

shambles *(sing)*; *Fam (affaires)* gear; *Fam* **mettre du b. dans qch** to make a shambles of sth

BCG [beseʒe] *nm Méd* BCG

BD [bede] *(abrév* **bande dessinée)** *nf* comic strip

bd *abrév* boulevard

béant, -e [beɑ̃, -ɑ̃t] *adj (gouffre)* yawning

béat, -e [bea, -at] *adj Hum (heureux)* blissful; *Péj (niais)* inane; **être b. d'admiration** to be open-mouthed in admiration ■ **béatement** *adv (sourire)* inanely

beau, belle [bo, bɛl] *(pl* **beaux, belles)**

bel is used before masculine singular nouns beginning with a vowel or h mute.

1 *adj* (**a**) *(femme, enfant, fleur, histoire)* beautiful; *(homme)* handsome, good-looking; *(spectacle, discours)* fine; *(maison, voyage, temps)* lovely; **une belle somme** a tidy sum; **se faire b.** to smarten oneself up; **c'est trop b. pour être vrai** it's too good to be true; **c'est le plus b. jour de ma vie!** it's the best day of my life!

(**b**) *(expressions)* **au b. milieu de** right in the middle of; **bel et bien** *(complètement)* well and truly

2 *adv* **il fait b.** the weather's nice; **j'ai b. crier...** it's no use (my) shouting...

3 *nm* **le b.** *(la beauté)* beauty

4 *nf* **belle** *(jeu, partie)* decider ■ **beau-fils** *(pl* **beaux-fils)** *nm (gendre)* son-in-law; *(après remariage)* stepson ■ **beau-frère** *(pl* **beaux-frères)** *nm* brother-in-law ■ **beau-père** *(pl* **beaux-pères)** *nm (père du conjoint)* father-in-law; *(après remariage)* stepfather ■ **beaux-arts** *nmpl* fine arts; **école des b., les B.** art school ■ **beaux-parents** *nmpl* parents-in-law

---

beaucoup [boku] *adv (intensément, en grande quantité)* a lot; **aimer b. qch** to like sth very much; **s'intéresser b. à qch** to be very interested in sth; **b.**

d'entre nous many of us; **b. de** *(quantité)* a lot of; *(nombre)* many, a lot of; **pas b. d'argent** not much money; **pas b. de gens** not many people; **j'en ai b.** *(quantité)* I have a lot; *(nombre)* I have lots; **b. plus/moins (que)** much more/less (than), a lot more/less (than); *(nombre)* many or a lot more/ a lot fewer (than)

beauté [bote] *nf (qualité, femme)* beauty

bébé [bebe] *nm* baby ■ **bébé-éprouvette** *(pl* **bébés-éprouvette)** *nm* test-tube baby

bec [bɛk] *nm (d'oiseau)* beak, bill; *(de pot)* lip; *(de flûte)* mouthpiece; *Fam (bouche)* mouth; *Fam* **clouer le b. à qn** to shut sb up; **b. verseur** spout ■ **bec-de-lièvre** *(pl* **becs-de-lièvre)** *nm* harelip

bêche [bɛʃ] *nf* spade ■ **bêcher** *vt* to dig

bedonnant, -e [bədɔnɑ̃, -ɑ̃t] *adj* pot-bellied, paunchy

bée [be] *adj f* **j'en suis resté bouche b.** I was speechless

beffroi [befrwa] *nm* belfry

bégayer [begeje] *vi* to stutter, to stammer

bègue [bɛg] **1** *adj* **être b.** to stutter, to stammer **2** *nmf* stutterer, stammerer

beige [bɛʒ] *adj & nm* beige

beignet [beɲɛ] *nm* fritter; *(au sucre, à la confiture)* doughnut

Beijing [beidʒiŋ] *nm ou f* Beijing

bel [bɛl] *voir* **beau**

bêler [bɛle] *vi* to bleat

belette [bəlɛt] *nf* weasel

Belgique [bɛlʒik] *nf* **la B.** Belgium ■ **belge 1** *adj* Belgian **2** *nmf* **B.** Belgian

bélier [belje] *nm (animal, machine)* ram; **le B.** *(signe)* Aries

belle [bɛl] *voir* **beau** ■ **belle-famille** *(pl* **belles-familles)** *nf* in-laws ■ **belle-fille** *(pl* **belles-filles)** *nf (épouse du fils)* daughter-in-law; *(après remariage)* stepdaughter ■ **belle-mère** *(pl* **belles-mères)** *nf (mère du conjoint)* mother-in-law; *(après remariage)* stepmother

■ **belle-sœur** *(pl* **belles-sœurs)** *nf* sister-in-law

belvédère [bɛlvedɛr] *nm (construction)* gazebo; *(sur site naturel)* viewpoint

bémol [bemɔl] *nm Mus* flat

bénédiction [benediksjɔ̃] *nf Rel & Fig* blessing

bénéfice [benefis] *nm (financier)* profit; *(avantage)* benefit; **accorder le b. du doute à qn** to give sb the benefit of the doubt

bénéficiaire [benefisjɛr] **1** *nmf (de chèque)* payee; *Jur* beneficiary **2** *adj (entreprise)* profit-making; *(compte)* in credit

bénéficier [benefisje] *vi* **b. de qch** *(profiter de)* to benefit from sth; *(avoir)* to have sth

bénéfique [benefik] *adj* beneficial (**à** to)

Bénélux [benelyks] *nm* **le B.** the Benelux

bénévolat [benevɔla] *nm* voluntary work

bénévole [benevɔl] **1** *adj (travail, infirmière)* voluntary **2** *nmf* volunteer, voluntary worker

bénin, -igne [benɛ̃, -iɲ] *adj (accident, opération)* minor; *(tumeur)* benign

bénir [benir] *vt* to bless; **que Dieu te bénisse!** God bless you! ■ **bénit, -e** *adj* **eau bénite** holy water

benne [bɛn] *nf (de camion)* tipping body; *(de téléphérique)* cable car; **b. à ordures** bin lorry

BEP [beəpe] *(abrév* **brevet d'études professionnelles)** *nm Scol* = vocational diploma taken at 18

BEPC [beəpese] *(abrév* **brevet d'études du premier cycle)** *nm Scol* = former school leaving certificate taken at 15

béquille [bekij] *nf (canne)* crutch; *(de moto)* stand

berceau, -x [bɛrso] *nm (de bébé)* cradle; *Fig (de civilisation)* birthplace

bercer [bɛrse] **1** *vt (bébé)* to rock **2 se bercer** *vpr* **se b. d'illusions** to delude oneself ■ **berceuse** *nf* lullaby

béret [bere] nm beret

berge [berʒ] nf (rive) bank

berger [berʒe] nm shepherd; **b. allemand** German shepherd, Br Alsatian ▪ **bergère** nf shepherdess

berline [berlin] nf (voiture) Br (fourdoor) saloon, Am sedan

berlingot [berlɛ̃go] nm (bonbon) Br boiled sweet, Am hard candy; (de lait) carton

bermuda [bermyda] nm Bermuda shorts

Bermudes [bermyd] nfpl les B. Bermuda

berner [berne] vt to fool

besogne [bəzɔɲ] nf job, task; Fig **aller vite en b.** to jump the gun

besoin [bəzwɛ̃] nm need; **avoir b. de qn/qch** to need sb/sth; **avoir b. de faire qch** to need to do sth; **au b., si b. est** if necessary, if need be

bestial, -e, -aux, -ales [bestjal, -o] adj bestial ▪ **bestiaux** nmpl livestock

bestiole [bestjɔl] nf (insecte) Br creepy-crawly, Am creepy-crawler

bétail [betaj] nm livestock

bête¹ [bɛt] adj stupid, silly

bête² [bɛt] nf animal; (insecte) bug; **b. féroce** wild animal; **b. noire** Br pet hate, Am pet peeve ▪ **bêtement** adv stupidly; **tout b.** quite simply ▪ **bêtise** nf (manque d'intelligence) stupidity; (action, parole) stupid thing; **faire une b.** to do something stupid; **dire des bêtises** to talk nonsense

béton [betɔ̃] nm (matériau) concrete; **mur en b.** concrete wall

bette [bɛt] nf Swiss chard

betterave [bɛtrav] nf (plante) Br beetroot, Am beet; **b. sucrière** sugar beet

beur [bœr] nmf = North African born in France of immigrant parents

beurre [bœr] nm butter ▪ **beurrer** vt to butter

bévue [bevy] nf slip-up

biais [bjɛ] nm (de mur) slant; (moyen) way; (aspect) angle; **regarder qn de b.** to look sideways at sb; **par le b. de** through

biaiser [bjeze] vi (ruser) to dodge the issue

bibelot [biblo] nm small ornament

biberon [bibrɔ̃] nm (feeding) bottle; **nourrir un bébé au b.** to bottle-feed a baby

bible [bibl] nf bible; **la B.** the Bible ▪ **biblique** adj biblical

bibliographie [bibljɔgrafi] nf bibliography

bibliothèque [bibljɔtɛk] nf (bâtiment, salle) library; (meuble) bookcase; **b. municipale** public library ▪ **bibliothécaire** nmf librarian

Bic® [bik] nm ballpoint, Br biro®

bicarbonate [bikarbɔnat] nm Chim bicarbonate; **b. de soude** bicarbonate of soda

biceps [bisɛps] nm biceps

biche [biʃ] nf (animal) doe, hind

bicolore [bikɔlɔr] adj two-coloured

bicyclette [bisiklɛt] nf bicycle; **faire de la b.** to go cycling

bidet [bidɛ] nm (cuvette) bidet

bidon [bidɔ̃] **1** nm (d'essence, d'huile) can; (de lait) churn; **b. d'essence** petrol can, jerry can **2** adj inv Fam (simulé) phoney, fake

bidonville [bidɔ̃vil] nf shantytown

bidule [bidyl] nm Fam (chose) whatsit; **B.** (personne) what's-his-name, f what's-her-name

BIEN [bjɛ̃] **1** adv (a) (convenablement) well; **il joue b.** he plays well; **je vais b.** I'm fine or well; **écoutez-moi b.!** listen carefully

(b) (moralement) right; **b. se conduire** to behave (well); **vous avez b. fait** you did the right thing; **tu ferais b. de te méfier** you would be wise to behave

(c) (très) very

(d) (beaucoup) a lot, a great deal; **b. plus/moins** much more/less; **b. des gens** a lot of people; **b. des fois** many times; **tu as b. de la chance** you're really lucky!; **merci b.!** thanks very much!

(e) (en intensif) **regarder qn b. en**

face to look sb right in the face; **je sais b.** I'm well aware of it; **je vous l'avais b. dit** I told you so!; **nous verrons b.** we'll see!; **c'est b. fait pour lui** it serves him right; **c'est b. ce que je pensais** that's what I thought **(f)** *(locutions)* **b. que...** (+ *subjunctive*) although, though; **b. entendu, b. sûr** of course; **b. sûr que non!** of course, not!; **b. sûr que je viendrai!** of course, I'll come!

2 *adj inv (satisfaisant)* good; *(à l'aise)* comfortable; *(en forme)* well; *(moral)* decent; *(beau)* attractive; **être b. avec qn** *(en bons termes)* to be on good terms with sb; **on est b. ici** it's nice here; **ce n'est pas b. de mentir** it's not nice to lie; **elle est b. sur cette photo** she looks good on this photo

3 *exclam* fine!, right!; **eh b.!** well!

4 *nm Phil & Rel* good; *(chose, capital)* possession; *Jur* asset; **le b. et le mal** good and evil; *Jur* **biens** property; **faire le b.** to do good; **ça te fera du b.** it will do you good; **dire du b. de qn** to speak well of sb; **c'est pour ton b.** it's for your own good; **biens de consommation** consumer goods; **biens immobiliers** real estate or property ■ **bien-aimé, -e** *(mpl* **bien-aimés,** *fpl* **bien-aimées)** *adj & nmf* beloved ■ **bien-être** *nm* well-being

bienfaisance [bjɛ̃fəzɑ̃s] *nf* œuvre de b. charity

bienfaisant, -e [bjɛ̃fəzɑ̃, -ɑ̃t] *adj (remède)* beneficial; *(personne)* charitable

bienfait [bjɛ̃fɛ] *nm (acte)* kindness; *(avantage)* benefit

bienfaiteur, -trice [bjɛ̃fɛtœr, -tris] *nmf* benefactor, *f* benefactress

bien-fondé [bjɛ̃fɔ̃de] *nm* validity

bienheureux, -euse [bjɛ̃nœrø, -øz] *adj* blissful; *Rel* blessed

bienséance [bjɛ̃seɑ̃s] *nf* propriety

bientôt [bjɛ̃to] *adv* soon; **à b.!** see you soon!

bienveillant, -e [bjɛ̃vɛjɑ̃, -ɑ̃t] *adj* kind ■ **bienveillance** *nf* kindness

bienvenu, -e¹ [bjɛ̃vny] **1** *adj (repos, explication)* welcome **2** *nmf* **soyez le b.!** welcome!

bienvenue² [bjɛ̃vny] *nf* welcome; **souhaiter la b. à qn** to welcome sb

bière¹ [bjɛr] *nf (boisson)* beer; **b. blonde** lager; **b. brune** *Br* brown ale, *Am* dark beer; **b. pression** *Br* draught beer, *Am* draft beer

bière² [bjɛr] *nf (cercueil)* coffin

biffer [bife] *vt* to cross out

bifteck [biftɛk] *nm* steak; **b. haché** *Br* mince, *Am* mincemeat

bifurquer [bifyrke] *vi (route, chemin)* to fork; *(automobiliste)* to turn off ■ **bifurcation** *nf* fork

bigamie [bigami] *nf* bigamy

bigarré, -e [bigare] *adj (étoffe)* multi-coloured; *(foule)* motley

bigorneau, -x [bigɔrno] *nm* winkle

bigoudi [bigudi] *nm* (hair) curler or roller

bijou, -x [biʒu] *nm* jewel; *Fig* gem ■ **bijouterie** *nf (boutique) Br* jeweller's shop, *Am* jewelry shop; *(commerce, fabrication)* jeweller's trade ■ **bijoutier, -ère** *nmf Br* jeweller, *Am* jeweler

bilan [bilɑ̃] *nm (de situation)* assessment; *(résultats)* results; *(d'un accident)* toll; *Com* **déposer son b.** to file for bankruptcy; *Fin* **b. (comptable)** balance sheet

bilatéral, -e, -aux, -ales [bilateral, -o] *adj* bilateral

bile [bil] *nf* bile

bilingue [bilɛ̃g] *adj* bilingual

billard [bijar] *nm (jeu)* billiards; *(table)* billiard table; **b. américain** pool; **b. électrique** pinball

bille [bij] *nf (de verre)* marble; *(de billard)* billiard ball

billet [bijɛ] *nm* ticket; **b. (de banque)** *Br* (bank)note, *Am* bill; **b. d'avion/de train** plane/train ticket; **b. de première/seconde** first-class/second-class ticket; **b. simple** single ticket, *Am* one-way ticket; **b. aller retour** return ticket, *Am* round trip ticket

billetterie [bijɛtri] *nf (lieu)* ticket

office; **b. automatique** *(de billet de transport)* ticket machine

billion [biljɔ̃] *nm* trillion

bimensuel, -elle [bimɑ̃sɥɛl] *adj* bi-monthly, *Br* fortnightly

bimoteur [bimɔtœr] *adj* twin-engined

binaire [biner] *adj Math* binary

biner [bine] *vt* to hoe

binocle [binɔkl] *nm* pince-nez

biochimie [bjɔʃimi] *nf* biochemistry

biodégradable [bjɔdegradabl] *adj* biodegradable

biodiversité [bjɔdiversite] *nf* biodiversity

biographie [bjɔgrafi] *nf* biography ■ **biographique** *adj* biographical

bio-industrie [bjɔɛ̃dystri] *(pl* **bio-industries)** *nf* biotechnology industry

biologie [bjɔlɔʒi] *nf* biology ■ **biologique** *adj* biological; *(sans engrais chimiques)* organic ■ **biologiste** *nmf* biologist

biotechnologie [bjɔtɛknɔlɔʒi] *nf* biotechnology

bip [bip] *nm (son)* beep; *(appareil)* beeper

bipède [biped] *nm* biped

Birmanie [birmani] *nf* **la B.** Burma ■ **birman, -e 1** *adj* Burmese **2** *nmf* **B., Birmane** Burmese

bis¹ [bis] *adv (au théâtre)* encore; *(en musique)* repeat; **4 bis** *(adresse)* ≃ 4A

bis², bise¹ [bi, biz] *adj Br* greyish-brown, *Am* grayish-brown

biscornu, -e [biskɔrny] *adj (objet)* oddly shaped; *Fam (idée)* cranky

biscotte [biskɔt] *nf* rusk

biscuit [biskɥi] *nm Br* biscuit, *Am* cookie

bise² [biz] *nf (vent)* north wind

bise³ [biz] *nf Fam (baiser)* kiss; **faire la b. à qn** to kiss sb on both cheeks

bisexuel, -elle [bisɛksɥɛl] *adj* bisexual

bison [bizɔ̃] *nm* bison

bisou [bizu] *nm Fam* kiss

bissextile [bisɛkstil] *adj f* **année b.** leap year

bistro(t) [bistro] *nm Fam* bar

bitume [bitym] *nm (revêtement)* asphalt

bizarre [bizar] *adj* odd

blafard, -e [blafar, -ard] *adj* pallid

blague [blag] *nf (plaisanterie)* joke; **faire une b. à qn** to play a joke on sb ■ **blaguer** [blage] *vi Fam* to joke ■ **blagueur, -euse** *nmf Fam* joker

blaireau, -x [blero] *nm (animal)* badger; *(brosse)* shaving brush

blâme [blɑm] *nm (reproche)* blame; *(sanction)* reprimand ■ **blâmer** *vt (désapprouver)* to blame; *(sanctionner)* to reprimand

blanc, blanche [blɑ̃, blɑ̃ʃ] **1** *adj* white; *(peau)* pale; *(page)* blank **2** *nm (couleur)* white; *(espace)* blank; *(vin)* white wine; **(article de) b.** *(linge)* linen; **en b.** *(chèque)* blank; **tirer à b.** to fire blanks; **b. d'œuf** egg white; **b. de poulet** chicken breast **3** *nf (note de musique) Br* minim, *Am* half-note **4** *nmf* **B.** *(personne)* White man, *f* White woman; **les B.** the Whites ■ **blanchâtre** *adj* whitish ■ **blancheur** *nf* whiteness

blanchiment [blɑ̃ʃimɑ̃] *nm (d'argent)* laundering

blanchir [blɑ̃ʃir] **1** *vt* to whiten; *(mur)* to whitewash; *(linge)* to launder; *Culin* to blanch; *Fig (argent)* to launder; **b. qn** *(disculper)* to clear sb **2** *vi* to turn white ■ **blanchisserie** *nf (lieu)* laundry ■ **blanchisseur, -euse** *nmf* laundryman, *f* laundrywoman

blanquette [blɑ̃kɛt] *nf* **b. de veau** = blanquette of veal; **b. de Limoux** = sparkling white wine from Limoux

blasé, -e [blaze] *adj* blasé

blason [blazɔ̃] *nm* coat of arms

blasphème [blasfɛm] *nm* blasphemy ■ **blasphémer** *vti* to blaspheme

blatte [blat] *nf* cockroach

blazer [blazœr] *nm* blazer

bld *(abrév* **boulevard)** Blvd

blé [ble] *nm* wheat, *Br* corn

blême [blɛm] *adj* sickly pale; **b. de colère** livid ■ **blêmir** *vi* to turn pale

blesser [blese] **1** vt (dans un accident) to injure, to hurt; (par arme) to wound; (offenser) to hurt

2 se blesser vpr (par accident) to hurt or injure oneself; (avec une arme) to wound oneself; **se b. au bras** to hurt one's arm ■ **blessant, -e** adj hurtful ■ **blessé, -e** nmf (victime d'accident) injured person; (victime d'agression) wounded person; **les blessés** the injured/wounded ■ **blessure** nf (dans un accident) injury; (par arme) wound

blette [blɛt] nf = **bette**

bleu, -e [blø] (mpl **-s**) **1** adj blue; (steak) very rare **2** n (couleur) blue; (ecchymose) bruise; (fromage) blue cheese; Fam (novice) novice; **b. de travail** Br overalls, Am overall; **b. ciel** sky blue; **b. marine** navy blue; **b. roi** royal blue

bleuet [bløɛ] nm (plante) cornflower

blinder [blɛ̃de] vt (véhicule) to armourplate ■ **blindé, -e 1** adj Mil armoured, armour-plated; (voiture) bulletproof **2** nm Mil armoured vehicle

bloc [blɔk] nm (de pierre, de bois) block; (de papier) pad; (de maison) & Pol bloc; **en b.** (démissionner) all together; **à b.** (visser, serrer) as tightly as possible; **b. opératoire** operating theatre ■ **bloc-notes** (pl **blocs-notes**) nm notepad

blocage [blɔkaʒ] nm (de mécanisme) jamming; (de freins, de roues) locking

blocus [blɔkys] nm blockade; **lever le b.** to raise the blockade

blond, -e [blɔ̃, -ɔ̃d] **1** adj (cheveux, personne) blond; (sable) golden **2** nm (homme) fair-haired or blond man; (couleur) blond; **b. cendré** ash blond; **b. vénitien** strawberry blond **3** nf (femme) fair-haired woman, blonde ■ **blondeur** nf fairness, blondness

bloquer [blɔke] vt (route, ballon, compte) to block; (porte, mécanisme) to jam; (roue) to lock; (salaires, prix, crédits) to freeze; (grouper) to group together; **b. le passage à qn** to block sb's way; **bloqué par la neige** snowbound

2 se bloquer vpr (machine) to get stuck

blottir [blɔtir] **se blottir** vpr to snuggle up; **se b. contre qn** to snuggle up to sb

blouse [bluz] nf (tablier) overall; (corsage) blouse; **b. blanche** (de médecin, de biologiste) white coat ■ **blouson** nm short jacket; **b. en cuir** leather jacket; **b. d'aviateur** bomber jacket

bluff [blœf] nm bluff ■ **bluffer** vi (aux cartes) & Fam to bluff

boa [bɔa] nm (serpent, tour de cou) boa

bobard [bɔbar] nm Fam tall story

bobine [bɔbin] nf (de ruban, de fil) reel; (de machine à coudre) bobbin; (de film, de papier) roll; (de machine à écrire) spool; Él coil

bocal, -aux [bɔkal, -o] nm jar; (aquarium) bowl

bœuf [bœf] (pl **bœufs** [bø]) nm (animal) bullock; (de trait) ox (pl oxen); (viande) beef

bogue [bɔg] nm Ordinat bug

bohème [bɔɛm] adj & nmf bohemian ■ **bohémien, -enne** adj & nmf gypsy

boire* [bwar] **1** vt (sujet: personne) to drink; (sujet: plante) to soak up

2 vi (sujet: personne) to drink; (sujet: plante) to soak in; Fam **b. un coup** to have a drink

3 se boire vpr to be drunk

4 nm **le b. et le manger** food and drink

bois [bwa] nm (matériau, forêt) wood; (de raquette) frame; **en** ou **de b.** wooden; **les b.** (d'un cerf) the antlers; (d'un orchestre) woodwind instruments; **b. de chauffage** firewood; **b. de construction** timber ■ **boisé, -e** adj wooded ■ **boiseries** nfpl Br panelling, Am paneling

boisson [bwasɔ̃] nf drink

boit [bwa] voir **boire**

boîte [bwat] nf (a) (récipient) box; **b. d'allumettes** (pleine) box of matches; (vide) matchbox; **des haricots en b.** canned or Br tinned beans; **b. à bijoux** jewel box; **b. à gants** glove compartment; **b. à** ou **aux lettres** Br postbox, *Am* mailbox; **b. de conserve** can, *Br* tin; *Aut* **b. de vitesses** gearbox; **b. postale** Post Office Box; **b. vocale** voice mail (**b**) *Fam (entreprise)* firm; **b. de nuit** nightclub ■ **boîtier** *nm (de montre)* case

boiter [bwate] *vi* to limp ■ **boiteux, -euse** *adj (personne)* lame; *Fig (raisonnement)* shaky

boive [bwav] *subjonctif de* **boire**

bol [bɔl] *nm (récipient, contenu)* bowl

bolide [bɔlid] *nm (voiture)* racing car

Bolivie [bɔlivi] *nf* **la B.** Bolivia ■ **bolivien, -enne 1** *adj* Bolivian **2** *nmf* **B., Bolivienne** Bolivian

bombardement [bɔ̃bardəmɑ̃] *nm (avec des bombes)* bombing; *(avec des obus)* shelling

bombarder [bɔ̃barde] *vt (avec des bombes)* to bomb; *(avec des obus)* to shell; **b. qn de questions** to bombard sb with questions ■ **bombardier** *nm (avion)* bomber

bombe [bɔ̃b] *nf* (**a**) *(explosif)* bomb; *Fig* **faire l'effet d'une b.** to be a bombshell (**b**) *(atomiseur)* spray (can) (**c**) *(chapeau)* riding hat

bomber [bɔ̃be] **1** *vt* **b. le torse** to throw out one's chest **2** *vi (mur)* to bulge; *(planche)* to warp

BON¹, BONNE¹ [bɔ̃, bɔn] **1** *adj* (**a**) *(satisfaisant)* good; **c'est b.** *(d'accord)* that's fine

(**b**) *(agréable)* nice, good; **passer une bonne soirée** to spend a pleasant evening; **b. anniversaire!** happy birthday!; **bonne année!** Happy New Year!

(**c**) *(charitable)* kind, good *(avec qn* to sb)

(**d**) *(correct)* right

(**e**) *(apte)* fit; **b. à manger** fit to eat; **elle n'est bonne à rien** she's useless

(**f**) *(prudent)* wise, good; **juger b. de partir** to think it wise to leave

(**g**) *(compétent)* good; **b. en français** good at French

(**h**) *(profitable) (investissement, conseil,*

idée) good; **c'est b. à savoir** it's worth knowing

(**i**) *(valable)* valid

(**j**) *(en intensif)* **un b. rhume** a bad cold; **dix bonnes minutes** ten good minutes; **j'ai mis un b. moment à comprendre** it took me a while to understand

(**k**) *(locutions)* **à quoi b.?** what's the point?; **quand b. vous semble** whenever you like; **pour de b.** *(partir, revenir)* for good; **tenir b.** *(personne)* to hold out; **elle est bien bonne!** that's a good one!

2 *nm* **avoir du b.** to have some good points; **un b. à rien** good-for-nothing; **les bons et les méchants** the goodies and the baddies

3 *adv* **sentir b.** to smell good; **il fait b.** it's nice and warm

4 *exclam* **b.! on y va?** right, shall we go?; **ah b., je ne le savais pas** really? I didn't know; **ah b.?** is that so?

bon² [bɔ̃] *nm (papier)* coupon, *Br* voucher; *Fin (titre)* bond; **b. d'achat** gift voucher; **b. de réduction** money-off coupon

bonbon [bɔ̃bɔ̃] *nm Br* sweet, *Am* candy

bonbonne [bɔ̃bɔn] *nf (bouteille)* demijohn; *(de gaz)* cylinder

bond [bɔ̃] *nm* leap, jump; *(de balle)* bounce; **faire un b.** to leap up; **se lever d'un b.** *(du lit)* to jump out of bed; *(d'une chaise)* to leap up; **faire faux b. à qn** to leave sb in the lurch

bonde [bɔ̃d] *nf (bouchon)* plug; *(trou)* plughole

bondé, -e [bɔ̃de] *adj* packed, crammed

bondir [bɔ̃dir] *vi* to leap, to jump; **b. sur qn/qch** to pounce on sb/sth

bonheur [bɔnœr] *nm (bien-être)* happiness; *(chance)* good fortune; **porter b. à qn** to bring sb luck; **par b.** luckily

bonhomie [bɔnɔmi] *nf* good-naturedness

bonhomme [bɔnɔm] *(pl* **bonshommes** [bɔ̃zɔm]*) nm* fellow, guy; **b. de neige** snowman

bonjour [bɔ̃ʒur] *nm & exclam (le matin)* hello, good morning; *(l'après-midi)* hello, good afternoon

bonne¹ [bɔn] *voir* **bon¹**

bonne² [bɔn] *nf (domestique)* maid; **b. d'enfants** nanny

bonnement [bɔnmɑ̃] *adv* **tout b.** simply

bonnet [bɔnɛ] *nm (coiffure)* hat; *(de soutien-gorge)* cup; *Fam* **gros b.** bigshot; *(de bain)* bathing cap ▪ **bonneterie** *nf (bas)* hosiery

bonniche [bɔniʃ] *nf* = **boniche**

bonsoir [bɔ̃swar] *nm & exclam (en rencontrant quelqu'un)* hello, good evening; *(en partant)* goodbye; *(au coucher)* goodnight

bonté [bɔ̃te] *nf* kindness, goodness

bonus [bɔnys] *nm (de salaire)* bonus; *(d'assurance)* no-claims bonus

bord [bɔr] *nm (limite)* edge; *(de chapeau)* brim; *(de verre)* rim; **le b. du trottoir** *Br* the kerb, *Am* the curb; **au b. de la route** at the side of the road; **au b. de la rivière** beside the river; **au b. de la mer** at the seaside; **au b. des larmes** on the verge of tears; **à b. d'un bateau/d'un avion** on board a boat/a plane; **monter à b.** to go on board; **par-dessus b.** overboard

bordeaux [bɔrdo] **1** *nm (vin)* Bordeaux (wine); *(rouge)* claret **2** *adj inv* burgundy

bordée [bɔrde] *nf Naut (salve)* broadside; *Fig (d'injures)* torrent

border [bɔrde] *vt (lit)* to tuck in; *(sujet: arbres)* to line

bordereau, -x [bɔrdəro] *nm Fin & Com* note

bordure [bɔrdyr] *nf (bord)* edge; *(de vêtement)* border; **en b. de route** by the roadside

borgne [bɔrɲ] *adj (personne)* one-eyed

borne [bɔrn] *nf (limite)* boundary marker; *(pierre)* boundary stone; *Él* terminal; *Fam (kilomètre)* kilometer; *Fig* **sans bornes** boundless; *Fig* **dépasser les bornes** to go too far

borné, -e [bɔrne] *adj (personne)* narrow-minded; *(esprit)* narrow

borner [bɔrne] **1** *vt (terrain)* to mark out **2 se borner** *vpr* **se b. à qch/à faire qch** *(personne)* to restrict oneself to sth/to doing sth; **se b. à qch** *(chose)* to be limited to sth

Bosnie [bɔzni] *nf* **la B.** Bosnia

bosquet [bɔskɛ] *nm* grove

bosse [bɔs] *nf (de bossu, de chameau)* hump; *(enflure)* bump, lump; *(de terrain)* bump

bosseler [bɔsle] *vt (déformer)* to dent

bosser [bɔse] *vi Fam* to work

bosseur, -euse [bɔsœr, -øz] *nmf Fam* hard-worker

bossu, -e [bɔsy] **1** *adj (personne)* hunchbacked **2** *nmf* hunchback

botanique [bɔtanik] **1** *adj* botanical **2** *nf* botany

botte [bɔt] *nf (chaussure)* boot; *(de fleurs, de radis)* bunch; **bottes en caoutchouc** rubber boots ▪ **botter** *vt* **botté de cuir** wearing leather boots; *Fam* **b. le derrière à qn** to boot sb up the backside ▪ **bottillon** *nm,* **bottine** *nf* ankle boot

Bottin® [bɔtɛ̃] *nm* phone book

bouc [buk] *nm (animal)* billy goat; *(barbe)* goatee; **b. émissaire** scapegoat

boucan [bukɑ̃] *nm Fam* din, row; **faire du b.** to kick up a row

bouche [buʃ] *nf* mouth; **de b. à oreille** by word of mouth; **b. d'égout** manhole; **b. d'incendie** *Br* fire hydrant, *Am* fireplug ▪ **bouchée** *nf* mouthful ▪ **bouche-à-bouche** *nm* mouth-to-mouth resuscitation

boucher¹ [buʃe] **1** *vt (fente, trou)* to fill in; *(conduite, fenêtre)* to block up; *(vue, rue, artère)* to block; *(bouteille)* to cork **2 se boucher** *vpr (conduite)* to get blocked up; **se b. le nez** to hold one's nose ▪ **bouché, -e** *adj (conduite)* blocked; *Fam (personne)* dense; **j'ai le nez b.** my nose is stuffed up ▪ **bouche-trou** *(pl* **bouche-trous)** *nm Fam* stopgap

boucher², -ère [buʃe, -ɛr] *nmf* butcher ■ **boucherie** *nf* butcher's (shop); *Fig (carnage)* butchery

bouchon [buʃɔ̃] *nm* (**a**) *(à vis)* cap, top; *(de tonneau)* stopper; *(de liège)* cork; *(de canne à pêche)* float (**b**) *(embouteillage)* traffic jam ■ **bouchonner** *vt Fam* **ça bouchonne** *(sur la route)* there's congestion

boucle [bukl] *nf (de ceinture)* buckle; *(de cheveu)* curl; *(méandre)* loop; **b. d'oreille** earring

boucler [bukle] **1** *vt (ceinture, valise)* to buckle; *(quartier)* to seal off; **b. ses valises** *(se préparer à partir)* to pack one's bags **2** *vi (cheveux)* to be curly ■ **bouclé, -e** *adj (cheveux)* curly

bouclier [buklije] *nm* shield

bouddhiste [budist] *adj & nmf* Buddhist

bouder [bude] **1** *vi* to sulk **2** *vt (personne)* to refuse to talk to; **b. une élection** to refuse to vote ■ **boudeur, -euse** *adj* sulky

boudin [budɛ̃] *nm* **b. noir** *Br* black pudding, *Am* blood sausage; **b. blanc** white pudding

boue [bu] *nf* mud ■ **boueux, -euse** *adj* muddy

bouée [bwe] *nf Naut* buoy; **b. de sauvetage** lifebelt; **b. (gonflable)** *(d'enfant)* (inflatable) rubber ring

bouffe [buf] *nf Fam (nourriture)* grub

bouffée [bufe] *nf (de fumée)* puff; *(de parfum)* whiff; *Fig (de colère)* outburst; *Méd* **b. de chaleur** *Br* hot flush, *Am* hot flash

bouffer¹ [bufe] *vti Fam (manger)* to eat

bouffer² [bufe] *vi (manche, jupe)* to puff out ■ **bouffi, -e** *adj (yeux, visage)* puffy

bouffon, -onne [bufɔ̃, -ɔn] **1** *adj* farcical **2** *nm* buffoon ■ **bouffonneries** *nfpl (actes)* antics

bougeoir [buʒwar] *nm* candlestick

bougeotte [buʒɔt] *nf Fam* **avoir la b.** to be fidgety

bouger [buʒe] **1** *vti* to move; **rester sans b.** to keep still **2 se bouger** *vpr*

Fam (se déplacer) to move; *(s'activer)* to get a move on

bougie [buʒi] *nf (en cire)* candle; *(de moteur)* spark plug

bougonner [bugɔne] *vi Fam* to grumble

bouillabaisse [bujabɛs] *nf* bouillabaisse, = Provençal fish soup

bouilli, -e¹ [buji] *adj* boiled

bouillie² [buji] *nf (pour bébé)* baby food; *(à base de céréales)* baby cereal

bouillir* [bujir] *vi* to boil; **faire b. qch** to boil sth; **b. de colère** to be seething (with anger) ■ **bouillant, -e** *adj (qui bout)* boiling; *(très chaud)* boiling hot

bouilloire [bujwar] *nf* kettle

bouillon [bujɔ̃] *nm (aliment)* stock; *(bulles)* bubbles ■ **bouillonner** *vi* to bubble

bouillotte [bujɔt] *nf* hot-water bottle

boulanger, -ère [bulɑ̃ʒe, -ɛr] *nmf* baker ■ **boulangerie** *nf* baker's (shop)

boule [bul] *nf (sphère)* ball; **boules** *(jeu)* bowls; **b. de neige** snowball; *Fig* **faire b. de neige** to snowball; **boules Quiès®** earplugs

bouledogue [buldɔg] *nm* bulldog

boulet [bulɛ] *nm (de forçat)* ball and chain; **b. de canon** cannonball

boulette [bulɛt] *nf (de papier)* ball; *(de viande)* meatball

boulevard [bulvar] *nm* boulevard

bouleverser [bulvɛrse] *vt (émouvoir)* to move deeply; *(perturber)* to distress; *(projets, habitudes)* to disrupt; *(vie)* to turn upside down ■ **bouleversant, -e** *adj (émouvant)* deeply moving, *(perturbant)* deeply moving ■ **bouleversement** *nm (de la vie)*

boulimie [bulimi] *nf Méd* bulimia ■ **boulimique** *adj* **être b.** to have bulimia

boulon [bulɔ̃] *nm* bolt

boulot¹ [bulo] *nm Fam (emploi)* job; *(travail)* work

boulot², -otte [bulo, -ɔt] *adj Fam* tubby

bouquet [bukɛ] *nm (fleurs)* bunch of flowers; *(d'arbres)* clump; *(de vin)* bouquet; *Fig* **c'est le b.!** that takes the *Br* biscuit *or Am* cake!

bouquin [bukɛ̃] *nm Fam* book ■ **bouquiner** *vti Fam* to read ■ **bouquiniste** *nmf* second-hand bookseller

bourbier [burbje] *nm (lieu, situation)* quagmire

bourde [burd] *nf Fam (gaffe)* blunder; **faire une b.** to put one's foot in it

bourdon [burdɔ̃] *nm (insecte)* bumblebee ■ **bourdonnement** *nm (d'insecte)* buzz(ing) ■ **bourdonner** *vi (insecte, oreilles)* to buzz

bourg [bur] *nm* market town ■ **bourgade** *nf* village

bourgeois, -e [burʒwa, -waz] **1** *adj* middle-class **2** *nmf* middle-class person ■ **bourgeoisie** *nf* middle class

bourgeon [burʒɔ̃] *nm* bud ■ **bourgeonner** *vi* to bud

bourgogne [burgɔɲ] *nm (vin)* Burgundy

bourrage [buraʒ] *nm Fam* **b. de crâne** brainwashing

bourrasque [burask] *nf* squall, gust of wind

bourratif, -ive [buratif, -iv] *adj Fam* stodgy

bourre [bur] *nf (pour rembourrer)* stuffing

bourreau, -x [buro] *nm* executioner; **b. de travail** workaholic

bourrelet [burlɛ] *nm (contre les courants d'air)* weather strip; **b. de graisse** spare *Br* tyre *or Am* tire

bourrer [bure] **1** *vt (coussin)* to stuff (**de** with); *(sac)* to cram (**de** with); *(pipe)* to fill; **b. qn de qch** *(gaver)* to fill sb up with sth **2 se bourrer** *vpr* **se b. de qch** *(se gaver)* to stuff oneself up with ■ **bourré, -e** *adj* (a) *(plein)* **b. à craquer** full to bursting (b) *Fam (ivre)* plastered

bourrique [burik] *nf* she-ass; *Fam* **faire tourner qn en b.** to drive sb crazy

bourru, -e [bury] *adj* surly

bourse [burs] *nf (sac)* purse; *Scol & Univ* **b. (d'étude)** grant; **la B.** the Stock Exchange ■ **boursier, -ère 1** *adj* opération boursière Stock Exchange transaction **2** *nmf (élève, étudiant)* grant holder

boursouflé, -e [bursufle] *adj (visage, yeux)* puffy

bous [bu] *voir* **bouillir**

bousculer [buskyle] **1** *vt (pousser)* to jostle; *(presser)* to rush; *Fig (habitudes)* to disrupt **2 se bousculer** *(foule)* to push and shove ■ **bousculade** *nf (agitation)* pushing and shoving

bousiller [buzije] *vt Fam* to wreck

boussole [busɔl] *nf* compass

bout¹ [bu] *voir* **bouillir**

bout² [bu] *nm (extrémité)* end; *(de langue, de doigt)* tip; *(morceau)* bit; **faire un b. de chemin** to go part of the way; **d'un b. à l'autre** from one end to the other; **au b. de la rue** at the end of the street; **au b. d'un moment** after a while; *Fam* **au b. du fil** *(au téléphone)* on the other end; **jusqu'au b.** *(lire, rester)* (right) to the end; **à b. de forces** exhausted; **à b. de souffle** out of breath; **pousser qn à b.** to push sb too far

boutade [butad] *nf (plaisanterie)* quip

boute-en-train [butɑ̃trɛ̃] *nm inv (personne)* live wire

bouteille [butɛj] *nf* bottle; *(de gaz)* cylinder

boutique [butik] *nf Br* shop, *Am* store; *(de couturier)* boutique; **fermer b.** to shut up shop ■ **boutiquier, -ère** *nmf Br* shopkeeper, *Am* storekeeper

bouton [butɔ̃] *nm (bourgeon)* bud; *(au visage)* spot; *(de vêtement)* button; *(de porte, de télévision)* knob; **b. de manchette** cufflink ■ **bouton-d'or** *(pl* **boutons-d'or)** *nm* buttercup ■ **boutonner** *vt,* **se boutonner** *vpr (vêtement)* to button (up) ■ **boutonnière** *nf* buttonhole

bouture [butyr] *nf* cutting

bovins [bɔvɛ̃] *nmpl* cattle

bowling [boliŋ] *nm (jeu) Br* tenpin bowling, *Am* tenpins; *(lieu)* bowling alley

box [bɔks] *(pl* **boxes)** *nm (d'écurie)* stall;

(de dortoir) cubicle; *(garage)* lock-up garage; *Jur* **b. des accusés** dock

boxe [bɔks] *nf* boxing ■ **boxer** *vi* to box ■ **boxeur** *nm* boxer

boyau, -x [bwajo] *nm (intestin)* gut; *(corde)* catgut; *(de vélo)* tubular *Br* tyre *or Am* tire; *(de mine)* narrow gallery

boycotter [bɔjkɔte] *vt* to boycott ■ **boycottage** *nm* boycott

BP [bepe] *(abrév* **boîte postale)** *nf* PO Box

bracelet [braslɛ] *nm (bijou)* bracelet; *(rigide)* bangle; *(de montre) Br* strap, *Am* band ■ **bracelet-montre** *(pl* **bracelets-montres)** *nm* wristwatch

braconner [brakɔne] *vi* to poach ■ **braconnier** *nm* poacher

brader [brade] *vt* to sell off cheaply ■ **braderie** *nf* clearance sale

braguette [bragɛt] *nf (de pantalon)* fly, *Br* flies

braille [braj] *nm* Braille; **en b.** in Braille

brailler [braje] *vti* to yell

braire* [brɛr] *vi (âne)* to bray

braises [brɛz] *nfpl* embers ■ **braiser** *vt Culin* to braise

brancard [brɑ̃kar] *nm (civière)* stretcher; *(de charrette)* shaft

branche [brɑ̃ʃ] *nf (d'arbre, de science)* branch; *(de lunettes)* side piece ■ **branchages** *nmpl (des arbres)* branches; *(coupés)* cut branches

brancher [brɑ̃ʃe] **1** *vt (à une prise)* to plug in; *(à un réseau)* to connect **2 se brancher** *vpr* **se b. sur** *(station de radio)* to tune in to ■ **branchement** *nm (fils)* connection

brandir [brɑ̃dir] *vt* to brandish

branle [brɑ̃l] *nm* **mettre qch en b.** *(mécanisme, procédure)* to set sth in motion ■ **branlant, -e** *adj (chaise, escalier)* rickety ■ **branler** *vi (chaise, escalier)* to be rickety

braquer [brake] **1** *vt (diriger)* to point *(* **sur** at); *(regard)* to fix *(* **sur** on); *Fam (banque)* to hold up; **b. qn contre qn/qch** to turn sb against sb/sth **2** *vi Aut* to turn the steering wheel

braquet [brakɛ] *nm* gear ratio

bras [bra] *nm* arm; **b. dessus b. dessous** arm in arm; **les b. croisés** with one's arms folded; *Fig* **b. droit** *(assistant)* right-hand man

brasier [brazje] *nm* blaze, inferno

brassard [brasar] *nm* armband

brasse [bras] *nf (nage)* breaststroke; *(mouvement)* stroke; **b. papillon** butterfly stroke

brassée [brase] *nf* armful

brasser [brase] *vt (mélanger)* to mix; *(bière)* to brew ■ **brassage** *nm (mélange)* mixing; *(de la bière)* brewing

brasserie [brasri] *nf (usine)* brewery; *(café)* brasserie

brassière [brasjɛr] *nf (de bébé) Br* vest, *Am* undershirt

bravade [bravad] *nf* bravado

brave [brav] **1** *adj (courageux)* brave; *(bon)* good **2** *nm (héros)* brave man

braver [brave] *vt (personne)* to defy; *(danger)* to brave

bravo [bravo] *exclam* bravo!

bravoure [bravur] *nf* bravery

break [brɛk] *nm (voiture) Br* estate car, *Am* station wagon

brebis [brəbi] *nf* ewe; *Fig* **b. galeuse** black sheep

brèche [brɛʃ] *nf* gap; *(dans la coque d'un bateau)* hole

bréchet [breʃɛ] *nm* breastbone

bredouille [brəduj] *adj* empty-handed

bredouiller [brəduje] *vti* to mumble

bref, brève [brɛf, brɛv] **1** *adj* brief, short **2** *adv* in short; **enfin b....** in a word...

Brésil [brezil] *nm* **le B.** Brazil ■ **brésilien, -enne 1** *adj* Brazilian **2** *nmf* **B., Brésilienne** Brazilian

Bretagne [brətaɲ] *nf* **la B.** Brittany ■ **breton, -onne 1** *adj* Breton **2** *nmf* **B., Bretonne** Breton

bretelle [brətɛl] *nf* strap; **bretelles** *(de pantalon) Br* braces, *Am* suspenders; **b. (d'accès)** *(route)* access road

breuvage [brœvaʒ] *nm* potion

brève [brɛv] *voir* **bref**

brevet [brəvɛ] nm (certificat) certificate; (diplôme) diploma; Scol **b. des collèges** = exam taken at 14; **b. de technicien supérieur** = advanced vocational training certificate; **b. (d'invention)** patent ■ **breveter** vt to patent

bric-à-brac [brikabrak] nm inv (vieux objets) odds and ends

bricole [brikɔl] nf (objet, futilité) trifle

bricoler [brikɔle] **1** vt (construire) to put together; (réparer) to fix **2** vi to do-it-yourself ■ **bricolage** nm (travail) DIY, do-it-yourself; **faire du b.** to do some DIY ■ **bricoleur, -euse 1** adj **être b.** to be good with one's hands **2** nmf handyman, f handywoman

bride [brid] nf (de cheval) bridle ■ **brider** vt (cheval) to bridle; (personne, désir) to curb; **avoir les yeux bridés** to have slanting eyes

bridge [bridʒ] nm (jeu, prothèse) bridge

brièvement [brievmɑ̃] adv briefly ■ **brièveté** nf brevity

brigade [brigad] nf (de gendarmerie) squad; Mil brigade ■ **brigadier** nm (de police) police sergeant; Mil corporal

brigand [brigɑ̃] nm (bandit) brigand

briguer [brige] vt (honneur, poste) to sollicit

brillant, -e [brijɑ̃, -ɑ̃t] **1** adj (luisant) shining; (couleur) bright; (cheveux, cuir) shiny; Fig (remarquable) brilliant **2** nm (éclat) shine; (diamant) diamond; **b. à lèvres** lip gloss ■ **brillamment** [-amɑ̃] adv brilliantly

briller [brije] vi to shine; **faire b. qch** to polish sth

brimer [brime] vt to bully ■ **brimades** nfpl (vexations) bullying

brin [brɛ̃] nm (d'herbe) blade; (de muguet) spray; (de fil) strand; Fig **un b. de qch** a bit of sth; **faire un b. de toilette** to have a quick wash

brindille [brɛ̃dij] nf twig

bringue¹ [brɛ̃g] nf Fam **faire la b.** to go on a binge

bringue² [brɛ̃g] nf Fam **grande b.** (fille) beanpole

brio [brijo] nm brilliance

brioche [brijɔʃ] nf brioche ■ **brioché** adj **pain b.** = milk bread

brique [brik] nf (de construction) brick; **mur de briques** brick wall

briquer [brike] vt (nettoyer) to scrub down

briquet [brikɛ] nm (cigarette) lighter

bris [bri] nm (de verre) breaking; **b. de glaces** broken windows

brise [briz] nf breeze

briser [brize] **1** vt to break; (opposition, résistance) to crush; (espoir, carrière) to wreck; (fatiguer) to exhaust **2 se briser** vpr to break ■ **brise-glace** nm inv (navire) ice breaker ■ **brise-lames** nm inv breakwater

britannique [britanik] **1** adj British **2** nmf B. Briton; **les Britanniques** the British

broc [bro] nm pitcher, jug

brocante [brɔkɑ̃t] nf (commerce) second-hand trade ■ **brocanteur** nm secondhand dealer

broche [brɔʃ] nf (pour rôtir) spit; (bijou) brooch; (pour fracture) pin; **faire cuire qch à la b.** to spit-roast sth ■ **brochette** nf (tige) skewer; (plat) kebab

broché, -e [brɔʃe] adj **livre b.** paperback

brochet [brɔʃɛ] nm pike

brochure [brɔʃyr] nf brochure, pamphlet

brocolis [brɔkɔli] nmpl broccoli

broder [brɔde] vt to embroider (**de** with) ■ **broderie** nf (activité) embroidery

broncher [brɔ̃ʃe] vi **il n'a pas bronché** he didn't bat an eyelid

bronches [brɔ̃ʃ] nfpl bronchial tubes ■ **bronchite** nf bronchitis; **avoir une b.** to have bronchitis

bronze [brɔ̃z] nm bronze

bronzer [brɔ̃ze] vi to tan ■ **bronzage** nm (sun)tan

brosse [brɔs] nf brush; **donner un**

coup de b. à qch to give sth a brush;
cheveux en b. crew cut; **b. à dents**
toothbrush ■ **brosser 1** *vt* (*tapis*, *cheveux*) to brush; **b. un tableau de qch**
to give an outline of sth **2 se brosser**
vpr **se b.** **les dents/les cheveux** to
brush one's teeth/one's hair

brouette [bruɛt] *nf* wheelbarrow

brouhaha [bruaa] *nm* hubbub

brouillard [brujar] *nm* fog; **il y a du b.**
it's foggy

brouiller [bruje] **1** *vt* (*idées*) to muddle
up; (*vue*) to blur; (*émission*) to jam **2 se**
brouiller *vpr* (*vue*) to become blurred;
(*personnes*) to fall out (**avec** with)
■ **brouillé, -e** *adj* (*teint*) blotchy; **être**
b. avec qn to have fallen out with sb

brouillon, -onne [brujɔ̃, -ɔn] **1** *adj*
(*mal organisé*) disorganized; (*mal présenté*) untidy **2** *nm* rough draft; (**papier**) **b.** *Br* scrap paper, *Am* scratch
paper

broussailles [brusaj] *nfpl* scrub

brousse [brus] *nf* **la b.** the bush

brouter [brute] *vti* to graze

broyer [brwaje] *vt* to grind; (*doigt*,
bras) to crush

bru [bry] *nf* daughter-in-law

brugnon [bryɲɔ̃] *nm* nectarine

bruine [brɥin] *nf* drizzle ■ **bruiner** *v*
impersonnel to drizzle; **il bruine** it's
drizzling

bruissement [brɥismɑ̃] *nm* (*de feuilles*) rustle, rustling

bruit [brɥi] *nm* noise, sound; (*nouvelle*) rumour; **faire du b.** to make a
noise ■ **bruitage** *nm Cin* sound effects

brûlant, -e [brylɑ̃, -ɑ̃t] *adj* (*objet*,
soupe) burning hot; (*soleil*) scorching;
Fig (*sujet*) burning

brûlé, -e [bryle] *nm* odeur de b. burnt
smell; **sentir le b.** to smell burnt

brûle-pourpoint [brylpurpwɛ̃] **à**
brûle-pourpoint *adv* point-blank

brûler [bryle] **1** *vt* (*sujet: flamme*, *acide*)
to burn; (*feu rouge*) to go through **2** *vi*
to burn **3 se brûler** *vpr* to burn oneself;
se b. la langue to burn one's tongue

brûlure [brylyr] *nf* burn

brume [brym] *nf* mist, haze ■ **brumeux, -euse** *adj* misty, hazy

brun, -e [brœ̃, bryn] **1** *adj* (*cheveux*)
dark, brown; (*personne*) dark-haired;
être b. de peau to be dark-skinned
2 *nm* (*couleur*) brown
3 *nmf* dark-haired man, *f* dark-haired
woman ■ **brunette** *nf* brunette ■ **bru-
nir** *vi* (*personne*, *peau*) to tan; (*cheveux*) to darken

brushing® [brœʃiŋ] *nm* blow-dry;
faire un b. à qn to blow-dry sb's hair

brusque [brysk] *adj* abrupt ■ **brusquement** [-əmɑ̃] *adv* abruptly ■ **brus-
quer** *vt* (*décision*) to rush ■ **brusquerie**
nf abruptness

brut, -e [bryt] *adj* (*pétrole*) crude; (*diamant*) rough; (*poids*, *salaire*) gross;
(*champagne*) extra-dry; **à l'état b.** in
its raw state

brutal, -e, -aux, -ales [brytal, -o] *adj*
(*personnes*, *manières*, *paroles*) brutal;
(*franchise*, *réponse*) crude, blunt;
(*changement*) abrupt; **être b. avec qn**
to be rough with sb ■ **brutalement**
adv (*violemment*) brutally; (*avec brusquerie*) bluntly; (*soudainement*) abruptly ■ **brutaliser** *vt* to ill-treat
■ **brutalité** *nf* (*violence*, *acte*) brutal-
ity; (*soudaineté*) abruptness ■ **brute**
nf brute

Bruxelles [brysɛl] *nm ou f* Brussels

bruyant, -e [brɥijɑ̃, -ɑ̃t] *adj* noisy
■ **bruyamment** [-amɑ̃] *adv* noisily

bruyère [brɥjɛr] *nf* (*plante*) heather;
(*terrain*) heath

BTS [beteɛs] (*abrév* brevet de technicien supérieur) *nm* = advanced vocational training certificate

bu, -e [by] *pp de* **boire**

buanderie [bɥɑ̃dri] *nf* (*lieu*) laundry

bûche [byʃ] *nf* log; **b. de Noël** Yule log
■ **bûcher** *nm* (*à bois*) woodshed; (*de*
supplice) stake

bûcheron [byʃrɔ̃] *nm* woodcutter

bûcheur, -euse [byʃœr, -øz] *nmf Br*
swot, *Am* grind

budget [bydʒɛ] *nm* budget ■ **budgé-
taire** *adj* budgetary; (*année*) financial

buée [bɥe] *nf (sur vitre)* condensation; *(sur miroir)* mist

buffet [byfɛ] *nm (meuble bas)* sideboard; *(meuble haut)* dresser; *(repas)* buffet

buffle [byfl] *nm* buffalo

buisson [bɥisɔ̃] *nm* bush

buissonnière [bɥisɔnjɛr] *adj f* **faire l'école b.** *Br* to play truant, *Am* to play hookey

bulbe [bylb] *nm* bulb

Bulgarie [bylgari] *nf* **la B.** Bulgaria ■ **bulgare 1** *adj* Bulgarian **2** *nmf* **B.** Bulgarian

bulldozer [byldozœr] *nm* bulldozer

bulle [byl] *nf (d'air, de savon)* bubble; *(de bande dessinée)* balloon; **faire des bulles** to blow bubbles

bulletin [byltɛ̃] *nm (communiqué, revue)* bulletin; **b. d'informations** news bulletin; **b. de paie** *ou* **de salaire** *Br* pay slip, *Am* pay stub; **b. de santé** medical bulletin; **b. de vote** ballot paper; **b. météo** weather report; **b. scolaire** *Br* school report, *Am* report card

bureau, -x [byro] *nm (table)* desk; *(lieu)* office; *(comité)* committee; **b. de change** bureau de change; **b. de poste** post office; **b. de tabac** *Br* tobacconist's (shop), *Am* tobacco store

bureaucratie [byrokrasi] *nf* bureaucracy ■ **bureaucratique** *adj* bureaucratic

Bureautique® [byrotik] *nf* office automation

burette [byrɛt] *nf (pour huile)* oilcan; *(de chimiste)* burette

burin [byrɛ̃] *nm (de graveur)* burin; *(pour découper)* (cold) chisel

buriné, -e [byrine] *adj (visage)* seamed

burlesque [byrlɛsk] *adj (idée)* ludicrous; *(genre)* burlesque

bus¹ [bys] *nm* bus

bus² [by] *pt de* **boire**

buste [byst] *nm (torse)* chest; *(sculpture)* bust ■ **bustier** *nm (corsage)* bustier

but¹ [by(t)] *nm (objectif)* aim, goal; *(intention)* purpose; *Sport* goal

but² [by] *pt de* **boire**

butane [bytan] *nm* butane

buter [byte] **1** *vt* **b. qn** to put sb's back up **2** *vi* **b. contre qch** *(cogner)* to bump into sth; *(trébucher)* to stumble over sth; *Fig (difficulté)* to come up against sth **3 se buter** *vpr (s'entêter)* to digone's heels in ■ **buté, -e** *adj* obstinate

butin [bytɛ̃] *nm (de voleur)* loot; *(de pillards)* spoils; *(d'armée)* booty

butoir [bytwar] *nm (pour train)* buffer; *(de porte)* stopper, *Br* stop

buvard [byvar] *nm* blotting paper

buvette [byvɛt] *nf* refreshment bar

buveur, -euse [byvœr, -øz] *nmf* drinker; **un grand b.** a heavy drinker

buviez [byvje] *voir* **boire**

Cc

C, c [se] *nm inv* C, c

c' [s] *voir* **ce²**

ÇA [sa] *(abrév* **cela)** *pron démonstratif (pour désigner)* that; *(plus près)* this; *(sujet indéfini)* it, that; **où/quand ça?** where?/when?; **ça dépend** it depends; **ça va?** how are things?; **ça va!** fine!, OK!; **c'est ça** that's right

çà [sa] **çà et là** *adv* here and there

cabane [kaban] *nf (baraque)* hut; *(en rondin)* cabin; *(de jardin)* shed; **c. à outils** tool shed

cabaret [kabarɛ] *nm* cabaret

cabillaud [kabijo] *nm* (fresh) cod

cabine [kabin] *nf (de bateau)* cabin; **c. d'essayage** fitting room; **c. de pilotage** cockpit; **c. téléphonique** phone box

cabinet [kabinɛ] *nm (de médecin) Br* surgery, *Am* office; *(d'avocat)* firm; *(de ministre)* departmental staff; **c. de toilette** (small) bathroom; *Fam* **les cabinets** *Br* the loo, *Am* the john

câble [kɑbl] *nm* cable; *TV* **le c.** cable ■ **câbler** *vt TV (ville, quartier)* to install cable television in

cabrer [kabre] **se cabrer** *vpr (cheval)* to rear (up)

cabriole [kabriɔl] *nf (saut)* caper; **faire des cabrioles** to caper about

cabriolet [kabriɔlɛ] *nm (auto)* convertible

cacah(o)uète [kakawɛt] *nf* peanut

cacao [kakao] *nm (poudre)* cocoa

cache [kaʃ] *nf* hiding place ■ **cache-cache** *nm inv* **jouer à c.** to play hide and seek ■ **cache-nez** *nm inv* scarf

cachemire [kaʃmir] *nm (laine)* cashmere

cacher [kaʃe] **1** *vt* to hide (à from) **2** **se cacher** *vpr* to hide

cachet [kaʃɛ] *nm (sceau)* seal; *(de fabrication)* stamp; *(comprimé)* tablet; *(d'acteur)* fee; *(originalité)* character; **c. de la poste** postmark ■ **cacheter** *vt* to seal

cachette [kaʃɛt] *nf* hiding place; **en c.** in secret

cachot [kaʃo] *nm* dungeon

cachotteries [kaʃɔtri] *nfpl* **faire des cachotteries** to be secretive

cactus [kaktys] *nm* cactus

cadavre [kadavr] *nm* corpse ■ **cadavérique** *adj (teint)* deathly pale

caddie® [kadi] *nm Br* trolley, *Am* cart

cadeau, -x [kado] *nm* present, gift; **faire un c. à qn** to give sb a present

cadenas [kadnɑ] *nm* padlock

cadence [kadɑ̃s] *nf (taux, vitesse)* rate; *(de chanson)* rhythm

cadet, -ette [kadɛ, -ɛt] **1** *adj (de deux)* younger; *(de plus de deux)* youngest **2** *nmf (de deux)* younger (one); *(de plus de deux)* youngest (one); *Sport* junior

cadran [kadrɑ̃] *nm (de téléphone)* dial; *(de montre)* face; **c. solaire** sundial

cadre [kadr] *nm* (**a**) *(de photo, de vélo)* frame; *(décor)* setting; **dans le c. de** within the framework of (**b**) *(d'entreprise)* executive; **les cadres** the management; *Mil* the officers

cadrer [kadre] **1** *vt (photo)* to centre **2** *vi (correspondre)* to tally (**avec** with)

caduc, caduque [kadyk] *adj (feuille)* deciduous

cafard [kafar] *nm (insecte)* cockroach

café [kafe] *nm (produit, boisson)* coffee; *(bar)* café; **c. au lait, c. crème** *Br* white coffee, *Am* coffee with milk; **c. noir** black coffee; **c. soluble** *ou* **instantané** instant coffee ■ **caféine** *nf* caffeine ■ **cafétéria** *nf* cafeteria ■ **cafetier** *nm* café owner ■ **cafetière** *nf (récipient)* coffeepot; *(électrique)* coffee machine

cage [kaʒ] *nf (d'oiseau, de zoo)* cage; *(d'ascenseur)* shaft; *Sport* goal; **c. d'escalier** stairwell

cageot [kaʒo] *nm* crate

cagneux [kaɲø] *adj* **avoir les genous c.** to have knock-knees

cagnotte [kaɲɔt] *nf (caisse commune)* kitty; *(de jeux)* pool

cagoule [kagul] *nf (de bandit)* hood; *(d'enfant)* *Br* balaclava, *Am* ski mask

cahier [kaje] *nm* notebook; *(d'écolier)* exercise book; **c. de brouillon** *Br* rough book, *Am* ≃ scratch pad; *Scol* **c. d'appel** register

cahin-caha [kaɛ̃kaa] *adv Fam* **aller c.** *(se déplacer)* to struggle along

caille [kaj] *nf (oiseau)* quail

cailler [kaje] *vi (lait)* to curdle ■ **caillot** *nm (de sang)* clot

caillou, -x [kaju] *nm* stone; *(sur la plage)* pebble

Caire [kɛr] *nm* **le C.** Cairo

caisse [kɛs] *nf* (**a**) *(boîte)* case; *(d'outils)* box; *(cageot)* crate (**b**) *(de magasin)* cash desk; *(de supermarché)* checkout; **c. enregistreuse** cash register **c. d'épargne** savings bank; **caissier, -ère** [kesje, -ɛr] *nmf* cashier; *(de supermarché)* checkout operator

cajoler [kaʒɔle] *vt* to cuddle

cajou [kaʒu] *nm* **noix de c.** cashew nut

calamité [kalamite] *nf (fléau)* calamity; *(malheur)* great misfortune

calcaire [kalkɛr] **1** *adj (eau)* hard; *(terrain)* chalky **2** *nm Géol* limestone; *(dépôt)* fur

calciné, -e [kalsine] *adj* burnt to a cinder

calcium [kalsjɔm] *nm* calcium

calcul [kalkyl] *nm* (**a**) *(opérations, estimation)* calculation; *Scol* **le c.** arithmetic; **faire un c.** to make a calculation (**b**) *Méd* stone; **c. rénal** kidney stone

calculatrice [kalkylatris] *nf* **c. (de poche)** (pocket) calculator

calculer [kalkyle] *vt (prix, superficie)* to calculate; *(chances, conséquences)* to weigh (up)

calculette [kalkylɛt] *nf* (pocket) calculator

cale [kal] *nf* (**a**) *(de meuble, de porte)* wedge (**b**) *(de navire)* hold

caleçon [kalsɔ̃] *nm* boxer shorts

calembour [kalɑ̃bur] *nm* pun, play on words

calendrier [kalɑ̃drije] *nm (mois et jours)* calendar; *(programme)* timetable

calepin [kalpɛ̃] *nm* notebook

caler [kale] **1** *vt (meuble, porte)* to wedge; *(chargement)* to secure **2** *vi (moteur)* to stall **3 se caler** *vpr (dans un fauteuil)* to settle oneself comfortably

calfeutrer [kalføtre] *vt (brèches)* to block up

calibre [kalibr] *nm (diamètre)* calibre; *(d'œuf, de fruit)* grade; *(outil)* gauge

Californie [kaliforni] *nf* **la C.** California

californchon [kalifurʃɔ̃] **à califourchon** *adv* astride; **se mettre à c. sur qch** to sit astride sth

câlin, -e [kalɛ̃, -in] **1** *adj* affectionate **2** *nm* cuddle; **faire un c. à qn** to give sb a cuddle

calmant [kalmɑ̃] *nm (pour les nerfs)* sedative

calmar [kalmar] *nm* squid

calme [kalm] **1** *adj (flegmatique)* calm, cool; *(tranquille)* quiet; *(mer)* calm **2** *nm* calm(ness); **garder/perdre son c.** to keep/lose one's calm; **du c.!** *(taisez-vous)* keep quiet!; *(pas de panique)* keep calm!

calmer [kalme] **1** *vt (douleur)* to soothe; *(inquiétude)* to calm; *(faim)* to appease; **c. qn** to calm sb down **2 se calmer** *vpr (personne)* to calm down; *(vent)* to die down; *(mer)* to become calm; *(douleur)* to subside

calomnie [kalɔmni] *nf (en paroles)* slander; *(par écrit)* libel ▪ **calomnier** *vt (en paroles)* to slander; *(par écrit)* to libel ▪ **calomnieux, -euse** *adj (paroles)* slanderous; *(écrits)* libellous

calorie [kalɔri] *nf* calorie

calotte [kalɔt] *nf (chapeau rond)* skull-cap

calque [kalk] *nm (copie)* tracing; **(papier-)c.** tracing paper

calvaire [kalvɛr] *nm Rel* calvary; *Fig* ordeal

calvitie [kalvisi] *nf* baldness

camarade [kamarad] *nmf* friend; **c. de classe** classmate; **c. d'école** school friend; **c. de jeu** playmate ▪ **camaraderie** *nf* camaraderie

Cambodge [kɑ̃bɔdʒ] *nm* **le C.** Cambodia

cambouis [kɑ̃bwi] *nm* dirty oil

cambrer [kɑ̃bre] **1** *vt* to arch **2 se cambrer** *vpr* to arch one's back ▪ **cambrure** *nf (du pied, du dos)* arch

cambrioler [kɑ̃brijɔle] *vt Br* to burgle, *Am* to burglarize ▪ **cambriolage** *nm* burglary ▪ **cambrioleur, -euse** *nmf* burglar

camée [kame] *nm* cameo

caméléon [kameleɔ̃] *nm* chameleon

camelot [kamlo] *nm* street peddler *or Br* hawker, *Am* huckster ▪ **camelote** *nf (pacotille)* junk; *(marchandise)* stuff

camembert [kamɑ̃bɛr] *nm (fromage)* Camembert (cheese)

caméra [kamera] *nf* camera ▪ **cameraman** *(pl* -mans *ou* -men*)* *nm* cameraman

Caméscope® [kameskɔp] *nm* camcorder

camion [kamjɔ̃] *nm Br* lorry, *Am* truck; **c. de déménagement** *Br* removal van, *Am* moving van ▪ **camion-citerne** *(pl* camions-citernes*)* *nm Br* tanker, *Am* tank truck ▪ **camionnette** *nf* van ▪ **camionneur** *nm (conducteur) Br* lorry

driver, *Am* truck driver; *(entrepreneur) Br* haulier, *Am* trucker

camomille [kamɔmij] *nf (plante)* camomile; *(tisane)* camomile tea

camoufler [kamufle] *vt Mil* to camouflage ▪ **camouflage** *nm Mil* camouflage

camp [kɑ̃] *nm (campement)* camp; *(de parti, de jeu)* side; **c. de concentration** concentration camp; **c. de prisonniers** prison camp

campagne [kɑ̃paɲ] *nf* **(a)** *(par opposition à la ville)* country; *(paysage)* countryside; **à la c.** in the country; **en pleine c.** deep in the countryside **(b)** *Mil, Com & Pol* campaign; **c. de presse/publicité** press/publicity campaign ▪ **campagnard, -e** *adj* country

camper [kɑ̃pe] **1** *vi* to camp **2** *vt (chapeau)* to plant **3 se camper** *vpr* to plant oneself **(devant** in front of) ▪ **campeur, -euse** *nmf* camper

camping [kɑ̃piŋ] *nm (activité)* camping; *(terrain)* camp(ing) site; **faire du c.** to go camping; **c. sauvage** unauthorized camping ▪ **camping-car** *(pl* camping-cars*)* *nm* camper

campus [kɑ̃pys] *nm* campus

Canada [kanada] *nm* **le C.** Canada ▪ **canadien, -enne 1** *adj* Canadian **2** *nmf* **C., Canadienne** Canadian

canal, -aux [kanal, -o] *nm (cours d'eau)* canal; *(conduite)* conduit; *Fig* channel

canaliser [kanalize] *vt (rivière, fleuve)* to canalize; *Fig (foule, énergie)* to channel ▪ **canalisation** *nf (conduite)* pipe

canapé [kanape] *nm* **(a)** *(siège)* sofa, couch **(b)** *(pour l'apéritif)* canapé ▪ **canapé-lit** *(pl* canapés-lits*)* *nm* sofa bed

canard [kanar] *nm* duck; *(mâle)* drake; *Fam (journal)* rag

canari [kanari] *nm* canary

cancaner [kɑ̃kane] *vi* to gossip

cancans [kɑ̃kɑ̃] *nmpl* gossip

cancer [kɑ̃ser] *nm (maladie)* cancer; **c.**

de l'estomac stomach cancer; **avoir un c.** to have cancer; **le C.** *(signe)* Cancer ■ **cancéreux, -euse 1** *adj* cancerous **2** *nmf* cancer patient ■ **cancérigène** *adj* carcinogenic

candeur [kɑ̃dœr] *nf* guilelessness

candidat, -e [kɑ̃dida, -at] *nmf (d'examen, d'élection)* candidate **(à** for); *(de poste)* applicant **(à** for); **être c. aux élections** to stand for election ■ **candidature** *nf (à un poste)* application **(à** for); *(aux élections)* candidature **(à** for); **poser sa c.** to apply **(à** for); **c. spontanée** unsolicited application

candide [kɑ̃did] *adj* guileless

cane [kan] *nf* (female) duck ■ **caneton** *nm* duckling

canette [kanɛt] *nf (boîte)* can

canevas [kanva] *nm (toile)* canvas

caniche [kaniʃ] *nm* poodle

canicule [kanikyl] *nf* heatwave

canif [kanif] *nm* penknife

canine [kanin] **1** *adj f (espèce, race)* canine **2** *nf (dent)* canine (tooth)

caniveau, -x [kanivo] *nm* gutter

canne [kan] *nf (tige)* cane; *(pour marcher)* (walking) stick; **c. à pêche** fishing rod; **c. à sucre** sugar cane

cannelle [kanɛl] *nf* cinnamon

cannette [kanɛt] *nf* = **canette**

cannibale [kanibal] *nmf* cannibal

canoë-kayak [kanɔekajak] *nm* canoeing

canon¹ [kanɔ̃] *nm* gun; *(ancien, à boulets)* cannon; *(de fusil)* barrel

canon² [kanɔ̃] *nm Rel & Fig (règle)* canon

canot [kano] *nm* boat; **c. de sauvetage** lifeboat; **c. pneumatique** rubber dinghy

cantatrice [kɑ̃tatris] *nf* opera singer

cantine [kɑ̃tin] *nf* **(a)** *(réfectoire)* canteen; *(d'école)* dining hall **(b)** *(coffre)* trunk

canton [kɑ̃tɔ̃] *nm (en France)* canton *(division of a department)*; *(en Suisse)* canton *(semi-autonomous region)*

cantonade [kɑ̃tɔnad] **à la cantonade** *adv* to everyone present

cantonner [kɑ̃tɔne] **1** *vt (troupes)* to quarter; **c. qn dans/à** to confine sb to **2 se cantonner** *vpr* **se c. dans/à** to confine oneself to ■ **cantonnement** *nm (lieu)* quarters

canular [kanylar] *nm Fam* hoax

CAO [seao] *(abrév* **conception assistée par ordinateur)** *Ordinat* CAD

caoutchouc [kautʃu] *nm* rubber; *(élastique)* rubber band

CAP [seape] *(abrév* **certificat d'aptitude professionnelle)** *nm Scol* = vocational training certificate

cap [kap] *nm Géog* cape, headland; *Naut (direction)* course

capable [kapabl] *adj* capable, able; **c. de qch** capable of sth; **c. de faire qch** able to do sth, capable of doing sth ■ **capacité** *nf* capacity; *(aptitude)* ability

CAPES [kapes] *(abrév* **certificat d'aptitude professionnelle à l'enseignement secondaire)** *nm* = postgraduate teaching certificate

capillaire [kapiler] *adj* **huile/lotion c.** hair oil/lotion

capitaine [kapiten] *nm* captain

capital, -e, -aux, -ales [kapital, -o] **1** *adj (essentiel)* major **2** *adj f* **lettre capitale** capital letter **3** *nm Fin* capital ■ **capitale** *nf (lettre, ville)* capital

capitalisme [kapitalism] *nm* capitalism ■ **capitaliste** *adj & nmf* capitalist

capiteux, -euse [kapitø, -øz] *adj (parfum)* heady

capitonné, -e [kapitɔne] *adj* padded

capituler [kapityle] *vi* to surrender ■ **capitulation** *nf* surrender

caporal, -aux [kapɔral, -o] *nm Mil* corporal

capot [kapo] *nm Aut Br* bonnet, *Am* hood

capote [kapɔt] *nf Aut (de décapotable)* top, *Br* hood

capoter [kapɔte] *vi (véhicule)* to overturn

câpre [kɑpr] *nf* caper

caprice [kapris] *nm* whim; **faire un c.** to throw a tantrum ■ **capricieux,**

-euse *adj (personne)* capricious

Capricorne [kaprikɔrn] *nm* le C. *(signe)* Capricorn

capsule [kapsyl] *nf (spatiale, de médicament)* capsule; *(de bouteille)* cap

capter [kapte] *vt (signal, radio)* to pick up; *(attention)* to capture

captif, -ive [kaptif, -iv] *adj & nmf* captive ■ **captivité** *nf* captivity; **en c.** in captivity

captiver [kaptive] *vt* to captivate ■ **captivant, -e** *adj* captivating

capture [kaptyr] *nf* capture ■ **capturer** *vt* to capture

capuche [kapyʃ] *nf* hood ■ **capuchon** *nm (de manteau)* hood; *(de stylo, de tube)* cap, top

caqueter [kakte] *vi (poule)* to cackle

car¹ [kar] *conj* because, for

car² [kar] *nm* bus, *Br* coach; **c. de police** police van

carabine [karabin] *nf* rifle; **c. à air comprimé** air gun

caractère¹ [karaktɛr] *nm (lettre)* character; **en caractères gras** in bold characters; **caractères d'imprimerie** block letters

caractère² [karaktɛr] *nm (tempérament, nature)* character, nature; **avoir bon c.** to be good-natured; **avoir mauvais c.** to be bad-tempered

caractériser [karakterize] **1** *vt* to characterize **2 se caractériser** *upr* **se c. par** to be characterized by

caractéristique [karakteristik] *adj & nf* characteristic

carafe [karaf] *nf (pour l'eau, le vin)* carafe

carambolage [karãbɔlaʒ] *nm* pile-up

caramel [karamɛl] *nm* caramel ■ **caraméliser** *vti* to caramelize

carapace [karapas] *nf (de tortue) & Fig* shell

carat [kara] *nm* carat; **or à 18 carats** 18-carat gold

caravane [karavan] *nf (pour camper) Br* caravan, *Am* trailer; *(dans le désert)* caravan ■ **caravaning** *nm* caravanning; **faire du c.** to go caravanning

carbone [karbɔn] *nm* carbon; **(papier) c.** carbon (paper) ■ **carbonique** *adj* **gaz c.** carbon dioxide; **neige c.** dry ice

carbonisé, -e [karbɔnize] *adj (nourriture)* burnt to a cinder

carburant [karbyrã] *nm* fuel ■ **carburateur** *nm Aut Br* carburettor, *Am* carburetor

carcasse [karkas] *nf (os)* carcass; *(d'immeuble)* shell

carcéral, -e, -aux, -ales [karseral, -o] *adj* prison

cardiaque [kardjak] **1** *adj (arrêt, massage)* cardiac; **être c.** to have a heart condition **2** *nmf* heart patient

cardigan [kardigã] *nm* cardigan

cardinal, -e, -aux, -ales [kardinal, -o] **1** *adj (nombre, point, vertu)* cardinal **2** *nm Rel* cardinal

cardiologie [kardjɔlɔʒi] *nf* cardiology

carême [karɛm] *nm Rel* le C. Lent; **faire c.** to fast

carence [karãs] *nf (manque)* deficiency

caresse [karɛs] *nf* caress; **faire des caresses à qn** to caress sb

caresser [karese] *vt (personne)* to caress; *(animal)* to stroke; *Fig (espoir)* to cherish

cargaison [kargɛzɔ̃] *nf* cargo

caricature [karikatyr] *nf* caricature

carie [kari] *nf* **c. (dentaire)** tooth decay; **avoir une c.** to have a cavity

carillon [karijɔ̃] *nm (sonnerie)* chimes; *(horloge)* chiming clock; *(de porte)* door chime

caritatif, -ive [karitatif, -iv] *adj* charitable

carlingue [karlɛ̃g] *nf (d'avion)* cabin

carnage [karnaʒ] *nm* carnage

carnassier, -ère [karnasje, -ɛr] **1** *adj* flesh-eating **2** *nm* carnivore

carnaval, -als [karnaval] *nm* carnival

carnet [karnɛ] *nm* notebook; *(de tickets)* = book of tickets; **c. d'adresses** address book; **c. de chèques** cheque book; **c. de notes** *Br* school report, *Am* report card

carnivore [karnivɔr] **1** *adj* carnivorous **2** *nm* carnivore

carotte [karɔt] *nf* carrot

carpette [karpɛt] *nf* rug

carré, -e [kare] **1** *adj* square; *(épaules)* square, broad; **mètre c.** square metre **2** *nm* square; **avoir une coupe au c.** to have (one's hair in) a bob; *Culin* **c. d'agneau** rack of lamb

carreau, -x [karo] *nm (motif)* square; *(sur tissu)* check; *(de céramique)* tile; *(vitre)* (window) pane; *Cartes (couleur)* diamonds; **tissu à carreaux** check(ed) material

carrefour [karfur] *nm* crossroads *(sing)*

carrelage [karlaʒ] *nm (sol)* tiled floor; *(carreaux)* tiles

carrelet [karlɛ] *nm Br* plaice, *Am* flounder

carrément [karemɑ̃] *adv Fam (franchement)* straight out; *(très)* really

carrière [karjɛr] *nf* (a) *(lieu)* quarry (b) *(métier)* career; **faire c. dans** to make a career in

carrosse [karɔs] *nm Hist* (horse-drawn) carriage ▪ **carrosserie** *nf (de véhicule)* bodywork

carrure [karyr] *nf (de personne)* build; *(de vêtement)* width across the shoulders

cartable [kartabl] *nm* school bag

carte [kart] *nf* (a) *(carton, document officiel, informatisé)* & *Ordinat* card; *(géographique)* map; *(marine, météo)* chart; *Fig* **avoir c. blanche** to have a free hand; **c. (à jouer)** (playing) card; **jouer aux cartes** to play cards; **c. à puce** smart card; **c. de crédit** credit card; **c. d'identité** identity card; **c. de séjour** residence permit; **c. de téléphone** phonecard; **c. de visite** *Br* visiting card, *Am* calling card; *(professionnelle)* business card; **c. de vœux** greetings card; **c. postale** postcard; **c. routière** road map (b) *(de restaurant)* menu; **manger à la c.** to eat to the à la carte; **c. des vins** wine list

cartel [kartɛl] *nm Écon* cartel

cartomancien, -enne [kartɔmɑ̃sjɛ̃, -ɛn] *nmf* fortune-teller *(who uses cards)*

carton [kartɔ̃] *nm (matière)* cardboard; *(boîte)* cardboard box; **c. à dessin** portfolio; *(au football)* **c. jaune/rouge** yellow/red card ▪ **cartonné** *adj* **livre c.** hardback

cartouche [kartuʃ] *nf* cartridge; *(de cigarettes)* carton

cas [kɑ] *nm* case; **en tout c.** in any case; **en c. de besoin** if need be; **en c. d'accident** in the event of an accident; **en c. d'urgence** in an emergency; **au c. où elle tomberait** if she should fall

casanier, -ère [kazanje, -ɛr] *adj* stay-at-home

cascade [kaskad] *nf* (a) *(d'eau)* waterfall; **en c.** in succession (b) *(de cinéma)* stunt ▪ **cascadeur, -euse** *nmf* stunt man, *f* stunt woman

case [kaz] *nf* (a) *(de tiroir)* compartment; *(d'échiquier)* square; *(de formulaire)* box (b) *(hutte)* hut

caser [kaze] *Fam* **1** *vt (placer)* to fit in **2 se caser** *vpr (se marier)* to get married and settle down

caserne [kazɛrn] *nf* barracks; **c. de pompiers** fire station

casier [kazje] *nm* compartment; *(pour courrier)* pigeonhole; *(pour vêtements)* locker; **c. à bouteilles** bottle rack; *Jur* **c. judiciaire** criminal *or* police record

casino [kazino] *nm* casino

casque [kask] *nm* helmet; **c. (à écouteurs)** headphones

casquette [kaskɛt] *nf* cap

cassation [kɑsasjɔ̃] *nf Jur* annulment

casse [kɑs] *nf (objets cassés)* breakages; **aller à la c.** to go for scrap

casser [kɑse] **1** *vt* (a) *(briser)* to break; *(noix)* to crack; *(voix)* to strain; *Fam* **c. les pieds à qn** to get on sb's nerves (b) *Jur (verdict)* to quash; *(mariage)* to annul **2** *vi* to break **3 se casser** *vpr* to break; **se c. la jambe** to break one's leg; *Fam* **se c. la figure** *(tomber)* to fall flat on one's face

■ **cassant, -e** *adj (fragile)* brittle; *(brusque)* curt, abrupt ■ **casse-cou** *nmf inv (personne)* daredevil ■ **casse-croûte** *nm inv Fam* snack ■ **casse-noisettes, casse-noix** [kɑsnwa] *nm inv* nutcrackers ■ **casse-pieds** *nmf inv Fam (personne)* pain (in the neck) ■ **casse-tête** *nm inv (problème)* headache; *(jeu)* puzzle ■ **casseur** *nm (manifestant)* rioter

casserole [kɑsrɔl] *nf* (sauce)pan

cassette [kɑsɛt] *nf (magnétique)* cassette, tape; **enregistrer qch sur c.** to tape sth; **c. video** video cassette

cassis [kɑsis] *nm (fruit)* blackcurrant; *(boisson)* blackcurrant liqueur

cassoulet [kɑsulɛ] *nm* cassoulet, = stew of beans, pork and goose

cassure [kɑsyr] *nf* break

castagnettes [kɑstaɲɛt] *nfpl* castanets

caste [kɑst] *nf* caste

castor [kɑstɔr] *nm* beaver

castrer [kɑstre] *vt* to castrate; *(chat, chien)* to neuter

catalogue [katalɔg] *nm Br* catalogue, *Am* catalog ■ **cataloguer** *vt Br* to catalogue, *Am* to catalog; *Fig & Péj* to label

catalyseur [katalizœr] *nm Chim & Fig* catalyst

catalytique [katalitik] *adj Aut* **pot c.** catalytic converter

catapulte [katapylt] *nf* catapult

catastrophe [katastrɔf] *nf* disaster, catastrophe ■ **catastrophique** *adj* disastrous, catastrophic

catch [katʃ] *nm* wrestling ■ **catcheur, -euse** *nmf* wrestler

catéchisme [kateʃism] *nm Rel* catechism

catégorie [kategɔri] *nf* category; *(d'hôtel)* grade

catégorique [kategɔrik] *adj* categorical; **c'est lui, je suis c.** I'm positive it's him

cathédrale [katedral] *nf* cathedral

catholicisme [katɔlisism] *nm* Catholicism ■ **catholique** *adj & nmf (Roman)* Catholic

catimini [katimini] **en catimini** *adv* on the sly

cauchemar [koʃmar] *nm aussi Fig* nightmare; **faire un c.** to have a nightmare

cause [koz] *nf (origine)* cause; *(procès, parti)* case; **à c. de qn/qch** because of sb/sth

causer¹ [koze] *vt (provoquer)* to cause

causer² [koze] *vi (bavarder)* to chat *(de* about*); (cancaner)* to talk ■ **causerie** *nf* talk

caustique [kostik] *adj (substance, esprit)* caustic

caution [kosjɔ̃] *nf (d'appartement)* deposit; *Jur* bail; *(personne)* guarantor; *Fig (appui)* backing; *Jur* **sous c.** on bail ■ **cautionner** *vt Fig (approuver)* to back

cavalier, -ère [kavalje, -ɛr] **1** *nmf (à cheval)* rider; *Échecs* knight; *(de bal)* partner, escort; *Fig* **faire c. seul** to go it alone **2** *adj (manière, personne)* cavalier

cave [kav] *nf* cellar ■ **caveau, -x** *nm (sépulture)* burial vault

caverne [kavɛrn] *nf* cave, cavern; **homme des cavernes** caveman

caviar [kavjar] *nm* caviar

cavité [kavite] *nf* hollow, cavity

CCP [sesepe] *(abrév* **compte chèque postal)** *nm Br* ≃ PO Giro account, *Am* ≃ Post Office checking account

CD [sede] *(abrév* **disque compact)** *nm* CD

CD-Rom [sederɔm] *nm inv Ordinat* CD-Rom

CE [sea] **1** *(abrév* **cours élémentaire)** *nm Scol* **CE1** = second year of primary school; **CE2** = third year of primary school **2** *(abrév* **Communauté européenne)** *nf* EC

CE¹, CETTE, CES [sǝ, sɛt, se]

cet is used before a masculine singular adjective beginning with a vowel or mute h.

adj démonstratif this, that, *pl* these, those; **cet homme** this/that man; **cet**

homme-ci this man; **cet homme-là** that man

CE² [sə]

ce becomes **c'** before a vowel.

pron démonstratif (**a**) *(pour désigner, pour qualifier)* it, that; **c'est facile** it's easy; **c'est exact** that's right; **c'est mon père** that's my father; *(au téléphone)* it's my father; **ce sont eux qui…** they are the people who…; **qui est-ce?** *(en général)* who is it?; *(en désignant)* who is that?; **ce faisant** in so doing; **sur ce** thereupon (**b**) *(après une proposition)* **ce que…, ce qui…** what…; **je sais ce qui est bon/ce que tu veux** I know what is good/what you want; **ce que c'est beau!** it's so beautiful!

ceci [səsi] *pron démonstratif* this; **c. étant dit** having said this

cécité [sesite] *nf* blindness

céder [sede] **1** *vt (donner)* to give up (**à** to); *(par testament)* to leave (**à** to); **'cédez le passage'** *Br* 'give way', *Am* 'yield'; **'à céder'** 'for sale' **2** *vi (personne)* to give in (**à/devant** to); *(branche, chaise)* to give way

cédérom [sederɔm] *nm Ordinat* CD-ROM

cèdre [sɛdr] *nm (arbre, bois)* cedar

CEI [seøi] *(abrév Communauté d'États Indépendants) nf* CIS

ceinture [sɛtyr] *nf (accessoire)* belt; *(taille)* waist; **c. de sécurité** *(de véhicule)* seatbelt

cela [s(ə)la] *pron démonstratif (pour désigner)* that; *(sujet indéfini)* it, that; **m'attriste que…** it saddens me that…; **quand/comment c.?** when?/how?

célèbre [selɛbr] *adj* famous ■ **célébrité** *nf* fame; *(personne)* celebrity

célébrer [selebre] *vt* to celebrate ■ **célébration** *nf* celebration (**de** of)

céleri [selri] *nm* celery

céleste [selɛst] *adj* celestial, heavenly

célibat [seliba] *nm (de prêtre)* celibacy ■ **célibataire 1** *adj (non marié)* single, unmarried **2** *nmf* bachelor, *f* single woman

celle *voir* **celui**

cellier [selje] *nm* storeroom

Cellophane® [selɔfan] *nf* cellophane®; **sous c.** cellophane®-wrapped

cellule [selyl] *nf (de prison) & Biol* cell ■ **cellulaire** *adj Biol* cell; **téléphone c.** cellular phone

celte [sɛlt] *adj* Celtic

celui, celle, ceux, celles [səlɥi, sɛl, sø, sɛl] *pron démonstratif* the one, *pl* those, the ones; **c. de Jean** Jean's (one); **ceux de Jean** Jean's (ones), those of Jean; **c. qui appartient à Jean** the one that belongs to Jean; **c.-ci** this one; *(le dernier)* the latter; **c.-là** that one; *(le premier)* the former

cendre [sɑ̃dr] *nf* ash

cendrier [sɑ̃drije] *nm* ashtray

censé, -e [sɑ̃se] *adj* **être c. faire qch** to be supposed to do sth

censeur [sɑ̃sœr] *nm (de films, de journaux)* censor; *(de lycée) Br* deputy head, *Am* assistant principal ■ **censure** *nf (activité)* censorship; *(comité)* board of censors ■ **censurer** *vt (film)* to censor

cent [sɑ̃] *adj & nm* a hundred; **c. pages** a or one hundred pages; **deux cents pages** two hundred pages; **cinq pour c.** five per cent ■ **centaine** *nf* **une c. (de)** about a hundred; **des centaines de** hundreds of ■ **centenaire 1** *adj* hundred-year-old; **être c.** to be a hundred **2** *nmf* centenarian **3** *nm (anniversaire)* centenary ■ **centième** *adj & nmf* hundredth

centigrade [sɑ̃tigrad] *adj* centigrade

centimètre [sɑ̃timɛtr] *nm* centimetre; *(ruban)* tape measure

central, -e, -aux, -ales [sɑ̃tral, -o] **1** *adj* central **2** *nm* **c. téléphonique** telephone exchange ■ **centrale** *nf* **c. électrique** *Br* power station, *Am* power plant; **c. nucléaire** nuclear *Br* power station *or Am* power plant ■ **centraliser** *vt* to centralize

centre [sātr] nm centre; **c. aéré** outdoor activity centre; **c. commercial** shopping centre; **c. hospitalo-universitaire** ≃ teaching hospital ■ **centre-ville** (pl **centres-villes**) nm town centre; (de grande ville) Br city centre, Am downtown ■ **centrer** vt to centre

centuple [sātypl] nm **x est le c. de y** x is a hundred times y; **au c.** a hundredfold

cependant [səpādā] conj however, yet

céramique [seramik] nf (matière) ceramic; (art) ceramics (sing); **de** ou **en c.** ceramic

cercle [serkl] nm (forme, groupe) circle; **le c. polaire arctique** the Arctic Circle; **c. vicieux** vicious circle

cercueil [serkœj] nm coffin

céréale [sereal] nf cereal

cérébral, -e, -aux, -ales [serebral, -o] adj cerebral

cérémonie [seremɔni] nf ceremony

cerf [ser] nm stag ■ **cerf-volant** (pl **cerfs-volants**) nm (jeu) kite

cerise [səriz] nf cherry ■ **cerisier** nm cherry tree

cerne [sern] nm ring ■ **cerner** vt to surround; (problème) to define; **avoir les yeux cernés** to have rings under one's eyes

certain, -e [sertɛ̃, -ɛn] **1** adj (sûr) certain; **il est c. que tu réussiras** you're certain to succeed; **je suis c. de réussir** I'm certain I'll be successful or of being successful; **être c. de qch** to be certain of sth

2 adj indéfini (avant nom) certain; **un c. temps** a while

3 pron indéfini **certains pensent que...** some people think that...; **certains d'entre nous** some of us ■ **certainement** adv most probably

certificat [sertifika] nm certificate

certifier [sertifje] vt to certify; **je te certifie que...** I assure you that...

certitude [sertityd] nf certainty; **avoir la c. que...** to be certain that...

cerveau, -x [servo] nm (organe) brain;

(intelligence) mind, brain(s); Fam (de projet) mastermind

cervelle [servel] nf (substance) brain; (plat) brains

CES [seaes] (abrév **collège d'enseignement secondaire**) nm Anciennement = secondary school for pupils aged 12 to 15

ces voir **ce¹**

César [sezar] nm Cin = French cinema award

césarienne [sezarjen] nf Méd Caesarean (section)

cesse [ses] nf **sans c.** constantly

cesser [sese] vti to stop; **faire c. qch** to put a stop to sth; **c. de faire qch** to stop doing sth ■ **cessez-le-feu** nm inv cease-fire

c'est-à-dire [setadir] conj that is (to say)

cet, cette voir **ce¹**

ceux voir **celui**

chacun, -e [ʃakœ̃, -yn] pron indéfini each (one), every one; (tout le monde) everyone; **(à) c. son tour!** wait your turn!

chagrin [ʃagrɛ̃] nm grief, sorrow; **avoir du c.** to be upset ■ **chagriner** vt (peiner) to grieve; (contrarier) to bother

chahut [ʃay] nm Fam racket ■ **chahuter** Fam **1** vi to make a racket **2** vt (professeur) to bait

chaîne [ʃen] nf (attache, décoration, série) chain; (de montagnes) chain, range; **réaction en c.** chain reaction; **travailler à la c.** to work on the assembly line; Aut **chaînes** (snow) chains; **c. de montage** assembly line; **c. de télévision** television channel; **c. (hi-fi)** hifi (system) ■ **chaînette** nf (small) chain ■ **chaînon** nm link

chair [ʃer] nf flesh; (couleur) **c.** flesh-coloured; **en c. et en os** in the flesh; **avoir la c. de poule** to have Br goose pimples or Am goose bumps

chaire [ʃer] nf (d'université) chair; (d'église) pulpit

chaise [ʃez] nf chair; **c. longue** deck-chair; **c. roulante** wheelchair

châle [ʃɑl] *nm* shawl

chalet [ʃalɛ] *nm* chalet

chaleur [ʃalœr] *nf* heat; *(de personne, de couleur, de voix)* warmth; **coup de c.** heatstroke ■ **chaleureux, -euse** *adj* warm

challenge [ʃalɑ̃ʒ] *nm* Sport tournament; *(défi)* challenge

chaloupe [ʃalup] *nf* launch

chalumeau, -x [ʃalymo] *nm* blowtorch; *Br* blowlamp

chalutier [ʃalytje] *nm* trawler

chamailler [ʃamaje] **se chamailler** *upr* to squabble

chambre [ʃɑ̃br] *nf* bedroom; *(de tribunal)* division; **c. (d'hôtel)** (hotel) room; **c. à coucher** *(pièce)* bedroom; *(mobilier)* bedroom suite; **c. d'ami** spare room; **c. d'hôte** ≃ guest house; **C. de commerce** Chamber of Commerce; *Pol* **C. des députés** = lower chamber of Parliament ■ **chambrer** *vt (vin)* to bring to room temperature

chameau, -x [ʃamo] *nm* camel

champ [ʃɑ̃] *nm (étendue)* & *El, Ordinat* field; *Fig (portée)* scope; *Fig* **laisser le c. libre à qn** to leave the field free for sb; **c. de bataille** battlefield; **c. de courses** *Br* racecourse, *Am* racetrack

champagne [ʃɑ̃paɲ] *nm* champagne

champêtre [ʃɑ̃pɛtr] *adj* rustic

champignon [ʃɑ̃piɲɔ̃] *nm (végétal)* mushroom; *Méd* fungus; **c. de Paris** button mushroom; **c. vénéneux** toadstool, poisonous mushroom

champion, -onne [ʃɑ̃pjɔ̃, -ɔn] 1 *nmf* champion 2 *adj* **l'équipe championne du monde** the world champions ■ **championnat** *nm* championship

chance [ʃɑ̃s] *nf (sort favorable)* luck; *(possibilité)* chance; **avoir de la c.** to be lucky; **ne pas avoir de c.** to be unlucky; **par c.** luckily ■ **chanceux, -euse** *adj* lucky

chanceler [ʃɑ̃sle] *vi* to stagger

chancelier [ʃɑ̃səlje] *nm Pol* chancellor

chandail [ʃɑ̃daj] *nm* sweater

Chandeleur [ʃɑ̃dlœr] *nf* **la C.** Candlemas

chandelier [ʃɑ̃dəlje] *nm (à une branche)* candlestick; *(à plusieurs branches)* candelabra

chandelle [ʃɑ̃dɛl] *nf* candle

change [ʃɑ̃ʒ] *nm Fin* exchange

changer [ʃɑ̃ʒe] 1 *vt (modifier, remplacer, convertir)* to change; **c. qch de place** to move sth
2 *vi* to change; **c. de voiture/d'adresse** to change one's car/address; **c. de vitesse/de couleur** to change gear/colour
3 **se changer** *upr* to change (one's clothes); **se c. en qch** to change into sth ■ **changeant, -e** *adj (temps)* unsettled ■ **changement** *nm* change; *Aut* **c. de vitesse** *(levier) Br* gear lever, *Am* gear shift

chanson [ʃɑ̃sɔ̃] *nf* song ■ **chant** *nm (art)* singing; *(chanson)* song; **c. de Noël** Christmas carol

chanter [ʃɑ̃te] 1 *vt (chanson)* to sing; *(exploits)* to sing of 2 *vi (personne, oiseau)* to sing; *(coq)* to crow; **faire c. qn** to blackmail sb ■ **chantage** *nm* blackmail ■ **chanteur, -euse** *nmf* singer

chantier [ʃɑ̃tje] *nm* (building) site; *(sur route)* roadworks; **mettre qch en c.** to get sth under way; **c. naval** shipyard

chantilly [ʃɑ̃tiji] *nf* whipped cream

chantonner [ʃɑ̃tɔne] *vti* to hum

chaos [kao] *nm* chaos ■ **chaotique** *adj* chaotic

chapeau, -x [ʃapo] *nm* hat; **c. de paille** straw hat; **c. melon** bowler hat

chapelle [ʃapɛl] *nf* chapel; **c. ardente** chapel of rest

chapelure [ʃaplyr] *nf* breadcrumbs

chapiteau, -x [ʃapito] *nm (de cirque)* big top; *(pour expositions)* tent, *Br* marquee

chapitre [ʃapitr] *nm* chapter

chaque [ʃak] *adj* each, every

char [ʃar] *nm (romain)* chariot; *(de carnaval)* float; *Mil* **c. (d'assaut)** tank

charabia [ʃarabja] *nm Fam* gibberish

charbon [ʃarbɔ̃] *nm* coal; **c. de bois** charcoal

charcuterie [ʃarkytri] *nf (magasin)* pork butcher's shop; *(aliments)* cooked (pork) meats ■ **charcutier, -ère** *nmf* pork butcher

chardon [ʃardɔ̃] *nm (plante)* thistle

charge [ʃarʒ] *nf (poids)* load; *(responsabilité)* responsibility; *(d'une arme) & Él, Mil* charge; *(fonction)* office; **être en c. de qch** to be in charge of sth; **prendre qn/qch en c.** to take charge of sb/sth; **être à la c. de qn** *(personne)* to be dependent on sb; *(frais)* to be payable by sb; **charges sociales** *Br* national insurance contributions, *Am* Social Security contributions

charger [ʃarʒe] **1** *vt (véhicule, marchandises, arme) & Ordinat* to load; *(batterie) & Mil* to charge; **c. qn de qch** to entrust sb with; **c. qn de faire qch** to give sb the responsibility of doing sth
2 *vi Ordinat* to load up; *Mil* to charge **3 se charger** *vpr (s'encombrer)* to weigh oneself down; **se c. de qn/qch** to take care of sb/sth; **se c. de faire qch** to undertake to do sth ■ **chargé, -e 1** *adj (véhicule)* loaded (**de** with); *(arme)* loaded; *(journée, programme)* busy; **être c. de faire qch** to be responsible for doing sth **2** *nmf* **c. de cours** = part-time lecturer ■ **chargement** *nm (action)* loading; *(marchandises)* load; *(de bateau)* cargo

chariot [ʃarjo] *nm (de supermarché) Br* trolley, *Am* cart; *(de ferme)* waggon; *(de machine à écrire)* carriage; **c. à bagages** luggage trolley

charisme [karism] *nm* charisma

charitable [ʃaritabl] *adj* charitable (**envers** towards)

charité [ʃarite] *nf (vertu)* charity; **faire la c.** to give to charity

charme [ʃarm] *nm (attrait)* charm; *(magie)* spell

charmer [ʃarme] *vt* to charm ■ **charmant, -e** *adj* charming ■ **charmeur,**

-euse 1 *adj (sourire, air)* charming **2** *nmf* charmer

charnel, -elle [ʃarnɛl] *adj* carnal

charnier [ʃarnje] *nm* mass grave

charnière [ʃarnjɛr] *nf* hinge

charnu, -e [ʃarny] *adj* fleshy

charpente [ʃarpɑ̃t] *nf* framework; *(de personne)* build ■ **charpentier** *nm* carpenter

charpie [ʃarpi] *nf* **mettre qch en c.** to tear sth to shreds

charrette [ʃarɛt] *nf* cart

charrier [ʃarje] *vt (transporter)* to cart; *(rivière)* to carry along

charrue [ʃary] *nf Br* plough, *Am* plow

charter [ʃartɛr] *nm (vol)* charter (flight); *(avion)* charter plane

chasse¹ [ʃas] *nf (activité)* hunting; *(événement)* hunt; *(poursuite)* chase; **aller à la c.** to go hunting; **c. à courre** hunting; **c. au trésor** treasure hunt; **c. gardée** private hunting ground

chasse² [ʃas] *nf* **c. d'eau** flush; **tirer la c.** to flush the toilet

chassé-croisé [ʃasekrwaze] *(pl chassés-croisés) nm (de personnes)* comings and goings

chasser [ʃase] **1** *vt (animal)* to hunt; *(faisan, perdrix)* to shoot; **c. qn** *(expulser)* to chase sb away; *(employé)* to dismiss sb **2** *vi* to hunt ■ **chasse-neige** *nm inv Br* snowplough, *Am* snowplow ■ **chasseur, -euse 1** *nmf* hunter; **c. de têtes** headhunter **2** *nm (d'hôtel) Br* pageboy, *Am* bellboy; *(avion)* fighter

châssis [ʃasi] *nm* frame; *(d'automobile)* chassis

chat [ʃa] *nm* cat; **c. sauvage** wildcat

châtaigne [ʃatɛɲ] *nf* chestnut ■ **châtaignier** *nm* chestnut tree ■ **châtain** *adj (cheveux)* (chestnut) brown; *(personne)* brown-haired

château, -x [ʃato] *nm (forteresse)* castle; *(manoir)* mansion

châtiment [ʃatimɑ̃] *nm* punishment; **c. corporel** corporal punishment

chaton [ʃatɔ̃] *nm* (**a**) *(chat)* kitten (**b**) *(de bague)* bezel (**c**) *(d'arbre)* catkin

chatouiller [ʃatuje] *vt* to tickle

■ **chatouilleux, -euse** adj ticklish

chatoyer [ʃatwaje] vi to shimmer; (pierre) to sparkle

châtrer [ʃatre] vt to castrate

chatte [ʃat] nf (female) cat

chaud, -e [ʃo, ʃod] **1** adj (**a**) (modérément) warm; (intensément) hot (**b**) Fig (couleur) warm; (voix) sultry **2** nm **avoir c.** to be hot; **il fait c.** it's hot ■ **chaudement** adv (s'habiller, féliciter) warmly

chaudière [ʃodjer] nf boiler

chauffage [ʃofaʒ] nm heating; (de voiture) heater

chauffard [ʃofar] nm reckless driver

chauffer [ʃofe] **1** vt to heat (up); (moteur) to warm up **2** vi to heat (up); (s'échauffer) (moteur) to overheat; **faire c. qch** to heat sth up **3** se chauffer vpr to warm oneself ■ **chauffant, -e** adj **couverture chauffante** electric blanket; **plaque chauffante** hot plate ■ **chauffé, -e** adj (piscine) heated ■ **chauffe-eau** nm inv water heater; **c. électrique** immersion heater ■ **chauffe-plat** (pl **chauffe-plats**) nm hotplate ■ **chaufferie** nf boiler room

chauffeur [ʃofœr] nm (de véhicule) driver; (employé) chauffeur; **c. de taxi** taxi driver

chaume [ʃom] nm (pour toits) thatch; **toit de c.** thatched roof ■ **chaumière** nf toit de chaume) thatched cottage; (maison pauvre) cottage

chaussée [ʃose] nf road(way)

chausser [ʃose] **1** vt (chaussures, lunettes, skis) to put on; **c. qn** to put shoes on sb; **c. du 40** to take a size 40 shoe **2** se chausser vpr to put one's shoes on

chaussette [ʃoset] nf sock

chausson [ʃosɔ̃] nm (pantoufle) slipper; (de danse) ballet shoe; (de bébé) bootee; Culin **c. aux pommes** apple turnover

chaussure [ʃosyr] nf shoe; **chaussures de ski** ski boots

chauve [ʃov] **1** adj bald **2** nm bald (-headed) man

chauve-souris [ʃovsuri] (pl **chauves-souris**) nf bat

chauvin, -e [ʃovɛ̃, -in] **1** adj chauvinistic **2** nmf chauvinist

chaux [ʃo] nf lime; **blanchir qch à la c.** to whitewash sth

chavirer [ʃavire] vti (bateau) to capsize

chef [ʃef] nm (**a**) (de groupe) leader; (de tribu) chief; **rédacteur en c.** editor in chief; **le c. du gouvernement** the head of government; **c. d'entreprise** company head; **c. d'État** head of state; **c. d'orchestre** conductor (**b**) (cuisinier) chef

chef-d'œuvre [ʃedœvr] (pl **chefs-d'œuvre**) nm masterpiece

chef-lieu [ʃefljø] (pl **chefs-lieux**) nm = administrative centre of a 'département'

chemin [ʃəmɛ̃] nm (route étroite) path, track; (itinéraire) way (**de** to); **à mi-c.** half-way; **en c., c. faisant** on the way; **c. de grande randonnée** hiking trail; **c. de terre** track ■ **chemin de fer** (pl **chemins de fer**) nm Br railway, Am railroad

cheminée [ʃəmine] nf (âtre) fireplace; (encadrement) mantelpiece; (sur le toit) chimney

cheminot [ʃəmino] nm Br railwayman, Am railroader

chemise [ʃəmiz] nf (vêtement) shirt; (classeur) folder; **c. de nuit** (de femme) nightdress ■ **chemisier** nm (corsage) blouse

chenal, -aux [ʃənal, -o] nm channel

chêne [ʃen] nm (arbre, bois) oak

chenil [ʃəni(l)] nm Br kennels, Am kennel

chenille [ʃənij] nf (insecte) caterpillar; (de char) caterpillar track

chèque [ʃɛk] nm Br cheque, Am check; **faire un c. à qn** to write sb a cheque; **payer qch par c.** to pay sth by cheque; **c. de voyage** traveller's cheque, Am traveler's check ■ **chèque-repas** (pl **chèques-repas**), **chèque-restaurant** (pl **chèques-restaurants**) nm Br luncheon voucher,

Am meal ticket ▪ **chéquier** *nm Br* cheque book, *Am* checkbook

cher, chère [ʃɛr] **1** *adj* (**a**) *(aimé)* dear (à to); **C. Monsieur** *(dans une lettre)* Dear Mr X; *(officiel)* Dear Sir (**b**) *(coûteux)* expensive, dear **2** *adv* **coûter c.** to be expensive **3** *nmf* **mon c., ma chère** my dear ▪ **chèrement** *adv (à un prix élevé)* dearly

chercher [ʃɛrʃe] **1** *vt* to look for; *(dans ses souvenirs)* to try to think of; *(dans un dictionnaire)* to look up; **aller c. qn/qch** to (go and) fetch sb/sth; **c. à faire qch** to try to do sth **2 se chercher** *vpr (chercher son identité)* to try to find oneself ▪ **chercheur, -euse** *nmf (scientifique)* researcher; **c. d'or** gold digger

chérir [ʃerir] *vt* to cherish ▪ **chéri, -e** *adj* dear

cherté [ʃɛrte] *nf* high cost

chétif, -ive [ʃetif, -iv] *adj (personne)* puny

cheval, -aux [ʃəval, -o] *nm* horse; **à c.** on horseback; **faire du c.** *Br* to go horse riding, *Am* to go horseback riding; **c. de course** racehorse; *Aut* **c. (-vapeur)** horsepower

chevalet [ʃəvalɛ] *nm (de peintre)* easel

chevalier [ʃəvalje] *nm* knight

chevalière [ʃəvaljɛr] *nf* signet ring

chevaline [ʃəvalin] *adj f* **boucherie c.** horse butcher's (shop)

chevaucher [ʃəvoʃe] **1** *vt* to straddle **2** *vi* **se chevaucher** *vpr* to overlap

chevelu, -e [ʃəvly] *adj* long-haired ▪ **chevelure** *nf (head of) hair*

chevet [ʃəvɛ] *nm* bedhead; **rester au c. de qn** to stay at sb's bedside

cheveu, -x [ʃəvø] *nm* **un c.** a hair; **cheveux** hair; **avoir les cheveux noirs** to have black hair

cheville [ʃəvij] *nf (partie du corps)* ankle

chèvre [ʃɛvr] **1** *nf* goat **2** *nm* goat's cheese

chevreau, -x [ʃəvro] *nm* kid

chèvrefeuille [ʃɛvrəfœj] *nm* honeysuckle

chevreuil [ʃəvrœj] *nm* roe deer; *(viande)* venison

chevronné, -e [ʃəvrɔne] *adj* experienced

chez [ʃe] *prép* **c. qn** at sb's house; **il n'est pas c. lui** he isn't at home; **elle est rentrée c. elle** she's gone home; **c. Mme Dupont** *(adresse)* c/o Mme Dupont ▪ **chez-soi** *nm inv* **son petit c.** one's own little home

chic [ʃik] **1** *adj inv* smart, stylish; *(gentil)* decent **2** *nm (élégance)* style; **avoir le c. pour faire qch** to have the knack of doing sth

chicaner [ʃikane] *vi* **c. sur qch** to quibble over sth

chicorée [ʃikɔre] *nf (en poudre)* chicory

chien, chienne [ʃjɛ̃, ʃjɛn] *nmf* dog, *f* bitch; *Fam* **quel temps de c.!** what foul weather!; **c. d'aveugle** guide dog; **c. de berger** sheepdog; **c. de garde** guard dog; **c. policier** police dog

chiendent [ʃjɛ̃dã] *nm (plante)* couch grass

chiffon [ʃifɔ̃] *nm* rag; **passer un coup de c. sur qch** to give sth a dust; **c. (de poussière)** *Br* duster, *Am* dustcloth

chiffonner [ʃifɔne] *vt* to crumple; *Fig (ennuyer)* to bother

chiffre [ʃifr] *nm (nombre)* figure, number; *(total)* total; **chiffres romains/arabes** Roman/Arabic numerals; **c. d'affaires** turnover ▪ **chiffrer 1** *vt (montant)* to work out; *(réparations)* to assess **2 se chiffrer** *vpr* **se c. à** to amount to

chignon [ʃiɲɔ̃] *nm* bun, chignon

Chili [ʃili] *nm* **le C.** Chile ▪ **chilien, -enne 1** *adj* Chilean **2** *nmf* **C., Chilienne** Chilean

chimie [ʃimi] *nf* chemistry ▪ **chimique** *adj* chemical ▪ **chimiste** *nmf (research)* chemist

chimiothérapie [ʃimjɔterapi] *nf Méd* chemotherapy

chimpanzé [ʃɛ̃pãze] *nm* chimpanzee

Chine [ʃin] *nf* **la C.** China ▪ **chinois, -e 1** *adj* Chinese **2** *nmf* **C., Chinoise**

Chinese; **les C.** the Chinese **3** *nm (langue)* Chinese

chiot [ʃjo] *nm* puppy, pup

chipoter [ʃipɔte] *vi (contester)* to quibble (**sur** about)

chips [ʃips] *nf Br* (potato) crisp, *Am* (potato) chip

chiromancien, -enne [kirɔmɑ̃sjɛ̃, -ɛn] *nmf* palmist

chirurgie [ʃiryrʒi] *nf* surgery; **c. esthétique** plastic surgery ■ **chirurgical, -e, -aux, -ales** *adj* surgical ■ **chirurgien, -enne** *nmf* surgeon ■ **chirurgien-dentiste** *(pl* **chirurgiens-dentistes)** *nm* dental surgeon

chlem [ʃlɛm] *nm Sport* **le grand c.** the grand slam

chlore [klɔr] *nm* chlorine

choc [ʃɔk] **1** *nm (coup)* impact; *(forte émotion)* shock; *(conflit)* clash; **faire un c. à qn** to give sb a shock; **c. pétrolier** oil crisis **2** *adj* **image-c.** shocking image; **'prix-chocs'** 'drastic reductions'

chocolat [ʃɔkɔla] **1** *nm* chocolate; **gâteau au c.** chocolate cake; **c. à croquer** *Br* plain chocolate, *Am* bittersweet chocolate; **c. au lait** milk chocolate **2** *adj inv* chocolate(-coloured) ■ **chocolaté, -e** *adj* chocolate

chœur [kœr] *nm (chanteurs, nef)* choir; *(d'opéra)* chorus; **en c.** *(chanter)* in chorus; *(répéter)* (all) together

choisir [ʃwazir] *vt* to choose, to pick; **c. de faire qch** to choose to do sth ■ **choisi, -e** *adj (œuvres)* selected; *(langage)* careful

choix [ʃwa] *nm* choice; *(assortiment)* selection; **avoir le c.** to have a choice

cholestérol [kɔlesterɔl] *nm Méd* cholesterol

chômer [ʃome] *vi* **vous n'avez pas chômé!** you've not been idle!; **jour chômé** (public) holiday ■ **chômage** *nm* unemployment; **être au c.** to be unemployed ■ **chômeur, -euse** *nmf* unemployed person; **les chômeurs** the unemployed

choquer [ʃoke] *vt (scandaliser)* to

shock ■ **choquant, -e** *adj* shocking

choral, -e, -aux *ou* **-als, -ales** [kɔral] *adj* choral ■ **chorale** *nf (club)* choral society; *(chanteurs)* choir ■ **choriste** *nmf* chorister

chorégraphe [kɔregraf] *nmf* choreographer

chose [ʃoz] *nf* thing; **avant toute c.** first of all

chou, -x [ʃu] *nm* cabbage; **choux de Bruxelles** Brussels sprouts; **c. à la crème** cream puff ■ **chou-fleur** *(pl* **choux-fleurs)** *nm* cauliflower

choucroute [ʃukrut] *nf* sauerkraut

chouette [ʃwɛt] **1** *nf (oiseau)* owl **2** *adj Fam (chic)* great **3** *exclam* great!

choyer [ʃwaje] *vt* to pamper

chrétien, -enne [kretjɛ̃, -ɛn] *adj & nmf* Christian ■ **Christ** [krist] *nm* **le C.** Christ ■ **christianisme** *nm* Christianity

chrome [krom] *nm* chromium; **chromes** *(de voitures)* chrome

chronique¹ [krɔnik] *adj (malade, chômage)* chronic

chronique² [krɔnik] *nf (de journal)* column; *(annales)* chronicle

chronologie [krɔnɔlɔʒi] *nf* chronology ■ **chronologique** *adj* chronological

chronomètre [krɔnɔmɛtr] *nm* chronometer; *(pour le sport)* stopwatch ■ **chronométrer** *vt* to time

chrysanthème [krizɑ̃tɛm] *nm* chrysanthemum

chuchoter [ʃyʃote] *vti* to whisper ■ **chuchotement** *nm* whisper

chuinter [ʃwɛte] *vi (siffler)* to hiss

chut [ʃyt] *exclam* sh!, shush!

chute [ʃyt] *nf* fall; *(d'histoire drôle)* punchline; *(de tissu)* scrap; **c. de neige** snowfall; **c. libre** free fall ■ **chuter** *vi (diminuer)* to fall, to drop; *Fam (tomber)* to fall

Chypre [ʃipr] *nm ou f* Cyprus ■ **chypriote 1** *adj* Cypriot **2** *nmf* **C.** Cypriot

ci [si] *pron démonstratif* **comme ci comme ça** so so

-ci [si] *adv* **(a) par-ci, par-là** here and

there (**b**) *voir* **ce¹, celui** ■ **ci-après** *adv* below ■ **ci-contre** *adv* opposite ■ **ci-dessous** *adv* below ■ **ci-dessus** *adv* above ■ **ci-gît** *adv* here lies… *(on gravestones)* ■ **ci-joint, -e** *(mpl* **ci-joints,** *fpl* **ci-jointes) 1** *adj* **le document c.** the enclosed document **2** *adv* **vous trouverez c. copie de…** please find enclosed a copy of…

cible [sibl] *nf* target

ciboulette [sibulɛt] *nf* chives

cicatrice [sikatris] *nf* scar

cicatriser [sikatrize] *vti,* **se cicatriser** *vpr* to heal ■ **cicatrisation** *nf* healing

cidre [sidr] *nm* cider

Cie *(abrév* **compagnie)** Co

ciel [sjɛl] *nm* **(a)** *(pl* **ciels)** sky; **à c. ouvert** open-air **(b)** *(pl* **cieux** [sjø]) *(paradis)* heaven

cierge [sjɛrʒ] *nm Rel* candle

cigale [sigal] *nf* cicada

cigare [sigar] *nm* cigar ■ **cigarette** *nf* cigarette

cigogne [sigɔɲ] *nf* stork

cil [sil] *nm* eyelash

cime [sim] *nf (d'arbre)* top; *(de montagne)* peak

ciment [simã] *nm* cement

cimetière [simtjɛr] *nm* cemetery; *(d'église)* graveyard

cinéaste [sineast] *nmf* film maker ■ **ciné-club** *(pl* **ciné-clubs)** *nm* film club ■ **cinéphile** *nmf Br* film *or Am* movie enthusiast

cinéma [sinema] *nm (art, industrie) Br* cinema, *Am* movies; *(salle) Br* cinema, *Am* movie theater; **faire du c.** to be a film actor/actress; **aller au c.** to go to the *Br* cinema *orAm* movies ■ **cinématographique** *adj* film; **industrie c.** film industry

cinglé, -e [sɛ̃gle] *adj Fam* crazy

cingler [sɛ̃gle] *vt* to lash ■ **cinglant, -e** *adj (pluie)* lashing; *(remarque)* cutting

cinq [sɛ̃k] **1** *adj inv* five **2** *nm inv* five ■ **cinquième** *adj & nmf* fifth; **un c. a** fifth

cinquante [sɛ̃kɑ̃t] *adj & nm inv* fifty ■ **cinquantaine** *nf* **une c. (de)** about

fifty; **avoir la c.** to be about fifty ■ **cinquantenaire** *nm (anniversaire)* fiftieth anniversary ■ **cinquantième** *adj & nmf* fiftieth

cintre [sɛ̃tr] *nm* coathanger

cirage [siraʒ] *nm (shoe)* polish

circonscription [sirkɔ̃skripsjɔ̃] *nf* division, district; **c. (électorale)** *Br* constituency, *Am* district

circonscrire* [sirkɔ̃skrir] *vt (encercler)* to encircle; *(incendie)* to contain

circonspect, -e [sirkɔ̃spɛ, -ɛkt] *adj* cautious, circumspect

circonstance [sirkɔ̃stɑ̃s] *nf* circumstance; **en pareilles circonstances** under such circumstances

circuit [sirkɥi] *nm Él & Sport* circuit; *(chemin)* way; **c. automobile** racing circuit; **c. touristique** (organized) tour

circulaire [sirkylɛr] **1** *adj* circular **2** *nf (lettre)* circular

circulation [sirkylɑsjɔ̃] *nf (du sang, de l'information, de billets)* circulation; *(d'autos)* traffic; **c. routière/aérienne** road/air traffic ■ **circuler** *vi (sang, air, information)* to circulate; *(voyageur)* to travel; *(train, bus)* to run

cire [sir] *nf* wax; *(pour meubles)* polish ■ **ciré** *nm (vêtement)* oilskin(s) ■ **cirer** *vt* to polish ■ **cireux, -euse** *adj* waxy

cirque [sirk] *nm (spectacle)* circus

cisailles [sizaj] *nfpl (garden)* shears ■ **ciseau, -x** *nm (de menuisier)* chisel; **(une paire de) ciseaux** (a pair of) scissors

ciseler [sizle] *vt* to chisel; *(or, argent)* to chase

citadelle [sitadɛl] *nf* citadel ■ **citadin, -e 1** *adj* city **2** *nmf* city dweller

cité [site] *nf (ville)* city; *(immeubles) Br* housing estate, *Am* housing development; **c. universitaire** *(students')* halls of residence, *Am* university dormitory complex

citer [site] *vt (auteur, texte)* to quote; *(énumérer)* to name ■ **citation** *nf* quotation

citerne [sitɛrn] *nf* tank

citoyen, -enne [sitwajɛ̃, -ɛn] *nmf* citizen ■ **citoyenneté** *nf* citizenship

citron [sitrɔ̃] *nm* lemon; **c. pressé** = freshly squeezed lemon juice served with water and sugar; **c. vert** lime ■ **citronnade** *nf Br* lemon squash, *Am* lemonade

citrouille [sitruj] *nf* pumpkin

civet [sive] *nm* stew

civière [sivjɛr] *nf* stretcher

civil, -e [sivil] **1** *adj (guerre, mariage, droits)* civil; *(non militaire)* civilian; *(courtois)* civil; **année civile** calendar year **2** *nm* civilian; **dans le c.** in civilian life; **en c.** *(policier)* in plain clothes ■ **civilité** *nf* civility

civilisation [sivilizasjɔ̃] *nf* civilization ■ **civilisé, -e** *adj* civilized

civique [sivik] *adj* civic; *Scol* **instruction c.** civics

clair, -e [klɛr] **1** *adj (net, limpide, évident)* clear; *(éclairé, pâle)* light; **bleu/ vert c.** light blue/green **2** *adv (voir)* clearly; **il fait c.** it's light **3** *nm* **en c.** in plain language; **c. de lune** moonlight

clairière [klɛrjɛr] *nf* clearing

clairon [klɛrɔ̃] *nm* bugle; *(soldat)* bugler

clairsemé, -e [klɛrsəme] *adj (auditoire, population)* sparse

clairvoyant, -e [klɛrvwajɑ̃, -ɑ̃t] *adj* perceptive

clameur [klamœr] *nf* clamour

clan [klɑ̃] *nm (tribu)* clan; *Péj (groupe)* clique

clandestin, -e [klɑ̃dɛstɛ̃, -in] *adj (rencontre)* clandestine; *(mouvement)* underground; *(travailleur)* illegal

clapier [klapje] *nm (rabbit)* hutch

clapoter [klapɔte] *vi (vagues)* to lap

claque [klak] *nf Fam* slap

claquer [klake] **1** *vt (porte)* to slam **2** *vi (porte)* to slam; *(drapeau)* to flap; *(talons)* to click; *(coup de feu)* to ring out; **elle claque des dents** her teeth are chattering **3 se claquer** *vpr* **se c. un muscle** to pull a muscle ■ **claquement** *nm (de porte)* slam(ming)

claquettes [klakɛt] *nfpl* tap dancing;

faire des c. to do tap dancing

clarifier [klarifje] *vt* to clarify ■ **clarification** *nf* clarification

clarinette [klarinɛt] *nf* clarinet

clarté [klarte] *nf (lumière)* light; *(transparence)* clearness; *Fig (d'explications)* clarity; **avec c.** clearly

classe [klas] *nf (catégorie, leçon, élèves)* class; **en c. de sixième** *Br* in the first year, *Am* in fifth grade; **aller en c.** to go to school; **avoir de la c.** *(personne)* to have class; **(salle de) c.** classroom; **de première c.** *(billet, compartiment)* first-class; **c. ouvrière/ moyenne** working/middle class; **sociale** social class

classer [klase] **1** *vt (objets)* to classify; *(papiers)* to file; **c. une affaire** to consider a matter closed

  2 se classer *vpr* **se c. parmi les meileurs** to rank among the best; *Sport* **se c. troisième** to be placed third ■ **classé, -e** *adj (monument)* listed; *(au tennis)* seeded ■ **classement** *nm* classification; *(de papiers)* filing; *(rang)* place; *Sport* table ■ **classeur** *nm (meuble)* filing cabinet; *(portefeuille)* ring binder

classifier [klasifje] *vt* to classify ■ **classification** *nf* classification

classique [klasik] **1** *adj (période)* classical; *(typique, conventionnel)* classic **2** *nm (œuvre)* classic; *(auteur)* classical author

claustrophobe [klostrɔfɔb] *adj* claustrophobic

clavecin [klavsɛ̃] *nm* harpsichord

clavicule [klavikyl] *nf* collarbone

clavier [klavje] *nm* keyboard

clé, clef [kle] **1** *nf (de porte)* key; *(outil) Br* spanner, *Am* wrench; **fermer qch à c.** to lock sth; **c. de contact** ignition key; *Mus* **c. de sol** treble clef; *Fig* **c. de voûte** cornerstone **2** *adj* key; **poste c.** key post

clément, -e [klemɑ̃, -ɑ̃t] *adj (juge)* clement; *(temps)* mild ■ **clémence** *nf (de juge)* clemency; *(de temps)* mildness

clémentine [klemɑ̃tin] *nf* clementine

clerc [klɛr] *nm Rel* cleric; **c. de notaire** ≃ solicitor's clerk ■ **clergé** *nm* clergy ■ **clérical, -e, -aux, -ales** *adj* clerical

cliché [kliʃe] *nm (photo)* photo; *(negative)* negative; *(idée)* cliché

client, -e [klijɑ̃, -ɑ̃t] *nmf (de magasin)* customer; *(d'avocat)* client; *(d'hôtel)* guest; *(de taxi)* fare ■ **clientèle** *nf (de magasin)* customers; *(d'avocat)* practice

cligner [kliɲe] *vi* **c. des yeux** to blink; **c. de l'œil** to wink

clignoter [kliɲɔte] *vi (lumière, voyant)* to flash ■ **clignotant** *nm (de voiture) Br* indicator, *Am* flasher; **mettre son c.** to indicate

climat [klima] *nm (de région) & Fig* climate ■ **climatique** *adj* climatic

climatisation [klimatizasjɔ̃] *nf* air-conditioning ■ **climatisé, -e** *adj* air-conditioned

clin d'œil [klɛ̃dœj] *(pl* **clins d'œil)** *nm* wink; **faire un c. à qn** to wink at sb; **en un c.** in a flash

clinique [klinik] *nf (hôpital)* clinic

clinquant, -e [klɛ̃kɑ̃, -ɑ̃t] *adj* flashy

clip [klip] *nm (vidéo)* (music) video

cliquer [klike] *vi Ordinat* to click

cliqueter [klikte] *vi (monnaie, clefs)* to jingle ■ **cliquetis** *nm (de monnaie, de clefs)* jingling

clivage [klivaʒ] *nm (de société)* divide; *(de parti)* split

clochard, -e [klɔʃar, -ard] *nmf* tramp

cloche [klɔʃ] *nf (d'église)* bell; **c. à fromage** covered cheese dish ■ **clocher 1** *nm (d'église)* bell tower, steeple **2** *vi Fam* **il y a quelque chose qui cloche** there's something wrong somewhere

cloche-pied [klɔʃpje] ■ **à cloche-pied** *adv* **sauter à c.** to hop

cloison [klwazɔ̃] *nf (entre pièces)* partition

cloître [klwatr] *nm (de monastère)* cloister; *(pour moines)* monastery; *(pour religieuses)* convent

clone [klon] *nm Biol* clone

clopin-clopant [klɔpɛ̃klɔpɑ̃] *adv* **aller c.** to hobble along

cloque [klɔk] *nf (au pied)* blister

clore* [klɔr] *vt (réunion)* to conclude; *(débat)* to close; *Ordinat* **c. une session** to log off

clos, -e [klo, kloz] **1** *adj (porte, volets)* closed; **l'incident est c.** the matter is closed; **espace c.** enclosed space **2** *nm* enclosure

clôture [klotyr] *nf (barrière)* fence; *(de réunion)* conclusion; *(de débat)* closing; *(de Bourse)* close ■ **clôturer** *vt (terrain)* to enclose

clou [klu] *nm (pointe)* nail; *(de spectacle)* main attraction; **les clous** *(passage) Br* the pedestrian crossing, *Am* the crosswalk; **c. de girofle** clove ■ **clouer** *vt (au mur)* to nail up; *(ensemble)* to nail together; **cloué au lit** confined to (one's) bed

clown [klun] *nm* clown; **faire le c.** to clown around

club [klœb] *nm* club

cm *(abrév* **centimètre)** cm

coalition [kɔalisjɔ̃] *nf* coalition

cobaye [kɔbaj] *nm (animal) & Fig* guinea pig

cocaïne [kɔkain] *nf* cocaine

coccinelle [kɔksinɛl] *nf (insecte) Br* ladybird, *Am* ladybug; *(voiture)* Beetle

cocher¹ [kɔʃe] *vt Br* to tick, *Am* to check

cocher² [kɔʃe] *nm* coachman

cochon, -onne [kɔʃɔ̃, -ɔn] **1** *nm (animal)* pig; *(viande)* pork; **c. d'Inde** guinea pig **2** *nmf (personne sale)* pig **3** *adj (histoire, film)* dirty ■ **cochonnerie** *nf (chose sans valeur)* trash, *Br* rubbish; *(obscénité)* smutty remark; **manger des cochonneries** to eat junk food

cocktail [kɔktɛl] *nm (boisson)* cocktail; *(réunion)* cocktail party; **c. de fruits** fruit cocktail

coco [kɔko] *nm* **noix de c.** coconut

cocu, -e [kɔky] **1** *adj* **il est c.** his wife's cheating on him **2** *nm* cuckold

code [kɔd] *nm (symboles, lois) & Ordinat* code; **passer le c.** *(du permis de* *conduire)* = to sit the written part of one's driving test; **codes** *Br* dipped headlights, *Am* low beams; **le c. de la route** *Br* the Highway Code, *Am* the traffic regulations; *Jur* **c. civil/pénal** civil/penal code; **c. confidentiel** security code; *(de carte bancaire)* PIN; **c. postal** *Br* postcode, *Am* zip code ∎ **code-barres** *(pl* **codes-barres)** *nm* bar code ∎ **coder** *vt* to code

coéquipier, -ère [kɔekipje, -ɛr] *nmf* team-mate

cœur [kœr] *nm* heart; *Cartes (couleur)* hearts; **avoir mal au c.** to feel sick; **par c.** (off) by heart; **de bon c.** *(volontiers)* willingly; *(rire)* heartily

coexister [kɔegziste] *vi* to coexist

coffre [kɔr] *nm (meuble)* chest; *(pour objets de valeur)* safe; *(de voiture) Br* boot, *Am* trunk; **c. à bagages** *(d'avion)* baggage compartment; **c. à jouets** toy box ∎ **coffre-fort** *(pl* **coffres-forts)** *nm* safe ∎ **coffret** *nm (petit coffre)* box; **c. à bijoux** *Br* jewellery or *Am* jewelry box

cogner [kɔɲe] **1** *vt (heurter)* to knock **2** *vi (buter)* to bang **(sur/contre** on) **3 se cogner** *vpr* to bang oneself; **se c. la tête contre qch** to bang one's head on sth; **se c. à qch** to bang into sth

cohabiter [kɔabite] *vi* to live together; **c. avec qn** to live with sb

cohérent, -e [kɔerɑ̃, -ɑ̃t] *adj (discours)* coherent; *(attitude)* consistent ∎ **cohérence** *nf (de discours)* coherence; *(d'attitude)* consistency ∎ **cohésion** *nf* cohesion

cohue [kɔy] *nf* crowd

coiffe [kwaf] *nf* headdress

coiffer [kwafe] **1** *vt Fig (surmonter)* to cap; *(service)* to head; **c. qn de qch** to put sth on sb's head; **elle est bien coiffée** her hair is lovely **2 se coiffer** *vpr* to do one's hair; **se c. de qch** to put sth on

coiffeur, -euse[1] [kwafœr, -øz] *nmf* hairdresser ∎ **coiffeuse[2]** *nf (meuble)* dressing table ∎ **coiffure** *nf (chapeau)* headgear; *(coupe de cheveux)* hairstyle

coin [kwɛ̃] *nm (angle)* corner; *(endroit)* spot; *(cale)* wedge; **faire le c.** to be on the corner; **dans le c.** in the area; *Fam* **le petit c.** *(toilettes)* the smallest room in the house

coincer [kwɛ̃se] **1** *vt (mécanisme, tiroir)* to jam; *(caler)* to wedge **2** *vi (mécanisme, tiroir)* to jam **3 se coincer** *vpr (mécanisme)* to jam; **se c. le doigt dans la porte** to catch one's finger in the door ∎ **coincé, -e** *adj (mécanisme, tiroir)* stuck, jammed

coïncider [kɔɛ̃side] *vi* to coincide **(avec** with) ∎ **coïncidence** *nf* coincidence

col [kɔl] *nm (de chemise)* collar; *Géog* col; **c. en V** V-neck; **c. roulé** *Br* polo neck, *Am* turtleneck

colère [kɔlɛr] *nf* anger; **être en c. (contre qn)** to be angry (with sb); **se mettre en c.** to get angry **(contre** with) ∎ **coléreux, -euse** *adj (personne)* quick-tempered

colimaçon [kɔlimasɔ̃] **en colimaçon** *adv* **escalier en c.** spiral staircase

colin [kɔlɛ̃] *nm (merlu)* hake; *(lieu noir)* coley

colique [kɔlik] *nf Br* diarrhoea, *Am* diarrhea

colis [kɔli] *nm* parcel

collaborer [kɔlabɔre] *vi* collaborate **(avec** with); **c. à qch** *(projet)* to take part in sth ∎ **collaborateur, -trice** *nmf (aide)* assistant ∎ **collaboration** *nf (aide)* collaboration

collage [kɔlaʒ] *nm (œuvre, jeu)* collage

collant, -e [kɔlɑ̃, -ɑ̃t] **1** *adj (papier)* sticky; *(vêtement)* skin-tight **2** *nm Br* tights, *Am* pantihose

colle [kɔl] *nf (transparente)* glue; *(blanche)* paste; *Fam (question)* poser; *Fam (retenue)* detention

collecte [kɔlɛkt] *nf* collection ∎ **collecter** *vt* to collect

collectif, -ive [kɔlɛktif, -iv] *adj* collective ∎ **collectivité** *nf (groupe)* community

collection [kɔlɛksjɔ̃] *nf (ensemble)* collection; **faire la c. de qch** to collect sth ■ **collectionner** vt to collect ■ **collectionneur, -euse** nmf collector

collège [kɔlɛʒ] nm (école) school ■ **collégien** nm schoolboy ■ **collégienne** nf schoolgirl

collègue [kɔlɛg] nmf colleague

coller [kɔle] **1** vt (timbre) to stick; (à la colle transparente) to glue; (à la colle blanche) to paste; (enveloppe) to stick (down); (deux objets) to stick together; (affiche) to stick up; Fam **c. un élève** (en punition) to keep a pupil in; Fam **être collé** (à un examen) to fail
2 se coller vpr **se c. contre un mur** to flatten oneself against a wall

collier [kɔlje] nm (bijou) necklace; (de chien) collar

colline [kɔlin] nf hill

collision [kɔlizjɔ̃] nf (de véhicules) collision; **entrer en c. avec qch** to collide with sth

colloque [kɔlɔk] nm (conférence) seminar

colmater [kɔlmate] vt to fill in

colombe [kɔlɔ̃b] nf dove

Colombie [kɔlɔ̃bi] nf **la C.** Columbia ■ **colombien, -enne 1** adj Columbian **2** nmf **C., Colombienne** Columbian

colon [kɔlɔ̃] nm (pionnier) settler, colonist

colonel [kɔlɔnɛl] nm (d'infanterie) colonel

colonial, -e, -aux, -ales [kɔlɔnjal, -jo] adj colonial

colonie [kɔlɔni] nf colony; **c. de vacances** Br (children's) holiday camp, Am summer camp

coloniser [kɔlɔnize] vt to colonize

colonne [kɔlɔn] nf column; Anat **c. vertébrale** spine

colorer [kɔlɔre] vt to colour; **c. qch en vert** to colour sth green ■ **colorant, -e** nm (pour teindre) colorant; (alimentaire) colouring ■ **colorier** vt (dessin) to colour (in) ■ **coloris** nm (nuance) shade

colosse [kɔlɔs] nm giant ■ **colossal, -e, -aux, -ales** adj colossal

colporter [kɔlpɔrte] vt (marchandises) to hawk; (rumeur) to spread

colza [kɔlza] nm rape

coma [kɔma] nm coma; **être dans le c.** to be in a coma

combat [kɔ̃ba] nm (bataille) & Fig fight; **c. de boxe** boxing match ■ **combatif, -ive** adj combative

combattre* [kɔ̃batr] **1** vt (personne, incendie) to fight (against); (maladie) to fight **2** vi to fight ■ **combattant, -e 1** adj (troupes) fighting **2** nmf combattant; **anciens combattants** veterans

combien [kɔ̃bjɛ̃] **1** adv (**a**) (en quantité) how much; (en nombre) how many; **c. d'argent** how much money; **c. de temps** how long; **c. de gens** how many people; **c. y a-t-il d'ici à...?** how far is it to...? (**b**) (comme) how; **tu verras c. il est bête** you'll see how silly he is **2** nm inv Fam **le c. sommes-nous?** what's the date?

combinaison [kɔ̃binɛzɔ̃] nf (assemblage) combination; (vêtement de travail) Br boiler suit, Am coveralls; **c. de ski** ski suit

combiner [kɔ̃bine] **1** vt (unir) to combine **2 se combiner** vpr to combine ■ **combiné** nm (de téléphone) receiver

comble [kɔ̃bl] **1** adj (salle, bus) packed; Théât **faire salle c.** to have a full house **2** nm **le c. du bonheur** the height of happiness; **c'est un** ou **le c.!** that's the last straw!

combler [kɔ̃ble] vt (trou) to fill in; (lacune) to fill; (désir) to satisfy

combustible [kɔ̃bystibl] **1** adj combustible **2** nm fuel ■ **combustion** nf combustion

comédie [kɔmedi] nf comedy; **jouer la c.** to act; **c. musicale** musical ■ **comédien** nm actor ■ **comédienne** nf actress

comestible [kɔmɛstibl] adj edible

comète [kɔmɛt] nf comet

comique [kɔmik] **1** adj (amusant) funny, comical; (acteur, rôle) comedy **2** nm (genre) comedy; (acteur) comic actor

comité [kɔmite] nm committee; **c.**

d'entreprise works council

commandant [kɔmɑ̃dɑ̃] *nm (de navire)* captain; *(grade) (dans l'infanterie)* major; *(dans l'aviation)* squadron leader; *Aviat* **c. de bord** captain

commande [kɔmɑ̃d] *nf (a) (achat)* order; **sur c.** to order; **passer une c.** to place an order (**b**) *Tech (action, manette)* control; *Ordinat* command; **c. à distance** remote control; **à c. vocale** voice-activated

commandement [kɔmɑ̃dmɑ̃] *nm (ordre, autorité)* command; *Rel* Commandment

commander [kɔmɑ̃de] **1** *vt (diriger, exiger)* to command; *(marchandises)* to order (**à** from) **2** *vi* **c. à qn de faire qch** to command sb to do sth

commando [kɔmɑ̃do] *nm* commando

COMME [kɔm] **1** *adv* (**a**) *(devant nom, pronom)* like; **c. moi/elle** like me/her; **c. cela** like that; **qu'as-tu c. diplômes?** what do you have in the way of certificates?; **les femmes c. les hommes** men and women alike; **P c. pomme** p as in 'pomme'
(**b**) *(devant proposition)* as; **il écrit c. il parle** he writes as he speaks; **c. si** as if; **c. pour faire qch** as if to do sth
2 *adv (exclamatif)* **regarde c. il pleut!** look how it's raining!; **c. c'est petit!** isn't it small!
3 *conj (cause)* as, since; **c. tu es mon ami…** as *or* since you're my friend…; **c. elle entrait** (just) as she was coming in

commémorer [kɔmemɔre] *vt* to commemorate ■ **commémoration** *nf* commemoration

commencer [kɔmɑ̃se] *vti* to begin, to start (**à** faire to do, doing; **par qch** with sth; **par faire** by doing); **pour c.** to begin with ■ **commencement** *nm* beginning, start; **au c.** at the beginning *or* start

comment [kɔmɑ̃] *adv* how; **c. le sais-tu?** how do you know?; **c. t'appelles-tu?** what's your name?; **c. est-il?** what

is he like?; **c. va-t-il?** how is he?; **c. faire?** what's to be done?; **c.?** *(pour faire répéter)* pardon?

commentaire [kɔmɑ̃ter] *nm (remarque)* comment; *(de radio, de télévision)* commentary ■ **commentateur, -trice** *nmf* commentator ■ **commenter** *vt* to comment (up)on

commérages [kɔmeraʒ] *nmpl* gossip

commerçant, -e [kɔmersɑ̃, -ɑ̃t] **1** *nmf* trader; *(de magasin)* shopkeeper **2** *adj* **rue commerçante** shopping street

commerce [kɔmers] *nm (activité, secteur)* trade; *(affaires, magasin)* business; **c. de proximité** *Br* local shop, *Am* local store ■ **commercial, -e, -aux, -ales** *adj* commercial ■ **commercialisation** *nf* marketing ■ **commercialiser** *vt* to market

commère [kɔmer] *nf* gossip

commettre* [kɔmetr] *vt (meurtre)* to commit; *(erreur)* to make

commis [kɔmi] *nm (de magasin)* shop assistant; *(de bureau)* clerk

commissaire [kɔmiser] *nm (de course)* steward; **c. (de police)** *Br* ≃ police superintendent, *Am* ≃ police captain ■ **commissariat** *nm* **c. (de police)** (central) police station

commission [kɔmisjɔ̃] *nf (course)* errand; *(message)* message; *(comité)* commission, committee; *Com (pourcentage)* commission (**sur** on); **faire les commissions** to go shopping

commode [kɔmɔd] **1** *adj (pratique)* handy; **pas c.** *(pas aimable)* awkward; *(difficile)* tricky **2** *nf Br* chest of drawers, *Am* dresser ■ **commodité** *nf* convenience

commun, -e [kɔmœ̃, -yn] **1** *adj (non exclusif, répandu, vulgaire)* common; *(cuisine)* shared; *(démarche)* joint; **peu c.** uncommon; **ami c.** mutual friend; **en c.** in common; **mettre qch en c.** to share sth **2** *nm* **hors du c.** out of the ordinary

communauté [kɔmynote] *nf (collectivité)* community; **la C. (économique) européenne** the (European) Economic

Community; **la C. d'États indépendants** the Commonwealth of Independent States ∎ **communautaire** *adj (de la CE)* Community; **vie c.** community life

commune [kɔmyn] *nf (municipalité)* commune ∎ **communal, -e, -aux, -ales** *adj Br* ≃ council, *Am* ≃ district; **école communale** ≃ local *Br* primary *or Am* grade school

communicatif, -ive [kɔmynikatif, -iv] *adj (personne)* communicative; *(rire)* infectious

communication [kɔmynikasjɔ̃] *nf* communication; **c. téléphonique** telephone call; **je vous passe la c.** I'll put you through; **la c. est mauvaise** the line is bad

communion [kɔmynjɔ̃] *nf* communion; *Rel* (Holy) Communion

communiquer [kɔmynike] **1** *vt* to communicate (**à** to); *(maladie)* to pass on (**à** to) **2** *vi (personne, pièces)* to communicate (**avec** with) **3 se communiquer** *vpr* to spread (**à** to) ∎ **communiqué** *nm (avis)* communiqué; **c. de presse** press release

communisme [kɔmynism] *nm* communism ∎ **communiste** *adj & nmf* communist

commutateur [kɔmytatœr] *nm (bouton)* switch

compact, -e [kɔ̃pakt] **1** *adj (foule, amas)* dense; *(appareil)* compact **2** *nm (CD)* compact disc

compagne [kɔ̃paɲ] *nf (camarade)* companion; *(concubine)* partner

compagnie [kɔ̃paɲi] *nf (présence, société, soldats)* company; **tenir c. à qn** to keep sb company

compagnon [kɔ̃paɲɔ̃] *nm* companion; *(concubin)* partner; **c. de jeu** playmate; **c. de route** travelling companion

comparaître* [kɔ̃paretr] *vi (devant tribunal)* to appear (in court) (**devant** before)

comparer [kɔ̃pare] *vt* to compare (**à** to, with) ∎ **comparable** *adj* comparable (**à** to, with) ∎ **comparaison** *nf*

comparison (**avec** with); **en c. de...** in comparison with...

compartiment [kɔ̃partimɑ̃] *nm* compartment; **c. à bagages** *(de car)* luggage compartment; **c. fumeurs** smoking compartment

compas [kɔ̃pa] *nm Math Br* (pair of) compasses, *Am* compass; *Naut* compass

compassion [kɔ̃pasjɔ̃] *nf* compassion

compatible [kɔ̃patibl] *adj* compatible (**avec** with) ∎ **compatibilité** *nf* compatibility

compatir [kɔ̃patir] *vi* to sympathize ∎ **compatissant, -e** *adj* compassionate, sympathetic

compatriote [kɔ̃patrijɔt] *nmf* compatriot

compenser [kɔ̃pɑ̃se] **1** *vt (perte, défaut)* to make up for, to compensate for **2** *vi* to compensate ∎ **compensation** *nf (de perte)* compensation; **en c.** in compensation (**de** for)

compétent, -e [kɔ̃petɑ̃, -ɑ̃t] *adj* competent ∎ **compétence** *nf* competence; **compétences** *(connaissances)* skills, abilities

compétition [kɔ̃petisjɔ̃] *nf (rivalité)* competition; *(épreuve sportive)* event; **être en c. avec qn** to compete with sb; **sport de c.** competitive sport ∎ **compétitif, -ive** *adj* competitive

compiler [kɔ̃pile] *vt* to compile

complaire* [kɔ̃pler] **se complaire** *vpr* **se c. dans qch/à faire qch** to delight in sth/in doing sth

complaisant, -e [kɔ̃plɛzɑ̃, -ɑ̃t] *adj (bienveillant)* kind, obliging; *(satisfait)* complacent ∎ **complaisance** *nf (bienveillance)* kindness; *(vanité)* complacency

complément [kɔ̃plemɑ̃] *nm (reste)* rest; *Gram* complement; **un c. d'information** additional information; **c. d'objet direct/indirect** direct/indirect object ∎ **complémentaire** *adj* complementary; *(détails)* additional

complet, -ète [kɔ̃ple, -et] **1** *adj (entier,*

absolu) complete; *(train, hôtel, théâtre)* full; *(pain)* wholemeal **2** *nm (costume)* suit

compléter [kɔ̃plete] **1** *vt (collection, formation)* to complete; *(formulaire)* to fill in; *(somme)* to make up **2 se compléter** *vpr* to complement each other

complexe [kɔ̃plɛks] **1** *adj* complex **2** *nm (sentiment, construction)* complex; **avoir des complexes** to have a hang-up ■ **complexé, -e** *adj Fam* hung up (**par** about) ■ **complexité** *nf* complexity

complication [kɔ̃plikasjɔ̃] *nf (ennui)* & *Méd* complication; *(complexité)* complexity

complice [kɔ̃plis] **1** *nm* accomplice **2** *adj (regard)* knowing; *(silence)* conniving; **être c. de qch** to be a party to sth ■ **complicité** *nf* complicity

compliment [kɔ̃plimã] *nm* compliment; **faire des compliments à qn** to pay sb compliments ■ **complimenter** *vt* to compliment (**sur** on)

compliquer [kɔ̃plike] **1** *vt* to complicate **2 se compliquer** *vpr (situation)* to get complicated; **se c. la vie** to make life complicated for oneself ■ **compliqué, -e** *adj* complicated

complot [kɔ̃plo] *nm* conspiracy (**contre** against)

comporter [kɔ̃pɔrte] **1** *vt (contenir)* to contain; *(être constitué de)* to consist of **2 se comporter** *vpr (personne)* to behave ■ **comportement** [-əmã] *nm* behaviour

composer [kɔ̃poze] **1** *vt (faire partie de)* to make up; *(musique, poème)* to compose; *(numéro de téléphone)* to dial; *Typ* to set; **être composé de qch** to be made up *or* composed of sth **2** *vi (étudiant)* to take a test **3 se composer** *vpr* **se c. de qch** to be made up *or* composed of sth ■ **composant** *nm* component ■ **composante** *nf* component

compositeur, -trice [kɔ̃pozitœr, -tris] *nmf (musicien)* composer; *(typographe)* typesetter

composition [kɔ̃pozisjɔ̃] *nf (de musique, de poème)* composing; *Typ* typesetting; *(éléments)* composition; *(d'aliment)* ingredients; *(examen)* test

composter [kɔ̃pɔste] *vt (billet)* to cancel

compote [kɔ̃pɔt] *nf Br* stewed fruit, *Am* sauce; **c. de pommes** *Br* stewed apples, *Am* applesauce

compréhensible [kɔ̃preãsibl] *adj (justifié)* understandable; *(clair)* comprehensible ■ **compréhensif, -ive** *adj* understanding ■ **compréhension** *nf* understanding

comprendre* [kɔ̃prãdr] **1** *vt (par l'esprit, par les sentiments)* to understand; *(être composé de)* to consist of; *(comporter)* to include; **mal c. qch** to misunderstand sth; **je n'y comprends rien** I can't make head or tail of it **2 se comprendre** *vpr* **ça se comprend** that's understandable

compresse [kɔ̃prɛs] *nf* compress

comprimé [kɔ̃prime] *nm (médicament)* tablet

comprimer [kɔ̃prime] *vt (gaz, artère)* to compress

compris, -e [kɔ̃pri, -iz] *pp voir* **comprendre 2** *adj (inclus)* included (**dans** in); **y c.** including

compromettre* [kɔ̃prɔmɛtr] *vt (personne)* to compromise; *(sécurité)* to jeopardize ■ **compromis** *nm* compromise

comptabiliser [kɔ̃tabilize] *vt (compter)* to count

comptabilité [kɔ̃tabilite] *nf (comptes)* accounts; *(science)* book-keeping, accounting; *(service)* accounts department ■ **comptable** *nmf* accountant

comptant [kɔ̃tã] **1** *adv* **payer c.** to pay (in) cash **2** *nm* **acheter au c.** to buy for cash

COMPTE [kɔ̃t] *nm* (**a**) *(de banque, de commerçant)* account; *(calcul)* calculation; **avoir un c. en banque** to have a bank account; **faire ses comptes** to do one's accounts; **c. chèque** *Br*

current account, *Am* checking account; **c. à rebours** countdown

(b) *(expressions)* **en fin de c.** all things considered; **tenir c. de qch** to take sth into account; **c. tenu de qch** considering sth; **se rendre c. de qch** to realize sth; **rendre c. de qch** *(exposer)* to report on sth; *(justifier)* to account for sth; **travailler à son c.** to be self-employed; *Fig* **être loin du c.** to be wide of the mark ■ **compte-gouttes** *nm inv* dropper; *Fig* **au c.** in dribs and drabs

compter [kɔ̃te] **1** *vt (calculer)* to count; *(prévoir)* to allow; *(include)* to include; **c. faire qch** *(espérer)* to expect to do sth; *(avoir l'intention de)* to intend to do sth; **c. qch à qn** *(facturer)* to charge sb for sth; **sans c....** *(sans parler de)* not to mention…

2 *vi (calculer, être important)* to count; **c. sur qn/qch** to count or rely on sb/sth; **à c. de demain** as from tomorrow

3 se compter *upr* **ses membres se comptent par milliers** it has thousands of members ■ **compteur** *nm* meter; **c. de gaz** gas meter; *Aut* **c. kilométrique** *Br* milometer, *Am* odometer; *Aut* **c. de vitesse** speedometer

compte rendu [kɔ̃trɑ̃dy] *(pl* **comptes rendus)** *nm* report; *(de livre, de film)* review

comptoir [kɔ̃twar] *nm (de magasin)* counter; *(de café)* bar

comte [kɔ̃t] *nm (noble)* count; *(en Grande-Bretagne)* earl ■ **comtesse** *nf* countess

concéder [kɔ̃sede] *vt (victoire, but)* to concede; **c. qch à qn** to grant sb sth

concentrer [kɔ̃sɑ̃tre] **1** *vt* to concentrate; *(attention)* to focus **2 se concentrer** *upr (réfléchir)* to concentrate ■ **concentration** *nf* concentration ■ **concentré, -e 1** *adj (lait)* condensed; *(attentif)* concentrating (hard) **2** *nm* **c. de tomates** tomato purée

concept [kɔ̃sɛpt] *nm* concept ■ **conception** *nf (d'idée)*

(création) design; **c. assistée par ordinateur** computer-aided design

concerner [kɔ̃serne] *vt* to concern; **en ce qui me concerne** as far as I'm concerned ■ **concernant** *prép* concerning

concert [kɔ̃ser] *nm (de musique)* concert

concerter [kɔ̃serte] **se concerter** *upr* to consult together ■ **concertation** *nf* consultation

concession [kɔ̃sesjɔ̃] *nf (compromis)* concession (à to); *(terrain)* plot ■ **concessionnaire** *nmf* dealer

concevoir* [kɔ̃səvwar] **1** *vt (enfant, plan, idée)* to conceive; *(produit)* to design; *(comprendre)* to understand **2 se concevoir** *upr* ça se conçoit that's understandable ■ **concevable** *adj* conceivable

concierge [kɔ̃sjerʒ] *nmf* caretaker, *Am* janitor

concilier [kɔ̃silje] *vt (choses)* to reconcile

concis, -e [kɔ̃si, -is] *adj* concise

conclure* [kɔ̃klyr] *vt (terminer)* to conclude; *(accord)* to finalize; *(marché)* to clinch ■ **concluant, -e** *adj* conclusive ■ **conclusion** *nf* conclusion; **tirer une c. de qch** to draw a conclusion from sth

concombre [kɔ̃kɔ̃br] *nm* cucumber

concorder [kɔ̃korde] *vi (preuves, dates, témoignages)* to tally (**avec** with)

concourir* [kɔ̃kurir] *vi Sport* to compete (**pour** for); *(converger)* to converge; **c. à qch/faire qch** to contribute to sth/do sth

concours [kɔ̃kur] *nm (examen)* competitive examination; *(jeu)* competition; *(aide)* assistance; **c. de beauté** beauty contest

concret, -ète [kɔ̃kre, -et] *adj* concrete ■ **concrétiser 1** *vt (rêve)* to realize; *(projet)* to carry out **2 se concrétiser** *upr* to materialize

conçu, -e [kɔ̃sy] **1** *pp de* **concevoir 2** *adj* **c. pour faire qch** designed to do sth

concubine [kɔ̃kybin] *nf Jur* cohabitant ▪ **concubinage** *nm* cohabitation; **vivre en c.** to cohabit

concurrent, -e [kɔ̃kyrɑ̃, -ɑ̃t] *nmf* competitor ▪ **concurrence** *nf* competition; **faire c. à** to compete with; **jusqu'à c. de 100 euros** up to the amount of 100 euros ▪ **concurrencer** *vt* to compete with

condamnation [kɔ̃danasjɔ̃] *nf Jur (jugement)* conviction (**pour** for); *(peine)* sentence (**à** to); *(critique)* condemnation; **c. à mort** death sentence

condamner [kɔ̃dane] *vt (blâmer)* to condemn; *Jur* to sentence (**à** to); *(porte)* to block up; **c. qn à une amende** to fine sb; **c. qn à qch** *(forcer à)* to force sb into sth ▪ **condamné, -e 1** *adj (malade)* terminally ill **2** *nmf (prisonnier)* convicted person

condensation [kɔ̃dɑ̃sasjɔ̃] *nf* condensation

condescendant, -e [kɔ̃desɑ̃dɑ̃, -ɑ̃t] *adj* condescending

condition [kɔ̃disjɔ̃] *nf (état, stipulation, sort)* condition; *(classe sociale)* station; **conditions** *(circonstances)* conditions; *(de contrat)* terms; **à c. de faire qch, à c. que l'on fasse qch** providing *or* provided (that) one does sth ▪ **conditionnel, -elle 1** *adj* conditional **2** *nm Gram* conditional

conditionner [kɔ̃disjɔne] *vt (être la condition de)* to govern; *(emballer)* to package; *(personne)* to condition ▪ **conditionnement** *nm (emballage)* packaging; *(de personne)* conditioning

condoléances [kɔ̃dɔleɑ̃s] *nfpl* condolences

conducteur, -trice [kɔ̃dyktœr, -tris] **1** *nmf (de véhicule, de train)* driver **2** *adj Él* **fil c.** lead (wire)

conduire* [kɔ̃dɥir] **1** *vt (troupeau)* to lead; *(voiture)* to drive; *(moto)* to ride; *(électricité)* to conduct; **c. qn à** *(accompagner)* to take sb to **2** *vi (en voiture)* to drive; **c. à** *(lieu)* to lead to **3** **se conduire** *upr* to behave

conduit [kɔ̃dɥi] *nm (tuyau)* pipe

conduite [kɔ̃dɥit] *nf (de véhicule)* driving (**de** of); *(d'entreprise)* management; *(tuyau)* pipe; *(comportement)* conduct, behaviour; **c. à gauche/droite** *(volant)* left-hand/right-hand drive; **c. de gaz** gas main

cône [kon] *nm* cone

confection [kɔ̃fɛksjɔ̃] *nf (réalisation)* making (**de** of); *(industrie)* clothing industry; **vêtements de c.** ready-to-wear clothes ▪ **confectionner** *vt* to make

confédération [kɔ̃federasjɔ̃] *nf* confederation

conférence [kɔ̃ferɑ̃s] *nf (réunion)* conference; *(exposé)* lecture; **c. de presse** press conference

conférer [kɔ̃fere] *vt (titre)* to confer (**à** on)

confesser [kɔ̃fese] *Rel* **1** *vt* to confess **2** **se confesser** *upr* to confess (**à** to) ▪ **confession** *nf* confession

confettis [kɔ̃feti] *nmpl* confetti

confiance [kɔ̃fjɑ̃s] *nf* confidence; **faire c. à qn, avoir c. en qn** to trust sb; **de c.** *(mission)* of trust; *(personne)* trustworthy; **c. en soi** self-confidence; **avoir c. en soi** to be self-confident ▪ **confiant, -e** *adj (qui fait confiance)* trusting; *(optimiste)* confident; *(qui a confiance en soi)* self-confident

confidence [kɔ̃fidɑ̃s] *nf* confidence; **faire une c. à qn** to confide in sb ▪ **confident, -e** *nmf* confidant, *f* confidante ▪ **confidentiel, -elle** *adj* confidential

confier [kɔ̃fje] **1** *vt* **c. qch à qn** *(laisser)* to entrust sb with sth; *(dire)* to confide sth to sb **2** **se confier** *upr* **se c. à qn** to confide in sb

configuration [kɔ̃figyrasjɔ̃] *nf (disposition)* layout; *Ordinat* configuration

confiner [kɔ̃fine] **1** *vt* to confine **2** *vi* **c. à** to border on **3** **se confiner** *upr* **se c. chez soi** to shut oneself up indoors

confins [kɔ̃fɛ̃] *nmpl* confines; **aux c. de** on the edge of

confirmation [kɔ̃firmasjɔ̃] *nf* confirmation

confirmer [kɔ̃firme] **1** *vt* to confirm (**que** that) **2 se confirmer** *vpr (nouvelle)* to be confirmed; *(tendance)* to continue

confiserie [kɔ̃fizri] *nf (magasin)* Br sweetshop, *Am* candy store; **confiseries** *(bonbons)* Br sweets, *Am* candy ■ **confiseur** *nm* confectioner

confisquer [kɔ̃fiske] *vt* to confiscate (**à qn** from sb)

confit, -e [kɔ̃fi] **1** *adj (fruits)* candied **2** *nm* **c. d'oie** potted goose

confiture [kɔ̃fityr] *nf* jam; **c. de fraises** strawberry jam

conflit [kɔ̃fli] *nm* conflict; **conflits sociaux** industrial disputes ■ **conflictuel, -elle** *adj (intérêts)* conflicting

confondre [kɔ̃fɔ̃dr] **1** *vt (choses, personnes)* to mix up, to confuse; *(consterner)* to astound; *(démasquer)* to confound; **c. qn/qch avec qn/qch** to mistake sb/sth for sb/sth **2 se confondre** *vpr (couleurs, intérêts)* to merge; **se c. en excuses** to apologize profusely

conforme [kɔ̃fɔrm] *adj* **c. à** in accordance with; *(modèle)* true to ■ **conformément** *adv* **c. à** in accordance with

conformer [kɔ̃fɔrme] **1** *vt* to model **2 se conformer** *vpr* to conform (**à** to)

conformiste [kɔ̃fɔrmist] *adj & nmf* conformist

conformité [kɔ̃fɔrmite] *nf* conformity (**à** with)

confort [kɔ̃fɔr] *nm* comfort ■ **confortable** *adj* comfortable

confrère [kɔ̃frɛr] *nm (de profession)* colleague

confronter [kɔ̃frɔ̃te] *vt (personnes)* to confront; *(expériences, résultats)* to compare; **confronté à** *(difficulté)* confronted with ■ **confrontation** *nf (face-à-face)* confrontation; *(comparaison)* comparison

confus, -e [kɔ̃fy, -yz] *adj (esprit, situation, explication)* confused; *(gêné)* embarrassed ■ **confusion** *nf (désordre, méprise)* confusion; *(gêne)* embarrassment

congé [kɔ̃ʒe] *nm (vacances)* Br holiday, *Am* vacation; *(arrêt de travail)* leave; *(avis de renvoi)* notice; **donner son c. à qn** *(employé, locataire)* to give notice to sb; **c. de maladie** sick leave; **c. de maternité** maternity leave; **c. de paternité** paternity leave; **congés payés** Br paid holidays, *Am* paid vacation

congédier [kɔ̃ʒedje] *vt* to dismiss

congeler [kɔ̃ʒle] *vt* to freeze ■ **congélateur** *nm* freezer

congère [kɔ̃ʒɛr] *nf* snowdrift

Congo [kɔ̃go] *nm* **le C.** Congo ■ **congolais, -e 1** *adj* Congolese **2** *nmf* **C., Congolaise** Congolese

congratuler [kɔ̃ɡratyle] *vt* to congratulate (**sur** on)

congrès [kɔ̃grɛ] *nm* conference; **le C.** *(aux États-Unis)* the Congress

conique [kɔnik] *adj* conical

conjoint, -e [kɔ̃ʒwɛ̃, -wɛt] **1** *adj* joint **2** *nm* spouse; **conjoints** husband and wife

conjonction [kɔ̃ʒɔ̃ksjɔ̃] *nf (union)* union; *Gram* conjunction

conjonctivite [kɔ̃ʒɔ̃ktivit] *nf Méd* conjunctivitis

conjoncture [kɔ̃ʒɔ̃ktyr] *nf* circumstances

conjugal, -e, -aux, -ales [kɔ̃ʒyɡal, -o] *adj (bonheur)* marital; *(vie)* married; *(devoir)* conjugal

conjuguer [kɔ̃ʒyɡe] **1** *vt (verbe)* to conjugate; *(efforts)* to combine **2 se conjuguer** *vpr (verbe)* to be conjugated ■ **conjugaison** *nf Gram* conjugation

conjurer [kɔ̃ʒyre] *vt (danger)* to avert; *(mauvais sort)* to ward off; **c. qn de faire qch** to beg sb to do sth ■ **conjuré, -e** *nmf* conspirator

connaissance [kɔnɛsɑ̃s] *nf (savoir)* knowledge; *(personne)* acquaintance; **à ma c.** to my knowledge; **avoir c. de qch** to be aware of sth; **faire c. avec qn** to get to know sb; **perdre/**

reprendre c. to lose/regain consciousness; **sans c.** unconscious ∎ **connaisseur** *nm* connoisseur

connaître* [kɔnɛtr] **1** *vt (personne, endroit, faits)* to know; *(rencontrer)* to meet; *(famine, guerre)* to experience; **faire c. qch** to make sth known; **faire c. qn** *(présenter)* to introduce sb; *(rendre célèbre)* to make sb known **2 se connaître** *upr* **nous nous connaissons déjà** we've met before; **s'y c. en qch** to know all about sth

connecter [kɔnɛkte] *vt (appareil électrique)* to connect; *Ordinat* **connecté on line** ∎ **connexion** *nf* connection

connu, -e [kɔny] **1** *pp de* **connaître** **2** *adj (célèbre)* well-known

conquérir* [kɔkerir] *vt (pays, sommet)* to conquer; *(marché)* to capture ∎ **conquérant, -e** *nmf* conqueror ∎ **conquête** *nf* conquest

consacrer [kɔsakre] **1** *vt (temps)* to devote (**à** to); *(église)* to consecrate; *(entériner)* to establish **2 se consacrer** *upr* **se c. à** to devote oneself to

consciemment [kɔsjamɑ] *adv* consciously

conscience [kɔsjɑ̃s] *nf* (**a**) *(esprit)* consciousness; **avoir/prendre c. de qch** to be/become aware of sth; **perdre c.** to lose consciousness (**b**) *(morale)* conscience; **avoir bonne/ mauvaise c.** to have a clear/guilty conscience ∎ **consciencieux, -euse** *adj* conscientious

conscient, -e [kɔsjɑ̃, -ɑ̃t] *adj (lucide)* conscious; **c. de qch** aware or conscious of sth

conscrit [kɔskri] *nm* conscript

consécutif, -ive [kɔsekytif, -iv] *adj* consecutive; **c. à** following upon

conseil [kɔsɛj] *nm* (**a**) **un c.** *(recommandation)* a piece of advice; **des conseils** advice (**b**) *(assemblée)* council, committee; **c. d'administration** board of directors; *Scol* **c. de classe** = staff meeting with participation of class representatives; *Pol* **c. des ministres** cabinet meeting

conseiller[1] [kɔseje] *vt (guider)* to advise; **c. qch à qn** to recommend sth to sb; **c. à qn de faire qch** to advise sb to do sth

conseiller[2]**, -ère** [kɔseje, -ɛr] *nmf (expert)* consultant, adviser; **c. d'orientation** careers adviser

consentir* [kɔsɑ̃tir] **1** *vi* **c. à qch/à faire qch** to consent to sth/to do sth **2** *vt (prêt)* to grant (**à** to) ∎ **consentement** *nm* consent

conséquence [kɔsekɑ̃s] *nf* consequence; **en c.** accordingly; **sans c.** *(sans importance)* of no importance

conservateur, -trice [kɔservatœr, -tris] **1** *adj* & *nmf Pol* Conservative **2** *nmf (de musée)* curator; *(de bibliothèque)* librarian **3** *nm (alimentaire)* preservative

conservatoire [kɔservatwar] *nm* school, academy

conserve [kɔserv] *nf* **conserves** canned *or Br* tinned food; **en c.** canned, *Br* tinned

conserver [kɔserve] **1** *vt* to keep; *(fruits, tradition)* to preserve **2 se conserver** *upr (aliment)* to keep

considérable [kɔsiderabl] *adj* considerable

considérer [kɔsidere] *vt* to consider (**que** that); **tout bien considéré** all things considered ∎ **considération** *nf (respect)* regard, esteem; **prendre qch en c.** to take sth into consideration

consigne [kɔsiɲ] *nf (instructions)* orders; *(de bouteille)* deposit; **c. (à bagages)** *Br* left-luggage office, *Am* checkroom; **c. automatique** lockers ∎ **consigner** *vt (bouteille)* to charge a deposit on; *(bagages) Br* to deposit in the left-luggage office, *Am* to check; *(écrire)* to record; *(punir) (soldat)* to confine to barracks

consistant, -e [kɔsistɑ̃, -ɑ̃t] *adj (sauce, bouillie)* thick; *(repas)* substantial ∎ **consistance** *nf* consistency

consister [kɔsiste] *vi* **c. en qch** to consist of sth; **c. à faire qch** to consist in doing sth

consœur [kɔ̃sœr] nf female colleague

console [kɔ̃sɔl] nf (d'ordinateur, de jeux) console

consoler [kɔ̃sɔle] **1** vt to comfort, to console **2 se consoler** vpr **se c. de qch** to get over sth ■ **consolation** nf comfort, consolation

consolider [kɔ̃sɔlide] vt (mur, position) to strengthen ■ **consolidation** nf strengthening

consommateur, -trice [kɔ̃sɔmatœr, -tris] nmf consumer; (au café) customer ■ **consommation** nf (de nourriture, d'électricité) consumption; (de voiture, (boisson) drink

consommer [kɔ̃sɔme] **1** vt (aliment, carburant) to consume; (mariage) to consummate **2** vi (au café) to drink

consonne [kɔ̃sɔn] nf consonant

consortium [kɔ̃sɔrsjɔm] nm (entreprises) consortium

conspirer [kɔ̃spire] vi (comploter) to conspire (**contre** against); **c. à faire qch** (concourir) to conspire to do sth ■ **conspirateur, -trice** nmf conspirator ■ **conspiration** nf conspiracy

constant, -e [kɔ̃stɑ̃, -ɑ̃t] **1** adj constant **2** nf **constante** Math constant ■ **constamment** [-amɑ̃] adv constantly ■ **constance** nf constancy

constat [kɔ̃sta] nm (official) report

constater [kɔ̃state] vt (observer) to note (**que** that); Jur (enregistrer) to record; (décès) to certify ■ **constatation** nf (remarque) observation

constellation [kɔ̃stelasjɔ̃] nf constellation

consterner [kɔ̃sterne] vt to dismay

constipation [kɔ̃stipasjɔ̃] nf constipation

constituer [kɔ̃stitɥe] **1** vt (composer) to make up; (équivaloir à) to constitute; (former) to form; **constitué de** made up of **2 se constituer** vpr **se c. prisonnier** to give oneself up

constitution [kɔ̃stitysjɔ̃] nf (santé, lois) constitution; (de gouvernement) formation ■ **constitutionnel, -elle** adj constitutional

constructeur [kɔ̃stryktœr] nm (bâtisseur) builder; (fabricant) maker (**de** of); **c. automobile** car manufacturer ■ **constructif, -ive** adj constructive ■ **construction** nf (de pont, de route, de maison) building, construction (**de** of); (édifice) building; **en c.** under construction

construire* [kɔ̃strɥir] vt (maison, route) to build

consul [kɔ̃syl] nm consul ■ **consulat** nm consulate

consulter [kɔ̃sylte] **1** vt to consult **2** vi (médecin) to see patients, Br to take surgery **3 se consulter** vpr (discuter) to confer ■ **consultation** nf consultation

consumer [kɔ̃syme] vt (brûler) to consume

contact [kɔ̃takt] nm contact; **être en c. avec qn** to be in contact with sb; **prendre c.** to get in touch (**avec** with); Aut **mettre/couper le c.** to switch on/off ■ **contacter** vt to contact

contagieux, -euse [kɔ̃taʒjø, -øz] adj (maladie, personne) contagious

contaminer [kɔ̃tamine] vt to contaminate ■ **contamination** nf contamination

conte [kɔ̃t] nm tale; **c. de fées** fairy tale

contempler [kɔ̃tɑ̃ple] vt to gaze at, to contemplate

contemporain, -e [kɔ̃tɑ̃pɔrɛ̃, -ɛn] adj & nmf contemporary

contenance [kɔ̃tnɑ̃s] nf (**a**) (de récipient) capacity (**b**) (allure) bearing

contenir* [kɔ̃tnir] vt (renfermer) to contain; (contrôler) to hold back, to contain ■ **conteneur** nm container

content, -e [kɔ̃tɑ̃, -ɑ̃t] **1** adj pleased, happy (**de** with; **de faire** to do); **être c. de soi** to be pleased with oneself **2** nm **avoir son c.** to have had one's fill (**de** of)

contenter [kɔ̃tɑ̃te] **1** vt (satisfaire) to satisfy; (faire plaisir à) to please **2 se contenter** vpr **se c. de qch** to content oneself with sth ■ **contentement** nm contentment, satisfaction

contentieux [kɔ̃tɑ̃sjø] *nm (querelles)* dispute; *Jur* litigation; *(service)* legal department

contenu [kɔ̃tny] *nm (de paquet, de bouteille)* contents; *(de lettre, de film)* content

conter [kɔ̃te] *vt* to tell (**à** to) ■ **conteur, -euse** storyteller

contestable [kɔ̃testabl] *adj* debatable

contestation [kɔ̃testasjɔ̃] *nf* protest

conteste [kɔ̃test] **sans conteste** *adv* indisputably

contester [kɔ̃teste] **1** *vt* to dispute **2** *vi* **faire qch sans c.** to do sth without protest ■ **contesté, -e** *adj (théorie, dirigeant)* controversial

contexte [kɔ̃tekst] *nm* context

contigu, -ë [kɔ̃tigy] *adj (maisons)* adjoining; **c. à qch** adjoining sth

continent [kɔ̃tinɑ̃] *nm* continent; *(opposé à une île)* mainland ■ **continental, -e, -aux, -ales** *adj (climat, plateau)* continental

contingent [kɔ̃tɛ̃ʒɑ̃] *nm Mil* contingent; *(quota)* quota

continu, -e [kɔ̃tiny] *adj* continuous ■ **continuel, -elle** *adj (ininterrompu)* continuous; *(qui se répète)* continual ■ **continuellement** *adv (de façon ininterrompue)* continuously; *(de façon répétitive)* continually

continuer [kɔ̃tinɥe] **1** *vt (études, efforts, politique)* to continue, to carry on with; **c. à** *ou* **de faire qch** to continue *or* carry on doing sth **2** *vi* to continue, to go on ■ **continuation** *nf* continuation

continuité [kɔ̃tinɥite] *nf* continuity

contour [kɔ̃tur] *nm* outline

contourner [kɔ̃turne] *vt* to go round; *Fig (difficulté, loi)* to get round

contraceptif, -ive [kɔ̃traseptif, -iv] *adj & nm* contraceptive

contracter [kɔ̃trakte] **1** *vt (muscle, habitude, dette)* to contract **2 se contracter** *vpr (muscle)* to contract; *(personne)* to tense up ■ **contraction** *nf* contraction

contractuel, -elle [kɔ̃traktɥel] **1** *adj*

(politique) contractual **2** *nmf Br* ≃ traffic warden, *Am* ≃ traffic policeman, *f* traffic policewoman

contradiction [kɔ̃tradiksjɔ̃] *nf* contradiction; **être en c. avec qch** to contradict sth ■ **contradictoire** *adj* contradictory

contraindre* [kɔ̃trɛ̃dr] **1** *vt* to compel, to force (**à faire** to do) **2 se contraindre** *vpr* to compel *or* force oneself (**à faire** to do) ■ **contraignant, -e** *adj* restricting ■ **contrainte** *nf (obligation, limitation)* constraint; **sous la c.** under duress

contraire [kɔ̃trer] **1** *adj (opposé)* conflicting; **c. à qch** contrary to sth; **en sens c.** in the opposite direction **2** *nm* opposite; **(bien) au c.** on the contrary ■ **contrairement** *adv* **c. à** contrary to; **c. à qn** unlike sb

contrarier [kɔ̃trarje] *vt (projet, action)* to thwart; *(personne)* to annoy ■ **contrariant, -e** *adj (situation)* annoying; *(personne)* contrary ■ **contrariété** *nf* annoyance

contraste [kɔ̃trast] *nm* contrast ■ **contraster** *vi* to contrast (**avec** with)

contrat [kɔ̃tra] *nm* contract

contravention [kɔ̃travɑ̃sjɔ̃] *nf (amende)* fine; *(pour stationnement interdit)* (parking) ticket

contre [kɔ̃tr] **1** *prép* against; *(en échange de)* (in exchange) for; **échanger qch c. qch** to exchange sth for sth; **fâché c. qn** angry with sb; **six voix c. deux** six votes to two; **Nîmes c. Arras** *(match)* Nîmes versus *or* against Arras; **sirop c. la toux** cough mixture; *Fam* **par c.** on the other hand **2** *nm (au volley, au basket)* block ■ **contre-attaque** *nf* counter-attack ■ **contre-attaquer** *vt* to counter-attack

contrebalancer [kɔ̃trəbalɑ̃se] *vt* to counterbalance; *Fig (compenser)* to offset

contrebande [kɔ̃trəbɑ̃d] *nf (activité)* smuggling; *(marchandises)* contraband; **tabac de c.** smuggled tobacco;

faire de la c. to smuggle goods ■ **contrebandier, -ère** *nmf* smuggler

contrebas [kɔ̃trəba] **en contrebas** *adv & prép* (down) below; **en c. de** below

contrebasse [kɔ̃trəbas] *nf (instrument)* double-bass

contrecarrer [kɔ̃trəkare] *vt* to thwart

contrecœur [kɔ̃trəkœr] **à contrecœur** *adv* reluctantly

contrecoup [kɔ̃trəku] *nm* repercussions

contre-courant [kɔ̃trəkurɑ̃] **à contre-courant** *adv (nager)* against the current

contredire* [kɔ̃trədir] **1** *vt* to contradict **2 se contredire** *vpr (soi-même)* to contradict oneself; *(l'un l'autre)* to contradict each other

contrée [kɔ̃tre] *nf Littéraire (region)* region; *(pays)* land

contre-espionnage [kɔ̃trɛspjɔnaʒ] *nm* counter-espionage

contrefaçon [kɔ̃trəfasɔ̃] *nf (pratique)* counterfeiting; *(produit)* fake ■ **contrefaire*** *vt (écriture)* to disguise; *(argent)* to counterfeit; *(signature)* to forge

contre-jour [kɔ̃trəʒur] **à contre-jour** *adv* against the light

contremaître [kɔ̃trəmetr] *nm* foreman

contre-offensive [kɔ̃trɔfɑ̃siv] *(pl* **contre-offensives)** *nf* counter-offensive

contrepartie [kɔ̃trəparti] *nf* compensation; **en c.** in return *(de* for)

contre-pied [kɔ̃trəpje] *nm Sport* **prendre son adversaire à c.** to wrongfoot one's opponent

contreplaqué [kɔ̃trəplake] *nm* plywood

contrepoids [kɔ̃trəpwa] *nm* counterbalance

contrepoison [kɔ̃trəpwazɔ̃] *nm* antidote

contrer [kɔ̃tre] *vt (personne, attaque)* to counter

contresens [kɔ̃trəsɑ̃s] *nm* misinterpretation; *(en traduisant)* mistranslation; **prendre une rue à c.** to go

down/up a street the wrong way

contresigner [kɔ̃trəsiɲe] *vt* to countersign

contretemps [kɔ̃trətɑ̃] *nm* hitch, mishap

contrevenir* [kɔ̃trəvnir] *vi* **c. à** to contravene

contribuable [kɔ̃tribɥabl] *nmf* taxpayer

contribuer [kɔ̃tribɥe] *vi* to contribute *(à* to); **c. à faire qch** to help (to) do sth

contribution [kɔ̃tribysjɔ̃] *nf* contribution *(à* to); *(impôt)* tax; **contributions** *(administration)* tax office

contrôle [kɔ̃trol] *nm (vérification)* checking *(de* of); *(surveillance)* monitoring; *(maîtrise)* control; *Scol* test; **avoir le c. de qch** to have control of sth; **le c. des naissances** birth control; **c. de soi** self-control; **c. fiscal** tax inspection

contrôler [kɔ̃trole] **1** *vt (vérifier)* to check; *(surveiller)* to monitor; *(maîtriser)* to control **2 se contrôler** *vpr* to control oneself ■ **contrôleur, -euse** *nmf (de train, de bus)* Br (ticket) inspector, Am conductor; **c. aérien** air-traffic controller

controverse [kɔ̃trɔvers] *nf* controversy ■ **controversé, -e** *adj* controversial

contumace [kɔ̃tymas] **par contumace** *adv Jur* in absentia

contusion [kɔ̃tyzjɔ̃] *nf* bruise

convaincre* [kɔ̃vɛkr] *vt* to convince *(de* of); **c. qn de faire qch** to persuade sb to do sth ■ **convaincant, -e** *adj* convincing ■ **convaincu, -e** *adj* convinced *(de* of; **que** that); *(partisan)* committed

convalescent, -e [kɔ̃valesɑ̃, -ɑ̃t] *adj & nmf* convalescent ■ **convalescence** *nf* convalescence

convenable [kɔ̃vnabl] *adj (approprié)* suitable; *(acceptable, décent)* decent

convenance [kɔ̃vnɑ̃s] *nf* **faire qch à sa c.** to do sth at one's own convenience

convenir* [kɔ̃vnir] **1** *vi* **c. à** *(être fait pour)* to be suitable for; *(plaire à, aller* *à*) to suit; **c. de qch** *(lieu, prix)* to agree upon sth; **c. de faire qch** to agree to do sth; **c. que...** to admit that...

2 *v impersonnel* **il convient de...** it is advisable to...; *(selon les usages)* it is proper to...; **il fut convenu que...** *(décidé)* it was agreed that... ■ **convenu, -e** *adj (décidé)* agreed

convention [kɔ̃vɑ̃sjɔ̃] *nf (accord)* agreement; *(règle)* convention; **c. collective** collective agreement

conventionné, -e [kɔ̃vɑ̃sjɔne] *adj (médecin, clinique)* attached to the health system, *Br* ≃ NHS; **médecin non c.** private doctor

conventionnel, -elle [kɔ̃vɑ̃sjɔnɛl] *adj* conventional

convergence [kɔ̃vɛrʒɑ̃s] *nf* convergence ■ **converger** *vi* to converge (**vers** on)

conversation [kɔ̃vɛrsasjɔ̃] *nf* conversation

conversion [kɔ̃vɛrsjɔ̃] *nf (changement)* conversion (**en** into); *(à une doctrine)* conversion (**à** to) ■ **convertible 1** *adj* convertible (**en** into) **2** *nm* sofa bed ■ **convertir 1** *vt (changer)* to convert (**en** into); *(à une doctrine)* to convert (**à** to) **2 se convertir** *upr (à une doctrine)* to be converted (**à** to)

conviction [kɔ̃viksjɔ̃] *nf (certitude, croyance)* conviction; **avoir la c. que...** to be convinced that...

convier [kɔ̃vje] *vt Formel* to invite (**à** to; **à faire** to do)

convive [kɔ̃viv] *nmf* guest

convivial, -e, -aux, -ales [kɔ̃vivjal, -jo] *adj* convivial; *Ordinat* user-friendly

convoi [kɔ̃vwa] *nm (véhicules, personnes)* convoy; *(train)* train; **c. funèbre** funeral procession

convoiter [kɔ̃vwate] *vt (poste, richesses)* to covet

convoquer [kɔ̃vɔke] *vt (employé, postulant)* to call in; **c. qn à un examen** to notify sb of an examination ■ **convocation** *nf (lettre)* notice to attend; **c. à**

un examen notification of an examination

convoyer [kɔ̃vwaje] *vt (troupes)* to convoy; *(fonds)* to transport under armed guard

convulsion [kɔ̃vylsjɔ̃] *nf* convulsion

coopérer [kɔɔpere] *vi* to cooperate (**à** in, **avec** with) ■ **coopératif, -ive** *adj & nf* cooperative ■ **coopération** *nf* cooperation (**entre** between); *Pol* overseas development

coordonner [kɔɔrdɔne] *vt* to coordinate (**à** *ou* **avec** with) ■ **coordination** *nf* coordination ■ **coordonnées** *nfpl (adresse, téléphone)* address and phone number

copain [kɔpɛ̃] *nm Fam (camarade)* pal; *(petit ami)* boyfriend

copeau, -x [kɔpo] *nm (de bois)* shaving

copie [kɔpi] *nf (manuscrit, double)* copy; *Scol (devoir, examen)* paper

copier [kɔpje] *vt (texte, musique, document) & Scol (à un examen)* to copy (**sur** from) ■ **copieur, -euse 1** *nmf (élève)* copier **2** *nm (machine)* photocopier

copieux, -euse [kɔpjø, -øz] *adj (repas)* copious; *(portion)* generous

copine [kɔpin] *nf Fam (camarade)* pal; *(petite amie)* girlfriend

copropriété [kɔprɔprijete] *nf* joint ownership

coq [kɔk] *nm* cock, *Am* rooster

coque [kɔk] *nf (de noix)* shell; *(de navire)* hull; *(fruit de mer)* cockle

coquelet [kɔklɛ] *nm* cockerel

coquelicot [kɔkliko] *nm* poppy

coqueluche [kɔklyʃ] *nf (maladie)* whooping cough

coquet, -ette [kɔkɛ, -ɛt] *adj (intérieur)* charming; *Fam (somme)* tidy

coquetier [kɔktje] *nm* egg-cup

coquille [kɔkij] *nf* shell; *(faute d'imprimerie)* misprint; *Culin* **c. Saint-Jacques** scallop ■ **coquillage** *nm (mollusque)* shellfish *inv; (coquille)* shell

coquin, -e [kɔkɛ̃, -in] **1** *adj (sourire, air)* mischievous; *(sous-vêtements)* naughty **2** *nmf* rascal

cor [kɔr] *nm* (*instrument*) horn; (*durillon*) corn

corail, -aux [kɔraj, -o] *nm* coral

Coran [kɔrɑ̃] *nm* le C. the Koran

corbeau, -x [kɔrbo] *nm* (*oiseau*) crow

corbeille [kɔrbɛj] *nf* (**a**) (*panier*) basket; **c. à pain** breadbasket; **c. à papier** wastepaper basket (**b**) (*à la Bourse*) trading floor (**c**) *Théât* dress circle

corbillard [kɔrbijar] *nm* hearse

corde [kɔrd] *nf* (*lien*) rope; (*de raquette, de violon*) string; **c. à linge** washing *or* clothes line; **c. à sauter** *Br* skipping rope, *Am* jump-rope; **cordes vocales** vocal cords ■ **cordée** *nf* roped party ■ **corder** *vt* (*raquette*) to string

cordial, -e, -aux, -ales [kɔrdjal, -o] **1** *adj* (*accueil, personne*) cordial **2** *nm* (*remontant*) tonic

cordon [kɔrdɔ̃] *nm* (*de tablier, de sac*) string; (*de rideau*) cord; (*de policiers*) cordon; *Anat* **c. ombilical** umbilical cord ■ **cordon-bleu** (*pl* **cordons-bleus**) *nm Fam* gourmet cook

cordonnier [kɔrdɔnje] *nm* shoe repairer ■ **cordonnerie** *nf* (*boutique*) shoe repairer's shop

Corée [kɔre] *nf* la C. Korea ■ **coréen, -enne** *adj* Korean **2** *nmf* C., Coréenne Korean

coriace [kɔrjas] *adj* (*viande, personne*) tough

corne [kɔrn] *nf* (*d'animal, matière, instrument*) horn; (*au pied, à la main*) hard skin; **c. de brume** foghorn

corneille [kɔrnɛj] *nf* crow

cornemuse [kɔrnəmyz] *nf* bagpipes

corner[1] [kɔrne] *vt* (*page*) to turn down the corner of; (*abîmer*) to make dog-eared

corner[2] [kɔrnɛr] *nm* (*au football*) corner; **tirer un c.** to take a corner

cornet [kɔrnɛ] *nm* (*glace*) cone, *Br* cornet

corniche [kɔrniʃ] *nf* (*de rocher*) ledge; (*route*) coast road; (*en haut d'un mur*) cornice

cornichon [kɔrniʃɔ̃] *nm* gherkin

cornu, -e [kɔrny] *adj* (*diable, animal*) horned

corporation [kɔrpɔrasjɔ̃] *nf* corporate body

corporel, -elle [kɔrpɔrɛl] *adj* (*besoin*) bodily; (*hygiène*) personal

corps [kɔr] *nm* (*organisme, cadavre*) & *Chim* body; (*partie principale*) main part; **c. et âme** body and soul; **c. d'armée/diplomatique** army/diplomatic corps; **c. enseignant** teaching profession; **c. gras** fat

corpulent, -e [kɔrpylɑ̃, -ɑ̃t] *adj* stout, corpulent

correct, -e [kɔrɛkt] *adj* (*exact, courtois*) correct; *Fam* (*acceptable*) reasonable ■ **correctement** *adv* (*sans faire de fautes, décemment*) correctly; *Fam* (*de façon acceptable*) reasonably

correcteur, -trice [kɔrɛktœr, -tris] **1** *adj* **verres correcteurs** corrective lenses **2** *nmf* (*d'examen*) examiner; (*en typographie*) proofreader **3** *nm Ordinat* **c. d'orthographe** spellchecker

correction [kɔrɛksjɔ̃] *nf* (*rectification*) correction; (*punition*) beating; (*décence, courtoisie*) correctness; *Scol* (*de devoirs, d'examens*) marking

correctionnel, -elle [kɔrɛksjɔnɛl] **1** *adj* **tribunal c.** criminal court **2** *nf* **correctionnelle** criminal court; **passer en c.** to go before a criminal court

correspondance [kɔrɛspɔ̃dɑ̃s] *nf* (*relation, lettres*) correspondence; (*de train, d'autocar*) *Br* connection, *Am* transfer

correspondre [kɔrɛspɔ̃dr] *vi* **c. à qch** to correspond to sth; **c. avec qn** (*par lettres*) to correspond with sb ■ **correspondant, -e 1** *adj* corresponding (**à** to) **2** *nmf* (*reporter*) correspondent; (*par lettres*) pen friend, pen pal; (*au téléphone*) caller; **c. de guerre** war correspondent

corrida [kɔrida] *nf* bullfight

corridor [kɔridɔr] *nm* corridor

corriger [kɔriʒe] **1** *vt* (*texte, erreur, myopie, injustice*) to correct; (*exercice, devoir*) to mark; **c. qn** to give sb a beating; **c. qn de qch** to cure sb of sth **2 se corriger** *vpr* to mend one's ways; **se c. de qch** to cure oneself of sth ■ **corrigé** *nm (d'exercice)* correct answers (**de** to)

corrompre* [kɔrɔ̃pr] *vt (personne, goût)* to corrupt; *(soudoyer)* to bribe ■ **corrompu, -e** *adj* corrupt ■ **corruption** *nf* corruption

corrosion [kɔrozjɔ̃] *nf* corrosion ■ **corrosif, -ive** *adj* corrosive

corsage [kɔrsaʒ] *nm* blouse

Corse [kɔrs] *nf* **la C.** Corsica ■ **corse 1** *adj* Corsican **2** *nmf* **C.** Corsican

corser [kɔrse] **1** *vt (plat)* to spice up; *Fig (récit)* to liven up **2 se corser** *vpr* **ça se corse** things are getting complicated ■ **corsé, -e** *adj (café)* full-flavoured; *Fig (histoire)* spicy

corset [kɔrse] *nm* corset

cortège [kɔrtɛʒ] *nm (défilé)* procession

corvée [kɔrve] *nf* chore; *Mil* fatigue duty

cosmétique [kɔsmetik] *adj & nm* cosmetic

cosmique [kɔsmik] *adj* cosmic ■ **cosmonaute** *nmf* cosmonaut

cosmopolite [kɔsmɔpɔlit] *adj* cosmopolitan

cossu, -e [kɔsy] *adj (personne)* well-to-do; *(maison, intérieur)* opulent

costaud [kɔsto] *adj* sturdy

costume [kɔstym] *nm (habit)* costume; *(complet)* suit

cotation [kɔtasjɔ̃] *nf* **c. (en Bourse)** quotation (on the Stock Exchange)

cote [kɔt] *nf (marque de classement)* classification mark; *(valeur)* quotation; *(liste)* share index; *(de cheval)* odds; *(altitude)* altitude

coté, -e [kɔte] *adj* **bien c.** highly rated; **c. en Bourse** quoted on the Stock Market

côte [kot] *nf* (**a**) *(os)* rib; **à côtes** *(étoffe)* ribbed; **à c.** side by side; **c. d'agneau/de porc** lamb/pork chop; **c. de bœuf** rib of beef (**b**) *(de montagne)* slope (**c**) *(littoral)* coast; **la C.**

d'Azur the French Riviera

côté [kote] *nm* side; **de l'autre c.** on the other side (**de** of); *(partir)* the other way; **de ce c.** *(passer)* this way; **du c. de** *(près de)* near; **à c.** close by, nearby; *(pièce)* in the other room; *(maison)* next door; **la maison d'à c.** the house next door; **à c. de qn/qch** next to sb/sth; *(en comparaison de)* compared to sb/sth; **passer à c.** *(balle)* to fall wide (**de** of); **mettre qch de c.** to put sth aside

coteau, -x [kɔto] *nm* hill; *(versant)* hillside

côtelé, -e [kotle] *adj* **velours c.** corduroy

côtelette [kotlɛt] *nf (d'agneau, de porc)* chop

coter [kɔte] *vt (prix, action)* to quote

côtier, -ère [kotje, -ɛr] *adj* coastal; *(pêche)* inshore

cotiser [kɔtize] **1** *vi (à un cadeau, pour la retraite)* to contribute (**à** to; **pour** towards) **2 se cotiser** *vpr Br* to club together, *Am* to club in ■ **cotisation** *nf (de club)* dues, subscription; *(de retraite, de chômage)* contribution

coton [kɔtɔ̃] *nm* cotton; **c. hydrophile** *Br* cotton wool, *Am* absorbent cotton

côtoyer [kotwaje] *vt (personnes)* to mix with

cou [ku] *nm* neck

couchage [kuʃaʒ] *nm* **sac de c.** sleeping bag

couchant [kuʃɑ̃, -ɑ̃t] **1** *adj m* **soleil c.** setting sun **2** *nm* **le c.** *(ouest)* the west

couche [kuʃ] *nf* (**a**) *(épaisseur)* layer; *(de peinture)* coat; **la c. d'ozone** the ozone layer (**b**) *(linge de bébé) Br* nappy, *Am* diaper ■ **couche-culotte** *(pl* **couches-culottes**) *nf Br* disposable nappy, *Am* disposable diaper

coucher [kuʃe] **1** *nm (moment)* bedtime; **l'heure du c.** bedtime; **au c.** at bedtime; **c. de soleil** sunset

2 *vt (allonger)* to lay down; **c. qn** to put sb to bed

3 *vi* to sleep (**avec** with)

4 se coucher *vpr (personne)* to go to

bed; *(s'allonger)* to lie down; *(soleil)* to set, to go down; **aller se c.** to go to bed ■ **couché, -e** *adj* **être c.** to be in bed; *(étendu)* to be lying (down)

couchette [kuʃɛt] *nf (de train)* couchette; *(de bateau)* bunk

coude [kud] *nm* elbow; *(tournant)* bend; **donner un coup de c. à qn** to nudge sb

cou-de-pied [kudpje] *(pl* **cous-de-pied)** *nm* instep

coudre* [kudr] *vti* to sew

couette¹ [kwɛt] *nf (édredon)* duvet

couette² [kwɛt] *nf Fam (coiffure)* bunch

couffin [kufɛ̃] *nm (de bébé) Br* Moses basket, *Am* bassinet

coulée [kule] *nf* **c. de lave** lava flow

couler [kule] **1** *vt* (**a**) *(métal, statue)* to cast; *(liquide, ciment)* to pour (**b**) *(navire)* to sink **2** *vi* (**a**) *(eau, rivière)* to flow; *(nez, sueur)* to run; *(robinet)* to leak (**b**) *(bateau, nageur)* to sink

couleur [kulœr] *nf (teinte) Br* colour, *Am* color; *(colorant)* paint; *(pour cheveux)* dye; *Cartes* suit; **de quelle c. est…?** what colour is…?; **télévision c. ou en couleurs** colour television (set)

couleuvre [kulœvr] *nf* grass snake

coulisse [kulis] *nf (de porte)* runner; **porte à c.** sliding door; *Théât* **les coulisses** the wings ■ **coulissant, -e** *adj* sliding

couloir [kulwar] *nm (de maison, de train)* corridor; *(en natation, en athlétisme)* lane; **c. de bus** bus lane

COUP [ku] *nm* (**a**) *(choc)* blow; *(essai)* attempt, go; **donner un c. à qn** to hit sb; **se donner un c. contre qch** to knock against sth; **donner un c. de couteau à qn** to knife sb; **c. de pied** kick; **donner un c. de pied à qn** to kick sb; **c. de poing** punch; **donner un c. de poing à qn** to punch sb; **c. de tête** header (**b**) *(action soudaine, événement soudain)* **c. de vent** gust of wind; **donner un c. de frein** to brake; **prendre un c.**

de soleil to get sunburned; *Fig* **ça a été le c. de foudre** it was love at first sight; **c. d'État** coup; **c. de théâtre** coup de théâtre (**c**) *(bruit)* **c. de feu** shot; **c. de fusil** shot; **c. de sifflet** whistle; **c. de tonnerre** clap of thunder; **l'horloge sonna deux coups** the clock struck two (**d**) *(expressions)* **après c.** after the event; **sur le c.** *(alors)* at the time; **tué sur le c.** killed outright; **tout à c., tout d'un c.** suddenly; **d'un seul c.** *(avaler)* in one go; *(soudain)* all of a sudden; **du premier c.** at the first attempt; **sous le c. de la colère** in a fit of anger; **tenir le c.** to hold out; **tomber sous le c. de la loi** to be an offence; **c. d'envoi** *(au football, au rugby)* kickoff; **c. de maître** masterstroke; **c. droit** *(au tennis)* forehand; **c. franc** *(au football)* free kick; **c. monté** put-up job

coupable [kupabl] **1** *adj* guilty (**de** of); *(négligence)* culpable; **se sentir c.** to feel guilty **2** *nmf* culprit

coupant, -e [kupɑ̃, -ɑ̃t] *adj* sharp

coupe¹ [kup] *nf (trophée)* cup; *(récipient)* bowl; **la C. du Monde** the World Cup; **c. à champagne** champagne glass

coupe² [kup] *nf (de vêtement)* cut; *(plan)* section; **c. de cheveux** haircut ■ **coupe-papier** *nm inv* paper knife ■ **coupe-vent** *nm inv (blouson) Br* windcheater, *Am* Windbreaker ®

couper [kupe] **1** *vt (trancher, supprimer)* to cut; *(arbre)* to cut down; **c. la parole à qn** to interrupt sb; **nous avons été coupés** *(au téléphone)* we were cut off

2 *vi (être tranchant)* to be sharp; *(aux cartes)* to cut; *(prendre un raccourci)* to take a short cut; **ne coupez pas!** *(au téléphone)* hold the line!

3 se couper *vpr (routes)* to intersect; **se c. au doigt** to cut one's finger; **se c. les cheveux** to cut one's hair ■ **coupé** *nm (voiture)* coupé

couperet [kupre] *nm (de boucher)* cleaver; *(de guillotine)* blade

couple [kupl] *nm* couple

couplet [kuplɛ] *nm* verse

coupole [kupɔl] *nf* dome

coupon [kupɔ̃] *nm* (*tissu*) remnant; **c. de réduction** money-off coupon; **c.-réponse** reply coupon

coupure [kupyr] *nf* (*blessure*) cut; **5 000 euros en petites coupures** 5,000 euros in small notes; **c. d'électricité** *ou* **de courant** blackout, *Br* power cut; **c. de presse** newspaper cutting

cour [kur] *nf* (**a**) (*de maison, de ferme*) yard; **c. de récréation** *Br* playground, *Am* schoolyard (**b**) (*de roi, tribunal*) court; **c. d'appel** court of appeal (**c**) **faire la c. à qn** to court sb

courage [kuraʒ] *nm* courage; **bon c.!** good luck! ■ **courageux, -euse** *adj* (*brave*) courageous; (*énergique*) spirited

couramment [kuramɑ̃] *adv* (*parler*) fluently; (*généralement*) commonly

courant, -e [kurɑ̃, -ɑ̃t] **1** *adj* (*common*) common; (*en cours*) current **2** *nm* (*de rivière*) current; **être au c. de qch** to know about sth; **mettre qn au c. de qch** to tell sb about sth; **c. d'air** *Br* draught, *Am* draft; **c. électrique** electric current

courbature [kurbatyr] *nf* ache; **avoir des courbatures** to be aching (all over)

courbe [kurb] **1** *adj* curved **2** *nf* curve; **c. de niveau** contour line ■ **courber 1** *vt* to bend **2 se courber** *vpr* (*personne*) to bend down; **se c. en deux** to bend double

courgette [kurʒɛt] *nf Br* courgette, *Am* zucchini

courir* [kurir] **1** *vi* to run; (*à une course automobile*) to race; **c. après qn/qch** to run after sb/sth; **descendre une colline en courant** to run down a hill; **le bruit court que...** rumour has it that...
2 *vt* **c. un risque** to run a risk; **c. le 100 mètres** to run the 100 metres ■ **coureur, -euse** *nmf* (*sportif*) runner; (*cycliste*) cyclist; **c. automobile** racing

driver; **c. de jupons** womanizer

couronne [kurɔn] *nf* (*de roi, de reine*) crown; (*pour enterrement*) wreath; (*de dent*) crown ■ **couronnement** *nm* (*de roi*) coronation; *Fig* (*réussite*) crowning achievement ■ **couronner** *vt* (*roi*) to crown; (*auteur, ouvrage*) to award a prize to; **et pour c. le tout...** and to crown it all...

courrier [kurje] *nm* (*lettres*) mail, *Br* post; **par retour du c.** *Br* by return of post, *Am* by return mail; *Journ* **c. du cœur** problem page; **c. électronique** electronic mail, e-mail

courroie [kurwa] *nf* (*attache*) strap

cours [kur] *nm* (**a**) (*de rivière, d'astre*) course; (*de monnaie*) currency; *Fin* (*d'action*) price; **suivre son c.** to run its course; **avoir c.** (*monnaie*) to be legal tender; (*pratique*) to be current; **en c.** (*travail*) in progress; (*année*) current; (*affaires*) outstanding; **au c. de qch** in the course of sth; **c. d'eau** river, stream
(**b**) (*leçon*) class; (*série de leçons*) course; (*conférence*) lecture; (*établissement*) school; **suivre un c.** to take a course; **c. particulier** private lesson
(**c**) (*allée*) avenue

course¹ [kurs] *nf* (*action de courir*) running; *Sport* (*épreuve*) race; (*discipline*) racing; (*trajet en taxi*) journey; (*de projectile, de planète*) course; **les courses de chevaux** the races; **faire la c. avec qn** to race sb; **c. automobile** motor race; **c. cycliste** cycle race

course² [kurs] *nf* (*commission*) errand; **courses** (*achats*) shopping; **faire une c.** to get something from the shops; **faire les courses** to do the shopping

coursier, -ère [kursje, -ɛr] *nmf* messenger

court, -e [kur, kurt] **1** *adj* short **2** *adv* short; **à c. d'argent** short of money **3** *nm* **c. (de tennis)** tennis court ■ **court-circuit** (*pl* **courts-circuits**) *nm* short-circuit

courtier, -ère [kurtje, -ɛr] *nmf* broker

courtisan [kurtizɑ̃] *nm Hist* courtier

■ **courtiser** vt (femme) to court

courtois, -e [kurtwa, -az] adj courteous ■ **courtoisie** nf courtesy

couru, -e [kury] adj (spectacle, lieu) popular

cousin, -e [kuzɛ̃, -in] 1 nmf cousin; **c. germain** first cousin 2 nm (insecte) mosquito

coussin [kusɛ̃] nm cushion

cousu, -e [kuzy] adj sewn; **c. main** hand-sewn

coût [ku] nm cost; **le c. de la vie** the cost of living ■ **coûter** vti to cost; **ça coûte combien?** how much is it?, how much does it cost?

couteau, -x [kuto] nm knife; **c. à pain** breadknife; **c.-scie** serrated knife

coûteux, -euse [kutø, -øz] adj costly, expensive

coutume [kutym] nf (habitude, tradition) custom; **avoir c. de faire qch** to be accustomed to doing sth; **comme de c.** as usual

couture [kutyr] nf (activité) sewing, needlework; (raccord) seam; **faire de la c.** to sew ■ **couturier** nm fashion designer ■ **couturière** nf dressmaker

couvent [kuvã] nm (de religieuses) convent; (de moines) monastery; (pensionnat) convent school

couver [kuve] 1 vt (œufs) to sit on; (maladie) to be coming down with 2 vi (poule) to brood; (feu) Br to smoulder, Am to smolder ■ **couveuse** nf (pour nouveaux-nés) incubator

couvercle [kuvɛrkl] nm lid; (vissé) cap

couvert[1] [kuvɛr] nm (a) **mettre le c.** to set or Br lay the table; **table de cinq couverts** table set or Br laid for five; **couverts** (ustensiles) cutlery (b) **sous le c. de** (sous l'apparence de) under cover of; **se mettre à c.** to take cover

couvert[2], **-e** [kuvɛr, -ɛrt] 1 pp de **couvrir** 2 adj covered (**de** with or in); (ciel) overcast; **être bien c.** (habillé chaudement) to be warmly dressed

couverture [kuvɛrtyr] nf (de lit) blanket; (de livre, de magazine) cover; (de bâtiment) roofing; Journ coverage; **c. chauffante** electric blanket; **c. sociale** social security cover

couvrir* [kuvrir] 1 vt to cover (**de** with); (bruit) to drown 2 **se couvrir** vpr (s'habiller) to wrap up; (se coiffer) to cover one's head; (ciel) to cloud over ■ **couvre-feu** (pl **couvre-feux**) nm curfew ■ **couvre-lit** (pl **couvre-lits**) nm bedspread

cow-boy [kɔbɔj] (pl **cow-boys**) nm cowboy

crabe [krab] nm crab

crachat [kraʃa] nm gob of spit; **crachats** spit

cracher [kraʃe] 1 vt to spit out 2 vi (personne) to spit; (stylo) to splutter; (radio) to crackle

crachin [kraʃɛ̃] nm (fine) drizzle

craie [krɛ] nf (matière) chalk; (bâton) stick of chalk

craindre* [krɛ̃dr] vt (redouter) to be afraid of, to fear; (chaleur, froid) to be sensitive to; **c. de faire qch** to be afraid of doing sth; **je crains qu'elle ne soit partie** I'm afraid she's left; **ne craignez rien** (n'ayez pas peur) don't be afraid; (ne vous inquiétez pas) don't worry

crainte [krɛ̃t] nf fear; **de c. de faire qch** for fear of doing sth

craintif, -ive [krɛ̃tif, -iv] adj timid

crampe [krɑ̃p] nf cramp

crampon [krɑ̃pɔ̃] nm (de chaussure) stud; (pour l'alpinisme) crampon

cramponner [krɑ̃pɔne] **se cramponner** vpr to hold on; **se c. à qn/qch** to hold on to sb/sth

cran [krɑ̃] nm (a) (entaille) notch; (de ceinture) hole; **c. d'arrêt** ou **de sûreté** safety catch (b) (de cheveux) wave (c) Fam (courage) guts; **avoir du c.** to have guts (d) Fam **être à c.** (excédé) to be wound up

crâne [krɑn] nm skull

crapaud [krapo] nm toad

crapule [krapyl] nf villain, scoundrel

craquer [krake] 1 vt (allumette) to strike 2 vi (branche) to crack; (escalier) to creak; *(se casser)* to snap; *(se déchirer)* to rip ■ **craquements** *nmpl (de branches)* cracking; *(d'escalier)* creaking

crasse [kras] *nf* filth ■ **crasseux, -euse** *adj* filthy

cratère [kratɛr] *nm* crater

cravate [kravat] *nf* tie

crawlé [krole] *adj* m **dos c.** backstroke

crayon [krɛjɔ̃] *nm (en bois)* pencil; *(en cire)* crayon

créancier, -ère [kreɑ̃sje, -ɛr] *nmf* debtor

créateur, -trice [kreatœr, -tris] **1** *adj* creative **2** *nmf* creator ■ **création** *nf* creation; **1000 créations d'emplois** 1,000 new jobs

créature [kreatyr] *nf (être vivant)* creature

crèche [krɛʃ] *nf (de Noël)* manger, *Br* crib; *(garderie)* (day) nursery, *Br* crèche

crédible [kredibl] *adj* credible

crédit [kredi] *nm (prêt, influence)* credit; **crédits** *(somme d'argent)* funds; **à c. on** credit ■ **créditer** *vt (compte)* to credit **(de** with); *Fig* **c. qn de qch** to give sb credit for sth ■ **créditeur, -trice** *adj* **solde c.** credit balance; **être c.** to be in credit

crédule [kredyl] *adj* credulous ■ **crédulité** *nf* credulity

créer [kree] *vt* to create

crémaillère [kremajɛr] *nf* **pendre la c.** to have a housewarming (party)

crématorium [krematɔrjɔm] *nm Br* crematorium, *Am* crematory

crème [krɛm] **1** *nf (de lait, dessert, cosmétique)* cream; **c. Chantilly** whipped cream; **c. glacée** ice cream; **c. à raser** shaving cream **2** *adj inv* cream (-coloured) **3** *nm Fam* coffee with milk, *Br* white coffee ■ **crèmerie** *nf (magasin)* dairy ■ **crémeux, -euse** *adj* creamy

créneau, -x [kreno] *nm Com* niche; *TV & Radio* slot

créole [kreɔl] **1** *adj* creole **2** *nmf* Creole **3** *nm (langue)* Creole

crêpe [krɛp] **1** *nf* pancake, crêpe **2** *nm (tissu)* crepe ■ **crêperie** *nf* pancake restaurant

crépiter [krepite] *vi (feu)* to crackle ■ **crépitement** *nm (du feu)* crackling

crépu, -e [krepy] *adj* frizzy

crépuscule [krepyskyl] *nm* twilight

cresson [krɛsɔ̃] *nm* watercress

Crète [krɛt] *nf* **la C.** Crete

crête [krɛt] *nf (de montagne, d'oiseau, de vague)* crest

creuser [krøze] **1** *vt (trou, puits)* to dig; *(évider)* to hollow (out); *Fig (idée)* to look into **2** *vi* to dig **3 se creuser** *vpr (joues)* to become hollow; *Fam* **se c. la tête** *ou* **la cervelle** to rack one's brains

creux, -euse [krø, -øz] **1** *adj (tube, joues, arbre, paroles)* hollow; *(sans activité)* slack; **assiette creuse** soup plate **2** *nm* hollow; *(moment)* slack period

crevaison [krəvɛzɔ̃] *nf (de pneu)* flat, *Br* puncture

crevasse [krəvas] *nf (trou)* crack; *(de glacier)* crevasse

crever [krəve] **1** *vt (ballon, bulle)* to burst; *Fam (épuiser)* to wear out **2** *vi (bulle, ballon, pneu)* to burst ■ **crevé, -e** *adj (ballon, pneu)* burst; *Fam (épuisé)* worn out

crevette [krəvɛt] *nf (grise)* shrimp; *(rose)* prawn

cri [kri] *nm (de personne)* cry, shout; *(perçant)* scream; *(d'animal)* cry ■ **criard, -e** *adj (son)* shrill; *(couleur)* loud

crier [krije] **1** *vt (injure, ordre)* to shout **(à** to) **2** *vi (personne)* to shout, to cry out; *(fort)* to scream; *(parler très fort)* to shout; **c. au secours** to shout for help

crime [krim] *nm* crime; *(assassinat)* murder ■ **criminalité** *nf* crime ■ **criminel, -elle 1** *adj* criminal **2** *nmf* criminal; *(assassin)* murderer

crinière [krinjɛr] *nf* mane

crique [krik] *nf* creek

crise [kriz] *nf* crisis; *(de maladie)* attack; **c. de nerfs** fit of hysteria

crisper [krispe] **1** vt (poing) to clench; (muscle) to tense **2 se crisper** vpr (visage) to get tense; (personne) to get tense ■ **crispé, -e** adj (personne) tense

crisser [krise] vi (pneu, roue) to squeal; (neige) to crunch

cristal, -aux [kristal, -o] nm crystal; Tech **cristaux liquides** liquid crystal ■ **cristallin, -e** adj (eau, son) crystal-clear

critère [kriter] nm criterion

critique [kritik] **1** adj (situation, phase) critical **2** nf (reproche) criticism; (de film, de livre) review; **faire la c.** (de (film) to review **3** nm critic ■ **critiquer** vt to criticize

croasser [krɔase] vi to caw

Croatie [krɔasi] nf la C. Croatia

croc [krɔ] nm (crochet) hook; (dent) fang

croche [krɔʃ] nf Mus Br quaver, Am eighth (note)

croche-pied [krɔʃpje] nm trip; **faire un c. à qn** to trip sb up

crochet [krɔʃɛ] nm (pour accrocher, en boxe) hook; (aiguille) crochet hook; (parenthèse) square bracket; **faire du c.** to crochet; **faire un c.** (détour) to make a detour; (route) to make a sudden turn ■ **crocheter** vt (serrure) to pick

crochu, -e [krɔʃy] adj (nez) hooked; (doigts) claw-like

crocodile [krɔkɔdil] nm crocodile

croire* [krwar] **1** vt to believe; (penser) to think (**que** that); **j'ai cru la voir** I thought I saw her; **je crois que oui** I think or believe so

2 vi to believe (**à** ou **en** in)

3 se croire vpr **il se croit malin** he thinks he's smart

croisé¹ [krwaze] nm Hist crusader ■ **croisade** nf Hist crusade

croiser [krwaze] **1** vt (passer) to pass; (ligne) to cross; (espèce) to cross-breed; **c. les jambes** to cross one's legs; **c. les bras** to fold one's arms; Fig **c. les doigts** to keep one's fingers crossed

2 vi (navire) to cruise

3 se croiser vpr (voitures) to pass each other; (lignes, routes) to cross, to intersect; (lettres) to cross; (regards) to meet ■ **croisé², -e** adj (bras) folded; (veston) double-breasted ■ **croisement** nm (de routes) crossroads (sing), intersection; (d'animaux) crossing

croisière [krwazjer] nf cruise

croître* [krwatr] vi (plante) to grow; (augmenter) to grow, to increase (**de** by); (lune) to wax ■ **croissance** nf growth ■ **croissant, -e 1** adj (nombre) growing **2** nm crescent; (pâtisserie) croissant

croix [krwa] nf cross; **la C.-Rouge** the Red Cross

croquer [krɔke] **1** vt (manger) to crunch **2** vi (fruit) to be crunchy; **c. dans qch** to bite into sth ■ **croquant, -e** adj crunchy ■ **croque-monsieur** nm inv = toasted cheese and ham sandwich

croquis [krɔki] nm sketch

crosse [krɔs] nf (de fusil) butt; (de hockey) stick; (d'évêque) crook

crotte [krɔt] nf (de mouton, de lapin) droppings; **c. de chien** dog dirt ■ **crottin** nm dung

crouler [krule] vi (édifice) to crumble; **c. sous le travail** to be snowed under with work ■ **croulant, -e** adj (mur) crumbling

croupe [krup] nf rump

croupier [krupje] nm croupier

croupir [krupir] vi (eau) to stagnate

croustiller [krustije] vi to be crunchy; (pain) to be crusty ■ **croustillant, -e** adj crunchy; (pain) crusty; Fig (histoire) spicy

croûte [krut] nf (de pain) crust; (de fromage) rind; (de plaie) scab; Fam **casser la c.** to have a snack ■ **croûton** nm (de pain) end; **croûtons** (pour la soupe) croûtons

croyable [krwajabl] adj credible, believable ■ **croyance** nf belief (**en** in) ■ **croyant, -e 1** adj **être c.** to be a believer **2** nmf believer

CRS [seɛrɛs] (*abrév* **compagnie républicaine de sécurité**) *nm* = French riot policeman

cru¹, -e¹ [kry] *pp de* **croire**

cru², -e² [kry] **1** *adj* (*aliment*) raw; (*lait*) unpasteurized; (*lumière*) garish; (*propos*) crude; **monter à c.** to ride bareback **2** *nm* (*vignoble*) vineyard; **un grand c.** (*vin*) a vintage wine; **vin du c.** local wine

cruauté [kryote] *nf* cruelty (**envers** to)

cruche [kryʃ] *nf* pitcher, jug

crucial, -e, -aux, -ales [krysjal, -o] *adj* crucial

crucifier [krysifje] *vt* to crucify ■ **crucifix** *nm* crucifix ■ **crucifixion** *nf* crucifixion

crudités [krydite] *nfpl* (*légumes*) assorted raw vegetables

crue [kry] *nf* (*montée*) swelling; (*inondation*) flood; **en c.** (*rivière, fleuve*) in spate

cruel, -elle [kryɛl] *adj* cruel (**envers** *ou* **avec** to) ■ **cruellement** *adv* cruelly

crûment [krymɑ̃] *adv* (*sans détour*) bluntly; (*grossièrement*) crudely

crustacés [krystase] *nmpl* Culin shellfish *inv*

crypte [kript] *nf* crypt

crypté, -e [kripte] *adj* (*message*) & TV coded

Cuba [kyba] *n* Cuba ■ **cubain, -e 1** *adj* Cuban **2** *nmf* C., Cubaine Cuban

cube [kyb] **1** *nm* cube; (*de jeu*) building block **2** *adj* **mètre c.** cubic metre ■ **cubique** *adj* cubic

cueillir* [kœjir] *vt* to pick, to gather

cuiller, cuillère [kɥijer] *nf* spoon; (*mesure*) spoonful; **c. à café, petite c.** teaspoon; **c. à soupe** tablespoon ■ **cuillerée** *nf* spoonful; **c. à café** teaspoonful; **c. à soupe** tablespoonful

cuir [kɥir] *nm* leather; (*d'éléphant*) hide; **pantalon en c.** leather trousers; **c. chevelu** scalp

cuirassé [kɥirase] *nm* Naut battleship

cuire* [kɥir] **1** *vt* (*aliment, plat*) to cook; **c. qch à l'eau** to boil sth; **c. qch au four** to bake sth; (*viande*) to roast

sth **2** *vi* (*aliment*) to cook; **faire c. qch** to cook sth

cuisant, -e [kɥizɑ̃, -ɑ̃t] *adj* (*douleur*) burning; (*affront*) stinging

cuisine [kɥizin] *nf* (*pièce*) kitchen; (*art*) cookery, cooking; **faire la c.** to do the cooking ■ **cuisiner** *vti* to cook

cuisinier, -ère¹ [kɥizinje, -ɛr] *nmf* cook

cuisinière² [kɥizinjɛr] *nf* (*appareil*) stove, Br cooker

cuisse [kɥis] *nf* thigh; **c. de poulet** chicken leg; **cuisses de grenouilles** frogs' legs

cuisson [kɥisɔ̃] *nm* (*d'aliments*) cooking; (*de pain*) baking

cuit, -e [kɥi, kɥit] **1** *pp de* **cuire 2** *adj* cooked; **bien c.** well done

cuivre [kɥivr] *nm* (*rouge*) copper; (*jaune*) brass; Mus **les cuivres** the brass ■ **cuivré, -e** *adj* copper-coloured

culbuter [kylbyte] *vi* (*personne*) to take a tumble

cul-de-sac [kydsak] (*pl* **culs-de-sac**) *nm* dead end, Br cul-de-sac

culinaire [kyliner] *adj* culinary

culminer [kylmine] *vi* (*tension, crise*) to peak; **la montagne culmine à 3 000 mètres** the mountain is 3,000 metres at its highest point ■ **culminant** *adj* **point c.** (*de montagne*) highest point

culot [kylo] *nm* (*d'ampoule, de lampe*) base; Fam (*audace*) nerve, Br cheek

culotte [kylɔt] *nf* (*de femme*) knickers, Am panties; (*d'enfant*) pants; **culottes courtes** Br short trousers, Am short pants

culpabiliser [kylpabilize] **1** *vt* **c. qn** to make sb feel guilty **2** **se culpabiliser** *vpr* to feel guilty ■ **culpabilité** *nf* guilt

culte [kylt] **1** *nm* (*de dieu*) worship; (*religion*) religion **2** *adj* **film c.** cult film

cultiver [kyltive] **1** *vt* (*terre, amitié*) to cultivate; (*plantes*) to grow **2** **se cultiver** *vpr* to improve one's mind ■ **cultivateur, -trice** *nmf* farmer ■ **cultivé, -e**

adj (*terre*) cultivated; (*esprit, personne*) cultured, cultivated

culture [kyltyr] *nf* (**a**) (*action*) farming, cultivation; (*de plantes*) growing; **cultures** (*terres*) fields under cultivation; (*plantes*) crops (**b**) (*éducation, civilisation*) & *Biol* culture; **c. générale** general knowledge; **c. physique** physical training ■ **culturel, -elle** *adj* cultural

culturisme [kyltyrism] *nm* body-building

cumulatif, -ive *adj* cumulative ■ **cumuler** *vt* **c. deux fonctions** to hold two offices **cupide** [kypid] *adj* avaricious

cure [kyr] *nf* (*traitement*) (course of) treatment

curé [kyre] *nm* parish priest

curer [kyre] **1** *vt* to clean out **2 se curer** *vpr* **se c. les dents** to clean one's teeth ■ **cure-dents** *nm inv* toothpick

curieux, -euse [kyrjø, -øz] **1** *adj* (*bizarre*) curious; (*indiscret*) inquisitive, curious ■ *nmf* inquisitive person; (*badaud*) onlooker ■ **curiosité** *nf* curiosity; (*chose*) curio

curriculum vitae [kyrikylɔmvite] *nm inv Br* curriculum vitae, *Am* résumé

curseur [kyrsœr] *nm Ordinat* cursor

cutané, -e [kytane] *adj* **maladie cutanée** skin condition

cuti [kyti] *nf* skin test

cuve [kyv] *nf* tank; (*de fermentation*) vat ■ **cuvée** *nf* (*récolte*) vintage ■ **cuvette** *nf* (*récipient*) & *Géog* basin; (*des cabinets*) bowl

CV [seve] (*abrév* **curriculum vitae**) *nm Br* CV, *Am* résumé

cyanure [sjanyr] *nm* cyanide

cybercafé [siberkafe] *nm* cybercafé

cycle [sikl] *nm* (**a**) (*série, mouvement*) cycle (**b**) **premier/second c.** *Scol* = lower/upper classes in secondary school; *Univ* = first/last two years of a degree course (**c**) (*bicyclette*) cycle ■ **cyclable** *adj* **piste c.** cycle path

cyclisme [siklism] *nm* cycling ■ **cycliste 1** *nmf* cyclist **2** *adj* **course c.** cycle race

cyclomoteur [siklɔmɔtœr] *nm* moped

cyclone [siklon] *nm* cyclone

cygne [siɲ] *nm* swan

cylindre [silɛ̃dr] *nm* cylinder; (*rouleau*) roller ■ **cylindrée** *nf* (cubic) capacity ■ **cylindrique** *adj* cylindrical

cymbale [sɛ̃bal] *nf* cymbal

cynique [sinik] **1** *adj* cynical **2** *nmf* cynic

cyprès [sipre] *nm* cypress

cypriote [siprijɔt] **1** *adj* Cypriot **2** *nmf* **C.** Cypriot

Dd

D, d [de] **1** *nm inv* D, d **2** *(abrév route départementale)* = designation of a secondary road

dactylo [daktilo] *nf (personne)* typist; *(action)* typing

daigner [deɲe] *vt* **d. faire qch** to deign to do sth

daim [dɛ̃] *nm (animal)* fallow deer; *(mâle)* buck; *(cuir)* suede

dalle [dal] *nf (de pierre)* paving stone; *(de marbre)* slab

daltonien, -enne [daltɔnjɛ̃, -ɛn] *adj* colour-blind

dame [dam] *nf (femme)* lady; *Cartes* queen; *(au jeu de dames)* king; **dames** *(jeu) Br* draughts, *Am* checkers

damner [dane] *vt* to damn

Danemark [danmark] *nm* le D. Denmark ■ **danois, -e 1** *adj* Danish **2** *nmf* D., Danoise Dane **3** *nm (langue)* Danish

danger [dɑ̃ʒe] *nm* danger; **en d. in danger** ■ **dangereux, -euse** *adj* dangerous (**pour** to)

prép (**a**) *(changement de lieu)* into; *(à l'intérieur de)* inside (**b**) *(provenance)* from, out of; **boire d. un verre** to drink out of a glass (**c**) *(exprime la temporalité)* in; **d. deux jours** in two days' time (**d**) *(exprime une approximation)* **d. les dix euros** about ten euros

danse [dɑ̃s] *nf* dance; **la d.** *(art)* dancing; **d. classique** ballet ■ **danser** *vti* to dance ■ **danseur, -euse** *nmf* dancer

dard [dar] *nm (d'insecte)* sting

date [dat] *nf* date; **d. de naissance** date of birth; **d. limite** deadline; **d. limite de vente** sell-by date ■ **dater 1** *vt (lettre)* to date **2** *vi* **à d. du 15** as from the 15th

datte [dat] *nf* date

daube [dob] *nf* **bœuf en d.** braised beef stew

dauphin [dofɛ̃] *nm (animal)* dolphin

davantage [davɑ̃taʒ] *adv* more; **d. de temps/d'argent** more time/money

de becomes **d'** before vowel and h mute; **de + le = du**, **de + les = des**.

prép (**a**) *(complément de nom)* of; **le livre de Paul** Paul's book; **un livre de Flaubert** a book by Flaubert; **le train de Londres** the London train; **une augmentation de salaire** an increase in salary

(**b**) *(complément d'adjectif)* **digne de qn** worthy of sb; **content de qn/qch** pleased with sb/sth; **heureux de partir** happy to leave

(**c**) *(complément de verbe)* **parler de qn/qch** to speak of sb/sth; **se souvenir de qn/qch** to remember sb/sth; **décider de faire qch** to decide to do sth; **empêcher qn de faire qch** to stop sb from doing sth

(**d**) *(indique la provenance)* from; **venir de...** to come from...; **sortir de qch** to come out of sth; **le train de Londres** the train from London

(**e**) *(introduit l'agent)* **accompagné de qn** accompanied by sb; **entouré de qch** surrounded by *or* with sth (**f**) *(introduit le moyen)* **armé de qch** armed with sth

(**g**) *(introduit la manière)* **d'une voix douce** in a gentle voice

(**h**) *(introduit la cause)* **puni de son impatience** punished for his/her impatience; **mourir de faim** to die of hunger

(**i**) *(introduit le temps)* **travailler de nuit** to work by night; **six heures du matin** six o'clock in the morning

(**j**) *(mesure)* **avoir six mètres de haut, être haut de six mètres** to be six metres high; **homme de trente ans** thirty-year-old man; **gagner cent francs de l'heure** to earn a hundred francs an hour

DE² [də] *article partitif* some; **elle boit du vin** she drinks (some) wine; **il ne boit pas de vin** he doesn't drink (any) wine; **est-ce que vous buvez du vin?** do you drink (any) wine?

DE³ [də] *article indéfini* **de, des** some; **des fleurs** (some) flowers; **de jolies fleurs** (some) pretty flowers; **d'agréables soirées** (some) pleasant evenings

dé [de] *nm (à jouer)* dice; *(à coudre)* thimble

déballer [debale] *vt* to unpack

débarbouiller [debarbuje] **se débarbouiller** *vpr* to wash one's face

débardeur [debardœr] *nm (vêtement)* vest

débarquer [debarke] **1** *vt (passagers)* to land; *(marchandises)* to unload **2** *vi (passagers)* to disembark ■ **débarquement** *nm (de passagers, de troupes)* landing; *(de marchandises)* unloading

débarras [debara] *nm* storeroom ■ **débarrasser 1** *vt (chambre, table)* to clear (**de** of); **d. qn de qch** to relieve sb of sth **2 se débarrasser** *vpr* **se d. de qn/qch** to get rid of sb/sth

débat [deba] *nm* debate

débattre* [debatr] **1** *vt* to discuss, to debate; **d. de qch** to discuss sth **2 se débattre** *vpr* to struggle

débaucher [deboʃe] *vt* **d. qn** *(licencier)* to lay sb off; *(inciter à la débauche)* to corrupt sb

débit [debi] *nm Fin* debit; *(de fleuve)* flow; *(de personne)* delivery; **d. de tabac** *Br* tobacconist's (shop), *Am* tobacco store

débiter [debite] *vt (découper)* to cut up (**en** into); *(compte)* to debit; *Péj (dire)* to spout ■ **débiteur** *adj m* **solde d.** debit balance; **mon compte est d.** my account is in debit

débloquer [debloke] *vt (mécanisme)* to unjam; *(compte, prix)* to unfreeze

déboiser [debwaze] *vt (terrain)* to clear of trees

déboîter [debwate] **1** *vt (tuyau)* to disconnect **2** *vi (véhicule)* to pull out **3 se déboîter** *vpr* **se d. l'épaule** to dislocate one's shoulder

déborder [deborde] **1** *vi (fleuve, liquide)* to overflow; *(en bouillant)* to boil over **2** *vt (dépasser)* to stick out from; **débordé de travail** snowed under with work

débouché [debuʃe] *nm (carrière)* opening; *(de produit)* outlet

déboucher [debuʃe] **1** *vt (bouteille)* to uncork; *(bouchon vissé)* to uncap; *(lavabo, tuyau)* to unblock **2** *vi (surgir)* to emerge (**de** from); **d. sur** *(rue)* to lead out onto/into

debout [dəbu] *adv (personne)* standing; *(objet)* upright; **se mettre d.** to stand up; **rester d.** to stand; **être d.** *(hors du lit)* to be up

déboutonner [debutɔne] **1** *vt* to unbutton **2 se déboutonner** *vpr (personne)* to undo one's coat/jacket/*etc*

débraillé, -e [debraje] *adj* slovenly

débrancher [debrɑ̃ʃe] *vt* to unplug

débrayer [debreje] *vi* (**a**) *Aut* to release the clutch (**b**) *(se mettre en grève)* to stop work ■ **débrayage** (**a**) *Aut* declutching (**b**) *(grève)* stoppage

débris [debri] *nmpl (de voiture, d'avion)* debris

débrouiller [debruje] **1** *vt (fil, mystère)* to unravel **2 se débrouiller** *vpr Fam* to manage; **se d. pour faire qch** to manage to do sth ■ **débrouillard, -e** *adj Fam* resourceful

début [deby] *nm* beginning, start; **au d. (de)** at the beginning (of); **dès le d.** (right) from the start *or* beginning

débuter [debyte] *vi* to start, to begin (**par** with); *(dans une carrière)* to start out ■ **débutant, -e** *nmf* beginner

deçà [dəsa] **en deçà 1** *adv* (on) this side **2** *prép* **en d. de** (on) this side of

décadent, -e [dekadã, -ãt] *adj* decadent

décaféiné, -e [dekafeine] *adj* decaffeinated

décaler [dekale] **1** *vt (dans le temps)* to change the time of; *(dans l'espace)* to shift, to move **2 se décaler** *vpr* to move, to shift ■ **décalage** *nm (écart)* gap (**entre** between); **d. horaire** time difference; **souffrir du d. horaire** to have jet lag

décalquer [dekalke] *vt* to trace

décaper [dekape] *vt (avec un produit)* to strip; *(au papier de verre)* to sand (down); *(four)* to clean

décapiter [dekapite] *vt (personne)* to decapitate

décapotable [dekapɔtabl] *adj & nf* convertible

décapsuleur [dekapsylœr] *nm* bottle opener

décédé, -e [desede] *adj* deceased

déceler [desle] *vt (trouver)* to detect

décembre [desãbr] *nm* December

décence [desãs] *nf (de comportement)* propriety; *(d'habillement)* decency

décennie [deseni] *nf* decade

décent, -e [desã, -ãt] *adj (comportement)* proper; *(vêtements)* decent

décentralisation [desãtralizasjɔ̃] *nf* decentralization

déception [desepsjɔ̃] *nf* disappointment

décerner [deserne] *vt (prix)* to award (**à** to)

décès [dese] *nm* death

décevant, -e [desvã, -ãt] *adj* disappointing

décevoir* [desəvwar] *vt* to disappoint

déchaîner [defene] **1** *vt (colère, violence)* to unleash **2 se déchaîner** *vpr (tempête)* to rage; *(personne)* to fly into a rage (**contre** with)

décharge [defarʒ] *nf* **d. (électrique)** (electric) shock; **d. (publique)** *Br* (rubbish) dump, *Am* (garbage) dump

décharger [defarʒe] **1** *vt (camion, navire, cargaison)* to unload; **d. qn de qch** *(tâche, responsabilité)* to relieve sb of **2 se décharger** *vpr (batterie)* to go flat

déchausser [defose] **1** *vt* **d. qn** to take sb's shoes off **2 se déchausser** *vpr (personne)* to take one's shoes off

déchéance [defeãs] *nf (déclin)* decline

déchets [defe] *nmpl* scraps; **d. radioactifs** radioactive waste

déchiffrer [defifre] *vt (message, écriture)* to decipher

déchiqueté, -e [defikte] *adj (tissu)* torn to shreds

déchirer [defire] **1** *vt (accidentellement)* to tear; *(volontairement)* to tear up **2 se déchirer** *vpr (tissu, papier)* to tear

déchirure [defiryr] *nf* tear

déchoir* [defwar] *vi (personne)* to demean oneself

déchu, -e [defy] *adj* **être d. de qch** to be stripped of sth

décidé, -e [deside] *adj (personne, air)* determined; *(fixé)* settled; **être d. à faire qch** to be determined to do sth

décidément [desidemã] *adv* really

décider [deside] **1** *vt* **d. quand/que…** to decide when/that… **2** *vi* **d. de qch** to decide on sth; **d. de faire qch** to decide to do sth **3 se décider** *vpr* **se d. (à faire qch)** to make up one's mind (to do sth)

décimal, -e, -aux, -ales [desimal, -o] *adj* decimal

décimer [desime] *vt* to decimate

décimètre [desimetr] *nm* decimetre

décisif, -ive [desizif, -iv] *adj (bataille)* decisive; *(moment)* critical ■ **décision**

nf decision (**de faire** to do); **prendre une d.** to make a decision

déclaration [deklarɑsjɔ̃] *nf (annonce)* statement; *(de naissance, de décès)* registration; *(à la police)* report; **d. d'impôts** income tax return

déclarer [deklare] **1** *vt (annoncer)* to declare (**que** that); *(naissance, décès)* to register; **d. qn coupable** to find sb guilty (**de** of); **d. la guerre** to declare war (**à** on); **rien à d.** *(en douane)* nothing to declare **2 se déclarer** *vpr (incendie, maladie)* to break out

déclencher [deklɑ̃ʃe] **1** *vt (appareil)* to start; *(mécanisme)* to activate; *(sonnerie)* to set off; *(révolte)* to trigger off; *(attaque)* to launch **2 se déclencher** *vpr (alarme, sonnerie)* to go off; *(incendie)* to start

déclic [deklik] *nm (bruit)* click

déclin [deklɛ̃] *nm* decline; **être en d.** to be in decline

décliner [dekline] **1** *vi (forces)* to decline; *(jour)* to draw to a close **2** *vt (refuser)* to decline

décocher [dekɔʃe] *vt (flèche)* to shoot

décoder [dekɔde] *vt* to decode ▪ **décodeur** *nm* TV decoder

décoiffer [dekwafe] **1** *vt* **d. qn** to mess up sb's hair **2 se décoiffer** *vpr (se dépeigner)* to mess up one's hair; *(ôter son chapeau)* to remove one's hat

décoincer [dekwɛ̃se] *vt*, **se décoincer** *vpr (tiroir, mécanisme)* to loosen

décollage [dekɔlaʒ] *nm (d'avion)* take-off

décoller [dekɔle] **1** *vt (enlever)* to peel off **2** *vi (avion)* to take off **3 se décoller** *vpr* to peel off

décolleté, -e [dekɔlte] **1** *adj (robe)* low-cut **2** *nm (de robe)* low neckline

décolorer [dekɔlore] **1** *vt (cheveux)* to bleach **2 se décolorer** *vpr (tissu)* to fade; **se d. les cheveux** to bleach one's hair

décombres [dekɔ̃br] *nmpl* ruins, debris

décommander [dekɔmɑ̃de] **1** *vt (marchandises, invitation)* to cancel; *(invité)*

to put off **2 se décommander** *vpr* to cancel

décomposer [dekɔ̃poze] **1** *vt* Chim to decompose **2 se décomposer** *vpr (pourrir)* to decompose ▪ **décomposition** *nf* decomposition

décompression [dekɔ̃presjɔ̃] *nf* decompression

décompte [dekɔ̃t] *nm (soustraction)* deduction; *(détail)* breakdown ▪ **décompter** *vt* to deduct (**de** from)

déconcentrer [dekɔ̃sɑ̃tre] **se déconcentrer** *vpr* to lose concentration

déconcerter [dekɔ̃serte] *vt* to disconcert

décongeler [dekɔ̃ʒle] *vt* to thaw, defrost

décongestionner [dekɔ̃ʒestjɔne] *vt (rue, poumons)* to relieve congestion in

déconnecter [dekɔnekte] *vt (appareil, fil)* to disconnect

déconseiller [dekɔ̃seje] *vt* **d. qch à qn** to advise sb against sth; **d. à qn de faire qch** to advise sb against doing sth

déconsidérer [dekɔ̃sidere] *vt* to discredit

décontaminer [dekɔ̃tamine] *vt* to contaminate

décontracter [dekɔ̃trakte] **1** *vt (muscle)* to relax **2 se décontracter** *vpr* to relax ▪ **décontracté, -e** *adj (ambiance, personne)* relaxed; *(vêtement)* casual

décor [dekɔr] *nm (de maison)* decor; *(paysage)* surroundings; *Théât* **décors** scenery, set

décorer [dekɔre] *vt (maison, soldat)* to decorate (**de** with) ▪ **décorateur, -trice** *nmf (interior)* decorator; *Théât* stage designer ▪ **décoratif, -ive** *adj* decorative ▪ **décoration** *nf (action, ornement, médaille)* decoration

décortiquer [dekɔrtike] *vt (riz, orge)* to hull; *(crevette, noisette)* to shell

découdre* [dekudr] **1** *vt (ourlet, vêtement)* to unstitch; *(bouton)* to take off **2 se découdre** *vpr (ourlet, vêtement)* to come unstitched; *(bouton)* to come off

découler [dekule] *vi* d. de qch to follow from sth

découper [dekupe] *vt* (*viande*) to carve; (*gâteau, papier*) to cut up ■ **découpé, -e** *adj* (*irrégulier*) jagged

décourager [dekuraʒe] 1 *vt* (*dissuader*) to discourage (de faire from doing); (*démoraliser*) to dishearten, to discourage 2 se décourager *vpr* to get discouraged *or* disheartened ■ **découragement** *nm* discouragement

décousu, -e [dekuzy] *adj* (*ourlet, vêtement*) unstitched; *Fig* (*propos*) disjointed

découvert, -e [dekuvɛr, -ɛrt] 1 *adj* (*terrain*) open; (*tête, épaule*) bare 2 *nm* (de compte) overdraft

découverte [dekuvɛrt] *nf* discovery; faire une d. to make a discovery

découvrir* [dekuvrir] 1 *vt* (*trouver, apprendre à connaître*) to discover; (*secret*) to uncover; faire d. qch à qn to introduce sb to sth 2 se découvrir *vpr* (ciel) to clear

décrire* [dekrir] *vt* (*représenter*) to describe

décrocher [dekrɔʃe] 1 *vt* (*détacher*) to unhook; (*tableau, rideau*) to take down; d. (le téléphone) (*pour répondre*) to pick up the phone; (*pour ne pas être dérangé*) to take the phone off the hook 2 se décrocher *vpr* (*tableau, rideau*) to come unhooked

décroître* [dekrwatr] *vi* (*forces, nombre*) to decrease; (*jours*) to get shorter

décrypter [dekripte] *vt* to decipher

déçu, -e [desy] 1 *pp de* décevoir 2 *adj* disappointed

décupler [dekyple] *vti* to increase tenfold

dédaigner [dedɛɲe] *vt* (*offre, richesses*) to scorn; (*conseil*) to disregard ■ **dédaigneux, -euse** *adj* scornful, disdainful (de of)

dédain [dedɛ̃] *nm* scorn, disdain (pour/de for)

dedans [dədɑ̃] *adv* inside; de d. from

(the) inside; en d. on the inside; tomber d. (trou) to fall in (it)

dédicace [dedikas] *nf* dedication ■ **dédicacer** *vt* (*signer*) to sign (à for)

dédier [dedje] *vt* to dedicate (à to)

dédommager [dedɔmaʒe] *vt* to compensate (de for) ■ **dédommagement** *nm* compensation

dédouaner [dedwane] *vt* (*marchandises*) to clear through customs

déduire* [dedɥir] *vt* (*retirer*) to deduct (de from); (*conclure*) to deduce (de from) ■ **déductible** *adj* deductible ■ **déduction** *nf* (*raisonnement, décompte*) deduction

déesse [deɛs] *nf* goddess

défaillir* [defajir] *vi* (*s'évanouir*) to faint; (*faiblir*) to fail ■ **défaillance** *nf* (*évanouissement*) fainting fit; (*faiblesse*) weakness; (*panne*) failure; avoir une d. (*s'évanouir*) to faint; (*faiblir*) to feel weak

défaire* [defɛr] *vt* (*nœud*) to undo; (*valises*) to unpack 2 se défaire *vpr* (*nœud*) to come undone

défait, -e¹ [defɛ, -ɛt] *adj* (*lit*) unmade; (*visage*) haggard

défaite² [defɛt] *nf* defeat

défaut [defo] *nm* (de personne) fault, shortcoming; (de machine) defect; (de diamant, de raisonnement) flaw; à d. de qch for lack of sth; ou, à d.... or, failing that...; d. de fabrication manufacturing fault; d. de prononciation speech impediment

défavorable [defavɔrabl] *adj* unfavourable (à to) ■ **défavorisé, -e** *adj* (*milieu*) underprivileged ■ **défavoriser** *vt* to put at a disadvantage

défection [defɛksjɔ̃] *nf* (de soldat, d'espion) defection; faire d. (soldat, espion) to defect

défectueux, -euse [defɛktɥø, -øz] *adj* faulty, defective

défendre [defɑ̃dr] 1 *vt* (*protéger, soutenir*) to defend (contre against); d. à qn de faire qch to forbid sb to do sth; d. qch à qn to forbid sb sth 2 se défendre *vpr* to defend oneself

défense¹ [defɑ̃s] *nf (protection) Br* defence, *Am* defense; **sans d.** *Br* defenceless, *Am* defenseless; **'d. de fumer'** 'no smoking'

défense² [defɑ̃s] *nf (d'éléphant)* tusk

défenseur [defɑ̃sœr] *nm* defender

défensif, -ive [defɑ̃sif, -iv] **1** *adj* defensive **2** *nf* **sur la défensive** on the defensive

déferler [defɛrle] *vi (vagues)* to break

défi [defi] *nm* challenge (**à** to); **lancer un d. à qn** to challenge sb; **mettre qn au d. de faire qch** to defy sb to do sth

défiance [defjɑ̃s] *nf* mistrust

déficience [defisjɑ̃s] *nf* deficiency

déficit [defisit] *nm* deficit; **être en d.** to be in deficit; **d. commercial** trade deficit ■ **déficitaire** *adj (budget)* in deficit; *(entreprise)* loss-making; *(compte)* in debit

défier [defje] *vt (provoquer)* to challenge; *(danger, mort)* to defy; **d. qn de faire qch** to defy sb to do sth

défiguré, -e [defigyre] *adj (personne)* disfigured

défilé [defile] *nm (cortège)* procession; *(de manifestants)* march; *Mil* parade; *Géog* pass; **d. de mode** fashion show

définir [definir] *vt* to define ■ **défini, -e** *adj* definite ■ **définition** *nf* definition; *(de mots croisés)* clue

définitif, -ive [definitif, -iv] **1** *adj (version)* final; *(fermeture)* permanent **2** *nf* **en définitive** in the final analysis ■ **définitivement** *adv (partir, exclure)* for good

déflagration [deflagrasjɔ̃] *nf* explosion

défoncer [defɔ̃se] *vt (porte, mur)* to smash in; *(trottoir)* to break up ■ **défoncé, -e** *adj (route)* bumpy

déformation [defɔrmasjɔ̃] *nf (de membre)* deformation; *(de fait)* distortion

déformer [defɔrme] **1** *vt (membre)* to deform; *(vêtement, chaussures)* to put out of shape; *(image)* to distort; *(propos)* to twist **2 se déformer** *vpr* to lose

its shape ■ **déformé, -e** *adj (objet)* misshapen; *(corps)* deformed

défricher [defriʃe] *vt (terrain)* to clear

défriser [defrize] *vt (cheveux)* to straighten

défroisser [defrwase] *vt* to smooth out

défunt, -e [defœ̃, -œ̃t] **1** *adj (mort)* departed; **mon d. mari** my late husband **2** *nmf* **le d., la défunte** the deceased

dégager [degaʒe] *vt (passage, voie)* to clear (**de** of); *(odeur, chaleur)* to emit; **d. qn de** *(décombres)* to free sb from **2 se dégager** *vpr (odeur)* to be given off; *(ciel)* to clear; **se d. de qch** *(personne)* to free oneself from sth ■ **dégagé, -e** *adj (ciel)* clear; *(ton)* casual; *(vue)* open ■ **dégagement** *nm (action)* clearing; *(de chaleur)* emission

dégainer [degene] *vti* to draw

dégarnir [degarnir] **se dégarnir** *vpr (personne)* to go bald

dégâts [dega] *nmpl* damage

dégel [deʒɛl] *nm* thaw ■ **dégeler 1** *vt* to thaw; *(surgelé)* to defrost; *(crédits)* to unfreeze **2** *vi* to thaw; **faire d. qch** *(surgelé)* to defrost sth **3** *v impersonnel* **il dégèle** it's thawing **4 se dégeler** *vpr Fig (atmosphère)* to become less chilly

dégénérer [deʒenere] *vi* to degenerate (**en** into)

dégonfler [degɔ̃fle] **1** *vt (pneu)* to let the air out of **2 se dégonfler** *vpr (pneu)* to go flat ■ **dégonflé, -e** *adj (pneu)* flat

dégouliner [deguline] *vi* to trickle

dégourdir [degurdir] **se dégourdir** *vpr* **se d. les jambes** to stretch one's legs ■ **dégourdi, -e** *adj (malin)* smart

dégoût [degu] *nm* disgust

dégoûter [degute] *vt (moralement)* to disgust; *(physiquement)* to turn sb's stomach; **d. qn de qch** to put sb off sth ■ **dégoûtant, -e** *adj* disgusting ■ **dégoûté, -e** *adj* disgusted; **être d. de qch** to be sick of sth

dégradation [degradasjɔ̃] *nf (de matériel)* damage (**de** to)

dégrader [degrade] **1** *vt (matériel)* to

damage **2 se dégrader** *vpr (situation)* to deteriorate ■ **dégradant, -e** *adj* degrading

dégrafer [degrafe] **1** *vt (vêtement)* to undo **2 se dégrafer** *vpr (vêtement)* to come undone

degré [dəgre] *nm (d'angle, de température)* degree; *(d'alcool)* proof; *(d'échelle)* rung; **au plus haut d.** in the extreme

dégrèvement [degrɛvmɑ̃] *nm* **d. fiscal** tax relief

dégrossir [degrosir] *vt (travail)* to rough out

déguiser [degize] **1** *vt (pour tromper)* to disguise; **d. qn en qch** *(costumer)* to dress sb up as sth **2 se déguiser** *vpr (pour s'amuser)* to dress oneself up (**en** as) ■ **déguisement** *nm* disguise; *(de bal costumé)* fancy dress

déguster [degyste] *vt (savourer)* to savour ■ **dégustation** *nf* tasting

dehors [dəɔr] **1** *adv* outside; *(pas chez soi)* out; *(en plein air)* out of doors; **en d. de la ville** out of town; *Fig* **en d. de** *(excepté)* apart from **2** *nm (extérieur)* outside; **au d.** on the outside; *(se pencher)* out

déjà [deʒa] *adv* already; **est-il d. parti?** has he left yet *or* already?; **elle l'a d. vu** she's seen it before, she's already seen it

déjeuner [deʒœne] **1** *nm* lunch; **petit d.** breakfast **2** *vi (à midi)* to have lunch; *(le matin)* to have breakfast

déjouer [deʒwe] *vt (intrigue)* to foil

délabré, -e [delabre] *adj (bâtiment)* dilapidated

délacer [delase] **1** *vt (chaussure)* to untie **2 se délacer** *vpr (chaussure)* to come untied

délai [delɛ] *nm (laps de temps)* time allowed; *(sursis)* extension; **dans les plus brefs délais** as soon as possible; **dernier d.** final date

délaisser [delese] *vt (négliger)* to neglect

délasser [delase] *vt*, **se délasser** *vpr* to relax

délavé, -e [delave] *adj (tissu, jean)* faded; *(couleur, ciel)* watery

délayer [deleje] *vt (poudre)* to add water to; *(liquide)* to water down

délecter [delɛkte] **se délecter** *vpr* **se d. de qch** to take delight in sth

déléguer [delege] *vt* to delegate (**à** to) ■ **délégation** *nf* delegation ■ **délégué, -e** *nmf* delegate; *Scol* **d. de classe** = pupil elected to represent his or her class at class meetings

délibération [deliberasjɔ̃] *nf* deliberation

délibéré, -e [delibere] *adj (intentionnel)* deliberate

délicat, -e [delika, -at] *adj (santé, travail)* delicate; *(question)* tricky, delicate; *(peau)* sensitive; *(geste)* tactful ■ **délicatesse** *nf (tact)* tact

délice [delis] *nm* delight ■ **délicieux, -euse** *adj (mets)* delicious; *(parfum)* delightful

délier [delje] *vt* to untie

délimiter [delimite] *vt (terrain)* to mark off; *(sujet)* to define

délinquant, -e [delɛ̃kɑ̃, -ɑ̃t] *nmf* delinquent ■ **délinquance** *nf* delinquency

délire [delir] *nm Méd* delirium; *(exaltation)* frenzy

délit [deli] *nm Br* offence, *Am* offense

délivrer [delivre] *vt* (**a**) *(captif)* to rescue; **d. qn de qch** to rid sb of sth (**b**) *(marchandises)* to deliver; *(passeport)* to issue (**à** to) ■ **délivrance** *nf (soulagement)* relief; *(de passeport)* issue

déloger [deloʒe] *vt (envahisseur)* to drive out (**de** from)

déloyal, -e, -aux, -ales [delwajal, -o] *adj (personne)* disloyal; *(concurrence)* unfair

deltaplane [deltaplan] *nm* hangglider; **faire du d.** to go hang-gliding

déluge [delyʒ] *nm (de pluie)* downpour; *(de paroles)* flood; *(d'insultes)* torrent

demain [dəmɛ̃] *adv* tomorrow; **d. soir** tomorrow evening; **à d.!** see you tomorrow!

demande [dəmɑ̃d] nf (requête) request (**de** for); Écon demand; **faire une d. de qch** (prêt, permis) to apply for sth; **demandes d'emploi** (dans le journal) jobs wanted, Br situations wanted

demander [dəmɑ̃de] **1** vt (conseil) to ask for; (prix, raison) to ask; (nécessiter) to require; **d. son chemin/l'heure** to ask the way/the time; **d. qch à qn** to ask sb for sth; **d. à qn de faire qch** to ask sb to do sth; **d. qn en mariage** to propose (marriage) to sb

2 se demander upr to wonder, to ask oneself (**pourquoi** why; **si** if) ■ **demandeur, -euse** nmf **d. d'emploi** job seeker

démanger [demɑ̃ʒe] vti to itch ■ **démangeaisons** nfpl **avoir des d.** to be itching

démanteler [demɑ̃tle] vt to break up

démaquiller [demakije] **se démaquiller** upr to remove one's make-up ■ **démaquillant** nm cleanser

démarcation [demarkɑsjɔ̃] nf demarcation

démarche [demarʃ] nf (allure) walk, gait; (requête) step; **faire les démarches nécessaires pour...** to take the necessary steps to...

démarcheur, -euse [demarʃœr, -øz] nmf (vendeur) door-to-door salesman, f saleswoman

démarquer [demarke] vt (marchandises) to mark down

démarrer [demare] vi (moteur) to start; (voiture) to move off; Fig (entreprise) to get off the ground ■ **démarrage** nm (de moteur) starting; **au d.** when moving off; **d. en côte** hill start ■ **démarreur** nm Aut starter

démasquer [demaske] vt to unmask

démêler [demele] vt to untangle

déménager [demenaʒe] **1** vi to move **2** vt (meubles) to move ■ **déménagement** nm move ■ **déménageur** nm Br removal man, Am (furniture) mover

démener [demne] **se démener** upr (s'agiter) to thrash about

dément, -e [demɑ̃, -ɑ̃t] adj insane ■ **démentiel, -elle** adj insane

démentir [demɑ̃tir] vt (nouvelle, fait) to deny ■ **démenti** nm denial

démesuré, -e [deməzyre] adj excessive

démettre* [demetr] **1** vt **d. qn de ses fonctions** to remove sb from his/her post **2 se démettre** upr **se d. l'épaule** to dislocate one's shoulder

demeurant [dəmœrɑ̃] **au demeurant** adv (malgré tout) for all that

demeure [dəmœr] nf (belle maison) mansion

demeurer [dəmœre] vi (**a**) (aux être) (rester) to remain (**b**) (aux avoir) Formel (habiter) to reside

demi, -e [dəmi] **1** adj half; **une heure et demie** (90 minutes) an hour and a half; (à l'horloge) half past one, one-thirty

2 adv (**à**) **d. plein** half-full; **à d. nu** half-naked

3 nmf (moitié) half

4 nm (au football) midfielder; **un d.** (bière) a beer, Br a half(-pint); **d. de mêlée** (au rugby) scrum half

5 nf **à la demie** (à l'horloge) at half-past ■ **demi-cercle** (pl **demi-cercles**) nm semicircle ■ **demi-douzaine** (pl **demi-douzaines**) nf **une d.** (de) half a dozen ■ **demi-écrémé** adj semi-skimmed ■ **demi-finale** (pl **demi-finales**) nf Sport semi-final ■ **demi-frère** (pl **demi-frères**) nm half brother ■ **demi-heure** (pl **demi-heures**) nf **une d.** half an hour ■ **demi-journée** (pl **demi-journées**) nf half-day ■ **demi-pension** nf Br half-board, Am breakfast and one meal ■ **demi-pensionnaire** (pl **demi-pensionnaires**) nmf Br = pupil who has school dinners ■ **demi-sœur** (pl **demi-sœurs**) nf half sister ■ **demi-tarif** (pl **demi-tarifs**) nm half-price ■ **demi-tour** (pl **demi-tours**) nm Br about turn, Am about face; (en voiture) U-turn; **faire d.** (à pied) to turn back; (en voiture) to do a U-turn

démission [demisjɔ̃] *nf* resignation; **donner sa d.** to hand in one's resignation ■ **démissionner** *vi* to resign

démocrate [demɔkrat] **1** *adj* democratic **2** *nmf* democrat ■ **démocratie** [-asi] *nf* democracy ■ **démocratique** *adj* democratic

démodé, -e [demɔde] *adj* old-fashioned

démographie [demɔgrafi] *nf* demography

demoiselle [dəmwazɛl] *nf (jeune fille)* young lady; **d. d'honneur** bridesmaid

démolir [demɔlir] *vt (bâtiment)* to pull down, to demolish ■ **démolition** *nf* demolition

démon [demɔ̃] *nm* demon; **le d.** the Devil

démonstratif, -ive [demɔ̃stratif, -iv] *adj* demonstrative

démonstration [demɔ̃strasjɔ̃] *nf* demonstration

démonter [demɔ̃te] **1** *vt (mécanisme, tente)* to dismantle **2 se démonter** *vpr (mécanisme)* to come apart

démontrer [demɔ̃tre] *vt* to demonstrate

démoraliser [demɔralize] **1** *vt* to demoralize **2 se démoraliser** *vpr* to become demoralized

démordre [demɔrdr] *vi* **ne pas d. de qch** to stick to sth

démouler [demule] *vt (gâteau)* to turn out

démuni, -e [demyni] *adj* penniless

démunir [demynir] **se démunir** *vpr* **se d. de qch** to part with sth

démystifier [demistifje] *vt* to demystify

dénier [denje] *vt (responsabilité)* to deny; **d. qch à qn** to deny sb sth

dénigrer [denigre] *vt* to denigrate

dénivellation [denivelasjɔ̃] *nf* difference in level; **dénivellations** *(relief)* bumps

dénombrer [denɔ̃bre] *vt* to count

dénommer [denɔme] *vt* to name

dénoncer [denɔ̃se] **1** *vt (injustice, abus, malfaiteur)* to denounce (**à** to);

(élève) to tell on (**à** to) **2 se dénoncer** *vpr (malfaiteur)* to give oneself up (**à** to); *(élève)* to own up (**à** to)

dénoter [denɔte] *vt* to denote

dénouement [denumɑ̃] *nm (de livre)* ending; *(de pièce de théâtre)* dénouement; *(d'affaire)* outcome

dénouer [denwe] **1** *vt (nœud, corde)* to undo, to untie; *(cheveux)* to let down, to undo; *Fig (intrigue)* to unravel **2 se dénouer** *vpr (nœud)* to come undone; *(cheveux)* to come down

denrée [dɑ̃re] *nf* foodstuff; **denrées alimentaires** foodstuffs; **denrées périssables** perishable goods

dense [dɑ̃s] *adj* dense ■ **densité** *nf* density

dent [dɑ̃] *nf* tooth *(pl* teeth); *(de roue)* cog; *(de fourchette)* prong; **d. de lait/ sagesse** milk/wisdom tooth; **faire ses dents** *(enfant)* to be teething; **en dents de scie** serrated; *Fig (résultats)* uneven ■ **dentaire** *adj* dental

dentelé, -e [dɑ̃tle] *adj (côte, feuille)* jagged

dentelle [dɑ̃tɛl] *nf* lace

dentier [dɑ̃tje] *nm (set of)* false teeth, dentures

dentifrice [dɑ̃tifris] *nm* toothpaste

dentiste [dɑ̃tist] *nmf* dentist

dénuder [denyde] *vt* to (lay) bare ■ **dénudé, -e** *adj* bare

dénué, -e [denɥe] *adj* **d. d'intérêt** devoid of interest

dénuement [denɥmɑ̃] *nm* destitution; **dans le d.** poverty-stricken, destitute

déodorant [deɔdɔrɑ̃] *nm* deodorant

dépanner [depane] *vt (machine)* to repair ■ **dépannage** *nm (emergency)* repairs; **voiture/service de d.** breakdown vehicle/service ■ **dépanneur** *nm (de télévision)* repairman; *(de voiture)* breakdown mechanic ■ **dépanneuse** *nf (voiture) Br* breakdown lorry, *Am* wrecker

dépareillé, -e [depareje] *adj (chaussure)* odd

départ [depar] *nm* departure; *(de*

course) start; **les grands départs** = the mass exodus of people from major cities at the beginning of the holiday period; **point/ligne de d.** starting point/post; **au d.** at the outset, at the start; **au d. de Paris** *(excursion)* leaving from Paris

départager [departaʒe] *vt* to decide between

département [departəmɑ̃] *nm* department *(division of local government)* ■ **départemental, -e, -aux, -ales** *adj* departmental; **route départementale** secondary road, *Br* ≃ B road

départir* [departir] **se départir** *upr* **il ne s'est jamais départi de son calme** his calm never deserted him

dépasser [depase] **1** *vt (véhicule) Br* to overtake, *Am* to pass; *(endroit)* to go past; *(vitesse)* to exceed; **d. qn** *(en hauteur)* to be taller than sb **2** *vi (clou)* to stick out ■ **dépassé, -e** *adj (démodé)* outdated; *(incapable)* unable to cope

dépayser [depeize] *vt Br* to disorientate, *Am* to disorient

dépêche [depɛʃ] *nf* dispatch ■ **dépêcher 1** *vt* to dispatch **2 se dépêcher** *upr* to hurry (up); **se d. de faire qch** to hurry to do sth

dépendant, -e [depɑ̃dɑ̃, -ɑ̃t] dependent *(de* on) ■ **dépendance** *nf* dependence; **sous la d. de qn** under sb's domination ■ **dépendances** *nfpl (bâtiments)* outbuildings

dépendre [depɑ̃dr] *vi* to depend *(de* on *or* upon); **d. de** *(appartenir à)* to belong to; *(être soumis à)* to be dependent on

dépens [depɑ̃] *nmpl* **apprendre qch à ses d.** to learn sth to one's cost

dépense [depɑ̃s] *nf (frais)* expense, expenditure; **faire des dépenses** to spend money ■ **dépenser 1** *vt (argent)* to spend; *(forces)* to exert **2 se dépenser** *upr* to burn up energy

dépensier, -ère [depɑ̃sje, -ɛr] *adj* extravagant

dépérir [deperir] *vi (personne)* to waste away; *(plante)* to wither

dépeupler [depœple] **1** *vt* to depopulate **2 se dépeupler** *upr* to become depopulated

dépilatoire [depilatwar] *nm* hair-remover

dépister [depiste] *vt (maladie)* to detect ■ **dépistage** *nm (de maladie)* screening

dépit [depi] *nm* spite; **en d. de qn/qch** in spite of sb/sth

dépité, -e [depite] *adj* annoyed

déplacement [deplasmɑ̃] *nm (voyage)* trip; **être en d.** *(homme d'affaires)* to be on a business trip; **frais de d.** *Br* travelling *or Am* traveling expenses

déplacer [deplase] **1** *vt (objet)* to move **2 se déplacer** *upr (aiguille de montre)* to move; *(personne, animal)* to move (about); *(marcher)* to walk (around); *(voyager)* to travel ■ **déplacé, -e** *adj (mal à propos)* out of place; **personne déplacée** *(réfugié)* displaced person

déplaire* [deplɛr] **1** *vt* **d. à qn** to displease sb; **ça me déplaît** I don't like it **2 se déplaire** *upr* **il se déplaît à Paris** he doesn't like it in Paris ■ **déplaisant, -e** *adj* unpleasant

déplier [deplije] *vt* to open out, to unfold ■ **dépliant** *nm (prospectus)* leaflet

déplorer [deplɔre] *vt (regretter)* to deplore; **d. que...** (+ *subjunctive)* to deplore the fact that...; **d. la mort de qn** to mourn sb's death

déployer [deplwaje] *vt (ailes)* to spread; *(journal, carte)* to unfold; *(troupes)* to deploy ■ **déploiement** *nm (démonstration)* display; *(d'une armée)* deployment

dépoli, -e [depɔli] *adj* **verre d.** frosted glass

déporter [depɔrte] *vt* **d. qn** to send sb to a concentration camp

déposer [depoze] **1** *vt (poser)* to put down; *(gerbe)* to lay; *(projet de loi)* to introduce; *(souverain)* to depose; **d. qn** *(en voiture)* to drop sb off; **d. de l'argent sur un compte** to deposit money in an account; **d. une plainte contre qn** to lodge a complaint against sb *vi Jur* to testify; *(liquide)* to leave a deposit **3 se déposer** *vpr* to settle

dépositaire [depɔziter] *nmf (vendeur)* agent

déposséder [depɔsede] *vt* to deprive, to dispossess (**de** of)

dépôt [depo] *nm (de vin)* deposit, sediment; *(entrepôt)* depot; *(prison)* jail; **faire un d.** *(d'argent)* to make a deposit; **d. de munitions** munitions depot

dépouille [depuj] *nf (d'animal)* hide, skin; **d. mortelle** *(de personne)* mortal remains

dépouiller [depuje] **1** *vt (animal)* to skin; *(analyser)* to go through; **d. qn de qch** to deprive sb of sth; **d. un scrutin** to count the votes **2 se dépouiller** *vpr* **se d. de qch** to rid oneself of sth ■ **dépouillé, -e** *adj (style)* austere ■ **dépouillement** *nm (de documents)* analysis; *(privation)* deprivation; *(sobriété)* austerity; **d. du scrutin** counting of the votes

dépourvu, -e [depurvy] *adj* **d. de qch** devoid of sth; **prendre qn au d.** to catch sb off guard

dépoussiérer [depusjere] *vt* to dust

dépraver [deprave] *vt* to deprave

déprécier [depresje] **se déprécier** *vpr (valeurs, marchandises)* to depreciate

dépression [depresjɔ̃] *nf (creux, maladie)* depression; **d. économique** slump; **d. nerveuse** nervous breakdown; **faire de la d.** to be suffering from depression ■ **dépressif, -ive** *adj* depressive

déprimer [deprime] *vt* to depress ■ **déprimé, -e** *adj* depressed

DEPUIS [dəpɥi] **1** *prép* since; **d. lundi/2001** since Monday/2001; **j'habite ici d. un mois** I've been living here for a month; **d. quand êtes-vous là?, d. combien de temps êtes-vous là?** how long have you been here?; **d. peu/longtemps** for a short/long time **2** *adv* since (then), ever since **3** *conj* **d. que** since

député [depyte] *nm Pol* deputy, *Br* ≃

MP, *Am* ≃ representative; **d. du Parlement européen** Member of the European Parliament

déraciner [derasine] *vt (arbre, personne)* to uproot

dérailler [deraje] *vi (train)* to leave the rails; **faire d. un train** to derail a train

déranger [derɑ̃ʒe] **1** *vt (affaires)* to disturb; **je viendrai si ça ne te dérange pas** I'll come if that's all right with you; **ça vous dérange si je fume?** do you mind if I smoke? **2 se déranger** *vpr* to put oneself to a lot of trouble (**pour faire** to do); *(se déplacer)* to move; **ne te dérange pas!** don't bother! ■ **dérangement** *nm (gêne)* trouble; **en d.** *(téléphone)* out of order

déraper [derape] *vi (véhicule)* to skid; *(personne)* to slip

dérégler [deregle] **1** *vt (mécanisme)* to cause to malfunction **2 se dérégler** *vpr (mécanisme)* to go wrong

dérider [deride] *vt, se* **dérider** *vpr* to cheer up

dérision [derizjɔ̃] *nf* derision; **tourner qch en d.** to deride sth ■ **dérisoire** *adj (somme)* derisory

dérive [deriv] *nf Naut* drift; **à la d.** adrift

dériver [derive] **1** *vt (cours d'eau)* to divert **2** *vi Naut* to drift

dermatologue [dɛrmatɔlɔg] *nmf* dermatologist

dernier, -ère [dɛrnje, -ɛr] **1** *adj (ultime)* last; *(marquant la fin)* final; *(nouvelles, mode)* latest; *(étage)* top; *(degré)* highest; **le d. rang** the back *or* last row; **ces derniers mois** these past few months; **les dix dernières minutes** the last ten minutes; **en d.** last **2** *nmf* last; **ce d.** *(de deux)* the latter; *(de plusieurs)* the last-mentioned

dérober [derɔbe] **1** *vt (voler)* to steal (**à** from); *(cacher)* to hide (**à** from) **2 se dérober** *vpr (s'esquiver)* to slip away; *(éviter de répondre)* to dodge the issue

dérogation [derɔgasjɔ̃] *nf* exemption (**à** from)

déroger [derɔʒe] *vi* d. à une règle to depart from a rule

dérouler [derule] **1** *vt (tapis)* to unroll; *(fil)* to unwind **2 se dérouler** *upr (tapis)* to unroll; *(fil)* to unwind

déroute [derut] *nf (d'armée)* rout

dérouter [derute] *vt (avion, navire)* to divert, to reroute; *(poursuivant)* to throw off the scent; *Fig (étonner)* to throw

derrière [derjer] **1** *prép & adv* behind; d. moi behind me; **assis d.** *(dans une voiture)* sitting in the back; par d. *(attaquer)* from behind, from the rear **2** *nm (de maison)* back, rear; *(fesses)* behind; **roue de d.** back *or* rear wheel

des [de] *voir* de, un

dès [de] *prép* from; d. le début (right) from the start; d. maintenant from now on; d. le VIᵉ siècle as early as *or* as far back as the sixth century; d. lors *(dans le temps)* from then on; *(en conséquence)* consequently; d. leur arrivée as soon as they arrive/arrived; d. qu'elle viendra as soon as she comes

désabusé, -e [dezabyze] *adj* disillusioned

désaccord [dezakɔr] *nm* disagreement; être en d. avec qn to disagree with sb

désaffecté, -e [dezafɛkte] *adj* disused

désaffection [dezafɛksjɔ̃] *nf* disaffection (à l'égard de with)

désagréable [dezagreabl] *adj* unpleasant

désagrément [dezagremã] *nm (gêne)* trouble; *(souci, aspect négatif)* problem

désaltérer [dezaltere] **1** *vt* d. qn to quench sb's thirst **2 se désaltérer** *upr* to quench one's thirst

désamorcer [dezamɔrse] *vt (bombe, conflit)* to defuse

désapprouver [dezapruve] **1** *vt* to disapprove of **2** *vi* to disapprove ■ **désapprobateur, -trice** *adj* disapproving ■ **désapprobation** *nf* disapproval

désarmer [dezarme] **1** *vt (soldat, nation)* to disarm; *Fig* d. qn *(franchise, attitude)* to disarm sb **2** *vi (pays)* to disarm ■ **désarmement** *nm (de nation)* disarmament

désarroi [dezarwa] *nm* confusion

désastre [dezastr] *nm* disaster ■ **désastreux, -euse** *adj* disastrous

désavantage [dezavãtaʒ] *nm* disadvantage ■ **désavantager** *vt* to put at a disadvantage

désavouer [dezavwe] *vt (renier)* to disown

désaxé, -e [dezakse] *nmf* unbalanced person

desceller [desele] **1** *vt (pierre)* to loosen **2 se desceller** *upr* to come loose

descendant, -e [desãdã, -ãt] *nmf* descendant ■ **descendance** *nf (enfants)* descendants; *(origine)* descent

descendre [desãdr] **1** *(aux être)* *vi* to come/go down (de from); *(d'un train)* to get off (de from); *(d'un arbre)* to climb down (de from); *(marée)* to go out; d. à l'hôtel to put up at a hotel; d. de *(être issu de)* to be descended from

2 *(aux avoir)* *vt (escalier)* to come/go down; *(objet)* to bring/take down

descente [desãt] *nf (d'avion)* descent; *(en parachute)* drop; *(pente)* slope; *(de police)* raid (dans upon); d. de lit bedside rug

descriptif, -ive [deskriptif, -iv] *adj* descriptive ■ **description** *nf* description

désemparé, -e [dezãpare] *adj (personne)* at a loss

désemplir [dezãplir] *vi* ce magasin ne désemplit pas this shop is always crowded

désenchanté, -e [dezãʃãte] *adj* disillusioned ■ **désenchantement** *nm* disenchantment

déséquilibre [dezekilibr] *nm* imbalance; en d. unsteady ■ **déséquilibré, -e** **1** *adj* unbalanced **2** *nmf* unbalanced person ■ **déséquilibrer** *vt* to throw off balance

désert, -e [dezεr, -εrt] **1** *adj (lieu)* deserted; *(région)* uninhabited; **île déserte** desert island **2** *nm* desert ∎ **désertique** *adj* région d. desert region

déserter [dezεrte] *vti* to desert ∎ **désertion** *nf* desertion

désespérer [dezεspere] **1** *vt* to drive to despair **2** *vi* to despair (**de** of) **3 se désespérer** *upr* to despair ∎ **désespérant, -e** *adj (situation, personne)* hopeless ∎ **désespéré, -e** *adj (personne)* in despair; *(cas, situation, efforts)* desperate ∎ **désespérément** *adv* desperately

désespoir [dezεspwar] *nm* despair; **en d. de cause** in desperation

déshabiller [dezabije] *vt,* **se déshabiller** *upr* to undress

désherber [dezεrbe] *vti* to weed

déshériter [dezerite] *vt* to disinherit

déshonneur [dezɔnœr] *nm* dishonour

déshonorer [dezɔnɔre] *vt* to disgrace ∎ **déshonorant, -e** *adj* dishonourable

déshydrater [dezidrate] **1** *vt* to dehydrate **2 se déshydrater** *upr* to become dehydrated

désigner [deziɲe] *vt (montrer)* to point to; *(choisir)* to choose; *(nommer)* to appoint; **d. qn par son nom** to refer to sb by name ∎ **désignation** *nf* designation

désillusion [dezilyzjɔ̃] *nf* disillusion ∎ **désillusionner** *vt* to disillusion

désinfecter [dezɛ̃fεkte] *vt* to disinfect ∎ **désinfectant** *nm* disinfectant

désinformation [dezɛ̃fɔrmasjɔ̃] *nf* disinformation

désintégrer [dezɛ̃tegre] **se désintégrer** *upr* to disintegrate

désintéresser [dezɛ̃terese] **se désintéresser** *upr* **se d. de qch** to lose interest in sth ∎ **désintéressé, -e** *adj (altruiste)* disinterested ∎ **désintérêt** *nm* lack of interest

désintoxiquer [dezɛ̃tɔksike] *vt (alcoolique, drogué)* to treat for alcoholism/drug abuse

désinvolte [dezɛ̃vɔlt] *adj (dégagé)* casual; *(insolent)* offhand ∎ **désinvolture** *nf* casualness; *(insolence)* offhandedness

désir [dezir] *nm* desire ∎ **désirable** *adj* desirable ∎ **désirer** *vt* to wish; *(convoiter)* to desire

désireux, -euse [desirø, -øz] *adj* d. de faire qch anxious to do sth

désistement [dezistəmɑ̃] *nm* withdrawal

désister [deziste] **se désister** *upr* to withdraw

désobéir [dezɔbeir] *vi* to disobey; **d. à qn** to disobey sb ∎ **désobéissant, -e** *adj* disobedient

désobligeant, -e [dezɔbliʒɑ̃, -ɑ̃t] *adj* disagreeable

désodorisant [dezɔdɔrizɑ̃] *nm* air freshener

désœuvré, -e [dezœvre] *adj* idle

désoler [dezɔle] **1** *vt* to upset **2 se désoler** *upr* to be upset (**de** at) ∎ **désolant, -e** *adj* upsetting ∎ **désolé, -e** *adj (région)* desolate; *(affligé)* upset; **être d. que...** (+ *subjunctive*) to be sorry that...; **je suis d. de vous déranger** I'm sorry to disturb you

désolidariser [desɔlidarize] **se désolidariser** *upr* to dissociate oneself (**from**)

désordonné, -e [dezɔrdɔne] *adj (personne, chambre)* untidy

désordre [dezɔrdr] *nm (manque d'ordre)* mess; *(manque d'organisation)* disorder; **en d.** untidy, messy; **de graves désordres** *(émeutes)* serious disturbances

désorganiser [dezɔrganize] *vt* to disorganize ∎ **désorganisation** *nf* disorganization ∎ **désorganisé, -e** *adj* disorganized

désorienter [dezɔrjɑ̃te] *vt* **d. qn** to bewilder sb

désormais [dezɔrmε] *adv* from now on, in future

despote [dεspɔt] *nm* despot

desquels, desquelles [dekεl] *voir* **lequel**

dessaisir [desezir] **se dessaisir** *upr* se

d. de qch to relinquish sth
dessaler [desale] *vt (poisson)* to remove the salt from *(by soaking)*
desséher [deseʃe] **1** *vt (peau)* to dry up; *(végétation)* to wither **2 se desséher** *vpr (peau)* to dry up; *(végétation)* to wither
dessein [desɛ̃] *nm* intention; **à d.** intentionally
desserrer [desere] **1** *vt (ceinture)* to loosen; *(poing)* to unclench; *(frein)* to release **2 se desserrer** *vpr (ceinture)* to come loose
dessert [desɛr] *nm* dessert, *Br* pudding
desserte [desɛrt] *nf* **assurer la d. de** *(village)* to provide a service to
desservir [desɛrvir] *vt (table)* to clear (away); **d. qn** to do sb a disservice; **le car dessert ce village** the bus stops at this village; **ce quartier est bien desservi** this district is well served by public transport
dessin [desɛ̃] *nm* drawing; *(rapide)* sketch; *(motif)* design, pattern; *(contour)* outline; **d. animé** cartoon; **d. humoristique** *(de journal)* cartoon
dessinateur, -trice [desinatœr, -tris] *nmf* drawer; **d. industriel** *Br* draughtsman, *Am* draftsman
dessiner [desine] **1** *vt* to draw; *(rapidement)* to sketch; *(meuble, robe)* to design; *(indiquer)* to outline; **d. (bien) la taille** *(vêtement)* to show off the figure **2 se dessiner** *vpr (colline)* to stand out; *(projet)* to take shape
dessous [dəsu] **1** *adv* underneath; **en d.** underneath; **en d. de** below **2** *nm* underside; **des d.** *(sous-vêtements)* underwear ▪ **dessous-de-plat** *nm inv* table mat ▪ **dessous-de-table** *nm inv* bribe, *Br* backhander
dessus [dəsy] **1** *adv (marcher, écrire)* on it/them; *(monter)* on top (of it/them), on it/them; *(passer)* over it/them; **de d. la table** *or* **from the table 2** *nm* top; *(de chaussure)* upper; **avoir le d.** to have the upper hand; **reprendre le d.** *(se remettre)* to get over it

déstabiliser [destabilize] *vt* to destabilize
destin [dɛstɛ̃] *nm* fate, destiny ▪ **destinée** *nf* destiny
destinataire [dɛstinatɛr] *nmf* addressee
destination [dɛstinasjɔ̃] *nf (lieu)* destination; **trains à d. de...** trains to...; **arriver à d.** to reach one's destination
destiner [dɛstine] **1** *vt* **d. qch à qn** to intend sth for sb; **d. qn à** *(carrière, fonction)* to intend *or* destine sb for **2 se destiner** *vpr* **se d. à** *(carrière)* to intend to take up
destituer [dɛstitɥe] *vt (fonctionnaire)* to remove from office
destructeur, -trice [dɛstryktœr, -tris] *adj* destructive
destruction [dɛstryksjɔ̃] *nf* destruction
désuet, -ète [desɥe, -ɛt] *adj* obsolete ▪ **désuétude** *nf* **tomber en d.** *(expression)* to become obsolete
désunir [dezynir] *vt (famille, personnes)* to divide
détachant [detaʃɑ̃] *nm* stain remover
détachement [detaʃmɑ̃] *nm* **(a)** *(indifférence)* detachment **(b)** *(de fonctionnaire)* secondment; *(de troupes)* detachment
détacher¹ [detaʃe] **1** *vt (ceinture, vêtement)* to undo; *(mains)* to untie; *(ôter)* to take off; *(mots)* to pronounce clearly; **d. qn** *(libérer)* to untie sb; *(affecter)* to transfer sb (on assignment) (**à** to)
2 se détacher *vpr (chien, prisonnier)* to break loose; *(se dénouer)* to come undone; *(fragment)* to come off *(de qch* sth); **se d. de qn** to break away from sb; **se d. sur qch** *(ressortir)* to stand out against sth ▪ **détaché, -e** *adj (air, ton)* detached
détacher² [detaʃe] *vt (linge)* to remove the stains from
détail [detaj] *nm* detail; **en d.** in detail; **entrer dans les détails** to go into detail; **prix de d.** retail price
détaillant [detajɑ̃] *nm* retailer

détailler [detaje] vt (énumérer) to detail ■ **détaillé, -e** adj (récit, description) detailed; (facture) itemized

détaxer [detakse] vt to exempt from tax; **produit détaxé** duty-free article

détecter [detɛkte] vt to detect ■ **détecteur** nm (appareil) detector

détective [detɛktiv] nm **d. (privé)** (private) detective

déteindre* [detɛ̃dr] vi (couleur, tissu) to run

détendre [detɑ̃dr] **1** vt (corde) to slacken; (arc) to unbend; **d. qn** to relax sb **2 se détendre** vpr (corde) to slacken; (arc) to unbend; (atmosphère) to become less tense; (personne) to relax ■ **détendu, -e** adj (visage, atmosphère) relaxed; (ressort, câble) slack

détenir* [detənir] vt (record, pouvoir, titre, prisonnier) to hold; (secret, objet volé) to be in possession of ■ **détenteur, -trice** nmf (de record) holder ■ **détention** nf (d'armes) possession; (captivité) detention; **d. provisoire** detention pending trial, remand ■ **détenu, -e** nmf prisoner

détente [detɑ̃t] nf (**a**) (repos) relaxation; (entre deux pays) détente (**b**) (saut) spring (**c**) (gâchette) trigger

détergent [detɛrʒɑ̃] nm detergent

détériorer [deterjɔre] **1** vt to damage **2 se détériorer** vpr to deteriorate ■ **détérioration** nf damage (**de** to); (de situation) deterioration (**de** in)

détermination [determinasjɔ̃] nf (fermeté) determination

déterminer [detɛrmine] vt (préciser) to determine; (causer) to bring about ■ **déterminant, -e** adj decisive ■ **déterminé, -e** adj (précis) specific; (résolu) determined

déterrer [detere] vt to dig up

détester [detɛste] vt to hate, to detest; **d. faire qch** to hate doing or to do sth ■ **détestable** adj foul

détonation [detɔnasjɔ̃] nf explosion; (d'arme) bang

détonner [detɔne] vi (contraster) to clash

détour [detur] nm (crochet) detour; (de route) bend, curve

détourner [deturne] **1** vt (dévier) to divert; (avion) to hijack; (conversation, sens) to change; (fonds) to embezzle; (coup) to ward off; **d. la tête** to turn one's head away; **d. les yeux** to look away; **d. qn de** (son devoir) to take sb away from; (sa route) to lead sb away from **2 se détourner** vpr to turn away ■ **détourné, -e** adj (chemin, moyen) roundabout, indirect ■ **détournement** [-əmɑ̃] nm (de cours d'eau) diversion; **d. d'avion** hijack(ing); **d. de fonds** embezzlement

détracteur, -trice [detraktœr, -tris] nmf detractor

détraquer [detrake] **1** vt (mécanisme) to put out of order **2 se détraquer** vpr (machine) to go wrong

détresse [detrɛs] nf distress; **en d.** (navire) in distress

détriment [detrimɑ̃] **au détriment de** prép to the detriment of

détritus [detritys] nmpl Br rubbish, Am garbage

détroit [detrwa] nm strait

détromper [detrɔ̃pe] **1** vt **d. qn** to put sb right **2 se détromper** vpr **détrompez-vous!** don't you believe it!

détrôner [detrone] vt (souverain) to dethrone; (supplanter) to supersede

détruire* [detrɥir] vt (ravager) to destroy; (tuer) to kill

dette [dɛt] nf debt; **avoir des dettes** to be in debt; **faire des dettes** to run into debt

DEUG [dœg] (abrév **diplôme d'études universitaires générales**) nm = degree gained after two years' study at university

deuil [dœj] nm (affliction, vêtements) mourning; (décès) bereavement; **être en d.** to be in mourning

deux [dø] adj inv & nm inv two; **d. fois** twice; **mes d. sœurs** both my sisters, my two sisters; **tous (les) d.** both ■ **deux-pièces** nm inv (maillot de bain) bikini; *(appartement)* two-roomed *Br* flat *or Am* apartment ■ **deux-roues** *nm inv* two-wheeled vehicle

deuxième [døzjɛm] *adj & nmf* second

dévaler [devale] *vt (escalier)* to hurtle down

dévaliser [devalize] *vt (personne, banque)* to rob

dévaloriser [devalɔrize] **1** *vt (monnaie, diplôme)* to devalue **2 se dévaloriser** *vpr (monnaie)* to depreciate ■ **dévalorisation** *nf (de diplôme)* loss of value

dévaluer [devalɥe] *vt (monnaie)* to devalue ■ **dévaluation** *nf Fin* devaluation

devancer [dəvɑ̃se] *vt (concurrent)* to be ahead of; *(arriver avant)* to arrive before

devant [dəvɑ̃] **1** *prép & adv* in front (of); **passer d. une église** to go past a church; **marcher d. qn** to walk in front of sb; **assis d.** *(dans une voiture)* sitting in the front

2 *nm* front; **roue/porte de d.** front wheel/door; **prendre les devants** *(action)* to take the initiative

devanture [dəvɑ̃tyr] *nf (vitrine)* window; *(façade)* front

dévaster [devaste] *vt,* to devastate ■ **dévastation** *nf* devastation

développer [devlɔpe] *vt,* **se développer** *vpr* to develop ■ **développement** *nm (croissance); (de photo)* developing; **en plein d.** *(entreprise, pays)* growing fast

devenir* [dəvnir] *(aux être)* *vi* to become; **d. médecin** to become a doctor; **d. vieux** to get *or* grow old; **d. tout rouge** to go all red; **qu'est-elle devenue?** what has become of her?

dévergondé, -e [devergɔ̃de] *adj* shameless

déverser [deverse] **1** *vt (liquide)* to pour out; *(ordures)* to dump **2 se déverser** *vpr (liquide, rivière)* to empty (**dans** into)

dévêtir [devetir] *vt,* **se dévêtir** *vpr* to undress

dévier [devje] **1** *vt (circulation)* to divert; *(coup, rayons)* to deflect **2** *vi (balle)* to deflect; *(véhicule)* to veer **3 de sa route** to veer off course ■ **déviation** *nf (itinéraire) Br* diversion, *Am* detour

devin [dəvɛ̃] *nm* soothsayer

deviner [dəvine] *vt* to guess (**que** that) ■ **devinette** *nf* riddle

devis [dəvi] *nm* estimate

dévisager [devizaʒe] *vt* **d. qn** to stare at sb

devise [dəviz] *nf (légende)* motto; *(monnaie)* currency; **devises étrangères** foreign currency

dévisser [devise] **1** *vt* to unscrew **2 se dévisser** *vpr (bouchon)* to unscrew; *(par accident)* to come unscrewed

dévoiler [devwale] **1** *vt (statue)* to unveil; *Fig (secret)* to disclose **2 se dévoiler** *vpr (mystère)* to come to light

DEVOIR*¹ [dəvwar] *v aux* **(a)** *(indique la nécessité)* **je dois refuser** I must refuse, I have (got) to refuse; **j'ai dû refuser** I had to refuse

(b) *(indique une forte probabilité)* **il doit être tard** it must be late; **elle a dû oublier** she must have forgotten; **cela devait arriver** it had to happen

(c) *(indique l'obligation)* **tu dois apprendre tes leçons** you must learn your lessons; **vous devriez rester** you should stay, you ought to stay; **il aurait dû venir** he should have come, he ought to have come

(d) *(indique l'intention)* **elle doit venir** she's supposed to be coming, she's due to come; **le train devait arriver à midi** the train was due (to arrive) at noon; **je devais le voir** I was (due) to see him

devoir*² [dəvwar] **1** *vt* to owe; **d. qch à qn** to owe sb sth, to owe sth to sb

2 se devoir *vpr* **comme il se doit** as is proper

3 *nm (obligation)* duty; **présenter ses devoirs à qn** to pay one's respects to sb; *Scol* **devoirs** homework; **faire ses**

devoirs to do one's homework

dévorer [devɔre] *vt (manger)* to devour

dévotion [devosjɔ̃] *nf (adoration)* devotion

dévouer [devwe] **se dévouer** *upr (se sacrifier)* to volunteer; *(se consacrer)* to devote oneself (à to) ■ **dévoué, -e** *adj (ami, femme)* devoted (à to) ■ **dévouement** [-umã] *nm* devotion; *(de héros)* devotion to duty

dextérité [dɛksterite] *nf* dexterity, skill

diabète [djabɛt] *nm Méd* diabetes ■ **diabétique** *adj & nmf* diabetic

diable [djabl] *nm* devil; **le d.** the Devil ■ **diabolique** *adj* diabolical

diadème [djadɛm] *nm* tiara

diagnostic [djagnɔstik] *nm* diagnosis ■ **diagnostiquer** *vt* to diagnose

diagonal, -e, -aux, -ales [djagɔnal, -o] *adj* diagonal ■ **diagonale** *nf* diagonal (line); **en d.** diagonally

dialecte [djalɛkt] *nm* dialect

dialogue [djalɔg] *nm Br* dialogue, *Am* dialog; *(conversation)* conversation ■ **dialoguer** *vi* to communicate; *Ordinat* to interact

diamant [djamã] *nm* diamond

diamètre [djamɛtr] *nm* diameter

diapason [djapazɔ̃] *nm Mus (appareil)* tuning fork

diapositive [djapozitiv] *nf* slide

diarrhée [djare] *nf* diarrhoea

dictateur [diktatœr] *nm* dictator ■ **dictatorial, -e, -aux, -ales** *adj* dictatorial ■ **dictature** *nf* dictatorship

dicter [dikte] *vt* to dictate (à to) ■ **dictée** *nf* dictation

diction [diksjɔ̃] *nf* diction

dictionnaire [diksjɔner] *nm* dictionary

dièse [djɛz] *adj & nm Mus* sharp

diesel [djezɛl] *adj & nm* **(moteur) d.** diesel (engine)

diète [djɛt] *nf (partielle)* diet; *(totale)* fast; **être à la d.** to be on a diet/to be fasting

diététicien, -enne [djetetisjɛ̃, -ɛn]

nmf dietician ■ **diététique 1** *nf* dietetics *(sing)* **2** *adj* **aliment** *ou* **produit d.** health food; **magasin d.** health-food shop

dieu, -x [djø] *nm* god; **D.** God; **le bon D.** God

diffamation [difamasjɔ̃] *nf (en paroles)* slander; *(par écrit)* libel ■ **diffamatoire** *adj (paroles)* slanderous; *(écrit)* libellous

différé [difere] *nm* **en d.** *(émission)* prerecorded

différence [diferãs] *nf* difference (**de** in); **à la d. de qn/qch** unlike sb/sth; **faire la d. entre** to make a distinction between

différencier [diferãsje] **1** *vt* to differentiate (**de** from) **2 se différencier** *upr* to differ (**de** from)

différend [diferã] *nm* difference of opinion

différent, -e [diferã, -ãt] *adj* different; **différents** *(divers)* different, various; **d. de** different from ■ **différemment** [-amã] *adv* differently (**de** from)

différer [difere] **1** *vt (remettre)* to postpone; *(paiement)* to defer **2** *vi* to differ (**de** from)

difficile [difisil] *adj* difficult; *(exigeant)* fussy; **c'est d. à faire** it's hard *or* difficult to do ■ **difficilement** *adv* with difficulty

difficulté [difikylte] *nf* difficulty (**à faire** in doing); **en d.** in a difficult situation; **avoir de la d. à faire qch** to have difficulty (in) doing sth

difforme [difɔrm] *adj* deformed, misshapen ■ **difformité** *nf* deformity

diffus, -e [dify, -yz] *adj (lumière)* diffuse; *(impression)* vague

diffuser [difyze] *vt (émission)* to broadcast; *(nouvelle)* to spread; *(lumière, chaleur)* to diffuse ■ **diffusion** *nf (d'émission)* broadcasting; *(de lumière, de chaleur)* diffusion

digérer [diʒere] **1** *vt* to digest **2** *vi* to digest

digestif, -ive [diʒestif, -iv] **1** *adj (tube,*

sucs) digestive **2** *nmf* after-dinner liqueur

digestion [diʒεstjɔ̃] *nf* digestion

Digicode® [diʒikɔd] *nm* door code *(for entrance to building)*

digne [diɲ] *adj (air, attitude)* dignified; **d. de qn/qch** worthy of sb/sth; **d. d'admiration** worthy of *or* deserving of admiration ■ **dignement** [-əmɑ̃] *adv* with dignity

dignitaire [diɲiter] *nm* dignitary

dignité [diɲite] *nf* dignity

digue [dig] *nf* dike, dyke; *(en bord de mer)* sea wall

dilapider [dilapide] *vt* to squander

dilater [dilate] *vt*, **se dilater** *vpr (pupille)* to dilate

dilemme [dilεm] *nm* dilemma

diluer [dilɥe] *vt (liquide, substance)* to dilute (**dans** in)

dimanche [dimɑ̃ʃ] *nm* Sunday

dimension [dimɑ̃sjɔ̃] *nf (mesure, aspect)* dimension; *(taille)* size; **à deux dimensions** two-dimensional; **prendre les dimensions de qch** to measure sth up

diminuer [diminɥe] **1** *vt (réduire)* to reduce, to decrease; *(affaiblir)* to affect **2** *vi (réserves, nombre)* to decrease, to diminish; *(jours)* to get shorter; *(prix, profits)* to decrease, to drop ■ **diminution** *nf* reduction, decrease *(de* in)

diminutif [diminytif] *nm (nom)* diminutive

dinde [dɛ̃d] *nf (volaille, viande)* turkey ■ **dindon** *nm* turkey (cock)

dîner [dine] **1** *nm (repas du soir)* dinner; *(repas de midi)* lunch; *(soirée)* dinner party **2** *vi* to have dinner; *Belg & Can* to (have) lunch

dinosaure [dinozɔr] *nm* dinosaur

diplomate [diplɔmat] **1** *adj* diplomatic **2** *nmf* diplomat ■ **diplomatie** [-asi] *nf (tact)* diplomacy; *(carrière)* diplomatic service ■ **diplomatique** *adj* diplomatic

diplôme [diplom] *nm* diploma; *(d'université)* degree ■ **diplômé, -e 1** *adj*

qualified; *Univ* **être d. (de)** to be a graduate (of) **2** *nmf* holder of a diploma; *Univ* graduate

DIRE* [dir] **1** *nm* **au d. de** according to; **selon ses dires** according to him/her

2 *vt (mot)* to say; *(vérité, secret)* to tell; **d. des bêtises** to talk nonsense; **d. qch à qn** to tell sb sth, to say sth to sb; **d. à qn que...** to tell sb that..., to say to sb that...; **d. à qn de faire qch** to tell sb to do sth; **d. du mal/du bien de qn** to speak ill/well of sb; **on dirait un château** it looks like a castle; **on dirait du cabillaud** it tastes like cod; **autrement dit** in other words; **à vrai d.** to tell the truth

3 *se dire vpr* **il se dit malade** he says he's ill; **comment ça se dit en anglais?** how do you say that in English?

direct, -e [direkt] **1** *adj* direct **2** *Radio & TV* live broadcasting; **en d. (de)** live (from) ■ **directement** [-əmɑ̃] *adv (sans intermédiaire)* directly; *(sans détour)* straight

directeur, -trice [direktœr, -tris] **1** *nmf* director; *(de magasin, de service)* manager; *(de journal)* editor; *(d'école) Br* headmaster, *f* headmistress, *Am* principal **2** *adj (principe)* guiding; *(idées)* main; *(équipe)* management

direction [direksjɔ̃] *nf* **(a)** *(sens)* direction; **train en d. de Lille** train to Lille **(b)** *(de société, de club)* running, management; *(de parti)* leadership; *Aut* steering; **sous la d. de** under the supervision of; *(orchestre)* conducted by; **un poste de d.** a management post; **d. du personnel** personnel department

dirigeant, -e [diriʒɑ̃, -ɑ̃t] **1** *adj (classe)* ruling **2** *nm (de pays)* leader; *(d'entreprise, de club)* manager

diriger [diriʒe] **1** *vt (entreprise, club)* to run, to manage; *(pays, parti)* to lead; *(orchestre)* to conduct; *(travaux)* to supervise; *(acteur)* to direct; *(orienter)* to turn (**vers** to); *(arme, lumière)* to point (**sur** at); *(véhicule)* to steer **2 se diriger** *vpr* **se d. vers** *(lieu, objet)* to head for; *(personne)* to go up to; *(dans une carrière)* to go into

dis, disant [di, dizɑ̃] *voir* **dire**

discerner [disɛrne] *vt (voir)* to make out; *(différencier)* to distinguish (**de** from) ■ **discernement** [-əmɑ̃] *nm* discernment

disciple [disipl] *nm* disciple

discipline [disiplin] *nf (règle, matière)* discipline

discipliner [disipline] **1** *vt (enfant)* to control **2 se discipliner** *vpr* to discipline oneself ■ **discipliné, -e** *adj* well-disciplined

discontinu, -e [diskɔ̃tiny] *adj (ligne)* broken; *(bruit)* intermittent ■ **discontinuer** *vi* **sans d.** without stopping

discorde [diskɔrd] *nf* discord

discothèque [diskɔtɛk] *nf (organisme)* record library; *(club)* disco

discours [diskur] *nm* speech; *(écrit littéraire)* discourse; **faire un d.** to make a speech

discréditer [diskredite] **1** *vt* to discredit **2 se discréditer** *vpr (personne)* to discredit oneself

discret, -ète [diskrɛ, -ɛt] *adj (personne, manière)* discreet; *(vêtement)* simple ■ **discrètement** *adv (avec retenue)* discreetly; *(sobrement)* simply

discrétion [diskresjɔ̃] *nf* discretion; **laisser qch à la d. de qn** to leave sth to sb's discretion

discrimination [diskriminɑsjɔ̃] *nf* discrimination

disculper [diskylpe] *vt* to exonerate (**de** from)

discussion [diskysjɔ̃] *nf* discussion; **avoir une d.** to have a discussion (**sur** about)

discutable [diskytabl] *adj* questionable

discuter [diskyte] **1** *vt* to discuss; *(contester)* to question **2** *vi* to discuss; *(protester)* to argue; **d. de qch avec qn** to discuss sth with sb **3 se discuter** *vpr* **ça se discute** that's debatable

dise, disent [diz] *voir* **dire**

disgrace [disgrɑs] *nf* **tomber en d.** to fall into disfavour ■ **disgracier** *vt* to disgrace ■ **disgracieux, -euse** *adj* ungainly

disjoint, -e [disʒwɛ̃, -ɛt] *adj* separated

disjoncter [disʒɔ̃kte] *vi (circuit électrique)* to fuse ■ **disjoncteur** *nm* circuit breaker

dislocation [dislɔkɑsjɔ̃] *nf (de membre)* dislocation

disloquer [dislɔke] **1** *vt (membre)* to dislocate **2 se disloquer** *vpr* **se d. le bras** to dislocate one's arm

disons [dizɔ̃] *voir* **dire**

disparaître* [disparɛtr] *vi* to disappear; *(être porté manquant)* to go missing; *(mourir)* to die; *(coutume)* to die out; **faire d. qch** to get rid of sth ■ **disparition** *nf* disappearance; *(mort)* death ■ **disparu, -e** **1** *adj (personne)* missing; **être porté d.** to be reported missing **2** *nmf (absent)* missing person; *(mort)* departed

disparité [disparite] *nf* disparity (**entre** *ou* **de** between)

dispensaire [dispɑ̃sɛr] *nm* community health centre

dispense [dispɑ̃s] *nf (d'obligation)* exemption ■ **dispenser 1** *vt (soins, bienfaits)* to dispense; **d. qn de qch** to exempt sb from sth; **d. qn de faire qch** to exempt sb from doing sth **2** *vpr* **se d. de qch** to get out of sth; **se d. de faire qch** to get out of doing sth

disperser [dispɛrse] **1** *vt (papiers, foule)* to scatter; *(brouillard)* to disperse; *(collection)* to break up **2 se disperser** *vpr (foule)* to scatter, to disperse ■ **dispersion** *nf (d'armée, de manifestants, de brouillard)* dispersal

disponible [dispɔnibl] *adj (article, place, personne)* available ■ **disponibilité** *nf* availability; **disponibilités** *(fonds)* available funds

dispos [dispo] *adj m* **frais et d.** hale and hearty

disposé, -e [dispoze] *adj* **bien/mal d.**

in a good/bad mood; **d. à faire qch** disposed to do sth

disposer [dispoze] **1** *vt (objets)* to arrange; **d. qn à (faire) qch** to dispose sb to (do) sth **2** *vi* **d. de qch** to have sth at one's disposal **3 se disposer** *vpr* **se d. à faire qch** to prepare to do sth

dispositif [dispozitif] *nm (mécanisme)* device

disposition [dispozisjɔ̃] *nf* arrangement; *(tendance)* tendency (**à** to); *(de maison, de page)* layout; **être** *ou* **rester** *ou* **se tenir à la d. de qn** to be or remain at sb's disposal; **dispositions** *(aptitudes)* ability, aptitude (**pour** for)

disproportionné, -e [disprɔpɔrsjɔne] *adj* disproportionate

dispute [dispyt] *nf* quarrel ■ **disputer 1** *vt (match)* to play; *(rallye)* to compete in; *(combat de boxe)* to fight; *(droit)* to contest; **d. qch à qn** *(prix, première place)* to fight with sb for or over sth **2 se disputer** *vpr* to quarrel (**avec** with); *(match)* to take place; **se d. qch** to fight over sth

disqualifier [diskalifje] *vt (équipe, athlète)* to disqualify ■ **disqualification** *nf* disqualification

disque [disk] *nm (de musique)* record; *(cercle)* **Br** disc, **Am** disk; *Ordinat* disk; **Sport** discus; **d. compact** compact **Br** disc *or* **Am** disk; **d. dur** hard disk ■ **disquaire** *nmf* record dealer ■ **disquette** *nf Ordinat* floppy (disk), diskette

disséminer [disemine] *vt (graines, mines)* to scatter

disséquer [diseke] *vt* to dissect

dissertation [disertasjɔ̃] *nf* essay

dissident, -e [disidã, -ãt] *nmf* dissident

dissimuler [disimyle] **1** *vt (cacher)* to conceal (**à** from) **2 se dissimuler** *vpr* to be hidden ■ **dissimulation** *nf* concealment; *(duplicité)* deceit

dissiper [disipe] **1** *vt (nuages)* to disperse; *(brouillard)* to clear; *(malentendu)* to clear up; *(craintes)* to dispel; **d. qn** to lead sb astray **2 se dissiper** *vpr*

(nuage) to disperse; *(brume)* to clear; *(craintes)* to vanish; *(élève)* to misbehave ■ **dissipé, -e** *adj (élève)* unruly

dissocier [disɔsje] *vt* to dissociate (**de** from)

dissolu, -e [disɔly] *adj (vie)* dissolute

dissolution [disɔlysjɔ̃] *nf* dissolution

dissolvant [disɔlvã] *nm* solvent; *(pour vernis à ongles)* nail polish remover

dissoudre* [disudr] *vt*, **se dissoudre** *vpr* to dissolve

dissuader [disɥade] *vt* to dissuade (**de qch** from sth; **de faire** from doing) ■ **dissuasif, -ive** *adj* deterrent; **avoir un effet d.** to be a deterrent ■ **dissuasion** *nf* dissuasion; *Mil* **force de d.** deterrent

distance [distãs] *nf* distance; **à deux mètres de d.** two metres apart; **à d.** at *or* from a distance; **garder ses distances** to keep one's distance (**vis-à-vis de** from); **commandé à d.** remote-controlled

distancer [distãse] *vt* to outstrip; **se laisser d.** to fall behind

distant, -e [distã, -ãt] *adj* distant; *(personne)* aloof, distant; **d. de dix kilomètres** *(éloigné)* ten kilometres away; *(à intervalles)* ten kilometres apart

distendre [distãdr] *vt*, **se distendre** *vpr* to stretch

distiller [distile] *vt* to distil ■ **distillerie** *nf (lieu)* distillery

distinct, -e [distɛ̃, -ɛkt] *adj (différent)* distinct, separate (**de** from); *(net)* clear, distinct ■ **distinctif, -ive** *adj* distinctive ■ **distinction** *nf (différence, raffinement)* distinction

distinguer [distɛ̃ge] **1** *vt (différencier)* to distinguish; *(voir)* to make out; *(choisir)* to single out; **d. le bien du mal** to tell good from evil **2 se distinguer** *vpr (s'illustrer)* to distinguish oneself; **se d. de qn/qch (par)** to be distinguishable from sb/sth (by) ■ **distingué, -e** *adj (bien élevé, éminent)* distinguished

distorsion [distɔrsjɔ̃] *nf* distortion

distraction [distraksjɔ̃] *nf (étourderie)* absent-mindedness ■ **distraire*** 1 *vt (divertir)* to entertain; **d. qn** to distract sb (**de** from) **2 se distraire** *upr* to amuse oneself ■ **distrait, -e** *adj* absent-minded ■ **distrayant, -e** *adj* entertaining

distribuer [distribɥe] *vt (donner)* & *Com* to distribute; *(courrier)* to deliver; *(cartes)* to deal; *(tâches)* to allocate; *(eau)* to supply

distributeur [distribytœr] *nm Com* distributor; **d. automatique** vending machine; **d. de billets** *(de train)* ticket machine; *(de billets de banque)* cash machine

distribution [distribysjɔ̃] *nf* distribution; *(du courrier)* delivery; *(de l'eau)* supply; *(acteurs de cinéma)* cast; **d. des prix** prizegiving

district [distrikt] *nm* district

dit¹, dite [di, dit] **1** *pp de* **dire 2** *adj (convenu)* agreed; *(surnommé)* called

dit², dites [di, dit] *voir* **dire**

divaguer [divage] *vi (dérailler)* to rave

divan [divã] *nm* divan, couch

divergent, -e [diverʒã, -ãt] *adj (lignes)* divergent; *(opinions)* differing ■ **divergence** *nf (de lignes)* divergence; *(d'opinions)* difference ■ **diverger** *vi* to diverge (**de** from)

divers, -e [diver, -ers] *adj (varié)* varied; **divers(es)** *(plusieurs)* various

diversifier [diversifje] *vt,* **se diversifier** *upr* to diversify

diversion [diversjɔ̃] *nf* diversion; **faire d.** to create a diversion

diversité [diversite] *nf* diversity

divertir [divertir] **1** *vt* to entertain **2 se divertir** *upr* to enjoy oneself ■ **divertissement** *nm* entertainment, amusement

divin, -e [divɛ̃, -in] *adj* divine ■ **divinité** *nf* divinity

diviser [divize] *vt,* **se diviser** *upr* to divide (**en** into) ■ **division** *nf* division

divorce [divors] *nm* divorce ■ **divorcer** *vi* to get divorced; **d. d'avec qn** to divorce sb ■ **divorcé, -e 1** *adj* divorced

(d'avec from) **2** *nmf* divorcee

divulguer [divylge] *vt* to divulge

dix [dis] *([di]* before consonant, *[diz]* before vowel*) adj* & *nm* ten ■ **dix-huit** *adj* & *nm* eighteen ■ **dixième** *adj* & *nmf* tenth; **un d.** a tenth ■ **dix-neuf** *adj* & *nm* nineteen ■ **dix-sept** *adj* & *nm* seventeen

dizaine [dizen] *nf* **une d. (de)** about ten

do [do] *nm inv (note)* C

docile [dɔsil] *adj* docile

docteur [dɔktœr] *nm (en médecine, d'université)* doctor (**ès/en** of) ■ **doctorat** *nm* doctorate, ≃ PhD (**ès/en** in)

doctrine [dɔktrin] *nf* doctrine

document [dɔkymã] *nm* document ■ **documentaire** *adj* & *nm* documentary ■ **documentaliste** *nmf* archivist; *(à l'école)* (school) librarian

documentation [dɔkymãtasjɔ̃] *nf (documents)* documentation, *(brochures)* literature ■ **se documenter** *upr* to gather information *or* material (**sur** on)

dodu, -e [dɔdy] *adj* chubby, plump

doigt [dwa] *nm* finger; **d. de pied** toe; **petit d.** little finger, *Am* & *Scot* pinkie; **un d. de vin** a drop of wine; **montrer qn du d.** to point at sb

doigté [dwate] *nm Mus* fingering; *(savoir-faire)* tact

dois, doit [dwa] *voir* **devoir¹,²**

doléances [dɔleãs] *nfpl (plaintes)* grievances

dollar [dɔlar] *nm* dollar

domaine [dɔmen] *nm (terres)* estate, domain; *(matière)* field, domain; **être du d. public** to be in the public domain

dôme [dom] *nm* dome

domestique [dɔmestik] **1** *adj (vie, marché, produit)* domestic; **travaux domestiques** housework **2** *nmf* servant ■ **domestiquer** *vt* to domesticate

domicile [dɔmisil] *nm* home; *(demeure légale)* abode; **sans d. fixe** of no fixed abode; *Jur* **d. conjugal** marital home

dominateur, -trice [dɔminatœr, -tris] *adj* domineering ∎ **domination** *nf* domination

dominer [dɔmine] **1** *vt* to dominate; *(situation, sentiment)* to master; *(être supérieur à)* to surpass **2** *vi (être le plus fort)* to be dominant; *(être le plus important)* to predominate **3 se dominer** *vpr* to control oneself ∎ **dominant, -e** *adj* dominant

dommage [dɔmaʒ] *nm (tort)* harm; **dommages** *(dégâts)* damage; **quel d.!** what a pity, what a shame!; **c'est (bien) d. qu'elle ne soit pas venue** it's a (great) pity *or* shame she didn't come; **dommages-intérêts** damages

dompter [dɔ̃te] *vt (animal)* to tame

DOM-TOM [dɔmtɔm] *(abrév* **départements et territoires d'outre-mer)** *nmpl* = French overseas departments and territories

don [dɔ̃] *nm (cadeau, aptitude)* gift; *(à un musée, à une œuvre)* donation; **faire d. de qch** to give sth; **d. du sang** blood donation

donateur, -trice [dɔnatœr, -tris] *nmf* donor ∎ **donation** *nf* donation

donc [dɔ̃(k)] *conj* so, then; *(par conséquent)* so, therefore; **asseyez-vous d.!** *(intensif)* do sit down!

donjon [dɔ̃ʒɔ̃] *nm* keep

données [dɔne] *nfpl Ordinat* data

DONNER [dɔne] **1** *vt* to give; *(récolte, résultat)* to produce; *(cartes)* to deal; *(pièce, film)* to put on; **pourriez-vous me d. l'heure?** could you tell me the time?; **d. un coup à qn** to hit sb; **d. à manger à qn** *(animal, enfant)* to feed sb; **elle m'a donné de ses nouvelles** she told me how she was doing; **ça donne soif/faim** it makes you thirsty/hungry; **étant donné...** considering..., in view of...; **étant donné que...** seeing (that), considering (that)...; **à un moment donné** at some stage

2 *vi* **d. sur** *(fenêtre)* to overlook, to look out onto; *(porte)* to open onto

3 se donner *vpr (se consacrer)* to

devote oneself (**à** to); **se d. du mal** to go to a lot of trouble (**pour faire** to do)

donneur, -euse [dɔnœr, -øz] *nmf (de sang, d'organe)* donor

dont [dɔ̃] (= **de qui, duquel, de quoi**) *pron relatif (exprime la partie d'un tout) (personne)* of whom; *(chose)* of which; *(exprime l'appartenance) (personne)* whose, of whom; *(chose)* of which, whose; **une mère d. le fils est malade** a mother whose son is ill; **la fille d. il est fier** the daughter he is proud of *or* of whom he is proud; **les outils d. j'ai besoin** the tools I need; **la façon d. elle joue** the way (in which) she plays; **cinq enfants d. deux filles** five children two of whom are daughters, five children including two daughters; **voici ce d. il s'agit** here's what it's about

doper [dɔpe] **1** *vt* to dope **2 se doper** *vpr* to take drugs ∎ **dopage** *nm (action)* doping; *(de sportif)* drug-taking

dorénavant [dɔrenavɑ̃] *adv* from now on

dorer [dɔre] **1** *vt (objet)* to gild **2** *vi (à la cuisson)* to brown **3 se dorer** *vpr* **se d. au soleil** to sunbathe ∎ **doré, -e** *adj (objet)* gilt, gold; *(couleur)* golden

dormir* [dɔrmir] *vi* to sleep; *(être endormi)* to be asleep; *Fig (argent)* to lie idle

dortoir [dɔrtwar] *nm* dormitory

dos [do] *nm (de personne, d'animal)* back; *(de livre)* spine; **'voir au d.'** *(verso)* 'see over'

dose [doz] *nf* dose; *(dans un mélange)* proportion ∎ **doser** *vt (médicament, ingrédients)* to measure out

dossard [dɔsar] *nm (de sportif)* number *(worn by player or competitor)*

dossier [dɔsje] *nm (de siège)* back; *(documents)* file

dot [dɔt] *nf* dowry

doter [dɔte] *vt (équiper)* to equip (**de** with); **doté d'une grande intelligence** endowed with great intelligence

douane [dwan] *nf* customs; **passer la d.** to go through customs ∎ **douanier, -ère** *nmf* customs officer

doublage [dublaʒ] *nm (de film)* dubbing

double [dubl] **1** *adj* double; *(rôle, avantage)* twofold, double; **en d. exemplaire** in duplicate **2** *adv* double **3** *nm (de personne)* double; *(copie)* copy, duplicate; **le d. (de)** *(quantité)* twice as much (as); **je l'ai en d.** I have two of them

doubler [duble] **1** *vt (augmenter)* to double; *(vêtement)* to line; *(film)* to dub; *(acteur)* to dub the voice of; *(classe à l'école)* to repeat **2** *vi (augmenter)* to double **3** *vti (en voiture)* Br to overtake, Am to pass **4 se doubler** *upr* **se d. de** to be coupled with

doublure [dublyr] *nf (étoffe)* lining; *(au théâtre)* understudy; *(au cinéma)* stand-in

douce [dus] *voir* **doux** ■ **doucement** *adv (délicatement)* gently; *(bas)* softly; *(lentement)* slowly; *(sans bruit)* quietly ■ **douceur** *nf (de miel)* sweetness; *(de peau)* softness; *(de temps)* mildness; *(de personne)* gentleness

douche [duʃ] *nf* shower; **prendre une d.** to have *or* take a shower ■ **doucher se doucher** *upr* to have *or* take a shower

doué, -e [dwe] *adj* gifted, talented *(en* at*)*; **être d. pour qch** to have a gift for sth

douille [duj] *nf (d'ampoule)* socket; *(de cartouche)* case

douillet, -ette [duje, -ɛt] *adj (lit)* Br cosy, Am cozy

douleur [dulœr] *nf (mal)* pain; *(chagrin)* sorrow, grief ■ **douloureux, -euse** *adj* painful

doute [dut] *nm* doubt; **sans d.** no doubt, probably; **sans aucun d.** without (any) doubt; **mettre qch en d.** to cast doubt on sth

douter [dute] **1** *vi* to doubt; **d. de qn/ qch** to doubt sb/sth **2** *vt* **je doute qu'il soit assez fort** I doubt whether he's strong enough **3 se douter** *upr* **se d. de quelque chose** to suspect something

douteux, -euse [dutø, -øz] *adj (peu certain)* doubtful; *(louche, médiocre)* dubious

Douvres [duvr] *nm ou f* Dover

doux, douce [du, dus] *adj (miel, son)* sweet; *(peau, lumière)* soft; *(temps, climat)* mild; *(personne, pente)* gentle

douze [duz] *adj & nm* twelve ■ **douzaine** *nf (douze)* dozen; *(environ)* about twelve; **une d. d'œufs** a dozen eggs

dragée [draʒe] *nf* sugared almond

dragon [dragɔ̃] *nm (animal, personne acariâtre)* dragon

drainer [drene] *vt* to drain

drame [dram] *nm (genre littéraire)* drama; *(catastrophe)* tragedy ■ **dramatique 1** *adj* dramatic; **auteur d.** playwright, dramatist **2** *nf* drama

drap [dra] *nm (de lit)* sheet; *(tissu)* cloth; **d.-housse** fitted sheet; **d. de bain** bath towel

drapeau, -x [drapo] *nm* flag

dresser [drese] **1** *vt (échelle, statue)* to put up, to erect; *(liste)* to draw up; *(piège)* to set, to lay; *(animal)* to train; **d. les oreilles** to prick up one's ears **2 se dresser** *upr (personne)* to stand up; *(statue, montagne)* to rise up ■ **dressage** *nm* training ■ **dresseur, -euse** *nmf* trainer

drogue [drɔg] *nf (stupéfiant) & Péj (médicament)* drug; **d. dure/douce** hard/ soft drug ■ **drogué, -e** *nmf* drug addict ■ **droguer 1** *vt (victime)* to drug; *(malade)* to dose up **2 se droguer** *upr* to take drugs

droguerie [drɔgri] *nf* hardware Br shop *or* Am store ■ **droguiste** *nmf* hardware dealer

droit¹ [drwa] *nm (privilège)* right; *(d'inscription)* fee(s); **le d.** *(science juridique)* law; **avoir d. à qch** to be entitled to sth; **avoir le d. de faire qch** to be entitled to do sth, to have the right to do sth; **droits de douane** (customs) duty; **droits de l'homme** human rights

droit², droite¹ [drwa, drwat] **1** *adj*

(route, ligne) straight; *(angle)* right; *Fig (honnête)* upright **2** *adv* straight; **tout d.** straight *or* right ahead; **aller d. au but** to go straight to the point

droit³, droite² [drwa, drwat] *adj (côté, bras)* right

droite³ [drwat] *nf (ligne)* straight line

droite⁴ [drwat] *nf* **la d.** *(côté)* the right (side); *Pol* the right (wing); **à d.** *(tourner)* (to the) right; *(rouler, se tenir)* on the right, on the right(-hand) side; **de d.** *(fenêtre)* right-hand; *(candidat)* right-wing; **à d. de** on *or* to the right of

droitier, -ère [drwatje, -ɛr] **1** *adj* right-handed **2** *nmf* right-handed person

droiture [drwatyr] *nf* rectitude

drôle [drol] *adj* funny ■ **drôlement** *adv* funnily; *Fam (extrêmement)* terribly, dreadfully

dru, drue [dry] **1** *adj (herbe)* thick, dense **2** *adv* **tomber d.** *(pluie)* to pour down heavily; **pousser d.** to grow thickly

du [dy] *voir* **de¹,²**

dû, due [dy] **1** *adj* **d. à qch** due to sth; **en bonne et due forme** in due form **2** *nm* due

duc [dyk] *nm* duke ■ **duchesse** *nf* duchess

duel [dɥɛl] *nm* duel

dûment [dymɑ̃] *adv* duly

dune [dyn] *nf (sand)* dune

duo [dɥo] *nm Mus* duet

dupe [dyp] **1** *adj* **être d. de** to be taken in by; **il n'est pas d.** he's well aware of it **2** *nf* dupe ■ **duper** *vt* to fool, to dupe

duplex [dyplɛks] *nm Br* maisonette, *Am* duplex

duplicata [dyplikata] *nm inv* duplicate

duquel [dykɛl] *voir* **lequel**

dur, dure [dyr] **1** *adj (substance)* hard; *(difficile)* hard, tough; *(viande)* tough; *(hiver, ton)* harsh; *(personne)* hard, harsh; **d. d'oreille** hard of hearing **2** *adv (travailler)* hard ■ **durement** *adv* harshly ■ **dureté** *nf (de substance)* hardness; *(d'hiver, de ton)* harshness; *(de viande)* toughness

durable [dyrabl] *adj* lasting

durant [dyrɑ̃] *prép* during; **d. l'hiver** during the winter; **des heures d.** for hours and hours

durcir [dyrsir] *vti, se durcir vpr* to harden

durée [dyre] *nf (de film, d'événement)* length; *(période)* duration; **de longue d.** *(bonheur)* lasting; **de courte d.** *(attente)* short; *(bonheur)* short-lived

durer [dyre] *vi* to last

duvet [dyvɛ] *nm (d'oiseau)* down; *(sac)* sleeping bag

dynamique [dinamik] *adj* dynamic

dynamite [dinamit] *nf* dynamite

dynamo [dinamo] *nf* dynamo

dynastie [dinasti] *nf* dynasty

dyslexique [dislɛksik] *adj* dyslexic

Ee

E, e [ə] *nm inv* E, e

EAO [əao] *(abrév* **enseignement assisté par ordinateur)** *nm inv* CAL

eau, -x [o] *nf* water; **sports d'e. vive** whitewater sports; **e. de toilette** eau de toilette; **e. du robinet** tap water; **e. douce** fresh water ▪ **eau-de-vie** *(pl* **eaux-de-vie)** *nf* brandy

ébahir [ebair] *vt* to astound

ébattre [ebatr] **s'ébattre** *vpr* to frolic

ébaucher [eboʃe] *vt (tableau, roman)* to rough out

ébéniste [ebenist] *nm* cabinetmaker

éblouir [ebluir] *vt* to dazzle

éboueur [ebwœr] *nm Br* dustman, *Am* garbage collector

ébouillanter [ebujɑ̃te] **1** *vt* to scald **2 s'ébouillanter** *vpr* to scald oneself

ébouler [ebule] **s'ébouler** *vpr (falaise)* to collapse; *(tunnel)* to cave in ▪ **éboulement** *nm (écroulement)* collapse; *(de mine)* cave-in

ébouriffé, -e [eburife] *adj* dishevelled

ébranler [ebrɑ̃le] **1** *vt (mur, confiance, personne)* to shake **2 s'ébranler** *vpr (train, cortège)* to move off

ébrécher [ebreʃe] *vt (assiette)* to chip; *(lame)* to nick

ébriété [ebrijete] *nf* **en état d'é.** under the influence of drink

ébrouer [ebrue] **s'ébrouer** *vpr (chien)* to shake itself; *(cheval)* to snort

ébruiter [ebrɥite] *vt (nouvelle)* to spread

EBS [øbɛɛs] *(abrév* **encéphalite bovine spongiforme)** *nf* BSE

ébullition [ebylisjɔ̃] *nf* boiling; **être en é.** *(eau)* to be boiling; **porter qch à é.** to bring sth to the boil

écaille [ekaj] *nf (de poisson)* scale ▪ **écailler 1** *vt (poisson)* to scale **2 s'écailler** *vpr (peinture)* to peel (off)

écarquiller [ekarkije] *vt* **é. les yeux** to open one's eyes wide

écart [ekar] *nm (intervalle)* gap, distance; *(différence)* difference *(de* in; **entre** between); **faire le grand é.** to do the splits; **à l'é.** out of the way; **à l'é. de qch** away from sth

écartelé, -e [ekartəle] *adj* **é. entre** *(tiraillé)* torn between

écartement [ekartəmɑ̃] *nm (espace)* gap, distance *(de* between)

écarter [ekarte] **1** *vt (objets, personnes)* to move apart; *(jambes, doigts)* to spread; *(rideaux)* to draw (back); *(idée)* to brush aside; *(proposition)* to turn down; **é. qch de qch** to move sth away from sth

2 s'écarter *vpr* **(a)** *(se séparer) (personnes)* to move apart *(de* from); *(foule)* to part

(b) *(piéton)* to move away *(de* from); **s'é. du sujet** to wander from the subject ▪ **écarté, -e** *adj* **les jambes écartées** with his/her legs (wide) apart

ecclésiastique [eklezjastik] *nm* clergyman

écervelé, -e [esɛrvəle] **1** *adj* scatterbrained **2** *nmf* scatterbrain

échafaudage [eʃafodaʒ] *nm* scaffolding; **des échafaudages** scaffolding

échalote [eʃalɔt] *nf* shallot

échancré, -e [eʃɑ̃kre] *adj* low-cut ▪ **échancrure** *nf* low neckline

échange [eʃɑ̃ʒ] *nm* exchange; **en é.** in exchange (**de** for) ■ **échanger** *vt* to exchange (**contre** for)

échangeur [eʃɑ̃ʒœr] *nm* interchange

échantillon [eʃɑ̃tijɔ̃] *nm* sample

échapper [eʃape] **1** *vi* **é. à qn** to escape from sb; **son nom m'échappe** his/her name escapes me; **ça lui a échappé des mains** it slipped out of his/her hands

2 *vt* **il l'a échappé belle** he had a narrow escape

3 s'échapper *vpr (personne, gaz, eau)* to escape (**de** from) ■ **échappée** *nf (de cyclistes)* breakaway

écharde [eʃard] *nf* splinter

écharpe [eʃarp] *nf* scarf; *(de maire)* sash; **avoir le bras en é.** to have one's arm in a sling

échasse [eʃas] *nf (bâton)* stilt

échauffer [eʃofe] **1** *vt (moteur)* to overheat **2 s'échauffer** *vpr (sportif)* to warm up

échauffourée [eʃofure] *nf* clash, brawl, skirmish

échéance [eʃeɑ̃s] *nf (de facture, de dette)* date of payment; **à brève/longue é.** *(projet, emprunt)* short-/long-term

échéant [eʃeɑ̃] **le cas échéant** *adv* if need be

échec [eʃɛk] *nm* failure; **faire é. à qch** to hold sth in check; **les échecs** *(jeu)* chess; **é.! check!; é. et mat!** checkmate!

échelle [eʃɛl] *nf (a) (marches)* ladder (**b**) *(de carte)* scale; **à l'é. nationale** on a national scale

échelon [eʃlɔ̃] *nm (d'échelle)* rung; *(d'employé)* grade; *(d'organisation)* echelon; **à l'é. régional** on a regional level

échelonner [eʃlɔne] **1** *vt (paiements)* to spread **2 s'échelonner** *vpr* to be spread out

échevelé, -e [eʃəvle] *adj (ébouriffé)* dishevelled

échiquier [eʃikje] *nm (plateau)* chessboard

écho [eko] *nm (de son)* echo; **échos** *(de presse)* gossip column

échographie [ekɔgrafi] *nf (ultrasound)* scan; **passer une é.** to have a scan

échoir* [eʃwar] *vi* **é. à qn** to fall to sb

échouer [eʃwe] **1** *vi* to fail; **é. à** *(examen)* to fail **2** *vi*, **s'échouer** *vpr (navire)* to run aground

éclabousser [eklabuse] *vt* to splash, to spatter (**avec** with) ■ **éclaboussure** *nf* splash

éclair [eklɛr] **1** *nm* (**a**) *(lumière)* flash; *(d'orage)* flash of lightning (**b**) *(gâteau)* éclair **2** *adj inv* **visite é.** lightning visit

éclairage [eklɛraʒ] *nm* lighting

éclaircie [eklɛrsi] *nf* sunny spell

éclaircir [eklɛrsir] **1** *vt (couleur)* to lighten; *(mystère)* to clear up **2 s'éclaircir** *vpr (ciel)* to clear; *(mystère)* to be cleared up; **s'é. la voix** to clear one's throat ■ **éclaircissement** *nm (explication)* explanation

éclairer [eklɛre] **1** *vt (pièce)* to light (up); **é. qn** *(avec une lampe)* to give sb some light; *(informer)* to enlighten sb (**sur** about)

2 *vi (lampe)* to give light; **é. bien/mal** to give good/poor light

3 s'éclairer *vpr (visage)* to light up; **s'é. à la bougie** to use candlelight; **s'é. à l'électricité** to have electric lighting ■ **éclairé, -e** *adj (averti)* enlightened; **bien/mal é.** *(illuminé)* well-/badly lit

éclaireur, -euse [eklɛrœr, -øz] *nmf* *(boy)* scout, *(girl)* guide **2** *nm (soldat)* scout

éclat [ekla] *nm* (**a**) *(de lumière)* brightness; *(de phare)* glare; *(de diamant)* flash (**b**) *(de verre)* splinter; **é. de rire** burst of laughter

éclatant, -e [eklatɑ̃, -ɑ̃t] *adj (lumière, succès)* brilliant; **être é. de santé** to be glowing with health

éclater [eklate] *vi (pneu)* to burst; *(bombe)* to go off, to explode; *(verre)* to shatter; *(guerre)* to break out; *(orage, scandale)* to break; *(parti)* to break up; **é. de rire** to burst out laughing; **é. en sanglots** to burst into tears ■ **éclatement** *nm (de pneu)* bursting; *(de bombe)* explosion; *(de parti)* break-up

éclectique [eklɛktik] *adj* eclectic

éclipse [eklips] *nf* eclipse ■ **éclipser** *vt* to eclipse

éclore* [eklɔr] *vi (œuf)* to hatch; *(fleur)* to open (out), to blossom

écluse [eklyz] *nf (de canal)* lock

écœurer [ekœre] *vt* **é. qn** *(aliment)* to make sb feel sick; *(moralement)* to sicken sb ■ **écœurant, -e** *adj* disgusting, sickening ■ **écœurement** *nm (nausée)* nausea; *(indignation)* disgust

école [ekɔl] *nf* school; **à l'é.** at school; **faire é.** to gain a following; **les grandes écoles** = university-level colleges specializing in professional training; **é. de dessin** art school; **é. privée** private school, *Br* public school; **é. publique** *Br* state school, *Am* public school ■ **écolier, -ère** *nmf* schoolboy, *f* schoolgirl

écologie [ekɔlɔʒi] *nf* ecology ■ **écologique** *adj* ecological ■ **écologiste** *adj & nmf* environmentalist

économe [ekɔnɔm] *adj* thrifty, economical

économie [ekɔnɔmi] *nf (activité, vertu)* economy; **économies** *(argent)* savings; **faire des économies** to save (up) ■ **économique** *adj* **(a)** *(relatif à l'économie)* economic; **science é.** economics *(sing)* **(b)** *(avantageux)* economical

économiser [ekɔnɔmize] **1** *vt (forces, argent, énergie)* to save **2** *vi* to economize **(sur** on)

écoper [ekɔpe] *vi Fam* **é. de qch** *(punition, amende)* to get sth

écorce [ekɔrs] *nf (d'arbre)* bark; *(de fruit)* peel; **l'é. terrestre** the earth's crust

écorcher [ekɔrʃe] **1** *vt (érafler)* to graze; *Fig (mot)* to mispronounce **2** **s'écorcher** *vpr* to graze oneself; **s'é. le genou** to graze one's knee

Écosse [ekɔs] *nf* **l'É.** Scotland ■ **écossais, -e** *adj* Scottish; *(tissu)* tartan **2** *nmf* **É., Écossaise** Scot

écouler [ekule] **1** *vt (se débarrasser de)* to dispose of **2** **s'écouler** *vpr (eau)* to flow out, to run out; *(temps)* to pass ■ **écoulé, -e** *adj (passé)* past ■ **écoulement** *nm (de liquide)* flow; *(de marchandises)* sale

écourter [ekurte] *vt (séjour)* to cut short; *(texte, tige)* to shorten

écoute [ekut] *nf* listening; **être à l'é.** to be listening in **(de** to); **écoutes téléphoniques** phone tapping

écouter [ekute] **1** *vt* to listen to; **faire é. qch à qn** *(disque)* to play sb sth **2** **s'écouter** *vpr* **si je m'écoutais** if I did what I wanted ■ **écouteur** *nm (de téléphone)* earpiece; **écouteurs** *(casque)* headphones

écran [ekrɑ̃] *nm* screen; **à l'é.** on screen; **le petit é.** television; **é. publicitaire** commercial break; **é. total** sun block

écraser [ekraze] **1** *vt (broyer, vaincre)* to crush; *(fruit, insecte)* to squash; *(cigarette)* to put out; *(piéton)* to run over; **se faire é. par une voiture** to get run over by a car **2** **s'écraser** *vpr (avion)* to crash **(contre** into) ■ **écrasant, -e** *adj (victoire, chaleur)* overwhelming

écrémer [ekreme] *vt (lait)* to skim

écrevisse [ekrəvis] *nf* crayfish *inv*

écrier [ekrije] **s'écrier** *vpr* to exclaim, to cry out **(que** that)

écrin [ekrɛ̃] *nm (jewel)* case

écrire* [ekrir] **1** *vt* to write; *(noter)* to write down **2** *vi* to write **3** **s'écrire** *vpr (mot)* to be spelt; **comment ça s'écrit?** how do you spell it? ■ **écrit** *nm (document)* written document; *(examen)* written examination; **par é.** in writing

écriteau, -x [ekrito] *nm* notice, sign

écriture [ekrityr] *nf (système)* writing; *(calligraphie)* (hand)writing; *Com* **écritures** accounts; **les Écritures** *(la Bible)* the Scriptures

écrivain [ekrivɛ̃] *nm* writer

écrou [ekru] *nm (de boulon)* nut

écrouer [ekrue] *vt* to imprison

écrouler [ekrule] **s'écrouler** *upr (édifice, personne)* to collapse ■ **écroulement** *nm* collapse

écru, -e [ekry] *adj (beige)* écru; *(naturel)* unbleached

ÉCU [eky] *(abrév* **European Currency Unit)** *nm Anciennement* ECU

écueil [ekœj] *nm (rocher)* reef; *Fig (obstacle)* pitfall

écuelle [ekɥɛl] *nf* bowl

écume [ekym] *nf (de mer)* foam ■ **écumer 1** *vt (piller)* to plunder **2** *vi* to foam **(de rage** with anger)

écureuil [ekyrœj] *nm* squirrel

écurie [ekyri] *nf* stable

écusson [ekysɔ̃] *nm (en étoffe)* badge

écuyer, -ère [ekɥije, -ɛr] *nmf (cavalier)* rider

édifice [edifis] *nm* edifice ■ **édifier** *vt (bâtiment)* to erect; *(théorie)* to construct

Édimbourg [edɛ̃bur] *nm ou f* Edinburgh

éditer [edite] *vt (publier)* to publish; *Ordinat* to edit ■ **éditeur, -trice** *nmf (dans l'édition)* publisher ■ **édition** *nf (livre, journal)* edition; *(métier, diffusion)* publishing

éditorial, -aux [editorjal, -o] *nm (article)* editorial, *Br* leader ■ **éditorialiste** *nmf* editorial or *Br* leader writer

éducateur, -trice [edykatœr, -tris] *nmf* educator

éducatif, -ive [edykatif, -iv] *adj* educational

éducation [edykasjɔ̃] *nf (enseignement)* education; *(des parents)* upbringing; **avoir de l'é.** to have good manners; **l'É. nationale** ≃ the Department of Education; **é. physique** physical education *or* training ■ **éduquer** *vt (à l'école)* to educate; *(à la maison)* to bring up

EEE [əəə] *(abrév* **Espace économique européen)** *nm* EEA

effacé, -e [efase] *adj (modeste)* self-effacing

effacer [efase] **1** *vt (avec une gomme)* to rub out, to erase; *(avec un chiffon)* to wipe away; *Fig (souvenir)* to blot out, to erase **2 s'effacer** *upr (souvenir)* to fade; *(se placer en retrait)* to step aside

effarant, -e [efarɑ̃, -ɑ̃t] *adj* astounding

effaroucher [efaruʃe] **1** *vt* to scare away **2 s'effaroucher** *upr* to take fright

effectif, -ive [efɛktif, -iv] **1** *adj (réel)* effective **2** *nm (de classe)* size; *(employés)* staff ■ **effectivement** *adv (en effet)* actually

effectuer [efɛktɥe] *vt (expérience, geste difficile)* to carry out, to perform; *(paiement, trajet)* to make

efféminé, -e [efemine] *adj* effeminate

effervescent, -e [efɛrvesɑ̃, -ɑ̃t] *adj (médicament)* effervescent

effet [efɛ] *nm (résultat)* effect; *(impression)* impression **(sur** on); **en e.** indeed, in fact; **e. de serre** greenhouse effect; **e. secondaire** side effect; *Cin* **effets spéciaux** special effects

efficace [efikas] *adj (mesure)* effective; *(personne)* efficient ■ **efficacité** *nf (de mesure)* effectiveness; *(de personne)* efficiency

effilocher [efiloʃe] **s'effilocher** *upr* to fray

effleurer [eflœre] *vt (frôler)* to touch lightly; **e. qn** *(pensée)* to cross sb's mind

effondrer [efɔ̃dre] **s'effondrer** *upr (tomber, chuter)* to collapse; *(plan)* to fall through; *Fig (perdre ses forces)* to go to pieces; **s'e. en larmes** to break down and cry ■ **effondrement** *nm (chute)* collapse; *(sentiment)* dejection

efforcer [eforse] **s'efforcer** *upr* **s'e. de faire qch** to try hard to do sth

effort [efor] *nm* effort; **faire des efforts** to make an effort

effraction [efraksjɔ̃] *nf* **entrer par e.** to break in; **vol avec e.** housebreaking

effrayer [efreje] **1** *vt* to frighten, to scare **2 s'effrayer** *upr* to be frightened *or* scared ■ **effrayant, -e** *adj* frightening, scary

effriter [efrite] **s'effriter** *vpr* to crumble

effronté, -e [efrɔ̃te] *adj (personne)* impudent

effroyable [efrwajabl] *adj* dreadful

effusion [efyzjɔ̃] *nf* e. de sang bloodshed

égal, -e, -aux, -ales [egal, -o] **1** *adj* equal (**à** to); *(régulier)* even; **ça m'est é.** it's all the same to me **2** *nmf (personne)* equal ■ **également** *adv (au même degré)* equally; *(aussi)* also, as well ■ **égaler** *vt* to equal, to match (**en** in); **3 plus 4 égale(nt) 7** 3 plus 4 equals 7

égaliser [egalize] *vi Sport* to equalize

égalité [egalite] *nf* equality; *(régularité)* evenness; *(au tennis)* deuce; *Sport* **à é.** even, equal (in points) ■ **égalitaire** *adj* egalitarian

égard [egar] *nm* **à l'é. de** *(envers)* towards; **à cet é.** in this respect; **par é. pour qn** out of consideration for sb

égarer [egare] **1** *vt (objet)* to mislay; *(personne)* to mislead **2 s'égarer** *vpr (personne, lettre)* to get lost; *(objet)* to go astray

égayer [egeje] **1** *vt (pièce)* to brighten up; **é. qn** to cheer sb up **2 s'égayer** *vpr (s'animer)* to cheer up

église [egliz] *nf* church

égoïste [egɔist] **1** *adj* selfish **2** *nmf* selfish person

égorger [egɔrʒe] *vt* to cut or slit the throat of

égout [egu] *nm* sewer

égoutter [egute] **1** *vt* to drain **2** *vi*, **s'égoutter** *vpr* to drain ■ **égouttoir** *nm (panier)* drainer

égratigner [egratiɲe] **1** *vt* to scratch **2 s'égratigner** *vpr* to scratch oneself ■ **égratignure** *nf* scratch

Égypte [eʒipt] *nf* l'É. Egypt ■ **égyptien, -enne 1** *adj* Egyptian **2** *nmf* É., Égyptienne Egyptian

éjecter [eʒekte] *vt* to eject

élaborer [elabɔre] *vt (plan, idée)* to develop ■ **élaboration** *nf (de plan, d'idée)* development

élan [elɑ̃] *nm (vitesse)* momentum;

(course) run-up; **prendre son é.** to take a run-up

élancé, -e [elɑ̃se] *adj (personne)* slender

élancer [elɑ̃se] **1** *vi (abcès)* to give shooting pains **2 s'élancer** *vpr (bondir)* to rush forward; *Sport* to take a run-up ■ **élancement** *nm (douleur)* shooting pain

élargir [elarʒir] **1** *vt (chemin)* to widen; *(vêtement)* to let out **2 s'élargir** *vpr (sentier)* to widen out; *(vêtement)* to stretch

élastique [elastik] **1** *adj (tissu)* elastic **2** *nm (lien)* rubber band, *Br* elastic band; *(pour la couture)* elastic

élection [eleksjɔ̃] *nf* election; **é. partielle** by-election ■ **électeur, -trice** *nmf* voter, elector ■ **électoral, -e, -aux, -ales** *adj* campagne électorale election campaign; liste électorale electoral roll ■ **électorat** *nm (électeurs)* electorate, voters

électricien, -enne [elektrisjɛ̃, -ɛn] *nmf* electrician ■ **électricité** *nf* electricity ■ **électrifier** *vt (voie ferrée)* to electrify ■ **électrique** *adj (pendule, décharge)* & *Fig* electric; *(courant, fil)* electric(al)

électrocuter [elektrɔkyte] *vt* to electrocute

électroménager [elektrɔmenaʒe] **1** *adj m* appareil é. household electrical appliance **2** *nm* household appliances

électronique [elektrɔnik] **1** *adj* electronic **2** *nf* electronics *(sing)*

élégant, -e [elegɑ̃, -ɑ̃t] *adj (bien habillé)* smart, elegant ■ **élégance** *nf* elegance

élément [elemɑ̃] *nm (composante, personne)* & *Chim* element; *(de meuble)* unit

élémentaire [elemɑ̃ter] *adj* basic

éléphant [elefɑ̃] *nm* elephant

élevage [elvaʒ] *nm (production)* breeding (**de** of); *(ferme)* farm

élevé, -e [elve] *adj (haut)* high; *(noble)* noble; **bien/mal é.** well-/bad-mannered

élève [elɛv] nmf (à l'école) pupil

élever [elve] **1** vt (objection) to raise; (enfant) to bring up; 2 **s'élever** vpr (montagne) to rise; (monument) to stand; **s'é. à** (prix) to amount to; **s'é. contre** to rise up against

éleveur, -euse [elvœr, -øz] nmf breeder

éliminer [elimine] vt to eliminate ■ **éliminatoire** adj épreuve é. Sport qualifying round, heat; Scol qualifying exam; Scol note é. disqualifying mark ■ **éliminatoires** nfpl Sport qualifying rounds

élire* [elir] vt to elect (à to)

élite [elit] nf élite (de of)

elle [ɛl] pron personnel (a) (sujet) she; (chose, animal) it; **elles** they (b) (complément) her; (chose, animal) it; **elles** them ■ **elle-même** pron (personne) herself; (chose, animal) itself; **elles-mêmes** themselves

éloge [elɔʒ] nm (compliment) praise ■ **élogieux, -euse** adj laudatory

éloigné, -e [elwaɲe] adj (lieu) far away, remote, é. de (village, maison) far (away) from; (très différent) far removed from

éloignement [elwaɲəmã] nm (distance) remoteness, distance; (absence) separation (de from)

éloigner [elwaɲe] **1** vt (chose, personne) to move away (de from); (malade) to keep away; é. qn de qch (sujet, but) to take sb away from sth **2** **s'éloigner** vpr (partir) to move away (de from); (dans le passé) to become (more) remote; **s'é. de qch** (sujet, but) to wander from sth

éloquent, -e [elɔkã, -ãt] adj eloquent

élu, -e [ely] **1** pp de **élire 2** nmf Pol elected member or representative

élucider [elyside] vt to elucidate

Élysée [elize] nm (**le palais de**) **l'É.** the Élysée palace (French President's residence)

e-mail [imɛl] nm e-mail; envoyer un e. to send an e-mail (à to)

émail, -aux [emaj, -o] nm enamel

émanations [emanasjõ] nfpl des é. (odeurs) smells; (vapeurs) fumes

émanciper [emãsipe] **1** vt (femmes) to emancipate **2** **s'émanciper** vpr to become emancipated

émaner [emane] vt é. de qch to emanate from sth

emballer [ãbale] **1** vt (dans une boîte) to pack; (dans du papier) to wrap (up) **2** **s'emballer** vpr (cheval) to bolt; (moteur) to race ■ **emballage** nm (action) packing; (dans du papier) wrapping; (boîte) packaging; **papier d'e.** wrapping paper

embarcadère [ãbarkadɛr] nm landing stage

embarcation [ãbarkasjõ] nf (small) boat

embarquer [ãbarke] **1** vt (passagers) to take on board; (marchandises) to load **2** vi, **s'embarquer** vpr (go on) board ■ **embarquement** nm (de passagers) boarding

embarras [ãbara] nm (gêne) embarrassment; **dans l'e.** in an awkward situation; (financièrement) in financial difficulties

embarrasser [ãbarase] **1** vt (encombrer) to clutter up; (mettre mal à l'aise) to embarrass **2** **s'embarrasser** vpr **s'e. de qch** to burden oneself with sth ■ **embarrassant, -e** adj (paquet) cumbersome; (question) embarrassing

embauche [ãboʃ] nf (action) hiring; (travail) work ■ **embaucher** vt (ouvrier) to hire, to take on

embaumer [ãbome] **1** vt (parfumer) to give a sweet smell to **2** vi to smell sweet

embellir [ãbelir] **1** vt (pièce, personne) to make more attractive **2** vi (personne) to grow more attractive

embêter [ãbete] Fam **1** vt (agacer) to annoy; (ennuyer) to bore **2** **s'embêter** vpr (s'ennuyer) to get bored ■ **embêtant, -e** adj Fam annoying

emblée [ãble] **d'emblée** adv right away

emblème [ãblɛm] *nm* emblem

emboîter [ãbwate] **1** *vt* to fit together **2** **s'emboîter** *vpr* to fit together

embouchure [ãbuʃyr] *nf (de fleuve)* mouth

embourber [ãburbe] **s'embourber** *vpr (véhicule)* to get bogged down

embouteillage [ãbutejaʒ] *nm* traffic jam

emboutir [ãbutir] *vt (voiture)* to crash into

embranchement [ãbrãʃmã] *nm (de voie)* junction

embraser [ãbraze] **1** *vt* to set ablaze **2** **s'embraser** *vpr (prendre feu)* to flare up

embrasser [ãbrase] **1** *vt* **e. qn** *(donner un baiser à)* to kiss sb; *(serrer contre soi)* to embrace *or* hug sb **2** **s'embrasser** *vpr* to kiss (each other)

embrasure [ãbrazyr] *nf (de fenêtre, de porte)* aperture; **dans l'e. de la porte** in the doorway

embrayer [ãbreje] *vi Aut* to engage the clutch ∎ **embrayage** *nm (mécanisme, pédale)* clutch

embrouiller [ãbruje] **1** *vt (fils)* to tangle (up); **e. qn** to confuse sb, to get sb muddled **2** **s'embrouiller** *vpr* to get confused *or* muddled (**dans** in *or* with)

embroussaillé, -e [ãbrusaje] *adj (barbe, chemin)* bushy

embûches [ãbyʃ] *nfpl (difficultés)* traps, pitfalls

embuer [ãbɥe] *vt (vitre)* to mist up

embusquer [ãbyske] **s'embusquer** *vpr* to lie in ambush ∎ **embuscade** *nf* ambush

émeraude [emrod] *nf & adj inv* emerald

émerger [emerʒe] *vi* to emerge (**de** from)

émerveiller [emɛrveje] **1** *vt* to amaze, to fill with wonder **2** **s'émerveiller** *vpr* to marvel, to be filled with wonder (**de** at)

émettre* [emɛtr] *vt (lumière, son)* to give out, to emit; *(message radio)* to broadcast; *(monnaie)* to issue; *(vœu)* to express; *(chèque)* to draw; *(emprunt)* to float ∎ **émetteur** *nm Radio* transmitter

émeute [emøt] *nf* riot

émietter [emjete] *vt*, **s'émietter** *vpr (pain)* to crumble

émigrer [emigre] *vi (personne)* to emigrate ∎ **émigrant, -e** *nmf* emigrant ∎ **émigration** *nf* emigration ∎ **émigré, -e 1** *adj* **travailleur é.** migrant worker **2** *nmf* exile, émigré

éminent, -e [eminã, -ãt] *adj* eminent ∎ **éminence** *nf (colline)* hill; **son É.** *(cardinal)* his Eminence

émissaire [emiser] *nm* emissary

émission [emisjõ] *nf (de radio)* programme; *(diffusion)* transmission; *(de lumière, de son)* emission (**de** of)

emmanchure [ãmãʃyr] *nf* armhole

emmêler [ãmele] **1** *vt (fil, cheveux)* to tangle (up) **2** **s'emmêler** *vpr* to get tangled

emménager [ãmenaʒe] *vi* to move in; **e. dans** to move into

emmener [ãmne] *vt* to take (**à** to); *(prisonnier)* to take away; **e. qn faire une promenade** to take sb for a walk; **e. qn en voiture** to give sb a *Br* lift *or Am* ride

emmitoufler [ãmitufle] **s'emmitoufler** *vpr* to wrap (oneself) up (**dans** in)

émotion [emosjõ] *nf (sentiment)* emotion ∎ **émotif, -ive** *adj* emotional

émoussé, -e [emuse] *adj (pointe)* blunt

émouvoir* [emuvwar] **1** *vt (affecter)* to move, to touch **2** **s'émouvoir** *vpr* to be moved *or* touched ∎ **émouvant, -e** *adj* moving, touching

empailler [ãpaje] *vt (animal)* to stuff

empaqueter [ãpakte] *vt* to pack

emparer [ãpare] **s'emparer** *vpr* **s'e. de** *(lieu, personne, objet)* to seize; *(sujet: émotion)* to take hold of

empêcher [ãpeʃe] *vt* to prevent, to stop; **e. qn de faire qch** to prevent *or* stop sb from doing sth ∎ **empêchement** [-ɛʃmã] *nm* hitch; **il a/j'ai eu un e.** something came up

empereur [ɑ̃prœr] *nm* emperor

empester [ɑ̃peste] **1** *vt (tabac)* to stink of; *(pièce)* to stink out **2** *vi* to stink

empêtrer [ɑ̃petre] **s'empêtrer** *upr* to get entangled (**dans** in)

empiéter [ɑ̃pjete] *vi* **e. sur** to encroach (up)on

empiler [ɑ̃pile] **1** *vt* to pile up (**sur** on) **2** **s'empiler** *upr* to pile up (**sur** on); **s'e. dans** *(passagers)* to cram into

empire [ɑ̃pir] *nm (territoires)* empire; *(autorité)* hold, influence

empirer [ɑ̃pire] *vi* to worsen, to get worse

emplacement [ɑ̃plasmɑ̃] *nm (de construction)* site, location; *(de stationnement)* place

emplettes [ɑ̃plet] *nfpl* **faire des e.** to do some shopping

emplir [ɑ̃plir] *vt*, **s'emplir** *upr* to fill (**de** with)

emploi [ɑ̃plwa] *nm* **(a)** *(usage)* use; **e. du temps** timetable **(b)** *(travail)* job; **sans e.** unemployed

employer [ɑ̃plwaje] **1** *vt (utiliser)* to use; *(personne)* to employ **2** **s'employer** *upr (expression)* to be used ■ **employé, -e** *nmf* employee; **e. de banque** bank clerk; **e. de bureau** office worker ■ **employeur, -euse** *nmf* employer

empocher [ɑ̃pɔʃe] *vt* to pocket

empoigner [ɑ̃pwaɲe] *vt (saisir)* to grab

empoisonner [ɑ̃pwazɔne] **1** *vt (personne, aliment)* to poison **2** **s'empoisonner** *upr (par accident)* to be poisoned; *(volontairement)* to poison oneself ■ **empoisonnement** *nm* poisoning

emporter [ɑ̃pɔrte] **1** *vt (prendre)* to take (**avec soi** with one); *(transporter)* to take away; *(entraîner)* to carry along *or* away; *(par le vent)* to blow off *or* away; *(par les vagues)* to sweep away; **pizza à e.** takeaway pizza; **l'e. sur qn** to get the upper hand over sb **2** **s'emporter** *upr* to lose one's temper (**contre** with)

empreinte [ɑ̃prɛ̃t] *nf* mark; **e. digitale** fingerprint

empresser [ɑ̃prese] **s'empresser** *upr* **s'e. de faire qch** to hasten to do sth

emprise [ɑ̃priz] *nf* hold (**sur** over)

emprisonner [ɑ̃prizɔne] *vt* to imprison ■ **emprisonnement** *nm* imprisonment

emprunt [ɑ̃prœ̃] *nm (argent)* loan; **faire un e.** *(auprès d'une banque)* to take out a loan ■ **emprunter** *vt (argent, objet)* to borrow (**à qn** from sb); *(route)* to take

ému, -e [emy] **1** *pp de* **émouvoir 2** *adj (attendri)* moved; *(attristé)* upset; *(apeuré)* nervous; **une voix émue** a voice charged with emotion

EN¹ [ɑ̃] *prép* **(a)** *(indique le lieu)* in; *(indique la direction)* to

(b) *(indique le temps)* in

(c) *(indique le moyen)* by; *(indique l'état)* in; **en avion** by plane; **en fleur** in flower; **en congé** on leave

(d) *(indique la matière)* in; **en bois** made of wood, wooden; **chemise en Nylon®** nylon shirt; **c'est en or** it's (made of) gold

(e) *(domaine)* **étudiant en anglais** English student; **docteur en médecine** doctor of medicine

(f) *(comme)* **en cadeau** as a present; **en ami** as a friend

(g) *(+ participe présent)* **en souriant** smiling, with a smile; **en chantant** while singing; **en apprenant que... on** hearing that…; **sortir en courant** to run out

(h) *(transformation)* into; **traduire en français** to translate into French

EN² [ɑ̃] *pron* **(a)** *(indique la provenance)* from there; **j'en viens** I've just come from there

(b) *(remplace les compléments introduits par 'de')* **en parler** to talk about it; **il en est content** he's pleased with it/him/them; **il s'en souviendra** he'll remember it

(c) *(partitif)* some; **j'en ai** I have

some; **en veux-tu?** do you want some? **donne-m'en** give some to me

ENA [ena] *(abrév* **École nationale d'administration***) nf* = university-level college preparing students for senior positions in law and economics

encadrer [ãkadre] *vt (tableau)* to frame; *(mot)* to circle; *(personnel)* to manage; *(prisonnier)* to flank ■ **encadrement** *nm (de porte, de photo)* frame

encaisser [ãkese] *vt (argent)* to collect; *(chèque)* to cash

encart [ãkar] *nm* **e. publicitaire** insert

encastré, -e [ãkastre] *adj (cuisinière, lave-linge)* built-in

enceinte¹ [ãsɛ̃t] *adj f (femme)* pregnant

enceinte² [ãsɛ̃t] *nf (muraille)* (surrounding) wall; *(espace)* enclosure; **dans l'e. de** within, inside; **e. (acoustique)** speaker

encercler [ãserkle] *vt (lieu, ennemi)* to surround, to encircle; *(mot)* to circle

enchaîner [ãʃene] **1** *vt (animal, prisonnier)* to chain up; *(idées)* to link (up) **2** *vi (continuer à parler)* to continue **3 s'enchaîner** *vpr (idées)* to be linked (up) ■ **enchaînement** [-ɛnmã] *nm (succession)* chain, series; *(liaison)* link(ing) **(de** between *or* of)

enchanter [ãʃãte] *vt (ravir)* to delight, to enchant; *(ensorceler)* to bewitch ■ **enchanté, -e** *adj (ravi)* delighted **(de** with; **que** + *subjunctive* that); *(magique)* enchanted; **e. de faire votre connaissance!** pleased to meet you! ■ **enchantement** *nm (ravissement)* delight; *(sortilège)* magic spell

enchère [ãʃer] *nf (offre)* bid; **vente aux enchères** auction; **mettre qch aux enchères** to put sth up for auction, to auction sth

enchérir [ãʃerir] *vi* to make a higher bid; **e. sur qn** to outbid sb

enchevêtrer [ãʃvetre] **s'enchevêtrer** *vpr* to get entangled **(dans** in)

enclencher [ãklãʃe] *vt* to engage

enclin, -e [ãklɛ̃, -in] *adj* **e. à** inclined to

enclos [ãklo] *nm (terrain, clôture)* enclosure

encoche [ãkɔʃ] *nf* notch **(à** in)

encolure [ãkɔlyr] *nf (de cheval, de vêtement)* neck; *(tour du cou)* collar (size)

encombre [ãkɔ̃br] **sans encombre** *adv* without a hitch

encombrer [ãkɔ̃bre] **1** *vt (pièce, couloir)* to clutter up **(de** with); *(rue, passage)* to block; **e. qn** to hamper sb **2 s'encombrer** *vpr* **s'e. de qch** to load oneself down with sth ■ **encombrant, -e** *adj (paquet)* bulky, cumbersome ■ **encombré, -e** *adj (lignes téléphoniques, route)* jammed ■ **encombrement** [-əmã] *nm (d'objets)* clutter; *(embouteillage)* traffic jam; *(volume)* bulk(iness)

encontre [ãkɔ̃trə] **à l'encontre de** *prép* against

ENCORE [ãkɔr] *adv* **(a)** *(toujours)* still

(b) *(avec négation)* **pas e.** not yet; **je ne suis pas e. prêt** I'm not ready yet

(c) *(de nouveau)* again

(d) *(de plus, en plus)* **e. un café** another coffee; **e. une fois** (once) again, once more; **e. un** another (one), one more; **e. du pain** (some) more bread; **quoi e.?** what else?

(e) *(avec comparatif)* even, still; **e. mieux** even better, better still

(f) *(aussi)* **mais e.** but also

(g) **et e.** *(à peine)* if that, only just

(h) **e. que...** (+ *subjunctive)* although...

encourager [ãkuraʒe] *vt* to encourage **(à faire** to do) ■ **encourageant, -e** *adj* encouraging ■ **encouragement** *nm* encouragement

encrasser [ãkrase] **1** *vt* to clog up (with dirt) **2 s'encrasser** *vpr* to get clogged up

encre [ãkr] *nf* ink

encyclopédie [ãsiklɔpedi] *nf* encyclopedia

endetter [ãdete] **s'endetter** *vpr* to get

into debt ■ **endettement** *nm* debts

endimanché, -e [ãdimãʃe] *adj* in one's Sunday best

endive [ãdiv] *nf* chicory *inv*, endive

endoctriner [ãdɔktrine] *vt* to indoctrinate

endolori, -e [ãdɔlɔri] *adj* painful

endommager [ãdɔmaʒe] *vt* to damage

endormir* [ãdɔrmir] **1** *vt* (enfant) to put to sleep; (ennuyer) to send to sleep **2 s'endormir** *vpr* to fall asleep, to go to sleep ■ **endormi, -e** *adj* asleep, sleeping

endosser [ãdose] *vt* (vêtement) to put on; (chèque) to endorse

endroit [ãdrwa] *nm* (**a**) (lieu) place, spot; **par endroits** in places (**b**) (de tissu) right side; **à l'e.** (vêtement) the right way round

enduire* [ãdμir] *vt* to smear, to coat (**de** with) ■ **enduit** *nm* coating; (de mur) plaster

endurant, -e [ãdyrã, -ãt] *adj* hardy, tough ■ **endurance** *nf* stamina; **course d'e.** endurance race

endurcir [ãdyrsir] **1** *vt* **e. qn à** (douleur) to harden sb to **2 s'endurcir** *vpr* (moralement) to become hard; (physiquement) to toughen up

endurer [ãdyre] *vt* to endure, to bear

énergie [enɛrʒi] *nf* energy ■ **énergétique** *adj* **aliment é.** energy food; **ressources énergétiques** energy resources ■ **énergique** *adj* (personne) energetic; (mesure, ton) forceful

énerver [enɛrve] **1** *vt* **é. qn** (irriter) to get on sb's nerves; (rendre nerveux) to make sb nervous **2 s'énerver** *vpr* to get worked up ■ **énervé, -e** *adj* (agacé) irritated; (excité) on edge, agitated

enfance [ãfãs] *nf* childhood ■ **enfantillages** *nmpl* childish behaviour ■ **enfantin, -e** *adj* (voix, joie) childlike; (langage) childish; (simple) easy

enfant [ãfã] *nmf* child (*pl* children); **attendre un e.** to be expecting a baby; **e. unique** only child

enfer [ãfɛr] *nm* hell

enfermer [ãfɛrme] **1** *vt* (personne, chose) to shut up; **e. qn/qch à clef** to lock sb/sth up **2 s'enfermer** *vpr* **s'e. dans** (chambre) to shut oneself (up) in; **s'e. à clef** to lock oneself in

enfiler [ãfile] *vt* (aiguille) to thread; (perles) to string; *Fam* (vêtement) to slip on

enfin [ãfɛ̃] *adv* (à la fin) finally, at last; (en dernier lieu) lastly; (en somme) in a word; (de résignation) well; *Fam* **e. bref…** (en somme) in a word…; (mais) **e.!** for heaven's sake!

enflammer [ãflame] **1** *vt* to set fire to; (allumette) to light **2 s'enflammer** *vpr* to catch fire

enfler [ãfle] *vi* (membre) to swell (up) ■ **enflure** *nf* swelling

enfoncer [ãfõse] **1** *vt* (clou) to bang in; (porte) to smash in; **e. dans qch** (couteau, mains) to plunge into sth **2 s'enfoncer** *vpr* (s'enliser) to sink (dans into); (couteau) to go in; **s'e. dans** (pénétrer) to disappear into

enfouir* [ãfwir] *vt* to bury

enfourner [ãfurne] *vt* to put in the oven

enfreindre* [ãfrɛ̃dr] *vt* to infringe

enfuir* [ãfμir] **s'enfuir** *vpr* to run away (**de** from)

engager [ãgaʒe] **1** *vt* (discussion, combat) to start; (bijou) to pawn; (clef) to insert (**dans** into); **e. qn** (embaucher) to hire sb **2 s'engager** *vpr* (dans l'armée) to enlist; (prendre position) to commit oneself; (partie) to start; **s'e. à faire qch** to undertake to do sth; **s'e. dans** (voie) to enter; (affaire) to get involved in ■ **engagé, -e** *adj* (écrivain) committed ■ **engageant, -e** *adj* engaging ■ **engagement** *nm* (promesse) commitment; (de soldats) enlistment; (au football) kick-off; **prendre l'e. de faire qch** to undertake to do sth

engelure [ãʒlyr] *nf* chilblain

engendrer [ãʒãdre] *vt* (causer) to generate, to engender; (procréer) to father

engin [ɑ̃ʒɛ̃] *nm* (*machine*) machine; (*outil*) device; **e. explosif** explosive device; **e. spatial** spacecraft

englober [ɑ̃ɡlɔbe] *vt* to include

engloutir [ɑ̃ɡlutir] *vt* (*nourriture*) to wolf down; (*bateau, village*) to submerge

engorger [ɑ̃ɡɔrʒe] *vt* to block up, to clog

engouement [ɑ̃ɡumɑ̃] *nm* craze (**pour** for)

engouffrer [ɑ̃ɡufre] **s'engouffrer** *vpr* **s'e. dans** to rush into

engourdir [ɑ̃ɡurdir] **s'engourdir** *vpr* (*membre*) to go numb

engrais [ɑ̃ɡrɛ] *nm* fertilizer

engraisser [ɑ̃ɡrese] *vt* (*animal, personne*) to fatten up

engrenage [ɑ̃ɡrənaʒ] *nm Tech* gears; *Fig* chain; *Fig* **pris dans l'e.** caught in a trap

énigme [enigm] *nf* (*devinette*) riddle; (*mystère*) enigma ■ **énigmatique** *adj* enigmatic

enjamber [ɑ̃ʒɑ̃be] *vt* to step over; (*sujet: pont*) (*rivière*) to span ■ **enjambée** *nf* stride

enjeu, -x [ɑ̃ʒø] *nm* (*mise*) stake; *Fig* (*de pari, de guerre*) stakes

enjoliver [ɑ̃ʒɔlive] *vt* to embellish

enjoué, -e [ɑ̃ʒwe] *adj* playful

enlacer [ɑ̃lase] *vt* (*mêler*) to entwine; (*embrasser*) to clasp

enlaidir [ɑ̃ledir] **1** *vt* to make ugly **2** *vi* to grow ugly

enlevé, -e [ɑ̃lve] *adj* (*style, danse*) lively

enlever [ɑ̃l(ə)ve] **1** *vt* to remove; (*meubles*) to take away, to remove; (*vêtement, couvercle*) to take off, to remove; (*tapis*) to take up; (*rideau*) to take down; (*enfant*) to kidnap, to abduct; (*ordures*) to collect **2 s'enlever** *vpr* (*tache*) to come out; (*vernis*) to come off ■ **enlèvement** [-ɛvmɑ̃] *nm* (*d'enfant*) kidnapping, abduction; (*d'objet*) removal

enliser [ɑ̃lize] **s'enliser** *vpr* (*véhicule*) & *Fig* to get bogged down (**dans** in)

enneigé, -e [ɑ̃neʒe] *adj* snow-covered

ennemi, -e [enmi] **1** *nmf* enemy **2** *adj* (*personne*) hostile (**de** to)

ennui [ɑ̃nɥi] *nm* (*lassitude*) boredom; (*souci*) problem; **avoir des ennuis** (*soucis*) to be worried; (*problèmes*) to have problems

ennuyer [ɑ̃nɥije] **1** *vt* (*agacer*) to annoy; (*préoccuper*) to bother; (*lasser*) to bore **2 s'ennuyer** *vpr* to get bored ■ **ennuyé, -e** *adj* (*air*) bored ■ **ennuyeux, -euse** *adj* (*contrariant*) annoying; (*lassant*) boring

énoncer [enɔ̃se] *vt* to state

énorme [enɔrm] *adj* enormous, huge ■ **énormément** *adv* (*travailler, pleurer*) an awful lot; **je le regrette é.** I'm awfully sorry about it; **il n'a pas é. d'argent** he hasn't got a huge amount of money ■ **énormité** *nf* (*de demande, de crime, de somme*) enormity; (*faute*) glaring mistake

enquête [ɑ̃kɛt] *nf* (*de policiers, de journalistes*) investigation; (*judiciaire, administrative*) inquiry; (*sondage*) survey ■ **enquêter** *vi* (*policier, journaliste*) to investigate; **e. sur qch** to investigate sth

enraciner [ɑ̃rasine] **s'enraciner** *vpr* to take root; **enraciné dans** (*personne, souvenir*) rooted in

enrager [ɑ̃raʒe] *vi* to be furious (**de** faire about doing); **faire e. qn** to get on sb's nerves ■ **enragé, -e** *adj* (*chien*) rabid

enrayer [ɑ̃reje] **1** *vt* (*maladie*) to check **2 s'enrayer** *vpr* (*fusil*) to jam

enregistrer [ɑ̃r(ə)ʒistre] *vt* (*par écrit, sur bande*) to record; (*afficher*) to register; **faire e. ses bagages** (*à l'aéroport*) to check in, to check one's baggage in ■ **enregistrement** [-əmɑ̃] *nm* (*sur bande*) recording; **l'e. des bagages** (*à l'aéroport*) (*baggage*) check-in; **se présenter à l'e.** to check in

enrhumer [ɑ̃ryme] **s'enrhumer** *vpr* to catch a cold; **être enrhumé** to have a cold

enrichir [ɑ̃riʃir] **1** vt to enrich (**de** with) **2 s'enrichir** upr (personne) to get rich

enrober [ɑ̃rɔbe] vt to coat (**de** in)

enrouer [ɑ̃rwe] **s'enrouer** upr to get hoarse

enrouler [ɑ̃rule] **1** vt (fil) to wind **2 s'enrouler** upr **s'e. dans qch** (couvertures) to wrap oneself up in sth; **s'e. sur** ou **autour de qch** to wind round sth

ensabler [ɑ̃sable] **s'ensabler** upr (port) to silt up

ensanglanté, -e [ɑ̃sɑ̃glɑ̃te] adj blood-stained

enseignant, -e [ɑ̃sɛɲɑ̃, -ɑ̃t] **1** nmf teacher **2** adj **corps e.** teaching profession

enseigne [ɑ̃sɛɲ] nf (de magasin) sign; **e. lumineuse** neon sign **2** nm **e. de vaisseau** Br lieutenant, Am ensign

enseigner [ɑ̃seɲe] **1** vt to teach; **ens. qch à qn** to teach sb sth **2** vi to teach ■ **enseignement** [-ɛɲmɑ̃] nm education; (action, métier) teaching; **e. par correspondance** distance learning; **e. privé** private education; **e. public** Br state orAm public education

ensemble [ɑ̃sɑ̃bl] **1** adv together; **aller (bien) e.** (couleurs) to go (well) together; (personnes) to be well-matched **2** nm (d'objets) group, set; Math set; (vêtement) outfit; (harmonie) unity; **l'e. du personnel** (totalité) the whole (of the) staff; **l'e. des enseignants** all (of) the teachers; **dans l'e.** on the whole

ensevelir [ɑ̃səvlir] vt to bury

ensoleillé, -e [ɑ̃sɔleje] adj (endroit, journée) sunny

ensommeillé, -e [ɑ̃sɔmeje] adj sleepy

ensorceler [ɑ̃sɔrsəle] vt (envoûter, séduire) to bewitch

ensuite [ɑ̃sɥit] adv (puis) next, then; (plus tard) afterwards

ensuivre* [ɑ̃sɥivr] **s'ensuivre** v impersonnel **il s'ensuit que...** it follows that...

entailler [ɑ̃taje] vt (fendre) to notch;

(blesser) to gash, to slash

entamer [ɑ̃tame] vt (pain) to cut into; (bouteille, boîte) to open; (négociations) to enter into

entartrer [ɑ̃tartre] vt, **s'entartrer** upr (chaudière) Br to fur up, Am to scale

entasser [ɑ̃tase] vt, **s'entasser** upr (objets) to pile up, to heap up

entendre [ɑ̃tɑ̃dr] **1** vt to hear; (comprendre) to understand; **e. parler de qn/qch** to hear of sb/sth; **e. dire que...** to hear (it said) that...
2 s'entendre upr (être entendu) to be heard; (être compris) to be understood; **s'e.** (être d'accord) to agree (**sur** on); (bien) **s'e. avec qn** to get along or Br on with sb

entendu, -e [ɑ̃tɑ̃dy] adj (convenu) agreed; (sourire, air) knowing; **e.!** all right!; **bien e.** of course

entente [ɑ̃tɑ̃t] nf (accord) agreement, understanding; **(bonne) e.** (amitié) harmony

entériner [ɑ̃terine] vt to ratify

enterrer [ɑ̃tere] vt (défunt) to bury; Fig (projet) to scrap ■ **enterrement** [-ɛrmɑ̃] nm (ensevelissement) burial; (funérailles) funeral

en-tête [ɑ̃tɛt] (pl **en-têtes**) nm (de papier) heading; **papier à e.** headed paper, letterhead

entêter [ɑ̃tete] **s'entêter** upr to persist (**à faire** in doing) ■ **entêté, -e** adj stubborn

enthousiasme [ɑ̃tuzjasm] nm enthusiasm ■ **enthousiaste** adj enthusiastic

enticher [ɑ̃tiʃe] **s'enticher** upr **s'e. de qn/qch** to become infatuated with sb/sth

entier, -ère [ɑ̃tje, -ɛr] **1** adj (total) whole, entire; (intact) intact; (absolu) absolute, complete; (caractère) uncompromising; **le pays tout e.** the whole or entire country **2** nm **en e.** in its entirety, completely

entonner [ɑ̃tɔne] vt (air) to start singing

entonnoir [ɑ̃tɔnwar] nm funnel

entorse [ātɔrs] *nf Méd* sprain; **se faire une e. à la cheville** to sprain one's ankle

entortiller [ātɔrtije] **1** *vt* to wrap (**dans** in) **2 s'entortiller** *upr (lierre)* to coil (**autour de** round)

entourage [āturaʒ] *nm (proches)* circle of family and friends

entourer [āture] **1** *vt* to surround (**de** with); *(envelopper)* to wrap (**de** in); **entouré de** surrounded by **2 s'entourer** *upr* **s'e. de** to surround oneself with

entracte [ātrakt] *nm Br* interval, *Am* intermission

entraide [ātrɛd] *nf* mutual aid ■ **s'entraider** *upr* to help each other

entraînant, -e [ātrɛnā, -āt] *adj (musique)* lively

entraîner [ātrene] **1** *vt* (**a**) *(charrier)* to carry away; *(causer)* to bring about; *(dépenses)* to entail; **e. qn** *(emmener)* to lead sb away; *(de force)* to drag sb away; *(attirer)* to lure sb; **se laisser e.** to allow oneself to be led astray (**b**) *(athlète, cheval)* to train (**à** for) **2 s'entraîner** *upr* to train oneself (**à faire qch** to do sth); *Sport* to train ■ **entraînement** [-ɛnmā] *nm Sport* training; *(élan)* impulse ■ **entraîneur** [-ɛnœr] *nm (d'athlète)* coach; *(de cheval)* trainer

entraver [ātrave] *vt* to hinder, to hamper

entre [ātr] *prép* between; *(parmi)* among(st); **l'un d'e. vous** one of you; **se dévorer e. eux** *(réciprocité)* to devour each other

entrebâiller [ātrəbaje] *vt (porte)* to open slightly

entrecôte [ātrəkot] *nf* rib steak

entrecouper [ātrəkupe] *vt (entremêler)* to punctuate (**de** with)

entrée [ātre] *nf (action)* entry, entrance; *(porte)* entrance; *(vestibule)* entrance hall, entry; *(accès)* admission, entry (**de** to); *Ordinat* input; *(plat)* starter; **faire son e.** to make one's entrance; '**e. interdite**' 'no entry', 'no admittance'; '**e. libre**'

'admission free'; **e. de service** service or *Br* tradesmen's entrance; **e. des artistes** stage door

entrelacer [ātrəlase] *vt*, **s'entrelacer** *upr* to intertwine

entremêler [ātrəmele] *vt*, **s'entremêler** *upr* to intermingle

entremets [ātrəmɛ] *nm (plat)* dessert, *Br* sweet

entreposer [ātrəpoze] *vt* to store ■ **entrepôt** *nm* warehouse

entreprendre* [ātrəprādr] *vt (travail, voyage)* to undertake; **e. de faire qch** to undertake to do sth ■ **entreprenant, -e** [-ānā, -āt] *adj (dynamique)* enterprising; *(galant)* forward

entrepreneur [ātrəprənœr] *nm (en bâtiment)* contractor; *(chef d'entreprise)* entrepreneur

entreprise [ātrəpriz] *nf (firme)* company, firm

entrer [ātre] **1** *vi (aux être) (aller)* to go in, to enter; *(venir)* to come in, to enter; **e. dans** to go into; *(pièce)* to come/go into, to enter; **e. à l'université** to start university; **e. dans les détails** to go into detail; **entrez!** come in!

2 *vt (aux* **avoir***) Ordinat* **e. des données** to enter data (**dans** into)

entresol [ātrəsɔl] *nm* mezzanine floor

entre-temps [ātrətā] *adv* meanwhile

entretenir* [ātrətnir] **1** *vt (voiture, maison, famille)* to maintain; *(relations)* to keep; **e. qn de qch** to talk to sb about sth **2 s'entretenir** *upr* **s'e. de qch** to talk about sth *(avec* with) ■ **entretenu, -e** *adj* **bien/mal e.** *(maison)* well-kept/badly kept

entretien [ātrətjɛ̃] *nm (de route, de maison)* maintenance, upkeep; *(dialogue)* conversation; *(entrevue)* interview

entrevoir* [ātrəvwar] *vt (rapidement)* to catch a glimpse of; *(pressentir)* to foresee

entrevue [ātrəvy] *nf* interview

entrouvrir* [ātruvrir] *vt*, **s'entrouvrir** *upr* to half-open ■ **entrouvert, -e** *adj (porte, fenêtre)* half-open

énumérer [enymere] *vt* to list ■ **énumération** *nf* listing

envahir [ɑ̃vair] *vt (pays)* to invade; *(marché)* to flood; **e. qn** *(doute, peur)* to overcome sb ■ **envahissant, -e** *adj (personne)* intrusive ■ **envahisseur** *nm* invader

enveloppant, -e [ɑ̃vlɔpɑ̃, -ɑ̃t] *adj (séduisant)* captivating

enveloppe [ɑ̃vlɔp] *nf (pour lettre)* envelope

envelopper [ɑ̃vlɔpe] **1** *vt* to wrap (up) *(dans* in) **2 s'envelopper** *upr* to wrap oneself (up) *(dans* in)

envenimer [ɑ̃vnime] **s'envenimer** *upr (plaie)* to turn septic; *Fig* to become acrimonious

envergure [ɑ̃vergyr] *nf (d'avion, d'oiseau)* wingspan; *(de personne)* calibre; *(ampleur)* scope

envers [ɑ̃ver] **1** *prép Br* towards, *Am* toward(s), to; *(de tissu)* wrong side; **à l'e.** *(chaussette)* inside out; *(pantalon)* back to front; *(la tête en bas)* upside down

envie [ɑ̃vi] *nf (jalousie)* envy; *(désir)* desire; **avoir e. de qch** to want sth; **avoir e. de faire qch** to feel like doing sth ■ **envier** *vt* to envy *(qch à qn* sb sth) ■ **envieux, -euse** *adj* envious

environ [ɑ̃virɔ̃] *adv (à peu près)* about ■ **environs** *nmpl* outskirts, surroundings; **aux e. de qch** around sth, in the vicinity of sth

environnant, -e [ɑ̃virɔnɑ̃, -ɑ̃t] *adj* surrounding

environnement [ɑ̃virɔnmɑ̃] *nm* environment

envisager [ɑ̃vizaʒe] *vt (considérer)* to consider; *(projeter) Br* to envisage, *Am* to envision; **e. de faire qch** to consider doing sth

envoi [ɑ̃vwa] *nm (action)* sending; *(paquet)* package; *(marchandises)* consignment

envoler [ɑ̃vɔle] **s'envoler** *upr (oiseau)* to fly away; *(avion)* to take off; *(chapeau, papier)* to blow away; *Fig (espoir)* to vanish

envoûter [ɑ̃vute] *vt* to bewitch

envoyer* [ɑ̃vwaje] *vt* to send; *(lancer)* to throw; **e. chercher qn** to send for sb ■ **envoyé, -e** *nmf* envoy; **e. spécial** *(reporter)* special correspondent ■ **envoyeur** *nm* sender; **retour à l'e.** 'return to sender'

épais, -aisse [epe, -es] *adj* thick ■ **épaisseur** *nf* thickness; **avoir 1 mètre d'é.** to be 1 metre thick ■ **épaissir** [epesir] **1** *vt* to thicken **2** *vi,* **s'épaissir** *upr* to thicken; *(grossir)* to fill out; **le mystère s'épaissit** the mystery is deepening

épanouir [epanwir] **s'épanouir** *upr (fleur)* to bloom; *Fig (personne)* to blossom; *(visage)* to beam ■ **épanoui, -e** *adj (fleur, personne)* in full bloom; *(visage)* beaming ■ **épanouissement** *nm (de fleur)* full bloom; *(de personne)* blossoming

épargne [eparɲ] *nf (action, vertu)* saving; *(sommes)* savings ■ **épargnant, -e** *nmf* saver ■ **épargner** *vt (argent, provisions)* to save; *(ennemi)* to spare; **e. qch à qn** *(ennuis, chagrin)* to spare sb sth

éparpiller [eparpije] *vt,* **s'éparpiller** *upr* to scatter; *(efforts)* to dissipate

épaule [epol] *nf* shoulder ■ **épauler 1** *vt (fusil)* to raise (to one's shoulder); **e. qn** *(aider)* to back sb up **2** *vi* to take aim ■ **épaulette** *nf (de veste)* shoulder pad

épave [epav] *nf (bateau, personne)* wreck

épée [epe] *nf* sword

épeler [eple] *vt* to spell

éperon [eprɔ̃] *nm (de cavalier, de coq)* spur

épi [epi] *nm (de blé)* ear; *(de cheveux)* tuft of hair

épice [epis] *nf* spice ■ **épicé, -e** *adj (plat, récit)* spicy ■ **épicer** *vt* to spice

épicier, -ère [episje, -er] *nmf* grocer ■ **épicerie** *nf (magasin) Br* grocer's (shop), *Am* grocery (store); **é. fine** delicatessen

épidémie [epidemi] *nf* epidemic

épier [epje] *vt (observer)* to watch closely; *(occasion)* to watch out for; **é. qn** to spy on sb

épiler [epile] **s'épiler** *upr* to remove unwanted hair; **s'é. les jambes à la cire** to wax one's legs

épilogue [epilɔg] *nm* epilogue

épinards [epinar] *nmpl* spinach

épine [epin] *nf (de plante)* thorn; *(d'animal)* spine, prickle ▪ **épineux, -euse** *adj (tige, question)* thorny; *(poisson)* spiny

épingle [epɛ̃gl] *nf* pin; **é. à nourrice** safety pin; **é. à linge** *Br* clothes peg, *Am* clothes pin ▪ **épingler** *vt* to pin

Épiphanie [epifani] *nf* l'É. Epiphany

épique [epik] *adj* epic

épiscopal, -e, -aux, -ales [episkɔpal, -o] *adj* episcopal

épisode [epizɔd] *nm* episode ▪ **épisodique** *adj (intermittent)* occasional

épitaphe [epitaf] *nf* epitaph

éplucher [eplyʃe] *vt (carotte, pomme)* to peel ▪ **épluchure** *nf* peeling

éponge [epɔ̃ʒ] *nf* sponge; *Fig* **jeter l'é.** to throw in the towel ▪ **éponger 1** *vt (liquide)* to mop up; *(dette)* to absorb **2 s'éponger** *upr* **s'é. le front** to mop one's brow

époque [epɔk] *nf (date)* time, period; *(historique)* age; **meubles d'é.** period furniture; **à l'é.** at the *or* that time

épouse [epuz] *nf* wife

épouser [epuze] *vt* to marry

épousseter [epuste] *vt* to dust

épouvantable [epuvɑ̃tabl] *adj* appalling

épouvantail [epuvɑ̃taj] *nm (de jardin)* scarecrow

épouvante [epuvɑ̃t] *nf* terror ▪ **épouvanter** *vt* to terrify

époux [epu] *nm* husband; **les é.** the husband and wife

éprendre* [eprɑ̃dr] **s'éprendre** *upr* **s'é. de qn** to fall in love with sb

épreuve [eprœv] *nf (essai, examen)* test; *(sportive)* event; *(malheur)* ordeal, trial; *(photo)* print; **mettre qn à l'é.** to put sb to the test; **à toute é.**

(patience) unfailing; *(nerfs)* rock-solid; **à l'é. du feu** fireproof

éprouver [epruve] *vt (méthode, personne)* to test; *(sentiment)* to feel; *(difficultés)* to meet with ▪ **éprouvant, -e** *adj (pénible)* trying

éprouvette [epruvɛt] *nf* test tube

EPS [əpeɛs] *(abrév* **éducation physique et sportive)** *nf* PE

épuiser [epɥize] **1** *vt (personne, provisions, sujet)* to exhaust **2 s'épuiser** *upr (réserves, patience)* to run out; **s'é. à faire qch** to exhaust oneself doing sth ▪ **épuisant, -e** *adj* exhausting ▪ **épuisé, -e** *adj* exhausted; *(marchandise)* sold out; *(édition)* out of print

épuisette [epɥizɛt] *nf* landing net

épurer [epyre] *vt (eau, gaz)* to purify; *(minerai)* to refine ▪ **épuration** *nf* purification; *(de minerai)* refining

équateur [ekwatœr] *nm* equator; **sous l'é.** at the equator

équation [ekwasjɔ̃] *nf Math* equation

équerre [eker] *nf* **é. (à dessin)** *Br* set square, *Am* triangle

équestre [ekɛstr] *adj (statue, sports)* equestrian

équilibre [ekilibr] *nm* balance; **garder/perdre l'é.** to keep/lose one's balance

équilibrer [ekilibre] *vt (charge, composition, budget)* to balance

équinoxe [ekinɔks] *nm* equinox

équipage [ekipaʒ] *nm (de navire, d'avion)* crew

équipe [ekip] *nf* team; *(d'ouvriers)* gang; **faire é. avec qn** to team up with sb; **é. de nuit** night shift; **é. de secours** rescue team ▪ **équipier, -ère** *nmf* team member

équiper [ekipe] **1** *vt* to equip (**de** with) **2 s'équiper** *upr* to equip oneself (**de** with) ▪ **équipement** *nm* equipment

équitable [ekitabl] *adj* fair, equitable

équitation [ekitasjɔ̃] *nf Br* (horse) riding, *Am* (horseback) riding; **faire de l'é.** to go riding

équivalent, -e [ekivalɑ̃, -ɑ̃t] *adj & nm*

equivalent ■ **équivalence** nf equivalence ■ **équivaloir*** vi **é. à qch** to be equivalent to sth

équivoque [ekivɔk] **1** adj (ambigu) equivocal; (douteux) dubious **2** nf ambiguity

érable [erabl] nm (arbre, bois) maple

érafler [erafle] vt to graze, to scratch ■ **éraflure** nf graze, scratch

ère [ɛr] nf era; **avant notre è.** BC; **en l'an 800 de notre è.** in the year 800 AD

éreinter [erɛ̃te] **1** vt (fatiguer) to exhaust **2 s'éreinter** upr **s'é. à faire qch** to wear oneself out doing sth

ériger [eriʒe] **1** vt to erect **2 s'ériger** upr **s'é. en qch** to set oneself up as sth

érosion [erozjɔ̃] nf erosion ■ **éroder** vt to erode

errer [ere] vi to wander ■ **errant** adj m **chien/chat a.** stray dog/cat

erreur [erœr] nf (faute) mistake, error; **par e.** by mistake; **e. judiciaire** miscarriage of justice

érudit, -e [erydi, -it] **1** adj scholarly, erudite **2** nmf scholar ■ **érudition** nf scholarship, erudition

éruption [erypsjɔ̃] nf (de volcan) eruption; (de boutons) rash

es [ɛ] voir **être**

ès [ɛs] prép of; **licencié ès lettres** ≃ BA; **docteur ès lettres** ≃ PhD

escabeau, -x [ɛskabo] nm (marchepied) stepladder, Br (pair of) steps; (tabouret) stool

escadrille [ɛskadrij] nf Aviat (unité) flight

escadron [ɛskadrɔ̃] nm squadron

escalade [ɛskalad] nf climbing; (de prix, de violence) escalation ■ **escalader** vt to climb, to scale

escale [ɛskal] nf Aviat stopover; Naut (lieu) port of call; **faire e. à** (avion) to stop (over) at; (navire) to put in at; **vol sans e.** non-stop flight

escalier [ɛskalje] nm (marches) stairs; (cage) staircase; **l'é., les escaliers** the stairs; **e. mécanique** ou **roulant** escalator; **e. de secours** fire escape

escalope [ɛskalɔp] nf escalope

escamoter [ɛskamɔte] vt (faire disparaître) to make vanish; (esquiver) to dodge

escapade [ɛskapad] nf jaunt

escargot [ɛskargo] nm snail

escarpé, -e [ɛskarpe] adj steep ■ **escarpement** [-əmɑ̃] nm (côte) steep slope

escarpin [ɛskarpɛ̃] nm (soulier) pump, Br court shoe

esclave [ɛsklav] nmf slave ■ **esclavage** nm slavery

escompte [ɛskɔ̃t] nm discount; **taux d'e.** bank discount rate ■ **escompter** vt (espérer) to anticipate (**faire** doing), to expect (**faire** to do)

escorte [ɛskɔrt] nf escort ■ **escorter** vt to escort

escrime [ɛskrim] nf fencing; **faire de l'e.** to fence ■ **escrimeur, -euse** nmf fencer

escrimer [ɛskrime] **s'escrimer** upr **s'é. à faire qch** to struggle to do sth

escroc [ɛskro] nm crook, swindler ■ **escroquer** vt **e. qn** to swindle sb; **e. qch à qn** to swindle sb out of sth ■ **escroquerie** nf (action) swindling; (résultat) swindle

espace [ɛspas] nm space; **e. aérien** air space; **e. vert** garden, park ■ **espacer** [ɛspase] **1** vt to space out; **espacés d'un mètre** one metre apart **2 s'espacer** upr (maisons, visites) to become less frequent

espadrille [ɛspadrij] nf = rope-soled sandal

Espagne [ɛspaɲ] nf **l'E.** Spain ■ **espagnol, -e 1** adj Spanish **2** nmf **E., Espagnole** Spaniard **3** nm (langue) Spanish

espèce [ɛspɛs] nf (race) species; (genre) kind, sort ■ **espèces** nfpl (argent) cash; **en e.** in cash

espérance [ɛsperɑ̃s] nf hope; **e. de vie** life expectancy

espérer [ɛspere] **1** vt to hope for; **e. que...** to hope that...; **e. faire qch** to hope to do sth **2** vi to hope; **j'espère (bien)!** I hope so!

espiègle [ɛspjɛgl] *adj* mischievous

espion, -onne [ɛspjɔ̃, -ɔn] *nmf* spy
■ **espionnage** *nm* spying, espionage
■ **espionner 1** *vt* to spy on **2** *vi* to spy

espoir [ɛspwar] *nm* hope; **avoir l'e. de faire qch** to have hopes of doing sth

esprit [ɛspri] *nm* (*attitude, fantôme*) spirit; (*intellect*) mind; (*humour*) wit; **venir à l'e. de qn** to cross sb's mind; **avoir de l'e.** to be witty; **avoir l'e. large/étroit** to be broad-/narrow-minded

esquimau, -aude, -aux, -audes [ɛskimo, -od] **1** *adj* Eskimo, *Am* Inuit **2** *nmf* **E., Esquimaude** Eskimo, *Am* Inuit **3** *nm* **Esquimau®** (*glace*) *Br* ≃ choc-ice (*on a stick*), *Am* ≃ ice-cream bar

esquisse [ɛskis] *nf* (*croquis, plan*) sketch ■ **esquisser** *vt* to sketch; **e. un geste** to make a (slight) gesture

esquiver [ɛskive] **1** *vt* (*coup, problème*) to dodge **2 s'esquiver** *vpr* to slip away

essai [ɛsɛ] *nm* (*test*) test, trial; (*tentative, au rugby*) try; (*ouvrage*) essay; **à l'e.** (*objet*) on a trial basis

essaim [ɛsɛ̃] *nm* swarm

essayer [eseje] *vt* to try (**de faire** to do); (*vêtement*) to try on; (*méthode*) to try out ■ **essayage** [-ɛjaʒ] *nm* (*de vêtement*) fitting

essence [esɑ̃s] *nf* (*carburant*) *Br* petrol, *Am* gas; (*extrait*) *& Phil* essence; **e. sans plomb** unleaded; **e. ordinaire** *Br* two-star petrol, *Am* regular gas

essentiel, -elle [esɑ̃sjɛl] **1** *adj* essen-tial (**à/pour** for) **2** *nm* **l'e.** (*le plus im-portant*) the main thing; (*le minimum*) the essentials

essor [esɔr] *nm* (*d'oiseau*) flight; (*de pays, d'entreprise*) rapid growth; **en plein e.** booming; **prendre son e.** to take off

essorer [esɔre] *vt* (*dans une essoreuse*) to spin-dry; (*dans une machine à laver*) to spin

essouffler [esufle] **1** *vt* to make out of breath **2 s'essouffler** *vpr* to get out of breath

essuyer [esɥije] **1** *vt* (*objet, surface*) to wipe; (*liquide*) to wipe up; (*larmes*) to wipe away; (*défaite*) to suffer; (*refus*) to meet with; **e. la vaisselle** to dry the dishes **2 s'essuyer** *vpr* to wipe one-self; **s'e. les yeux** to wipe one's eyes ■ **essuie-glace** (*pl* **essuie-glaces**) *nm Br* windscreen wiper, *Am* windshield wiper

est¹ [ɛ] *voir* **être**

est² [ɛst] **1** *nm* east; **à l'e.** in the east; (*direction*) (to the) east (**de** of); **d'e.** (*vent*) east(erly); **de l'e.** eastern **2** *adj inv* (*côte*) east(ern)

estampe [ɛstɑ̃p] *nf* print

estampille [ɛstɑ̃pij] *nf* (*de produit*) mark; (*de document*) stamp

esthéticienne [ɛstetisjɛn] *nf* beauti-cian

estime [ɛstim] *nf* esteem, regard

estimer [ɛstime] **1** *vt* (*tableau*) to value (**à** at); (*prix, distance, poids*) to esti-mate; (*dommages, besoins*) to assess; (*juger*) to consider (**que** that); **e. qn** to esteem sb
2 s'estimer *vpr* **s'e. heureux** to con-sider oneself happy ■ **estimable** *adj* respectable ■ **estimation** *nf* (*de mobi-lier*) valuation; (*de prix, de distance, de poids*) estimation; (*de dommages, de besoins*) assessment

estival, -e, -aux, -ales [ɛstival, -o] *adj* **température estivale** summer temperature ■ **estivant, -e** *nmf Br* holidaymaker, *Am* vacationer

estomac [ɛstɔma] *nm* stomach

estomper [ɛstɔ̃pe] **1** *vt* (*rendre flou*) to blur **2 s'estomper** *vpr* to become blurred

estrade [ɛstrad] *nf* platform

estragon [ɛstragɔ̃] *nm* tarragon

esturgeon [ɛstyrʒɔ̃] *nm* sturgeon

et [e] *conj* and; **vingt et un** twenty-one; **et moi?** what about me?

établi [etabli] *nm* workbench

établir [etablir] **1** *vt* (*paix, relations, principe*) to establish; (*liste*) to draw up; (*record*) to set; (*démontrer*) to es-tablish, to prove **2 s'établir** *vpr* (*pour habiter*) to settle; (*pour exercer un* *métier)* to set up in business ∎ **établissement** *nm (de paix, de relations, de principe)* establishment; *(entreprise)* business, firm; **é. scolaire** school

étage [etaʒ] *nm (d'immeuble)* floor, *Br* storey, *Am* story; *(de fusée)* stage; **à l'é.** upstairs; **au premier é.** on the *Br* first *or Am* second floor; **maison à deux étages** *Br* two-storeyed *or Am* two-storied house

étagère [etaʒɛr] *nf* shelf; *(meuble)* shelving unit

étain [etɛ̃] *nm (métal)* tin; *(de gobelet)* pewter

étais, était [etɛ] *voir* **être**

étal [etal] *(pl* **étals)** *nm (au marché)* stall

étalage [etalaʒ] *nm* display; *(vitrine)* display window

étaler [etale] **1** *vt (disposer)* to lay out; *(en vitrine)* to display; *(beurre)* to spread; *(vacances, paiements)* to stagger **2 s'étaler** *upr* **s'é. sur** *(congés, paiements)* to be spread over ∎ **étalement** *nm (de vacances, de paiements)* staggering

étanche [etɑ̃ʃ] *adj* watertight; *(montre)* waterproof

étancher [etɑ̃ʃe] *vt (sang)* to stop the flow of; *(soif)* to quench

étang [etɑ̃] *nm* pond

étant [etɑ̃] *p près de* **être**

étape [etap] *nf (de voyage)* stage; *(lieu)* stop(over); **faire é. à** to stop off *or* over at; **par étapes** in stages

état [eta] *nm* (**a**) *(condition, manière d'être)* state; **à l'é. neuf** as new; **en bon é.** in good condition; **é. d'esprit** state *or* frame of mind; **é. des lieux** inventory of fixtures; **é. civil** register office (**b**) *(autorité centrale)* **É.** *(nation)* State

état-major [etamaʒɔr] *(pl* **états-majors)** *nm Mil* (general) staff; *(de parti)* senior staff

États-Unis [etazyni] *nmpl* **les É.** the United States; **les É. d'Amérique** the United States of America

étau, -x [eto] *nm (instrument) Br* vice, *Am* vise

été¹ [ete] *nm* summer

été² [ete] *pp de* **être**

éteindre* [etɛ̃dr] **1** *vt (feu, cigarette)* to put out, to extinguish; *(lampe)* to switch off; *(gaz)* to turn off **2** *vi* to switch off **3 s'éteindre** *upr (feu)* to go out; *(personne)* to pass away ∎ **éteint, -e** *adj (feu, bougie)* out; *(lampe, lumière)* off; *(volcan)* extinct

étendre [etɑ̃dr] **1** *vt (linge)* to hang out; *(agrandir)* to extend; **é. les bras** to stretch out one's arm; **é. qn** to stretch sb out **2 s'étendre** *upr (personne)* to lie down; *(plaine)* to stretch; *(feu)* to spread; **s'é. sur qch** *(sujet)* to dwell on sth

étendu, -e¹ [etɑ̃dy] *adj (forêt, vocabulaire)* extensive; *(personne)* lying

étendue² [etɑ̃dy] *nf (importance)* extent; *(surface)* area

éternel, -elle [etɛrnɛl] *adj* eternal ∎ **s'éterniser** *upr (débat)* to drag on endlessly; *Fam (visiteur)* to stay for ever ∎ **éternité** *nf* eternity

éternuer [etɛrnɥe] *vi* to sneeze

êtes [et] *voir* **être**

Éthiopie [etjɔpi] *nf* **l'É.** Ethiopia ∎ **éthiopien, -enne 1** *adj* Ethiopian **2** *nmf* **É., Éthiopienne** Ethiopian

ethnie [etni] *nf* ethnic group ∎ **ethnique** *adj* ethnic

étinceler [etɛ̃sle] *vi* to sparkle ∎ **étincelle** *nf* spark

étiqueter [etikte] *vt* to label ∎ **étiquette** *nf (marque)* label; *(protocole)* (diplomatic *or* court) etiquette

étirer [etire] **1** *vt* to stretch **2 s'étirer** *upr* to stretch (oneself)

étoffe [etɔf] *nf* material, fabric

étoffer [etɔfe] **1** *vt* to fill out; *(texte)* to make more meaty **2 s'étoffer** *upr (personne)* to fill out

étoile [etwal] *nf* star; **à la belle é.** in the open; **é. de mer** starfish; **é. filante** shooting star

étonner [etɔne] **1** *vt* to surprise **2 s'étonner** *upr* to be surprised (**de qch** at sth; **que** + *subjunctive* that) ∎ **étonnant, -e** *adj (ahurissant)* surprising;

(remarquable) amazing ■ **étonnement** *nm* surprise

étouffant, -e [etufã, -ãt] *adj (air)* stifling

étouffer [etufe] **1** *vt (tuer)* to suffocate; *Fig (révolte)* to stifle; *Fig (scandale)* to hush up **2** *vi* to suffocate **3** **s'étouffer** *upr (en mangeant)* to choke (avec on); *(mourir)* to suffocate

étourdi, -e [eturdi] **1** *adj* scatterbrained **2** *nmf* scatterbrain ■ **étourderie** *nf* absent-mindedness; **une é.** a thoughtless blunder

étourdissant, -e [eturdisã, -ãt] *adj (bruit)* deafening; *(beauté)* stunning

étourdissement [eturdismã] *nm (malaise)* dizzy spell

étrange [etrãʒ] *adj* strange, odd ■ **étranger, -ère 1** *adj (d'un autre pays)* foreign; *(non familier)* strange (à to) **2** *nmf (d'un autre pays)* foreigner; *(inconnu)* stranger; **à l'é.** abroad

étrangler [etrãgle] **1** *vt* **é. qn** *(tuer)* to strangle sb **2** **s'étrangler** *upr (de colère, en mangeant)* to choke ■ **étranglé, -e** *adj (voix)* choking

ÊTRE* [etr] **1** *vi* to be; **il est professeur** he's a teacher; **est-ce qu'elle vient?** is she coming?; **il vient, n'est-ce pas?** he's coming, isn't he?; **est-ce qu'il aime le thé?** does he like tea?; **nous sommes dix** there are ten of us; **nous sommes le dix** today is the tenth; **il a été à Paris** *(il y est allé)* he has been to Paris; **elle est de Paris** she's from Paris; **il est cinq heures** it's five (o'clock); **c'est à lire pour demain** this has to be read for tomorrow; **c'est à lui** it's his

2 *v aux (avec 'venir', 'partir' etc)* to have/to be; **elle est arrivée** she has arrived; **elle est née en 1999** she was born in 1999

3 *nm (personne)* being; **les êtres chers** the loved ones; **ê. humain** human being; **ê. vivant** living being

étreindre* [etrɛ̃dr] *vt* to grip; *(avec amour)* to embrace

étrennes [etren] *nfpl* New Year gift; *(gratification)* ≃ Christmas tip *or Br* box

étrier [etrije] *nm* stirrup

étroit, -e [etrwa, -at] *adj* narrow; *(vêtement)* tight; *(lien, collaboration)* close; **être à l'é.** to be cramped

étude [etyd] *nf (action, ouvrage)* study; *(de notaire)* office; *Scol (pièce)* study room; *(période)* study period; **à l'é.** *(projet)* under consideration; **faire des études de français** to study French; **faire une é. de marché** to do market research

étudiant, -e [etydjã, -ãt] **1** *nmf* student **2** *adj (vie)* student

étudier [etydje] *vti* to study

étui [etɥi] *nm (à lunettes, à cigarettes)* case; *(de revolver)* holster

eu, eue [y] *pp de* **avoir**

eurent [yr] *voir* **avoir**

euro [øro] *nm (monnaie)* Euro

euro- [øro] *préf* Euro-

eurodéputé [ørodepyte] *nm* Euro MP

Europe [ørɔp] *nf* **l'E.** Europe; **l'E. verte** European Union agriculture ■ **européen, -enne 1** *adj* European **2** *nmf* E., Européenne European

eut [y] *voir* **avoir**

euthanasie [øtanazi] *nf* euthanasia

eux [ø] *pron personnel (sujet)* they; *(complément)* them; *(réfléchi, emphase)* themselves ■ **eux-mêmes** *pron* themselves

évacuer [evakɥe] *vt (bâtiment)* to evacuate; *(liquide)* to drain off ■ **évacuation** *nf* evacuation

évader [evade] **s'évader** *upr* to escape (de from) ■ **évadé, -e** *nmf* escaped prisoner

évaluer [evalɥe] *vt (fortune)* to estimate; *(bien)* to value ■ **évaluation** *nf* estimation; *(de bien)* valuation

évangile [evãʒil] *nm* gospel; **l'É.** the Gospel

évanouir [evanwir] **s'évanouir** *upr (personne)* to faint; *Fig (espoir, crainte)* to vanish ■ **évanoui, -e** *adj* unconscious ■ **évanouissement** *nm (syncope)* fainting fit

évaporer [evapɔre] **s'évaporer** *vpr* to evaporate; *Fig (disparaître)* to vanish into thin air

évasé, -e [evaze] *adj (jupe)* flared

évasif, -ive [evazif, -iv] *adj* evasive

évasion [evazjɔ̃] *nf* escape (**de** from); *(de la réalité)* escapism; **é. fiscale** tax evasion

éveil [evɛj] *nm* awakening; **être en é.** to be alert

éveiller [eveje] **1** *vt (susciter)* to arouse **2 s'éveiller** *vpr* to awaken (**à** to) ■ **éveillé, -e** *adj* awake; *(vif)* alert

événement [evɛnmɑ̃] *nm* event

éventail [evɑ̃taj] *nm (instrument)* fan; *(choix)* range

éventuel, -elle [evɑ̃tɥɛl] *adj* possible ■ **éventualité** *nf* possibility ■ **éventuellement** *adv* possibly

évêque [evɛk] *nm* bishop

évertuer [evertɥe] **s'évertuer** *vpr* **s'é. à faire qch** to endeavour to do sth

éviction [eviksjɔ̃] *nf (de concurrent, de président)* ousting; *(de locataire)* eviction

évident, -e [evidɑ̃, -ɑ̃t] *adj* obvious (**que** that) ■ **évidemment** [-amɑ̃] *adv* obviously ■ **évidence** *nf* obviousness; **une é.** an obvious fact; **en é.** in a prominent position

évier [evje] *nm (kitchen)* sink

évincer [evɛ̃se] *vt (concurrent)* to oust (**de** from)

éviter [evite] *vt* to avoid (**de faire** doing); **é. qch à qn** to spare *or* save sb sth

évoluer [evɔlɥe] *vi (changer)* to develop; *(société, situation)* to evolve; *(se déplacer)* to move around ■ **évolué, -e** *adj (pays)* advanced; *(personne)* enlightened ■ **évolution** *nf (changement)* development; *Biol* evolution

évoquer [evɔke] *vt* to evoke

exact, -e [ɛgzakt] *adj (quantité, poids, nombre)* exact, precise; *(rapport, description)* exact, accurate; *(mot)* right, correct; *(ponctuel)* punctual ■ **exactement** [-amɑ̃] *adv* exactly ■ **exactitude** *nf (précision, fidélité)* exactness;

(justesse) correctness; *(ponctualité)* punctuality

ex æquo [ɛgzeko] **1** *adj inv Sport* **être classés e.** to tie, to be equally placed **2** *adv Sport* **être troisième e.** to tie for third place

exagérer [ɛgzaʒere] **1** *vt* to exaggerate **2** *vi (parler)* to exaggerate; *(agir)* to go too far ■ **exagération** *nf* exaggeration ■ **exagéré, -e** *adj* excessive

exalter [ɛgzalte] *vt (passionner)* to stir ■ **exaltant, -e** *adj* stirring ■ **exalté, -e** *adj (sentiment)* impassioned

examen [ɛgzamɛ̃] *nm* examination; **e. blanc** mock exam; **e. de la vue** eye test ■ **examinateur, -trice** *nmf* examiner ■ **examiner** *vt (considérer, regarder)* to examine

exaspérer [ɛgzaspere] *vt (personne)* to exasperate

exaucer [ɛgzose] *vt (désir)* to grant

excavation [ɛkskavasjɔ̃] *nf (trou, action)* excavation

excéder [ɛksede] *vt (dépasser)* to exceed; **é. qn** *(énerver)* to exasperate sb ■ **excédent** *nm* surplus, excess ■ **excédentaire** *adj* **poids e.** excess weight

excellent, -e [ɛksela, -ɑ̃t] *adj* excellent ■ **excellence** *nf* excellence ■ **exceller** *vi* to excel (**en** at)

excentrique [ɛksɑ̃trik] *adj & nmf* eccentric

excepté¹ [ɛksɛpte] *prép* except

excepté², -e *adj* except (for)

exception [ɛksɛpsjɔ̃] *nf* exception; **à l'e. de** except (for), with the exception of ■ **exceptionnel, -elle** *adj* exceptional

excès [ɛksɛ] *nm* excess; **e. de vitesse** speeding ■ **excessif, -ive** *adj* excessive

exciter [ɛksite] **1** *vt (faire naître)* to arouse; **e. qn** *(énerver)* to excite sb **2 s'exciter** *vpr (devenir nerveux)* to get excited ■ **excitant, -e** *nm* stimulant ■ **excitation** *nf (agitation)* excitement ■ **excité, -e** *adj* excited

exclamer [ɛksklame] **s'exclamer** *vpr* to

exclaim ■ **exclamation** nf exclamation

exclure* [ɛksklyr] vt (écarter) to exclude (de from); (chasser) to expel (de from) ■ **exclu, -e** adj (solution) out of the question; (avec une date) exclusive

exclusif, -ive [ɛksklyzif, -iv] adj (droit, modèle) exclusive ■ **exclusivité** nf Com exclusive rights; (dans la presse) scoop; **en e.** (film) having an exclusive showing (à at)

exclusion [ɛksklyzjɔ̃] nf exclusion; **à l'e. de** with the exception of

excursion [ɛkskyrsjɔ̃] nf trip, excursion; (de plusieurs jours) tour; **faire une e.** to go on a trip/tour

excuse [ɛkskyz] nf (prétexte) excuse; **excuses** (regrets) apology; **faire des excuses** to apologize (à to) ■ **excuser** 1 vt (justifier, pardonner) to excuse (qn d'avoir fait/qn de faire sb for doing) 2 **s'excuser** vpr to apologize (de for; auprès de to); **excusez-moi!, je m'excuse!** excuse me!

exécrer [ɛgzekre] vt to loathe ■ **exécrable** adj atrocious

exécuter [ɛgzekyte] 1 vt (tâche) to carry out; (jouer) to perform; **e. qn** to execute sb 2 **s'exécuter** vpr to comply ■ **exécutant, -e** nmf (ouvrier, employé) subordinate ■ **exécution** nf (de tâche) carrying out; (de musique) performance; (de condamné) execution

exécutif [ɛgzekytif] 1 adj m **pouvoir e.** executive power 2 nm **l'e.** the executive

exemplaire [ɛgzɑ̃plɛr] 1 adj exemplary 2 nm (livre) copy

exemple [ɛgzɑ̃pl] nm example; **par e.** for example, for instance; **donner l'e.** to set an example (à to)

exempt, -e [ɛgzɑ̃, -ɑ̃t] adj **e. de** (dispensé de) exempt from; (sans) free from ■ **exempter** [ɛgzɑ̃te] vt to exempt (de from) ■ **exemption** nf exemption

exercer [ɛgzɛrse] 1 vt (voix, droits) to exercise; (autorité, influence) to exert

(sur on); (profession) to practise; **e. qn à qch** to train sb in sth 2 vi (médecin) to practise 3 **s'exercer** vpr (s'entraîner) to train; **s'e. à qch** to practise sth; **s'e. à faire qch** to practise doing sth

exercice [ɛgzɛrsis] nm (physique) & Scol exercise; Mil drill; **en e.** (fonctionnaire) in office; (médecin) in practice; **prendre de l'e.** to exercise

exhiber [ɛgzibe] vt (documents, passeport) to produce; Péj (savoir, richesses) to show off, to flaunt

exiger [ɛgziʒe] vt (exiger) to demand (de from); (nécessiter) to require ■ **exigeant, -e** adj demanding, exacting ■ **exigence** nf (caractère) exacting nature; (condition) demand

exigu, -ë [ɛgzigy] adj cramped, tiny

exil [ɛgzil] nm exile ■ **exilé, -e** nmf (personne) exile ■ **exiler** 1 vt to exile 2 **s'exiler** vpr to go into exile

existence [ɛgzistɑ̃s] nf (fait d'exister) existence; (vie) life; **moyen d'e.** means of existence ■ **exister** 1 vi to exist 2 v impersonnel **il existe…** there is/are…

exode [ɛgzɔd] nm exodus

exonérer [ɛgzɔnere] vt to exempt (de from) ■ **exonération** nf exemption

exorbitant, -e [ɛgzɔrbitɑ̃, -ɑ̃t] adj exorbitant

exotique [ɛgzɔtik] adj exotic

expansif, -ive [ɛkspɑ̃sif, -iv] adj expansive

expansion [ɛkspɑ̃sjɔ̃] nf (de commerce, de pays, de gaz) expansion; **en (pleine) e.** (fast or rapidly) expanding

expatrier [ɛkspatrije] **s'expatrier** vpr to leave one's country

expédier [ɛkspedje] vt (envoyer) to send, to dispatch; (affaires, client) to deal promptly with ■ **expéditeur, -trice** nmf sender ■ **expéditif, -ive** adj hasty ■ **expédition** nf (envoi) dispatch; (voyage) expedition

expérience [ɛksperjɑ̃s] nf (connaissance) experience; (scientifique) experiment; **faire l'e. de qch** to experience sth; **avoir de l'e.** to have experience ■ **expérimental, -e, -aux, -ales** adj experimental

expérimenter [ɛksperimɑ̃te] vt (remède, vaccin) to try out (**sur** on) ■ **expérimenté, -e** adj experienced

expert, -e [ɛksper, -ɛrt] 1 adj expert, skilled (**en** in) 2 nm expert (**en** on or in); (d'assurances) valuer ■ **expert-comptable** (pl **experts-comptables**) nm Br ≃ chartered accountant, Am ≃ certified public accountant

expertise [ɛkspertiz] nf (évaluation) valuation; (rapport) expert's report; (compétence) expertise

expier [ɛkspje] vt (péchés) to expiate, to atone for

expirer [ɛkspire] 1 vti to breathe out 2 vi (mourir) to pass away; (finir, cesser) to expire ■ **expiration** nf (respiration) breathing out; (échéance) Br expiry, Am expiration

explication [ɛksplikasjɔ̃] nf explanation; (mise au point) discussion

explicite [ɛksplisit] adj explicit

expliquer [ɛksplike] 1 vt to explain (**à** to; **que** that) 2 **s'expliquer** vpr to explain oneself; (discuter) to talk things over (**avec** with); **s'e. qch** (comprendre) to understand sth ■ **explicatif, -ive** adj explanatory

exploit [ɛksplwa] nm feat

exploiter [ɛksplwate] vt (champs) to farm; (ferme) to run; (mine) to work; Fig & Péj (personne, situation) to exploit ■ **exploitant, -e** nmf e. **agricole** farmer ■ **exploitation** nf (de champs) farming; (de ferme) running; (de mine) working; Péj exploitation; **e. agricole** farm

explorer [ɛksplɔre] vt to explore ■ **explorateur, -trice** nmf explorer

exploser [ɛksploze] vi (gaz, bombe) to explode; **faire e. qch** to explode sth ■ **explosif, -ive** adj & nm explosive ■ **explosion** nf explosion; (de colère) outburst

exporter [ɛkspɔrte] vt to export (**vers** to; **de** from) ■ **exportateur, -trice** 1

nmf exporter 2 adj exporting ■ **exportation** nf (produit) export; (action) export(ation)

exposer [ɛkspoze] 1 vt (tableau) to exhibit; (marchandises) to display; (théorie) to set out; Phot (film) to expose 2 **s'exposer** vpr **s'e. au danger** to put oneself in danger; **s'e. à la critique** to lay oneself open to criticism ■ **exposé, -e** 1 adj **e. au sud** facing south 2 nm (compte rendu) account (**de** of); (présentation) talk; Scol paper

exposition [ɛkspozisjɔ̃] nf (d'objets d'art) exhibition; (de marchandises) display; Phot exposure (**à** to); (de maison) aspect

exprès¹ [ɛkspre] adv on purpose, intentionally; (spécialement) specially

exprès², -esse [ɛkspres] adj (ordre, condition) express ■ **expressément** adv expressly

exprès³ [ɛkspres] adj inv **lettre e.** special delivery letter

express [ɛkspres] adj & nm inv (train) express; (café) espresso

expressif, -ive [ɛkspresif, -iv] adj expressive ■ **expression** nf (phrase, mine) expression ■ **exprimer** 1 vt to express 2 **s'exprimer** vpr to express oneself

expulser [ɛkspylse] vt to expel (**de** from); (joueur) to send off ■ **expulsion** nf expulsion; (de joueur) sending off

exquis, -e [ɛkski, -iz] adj (nourriture) exquisite

extase [ɛkstaz] nf ecstasy ■ **s'extasier** vpr to be in raptures (**sur** over or about)

extensible [ɛkstɑ̃sibl] adj (métal) tensile; (tissu) stretch ■ **extension** nf (de muscle) stretching; (de durée, de contrat) extension

exténué, -e [ɛkstenɥe] adj exhausted

extérieur, -e [ɛksterjœr] 1 adj (monde) outside; (surface) outer, external; (signe) outward, external; (politique) foreign 2 nm outside, exterior; **à l'e. (de)** outside; **à l'e.** (match) away ■ **extérieurement** adv (dehors) externally;

(en apparence) outwardly ■ **extérioriser** *vt* to express

exterminer [εkstεrmine] *vt* to exterminate

externat [εkstεrna] *nm (école)* day school

externe [εkstεrn] **1** *adj* external **2** *nmf (élève)* day pupil; *Méd* = non-resident hospital medical student, *Am* extern

extincteur [εkstε̃ktœr] *nm* fire extinguisher ■ **extinction** *nf (de feu)* extinguishing; *(de race)* extinction; **e. de voix** loss of voice

extorquer [εkstɔrke] *vt* to extort (**à** from) ■ **extorsion** *nf* extortion; **e. de fonds** extortion

extradition [εkstradisjɔ̃] *nf* extradition ■ **extrader** *vt* to extradite

extraire* [εkstrεr] *vt* to extract (**de** from); *(charbon)* to mine ■ **extrait** *nm*

extract; **e. de naissance** birth certificate

extralucide [εkstralysid] *adj & nmf* clairvoyant

extraordinaire [εkstraɔrdinεr] *adj* extraordinary

extraterrestre [εkstraterestr] *adj & nmf* extraterrestrial

extravagant, -e [εkstravagɑ̃, -ɑ̃t] *adj (idée, comportement)* extravagant

extraverti, -e [εkstravεrti] *nmf* extrovert

extrême [εkstrεm] **1** *adj* extreme; *Pol* **l'e. droite/gauche** the far *or* extreme right/left **2** *nm* extreme ■ **Extrême-Orient** *nm* **l'E.** the Far East ■ **extrémiste** *adj & nmf* extremist ■ **extrémité** *nf (bout)* extremity, end; **extrémités** *(pieds et mains)* extremities

exulter [εgzylte] *vi* to exult, to rejoice

Ff

F, f [ɛf] *nm inv* F, f

fa [fa] *nm (note)* F

fabricant, -e [fabrikɑ̃, -ɑ̃t] *nmf* manufacturer ▪ **fabrication** *nf* manufacture

fabrique [fabrik] *nf* factory

fabriquer [fabrike] *vt (objet)* to make; *(en usine)* to manufacture

fabuleux, -euse [fabylø, -øz] *adj (légendaire, incroyable)* fabulous

façade [fasad] *nf* façade

face [fas] *nf (visage)* face; *(de cube, de montagne)* side; *(de pièce de monnaie)* head; **en f.** opposite; **en f. de** opposite, facing; *(en présence de)* in front of; **f. à** *(vis-à-vis)* facing; **f. à f.** face to face; **faire f. à qch** to face up to sth; **sauver/perdre la f.** to save/lose face

facette [faset] *nf (de diamant, de problème)* facet

fâcher [faʃe] **se fâcher** *vpr* to get angry (**contre** with); **se f. avec qn** to fall out with sb ▪ **fâché, -e** *adj (air)* angry; *(personnes)* on bad terms; **f. contre qn** angry with sb

facile [fasil] *adj* easy; **f. à vivre** easy to get along with ▪ **facilité** *nf (simplicité)* easiness; *(aisance)* ease ▪ **faciliter** *vt* to make easier, to facilitate

façon [fasɔ̃] *nf (manière)* way; **la f. dont elle parle** the way (in which) she talks; **de quelle f.?** how?; **de toute f.** anyway, anyhow; **de f.** à so as to; **de f. générale** generally speaking; **d'une f. ou d'une autre** one way or another; **à ma f.** my way, (in) my own way

façonner [fasɔne] *vt (former)* to shape; *(fabriquer)* to make

facteur [faktœr] *nm* **(a)** *(employé) Br* postman, *Am* mailman **(b)** *(élément)* factor

facture [faktyr] *nf Com* bill, invoice ▪ **facturer** *vt* to bill, to invoice

facultatif, -ive [fakyltatif, -iv] *adj (travail)* optional; *Scol* **matière facultative** optional subject

faculté [fakylte] *nf* **(a)** *(aptitude)* faculty **(b)** *(d'université)* faculty; **à la f.** *Br* at university, *Am* at school

fade [fad] *adj* insipid

faible [fɛbl] **1** *adj* weak, feeble; *(voix)* faint; *(chances)* slight; *(revenus)* small **2** *nm* weakling; **f. d'esprit** feeble-minded person ▪ **faiblesse** *nf (physique, morale)* weakness

faiblir [feblir] *vi (forces)* to weaken; *(courage, vue)* to fail; *(vent)* to drop

faïence [fajɑ̃s] *nf (matière)* earthenware; **faïences** *(objets)* earthenware

faille¹ [faj] *nf Géol* fault; *Fig* flaw

faille² [faj] *voir* **falloir**

faillir* [fajir] *vi* **il a failli tomber** he almost *or* nearly fell

faillite [fajit] *nf Com* bankruptcy; **faire f.** to go bankrupt

faim [fɛ̃] *nf* hunger; **avoir f.** to be hungry

fainéant, -e [feneɑ̃, -ɑ̃t] **1** *adj* idle **2** *nmf* idler

FAIRE* [fɛr] **1** *vt (faute, gâteau, voyage, promenade, repas)* to make; *(devoir, ménage, repas)* to do; *(rêve, chute)* to have; *(sourire)* to give; *(promenade, sieste)* to have, to take; *(guerre)* to wage, to make; **ça fait 10 mètres de large** it's 10 metres wide; **ça fait 10 euros** it's *or* that's 10 euros; **2 et 2 font 4** 2 and 2 are 4; **que f.?** what's to be done? **f. du tennis/du piano** to play tennis/the piano; **f. du droit** to study law; **f. du bien à qn** to do sb good; **f. du mal à qn** to hurt *or* harm sb; **ça ne fait rien** that doesn't matter; **comment as-tu fait pour…?** how did you manage to…?; **'oui', fit-elle** 'yes', she said

2 *vi (agir)* to do; *(paraître)* to look; **f. comme chez soi** to make oneself at home; **elle ferait bien de partir** she'd do well to leave

3 *v impersonnel* **il fait beau/froid** it's fine/cold; **il fait du vent** it's windy; **quel temps fait-il?** what's the weather like?; **ça fait deux ans que je ne l'ai pas vu** I haven't seen him for two years, it's (been) two years since I saw him

4 *v aux (+ infinitive)* **f. construire une maison** to have a house built (**à qn** for sb; **par qn** by sb); **f. souffrir qn** to make sb suffer

5 **se faire** *upr (fabrication)* to be made; *(activité)* to be done; **se f. couper les cheveux** to have one's hair cut; **se f. renverser** to get knocked down; **se f. des amis** to make friends; **il se fait tard** it's getting late; **comment se fait-il que…?** how is it that…?; **ça se fait beaucoup** people do that a lot; **se f. à qch** to get used to sth; **ne t'en fais pas!** don't worry! ■ **faire-part** *nm inv* announcement

fais, fait [fε] *voir* **faire**
faisable [fəzabl] *adj* feasible
faisan [fəzɑ̃] *nm* pheasant
faisceau, -x [fεso] *nm (rayons)* beam
fait, -e [fε, fεt] **1** *pp de* **faire** **2** *adj (fromage)* ripe; *(ongles)* polished; **tout f.** ready made **3** *nm (événement)* event; *(donnée, réalité)* fact; **du f. de** on account of; **au f.** *(à propos)* by the way; **en f.** in fact; **prendre qn sur le f.** to catch sb red-handed or in the act; *Journ* **faits divers** ≃ news in brief
faîte [fεt] *nm (haut)* top; *Fig (apogée)* height
faites [fεt] *voir* **faire**

falaise [falεz] *nf* cliff

FALLOIR* [falwar] **1** *v impersonnel* **il faut qn/qch** I/you/we/*etc* need sb/sth; **il te faut un stylo** you need a pen; **il faut partir** I/you/we/*etc* have to go; **il faut que je parte** I have to go; **il faudrait qu'elle reste** she ought to stay; **il faut un jour** it takes a day (**pour faire** to do); **comme il faut** *(adjectif)* proper; *(adverbe)* properly; **s'il le faut** if need be

2 **s'en falloir** *upr* **il s'en est fallu de peu qu'il ne pleure** he almost cried; **tant s'en faut** far from it

famé [fame] **mal famé, -e** *adj* disreputable
fameux, -euse [famø, -øz] *adj (célèbre)* famous
familial, -e, -aux, -ales [familjal, -o] *adj (atmosphère, ennuis)* family; *(entreprise)* family-run
familier, -ère [familje, -εr] *adj (connu)* familiar (**à** to); *(désinvolte)* informal (**avec** with); *(locution)* colloquial ■ **familiariser 1** *vt* to familiarize (**avec** with) **2 se familiariser** *upr* to familiarize oneself (**avec** with)
famille [famij] *nf* family
famine [famin] *nf* famine
fanatique [fanatik] **1** *adj* fanatical **2** *nmf* fanatic
faner [fane] **se faner** *upr (fleur, beauté)* to fade ■ **fané, -e** *adj* faded
fanfare [fɑ̃far] *nf (orchestre)* brass band
fantaisie [fɑ̃tezi] *nf (imagination)* imagination; **bijoux f.** costume jewellery
fantastique [fɑ̃tastik] *adj (imaginaire, excellent)* fantastic
fantôme [fɑ̃tom] **1** *nm* ghost, phantom **2** *adj* **ville/train f.** ghost town/train
faon [fɑ̃] *nm* fawn
farce¹ [fars] *nf (tour)* practical joke, prank; **faire une f. à qn** to play a practical joke *or* a prank on sb ■ **farceur, -euse** *nmf (blagueur)* practical joker

farce² [fars] nf Culin stuffing ■ **farcir** vt (poulet) to stuff

fardeau, -x [fardo] nm burden, load

farder [farde] **1** vt (maquiller) to make up **2 se farder** vpr (se maquiller) to put on one's make-up; **se f. les yeux** to put eyeshadow on

farine [farin] nf (de blé) flour

farouche [faruʃ] adj (personne) shy; (animal) timid; (haine) fierce

fart [far] nm wax

fascicule [fasikyl] nm (de publication) instalment; (brochure) brochure

fasciner [fasine] vt to fascinate ■ **fascination** nf fascination

fascisme [faʃism] nm fascism ■ **fasciste** adj & nmf fascist

fasse(s), fassent [fas] voir **faire**

faste [fast] **1** nm splendour **2** adj jour **f.** lucky day

fastidieux, -euse [fastidjø, -øz] adj tedious

fatal, -e, -als, -ales [fatal] adj (mortel) fatal; (inévitable) inevitable; (moment) fateful ■ **fataliste** adj fatalistic ■ **fatalité** nf (destin) fate ■ **fatidique** adj (jour, date) fateful

fatigant, -e [fatigɑ̃, -ɑ̃t] adj (épuisant) tiring; (ennuyeux) tiresome

fatigue [fatig] nf tiredness

fatiguer [fatige] **1** vt (épuiser) to tire; (yeux) to strain; (ennuyer) to bore **2** vi (personne) to get tired; (moteur) to labour **3 se fatiguer** vpr (s'épuiser, se lasser) to get tired (**de** of); **se f. à faire qch** to tire oneself out doing sth; **se f. les yeux** to strain one's eyes ■ **fatigué, -e** adj tired (**de** of)

faucher [foʃe] vt (herbe) to mow; (blé) to reap

faucon [fokɔ̃] nm hawk, falcon

faudra, faudrait [fodra, fodrɛ] voir **falloir**

faufiler [fofile] **se faufiler** vpr to work one's way (**dans** through or into; **entre** between)

faune [fon] nf wildlife, fauna

faussaire [fosɛr] nm forger

fausse [fos] voir **faux¹**

fausser [fose] vt (réalité) to distort

fausseté [foste] nf (hypocrisie) duplicity

faut [fo] voir **falloir**

faute [fot] nf (erreur) mistake; (responsabilité) & (au tennis) fault; (au football) foul; **c'est de ta f.** it's your fault; **f. de mieux** for want of anything better; **faire une f.** to make a mistake

fauteuil [fotœj] nm armchair; (de président) chair; **f. roulant** wheelchair

fautif, -ive [fotif, -iv] adj (personne) at fault; (erroné) faulty

fauve [fov] nm big cat

faux, fausse [fo, fos] **1** adj (pas vrai) false, untrue; (inexact) wrong; (inauthentique) false; (monnaie) forged; (tableau) fake; **faire une fausse couche** to have a miscarriage; **f. départ** false start

2 adv (chanter) out of tune

3 nm (tableau) fake; (document) forgery ■ **faux-filet** (pl **faux-filets**) nm sirloin ■ **faux-monnayeur** (pl **faux-monnayeurs**) nm counterfeiter

faveur [favœr] nf favour; **en f. de** (au profit de) in aid of; **être en f. de qch** to be in favour of sth ■ **favorable** adj favourable (**à** to) ■ **favori, -e** adj & nmf favourite ■ **favoriser** vt to favour

fax [faks] nm (appareil, message) fax ■ **faxer** vt (message) to fax

fécond, -e [fekɔ̃, -ɔ̃d] adj (femme, idée) fertile ■ **fécondité** nf fertility

fédéral, -e, -aux, -ales [federal, -o] adj federal ■ **fédération** nf federation

fée [fe] nf fairy ■ **féerique** adj (personnage, monde) fairy; (vision) enchanting

feindre* [fɛ̃dr] vt to feign; **f. de faire qch** to pretend to do sth ■ **feint, -e** adj feigned ■ **feinte** nf (ruse) ruse

fêler [fele] vt, **se fêler** vpr to crack

féliciter [felisite] vt to congratulate (**de** ou **sur** on) ■ **félicitations** nfpl congratulations (**pour** on)

félin [felɛ̃] nm feline

fêlure [felyr] nf crack

femelle [fəmɛl] adj & nf female

féminin, -e [feminɛ̃, -in] *adj (prénom, hormone)* female; *(trait, intuition, pronom)* feminine; *(mode)* women's ■ **féministe** *adj & nmf* feminist ■ **féminité** *nf* femininity

femme [fam] *nf* woman *(pl* women); *(épouse)* wife; **f. de ménage** cleaning lady, maid; **f. au foyer** housewife

fendiller [fɑ̃dije] **se fendiller** *vpr* to crack

fendre [fɑ̃dr] **1** *vt (bois, lèvre)* to split; *Fig (cœur)* to break **2 se fendre** *vpr (se fissurer)* to crack

fenêtre [fənɛtr] *nf* window

fenouil [fənuj] *nm* fennel

fente [fɑ̃t] *nf (de tirelire, de palissade)* slit; *(de rocher)* split, crack

féodal, -e, -aux, -ales [feɔdal, -o] *adj* feudal

fer [fɛr] *nm* iron; *(partie métallique)* metal (part); **barre de** *ou* **en f.** iron bar; **f. à cheval** horseshoe; **f. forgé** wrought iron; **f. à repasser** iron

fera, ferait *etc* [fəra, fərɛ] *voir* **faire**

férié [ferje] *adj m* **jour f.** (public) holiday

ferme¹ [fɛrm] *nf* farm; *(maison)* farm(-house)

ferme² [fɛrm] **1** *adj (fruit, beurre, décision)* firm; *(autoritaire)* firm (**avec with**) **2** *adv (travailler)* hard; **s'ennuyer f.** to be bored stiff

fermenter [fɛrmɑ̃te] *vi* to ferment

fermer [fɛrme] **1** *vt* to close, to shut; *(gaz, radio)* to turn *or* switch off; *(passage)* to block; **f. qch à clef** to lock sth; **f. un magasin** *(définitivement)* to close *or* shut (down) a shop **2** *vi*, **se fermer** *vpr* to close, to shut ■ **fermé, -e** *adj (porte, magasin)* closed, shut; *(route, circuit)* closed; *(gaz)* off

fermeté [fɛrmɑte] *nf* firmness

fermeture [fɛrmətyr] *nf* closing, closure; *(heure)* closing time; *(mécanisme)* catch; **f. annuelle** annual closing; **f. Éclair®** *Br* zip (fastener), *Am* zipper

fermier, -ère [fɛrmje, -ɛr] *nmf* farmer

fermoir [fɛrmwar] *nm* clasp

féroce [ferɔs] *adj* ferocious ■ **férocité** *nf* ferocity

feront [fərɔ̃] *voir* **faire**

ferraille [fɛraj] *nf* scrap iron; **mettre qch à la f.** to scrap sth

ferronnerie [fɛrɔnri] *nf* ironwork

ferroviaire [fɛrɔvjɛr] *adj* **compagnie f.** *Br* railway company, *Am* railroad company

ferry [fɛri] *(pl* **ferrys** *ou* **ferries)** *nm* ferry

fertile [fɛrtil] *adj (terre, imagination)* fertile ■ **fertiliser** *vt* to fertilize ■ **fertilité** *nf* fertility

ferveur [fɛrvœr] *nf* fervour

fesse [fɛs] *nf* buttock; **fesses** *Br* bottom, *Am* butt ■ **fessée** *nf* spanking

festin [fɛstɛ̃] *nm* feast

festival, -als [fɛstival] *nm* festival

festivités [fɛstivite] *nfpl* festivities

fête [fɛt] *nf (civile)* holiday; *(religieuse)* festival, feast; *(entre amis)* party; **jour de f.** (public) holiday; **les fêtes (de Noël et du nouvel an)** the Christmas holidays; **faire la f.** to have a good time; **c'est sa f.** it's his/her saint's day; **la f. des Mères** Mother's Day; **la f. du Travail** Labour Day ■ **fêter** *vt (événement)* to celebrate

feu, -x [fø] *nm* fire; *(de réchaud)* burner; *Aut, Naut & Aviat (lumière)* light; **en f.** on fire, ablaze; **faire du f.** to light *or* make a fire; **mettre le f. à qch** to set fire to sth; **prendre f.** to catch fire; **donner du f. à qn** to give sb a light; **avez-vous du f.?** have you got a light?; **faire cuire qch à f. doux** to cook sth on a low heat; **au f.!** (there's a fire!); *Aut* **f. rouge** *(lumière)* red light; *(objet)* traffic lights

feuille [fœj] *nf* leaf; *(de papier)* sheet; *(de journal)* newssheet; **f. de maladie** = form given by doctor to patient for claiming reimbursement from the Social Security; **f. de paie** *Br* pay slip, *Am* pay stub ■ **feuillage** *nm* leaves, foliage

feuilleté [fœjte] *nm* **f. au fromage** cheese pastry

feuilleter [fœjte] *vt (livre)* to flip through

feuilleton [fœjtɔ̃] *nm (roman, film)* serial; **f. télévisé** television serial

feutre [føtr] *nm* felt; **(crayon) f.** felt-tip(ped) pen

fève [fɛv] *nf* (broad) bean

février [fevrije] *nm* February

fiable [fjabl] *adj* reliable

fiancer [fjɑ̃se] **se fiancer** *upr* to become engaged **(avec to)** ■ **fiabilité** *nf* reliability ■ **fiançailles** *nfpl* engagement ■ **fiancé** *nm* fiancé; **fiancés** engaged couple ■ **fiancée** *nf* fiancée

fibre [fibr] *nf* fibre; **f. de verre** fibreglass; **fibres optiques** optical fibres

ficelle [fisɛl] *nf (de corde)* string; *(pain)* = long thin loaf ■ **ficeler** *vt* to tie up

fiche [fiʃ] *nf* **(a)** *(carte)* index card; *(papier)* form; **f. de paie** *Br* pay slip, *Am* pay stub **(b)** *Él (broche)* pin; *(prise)* plug ■ **fichier** *nm* card index, file; *Ordinat* file

ficher [fiʃe] *vt (enfoncer)* to drive in; *(mettre sur fiche)* to put on file

fictif, -ive [fiktif, -iv] *adj* fictitious ■ **fiction** *nf* fiction

fidèle [fidɛl] **1** *adj* faithful **(à** to) **2** *nmf* faithful supporter; **les fidèles** *(croyants)* the faithful; *(à l'église)* the congregation ■ **fidélité** *nf* fidelity, faithfulness

fier¹ [fje] **se fier** *upr* **se f. à qn/qch** to trust sb/sth

fier², fière [fjɛr] *adj* proud **(de** of) ■ **fierté** *nf* pride

fièvre [fjɛvr] *nf (maladie)* fever; **avoir de la f.** to have a temperature *or* a fever ■ **fiévreux, -euse** *adj* feverish

figer [fiʒe] **1** *vt (liquide)* to congeal **2 se figer** *upr (liquide)* to congeal; *Fig (sourire, personne)* to freeze

figue [fig] *nf* fig

figurant, -e [figyrɑ̃, -ɑ̃t] *nmf (de film)* extra

figure [figyr] *nf (visage)* face; *(personnage)* figure

figurer [figyre] **1** *vt* to represent **2** *vi* to appear **3 se figurer** *upr* to imagine; **figure-toi que...?** would you believe that...?

fil [fil] *nm* **(a)** *(de coton, de pensée)* thread; *(lin)* linen; **f. dentaire** dental floss **(b)** *(métallique)* wire; **f. de fer** wire **(c)** *(expressions)* **au f. de l'eau** with the current; **au bout du f.** *(au téléphone)* on the line

file [fil] *nf* line; *Aut (couloir)* lane; **f. d'attente** *Br* queue, *Am* line; **être en double f.** to be double-parked

filer [file] **1** *vt (coton)* to spin; **f. qn** to shadow sb **2** *vi (partir)* to rush off; *(aller vite)* to speed along; *(collant)* to run, *Br* to ladder

filet [file] *nm* **(a)** *(en maille)* net; **f. à provisions** string bag **(b)** *(d'eau)* trickle **(c)** *(de poisson, de viande)* fillet

filial, -e, -aux, -ales [filjal, -o] *adj* filial ■ **filiale** *nf* subsidiary (company)

filière [filjɛr] *nf (voie obligée)* channels; *(domaine d'études)* field of study; *(organisation clandestine)* network; **suivre la f. normale** to go through the official channels

fille [fij] *nf (enfant)* girl; *(descendante)* daughter; **petite f.** (little *or* young) girl; **jeune f.** girl, young lady ■ **fillette** *nf* little girl

film [film] *nm (œuvre)* film, movie; *(pour photo)* film; **f. muet** silent film; **f. policier** thriller ■ **filmer** *vt (personne, scène)* to film

fils [fis] *nm* son

filtre [filtr] *nm* filter; **bout f.** filter tip ■ **filtrer** **1** *vt (liquide, lumière)* to filter; *(personne, nouvelles)* to screen **2** *vi (liquide)* to filter (through); *(nouvelle)* to leak out

fin¹ [fɛ̃] *nf* **(a)** *(conclusion)* end; **mettre f. à qch** to put an end to sth; **prendre f.** to come to an end; **à la f.** in the end; **f. mai** at the end of May **(b)** *(but)* end, aim

fin², fine [fɛ̃, fin] **1** *adj (pointe, tissu)* fine; *(couche)* thin; *(visage, mets)* delicate; *(oreille)* sharp; *(intelligent)* subtle **2** *adv (couper, moudre)* finely

final, -e, -aux *ou* **-als, -ales** [final, -o] *adj* final ■ **finale** *nf Sport* final ■ **finaliste** *nmf Sport* finalist

finance [finãs] *nf* finance ■ **financement** *nm* financing ■ **financer** *vt* to finance

financier, -ère [finãsje, -ɛr] **1** *adj* financial **2** *nm* financier

finesse [fines] *nf (de pointe)* fineness; *(de taille)* thinness; *(de visage)* delicacy; *(intelligence)* subtlety

finir [finir] **1** *vt* to finish; *(discours, vie)* to end, to finish **2** *vi* to finish, to end; **f. de faire qch** to finish doing sth; **f. par faire qch** to end up doing sth; **f. par qch** to finish (up) *or* end (up) with sth ■ **fini, -e** *adj (produit)* finished; *(univers)* & *Math* finite

Finlande [fɛ̃lɑ̃d] *nf* **la F.** Finland ■ **finlandais, -e 1** *adj* Finnish **2** *nmf* **F., Finlandaise** Finn

firme [firm] *nf* firm

fisc [fisk] *nm Br* ≃ Inland Revenue, *Am* ≃ Internal Revenue ■ **fiscal, -e, -aux, -ales** *adj* **charges fiscales** taxes; **fraude fiscale** tax fraud *or* evasion ■ **fiscalité** *nf* tax system

fissure [fisyr] *nf* crack ■ **se fissurer** *vpr* to crack

fixation [fiksɑsjɔ̃] *nf (action)* fixing; *(dispositif)* fastening, binding; *(idée fixe)* fixation; **faire une f. sur qn/qch** to be fixated on sb/sth

fixe [fiks] *adj* fixed ■ **fixement** [-əmɑ̃] *adv* **regarder qn/qch f.** to stare at sb/sth

fixer [fikse] **1** *vt (attacher)* to fix (**à** to); *(date, règle)* to decide, to fix; **f. qn/qch du regard** to stare at sb/sth; **être fixé** *(décidé)* to be decided **2 se fixer** *vpr (regard)* to become fixed; *(s'établir)* to settle

flacon [flakɔ̃] *nm* small bottle

flageolet [flaʒɔlɛ] *nm (haricot)* flageolet bean

flagrant, -e [flagrɑ̃, -ɑ̃t] *adj (injustice)* flagrant, blatant; **pris en f. délit** caught in the act *or* red-handed

flair [flɛr] *nm (de chien)* (sense of) smell, scent; *(de personne)* intuition, flair ■ **flairer** *vt* to smell, to sniff at

flamand, -e [flamɑ̃, -ɑ̃d] **1** *adj* Flemish **2** *nmf* **F., Flamande** Fleming **3** *nm (langue)* Flemish

flamant [flamɑ̃] *nm* **f. rose** flamingo

flambant [flɑ̃bɑ̃] *adv* **f. neuf** brand new

flambeau, -x [flɑ̃bo] *nm* torch

flamber [flɑ̃be] *vi* to blaze

flamboyer [flɑ̃bwaje] *vi* to blaze

flamme [flɑm] *nf* flame; **en flammes** on fire

flan [flɑ̃] *nm* baked custard

flanc [flɑ̃] *nm* side; *(d'armée, d'animal)* flank

Flandre [flɑ̃dr] *nf* **la F., les Flandres** Flanders

flâner [flɑne] *vi* to stroll

flanquer [flɑ̃ke] *vt* to flank (**de** with)

flaque [flak] *nf (d'eau)* puddle

flash [flaʃ] *(pl* **flashes)** *nm Phot* flashlight; *Radio & TV* **f. d'informations** (news)flash

flatter [flate] *vt* to flatter ■ **flatterie** *nf* flattery ■ **flatteur, -euse** *adj* flattering

fléau, -x [fleo] *nm (catastrophe)* scourge

flèche [flɛʃ] *nf (projectile)* arrow; *(d'église)* spire; **monter en f.** *(prix)* to shoot up ■ **fléchette** *nf* dart; **fléchettes** *(jeu)* darts

fléchir [fleʃir] **1** *vt (ployer)* to bend **2** *vi (ployer)* to bend; *(faiblir)* to give way; *(baisser)* to fall

flétrir [fletrir] *vt,* **se flétrir** *vpr* to wither

fleur [flœr] *nf* flower; *(d'arbre, d'arbuste)* blossom; **en fleur(s)** in flower, in bloom; *(arbre)* in blossom

fleurir [flœrir] **1** *vt (table)* to decorate with flowers; *(tombe)* to lay flowers on **2** *vi (plante)* to flower, to bloom; *(arbre)* to blossom; *Fig (prospérer)* to flourish ■ **fleuri, -e** *adj (fleur, jardin)* in bloom; *(tissu)* floral

fleuriste [flœrist] *nmf* florist

fleuve [flœv] *nm* river

flexible [flɛksibl] *adj* flexible ■ **flexibilité** *nf* flexibility

flocon [flɔkɔ̃] *nm* flake; **f. de neige** snowflake

floraison [flɔrezɔ̃] *nf* flowering; **en pleine f.** in full bloom ∎ **floral, -e, -aux, -ales** *adj* floral

flore [flɔr] *nf* flora

florissant, -e [flɔrisɑ̃, -ɑ̃t] *adj* flourishing

flot [flo] *nm (de larmes)* flood, stream; **les flots** *(la mer)* the waves; **à f.** *(bateau)* afloat; *Fig* **couler à flots** *(argent, vin)* to flow freely

flotte [flɔt] *nf (de bateaux, d'avions)* fleet

flotter [flɔte] *vi (bateau)* to float; *(drapeau)* to fly ∎ **flotteur** *nm* float

flou, -e [flu] *adj (image)* fuzzy, blurred; *(idée)* vague

fluet, -ette [flyɛ, -ɛt] *adj* thin, slender

fluide [flɥid] *adj & nm (liquide)* fluid

fluorescent, -e [flyɔresɑ̃, -ɑ̃t] *adj* fluorescent

flûte [flyt] *nf (instrument)* flute; *(verre)* champagne glass ∎ **flûtiste** *nmf Br* flautist, *Am* flutist

flux [fly] *nm (abondance)* flow; **f. et reflux** ebb and flow

foi [fwa] *nf* faith; **être de bonne/mauvaise f.** to be sincere/insincere

foie [fwa] *nm* liver; **f. gras** foie gras; **crise de f.** bout of indigestion

foin [fwɛ̃] *nm* hay

foire [fwar] *nf* fair

fois [fwa] *nf* time; **une f.** once; **deux f.** twice; **trois f.** three times; **deux f. trois** two times three; **chaque f. que...** whenever...; each time *(that)*...; **une f. qu'il sera arrivé** once he has arrived; **à la f.** at the same time, at once; **il était une fois...** once upon a time there was...

foisonner [fwazɔne] *vi* to abound *(de* ou **en** in)

fol [fɔl] *voir* **fou**

folie [fɔli] *nf* madness; **aimer qn à la f.** to be madly in love with sb

folklore [fɔlklɔr] *nm* folklore ∎ **folklorique** *adj (costume)* traditional; *(musique, danse)* folk

folle [fɔl] *voir* **fou**

foncé, -e [fɔ̃se] *adj* dark

foncer [fɔ̃se] **1** *vi (aller vite)* to tear or charge along; **f. sur qn/qch** to swoop on sb/sth **2** *vti (couleur)* to darken

foncier, -ère [fɔ̃sje, -ɛr] *adj (taxe)* land

fonction [fɔ̃ksjɔ̃] *nf* function; *(emploi)* office; **en f. de** according to; **faire f. de** *(personne)* to act as; *(objet)* to serve or act as; **prendre ses fonctions** to take up one's duties; **la f. publique** the civil service ∎ **fonctionnaire** *nmf* civil servant; **haut f.** high-ranking civil servant ∎ **fonctionnel, -elle** *adj* functional

fonctionner [fɔ̃ksjɔne] *vi (machine)* to work, to function; **faire f. qch** to operate sth ∎ **fonctionnement** *nm (de machine)* working; **en état de f.** in working order

fond [fɔ̃] *nm (de boîte, de jardin, de vallée)* bottom; *(de salle, d'armoire)* back; *(arrière-plan)* background; **au f. de** *(boîte, jardin)* at the bottom of; *(salle)* at the back of; *Fig* **au f., dans le f.** basically; **à f.** *(connaître)* thoroughly; **de f. en comble** from top to bottom; **course de f.** long-distance race; **ski de f.** cross-country skiing; **bruits de f.** background noise; **f. sonore** background music

fondamental, -e, -aux, -ales [fɔ̃damɑ̃tal, -o] *adj* fundamental, basic

fonder [fɔ̃de] **1** *vt (ville)* to found; *(commerce)* to set up; *(famille)* to start; **f. qch sur qch** to base sth on sth **2 se fonder** *vpr* **se f. sur qch** *(sujet: théorie)* to be based on sth ∎ **fondateur, -trice** *nmf* founder ∎ **fondation** *nf (création, œuvre)* foundation *(de* of); **fondations** *(de bâtiment)* foundations ∎ **fondement** *nm* foundation

fondre [fɔ̃dr] **1** *vt (métal)* to melt down; *(neige)* to melt; **faites f. le chocolat** melt the chocolate **2** *vi (se liquéfier)* to melt; **f. en larmes** to burst into tears; **f. sur qch** to swoop on sth **3 se fondre** *vpr* **se f. dans qch** *(disparaître* to merge into sth ■ **fondant, -e** *adj* *(aliment)* which melts in the mouth

fonds [fɔ̃] **1** *nm* *(organisme)* fund; *(de bibliothèque)* collection; **f. de commerce** business; **F. monétaire international** International Monetary Fund **2** *nmpl* *(argent)* funds; **être en f.** to be in funds

font [fɔ̃] *voir* **faire**

fontaine [fɔ̃tɛn] *nf* *(construction)* fountain; *(source)* spring

fonte [fɔ̃t] *nf* (a) *(de neige)* melting; *(d'acier)* smelting (b) *(alliage)* cast iron; **en f.** *(poêle)* cast-iron (c) *Typ* font

football [futbol] *nm* *Br* football, *Am* soccer ■ **footballeur, -euse** *nmf Br* footballer, *Am* soccer player

forage [fɔraʒ] *nm* drilling, boring

forain [fɔrɛ̃] *nm* fairground stallholder

force [fɔrs] *nf* *(violence)* & *Phys* force; *(vigueur)* strength; **de toutes ses forces** with all one's strength; **de f.** by force, forcibly; **à f. de faire qch** through doing sth; **les forces armées** the armed forces ■ **forcément** *adv* inevitably; **pas f.** not necessarily

forcer [fɔrse] **1** *vt (obliger)* to force; *(porte)* to force open; *(voix)* to strain; **f. qn à faire qch** to force sb to do sth **2** *vi (appuyer, tirer)* to force it; *(se surmener)* to overdo it **3 se forcer** *vpr* to force oneself (**à faire** to do)

forer [fɔre] *vt* to drill, to bore

forêt [fɔrɛ] *nf* forest

forfait [fɔrfɛ] *nm* (a) *(prix)* all-in price; *(de ski)* pass; **f. week-end** weekend package (b) *(crime)* heinous crime ■ **forfaitaire** *adj (indemnités)* basic; **prix f.** all-in price

forge [fɔrʒ] *nf* forge ■ **forger** *vt (métal, liens)* to forge; *Fig (caractère)* to form ■ **forgeron** [-ərɔ̃] *nm* (black)smith

formaliser [fɔrmalize] **se formaliser** *vpr* to take offence (**de** at)

formalité [fɔrmalite] *nf* formality

format [fɔrma] *nm* format

formater [fɔrmate] *vt Ordinat* to format

formation [fɔrmasjɔ̃] *nf (de roche, de mot)* formation; *(éducation)* education; **f. permanente** continuing education; **f. professionnelle** vocational training ■ **formateur, -trice 1** *adj* formative **2** *nmf* trainer

forme [fɔrm] *nf (contour)* shape, form; *(manière, santé)* form; **en f. de qch** in the shape of sth; **en f. de poire** pear-shaped; **sous f. de qch** in the form of sth; **en (pleine) f.** *(en bonne santé)* on (top) form

formel, -elle [fɔrmɛl] *adj (structure)* formal; *(personne, preuve)* positive; *(interdiction)* strict

former [fɔrme] **1** *vt (groupe, caractère)* to form; *(apprenti)* to train **2 se former** *vpr (apparaître)* to form; *(association, liens)* to be formed; *(apprendre son métier)* to train oneself

formidable [fɔrmidabl] *adj (fantastique)* great; *(gigantesque)* tremendous

formulaire [fɔrmylɛr] *nm* form

formule [fɔrmyl] *nf Math* formula; *(phrase)* expression; *(solution)* method; **nouvelle f.** *(menu)* new-style; **f. magique** magic formula ■ **formulation** *nf* formulation ■ **formuler** *vt* to formulate

fort¹, -e [fɔr, fɔrt] **1** *adj (vigoureux)* strong; *(gros, important)* large; *(pluie, mer, chute de neige)* heavy; *(voix)* loud; *(fièvre)* high; *(pente)* steep; **être f. en qch** *(doué)* to be good at sth **2** *adv (frapper, pleuvoir)* hard; *(parler)* loud(ly); *(serrer)* tight; **sentir f.** to have a strong smell; **respirer f.** to breathe heavily **3** *nm (spécialité)* strong point

fort² [fɔr] *nm Hist* & *Mil* fort ■ **forteresse** *nf* fortress

fortifié, -e [fɔrtifje] *adj (ville, camp)* fortified ■ **fortification** *nf* fortification

fortifier [fɔrtifje] *vt (mur, ville)* to fortify; *(corps)* to strengthen ■ **fortifiant** *nm* tonic

fortune [fɔrtyn] *nf (richesse, hasard)*

fortune; **faire f.** to make one's fortune

fosse [fos] *nf (trou)* pit; **f. d'orchestre** orchestra pit

fossé [fose] *nm* ditch; *(de château)* moat; *Fig (désaccord)* gulf

fossette [foset] *nf* dimple

fossoyeur [foswajœr] *nm* gravedigger

fou, folle [fu, fɔl]

> **fol** is used before masculine singular nouns beginning with a vowel or h mute.

1 *adj (personne, projet)* mad, insane; *(succès, temps)* tremendous; *(envie)* wild, mad; *(espoir)* foolish; **f. de qch** *(musique, personne)* mad about sth; **f. de joie** beside oneself with joy

2 *nm* madman, *f* madwoman

3 *nm (bouffon)* jester; *Échecs* bishop

foudre [fudr] *nf* la **f.** lightning ■ **foudroyant,-e** *adj (succès, vitesse)* staggering ■ **foudroyer** *vt* to strike; **f. qn du regard** to give sb a withering look

fouet [fwɛ] *nm* whip; *Culin* whisk; **coup de f.** lash (with a whip); **de plein f.** head-on ■ **fouetter** *vt* to whip; *(sujet: pluie)* to lash (against); **crème fouettée** whipped cream

fougère [fuʒɛr] *nf* fern

fougue [fug] *nf* fire, spirit ■ **fougueux, -euse** *adj* fiery, ardent

fouille [fuj] **1** *nf (de personne, de bagages)* search **2** *nfpl* **fouilles archéologiques** excavations, dig ■ **fouiller 1** *vt (personne, maison)* to search **2** *vi* **f. dans qch** *(tiroir)* to search through sth **3** *vti (creuser)* to dig

fouillis [fuji] *nm* jumble

foulard [fular] *nm* (head)scarf

foule [ful] *nf* crowd; **une f. de** *(objets)* a mass of

foulée [fule] *nf (de coureur, de cheval)* stride

fouler [fule] **1** *vt (sol)* to tread; **f. qch aux pieds** to trample sth underfoot **2 se fouler** *vpr* **se f. la cheville** to sprain one's ankle ■ **foulure** *nf* sprain

four [fur] *nm (de cuisine)* oven; *(de potier)* kiln; **petit f.** *(gâteau)* (small) fancy cake

fourche [furʃ] *nf (outil, embranchement)* fork; **faire une f.** to fork ■ **fourcher** *vi (arbre)* to fork ■ **fourchette** *nf (pour manger)* fork; *(de salaires)* bracket ■ **fourchu, -e** *adj* forked

fourgon [furgɔ̃] *nm (camion)* van; **f. cellulaire** *Br* prison van, *Am* patrol wagon

fourmi [furmi] *nf (insecte)* ant; **avoir des fourmis dans les jambes** to have pins and needles in one's legs ■ **fourmiller** *vi* to teem, to swarm (**de** with)

fourneau, -x [furno] *nm (de cuisine)* stove

fournir [furnir] *vt (approvisionner)* to supply (**en** with); *(alibi, preuve, document)* to provide; *(effort)* to make; **f. qch à qn** to provide sb with sth; **pièces à f.** required documents ■ **fourni, -e** *adj (barbe)* bushy; **bien f.** *(boutique)* well-stocked ■ **fournisseur** *nm (commerçant)* supplier; *Ordinat* **f. d'accès** access provider ■ **fournitures** *nfpl* **f. de bureau** office supplies; **f. scolaires** school stationery

fourrage [furaʒ] *nm* fodder

fourré, -e [fure] **1** *adj (vêtement)* furlined; *(gâteau)* jam-/cream-filled **2** *nm Bot* thicket

fourreau, -x [furo] *nm (gaine)* sheath

fourrer [fure] **1** *vt (vêtement)* to furline; *(gâteau)* to fill **2 se fourrer** *vpr Fam* to put oneself (**dans** in); **où est-il allé se f.?** where's he got to? ■ **fourretout** *nm inv (sac) Br* holdall, *Am* carryall

fourrière [furjɛr] *nf (lieu)* pound; **mettre à la f.** *(voiture)* to impound; *(chien)* to put in the pound

fourrure [furyr] *nf* fur

foyer [fwaje] *nm (maison)* home; *(d'étudiants)* residence; *(de travailleurs)* hostel; *(de théâtre)* foyer; *(de lunettes)* focus; *(de chaleur, d'infection)* source; *(d'incendie)* seat; *(âtre)* hearth; *(famille)* family

fracas [fraka] *nm* crash ■ **fracassant, -e** *adj (nouvelle, révélation)* shattering

■ **fracasser** *vt*, **se fracasser** *vpr* to smash

fraction [fraksjɔ̃] *nf* fraction; *(partie)* part ■ **fractionner** *vt*, **se fractionner** *vpr* to split (up)

fracture [fraktyr] *nf* fracture ■ **fracturer 1** *vt (porte)* to break open; *(os)* to fracture **2 se fracturer** *vpr* **se f. la jambe** to fracture one's leg

fragile [fraʒil] *adj (objet, matériau)* fragile; *(santé, équilibre)* delicate; *(personne) (physiquement)* frail; *(mentalement)* sensitive ■ **fragilité** *nf (d'objet, de matériau)* fragility; *(de personne) (physique)* frailty; *(mentale)* sensitivity

fragment [fragmɑ̃] *nm* fragment

fraîcheur [frɛʃœr] *nf (d'aliments)* freshness; *(de température)* coolness

frais¹, fraîche [frɛ, frɛʃ] **1** *adj (aliment, fleurs)* fresh; *(vent, air)* cool, fresh; *(nouvelles)* recent; *(peinture)* wet
2 *adv* **servir f.** *(vin)* to serve chilled
3 *nm* **mettre qch au f.** to put sth in a cool place; *(au réfrigérateur)* to refrigerate sth; **il fait f.** it's cool ■ **fraîchir** *vi (temps)* to freshen

frais² [frɛ] *nmpl* expenses; **à mes f.** at my (own) expense; **faire des f.** to go to great expense; **f. de scolarité** school fees

fraise [frɛz] *nf (fruit)* strawberry; *(de dentiste)* drill ■ **fraisier** *nm (plante)* strawberry plant; *(gâteau)* strawberry cream cake

framboise [frɑ̃bwaz] *nf* raspberry ■ **framboisier** *nm* raspberry bush

franc¹, franche [frɑ̃, frɑ̃ʃ] *adj* **(a)** *(sincère)* frank; *(visage)* open **(b)** *(net) (couleur)* pure **(c)** *(zone, ville, port)* free ■ **franchement** *adv (sincèrement)* frankly; *(vraiment)* really; *(sans ambiguïté)* clearly

franc² [frɑ̃] *nm Anciennement (monnaie)* franc

France *nf* **la F.** France ■ **français, -e 1** *adj* French **2** *nmf* **F.** Frenchman; **Française** Frenchwoman; **les F.** the French **3** *nm (langue)* French

franchir [frɑ̃ʃir] *vt (obstacle)* to get over; *(fossé)* to jump over; *(frontière, ligne d'arrivée)* to cross; *(porte)* to go through; *(distance)* to cover

franchise [frɑ̃ʃiz] *nf (sincérité)* frankness; *(exonération)* exemption; *Com* franchise; **f. postale** ≃ postage paid

franc-maçon [frɑ̃masɔ̃] *nm (pl* **francs-maçons)** *nm* freemason

francophone [frɑ̃kɔfɔn] **1** *adj* French-speaking **2** *nmf* French speaker

franc-parler [frɑ̃parle] *nm* **avoir son f.** to speak one's mind

frange [frɑ̃ʒ] *nf (de cheveux) Br* fringe, *Am* bangs; *(de vêtement)* fringe

frappe [frap] *nf (sur machine à écrire)* typing; *(sur ordinateur)* keying; **faute de f.** typing error

frapper [frape] **1** *vt (battre)* to strike, to hit; *(monnaie)* to mint; **f. qn** *(impressionner)* to strike sb; *(impôt, mesure)* to hit sb **2** *vi (donner un coup)* to strike, to hit; **f. du pied** to stamp (one's foot); **f. du poing sur la table** to bang (on) the table; **f. à une porte** to knock on a door; **'entrez sans f.'** 'go straight in' ■ **frappant, -e** *adj* striking ■ **frappé, -e** *adj (boisson)* chilled

fraternel, -elle [fraternɛl] *adj* fraternal, brotherly ■ **fraternité** *nf* fraternity, brotherhood

fraude [frod] *nf* fraud; **passer qch en f.** to smuggle sth in; **f. fiscale** tax evasion ■ **frauder 1** *vt* **f. le fisc** to evade tax **2** *vi* to cheat *(sur* on) ■ **fraudeur, -euse** *nmf* defrauder ■ **frauduleux, -euse** *adj* fraudulent

frayer [freje] **se frayer** *vpr* **se f. un chemin** to clear a way *(à travers/dans* through)

frayeur [frejœr] *nf* fright

fredonner [frədɔne] *vti* to hum

frein [frɛ̃] *nm* brake; **donner un coup de f.** to put on the brakes; **f. à main** handbrake ■ **freiner 1** *vt (véhicule)* to slow down; *(chute)* to break; *Fig (inflation)* to curb **2** *vi* to brake

frelaté, -e [frəlate] *adj (vin) & Fig* adulterated

frêle [frɛl] *adj* frail

frémir [fremir] *vi* (*personne*) to tremble (**de** with); (*feuilles*) to rustle; (*eau chaude*) to simmer ■ **frémissement** *nm* (*de peur*) shudder; (*de plaisir*) thrill; (*de colère*) quiver; (*de feuilles*) rustle; (*d'eau chaude*) simmering

frénétique [frenetik] *adj* frenzied

fréquent, -e [frekã, -ãt] *adj* frequent ■ **fréquence** *nf* frequency

fréquenter [frekãte] **1** *vt* (*lieu*) to frequent; **f. qn** to see sb regularly **2 se fréquenter** *upr* (*se voir régulièrement*) to see each other often socially ■ **fréquentation** *nf* (*de lieu*) frequenting; **fréquentations** (*relations*) company ■ **fréquenté, -e** *adj* **mal f.** disreputable, of ill repute; **bien f.** reputable, of good repute

frère [frɛr] *nm* brother

friable [frijabl] *adj* crumbly

friand, -e [frijã, -ãd] **1** *adj* **f. de qch** fond of sth **2** *nm* (*salé*) = small savoury pastry ■ **friandise** *nf* *Br* titbit, *Am* tidbit

friction [friksjɔ̃] *nf* (*massage*) rubdown; (*de cuir chevelu*) scalp massage; (*désaccord*) friction ■ **frictionner** *vt* (*partie du corps*) to rub; (*personne*) to rub down

Frigidaire® [friʒidɛr] *nm* fridge

frileux, -euse [frilø, -øz] *adj* **être f.** to feel the cold

friper [fripe] **1** *vt* to crumple **2 se friper** *upr* to get crumpled ■ **fripé, -e** *adj* crumpled

frire* [frir] **1** *vt* to fry **2** *vi* to fry; **faire f. qch** to fry sth

friser [frize] **1** *vt* (*cheveux*) to curl; (*effleurer*) to skim; **f. la catastrophe** to come within an inch of disaster **2** *vi* (*cheveux*) to curl; (*personne*) to have curly hair ■ **frisé, -e** *adj* (*cheveux*) curly; (*personne*) curly-haired

frisson [frisɔ̃] *nm* (*de froid, de peur*) shiver; (*de plaisir*) thrill ■ **frissonner** *vi* (*de froid, de peur*) to shiver

frit, -e [fri, -it] **1** *pp de* **frire 2** *adj* fried ■ **frites** *nfpl Br* chips, *Am* French fries

■ **friture** *nf* (*mode de cuisson*) frying; (*aliment*) fried food

frivole [frivol] *adj* frivolous

froid, -e [frwa, frwad] **1** *adj* cold **2** *nm* cold; **avoir f.** to be/catch cold; **il fait f.** it's cold

froisser [frwase] **1** *vt* (*tissu*) to crumple, to crease **2 se froisser** *upr* (*tissu*) to crease, to crumple; **se f. un muscle** to strain a muscle

frôler [frole] *vt* (*effleurer*) to brush against, to touch lightly; *Fig* (*catastrophe*) to come close to

fromage [frɔmaʒ] *nm* cheese; **f. de chèvre** goat's cheese; **f. blanc** soft cheese; **f. frais** fromage frais ■ **fromager, -ère** *nmf* (*fabricant*) cheesemaker; (*commerçant*) cheese seller ■ **fromagerie** *nf* (*magasin*) cheese shop

froment [frɔmã] *nm* wheat

froncer [frɔ̃se] *vt* (*tissu*) to gather; **f. les sourcils** to frown

front [frɔ̃] *nm* (*du visage*) forehead; (*avant*), *Mil & Pol* front; **de f.** (*heurter*) head-on; (*côte à côte*) abreast; (*à la fois*) (all) at once; **faire f. à qn/qch** to face up to sb/sth; **f. de mer** sea front ■ **frontal, -e, -aux, -ales** *adj* (*collision*) head-on

frontière [frɔ̃tjɛr] **1** *nf* (*de pays*) border **2** *adj inv* **ville f.** border town ■ **frontalier, -ère** *adj* **ville frontalière** border *or* frontier town

frotter [frɔte] **1** *vt* to rub; (*plancher*) to scrub; (*allumette*) to strike **2** *vi* to rub (**contre** against) **3 se frotter** *upr* to rub oneself; **se f. le dos** to scrub one's back

fructifier [fryktifje] *vi* (*arbre, capital*) to bear fruit ■ **fructueux, -euse** *adj* fruitful

frugal, -e, -aux, -ales [frygal, -o] *adj* frugal

fruit [frɥi] *nm* fruit; **des fruits** fruit; **un f.** a piece of fruit; **fruits de mer** seafood; **fruits secs** dried fruit ■ **fruité, -e** *adj* fruity ■ **fruitier** *adj m* **arbre f.** fruit tree

frustrer [frystre] *vt* **f. qn** to frustrate sb; **f. qn de qch** to deprive sb of sth ▪ **frustration** *nf* frustration ▪ **frustré, -e** *adj* frustrated

fuel [fjul] *nm* fuel oil

fugitif, -ive [fyʒitif, -iv] **1** *adj (passager)* fleeting **2** *nmf* runaway, fugitive

fugue [fyg] *nf* **faire une f.** *(enfant)* to run away ▪ **fuguer** *vi Fam* to run away

fuir* [fɥir] **1** *vt (pays)* to flee; *(personne)* to run away from; *(guerre)* to escape **2** *vi (s'échapper)* to run away *(devant* from); *(gaz, robinet, stylo)* to leak ▪ **fuite** *nf (évasion)* flight *(devant* from); *(de gaz)* leak; **en f.** on the run; **prendre la f.** to take flight

fulgurant, -e [fylgyrã, -ãt] *adj (progrès)* spectacular; *(douleur)* shooting

fumer [fyme] **1** *vt (cigarette, poisson)* to smoke; **f. la pipe** to smoke a pipe **2** *vi (fumeur, moteur)* to smoke; *(liquide brûlant)* to steam ▪ **fumé, -e** *adj (poisson, verre)* smoked ▪ **fumée** *nf* smoke; *(vapeur)* steam ▪ **fumeur, -euse** *nmf* smoker

fumeux, -euse [fymø, -øz] *adj Fig (idée)* hazy

fumier [fymje] *nm (engrais)* manure, dung

funambule [fynãbyl] *nmf* tightrope walker

funèbre [fynɛbr] *adj (lugubre)* gloomy; **marche f.** funeral march

funérailles *nfpl* funeral ▪ **funéraire** *adj* funeral

funiculaire [fynikyler] *nm* funicular

fur [fyr] **au fur et à mesure** *adv* as one goes along, progressively; **au f. et à mesure que...** as...

furent [fyr] *voir* **être**

furie [fyri] *nf (colère)* fury ▪ **furieux, -euse** *adj (en colère)* furious *(contre* with)

fuseau, -x [fyzo] *nm (pantalon)* ski pants; *(bobine)* spindle; **f. horaire** time zone

fusée [fyze] *nf* rocket

fuselage [fyzlaʒ] *nm (d'avion)* fuselage

fusible [fyzibl] *nm* fuse

fusil [fyzi] *nm* rifle, gun; *(de chasse)* shotgun ▪ **fusillade** *nf (tirs)* gunfire ▪ **fusiller** *vt (exécuter)* to shoot

fusion [fyzjõ] *nf* (**a**) *(de métal)* melting; *Phys* fusion; **métal en f.** molten metal (**b**) *(de sociétés)* merger ▪ **fusionner** *vti (sociétés)* to merge

fut [fy] *voir* **être**

futile [fytil] *adj (personne)* frivolous; *(prétexte)* trivial

futur, -ure [fytyr] **1** *adj* future; **future mère** mother-to-be **2** *nmf* **mon f./ma future** my intended **3** *nm (avenir)* future

fuyant [fɥijã] *p prés de* **fuir** ▪ **fuyant, -e** *adj (front)* receding; *(personne)* evasive ▪ **fuyard, -e** *nmf* runaway

Gg

G, g [ʒe] *nm inv* G, g

gabarit [gabaʀi] *nm (dimension)* size

gâcher [gɑʃe] *vt (gâter)* to spoil; *(gaspiller)* to waste ▪ **gâchis** *nm* waste

gâchette [gɑʃɛt] *nf* trigger

gadget [gadʒɛt] *nm* gadget

gadoue [gadu] *nf* mud

gag [gag] *nm* gag

gage [gaʒ] *nm (garantie)* guarantee; *(au jeu)* forfeit; *(preuve)* token

gagnant, -e [gaɲɑ̃, -ɑ̃t] **1** *adj (billet, cheval)* winning **2** *nmf* winner

gagner [gaɲe] **1** *vt (par le travail)* to earn; *(par le jeu)* to win; *(obtenir)* to gain; *(atteindre)* to reach; *(sujet: feu, épidémie)* to spread to; **g. sa vie** to earn one's living; **g. du temps** *(aller plus vite)* to save time; *(temporiser)* to gain time; **g. du terrain** to gain ground; **g. de la place** to save space **2** *vi (être vainqueur)* to win ▪ **gagne-pain** *nm inv* livelihood

gai, -e [ge] *adj* cheerful ▪ **gaieté** *nf* cheerfulness

gaillard [gajaʀ] *nm (homme)* fellow; **un grand g.** a strapping man

gain [gɛ̃] *nm (profit)* gain, profit; *(succès)* winning; **gains** *(à la Bourse)* profits; *(au jeu)* winnings

gaine [gɛn] *nf (étui)* sheath

gala [gala] *nm* gala

galant, -e [galɑ̃, -ɑ̃t] *adj (homme)* gallant; *(rendez-vous)* romantic ▪ **galanterie** *nf* gallantry

galaxie [galaksi] *nf* galaxy

galerie [galʀi] *nf (passage, salle)* gallery; *(de taupe)* tunnel; **g. d'art** art gallery; **g. marchande** (shopping) mall

galet [galɛ] *nm* pebble; **plage de galets** shingle beach

galette [galɛt] *nf (gâteau)* butter biscuit; *(crêpe)* buckwheat pancake; **g. des Rois** = Twelfth Night cake

Galles [gal] *nm* **pays de G.** Wales ▪ **gallois, -e 1** *adj* Welsh **2** *nmf* **G.** Welshman; **Galloise** Welshwoman **3** *nm (langue)* Welsh

galon [galɔ̃] *nm (ruban)* braid; *(de soldat)* stripe

galop [galo] *nm* gallop; **aller au g.** to gallop ▪ **galoper** *vi (cheval)* to gallop

gambader [gɑ̃bade] *vi* to leap *or* frisk about

Gambie [gɑ̃bi] *nf* **la G.** The Gambia

gamelle [gamɛl] *nf (de chien)* bowl; *(d'ouvrier)* billy(can); *(de soldat)* mess tin

gamin, -e [gamɛ̃, -in] *nmf (enfant)* kid

gamme [gam] *nf* Mus scale; *(éventail)* range; **téléviseur haut/bas de g.** top-of-the-range/bottom-of-the-range television

gang [gɑ̃g] *nm* gang

gant [gɑ̃] *nm* glove; **g. de toilette** ≃ facecloth

garage [gaʀaʒ] *nm (de voitures)* garage ▪ **garagiste** *nmf (mécanicien)* garage mechanic; *(propriétaire)* garage owner

garant, -e [gaʀɑ̃, -ɑ̃t] *nmf* Jur *(personne)* guarantor; **se porter g. de qn** to stand guarantor for sb; **se porter g. de qch** to vouch for sth

garantie [gaʀɑ̃ti] *nf* guarantee; Fig *(précaution)* safeguard; **sous g.** under guarantee ▪ **garantir** vt to guarantee; (emprunt) to secure; **g. à qn que…** to guarantee sb that…

garçon [garsɔ̃] nm boy; (jeune homme) young man; (serveur) waiter; **g. de café** waiter; **g. d'honneur** best man; **g. manqué** tomboy

garde [gard] **1** nm (gardien) guard; (soldat) guardsman; **g. du corps** bodyguard

2 nf (**a**) (d'enfants, de bagages) care, custody (**de** of); **avoir la g. de** to be in charge of; **prendre g.** to pay attention (**à qch** to sth); **être de g.** to be on duty; (soldat) to be on guard duty; **médecin de g.** duty doctor

(**b**) (escorte, soldats) guard

3 nm **g. de nuit** (de malade) night nurse ▪ **garde-à-vous** nm inv Mil (position of) attention; **se mettre au g.** to stand to attention ▪ **garde-chasse** (pl **gardes-chasses**) nm gamekeeper ▪ **garde-côte** (pl **gardes-côtes**) nm (bateau) coastguard vessel ▪ **garde-manger** nm inv (armoire) food safe; (pièce) pantry, Br larder ▪ **garde-robe** (pl **garde-robes**) nf wardrobe

garder [garde] **1** vt (conserver) to keep; (vêtement) to keep on; (habitude) to keep up; (surveiller) to look after; (défendre) to protect **2 se garder** vpr (aliment) to keep; **se g. de qch** to beware of sth; **se g. de faire qch** to take care not to do sth

garderie [gardəri] nf Br (day) nursery, Am daycare center

gardien, -enne [gardjɛ̃, -ɛn] nmf (d'immeuble, d'hôtel) caretaker, Am janitor; (de prison) (prison) guard, Br warder; (de zoo) keeper; (de musée) Br attendant, Am guard; **g. de but** (au football) goalkeeper; **gardienne d'enfants** child minder, baby-sitter; **g. de nuit** night watchman; **g. de la paix** policeman

gare [gar] nf (pour trains) station; **g. routière** bus or Br coach station

garer [gare] **1** vt (voiture) to park **2 se garer** vpr (automobiliste) to park

gargariser [gargarize] **se gargariser** vpr to gargle

gargouiller [garguje] vi (fontaine, eau) to gurgle; (ventre) to rumble

garnir [garnir] vt (décorer) to trim (**de** with); (équiper) to fit out (**de** with); (couvrir) to cover; (remplir) to fill ▪ **garniture** nf Culin garnish

garnison [garnizɔ̃] nf garrison

gaspiller [gaspije] vt to waste ▪ **gaspillage** nm waste

gastronomie [gastronomi] nf gastronomy

gâté, -e [gɑte] adj (dent, fruit) bad; **enfant g.** spoilt child

gâteau, -x [gɑto] nm cake; **g. sec** Br biscuit, Am cookie

gâter [gɑte] **1** vt to spoil **2 se gâter** vpr (aliment, dent) to go bad; (temps) to take a turn for the worst

gâteux, -euse [gɑtø, -øz] adj senile

gauche¹ [goʃ] **1** adj (côté, main) left **2** nf **la g.** (côté) the left (side); Pol the left (wing); **à g.** (tourner) (to the) left; (marcher) on the left, on the left(-hand) side; **de g.** (fenêtre, colonne) left-hand; (parti, politique) left-wing; **à g. de** on or to the left of ▪ **gaucher, -ère 1** adj left-handed **2** nmf left-hander ▪ **gauchiste** adj & nmf Pol (extreme) leftist

gauche² [goʃ] adj (maladroit) awkward

gaufre [gofr] nf waffle ▪ **gaufrette** nf wafer (biscuit)

gaver [gave] **1** vt (animal) to force-feed; Fig (personne) to stuff (**de** with) **2 se gaver** vpr to stuff oneself (**de** with)

gaz [gaz] nm inv gas; **masque à g.** gas mask; **g. carbonique** carbon dioxide; **g. d'échappement** exhaust fumes ▪ **gazeux, -euse** adj (état) gaseous; (boisson) fizzy, carbonated; (eau) sparkling

gazole [gazɔl] nm diesel oil

gazon [gazɔ̃] nm (herbe) grass; (surface) lawn

gazouiller [gazuje] vi (oiseau) to

chirp; *(bébé, ruisseau)* to babble

géant, -e [ʒeā, -āt] *adj & nmf* giant

geindre* [ʒɛ̃dr] *vi (gémir)* to moan

gel [ʒɛl] *nm* (**a**) *(temps, glace)* frost (**b**) *(pour cheveux)* gel ■ **gelé, -e** *adj* frozen; *Méd* frostbitten ■ **gelée** *nf* (**a**) frost; **g. blanche** ground frost (**b**) *(de fruits, de viande)* jelly ■ **geler 1** *vt* to freeze **2** *vi* to freeze; **on gèle ici** it's freezing here **3** *v impersonnel* **il gèle** it's freezing

Gémeaux [ʒemo] *nmpl* **les G.** *(signe)* Gemini

gémir [ʒemir] *vi* to groan, to moan ■ **gémissement** *nm* groan, moan

gênant, -e [ʒɛnā, -āt] *adj (objet)* cumbersome; *(présence, situation)* awkward; *(bruit, personne)* annoying

gencive [ʒāsiv] *nf* gum

gendarme [ʒādarm] *nm* gendarme, policeman ■ **gendarmerie** *nf (corps)* police force; *(local)* police headquarters

gendre [ʒādr] *nm* son-in-law

gène [ʒɛn] *nm Biol* gene

gêne [ʒɛn] *nf (trouble physique)* discomfort; *(confusion)* embarrassment; *(dérangement)* inconvenience

gêné, -e [ʒene] *adj (intimidé)* embarrassed; *(silence, sourire)* awkward

généalogie [ʒenealɔʒi] *nf* genealogy ■ **généalogique** *adj* genealogical; **arbre g.** family tree

gêner [ʒene] **1** *vt (déranger, irriter)* to bother; *(troubler)* to embarrass; *(mouvement)* to hamper; *(circulation)* to hold up; **ça ne me gêne pas** I don't mind **(si** if) **2 se gêner** *vpr (se déranger)* to put oneself out

général, -e, -aux, -ales [ʒeneral, -o] **1** *adj* general; **en g.** in general **2** *nm Mil* general ■ **généralité** *nf* generality

généralisation [ʒeneralizasjɔ̃] *nf* generalization ■ **généraliser 1** *vti* to generalize **2 se généraliser** *vpr* to become widespread ■ **généraliste** *nmf (médecin)* general practitioner, GP

générateur [ʒeneratœr] *nm Él* generator

génération [ʒenerasjɔ̃] *nf* generation

génératrice [ʒeneratris] *nf Él* generator

générer [ʒenere] *vt* to generate

généreux, -euse [ʒenerø, -øz] *adj* generous (**de** with)

générique [ʒenerik] **1** *nm (de film)* credits **2** *adj* **produit g.** generic product

générosité [ʒenerozite] *nf* generosity

génétique [ʒenetik] **1** *nf* genetics *(sing)* **2** *adj* genetic; **manipulation g.** genetic engineering ■ **génétiquement** *adv* **g. modifié** genetically modified

Genève [ʒənɛv] *nm ou f* Geneva

génial, -e, -aux, -ales [ʒenjal, -jo] *adj (personne, invention)* brilliant

génie [ʒeni] *nm* (**a**) *(aptitude, personne)* genius; **avoir le g. pour faire qch** to have a genius for doing sth (**b**) **g. civil** civil engineering; **g. génétique** genetic engineering (**c**) *(esprit)* genie, spirit

genou, -x [ʒ(ə)nu] *nm* knee; **être à genoux** to be kneeling (down); **se mettre à genoux** to kneel (down)

genre [ʒār] *nm (espèce)* kind, sort; *(attitude)* manner; *Beaux-Arts* genre; *Gram* gender; **le g. humain** mankind

gens [ʒā] *nmpl* people

gentil, -ille [ʒāti, -ij] *adj (aimable)* nice (**avec** to); *(sage)* good ■ **gentillesse** *nf* kindness; **avoir la g. de faire qch** to be kind enough to do sth ■ **gentiment** *adv (aimablement)* kindly; *(sagement)* nicely

géographie [ʒeɔgrafi] *nf* geography ■ **géographique** *adj* geographical

geôlier, -ère [ʒolje, -jɛr] *nmf* jailer

géologie [ʒeɔlɔʒi] *nf* geology ■ **géologique** *adj* geological

géomètre [ʒeɔmɛtr] *nm* surveyor

géométrie [ʒeɔmetri] *nf* geometry ■ **géométrique** *adj* geometric(al)

gérant, -e [ʒerā, -āt] *nmf* manager, *f* manageress

gerbe [ʒɛrb] *nf (de blé)* sheaf; *(de fleurs)* bunch; *(d'eau)* spray

gercer [ʒɛrse] *vi*, **se gercer** *vpr (peau, lèvres)* to chap ■ **gerçure** *nf* chap, crack

gérer [ʒere] *vt* to manage

germe [ʒɛrm] *nm (microbe)* germ; *(de plante)* shoot ■ **germer** *vi (graine)* to start to grow; *(pomme de terre)* to sprout

geste [ʒɛst] *nm* gesture; **faire un g.** *(bouger, agir)* to make a gesture; **ne pas faire un g.** *(ne pas bouger)* not to make a move

gestion [ʒɛstjɔ̃] *nf (action)* management ■ **gestionnaire** *nmf* administrator

Ghana [gana] *nm* **le G.** Ghana

gibier [ʒibje] *nm* game

giboulée [ʒibule] *nf* sudden shower; **giboulées de mars** ≃ April showers

gicler [ʒikle] *vi (liquide)* to spurt out; *(boue)* to splash up

gifle [ʒifl] *nf* slap in the face ■ **gifler** *vt* **g. qn** to slap sb in the face

gigantesque [ʒigɑ̃tɛsk] *adj* gigantic

gigot [ʒigo] *nm* leg of mutton/lamb

gilet [ʒile] *nm (cardigan)* cardigan; *(de costume)* Br waistcoat, Am vest; **g. pare-balles** bulletproof vest; **g. de sauvetage** life jacket

gingembre [ʒɛ̃ʒɑ̃br] *nm* ginger

girafe [ʒiraf] *nf* giraffe

giratoire [ʒiratwar] *adj Aut* **sens g.** Br roundabout, Am traffic circle

girofle [ʒirɔfl] *nm* **clou de g.** clove

gisement [ʒizmɑ̃] *nm (de minerai)* deposit; **g. de pétrole** oilfield

gitan, -e [ʒitɑ̃, -an] *nmf* gipsy

gîte [ʒit] *nm (abri)* resting place; **g. rural** gîte, = self-catering holiday cottage or apartment

givre [ʒivr] *nm* frost ■ **givré, -e** *adj* frost-covered

glace [glas] *nf* **(a)** *(eau gelée)* ice; *(crème glacée)* ice cream **(b)** *(vitre)* window; *(miroir)* mirror

glacer [glase] *vt (durcir)* to freeze; *(gâteau)* to ice ■ **glaçage** *nm (de gâteau)* icing ■ **glacé, -e** *adj (eau, pièce)* ice-cold, icy; *(vent)* freezing, icy;

(thé, café) iced; *(papier)* glazed

glacial, -e, -aux, -ales [glasjal, -o] *adj* icy

glacier [glasje] *nm* **(a)** *Géol* glacier **(b)** *(vendeur)* ice-cream seller

glacière [glasjɛr] *nf (boîte)* icebox

glaçon [glasɔ̃] *nm Culin* ice cube; *Géol* block of ice; *(sur toit)* icicle

glande [glɑ̃d] *nf* gland

glaner [glane] *vt (blé, renseignement)* to glean

glisse [glis] *nf* **sports de g.** = sports involving sliding and gliding motion, eg skiing, surfing etc

glisser [glise] **1** *vt (introduire)* to slip (**dans** into); *(murmurer)* to whisper **2** *vi (involontairement)* to slip; *(volontairement) (sur glace)* to slide; *(sur l'eau)* to glide; **ça glisse** it's slippery **3** **se glisser** *vpr* **se g. dans/sous qch** to slip into/under sth ■ **glissade** *nf (involontaire)* slip; *(volontaire)* slide ■ **glissant, -e** *adj* slippery ■ **glissement** *nm* **g. de terrain** landslide

glissière [glisjɛr] *nf Tech* runner, slide; **porte à g.** sliding door

global, -e, -aux, -ales [glɔbal, -o] *adj* total, global ■ **globalement** *adv* overall

globe [glɔb] *nm* globe; **g. terrestre** *(mappemonde)* globe

globuleux, -euse [glɔbylø, -øz] *adj* **yeux g.** protruding eyes

gloire [glwar] *nf (renom)* glory; *(personne célèbre)* celebrity ■ **glorieux, -euse** *adj* glorious ■ **glorifier 1** *vt* to glorify **2 se glorifier** *vpr* **se g. de qch** to glory in sth

glousser [gluse] *vi (poule)* to cluck; *(personne)* to chuckle

glouton, -onne [glutɔ̃, -ɔn] **1** *adj* greedy, gluttonous **2** *nmf* glutton

gluant, -e [glyɑ̃, -ɑ̃t] *adj* sticky

goal [gol] *nm (au football)* goalkeeper

gobelet [gɔblɛ] *nm* tumbler; *(de plastique, de papier)* cup

goéland [gɔelɑ̃] *nm (sea)*gull

golf [gɔlf] *nm* golf; *(terrain)* golf course ■ **golfeur, -euse** *nmf* golfer

golfe [gɔlf] *nm* gulf, bay

gomme [gɔm] *nf (pour effacer)* eraser, *Br* rubber ■ **gommer** *vt (effacer)* to rub out, to erase

gond [gɔ̃] *nm (de porte)* hinge

gondoler [gɔ̃dɔle] **1** *vi (planche)* to warp; *(papier)* to crinkle **2 se gondoler** *vpr (planche)* to warp; *(papier)* to crinkle

gonflable [gɔ̃flabl] *adj* inflatable

gonfler [gɔ̃fle] **1** *vt* to swell; *(pneu)* to inflate **2** *vi* to swell ■ **gonflé, -e** *adj* swollen ■ **gonflement** *nm* swelling

gorge [gɔrʒ] *nf* throat; *Géog* gorge; **avoir la g. serrée** to have a lump in one's throat

gorgé, -e [gɔrʒe] *adj* **g. de qch** *(saturé)* gorged with sth

gorgée [gɔrʒe] *nf* mouthful; **petite g.** sip

gorger [gɔrʒe] **1** *vt (remplir)* to stuff (de with) **2 se gorger** *vpr* **se g. de qch** to gorge oneself with sth

gorille [gɔrij] *nm (animal)* gorilla

gothique [gɔtik] *adj & nm* Gothic

goudron [gudrɔ̃] *nm* tar

gouffre [gufr] *nm* abyss

goulot [gulo] *nm (de bouteille)* neck; **boire au g.** to drink from the bottle

goulu, -e [guly] *adj* greedy

goupille [gupij] *nf (de grenade)* pin

gourde [gurd] *nf (à eau)* water bottle, flask

gourmand, -e [gurmã, -ãd] **1** *adj* fond of eating; **g. de qch** fond of sth **2** *nmf* hearty eater ■ **gourmandise** *nf* fondness for food; **gourmandises** *(mets)* delicacies

gourmet [gurmε] *nm* gourmet; **fin g.** gourmet

gousse [gus] *nf* **g. d'ail** clove of garlic

goût [gu] *nm* taste; **de bon g.** in good taste; **par g.** by choice; **avoir du g.** *(personne)* to have (good) taste; **avoir un g. de noisette** to taste of hazelnut

goûter [gute] **1** *vt (aliment)* to taste; *(apprécier)* to enjoy; **g. à qch** to taste (a little of) sth **2** *vi* to have an afternoon snack, *Br* to have tea **3** *nm* afternoon snack, *Br* tea

goutte [gut] *nf (de liquide)* drop; **couler g. à g.** to drip ■ **goutte-à-goutte** *nm inv Méd* drip ■ **gouttelette** *nf* droplet ■ **goutter** *vi* to drip

gouttière [gutjεr] *nf (le long du toit)* gutter; *(le long du mur)* drainpipe

gouvernail [guvεrnaj] *nm (pale)* rudder; *(barre)* helm

gouvernante [guvεrnãt] *nf* governess

gouvernants [guvεrnã] *nmpl* rulers

gouvernement [guvεrnəmã] *nm* government ■ **gouvernemental, -e, -aux, -ales** *adj* **politique gouvernementale** government policy

gouverner [guvεrne] *vti Pol & Fig* to govern, to rule ■ **gouverneur** *nm* governor

grâce [gras] **1** *nf (charme)* & *Rel* grace; *(acquittement)* pardon; **de bonne/mauvaise g.** with good/bad grace; **délai de g.** period of grace **2** *prép* **g. à** thanks to

gracier [grasje] *vt (condamné)* to pardon

gracieux, -euse [grasjø, -øz] *adj (élégant)* graceful; *(aimable)* gracious; *(gratuit)* gratuitous; **à titre g.** free (of charge) ■ **gracieusement** *adv (avec élégance)* gracefully; *(aimablement)* graciously; *(gratuitement)* free (of charge)

grade [grad] *nm (militaire)* rank; **monter en g.** to be promoted ■ **gradé** *nm Mil* non-commissioned officer

gradins [gradɛ̃] *nmpl (d'amphithéâtre)* rows of seats; *(de stade) Br* terraces, *Am* bleachers

graduel, -elle [graduɛl] *adj* gradual

graduer [gradue] *vt (règle)* to graduate; *(augmenter)* to increase gradually

graffiti [grafiti] *nmpl* graffiti

grain [grɛ̃] *nm* **(a)** *(de blé)* & *Fig* grain; *(de café)* bean; *(de poussière)* speck; **g. de beauté** mole; *(sur le visage)* beauty spot; **g. de raisin** grape **(b)** *(averse)* shower

graine [grεn] *nf* seed

graisse [grεs] *nf* fat; *(lubrifiant)* grease

■ **graisser** *vt* to grease ■ **graisseux, -euse** *adj (vêtement)* greasy, oily; *(tissu)* fatty

grammaire [gramɛr] *nf* grammar ■ **grammatical, -e, -aux, -ales** *adj* grammatical

gramme [gram] *nm* gram(me)

GRAND, -E [grɑ̃, grɑ̃d] **1** *adj* big, large; *(en hauteur)* tall; *(chaleur, découverte, âge, mérite, ami)* great; *(bruit)* loud; *(différence)* big, great; *(adulte)* grown-up, big; *(illustre)* great; **g. frère** *(plus âgé)* big brother; **le g. air** the open air; **il est g. temps que je parte** it's high time that I left; **il n'y avait pas g. monde** there were not many people

2 *adv* **g. ouvert** *(yeux, fenêtre)* wide open; **ouvrir g.** to open wide; **en g.** on a grand or large scale

3 *nmf (enfant)* senior; *(adulte)* grown-up ■ **grandement** *adv (beaucoup)* greatly; *(généreusement)* grandly ■ **grand-mère** *(pl* **grands-mères)** *nf* grandmother ■ **grand-père** *(pl* **grands-pères)** *nm* grandfather ■ **grands-parents** *nmpl* grandparents

grand-chose [grɑ̃ʃoz] *pron* **pas g.** not much

Grande-Bretagne [grɑ̃dbrətaɲ] *nf* **la G.** Great Britain

grandeur [grɑ̃dœr] *nf (importance, gloire)* greatness; *(dimension)* size; *(majesté, splendeur)* grandeur; **g. nature** life-size

grandiose [grɑ̃djoz] *adj* imposing

grandir [grɑ̃dir] **1** *vi (en taille)* to grow; *(en âge)* to grow up; **g. de 2 cm** to grow 2 cm **2** *vt* **g. qn** *(faire paraître plus grand)* to make sb look taller

grange [grɑ̃ʒ] *nf* barn

granit(e) [granit] *nm* granite

graphique [grafik] **1** *adj (signe, art)* graphic **2** *nm* graph; *Ordinat* graphic

grappe [grap] *nf (de fruits)* cluster; **g. de raisin** bunch of grapes

gras, grasse [grɑ, grɑs] **1** *adj (personne, ventre)* fat; *(aliment)* fatty;

(graisseux) greasy, oily; *(toux)* loose; **faire la grasse matinée** to have a lie-in **2** *nm (de viande)* fat ■ **grassement** *adv* **g. payé** handsomely paid ■ **grassouillet, -ette** *adj* plump

gratifier [gratifje] *vt* **g. qn de qch** to present sb with sth ■ **gratification** *nf (prime)* bonus

gratin [gratɛ̃] *nm (plat)* = baked dish with a cheese topping; **chou-fleur au g.** cauliflower cheese

gratis [gratis] *adv* free (of charge)

gratitude [gratityd] *nf* gratitude

gratte-ciel [gratsjɛl] *nm inv* skyscraper

gratter [grate] **1** *vt (avec un outil)* to scrape; *(avec les ongles, les griffes)* to scratch; *(effacer)* to scratch out; *Fam* **ça me gratte** it's itchy **2** *vi (tissu)* to be scratchy **3** *se gratter vpr* to scratch oneself

gratuit, -e [gratɥi, -it] *adj (billet, entrée)* free; *(acte)* gratuitous ■ **gratuité** *nf* **la g. de l'enseignement** free education ■ **gratuitement** *adv (sans payer)* free (of charge); *(sans motif)* gratuitously

gravats [grava] *nmpl* rubble, debris

grave [grav] *adj (maladie, faute)* serious; *(visage)* grave; *(voix)* deep, low; **ce n'est pas g.!** it's not important! ■ **gravement** *adv (malade)* seriously; *(dignement)* gravely

graver [grave] *vt (sur métal)* to engrave; *(sur bois)* to carve; *(disque)* to cut ■ **graveur** *nm* engraver

gravier [gravje] *nm* gravel ■ **gravillon** *nm* piece of gravel; **gravillons** gravel, *Br* (loose) chippings

gravir [gravir] *vt* to climb

gravité [gravite] *nf (de situation)* seriousness; *(solennité)* & *Phys* gravity; *Phys* **centre de g.** centre of gravity

graviter [gravite] *vi* to revolve (**autour** around)

gravure [gravyr] *nf (image)* print; *(action, art)* engraving; **g. sur bois** *(action)* woodcarving; *(objet)* woodcut

gré [gre] *nm* **de son plein g.** of one's

own free will; **de bon g.** willingly; **contre le g. de qn** against sb's will; **bon g. mal g.** whether we/you/*etc* like it or not; **de g. ou de force** one way or another

Grèce [grɛs] *nf* **la G.** Greece ▪ **grec, grecque 1** *adj* Greek **2** *nmf* **G., Grecque** Greek **3** *nm* (*langue*) Greek

greffe [grɛf] **1** *nf* (*de peau, d'arbre*) graft; (*d'organe*) transplant **2** *nm* Jur record office ▪ **greffer** *vt* (*peau*) & *Bot* to graft (**à** on to); (*organe*) to transplant ▪ **greffier** *nm* Jur clerk (of the court)

grêle¹ [grɛl] *nf* hail ▪ **grêler** *v impersonnel* to hail; **il grêle** it's hailing ▪ **grêlon** *nm* hailstone

grêle² [grɛl] *adj* (*jambes*) skinny; (*voix*) shrill

grelot [grəlo] *nm* (small) bell

grelotter [grələte] *vi* to shiver (**de** with)

grenade [grənad] *nf* (*fruit*) pomegranate; (*projectile*) grenade

grenier [grənje] *nm* (*de maison*) attic; (*pour le fourrage*) granary

grenouille [grənuj] *nf* frog

grès [grɛ] *nm* (*roche*) sandstone; (*poterie*) stoneware

grésiller [grezije] *vi* (*huile*) to sizzle

grève¹ [grɛv] *nf* (*arrêt du travail*) strike; **faire g.** to be on strike; **g. de la faim** hunger strike; **g. du zèle** *Br* work-to-rule, *Am* rule-book slowdown ▪ **gréviste** *nmf* striker

grève² [grɛv] *nf* (*de mer*) shore; (*de rivière*) bank

gribouiller [gribuje] *vti* to scribble

grief [grijɛf] *nm* (*plainte*) grievance; **faire g. de qch à qn** to hold sth against sb

grièvement [grijɛvmɑ̃] *adv* seriously, badly

griffe [grif] *nf* (*ongle*) claw; (*de couturier*) (designer) label; *Fig* (*style*) stamp ▪ **griffer** *vt* to scratch

griffonner [grifɔne] *vt* to scribble, to scrawl

grignoter [griɲɔte] *vti* to nibble

gril [gril] *nm* (*ustensile*) *Br* grill, *Am* broiler ▪ **grillade** *nf* (*viande*) *Br* grilled meat, *Am* broiled meat ▪ **grille-pain** *nm inv* toaster ▪ **griller 1** *vt* (*viande*) *Br* to grill, *Am* to broil; (*pain*) to toast; (*ampoule électrique*) to blow; *Fam* **g. un feu rouge** to jump the lights; **2** *vi* (*viande*) to grill; (*pain*) to toast

grille [grij] *nf* (*clôture*) railings; (*porte*) gate; (*de foyer*) grate; *Fig* (*de salaires*) scale ▪ **grillage** *nm* wire mesh *or* netting

grillon [grijɔ̃] *nm* cricket

grimace [grimas] *nf* (*pour faire rire*) (funny) face; (*de douleur*) grimace; **faire la g.** to pull a face ▪ **grimacer** *vi* to make a face; (*de douleur*) to wince (**de** with)

grimer [grime] **se grimer** *vpr* to put one's make-up on

grimper [grɛ̃pe] **1** *vi* to climb (**à qch** up sth) **2** *vt* (*escalier*) to climb

grincer [grɛ̃se] *vi* to creak; **g. des dents** to grind one's teeth ▪ **grincement** *nm* creaking

grincheux, -euse [grɛ̃ʃø, -øz] *adj* grumpy

grippe [grip] *nf* (*maladie*) flu, influenza; **prendre qn en g.** to take a strong dislike to sb ▪ **grippé, -e** *adj* **être g.** to have (the) flu

gripper [gripe] **se gripper** *vpr* (*moteur*) to seize up

gris, -e [gri, griz] **1** *adj* *Br* grey, *Am* gray; (*temps*) dull, grey; (*ivre*) tipsy **2** *nm* *Br* grey, *Am* gray ▪ **grisaille** *nf* (*caractère morne*) dreariness

grisonner [grizɔne] *vi* (*cheveux, personne*) to go *Br* grey *or Am* gray

grivois, -e [grivwa, -waz] *adj* bawdy

Groenland [grɔɛnlɑ̃d] *nm* **le G.** Greenland

grog [grɔg] *nm* hot toddy

grogner [grɔɲe] *vi* (*personne*) to grumble (**contre** at); (*cochon*) to grunt ▪ **grognement** *nm* (*de personne*) growl; (*de cochon*) grunt ▪ **grognon, -onne** *adj* grumpy

grommeler [grɔm(ə)le] *vti* to mutter

gronder [grɔ̃de] **1** *vt (réprimander)* to scold, to tell off **2** *vi (chien)* to growl; *(tonnerre)* to rumble

GROS, GROSSE [gro, gros] **1** *adj (corpulent, important)* big; *(gras)* fat; *(épais)* thick; *(effort, progrès)* great; *(somme, fortune)* large; *(rhume, mer)* heavy; *(faute)* serious, gross; *(traits, laine)* coarse; **g. mot** swearword **2** *adv* **risquer g.** to take a big risk; **écrire g.** to write big; **en g.** *(globalement)* roughly; *(écrire)* in big letters; *(vendre)* in bulk, wholesale **3** *nmf (personne)* fat man, f fat woman **4** *nm* **le g. de** the bulk of; **prix de g.** wholesale prices

groseille [grozɛj] *nf* redcurrant

grossesse [grosɛs] *nf* pregnancy

grosseur [grosœr] *nf (volume)* size; *(tumeur)* lump

grossier, -ère [grosje, -ɛr] *adj (tissu, traits)* rough, coarse; *(personne, manières)* rude, coarse; *(erreur)* gross; *(ruse, instrument)* crude ▪ **grossièrement** *adv (calculer)* roughly; *(répondre)* coarsely, rudely; *(se tromper)* grossly ▪ **grossièreté** *nf (incorrection, vulgarité)* coarseness; *(mot)* rude word

grossir [grosir] **1** *vt (sujet: verre, loupe)* to magnify **2** *vi (personne)* to put on weight; *(fleuve)* to swell; *(bosse, foule)* to get bigger ▪ **grossissement** *nm (augmentation de taille)* increase in size; *(de microscope)* magnification

grossiste [grosist] *nmf Com* wholesaler

grosso modo [grosomɔdo] *adv (en gros)* roughly

grotesque [grɔtɛsk] *adj* ludicrous

grotte [grɔt] *nf* cave

grouiller [gruje] *vi (se presser)* to swarm around; **g. de qch** to swarm with sth

groupe [grup] *nm* group; **g. sanguin** blood group ▪ **groupement** *nm (action)* grouping; *(groupe)* group ▪ **grouper 1** *vt* to group (together) **2**

se grouper *vpr (en association)* to form a group

grue [gry] *nf (machine, oiseau)* crane

grumeau, -x [grymo] *nm (dans une sauce)* lump

Guadeloupe [gwadlup] *nf* **la G.** Guadeloupe

Guatemala [gwatemala] *nm* **le G.** Guatemala

gué [ge] *nm* ford

guenon [gənɔ̃] *nf* female monkey

guépard [gepar] *nm* cheetah

guêpe [gɛp] *nf* wasp

guère [gɛr] *adv* **(ne...) g.** *(pas beaucoup)* not much; *(pas longtemps)* hardly, scarcely; **il n'a g. d'amis** he hasn't got many friends

guéri, -e [geri] *adj* cured

guérilla [gerija] *nf* guerrilla warfare

guérir [gerir] **1** *vt (personne, maladie)* to cure *(de* of*)*; *(blessure)* to heal **2** *vi (personne)* to get better, to recover; *(blessure)* to heal; *(rhume)* to get better **3** **se guérir** *vpr* to get better ▪ **guérison** *nf (rétablissement)* recovery ▪ **guérisseur, -euse** *nmf* faith healer

Guernesey [gɛrnze] *nf* Guernsey

guerre [gɛr] *nf* war; *(technique)* warfare; **en g.** at war *(avec* with*)*; **faire la g.** to wage *or* make war *(à* on *or* against*)*; *(soldat)* to fight; **crime de g.** war crime; **g. d'usure** war of attrition ▪ **guerrier, -ère 1** *adj* **danse guerrière** war dance; **chant g.** battle song; **2** *nmf* warrior

guet [gɛ] *nm* **faire le g.** to be on the lookout ▪ **guetter** *vt (occasion)* to watch out for; *(gibier)* to lie in wait for

guet-apens [gɛtapɑ̃] *(pl* guets-apens*)* *nm* ambush

gueule [gœl] *nf (d'animal, de canon)* mouth

gui [gi] *nm* mistletoe

guichet [giʃɛ] *nm (de gare, de banque)* window; **g. automatique** *(de banque)* cash dispenser ▪ **guichetier, -ère** *nmf (de banque) Br* counter clerk, *Am* teller; *(de gare)* ticket clerk

guide [gid] *nm (personne, livre)* guide;

g. touristique tourist guide ▪ **guider** *vt* to guide

guidon [gidɔ̃] *nm* handlebars

guignol [giɲɔl] *nm (spectacle)* ≃ Punch and Judy show

guillemets [gijmɛ] *nmpl Typ* inverted commas, quotation marks; **entre g.** in inverted commas, in quotation marks

guillotine [gijɔtin] *nf* guillotine ▪ **guillotiner** *vt* to guillotine

guimauve [gimov] *nf (confiserie)* marshmallow

guindé, -e [gɛ̃de] *adj (peu naturel)* stiff; *(style)* stilted

Guinée [gine] *nf* **la G.** Guinea

guirlande [girlɑ̃d] *nf* garland; **g. de Noël** piece of tinsel

guise [giz] *nf* **n'en faire qu'à sa g.** to do just as one pleases; **en g. de** by way of

guitare [gitar] *nf* guitar ▪ **guitariste** *nmf* guitarist

Guyane [gɥijan] *nf* **la G.** Guiana

gymnase [ʒimnɑz] *nm* gymnasium ▪ **gymnaste** *nmf* gymnast ▪ **gymnastique** *nf* gymnastics *(sing)*

gynécologue [ʒinekɔlɔg] *nmf Br* gynaecologist, *Am* gynecologist

Hh

H, h [aʃ] *nm inv* H, h

habile [abil] *adj* skilful, *Am* skillful (**à qch** at sth); **h. de ses mains** good with one's hands ■ **habileté** *nf* skill

habilité, -e [abilite] *adj* (legally) authorized (**à faire** to do)

habillé, -e [abije] *adj* dressed (**de** in; **en** as); *(costume, robe)* smart

habiller [abije] **1** *vt (vêtir)* to dress (**de** in); *(fournir en vêtements)* to clothe **2 s'habiller** *vpr* to dress, to get dressed; *(avec élégance)* to dress up ■ **habillement** *nm (vêtements)* clothes

habit [abi] *nm (tenue de soirée)* evening dress, tails; **habits** *(vêtements)* clothes

habitable [abitabl] *adj* (in)habitable; *(maison)* fit to live in

habitat [abita] *nm (d'animal, de plante)* habitat; *(conditions)* housing conditions

habitation [abitasjɔ̃] *nf (lieu)* dwelling; *(fait de résider)* living

habiter [abite] **1** *vt (maison, région)* to live in **2** *vi* to live (**à/en** in) ■ **habitant, -e** *nmf (de pays)* inhabitant ■ **habité, -e** *adj (région)* inhabited; *(maison)* occupied

habitude [abityd] *nf* habit; **avoir l'h. de qch** to be used to sth; **avoir l'h. de faire qch** to be used to doing sth; **prendre l'h. de faire qch** to get into the habit of doing sth; **d'h.** usually; **comme d'h.** as usual

habituel, -elle [abitɥɛl] *adj* usual, customary

habituer [abitɥe] **1** *vt* **h. qn à qch** to accustom sb to sth; **être habitué à qch/à faire qch** to be used to sth/to doing sth **2 s'habituer** *vpr* **s'h. à qn/qch** to get used to sb/sth ■ **habitué, -e** *nmf* regular

hache [ʼaʃ] *nf* axe, *Am* ax

hacher [ʼaʃe] *vt (au couteau)* to chop up; *(avec un appareil) Br* to mince, *Am* to grind ■ **haché, -e** *adj (viande) Br* minced, *Am* ground ■ **hachis** *nm* **h. Parmentier** ≃ cottage pie

hachurer [ʼaʃyre] *vt* to hatch

haie [ʼɛ] *nf (clôture)* hedge; *(en équitation)* fence; **400 mètres haies** *(épreuve d'athlétisme)* 400-metre hurdles; **h. d'honneur** guard of honour

haine [ʼɛn] *nf* hatred, hate ■ **haineux, -euse** *adj* full of hatred

haïr* [ʼair] *vt* to hate ■ **haïssable** *adj* hateful

hâle [ʼal] *nm* suntan ■ **hâlé, -e** *adj* suntanned

haleine [alɛn] *nf* breath; **reprendre h.** to get one's breath back

haleter [ʼalte] *vi* to pant, to gasp ■ **haletant, -e** *adj* panting, gasping

hall [ʼol] *nm (de maison)* entrance hall; *(d'hôtel)* lobby; **h. de gare** station concourse

halle [ʼal] *nf (couvered)* market; **les halles** the central food market

hallucination [alysinasjɔ̃] *nf* hallucination ■ **hallucinant, -e** *adj* extraordinary

halogène [alɔʒɛn] *nm (lampe)* halogen lamp

halte [ʼalt] *nf (arrêt)* stop; *Mil* halt; *(lieu)* stopping place; *Mil* halting place; **faire h.** to stop

haltère [altɛr] nm dumbbell ■ **haltérophile** nmf weightlifter ■ **haltérophilie** nf weightlifting

hamac ['amak] nm hammock

hamburger ['ãbœrgœr] nm (ham-) burger

hameau, -x ['amo] nm hamlet

hameçon [amsɔ̃] nm (fish-)hook

hamster ['amstɛr] nm hamster

hanche ['ãʃ] nf hip

handball ['ãdbal] nm Sport handball

handicap ['ãdikap] nm (physique, mental) disability; Fig handicap ■ **handicapé, -e** adj disabled **2** nmf disabled person; **h. physique/mental** physically/mentally handicapped person

hangar ['ãgar] nm (entrepôt) shed

hanter ['ãte] vt (sujet: fantôme, souvenir) to haunt ■ **hantise** nf avoir la h. de qch to really dread sth

harasser ['arase] vt to exhaust

harceler ['arsəle] vt (importuner) to harass; (insister auprès de) to pester ■ **harcèlement** nm harassment

hardi, -e ['ardi] adj bold

hargneux, -euse ['arɲø, -øz] adj bad-tempered

haricot ['ariko] nm bean; Culin h. de mouton mutton stew; **h. rouge** kidney bean; **h. vert** green bean, Br French bean

harmonica [armɔnika] nm harmonica, mouthorgan

harmonie [armɔni] nf harmony ■ **harmonieux, -euse** adj harmonious ■ **harmoniser** vt, **s'harmoniser** vpr to harmonize

harnais ['arnɛ] nm (de cheval, de bébé) harness

harpe ['arp] nf harp

harpon ['arpɔ̃] nm harpoon

hasard ['azar] nm le h. chance; un h. a coincidence; **par h.** by chance; **au h.** (choisir, répondre) at random; (marcher) aimlessly; **à tout h.** (par précaution) just in case; (pour voir) on the off chance ■ **hasarder 1** vt (remarque) to venture **2 se hasarder** vpr se h. dans

to venture into; **se h. à faire qch** to risk doing sth ■ **hasardeux, -euse** adj risky, hazardous

hâte ['ãt] nf haste; **à la h.** hastily; **en (toute) h.** hurriedly; **avoir h. de faire qch** to be eager to do sth ■ **hâter** vt (pas, départ) to hasten **2 se hâter** vpr to hurry (**de faire** to do) ■ **hâtif, -ive** adj (trop rapide) hasty

hausse ['os] nf rise (de in); **en h.** rising ■ **hausser** vt (prix, voix) to raise; (épaules) to shrug **2 se hausser** vpr se h. sur la pointe des pieds to stand on tiptoe

HAUT, -E ['o, 'ot] **1** adj high; (en taille) tall; **h. de 5 mètres** 5 metres high or tall; **à haute voix, à voix haute** aloud; **en haute mer** out at sea; **la mer est haute** it's high tide; **la haute couture** designer fashion; **un instrument de haute précision** a precision instrument; **un renseignement de la plus haute importance** news of the utmost importance; **haute trahison** high treason

2 adv (dans l'espace) & Mus high; (dans une hiérarchie) highly; (parler) loud, loudly; **tout h.** (lire, penser) out loud; **h. placé** (personne) in a high position; **plus h.** (dans un texte) above

3 nm (partie haute) top; **en h. de** at the top of; **en h.** (loger) upstairs; (regarder) up; (mettre) on (the) top; **d'en h.** (de la partie haute, du ciel) from high up, from up above; **avoir 5 mètres de h.** to be 5 metres high or tall; Fig **des hauts et des bas** ups and downs ■ **haut-parleur** (pl haut-parleurs) nm loudspeaker

hautain, -e ['otɛ̃, -ɛn] adj haughty

hautbois ['obwa] nm oboe

haut-de-forme ['odfɔrm] (pl hauts-de-forme) nm top hat

hautement [otmã] adv (très) highly ■ **hauteur** nf height; (colline) hill; Péj (orgueil) haughtiness; **à la h. de** (objet) level with; (rue) opposite; **arriver**

à la h. de qch *(mesurer)* to reach (the level of) sth; **il n'est pas à la h.** he isn't up to it

Haye ['ɛ] *nf* **La H.** The Hague

hebdomadaire [ɛbdɔmadɛr] *adj & nm* weekly

héberger [ebɛrʒe] *vt* to put up

hébreu, -x [ebrø] **1** *adj m* Hebrew **2** *nm (langue)* Hebrew

hectare [ɛktar] *nm* hectare *(= 2.47 acres)*

hélas ['elas] *exclam* unfortunately

héler ['ele] *vt (taxi)* to hail

hélice [elis] *nf (d'avion, de navire)* propeller

hélicoptère [elikɔptɛr] *nm* helicopter

helvétique [ɛlvetik] *adj* Swiss

hémisphère [emisfɛr] *nm* hemisphere

hémophilie [emɔfili] *nf Méd* haemophilia

hémorragie [emɔraʒi] *nf Méd* haemorrhage; *Fig (de capitaux)* drain; **faire une h.** to haemorrhage; **h. cérébrale** stroke

hémorroïdes [emɔrɔid] *nfpl* piles, haemorrhoids

hennir [enir] *vi (cheval)* to neigh

herbe [ɛrb] *nf* grass; **mauvaise h.** weed; *Culin* **fines herbes** herbs

herbivore [ɛrbivɔr] *adj* herbivorous

hérédité [eredite] *nf* heredity ■ **héréditaire** *adj* hereditary

hérésie [erezi] *nf* heresy ■ **hérétique 1** *adj* heretical **2** *nmf* heretic

hérisser ['erise] **1** *vt (poils)* to bristle up; *Fig* **h. qn** *(irriter)* to get sb's back up **2 se hérisser** *upr (animal, personne)* to bristle; *(poils, cheveux)* to stand on end ■ **hérissé, -e** *adj (cheveux)* bristly; **h. de** bristling with

hérisson ['erisɔ̃] *nm* hedgehog

hériter [erite] **1** *vt* to inherit *(qch de qn* sth from sb) **2** *vi* **h. de qch** to inherit sth ■ **héritage** *nm (biens)* inheritance; *Fig (culturel)* heritage; **faire un h.** to come into an inheritance ■ **héritier** *nm* heir *(de* to) ■ **héritière** *nf* heiress *(de* to)

hermétique [ɛrmetik] *adj* hermetically sealed; *Fig (obscur)* impenetrable

héros ['ero] *nm* hero ■ **héroïne** *nf (femme)* heroine; *(drogue)* heroin ■ **héroïque** *adj* heroic ■ **héroïsme** *nm* heroism

hésiter [ezite] *vi* to hesitate *(sur over or* about; *entre* between; *à faire* to do) ■ **hésitant, -e** *adj* hesitant ■ **hésitation** *nf* hesitation; **avec h.** hesitatingly

hétérogène [eterɔʒɛn] *adj* mixed

hêtre ['ɛtr] *nm (arbre, bois)* beech

HEURE [œr] *nf (mesure)* hour; *(moment)* time; **quelle h. est-il?** what time is it?; **il est six heures** it's six (o'clock); **six heures moins cinq** five to six; **six heures cinq** Br five past six, *Am* five after six; **à l'h.** *(arriver)* on time; *(être payé)* by the hour; **100 km à l'h.** 100 km an hour; **de bonne h.** early; **nouvelle de dernière h.** latest *or* lastminute news; **tout à l'h.** *(futur)* in a few moments, later; *(passé)* a moment ago; **à tout à l'h.!** *(au revoir)* see you soon!; **à toute h.** *(continuellement)* at all hours; **24 heures sur 24** 24 hours a day; **d'h. en h.** hourly, hour by hour; **faire des heures supplémentaires** to work *or* do overtime; **heures d'affluence, heures de pointe** *(circulation)* rush hour; *(dans les magasins)* peak period; **heures creuses** off-peak or slack periods; **h. d'été** Br summer time, *Am* daylight-saving time

heureux, -euse [œrø, -øz] **1** *adj* happy *(de* with); *(chanceux)* lucky, fortunate; *(issue)* successful **2** *adv (vivre, mourir)* happily ■ **heureusement** *adv (par chance)* fortunately, luckily *(pour* for); *(avec succès)* successfully

heurter ['œrte] **1** *vt (cogner)* to hit *(contre* against); *(entrer en collision avec)* to collide with; **h. qn** *(choquer)* to offend sb ■ **se heurter** *upr* to collide *(à ou contre* against); *Fig* **se h. à qch** to meet with sth

hexagone [ɛgzagɔn] *nm* hexagon; *Fig* **l'H.** France

hiberner [ibɛrne] *vi* to hibernate

hibou, -x [´ibu] *nm* owl

hier [ijɛr] *adv* yesterday; **h. soir** yesterday evening

hiérarchie [´jerarʃi] *nf* hierarchy

hi-fi [´ifi] *adj inv & nf inv* hi-fi

hilare [ilar] *adj* grinning ▪ **hilarant, -e** *adj* hilarious ▪ **hilarité** *nf* hilarity, mirth

hindou, -e [ɛ̃du] *adj & nmf* Hindu

hippie [´ipi] *nmf* hippie, hippy

hippique [ipik] *adj* **concours h.** horse show

hippodrome [ipɔdrom] *nm Br* racecourse, *Am* racetrack

hippopotame [ipɔpɔtam] *nm* hippopotamus

hirondelle [irɔ̃dɛl] *nf* swallow

hisser [´ise] **1** *vt* to hoist up **2 se hisser** *vpr* to heave oneself up

histoire [istwar] *nf (science, événements)* history; *(récit)* story

historien, -enne [istɔrjɛ̃, -ɛn] *nmf* historian

historique [istɔrik] **1** *adj (concernant l'histoire)* historical; *(important)* historic **2** *nm* historical account

hiver [ivɛr] *nm* winter ▪ **hivernal, -e, -aux, -ales** *adj* winter; *(temps)* wintry

HLM [´aʃɛlɛm] *(abrév* **habitation à loyer modéré)** *nm ou f Br* ≃ council flats, *Am* ≃ low-rent apartment building

hocher [´ɔʃe] *vt* **h. la tête** *(pour dire oui)* to nod; *(pour dire non)* to shake one's head

hockey [´ɔkɛ] *nm* hockey; **h. sur glace** ice hockey; **h. sur gazon** *Br* hockey, *Am* field hockey

hold-up [´ɔldœp] *nm inv* hold-up

Hollande [´ɔlɑ̃d] *nf* **la H.** Holland ▪ **hollandais, -e 1** *adj* Dutch **2** *nmf* **H.** Dutchman; **Hollandaise** Dutchwoman; **les H.** the Dutch **3** *nm (langue)* Dutch

homard [´ɔmar] *nm* lobster

homéopathie [ɔmeɔpati] *nf* homeopathy

homicide [ɔmisid] *nm* homicide; **h. involontaire** *ou* **par imprudence** manslaughter; **h. volontaire** murder

hommage [ɔmaʒ] *nm* homage (**à** to); **rendre h. à qn** to pay homage to sb; **faire qch en h. à qn** to do sth as a tribute to sb *or* in homage to sb

homme [ɔm] *nm* man *(pl* men); **l'h.** *(genre humain)* man(kind); **les vêtements d'h.** men's clothes; **h. d'affaires** businessman; **h. politique** politician ▪ **homme-grenouille** *(pl* **hommes-grenouilles)** *nm* frogman

homogène [ɔmɔʒɛn] *adj* homogeneous

homologue [ɔmɔlɔg] *nmf* counterpart, opposite number

homologuer [ɔmɔlɔge] *vt (décision, accord, record)* to ratify

homonyme [ɔmɔnim] *nm (mot)* homonym

homosexuel, -elle [ɔmɔsɛksɥɛl] *adj & nmf* homosexual

Hongrie [´ɔ̃gri] *nf* **la H.** Hungary ▪ **hongrois, -e 1** *adj* Hungarian **2** *nmf* **H., Hongroise** Hungarian **3** *nm (langue)* Hungarian

honnête [ɔnɛt] *adj (intègre)* honest; *(vie, gens)* decent; *(prix)* fair ▪ **honnêtement** *adv (avec intégrité)* honestly; *(raisonnablement)* decently ▪ **honnêteté** *nf (intégrité)* honesty

honneur [ɔnœr] *nm* honour; **en l'h. de qn** in honour of sb; **invité d'h.** guest of honour

honorable [ɔnɔrabl] *adj* honourable; *Fig (résultat, salaire)* respectable

honoraires [ɔnɔrɛr] *nmpl* fees

honorer [ɔnɔre] *vt* to honour (**de** with); **h. qn** *(conduite)* to be a credit to sb ▪ **honorifique** *adj* honorary

honte [´ɔ̃t] *nf* shame; **avoir h.** to be *or* feel ashamed (**de qch/de faire qch** of sth/to do *or* of doing sth); **faire h. à qn** to put sb to shame ▪ **honteux, -euse** *adj (personne)* ashamed (**de** of); *(conduite, acte)* shameful

hôpital, -aux [ɔpital, -o] *nm* hospital; **à l'h.** *Br* in hospital, *Am* in the hospital

hoquet [ɔkɛ] *nm* hiccup; **avoir le h.** to have the hiccups

horaire [ɔrɛr] **1** *adj (salaire)* hourly; *(vitesse)* per hour **2** *nm* timetable, schedule; **horaires de travail** working hours

horizon [ɔrizɔ̃] *nm* horizon; *(vue, paysage)* view; **à l'h.** on the horizon ■ **horizontal, -e, -aux, -ales** *adj* horizontal

horloge [ɔrlɔʒ] *nf* clock

hormone [ɔrmɔn] *nf* hormone

horoscope [ɔrɔskɔp] *nm* horoscope

horreur [ɔrœr] *nf* horror; **avoir h. de qch** to hate *or* loathe sth; **quelle h.!** how horrible!

horrible [ɔribl] *adj (effrayant)* horrible; *(laid)* hideous ■ **horriblement** [-əmã] *adv (défiguré)* horribly; *(cher, froid)* terribly

horrifié, -e [ɔrifje] *adj* horrified

hors [ɔr] *prép* **h. de** *(maison, boîte)* outside; *Fig (danger, haleine)* out of; *(au football)* **être h. jeu** to be offside ■ **hors-bord** *nm inv* speedboat ■ **hors-d'œuvre** *nm inv (plat)* hors-d'œuvre, starter ■ **hors-jeu** *nm inv (au football)* offside ■ **hors-la-loi** *nm inv* outlaw ■ **hors-piste** *nm inv* Ski off-piste skiing ■ **hors service** *adj inv (appareil)* out of order ■ **hors taxe** *adj inv (magasin, objet)* duty-free

horticulteur, -trice [ɔrtikyltœr, -tris] *nmf* horticulturist ■ **horticulture** *nf* horticulture

hospice [ɔspis] *nm (asile)* home

hospitalier, -ère [ɔspitalje, -ɛr] *adj (accueillant)* hospitable; **centre h.** hospital (complex); **personnel h.** hospital staff ■ **hospitaliser** *vt* to hospitalize ■ **hospitalité** *nf* hospitality

hostile [ɔstil] *adj* hostile (**à** *to or* towards); ■ **hostilité** *nf* hostility (**envers** *to or* towards)

hôte [ot] **1** *nm (qui reçoit)* host **2** *nm (invité)* guest ■ **hôtesse** *nf* hostess; **h. de l'air** air hostess

hôtel [otɛl] *nm* hotel; **h. particulier** mansion, town house; **h. de ville** *Br* town hall, *Am* city hall ■ **hôtelier,**

-ère **1** *nmf* hotel-keeper, hotelier **2** *adj* **industrie hôtelière** hotel industry ■ **hôtellerie** *nf (auberge)* inn; *(métier)* hotel trade

hotte [ɔt] *nf (panier)* basket *(carried on back)*; *(de cheminée)* hood; **h. aspirante** extractor hood

houille [uj] *nf* coal; **h. blanche** hydro-electric power ■ **houiller, -ère** *adj* **bassin h.** coalfield

houleux, -euse [ulø, -øz] *adj (mer)* rough; *Fig (réunion)* stormy

housse ['us] *nf (protective)* cover

houx ['u] *nm* holly

hublot ['yblo] *nm (de navire, d'avion)* porthole

huer ['ɥe] *vt* to boo ■ **huées** *nfpl* boos

huile [ɥil] *nf* oil; **h. d'arachide/d'olive** groundnut/olive oil; **h. essentielle** essential oil; **h. solaire** suntan oil ■ **huiler** *vt* to oil ■ **huileux, -euse** *adj* oily

huis [ɥi] *nm* **à h. clos** behind closed doors; *Jur* in camera

huissier [ɥisje] *nm (portier)* usher; *Jur* bailiff

huit [ɥit, 'ɥi *before consonant]* *adj &* *nm inv* eight; **h. jours** a week ■ **huitième** *adj, nm & nmf* eighth; **un h.** an eighth; *Sport* **h. de finale** last sixteen

huître [ɥitr] *nf* oyster

humain, -e [ymɛ̃, -ɛn] **1** *adj (relatif à l'homme)* human; *(compatissant)* humane **2** *nmpl* **les humains** humans ■ **humainement** *adv (relatif à l'homme)* humanly; *(avec bonté)* humanely ■ **humanitaire** *adj* humanitarian ■ **humanité** *nf (genre humain, sentiment)* humanity

humble [œbl] *adj* humble

humecter [ymɛkte] *vt* to moisten

humer ['yme] *vt (respirer)* to breathe in; *(sentir)* to smell

humeur [ymœr] *nf (disposition)* mood; **être de bonne/mauvaise h.** to be in a good/bad mood

humide [ymid] *adj (linge)* damp, wet; *(climat, temps)* humid ■ **humidifier** *vt* to humidify ■ **humidité** *nf (de maison)* dampness; *(de climat)* humidity

humilier [ymilje] *vt* to humiliate ■ **humiliant, -e** *adj* humiliating ■ **humiliation** *nf* humiliation ■ **humilité** *nf* humility

humour [ymur] *nm* humour; **avoir le sens de l'h.** to have a sense of humour ■ **humoriste** *nmf* humorist ■ **humoristique** *adj (récit, ton)* humorous

hurler ['yrle] **1** *vt (slogans, injures)* to yell **2** *vi (loup, vent)* to howl; *(personne)* to scream ■ **hurlement** [-əmɑ̃] *nm (de loup, de vent)* howl; *(de personne)* scream

hutte ['yt] *nf* hut

hybride [ibrid] *adj & nm* hybrid

hydrater [idrate] *vt (peau)* to moisturize

hydraulique [idrolik] *adj* hydraulic

hydravion [idravjɔ̃] *nm* seaplane

hydrocarbure [idrokarbyr] *nm* hydrocarbon

hydrophile [idrɔfil] *adj* **coton h.** *Br* cotton wool, *Am* (absorbent) cotton

hyène [jɛn] *nf* hyena

hygiène [iʒjɛn] *nf* hygiene ■ **hygiénique** *adj* hygienic; *(serviette, conditions)* sanitary

hymne [imn] *nm* hymn; **h. national** national anthem

hypermarché [ipɛrmarʃe] *nm* hypermarket

hypermétrope [ipɛrmetrɔp] *adj* long-sighted

hypnose [ipnoz] *nf* hypnosis ■ **hypnotiser** *vt* to hypnotize

hypocrisie [ipɔkrizi] *nf* hypocrisy ■ **hypocrite 1** *adj* hypocritical **2** *nmf* hypocrite

hypodermique [ipɔdɛrmik] *adj* hypodermic

hypothèque [ipɔtek] *nf* mortgage

hypothèse [ipɔtez] *nf* hypothesis; **dans l'h. où...** supposing (that)...

Ii

I, i [i] *nm inv* I, i

iceberg [isbɛrg, ajsbɛrg] *nm* iceberg

ici [isi] *adv* here; **par i.** *(passer)* this way; *(habiter)* around here; **jusqu'i.** *(temps)* up to now; *(lieu)* as far as this or here; **d'i. à mardi** by Tuesday; **d'i. peu** before long

icône [ikon] *nf Rel & Ordinat* icon

idéal, -e, -aux *ou* **-als, -ales** [ideal, -o] **1** *adj* ideal **2** *n* ideal; **l'i. serait de/ que...** the ideal *or* best solution would be to/if... ■ **idéaliser** *vt* to idealize ■ **idéaliste 1** *adj* idealistic **2** *nmf* idealist

idée [ide] *nf* idea *(de* of; *que* that); **i. fixe** obsession

identifier [idãtifje] *vt*, **s'identifier** *vpr* to identify *(à* with) ■ **identification** *nf* identification

identique [idãtik] *adj* identical *(à* to)

identité [idãtite] *nf* identity

idéologie [ideɔlɔʒi] *nf* ideology

idiot, -e [idjo, -ɔt] **1** *adj* silly, idiotic **2** *nmf* idiot

idole [idɔl] *nf* idol

idyllique [idilik] *adj* idyllic

igloo [iglu] *nm* igloo

ignare [iɲar] **1** *adj* ignorant **2** *nmf* ignoramus

ignoble [iɲɔbl] *adj* vile

ignorant, -e [iɲɔrɑ̃, -ɑ̃t] *adj* ignorant *(de* of) ■ **ignorance** *nf* ignorance

ignorer [iɲɔre] *vt* not to know; **j'ignore si...** I don't know if...; **je n'ignore pas les difficultés** I am not unaware of the difficulties; **i. qn** *(mépriser)* to ignore sb ■ **ignoré, -e** *adj (inconnu)* unknown

il [il] *pron personnel (personne)* he; *(chose, animal, impersonnel)* it; **il est** he/it is; **il pleut** it's raining; **il est vrai que...** it's true that...; **il y a...** there is/ are...; **il y a six ans** six years ago; **il y a une heure qu'il travaille** he has been working for an hour; **qu'est-ce qu'il y a?** what's the matter?, what's wrong?; **il n'y a pas de quoi!** don't mention it!

île [il] *nf* island; **les îles Anglo-Normandes** the Channel Islands; **les îles Britanniques** the British Isles

illégal, -e, -aux, -ales [il(l)egal, -o] *adj* illegal

illégitime [il(l)eʒitim] *adj (enfant, revendication)* illegitimate; *(demande)* unwarranted

illettré, -e [il(l)etre] *adj & nmf* illiterate

illicite [il(l)isit] *adj* unlawful, illicit

illimité, -e [il(l)imite] *adj* unlimited

illisible [il(l)izibl] *adj (écriture)* illegible; *(livre)* & *Ordinat* unreadable

illogique [il(l)ɔʒik] *adj* illogical

illuminer [il(l)ymine] **1** *vt* to light up, to illuminate **2 s'illuminer** *vpr (visage, ciel)* to light up ■ **illumination** *nf (action, lumière)* illumination ■ **illuminé, -e** *adj (monument)* floodlit

illusion [il(l)yzjɔ̃] *nf* illusion *(sur* about); **se faire des illusions** to delude oneself *(sur* about); **i. d'optique** optical illusion ■ **illusionniste** *nmf* conjurer ■ **illusoire** *adj* illusory

illustrer [il(l)ystre] **1** *vt (livre, récit)* to illustrate *(de* with) **2 s'illustrer** *vpr* to distinguish oneself *(par* by) ■ **illustration** *nf* illustration ■ **illustré, -e** *adj* *(livre, magazine)* illustrated

îlot [ilo] *nm (île)* small island; *(maisons)* block

ils [il] *pron personnel mpl* they; **i. sont ici** they are here

image [imaʒ] *nf* picture; *(ressemblance, symbole)* image; *(dans une glace)* reflection; *Ordinat* **i. de synthèse** computer-generated image ■ **imagé, -e** *adj (style)* colourful, full of imagery

imaginable [imaʒinabl] *adj* imaginable ■ **imaginaire** *adj* imaginary ■ **imaginatif, -ive** *adj* imaginative

imagination [imaʒinɑsjɔ̃] *nf* imagination

imaginer [imaʒine] **1** *vt (se figurer)* to imagine; *(inventer)* to devise **2 s'imaginer** *vpr (se figurer)* to imagine **(que** that); *(se voir)* to picture oneself

imbattable [ɛ̃batabl] *adj* unbeatable

imbécile [ɛ̃besil] **1** *adj* idiotic **2** *nmf* idiot, imbecile ■ **imbécillité** *nf (état)* imbecility; **une i.** *(action, parole)* an idiotic thing

imberbe [ɛ̃bɛrb] *adj* beardless

imbiber [ɛ̃bibe] *vt* to soak **(de** with or in)

imbriquer [ɛ̃brike] **s'imbriquer** *vpr (s'emboîter)* to overlap

imbu, -e [ɛ̃by] *adj* **i. de soi-même** full of oneself

imbuvable [ɛ̃byvabl] *adj* undrinkable

imiter [imite] *vt* to imitate; *(signature)* to forge; **i. qn** *(pour rire)* to mimic sb; *(faire comme)* to do the same as sb; *(imitateur professionnel)* to impersonate sb ■ **imitateur, -trice** *nmf* imitator; *(professionnel)* impersonator ■ **imitation** *nf* imitation

immaculé, -e [imakyle] *adj (sans tache, sans péché)* immaculate

immangeable [ɛ̃mɑ̃ʒabl] *adj* inedible

immanquable [ɛ̃mɑ̃kabl] *adj* inevitable

immatriculer [imatrikyle] *vt* to register; **se faire i.** to register ■ **immatriculation** *nf* registration

immédiat, -e [imedja, -jat] **1** *adj* immediate **2** *nm* **dans l'i.** for the time being ■ **immédiatement** *adv* immediately

immense [imɑ̃s] *adj* immense ■ **immensément** *adv* immensely ■ **immensité** *nf* immensity

immerger [imɛrʒe] *vt* to immerse ■ **immersion** *nf* immersion **(dans** in)

immeuble [imœbl] *nm* building; *(appartements) Br* block of flats, *Am* apartment block

immigrant, -e [imigrɑ̃, -ɑ̃t] *nmf* immigrant ■ **immigration** *nf* immigration ■ **immigré, -e** *adj & nmf* immigrant; **travailleur i.** immigrant worker

imminent, -e [iminɑ̃, -ɑ̃t] *adj* imminent

immiscer [imise] **s'immiscer** *vpr* to interfere **(dans** in)

immobile [imɔbil] *adj* still, motionless

immobilier, -ère [imɔbilje, -ɛr] **1** *adj* **marché i.** property market **2** *nm* **l'i.** *Br* property, *Am* real estate

immobiliser [imɔbilize] **1** *vt (blessé)* to immobilize; *(train)* to bring to a stop; *(voiture) (avec un sabot)* to clamp **2 s'immobiliser** *vpr* to come to a stop

immonde [i(m)mɔ̃d] *adj (sale)* foul, *(ignoble, laid)* vile

immoral, -e, -aux, -ales [i(m)mɔral, -o] *adj* immoral ■ **immoralité** *nf* immorality

immortel, -elle [i(m)mɔrtɛl] *adj* immortal ■ **immortaliser** *vt* to immortalize ■ **immortalité** *nf* immortality

immuable [i(m)mɥabl] *adj* immutable, unchanging

immuniser [i(m)mynize] *vt* to immunize **(contre** against) ■ **immunitaire** *adj Méd (déficience, système)* immune ■ **immunité** *nf* immunity

impact [ɛ̃pakt] *nm* impact **(sur** on)

impair, -e [ɛ̃pɛr] **1** *adj (nombre)* odd, uneven **2** *nm (maladresse)* blunder

imparable [ɛ̃parabl] *adj (coup)* unavoidable

impardonnable [ɛ̃pardɔnabl] *adj* unforgivable

imparfait, -e [ɛ̃parfɛ, -ɛt] *adj (connaissance)* imperfect

impartial, -e, -aux, -ales [ɛ̃parsjal, -o] *adj* impartial, unbiased ■ **impartialité** *nf* impartiality

impartir [ɛ̃partir] *vt* **dans le temps qui nous est imparti** within the allotted time

impasse [ɛ̃pas] *nf (rue)* dead end; *Fig (situation)* impasse; **être dans une i.** to be deadlocked

impassible [ɛ̃pasibl] *adj* impassive

impatient, -e [ɛ̃pasjɑ̃, -ɑ̃t] *adj* impatient; **i. de faire qch** impatient to do sth ■ **impatience** *nf* impatience ■ **impatienter 1** *vt* to annoy **2 s'impatienter** *vpr* to get impatient

impayé, -e [ɛ̃peje] *adj* unpaid

impeccable [ɛ̃pekabl] *adj* impeccable

impénétrable [ɛ̃penetrabl] *adj (forêt, mystère)* impenetrable

impensable [ɛ̃pɑ̃sabl] *adj* unthinkable

impératif, -ive [ɛ̃peratif, -iv] *adj (consigne, besoin)* imperative; *(ton)* imperious

impératrice [ɛ̃peratris] *nf* empress

imperceptible [ɛ̃persɛptibl] *adj* imperceptible *(à* to)

imperfection [ɛ̃pɛrfɛksjɔ̃] *nf* imperfection

impérial, -e, -aux, -ales [ɛ̃perjal, -o] *adj* imperial ■ **impérialisme** *nm* imperialism

impérieux, -euse [ɛ̃perjø, -øz] *adj (autoritaire)* imperious; *(besoin)* pressing

impérissable [ɛ̃perisabl] *adj (souvenir)* enduring

imperméable [ɛ̃pɛrmeabl] **1** *adj* impervious *(à* to); *(tissu, manteau)* waterproof **2** *nm* raincoat

impersonnel, -elle [ɛ̃pɛrsɔnɛl] *adj* impersonal

impertinent, -e [ɛ̃pɛrtinɑ̃, -ɑ̃t] *adj* impertinent *(envers* to) ■ **impertinence** *nf* impertinence

imperturbable [ɛ̃pɛrtyrbabl] *adj (personne)* imperturbable

impitoyable [ɛ̃pitwajabl] *adj* merciless

implacable [ɛ̃plakabl] *adj (personne, vengeance)* implacable; *(avancée)* relentless

implanter [ɛ̃plɑ̃te] **1** *vt (installer)* to establish; *(chirurgicalement)* to implant **2 s'implanter** *vpr* to become established ■ **implantation** *nf* establishment

implicite [ɛ̃plisit] *adj* implicit

impliquer [ɛ̃plike] *vt (entraîner)* to imply; **i. que…** to imply that…; **i. qn** to implicate sb *(dans* in) ■ **implication** *nf (conséquence)* implication; *(participation)* involvement

implorer [ɛ̃plɔre] *vt* to implore *(qn de faire* sb to do)

impoli, -e [ɛ̃pɔli] *adj* rude, impolite

impolitesse [ɛ̃pɔlites] *nf* impoliteness, rudeness

impopulaire [ɛ̃pɔpylɛr] *adj* unpopular

import [ɛ̃pɔr] *nm* import

important, -e [ɛ̃pɔrtɑ̃, -ɑ̃t] **1** *adj (personnage, événement)* important; *(quantité, somme, ville)* large; *(dégâts, retard)* considerable **2** *nm* **l'i., c'est de…** the important thing is to… ■ **importance** *nf* importance; *(taille)* size; *(de dégâts)* extent; **ça n'a pas d'i.** it doesn't matter

importer¹ [ɛ̃pɔrte] **1** *vi* to matter *(à* to) **2** *v impersonnel* **il importe de faire qch** it's important to do sth; **il importe que vous y soyez** it is important that you're there; **peu importe, n'importe** it doesn't matter; **n'importe qui/ quoi/où/quand/comment** anyone/ anything/anywhere/any time/anyhow

importer² [ɛ̃pɔrte] *vt (marchandises)* to import *(de* from) ■ **importateur, -trice 1** *adj* importing **2** *nmf* importer ■ **importation** *nf (objet)* import; *(action)* importing, importation

importun, -e [ɛ̃pɔrtœ̃, -yn] **1** *adj*

(personne, question) importunate **2** *nmf* nuisance

imposer [ɛ̃poze] **1** *vt (condition)* to impose; *(taxer)* to tax; **i. qch à qn** to impose sth on sb **2** *vi* **en i. à qn** to impress sb **3 s'imposer** *vpr (faire reconnaître sa valeur)* to assert oneself; *(gagner)* to win; *(être nécessaire)* to be essential; *Péj (chez quelqu'un)* to impose; **s'i. de faire qch** to make it a rule to do sth ■ **imposant, -e** *adj* imposing

impossible [ɛ̃posibl] **1** *adj* impossible **(à faire** to do); **il est i. que...** *(+ subjunctive)* it is impossible that... **2** *nm* **tenter l'i.** to attempt the impossible ■ **impossibilité** *nf* impossibility

imposteur [ɛ̃pɔstœr] *nm* impostor ■ **imposture** *nf* deception

impôt [ɛ̃po] *nm* tax; **(service des) impôts** tax authorities; **impôts locaux** local taxes; **i. sur le revenu** income tax

impraticable [ɛ̃pratikabl] *adj (chemin)* impassable; *(projet)* impracticable

imprécis, -e [ɛ̃presi, -iz] *adj* imprecise ■ **imprécision** *nf* imprecision

imprégner [ɛ̃preɲe] **1** *vt* to impregnate **(de** with); *Fig* **être imprégné de qch** to be full of sth **2 s'imprégner** *vpr* to become impregnated **(de** with)

imprenable [ɛ̃prənabl] *adj (forteresse)* impregnable; *(vue)* unobstructed

impression [ɛ̃presjɔ̃] *nf* **(a)** *(sensation)* impression; **avoir l'i. que...** to have the impression that...; **faire bonne i. à qn** to make a good impression on sb **(b)** *(de livre)* printing

impressionner [ɛ̃presjɔne] *vt (bouleverser)* to upset; *(frapper)* to impress ■ **impressionnable** *adj* easily upset ■ **impressionnant, -e** *adj* impressive

imprévisible [ɛ̃previzibl] *adj (temps, réaction, personne)* unpredictable; *(événement)* unforeseeable ■ **imprévu, -e 1** *adj* unexpected, unforeseen **2** *nm* **en cas d'i.** in case of anything unexpected

imprimer [ɛ̃prime] *vt (livre, tissu)* to print; *Ordinat* to print (out) ■ **imprimante** *nf* printer ■ **imprimé** *nm (formulaire)* printed form ■ **imprimerie** *nf (technique)* printing; *(lieu)* Br printing works, *Am* print shop ■ **imprimeur** *nm* printer

improbable [ɛ̃prɔbabl] *adj* improbable, unlikely

impropre [ɛ̃prɔpr] *adj* inappropriate; **i. à qch** unfit for sth; **i. à la consommation** unfit for human consumption

improviser [ɛ̃prɔvize] *vt & vi* to improvise ■ **improvisation** *nf* improvisation

improviste [ɛ̃prɔvist] **à l'improviste** *adv* unexpectedly

imprudent, -e [ɛ̃prydɑ̃, -ɑ̃t] *adj (personne, action)* rash; **il est i. de...** it is unwise to... ■ **imprudemment** [-amɑ̃] *adv* rashly ■ **imprudence** *nf* rashness

impudique [ɛ̃pydik] *adj* shameless

impuissant, -e [ɛ̃pɥisɑ̃, -ɑ̃t] *adj* powerless; *Méd* impotent

impulsif, -ive [ɛ̃pylsif, -iv] *adj* impulsive ■ **impulsion** *nf* impulse

impunément [ɛ̃pynemɑ̃] *adv* with impunity ■ **impuni, -e** *adj* unpunished

impur, -e [ɛ̃pyr] *adj* impure ■ **impureté** *nf* impurity

imputer [ɛ̃pyte] *vt* to attribute **(à** to); *(frais)* to charge **(à** to)

inabordable [inabɔrdabl] *adj (prix)* prohibitive; *(lieu)* inaccessible; *(personne)* unapproachable

inacceptable [inaksɛptabl] *adj* unacceptable

inaccessible [inaksesibl] *adj (lieu)* inaccessible; *(personne)* unapproachable

inachevé, -e [inaʃve] *adj* unfinished

inactif, -ive [inaktif, -iv] *adj (personne)* inactive; *(remède)* ineffective ■ **inaction** *nf* inaction ■ **inactivité** *nf* inactivity

inadapté, -e [inadapte] *adj (socialement)* maladjusted; *(physiquement, mentalement)* handicapped; *(matériel)* unsuitable **(à** for) **2** *nmf (socialement)* maladjusted person

inadmissible [inadmisibl] *adj* inadmissible

inadvertance [inadvɛrtɑ̃s] *par inadvertance adv* inadvertently

inamical, -e, -aux, -ales [inamikal, -o] *adj* unfriendly

inanimé, -e [inanime] *adj (mort)* lifeless; *(évanoui)* unconscious; *(matière)* inanimate

inaperçu, -e [inapɛrsy] *adj* **passer i.** to go unnoticed

inappréciable [inapresjabl] *adj* invaluable

inapte [inapt] *adj (intellectuellement)* unsuited *(à* for); *(médicalement)* unfit *(à* for) ▪ **inaptitude** *nf (intellectuelle)* inaptitude; *(médicale)* unfitness *(à* for)

inattendu, -e [inatɑ̃dy] *adj* unexpected

inattention [inatɑ̃sjɔ̃] *nf* lack of attention

inaudible [inodibl] *adj* inaudible

inaugurer [inogyre] *vt (édifice)* to inaugurate ▪ **inaugural, -e, -aux, -ales** *adj* inaugural

inavouable [inavwabl] *adj* shameful

incalculable [ɛ̃kalkylabl] *adj* incalculable

incapable [ɛ̃kapabl] *adj* incapable; **i. de faire qch** incapable of doing sth ▪ **incapacité** *nf (impossibilité)* inability *(de faire* to do); *(invalidité)* disability; **être dans l'i. de faire qch** to be unable to do sth

incarcérer [ɛ̃karsere] *vt* to incarcerate ▪ **incarcération** *nf* incarceration

incarnation [ɛ̃karnɑsjɔ̃] *nf* incarnation

incarné, -e [ɛ̃karne] *adj (ongle)* ingrown

incarner [ɛ̃karne] *vt* to embody

incassable [ɛ̃kɑsabl] *adj* unbreakable

incendie [ɛ̃sɑ̃di] *nm* fire; **i. criminel** arson; **i. de forêt** forest fire ▪ **incendiaire 1** *adj (bombe)* incendiary **2** *nmf* arsonist ▪ **incendier** *vt* to set on fire

incertain, -e [ɛ̃sɛrtɛ̃, -ɛn] *adj (résultat)* uncertain; *(temps)* unsettled; *(personne)* indecisive ▪ **incertitude** *nf* uncertainty

incessamment [ɛ̃sesamɑ̃] *adv* very soon

incessant, -e [ɛ̃sesɑ̃, -ɑ̃t] *adj* incessant

inchangé, -e [ɛ̃ʃɑ̃ʒe] *adj* unchanged

incidence [ɛ̃sidɑ̃s] *nf (influence)* impact *(sur* on); *Méd* incidence

incident [ɛ̃sidɑ̃] *nm* incident; *(accroc)* hitch; **i. de parcours** minor setback

incinérer [ɛ̃sinere] *vt (ordures)* to incinerate; *(cadavre)* to cremate ▪ **incinération** *nf (d'ordures)* incineration; *(de cadavre)* cremation

inciser [ɛ̃size] *vt (peau)* to make an incision in; *(abcès)* to lance ▪ **incision** *nf (entaille)* incision

incisif, -ive¹ [ɛ̃sizif, -iv] *adj* incisive

incisive² [ɛ̃siziv] *nf (dent)* incisor (tooth)

inciter [ɛ̃site] *vt* to encourage *(à faire* to do) ▪ **incitation** *nf* incitement *(à* to)

incliner [ɛ̃kline] **1** *vt (pencher)* to tilt; **i. la tête** *(approuver)* to nod; *(saluer)* to bow one's head **2** **s'incliner** *vpr (se pencher)* to lean forward; *(pour saluer)* to bow; *Fig (se soumettre)* to give in *(devant* to) ▪ **inclinaison** *nf* incline, slope ▪ **inclination** *nf (tendance)* inclination

inclure* [ɛ̃klyr] *vt* to include; *(dans un courrier)* to enclose *(dans* with) ▪ **inclus, -e** *adj* **du 4 au 10 i.** from the 4th to the 10th inclusive; **jusqu'à lundi i.** *Br* up to and including Monday, *Am* through Monday ▪ **inclusion** *nf* inclusion

incognito [ɛ̃kɔɲito] *adv* incognito

incohérent, -e [ɛ̃kɔerɑ̃, -ɑ̃t] *adj (propos)* incoherent; *(histoire)* inconsistent ▪ **incohérence** *nf (de propos)* incoherence; *(d'histoire)* inconsistency

incolore [ɛ̃kɔlɔr] *adj* colourless; *(vernis, verre)* clear

incomber [ɛ̃kɔ̃be] *vi* **i. à qn** *(devoir)* to fall to sb; **il lui incombe de faire qch** it falls to him/her to do sth

incommoder [ɛ̃kɔmɔde] *vt* to bother

incomparable [ɛ̃kɔ̃parabl] *adj* matchless

incompatible [ɛ̃kɔ̃patibl] *adj* incompatible (**avec** with)

incompétent, -e [ɛ̃kɔ̃petɑ̃, -ɑ̃t] *adj* incompetent ■ **incompétence** *nf* incompetence

incomplet, -ète [ɛ̃kɔ̃plɛ, -ɛt] *adj* incomplete

incompréhensible [ɛ̃kɔ̃preɑ̃sibl] *adj* incomprehensible ■ **incompréhension** *nf* incomprehension

incompris, -e [ɛ̃kɔ̃pri, -iz] **1** *adj* misunderstood **2** *nmf* **être un i.** to be misunderstood

inconcevable [ɛ̃kɔ̃səvabl] *adj* inconceivable

inconciliable [ɛ̃kɔ̃siljabl] *adj (théorie)* irreconcilable; *(activité)* incompatible

inconditionnel, -elle [ɛ̃kɔ̃disjɔnɛl] *adj* unconditional; *(supporter)* staunch

inconfortable [ɛ̃kɔ̃fɔrtabl] *adj* uncomfortable

inconnu, -e [ɛ̃kɔny] **1** *adj* unknown (**de** to) **2** *nmf (étranger)* stranger; *(auteur)* unknown **3** *nm* **l'i.** the unknown **4** *nf Math* **inconnue** unknown (quantity)

inconscient, -e [ɛ̃kɔ̃sjɑ̃, -ɑ̃t] **1** *adj (sans connaissance)* unconscious; *(imprudent)* reckless; **i. de qch** unaware of sth **2** *nm* **l'i.** the unconscious ■ **inconsciemment** [-amɑ̃] *adv (dans l'inconscient)* subconsciously ■ **inconscience** *nf (perte de connaissance)* unconsciousness; *(irréflexion)* recklessness

inconséquence [ɛ̃kɔ̃sekɑ̃s] *nf (manque de prudence)* recklessness; *(manque de cohérence)* inconsistency

inconsidéré, -e [ɛ̃kɔ̃sidere] *adj* thoughtless

inconsistant, -e [ɛ̃kɔ̃sistɑ̃, -ɑ̃t] *adj (personne)* weak; *(film, roman)* flimsy; *(sauce, crème)* thin

inconsolable [ɛ̃kɔ̃sɔlabl] *adj* inconsolable

inconstant, -e [ɛ̃kɔ̃stɑ̃, -ɑ̃t] *adj* fickle

incontestable [ɛ̃kɔ̃tɛstabl] *adj* indisputable ■ **incontesté, -e** *adj* undisputed

incontournable [ɛ̃kɔ̃turnabl] *adj Fig (film)* unmissable; *(auteur)* who cannot be ignored

incontrôlé, -e [ɛ̃kɔ̃trole] *adj* unchecked ■ **incontrôlable** *adj (invérifiable)* unverifiable; *(indomptable)* uncontrollable

inconvenant, -e [ɛ̃kɔ̃vnɑ̃, -ɑ̃t] *adj* improper

inconvénient [ɛ̃kɔ̃venjɑ̃] *nm (désavantage)* drawback; **l'i., c'est que...** the annoying thing is that...

incorporer [ɛ̃kɔrpɔre] *vt (insérer)* to insert (**à** in); *(troupes)* to draft; **i. qch à qch** to blend sth into sth ■ **incorporation** *nf (mélange)* blending (**de qch dans qch** of sth into sth); *Mil* conscription

incorrect, -e [ɛ̃kɔrɛkt] *adj (inexact)* incorrect; *(grossier)* impolite; *(inconvenant)* improper ■ **incorrection** *nf (impolitesse)* impoliteness; *(propos)* impolite remark; *(faute de grammaire)* mistake

incorrigible [ɛ̃kɔriʒibl] *adj* incorrigible

incorruptible [ɛ̃kɔryptibl] *adj* incorruptible

incrédule [ɛ̃kredyl] *adj* incredulous ■ **incrédulité** *nf* incredulity

incriminer [ɛ̃krimine] *vt (personne)* to accuse

incroyable [ɛ̃krwajabl] *adj* incredible

incrusté, -e [ɛ̃kryste] *adj* **i. de** *(orné)* inlaid with

incubation [ɛ̃kybasjɔ̃] *nf* incubation

inculper [ɛ̃kylpe] *vt (accuser)* to charge (**de** with) ■ **inculpation** *nf* charge, indictment ■ **inculpé, -e** *nmf* **l'i.** the accused

inculquer [ɛ̃kylke] *vt* to instil (**à qn** in sb)

inculte [ɛ̃kylt] *adj (terre, personne)* uncultivated

incurable [ɛ̃kyrabl] *adj* incurable

incursion [ɛ̃kyrsjɔ̃] *nf* (*invasion*) incursion; *Fig* (*entrée soudaine*) intrusion

Inde [ɛ̃d] *nf* l'I. India

indécent, -e [ɛ̃desɑ̃, -ɑ̃t] *adj* indecent ■ **indécence** *nf* indecency

indéchiffrable [ɛ̃deʃifrabl] *adj* (*illisible*) undecipherable

indécis, -e [ɛ̃desi, -iz] *adj* (*personne*) (*de caractère*) indecisive; (*ponctuellement*) undecided ■ **indécision** *nf* (*de caractère*) indecisiveness; (*ponctuelle*) indecision

indéfendable [ɛ̃defɑ̃dabl] *adj* indefensible

indéfini, -e [ɛ̃defini] *adj* (*illimité*) indefinite; (*imprécis*) undefined ■ **indéfiniment** *adv* indefinitely ■ **indéfinissable** *adj* indefinable

indélébile [ɛ̃delebil] *adj* indelible

indélicat, -e [ɛ̃delika, -at] *adj* (*grossier*) insensitive; (*malhonnête*) unscrupulous

indemne [ɛ̃dɛmn] *adj* unhurt, unscathed

indemniser [ɛ̃dɛmnize] *vt* to compensate (**de** for) ■ **indemnisation** *nf* compensation ■ **indemnité** *nf* (*dédommagement*) compensation; (*allocation*) allowance; **i. de licenciement** redundancy payment

indéniable [ɛ̃denjabl] *adj* undeniable

indépendant, -e [ɛ̃depɑ̃dɑ̃, -ɑ̃t] *adj* independent (**de** of); (*chambre*) self-contained; (*travailleur*) self-employed ■ **indépendamment** [-amɑ̃] *adv* independently; **i. de** apart from ■ **indépendance** *nf* independence

indescriptible [ɛ̃deskriptibl] *adj* indescribable

indésirable [ɛ̃dezirabl] *adj & nmf* undesirable

indestructible [ɛ̃destryktibl] *adj* indestructible

indéterminé, -e [ɛ̃determine] *adj* (*date, heure*) unspecified; (*raison*) unknown

index [ɛ̃dɛks] *nm* (*doigt*) forefinger, index finger; (*liste*) & *Ordinat* index

indicateur, -trice [ɛ̃dikatœr, -tris] **1** *nm Tech* indicator, gauge; *Écon* indicator; (*espion*) informer **2** *adj* **panneau i.** road sign

indicatif, -ive [ɛ̃dikatif, -iv] **1** *adj* indicative (**de** of) **2** *nm Radio* theme tune; **i. téléphonique** *Br* dialling code, *Am* area code

indication [ɛ̃dikasjɔ̃] *nf* indication (**de** of); (*renseignement*) (piece of) information; (*directive*) instruction; **indications...** (*de médicament*) suitable for...

indice [ɛ̃dis] *nm* (*signe*) sign; (*d'enquête*) clue

indien, -enne [ɛ̃djɛ̃, -ɛn] **1** *adj* Indian **2** *nmf* I., Indienne Indian

indifférent, -e [ɛ̃diferɑ̃, -ɑ̃t] *adj* indifferent (**à** to) ■ **indifférence** *nf* indifference (**à** to)

indigène [ɛ̃diʒɛn] *adj & nmf* native

indigent, -e [ɛ̃diʒɑ̃, -ɑ̃t] *adj* destitute ■ **indigence** *nf* destitution

indigeste [ɛ̃diʒɛst] *adj* indigestible ■ **indigestion** *nf* **avoir une i.** to have a stomach upset

indignation [ɛ̃diɲasjɔ̃] *nf* indignation

indigne [ɛ̃diɲ] *adj* (*personne*) unworthy; (*conduite*) shameful; **i. de qn/qch** unworthy of sb/sth ■ **indignité** *nf* (*de personne*) unworthiness; (*de conduite*) shamefulness; (*action*) shameful act

indigner [ɛ̃diɲe] **1** *vt* **i. qn** to make sb indignant **2 s'indigner** *vpr* to be indignant (**de** at) ■ **indigné, -e** *adj* indignant

indiquer [ɛ̃dike] *vt* (*sujet: personne*) to point out; (*sujet: panneau*) to show, to indicate; (*sujet: compteur*) to read; (*donner*) (*date, adresse*) to give; **i. le chemin à qn** to tell sb the way ■ **indiqué, -e** *adj* (*conseillé*) advisable; **à l'heure indiquée** at the appointed time

indirect, -e [ɛ̃dirɛkt] *adj* indirect

indiscipline [ɛ̃disiplin] *nf* indiscipline ■ **indiscipliné, -e** *adj* unruly

indiscret, -ète [ɛ̃diskrɛ, -ɛt] *adj Péj (curieux)* inquisitive; *(qui parle trop)* indiscreet ■ **indiscrétion** *nf* indiscretion

indiscutable [ɛ̃diskytabl] *adj* indisputable

indispensable [ɛ̃dispɑ̃sabl] *adj* essential, indispensable (**à qch** for sth); **i. à qn** indispensable to sb

indisponible [ɛ̃disponibl] *adj* unavailable

indisposer [ɛ̃dispoze] *vt (contrarier)* to annoy; **i. qn** *(odeur, climat)* to make sb feel ill ■ **indisposé, -e** *adj (malade)* indisposed, unwell ■ **indisposition** *nf* indisposition

indistinct, -e [ɛ̃distɛ̃(kt), -ɛkt] *adj* indistinct ■ **indistinctement** [-ɛktəmɑ̃] *adv (voir, parler)* indistinctly; *(également)* equally

individu [ɛ̃dividy] *nm* individual; *Péj* individual, character

individualiste [ɛ̃dividɥalist] **1** *adj* individualistic **2** *nmf* individualist

individualité [ɛ̃dividɥalite] *nf* individuality

individuel, -elle [ɛ̃dividɥɛl] *adj* individual; *(maison)* detached

indivisible [ɛ̃divizibl] *adj* indivisible

Indochine [ɛ̃doʃin] *nf* **l'I.** Indo-China

indolent, -e [ɛ̃dolɑ̃, -ɑ̃t] *adj* lazy

indolore [ɛ̃dolɔr] *adj* painless

indomptable [ɛ̃dɔ̃(p)tabl] *adj (animal)* untamable

Indonésie [ɛ̃donezi] *nf* **l'I.** Indonesia

indue [ɛ̃dy] *adj f* **rentrer à des heures indues** to come home at all hours of the night

induire* [ɛ̃dɥir] *vt* **i. qn en erreur** to lead sb astray

indulgent, -e [ɛ̃dylʒɑ̃, -ɑ̃t] *adj* indulgent ■ **indulgence** *nf* indulgence

industrie [ɛ̃dystri] *nf* industry ■ **industrialisé, -e** *adj* industrialized ■ **industriel, -elle 1** *adj* industrial **2** *nm* industrialist

inébranlable [inebrɑ̃labl] *adj Fig (certitude, personne)* unshakeable

inédit, -e [inedi, -it] *adj (texte)* unpublished

inefficace [inefikas] *adj (mesure)* ineffective; *(personne)* inefficient ■ **inefficacité** *nf (de mesure)* ineffectiveness; *(de personne)* inefficiency

inégal, -e, -aux, -ales [inegal, -o] *adj (parts, lutte)* unequal; *(sol, humeur)* uneven; *Fig (travail)* inconsistent ■ **inégalable** *adj* incomparable ■ **inégalé, -e** *adj* unequalled ■ **inégalité** *nf (injustice)* inequality; *(physique)* disparity (**de** in); *(de sol)* unevenness

inéluctable [inelyktabl] *adj* inescapable

inepte [inɛpt] *adj (remarque, histoire)* inane; *(personne)* inept ■ **ineptie** [inɛpsi] *nf (de comportement, de film)* inanity; *(remarque)* stupid remark

inépuisable [inepɥizabl] *adj* inexhaustible

inespéré, -e [inɛspere] *adj* unhoped-for

inestimable [inɛstimabl] *adj (objet d'art)* priceless

inévitable [inevitabl] *adj* inevitable, unavoidable

inexact, -e [inɛgzakt] *adj (erroné)* inaccurate; *(calcul)* wrong ■ **inexactitude** *nf (caractère erroné, erreur)* inaccuracy; *(manque de ponctualité)* unpunctuality

inexcusable [inɛkskyzabl] *adj* inexcusable

inexistant, -e [inɛgzistɑ̃, -ɑ̃t] *adj* non-existent

inexpérience [inɛksperjɑ̃s] *nf* inexperience ■ **inexpérimenté, -e** *adj* inexperienced

inexplicable [inɛksplikabl] *adj* inexplicable ■ **inexpliqué, -e** *adj* unexplained

inexploré, -e [inɛksplore] *adj* unexplored

inexprimable [inɛksprimabl] *adj* inexpressible

inextricable [inɛkstrikabl] *adj* inextricable

infaillible [ɛ̃fajibl] *adj* infallible

infaisable [ɛ̃fəzabl] *adj (travail)* impossible

infâme [ɛ̃fɑm] *adj (personne)* despicable; *(acte)* unspeakable; *(taudis)* squalid; *(aliment)* revolting

infantile [ɛ̃fɑ̃til] *adj (maladie)* childhood; *Péj (comportement, personne)* infantile

infarctus [ɛ̃farktys] *nm Méd* heart attack

infatigable [ɛ̃fatigabl] *adj* tireless

infect, -e [ɛ̃fɛkt] *adj* foul

infecter [ɛ̃fɛkte] **1** *vt (atmosphère)* to contaminate; *Méd* to infect **2 s'infecter** *vpr* to become infected ■ **infection** *nf Méd* infection; *(odeur)* stench

inférieur, -e [ɛ̃ferjœr] **1** *adj (étagère, niveau)* bottom; *(étage, lèvre, membre)* lower; *(qualité, marchandises)* inferior; **i. à la moyenne** below average; **à l'étage i.** on the floor below **2** *nmf* inferior ■ **infériorité** *nf* inferiority

infernal, -e, -aux, -ales [ɛ̃fɛrnal, -o] *adj (de l'enfer)* & *Fig (chaleur, bruit)* infernal

infidèle [ɛ̃fidɛl] *adj* unfaithful (**à** to) ■ **infidélité** *nf* unfaithfulness, infidelity

infiltrer [ɛ̃filtre] **1** *vt (party)* to infiltrate **2 s'infiltrer** *vpr (liquide)* to seep (**dans** into); *(lumière)* to filter in; *Fig* **s'i. dans** *(groupe, esprit)* to infiltrate ■ **infiltration** *nf (de liquide, d'espions)* infiltration

infime [ɛ̃fim] *adj* tiny

infini [ɛ̃fini] **1** *adj* infinite **2** *nm Math* & *Phot* infinity; *Phil* infinite; **à l'i.** *(discuter)* ad infinitum; *Math* to infinity ■ **infiniment** *adv* infinitely; **je regrette i.** I'm very sorry ■ **infinité** *nf* **une i. de** an infinite number of

infirme [ɛ̃firm] **1** *adj* disabled **2** *nmf* disabled person ■ **infirmité** *nf* disability

infirmer [ɛ̃firme] *vt* to invalidate

infirmerie [ɛ̃firməri] *nf (d'école, de bateau)* sick room; *(de caserne, de prison)* infirmary ■ **infirmier** *nm* male nurse ■ **infirmière** *nf* nurse

inflammable [ɛ̃flamabl] *adj* (in)flammable

inflammation [ɛ̃flamasjɔ̃] *nf Méd* inflammation

inflation [ɛ̃flasjɔ̃] *nf Écon* inflation

infléchir [ɛ̃fleʃir] *vt (courber)* to bend; *(politique)* to change the direction of ■ **inflexion** *nf (de courbe, de voix)* inflection

inflexible [ɛ̃flɛksibl] *adj* inflexible

infliger [ɛ̃fliʒe] *vt* to inflict (**à** on); *(amende)* to impose (**à** on)

influence [ɛ̃flyɑ̃s] *nf* influence ■ **influençable** *adj* easily influenced ■ **influencer** *vt* to influence ■ **influent, -e** *adj* influential ■ **influer** *vi* **i. sur qch** to influence sth

informaticien, -enne [ɛ̃fɔrmatisjɛ̃, -ɛn] *nmf* computer scientist

information [ɛ̃fɔrmasjɔ̃] *nf* information; *(nouvelle)* piece of news; *Ordinat* data, information; *Radio* & *TV* **les informations** the news *(sing)*

informatique [ɛ̃fɔrmatik] **1** *nf (science)* computer science; *(technique)* data processing **2** *adj* **programme i.** computer program ■ **informatisation** *nf* computerization ■ **informatiser** *vt* to computerize

informe [ɛ̃fɔrm] *adj* shapeless

informer [ɛ̃fɔrme] **1** *vt* to inform (**de** of *or* about; **que** that) **2 s'informer** *vpr (se renseigner)* to inquire (**de** about; **si** if *or* whether)

inforoute [ɛ̃fɔrut] *nf* information superhighway

infortune [ɛ̃fɔrtyn] *nf* misfortune ■ **infortuné, -e** *adj* unfortunate

infraction [ɛ̃fraksjɔ̃] *nf (à un règlement)* infringement; *(délit) Br* offence, *Am* offense

infranchissable [ɛ̃frɑ̃ʃisabl] *adj (mur, fleuve)* impassable; *Fig (difficulté)* insurmountable

infrarouge [ɛ̃fraruʒ] *adj* infrared

infrastructure [ɛ̃frastryktyr] *nf (de bâtiment)* substructure; *(équipements)* infrastructure

infructueux, -euse [ɛ̃fryktɥø, -øz] *adj* fruitless

infuser [ɛ̃fyze] *vi (thé)* to brew; *(tisane)*

to infuse ■ **infusion** *nf (tisane)* herb tea

ingénier [ɛ̃ʒenje] **s'ingénier** *vpr* to strive (**à faire** to do)

ingénieur [ɛ̃ʒenjœr] *nm* engineer ■ **ingénierie** [-iri] *nf* engineering

ingénieux, -euse [ɛ̃ʒenjø, -øz] *adj* ingenious ■ **ingéniosité** *nf* ingenuity

ingénu, -e [ɛ̃ʒeny] *adj* ingenuous

ingérer [ɛ̃ʒere] **s'ingérer** *vpr* to interfere (**dans** in) ■ **ingérence** *nf* interference (**dans** in)

ingrat, -e [ɛ̃gra, -at] *adj (personne)* ungrateful (**envers** to); *(tâche)* thankless; *(sol)* barren; *(visage)* unattractive; **l'âge i.** the awkward age ■ **ingratitude** *nf* ingratitude

ingrédient [ɛ̃gredjɑ̃] *nm* ingredient

inhabitable [inabitabl] *adj* uninhabitable ■ **inhabité, -e** *adj* uninhabited

inhabituel, -elle [inabituɛl] *adj* unusual

inhérent, -e [inerɑ̃, -ɑ̃t] *adj* inherent (**à** in)

inhibé, -e [inibe] *adj* inhibited ■ **inhibition** *nf* inhibition

inhospitalier, -ère [inɔspitalje, -ɛr] *adj* inhospitable

inhumain, -e [inymɛ̃, -ɛn] *adj (cruel, terrible)* inhuman

inhumer [inyme] *vt* to bury

inimaginable [inimaʒinabl] *adj* unimaginable

inimitable [inimitabl] *adj* inimitable

inimitié [inimitje] *nf* enmity

ininflammable [inɛ̃flamabl] *adj* nonflammable

inintelligible [inɛ̃teliʒibl] *adj* unintelligible

ininterrompu, -e [inɛ̃terɔ̃py] *adj* continuous

initial, -e, -aux, -ales [inisjal, -o] *adj* initial ■ **initiale** *nf* initial

initialiser [inisjalize] *vt Ordinat (disque)* to initialize; *(ordinateur)* to boot

initiation [inisjasjɔ̃] *nf* initiation

initiative [inisjativ] *nf* initiative; **de ma propre i.** on my own initiative

initier [inisje] **1** *vt (former)* to introduce (**à** to); *(rituellement)* to initiate (**à** into) **2 s'initier** *vpr* **s'i. à qch** to start learning sth

injecter [ɛ̃ʒɛkte] *vt* to inject (**dans** into) ■ **injection** *nf* injection

injure [ɛ̃ʒyr] *nf* insult ■ **injurier** *vt* to insult, to abuse ■ **injurieux, -euse** *adj* abusive, insulting (**pour** to)

injuste [ɛ̃ʒyst] *adj (contraire à la justice)* unjust; *(non équitable)* unfair ■ **injustice** *nf* injustice

injustifiable [ɛ̃ʒystifjabl] *adj* unjustifiable ■ **injustifié, -e** *adj* unjustified

inlassable [ɛ̃lɑsabl] *adj* untiring

inné, -e [ine] *adj* innate, inborn

innocent, -e [inɔsɑ̃, -ɑ̃t] **1** *adj* innocent (**de** of) **2** *nmf (non coupable)* innocent person; *(idiot)* simpleton ■ **innocence** *nf* innocence ■ **innocenter** *vt* **i. qn** to clear sb (**de** of)

innombrable [inɔ̃brabl] *adj* countless, innumerable; *(foule)* huge

innommable [inɔmabl] *adj (conduite, actes)* unspeakable; *(nourriture, odeur)* vile

innover [inɔve] *vi* to innovate ■ **innovateur, -trice 1** *adj* innovative **2** *nmf* innovator ■ **innovation** *nf* innovation

inoccupé, -e [inɔkype] *adj* unoccupied

inoculer [inɔkyle] *vt* **i. qch à qn** to inoculate sb with sth; **i. qn contre qch** to inoculate sb against sth

inodore [inɔdɔr] *adj* odourless

inoffensif, -ive [inɔfɑ̃sif, -iv] *adj* harmless

inonder [inɔ̃de] *vt (lieu)* to flood; *Fig (marché)* to flood, to inundate (**de** with); **inondé de soleil** bathed in sunlight ■ **inondation** *nf* flood; *(action)* flooding

inopérable [inɔperabl] *adj* inoperable

inopiné, -e [inɔpine] *adj* unexpected

inopportun, -e [inɔpɔrtœ̃, -yn] *adj* inopportune

inoubliable [inubljabl] *adj* unforgettable

inouï, -e [inwi] *adj* incredible

Inox® [inɔks] *nm* stainless steel; **couteau en I.** stainless-steel knife ■ **inoxydable** *adj (couteau)* stainless-steel

inqualifiable [ɛ̃kalifjabl] *adj* unspeakable

inquiet, -ète [ɛ̃kjɛ, -ɛt] *adj* worried, anxious (**de** about)

inquiéter [ɛ̃kjete] **1** *vt (préoccuper)* to worry **2 s'inquiéter** *vpr* to worry (**de** about); **s'i. pour qn** to worry about sb ■ **inquiétant, -e** *adj* worrying

inquiétude [ɛ̃kjetyd] *nf* anxiety, worry

insaisissable [ɛ̃sezisabl] *adj* elusive

insalubre [ɛ̃salybr] *adj (climat, habitation)* insalubrious

insatiable [ɛ̃sasjabl] *adj* insatiable

insatisfait, -e [ɛ̃satisfɛ, -ɛt] *adj (personne)* dissatisfied

inscription [ɛ̃skripsjɔ̃] *nf (action)* entering; *(immatriculation)* registration; *(sur écriteau, mur, tombe)* inscription

inscrire* [ɛ̃skrir] **1** *vt (renseignements, date)* to write down; *(dans un journal, sur un registre)* to enter; *(graver)* to inscribe; **i. qn à un club** to *Br* enrol *or Am* enroll sb in a club

2 s'inscrire *vpr* to put one's name down; *(à une activité) Br* to enrol, *Am* to enroll (**à** at); *(à l'université)* to register (**à** at); **s'i. à un club** to join a club

insecte [ɛ̃sɛkt] *nm* insect

insécurité [ɛ̃sekyrite] *nf* insecurity

insensé, -e [ɛ̃sɑ̃se] *adj (projet, idée)* crazy; *(espoir)* wild

insensible [ɛ̃sɑ̃sibl] *adj (indifférent)* insensitive (**à** to); *(imperceptible)* imperceptible

inséparable [ɛ̃separabl] *adj* inseparable (**de** from)

insérer [ɛ̃sere] *vt* to insert (**dans** in) ■ **insertion** [ɛ̃sɛrsjɔ̃] *nf* insertion

insidieux, -euse [ɛ̃sidjø, -øz] *adj* insidious

insigne [ɛ̃siɲ] *nm* badge

insignifiant, -e [ɛ̃siɲifjɑ̃, -jɑ̃t] *adj* insignificant

insinuer [ɛ̃sinɥe] **1** *vt Péj* to insinuate (**que** that) **2 s'insinuer** *vpr (froid)* to

creep (**dans** into); *(personne)* to worm one's way (**dans** into)

insipide [ɛ̃sipid] *adj* insipid

insister [ɛ̃siste] *vi* to insist (**pour faire** on doing); **i. sur qch** to stress sth; **i. pour que...** (+ *subjunctive*) to insist that... ■ **insistance** *nf* insistence

insolation [ɛ̃sɔlasjɔ̃] *nf Méd* sunstroke

insolent, -e [ɛ̃sɔlɑ̃, -ɑ̃t] *adj (impoli)* insolent; *(luxe)* unashamed ■ **insolence** *nf* insolence

insolite [ɛ̃sɔlit] *adj* unusual, strange

insoluble [ɛ̃sɔlybl] *adj* insoluble

insomnie [ɛ̃sɔmni] *nf* insomnia ■ **insomniaque** *nmf* insomniac

insondable [ɛ̃sɔ̃dabl] *adj* unfathomable

insonoriser [ɛ̃sɔnɔrize] *vt* to soundproof

insouciant, -e [ɛ̃susjɑ̃, -ɑ̃t] *adj* carefree ■ **insouciance** *nf* carefree attitude

insoumis, -e [ɛ̃sumi, -iz] *adj (personne)* rebellious; *Mil* absentee

insoupçonnable [ɛ̃supsɔnabl] *adj* beyond suspicion

insoutenable [ɛ̃sutnabl] *adj (spectacle, odeur)* unbearable; *(théorie)* untenable

inspecter [ɛ̃spɛkte] *vt* to inspect ■ **inspecteur, -trice** *nmf* inspector ■ **inspection** *nf* inspection

inspirer [ɛ̃spire] **1** *vt* to inspire; **i. qch à qn** to inspire sb with sth **2** *vi* to breathe in **3 s'inspirer** *vpr* **s'i. de qn/ qch** to take one's inspiration from sb/ sth ■ **inspiration** *nf (idée)* inspiration; *(respiration)* breathing in ■ **inspiré, -e** *adj* inspired

instable [ɛ̃stabl] *adj* unstable; *(temps)* changeable ■ **instabilité** *nf* instability; *(de temps)* changeability

installer [ɛ̃stale] **1** *vt (appareil, meuble)* to install, to put in; *(étagère)* to put up; *(cuisine)* to fit out; **i. qn** *(dans une fonction, dans un logement)* to install sb (**dans** in)

2 s'installer *vpr (s'asseoir)* to settle

down; *(dans un bureau)* to install oneself; *(médecin)* to set oneself up; **s'i. à la campagne** to settle in the country ▪ **installation** *nf (de machine)* installation; *(de cuisine)* fitting out; *(emménagement)* move; **installations** *(appareils)* fittings; *(bâtiments)* facilities

instant [ɛstɑ̃] *nm* moment, instant; **à l'i.** a moment ago; **à l'i. où...** just as...; **pour l'i.** for the moment ▪ **instantané, -e 1** *adj* instantaneous; **café i.** instant coffee **2** *nm (photo)* snapshot

instar [ɛstar] *nm* **à l'i. de qn** after the fashion of sb

instaurer [ɛstore] *vt* to establish

instigateur, -trice [ɛstigatœr, -tris] *nmf* instigator

instinct [ɛstɛ̃] *nm* instinct; **d'i.** by instinct ▪ **instinctif, -ive** *adj* instinctive

instituer [ɛstitɥe] *vt* to establish

institut [ɛstity] *nm* institute; **i. de beauté** beauty salon

instituteur, -trice [ɛstitytœr, -tris] *nmf* Br primary or Am elementary school teacher

institution [ɛstitysjɔ̃] *nf (création)* establishment; *(coutume)* institution; *(école)* private school ▪ **institutionnel, -elle** *adj* institutional

instructif, -ive [ɛstryktif, -iv] *adj* instructive

instruction [ɛstryksjɔ̃] *nf (éducation)* education; *Mil* training; *Jur* preliminary investigation; **instructions** *(ordres)* instructions; **i. civique** civics *(sing)* ▪ **instructeur** *nm* instructor

instruire* [ɛstrɥir] **1** *vt* to teach, to educate; *Mil* to train; *Jur* to investigate; **i. qn de qch** to inform sb of sth **2** **s'instruire** *vpr* to educate oneself ▪ **instruit, -e** *adj* educated

instrument [ɛstrymɑ̃] *nm* instrument; **i. à vent** wind instrument ▪ **instrumental, -e, -aux, -ales** *adj* Mus instrumental

insu [ɛsy] **à l'insu de** *prép* without the knowledge of; **à mon/son i.** *(sans*

m'en/s'en apercevoir)* without my/his/her being aware of it

insuffisant, -e [ɛsyfizɑ̃, -ɑ̃t] *adj (en quantité)* insufficient; *(en qualité)* inadequate ▪ **insuffisance** *nf (manque)* insufficiency; *(de moyens)* inadequacy

insulaire [ɛsylɛr] **1** *adj* insular **2** *nmf* islander

insulte [ɛsylt] *nf* insult (**à** to) ▪ **insulter** *vt* to insult

insupportable [ɛsypɔrtabl] *adj* unbearable

insurger [ɛsyrʒe] **s'insurger** *vpr* to rise up (**contre** against)

insurmontable [ɛsyrmɔ̃tabl] *adj* insurmountable

insurrection [ɛsyrɛksjɔ̃] *nf* insurrection, uprising

intact, -e [ɛtakt] *adj* intact

intarissable [ɛtarisabl] *adj* inexhaustible

intégral, -e, -aux, -ales [ɛtegral, -o] *adj (paiement)* full; *(édition)* unabridged; **version intégrale** *(de film)* uncut version ▪ **intégralement** *adv* in full, fully ▪ **intégralité** *nf* whole (**de** of)

intègre [ɛtɛgr] *adj* upright, honest ▪ **intégrité** *nf* integrity

intégrer [ɛtegre] **1** *vt* to integrate (**dans** in); *(école)* to get into **2** **s'intégrer** *vpr* to become integrated ▪ **intégrante** *adj* **faire partie i. de qch** to be an integral part of sth ▪ **intégration** *nf (au sein d'un groupe)* integration

intégrisme [ɛtegrism] *nm* fundamentalism

intellectuel, -elle [ɛtelɛktɥel] *adj & nmf* intellectual

intelligent, -e [ɛteliʒɑ̃, -ɑ̃t] *adj* intelligent, clever ▪ **intelligence** *nf (faculté)* intelligence; **avoir l'i. de faire qch** to have the intelligence to do sth; *Ordinat* **i. artificielle** artificial intelligence

intelligible [ɛteliʒibl] *adj* intelligible

intempéries [ɛtɑ̃peri] *nfpl* **les i.** the bad weather

intempestif, -ive [ɛ̃tɑ̃pɛstif, -iv] *adj* untimely

intenable [ɛ̃tnabl] *adj (position)* untenable

intendant, -e [ɛ̃tɑ̃dɑ̃, -ɑ̃t] *nmf Scol* bursar

intense [ɛ̃tɑ̃s] *adj* intense; *(circulation)* heavy ■ **intensif, -ive** *adj* intensive ■ **intensité** *nf* intensity

intensifier [ɛ̃tɑ̃sifje] *vt,* **s'intensifier** *vpr* to intensify

intenter [ɛ̃tɑ̃te] *vt Jur* **i. un procès à qn** to institute proceedings against sb

intention [ɛ̃tɑ̃sjɔ̃] *nf* intention; *Jur* intent; **avoir l'i. de faire qch** to intend to do sth ■ **intentionné, -e** *adj* **bien i.** well-intentioned; **mal i.** ill-intentioned ■ **intentionnel, -elle** *adj* intentional

interactif, -ive [ɛ̃teraktif, -iv] *adj Ordinat* interactive

interaction [ɛ̃terɑksjɔ̃] *nf* interaction

intercaler [ɛ̃terkale] *vt* to insert

intercéder [ɛ̃tersede] *vt* to intercede (**auprès de** with; **en faveur de** on behalf of)

intercepter [ɛ̃tersɛpte] *vt* to intercept

interchangeable [ɛ̃terʃɑ̃ʒabl] *adj* interchangeable

interdire* [ɛ̃terdir] *vt* to forbid (**qch à qn** sb sth); *(film, meeting)* to ban; **i. à qn de faire qch** *(personne)* to forbid sb to do sth ■ **interdiction** *nf* ban (**de** on); **'i. de fumer'** 'no smoking' ■ **interdit, -e** *adj* **(a)** *(défendu)* forbidden; **'stationnement i.'** 'no parking' **(b)** *(étonné)* disconcerted

intéresser [ɛ̃terese] **1** *vt (captiver)* to interest; *(concerner)* to concern **2 s'intéresser** *vpr* **s'i. à qn/qch** to be interested in sb/sth ■ **intéressant, -e 1** *adj (captivant)* interesting; *(prix)* attractive **2** *nmf Péj* **faire l'i.** to show off ■ **intéressé, -e 1** *adj (avide)* self-interested; *(motif)* selfish; *(concerné)* concerned **2** *nmf* **l'i.** the person concerned

intérêt [ɛ̃terɛ] *nm* interest; *Fin* **intérêts** interest; **tu as i. à le faire** you'd

do well to do it; **sans i.** *(personne, film)* uninteresting

intérieur, -eure [ɛ̃terjœr] **1** *adj (escalier, paroi)* interior; *(cour, vie)* inner; *(poche)* inside; *(partie)* internal; *(vol)* internal, domestic; *(mer)* inland **2** *nm (de boîte, de maison)* inside (**de** of); *(de pays)* interior; *(maison)* home; **à l'i. (de)** inside; **d'i.** *(vêtement, jeux)* indoor

intérim [ɛ̃terim] *nm (travail temporaire)* temporary work; **président par i.** acting president ■ **intérimaire 1** *adj (fonction, employé)* temporary **2** *nmf (travailleur)* temporary worker; *(secrétaire)* temp

interlocuteur, -trice [ɛ̃terlɔkytœr, -tris] *nmf (de conversation)* speaker; *(de négociation)* negotiating partner; **mon i.** the person I am/was speaking to

intermède [ɛ̃termɛd] *nm* interlude

intermédiaire [ɛ̃termedjɛr] **1** *adj* intermediate **2** *nmf* intermediary; *Com* middleman; **par l'i. de** through; **sans i.** directly

interminable [ɛ̃terminabl] *adj* interminable

intermittent, -e [ɛ̃termitɑ̃, -ɑ̃t] *adj* intermittent ■ **intermittence** *nf* **par i.** intermittently

internat [ɛ̃terna] *nm (école)* boarding school; *(concours de médecine)* = entrance examination for *Br* a housemanship *or Am* an internship ■ **interne 1** *adj (douleur)* internal; *(oreille)* inner **2** *nmf (élève)* boarder; **i. des hôpitaux** *Br* house doctor, *Am* intern

international, -e, -aux, -ales [ɛ̃ternasjɔnal, -o] **1** *adj* international **2** *nm (footballeur)* international

interner [ɛ̃terne] *vt (prisonnier)* to intern; *(aliéné)* to commit ■ **internement** [-əmɑ̃] *nm (emprisonnement)* internment; *(d'aliéné)* confinement

Internet [ɛ̃ternet] *nm* Internet; **sur (l')i.** on the Internet ■ **internaute** *nmf* Internet surfer

interpeller [ɛ̃terpəle] *vt (appeler)* to

call out to; *(dans une réunion)* to question; **i. qn** *(police)* to take sb in for questioning ■ **interpellation** *nf* sharp address; *(dans une réunion)* question

interposer [ɛ̃tɛrpoze] **s'interposer** *vpr (intervenir)* to intervene (**dans** in)

interprète [ɛ̃tɛrprɛt] *nmf (traducteur)* interpreter; *(chanteur)* singer; *(musicien, acteur)* performer ■ **interprétariat** *nm* interpreting ■ **interprétation** *nf (de texte, de rôle, de rêve)* interpretation; *(traduction)* interpreting ■ **interpréter** *vt (texte, rôle, musique, rêve)* to interpret; *(chanter)* to sing

interroger [ɛ̃tɛrɔʒe] *vt* to question; *(élève)* to test; *Ordinat (banque de données)* to query ■ **interrogateur, -trice** *adj (air)* questioning ■ **interrogation** *nf (question)* question; *(de prisonnier)* questioning; *Scol* **i. écrite/orale** written/oral test ■ **interrogatoire** *nm* interrogation

interrompre* [ɛ̃tɛrɔ̃pr] **1** *vt* to interrupt **2 s'interrompre** *vpr* to break off ■ **interrupteur** *nm* switch ■ **interruption** *nf* interruption; *(de négociations)* breaking off; **sans i.** continuously; **i. volontaire de grossesse** termination

intersection [ɛ̃tɛrsɛksjɔ̃] *nf* intersection

intervalle [ɛ̃tɛrval] *nm (dans l'espace)* gap, space; *(dans le temps)* interval; **dans l'i.** *(entretemps)* in the meantime; **par intervalles** (every) now and then, at intervals

intervenir* [ɛ̃tɛrvənir] *vi (agir, prendre la parole)* to intervene; *(survenir)* to occur; **être intervenu** *(accord)* to be reached ■ **intervention** *nf* intervention; *(discours)* speech; **i. chirurgicale** operation

intervertir [ɛ̃tɛrvɛrtir] *vt* to invert

interview [ɛ̃tɛrvju] *nm ou f* interview ■ **interviewer** [-vjuve] *vt* to interview

intestin [ɛ̃tɛstɛ̃] *nm* intestine

intime [ɛ̃tim] **1** *adj* intimate; *(ami)* close; *(cérémonie)* quiet **2** *nmf* close friend ■ **intimement** [-əmã] *adv* intimately; **i. liés** *(problèmes)* closely linked

■ **intimité** *nf (familiarité)* intimacy; *(vie privée)* privacy; **dans l'i.** in private

intimider [ɛ̃timide] *vt* to intimidate

intituler [ɛ̃tityle] **1** *vt* to give a title to **2 s'intituler** *vpr* to be entitled

intolérable [ɛ̃tɔlerabl] *adj* intolerable ■ **intolérance** *nf* intolerance ■ **intolérant, -e** *adj* intolerant

intoxiquer [ɛ̃tɔksike] **1** *vt (empoisonner)* to poison **2 s'intoxiquer** *vpr* to poison oneself ■ **intoxication** *nf (empoisonnement)* poisoning; **i. alimentaire** food poisoning

intraitable [ɛ̃tretabl] *adj* uncompromising

intransigeant, -e [ɛ̃trãziʒã, -ãt] *adj* intransigent

intrépide [ɛ̃trepid] *adj* fearless, intrepid

intrigue [ɛ̃trig] *nf* intrigue; *(de film, roman)* plot ■ **intriguer 1** *vt* **i. qn** to intrigue sb **2** *vi* to scheme

introduire* [ɛ̃trɔdɥir] **1** *vt (insérer)* to insert (**dans** into); *(marchandises)* to bring in; *(réforme, mode)* to introduce; *(visiteur)* to show in **2 s'introduire** *vpr* **s'i. dans une maison** to get into a house ■ **introduction** *nf (texte, action)* introduction

introuvable [ɛ̃truvabl] *adj (produit)* unobtainable; *(personne)* nowhere to be found

introverti, -e [ɛ̃trɔvɛrti] *nmf* introvert

intrus, -e [ɛ̃try, -yz] *nmf* intruder ■ **intrusion** *nf* intrusion (**dans** into)

intuition [ɛ̃tɥisjɔ̃] *nf* intuition ■ **intuitif, -ive** *adj* intuitive

inuit [inɥit] **1** *adj inv* Inuit **2** *nmf inv* **I.** Inuit

inusable [inyzabl] *adj* hard-wearing

inusité, -e [inyzite] *adj (mot, forme)* uncommon

inutile [inytil] *adj (qui ne sert à rien)* useless; *(précaution, bagage)* unnecessary; **c'est i.** de crier it's pointless shouting ■ **inutilement** *adv* needlessly ■ **inutilité** *nf* uselessness

inutilisable [inytilizabl] *adj* unusable ■ **inutilisé, -e** *adj* unused

invaincu, -e [ɛ̃vɛ̃ky] adj Sport unbeaten

invalide [ɛ̃valid] 1 adj disabled 2 nmf disabled person

invalider [ɛ̃valide] vt to invalidate

invariable [ɛ̃varjabl] adj invariable

invasion [ɛ̃vazjɔ̃] nf invasion

invendable [ɛ̃vɑ̃dabl] adj unsellable ■ **invendu, -e** 1 adj unsold 2 nmpl **invendus** unsold articles; (journaux) unsold copies

inventaire [ɛ̃vɑ̃tɛr] nm Com (liste) inventory; **faire l'i.** to do the stocktaking (**de** of)

inventer [ɛ̃vɑ̃te] vt (créer) to invent; (concept) to think up; (histoire, excuse) to make up ■ **inventeur, -trice** nmf inventor ■ **inventif, -ive** adj inventive ■ **invention** nf invention

inverse [ɛ̃vɛrs] 1 adj (sens) opposite; (ordre) reverse; Math inverse 2 nm **l'i.** the reverse, the opposite ■ **inversement** [-əmɑ̃] adv conversely ■ **inverser** vt (ordre) to reverse ■ **inversion** nf inversion

investigation [ɛ̃vɛstigasjɔ̃] nf investigation

investir [ɛ̃vɛstir] 1 vt (capitaux) to invest (**dans** in); (édifice, ville) to besiege 2 vi to invest (**dans** in) ■ **investissement** nm Fin investment

invincible [ɛ̃vɛ̃sibl] adj invincible

invisible [ɛ̃vizibl] adj invisible

inviter [ɛ̃vite] vt to invite; **i. qn à faire qch** (prier) to request sb to do sth; (inciter) to urge sb to do sth; **i. qn à dîner** to invite sb to dinner ■ **invitation** nf invitation ■ **invité, -e** nmf guest

involontaire [ɛ̃vɔlɔ̃tɛr] adj (geste) involuntary; (témoin) unwilling

invoquer [ɛ̃vɔke] vt (argument) to put forward; (loi, texte) to refer to; (divinité) to invoke ■ **invocation** nf invocation (**à** to)

invraisemblable [ɛ̃vrɛsɑ̃blabl] adj (extraordinaire) incredible; (alibi) implausible ■ **invraisemblance** nf (improbabilité) unlikelihood; (d'alibi) implausibility

invulnérable [ɛ̃vylnerabl] adj invulnerable

ira, irait etc [ira, irɛ] voir **aller**[1]

Irak [irak] nm **l'I.** Iraq ■ **irakien, -enne** 1 adj Iraqi 2 nmf **I., Irakienne** Iraqi

Iran [irɑ̃] nm **l'I.** Iran ■ **iranien, -enne** 1 adj Iranian 2 nmf **I., Iranienne** Iranian

iris [iris] nm (plante) & Anat iris

Irlande [irlɑ̃d] nf **l'I.** Ireland; **l'I. du Nord** Northern Ireland ■ **irlandais, -e** 1 adj Irish 2 nmf **I.** Irishman; **Irlandaise** Irishwoman; **les I.** the Irish 3 nm (langue) Irish

ironie [ironi] nf irony ■ **ironique** adj ironic(al)

iront [irɔ̃] voir **aller**[1]

irrationnel, -elle [irasjɔnɛl] adj irrational

irréalisable [irealizabl] adj (projet) impracticable

irréaliste [irealist] adj unrealistic

irrécusable [irekyzabl] adj (preuve) indisputable; Jur (témoignage) unimpeachable

irréductible [iredyktibl] 1 adj (ennemi) implacable 2 nm diehard

irréel, -elle [ireɛl] adj unreal

irréfléchi, -e [irefleʃi] adj rash

irréfutable [irefytabl] adj irrefutable

irrégulier, -ère [iregylje, -ɛr] adj (rythme, verbe, procédure) irregular; (sol) uneven; (résultats) inconsistent ■ **irrégularité** nf irregularity; (de sol) unevenness

irrémédiable [iremedjabl] adj irreparable

irremplaçable [irɑ̃plasabl] adj irreplaceable

irréparable [ireparabl] adj (véhicule) beyond repair; (tort, perte) irreparable

irrépressible [irepresibl] adj irrepressible

irréprochable [ireprɔʃabl] adj irreproachable

irrésistible [irezistibl] adj (personne, charme) irresistible

irrésolu, -e [irezɔly] adj (personne) indecisive; (problème) unresolved

irrespirable [irespirabl] *adj (air)* unbreathable; *Fig (atmosphère)* unbearable

irresponsable [irespõsabl] *adj (personne)* irresponsible

irréversible [ireversibl] *adj* irreversible

irrévocable [irevɔkabl] *adj* irrevocable

irrigation [irigɑsjõ] *nf* irrigation

irriter [irite] **1** *vt* to irritate **2 s'irriter** *vpr (s'énerver)* to get irritated (**de** with; **contre** at); *(s'enflammer)* to become irritated ■ **irritable** *adj* irritable ■ **irritation** *nf (colère) & Méd* irritation

irruption [irypsjõ] *nf* **faire i. dans** to burst into

Islam [islam] *nm* **l'I.** Islam ■ **islamique** *adj* Islamic

Islande [islɑ̃d] *nf* **l'I.** Iceland ■ **islandais, -e 1** *adj* Icelandic **2** *nmf* **I., Islandaise** Icelander

isolant, -e [izɔlɑ̃, -ɑ̃t] **1** *adj* insulating **2** *nm* insulating material

isoler [izɔle] **1** *vt* to isolate (**de** from); *(du froid) & Él* to insulate **2 s'isoler** *vpr* to isolate oneself ■ **isolation** *nf* insulation ■ **isolé, -e** *adj (personne, endroit, maison)* isolated; *(du froid)* insulated; **i. de** cut off *or* isolated from ■ **isolement** *nm (de personne)* isolation; ■ **isolément** *adv (agir)* in isolation; *(interroger des gens)* individually

isoloir [izɔlwar] *nm Br* polling *or Am* voting booth

Israël [israel] *nm* Israel ■ **israélien, -enne 1** *adj* Israeli **2** *nmf* **I., Israélienne** Israeli ■ **israélite 1** *adj* Jewish **2** *nmf* Jew

issu, -e [isy] *adj* **être i. de** to come from

issue [isy] *nf (sortie)* exit; *Fig (solution)* way out; *(résultat)* outcome; **à l'i. de** at the end of; **i. de secours** emergency exit

isthme [ism] *nm* isthmus

Italie [itali] *nf* **l'I.** Italy ■ **italien, -enne 1** *adj* Italian **2** *nmf* **I., Italienne** Italian **3** *nm (langue)* Italian

italique [italik] **1** *adj (lettre)* italic **2** *nm* italics; **en i.** in italics

itinéraire [itinerer] *nm* route, itinerary

IUT [iyte] *(abrév* **institut universitaire de technologie)** *nm* = vocational higher education college

IVG [iveʒe] *(abrév* **interruption volontaire de grossesse)** *nf* abortion, termination

ivoire [ivwar] *nm* ivory; **statuette en i.** *ou* **d'i.** ivory statuette

ivre [ivr] *adj* drunk (**de** with); *Fig* **i. de joie** wild with joy ■ **ivresse** *nf* drunkenness; **en état d'i.** under the influence of drink ■ **ivrogne** *nmf* drunk(ard)

Jj

J, j [ʒi] *nm inv* J, j; **le jour J.** D-day

j' [ʒ] *voir* **je**

jadis [ʒadis] *adv Littéraire* in times past

jaillir [ʒajir] *vi (liquide)* to gush out; *(étincelles)* to shoot out

jalonner [ʒalɔne] *vt (marquer)* to mark out; *(border)* to line

jaloux, -ouse [ʒalu, -uz] *adj* jealous (**de** of) ■ **jalousie** *nf (sentiment)* jealousy

Jamaïque [ʒamaik] *nf* **la J.** Jamaica

jamais [ʒamɛ] *adv* (**a**) *(négatif)* never; **elle ne sort j.** she never goes out; **sans j. sortir** without ever going out (**b**) *(positif)* ever; **à tout j.** for ever; **si j.** if ever; **le film le plus drôle que j'aie j. vu** the funniest film I have ever seen

jambe [ʒɑ̃b] *nf* leg

jambon [ʒɑ̃bɔ̃] *nm* ham

janvier [ʒɑ̃vje] *nm* January

Japon [ʒapɔ̃] *nm* **le J.** Japan ■ **japonais, -e 1** *adj* Japanese **2** *nmf* **J., Japonaise** Japanese *inv*; **les J.** the Japanese **3** *nm (langue)* Japanese

jardin [ʒardɛ̃] *nm* garden; **j. d'enfants** kindergarten; **j. public** gardens ■ **jardinage** *nm* gardening ■ **jardinier** *nm* gardener

jargon [ʒargɔ̃] *nm* jargon

jasmin [ʒasmɛ̃] *nm* jasmine; **thé au j.** jasmine tea

jaune [ʒon] **1** *adj* yellow **2** *nm (couleur)* yellow; **j. d'œuf** (egg) yolk

Javel [ʒavɛl] **eau de Javel** *nf* bleach

javelot [ʒavlo] *nm* javelin

jazz [dʒaz] *nm* jazz

je [ʒə]

j' is used before a word beginning with a vowel or h mute.

pron personnel I; **je suis ici** I'm here

jean [dʒin] *nm (pair of)* jeans; **veste en j.** denim jacket

Jersey [ʒɛrzɛ] *nf* Jersey

jet [ʒɛ] *nm (de pierre)* throwing; *(de vapeur, de liquide)* jet; **j. d'eau** fountain

jetable [ʒətabl] *adj* disposable

jetée [ʒəte] *nf* pier, jetty

jeter [ʒəte] **1** *vt* to throw (**à** to; **dans** into); *(à la poubelle)* to throw away; *(sort)* to cast; **j. un coup d'œil à qn/ qch** to have a quick look at sb/sth **2 se jeter** *vpr (personne)* to throw oneself; **se j. sur qn** to throw oneself at sb; *Fig* to pounce on sb; **se j. sur qch** *(occasion)* to jump at sth; **se j. contre** *(véhicule)* to crash into; **se j. dans** *(fleuve)* to flow into

jeton [ʒətɔ̃] *nm (pièce)* token; *(au jeu)* chip

jeu, -x [ʒø] *nm* (**a**) *(amusement)* play; *(activité, au tennis)* game; *(d'acteur)* acting; **le j.** *(au casino)* gambling; **en j.** *(en cause)* at stake; *(forces)* at work; **j.-concours** competition; **j. électronique** computer game; **j. de hasard** game of chance; **j. de mots** play on words, pun; **jeux de société** board games; **j. télévisé** television game show; *(avec questions)* television quiz show; **j. vidéo** video game (**b**) *(série complète)* set; *(de cartes)* deck, *Br* pack; *(cartes en main)* hand; **j. d'échecs** *(boîte, pièces)* chess set (**c**) *Tech (de ressort, de verrou)* play

jeudi [ʒødi] *nm* Thursday

jeun [ʒœ̃] **à jeun 1** *adv* on an empty stomach **2** *adj* **être à j.** to have eaten no food

jeune [ʒœn] **1** *adj* young; *(apparence)* youthful; **jeunes gens** young people **2** *nmf* young person; **les jeunes** young people ▪ **jeunesse** *nf* youth; *(apparence)* youthfulness; **la j.** *(les jeunes)* the young

jeûner [ʒøne] *vi* to fast

joaillier, -ère [ʒɔaje, -ɛr] *nmf Br* jeweller, *Am* jeweler ▪ **joaillerie** *nf (bijoux) Br* jewellery, *Am* jewelry; *(magasin) Br* jewellery shop, *Am* jewelry store

jockey [ʒɔkɛ] *nm* jockey

jogging [dʒɔgiŋ] *nm Sport* jogging; *(survêtement)* jogging suit

joie [ʒwa] *nf* joy, delight; **avec j.** with pleasure, gladly

joindre* [ʒwɛ̃dr] **1** *vt (réunir)* to join; *(ajouter)* to add (**à** to); *(dans une enveloppe)* to enclose (**à** with); **j. qn** *(contacter)* to get in touch with sb
2 se joindre *vpr* **se j. à qn** to join sb ▪ **joint, -e1** *adj* **à pieds joints** with feet together; **pièces jointes** *(de lettre)* enclosures **2** *nm Tech (articulation)* joint; *(d'étanchéité)* seal; *(de robinet)* washer; **j. de culasse** gasket

joker [ʒɔkɛr] *nm Cartes* joker

joli, -e [ʒɔli] *adj* pretty

jonché [ʒɔ̃ʃe] *adj* **j. de** strewn with

jonction [ʒɔ̃ksjɔ̃] *nf* junction

jongler [ʒɔ̃gle] *vi* to juggle (**avec** with)

jonquille [ʒɔ̃kij] *nf* daffodil

Jordanie [ʒɔrdani] *nf* **la J.** Jordan

joue [ʒu] *nf (du visage)* cheek

jouer [ʒwe] *vt (musique, carte, rôle)* to play; *(pièce de théâtre)* to perform; *(film)* to show; *(parier)* to stake (**sur** on); *(cheval)* to bet on
2 *vi* to play; *(acteur)* to act; *(au tiercé)* to gamble; *(être important)* to count; **j. au tennis/aux cartes** to play tennis/ cards; **j. du piano/du violon** to play the piano/violin; **à toi de j.!** it's your turn (to play)!

3 se jouer *vpr (film, pièce)* to be on

jouet [ʒwɛ] *nm* toy

joueur, -euse [ʒwœr, -øz] *nmf* player; *(au tiercé)* gambler

jouir [ʒwir] *vi* **j. de qch** to enjoy sth

jour [ʒur] *nm (journée, date)* day; *(clarté)* daylight; *(éclairage)* light; **il fait j.** it's (day)light; **de j. en j.** day by day; **du j. au lendemain** overnight; **en plein j., au grand j.** in broad daylight; **de nos jours** nowadays, these days; *Fig* **sous un j. nouveau** in a different light; **mettre qch à j.** to bring sth up to date; **quel j. sommes-nous?** what day is it?; **il y a dix ans j. pour j.** ten years ago to the day; **le j. de l'an** New Year's Day

journal, -aux [ʒurnal, -o] *nm* (news)-paper; *(spécialisé)* journal; *(intime)* diary; **j. télévisé** (TV) news *(sing)* ▪ **journalisme** *nm* journalism ▪ **journaliste** *nmf* journalist

journalier, -ère [ʒurnalje, -ɛr] *adj* daily

journée [ʒurne] *nf* day; **pendant la j.** during the day(time); **toute la j.** all day (long)

jovial, -e, -aux, -ales [ʒɔvjal, -o] *adj* jovial, jolly

joyau, -x [ʒwajo] *nm* jewel

joyeux, -euse [ʒwajø, -øz] *adj* joyful; **j. anniversaire!** happy birthday!; **j. Noël!** merry *or Br* happy Christmas!

jubiler [ʒybile] *vi* to be jubilant

jucher [ʒyʃe] *vt, se jucher* *vpr* to perch (**sur** on)

judicieux, -euse [ʒydisjø, -øz] *adj* judicious

judo [ʒydo] *nm* judo

juge [ʒyʒ] *nm* judge; **j. de touche** *(au football)* linesman, assistant referee

jugé [ʒyʒe] **au jugé** *adv (calculer)* roughly

jugement [ʒyʒmɑ̃] *nm (opinion, discernement)* judgement; *(verdict)* sentence; **porter un j. sur qch** to pass judgement on sth; *Jur* **passer en j.** to stand trial

juger [ʒyʒe] **1** *vt (personne, question)*

to judge; *(au tribunal)* to try; *(estimer)* to consider (**que** that) **2** *vi* **j. de** to judge; **jugez de ma surprise!** imagine my surprise!

juif, juive [ʒ4if, ʒ4iv] **1** *adj* Jewish **2** *nmf/***J.** Jew

juillet [ʒ4ijɛ] *nm* July

juin [ʒ4ɛ̃] *nm* June

jumeau, -elle, -x, -elles [ʒymo, -ɛl] **1** *adj* **frère j.** twin brother; **sœur jumelle** twin sister; **lits jumeaux** twin beds **2** *nmf* twin ■ **jumeler** *vt (villes)* to twin ■ **jumelles** *nfpl (pour regarder)* binoculars

jument [ʒymɑ̃] *nf* mare

jungle [ʒœ̃gl] *nf* jungle

junior [ʒynjɔr] *nm & adj inv Sport* junior

jupe [ʒyp] *nf* skirt

jurer [ʒyre] **1** *vt (promettre)* to swear (**que** that; **de faire** to do) **2** *vi (dire un gros mot)* to swear (**contre** at); *(contraster)* to clash (**avec** with); **j. de qch** to swear to sth ■ **juré, -e 1** *adj* **ennemi j.** sworn enemy **2** *nm Jur* juror

juriste [ʒyrist] *nmf* legal expert

juron [ʒyrɔ̃] *nm* swearword

jury [ʒyri] *nm Jur* jury; *(d'examen)* board of examiners

jus [ʒy] *nm (de fruits)* juice; *(de viande)* gravy; **j. d'orange** orange juice

jusque [ʒysk] **1** *prép* **jusqu'à** *(espace)* as far as, (right) up to; *(temps)* until, (up) till, to; *(même)* even; **jusqu'en mai** until May; **jusqu'où?** how far?; **jusqu'ici** as far as this; *(temps)* up till now; **j. chez moi** as far as my place **2** *conj* **jusqu'à ce qu'il vienne** until he comes

juste [ʒyst] **1** *adj (équitable)* fair, just; *(exact)* right, correct; *(étroit)* tight; *(raisonnement)* sound; **un peu j.** *(quantité, qualité)* barely enough **2** *adv (deviner, compter)* correctly, right; *(chanter)* in tune; *(précisément, à peine)* just; **à trois heures j.** on the stroke of three; **un peu j.** *(mesurer, compter)* a bit on the short side ■ **justement** [-əmɑ̃] *adv (précisément)* exactly; *(avec justesse, avec justice)* justly; **j. j'allais t'appeler** I was just going to ring you

justesse [ʒystɛs] *nf (exactitude)* accuracy; **de j.** *(éviter, gagner)* just

justice [ʒystis] *nf (équité)* justice; **la j.** *(autorité)* the law; **rendre j. à qn** to do justice to sb

justifier [ʒystifje] **1** *vt* to justify **2 se justifier** *vpr* to justify oneself (**de** of) ■ **justification** *nf (explication)* justification; *(preuve)* proof

juteux, -euse [ʒytø, -øz] *adj* juicy

Kk

K, k [ka] *nm inv* K, k
kangourou [kãguru] *nm* kangaroo
karaté [karate] *nm* karate
karting [kartiŋ] *nm* karting
kasher [kaʃer] *adj inv Rel* kosher
kayak [kajak] *nm (bateau de sport)* canoe
Kenya [kenja] *nm* le K. Kenya
kermesse [kɛrmɛs] *nf* charity fair *or Br* fête; *(en Belgique)* village fair
kérosène [kerozɛn] *nm* kerosene
kidnapper [kidnape] *vt* to kidnap ■ **kidnappeur, -euse** *nmf* kidnapper
kilo [kilo] *nm* kilo ■ **kilogramme** *nm* kilogram(me)
kilomètre [kilɔmetr] *nm* kilometre ■ **kilométrage** *nm Aut* ≃ mileage ■ **kilométrique** *adj* borne k. ≃ milestone

kilo-octet [kilɔɔktɛ] *(pl* kilo-octets) *nm Ordinat* kilobyte
kilowatt [kilɔwat] *nm* kilowatt
kinésithérapeute [kineziterapøt] *nmf* physiotherapist
kiosque [kjɔsk] *nm (à fleurs)* kiosk, *Br* stall; k. à journaux news-stand
kit [kit] *nm (self-assembly)* kit; en k. in kit form
kiwi [kiwi] *nm (oiseau, fruit)* kiwi
Klaxon® [klaksɔn] *nm* horn ■ **klaxonner** *vi* to sound one's horn
km *(abrév* **kilomètre)** km
km/h *(abrév* **kilomètre-heure)** kph, ≃ mph
Koweït [kɔwɛjt] *nm* le K. Kuwait ■ **koweïtien, -enne 1** *adj* Kuwaiti **2** *nmf* K., Koweïtienne Kuwaiti

Ll

L, l [ɛl] *nm inv* L, l

l', la¹ [l, la] *voir* **le**

la² [la] *nm inv (note)* A

là [la] **1** *adv (là-bas)* there; *(ici)* here; **c'est là que...** *(lieu)* that's where...; **à 5 mètres de là** 5 metres away **2** *exclam* **oh là là!** oh dear! **3** *voir* **ce¹, celui**

là-bas [labɑ] *adv* over there

laboratoire [laboratwar] *nm* laboratory

labourer [labure] *vt (terre) Br* to plough, *Am* to plow

lac [lak] *nm* lake

lacet [lasɛ] *nm (de chaussure)* lace; **faire ses lacets** to tie one's laces

lâche [lɑʃ] **1** *adj (nœud)* loose, slack; *Péj (personne, acte)* cowardly **2** *nmf* coward ■ **lâcheté** *nf* cowardice; **une l.** *(action)* a cowardly act

lâcher [lɑʃe] **1** *vt (ne plus tenir)* to let go of; *(bombe)* to drop; *(poursuivant)* to shake off; *(dans une course)* to leave behind; **l. prise** to let go **2** *vi (corde)* to break

là-dedans [ladədɑ̃] *adv (lieu)* in there, inside

là-dessous [ladəsu] *adv* underneath

là-dessus [ladəsy] *adv* on there; *(monter)* on top

là-haut [lao] *adv* up there; *(à l'étage)* upstairs

laid, -e [lɛ, lɛd] *adj (physiquement)* ugly ■ **laideur** *nf* ugliness

laine [lɛn] *nf* wool; **de l., en l.** *Br* woollen, *Am* woolen ■ **lainage** *nm (vêtement)* jumper

laisse [lɛs] *nf* lead, leash

laisser [lese] **1** *vt* to leave; **l. qn partir** *(permettre)* to let sb go; **l. qch à qn** *(confier, donner)* to leave sth with sb **2 se laisser** *vpr* **se l. aller** to let oneself go; **se l. faire** to be pushed around

lait [lɛ] *nm* milk; **l. entier/demi-écrémé/écrémé** whole/semi-skimmed/skimmed milk ■ **laitier** *adj m* **produit l.** dairy product

laitue [lety] *nf* lettuce

lame [lam] *nf (de couteau, de rasoir)* blade; *(vague)* wave

lamelle [lamɛl] *nf* thin strip

lamenter [lamɑ̃te] **se lamenter** *vpr* to moan ■ **lamentable** *adj (mauvais)* terrible, deplorable; *(voix, cri)* mournful; *(personne)* pathetic

lampadaire [lɑ̃padɛr] *nm Br* standard lamp, *Am* floor lamp; *(de rue)* street lamp

lampe [lɑ̃p] *nf* lamp; **l. de poche** *Br* torch, *Am* flashlight

lance [lɑ̃s] *nf* spear

lancer [lɑ̃se] **1** *vt (jeter)* to throw (**à** to); *(fusée, produit)* to launch; *(appel)* to issue **2 se lancer** *vpr (se précipiter)* to rush; **se l. dans** *(aventure)* to launch into **3** *nm Sport* **l. du javelot** throwing the javelin; **l. franc** *(au basket)* free throw ■ **lancement** *nm (de fusée, de produit)* launch(ing)

landau, -s [lɑ̃do] *nm Br* pram, *Am* baby carriage

langage [lɑ̃gaʒ] *nm* language; *Ordinat* **l. machine/naturel** computer/natural language

langer [lɑ̃ʒe] *vt (bébé)* to change

langouste [lɑ̃gust] *nf* crayfish ■ **langoustine** *nf* langoustine

langue [lɑ̃g] *nf Anat* tongue; *Ling* language; **de l. anglaise/française** English-/French-speaking; **l. maternelle** mother tongue; **langues vivantes** modern languages ■ **languette** *nf (patte)* tongue

lanière [lanjɛr] *nf* strap; *(d'étoffe)* strip

lapin [lapɛ̃] *nm* rabbit

laque [lak] *nf (pour cheveux)* hair spray

laquelle [lakɛl] *voir* **lequel**

lard [lar] *nm (viande)* bacon ■ **lardon** *nm Culin* strip of bacon

large [larʒ] **1** *adj (route, porte, chaussure)* wide; *(considérable)* **l. de 6 mètres** 6 metres wide

2 *nm* **avoir 6 mètres de l.** to be 6 metres wide; **au l. de Cherbourg** off Cherbourg ■ **largement** [-əmɑ̃] *adv (répandu, critiqué)* widely; *(payer, servir)* generously; *(dépasser)* by a long way; **avoir l. le temps** to have plenty of time ■ **largeur** *nf (dimension)* width, breadth; **en l., dans la l.** widthwise

larguer [large] *vt (bombe)* to drop; *Naut* **l. les amarres** to cast off

larme [larm] *nf* tear; **en larmes** in tears; **rire aux larmes** to laugh till one cries

las, lasse [lɑ, lɑs] *adj* weary **(de** of) ■ **lassant, -e** *adj* tiresome ■ **lasser 1** *vt* to tire **2 se lasser** *upr* **se l. de qch/de faire qch** to get tired of sth/of doing sth

laser [lazɛr] *nm* laser

latéral, -e, -aux, -ales [lateral, -o] *adj* side

latin, -e [latɛ̃, -in] **1** *adj* Latin **2** *nmf* **L., Latine** Latin **3** *nm (langue)* Latin

lavabo [lavabo] *nm* washbasin; **lavabos** *(toilettes) Br* toilet(s), *Am* washroom

lavande [lavɑ̃d] *nf* lavender

lave [lav] *nf* lava

laver [lave] **1** *vt* to wash; **l. qch à l'eau froide** to wash sth in cold water **2 se**

laver *upr* to wash (oneself), *Am* to wash up; **se l. les mains** to wash one's hands ■ **lavable** *adj* washable ■ **lavage** *nm* washing ■ **lave-auto** *(pl* **lave-autos)** *nm Can* carwash ■ **lave-linge** *nm inv* washing machine ■ **laverie** *nf (automatique) Br* launderette, *Am* Laundromat® ■ **laveur de vitres** window *Br* cleaner *or Am* washer ■ **lave-vaisselle** *nm inv* dishwasher

---

1 *article défini* **(a)** *(pour définir le nom)* the; **le garçon** the boy; **la fille** the girl; **les petits** the little ones

(b) *(avec les notions)* **la vie** life; **la France** France; **les Français** the French; **les hommes** men; **aimer le café** to like coffee

(c) *(avec les parties du corps)* **il ouvrit la bouche** he opened his mouth; **se blesser au pied** to hurt one's foot; **avoir les cheveux blonds** to have blond hair

(d) *(distributif)* **10 euros le kilo** 10 euros a kilo

(e) *(dans les compléments de temps)* **elle vient le lundi** she comes on Mondays; **l'an prochain** next year

2 *pron (homme)* him; *(femme)* her; *(chose, animal)* it; **les** them; **je la vois** I see her/it; **je le vois** I see him/it; **je les vois** I see them

---

lécher [leʃe] *vt* to lick

leçon [ləsɔ̃] *nf* lesson

lecteur, -trice [lɛktœr, -tris] *nmf* reader; *Univ* foreign language assistant; **l. de cassettes/de CD** cassette/CD player; *Ordinat* **l. de disques** *ou* **de disquettes** disk drive ■ **lecture** *nf* reading

légal, -e, -aux, -ales [legal, -o] *adj* legal ■ **légaliser** *vt* to legalize ■ **légalité** *nf* legality **(de** of)

légende [leʒɑ̃d] *nf (histoire)* legend; *(de carte)* key; *(de photo)* caption

léger, -ère [leʒe, -er] **1** *adj* light; *(blessure, odeur)* slight; *(café, thé)* weak; *(bière, tabac)* mild; *(frivole)* frivolous; *(irréfléchi)* thoughtless

2 *adv* **manger l.** to have a light meal

3 *nf* **prendre qch à la légère** to make light of sth ■ **légèrement** *adv (inconsidérément)* lightly; *(un peu)* slightly ■ **légèreté** *nf (poids)* lightness; *(de blessure)* slightness; *(d'attitude)* thoughtlessness

légion [leʒjɔ̃] *nf Mil* legion ■ **légionnaire** *nm (de la Légion étrangère)* legionnaire

législatif, -ive [leʒislatif, -iv] *adj* legislative; *(élections)* parliamentary

légitime [leʒitim] *adj (action, enfant)* legitimate; *(héritier)* rightful; *(colère)* justified; **être en état de l. défense** to be acting in *Br* self-defence *or Am* self-defense

léguer [lege] *vt* to bequeath (**à** to)

légume [legym] *nm* vegetable

lendemain [lɑ̃dmɛ̃] *nm* **le l.** the next day; **le l.** de the day after; **le l. matin** the next morning

lent, -e [lɑ̃, lɑ̃t] *adj* slow

lentille [lɑ̃tij] *nf (plante, graine)* lentil; *(verre)* lens; **lentilles de contact** contact lenses

lequel, laquelle [ləkɛl, lakɛl] *(mpl* **lesquels,** *fpl* **lesquelles** [lekɛl]*)*

lequel and lesquel(le)s contract with **à** to form **auquel** and **auxquel(le)s**, and with **de** to form **duquel** and **desquel(le)s**.

1 *pron relatif (chose, animal)* which; *(personne)* who; *(indirect)* whom; **dans l.** in which; **parmi lesquels** *(choses, animaux)* among which; *(personnes)* among whom

2 *pron interrogatif* which (one); **l. préférez-vous?** which (one) do you prefer?

les [le] *voir* **le**

lessive [lesiv] *nf (produit)* washing powder; *(liquide)* liquid detergent; *(linge)* washing; **faire la l.** to do the washing

lettre [letr] *nf (missive, caractère)* letter; **les lettres** *(discipline)* arts, humanities

leur [lœr] **1** *adj possessif* their; **l. chat** their cat; **leurs voitures** their cars **2** *pron possessif* **le l., la l., les leurs** theirs **3** *pron personnel (indirect)* to them; **donne-l. ta carte** give them your card

lever [lave] **1** *vt (objet)* to lift, to raise; *(blocus, immunité)* to lift; *(séance)* to close; *(impôts)* to levy

2 *vi (pâte)* to rise

3 se lever *vpr* to get up; *(soleil)* to rise; *(jour)* to break; *(brouillard)* to clear, to lift

4 *nm* **le l. du soleil** sunrise; *Théât* **l. de rideau** curtain up ■ **levé, -e** *adj* **être l.** *(debout)* to be up ■ **levée** *nf (d'interdiction)* lifting; *(du courrier)* collection

levier [ləvje] *nm* lever; *Aut* **l. de vitesse** *Br* gear lever, *Am* gearshift

lèvre [levr] *nf* lip

lévrier [levrije] *nm* greyhound

levure [ləvyr] *nf* yeast

lézard [lezar] *nm* lizard ■ **lézarder se lézarder** *vpr* to crack

liaison [ljezɔ̃] *nf (rapport)* connection; *(entre mots)* & *Mil* liaison; **l. aérienne/ferroviaire** air/rail link; **l. amoureuse** love affair

Liban [libɑ̃] *nm* **le L.** (the) Lebanon ■ **libanais, -e 1** *adj* Lebanese **2** *nmf* **L., Libanaise** Lebanese

libeller [libele] *vt (chèque)* to make out

libéral, -e, -aux, -ales [liberal, -o] *adj & nmf* liberal

libérer [libere] **1** *vt (prisonnier)* to free, to release; *(pays)* to liberate (**de** from); *(chambre)* to vacate **2 se libérer** *vpr* to free oneself (**de** from); **je n'ai pas pu me l.** I couldn't get away ■ **libération** *nf (de prisonnier)* release; *(de pays)* liberation

liberté [liberte] *nf* freedom, liberty; **mettre qn en l.** to set sb free

libraire [librer] *nmf* bookseller ■ **librairie** *nf (magasin)* bookshop

libre [libr] *adj (personne, siège)* free (**de qch** from sth; **de faire** to do);

(voie) clear; **radio l.** independent radio
■ **libre-échange** *nm Écon* free trade
■ **libre-service** *(pl* libres-services) *nm*
(système, magasin) self-service

Libye [libi] *nf* la L. Libya ■ **libyen,**
-enne 1 *adj* Libyan **2** *nmf* L., Libyenne
Libyan

licence [lisɑ̃s] *nf Sport* permit; *Com Br*
licence, *Am* license; *Univ* (bachelor's)
degree; **l. ès lettres/sciences** arts/
science degree

licencier [lisɑ̃sje] *vt (employé)* to lay
off, *Br* to make redundant ■ **licencie-**
ment *nm* lay-off, *Br* redundancy

lien [ljɛ̃] *nm (rapport)* link, connection; *(attache)* bond; **l. de parenté**
family relationship; *Ordinat* **l. hyper-**
texte hypertext link

lier [lje] **1** *vt (attacher)* to tie up;
(contrat) to be binding on; *(personnes)*
to bind together; *(paragraphes)* to
connect, to link; **l. qn** *(unir, engager)*
to bind sb; **être très lié avec qn** to be
great friends with sb **2 se lier** *vpr* **se l.**
d'amitié to become friends

lierre [ljɛr] *nm* ivy

lieu[1], **-x** [ljø] *nm* place; **les lieux** *(lo-*
caux) the premises; **être sur les lieux**
to be on the spot; **avoir l.** to take
place; **au l. de qch** instead of sth; **au**
l. de faire qch instead of doing sth;
en dernier l. lastly; **l. de naissance**
place of birth; **l. public** public place

lieu[2], **-s** [ljø] *nm (poisson)* **l. noir** coal-
fish

lieutenant [ljøtnɑ̃] *nm* lieutenant

lièvre [ljɛvr] *nm* hare

ligne [liɲ] *nf (trait)* line; *(silhouette)* figure; *(rangée)* row, line; **les grandes li-**
gnes *(de train)* the main lines; *Fig*
(idées principales) the broad outline;
aller à la l. to begin a new paragraph;
Fig **sur toute la l.** completely; **l. d'au-**
tobus bus service; *(parcours)* bus
route; **l. de chemin de fer** *Br* railway
or Am railroad line; *Sport* **l. de touche**
touchline

ligoter [ligɔte] *vt* to tie up (**à** to)

liguer [lige] **se liguer** *vpr (États)* to

form a league (**contre** against); *(per-*
sonnes) to gang up (**contre** against)

lilas [lila] *nm & adj inv* lilac

limace [limas] *nf* slug

limande [limɑ̃d] *nf* dab

lime [lim] *nf (outil)* file; **l. à ongles** nail
file

limitation [limitasjɔ̃] *nf* limitation; **l.**
de vitesse speed limit

limite [limit] **1** *nf* limit (**à** to); *(de pro-*
priété) boundary; **sans l.** unlimited,
limitless; **dans la l. des stocks disponi-**
bles while stocks last **2** *adj (vitesse,*
âge) maximum

limiter [limite] **1** *vt (restreindre)* to
limit, to restrict (**à** to); *(territoire)* to
bound **2 se limiter** *vpr* **se l. à qch/à**
faire qch to limit *or* restrict oneself to
sth/to doing sth

limoger [limɔʒe] *vt* to dismiss

limonade [limɔnad] *nf (boisson)* lemonade

limpide [lɛ̃pid] *adj (eau, explication)*
clear, crystal-clear

lin [lɛ̃] *nm (tissu)* linen

linge [lɛ̃ʒ] *nm (vêtements)* linen; *(à la-*
ver) washing; **l. de corps** underwear
■ **lingerie** *nf (de femmes)* underwear

lingot [lɛ̃go] *nm* **l. d'or** gold bar

lion [ljɔ̃] *nm* lion; **le L.** *(signe)* Leo

liqueur [likœr] *nf* liqueur

liquide [likid] **1** *adj* liquid **2** *nm* liquid;
(argent) cash; **payer en l.** to pay cash

liquider [likide] *vt (stock)* to clear ■ **li-**
quidation *nf (de stock)* clearing; *Com* **l.**
totale stock clearance

lire[1]* [lir] **1** *vt* to read; **l. qch à qn** to
read sth to sb **2** *vi* to read

lire[2] [lir] *nf (monnaie)* lira

lis, lisant, lise(nt) *etc* [li, lizɑ̃, liz]
voir **lire**[1]

lisible [lizibl] *adj (écriture)* legible

lisière [lizjɛr] *nf* edge

lisse [lis] *adj* smooth

liste [list] *nf* list; **l. d'attente** waiting
list; **l. électorale** electoral roll

lit[1] [li] *nm* bed; **se mettre au l.** to go to
bed; **faire son l.** to make one's bed; **l. de**
camp *Br* camp bed, *Am* cot; **l. d'enfant**

Br cot, *Am* crib; **lits superposés** bunk beds

lit² [li] *voir* **lire¹**

litière [litjɛr] *nf (d'animal)* litter

litige [litiʒ] *nm (conflit)* dispute

litre [litr] *nm Br* litre, *Am* liter

littéraire [literɛr] *adj* literary ■ **littérature** *nf* literature

littoral, -e, -aux, -ales [litɔral, -o] **1** *adj* coastal **2** *nm* coast(line)

livraison [livrɛzɔ̃] *nf* delivery

livre [livr] **1** *nm* book; *Naut* **l. de bord** logbook; **l. de poche** paperback (book) **2** *nf (monnaie, poids)* pound

livrer [livre] **1** *vt (marchandises)* to deliver (à to); **l. qn à la police** to hand sb over to the police **2 se livrer** *vpr (se rendre)* to give oneself up (à to) ■ **livreur, -euse** *nmf* delivery man, *f* delivery woman

livret [livrɛ] *nm (livre)* booklet; **l. d'épargne** bankbook, *Br* passbook; **l. scolaire** school report book

local, -e, -aux, -ales [lɔkal, -o] **1** *adj* local **2** *nm (pièce)* room; **locaux** *(bâtiment)* premises

localité [lɔkalite] *nf* locality

locataire [lɔkatɛr] *nmf* tenant; *(chez le propriétaire)* lodger, *Am* roomer

location [lɔkasjɔ̃] *nf (de maison) (par le locataire)* renting; *(par le propriétaire)* renting out, *Br* letting; *(de voiture)* renting, *Br* hiring; *(logement)* rented *Br* accommodation *or Am* accommodations; *(loyer)* rent; *(pour spectacle)* booking; **bureau de l.** booking office; **en l.** on hire; **voiture de l.** rented *or Br* hired car

locomotion [lɔkɔmosjɔ̃] *nf* **moyen de l.** means of transport

locomotive [lɔkɔmɔtiv] *nf (de train)* engine

loge [lɔʒ] *nf (de concierge)* lodge; *(d'acteur)* dressing-room; *Théât (de spectateur)* box

loger [lɔʒe] **1** *vt (recevoir, mettre)* to accommodate; *(héberger)* to put up; **être logé et nourri** to have board and lodging

2 *vi (temporairement)* to stay; *(en permanence)* to live

3 se loger *vpr* **trouver à se l.** to find somewhere to live; *(temporairement)* to find somewhere to stay ■ **logement** *nm (habitation)* lodging, *Br* accommodation, *Am* accommodations; **le l.** housing

logiciel [lɔʒisjɛl] *nm Ordinat* software *inv*

logique [lɔʒik] **1** *adj* logical **2** *nf* logic

loi [lwa] *nf* law; **faire la l.** to lay down the law (à to)

loin [lwɛ̃] *adv* far (away *or* off) *(de* from); **Nice est l. de Paris** Nice is a long way away from Paris; **plus l.** further, farther; **au l.** in the distance, far away; **de l.** from a distance ■ **lointain, -e** *adj* distant, far-off; *(rapport)* remote

loisirs [lwazir] *nmpl (temps libre)* spare time, leisure (time); *(distractions)* leisure *or* spare-time activities

Londres [lɔ̃dr] *nm ou f* London ■ **londonien, -enne 1** *adj* London, of London **2** *nmf* **L., Londonienne** Londoner

long, longue [lɔ̃, lɔ̃g] **1** *adj* long; **l. de 2 mètres** 2 metres long

2 *nm* **avoir 2 mètres de l.** to be 2 metres long; **le l. de qch** along sth; **de l. en large** *(marcher)* up and down

3 *adv* **en savoir l. sur qch** to know a lot about sth ■ **long-courrier** *(pl* **long-courriers)** *nm (avion)* long-haul aircraft

longer [lɔ̃ʒe] *vt (sujet: personne, voiture)* to go along; *(mur, côte)* to hug; *(sujet: sentier, canal)* to run alongside

longtemps [lɔ̃tɑ̃] *adv* (for) a long time; **trop l.** too long; **aussi l. que** as long as

longue [lɔ̃g] *voir* **long** ■ **longuement** *adv (expliquer)* at length; *(réfléchir)* for a long time ■ **longueur** *nf* length; *Radio* **l. d'onde** wavelength ■ **longue-vue** *(pl* **longues-vues)** *nf* telescope

lopin [lɔpɛ̃] *nm* **l. de terre** plot *or* patch of land

loquet [lɔkɛ] *nm* latch

lorgner [lɔrɲe] *vt (regarder)* to eye; *(convoiter)* to have one's eye on

lors [lɔr] *adv* **l. de** at the time of; **dès l.** from then on; **dès l. que** *(puisque)* since

lorsque [lɔrsk(ə)] *conj* when

losange [lɔzɑ̃ʒ] *nm (forme)* diamond

lot [lo] *nm (de marchandises)* batch; *(de loterie)* prize; **gros l.** jackpot

loterie [lɔtri] *nf* lottery

lotion [losjɔ̃] *nf* lotion

lotissement [lɔtismɑ̃] *nm (terrain)* building plot; *(habitations)* housing *Br* estate *or Am* development

loto [lɔto] *nm (jeu)* lotto; *(jeu national)* national lottery

louange [lwɑ̃ʒ] *nf* praise

louche[1] [luʃ] *nf (cuillère)* ladle

louche[2] [luʃ] *adj (suspect)* dodgy

loucher [luʃe] *vi* to squint

louer[1] [lwe] *vt (prendre en location) (maison, appartement)* to rent; *(voiture)* to rent, *Br* to hire; *(donner en location) (logement)* to rent out, *Br* to let; *(voiture)* to rent out, *Br* to hire out; *(réserver)* to book; **maison/chambre à l.** house/room to rent *or Br* to let

louer[2] [lwe] **1** *vt (exalter)* to praise *(de* for) **2 se louer** *vpr* **se l. de qch** to be highly satisfied with sth

loup [lu] *nm* wolf

loupe [lup] *nf* magnifying glass

lourd, -e [lur, lurd] **1** *adj* heavy *(de* with); *(temps)* close **2** *adv* **peser l.** *(personne, objet)* to be heavy ■ **lourdement** [-əmɑ̃] *adv* heavily ■ **lourdeur** *nf* heaviness; **avoir des lourdeurs d'estomac** to feel bloated

loyal, -e, -aux, -ales [lwajal, -o] *adj (honnête)* fair *(envers* to); *(dévoué)* loyal *(envers* to) ■ **loyauté** *nf (honnêteté)* fairness; *(dévouement)* loyalty *(envers* to)

loyer [lwaje] *nm* rent

lu [ly] *(pp de* **lire**[1])

lubrifier [lybrifje] *vt* to lubricate

lucarne [lykarn] *nf (fenêtre)* dormer window; *(de toit)* skylight

lucide [lysid] *adj* lucid ■ **lucidité** *nf* lucidity

lucratif, -ive [lykratif, -iv] *adj* lucrative

lueur [lɥœr] *nf (lumière) & Fig* glimmer

luge [lyʒ] *nf Br* sledge, *Am* sled, toboggan

LUI [lɥi] *pron personnel* **(a)** *(objet indirect)* (to) him; *(femme)* (to) her; *(chose, animal)* (to) it; **je le l. ai montré** I showed it to him/her **(b)** *(complément direct)* him; **elle n'aime que l.** she only loves him **(c)** *(après une préposition)* him; **pour/avec l.** for/with him; **elle pense à l.** she thinks of him; **ce livre est à l.** this book is his **(d)** *(dans les comparaisons)* **elle est plus grande que l.** she's taller than he is *or* than him **(e)** *(sujet)* **l., il ne viendra pas** *(emphatique)* HE won't come; **c'est l. qui me l'a dit** he is the one who told me ■ **lui-même** *pron* himself; *(chose, animal)* itself

luire* [lɥir] *vi* to shine ■ **luisant, -e** *adj (métal)* shiny

lumière [lymjɛr] *nf* light; **à la l. de** by the light of

lumineux, -euse [lyminø, -øz] *adj (idée, ciel)* bright, brilliant; *(cadran)* luminous

lunaire [lynɛr] *adj* lunar

lundi [lœdi] *nm* Monday

lune [lyn] *nf* moon; **l. de miel** honeymoon

lunette [lynɛt] *nf (astronomique)* telescope; **lunettes** *(de vue)* glasses, spectacles; *(de protection, de plongée)* goggles; **l. arrière** *(de voiture)* rear window; **lunettes de soleil** sunglasses

lustre [lystr] *nm (lampe)* chandelier; *(éclat)* lustre

lutte [lyt] *nf* fight, struggle; *Sport* wrestling ■ **lutter** *vi* to fight, to struggle; *Sport* to wrestle

luxation [lyksasjɔ̃] *nf Méd* dislocation

luxe [lyks] *nm* luxury; **modèle de l.** de luxe model ∎ **luxueux, -euse** *adj* luxurious

Luxembourg [lyksɑ̄bur] *nm* **le L.** Luxembourg

lycée [lise] *nm Br* ≃ secondary school, *Am* ≃ high school; **l. technique** *ou* **professionnel** vocational *or* technical school ∎ **lycéen, -enne** *nmf* pupil *(at a lycée)*

Mm

M¹, m¹ [ɛm] *nm inv* M, m

m' [m] *voir* **me**

M² (*abrév* **Monsieur**) Mr

m² (*abrév* **mètre(s)**) m

ma [ma] *voir* **mon**

macérer [masere] *vti* to steep

mâcher [mɑʃe] *vt* to chew

machine [maʃin] *nf (appareil)* machine; **m. à calculer** calculator; **m. à coudre** sewing machine; **m. à écrire** typewriter; **m. à laver** washing machine; **m. à laver la vaisselle** dishwasher; **m. à** *ou* **de traitement de texte** word processor ■ **machiniste** *nm (conducteur)* driver

mâchoire [mɑʃwar] *nf* jaw

mâchonner [mɑʃɔne] *vt* to chew

maçon [masɔ̃] *nm (de briques)* bricklayer; *(de pierres)* mason ■ **maçonnerie** *nf (travaux)* building work; *(ouvrage de briques)* brickwork; *(de pierres)* masonry, stonework

Madagascar [madagaskar] *nf* Madagascar

madame [madam] *(pl* **mesdames**) *nf (en apostrophe)* madam; **bonjour mesdames** good morning(, ladies); **M. Legras** Mrs Legras; **M.** *(dans une lettre)* Dear Madam

madeleine *nf (small)* sponge cake

mademoiselle [madmwazɛl] *(pl* **mesdemoiselles**) *nf (avant nom)* Miss; **M. Legras** Miss Legras; **M.** *(dans une lettre)* Dear Madam

magasin [magazɛ̃] *nm Br* shop, *Am* store; *(entrepôt)* warehouse; *(d'arme)* & *Phot* magazine; **grand m.** department store; **en m.** in stock

magazine [magazin] *nm (revue)* magazine

magie [maʒi] *nf* magic ■ **magicien, -enne** *nmf* magician ■ **magique** *adj (surnaturel)* magic; *(enchanteur)* magical

magistrat [maʒistra] *nm* magistrate

magnanime [maɲanim] *adj* magnanimous

magnat [maɲa] *nm* tycoon, magnate

magnésium [maɲezjɔm] *nm* magnesium

magnétique [maɲetik] *adj* magnetic

magnétophone [maɲetɔfɔn] *nm* tape recorder; **m. à cassettes** cassette recorder

magnétoscope [maɲetɔskɔp] *nm Br* video (recorder), *Am* VCR

magnifique [maɲifik] *adj* magnificent

mai [mɛ] *nm* May

maigre [mɛgr] *adj (personne, corps)* thin; *(viande)* lean; *(fromage)* low-fat; *(salaire)* meagre ■ **maigrir** *vi* to get thinner

maillot [majo] *nm (de sportif)* jersey, shirt; **m. de bain** *(de femme)* swimsuit; *(d'homme)* (swimming) trunks; **m. jaune** *(du Tour de France)* yellow jersey

main [mɛ̃] **1** *nf* hand; **à la m.** *(faire, écrire)* by hand; **tenir qch à la m.** to hold sth in one's hand; **en mains propres** in person; **donner la m. à qn** to hold sb's hand; **haut les mains!** hands up! **2** *adj* **fait m.** hand-made ■ **main-d'œuvre** *(pl* **mains-d'œuvre**) *nf* labour

maintenant [mɛ̃tnɑ̃] *adv* now; *(de nos jours)* nowadays; **m. que...** now that…; **dès m.** from now on

maintenir* [mɛ̃tnir] **1** vt (conserver) to keep, to maintain; (retenir) to hold in position; (affirmer) to maintain (**que** that) **2 se maintenir** vpr (durer) to remain ■ **maintien** nm (action) maintenance (**de** of); (allure) bearing

maire [mɛr] nm mayor ■ **mairie** nf Br town hall, Am city hall; (administration) Br town council, Am city hall

mais [mɛ] conj but; **m. oui, m. si** of course; **m. non** definitely not

maïs [mais] nm Br maize, Am corn

maison [mɛzɔ̃] **1** nf (bâtiment, famille) house; (foyer) home; (entreprise) company; **à la m.** at home; **rentrer à la m.** to go/come (back) home; **m. de la culture** arts centre; **m. d'édition** publishing house; **m. de retraite** old people's home; **m. de santé** nursing home **2** adj inv (artisanal) home-made

maître [mɛtr] nm master; **être m. de la situation** to be in control of the situation; **m. d'hôtel** (de restaurant) head waiter; **m. de maison** host; **m. chanteur** blackmailer; **m. nageur (sauveteur)** swimming instructor (and lifeguard)

maîtresse [mɛtrɛs] **1** nf mistress; **être m. de la situation** to be in control of the situation; **m. d'école** teacher; **m. de maison** hostess **2** adj f (idée, poutre) main; (carte) master

maîtrise [mɛtriz] nf (contrôle, connaissance) mastery (**de** of); (diplôme) ≃ master's degree (**de** in); **m. de soi** self-control ■ **maîtriser 1** vt (incendie, passion) to control; (peur) to overcome; (sujet) to master; (véhicule) to have under control; **m. qn** to overpower sb **2 se maîtriser** vpr to control oneself

majesté [maʒɛste] nf majesty; **Votre M.** (titre) Your Majesty

majeur, -e [maʒœr] **1** adj (important) & Mus major; **Jur être m.** to be of age; **la majeure partie de** most of **2** nm (doigt) middle finger

majorer [maʒɔre] vt to increase

majorette [maʒɔrɛt] nf (drum) major-

ette

majoritaire [maʒɔritɛr] adj majority; **être m.** to be in the majority

majorité [maʒɔrite] nf majority (**de** of); (gouvernement) government, party in office; **en m.** (pour la plupart) in the main

Majorque [maʒɔrk] nf Majorca

majuscule [maʒyskyl] **1** adj capital **2** nf capital letter

MAL, MAUX [mal, mo] **1** nm (douleur) pain; (préjudice) harm; (maladie) illness; (malheur) misfortune; Phil **m.** evil; **avoir m. à la tête/à la gorge** to have a headache/sore throat; **ça me fait m., j'ai m.** it hurts (me); **avoir le m. de mer** to be seasick; **faire du m. à qn** to harm sb; **avoir du m. à faire qch** to have trouble doing sth; **avoir le m. du pays** to be homesick; **m. de gorge** sore throat; **m. de tête** headache **2** adv (avec médiocrité) badly; (incorrectement) wrongly; (mal à l'aise) **aller m.** (personne) to be ill; **m. comprendre** to misunderstand; **se trouver m.** to faint; Fam **pas m.** (beaucoup) quite a lot (**de** of)

malade [malad] **1** adj ill, sick; (arbre, dent) diseased; **être m. du cœur** to have a bad heart **2** nmf sick person; (de médecin) patient; **les malades** the sick ■ **maladie** nf illness, disease

maladroit, -e [maladrwa, -at] adj (malhabile) clumsy, awkward; (indélicat) tactless ■ **maladresse** nf (manque d'habileté) clumsiness, awkwardness; (indélicatesse) tactlessness; (bévue) blunder

malaise [malɛz] nm (angoisse) uneasiness, malaise; (indisposition) feeling of sickness; (étourdissement) dizzy spell; **avoir un m.** to feel faint

Malaisie [malɛzi] nf **la M.** Malaysia

malchance [malʃɑ̃s] nf bad luck; **jouer de m.** to have no luck at all ■ **malchanceux, -euse** adj unlucky

mâle [mal] **1** adj (du sexe masculin) male; (viril) manly **2** nm male

malédiction [malediksjɔ̃] *nf* curse

maléfique [malefik] *adj* evil

malencontreux, -euse [malɑ̃kɔ̃trø, -øz] *adj* unfortunate

malentendant, -e [malɑ̃tɑ̃dɑ̃, -ɑ̃t] *nmf* person who is hard of hearing

malentendu [malɑ̃tɑ̃dy] *nm* misunderstanding

malfaçon [malfasɔ̃] *nf* defect

malfaisant, -e [malfəzɑ̃, -ɑ̃t] *adj* harmful

malfaiteur [malfɛtœr] *nm* criminal

malgré [malgre] *prép* in spite of; **m. tout** for all that, after all

malhabile [malabil] *adj* clumsy

malheur [malœr] *nm (drame)* misfortune; *(malchance)* bad luck; **par m.** unfortunately; **porter m. à qn** to bring sb bad luck ■ **malheureusement** *adv* unfortunately ■ **malheureux, -euse 1** *adj (triste)* unhappy, miserable; *(malchanceux)* unlucky **2** *nmf (infortuné)* poor wretch; *(indigent)* needy person

malhonnête [malɔnɛt] *adj* dishonest ■ **malhonnêteté** *nf* dishonesty

malice [malis] *nf* mischievousness ■ **malicieux, -euse** *adj* mischievous

malin, -igne [malɛ̃, -iɲ] *adj (astucieux)* clever, smart; *Méd (tumeur)* malignant

malintentionné, -e [malɛ̃tɑ̃sjɔne] *adj* ill-intentioned (**à l'égard de** towards)

malle [mal] *nf (coffre)* trunk; *(de véhicule) Br* boot, *Am* trunk

mallette [malɛt] *nf* briefcase

malmener [malməne] *vt* to manhandle, to treat badly

malnutrition [malnytrisjɔ̃] *nf* malnutrition

malpoli, -e [malpɔli] *adj Fam* rude

malsain, -e [malsɛ̃, -ɛn] *adj* unhealthy

Malte [malt] *nf* Malta ■ **maltais, -e** [maltɛ] *adj* Maltese **2** *nmf* **M., Maltaise** Maltese

maltraiter [maltrete] *vt* to ill-treat

malveillant, -e [malvɛjɑ̃, -ɑ̃t] *adj* malevolent

maman [mamɑ̃] *nf Br* mum, *Am* mom

mamie [mami] *nf* grandma, granny

mammifère [mamifɛr] *nm* mammal

Manche [mɑ̃ʃ] *nf* **la M.** the Channel

manche¹ [mɑ̃ʃ] *nf (de vêtement)* sleeve; *Sport & Cartes* round ■ **manchette** *nf (de chemise)* cuff; *(de journal)* headline

manche² [mɑ̃ʃ] *nm (d'outil)* handle; **m. à balai** broomstick; *(d'avion, d'ordinateur)* joystick

manchot, -e [mɑ̃ʃo, -ɔt] **1** *adj* one-armed **2** *nmf* one-armed person

mandarine [mɑ̃darin] *nf (fruit)* mandarin (orange)

mandat [mɑ̃da] *nm (de député)* mandate; *(de président)* term of office; **m. postal** *Br* postal order, *Am* money order

manège [manɛʒ] *nm (de foire)* merry-go-round, *Br* roundabout; *Équitation* riding school

manette [manɛt] *nf* lever

manger [mɑ̃ʒe] **1** *vt* to eat; *(corroder)* to eat into **2** *vi* to eat; **donner à m. à qn** to give sb sth to eat **3** *nm (nourriture)* food ■ **mangeable** *adj (médiocre)* eatable

mangue [mɑ̃g] *nf* mango

maniaque [manjak] *adj* fussy

manie [mani] *nf (habitude)* odd habit; *(idée fixe)* mania (**de** for)

manier [manje] *vt* to handle ■ **maniable** *adj (outil)* handy; *(véhicule)* easy to handle

manière [manjɛr] *nf* way, manner; **la m. dont elle parle** the way (in which) she talks; **manières** *(politesse)* manners; **de toute m.** anyway, anyhow; **de cette m.** (in) this way; **à la m. de** in the style of; **d'une m. générale** generally speaking ■ **maniéré, -e** *adj* affected

manifeste [manifɛst] **1** *adj* manifest, obvious **2** *nm Pol* manifesto

manifester [manifɛste] **1** *vt (exprimer)* to show **2** *vi (protester)* to demonstrate **3** **se manifester** *vpr (maladie)* to show *or* manifest itself; *(personne)* to make oneself known ■ **manifestant,**

-e *nmf* demonstrator ■ **manifestation** *nf* (*défilé*) demonstration; (*réunion, fête*) event

manipuler [manipyle] *vt* (*appareils, produits*) to handle ■ **manipulation** *nf* (*d'appareils, de produits*) handling; **manipulations génétiques** genetic engineering

manivelle [manivεl] *nf* crank

mannequin [mankε̃] *nm* (*personne*) model; (*statue*) dummy

manœuvre [manœvr] **1** *nm* (*ouvrier*) unskilled worker **2** *nf* (*opération*) & *Mil Br* manoeuvre, *Am* maneuver ■ **manœuvrer 1** *vt* (*véhicule, personne*) *Br* to manoeuvre, *Am* to maneuver; (*machine*) to operate **2** *vi Br* to manoeuvre, *Am* to maneuver

manoir [manwar] *nm* manor house

manque [mɑ̃k] *nm* (*insuffisance*) lack (**de** of); (*lacune*) gap; **par m. de qch** through lack of sth; **être en m.** (*drogué*) to have withdrawal symptoms

manquer [mɑ̃ke] **1** *vt* (*cible, train, chance*) to miss; (*échouer*) to fail **2** *vi* (*faire défaut*) to be lacking; (*être absent*) to be missing; (*échouer*) to fail; **m. de** (*pain, argent*) to be short of; (*attention, cohérence*) to lack; **tu me manques** I miss you; **ne m. de rien** to have all one needs **3** *v impersonnel* **il manque/il nous manque dix tasses** there are/we are ten cups short; **il manque quelques pages** there are a few pages missing ■ **manquant, -e** *adj* missing ■ **manqué, -e** *adj* (*occasion*) missed; (*tentative*) unsuccessful

mansarde [mɑ̃sard] *nf* attic

manteau, -x [mɑ̃to] *nm* coat

manucure [manykyr] *nmf* (*personne*) manicurist

manuel, -elle [manɥεl] **1** *adj* (*travail*) manual **2** *nm* (*livre*) handbook, manual; **m. scolaire** textbook

manufacture [manyfaktyr] *nf* factory ■ **manufacturé, -e** *adj* (*produit*) manufactured

manuscrit [manyskri] *nm* manuscript;

(*tapé à la machine*) typescript

maquereau, -x [makro] *nm* (*poisson*) mackerel

maquiller [makije] **1** *vt* (*personne, visage*) to make up **2 se maquiller** *vpr* to put one's make-up on ■ **maquillage** *nm* (*fard*) make-up

maraîcher, -ère [marεʃe, -εr] **1** *nmf Br* market gardener, *Am* truck farmer **2** *adj* **culture maraîchère** *Br* market gardening, *Am* truck farming

marais [marε] *nm* marsh

marathon [maratɔ̃] *nm* marathon

marbre [marbr] *nm* marble ■ **marbré, -e** *adj* (*surface*) marbled; **gâteau m.** marble cake

marc [mar] *nm* **m. de café** coffee grounds

marchand, -e [marʃɑ̃, -ɑ̃d] **1** *nmf Br* shopkeeper, *Am* storekeeper; (*de vins*) merchant; (*de voitures, de meubles*) dealer; **m. de journaux** (*dans la rue*) newsvendor; (*dans un magasin*) *Br* newsagent, *Am* newsdealer **2** *adj* **valeur marchande** market value

marchander [marʃɑ̃de] **1** *vt* (*objet, prix*) to haggle over **2** *vi* to haggle

marchandises [marʃɑ̃diz] *nfpl* goods, merchandise

marche [marʃ] *nf* (**a**) (*d'escalier*) step, stair (**b**) (*action*) walking; (*promenade*) walk; *Mus* march; **un train en m.** a moving train; **la bonne m. de** (*opération*) the smooth running of; **mettre qch en m.** to start sth (up); **faire m. arrière** (*en voiture*) *Br* to reverse, *Am* to back up; *Fig* to backtrack; **fermer la m.** to bring up the rear; **m. à suivre** procedure

marché [marʃe] **1** *nm* (*lieu*) & *Écon* market; (*contrat*) deal; **faire son** *ou* **le m.** to go shopping; **vendre qch au m. noir** to sell sth on the black market; **le m. du travail** the labour market; **le M. commun** the Common Market; **le M. unique européen** the Single European Market; **m. des changes** foreign exchange market **2** *adj inv* **être bon m.** to be cheap;

c'est meilleur m. it's cheaper

marcher [marʃe] *vi (personne)* to walk; *(machine)* to run; *(plans)* to work; **faire m. qch** to operate sth ▪ **marcheur, -euse** *nmf* walker

mardi [mardi] *nm* Tuesday; **M. gras** ShroveTuesday

mare [mar] *nf (étang)* pond

marécage [mareka3] *nm* marsh

maréchal, -aux [mareʃal, -o] *nm* **m. de France** field marshal ▪ **maréchal-ferrant** *(pl* **maréchaux-ferrants)** *nm* blacksmith

marée [mare] *nf* tide; *(poissons)* fresh seafood; **m. haute/basse** high/low tide; **m. noire** oil slick

margarine [margarin] *nf* margarine

marge [mar3] *nf (de page)* margin; **en m. de** *(en dehors de)* on the fringes of; **avoir de la m.** to have some leeway; **m. de manœuvre** room for *Br* manoeuvre *or Am* maneuver ▪ **marginal, -e, -aux, -ales 1** *adj (secondaire)* marginal; *(personne)* on the fringes of society **2** *nmf* dropout

marguerite [margərit] *nf (fleur)* daisy

mari [mari] *nm* husband

mariage [marja3] *nm (union)* marriage; *(cérémonie)* wedding; *Fig (de couleurs)* blend

marier [marje] **1** *vt (couleurs)* to blend; **m. qn** *(sujet: prêtre, maire)* to marry sb; *(sujet: père)* to marry sb off **2 se marier** *vpr* to get married; **se m. avec qn** to get married to sb, to marry sb ▪ **marié, -e 1** *adj* married **2** *nm (bride)-* groom; **les mariés** the bride and groom ▪ **mariée** *nf* bride

marin, -e [marɛ̃, -in] **1** *adj (flore)* marine; *(mille)* nautical; **air m.** sea air **2** *nm* sailor, seaman; **m. pêcheur** (deep-sea) fisherman ▪ **marine 1** *nf* **m. de guerre** navy; **m. marchande** merchant navy **2** *adj & nm inv* **bleu m.** *(couleur)* navy (blue)

mariner [marine] *vti Culin* to marinate

marionnette [marjɔnɛt] *nf* puppet; *(à fils)* marionette

maritalement [maritalmɑ̃] *adv* **vivre**

m. to cohabit

maritime [maritim] *adj (droit, climat)* maritime; **port m.** seaport; **gare m.** harbour station; *Can* **les Provinces maritimes** the Maritime Provinces

marmelade [marmǝlad] *nf Br* stewed fruit, *Am* fruit compote

marmite [marmit] *nf* (cooking) pot

Maroc [marɔk] *nm* **le M.** Morocco ▪ **marocain, -e 1** *adj* Moroccan **2** *nmf* **M., Marocaine** Moroccan

maroquinerie [marɔkinri] *nf (magasin)* leather goods shop

marque [mark] *nf (trace, signe)* mark; *(de confiance)* sign; *(de produit)* brand; *(de voiture)* make; *Sport (points)* score; **de m.** *(hôte, visiteur)* distinguished; *(produit)* of quality; **m. déposée** (registered) trademark

marquer [marke] **1** *vt (par une marque)* to mark; *(écrire)* to note down; *(indiquer)* to show; *Sport (point, but)* to score; **m. les points** to keep (the) score **2** *vi (laisser une trace)* to leave a mark; *(date, événement)* to stand out; *Sport* to score ▪ **marquant, -e** *adj (remarquable)* outstanding; *(épisode)* significant ▪ **marqué, -e** *adj (différence, accent)* marked; *(visage)* lined ▪ **marqueur** *nm (stylo)* marker

marquis [marki] *nm* marquis ▪ **marquise** *nf* (**a**) *(personne)* marchioness (**b**) *(auvent)* canopy

marraine [marɛn] *nf* godmother

marre [mar] *adv Fam* **en avoir m.** to be fed up (**de** with)

marron [marɔ̃] **1** *nm (fruit)* chestnut; *(couleur)* (chestnut) brown **2** *adj inv* *(couleur)* (chestnut) brown ▪ **marronnier** *nm* (horse) chestnut tree

mars [mars] *nm* March

marteau, -x [marto] *nm* hammer; **m. piqueur** pneumatic drill ▪ **marteler** *vt* to hammer

martial, -e, -aux, -ales [marsjal, -o] *adj* martial; **cour martiale** court martial

Martinique [martinik] *nf* **la M.** Martinique ▪ **martiniquais, -e 1** *adj* Martinican **2** *nmf* **M., Martiniquaise**

Martinican

martyriser [martirize] *vt* to torture; *(enfant)* to batter

masculin, -e [maskylɛ̃, -in] **1** *adj (sexe, mode)* male; *(caractère, femme, nom)* masculine **2** *nm (en grammaire)* masculine

masochiste [mazɔʃist] **1** *adj* masochistic **2** *nmf* masochist

masque [mask] *nm* mask; **m. à gaz** gas mask ■ **masquer** *vt (dissimuler)* to mask (**à** from); *(cacher à la vue)* to block off

massacre [masakr] *nm (tuerie)* massacre ■ **massacrer** *vt* to massacre

massage [masaʒ] *nm* massage

masse [mas] *nf* (**a**) *(volume)* mass; *(gros morceau, majorité)* bulk (**de** of); **de m.** *(culture, communication)* mass; **en m.** en masse (**b**) *Él Br* earth, *Am* ground

masser [mase] **1** *vt (rassembler)* to assemble; *(pétrir)* to massage **2 se masser** *upr (foule)* to form ■ **masseur** *nm* masseur ■ **masseuse** *nf* masseuse

massif, -ive [masif, -iv] *adj* massive; *(or, chêne)* solid **2** *nm (d'arbres, de fleurs)* clump; *Géog* massif

mastic [mastik] *nm (pour vitres)* putty; *(pour bois)* filler ■ **mastiquer** *vt (mâcher)* to chew

mat¹, mate [mat] *adj (papier, couleur)* matt

mat² [mat] *adj m inv & nm* Échecs (check-)mate; **faire m.** to (check)mate

mât [mɑ] *nm (de navire)* mast; *(poteau)* pole

match [matʃ] *nm Sport Br* match, *Am* game; **m. nul** draw; **faire m. nul** to draw; **m. aller** first leg; **m. retour** return leg

matelas [matla] *nm* mattress; **m. pneumatique** air bed

matelot [matlo] *nm* sailor

mater [mate] *vt (dominer)* to bring to heel

matérialiser [materjalize] *vt*, **se matérialiser** *upr* to materialize

matérialiste [materjalist] **1** *adj* mate-

rialistic **2** *nmf* materialist

matériau, -x [materjo] *nm* material; **matériaux** *(de construction)* building material(s)

matériel, -elle [materjεl] **1** *adj (confort, dégâts, besoins)* material; *(problème)* practical **2** *nm (de camping)* equipment; *Ordinat* **m. informatique** computer hardware ■ **matériellement** *adv* materially; **m. impossible** physically impossible

maternel, -elle [matεrnεl] **1** *adj (amour, femme)* maternal; *(langue)* native **2** *adj & nf (école)* maternelle *Br* nursery school, *Am* kindergarten ■ **maternité** *nf (hôpital)* maternity hospital

mathématiques [matematik] *nfpl* mathematics *(sing)* ■ **maths** *nfpl Fam Br* maths, *Am* math

matière [matjεr] *nf (à l'école)* subject; *(de livre)* subject matter; *(substance)* material; *Phys* **la m.** matter; **en m. de qch** as regards sth; **m. première** raw material; **matières grasses** fat

Matignon [matiɲɔ̃] *nm (l'hôtel)* **M.** = the French Prime Minister's offices

matin [matɛ̃] *nm* morning; **le m.** *(chaque matin)* in the morning(s); **le mardi matin** every Tuesday morning; **tous les matins** every morning; **le 8 au m.** on the morning of the 8th; **à sept heures du m.** at seven in the morning; **au petit m.** very early (in the morning) ■ **matinal, -e, -aux, -ales** *adj (heure)* early; **être m.** to be an early riser

matinée [matine] *nf* morning; *Théât & Cin* matinée; **dans la m.** in the course of the morning

matraque [matrak] *nf* bludgeon; *(de policier) Br* truncheon, *Am* nightstick ■ **matraquage** *nm* **m. publicitaire** hype

matrimonial, -e, -aux, -ales [matrimɔnjal, -o] *adj* matrimonial

maturité [matyrite] *nf* maturity; **arriver à m.** *(fromage, vin)* to mature; *(fruit)* to ripen

maudire* [modir] *vt* to curse ■ **mau-**

dit, -e *adj (damné)* cursed

Maurice [mɔris] *nf* **l'île M.** Mauritius

maussade [mosad] *adj (personne)* sullen; *(temps)* gloomy

mauvais, -e [move, -ɛz] **1** *adj* bad; *(santé, vue)* poor; *(méchant)* nasty; *(mal choisi)* wrong; *(mer)* rough; **plus m. que...** worse than...; **le plus m.** the worst; **être m. en anglais** to be bad at English; **être en mauvaise santé** to be in bad *or* ill *or* poor health **2** *adv* **il fait m.** the weather's bad; **ça sent m.** it smells bad **3** *nm* **le bon et le m.** the good and the bad

mauve [mov] *adj & nm (couleur)* mauve

maux [mo] *pl de* **mal**

maximum [maksimɔm] *(pl* **maxima** [-a] *ou* **maximums**) **1** *nm* maximum; **faire le m.** to do one's very best; **au m.** at the most **2** *adj* maximum

mayonnaise [majɔnɛz] *nf* mayonnaise

mazout [mazut] *nm (fuel)* oil

me [mə]

> **m'** is used before a vowel or mute h.

pron personnel **(a)** *(complément direct)* me; **il me voit** he sees me **(b)** *(complément indirect)* (to) me; **elle me parle** she speaks to me; **tu me l'as dit** you told me **(c)** *(réfléchi)* myself; **je me lave** I wash myself **(d)** *(avec les pronominaux)* **je me suis trompé** I made a mistake

mécanicien [mekanisjɛ̃] *nm* mechanic; *(de train)* Br train driver, Am engineer

mécanique [mekanik] **1** *adj* mechanical **2** *nf (science)* mechanics *(sing)*; *(mécanisme)* mechanism ■ **mécanisme** *nm* mechanism

mécène [mesɛn] *nm* patron (of the arts)

méchant, -e [meʃɑ̃, -ɑ̃t] *adj (personne, remarque)* nasty; *(enfant)* naughty; *(chien)* vicious; **'attention! chien m.'** 'beware of the dog' ■ **méchanceté** *nf* nastiness; **une m.** *(parole)*

a nasty remark; *(acte)* a nasty action

mèche [mɛʃ] *nf* **(a)** *(de cheveux)* lock **(b)** *(de bougie)* wick; *(de pétard)* fuse; *(de perceuse)* bit

méconnaître* [mekɔnɛtr] *vt (fait)* to fail to take into account; *(talent)* to fail to recognize ■ **méconnaissable** *adj* unrecognizable ■ **méconnu, -e** *adj* unrecognized

mécontent, -e [mekɔ̃tɑ̃, -ɑ̃t] *adj (insatisfait)* displeased (**de** with); *(contrarié)* annoyed ■ **mécontenter** *vt (ne pas satisfaire)* to displease; *(contrarier)* to annoy

Mecque [mɛk] *nf* **La M.** Mecca

médaille [medaj] *nf (décoration, bijou) & Sport* medal; *(portant le nom)* pendant *(with name engraved on it)*; *(de chien)* name tag; *Sport* **être m. d'or/ d'argent** to be a gold/silver medallist ■ **médaillé, -e** *nmf* medal holder ■ **médaillon** *nm (bijou)* locket; *(de viande)* medallion

médecin [medsɛ̃] *nm* doctor, physician; **m. généraliste** general practitioner; **m. traitant** consulting physician ■ **médecine** *nf* medicine; **médecines douces** alternative medicine; **étudiant en m.** medical student ■ **médical, -e, -aux, -ales** *adj* medical ■ **médicament** *nm* medicine ■ **médicinal, -e, -aux, -ales** *adj* medicinal

média [medja] *nm* medium; **les médias** the media ■ **médiatique** *adj* **campagne m.** media campaign ■ **médiatiser** *vt* to give media coverage to

médiateur, -trice [medjatœr, -tris] *nmf* mediator

médiéval, -e, -aux, -ales [medjeval, -o] *adj* medieval

médiocre [medjɔkr] *adj* mediocre ■ **médiocrité** *nf* mediocrity

médire* [medir] *vi* **m. de qn** to speak ill of sb ■ **médisance** *nf (action)* gossiping; **médisances** *(propos)* gossip

méditer [medite] **1** *vt (réfléchir à)* to contemplate **2** *vi* to meditate (**sur** on) ■ **méditation** *nf* meditation

Méditerranée [mediterane] *nf* **la M.** the Mediterranean ■ **méditerranéen, -enne** *adj* Mediterranean

médium [medjɔm] *nmf (voyant)* medium

méduse [medyz] *nf* jellyfish

méfiance [mefjɑ̃s] *nf* distrust, mistrust

méfier [mefje] **se méfier** *vpr* to be careful; **se m. de qn** not to trust sb; **se m. de qch** to watch out for sth; **méfie-toi!** watch out!, beware! ■ **méfiant, -e** *adj* suspicious, distrustful

mégaoctet [megaɔktɛ] *nm* Ordinat megabyte

mégarde [megard] **par mégarde** *adv* inadvertently

mégot [mego] *nm* cigarette butt *or* end

meilleur, -e [mɛjœr] **1** *adj* better (**que** than); **le m. résultat/moment** the best result/moment **2** *nmf* **le m., la meilleure** the best (one) **3** *adv* **il fait m.** it's warmer

mél [mɛl] *nm (courrier)* e-mail

mélancolie [melɑ̃kɔli] *nf* melancholy ■ **mélancolique** *adj* melancholy

mélange [melɑ̃ʒ] *nm (résultat)* mixture; *(opération)* mixing ■ **mélanger 1** *vt (mêler)* to mix; *(brouiller)* to mix up **2 se mélanger** *vpr (s'incorporer)* to mix; *(idées)* to get mixed up

mêler [mele] **1** *vt* to mix (**à** with); *(odeurs, thèmes)* to combine; **m. qn à qch** *(affaire, conversation)* to involve sb in sth

2 se mêler *vpr* to combine (**à** with); **se m. à qch** *(foule)* to mingle with sth; *(conversation)* to join in sth; **se m. de qch** to get involved in sth; **mêle-toi de tes affaires!** mind your own business! ■ **mêlé, -e** *adj* mixed (**de** with) ■ **mêlée** *nf (au rugby)* scrum(mage)

mélodie [melɔdi] *nf* melody

mélodramatique [melɔdramatik] *adj* melodramatic

melon [mǝlɔ̃] *nm (fruit)* melon; **(chapeau) m.** *Br* bowler (hat), *Am* derby

membre [mɑ̃br] *nm (bras, jambe)* limb; *(de groupe)* member

MÊME [mɛm] **1** *adj (identique)* same; **en m. temps** at the same time (**que** as); **le m. jour** the same day; **le jour m.** *(exact)* the very day; **lui-m./vous-m.** himself/yourself

2 *pron* **le/la m.** the same (one); **j'ai les mêmes** I have the same (ones); **cela revient au m.** it amounts to the same thing

3 *adv (y compris, aussi)* even; **m. si…** even if…; **ici m.** in this very place; **tout de m.,** *Fam* **quand m.** all the same; **de m.** likewise; **de m. que…** just as…; **être à m. de faire qch** to be in a position to do sth

mémoire [memwar] **1** *nf* memory; **de m.** *(citer)* from memory; **à la m. de** in memory of; Ordinat **m. morte/vive** read-only/random access memory **2** *nm (rapport)* report; *Univ* dissertation; **Mémoires** *(chronique)* memoirs ■ **mémorable** *adj* memorable

mémorial, -aux [memɔrjal, -o] *nm (monument)* memorial

menaçant, -e [mǝnasɑ̃, -ɑ̃t] *adj* threatening

menace [mǝnas] *nf* threat ■ **menacer** *vt* to threaten (**de faire** to do)

ménage [menaʒ] *nm (entretien)* housekeeping; *(couple)* couple, household; **faire le m.** to do the housework

ménager¹, -ère [menaʒe, -ɛr] **1** *adj (équipement)* household **2** *nf* **ménagère** *(femme)* housewife

ménager² [menaʒe] **1** *vt (argent)* to use sparingly; *(forces)* to save; *(sortie)* to provide; **m. qn** to treat sb carefully; **ne pas m. sa peine** to put in a lot of effort **2 se ménager** *vpr (prendre soin de soi)* to look after oneself; *(se réserver)* to set aside

ménagerie [menaʒri] *nf* menagerie

mendier [mɑ̃dje] **1** *vt* to beg for **2** *vi* to beg ■ **mendiant, -e** *nmf* beggar

mener [mǝne] **1** *vt (personne)* to take (**à** to); *(course, vie)* to lead; *(enquête)* to carry out; *Fig* **m. qch à bien** to carry sth through **2** *vi Sport* to lead; **m. à un lieu** to lead to a place ■ **meneur, -euse** *nmf (de révolte)* ringleader

méningite [menɛʒit] *nf* meningitis

menottes [mənɔt] *nfpl* handcuffs

mensonge [mãsɔ̃ʒ] *nm (propos)* lie; *(action)* lying ■ **mensonger, -ère** *adj (propos)* untrue; *(publicité)* misleading

mensuel, -elle [mãsɥɛl] **1** *adj* monthly **2** *nm (revue)* monthly ■ **mensualité** *nf* monthly payment

mensurations [mãsyrasjɔ̃] *nfpl* measurements

mental, -e, -aux, -ales [mãtal, -o] *adj* mental ■ **mentalité** *nf* mentality

menthe [mãt] *nf* mint

mention [mãsjɔ̃] *nf (fait de citer)* mention; *(à un examen)* ≃ distinction; *Scol* **m. passable/assez bien/bien/très bien** ≃ C/B/A; **faire m. de qch** to mention sth; **'rayez les mentions inutiles'** 'delete as appropriate' ■ **mentionner** *vt* to mention

mentir* [mãtir] *vi* to lie (**à** to) ■ **menteur, -euse 1** *adj* lying **2** *nmf* liar

menton [mãtɔ̃] *nm* chin

menu¹ [məny] *nm (de restaurant)* set menu; *Ordinat* menu; **par le m.** in detail

menu², -e [məny] **1** *adj (petit)* tiny; *(mince)* slim **2** *adv (hacher)* small, finely

menuisier [mənɥizje] *nm* carpenter, joiner ■ **menuiserie** *nf (atelier)* joiner's workshop; *(boiseries)* woodwork

mépris [mepri] *nm* contempt (**pour** for), scorn (**pour** for); **au m. de qch** without regard to sth ■ **méprisable** *adj* despicable ■ **méprisant, -e** *adj* contemptuous, scornful ■ **mépriser** *vt* to despise

méprise [mepriz] *nf* mistake

mer [mɛr] *nf* sea; *(marée)* tide; **en (haute) m.** at sea; **par m.** by sea; **aller à la m.** to go to the seaside; **prendre la m.** to set sail

mercatique [mɛrkatik] *nf* marketing

mercenaire [mɛrsənɛr] *nm* mercenary

mercerie [mɛrsəri] *nf (magasin) Br* haberdasher's, *Am* notions store

merci [mɛrsi] **1** *exclam* thank you, thanks (**de** *ou* **pour** for); **non m.** no thank you; **m. bien** thanks very much **2** *nf* **à la m. de qn/qch** at the mercy of sb/sth; **sans m.** merciless

mercredi [mɛrkrədi] *nm* Wednesday

mercure [mɛrkyr] *nm* mercury

mère [mɛr] *nf* mother; *Com* **maison m.** parent company; **m. porteuse** surrogate mother

méridional, -e, -aux, -ales [meridjɔnal, -o] **1** *adj* southern **2** *nmf* southerner

mérite [merit] *nm* merit; *(honneur)* credit; **avoir du m. à faire qch** to deserve credit for doing sth ■ **mériter** *vt (être digne de)* to deserve; *(demander)* to be worth; **m. réflexion** to be worth thinking about; **ce livre mérite d'être lu** this book is worth reading

merle [mɛrl] *nm* blackbird

merlu [mɛrly] *nm* hake

merveille [mɛrvɛj] *nf* wonder, marvel; **à m.** wonderfully (well)

merveilleux, -euse [mɛrvejø, -øz] *adj* wonderful, *Br* marvellous, *Am* marvelous

mes [me] *voir* **mon**

mésaventure [mezavãtyr] *nf* misadventure

mesdames [medam] *pl de* **madame**

mesdemoiselles [medmwazɛl] *pl de* **mademoiselle**

mésestimer [mezɛstime] *vt* to underestimate

mesquin, -e [mɛskɛ̃, -in] *adj* mean, petty ■ **mesquinerie** *nf* meanness, pettiness; **une m.** an act of meanness

mess [mɛs] *nm inv Mil (salle)* mess

message [mesaʒ] *nm* message; **m. publicitaire** advertisement ■ **messager, -ère** *nmf* messenger ■ **messagerie** *nf* courier company; **m. électronique** electronic mail service; **m. vocale** voice mail

messe [mɛs] *nf (office, musique)* mass;

aller à la m. to go to mass
messeigneurs [meseɲœr] *pl de* **monseigneur**
messieurs [mesjø] *pl de* **monsieur**
mesure [məzyr] *nf (dimension)* measurement; *(moyen)* measure; *(retenue)* moderation; *Mus (temps)* time; *Mus (division)* bar; **sur m.** *(vêtement)* made to measure; **être en m. de faire qch** to be in a position to do sth; **prendre des mesures** to take measures; **à m. que… as…; dans la m. où… in so far as…; dans la m. du possible** as far as possible

mesurer [məzyre] **1** *vt (dimension, taille)* to measure; *(déterminer)* to assess **2** *vi* **m. 1 mètre 83** *(personne)* ≃ to be 6 feet tall; *(objet)* ≃ to measure 6 feet **3 se mesurer** *vpr* **se m. à** *ou* **avec qn** to pit oneself against sb

met [me] *voir* **mettre**

métal, -aux [metal, -o] *nm* metal ■ **métallique** *adj (éclat, reflet)* metallic ■ **métallisé, -e** *adj* **bleu m.** metallic blue

métallurgie [metalyrʒi] *nf (industrie)* steel industry; *(science)* metallurgy ■ **métallurgiste** *nm* metalworker

métamorphoser [metamɔrfoze] *vt*, **se métamorphoser** *vpr* to transform (en into)

météo [meteo] *nf Fam (bulletin)* weather forecast

météorologie [meteɔrɔlɔʒi] *nf (science)* meteorology; *(service)* weather bureau ■ **météorologique** *adj* meteorological; **bulletin m.** weather report

méthode [metɔd] *nf (manière, soin)* method; *(livre)* course ■ **méthodique** *adj* methodical

méticuleux, -euse [metikylø, -øz] *adj* meticulous

métier [metje] *nm (manuel, commercial)* trade; *(intellectuel)* profession; *(savoir-faire)* experience; **homme de m.** specialist; **tailleur de son m.** tailor by trade; **être du m.** to be in the business; **m. à tisser** loom

métrage [metraʒ] *nm (action)* measur-

ing; *(tissu)* length; **long m.** feature film; **court m.** short film

mètre [metr] *nm (mesure) Br* metre, *Am* meter; **m. carré/cube** square/cubic metre ■ **métrique** *adj (système)* metric

métro [metro] *nm Br* underground, *Am* subway

métropole [metrɔpɔl] *nf (ville)* metropolis; *(pays)* mother country ■ **métropolitain, -e** *adj* metropolitan

mets [me] *nm (aliment)* dish

metteur [metœr] *nm* **m. en scène** director

METTRE* [metr] **1** *vt* to put; *(vêtement, lunettes)* to put on; *(chauffage, radio)* to switch on; *(réveil)* to set (à for); **j'ai mis une heure** it took me an hour; **m. qn en colère** to make sb angry; **m. qn à l'aise** to put sb at ease; **m. qch plus fort** to turn sth up; **m. de la musique** to put some music on; **mettons que… (+ subjunctive)** let's suppose that…

2 se mettre *vpr (se placer)* to put oneself; *(debout)* to stand; *(assis)* to sit; *(objet)* to go; **se m. en pyjama** to get into one's pyjamas; **se m. à table** to sit (down) at the table; **se m. à l'aise** to make oneself comfortable; **se m. au salon** to go into the dining room; **se m. au travail** to start work; **se m. à faire qch** to start doing sth; **le temps s'est mis au beau** the weather has turned fine

meuble [mœbl] *nm* piece of furniture; **meubles** furniture ■ **meublé** *nm* furnished *Br* flat *or Am* apartment ■ **meubler** *vt* to furnish

meule [møl] *nf (d'herbe)* stack; *(de moulin)* millstone; **m. de foin** haystack

meunier, -ère [mønje, -ɛr] *nmf* miller

meurt [mœr] *voir* **mourir**

meurtre [mœrtr] *nm* murder ■ **meurtrier, -ère 1** *nmf* murderer **2** *adj* murderous; *(épidémie)* deadly

meurtrir [mœrtrir] *vt* to bruise

meute [møt] *nf* pack

Mexique [mɛksik] *nm* **le M.** Mexico ■ **mexicain, -e 1** *adj* Mexican **2** *nmf* **M., Mexicaine** Mexican

mi [mi] *nm inv (note)* E

mi- [mi] *préf* **la mi-mars** mid March; **à mi-distance** midway; **cheveux mi-longs** shoulder-length hair

miauler [mjole] *vi (chat)* to miaow

mi-chemin [miʃmɛ̃] **à mi-chemin** *adv* halfway

mi-clos, -e [miklo, -oz] *(mpl* **mi-clos,** *fpl* **mi-closes)** *adj* half-closed

micro [mikro] *nm (microphone)* mike ■ **microphone** *nm* microphone

microbe [mikrɔb] *nm* germ, microbe

microfilm [mikrɔfilm] *nm* microfilm

micro-informatique [mikroɛ̃fɔrmatik] *nf* microcomputing

micro-ondes [mikrɔɔ̃d] *nm inv* microwave; **four à m.** microwave oven

micro-ordinateur [mikroɔrdinatœr] *(pl* **micro-ordinateurs)** *nm* microcomputer

microprocesseur [mikroprɔsɛsœr] *nm Ordinat* microprocessor

microscope [mikrɔskɔp] *nm* microscope ■ **microscopique** *adj* microscopic

midi [midi] *nm* (**a**) *(heure)* twelve o'clock, midday; *(heure du déjeuner)* lunchtime; **entre m. et deux heures** at lunchtime (**b**) *(sud)* south; **le M.** the South of France

mie [mi] *nf (de pain)* soft part

miel [mjɛl] *nm* honey

mien, mienne [mjɛ̃, mjɛn] **1** *pron possessif* **le m., la mienne** mine, *Br* my one; **les miens, les miennes** mine, *Br* my ones; **les deux miens** my two **2** *nmpl* **les miens** *(ma famille)* my family

miette [mjɛt] *nf (de pain)* crumb

mieux [mjø] **1** *adv* better (**que** than); **aller m.** to be (feeling) better; **de m. en m.** better and better; **le/la/les m.** *(de plusieurs)* the best; *(de deux)* the better; **le m. serait de...** the best thing would be to...; **le plus tôt sera le m.** the sooner the better

2 *adj inv* better; *(plus beau)* better-looking; **si tu n'as rien de m. à faire** if you've got nothing better to do

3 *nm (amélioration)* improvement; **faire de son m.** to do one's best; **faites au m.** do the best you can

mignon, -onne [miɲɔ̃, -ɔn] *adj (charmant)* cute

migraine [migrɛn] *nf* headache; *Méd* migraine

migration [migrɑsjɔ̃] *nf* migration

mijoter [miʒɔte] **1** *vt (avec soin)* to cook (lovingly); *(lentement)* to simmer **2** *vi* to simmer

mil [mil] *adj inv* **l'an deux m.** the year two thousand

milieu, -x [miljø] *nm (centre)* middle; *(cadre, groupe social)* environment; *(entre extrêmes)* middle course; *Phys* medium; **milieux littéraires** literary circles; **au m. de** in the middle of; **le juste m.** the happy medium; **le m.** *(la pègre)* the underworld

militaire [militɛr] **1** *adj* military **2** *nm* serviceman; *(de l'armée de terre)* soldier

militer [milite] *vi (personne)* to campaign (**pour** for; **contre** against)

mille [mil] **1** *adj inv & nm inv* thousand; **m. hommes** a *or* one thousand men; **deux m.** two thousand; **je vous le donne en m.!** you'll never guess! **2** *nm (de cible)* bull's eye; *(marin)* nautical mile ■ **mille-feuille** *(pl* **mille-feuilles)** *nm Br* ≃ vanilla slice, *Am* ≃ napoleon ■ **millième** *adj, nm & nmf* thousandth; **un m.** a thousandth ■ **millier** *nm* thousand; **un m. (de)** a thousand or so; **par milliers** in their thousands

millénaire [milenɛr] *nm* millennium

milliard [miljar] *nm* billion ■ **milliardaire** *adj & nmf* billionaire

millimètre [milimɛtr] *nm* millimetre

million [miljɔ̃] *nm* million; **un m. de francs** a million francs; **deux millions** two million; **par millions** in millions ■ **millionnaire** *nmf* millionaire

mime [mim] **1** *nm (art)* mime **2** *nmf (artiste)* mime ■ **mimer** *vti (exprimer)* to mime

minable [minabl] *adj (lieu, personne)* shabby

mince [mɛ̃s] *adj* thin; *(élancé)* slim; *(insuffisant)* slight ■ **minceur** *nf* thinness; *(sveltesse)* slimness ■ **mincir** *vi* to get slimmer

mine [min] *nf* (a) *(physionomie)* look; **avoir bonne/mauvaise m.** to look well/ill (b) *(gisement) & Fig* mine; **m. de charbon** coalmine (c) *(de crayon)* lead (d) *(engin explosif)* mine

miner [mine] *vt (terrain)* to mine; *Fig (saper)* to undermine; **m. qn** *(chagrin, maladie)* to wear sb down

minerai [minrɛ] *nm* ore

minéral, -e, -aux, -ales [mineral, -o] *adj & nm* mineral

minéralogique [mineralɔʒik] *adj* **plaque m.** *(de véhicule) Br* number or *Am* license plate

mineur, -e [minœr] **1** *nm (ouvrier)* miner; **m. de fond** underground worker **2** *adj (secondaire) & Mus* minor; *(de moins de 18 ans)* underage **3** *nmf Jur* minor ■ **minière** *adj f* **industrie minière** mining industry

miniature [minjatyr] **1** *nf* miniature **2** *adj* **train m.** miniature train

minigolf [minigɔlf] *nm* crazy golf

minijupe [miniʒyp] *nf* miniskirt

minimum [minimɔm] *(pl* **minima** [-a] *ou* **minimums)** **1** *nm* minimum; **le m. de** *(force)* the minimum (amount of); **faire le m.** to do the bare minimum; **en un m. de temps** in as short a time as possible; **au m.** at the very least; **le m. vital** a minimum to live on; **les minima sociaux** = basic income support **2** *adj* minimum

ministère [minister] *nm (département)* ministry; *(gouvernement)* government, cabinet; **m. des Affaires étrangères** *Br* ≃ Foreign Office, *Am* ≃ State Department; **m. de l'Intérieur** *Br* ≃ Home Office, *Am* ≃ Department of the Interior ■ **ministériel, -elle** *adj*

ministerial

ministre [ministr] *nm Pol & Rel* secretary, *Br* minister; **m. des Affaires étrangères** *Br* ≃ Foreign Secretary, *Am* ≃ Secretary of State; **m. de l'Intérieur** *Br* ≃ Home Secretary, *Am* ≃ Secretary of the Interior

Minitel® [minitel] *nm* = consumer information network accessible via home computer terminal

minorité [minɔrite] *nf* minority ■ **minoritaire** *adj* **être m.** to be in the minority

minuit [minɥi] *nm* midnight, twelve o'clock

minuscule [minyskyl] **1** *adj (petit)* tiny, minute **2** *adj & nf (lettre)* **m.** small letter

minute [minyt] *nf* minute; **à la m.** *(tout de suite)* this (very) minute; **d'une m. à l'autre** any minute (now) ■ **minuterie** *nf (d'éclairage)* time switch

minutie [minysi] *nf* meticulousness ■ **minutieux, -euse** *adj* meticulous

mirabelle [mirabɛl] *nf* mirabelle plum

miracle [mirakl] *nm* miracle; **par m.** miraculously ■ **miraculeux, -euse** *adj* miraculous

mirage [miraʒ] *nm* mirage

mire [mir] *nf* **point de m.** *(cible) & Fig* target

miroir [mirwar] *nm* mirror

mis, mise¹ [mi, miz] **1** *pp de* **mettre 2** *adj* **bien m.** *(vêtu)* well-dressed

mise² [miz] *nf* (a) *(placement)* putting; **m. au point** *(de rapport)* finalization; *Phot* focusing; *(de moteur)* tuning; *(de technique)* perfecting; *Fig (clarification)* clarification; **m. en garde** warning; **m. en scène** *Théât* production; *Cin* direction (b) *(argent)* stake (c) **être de m.** to be acceptable

miser [mize] *vt (argent)* to stake (**sur** on); **m. sur qn/qch** *(parier)* to bet on sb/sth; *(compter sur)* to count on sb/sth

misère [mizɛr] *nf* extreme poverty; **être dans la m.** to be poverty-stricken ■ **misérable 1** *(pitoyable)* miserable; *(pauvre)* destitute; *(existence)* wretched; *(logement, quartier)* seedy, slummy **2** *nmf (indigent)* poor wretch; *(scélérat)* scoundrel

missile [misil] *nm* missile

mission [misjɔ̃] *nf (tâche, organisation)* mission; *(d'employé)* task; **partir en m.** *(cadre)* to go away on business; *(diplomate)* to go off on a mission ■ **missionnaire** *nmf & adj* missionary

mistral [mistral] *nm* **le m.** the mistral

mite [mit] *nf* moth

mi-temps [mitɑ̃] **1** *nf inv Sport (pause)* half-time; *(période)* half **2** *nm inv* part-time job; **travailler à m.** to work part-time

mitigé, -e [mitiʒe] *adj (accueil)* luke-warm

mitoyen, -enne [mitwajɛ̃, -ɛn] *adj* common, shared

mitraillette [mitrajɛt] *nf* submachine gun

mitrailleur [mitrajœr] *adj m* **fusil m.** machine gun

mitrailleuse [mitrajøz] *nf* machine gun

mi-voix [mivwa] **à mi-voix** *adv* in a low voice

mixer¹ [mikse] *vt (à la main)* to mix; *(au mixer)* to blend

mixer², mixeur [miksœr] *nm (pour mélanger)* (food) mixer; *(pour rendre liquide)* liquidizer

mixte [mikst] *adj* mixed; *(école)* co-educational, *Br* mixed

mixture [mikstyr] *nf* mixture

MJC [ɛmʒise] *(abrév* **maison des jeunes et de la culture)** *nf =* youth club and arts centre

Mlle *(abrév* **Mademoiselle)** Miss

MM *(abrév* **Messieurs)** Messrs

mm *(abrév* **millimètre(s))** mm

Mme *(abrév* **Madame)** Mrs

mobile [mɔbil] **1** *adj (pièce, cible)* moving; *(panneau)* movable; *(personne)* mobile; *(feuillets)* loose **2** *nm (décoration)* mobile; *(motif)* motive **(de** for)

mobilier [mɔbilje] *nm* furniture

mobiliser [mɔbilize] *vt,* **se mobiliser** *vpr* to mobilize

Mobylette® [mɔbilɛt] *nf* moped

mode¹ [mɔd] *nf (tendance)* fashion; *(industrie)* fashion industry; **à la m.** fashionable; **à la m. de** in the manner of

mode² [mɔd] *nm (manière)* mode; **m. d'emploi** instructions; **m. de transport** mode of transport; **m. de vie** way of life

modèle [mɔdɛl] **1** *nm (schéma, exemple, personne)* model; *(au tricot)* pattern; **grand/petit m.** *(de vêtement)* large/small size; **m. déposé** registered design **2** *adj* **élève m.** model pupil ■ **modeler** [mɔdle] *vt* to model *(sur* on) **2 se modeler** *vpr* **se m. sur qn** to model oneself on sb

modem [mɔdɛm] *nm Ordinat* modem

modérer [mɔdere] **1** *vt (passions, désirs)* to moderate, to restrain; *(vitesse)* to reduce **2 se modérer** *vpr* to calm down ■ **modération** *nf (retenue)* moderation; *(réduction)* reduction; **avec m.** in moderation ■ **modéré, -e** *adj* moderate

moderne [mɔdɛrn] *adj* modern ■ **moderniser** *vt,* **se moderniser** *vpr* to modernize ■ **modernité** *nf* modernity

modeste [mɔdɛst] *adj* modest ■ **modestie** *nf* modesty

modifier [mɔdifje] **1** *vt* to alter, to modify **2 se modifier** *vpr* to alter ■ **modification** *nf* alteration, modification; **apporter une m. à qch** to make an alteration to sth

modulation [mɔdylɑsjɔ̃] *nf (de son, d'amplitude)* modulation; *Radio* **m. de fréquence** frequency modulation

moelle [mwal] *nf (d'os)* marrow; **m. épinière** spinal cord; **m. osseuse** bone marrow

moelleux, -euse [mwalø, -øz] *adj (lit, tissu)* soft

mœurs [mœr(s)] *nfpl (morale)* morals; *(habitudes)* customs; **entrer dans les m.** to become part of everyday life

moi [mwa] **1** *pron personnel* **(a)** *(après une préposition)* me; **pour/avec m.** for/with me; *Fam* **un ami à m.** a friend of

mine
  (**b**) *(complément direct)* me; **laissez-m.** leave me
  (**c**) *(complément indirect)* (to) me; **montrez-le-m.** show it to me, show me it
  (**d**) *(sujet)* I; **c'est m. qui vous le dis!** I'm telling you!; **il est plus grand que m.** he's taller than I am *or* than me
  2 *nm inv* self, ego ■ **moi-même** *pron* myself

moindre [mwɛ̃dr] *adj (comparatif)* lesser; *(prix)* lower; *(quantité)* smaller; **le/la m.** *(superlatif)* the least; **la m. erreur** the slightest mistake; **dans les moindres détails** in the smallest detail; **c'est la m. des choses** it's the least I/we/*etc* can do

moineau, -x [mwano] *nm* sparrow

MOINS [mwɛ̃] **1** ([mwɛz] *before vowel) adv (comparatif)* less (**que** than); **m. de** *(temps, travail)* less (**que** than); *(gens, livres)* fewer (**que** than); **le/la/les m.** *(superlatif)* the least; **le m. grand, la m. grande, les m. grand(e)s** the smallest); **au m., du m.** at least; **qch de m., qch en m.** *(qui manque)* sth missing; **dix ans de m.** ten years less; **en m.** *(personne, objet)* less; *(personnes, objets)* fewer; **les m. de vingt ans** those under twenty, the under-twenties; **à m. que…** (+ *subjunctive)* unless…
  2 *prép Math* minus; **deux heures m. cinq** five to two; **il fait m. 10 (degrés)** it's minus 10 (degrees)

mois [mwa] *nm* month; **au m. de juin** in (the month of) June

moisir [mwazir] *vi* to go *Br* mouldy *or Am* moldy ■ **moisi, -e 1** *adj Br* mouldy, *Am* moldy **2** *nm Br* mould, *Am* mold; *(sur un mur)* mildew; **sentir le m.** to smell musty ■ **moisissure** *nf Br* mould, *Am* mold

moisson [mwasɔ̃] *nf* harvest; **faire la m.** to harvest ■ **moissonner** *vt (céréales)* to harvest; *(champ)* to reap ■ **moissonneuse-batteuse** *(pl* **moissonneuses-batteuses)** *nf* combine

harvester

moite [mwat] *adj* sticky

moitié [mwatje] *nf* half; **la m. de la pomme** half (of) the apple; **à m.** *(remplir)* halfway; **à m. plein/vide** half-full/-empty; **à m. prix** (at) half-price

moka [mɔka] *nm (café)* mocha; *(gâteau)* coffee cake

mol [mɔl] *voir* **mou**

molaire [mɔlɛr] *nf* molar

molécule [mɔlekyl] *nf* molecule

molester [mɔleste] *vt* to manhandle

molle [mɔl] *voir* **mou**

mollet¹ [mɔlɛ] *nm (de jambe)* calf

mollet² [mɔlɛ] *adj* **œuf m.** soft-boiled egg

mollusque [mɔlysk] *nm* mollusc

moment [mɔmɑ̃] *nm (instant, durée)* moment; **un petit m.** a little while; **en ce m.** at the moment; **pour le m.** for the moment, for the time being; **sur le m.** at the time; **à ce m.-là** *(à ce moment précis)* at that (very) moment, at that time; *(dans ce cas)* then; **à un m. donné** at one point; **le m. venu** *(dans le future)* when the time comes; **d'un m. à l'autre** any moment; **dans ces moments-là** at times like these!; **par moments** at times; **au m. de partir** when just about to leave; **au m. où…** just as…; **jusqu'au m. où…** until…; **du m. que…** *(puisque)* seeing that… ■ **momentané, -e** *adj (temporaire)* momentary; *(bref)* brief ■ **momentanément** *adv (temporairement)* temporarily; *(brièvement)* briefly

mon, ma, mes [mɔ̃, ma, me]

ma becomes **mon** [mɔ̃n] before a vowel or mute h.

adj possessif my; **m. père** my father; **ma mère** my mother; **m. ami(e)** my friend; **mes parents** my parents

Monaco [mɔnako] *nm* Monaco

monarque [mɔnark] *nm* monarch ■ **monarchie** *nf* monarchy

monastère [mɔnastɛr] *nm* monastery

mondain, -e [mɔ̃dɛ̃, -ɛn] *adj* **réunion mondaine** society gathering ■ **mondanités** *nfpl (événements)* social life;

(conversations) social chitchat

monde [mɔ̃d] *nm* world; *(gens)* people; **dans le m. entier** worldwide, all over the world; **tout le m.** everybody; **il y a du m.** there are a lot of people; **venir au m.** to come into the world ■ **mondial, -e, -aux, -ales** *adj (crise, renommée)* worldwide; **guerre mondiale** world war ■ **mondialisation** *nf* globalization

monégasque [monegask] **1** *adj* Monégasque **2** *nmf* **M.** Monegasque

monétaire [moneter] *adj* monetary

mongolien, -enne [mɔ̃goljɛ̃, -ɛn] **1** *adj* **être m.** to have Down's syndrome **2** *nmf* person with Down's syndrome

moniteur, -trice [monitœr, -tris] **1** *nmf (de colonie)* Br assistant, Am camp counselor **2** *nm* Ordinat *(écran)* monitor

monnaie [monɛ] *nf (argent)* money; *(de)* currency; *(pièces)* change; **petite m.** small change; **faire de la m.** to get change; **avoir la m. de 100 euros** to have change for 100 euros; **m. électronique** plastic money; **m. unique** single currency

monoparentale [monoparɑ̃tal] *adj f* **famille m.** one-parent family

monoplace [monoplas] *adj & nmf* single-seater

monopole [monopol] *nm* monopoly; **avoir le m. de qch** to have a monopoly on sth ■ **monopoliser** *vt* to monopolize

monoski [monoski] *nm* mono-ski; **faire du m.** to mono-ski

monotone [monoton] *adj* monotonous ■ **monotonie** *nf* monotony

monseigneur [mɔ̃sɛɲœr] *(pl* **messeigneurs)** *nm (évêque)* His/Your Lordship; *(prince)* His/Your Highness

monsieur [məsjø] *(pl* **messieurs)** *nm (homme quelconque)* gentleman; **M. Legras** Mr Legras; **bonsoir, messieurs-dames!** good evening!; **M.** *(dans une lettre)* Dear Sir

monstre [mɔ̃str] *nm* monster; **m. sacré** giant ■ **monstrueux, -euse** *adj (mal formé, scandaleux)* monstrous;

(énorme) huge

mont [mɔ̃] *nm* mount

montage [mɔ̃taʒ] *nm Tech* assembling; Cin editing; *(image truquée)* montage

montagne [mɔ̃taɲ] *nf* mountain; **la m.** *(zone)* the mountains; **à la m.** in the mountains; **en haute m.** high in the mountains; **montagnes russes** *(attraction foraine)* rollercoaster ■ **montagnard, -e** *nmf* mountain dweller ■ **montagneux, -euse** *adj* mountainous

montant, -e 1 *adj (marée)* rising; *(col)* stand-up **2** *nm (somme)* amount; *(de barrière)* post; **montants compensatoires** subsidies

monte-charge [mɔ̃tʃarʒ] *(pl* **monte-charges)** *nm* service Br lift or Am elevator

montée [mɔ̃te] *nf (ascension)* climb, ascent; *(chemin)* slope; *(des prix, du fascisme)* rise; **la m. des eaux** the rise in the water level

monter [mɔ̃te] **1** *(aux avoir) vt (côte)* to climb up); *(objet)* to bring/take up); *(cheval)* to ride; *(son)* to turn up; *(tente)* to put up; *(machine)* to assemble; *(pièce de théâtre)* to stage; **m. l'escalier** to go/come upstairs *or* up the stairs

2 *(aux* **être)** *vi (personne)* to go/come up; *(prix)* to rise; *(marée)* to come in; *(avion)* to climb; **faire m. qn** to show sb up; **m. dans un véhicule** to get in(to) a vehicle; **m. sur qch** to climb onto sth; **m. sur** *ou* **à une échelle** to climb up a ladder; **m. en courant** to run up; Sport **m. à cheval** to ride (a horse)

3 *se monter upr* **se m. à** *(s'élever à)* to amount to

monteur, -euse [mɔ̃tœr, -øz] *nmf* Cin editor

montre [mɔ̃tr] *nf (instrument)* (wrist-)watch; Sport & Fig **course contre la m.** race against the clock

Montréal [mɔ̃real] *nm ou f* Montreal

montrer [mɔ̃tre] **1** *vt* to show (**à** to); **m. qn/qch du doigt** to point at sb/sth; **m.**

le chemin à qn to show sb the way **2 se montrer** *vpr* to show oneself; **se m. courageux** to be courageous

monture [mɔ̃tyr] *nf* (*de lunettes*) frame; (*de bijou*) setting

monument [mɔnymɑ̃] *nm* monument; **m. historique** ancient monument; **m. aux morts** war memorial ▪ **monumental, -e, -aux, -ales** *adj* (*imposant, énorme*) monumental

moquer [mɔke] **se moquer** *vpr* **se m. de qn** to make fun of sb; **se m. de qch** (*rire de*) to make fun of sth; (*ne pas se soucier*) not to care about sth ▪ **moquerie** *nf* mockery ▪ **moqueur, -euse** *adj* mocking

moquette [mɔkɛt] *nf Br* fitted carpet, *Am* wall-to-wall carpeting

moral, -e, -aux, -ales [mɔral, -o] **1** *adj* moral **2** *nm* **avoir le m.** to be in good spirits ▪ **morale** *nf* (*d'histoire*) moral; (*principes*) morals; (*règles*) morality; **faire la m. à qn** to lecture sb ▪ **moralité** *nf* (*mœurs*) morality; (*de récit*) moral

morceau, -x [mɔrso] *nm* piece, bit; (*de sucre*) lump; (*de viande*) cut; **tomber en morceaux** to fall to pieces ▪ **morceler** *vt* (*terrain*) to divide up

mordiller [mɔrdije] *vt* to nibble

mordre [mɔrdr] **1** *vti* to bite; **m. qn au bras** to bite sb's arm; **2 se mordre** *vpr Fig* **se m. les doigts d'avoir fait qch** to kick oneself for doing sth

mordu, -e [mɔrdy] *pp de* **mordre**

morgue [mɔrg] *nf* (*d'hôpital*) mortuary; (*pour corps non identifiés*) morgue

moribond, -e [mɔribɔ̃, -ɔ̃d] **1** *adj* dying **2** *nmf* dying person

morne [mɔrn] *adj* (*temps*) dismal; (*silence*) gloomy; (*personne*) glum

morose [mɔroz] *adj* morose

mors [mɔr] *nm* (*de harnais*) bit

morse [mɔrs] *nm* (*code*) Morse (code)

morsure [mɔrsyr] *nf* bite

mort¹ [mɔr] *nf* death; **se donner la m.** to take one's own life; **un silence de m.** a deathly silence ▪ **mortalité** *nf* death rate, mortality ▪ **mortel, -elle**

1 *adj* (*hommes, ennemi, danger*) mortal; (*accident*) fatal **2** *nmf* mortal ▪ **mortellement** *adv* (*blessé*) fatally

mort², morte [mɔr, mɔrt] **1** *adj* (*personne, plante, ville*) dead; **m. de fatigue** dead tired; **m. de froid** numb with cold; **m. de peur** frightened to death; **m. ou vif** dead or alive **2** *nmf* dead man, *f* dead woman; **les morts** the dead; **de nombreux morts** (*victimes*) many deaths; **le jour** *ou* **la fête des Morts** All Souls' Day ▪ **morte-saison** (*pl* **mortes-saisons**) *nf* off-season ▪ **mort-né, -e** (*mpl* **mort-nés**, *fpl* **mort-nées**) *adj* (*enfant*) stillborn

morue [mɔry] *nf* cod

mosaïque [mɔzaik] *nf* mosaic

Moscou [mɔsku] *nm ou f* Moscow

mot [mo] *nm* word; **envoyer un m. à qn** to drop sb a line; **m. à m.** word for word; **avoir le dernier m.** to have the last word; **mots croisés** crossword (puzzle); **m. de passe** password

motel [mɔtɛl] *nm* motel

moteur¹ [mɔtœr] *nm* (*de véhicule*) engine; (*électrique*) motor

moteur², -trice [mɔtœr, -tris] **1** *adj* (*nerf, muscle*) motor; **voiture à quatre roues motrices** four-wheel drive (car) **2** *nf* **motrice** (*de train*) engine

motif [mɔtif] *nm* (*raison*) reason (**de** for); (*dessin*) pattern

motiver [mɔtive] *vt* (*inciter, causer*) to motivate; (*justifier*) to justify ▪ **motivation** *nf* motivation ▪ **motivé, -e** *adj* motivated

moto [mɔto] *nf* motorbike ▪ **motocycliste** *nmf* motorcyclist

motte [mɔt] *nf* (*de terre*) lump, clod; (*de beurre*) block

mou, molle [mu, mɔl]

mol is used before masculine singular nouns beginning with a vowel or h mute.

adj soft; (*sans énergie*) feeble ▪ **mollesse** *nf* (*de matelas*) softness; (*de personne*) lethargy

mouche [muʃ] *nf* (*insecte*) fly; **faire m.** to hit the bull's-eye ▪ **moucheron** *nm* midge

moucher [muʃe] **1** vt **m. qn** to wipe sb 's nose **2 se moucher** vpr to blow one's nose

moucheté, -e [muʃte] adj speckled

mouchoir [muʃwar] nm handkerchief; **m. en papier** tissue

moudre* [mudr] vt to grind

mouette [mwet] nf (sea)gull

moufle [mufl] nf mitten, mitt

mouiller [muje] **1** vt to wet **2** vi Naut to anchor **3 se mouiller** vpr to get wet ■ **mouillé, -e** adj wet (**de** with)

moule¹ [mul] nm Br mould, Am mold; **m. à gâteaux** cake tin ■ **moulage** (objet) cast ■ **moulant, -e** adj (vêtement) tight-fitting ■ **mouler** vt Br to mould, Am to mold; (statue) to cast

moule² [mul] nf (mollusque) mussel

moulin [mulɛ̃] nm mill; **m. à café** coffee grinder; **m. à vent** windmill

moulinet [mulinɛ] nm (de canne à pêche) reel

moulu, -e [muly] **1** pp de **moudre 2** adj (café) ground

mourir* [murir] (aux être) vi to die (**de** of or from); **m. de froid** to die of exposure; Fig **m. de fatigue** to be dead tired; Fig **m. de peur** to be frightened to death; Fig **je meurs de faim!** I'm starving! ■ **mourant, -e 1** adj dying; (voix) faint **2** nmf dying person

mousse [mus] **1** nf (plante) moss; (écume) foam; (de bière) head; (de savon) lather; **m. à raser** shaving foam; Culin **m. au chocolat** chocolate mousse **2** nm (marin) ship's boy ■ **mousser** vi (bière) to froth; (savon) to lather ■ **mousseux, -euse 1** adj (vin) sparkling **2** nm sparkling wine

moustache [mustaʃ] nf (d'homme) moustache, Am mustache; (de chat) whiskers ■ **moustachu, -e** adj with a Br moustache or Am mustache

moustique [mustik] nm mosquito ■ **moustiquaire** nf mosquito net; (en métal) screen

moutarde [mutard] nf mustard

mouton [mutɔ̃] nm sheep inv; (viande)

mutton; **moutons** (écume) Br white horses, Am whitecaps; (poussière) fluff; **peau de m.** sheepskin

mouvement [muvmɑ̃] nm (geste, groupe, déplacement) movement; (élan) impulse; (de gymnastique) exercise; **en m.** in motion; **m. de colère** fit of anger; **mouvements sociaux** workers' protest movements ■ **mouvementé, -e** adj (vie, voyage) eventful

mouvoir* [muvwar] vi, **se mouvoir** vpr to move; **mû par** (mécanisme) driven by

MOYEN¹, -ENNE [mwajɛ̃, -ɛn] **1** adj average; (format, entreprise) medium(-sized)

2 nf **moyenne** average; **en moyenne** on average; **la moyenne d'âge** the average age; **avoir la moyenne** (à un examen) Br to get a pass mark, Am to get a pass; (à un devoir) to get 50 percent, Br to get half marks; **le M. Âge** the Middle Ages

moyen² [mwajɛ̃] nm (procédé, façon) means, way (**de faire** of doing or to do); **moyens** (capacités mentales) ability; (argent, ressources) means; **je n'ai pas les moyens** (argent) I can't afford it; **au m. de qch** by means of sth

Mozambique [mɔzɑ̃bik] nm **le M.** Mozambique

MST [emeste] (abrév **maladie sexuellement transmissible**) nf STD

muer [mɥe] **1** vi (animal) Br to moult, Am to molt; (voix) to break **2 se muer** vpr **se m. en qch** to change into sth

muet, muette [mɥe, mɥet] **1** adj (infirme) dumb; (de surprise) speechless; (film) silent **2** nmf mute

muguet [mɥge] nm lily of the valley

mule [myl] nf (pantoufle, animal) mule ■ **mulet** nm (équidé) mule; (poisson) mullet

multicolore [myltikɔlɔr] adj Br multicoloured, Am multicolored

multinationale [myltinasjɔnal] nf multinational

multiple [myltipl] *adj (nombreux)* numerous; *(varié)* multiple ■ **multiplication** *nf (calcul)* multiplication; *(augmentation)* increase ■ **multiplier 1** *vt* to multiply **2 se multiplier** *vpr* to increase; *(se reproduire)* to multiply

multitude [myltityd] *nf* multitude

municipal, -e, -aux, -ales [mynisipal, -o] *adj* municipal ■ **municipalité** *nf (maires et conseillers)* local council; *(commune)* municipality

munir [mynir] **1** *vt* **m. de qch** *(personne)* to provide with sth **2 se munir** *vpr* **se m. de qch** to take sth

munitions [mynisjɔ̃] *nfpl* ammunition

mur [myr] *nm* wall; *Fig* **au pied du m.** with one's back to the wall; **m. du son** sound barrier ■ **muraille** *nf (high)* wall ■ **mural, -e, -aux, -ales** *adj* **carte murale** wall map; **peinture murale** mural (painting) ■ **murer** *vt (porte)* to wall up

mûr, mûre¹ [myr] *adj (fruit)* ripe; *(personne)* mature; **d'âge m.** middle-aged ■ **mûrir** *vti (fruit)* to ripen; *(personne)* to mature

mûre² [myr] *nf (baie)* blackberry

muret [myrɛ] *nm* low wall

murmure [myrmyr] *nm* murmur ■ **murmurer** *vti* to murmur

muscle [myskl] *nm* muscle ■ **musclé, -e** *adj (bras)* muscular ■ **musculaire** *adj (force, douleur)* muscular ■ **musculature** *nf* muscles

museau, -x [myzo] *nm (de chien, de chat)* muzzle ■ **museler** *vt (animal, presse)* to muzzle

musée [myze] *nm* museum; **m. de peinture** art gallery ■ **muséum** *nm* natural history museum

music-hall [myzikol] *(pl* **music-halls***) nm (genre, salle)* music hall

musique [myzik] *nf* music ■ **musical, -e, -aux, -ales** *adj* musical ■ **musicien, -enne 1** *nmf* musician **2** *adj* musical

musulman, -e [myzylmɑ̃, -an] *adj & nmf* Muslim, Moslem

muter [myte] *vt* to transfer ■ **mutant, -e** *adj & nmf* mutant ■ **mutation** *nf (d'employé)* transfer; *Biol* mutation

mutiler [mytile] *vt* to mutilate, to maim; **être mutilé** to be disabled

mutin [mytɛ̃] *nm (rebelle)* mutineer ■ **mutinerie** *nf* mutiny

mutisme [mytism] *nm* silence

mutuel, -elle [mytɥɛl] **1** *adj (réciproque)* mutual **2** *nf* **mutuelle** mutual insurance company ■ **mutuellement** *adv* each other

myope [mjɔp] *adj* shortsighted

myrtille [mirtij] *nf (baie)* bilberry

mystère [mistɛr] *nm* mystery ■ **mystérieux, -euse** *adj* mysterious

mystique [mistik] **1** *adj* mystical **2** *nmf (personne)* mystic

mythe [mit] *nm* myth ■ **mythique** *adj* mythical ■ **mythologie** *nf* mythology ■ **mythologique** *adj* mythological

Nn

N¹, n [ɛn] *nm inv* N, n

N² (*abrév* **route nationale**) M

n' [n] *voir* **ne**

nacelle [nasɛl] *nf (de ballon)* basket

nacre [nakr] *nf* mother-of-pearl ■ **nacré, -e** *adj* pearly

nage [naʒ] *nf (swimming)* stroke; **traverser une rivière à la n.** to swim across a river; **n. libre** freestyle

nageoire [naʒwar] *nf (de poisson)* fin; *(de dauphin)* flipper

nager [naʒe] *vti* to swim ■ **nageur, -euse** *nmf* swimmer

naïf, naïve [naif, naiv] *adj* naïve

nain, naine [nɛ̃, nɛn] *adj & nmf* dwarf

naissance [nɛsɑ̃s] *nf (de personne, d'animal)* birth; *(enfant)* to give birth to; **de n.** from birth

naître* [nɛtr] *vi* to be born; *(sentiment, difficulté)* to arise (**de** from); *(idée)* to originate

naïveté [naivte] *nf* naïvety

nantir [nɑ̃tir] *vt* **n. qn de qch** to provide sb with sth ■ **nanti, -e 1** *adj* well-to-do **2** *nmpl Péj* **les nantis** the well-to-do

nappe [nap] *nf (de table)* tablecloth; **n. de brouillard** fog patch; **n. d'eau** expanse of water; **n. de pétrole** layer of oil; *(de marée noire)* oil slick

napper [nape] *vt* to coat (**de** with)

narguer [narge] *vt* to taunt

narine [narin] *nf* nostril

narquois, -e [narkwa, -az] *adj* sneering

nasal, -e, -aux, -ales [nazal, -o] *adj* nasal

nasillard, -e [nazijar, -ard] *adj (voix)* nasal

natal, -e, -als, -ales [natal] *adj* native

natalité [natalite] *nf* birth rate

natation [natasjɔ̃] *nf* swimming

natif, -ive [natif, -iv] *adj & nmf* native; **être n. de** to be a native of

nation [nasjɔ̃] *nf* nation; **les Nations unies** the United Nations ■ **national, -e, -aux, -ales** *adj* national ■ **nationale** *nf (route) Br* ≃ A road, *Am* ≃ highway ■ **nationaliser** *vt* to nationalize ■ **nationaliste 1** *adj* nationalistic **2** *nmf* nationalist ■ **nationalité** *nf* nationality

natte [nat] *nf (de cheveux) Br* plait, *Am* braid

naturaliser [natyralize] *vt* to naturalize ■ **naturalisation** *nf* naturalization

nature [natyr] **1** *nf (univers, caractère)* nature; *(campagne)* country; **contre n.** unnatural; **en pleine n.** in the middle of the country; **payer en n.** to pay in kind; **n. morte** still life **2** *adj inv (omelette, yaourt)* plain; *(thé)* without milk

naturel, -elle [natyrɛl] **1** *adj (naturel, mort naturelle* death from natural causes **2** *nm (caractère)* nature; *(simplicité)* naturalness ■ **naturellement** *adv* naturally

naufrage [nofraʒ] *nm (ship)wreck; **faire n.** *(bateau)* to be wrecked; *(marin)* to be shipwrecked

nausée [noze] *nf* nausea, sickness; **avoir la n.** to feel sick

nautique [notik] *adj* nautical

naval, -e, -als, -ales [naval] *adj* naval

navet [navɛ] *nm (légume)* turnip

navette [navɛt] *nf (véhicule)* shuttle; **faire la n.** *(véhicule, personne)* to shuttle back and forth (**entre** between); **n. spatiale** space shuttle

navigable [navigabl] *adj (fleuve)* navigable

navigant, -e [navigɑ̃, -ɑ̃t] *adj Aviat* **personnel n.** flight crew

navigateur [navigatœr] *nm (marin)* navigator ▪ **navigation** *nf* navigation

naviguer [navige] *vi (bateau)* to sail; **n. sur Internet** to surf the Net

navire [navir] *nm* ship

navrer [navre] *vt* to appal ▪ **navrant, -e** *adj* appalling ▪ **navré, -e** *adj (air)* distressed; **je suis n.** I'm terribly sorry

ne [nə]

n' before vowel or mute h; used to form negative verb with **pas, jamais, personne, rien** etc.

adv ne... pas not; **il ne boit pas** he does not *or* doesn't drink; **elle n'ose (pas)** she doesn't dare; **ne... que** only; **je crains qu'il ne parte** I'm afraid he'll leave

né, -e [ne] **1** *pp de* **naître** born; **il est né en 2001** he was born in 2001; **née Dupont** née Dupont **2** *adj* born; **c'est un poète-né** he's a born poet

néanmoins [neɑ̃mwɛ̃] *adv* nevertheless

néant [neɑ̃] *nm* nothingness; *(sur formulaire)* ≃ none

nécessaire [neseser] **1** *adj* necessary **2** *nm* **le n.** the necessities; **faire le n.** to do what's necessary; **n. de toilette** toilet bag

nécessité [nesesite] *nf* necessity ▪ **nécessiter** *vt* to require, to necessitate

nectarine [nɛktarin] *nf* nectarine

néerlandais, -e [neɛrlɑ̃dɛ, -ɛz] **1** *adj* Dutch **2** *nmf* **N.** Dutchman; **Néerlandaise** Dutchwoman **3** *nm (langue)* Dutch

nef [nɛf] *nf (d'église)* nave

néfaste [nefast] *adj* harmful (**à** to)

négatif, -ive [negatif, -iv] **1** *adj* negative **2** *nm (de photo)* negative

négligeable [negliʒabl] *adj* negligible; **non n.** *(quantité)* significant

négligent, -e [negliʒɑ̃, -ɑ̃t] *adj* careless, negligent ▪ **négligence** *nf (défaut)* carelessness, negligence

négliger [negliʒe] *vt (personne, travail, conseil)* to neglect; **n. de faire qch** to neglect to do sth **2 se négliger** *vpr* to neglect oneself ▪ **négligé, -e** *adj (tenue)* untidy; *(travail)* careless

négocier [negɔsje] *vti* to negotiate ▪ **négociable** *adj* negotiable ▪ **négociant, -e** *nmf* merchant, dealer ▪ **négociateur, -trice** *nmf* negotiator ▪ **négociation** *nf* negotiation

neige [nɛʒ] *nf* snow; **aller à la n.** to go skiing; **n. fondue** sleet ▪ **neiger** *v impersonnel* to snow; **il neige** it's snowing

néon [neɔ̃] *nm (gaz)* neon; *(enseigne)* neon sign; **éclairage au n.** neon lighting

néo-zélandais, -e [neozelɑ̃dɛ, -ɛz] *(mpl* **néo-zélandais,** *fpl* **néo-zélandaises) 1** *adj* New Zealand **2** *nmf* **N., Néo-Zélandaise** New Zealander

nerf [nɛr] *nm* nerve ▪ **nerveux, -euse** *adj* nervous ▪ **nervosité** *nf* nervousness

n'est-ce pas [nɛspɑ] *adv* isn't he?/ don't you?/won't they?/*etc;* **tu viendras, n.?** you'll come, won't you?; **il fait beau, n.?** the weather's nice, isn't it?

Net [nɛt] *nm* **le N.** the Net

net, nette [nɛt] **1** *adj (propre)* clean; *(image, refus)* clear; *(écriture)* neat; *(prix, salaire)* net; **n. d'impôt** net of tax **2** *adv (casser, couper)* clean; *(tuer)* outright; *(refuser)* flatly; **s'arrêter n.** to stop dead ▪ **nettement** *adv (avec précision)* clearly; *(incontestablement)* definitely; **il va n. mieux** he's much better ▪ **netteté** *nf (propreté, précision)* cleanness; *(de travail)* neatness

nettoyer [netwaje] **1** *vt* to clean **2 se nettoyer** *vpr* **se n. les oreilles** to clean one's ears ▪ **nettoyage** *nm* cleaning; **n. à sec** dry-cleaning

neuf¹, neuve [nœf, nœv] **1** *adj* new; **quoi de n.?** what's new? **2** *nm* **remettre qch à n.** to make sth as good as new

neuf² [nœf, nœv *before* **heures, ans**] *adj & nm* nine ■ **neuvième** *adj & nmf* ninth

neutre [nøtr] **1** *adj (pays, personne)* neutral **2** *nm* **É**l neutral ■ **neutraliser** *vt* to neutralize ■ **neutralité** *nf* neutrality

neveu, -x [nəvø] *nm* nephew

nez [ne] *nm* nose; **n. à n.** face to face (**avec** with); **rire au n. de qn** to laugh in sb's face; **parler du n.** to speak through one's nose

ni [ni] *conj* **ni... ni...** neither... nor...; **ni Pierre ni Paul ne sont venus** neither Pierre nor Paul came; **il n'a ni faim ni soif** he's neither hungry nor thirsty; **sans manger ni boire** without eating or drinking; **ni l'un(e) ni l'autre** neither (of them)

Nicaragua [nikaragwa] *nm* **le N.** Nicaragua

niche [niʃ] *nf (de chien) Br* kennel, *Am* doghouse; *(cavité)* niche, recess

nicher [niʃe] **1** *vi (oiseau)* to nest **2 se nicher** *vpr (oiseau)* to nest ■ **nichée** *nf (chiens)* litter; *(oiseaux)* brood

nickel [nikɛl] *nm (métal)* nickel

nicotine [nikɔtin] *nf* nicotine

nid [ni] *nm* nest

nièce [njɛs] *nf* niece

nier [nje] **1** *vt* to deny (**que** that) **2** *vi (accusé)* to deny the charge

Niger [niʒɛr] *nm* **le N.** *(pays)* Niger

Nigéria [niʒerja] *nm* **le N.** Nigeria

Nil [nil] *nm* **le N.** the Nile

n'importe [nɛ̃pɔrt] *voir* **importer¹**

nippon, -one *ou* **-onne** [nipɔ̃, -ɔn] *adj* Japanese

niveau, -x [nivo] *nm (hauteur, étage, degré)* level; *Scol* standard; **au n. de la mer** at sea level; **n. de vie** standard of living ■ **niveler** *vt (surface)* to level

noble [nɔbl] **1** *adj* noble **2** *nmf* nobleman, *f* noblewoman ■ **noblesse** *nf (caractère, classe)* nobility

noce [nɔs] *nf* wedding; **noces d'or** golden wedding

nocif, -ive [nɔsif, -iv] *adj* harmful ■ **nocivité** *nf* harmfulness

nocturne [nɔktyrn] **1** *adj (animal)* nocturnal **2** *nf (de magasin)* late-night opening; *Sport* **(match en) n.** evening match

Noël [nɔɛl] *nm* Christmas; **arbre de N.** Christmas tree; **le père N.** Father Christmas, Santa Claus

nœud [nø] *nm* **(a)** *(entrecroisement)* knot; *(ruban)* bow; **n. papillon** bow tie (**b**) *Naut (vitesse)* knot

noir, -e [nwar] **1** *adj* black; *(sombre)* dark; *(idées)* gloomy; *(misère)* dire; **il fait n.** it's dark; **film n.** film noir **2** *nm (couleur)* black; *(obscurité)* dark; **N.** *(homme)* Black (man); **3** *nf* **noire** *(note) Br* crotchet, *Am* quarter note; **Noire** *(femme)* Black (woman) ■ **noircir** **1** *vt* to blacken **2** *vi* to turn black

noisette [nwazɛt] *nf* hazelnut

noix [nwa] *nf (du noyer)* walnut; **n. de coco** coconut

nom [nɔ̃] *nm* name; *Gram* noun; **au n. de qn** on sb's behalf; **n. de famille** surname; **n. de jeune fille** maiden name

nomade [nɔmad] **1** *adj* nomadic **2** *nmf* nomad

nombre [nɔ̃br] *nm* number; **être au** *ou* **du n. de** to be among; **ils sont au n. de dix** there are ten of them; **le plus grand n. de** the majority of; **bon n. de** a good many; *Math* **n. premier** prime number

nombreux, -euse [nɔ̃brø, -øz] *adj (amis, livres)* numerous, many; *(famille, collection)* large; **peu n.** few; **venir n.** to come in large numbers

nombril [nɔ̃bri] *nm* navel

nominal, -e, -aux, -ales [nɔminal, -o] *adj* nominal

nomination [nɔminasjɔ̃] *nf (à un poste)* appointment; *(pour récompense)* nomination

nommer [nɔme] **1** *vt (appeler)* to name; **n. qn** *(désigner)* to appoint sb (**à un poste** to a post); **n. qn président**

to appoint sb chairman **2 se nommer** *vpr (s'appeler)* to be called

non [nɔ̃] *adv* no; **tu viens ou n.?** are you coming or not?; **n. seulement** not only; **n. (pas) que...** (*+ subjunctive*) not that...; **n. loin** not far; **je crois que n.** I don't think so; **(ni) moi n. plus** neither do/am/can/*etc* I

nonante [nɔnɑ̃t] *adj & nm (en Belgique, en Suisse)* ninety

nonchalant, -e [nɔ̃ʃalɑ̃, -ɑ̃t] *adj* nonchalant

non-fumeur, -euse [nɔ̃fymœr, -øz] **1** *adj* non-smoking **2** *nmf* non-smoker

non-retour [nɔ̃rətur] *nm* point de n. point of no return

non-violence [nɔ̃vjɔlɑ̃s] *nf* non-violence

non-voyants [nɔ̃vwajɑ̃] *nmpl* **les n.** the unsighted

nord [nɔr] **1** *nm* north; **au n.** in the north; *(direction)* (to the) north (**de** of); *(vent, direction)* northerly; *(ville)* northern; *(gens)* from/in the north; **l'Afrique du N.** North Africa; **l'Europe du N.** Northern Europe; **le grand N.** the Frozen North **2** *adj inv (côte)* north; *(régions)* northern ▪ **nord-africain, -e** (*mpl* **nord-africains**, *fpl* **nord-africaines**) **1** *adj* North African **2** *nmf* **N., Nord-Africaine** North African ▪ **nord-américain, -e** (*mpl* **nord-américains**, *fpl* **nord-américaines**) **1** *adj* North American **2** *nmf* **N., Nord-Américaine** North American ▪ **nord-est** *nm & adj inv* northeast ▪ **nord-ouest** *nm & adj inv* northwest

nordique [nɔrdik] **1** *adj* Scandinavian **2** *nmf* **N.** Scandinavian; *Can* Northern Canadian

normal, -e, -aux, -ales [nɔrmal, -o] *adj* normal ▪ **normale** *nf* norm; **au-dessus/au-dessous de la n.** above/below average; *Fam* **N. Sup** = university-level college preparing students for senior posts in teaching ▪ **normalement** *adv* normally ▪ **normaliser** *vt (uniformiser)* to standardize; *(relations)* to normalize

normand, -e [nɔrmɑ̃, -ɑ̃d] **1** *adj* Norman **2** *nmf* **N., Normande** Norman ▪ **Normandie** *nf* la N. Normandy

norme [nɔrm] *nf* norm; **normes de sécurité** safety standards

Norvège [nɔrvɛʒ] *nf* **la N.** Norway ▪ **norvégien, -enne 1** *adj* Norwegian **2** *nmf* **N., Norvégienne** Norwegian **3** *nm (langue)* Norwegian

nos [no] *voir* **notre**

nostalgie [nɔstalʒi] *nf* nostalgia ▪ **nostalgique** *adj* nostalgic

notable [nɔtabl] *adj & nm* notable

notaire [nɔter] *nm* lawyer, *Br* notary (public)

notamment [nɔtamɑ̃] *adv* notably

note [nɔt] *nf (annotation, communication) & Mus* note; *Scol Br* mark, *Am* grade; *(facture) Br* bill, *Am* check; **prendre n. de qch** to make a note of sth; **prendre des notes** to take notes; **n. de frais** expenses

noter [nɔte] *vt (remarquer)* to note; *(écrire)* to note down; *(devoir) Br* to mark, *Am* to grade

notice [nɔtis] *nf (mode d'emploi)* instructions; *(de médicament)* directions

notifier [nɔtifje] *vt* **n. qch à qn** to notify sb of sth

notion [nɔsjɔ̃] *nf* notion; **notions** *(éléments)* rudiments; **avoir des notions de qch** to know the basics of sth

notoriété [nɔtɔrjete] *nf (renom)* fame; **il est de n. publique que...** it's common knowledge that...

notre, nos [nɔtr, no] *adj possessif* our

nôtre [notr] **1** *pron possessif* **le/la n., les nôtres** ours **2** *nmpl* **les nôtres** *(parents)* our family

nouer [nwe] **1** *vt (lacets)* to tie; *(cravate)* to knot; *Fig (relation)* to establish **2 se nouer** *vpr (intrigue)* to take shape

nougat [nuga] *nm* nougat

nouilles [nuj] *nfpl* noodles

nourrice [nuris] *nf (assistante maternelle)* (children's) nurse, *Br* childminder; *(qui allaite)* wet nurse

nourrir [nurir] **1** vt (alimenter) to feed; Fig (espoir) to cherish **2 se nourrir** vpr to eat; **se n. de qch** to feed on sth

nourrisson [nurisɔ̃] nm infant

nourriture [nurityr] nf food

nous [nu] pron personnel (**a**) (sujet) we; **n. sommes ici** we are here (**b**) (complément direct) us; **il n. connaît** he knows us (**c**) (complément indirect) (to) us; **il n. l'a donné** he gave it to us, he gave us it (**d**) (réfléchi) ourselves; **n. n. lavons** we wash ourselves; **n. n. habillons** we get dressed (**e**) (réciproque) each other; **n. n. détestons** we hate each other ∎ **nous-mêmes** pron ourselves

nouveau, -elle¹, -x, -elles [nuvo, -ɛl]

nouvel is used before masculine singular nouns beginning with a vowel or mute h.

1 adj new; (mode) latest; **on craint de nouvelles inondations** (d'autres) further flooding is feared **2** nmf (à l'école) new boy, f new girl **3** nm **du n.** something new **4** adv **de n.**, **à n.** again ∎ **nouveau-né, -e** (mpl **nouveau-nés**, fpl **nouveau-nées**) **1** adj newborn **2** nmf newborn baby

nouveauté [nuvote] nf novelty; **nouveautés** (livres) new books; (disques) new releases

nouvelle² [nuvɛl] nf (**a**) **une n.** (annonce) a piece of news; **la n. de sa mort** the news of his/her death; **les nouvelles** the news (sing); **avoir des nouvelles de qn** (directement) to have heard from sb (**b**) (récit) short story

Nouvelle-Calédonie [nuvɛlkaledɔni] nf **la N.** New Caledonia

Nouvelle-Zélande [nuvɛlzelɑ̃d] nf **la N.** New Zealand

novateur, -trice [nɔvatœr, -tris] adj innovative

novembre [nɔvɑ̃br] nm November

noyade [nwajad] nf drowning

noyau, -x [nwajo] nm (de fruit) stone, Am pit; (d'atome, de cellule) nucleus; (groupe) group; **n. dur** (de groupe) hard core

noyauter [nwajote] vt to infiltrate

noyé, -e [nwaje] nmf drowned person

noyer¹ [nwaje] **1** vt (personne) to drown; (terres) to flood **2 se noyer** vpr to drown; **se n. dans les détails** to get bogged down in details

noyer² [nwaje] nm (arbre) walnut tree

nu, -e [ny] **1** adj (personne, vérité) naked; (mains, chambre) bare; **tout nu** (stark) naked, (in the) nude; **tête nue, nu-tête** bare-headed; **aller pieds nus** to go barefoot **2** nm nude; **mettre qch à nu** to expose sth

nuage [nɥaʒ] nm cloud; Fig **être dans les nuages** to have one's head in the clouds ∎ **nuageux, -euse** adj (ciel) cloudy

nuance [nɥɑ̃s] nf (de couleur) shade; (de sens) nuance; (de regret) tinge ∎ **nuancé, -e** adj (jugement) qualified ∎ **nuancer** vt (pensée) to qualify

nucléaire [nykleɛr] **1** adj nuclear **2** nm nuclear energy

nudiste [nydist] nmf nudist ∎ **nudité** nf (de personne) nudity, nakedness

nuée [nɥe] nf **une n. de** (foule) a horde of; (groupe compact) a cloud of

nuire* [nɥir] vi **n. à qn/qch** to harm sb/sth ∎ **nuisible** adj harmful (**à** to)

nuit [nɥi] nf night; (obscurité) dark(-ness); **la n.** (se promener) at night; **cette n.** (hier) last night; (aujourd'hui) tonight; **avant la n.** before nightfall; **il fait n.** it's dark; **il fait n. noire** it's pitch-black; **bonne n.!** good night! ∎ **nuitée** nf overnight stay

nul, nulle [nyl] **1** adj (médiocre) hopeless, useless; (risque) non-existent, nil; Jur (non valable) null (and void); **être n. en qch** to be hopeless at sth **2** adj indéfini Littéraire (aucun) no; **sans n. doute** without any doubt **3** pron indéfini m Littéraire (aucun) no one ∎ **nulle part** adv nowhere; **n. ailleurs** nowhere else

numérique [nymerik] adj numerical;

(montre, clavier, données) digital
numéro [nymero] *nm (chiffre)* number; *(de journal)* issue, number; *(au cirque)* act; *Tél* **n. vert** *Br* ≃ Freefone® number, *Am* ≃ toll-free number; **n. de téléphone** telephone number ■ **numéroter** *vt (pages, sièges)* to number

nuptial, -ale, -aux, -ales [nypsjal, -jo] *adj (chambre)* bridal; **cérémonie nuptiale** wedding ceremony
nuque [nyk] *nf* back of the neck
nutrition [nytrisjɔ̃] *nf* nutrition
Nylon® [nilɔ̃] *nm (fibre)* nylon; **chemise en N.** nylon shirt

Oo

O, o [o] *nm inv* O, o

obéir [ɔbeir] *vi* to obey; **o. à qn/qch** to obey sb/sth ▪ **obéissance** *nf* obedience (**à** to) ▪ **obéissant, -e** *adj* obedient

obèse [ɔbɛz] *adj* obese ▪ **obésité** [ɔbesite] *nf* obesity

objecter [ɔbʒɛkte] *vt* **o. que...** to object that... ▪ **objecteur** *nm* **o. de conscience** conscientious objector ▪ **objection** *nf* objection; **si vous n'y voyez pas d'o.** if you have no objections

objectif, -ive [ɔbʒɛktif, -iv] **1** *adj* objective **2** *nm (but)* objective; *(d'appareil photo)* lens ▪ **objectivité** *nf* objectivity

objet [ɔbʒɛ] *nm (chose, sujet, but)* object; **faire l'o. de** *(étude, critiques)* to be the subject of; *(soins, surveillance)* to be given; **o. d'art** objet d'art; **objets trouvés** *(bureau) Br* lost property, *Am* lost and found

obligation [ɔbligɑsjɔ̃] *nf (contrainte)* obligation; *Fin* bond; **se trouver dans l'o. de faire qch** to be obliged to do sth; **sans o. d'achat** no purchase necessary ▪ **obligatoire** *adj* compulsory, obligatory

obliger [ɔbliʒe] **1** *vt (contraindre)* to force (**à faire** to do); **être obligé de faire qch** to be obliged to do sth **2 s'obliger** *vpr* **s'o. à faire qch** to force oneself to do sth ▪ **obligé, -e** *adj (obligatoire)* necessary

oblique [ɔblik] *adj* oblique

oblitéré, -e [ɔblitere] *adj (timbre)* used

obscène [ɔpsɛn] *adj* obscene ▪ **obscénité** *nf* obscenity

obscur, -e [ɔpskyr] *adj (sombre)* dark; *(confus, inconnu)* obscure ▪ **obscurcir 1** *vt (rendre sombre)* to darken; *(rendre confus)* to obscure **2 s'obscurcir** *vpr (ciel)* to darken ▪ **obscurité** *nf (noirceur)* darkness; **dans l'o.** in the dark

obséder [ɔpsede] *vt* to obsess ▪ **obsédant, -e** *adj* haunting; *(pensée)* obsessive

obsèques [ɔpsɛk] *nfpl* funeral

observateur, -trice [ɔpsɛrvatœr, -tris] **1** *adj* observant **2** *nmf* observer

observation [ɔpsɛrvasjɔ̃] *nf (étude, remarque)* observation; *(reproche)* remark; *(respect)* observance

observatoire [ɔpsɛrvatwar] *nm* observatory

observer [ɔpsɛrve] *vt (regarder, respecter)* to observe; *(remarquer)* to notice; **faire o. qch à qn** to point sth out to sb

obsession [ɔpsesjɔ̃] *nf* obsession ▪ **obsessionnel, -elle** *adj* obsessional

obstacle [ɔpstakl] *nm* obstacle; **faire o. à qch** to stand in the way of sth

obstétricien, -enne [ɔpstetrisjɛ̃, -ɛn] *nmf* obstetrician

obstiner [ɔpstine] **s'obstiner** *vpr* to persist (**à faire** in doing) ▪ **obstination** *nf* stubbornness, obstinacy ▪ **obstiné, -e** *adj* stubborn, obstinate

obstruction [ɔpstryksjɔ̃] *nf* obstruction ▪ **obstruer** *vt* to obstruct

obtempérer [ɔptɑ̃pere] *vi* **o. à qch** to comply with sth

obtenir* [ɔptənir] *vt* to get, to obtain ▪ **obtention** *nf* obtaining

obus [ɔby] *nm (projectile)* shell

occasion [ɔkazjɔ̃] *nf* (**a**) *(chance)* chance, opportunity (**de faire** to do); *(moment)* occasion; **à l'o.** when the occasion arises; **à l'o. de qch** on the occasion of sth; **pour les grandes occasions** for special occasions (**b**) *(affaire)* bargain; *(objet non neuf)* second-hand item; **d'o.** second-hand

occasionner [ɔkazjɔne] *vt* to cause; **o. qch à qn** to cause sb sth

occident [ɔksidɑ̃] *nm* **l'O.** the West ■ **occidental, -e, -aux, -ales** *adj Géog & Pol* western **2** *nmpl Pol* **les Occidentaux** Westerners

occulte [ɔkylt] *adj* occult

occupant, -e [ɔkypɑ̃, -ɑ̃t] **1** *adj (armée)* occupying **2** *nmf (habitant)* occupant **3** *nm Mil* **l'o.** the occupying forces

occupation [ɔkypasjɔ̃] *nf (activité, travail)* & *Mil* occupation

occupé, -e [ɔkype] *adj* busy (**à faire** doing); *(place, maison)* occupied; *(ligne téléphonique) Br* engaged, *Am* busy

occuper [ɔkype] **1** *vt (bâtiment, pays)* to occupy; *(place)* to take up, to occupy; *(poste)* to hold; **o. qn** *(jeu, travail)* to keep sb busy *or* occupied **2 s'occuper** *vpr* to keep oneself busy (**à faire** doing); **s'o. de** *(affaire, problème)* to deal with; **s'o. de qn** *(malade)* to take care of sb; *(client)* to see to sb

océan [ɔseɑ̃] *nm* ocean; **l'o. Atlantique/Pacifique** the Atlantic/Pacific Ocean

octante [ɔktɑ̃t] *adj & nm inv (en Belgique, en Suisse)* eighty

octet [ɔkte] *nm Ordinat* byte; **milliard d'octets** gigabyte

octobre [ɔktɔbr] *nm* October

octogonal, -e, -aux, -ales [ɔktɔgɔnal, -o] *adj* octagonal

oculaire [ɔkyler] *adj* **témoin o.** eyewitness ■ **oculiste** *nmf* eye specialist

odeur [ɔdœr] *nf* smell; *(de fleur)* scent ■ **odorat** *nm* sense of smell

odieux, -euse [ɔdjø, -øz] *adj* odious

œil [œj] *(pl* **yeux** [jø]*) nm* eye; **avoir les yeux verts** to have green eyes; **avoir de grands yeux** to have big eyes; **lever/baisser les yeux** to look up/down; **coup d'o.** *(regard)* look, glance; **jeter un coup d'o. sur qch** to have a look at sth; **à vue d'o.** visibly; **regarder qn dans les yeux** to look sb in the eye; *Fig* **o. au beurre noir** black eye

œillères [œjer] *nfpl (de cheval) Br* blinkers, *Am* blinders

œillet [œje] *nm (fleur)* carnation

œuf [œf] *(pl* **œufs** [ø]*) nm* egg; **œufs** *(de poissons)* (hard) roe; **o. à la coque** boiled egg; **o. sur le plat** fried egg; **o. dur** hard-boiled egg; **œufs brouillés** scrambled eggs; **o. de Pâques** Easter egg

œuvre [œvr] *nf (travail, livre)* work; **o. d'art** work of art; **o. de charité** *(organisation)* charity

offense [ɔfɑ̃s] *nf* insult ■ **offensant, -e** *adj* offensive ■ **offenser 1** *vt* to offend **2 s'offenser** *vpr* **s'o. de qch** to take *Br* offence *or Am* offense at sth

offensif, -ive [ɔfɑ̃sif, -iv] **1** *adj* offensive **2** *nf* **offensive** offensive; **passer à l'o.** to go on the offensive

offert, -e [ɔfer, -ert] *pp de* **offrir**

office [ɔfis] *nm* (**a**) *Rel* service (**b**) *(pièce) (établissement)* office, bureau; **o. du tourisme** tourist information centre (**d**) *(charge)* office; **d'o.** without having any say; **faire o. de qch** to serve as sth

officiel, -elle [ɔfisjel] *adj & nm* official

officier [ɔfisje] *nm (dans l'armée)* officer

officieux, -euse [ɔfisjø, -øz] *adj* unofficial

offre [ɔfr] *nf* offer; *(aux enchères)* bid; *Écon* **l'o. et la demande** supply and demand; *Fin* **o. publique d'achat** takeover bid; **offres d'emploi** *(de journal)* job vacancies, *Br* situations vacant ■ **offrande** *nf* offering

offrir* [ɔfrir] **1** *vt (donner)* to give;

(*proposer*) to offer; **o. qch à qn** (*donner*) to give sb sth, to give sth to sb; (*proposer*) to offer sth to sb, to offer sth to sb; **o. de faire qch** to offer to do sth **2** s'**offrir** *vpr* (*cadeau*) to treat oneself to; (*se proposer*) to offer oneself (**comme** as) ■ **offrant** *nm* **au plus o.** to the highest bidder

OGM [ɔʒeɛm] (*abrév* **organisme génétiquement modifié**) *nm* GMO

oie [wa] *nf* goose (*pl* geese)

oignon [ɔɲɔ̃] *nm* (*légume*) onion

oiseau, -x [wazo] *nm* bird; **o. de proie** bird of prey

oisif, -ive [wazif, -iv] *adj* idle ■ **oisiveté** *nf* idleness

oléoduc [ɔleɔdyk] *nm* pipeline

olive [ɔliv] **1** *nf* olive **2** *adj inv* **vert o.** olive (green) ■ **olivier** *nm* (*arbre*) olive tree

olympique [ɔlɛ̃pik] *adj* Olympic; **les jeux Olympiques** the Olympic games

ombilical, -e, -aux, -ales [ɔ̃bilikal, -o] *adj* umbilical

ombrage [ɔ̃braʒ] *nm* (*ombre*) shade

ombre [ɔ̃br] *nf* (*forme*) shadow; (*zone sombre*) shade; **30° à l'o.** 30° in the shade; **sans l'o. d'un doute** without the shadow of a doubt; **pas l'o. d'un reproche/remords** not a trace of blame/remorse

ombrelle [ɔ̃brɛl] *nf* sunshade, parasol

omelette [ɔmlɛt] *nf* omelette; **o. norvégienne** baked Alaska

omettre* [ɔmɛtr] *vt* to omit (**de faire** to do) ■ **omission** *nf* omission

omnibus [ɔmnibys] *adj & nm* (**train**) *n* slow train (*stopping at all stations*)

omnipotent, -e [ɔmnipɔtɑ̃, -ɑ̃t] *adj* omnipotent

omniprésent, -e [ɔmniprezɑ̃, ɑ̃t] *adj* omnipresent

omnisports [ɔmnispɔr] *adj inv* **centre o.** sports centre

omnivore [ɔmnivɔr] *adj* omnivorous

on [ɔ̃] (*sometimes* l'**on** [lɔ̃]) *pron indéfini* (*les gens*) they, people; (*nous*) we, one; (*vous*) you, one; **on m'a dit que...** I

was told that...; **on me l'a donné** somebody gave it to me

oncle [ɔ̃kl] *nm* uncle

onctueux, -euse [ɔ̃ktɥø, -øz] *adj* smooth

onde [ɔ̃d] *nf* (*à la radio*) & *Phys* wave; **grandes ondes** long wave; **ondes courtes/moyennes** short/medium wave; **o. de choc** shock wave

ondée [ɔ̃de] *nf* sudden downpour

on-dit [ɔ̃di] *nm inv* rumour, hearsay

ondoyer [ɔ̃dwaje] *vi* to undulate

ondulé, -e [ɔ̃dyle] *adj* wavy

onduler [ɔ̃dyle] *vi* to undulate; (*cheveux*) to be wavy

onéreux, -euse [ɔnerø, -øz] *adj* costly

ONG [ɔɛnʒe] (*abrév* **organisation non gouvernementale**) *nf* NGO

ongle [ɔ̃gl] *nm* (finger)nail

ont [ɔ̃] *voir* **avoir**

ONU [ɔny] (*abrév* **Organisation des Nations unies**) *nf* UN

onze [ɔ̃z] *adj & nm* eleven ■ **onzième** *adj & nm* eleventh

OPA [ɔpea] (*abrév* **offre publique d'achat**) *nf Fin* takeover bid

opaque [ɔpak] *adj* opaque

opéra [ɔpera] *nm* (*musique*) opera; (*édifice*) opera house

opérateur, -trice [ɔperatœr, -tris] *nmf* (*personne*) operator; *Cin* cameraman

opération [ɔperasjɔ̃] *nf* (*action*) & *Méd, Mil & Math* operation ■ **opérationnel, -elle** *adj* operational

opérer [ɔpere] **1** *vt* (*exécuter*) to carry out; (*choix*) to make; (*patient*) to operate on (**de** for); **se faire o.** to have an operation **2** *vi* (*agir*) to work; (*procéder*) to proceed; (*chirurgien*) to operate

ophtalmologue [ɔftalmɔlɔg] *nmf* ophthalmologist

opiniâtre [ɔpinjɑtr] *adj* stubborn

opinion [ɔpinjɔ̃] *nf* opinion (**sur** about *or* on); **mon o. est faite** my mind is made up; **o. publique** public opinion

opportun, -e [ɔpɔrtœ̃, -yn] *adj* opportune, timely ■ **opportunité** *nf* timeliness

opposant, -e [ɔpozɑ̃, -ɑ̃t] *nmf* opponent (à of)

opposé, -e [ɔpoze] **1** *adj* (*direction*) opposite; (*intérêts*) conflicting; (*armées, équipe*) opposing; **être o. à qch** to be opposed to sth **2** *nm* **l'o.** the opposite (**de** of); **à l'o.** (*côté*) on the opposite side (**de** to); **à l'o. de** (*contrairement à*) contrary to

opposer [ɔpoze] **1** *vt* (*résistance, argument*) to put up (**à** against); **o. qn à qn** to set sb against sb; **match qui oppose...** match between... **2 s'opposer** *vpr* (*équipes*) to confront each other; **s'o. à qch** to be opposed to sth; **je m'y oppose** I'm opposed to it

opposition [ɔpozisjɔ̃] *nf* opposition (**à** to); **faire o.** to oppose; (*chèque*) to stop; **par o. à** as opposed to

oppresser [ɔprese] *vt* (*gêner*) to oppress ■ **oppressant, -e** *adj* oppressive ■ **oppresseur** *nm* oppressor ■ **oppression** *nf* oppression ■ **opprimer** *vt* (*peuple, nation*) to oppress ■ **opprimés** *nmpl* **les o.** the oppressed

opter [ɔpte] *vi* **o. pour qch** to opt for sth

opticien, -enne [ɔptisjɛ̃, -ɛn] *nmf* optician

optimal, -e, -aux, -ales [ɔptimal, -o] *adj* optimal

optimiser [ɔptimize] *vt* to optimize

optimisme [ɔptimism] *nm* optimism ■ **optimiste 1** *adj* optimistic **2** *nmf* optimist

option [ɔpsjɔ̃] *nf* (*choix*) option; (*chose*) optional extra; *Scol Br* optional subject, *Am* elective (subject)

optique [ɔptik] **1** *adj* (*nerf*) optic; (*verre, fibres*) optical **2** *nf* optics (*sing*); **d'o.** (*instrument, appareil*) optical

opulent, -e [ɔpylɑ̃, -ɑ̃t] *adj* opulent ■ **opulence** *nf* opulence

or[1] [ɔr] *nm* gold; **montre en or** gold watch; **règle/âge d'or** golden rule/age; **cœur d'or** heart of gold; **mine**

d'or gold mine; **affaire en or** bargain; **or noir** (*pétrole*) black gold

or[2] [ɔr] *conj* (*cependant*) now, well

orage [ɔraʒ] *nm* (thunder)storm ■ **orageux, -euse** *adj* stormy

oral, -e, -aux, -ales [ɔral, -o] **1** *adj* oral **2** *nm Scol & Univ* oral

orange [ɔrɑ̃ʒ] **1** *nf* orange; **o. pressée** (fresh) orange juice **2** *adj & nm inv* (*couleur*) orange ■ **oranger** *nm* orange tree

orateur [ɔratœr] *nm* speaker, orator

orbite [ɔrbit] *nf* (*d'astre*) orbit; (*d'œil*) socket; **mettre qch sur o.** (*fusée*) to put sth into orbit

orchestre [ɔrkɛstr] *nm* (*classique*) orchestra; (*de jazz*) band; *Théât* (*places*) *Br* stalls, *Am* orchestra ■ **orchestrer** *vt* (*organiser*) & *Mus* to orchestrate

ordinaire [ɔrdinɛr] *adj* (*habituel, normal*) ordinary, *Am* regular; (*médiocre*) ordinary, average; **d'o., à l'o.** usually; **comme d'o., comme à l'o.** as usual

ordinateur [ɔrdinatœr] *nm* computer; **o. individuel** personal computer; **o. portable** laptop

ordonnance [ɔrdɔnɑ̃s] *nf* (*de médecin*) prescription; (*disposition*) arrangement

ordonner [ɔrdɔne] *vt* (**a**) (*commander*) to order (**que** + *subjunctive* that); **o. à qn de faire qch** to order sb to do sth (**b**) (*ranger*) to organize (**c**) (*prêtre*) to ordain; **il a été ordonné prêtre** he has been ordained (as) a priest ■ **ordonné, -e** *adj* (*personne, maison*) tidy

ordre [ɔrdr] *nm* (*organisation, discipline, catégorie, commandement*) order; (*absence de désordre*) tidiness; **en o.** (*chambre*) tidy; **mettre de l'o. dans qch** to tidy sth up; **rentrer dans l'o.** to return to normal; **jusqu'à nouvel o.** until further notice; **de l'o. de** (*environ*) of the order of; **du même o.** of the same order; **de premier o.** first-rate; **par o. d'âge** in order of age; **assurer le maintien de l'o.** to maintain order; *Rel* **entrer dans les ordres** to take holy orders; **o. du jour** agenda; **l'o. public** law and order

ordures [ɔrdyr] *nfpl (déchets) Br* rubbish, *Am* garbage; **mettre qch aux o.** to throw sth out (in the *Br* rubbish or *Am* garbage)

oreille [ɔrɛj] *nf* ear; **faire la sourde o.** to turn a deaf ear

oreiller [ɔrɛje] *nm* pillow

oreillons [ɔrɛjɔ̃] *nmpl (maladie)* mumps

ores et déjà [ɔrzedeʒa] **d'ores et déjà** *adv* already

orfèvrerie [ɔrfɛvrəri] *nf (magasin)* goldsmith's/silversmith's shop; *(objets)* gold/silver plate

organe [ɔrgan] *nm Anat & Fig* organ; ■ **organisme** *nm (corps)* body; *Biol* organism; *(bureaux)* organization

organisateur, -trice [ɔrganizatœr, -tris] *nmf* organizer

organisation [ɔrganizasjɔ̃] *nf (arrangement, association)* organization

organiser [ɔrganize] **1** *vt* to organize **2 s'organiser** *upr* to get organized ■ **organisé, -e** *adj* organized

orge [ɔrʒ] *nf* barley

orgue [ɔrg] **1** *nm* organ **2** *nfpl* **orgues** organ

orgueil [ɔrgœj] *nm* pride ■ **orgueilleux, -euse** *adj* proud

orient [ɔrjɑ̃] *nm* **l'O.** the Orient, the East; **en O.** in the East ■ **oriental, -e, -aux, -ales 1** *adj (côte, région)* eastern; *(langue)* oriental **2** *nmf* **O., Orientale** Oriental

orientation [ɔrjɑ̃tasjɔ̃] *nf (de position)* orientation; *(d'antenne)* positioning; *(de maison)* aspect; **avoir le sens de l'o.** to have a good sense of direction; **o. professionnelle** careers guidance

orienter [ɔrjɑ̃te] **1** *vt (bâtiment)* to orientate; *(canon, télescope)* to point (**vers** at); **o. ses recherches sur** to direct one's research on **2 s'orienter** *upr* to get one's bearings; **s'o. vers** *(carrière)* to specialize in ■ **orienté, -e** *adj (peu objectif)* slanted; **o. à l'ouest** *(appartement)* facing west

orifice [ɔrifis] *nm* opening

originaire [ɔriʒiner] *adj* **être o. de** *(natif)* to be a native of

original, -e, -aux, -ales [ɔriʒinal, -o] **1** *adj (idée, artiste, version)* original **2** *nm (texte, tableau)* original **3** *nmf (personne)* eccentric ■ **originalité** *nf* originality

origine [ɔriʒin] *nf* origin; **à l'o.** originally; **être à l'o. de qch** to be at the origin of sth; **d'o.** *(pneu)* original; **être d'o. française** to be of French origin ■ **originel, -elle** *adj* original

ornement [ɔrnəmɑ̃] *nm* ornament ■ **ornemental, -e, -aux, -ales** *adj* ornamental

orner [ɔrne] *vt* to decorate (**de** with)

orphelin, -e [ɔrfelɛ̃, -in] *nmf* orphan ■ **orphelinat** *nm* orphanage

orteil [ɔrtɛj] *nm* toe

orthodoxe [ɔrtɔdɔks] *adj* orthodox

orthographe [ɔrtɔgraf] *nf* spelling ■ **orthographier** *vt* to spell; **mal o. qch** to misspell sth

ortie [ɔrti] *nf* nettle

os [ɔs, *pl* o *ou* os] *nm* bone

oscar [ɔskar] *nm (récompense)* Oscar

osciller [ɔsile] *vi Tech* to oscillate; *(pendule)* to swing; *(aiguille, flamme)* to flicker; *Fig (varier)* to fluctuate (**entre** between)

oser [oze] *vt* to dare; **o. faire qch** to dare (to) do sth ■ **osé, -e** *adj* daring

osier [ozje] *nm* wicker; **panier d'o.** wicker basket

ossements [ɔsmɑ̃] *nmpl* bones

osseux, -euse [ɔsø, -øz] *adj (maigre)* bony

otage [ɔtaʒ] *nm* hostage; **prendre qn en o.** to take sb hostage

OTAN [ɔtɑ̃] *(abrév* **Organisation du traité de l'Atlantique Nord)** *nf* NATO

ôter [ote] *vt* to take away, to remove (**à qn** from sb); *(vêtement)* to take off; *(déduire)* to take (away)

otite [ɔtit] *nf* ear infection

ou [u] *conj* or; **ou elle ou moi** either her or me

où [u] *adv & pron relatif* where; **le jour**

où... the day when...; **la table où...** the table on which...; **l'état où...** the condition in which...; **par où?** which way?; **d'où?** where from?; **le pays d'où je viens** the country from which I come

ouate [wat] *nf (pour pansement)* Br cotton wool, *Am* absorbent cotton

oubli [ubli] *nm (trou de mémoire)* oversight; *(lacune)* omission; **tomber dans l'o.** to fall into oblivion

oublier [ublije] *vt* to forget (**de faire** to do); *(omettre)* to leave out

oubliettes [ublijet] *nfpl (de château)* dungeons

ouest [west] **1** *nm* west; **à l'o.** in the west; *(direction)* (to the) west (**de** of); **d'o.** *(vent)* west(erly); **de l'o.** western **2** *adj inv (côte)* west; *(région)* western

Ouganda [ugãda] *nm* l'O. Uganda

oui [wi] **1** *adv* yes; **ah, ça o.!** oh yes (indeed!); **je crois que o.** I think so **2** *nm inv* **pour un o. pour un non** for the slightest thing

ouï-dire [widir] *nm* hearsay; **par o.** by hearsay

ouïe [wi] *nf* hearing

ouïes [wi] *nfpl (de poisson)* gills

ouragan [uragã] *nm* hurricane

ourlet [urlɛ] *nm* hem

ours [urs] *nm* bear; **o. blanc** polar bear; **o. en peluche** teddy bear ■ **ourse** *nf* she-bear; **la Grande O.** the Great Bear

oursin [ursɛ̃] *nm* sea urchin

outil [uti] *nm* tool ■ **outillage** *nm* tools; *(d'usine)* equipment ■ **outiller** *vt* to equip

outrage [utraʒ] *nm* insult (**à** to)

outrance [utrãs] *nf (excès)* excess; **à o.** to excess ■ **outrancier, -ère** *adj* excessive

outre [utr] **1** *prép* besides; **o. mesure** unduly **2** *adv* **en o.** besides; **passer o.**

to take no notice (**à** of) ■ **outre-Manche** *adv* across the Channel ■ **outremer** *adv* overseas; **d'o.** *(marché)* overseas; **territoires d'o.** overseas territories

outré, -e [utre] *adj (révolté)* outraged; *(excessif)* exaggerated

outrepasser [utrəpase] *vt* to go beyond, to exceed

ouvert, -e [uver, -ɛrt] **1** *pp de* **ouvrir 2** *adj* open; *(robinet, gaz)* on ■ **ouverture** *nf* opening; *(trou)* hole

ouvrable [uvrabl] *adj* **jour o.** working *or Am* work day

ouvrage [uvraʒ] *nm (travail, livre, objet)* work; *(couture)* (needle)work; **un o.** *(travail)* a piece of work

ouvreuse [uvrøz] *nf* usherette

ouvrier, -ère [uvrije, -ɛr] **1** *nmf* worker; **o. qualifié/spécialisé** skilled/ semi-skilled worker; **o. agricole** farm worker **2** *adj (quartier)* working-class

ouvrir* [uvrir] **1** *vt* to open; *(gaz, radio)* to turn on; *(hostilités)* to begin; *(appétit)* to whet **2** *vi* to open **3** **s'ouvrir** *vpr (porte, boîte, fleur)* to open ■ **ouvre-boîtes** *nm inv* Br tin opener, *Am* can opener ■ **ouvre-bouteilles** *nm inv* bottle opener

ovale [oval] *adj & nm* oval

ovation [ovasjɔ̃] *nf* (standing) ovation

ovni [ovni] *(abrév objet volant non identifié) nm* UFO

oxyder [ɔkside] *vt,* **s'oxyder** *vpr* to oxidize

oxygène [ɔksiʒɛn] *nm* oxygen; **masque/tente à o.** oxygen mask/tent ■ **oxygéné, -e** *adj* **eau oxygénée** (hydrogen) peroxide; **cheveux blonds oxygénés** peroxide blonde hair, bleached hair

ozone [ozon] *nm Chim* ozone

Pp

P, p [pe] *nm inv* P, p
pacifique [pasifik] **1** *adj (manifestation)* peaceful; *(personne, peuple)* peace-loving; *(côte)* Pacific **2** *nm* **le P.** the Pacific
pacifiste [pasifist] *adj & nmf* pacifist
pacte [pakt] *nm* pact
pagaie [page] *nf* paddle
pagaïe, pagaille [pagaj] *nf Fam (désordre)* mess; **semer la p.** to cause chaos
pagayer [pageje] *vi* to paddle
page [paʒ] *nf (de livre)* page; *Ordinat* **p. d'accueil** home page; **les Pages Jaunes®** *(de l'annuaire)* the Yellow Pages®; *Radio* **p. de publicité** commercial break
paie [pɛ] *nf* pay, wages
paiement [pemã] *nm* payment
païen, -enne [pajɛ̃, -ɛn] *adj & nmf* pagan, heathen
paillasson [pajasɔ̃] *nm* (door)mat
paille [paj] *nf* straw; *(pour boire)* (drinking) straw
paillette [pajɛt] *nf (d'habit)* sequin; **paillettes** *(de savon, lessive)* flakes; *(d'or)* gold dust
pain [pɛ̃] *nm* bread; **un p.** a loaf (of bread); **petit p.** roll; **p. au chocolat** = chocolate-filled pastry; **p. complet** wholemeal bread; **p. d'épices** ≃ gingerbread; **p. grillé** toast; **p. de mie** sandwich loaf
pair, -e [pɛr] **1** *adj (numéro)* even **2** *nm (personne)* peer; **hors p.** unrivalled; **aller de p.** to go hand in hand (**avec** with); **au p.** *(étudiante)* au pair; **travailler au p.** to work as an au pair

paire [pɛr] *nf* pair (**de** of)
paisible [pezibl] *adj (vie, endroit)* peaceful; *(caractère, personne)* quiet
paître* [pɛtr] *vi* to graze
paix [pɛ] *nf* peace; **en p.** *(vivre, laisser)* in peace (**avec** with)
Pakistan [pakistã] *nm* **le P.** Pakistan ∎ **pakistanais, -e 1** *adj* Pakistani **2** *nmf* **P., Pakistanaise** Pakistani
palace [palas] *nm* luxury hotel
palais [palɛ] *nm (château)* palace; *Anat* palate; **P. de justice** law courts; **p. des sports** sports centre
pâle [pal] *adj* pale
Palestine [palestin] *nf* **la P.** Palestine ∎ **palestinien, -enne 1** *adj* Palestinian **2** *nmf* **P., Palestinienne** Palestinian
palette [palɛt] *nf (de peintre)* palette; *(pour marchandises)* pallet
pâleur [palœr] *nf (de lumière)* paleness; *(de personne)* pallor
palier [palje] *nm (niveau)* level; *(d'escalier)* landing; *(phase)* plateau; **par paliers** in stages
pâlir [palir] *vi* to turn pale (**de** with)
palissade [palisad] *nf* fence
pallier [palje] **1** *vt (difficultés)* to alleviate **2** *vi* **p. à qch** to compensate for sth
palmarès [palmares] *nm* prize list; *(de chansons)* charts
palme [palm] *nf (de palmier)* palm (branch); *(de nageur)* flipper
palmier [palmje] *nm* palm (tree)
palourde [palurd] *nf* clam
palper [palpe] *vt* to feel ∎ **palpable** *adj* palpable
palpiter [palpite] *vi (cœur)* to flutter; *(plus fort)* to throb

pamplemousse [pãpləmus] *nm* grapefruit

panaché, -e [panaʃe] **1** *adj* multicoloured; **p. de blanc** streaked with white **2** *nm* shandy

Panama [panama] *nm* **le P.** Panama

pancarte [pãkart] *nf* sign, notice; *(de manifestant)* placard

pané, -e [pane] *adj (poisson)* breaded

panier [panje] *nm (ustensile, contenu)* basket; **p. à linge** *Br* linen basket, *Am* (clothes) hamper

panique [panik] **1** *nf* panic; **pris de p.** panic-stricken **2** *adj* **peur p.** panic

panne [pan] *nf* breakdown; **tomber en p.** to break down; **être en p.** to have broken down; **tomber en p. sèche** to run out of *Br* petrol *or Am* gas; **p. d'électricité** blackout, *Br* power cut

panneau, -x [pano] *nm (écriteau)* sign, notice, board; *(de porte)* panel; **p. d'affichage** *Br* notice board, *Am* bulletin board; **p. de signalisation** road sign ■ **panonceau, -x** *nm (enseigne)* sign

panoplie [panɔpli] *nf (jouet)* outfit; *(gamme)* set

panorama [panɔrama] *nm* panorama ■ **panoramique** *adj* panoramic; *Cin* **écran p.** wide screen

panser [pãse] *vt (main)* to bandage; *(plaie)* to dress; **p. qn** to dress sb's wounds ■ **pansement** *nm* dressing; **faire un p. à qn** to put a dressing on sb; **p. adhésif** *Br* sticking plaster, *Am* Band-aid®

pantalon [pãtalɔ̃] *nm Br* trousers, *Am* pants; **deux pantalons** two pairs of *Br* trousers *or Am* pants

panthère [pãter] *nf* panther

pantoufle [pãtufl] *nf* slipper

paon [pã] *nm* peacock

papa [papa] *nm* dad(dy)

pape [pap] *nm* pope

papeterie [papetri] *nf (magasin)* stationer's shop; *(articles)* stationery; *(fabrique)* paper mill

papi [papi] *nm* = **papy**

papier [papje] *nm (matière)* paper; **un**

p. *(feuille)* a piece of paper; *(formulaire)* a form; *(de journal)* an article; **p. hygiénique** toilet paper; **papiers d'identité** identity papers; **p. à lettres** writing paper; **p. peint** wallpaper

papillon [papijɔ̃] *nm (insecte)* butterfly; **p. de nuit** moth

papy [papi] *nm* grand(d)ad

Pâque [pɑk] *nf Rel* **la P. juive, P.** Passover

paquebot [pakbo] *nm* liner

pâquerette [pakret] *nf* daisy

Pâques [pɑk] *nm sing & nfpl* Easter

paquet [pake] *nm (sac)* packet; *(de sucre)* bag; *(de cigarettes)* packet, *Am* pack; *Br (postal)* parcel, package

PAR [par] *prép* **(a)** *(indique l'agent, la manière, le moyen)* by; **frappé p. qn** hit by sb; **p. mer** by sea; **p. le train** by train; **p. la force** by *or* through force; **commencer p. qch** *(récit)* to begin with sth; **p. erreur** by mistake; **p. chance** by a stroke of luck

(b) *(à travers)* through; **p. la porte** through the door; **jeter/regarder p. la fenêtre** to throw/look out (of) the window; **p. ici/là** *(aller)* this/that way; *(habiter)* around here/there; **p. les rues** through the streets

(c) *(à cause de)* out of, from; **p. pitié** out of pity

(d) *(pendant)* **p. ce froid** in this cold; **p. le passé** in the past

(e) *(distributif)* **dix fois p. an/mois** ten times a *or* per year/month; **50 euros p. personne** 50 euros per person; **deux p. deux** two by two; **p. deux fois** twice

(f) *(avec 'trop')* **p. trop aimable** far too kind

parachute [paraʃyt] *nm* parachute; **p. ascensionnel** parascending ■ **parachutisme** *nm* parachute jumping ■ **parachutiste** *nmf* parachutist; *(soldat)* paratrooper

parade [parad] *nf (défilé)* parade; *(étalage)* show

paradis [paradi] *nm* heaven

paradoxe [paradɔks] *nm* paradox

parafer [parafe] *vt* = **parapher**

paraffine [parafin] *nf* paraffin (wax)

parages [paraʒ] *nmpl Naut* waters; **dans les p. de** in the vicinity of

paragraphe [paragraf] *nm* paragraph

Paraguay [paragwe] *nm* **le P.** Paraguay

paraître* [parɛtr] **1** *vi* (*sembler*) to seem, to appear; (*apparaître*) to appear; (*livre*) to come out, to be published **2** *v impersonnel* **il paraît qu'il va partir** it appears or seems (that) he's leaving; **à ce qu'il paraît** apparently

parallèle [paralɛl] **1** *adj* parallel (**à** with *or* to); (*police, marché*) unofficial **2** *nf* parallel (line) **3** *nm* (*comparaison*) & *Géog* parallel; **mettre qch en p. avec qch** to draw a parallel between sth and sth ◾ **parallèlement** *adv* **p. à** parallel to; (*simultanément*) at the same time as

paralyser [paralize] *vt Br* to paralyse, *Am* to paralyze ◾ **paralysie** *nf* paralysis ◾ **paralytique** *adj* & *nmf* paralytic

paramédical, -e, -aux, -ales [paramedikal, -o] *adj* paramedical

paramilitaire [paramiliter] *adj* paramilitary

parapente [parapɑ̃t] *nm* (*activité*) paragliding; **faire du p.** to go paragliding

parapet [parapɛ] *nm* parapet

parapher [parafe] *vt* to initial

parapluie [paraplɥi] *nm* umbrella

parasite [parazit] **1** *nm* (*organisme, personne*) parasite; **parasites** (*à la radio*) interference **2** *adj* parasitic

parasol [parasɔl] *nm* sunshade, parasol; (*de plage*) beach umbrella

paratonnerre [paratɔner] *nm* lightning *Br* conductor *or Am* rod

paravent [paravɑ̃] *nm* screen

parc [park] *nm* (*jardin*) park; (*de château*) grounds; (*de bébé*) playpen; **p. d'attractions** amusement park; **p. de stationnement** *Br* car park, *Am* parking lot; **p. naturel** nature reserve

parcelle [parsɛl] *nf* small piece; (*terrain*) plot

parce que [parsəkə] *conj* because

parchemin [parʃəmɛ̃] *nm* parchment

par-ci, par-là [parsiparla] *adv* here, there and everywhere

parcmètre [parkmetr] *nm* (parking) meter

parcourir* [parkurir] *vt* (*lieu*) to walk round; (*pays*) to travel through; (*mer*) to sail; (*distance*) to cover; (*texte*) to glance through; **p. qch des yeux** *ou* **du regard** to glance at sth; **il reste 2 km à p.** there are 2 km to go ◾ **parcours** *nm* (*itinéraire*) route; **p. de golf** (*terrain*) golf course

par-delà [pardəla] *prép & adv* beyond

par-derrière [parderjer] **1** *prép* behind **2** *adv* (*attaquer*) from behind; (*se boutonner*) at the back; **passer p.** to go in the back door

par-dessous [pardəsu] *prép & adv* underneath

pardessus [pardəsy] *nm* overcoat

par-dessus [pardəsy] **1** *prép* over; **p. tout** above all **2** *adv* over

par-devant [pardəvɑ̃] *adv* (*attaquer*) from the front; (*se boutonner*) at the front

pardon [pardɔ̃] *nm* forgiveness; **p.!** (*excusez-moi*) sorry!; (*pour demander*) excuse me?, *Am* pardon me?; **demander p.** to apologize (**à** to) ◾ **pardonner** *vt* to forgive; **p. qch à qn** to forgive sb for sth; **elle m'a pardonné d'avoir oublié** she forgave me for forgetting

pare-balles [parbal] *adj inv* **gilet p.** bulletproof *Br* jacket *or Am* vest

pare-brise [parbriz] *nm inv Br* windscreen, *Am* windshield

pare-chocs [parʃɔk] *nm inv* bumper

pareil, -eille [parɛj] **1** *adj* (**a**) (*identique*) the same; **p. à** the same as (**b**) (*tel*) such; **en p. cas** in such cases **2** *adv Fam* the same **3** *nmf* (*personne*) equal; **sans p.** unparalleled, unique **4** *nf* **rendre la pareille à qn** (*se venger*) to get one's own back on sb ◾ **pareillement** *adv* (*de la même manière*) in the same way; *(aussi)* likewise

parent, -e [parɑ̃, -ɑ̃t] **1** *nmf (oncle, tante, cousin)* relative, relation **2** *nmpl* **parents** *(père et mère)* parents **3** *adj* related (**de** to) ■ **parental, -e, -aux, -ales** *adj* parental ■ **parenté** *nf* relationship; **avoir un lien de p.** to be related

parenthèse [parɑ̃tɛz] *nf (signe)* bracket, parenthesis; **entre parenthèses** in brackets

parer[1] [pare] **1** *vt (coup)* to parry **2** *vi* **p. à toute éventualité** to prepare for any contingency

parer[2] [pare] *vt (orner)* to adorn (**de** with)

paresseux, -euse [paresø, -øz] **1** *adj* lazy **2** *nmf* lazy person

parfaire* [parfɛr] *vt* to finish off ■ **parfait, -e** *adj* perfect ■ **parfaitement** *adv (sans fautes, complètement)* perfectly; *(certainement)* certainly

parfois [parfwa] *adv* sometimes

parfum [parfœ̃] *nm (essence)* perfume; *(senteur)* fragrance; *(de glace)* flavour ■ **parfumer 1** *vt (embaumer)* to scent; *(glace)* to flavour (**à** with) **2 se parfumer** *upr* to put perfume on ■ **parfumerie** *nf (magasin)* perfumery

pari [pari] *nm* bet; **faire un p.** to make a bet; **p. mutuel** *Br* ≃ tote, *Am* ≃ pari-mutuel ■ **parier** *vti* to bet (**sur** on; **que** that); **il y a fort à p. que...** the odds are that...

Paris [pari] *nm ou f* Paris ■ **parisien, -enne 1** *adj* Parisian **2** *nmf* **P.**, **Parisienne** Parisian

parking [parkiŋ] *nm Br* car park, *Am* parking lot; **'p. payant'** *Br* ≃ 'pay-and-display car park'

parlement [parləmɑ̃] *nm* **le P.** Parliament ■ **parlementaire 1** *adj* parliamentary **2** *nmf* member of parliament

parlementer [parləmɑ̃te] *vi* to negotiate (**avec** with)

parler [parle] **1** *vi* to talk, to speak (**de** about or of; **à** to); **sans p. de...** not to mention...

2 *vt (langue)* to speak; **p. affaires** to talk business

3 se parler *upr (langue)* to be spoken; *(l'un l'autre)* to speak to each other

4 *nm* speech; *(régional)* dialect

parloir [parlwar] *nm* visiting room

parmi [parmi] *prép* among(st)

paroi [parwa] *nf* wall; *(de rocher)* (rock) face

paroisse [parwas] *nf* parish

parole [parɔl] *nf (mot, promesse)* word; *(faculté, langage)* speech; **paroles** *(de chanson)* words, lyrics; **adresser la p. à qn** to speak to sb; **prendre la p.** to speak; **tenir p.** to keep one's word

parquet [parkɛ] *nm (sol)* wooden floor

parrain [parɛ̃] *nm Rel* godfather; *(de sportif, de club)* sponsor ■ **parrainer** *vt (sportif, membre)* to sponsor

pars [par] *voir* **partir**

parsemer [parsəme] *vt* to scatter (**de** with)

part[1] [par] *voir* **partir**

part[2] [par] *nf (portion)* share, part; *(de gâteau)* slice; **prendre p. à** *(activité)* to take part in; **faire p. de qch à qn** to inform sb of sth; **de toutes parts** on all sides; **de p. et d'autre** on both sides; **d'une p.... d'autre p....** on the one hand... on the other hand...; **de la p. de qn** from sb; **c'est de la p. de qui?** *(au téléphone)* who's calling?; **pour ma p.** as for me; **à p.** *(mettre)* aside; *(excepté)* apart from; *(personne)* different; **prendre qn à p.** to take sb aside

partage [partaʒ] *nm (action)* dividing up; *(de gâteau, de responsabilités)* sharing out; **faire le p. de qch** to divide sth up

partager [partaʒe] **1** *vt (avoir en commun)* to share (**avec** with); *(répartir)* to divide (up); **p. qch en deux** to divide sth in two; **p. l'avis de qn** to share sb's opinion

2 se partager *upr (bénéfices)* to share (between themselves); **se p. entre** to divide one's time between ■ **partagé, -e** *adj (amour)* mutual; **les avis sont partagés** opinions are divided

partance [partɑ̃s] **en partance** *adv*

(train) about to depart; **en p. pour...** for...

partenaire [partənɛr] *nmf* partner ■ **partenariat** *nm* partnership

parterre [partɛr] *nm (de fleurs)* flower bed; *Théât Br* stalls, *Am* orchestra; *Fam (sol)* floor

parti [parti] *nm (camp)* side; **tirer p. de qch** to make good use of sth; **p. (politique)** (political) party

partial, -e, -aux, -ales [parsjal, -o] *adj* biased ■ **partialité** *nf* bias

participer [partisipe] *vi* **p. à** *(jeu)* to take part in, to participate in; *(bénéfices, joie)* to share (in); *(financièrement)* to contribute to ■ **participant, -e** *nmf* participant ■ **participation** *nf* participation; *(d'élection)* turnout; **p. aux frais** contribution towards costs

particularité [partikylarite] *nf* peculiarity

particule [partikyl] *nf* particle

particulier, -ère [partikylje, -ɛr] **1** *adj (propre)* characteristic (**à** of); *(remarquable)* unusual; *(soin, intérêt)* particular; *(maison, voiture, leçon)* private; *Péj (bizarre)* peculiar; **en p.** *(surtout)* in particular; *(à part)* in private; **cas p.** special case **2** *nm* private individual; **vente de p. à p.** private sale ■ **particulièrement** *adv* particularly; **tout p.** especially

partie [parti] *nf (morceau)* part; *(jeu)* game; *(domaine)* field; **en p.** partly, in part; **en grande p.** mainly; **faire p. de** to be a part of; *(club)* to belong to; *(comité)* to be in ■ **partiel, -elle** *adj* partial

partir* [partir] *(aux être) vi (s'en aller)* to go, to leave; *(se mettre en route)* to set off; *(s'éloigner)* to go away; *(coup de feu)* to go off; *(tache)* to come out; *(peinture)* to come off; **p. en voiture** to go by car, to drive; **p. en courant** to run off; **p. de** *(lieu)* to leave from; *(commencer par)* to start (off) with; **à p. de** *(date, prix)* from

partisan [partizɑ̃] **1** *nm* supporter; *(combattant)* partisan **2** *adj (esprit)* partisan; **être p. de qch/de faire qch** to be in favour of sth/of doing sth

partition [partisjɔ̃] *nf Mus* score

partout [partu] *adv* everywhere; **p. où je vais** everywhere *or* wherever I go; **un peu p.** all over the place

paru, -e [pary] *pp de* **paraître** ■ **parution** *nf* publication

parure [paryr] *nf (ensemble)* set

parvenir* [parvənir] *(aux être) vi* **p. à** *(lieu)* to reach; *(objectif)* to achieve; **p. à faire qch** to manage to do sth

PAS¹ [pɑ] *adv (de négation)* **(ne...) p.** not; **je ne sais p.** I do not *or* don't know; **je n'ai p. compris** I didn't understand; **je voudrais ne p. sortir** I would like not to go out; **p. de pain** no bread; **p. du tout** not at all; **elle chantera – p. moi!** she'll sing – no I won't!

pas² [pɑ] *nm* **(a)** *(enjambée)* step; *(allure)* pace; *(bruit)* footstep; *(trace)* footprint; **p. à p.** step by step; **à p. de loup** stealthily; **à deux p. (de)** close by; **aller au p.** to go at a walking pace; **rouler au p.** *(véhicule)* to crawl along; **faire un faux p.** *(en marchant)* to trip; **revenir sur ses p.** to retrace one's steps; **marcher à grands p.** to stride along **(b)** *(de vis)* pitch **(c)** **le p. de Calais** the Straits of Dover

passable [pɑsabl] *adj* passable, fair

passage [pɑsaʒ] *nm (chemin, extrait)* passage; *(ruelle)* alley(way); *(traversée)* crossing; **être de p. dans une ville** to be passing through a town; **p. clouté** *ou* **pour piétons** *Br* (pedestrian) crossing, *Am* crosswalk; **p. souterrain** *Br* subway, *Am* underpass; **p. à niveau** *Br* level crossing, *Am* grade crossing; **'p. interdit'** 'no through traffic'; **'cédez le p.'** *(au carrefour) Br* 'give way', *Am* 'yield'

passager, -ère [pɑsaʒe, -ɛr] **1** *adj* momentary **2** *nmf* passenger; **p. clandestin** stowaway

passant, -e [pɑsɑ̃, -ɑ̃t] **1** *adj (rue)* busy **2** *nmf* passer-by **3** *nm (de ceinture)* loop

passe [pɑs] *nf (au football)* pass; *Fig* **une mauvaise p.** a bad patch

passé, -e [pɑse] **1** *adj (temps)* past; *(couleur)* faded; **la semaine passée** last week; **il est dix heures passées** it's after *or Br* gone ten o'clock; **p. de mode** out of fashion **2** *nm (temps, vie passée)* past; **par le p.** in the past **3** *prép* after; **p. huit heures** after eight o'clock

passe-montagne [pɑsmɔ̃taɲ] *(pl* **passe-montagnes)** *nm Br* balaclava, *Am* ski mask

passe-partout [pɑspartu] *nm inv* master key

passeport [pɑspɔr] *nm* passport

PASSER [pɑse] **1** *(aux avoir)* vt *(pont, frontière)* to go over; *(porte, douane)* to go through; *(ballon)* to pass; *(vêtement)* to slip on; *(film)* to show; *(disque)* to play; *(vacances)* to spend; *(examen)* to take; *(commande)* to place; *(visite médicale)* to have; *(omettre)* to leave out; **p. qch à qn** *(prêter)* to pass sth to sb; *Aut* **p. la seconde** to change into second; **p. son temps à faire qch** to spend one's time doing sth **2** *(aux être)* vi *(se déplacer)* to go past; *(disparaître)* to go; *(facteur)* to come; *(temps)* to pass (by), to go by; *(film, programme)* to be on; *(douleur)* to pass; *(courant)* to flow; **laisser p. qn** to let sb through; **p. de qch à qch** to go from sth to sth; **p. devant qn/qch** to go past sb/sth; **p. par Paris** to pass through Paris; **p. chez le boulanger** to go round to the baker's; **p. à la radio** to be on the radio; **p. pour** *(riche)* to be taken for; **faire p. qn pour** to pass sb off as; **faire p. qch sous/dans qch** to slide/push sth under/into sth; **p. sur** *(détail)* to pass over **3** **se passer** *vpr (se produire)* to happen; **se p. de qch** to do without sth/sb; **ça s'est bien passé** it went off well

passerelle [pɑsrɛl] *nf (pont)* footbridge; **p. d'embarquement** *(de navire)* gangway; *(d'avion)* steps

passe-temps [pɑstɑ̃] *nm inv* pastime

passeur, -euse [pɑsœr, -øz] *nmf (batelier)* ferryman, *f* ferrywoman; *(contrebandier)* smuggler

passif, -ive [pɑsif, -iv] *adj* passive

passion [pɑsjɔ̃] *nf* passion; **avoir la p. des voitures** to have a passion for cars

passionner [pɑsjɔne] **1** *vt* to fascinate **2 se passionner** *vpr* **se p. pour qch** to have a passion for sth ■ **passionnant, -e** *adj* fascinating ■ **passionné, -e** *adj* passionate; **p. de qch** passionately fond of sth

passivité [pɑsivite] *nf* passiveness, passivity

passoire [pɑswar] *nf (pour liquides)* sieve; *(à thé)* strainer; *(à légumes)* colander

pastel [pastɛl] *adj inv & nm* pastel

pastèque [pastɛk] *nf* watermelon

pasteurisé, -e [pastœrize] *adj* pasteurized

pastille [pastij] *nf* pastille; *(médicament)* lozenge

patauger [patoʒe] *vi (s'embourber)* to squelch; *(barboter)* to splash about

pâte [pɑt] *nf (pour tarte)* pastry; *(pour pain)* dough; *(pour gâteau)* mixture; **p. d'amandes** marzipan; **p. feuilletée** puff pastry; **pâtes (alimentaires)** pasta

pâté [pɑte] *nm (charcuterie)* pâté; *(tache d'encre)* blot; **p. en croûte** ≃ meat pie; **p. de maisons** block of houses

pâtée [pɑte] *nf (pour chien)* dog food; *(pour chat)* cat food

paternel, -elle [patɛrnɛl] *adj* paternal ■ **paternité** *nf (état)* paternity, fatherhood; *(de livre)* authorship

pathétique [patetik] *adj* moving

pathologique [patɔlɔʒik] *adj* pathological

patience [pasjɑ̃s] *nf* patience; **avoir de la p.** to be patient; **perdre p.** to lose patience

patient, -e [pasjɑ̃, -ɑ̃t] **1** *adj* patient **2** *nmf (malade)* patient ■ **patienter** *vi* to wait

patin [patɛ̃] *nm* (*de patineur*) skate; **p. à glace** ice skate; **p. à roulettes** roller skate

patiner [patine] *vi Sport* to skate; (*véhicule*) to skid ■ **patinage** *nm Sport* skating; **p. artistique** figure skating ■ **patineur, -euse** *nmf* skater ■ **patinoire** *nf* skating rink, ice rink

pâtir [patir] *vi* **p. de** to suffer because of

pâtisserie [patisri] *nf* (*gâteau*) pastry, cake; (*magasin*) cake shop; (*art*) pastry-making ■ **pâtissier, -ère 1** *nmf* pastry cook; (*commerçant*) confectioner **2** *adj* **crème pâtissière** confectioner's custard

patrie [patri] *nf* homeland

patrimoine [patrimwan] *nm* heritage; (*biens*) property

patriote [patrijɔt] **1** *adj* patriotic **2** *nmf* patriot ■ **patriotique** *adj* patriotic ■ **patriotisme** *nm* patriotism

patron, -onne [patrɔ̃, -ɔn] **1** *nmf* (*chef*) boss; (*propriétaire*) owner (**de** of); (*gérant*) manager, *f* manageress; (*de bar*) landlord, *f* landlady **2** *nm Couture* pattern

patronat [patrɔna] *nm* employers ■ **patronal, -e, -aux, -ales** *adj* employers'

patrouille [patruj] *nf* patrol ■ **patrouiller** *vi* to patrol

patte [pat] *nf* (**a**) (*membre*) leg; (*de chat, de chien*) paw (**b**) (*languette*) tab; (*de poche*) flap ■ **pattes** *nfpl* (*favoris*) sideburns

pâturage [patyraʒ] *nm* pasture

paume [pom] *nf* palm

paupière [popjɛr] *nf* eyelid

paupiette [popjɛt] *nf* **p. de veau** veal olive

pause [poz] *nf* (*arrêt*) break; (*en parlant*) pause

pauvre [povr] **1** *adj* (*personne, sol, excuse*) poor; (*meubles*) shabby; **p. en** (*calories*) low in; (*ressources*) low on **2** *nmf* poor man, *f* poor woman; **les pauvres** the poor ■ **pauvreté** [-əte] *nf* poverty

pavaner [pavane] **se pavaner** *vpr* to strut about

paver [pave] *vt* to pave ■ **pavé** *nm* paving stone

pavillon [pavijɔ̃] *nm* (**a**) (*maison*) detached house; (*d'hôpital*) wing; (*d'exposition*) pavilion (**b**) (*drapeau*) flag

payable [pejabl] *adj* payable

paye [pɛj] *nf* pay, wages ■ **payement** *nm* = **paiement**

payer [peje] **1** *vt* (*personne, somme*) to pay; (*service, objet*) to pay for; (*récompenser*) to repay; **se faire p.** to get paid **2** *vi* to pay ■ **payant, -e** [pejɑ̃, -ɑ̃t] *adj* (*hôte, spectateur*) paying

pays [pei] *nm* country; (*région*) region; **du p.** (*vin, gens*) local

paysage [peizaʒ] *nm* landscape, scenery

paysan, -anne [peizɑ̃, -an] **1** *nmf* farmer **2** *adj* **coutume paysanne** rural *or* country custom; **le monde p.** the farming community

Pays-Bas [peiba] *nmpl* **les P.** the Netherlands

P-DG [pedeʒe] (*abrév* **président-directeur général**) *nm Br* (chairman and) managing director, *Am* chief executive officer

péage [peaʒ] *nm* (*droit*) toll; (*lieu*) tollbooth; **pont à p.** toll bridge; *TV* **chaîne à p.** pay channel

peau, -x [po] *nf* skin; (*de fruit*) peel, skin; (*cuir*) hide ■ **Peau-Rouge** (*pl* **Peaux-Rouges**) *nmf* Red Indian

péché [peʃe] *nm* sin ■ **pécher** *vi* to sin

pêche¹ [pɛʃ] *nf* (*activité*) fishing; (*poissons*) catch; **p. à la ligne** angling; **aller à la p.** to go fishing ■ **pêcher** [peʃe] **1** *vt* (*attraper*) to catch; (*chercher à prendre*) to fish for **2** *vi* to fish ■ **pêcheur** *nm* fisherman; (*à la ligne*) angler

pêche² [pɛʃ] *nf* (*fruit*) peach ■ **pêcher** [peʃe] *nm* (*arbre*) peach tree

pectoraux [pɛktɔro] *nmpl* chest muscles

pédagogie [pedagɔʒi] *nf* (*discipline*) pedagogy ■ **pédagogique** *adj* educational ■ **pédagogue** *nmf* teacher

pédale [pedal] *nf (de voiture, de piano)* pedal; **p. de frein** brake pedal

Pédalo® [pedalo] *nm* pedal boat, pedalo

pédestre [pedɛstr] *adj* **randonnée p.** hike

pédiatre [pedjatr] *nmf* paediatrician

pédicure [pedikyr] *nmf Br* chiropodist, *Am* podiatrist

pègre [pɛgr] *nf* **la p.** the underworld

peigne [pɛɲ] *nm* comb; **se donner un coup de p.** to give one's hair a comb ■ **peigner 1** *vt (cheveux)* to comb; **p. qn** to comb sb's hair **2 se peigner** *vpr* to comb one's hair

peignoir [pɛɲwar] *nm Br* dressing gown, *Am* bathrobe; **p. de bain** bathrobe

peindre* [pɛ̃dr] **1** *vt* to paint **2** *vi* to paint

peine [pɛn] *nf* (**a**) *(châtiment)* punishment; **p. de mort** death penalty; **p. de prison** prison sentence; **'défense d'entrer sous p. d'amende'** 'trespassers will be prosecuted'
(**b**) *(chagrin)* sorrow; **avoir de la p. to** be upset; **faire de la p. à qn** to upset sb
(**c**) *(effort)* trouble; *(difficulté)* difficulty; **se donner de la p. ou beaucoup de p.** to go to a lot of trouble (**pour faire** to do); **avec p.** with difficulty; **ça vaut la p. d'attendre** it's worth waiting; **ce n'est pas ou ça ne vaut pas la p.** it's not worth it
(**d**) **à p.** hardly, scarcely; **à p. arrivée, elle...** no sooner had she arrived than she... ■ **peiner 1** *vt* to upset **2** *vi* to labour

peintre [pɛ̃tr] *nm (artiste)* painter; **p. en bâtiment** painter and decorator ■ **peinture** *nf (tableau, activité)* painting; *(matière)* paint; **p. à l'huile** oil painting; **'p. fraîche'** 'wet paint'

Pékin [pekɛ̃] *nm ou f* Peking, Beijing

pelage [pəlaʒ] *nm* coat, fur

pelé, -e [pəle] *adj* bare

peler [pəle] **1** *vt* to peel **2** *vi (personne, peau)* to peel

pelle [pɛl] *nf* shovel; *(d'enfant)* spade; **p. à tarte** cake server

pellicule [pelikyl] *nf (pour photos)* film; *(couche)* thin layer; **pellicules** *(de cheveux)* dandruff

pelote [plɔt] *nf (de laine)* ball; *(à épingles)* pincushion; *Sport* **p. basque** pelota

peloton [p(ə)lɔtɔ̃] *nm (de ficelle)* ball; *(de cyclistes)* pack; *Mil* platoon; **p. d'exécution** firing squad

pelotonner [plɔtɔne] **se pelotonner** *vpr* to curl up (into a ball)

pelouse [pəluz] *nf* lawn

peluche [pəlyʃ] *nf (tissu)* plush; **(jouet en) p.** soft toy; **peluches** *(de pull)* fluff, lint

pelure [pəlyr] *nf (de légumes)* peelings; *(de fruits)* peel

pénal, -e, -aux, -ales [penal, -o] *adj* penal ■ **pénaliser** *vt* to penalize ■ **pénalité** *nf* penalty

penalty [penalti] *nm Sport* penalty

penchant [pɑ̃ʃɑ̃] *nm (préférence)* penchant (**pour** for); *(tendance)* propensity *(pour* for)

penché, -e [pɑ̃ʃe] *adj* leaning

pencher [pɑ̃ʃe] **1** *vt (objet)* to tilt; *(tête)* to lean **2** *vi (arbre)* to lean over **3 se pencher** *vpr* to lean over; **se p. par la fenêtre** to lean out of the window; **se p. sur qch** *(problème)* to examine sth

pendaison [pɑ̃dɛzɔ̃] *nf* hanging

pendant¹ [pɑ̃dɑ̃] *prép (au cours de)* during; **p. deux mois** for two months; **p. tout le trajet** for the whole journey; **p. que...** while...

pendant², -e 1 *adj* hanging; *(langue)* hanging out **2** *nm* **le p. de** the companion piece to

pendentif [pɑ̃dɑ̃tif] *nm (collier)* pendant

penderie [pɑ̃dri] *nf Br* wardrobe, *Am* closet

pendre [pɑ̃dr] **1** *vti* to hang (**à** from); **p. qn** to hang sb **2 se pendre** *vpr (se suicider)* to hang oneself; *(se suspendre)* to hang (**à** from) ■ **pendu, -e** *adj (objet)* hanging (**à** from)

pendule [pɑ̃dyl] **1** nf clock **2** nm (balancier) pendulum

pénétrer [penetre] **1** vi **p. dans** to enter; (profondément) to penetrate (into) **2** vt (sujet: pluie) to penetrate **3 se pénétrer** vpr **se p. d'une idée** to become convinced of an idea ▪ **pénétration** nf penetration

pénible [penibl] adj (difficile) difficult; (douloureux) painful, distressing; (ennuyeux) tiresome ▪ **péniblement** [-əmɑ̃] adv with difficulty

péniche [peniʃ] nf barge

pénicilline [penisilin] nf penicillin

péninsule [penɛ̃syl] nf peninsula

pénitencier [penitɑ̃sje] nm prison, Am penitentiary

pensée [pɑ̃se] nf (idée) thought; **à la p. de faire qch** at the thought of doing sth

penser [pɑ̃se] **1** vi (réfléchir) to think (**à** of or about); **p. à qn/qch** to think of or about sb/sth; **p. à faire qch** (ne pas oublier) to remember to do sth; **pensestu!** what an idea!
2 vt (estimer) to think (**que** that); (concevoir) to think out; **je pensais rester** I was thinking of staying; **que pensez-vous de…?** what do you think of or about…?; **p. du bien de qn/qch** to think highly of sb/sth ▪ **pensif, -ive** adj thoughtful, pensive

pension [pɑ̃sjɔ̃] nf (**a**) (école) boarding school; **mettre un enfant en p.** to send a child to boarding school (**b**) (hôtel) **p. de famille** boarding house; **p. complète** Br full board, Am American plan (**c**) (allocation) pension; **p. alimentaire** maintenance, alimony ▪ **pensionnaire** nmf (élève, résident) boarder ▪ **pensionnat** nm boarding school

pente [pɑ̃t] nf slope; **être en p.** to be sloping

Pentecôte [pɑ̃tkot] nf Rel Br Whitsun, Am Pentecost

pénurie [penyri] nf shortage (**de** of)

pépé [pepe] nm grandpa

pépin [pepɛ̃] nm (de fruit) Br pip, Am seed, pit

pépinière [pepinjɛr] nf (pour plantes) nursery

pépite [pepit] nf (d'or) nugget; **p. de chocolat** chocolate chip

perçant, -e [pɛrsɑ̃, -ɑ̃t] adj (cri, froid) piercing; (vue) sharp

percée [pɛrse] nf (ouverture) opening; Mil, Sport & Tech breakthrough

perceptible [pɛrsɛptibl] adj perceptible (**à** to)

perception [pɛrsɛpsjɔ̃] nf (**a**) (bureau) tax office; (d'impôt) collection (**b**) (sensation) perception

percer [pɛrse] **1** vt (trouer) to pierce; (avec une perceuse) to drill; (trou, ouverture) to make; (abcès) to lance; (mystère) to solve; **p. une dent** (bébé) to cut a tooth; **p. qch à jour** to see through sth **2** vi (soleil) to break through; (abcès) to burst; (acteur) to make a name for oneself ▪ **perceuse** nf drill

percevoir* [pɛrsəvwar] vt (**a**) (sensation) to perceive; (son) to hear (**b**) (impôt) to collect

perche [pɛrʃ] nf (bâton) pole

percher [pɛrʃe] **1** vi (oiseau) to perch **2 se percher** vpr (oiseau, personne) to perch

percuter [pɛrkyte] **1** vt (véhicule) to crash into **2** vi **p. contre** to crash into **3 se percuter** vpr to crash into each other

perdant, -e [pɛrdɑ̃, -ɑ̃t] **1** adj losing **2** nmf loser

perdre [pɛrdr] **1** vt to lose; (habitude) to get out of; **p. qn/qch de vue** to lose sight of sb/sth **2** vi to lose **3 se perdre** vpr (s'égarer) to get lost; (disparaître) to die out; **se p. dans les détails** to get lost in details ▪ **perdu, -e** adj (égaré) lost; (gaspillé) wasted; (malade) finished; (lieu) out-of-the-way

père [pɛr] nm father; **de p. en fils** from father to son; Rel **mon p.** father; **p. de famille** father

péremption [perɑ̃psjɔ̃] nf **date de p.** use-by date

perfection [pɛrfɛksjɔ̃] nf perfection; **à la p.** to perfection

perfectionner [pɛrfɛksjɔne] **1** vt to improve, to perfect **2 se perfectionner** vpr **se p. en anglais** to improve one's English ▪ **perfectionné, -e** adj advanced ▪ **perfectionnement** nm improvement (**de** in; **par rapport à** on); **cours de p.** proficiency course

perfectionniste [pɛrfɛksjɔnist] nmf perfectionist

perforer [pɛrfɔre] vt (pneu, intestin) to perforate; (billet) to punch; **carte perforée** punch card

performance [pɛrfɔrmɑ̃s] nf performance ▪ **performant, -e** adj highly efficient

perfusion [pɛrfyzjɔ̃] nf drip; **être sous p.** to be on a drip

péril [peril] nm danger, peril; **à tes risques et périls** at your own risk; **mettre qch en p.** to endanger sth ▪ **périlleux, -euse** adj dangerous, perilous

périmé, -e [perime] adj (billet) expired; (nourriture) past its sell-by date

période [perjɔd] nf period ▪ **périodique 1** adj periodic **2** nm (revue) periodical

périphérie [periferi] nf (limite) periphery; (banlieue) outskirts

périphérique [periferik] **1** adj peripheral; **radio p.** = radio station broadcasting from outside France **2** nm & adj (boulevard) p. Br ring road, Am beltway

périr [perir] vi to perish ▪ **périssable** adj (denrée) perishable

perle [pɛrl] nf (bijou) pearl; (de bois, de verre) bead

permanent, -e [pɛrmanɑ̃, -ɑ̃t] **1** adj permanent; Cin (spectacle) continuous; (comité) standing **2** nf permanente perm ▪ **permanence** nf permanence; (salle d'étude) study room; (service, bureau) duty office; **être de p.** to be on duty; **en p.** permanently

perméable [pɛrmeabl] adj permeable (**à** to)

permettre* [pɛrmɛtr] **1** vt to allow, to permit; **p. à qn de faire qch** to allow sb to do sth; **vous permettez?** may I? **2 se permettre** vpr **se p. de faire qch** to take the liberty of doing sth; **je ne peux pas me le p.** I can't afford it

permis, -e [pɛrmi, -iz] **1** adj allowed, permitted **2** nm Br licence, Am license, permit; **p. de conduire** Br driving licence, Am driver's license; **passer son p. de conduire** to take one's driving test

permission [pɛrmisjɔ̃] nf permission; Mil leave; Mil **en p.** on leave; **demander la p.** to ask permission (**de faire** to do)

permuter [pɛrmyte] **1** vt (lettres, chiffres) to transpose **2** vi to exchange posts

Pérou [peru] nm **le P.** Peru

perpendiculaire [pɛrpɑ̃dikylɛr] adj & nf perpendicular (**à** to)

perpétrer [pɛrpetre] vt to perpetrate

perpétuel, -elle [pɛrpetɥɛl] adj perpetual; (membre) permanent ▪ **perpétuer** vt to perpetuate ▪ **perpétuité** adv **à p.** in perpetuity; **condamnation à p.** life sentence

perplexe [pɛrplɛks] adj perplexed, puzzled

perquisition [pɛrkizisjɔ̃] nf search ▪ **perquisitionner** vi to make a search

perron [pɛrɔ̃] nm steps (leading to a building)

perroquet [pɛrɔke] nm parrot

perruche [peryʃ] nf Br budgerigar, Am parakeet

perruque [peryk] nf wig

persan, -e [pɛrsɑ̃, -an] **1** adj Persian **2** nm (langue) Persian

persécuter [pɛrsekyte] vt to persecute ▪ **persécution** nf persecution

persévérer [pɛrsevere] vi to persevere (**dans** in) ▪ **persévérance** nf perseverance ▪ **persévérant, -e** adj persevering

persil [pɛrsi] nm parsley

Persique [pɛrsik] adj **le golfe P.** the Persian Gulf

persister [pɛrsiste] vi to persist (**à**

faire in doing; **dans qch** in sth ■ **persistance** *nf* persistence

personnage [pɛrsɔnaʒ] *nm (de fiction, individu)* character; *(personnalité)* important person; **p. célèbre** celebrity; **p. officiel** VIP

personnaliser [pɛrsɔnalize] *vt* to personalize; *(voiture)* to customize

personnalité [pɛrsɔnalite] *nf (caractère, personnage)* personality; **avoir de la p.** to have lots of personality

personne [pɛrsɔn] **1** *nf (être)* person; **deux personnes** two people; **p. âgée** elderly person; **en p.** in person **2** *pron indéfini (de négation)* **(ne...) p.** nobody, no one; **je ne vois p.** I don't see anybody *or* anyone; **p. ne saura** nobody *or* no one will know

personnel, -elle [pɛrsɔnɛl] **1** *adj* personal; *(joueur, jeu)* individualistic **2** *nm (de firme, d'école)* staff; *(d'usine)* workforce; **manquer de p.** to be understaffed; **p. au sol** ground personnel

personnifier [pɛrsɔnifje] *vt* to personify ■ **personnification** *nf* personification

perspective [pɛrspɛktiv] *nf (de dessin)* perspective; *(idée)* prospect *(de* of); *Fig (point de vue)* viewpoint; **perspectives d'avenir** future prospects

perspicace [pɛrspikas] *adj* shrewd ■ **perspicacité** *nf* shrewdness

persuader [pɛrsɥade] *vt* **p. qn (de qch)** to persuade sb (of sth); **p. qn de faire qch** to persuade sb to do sth; **être persuadé de qch/que...** to be convinced of sth/that... ■ **persuasif, -ive** *adj* persuasive ■ **persuasion** *nf* persuasion

perte [pɛrt] *nf* loss; *(destruction)* ruin; **une p. de temps** a waste of time; **à p. de vue** as far as the eye can see; **vendre qch à p.** to sell sth at a loss

pertinent, -e [pɛrtinɑ̃, -ɑ̃t] *adj* relevant, pertinent ■ **pertinemment** [-amɑ̃] *adv* **savoir qch p.** to know sth for a fact ■ **pertinence** *nf* relevance, pertinence

perturber [pɛrtyrbe] *vt (trafic, cérémonie)* to disrupt; *(personne)* to disturb ■ **perturbateur, -trice** **1** *adj* disruptive **2** *nmf* troublemaker ■ **perturbation** *nf* disruption

péruvien, -enne [peryvjɛ̃, -jɛn] **1** *adj* Peruvian **2** *nmf* **P., Péruvienne** Peruvian

pervers, -e [pɛrvɛr, -ɛrs] **1** *adj* perverse **2** *nmf* pervert ■ **perversion** *nf* perversion ■ **perversité** *nf* perversity ■ **pervertir** *vt* to pervert

pesant, -e [pəzɑ̃, -ɑ̃t] **1** *adj* heavy, weighty **2** *nm* **valoir son p. d'or** to be worth one's weight in gold ■ **pesanteur** *nf* heaviness; *Phys* gravity

pesée [pəze] *nf* weighing; *(pression)* force

peser [pəze] **1** *vt* to weigh **2** *vi* to weigh; **p. 2 kilos** to weigh 2 kilos; **p. lourd** to be heavy; *Fig (argument)* to carry weight; **p. sur** *(appuyer)* to press on; *(influer)* to bear upon; **p. sur qn** *(menace)* to hang over sb ■ **pèse-personne** *(pl* **pèse-personnes)** *nm (bathroom)* scales

pessimisme [pesimism] *nm* pessimism ■ **pessimiste 1** *adj* pessimistic **2** *nmf* pessimist

pester [pɛste] *vi* **p. contre qn/qch** to curse sb/sth

pétale [petal] *nm* petal

pétanque [petɑ̃k] *nf (jeu)* ≃ bowls

pétard [petar] *nm (feu d'artifice)* firecracker, *Br* banger

pétiller [petije] *vi (yeux, vin)* to sparkle ■ **pétillant, -e** *adj (gazeux)* sparkling

petit, -e [pəti, -it] **1** *adj* small, little; *(taille, distance)* short; *(bruit, coup)* slight; *(somme)* small; *(accident)* minor; *(mesquin)* petty; **tout p.** tiny; **mon p. frère** my little brother

2 *nmf (little)* boy, *f (little)* girl; *(personne)* small person; *Scol* junior; **petits** *(d'animal)* young; *(de chien)* pups; *(de chat)* kittens

3 *adv* **écrire p.** to write small; **p. à p.** little by little ■ **petite-fille** *(pl* **petites-filles)** *nf* granddaughter ■ **petit-fils** *(pl*

petits-fils) *nm* grandson ■ **petits-enfants** *nmpl* grandchildren

pétition [petisjɔ̃] *nf* petition

pétrifier [petrifje] *vt* to petrify

pétrir [petrir] *vt* to knead

pétrole [petrol] *nm* oil, petroleum ■ **pétrolier, -ère 1** *adj* industrie pétrolière oil industry **2** *nm* oil tanker ■ **pétrolifère** *adj* gisement p. oilfield

PEU [pø] **1** *adv (avec un verbe)* not much; *(avec un adjectif, un adverbe)* not very; *(un petit nombre)* few; **elle mange p.** she doesn't eat much; **p. intéressant/souvent** not very interesting/often; **p. ont compris** few understood; **p. de sel/de temps** not much salt/time, little salt/time; **p. de gens/de livres** few people/books; **p. à p.** little by little, gradually; **à p. près** more or less; **p. après/avant** shortly after/before; **sous p.** shortly; **pour p. que…** *(+ subjunctive)* if by chance… **2** *nm* **un p.** a little, a bit; **un p. grand** a bit big; **un p. de fromage** a little cheese, a bit of cheese; **un (tout) petit p.** a (tiny) little bit; **le p. de fromage que j'ai** the little cheese I have; **reste encore un p.** stay a little longer

peuplade [pøplad] *nf* tribe

peuple [pœpl] *nm (nation, citoyens)* people; **les gens du p.** ordinary people

peupler [pœple] *vt (habiter)* to inhabit ■ **peuplé, -e** *adj (région)* inhabited (**de** by); **très/peu p.** highly/sparsely populated

peuplier [pøplije] *nm (arbre, bois)* poplar

peur [pœr] *nf* fear; **avoir p.** to be afraid *or* frightened (**de qn/qch** of sb/sth; **de faire qch** to do sth *or* of doing sth); **faire p. à qn** to frighten *or* scare sb; **de p. qu'il ne parte** for fear that he would leave; **de p. de faire qch** for fear of doing sth ■ **peureux, -euse** *adj* easily fearful

peut [pø] *voir* **pouvoir 1**

peut-être [pøtɛtr] *adv* perhaps,

maybe; **p. qu'il viendra, p. viendra-t-il** perhaps *or* maybe he'll come; **p. que oui** perhaps; **p. que non** perhaps not

peuvent, peux [pœv, pø] *voir* **pouvoir 1**

phare [far] **1** *nm (pour bateaux)* lighthouse; *(de véhicule)* headlight; **faire un appel de phares** to flash one's lights **2** *adj* épreuve-p. star event

pharmacie [farmasi] *nf (magasin)* Br chemist, *Am* drugstore; *(armoire)* medicine cabinet ■ **pharmaceutique** *adj* pharmaceutical ■ **pharmacien, -enne** *nmf Br* chemist, pharmacist, *Am* druggist

phase [faz] *nf* phase

phénomène [fenɔmɛn] *nm* phenomenon

philharmonique [filarmɔnik] *adj* philharmonic

Philippines [filipin] *nfpl* les P. the Philippines

philosophe [filozof] **1** *nmf* philosopher **2** *adj* philosophical ■ **philosopher** *vi* to philosophize (**sur** about) ■ **philosophie** *nf* philosophy ■ **philosophique** *adj* philosophical

photo [foto] **1** *nf (cliché)* photo; *(art)* photography; **prendre une p. de qn/qch, prendre qn/qch en p.** to take a photo of sb/sth; **p. d'identité** ID photo **2** *adj inv* appareil p. camera ■ **photogénique** *adj* photogenic ■ **photographe** *nmf* photographer ■ **photographie** *nf (art)* photography; *(cliché)* photograph ■ **photographier** *vt* to photograph; **se faire p.** to have one's photo taken ■ **photographique** *adj* photographic

photocopie [fotokɔpi] *nf* photocopy ■ **photocopier** *vt* to photocopy ■ **photocopieur** *nm*, **photocopieuse** [fotokɔpjøz] *nf* photocopier

Photomaton® [fotomatɔ̃] *nm* photo booth

phrase [fraz] *nf* sentence

physicien, -enne [fizisjɛ̃, -ɛn] *nmf* physicist

physique [fizik] **1** *adj* physical **2** *nm* (de personne) physique **3** *nf* (science) physics (*sing*)

pianiste [pjanist] *nmf* pianist

piano [pjano] *nm* piano; **p. droit/à queue** upright/grand piano ■ **pianoter** *vi* **p. sur qch** (table) to drum one's fingers on sth

pic [pik] *nm* (cime) peak; (outil) pick(-axe); (oiseau) woodpecker; **couler à p.** to sink like a stone; **tomber à p.** (falaise) to go straight down; **p. à glace** ice pick

pichet [piʃɛ] *nm Br* jug, *Am* pitcher

picorer [pikɔre] *vt* to peck

picoter [pikɔte] *vt* **j'ai la gorge qui (me) picote** I've got a tickle in my throat

pièce [pjɛs] *nf* (de maison) room; (morceau, objet) piece; (de pantalon) patch; (de dossier) document; **p. (de monnaie)** coin; **p. (de théâtre)** play; **5 euros la p.** 5 euros each; **mettre qch en pièces** to tear sth to pieces; **p. d'identité** proof of identity; **pièces détachées** *ou* **de rechange** spare parts

pied [pje] *nm* (de personne) foot (*pl* feet); (de lit, d'arbre, de colline) foot; (de meuble) leg; (de verre, de lampe) base; **à p.** on foot; **aller à p.** to walk, to go on foot; **au p. de** at the foot *or* bottom of; **sur un p. d'égalité** on an equal footing; **avoir p.** to be within one's depth; **mettre qch sur p.** to set sth up

piédestal, -aux [pjedɛstal, -o] *nm* pedestal

piège [pjɛʒ] *nm* (pour animal) & *Fig* trap ■ **piéger** *vt* (animal) to trap; (voiture) to booby-trap; **voiture/lettre piégée** car/letter bomb

pierre [pjɛr] *nf* stone; (de bijou) gem, stone; **p. précieuse** precious stone, gem ■ **pierreries** *nfpl* gems, precious stones ■ **pierreux, -euse** *adj* stony

piétiner [pjetine] **1** *vt* **p. qch** (en trépignant) to stamp on sth; (en marchant) to trample on sth **2** *vi* (ne pas avancer) to stand around; **p. d'impatience** to

stamp one's feet impatiently

piéton [pjetɔ̃] *nm* pedestrian ■ **piétonne, piétonnière** [pjetɔnjɛr] *adj f* **rue p.** pedestrian(ized) street; **zone p.** pedestrian precinct

pigeon [piʒɔ̃] *nm* pigeon

pile [pil] **1** *nf* (**a**) **p. (électrique)** battery; **radio à piles** battery radio (**b**) (tas) pile; **en p.** in a pile (**c**) (de pièce) **p. ou face?** heads or tails?; **jouer à p. ou face** to toss for it **2** *adv Fam* **s'arrêter p.** to stop dead; *Fam* **à deux heures p.** at two on the dot

piler [pile] *vt* (broyer) to crush; (amandes) to grind

pilier [pilje] *nm* pillar

piller [pije] *vt* to loot, to pillage ■ **pillage** *nm* looting, pillaging

pilon [pilɔ̃] *nm* (de poulet) drumstick

pilonner [pilɔne] *vt* (bombarder) to bombard

pilote [pilɔt] **1** *nm* (d'avion, de bateau) pilot; (de voiture) driver; **p. automatique** automatic pilot; **p. de chasse** fighter pilot; **p. d'essai** test pilot; **p. de ligne** airline pilot **2** *adj* usine(-)p. pilot factory ■ **pilotage** *nm* piloting ■ **piloter** *vt* (avion) to fly, to pilot; (bateau) to pilot; (voiture) to drive

pilule [pilyl] *nf* pill; **prendre la p.** to be on the pill

piment [pimɑ̃] *nm* chilli ■ **pimenté, -e** *adj* (épicé) spicy

pin [pɛ̃] *nm* (arbre, bois) pine; **pomme de p.** pine cone; (de sapin) fir cone

pince [pɛ̃s] *nf* (outil) pliers; (sur vêtement) dart; (de crustacé) pincer; **p. à épiler** tweezers; **p. à linge** (clothes) *Br* peg *or Am* pin

pincé, -e [pɛ̃se] *adj* (air) stiff; (sourire) tight-lipped

pinceau, -x [pɛ̃so] *nm* (paint)brush

pincer [pɛ̃se] **1** *vt* to pinch **2 se pincer** *vpr* **se p. le doigt** to get one's finger caught (**dans** in); **se p. le nez** to hold one's nose ■ **pincée** *nf* pinch (**de** of)

ping-pong [piŋpɔ̃g] *nm* table tennis, Ping-Pong®

pintade [pɛ̃tad] *nf* guinea fowl

pioche [pjɔʃ] *nf (outil)* pick(axe); *Cartes* stock, pile ■ **piocher** *vt (creuser)* to dig *(with a pick)*; **p. une carte** to draw a card

pion [pjɔ̃] *nm (au jeu de dames)* piece; *Échecs & Fig* pawn

pionnier [pjɔnje] *nm* pioneer

pipe [pip] *nf (de fumeur)* pipe

pipeau, -x [pipo] *nm (flûte)* pipe

piquant, -e [pikɑ̃, -ɑ̃t] **1** *adj (au goût)* spicy, hot; *(plante, barbe)* prickly; *(détail)* spicy **2** *nm (de plante)* prickle, thorn; *(d'animal)* spine

pique [pik] **1** *nm Cartes (couleur)* spades **2** *nf (allusion)* cutting remark; *(arme)* pike

pique-nique [piknik] *(pl* **pique-niques**) *nm* picnic ■ **pique-niquer** *vi* to picnic

piquer [pike] **1** *vt (percer)* to prick; *(langue, yeux)* to sting; *(sujet: moustique)* to bite; **p. qch dans** *(enfoncer)* to stick sth into; **la fumée me pique les yeux** the smoke is making my eyes sting **2** *vi (moutarde)* to be hot **3** **se piquer** *vpr* to prick oneself; **se p. au doigt** to prick one's finger

piquet [pikɛ] *nm (pieu)* stake, post; *(de tente)* peg; **p. de grève** picket

piqûre [pikyʀ] *nf (d'abeille)* sting; *(de moustique)* bite; *(d'épingle)* prick; *(de tissu)* stitching; *(de rouille)* spot; *Méd* injection; **faire une p. à qn** to give sb an injection

pirate [piʀat] **1** *nm (des mers)* pirate; **p. de l'air** hijacker; **p. informatique** hacker **2** *adj* **radio p.** pirate radio; **édition/CD p.** pirated edition/CD ■ **pirater** *vt (enregistrement)* to pirate; *Ordinat* to hack

pire [piʀ] **1** *adj* worse *(que* than); **c'est de p. en p.** it's getting worse and worse **2** *nmf* **le/la p.** the worst (one); **le p. de tout** the worst thing of all; **au p.** at (the very) worst; **s'attendre au p.** to expect the (very) worst

pirogue [piʀɔg] *nf* canoe, dugout

pis¹ [pi] *nm (de vache)* udder

pis² [pi] *adv* **aller de mal en p.** to go from bad to worse

piscine [pisin] *nf* swimming pool

pistache [pistaʃ] *nf* pistachio

piste [pist] *nf (traces)* track, trail; *(indices)* lead; *(de magnétophone) & Sport* track; *(de cirque)* ring; *(de ski)* run, piste; *(pour chevaux) Br* racecourse, *Am* racetrack; *Sport* **tour de p.** lap; **p. d'atterrissage** runway; **p. cyclable** *Br* cycle path, *Am* bicycle path; **p. de danse** dance floor

pistolet [pistɔlɛ] *nm* gun, pistol; *(de peintre)* spray gun; **p. à eau** water pistol

pitié [pitje] *nf* pity; **avoir de la p. pour qn** to pity sb; **il me fait p.** I feel sorry for him; **être sans p.** to be ruthless ■ **pitoyable** *adj (piteux) = * **piteux, -euse** *adj* pitiful; **en p. état** in a sorry state

piton [pitɔ̃] *nm (d'alpiniste)* piton; **p. (rocheux)** (rocky) peak

pittoresque [pitɔʀɛsk] *adj* picturesque

pivoter [pivɔte] *vi* to pivot, to swivel; **faire p. qch** to swivel sth round

pizza [pidza] *nf* pizza ■ **pizzeria** *nf* pizzeria

placard [plakaʀ] *nm (armoire) Br* cupboard, *Am* closet; **p. publicitaire** large display advertisement

place [plas] *nf (endroit, rang) & Sport* place; *(lieu public)* square; *(espace)* room; *(siège)* seat; *(emploi)* job, post; **à la p.** instead *(de* of); **à votre p.** in your place; **se mettre à la p. de qn** to put oneself in sb's position; **sur p.** on the spot; **en p.** *(objet)* in place; **mettre qch en p.** to put sth in place; **changer de p.** to change places; **faire de la p.** to make room *(à* for); **faire p. à qn/qch** to give way to sb/sth; **prendre p.** to take a seat; **p. de parking** parking space; **p. de train/bus** train/bus fare; **p. assise** seat

placer [plase] **1** *vt (mettre)* to put, to place; *(faire asseoir)* to seat; *(trouver un emploi à)* to place; *(argent)* to invest *(dans* in) **2** **se placer** *vpr (debout)* to stand; *(s'asseoir)* to sit ■ **placé, -e** *adj (objet) & Sport* placed; **bien/mal p.**

pour faire qch well/badly placed to do sth ■ **placement** *nm (d'argent)* investment

plafond [plafɔ̃] *nm* ceiling ■ **plafonner** *vi (prix)* to peak; *(salaires)* to have reached a ceiling (**à** of) ■ **plafonnier** *nm* ceiling light

plage [plaʒ] *nf (grève)* beach; *(surface)* area; *(de disque)* track; **p. de sable** sandy beach; **p. horaire** time slot

plaider [plede] *vti Jur (défendre)* to plead; **p. coupable** to plead guilty ■ **plaidoyer** *nm Jur* speech for the *Br* defence *orAm* defense

plaie [plɛ] *nf (blessure)* wound

plaindre* [plɛ̃dr] **1** *vt* to feel sorry for, to pity **2 se plaindre** *vpr (protester)* to complain (**de** about; **que** that); **se p. de** *(douleur)* to complain of ■ **plainte** *nf* complaint; *(gémissement)* moan; **porter p. contre qn** to lodge a complaint against sb

plaine [plɛn] *nf* plain

plaintif, -ive [plɛ̃tif, -iv] *adj* plaintive

plaire* [plɛr] **1** *vi* **elle me plaît** I like her; **ça me plaît** I like it **2** *v impersonnel* **il me plaît de le faire** I like doing it; **s'il vous/te plaît** please; **comme il vous plaira** as you like it **3 se plaire** *vpr (l'un l'autre)* to like each other; **se p. à Paris** to like it in Paris

plaisance [plɛzɑ̃s] *nf* **navigation de p.** yachting

plaisant, -e [plɛzɑ̃, -ɑ̃t] **1** *adj (drôle)* amusing; *(agréable)* pleasing **2** *nm* **mauvais p.** joker ■ **plaisanter** *vi* to joke (**sur** about) ■ **plaisanterie** *nf* joke; **par p.** for a joke ■ **plaisantin** *nm* joker

plaisir [plɛzir] *nm* pleasure; **faire p. à qn** to please sb; **pour le p.** for the fun of it; **au p. (de vous revoir)** see you again sometime; **faites-moi le p. de…** would you be good enough to…

plan [plɑ̃] *nm (projet, dessin, organisation)* plan; *(de ville)* map; *Math* plane; **au premier p.** in the foreground; *Phot* **au second p.** in the background; **sur le p. politique, au p. politique** from the political viewpoint; **sur le même p.** on the same level; **de premier p.** of importance, major; *Phot & Cin* **gros p.** close-up; **p. d'eau** stretch of water; *Fin* **p. d'épargne** savings plan

planche [plɑ̃ʃ] *nf (en bois)* plank; *(plus large)* board; *(illustration)* plate; **faire la p.** to float on one's back; **p. à dessin** drawing board; **p. à roulettes** skateboard; **p. à voile** sailboard; **faire de la p. à voile** to go windsurfing

plancher [plɑ̃ʃe] *nm* floor

planer [plane] *vi (oiseau, planeur)* to glide

planète [planɛt] *nf* planet

planeur [planœr] *nm (avion)* glider

planifier [planifje] *vt* to plan

plant [plɑ̃] *nm (de plante)* seedling

plantation [plɑ̃tasjɔ̃] *nf (action)* planting; *(exploitation agricole)* plantation

plante [plɑ̃t] *nf Bot* plant; **jardin des plantes** botanical gardens; **p. du pied** sole (of the foot)

planter [plɑ̃te] *vt (fleur, arbre)* to plant; *(clou, couteau)* to drive in; *(tente)* to put up; *(mettre)* to put (**sur** on; **contre** against)

plaque [plak] *nf* plate; *(de verre, de métal)* sheet, plate; *(de verglas)* sheet; *(de marbre)* slab; *(de chocolat)* bar; *(commémorative)* plaque; *(sur la peau)* blotch; **p. chauffante** hotplate; *Aut* **p. minéralogique, p. d'immatriculation** *Br* number *orAm* license plate

plaquer [plake] **1** *vt (métal, bijou)* to plate; *(bois)* to veneer; *(cheveux)* to plaster down; *(au rugby)* to tackle; *(aplatir)* to flatten (**contre** against) **2 se plaquer** *vpr* **se p. contre** to flatten oneself against ■ **plaqué, -e 1** *adj (bijou)* plated; **p. or** gold-plated **2** *nm* **p. or** gold plate

plasma [plasma] *nm Biol* plasma

plastic [plastik] *nm* plastic explosive ■ **plastiquer** *vt* to bomb

plastifier [plastifje] *vt* to laminate

plastique [plastik] *adj & nm* plastic

plat, -e [pla, plat] **1** *adj* flat; *(mer)* calm,

smooth; (*ennuyeux*) flat, dull; **à p. ven-tre** flat on one's face; **à p.** (*pneu, batterie*) flat; **poser qch à p.** to lay sth (down) flat

2 *nm* (**a**) (*de la main*) flat (**b**) (*récipient, nourriture*) dish; (*partie du repas*) course; **p. de résistance** main course ■ **plate-bande** (*pl* **plates-bandes**) *nf* flower bed ■ **plate-forme** (*pl* **plates-formes**) *nf* platform; **p. pétrolière** oil rig

plateau, -x [plato] *nm* tray; (*de balance*) pan; *TV & Cin* set; *Géog* plateau; **p. à fromages** cheeseboard

platine¹ [platin] **1** *nm* (*métal*) platinum **2** *adj inv* platinum; **blond p.** platinum blond

platine² [platin] *nf* (*d'électrophone, de magnétophone*) deck; **p. laser** CD player

platitude [platityd] *nf* (*propos*) platitude

plâtre [platr] *nm* (*matière*) plaster; **un p.** (*de jambe cassée*) a plaster cast; **les plâtres** (*de maison*) the plasterwork ■ **plâtrer** *vt* (*mur*) to plaster; (*membre*) to put in plaster

plausible [plozibl] *adj* plausible

play-back [plebak] *nm inv* **chanter en p.** to mime

plein, -e [plɛ̃, plɛn] **1** *adj* (*rempli, complet*) full; (*solide*) solid; **p. de** full of; **p. à craquer** full to bursting; **en pleine mer** out at sea, on the open sea; **en pleine figure** right in the face; **en pleine nuit** in the middle of the night; **en p. jour** in broad daylight; **en p. hiver** in the depths of winter; **en p. soleil** in the full heat of the sun; **être en p. travail** to be hard at work; **à la pleine lune** at full moon; **travailler à p. temps** to work full-time; **p. sud** due south; **p. tarif** full price; (*de transport*) full fare

2 *adv* **de l'argent p. les poches** pockets full of money; **du chocolat p. la figure** chocolate all over one's face

3 *nm* *Aut* **faire le p. (d'essence)** to fill up (the tank)

pleurer [plœre] **1** *vi* to cry, to weep (**sur** over) **2** *vt* (*personne*) to mourn (for) ■ **pleurs** *mpl* **en p.** in tears

pleuvoir* [pløvwar] **1** *v impersonnel* to rain; **il pleut** it's raining; *Fig* **il pleut des cordes** it's raining cats and dogs **2** *vi* (*coups*) to rain down (**sur** on)

Plexiglas® [plɛksiglas] *nm* *Br* Perspex®, *Am* Plexiglas®

pli [pli] *nm* (**a**) (*de papier, de rideau, de la peau*) fold; (*de jupe, de robe*) pleat; (*de pantalon, de bouche*) crease; (**faux**) **p.** crease; **mise en plis** set (*hairstyle*) (**b**) (*enveloppe*) envelope; (*lettre*) letter (**c**) *Cartes* trick

plier [plije] **1** *vt* (*draps, vêtements*) to fold; (*parapluie*) to fold up; (*courber*) to bend; **p. bagages** to pack one's bags (and leave) **2** *vi* (*branche*) to bend **3 se plier** *vpr* (*lit, chaise*) to fold up; **se p. à** to submit to ■ **pliable** *adj* foldable ■ **pliage** *nm* (*manière*) fold; (*action*) folding ■ **pliant, -e 1** *adj* (*chaise*) folding **2** *nm* folding stool

plisser [plise] *vt* (*lèvres*) to pucker; (*front*) to wrinkle; (*yeux*) to screw up ■ **plissé, -e** *adj* (*jupe*) pleated

plomb [plɔ̃] *nm* (*métal*) lead; (*fusible*) *Br* fuse, *Am* fuze; (*pour rideau*) lead weight; **plombs** (*de chasse*) lead shot; *Fig* **de p.** (*sommeil*) heavy; (*soleil*) blazing

plomber [plɔ̃be] *vt* (*dent*) to fill; (*mettre des plombs à*) to weigh with lead ■ **plombage** *nm* (*de dent*) filling

plombier [plɔ̃bje] *nm* plumber ■ **plomberie** *nf* (*métier, installations*) plumbing

plonger [plɔ̃ʒe] **1** *vi* (*personne*) to dive (**dans** into); (*oiseau, avion*) to dive (**sur** onto) **2** *vt* (*enfoncer*) to plunge (**dans** into) **3 se plonger** *vpr* **se p. dans** (*lecture*) to immerse oneself in; **plongé dans l'obscurité** plunged in darkness ■ **plongée** *nf* diving; (*de sous-marin*) dive; **p. sous-marine** skin *or* scuba diving ■ **plongeoir** *nm* diving board ■ **plongeon** *nm* dive; **faire un p.** to dive ■ **plongeur, -euse** *nmf* (*nageur*) diver

plu [ply] *pp de* **plaire, pleuvoir**

pluie [plчi] *nf* rain; **sous la p.** in the rain; **p. fine** drizzle

plume [plym] *nf (d'oiseau)* feather; *(de stylo)* nib ▪ **plumer** *vt (volaille)* to pluck

plupart [plypar] **la plupart** *nf* most; **la p. du temps** most of the time; **la p. d'entre eux** most of them; **pour la p.** mostly

PLUS¹ [ply] ([plyz] *before vowel,* [plys] *in end position*) *adv* (**a**) *(comparatif)* more (**que** than); **p. d'un kilo/de dix** more than a kilo/ten; **p. de thé** more tea; **p. beau/rapidement** more beautiful/quickly (**que** than); **p. tard** later; **p. petit** smaller; **de p. en p.** more and more; **de p. en p. vite** quicker and quicker; **p. ou moins** more or less; **en p.** in addition (**de** to); **au p.** at most; **de p.** more (**que** than); *(en outre)* moreover; **les enfants de p. de dix ans** children over ten; **j'ai dix ans de p. qu'elle** I'm ten years older than she is; **il est p. de cinq heures** it's after five (o'clock); **p. il crie, p. il s'enroue** the more he shouts, the more hoarse he gets

(**b**) *(superlatif)* **le p.** (the) most; **le p. beau** the most beautiful (**de** in); *(de deux)* the more beautiful; **le p. grand** the biggest (**de** in); *(de deux)* the bigger; **j'ai le p. de livres** I have (the) most books; **j'en ai le p.** I have the most

PLUS² [ply] *adv (négation)* (**ne…**) **p.** no more; **il n'a p. de pain** he has no more bread, he doesn't have any more bread; **il n'y a p. rien** there's nothing left; **elle ne le fait p.** she no longer does it, she doesn't do it any more *or* any longer; **je ne la reverrai p.** I won't see her again; **je ne voyagerai p. jamais** I'll never travel again

plus³ [plys] **1** *conj* plus; **deux p. deux font quatre** two plus two are four; **il fait p. 2** *(degrés)* it's 2 degrees above

freezing **2** *nm* **le signe p.** the plus sign

plusieurs [plyzjœr] *adj & pron* several

plutôt [plyto] *adv* rather (**que** than)

pluvieux, -euse [plyvjø, -jøz] *adj* rainy, wet

pneu [pnø] *(pl* **pneus**) *nm (de roue)* Br tyre, *Am* tire ▪ **pneumatique** *adj (gonflable)* inflatable

poche [pɔʃ] *nf (de vêtement)* pocket; *(de kangourou)* pouch ▪ **pochette** *nf (sac)* bag; *(d'allumettes)* book; *(de disque)* sleeve; *(sac à main)* (clutch) bag; *(mouchoir)* pocket handkerchief

pocher [pɔʃe] *vt (œufs)* to poach

poêle [pwal] **1** *nm (chauffage)* stove **2** *nf* **p. (à frire)** frying pan

poème [pɔɛm] *nm* poem ▪ **poésie** *nf (art)* poetry; *(poème)* poem ▪ **poète** *nm* poet

poids [pwa] *nm* weight; *Sport* shot; **au p.** by weight; **prendre/perdre du p.** to gain/lose weight; **p. lourd** *(camion)* Br lorry, *Am* truck; *(en boxe)* heavyweight; **p. plume** *(en boxe)* featherweight

poignant, -e [pwaɲɑ̃, -ɑ̃t] *adj* poignant

poignard [pwaɲar] *nm* dagger; **coup de p.** stab ▪ **poignarder** *vt* to stab

poignée [pwaɲe] *nf (quantité)* handful (**de** of); *(de porte, de casserole)* handle; *(d'épée)* hilt; **p. de main** handshake

poignet [pwaɲe] *nm* wrist; *(de chemise)* cuff

poil [pwal] *nm* hair; *(pelage)* coat; **poils** *(de brosse)* bristles; *(de tapis)* pile; **p. à gratter** itching powder ▪ **poilu, -e** *adj* hairy

poinçonner [pwɛ̃sɔne] *vt (billet)* to punch; *(bijou)* to hallmark

poing [pwɛ̃] *nm* fist

POINT [pwɛ̃] *nm (lieu, score, question)* point; *(sur i, à l'horizon)* dot; *(tache)* spot; *(de notation)* mark; *(de couture)* stitch; **être sur le p. de faire qch** to be about to do sth; **p. (du steak)** medium; **déprimé au p. que…** depressed to such an extent that…; **mettre au p.** *(appareil photo)* to focus; *(moteur)* to tune; *(technique)* to perfect; **être au p.** to be up to scratch; **au p. où j'en suis...** at the stage I've reached...; **au plus haut p.** extremely; **p. de côté** stitch; **p. de départ** starting point; **p. de vue** *(opinion)* point of view, viewpoint; *(endroit)* viewing point; **p. faible/fort** weak/strong point

pointe [pwɛ̃t] *nf (extrémité)* tip, point; *(clou)* nail; *Géog* headland; *Fig (maximum)* peak; **une p. d'humour** a touch of humour; **sur la p. des pieds** on tiptoe; **en p.** pointed; **de p.** *(technologie, industrie)* state-of-the-art; **vitesse de p.** top speed; *Fig* **à la p. de** *(progrès)* in or at the forefront of; **faire des pointes** *(danseuse)* to dance on points; **p. de vitesse** burst of speed

pointer [pwɛ̃te] **1** *vt (cocher)* *Br* to tick off, *Am* to check (off); *(braquer)* to point **(sur/vers** at) **2** *vi (employé)* *(à l'arrivée)* to clock in; *(à la sortie)* to clock out

pointillé [pwɛ̃tije] *nm* dotted line

pointu, -e [pwɛ̃ty] *adj (en pointe)* pointed; *(voix)* shrill; *Fig (spécialisé)* specialized

pointure [pwɛ̃tyr] *nf* size

poire [pwar] *nf (fruit)* pear ■ **poirier** *nm* pear tree

poireau, -x [pwaro] *nm* leek

pois [pwa] *nm (légume)* pea; *(dessin)* (polka) dot; **à p.** *(vêtement)* polkadot; **petits p.** *Br* (garden) peas, *Am* peas; **p. de senteur** sweet pea; **p. chiche** chickpea

poison [pwazɔ̃] *nm* poison

poisson [pwasɔ̃] *nm* fish; **les Poissons** *(signe)* Pisces; **p. d'avril** April fool; **p. rouge** goldfish ■ **poissonnerie** *nf* fish shop ■ **poissonnier, -ère** *nmf* fishmonger

poitrine [pwatrin] *nf* chest; *(seins)* bust; *Culin (de veau)* breast

poivre [pwavr] *nm* pepper ■ **poivrer** *vt* to pepper ■ **poivrière** *nf* pepper pot

poivron [pwavrɔ̃] *nm* pepper

pôle [pol] *nm Géog* pole; **p. Nord/Sud** North/South Pole ■ **polaire** *adj* polar

polémique [pɔlemik] **1** *adj* polemical **2** *nf* heated debate

poli, -e [pɔli] *adj (courtois)* polite **(avec** to or with); *(lisse)* polished

police [pɔlis] *nf* police; *Typ & Ordinat* **p. de caractères** font; **p. secours** emergency services ■ **policier, -ère 1** *adj* **enquête policière** police inquiry; **roman p.** detective novel **2** *nm* policeman, detective

polir [pɔlir] *vt* to polish

politesse [pɔlites] *nf* politeness

politique [pɔlitik] **1** *adj* political **2** *nf (activité, science)* politics *(sing)*; *(mesure)* policy; **faire de la p.** to be in politics **3** *nmf* politician ■ **politicien, -enne** *Péj* politician

pollen [pɔlen] *nm* pollen

polluer [pɔlɥe] *vt* to pollute ■ **polluant** *nm* pollutant ■ **pollueur, -euse** *1* *adj* polluting **2** *nmf* polluter ■ **pollution** *nf* pollution

Pologne [pɔlɔɲ] *nf* **la P.** Poland ■ **polonais, -e 1** *adj* Polish **2** *nmf* **P., Polonaise** Pole **3** *nm (langue)* Polish

polycopier [pɔlikɔpje] *vt* to duplicate

polyester [pɔljɛstɛr] *nm* polyester

polygame [pɔligam] *adj* polygamous

Polynésie [pɔlinezi] *nf* **la P.** Polynesia

polyvalent, -e [pɔlivalɑ̃, -ɑ̃t] **1** *adj (salle)* multi-purpose; *(personne)* versatile **2** *adj & nf (école)* **polyvalente** *Br* = secondary school, *Am* = high school

pommade [pɔmad] *nf* ointment

pomme [pɔm] *nf* **(a)** *(fruit)* apple; *Anat* **p. d'Adam** Adam's apple; **p. de terre** potato; **pommes chips** *Br* (potato) crisps, *Am* (potato) chips; **pommes frites** *Br* chips, *Am* (French) fries; **pommes vapeur** steamed potatoes **(b)** *(d'arrosoir)* rose ■ **pommier** *nm* apple tree

pompe¹ [pɔ̃p] **1** *nf (machine)* pump; **p. à essence** *Br* petrol or *Am* gas station; **p. à vélo** bicycle pump **2** *nfpl* **pompes funèbres** undertaker's; **entrepreneur des pompes funèbres** *Br* undertaker, *Am* mortician

pompe² [pɔ̃p] *nf* **en grande p.** with great ceremony

pomper [pɔ̃pe] **1** *vt (eau, air)* to pump; *(faire monter)* to pump up; *(évacuer)* to pump out **2** *vi* to pump

pompeux, -euse [pɔ̃pø, -øz] *adj* pompous

pompier [pɔ̃pje] *nm* fireman; **voiture des pompiers** fire engine

pompiste [pɔ̃pist] *nmf Br* petrol *or Am* gas station attendant

ponce [pɔ̃s] *nf* **pierre p.** pumice stone

ponctuel, -elle [pɔ̃ktɥɛl] *adj (à l'heure)* punctual; *(unique) Br* one-off, *Am* one-of-a-kind ▪ **ponctualité** *nf* punctuality

ponctuer [pɔ̃ktɥe] *vt* to punctuate (**de** with)

pondre [pɔ̃dr] *vt (œuf)* to lay

poney [pɔne] *nm* pony

pont [pɔ̃] *nm* bridge; *(de bateau)* deck; *Fig* **faire le p.** to make a long weekend of it ▪ **pont-levis** *(pl* **ponts-levis**) *nm* drawbridge

populaire [pɔpylɛr] *adj (personne, gouvernement)* popular; *(quartier, milieu)* working-class; *(expression)* vernacular ▪ **populariser** *vt* to popularize ▪ **popularité** *nf* popularity (**auprès de** with)

population [pɔpylasjɔ̃] *nf* population

porc [pɔr] *nm (animal)* pig; *(viande)* pork

porcelaine [pɔrsəlɛn] *nf* china, porcelain

porche [pɔrʃ] *nm* porch

pornographie [pɔrnɔgrafi] *nf* pornography

port [pɔr] *nm* (**a**) *(pour bateaux)* port, harbour; *Ordinat* port (**b**) *(d'armes)* carrying; *(de barbe)* wearing; *(prix)* carriage, postage; *(attitude)* bearing

portable [pɔrtabl] **1** *adj (ordinateur)* portable; *(téléphone)* mobile **2** *nm (ordinateur)* laptop; *(téléphone)* mobile

portail [pɔrtaj] *nm (de jardin)* gate; *(de cathédrale)* portal

portant, -e [pɔrtɑ̃, -ɑ̃t] *adj* **bien p.** in good health

portatif, -ive [pɔrtatif, -iv] *adj* portable

porte [pɔrt] *nf* door, *(de jardin, de ville, de slalom)* gate; **mettre qn à la p.** *(jeter dehors)* to throw sb out; *(renvoyer)* to fire sb; **p. d'embarquement** *(d'aéroport)* (departure) gate; **p. d'entrée** front door

portée [pɔrte] *nf* (**a**) *(de fusil)* range; *Fig* scope; **à la p. de qn** within reach of sb; **à p. de la main** within reach; **hors de p.** out of reach (**b**) *(animaux)* litter (**c**) *(impact)* significance (**d**) *Mus* stave

portefeuille [pɔrtəfœj] *nm Br* wallet, *Am* billfold; *(de ministre, d'actions)* portfolio

portemanteau, -x [pɔrtmɑ̃to] *nm (sur pied)* coat stand; *(crochet)* coat rack

porter [pɔrte] **1** *vt* to carry; *(vêtement, lunettes)* to wear; *(moustache, barbe)* to have; *(trace, responsabilité, fruits)* to bear; *(regard)* to cast; *(inscrire)* to enter; **p. qch à qn** to take/bring sth to sb; **p. bonheur/malheur** to bring good/bad luck; **p. son attention sur qch** to turn one's attention to sth; **tout (me) porte à croire que...** everything leads me to believe that...; **se faire p. malade** to report sick

2 *vi (voix)* to carry; *(coup)* to strike home; **p. sur** *(concerner)* to be about **3** **se porter** *vpr (vêtement)* to be worn; **se p. bien** to be well; **comment te portes-tu?** how are you?; **se p. candidat** *Br* to stand *or Am* to run as a candidate ▪ **porté, -e** *adj* **p. à croire** inclined to believe; **p. sur qch** fond of sth ▪ **porte-bonheur** *nm inv (lucky)* charm ▪ **porte-clefs** *nm inv* key ring ▪ **porte-monnaie** *nm inv* purse ▪ **porte-parole** *nmf inv* spokesperson (**de** for) ▪ **porte-voix** *nm inv* megaphone

porteur, -euse [pɔrtœr, -øz] **1** *nm (de bagages)* porter **2** *nmf (malade)* carrier; *(de nouvelles, de chèque)* bearer

portier [pɔrtje] nm doorkeeper, porter ■ **portière** nf (de véhicule, de train) door ■ **portillon** nm gate

portion [pɔrsjɔ̃] nf portion

Porto Rico [pɔrtoriko] nm ou f Puerto Rico

portrait [pɔrtrɛ] nm (peinture, dessin, photo) portrait; (description) description; **faire le p. de qn** to do sb's portrait ■ **portrait-robot** (pl **portraits-robots**) nm identikit picture, Photofit®

Portugal [pɔrtygal] nm **le P.** Portugal ■ **portugais, -e 1** adj Portuguese **2** nmf **P., Portugaise** Portuguese inv; **les P.** the Portuguese **3** nm (langue) Portuguese

pose [poz] nf (a) (de rideau, de papier peint) putting up; (de moquette) laying (b) (pour photo, portrait) pose; Phot exposure; **prendre la p.** to pose

posé, -e [poze] adj (calme) composed, staid

poser [poze] **1** vt to put down; (papier peint, rideaux) to put up; (mine, moquette, fondations) to lay; (bombe) to plant; (conditions, principe) to lay down; **p. qch sur qch** to put sth on sth; **p. une question à qn** to ask sb a question; **p. sa candidature** (à une élection) to put oneself forward as a candidate; (à un emploi) to apply (à for)

2 vi (modèle) to pose (**pour** for)

3 se poser vpr (oiseau, avion) to land; (problème, question) to arise; **se p. sur** (sujet: regard) to rest on; **se p. des questions** to ask oneself questions

positif, -ive [pozitif, -iv] adj positive

position [pozisjɔ̃] nf position; Fig **prendre p.** to take a stand (**contre** against)

posséder [posede] vt (biens, talent) to possess; (sujet) to have a thorough knowledge of; (langue) to have mastered ■ **possession** nf possession; **en p. de qch** in possession of sth; **prendre p. de qch** to take possession of sth

possibilité [posibilite] nf possibility;

avoir la p. de faire qch to have the chance or opportunity of doing sth

possible [posibl] **1** adj possible (à faire to do); **il (nous) est p. de le faire** it is possible (for us) to do it; **il est p. que...** (+ subjunctive) it is possible that...; **si p.** if possible; **le plus tôt p.** as soon as possible; **autant que p.** as far as possible; **le plus p.** as much/as many as possible; **le moins de détails p.** as few details as possible **2** nm **faire (tout) son p.** to do one's utmost (**pour faire** to do)

postal, -e, -aux, -ales [postal, -o] adj postal; (train) mail

poste¹ [post] nf (service) mail, Br post; (bureau) post office; **la P.** the postal services; **par la p.** by mail, Br by post; **p. aérienne** airmail; **p. restante** Br poste restante, Am general delivery

poste² [post] nm (a) (lieu, emploi) post; **être à son p.** to be at one's post; **p. d'essence** Br petrol or Am gas station; **p. d'incendie** fire point; **p. de police** police station; **p. de secours** first-aid post (b) **p. (de radio/télévision)** radio/television set (c) (de standard) extension

poster¹ [poste] vt (lettre) to mail, Br to post

poster² [poste] **1** vt (sentinelle, troupes) to post, to station **2 se poster** vpr to take up a position

poster³ [poster] nm poster

postérieur, -e [posterjœr] adj (dans le temps) later; (de derrière) back; **p. à** after

postérité [posterite] nf posterity

postier, -ère [postje, -ɛr] nmf postal worker

postillonner [postijone] vi to splutter

postuler [postyle] **1** vt Math to postulate **2** vi **à un emploi** to apply for a job ■ **postulant, -e** nmf applicant (à for)

posture [postyr] nf posture

pot [po] nm pot; (en verre) jar; (de bébé) potty; **p. d'échappement** Br exhaust pipe, Am tail pipe

potable [pɔtabl] *adj* drinkable; **eau p.** drinking water

potage [pɔtaʒ] *nm* soup

potager, -ère [pɔtaʒe, -ɛr] **1** *adj* **jardin p.** vegetable garden; **plante potagère** vegetable **2** *nm* vegetable garden

pot-au-feu [pɔtofø] *nm inv* = boiled beef with vegetables

pot-de-vin [podvɛ̃] (*pl* **pots-de-vin**) *nm* bribe

poteau, -x [pɔto] *nm* post; **p. électrique** electricity pylon; **p. indicateur** signpost; **p. télégraphique** telegraph pole

potelé, -e [pɔtle] *adj* plump, chubby

potence [pɔtɑ̃s] *nf* (*gibet*) gallows (*sing*)

potentiel, -elle [pɔtɑ̃sjɛl] *adj & nm* potential

poterie [pɔtri] *nf* (*art, objets*) pottery; (*objet*) piece of pottery ■ **potier, -ère** *nmf* potter

potion [posjɔ̃] *nf* potion

potiron [pɔtirɔ̃] *nm* pumpkin

pot-pourri [popuri] (*pl* **pots-pourris**) *nm* (*chansons*) medley

pou, -x [pu] *nm* louse (*pl* lice)

poubelle [pubɛl] *nf* *Br* dustbin, *Am* garbage can; **mettre qch à la p.** to throw sth out

pouce [pus] *nm* (*doigt*) thumb

poudre [pudr] *nf* (*poussière, explosif*) powder; **en p.** (*lait*) powdered; (*chocolat*) drinking; **p. à récurer** scouring powder ■ **poudrer 1** *vt* to powder **2 se poudrer** *vpr* to powder one's face ■ **poudreux, -euse 1** *adj* powdery **2** *nf* **poudreuse** (*neige*) powder snow

poulain [pulɛ̃] *nm* foal

poule¹ [pul] *nf* (*animal*) hen; *Culin* fowl

poule² [pul] *nf* (*groupe*) group

poulet [pulɛ] *nm* (*animal*) chicken

poulie [puli] *nf* pulley

pouls [pu] *nm Méd* pulse; **prendre le p. de qn** to take sb's pulse

poumon [pumɔ̃] *nm* lung; **à pleins poumons** (*respirer*) deeply

poupée [pupe] *nf* doll

POUR [pur] **1** *prép* for; **p. toi/moi** for you/me; **faites-le p. lui** do it for him, do it for his sake; **partir p. Paris/l'Italie** to leave for Paris/Italy; **elle part p. cinq ans** she's leaving for five years; **elle est p.** she's all for it, she's in favour of it; **p. faire qch** (in order) to do sth; **p. que tu le voies** so (that) you may see it; **p. quoi faire?** what for?; **assez grand p. faire qch** big enough to do sth; **p. affaires** on business; **p. cela** for that reason; **p. ma part** as for me; **jour p. jour/heure p. heure** to the day/hour; **dix p. cent** ten percent

2 *nm* **le p. et le contre** the pros and cons

pourboire [purbwar] *nm* tip

pourcentage [pursɑ̃taʒ] *nm* percentage

pourchasser [purʃase] *vt* to pursue

pourparlers [purparle] *nmpl* negotiations, talks

pourquoi [purkwa] **1** *adv & conj* why; **p. pas?** why not? **2** *nm inv* reason (**de** for); **le p. et le comment** the whys and wherefores

pourra, pourrait [pura, purɛ] *voir* **pouvoir 1**

pourrir [purir] *vti* to rot ■ **pourri, -e** *adj* (*fruit, temps*) rotten ■ **pourriture** *nf* rot

poursuite [pursɥit] *nf* (*chasse*) pursuit; (*continuation*) continuation; **se lancer à la p. de qn** to set off in pursuit of sb **2** *nfpl Jur* **poursuites (judiciaires)** legal proceedings (**contre** against); **engager des poursuites contre qn** to start proceedings against sb

poursuivre* [pursɥivr] **1** *vt* (*chercher à atteindre*) to pursue; (*sujet: idée, crainte*) to haunt; (*sujet: malchance*) to dog; (*harceler*) to pester; (*continuer*) to continue, to go on with; *Jur* **p. qn (en justice)** to bring proceedings against sb; (*au criminel*) to prosecute sb **2 se poursuivre** *vpr* to continue, to go on

pourtant [purtɑ̃] *adv* yet, nevertheless; **et p.** and yet

pourtour [purtur] *nm* perimeter

pourvoir* [purvwar] **1** *vt* to provide (**de** with); **être pourvu de** to be provided with **2** *vi* **p. à** (*besoins*) to provide for **3 se pourvoir** *upr Jur* **se p. en cassation** to take one's case to the Court of Appeal ■ **pourvoyeur, -euse** *nmf* supplier

pourvu [purvy] **pourvu que** *conj* (**a**) (*condition*) provided (that) (**b**) (*souhait*) **p. qu'elle soit là!** I just hope (that) she's there!

pousse [pus] *nf* (*croissance*) growth; (*bourgeon*) shoot, sprout

poussée [puse] *nf* (*pression*) pressure; (*coup*) push; (*d'ennemi*) thrust, push; (*de fièvre*) outbreak

pousser [puse] **1** *vt* (*presser*) to push; (*moteur*) to drive hard; **p. qn à qch** to drive sb to sth; **p. qn à faire qch** (*sujet: faim*) to drive sb to do sth; (*sujet: personne*) to urge sb to do sth; **p. un cri** to shout; **p. un soupir** to sigh

2 *vi* (*presser*) to push; (*croître*) to grow; **faire p. qch** (*plante*) to grow sth; **se laisser p. les cheveux** to let one's hair grow

3 se pousser *upr* (*pour faire de la place*) to move over ■ **poussé, -e** *adj* (*études*) thorough

poussette [puset] *nf Br* pushchair, *Am* stroller

poussière [pusjɛr] *nf* dust; **une p.** a speck of dust ■ **poussiéreux, -euse** *adj* dusty

poussin [pusɛ̃] *nm* (*animal*) chick

poutre [putr] *nf* (*en bois*) beam; (*en acier*) girder

POUVOIR* [puvwar] **1** *v aux* (*être capable de*) can, to be able to; (*avoir la permission*) can, may, to be allowed; **tu peux entrer** you may *or* can come in

2 *v impersonnel* **il peut neiger** it may snow; **il se peut qu'elle parte** she might leave

3 *nm* (*puissance, attributions*) power; **au p.** (*parti*) in power; **p. d'achat** purchasing power; **les pouvoirs publics** the authorities

poux [pu] *pl de* **pou**

prairie [preri] *nf* meadow

praline [pralin] *nf* praline

pratique [pratik] **1** *adj* (*méthode, personne*) practical; (*outil*) handy **2** *nf* (*application, procédé, coutume*) practice; (*expérience*) practical experience; **la p. de la natation/du golf** swimming/golfing; **mettre qch en p.** to put sth into practice; **dans la p.** (*en réalité*) in practice ■ **pratiquement** *adv* (*presque*) practically; (*en réalité*) in practice

pratiquer [pratike] **1** *vt* (*religion*) *Br* to practise, *Am* to practice; (*activité*) to take part in; (*langue*) to use; (*sport*) to play; **p. la natation** to go swimming **2** *vi* (*médecin, avocat*) *Br* to practise, *Am* to practice ■ **pratiquant, -e 1** *adj* practising **2** *nmf* practising Christian/Jew/Muslim/*etc*

pré [pre] *nm* meadow

préalable [prealabl] **1** *adj* prior, previous; **p. à** prior to **2** *nm* precondition, prerequisite; **au p.** beforehand

préavis [preavi] *nm* (*advance*) notice (**de** of); **p. de grève** strike notice; **p. de licenciement** notice of dismissal

précaire [prekɛr] *adj* precarious; (*santé*) delicate ■ **précarité** *nf* precariousness; **p. de l'emploi** lack of job security

précaution [prekosjɔ̃] *nf* (*mesure*) precaution; (*prudence*) caution; **par p.** as a precaution; **pour plus de p.** to be on the safe side; **prendre des précautions** to take precautions

précédent, -e [presedɑ̃, -ɑ̃t] **1** *adj* previous **2** *nmf* previous one **3** *nm* precedent; **sans p.** unprecedented ■ **précéder** *vti* to precede

prêcher [preʃe] *vti* to preach

précieux, -euse [presjø, -øz] *adj* precious

précipice [presipis] *nm* chasm, abyss; (*de ravin*) precipice

précipiter [presipite] **1** *vt* (*hâter*) to hasten; (*jeter*) to hurl down **2 se précipiter** *upr* (*se jeter*) to rush (**vers/sur**

towards/at); *(se hâter)* to rush; **les événements se sont précipités** things started happening quickly ▪ **précipitamment** [-amã] *adv* hastily ▪ **précipitation** *nf* haste; **précipitations** *(pluie)* precipitation ▪ **précipité, -e** *adj* hasty

précis, -e [presi, -iz] **1** *adj* precise, exact; *(mécanisme)* accurate, precise; **à deux heures précises** at two o'clock sharp *or* precisely **2** *nm (résumé)* summary; *(manuel)* handbook ▪ **précision** *nf* precision; *(de mécanisme, d'information)* accuracy; *(détail)* detail; **donner des précisions sur qch** to give precise details about sth; **demander des précisions sur qch** to ask for further information about sth

préciser [presize] **1** *vt* to specify (**que** that) **2 se préciser** *vpr* to become clear(er)

précoce [prekɔs] *adj (fruit, été)* early; *(enfant)* precocious

préconiser [prekɔnize] *vt* to advocate (**que** that)

précurseur [prekyrsœr] **1** *nm* forerunner, precursor **2** *adj* **signe p.** forewarning

prédécesseur [predesesœr] *nm* predecessor

prédestiné, -e [predestine] *adj* predestined (**à faire** to do)

prédilection [predileksjɔ̃] *nf* predilection; **de p.** favourite

prédire* [predir] *vt* to predict (**que** that) ▪ **prédiction** *nf* prediction

prédisposer [predispoze] *vt* to predispose (**à qch** to sth; **à faire** to do) ▪ **prédisposition** *nf* predisposition (**à** to)

préfabriqué, -e [prefabrike] *adj* prefabricated

préface [prefas] *nf* preface (**de** to)

préfecture [prefɛktyr] *nf* prefecture; **la P. de police** police headquarters

préférable [preferabl] *adj* preferable (**à** to)

préférence [preferãs] *nf* preference (**pour** for); **de p.** preferably; **de p. à** in preference to ▪ **préférentiel, -elle** *adj* preferential

préférer [prefere] *vt* to prefer (**à** to); **p. faire qch** to prefer to do sth; **je préférerais rester** I would rather stay, I would prefer to stay ▪ **préféré, -e** *adj & nmf* favourite

préfet [prefɛ] *nm* prefect *(chief administrator in a 'département')*; **p. de police** = chief commissioner of police

préhistorique [preistɔrik] *adj* prehistoric

préjudice [preʒydis] *nm (à une cause)* prejudice; *(à une personne)* harm; **porter p. à qn** to do sb harm

préjugé [preʒyʒe] *nm* prejudice; **avoir des préjugés** to be prejudiced (**contre** against)

prélasser [prelase] **se prélasser** *vpr* to lounge

prélever [prel(ə)ve] *vt (échantillon)* to take (**sur** from); *(somme)* to deduct (**sur** from) ▪ **prélèvement** *nm (d'échantillon)* taking; *(de somme)* deduction; **p. automatique** *Br* direct debit, *Am* automatic deduction; **prélèvements obligatoires** = tax and social security contributions

préliminaire [preliminɛr] **1** *adj* preliminary **2** *nmpl* **préliminaires** preliminaries

prélude [prelyd] *nm* prelude (**à** to)

prématuré, -e [prematyre] **1** *adj* premature **2** *nmf* premature baby

préméditer [premedite] *vt* to premeditate ▪ **préméditation** *nf* premeditation; **meurtre avec p.** premeditated murder

premier, -ère [prəmje, -ɛr] **1** *adj* first; *(enfance)* early; *(page de journal)* front; *(qualité)* prime; *(état)* original; *(danseuse, rôle)* leading; *(marche)* bottom; **le p. rang** the front row; **les trois premiers mois** the first three months; **à la première occasion** at the earliest opportunity; **en p.** firstly; **P. ministre** Prime Minister

2 *nm (étage) Br* first *or Am* second floor; **le p. juin** June the first; **le p. de l'an** New Year's Day

3 *nmf* first (one); **arriver le p.** *ou* **en p.** to arrive first

4 *nf* **première** *(wagon, billet)* first class; *(vitesse)* first (gear); *(événement historique)* first; *(de chaussure)* insole; *Théât* opening night; *Cin* première; *Scol Br* ≃ lower sixth, *Am* ≃ eleventh grade

prémonition [premɔnisjɔ̃] *nf* premonition

prénatal, -e, -als, -ales [prenatal] *adj Br* antenatal, *Am* prenatal

PRENDRE* [prɑ̃dr] **1** *vt* to take (**à qn** from sb); *(attraper)* to catch; *(repas, boisson, douche)* to have; *(nouvelles)* to get; *(air)* to put on; *(bonne)* to take on; **p. qch dans un tiroir** to take sth out of a drawer; **p. qn pour** to take sb for; **p. feu** to catch fire; **p. du temps/ une heure** to take time/an hour; **p. de la place** to take up room; **p. du poids/ de la vitesse** to put on weight/gather speed; **p. l'eau** *(bateau, chaussure)* to be leaking

2 *vi (feu)* to catch; *(ciment, gelée)* to set; *(greffe, vaccin, plante)* to take; *(mode)* to catch on; **p. sur soi** to restrain oneself

3 se prendre *upr (médicament)* to be taken; *(s'accrocher)* to get caught; **se p. les pieds dans qch** to get one's feet caught in sth; **s'y p. bien avec qn** to know how to handle sb; **s'en p. à qn** to take it out on sb

prénom [prenɔ̃] *nm* first name ■ **prénommer** *vt* to name; **il se prénomme Daniel** his first name is Daniel

préoccuper [preɔkype] **1** *vt (inquiéter)* to worry; **se préoccuper** *upr* **se p. de qn/qch** to concern oneself with sb/ sth ■ **préoccupant, -e** *adj* worrying ■ **préoccupation** *nf* preoccupation, concern ■ **préoccupé, -e** *adj* worried (**par** about)

préparatifs [preparatif] *nmpl* preparations (**de** for) ■ **préparation** *nf* preparation ■ **préparatoire** *adj* preparatory

préparer [prepare] **1** *vt* to prepare (**qch pour** sth for); *(examen)* to study for; **p. qch à qn** to prepare sth for sb; **plats tout préparés** ready-cooked meals

2 se préparer *upr (être imminent)* to be in the offing; *(s'apprêter)* to prepare oneself (**à** *ou* **pour qch** for sth); **se p. à faire qch** to prepare to do sth; **se p. qch** *(boisson)* to make oneself sth

préposé, -e [prepoze] *nmf* employee; *(facteur)* postman, *f* postwoman

préretraite [preretret] *nf* early retirement

près [prɛ] *adv* **p. de qn/qch** near sb/ sth, close to sb/sth; **p. de deux ans** nearly two years; **p. de partir** about to leave; **tout p.** nearby (**de qn/qch** sb/sth), close by (**de qn/qch** sb/sth); **de p.** *(suivre, examiner)* closely; **p. les uns des autres** *sic*... [see note]; **p.** de chose **p.** more or less; **à cela p.** except for that; **voici le chiffre à un euro p.** here is the figure, give or take a euro; **calculer au euro p.** to calculate to the nearest euro

présage [preza3] *nm* omen, sign ■ **présager** *vt* **ça ne présage rien de bon** it doesn't bode well

presbyte [presbit] *adj* long-sighted

presbytère [presbiter] *nm* presbytery

prescrire* [preskrir] *vt (médicament)* to prescribe ■ **prescription** *nf (ordonnance)* prescription

présence [prezɑ̃s] *nf* presence; *(à l'école)* attendance (**à** at); **en p. de** in the presence of; **faire acte de p.** to put in an appearance; **p. d'esprit** presence of mind

présent, -e [prezɑ̃, -ɑ̃t] **1** *adj (non absent, actuel)* present **2** *nm (temps)* present; **à p.** at present, now; **dès à p.** as from now

présenter [prezɑ̃te] **1** *vt (montrer)* to show, to present; *(facture)* to submit; *(arguments)* to present; **p. qn à qn** to introduce sb to sb

2 se présenter *upr (dire son nom)* to introduce oneself (**à** to); *(chez qn)* to show up; *(occasion)* to arise; **se p. à**

(examen) to take, *Br* to sit for; *(élections)* to run in; *(emploi)* to apply for; *(autorités)* to report to; **ça se présente bien** it looks promising ■ **présentable** *adj* presentable ■ **présentateur, -trice** *nmf* presenter ■ **présentation** *nf* presentation; *(de personnes)* introduction; **faire les présentations** to make the introductions; **p. de mode** fashion show

préserver [prezεrve] *vt* to protect, to preserve (**de** from) ■ **préservation** *nf* protection, preservation

présidence [prezidãs] *nf (de nation)* presidency; *(de firme)* chairmanship ■ **président, -e** *nmf (de nation)* president; *(de firme)* chairman, *f* chairwoman; **p.-directeur général** *Br* (chairman and) managing director, *Am* chief executive officer; **p. du jury** *(d'examen)* chief examiner; *(de tribunal)* foreman of the jury ■ **présidentiel, -elle** *adj* presidential

présider [prezide] *vt (réunion)* to chair; *(conseil)* to preside over

presque [prεsk] *adv* almost, nearly; **p. jamais/rien** hardly ever/anything

presqu'île [prεskil] *nf* peninsula

pressant, -e [prεsã, -ãt] *adj* urgent, pressing

presse [prεs] *nf Tech* press; *Typ* (printing) press; **la p.** *(journaux)* the press

pressé, -e [prεse] *adj (personne)* in a hurry; *(air)* hurried

pressentir* [presãtir] *vt (deviner)* to sense (**que** that) ■ **pressentiment** *nm* presentiment; *(de malheur)* foreboding

pressing [presiŋ] *nm* dry cleaner's

pression [prεsjõ] *nf Tech* pressure; *(bouton)* snap (fastener); **faire p. sur qn** to put pressure on sb, to pressurize sb

pressuriser [presyrize] *vt (avion)* to pressurize

prestataire [prεstatεr] *nmf Ordinat* **p. d'accès** access provider

prestation [prεstasjõ] *nf* (**a**) *(allocation)* benefit; **prestations** *(services)*

services; **prestations sociales** *Br* social security benefits, *Am* welfare payments (**b**) *(de comédien)* performance

prestidigitateur, -trice [prεstidiʒitatœr, -tris] *nmf* conjurer ■ **prestidigitation** *nf* **tour de g.** conjuring trick

prestige [prεstiʒ] *nm* prestige ■ **prestigieux, -euse** *adj* prestigious

présumer [prezyme] *vt* to presume (**que** that); **p. de qch** to overestimate sth

prêt¹, -e [prε, prεt] *adj (préparé)* ready (**à faire** to do; **à qch** for sth); **être fin p.** to be all set ■ **prêt-à-porter** *nm* ready-to-wear clothes

prêt² [prε] *nm (somme)* loan

prétendre [pretãdr] **1** *vt (déclarer)* to claim (**que** that); *(vouloir)* to intend (**faire** to do); **à ce qu'il prétend** according to him **2** *vi* **p. à** *(titre)* to lay claim to **3 se prétendre** *vpr* to claim to be ■ **prétendu, -e** *adj (progrès)* so-called; *(coupable)* alleged

prétentieux, -euse [pretãsjø, -øz] *adj* pretentious ■ **prétention** *nf (vanité)* pretension; *(revendication, ambition)* claim; **sans p.** *(film, robe)* unpretentious

prêter [prεte] **1** *vt (argent, objet)* to lend (**à** to); *(aide)* to give (**à** to); *(propos, intention)* to attribute (**à** to); **p. attention** to pay attention (**à** to); **p. serment** to take an oath; **p. main-forte à qn** to lend sb a hand **2** *vi* **p. à confusion** to give rise to confusion **3 se prêter** *vpr* **se p. à** *(consentir)* to agree to; *(convenir)* to lend itself to

prétexte [pretεkst] *nm* excuse, pretext; **sous p. de/que** on the pretext of/that; **sous aucun p.** under no circumstances ■ **prétexter** *vt* to plead (**que** that)

prêtre [prεtr] *nm* priest

preuve [prœv] *nf* piece of evidence; **preuves** evidence; **faire p. de qch** to prove sth; **faire p. de courage** to show courage; **faire ses preuves** *(personne)* to prove oneself; *(méthode)* to be tried and tested

prévaloir* [prevalwar] *vi* to prevail (**sur** over)

prévenant, -e [prevnã, -ãt] *adj* considerate

prévenir* [prevnir] *vt* (**a**) *(mettre en garde)* to warn; *(aviser)* to inform (**de** of *or* about) (**b**) *(maladie)* to prevent; *(accident)* to avert ■ **préventif, -ive** *adj* preventive ■ **prévention** *nf* prevention; **p. routière** road safety

prévisible [previzibl] *adj* foreseeable

prévision [previzjɔ̃] *nf* forecast; **en p. de** in expectation of; **prévisions météorologiques** weather forecast

prévoir* [prevwar] *vt* (*météo*) to forecast; *(difficultés, retard, réaction)* to expect; *(organiser)* to plan; **la réunion est prévue pour demain** the meeting is scheduled for tomorrow; **comme prévu** as planned; **plus tôt que prévu** earlier than expected; **prévu pour** *(véhicule, appareil)* designed for

prévoyant, -e [prevwajã, -ãt] *adj* farsighted ■ **prévoyance** *nf* foresight

prier [prije] **1** *vi Rel* to pray **2** *vt* (*Dieu*) to pray to; *(supplier)* to beg; **p. qn de faire qch** to ask sb to do sth; **je vous en prie** *(faites-le)* please; *(en réponse à 'merci')* don't mention it

prière [prijer] *nf Rel* prayer; *(demande)* request

primaire [primer] **1** *adj* primary; **école p.** *Br* primary school, *Am* elementary school **2** *nm Scol Br* primary or*Am* elementary education; **entrer en p.** to be at *Br* primary or *Am* elementary school

prime [prim] **1** *nf* (*sur salaire*) bonus; *(d'État)* subsidy; **en p.** *(cadeau)* as a free gift; **p. (d'assurance)** *(insurance)* premium; **p. de fin d'année** ≃ Christmas bonus; **p. de licenciement** severance allowance; **p. de transport** transport allowance **2** *adj* **de p. abord** at the very first glance

primé, -e [prime] *adj* (*film, animal*) prizewinning

primer [prime] *vi* to come first; **p. sur qch** to take precedence over sth

primitif, -ive [primitif, -iv] *adj* (*société, art*) primitive; *(état, sens)* original

primordial, -e, -aux, -ales [primɔrdjal, -jo] *adj* vital (**de faire** to do)

prince [prɛ̃s] *nm* prince ■ **princesse** *nf* princess ■ **princier, -ère** *adj* princely ■ **principauté** *nf* principality

principal, -e, -aux, -ales [prɛ̃sipal, -o] **1** *adj* main, principal; *(rôle)* leading **2** *nm* (*de collège*) principal, *Br* headmaster, *f* headmistress; **le p.** *(l'essentiel)* the main thing

principe [prɛ̃sip] *nm* principle; **en p.** theoretically, in principle; **par p.** on principle

printemps [prɛ̃tã] *nm* spring; **au p.** in the spring

priorité [priorite] *nf* priority (**sur** over); *Aut* right of way; *Aut* **avoir la p.** to have (the) right of way; *Aut* **p. à droite** right of way to traffic coming from the right; **'cédez la p.'** *Br* 'give way', *Am* 'yield'; **en p.** as a matter of priority ■ **prioritaire** *adj* **secteur p.** priority sector; **être p.** to have priority; *Aut* to have (the) right of way

pris, -e¹ [pri, priz] **1** *pp de* **prendre 2** *adj* (*place*) taken; **avoir le nez p.** to have a blocked nose; **être p.** *(occupé)* to be busy; *(candidat)* to be accepted; **p. de** *(peur)* seized with; **p. de panique** panic-stricken

prise² [priz] *nf* (*action*) taking; *(objet saisi)* catch; *(manière d'empoigner)* grip; *(de judo)* hold; *(de tabac)* pinch; **lâcher p.** to lose one's grip; **p. de sang** blood test; *Él* **p. (de courant)** *(mâle)* plug; *(femelle)* socket; *Él* **p. multiple** adaptor; **p. d'otages** hostage-taking

prison [prizɔ̃] *nf* prison, jail; *(peine)* imprisonment; **mettre qn en p.** to put sb in prison, to jail sb ■ **prisonnier, -ère** *nmf* prisoner; **faire qn p.** to take sb prisoner; **p. de guerre** prisoner of war

privation [privasjɔ̃] *nf* deprivation (**de** of); **privations** *(manque)* hardship

privatiser [privatize] *vt* to privatize

■ **privatisation** *nf* privatization

privé, -e [prive] **1** *adj* private **2** *nm* **le p.** the private sector; *Scol* the private education system; **en p.** in private; **dans le p.** privately; *(travailler)* in the private sector

priver [prive] **1** *vt* to deprive (**de** of) **2 se priver** *vpr* **se p. de** to do without, to deprive oneself of

privilège [privilɛʒ] *nm* privilege ■ **privilégié, -e** *adj* privileged

prix [pri] *nm (coût)* price; *(récompense)* prize; **à tout p.** at all costs; **hors de p.** exorbitant; **attacher du p. à qch** to attach importance to sth

probable [prɔbabl] *adj* likely, probable; **peu p.** unlikely ■ **probabilité** *nf* probability, likelihood; **selon toute p.** in all probability

probant, -e [prɔbɑ̃, -ɑ̃t] *adj* conclusive

probité [prɔbite] *nf* integrity

problème [prɔblɛm] *nm* problem ■ **problématique** *adj* problematic

procédé [prɔsede] *nm (technique)* process; *(méthode)* method

procéder [prɔsede] *vi (agir)* to proceed; **p. à** *(enquête, arrestation)* to carry out; **p. par élimination** to follow a process of elimination ■ **procédure** *nf (méthode)* procedure; *(règles juridiques)* procedure; *(procès)* proceedings

procès [prɔsɛ] *nm (criminel)* trial; *(civil)* lawsuit; **faire un p. à qn** to take sb to court

procession [prɔsesjɔ̃] *nf* procession

processus [prɔsesys] *nm* process

procès-verbal [prɔsɛverbal] *(pl* **procès-verbaux** [-o]) *nm* **1** *(amende)* fine

prochain, -e [prɔʃɛ̃, -ɛn] *adj* next; *(mort, arrivée)* impending ■ **prochainement** *adv* shortly, soon

proche [prɔʃ] *adj (dans l'espace)* near, close; *(dans le temps)* near, imminent; *(parent, ami)* close; **p. de** near (to), close to; **de p. en p.** step by step; **le P.-Orient** the Middle East ■ **proches** *nmpl* close relations

proclamer [prɔklame] *vt* to proclaim (**que** that) ■ **proclamation** *nf* proclamation

procréer [prɔkree] *vi* to procreate ■ **procréation** *nf* procreation; **p. médicalement assistée** assisted conception

procuration [prɔkyrasjɔ̃] *nf* power of attorney; **par p.** by proxy

procurer [prɔkyre] **1** *vt* **p. qch à qn** *(sujet: personne)* to get sth for sb; *(sujet: chose)* to bring sb sth **2 se procurer** *vpr* **se p. qch** to obtain sth

prodige [prɔdiʒ] *nm (miracle)* wonder; *(personne)* prodigy; **tenir du p.** to be extraordinary ■ **prodigieux, -euse** *adj* prodigious

prodiguer [prɔdige] *vt* **p. qch à qn** to lavish sth on sb; **p. des conseils à qn** to pour out advice to sb

production [prɔdyksjɔ̃] *nf* production; *(produit)* product; *(d'usine)* output ■ **producteur, -trice 1** *nmf* producer **2** *adj* producing; **pays p. de pétrole** oil-producing country ■ **productif, -ive** *adj* productive ■ **productivité** *nf* productivity

produire* [prɔdɥir] **1** *vt (marchandise, émission, gaz)* to produce; *(effet, résultat)* to produce, to bring about **2 se produire** *vpr (événement)* to happen, to occur; *(acteur)* to perform ■ **produit** *nm (article)* product; *(de vente, de collecte)* proceeds; **p. de beauté** cosmetic; **p. chimique** chemical; **produits ménagers** cleaning products

profane [prɔfan] **1** *adj* secular **2** *nmf* lay person

profaner [prɔfane] *vt* to desecrate

proférer [prɔfere] *vt* to utter

professer [prɔfese] *vt* to profess (**que** that)

professeur [prɔfesœr] *nm* teacher; *(à l'université)* professor; **p. principal** *Br* class *or* form teacher, *Am* homeroom teacher

profession [prɔfesjɔ̃] *nf* occupation, profession; *(manuelle)* trade; **sans p.** not gainfully employed; **p. libérale**

profession ■ **professionnel, -elle** *adj* professional; *(enseignement)* vocational **2** *nmf* professional

profil [pʀɔfil] *nm* profile; **de p.** (viewed) from the side ■ **se profiler** *vpr* to be outlined (**sur** against)

profit [pʀɔfi] *nm* profit; **tirer p. de qch** to benefit from sth; **mettre qch à p.** to put sth to good use ■ **profitable** *adj* profitable (**à** to) ■ **profiter** *vi* **p. de** to take advantage of; **p. de la vie** to make the most of life; **p. à qn** to benefit sb, to be of benefit to sb

profond, -e [pʀɔfɔ̃, -ɔ̃d] **1** *adj* deep; *(joie, erreur)* profound; *(cause)* underlying; **p. de 2 mètres** 2 metres deep **2** *adv* deep ■ **profondément** *adv* deeply; *(dormir)* soundly; *(triste, ému)* profoundly; *(creuser)* deep ■ **profondeur** *nf* depth; **faire 6 mètres de p.** to be 6 metres deep; **à 6 mètres de p.** at a depth of 6 metres

profusion [pʀɔfyzjɔ̃] *nf* profusion; **à p.** in profusion

programmable [pʀɔgʀamabl] *adj* programmable ■ **programmation** *nf* Radio & TV programme planning; Ordinat programming

programmateur [pʀɔgʀamatœʀ] *nm* Tech automatic control (device)

programme [pʀɔgʀam] *nm* Br programme, Am program; *(de parti politique)* manifesto; Scol curriculum; *(d'un cours)* syllabus; Ordinat program ■ **programmer** *vt* Ordinat to program; Radio, TV & Cin to schedule ■ **programmeur, -euse** *nmf* (computer) programmer

progrès [pʀɔgʀɛ] *nm & nmpl* progress; **faire des p.** to make (good) progress ■ **progresser** *vi* to progress ■ **progressif, -ive** *adj* progressive ■ **progression** *nf* progression ■ **progressiste** *adj & nmf* progressive ■ **progressivement** *adv* progressively

prohiber [pʀɔibe] *vt* to prohibit, to forbid ■ **prohibitif, -ive** *adj* prohibitive ■ **prohibition** *nf* prohibition

proie [pʀwa] *nf* prey; **être la p. des**

flammes to be consumed by fire

projecteur [pʀɔʒɛktœʀ] *nm (de monument, de stade)* floodlight; *(de prison, d'armée)* searchlight; Théât spotlight; Cin projector

projectile [pʀɔʒɛktil] *nm* missile

projection [pʀɔʒɛksjɔ̃] *nf (d'objet, de film)* projection; *(séance)* screening

projet [pʀɔʒɛ] *nm (intention)* plan; *(étude)* project; **faire des projets d'avenir** to make plans for the future; **p. de loi** bill

projeter [pʀɔʒte] *vt (lancer)* to project; *(liquide, boue)* to splash; *(lumière)* to flash; *(film)* to show; *(ombre)* to cast; *(prévoir)* to plan; **p. de faire qch** to plan to do sth

proliférer [pʀɔlifeʀe] *vi* to proliferate ■ **prolifération** *nf* proliferation

prolonger [pʀɔlɔ̃ʒe] **1** *vt (vie, débat, séjour)* to prolong; *(mur, route)* to extend **2 se prolonger** *vpr (séjour)* to be prolonged; *(réunion)* to go on; *(rue)* to continue ■ **prolongation** *nf (de séjour)* extension; **prolongations** *(au football)* extra time ■ **prolongement** *nm (de rue)* continuation; *(de mur)* extension; **prolongements** *(d'affaires)* repercussions

promenade [pʀɔmnad] *nf (à pied)* walk; *(courte)* stroll; *(avenue)* promenade; **faire une p.** to go for a walk; **faire une p. à cheval** to go for a ride

promener [pʀɔmne] **1** *vt (personne, chien)* to take for a walk; *(visiteur)* to show around; **p. qch sur qch** *(main, regard)* to run sth over sth **2 se promener** *vpr (à pied)* to go for a walk ■ **promeneur, -euse** *nmf* stroller, walker

promesse [pʀɔmɛs] *nf* promise; **tenir sa p.** to keep one's promise

promettre* [pʀɔmɛtʀ] **1** *vt* to promise (**qch à qn** sb sth; **que** that); **p. de faire qch** to promise to do sth; **c'est promis** it's a promise **2** *vi* Fig to be promising **3 se promettre** *vpr* **se p. qch** *(à soi-même)* to promise oneself sth; *(l'un l'autre)* to promise each other sth

■ **prometteur, -euse** *adj* promising

promoteur [prɔmɔtœr] *nm* **p. (immobilier)** property developer

promotion [prɔmɔsjɔ̃] *nf* (**a**) *(avancement)* & *Com* promotion; **en p.** *(produit)* on (special) offer; **p. sociale** upward mobility (**b**) *(d'une école)* Br year, *Am* class ■ **promouvoir*** *vt (personne, produit)* to promote; **être promu** *(employé)* to be promoted (**à** to)

prompt, -e [prɔ̃, prɔ̃t] *adj* prompt; **p. à faire qch** quick to do sth

promulguer [prɔmylge] *vt* to promulgate

prononcer [prɔnɔ̃se] **1** *vt (articuler)* to pronounce; *(dire)* to utter; *(discours)* to deliver; *(jugement)* to pronounce **2 se prononcer** *vpr (mot)* to be pronounced; *(personne)* to give one's opinion (**sur** about *or* on); **se p. pour/contre qch** to come out in favour of/against sth ■ **prononcé, -e** *adj* pronounced, marked ■ **prononciation** *nf* pronunciation

pronostic [prɔnɔstik] *nm* forecast; *Méd* prognosis ■ **pronostiquer** *vt* to forecast

propagande [prɔpagɑ̃d] *nf* propaganda

propager [prɔpaʒe] *vt*, **se propager** *vpr* to spread ■ **propagation** *nf* spreading

prophète [prɔfɛt] *nm* prophet ■ **prophétie** [-fesi] *nf* prophecy ■ **prophétique** *adj* prophetic

propice [prɔpis] *adj* favourable (**à** to); **le moment p.** the right moment

proportion [prɔpɔrsjɔ̃] *nf* proportion; **en p. de** in proportion to; **hors de p.** out of proportion (**avec** to) ■ **proportionné, -e** *adj* proportionate (**à** to); **bien p.** well-proportioned ■ **proportionnel, -elle 1** *adj* proportional (**à** to) **2** *nf* **proportionnelle** *(scrutin)* proportional representation

propos [prɔpo] *nm (sujet)* subject; *(intention)* purpose; **des p.** *(paroles)* talk, words; **à p. de qn/qch** about sb/sth; **à p.** *(arriver)* at the right time; **à p. by the way

proposer [prɔpoze] **1** *vt (suggérer)* to suggest, to propose (**qch à qn** sth to sb; **que** + *subjunctive*); *(offrir)* to offer (**qch à qn** sb sth; **de faire** to do); **je te propose de rester** I suggest (that) you stay **2 se proposer** *vpr* to offer one's services; **se p. pour faire qch** to offer to do sth; **se p. de faire qch** to propose to do sth ■ **proposition** *nf* suggestion, proposal; *(offre)* offer; **faire une p. à qn** to make a suggestion to sb

propre¹ [prɔpr] **1** *adj* clean; *(soigné)* neat; **p. comme un sou neuf** spick and span **2** *nm* **mettre qch au p.** to make a fair copy of sth ■ **proprement** [-əmɑ̃] *adv (avec propreté)* cleanly; *(avec soin)* neatly ■ **propreté** [-əte] *nf* cleanliness; *(soin)* neatness

propre² [prɔpr] **1** *adj (à soi)* own; **mon p. argent** my own money; **être p. à qn/qch** *(particulier)* to be characteristic of sb/sth; **au sens p.** literally **2** *nm* **le p. de** *(qualité)* the distinctive quality of; **au p.** *(au sens propre)* literally ■ **proprement** [-əmɑ̃] *adv (strictement)* strictly; **à p. parler** strictly speaking; **le village p. dit** the village proper

propriétaire [prɔprijetɛr] *nmf* owner; *(de location)* landlord, *f* landlady; **p. foncier** landowner

propriété [prɔprijete] *nf (fait de posséder)* ownership; *(chose possédée)* property; *(caractéristique)* property; **p. privée** private property

propulser [prɔpylse] *vt* to propel

proscrire* [prɔskrir] *vt* to proscribe, to ban

prospecter [prɔspɛkte] *vt (sol)* to prospect; *(clients)* to canvass

prospectus [prɔspɛktys] *nm* leaflet

prospère [prɔspɛr] *adj* prosperous; *(santé)* glowing ■ **prospérer** *vi* to prosper ■ **prospérité** *nf* prosperity

prosterner [prɔstɛrne] **se prosterner** *vpr* to prostrate oneself (**devant** before)

prostituée [prɔstitɥe] *nf* prostitute ■ **prostitution** *nf* prostitution

protecteur, -trice [prɔtektœr, -tris] **1** *nmf* protector; *(mécène)* patron **2** *adj (geste, crème)* protective ∎ **protection** *nf* protection; **de p.** *(écran)* protective; **assurer la p. de qn** to ensure sb's safety ∎ **protectionnisme** *nm Écon* protectionism

protéger [prɔteʒe] **1** *vt* to protect (**de** from; **contre** against) **2 se protéger** *vpr* to protect oneself ∎ **protégé** *nm* protégé ∎ **protégée** *nf* protégée

protestant, -e [prɔtestɑ̃, -ɑ̃t] *adj & nmf* Protestant

protester [prɔteste] *vi* to protest (**contre** against); **p. de son innocence** to protest one's innocence ∎ **protestataire** *nmf* protester ∎ **protestation** *nf* protest (**contre** against); **en signe de p.** as a protest

prothèse [prɔtɛz] *nf* prosthesis; **p. auditive** hearing aid; **p. dentaire** false teeth

protocole [prɔtɔkɔl] *nm* protocol

prototype [prɔtɔtip] *nm* prototype

prouesse [prues] *nf* feat

prouver [pruve] *vt* to prove (**que** that)

Provence [prɔvɑ̃s] *nf* **la P.** Provence ∎ **provençal, -e, -aux, -ales 1** *adj* Provençal **2** *nmf* **P., Provençale** Provençal

provenir* [prɔvənir] *vi* **p. de** to come from ∎ **provenance** *nf* origin; **en p. de** from

proverbe [prɔvɛrb] *nm* proverb

providence [prɔvidɑ̃s] *nf* providence ∎ **providentiel, -elle** *adj* providential

province [prɔvɛ̃s] *nf* province; **la p.** the provinces; **en p.** in the provinces; **de p.** *(ville)* provincial ∎ **provincial, -e, -aux, -ales** *adj & nmf* provincial

proviseur [prɔvizœr] *nm Br* headmaster, *f* headmistress, *Am* principal

provision [prɔvizjɔ̃] *nf* (**a**) *(réserve)* supply, stock; **provisions** *(nourriture)* shopping; **sac à provisions** shopping bag; **faire des provisions de qch** to stock up on sth (**b**) *(somme)* credit; *(acompte)* deposit

provisoire [prɔvizwar] *adj* temporary; **à titre p.** temporarily

provoquer [prɔvɔke] *vt (incendie, mort)* to cause; *(réaction)* to provoke; *(colère, désir)* to arouse ∎ **provocant, -e** *adj* provocative ∎ **provocateur** *nm* troublemaker ∎ **provocation** *nf* provocation

proximité [prɔksimite] *nf* closeness, proximity; **à p.** close by; **à p. de** close to; **de p.** local

prude [pryd] **1** *adj* prudish **2** *nf* prude

prudent, -e [prydɑ̃, -ɑ̃t] *adj (personne)* cautious, careful; *(décision)* sensible ∎ **prudence** *nf* caution, care; **par p.** as a precaution

prune [pryn] *nf (fruit)* plum ∎ **prunier** *nm* plum tree

pruneau, -x [pryno] *nm* prune

pseudonyme [psødɔnim] *nm* pseudonym

psychanalyse [psikanaliz] *nf* psychoanalysis ∎ **psychanalyste** *nmf* psychoanalyst

psychiatre [psikjatr] *nmf* psychiatrist ∎ **psychiatrie** *nf* psychiatry ∎ **psychiatrique** *adj* psychiatric

psychique [psiʃik] *adj* psychic

psychologie [psikɔlɔʒi] *nf* psychology ∎ **psychologique** *adj* psychological ∎ **psychologue** *nmf* psychologist

psychose [psikoz] *nf* psychosis

pu [py] *pp de* **pouvoir 1**

puant, -e [pɥɑ̃, pɥɑ̃t] *adj* stinking ∎ **puanteur** *nf* stink, stench

public, -ique [pyblik] **1** *adj* public; **dette publique** national debt **2** *nm (de spectacle)* audience; **le grand p.** the general public; **film grand p.** film suitable for the general public; **en p.** in public; *(émission)* before a live audience

publication [pyblikasjɔ̃] *nf (action, livre)* publication ∎ **publier** *vt* to publish

publicité [pyblisite] *nf (secteur)* advertising; *(annonce)* advertisement, advert; *Radio & TV* commercial; **agence de p.** advertising agency; **faire de la**

p. pour qch to advertise sth ■ **publicitaire 1** *adj* film **p.** promotional film **2** *nmf* advertising executive

puce [pys] *nf (insecte)* flea; *Ordinat* (micro-)chip; **le marché aux puces, les puces** the flea market

pudeur [pydœr] *nf* modesty; **par p.** out of a sense of decency ■ **pudibond, -e** *adj* prudish ■ **pudique** *adj* modest

puer [pɥe] **1** *vt* to stink of **2** *vi* to stink

puériculture [pɥerikyltyr] *nf* child care ■ **puéricultrice** *nf* nursery nurse

puéril, -e [pɥeril] *adj* puerile ■ **puérilité** *nf* puerility

puis [pɥi] *adv* then; **et p.** *(ensuite)* and then; *(en plus)* and besides

puiser [pɥize] **1** *vt* to draw **(à/dans** from) **2** *vi* **p. dans qch** to dip into sth

puisque [pɥisk(ə)] *conj* since, as

puissant, -e [pɥisɑ̃, -ɑ̃t] *adj* powerful ■ **puissance** *nf (force, nation) & Math* power; **en p.** *(meurtrier)* potential; *Math* **dix p. quatre** ten to the power of four

puisse(s), puissent [pɥis] *voir* **pouvoir 1**

puits [pɥi] *nm* well; *(de mine)* shaft; **p. de pétrole** oil well

pull-over [pylɔver] *(pl* pull-overs), **pull** [pyl] *nm* sweater, *Br* jumper

pulluler [pylyle] *vi (abonder)* to swarm

pulmonaire [pylmɔner] *adj* pulmonary

pulpe [pylp] *nf (de fruits)* pulp

pulvériser [pylverize] *vt (vaporiser)* to spray; *(broyer)* to pulverize ■ **pulvérisateur** *nm* spray

punaise [pynez] *nf (insecte)* bug; *(clou)* *Br* drawing pin, *Am* thumbtack

punir [pynir] *vt* to punish; **p. qn de qch** *(bêtise, crime)* to punish sb for sth ■ **punition** *nf* punishment

pupille [pypij] **1** *nf (de l'œil)* pupil **2** *nmf (enfant)* ward

pupitre [pypitr] *nm (d'écolier)* desk; *(d'orateur)* lectern

pur, -e [pyr] *adj* pure; *(alcool)* neat, straight ■ **pureté** *nf* purity

purée [pyre] *nf* purée; **p. (de pommes de terre)** mashed potatoes, *Br* mash

purge [pyrʒ] *nf (à des fins médicales, politiques)* purge

purger [pyrʒe] *vt (patient)* to purge; *(radiateur)* to bleed; *(peine de prison)* to serve

purifier [pyrifje] *vt* to purify ■ **purification** *nf* purification; **p. ethnique** ethnic cleansing

puriste [pyrist] *nmf* purist

puritain, -e [pyritɛ̃, -ɛn] *adj & nmf* puritan

pur-sang [pyrsɑ̃] *nm inv* thoroughbred

pus¹ [py] *nm (liquide)* pus, matter

pus², put [py] *voir* **pouvoir 1**

putréfier [pytrefje] *vt*, **se putréfier** *vpr* to putrefy

puzzle [pœzl] *nm (jigsaw)* puzzle

pyjama [piʒama] *nm Br* pyjamas, *Am* pajamas; **un p.** a pair of *Br* pyjamas *orAm* pajamas

pyramide [piramid] *nf* pyramid

Pyrénées [pirene] *nfpl* **les P.** the Pyrenees

Pyrex® [pireks] *nm* Pyrex®; **plat en P.** Pyrex® dish

pyromane [pirɔman] *nmf* arsonist

Qq

Q, q [ky] *nm inv* Q, q

qu' [k] *voir* **que**

quadrillage [kadrijaʒ] *nm (de carte)* grid

quadriller [kadrije] *vt (quartier, ville)* to put under tight surveillance; *(papier)* to mark into squares ▪ **quadrillé, -e** *adj (papier)* squared

quadrupède [k(w)adrypɛd] *adj & nm* quadruped

quadruple [k(w)adrypl] **1** *adj* fourfold **2** *nm* le q. (de) *(quantité)* four times as much (as); *(nombre)* four times as many (as) ▪ **quadrupler** *vti* to quadruple ▪ **quadruplés, -es** *nmfpl* quadruplets

quai [kɛ] *nm (de port)* quay; *(de fleuve)* embankment; *(de gare, de métro)* platform

qualification [kalifikasjɔ̃] *nf (action, d'équipe, de sportif)* qualification; *(désignation)* description

qualifier [kalifje] **1** *vt (équipe)* to qualify (**pour qch** for sth; **pour faire** to do); *(décrire)* to describe (**de** as) **2 se qualifier** *vpr (équipe)* to qualify (**pour** for) ▪ **qualifié, -e** *adj (équipe)* that has qualified; **q. pour faire qch** qualified to do sth

qualité [kalite] *nf (de personne, de produit)* quality; *(occupation)* occupation; **produit de q.** quality product; **de bonne q.** of good quality; **en q. de** in his/her/*etc* capacity as

quand [kɑ̃] *conj & adv* when; **q. je viendrai** when I come

quant [kɑ̃] **quant à** *prép* as for

quantité [kɑ̃tite] *nf* quantity; **une q.,**

des quantités *(beaucoup)* a lot (**de** of)

quarante [karɑ̃t] *adj & nm inv* forty; **un q.-cinq tours** *(disque)* a single ▪ **quarantaine** *nf* (a) **une q. (de)** *(nombre)* (about) forty; **avoir la q.** *(âge)* to be about forty (b) *Méd* quarantine; **mettre qn en q.** to quarantine sb ▪ **quarantième** *adj & nmf* fortieth

quart [kar] *nm* (a) *(fraction)* quarter; **q. de litre** quarter litre, quarter of a litre; **q. d'heure** quarter of an hour; **une heure et q.** an hour and a quarter; **il est une heure et q.** it's a quarter *Br* past *or Am* after one; **une heure moins le q.** quarter to one; *Sport* **quarts de finale** quarter finals (b) *Naut* **être de q.** to be on watch ▪ **quart-monde** *nm* **le q.** the least-developed countries

quartier [kartje] *nm* (a) *(de ville)* district; **de q.** local; **q. général** headquarters (b) *(de lune)* quarter; *(de pomme)* piece; *(d'orange)* segment (c) *(expression)* **avoir q. libre** to be free

quartz [kwarts] *nm* quartz; **montre à q.** quartz watch

quasi [kazi] *adv* almost

quasiment [kazimɑ̃] *adv* almost

quatorze [katɔrz] *adj & nm inv* fourteen ▪ **quatorzième** *adj & nmf* fourteenth

quatre [katr] *adj & nm inv* four ▪ **quatrième** *adj & nmf* fourth

quatre-vingt [katrəvɛ̃] *adj & nm* eighty; **quatre-vingts ans** eighty years; **q.-un** eighty-one; **page q.** page eighty ▪ **quatre-vingt-dix** *adj & nm inv* ninety

QUE [kə]

> **que** becomes **qu'** before a vowel or mute h.

1 *conj* (**a**) *(complétif)* that; **je pense qu'elle restera** I think (that) she'll stay; **qu'elle vienne ou non** whether she comes or not; **qu'il s'en aille!** let him leave!; **ça fait un an q. je suis là** I've been here for a year

(**b**) *(de comparaison)* than; *(avec 'aussi', 'même', 'tel', 'autant')* as; **plus/moins âgé q. lui** older/younger than him; **aussi sage/fatigué q. toi** as wise/tired as you; **le même q. Pauline** the same as Pauline

(**c**) **(ne...) que** only; **tu n'as qu'un stylo** you only have one pen

2 *adv* **(ce) qu'il est bête!** *(comme)* he's really stupid!

3 *pron relatif (chose)* that, which; *(personne)* than, whom; *(temps)* when; **le livre q. j'ai** the book (that *or* which) I have; **l'ami q. j'ai** the friend (that *or* whom) I have

4 *pron interrogatif* what; **q. fait-il?, qu'est-ce qu'il fait?** what is he doing?; **q. préférez-vous?** which do you prefer?

Québec [kebɛk] *nm* **le Q.** Quebec

quel, quelle [kɛl] **1** *adj interrogatif (chose)* what, which; *(personne)* which; **q. livre préférez-vous?** which *or* what book do you prefer?; **q. est cet homme?** who is that man?; **je sais q. est ton but** I know what your aim is; **je ne sais à q. employé m'adresser** I don't know which clerk to ask

2 *pron interrogatif* which (one); **q. est le meilleur?** which (one) is the best?

3 *adj exclamatif* **q. idiot!** what a fool!

4 *adj relatif* **q. qu'il soit** *(chose)* whatever it may be; *(personne)* whoever it *or* he may be

quelconque [kɛlkɔ̃k] **1** *adj indéfini* any; **donne-moi un livre q.** give me any book **2** *adj (insignifiant)* ordinary

quelque [kɛlk] **1** *adj indéfini* some; **quelques** some, a few; **les quelques**

amies qu'elle a the few friends she has **2** *adv (environ)* about, some; **q. peu** somewhat; *Fam* **100 euros et q.** 100 euros and a bit

quelque chose [kɛlkəʃoz] *pron indéfini* something; **q. d'autre** something else; **q. de grand** something big; **q. de plus pratique/de moins lourd** something more practical/less heavy

quelquefois [kɛlkəfwa] *adv* sometimes

quelque part [kɛlkəpar] *adv* somewhere; *(dans les questions)* anywhere

quelques-uns, -unes [kɛlkəzœ̃, -yn] *pron* some

quelqu'un [kɛlkœ̃] *pron indéfini* someone, somebody; *(dans les questions)* anyone, anybody; **q. d'intelligent** someone clever

querelle [kərɛl] *nf* quarrel; **chercher q. à qn** to try to pick a fight with sb ■ **se quereller** *vpr* to quarrel

question [kɛstjɔ̃] *nf (interrogation)* question; *(affaire)* matter, question; **il n'en est pas q.** it's out of the question; **en q.** in question ■ **questionnaire** *nm* questionnaire ■ **questionner** *vt* to question **(sur** about)

quête [kɛt] *nf* (**a**) *(collecte)* collection; **faire la q.** to collect money (**b**) *(recherche)* quest (**de** for); **en q. de** in quest *or* search of ■ **quêter** [kete] **1** *vt* to seek **2** *vi* to collect money

queue [kø] *nf* (**a**) *(d'animal)* tail; *(de fleur, de fruit)* stalk; *(de train)* rear; **à la q. leu leu** in single file; **q. de cheval** *(coiffure)* ponytail (**b**) *(file)* *Br* queue, *Am* line; **faire la q.** *Br* to queue up, *Am* to stand in line

QUI [ki] **1** *pron interrogatif (personne)* who; *(en complément)* whom; **q. (est-ce qui) est là?** who's there?; **q. désirez-vous voir?, q. est-ce que vous désirez voir?** who(m) do you want to see?; **à q. est ce livre?** whose book is this?; **je demande q. a téléphoné** I'm asking who phoned

2 *pron relatif* (**a**) *(sujet) (personne)*

who, that; *(chose)* which, that; **l'hom- me q. est là** the man who's here *or* that's here; **la maison q. se trouve en face** the house which is *or* that's opposite

(**b**) *(sans antécédent)* **q. que vous soyez** whoever you are

(**c**) *(après une préposition)* **la femme de q. je parle** the woman I'm talking about

quiconque [kikɔ̃k] *pron (sujet)* who- ever; *(complément)* anyone

quille [kij] *nf (de navire)* keel; *(de jeu)* (bowling) pin, *Br* skittle; **jouer aux quilles** to bowl, *Br* to play skittles

quincaillerie [kɛ̃kajri] *nf (magasin)* hardware shop; *(objets)* hardware

quinquennal, -e, -aux, -ales [kɛ̃- kenal, -o] *adj* **plan q.** five-year plan ■ **quinquennat** *nm Pol* five-year term (of office)

quintuple [kɛ̃typl] **1** *adj* **q. de** fivefold **2** *nm* **le q. (de)** *(quantité)* five times as much (as); *(nombre)* five times as many (as) ■ **quintupler** *vti* to increase fivefold

quinze [kɛ̃z] *adj & nm inv* fifteen; **q. jours** two weeks, *Br* a fortnight ■ **quinzaine** *nf* **une q. (de)** (about)

fifteen; **une q. (de jours)** two weeks, *Br* a fortnight ■ **quinzième** *adj & nmf* fifteenth

quittance [kitɑ̃s] *nf (reçu)* receipt

quitte [kit] *adj* quits (**envers** with); **q. à faire qch** even if it means doing sth; **en être q. pour qch** to get off with sth

quitter [kite] **1** *vt (personne, lieu, pos- te)* to leave; **ne pas q. qn des yeux** to keep one's eyes on sb **2** *vi* **ne quittez pas!** *(au téléphone)* hold the line! **3 se quitter** *vpr* to part; **ils ne se quittent plus** they are inseparable

QUOI [kwa] *pron* what; *(après une préposition)* which; **à q. penses-tu?** what are you thinking about?; **après q.** after which; **de q. manger** some- thing to eat; *(assez)* enough to eat; **de q. écrire** something to write with; **q. que je dise** whatever I say; **q. qu'il en soit** be that as it may; **il n'y a pas de q.!** *(en réponse à 'merci')* don't mention it!; **q.?** what?

quoique [kwak] *conj* (al)though; **quoi- qu'il soit pauvre** (al)though he's poor

quota [kwɔta] *nm* quota

quotidien, -enne [kɔtidjɛ̃, -ɛn] **1** *adj* daily **2** *nm* daily (paper)

Rr

R, r [ɛr] *nm inv* R, r

rabâcher [rabɑʃe] **1** *vt* to repeat endlessly **2** *vi* to say the same thing over and over again

rabais [rabɛ] *nm* reduction, discount ■ **rabaisser 1** *vt* (dénigrer) to belittle **2 se rabaisser** *upr* to belittle oneself

rabattre* [rabatr] **1** *vt* (col) to turn down; (couvercle) to close **2 se rabattre** *upr* (se refermer) to close; (véhicule) to pull back in; *Fig* **se r. sur qch** to fall back on sth

rabbin [rabɛ̃] *nm* rabbi

rabougri, -e [rabugri] *adj* (personne, plante) stunted

raccommoder [rakɔmɔde] *vt* (linge) to mend; (chaussette) to darn

raccompagner [rakɔ̃paɲe] *vt* to take back

raccord [rakɔr] *nm* (dispositif) connection; (de papier peint) join; (de peinture) touch-up ■ **raccordement** [-əmɑ̃] *nm* (action, lien) connection ■ **raccorder** *vt*, **se raccorder** *upr* to link up (**à** to)

raccourcir [rakursir] **1** *vt* to shorten **2** *vi* to get shorter ■ **raccourci** *nm* short cut; **en r.** in brief

raccrocher [rakrɔʃe] **1** *vt* (objet tombé) to hang back up; (téléphone) to put down **2** *vi* (au téléphone) to hang up **3 se raccrocher** *upr* **se r. à qch** to catch hold of sth; *Fig* to cling to sth

race [ras] *nf* (ethnie) race; (animale) breed; **chien de r.** pedigree dog ■ **racial, -e, -aux, -ales** *adj* racial ■ **racisme** *nm* racism ■ **raciste** *adj & nmf* racist

rachat [raʃa] *nm* (de voiture, d'appartement) repurchase; (de firme) buy-out ■ **racheter 1** *vt* (acheter davantage) to buy some more; (remplacer) to buy another; (firme) to buy out; (faute) to make up for **2 se racheter** *upr* to make amends, to redeem oneself

racine [rasin] *nf* (de plante, de personne) & *Math* root

racler [rɑkle] **1** *vt* to scrape; (peinture, boue) to scrape off **2 se racler** *upr* **se r. la gorge** to clear one's throat ■ **raclette** *nf* (outil) scraper; (plat) raclette (Swiss dish consisting of potatoes and melted cheese)

raconter [rakɔ̃te] *vt* (histoire, mensonge) to tell; (événement) to tell about; **r. qch à qn** (histoire) to tell sb sth; (événement) to tell sb about sth; **r. à qn que...** to tell sb that... ■ **racontars** *nmpl* gossip

radar [radar] *nm* radar; **contrôle r.** radar speed check

rade [rad] *nf* harbour

radeau, -x [rado] *nm* raft

radiateur [radjatœr] *nm* radiator; **r. électrique** electric heater

radiation [radjasjɔ̃] *nf* *Phys* radiation; (suppression) removal (**de** from) ■ **radier** *vt* to strike off (**de** from)

radical, -e, -aux, -ales [radikal, -o] *adj* radical

radieux, -euse [radjø, -øz] *adj* (personne, visage, soleil) radiant; (temps) glorious

radio [radjo] **1** *nf* (**a**) (poste) radio; (station) radio station; **à la r.** on the radio (**b**) *Méd* X-ray; **passer une r. to**

have an X-ray **2** *nm (opérateur)* radio operator ■ **radio-réveil** *(pl* **radios-réveils)** *nm* radio alarm, clock radio

radioactif, -ive [radjoaktif, -iv] *adj* radioactive ■ **radioactivité** *nf* radioactivity

radiodiffuser [radjodifyse] *vt* to broadcast ■ **radiodiffusion** *nf* broadcasting

radiographie [radjografi] *nf (photo)* X-ray; *(technique)* radiography ■ **radiographier** *vt* to X-ray ■ **radiologie** *nf Méd* radiology ■ **radiologue** *nmf (technicien)* radiographer; *(médecin)* radiologist

radiophonique [radjofɔnik] *adj* **émission r.** radio broadcast

radis [radi] *nm* radish

radoucir [radusir] **se radoucir** *vpr (personne)* to calm down; *(temps)* to become milder

rafale [rafal] *nf (vent)* gust; *(de mitrailleuse)* burst

raffermir [rafermir] **1** *vt (autorité)* to strengthen; *(muscles)* to tone up **2 se raffermir** *vpr (muscle)* to become stronger

raffiné, -e [rafine] *adj* refined ■ **raffinement** *nm* refinement

raffiner [rafine] *vt* to refine ■ **raffinage** *nm* refining

raffinerie [rafinri] *nf* refinery

rafle [rafl] *nf* raid

rafraîchir [rafrɛʃir] **1** *vt (rendre frais)* to chill; *(pièce)* to air; *(raviver)* to freshen up **2** *vi* to cool down **3 se rafraîchir** *vpr (temps)* to get cooler; *(se laver)* to freshen up ■ **rafraîchissant, -e** *adj* refreshing ■ **rafraîchissement** *nm (boisson)* cold drink

rage [raʒ] *nf (colère)* rage; *(maladie)* rabies; **faire r.** *(incendie, tempête)* to rage

ragoût [ragu] *nm Culin* stew

raid [rɛd] *nm* raid

raide [rɛd] **1** *adj (rigide, guindé)* stiff; *(côte)* steep; *(cheveux)* straight **2** *adv (grimper)* steeply; **tomber r.** to fall to the ground ■ **raideur** *nf (rigidité)* stiffness; *(de côte)* steepness ■ **raidir 1** *vt*

(bras, jambe) to brace; *(corde)* to tauten **2 se raidir** *vpr (membres)* to stiffen; *(corde)* to tauten; *(personne)* to tense up

raie [rɛ] *nf (motif)* stripe; *(de cheveux)* Br parting, Am part

rail [raj] *nm* rail; **le r.** *(chemins de fer)* rail; **r. de sécurité** crash barrier

raisin [rezɛ̃] *nm* **raisin(s)** grapes; **r. sec** raisin

raison [rezɔ̃] *nf* **(a)** *(faculté, motif)* reason; **la r. de mon absence** the reason for my absence; **la r. pour laquelle…** the reason (why)…; **en r. de** *(cause)* on account of; **à r. de** *(proportion)* at the rate of; **à plus forte r.** all the more so

(b) avoir r. to be right **(de faire** to do or in doing); **donner r. à qn** to agree with sb

raisonnable [rezɔnabl] *adj* reasonable

raisonner [rezɔne] *vi (penser)* to reason ■ **raisonnement** *nm (faculté, activité)* reasoning; *(argumentation)* argument

rajeunir [raʒœnir] **1** *vt (moderniser)* to modernize; **r. qn** *(faire paraître plus jeune)* to make sb look younger; *(donner moins que son âge à)* to underestimate how old sb is **2** *vi* to look younger ■ **rajeunissement** *nm (après traitement)* rejuvenation; *(de population)* decrease in age

rajouter [raʒute] *vt* to add **(à** to)

rajuster [raʒyste] *vt (vêtements, lunettes)* to straighten, to adjust

ralentir [ralɑ̃tir] *vti* to slow down ■ **ralenti** *nm Cin & TV* slow motion; **au r.** in slow motion; *(travailler)* at a slower pace; **tourner au r.** *(moteur, usine)* Br to tick over, Am to turn over ■ **ralentissement** *nm* slowing down; *(embouteillage)* hold-up

rallier [ralje] **1** *vt (réunir)* to rally; *(regagner)* to return to; **r. qn à qch** *(convertir)* to win sb over to sth **2 se rallier** *vpr* **se r. à** *(avis)* to come round to; *(cause)* to rally to

rallonge [ralɔ̃ʒ] *nf* (*de table*) extension; (*fil électrique*) extension (lead) ∎ **rallonger** *vti* to lengthen

rallumer [ralyme] **1** *vt* (*feu, pipe*) to light again; (*lampe*) to switch on again **2 se rallumer** *vpr* (*lumière*) to come back on; (*incendie*) to flare up again

ramasser [ramɑse] **1** *vt* (*prendre, réunir*) to pick up; (*ordures, copies*) to collect; (*fruits, coquillages*) to gather
  2 se ramasser *vpr* (*se pelotonner*) to curl up; (*se relever*) to pick oneself up ∎ **ramassage** (*d'ordures*) collection; **r. scolaire** school bus service

rame [ram] *nf* (*aviron*) oar; (*de métro*) train ∎ **ramer** *vi* to row ∎ **rameur, -euse** *nmf* rower

ramener [ramne] *vt* (*amener*) to bring back; (*raccompagner*) to take back; (*ordre, calme*) to restore; **r. qch à qch** to reduce sth to sth; **r. qn à la vie** to bring sb back to life

ramollir [ramɔlir] *vt, se ramollir vpr* to soften

ramoner [ramɔne] *vt* (*cheminée*) to sweep

rampe [rɑ̃p] *nf* (*d'escalier*) banister; (*pente*) slope; **r. d'accès** (*de pont*) access ramp

ramper [rɑ̃pe] *vi* to crawl

rancœur [rɑ̃kœr] *nf* rancour, resentment

rançon [rɑ̃sɔ̃] *nf* ransom ∎ **rançonner** *vt* to hold to ransom

rancune [rɑ̃kyn] *nf* spite; **garder r. à qn** to bear sb a grudge ∎ **rancunier, -ère** *adj* spiteful

randonnée [rɑ̃dɔne] *nf* (*à pied*) hike; (*en vélo*) ride

rang [rɑ̃] *nm* (*rangée*) row; (*classement, grade*) rank; **par r. de taille** in order of size; **de haut r.** high-ranking; **se mettre en r.** to line up (**par trois** in threes) ∎ **rangée** *nf* row

ranger [rɑ̃ʒe] **1** *vt* (*papiers, vaisselle*) to put away; (*chambre*) to tidy (up); (*classer*) to rank (**parmi** among) **2 se ranger** *vpr* (*se disposer*) to line up;

(*s'écarter*) to stand aside ∎ **rangé, -e** *adj* (*chambre*) tidy; (*personne*) steady ∎ **rangement** *nm* putting away; (*de chambre*) tidying (up); **rangements** (*placards*) storage space

ranimer [ranime] *vt* (*personne*) (*après évanouissement*) to bring round; (*après arrêt cardiaque*) to resuscitate; (*feu*) to rekindle; (*souvenir*) to reawaken; (*débat*) to revive

rapace [rapas] **1** *nm* (*oiseau*) bird of prey **2** *adj* (*personne*) grasping

rapatrier [rapatrije] *vt* to repatriate

râpé, -e [rɑpe] *adj* (*fromage, carottes*) grated ∎ **râper** *vt* (*fromage*) to grate; (*bois*) to rasp

rapetisser [raptise] **1** *vt* (*rendre plus petit*) to make smaller; (*faire paraître plus petit*) to make look smaller **2** *vi* (*vêtement, personne*) to shrink

rapide [rapid] **1** *adj* fast; (*progrès*) rapid; (*esprit, lecture*) quick **2** *nm* (*train*) express (train); (*de fleuve*) rapid ∎ **rapidité** *nf* speed

rappel [rapɛl] *nm* (*de diplomate*) recall; (*d'événement, de promesse*) reminder; (*au théâtre*) curtain call; (*vaccin*) booster; **descendre en r.** (*en alpinisme*) to abseil down

rappeler [raple] **1** *vt* (*pour faire revenir, au téléphone*) to call back; (*souvenir, diplomate*) to recall; **r. qch à qn** to remind sb of sth **2** *vi* (*au téléphone*) to call back **3 se rappeler** *vpr* **se r. qn/qch** to remember sb/sth; **se r. que...** to remember that...

rapport [rapɔr] *nm* (**a**) (*lien*) connection, link; **par r. à** compared with; **rapports** (*entre personnes*) relations; **rapports (sexuels)** (sexual) intercourse (**b**) (*profit*) return, yield (**c**) (*compte rendu*) report

rapporter [rapɔrte] **1** *vt* (*rendre*) to bring back; (*remporter*) to take back; (*raconter*) to report; (*profit*) to yield; **r. de l'argent** to be profitable; (*moralement*) to bring sb sth; **on rapporte que...** it is reported that...
  2 *vi* (*chien*) to retrieve

3 se rapporter *vpr* **se r. à qch** to relate to sth; **s'en r. à qn/qch** to rely on sb/sth

rapprocher [raprɔʃe] **1** *vt* (*objet*) to move closer (**de** to); (*réconcilier*) to bring together; (*comparer*) to compare (**de** *or* with)

2 se rapprocher *vpr* to get closer (**de** to); (*se réconcilier*) to be reconciled; (*ressembler*) to be similar (**de** to) ▪ **rapproché, -e** *adj* close; (*yeux*) close-set ▪ **rapprochement** *nm* (*réconciliation*) reconciliation; (*rapport*) connection

rapt [rapt] *nm* abduction

raquette [raket] *nf* (*de tennis*) racket; (*de ping-pong*) bat; (*de neige*) snowshoe

rare [rɑr] *adj* rare; (*argent, main-d'œuvre*) scarce; (*barbe, végétation*) sparse; **c'est r. qu'il pleuve ici** it rarely rains here ▪ **rarement** *adv* rarely, seldom ▪ **rareté** *nf* (*objet rare*) rarity; (*de main-d'œuvre*) scarcity; (*de phénomène*) rareness

ras, -e [rɑ, rɑz] **1** *adj* (*cheveux*) close-cropped; (*herbe, barbe*) short; (*mesure*) full; **à r. bord** to the brim; **pull (au) r. du cou** crew-neck sweater **2** *nm* **au r. de, à r. de** level with; **voler au r. du sol** to fly close to the ground **3** *adv* (*coupé*) short

raser [rɑze] **1** *vt* (*menton, personne*) to shave; (*barbe, moustache*) to shave off; (*démolir*) to raze to the ground; (*frôler*) to skim **2 se raser** *vpr* to shave ▪ **rasé, -e** *adj* **être bien r.** to be clean-shaven

rasoir [rɑzwar] *nm* razor; (*électrique*) shaver

rassasier [rasazje] *vt* (*faim, curiosité*) to satisfy

rassembler [rasɑ̃ble] **1** *vt* (*gens, objets*) to gather (together) **2 se rassembler** *vpr* to gather, to assemble ▪ **rassemblement** [-əmɑ̃] *nm* (*action, groupe*) gathering

rasseoir* [raswar] **se rasseoir** *vpr* to sit down again

rassis, -e [rɑsi, -iz] *adj* (*pain*) stale

rassurer [rasyre] **1** *vt* to reassure **2 se rassurer** *vpr* **rassure-toi** don't worry ▪ **rassurant, -e** *adj* reassuring

rat [ra] *nm* rat

ratatiner [ratatine] **se ratatiner** *vpr* to shrivel up

ratatouille [ratatuj] *nf* *Culin* **r. (niçoise)** ratatouille

râteau, -x [rɑto] *nm* rake

râtelier [rɑtəlje] *nm* (*pour outils, pour armes*) rack

rater [rate] *vt* (*bus, cible, occasion*) to miss; (*travail, gâteau*) to ruin; (*examen*) to fail; (*vie*) to waste ▪ **raté, -e** *nmf* loser

ratifier [ratifje] *vt* to ratify

ration [rɑsjɔ̃] *nf* ration ▪ **rationnement** *nm* rationing

rationaliser [rasjɔnalize] *vt* to rationalize

rationnel, -elle [rasjɔnɛl] *adj* rational

ratisser [ratise] *vt* (*allée*) to rake; (*feuilles*) to rake up

rattacher [rataʃe] **1** *vt* (*lacets*) to tie up again; (*région*) to unite (**à** with) **2 se rattacher** *vpr* **se r. à** to be linked to

rattraper [ratrape] **1** *vt* to catch; (*prisonnier*) to recapture; **r. qn** (*rejoindre*) to catch up with sb; **r. le temps perdu** to make up for lost time **2 se rattraper** *vpr* (*se retenir*) to catch oneself in time; (*après une faute*) to make up for it; **se r. à qch** to catch hold of sth ▪ **rattrapage** *nm* *Scol* **cours de r.** remedial class

raturer [ratyre] *vt* to cross out, to delete

rauque [rok] *adj* (*voix*) hoarse

ravages [ravaʒ] *nmpl* devastation; (*du temps, de maladie*) ravages; **faire des r.** to wreak havoc; (*femme*) to break hearts ▪ **ravager** *vt* to devastate

ravaler [ravale] *vt* (*façade*) to clean

ravi, -e [ravi] *adj* delighted (**de** with; **de faire** to do; **que** that)

ravin [ravɛ̃] *nm* ravine

ravir [ravir] *vt* (*emporter*) to snatch (**à**

from); *(plaire à)* to delight; **chanter à r.** to sing delightfully ■ **ravissement** *nm* (*extase*) ecstasy ■ **ravisseur, -euse** *nmf* kidnapper

raviser [ravize] **se raviser** *vpr* to change one's mind

ravitailler [ravitaje] **1** *vt* (*personnes*) to supply; *(avion)* to refuel **2 se ravitailler** *vpr* to get in supplies ■ **ravitaillement** *nm* (*action*) supplying; *(d'avion)* refuelling; *(denrées)* supplies

raviver [ravive] *vt* (*feu, sentiment*) to rekindle; *(douleur)* to revive; *(couleur)* to brighten up

rayer [reje] *vt* (*érafler*) to scratch; *(mot)* to cross out ■ **rayé, -e** *adj* (*verre, disque*) scratched; *(tissu, pantalon)* striped ■ **rayure** *nf* (*éraflure*) scratch; *(motif)* stripe; **à rayures** striped

rayon [rɛjɔ̃] *nm* (**a**) *(de lumière)* ray; *(de cercle)* radius; *(de roue)* spoke; **dans un r. de** within a radius of; **r. X** X-ray; **r. de soleil** sunbeam (**b**) *(d'étagère)* shelf; *(de magasin)* department; *(de ruche)* honeycomb ■ **rayonnage** *nm* shelving, shelves

rayonner [rɛjɔne] *vi* (*avenue, douleur*) to radiate; *(dans une région)* to travel around *(from a central base)*; *(soleil)* to beam; *Fig* **r. de joie** to beam with joy ■ **rayonnant, -e** *adj* (*soleil*) radiant; *Fig (visage)* beaming (**de** with) ■ **rayonnement** *nm* (*du soleil*) radiance; *(influence)* influence

raz de marée [radmare] *nm inv* tidal wave; **r. électoral** landslide

ré [re] *nm inv* (*note*) D

réacteur [reaktœr] *nm* (*d'avion*) jet engine; *(nucléaire)* reactor

réaction [reaksjɔ̃] *nf* reaction; **moteur à r.** jet engine

réagir [reaʒir] *vi* to react (**contre** against; **à** to); *Fig (se secouer)* to shake oneself out of it

réaliser [realize] **1** *vt* (*projet*) to realize; *(rêve, ambition) Br* to fulfil, *Am* to fulfill; *(bénéfices)* to make; *(film)* to direct; *(comprendre)* to realize (**que** that)

2 se réaliser *vpr* (*vœu*) to come true; *(personne) Br* to fulfil *or Am* fulfill oneself ■ **réalisable** *adj* (*plan*) workable; *(rêve)* attainable ■ **réalisateur, -trice** *nmf* (*de film*) director ■ **réalisation** *nf* (*de projet*) realization; *(de rêve)* fulfilment; *(de film)* direction

réalité [realite] *nf* reality; **en r.** in reality

réanimation [reanimɑsjɔ̃] *nf* resuscitation; **(service de) r.** intensive care unit ■ **réanimer** *vt* to resuscitate

rebattu, -e [rəbaty] *adj* (*sujet*) hackneyed

rebelle [rəbɛl] **1** *adj* (*personne*) rebellious; *(mèche)* unruly **2** *nmf* rebel ■ **se rebeller** *vpr* to rebel (**contre** against) ■ **rébellion** *nf* rebellion

rebondir [rəbɔ̃dir] *vi* to bounce; *(par ricochet)* to rebound

rebondissement [rəbɔ̃dismɑ̃] *nm* new development (**de** in)

rebord [rəbɔr] *nm* edge; *(de plat)* rim; *(de vêtement)* hem; **r. de fenêtre** windowsill

reboucher [rəbuʃe] *vt* (*flacon*) to put the top back on; *(trou)* to fill in again

rebours [rəbur] **à rebours** *adv* the wrong way

rébus [rebys] *nm* rebus

rebut [rəby] *nm* **mettre qch au r.** to throw sth out

rebuter [rəbyte] *vt* (*décourager*) to put off

récapituler [rekapityle] *vti* to recapitulate

recel [rəsɛl] *nm* receiving stolen goods ■ **receler, recéler** *vt* (*mystère, secret*) to conceal; *(objet volé)* to receive; *(criminel)* to harbour

recenser [rəsɑ̃se] *vt* (*population*) to take a census of ■ **recensement** *nm* (*de population*) census

récent, -e [resɑ̃, -ɑ̃t] *adj* recent

récepteur [reseptœr] *nm* (*téléphone*) receiver ■ **réceptif, -ive** *adj* receptive (**à** to) ■ **réception** *nf* (*accueil, soirée*) & *Radio* reception; *(de lettre)* receipt; *(d'hôtel)* reception (desk); **dès r. de**

on receipt of; **avec accusé de r.** with acknowledgement of receipt ■ **réceptionniste** *nmf* receptionist

récession [resesjɔ̃] *nf Écon* recession

recette [rəsɛt] *nf Culin & Fig* recipe (**de** for); *(argent, bénéfice)* takings; **recettes** *(gains)* takings

recevoir* [rəsəvwar] **1** *vt (amis, lettre, proposition, coup de téléphone)* to receive; *(gifle, coup)* to get; *(client)* to see; *(candidat)* to admit; *(station de radio)* to pick up; **r. la visite de qn** to have a visit from sb; **être reçu à un examen** to pass an exam; **être reçu premier** to come first
2 *vi (faire une fête)* to have guests ■ **receveur, -euse** *nmf (de bus)* (bus) conductor; **r. des Postes** postmaster, *f* postmistress

rechange [rəʃɑ̃ʒ] **de rechange** *adj (pièce)* spare

recharge [rəʃarʒ] *nf (de stylo)* refill ■ **rechargeable** *adj (briquet)* refillable; *(pile)* rechargeable ■ **recharger** *vt (fusil, appareil photo, camion)* to reload; *(briquet, stylo)* to refill; *(pile)* to recharge

réchaud [reʃo] *nm* (portable) stove

réchauffer [reʃofe] **1** *vt (personne, aliment)* to warm up **2 se réchauffer** *vpr (personne)* to get warm ■ **réchauffement** *nm (de température)* rise (**de** in); **le r. de la planète** global warming

rêche [rɛʃ] *adj* rough

recherche [rəʃɛrʃ] *nf* (a) *(quête)* search (**de** for); **à la r. de** in search of (b) *(scientifique)* research (**sur** into); **faire de la r.** to do research (c) **recherches** *(de police)* search, hunt; **faire des recherches** to make inquiries (d) *(raffinement)* elegance

rechercher [rəʃɛrʃe] *vt (personne, objet)* to search for; *(emploi)* to look for; *(honneurs)* to seek ■ **recherché, -e** *adj* (a) *(très demandé)* in demand; *(rare)* sought-after; **r. pour meurtre** wanted for murder (b) *(élégant)* elegant

rechute [rəʃyt] *nf* relapse ■ **rechuter** *vi* to have a relapse

récidive [residiv] *nf (de malfaiteur)* repeat *Br* offence *or Am* offense; *(de maladie)* recurrence (**de** of) ■ **récidiver** *vi (malfaiteur)* to reoffend ■ **récidiviste** *nmf (malfaiteur)* repeat offender

récif [resif] *nm* reef

récipient [resipjɑ̃] *nm* container

réciproque [resiprɔk] *adj (sentiments)* mutual; *(concessions)* reciprocal

récit [resi] *nm (histoire)* story; *(compte rendu)* account; **faire le r. de qch** to give an account of sth

récital, -als [resital] *nm* recital

réciter [resite] *vt* to recite

réclame [reklam] *nf (publicité)* advertising; *(annonce)* advertisement; **en r.** on special offer

réclamer [reklame] **1** *vt (demander)* to ask for; *(exiger)* to demand; *(nécessiter)* to require **2** *vi* to complain ■ **réclamation** *nf* complaint; **(bureau des) réclamations** complaints department

réclusion [reklyzjɔ̃] *nf* **r. (criminelle) à perpétuité** life imprisonment

recoin [rəkwɛ̃] *nm (de lieu)* nook

recoller [rəkɔle] *vt (objet cassé)* to stick back together

récolte [rekɔlt] *nf (action)* harvesting; *(produits)* harvest; **faire la r.** to harvest the crops ■ **récolter** *vt* to harvest

recommandable [rəkɔmɑ̃dabl] *adj* **peu r.** disreputable

recommandation [rəkɔmɑ̃dasjɔ̃] *nf (appui, conseil)* recommendation

recommander [rəkɔmɑ̃de] *vt (appuyer)* to recommend (**à** to; **pour** for); **r. à qn de faire qch** to advise sb to do sth ■ **recommandé, -e 1** *adj (lettre)* registered **2** *nm* **en r.** registered

recommencer [rəkɔmɑ̃se] *vti* to start or begin again ■ **recommencement** *nm* renewal (**de** of)

récompense [rekɔ̃pɑ̃s] *nf* reward (**pour** *ou* **de** for); *(prix)* award ■ **récompenser** *vt* to reward (**de** *ou* **pour** for)

réconcilier [rekɔ̃silje] **1** *vt* to reconcile (**avec** with) **2 se réconcilier** *vpr* to become reconciled, *Br* to make it up (**avec** with) ▪ **réconciliation** nf reconciliation

reconduire* [rəkɔ̃dɥir] vt (contrat) to renew; **r. qn (à la porte)** to show sb out ▪ **reconduction** nf (de contrat) renewal

réconfort [rekɔ̃fɔr] nm comfort ▪ **réconfortant, -e** adj comforting ▪ **réconforter** vt to comfort

reconnaissable [rəkɔnɛsabl] adj recognizable (**à qch** by sth)

reconnaissant, -e [rəkɔnɛsɑ̃, -ɑ̃t] adj grateful (**à qn de qch** to sb for sth) ▪ **reconnaissance** nf (gratitude) gratitude (**pour** for); (de droit, de gouvernement) recognition; Mil reconnaissance; **r. de dette** IOU

reconnaître* [rəkɔnɛtr] 1 vt (identifier, admettre) to recognize (**à qch** by sth); (enfant, erreur) to acknowledge; Mil (terrain) to reconnoitre; **être reconnu coupable** to be found guilty
2 **se reconnaître** vpr (soi-même) to recognize oneself; (l'un l'autre) to recognize each other ▪ **reconnu, -e** adj recognized

reconquérir* [rəkɔ̃kerir] vt (territoire) to reconquer

reconsidérer [rəkɔ̃sidere] vt to reconsider

reconstituer [rəkɔ̃stitɥe] vt (armée, parti) to reconstitute; (crime) to reconstruct ▪ **reconstitution** nf (de crime) reconstruction; **r. historique** historical reconstruction

reconstruire* [rəkɔ̃strɥir] vt to rebuild ▪ **reconstruction** nf rebuilding

reconvertir [rəkɔ̃vertir] 1 vt (entreprise) to convert; (personne) to retrain 2 **se reconvertir** vpr (personne) to retrain ▪ **reconversion** nf (d'usine) conversion; (de personne) retraining

recopier [rəkɔpje] vt (mettre au propre) to copy out; (faire un double de) to recopy

record [rəkɔr] nm & adj inv record

recoucher [rəkuʃe] se recoucher vpr to go back to bed

recoudre* [rəkudr] vt (bouton) to sew

back on; (vêtement, plaie) to stitch up

recouper [rəkupe] 1 vt (couper de nouveau) to recut; (confirmer) to confirm 2 **se recouper** vpr (témoignages) to tally ▪ **recoupement** nm crosscheck; **par r.** by crosschecking

recourber [rəkurbe] vt, **se recourber** vpr to bend ▪ **recourbé, -e** adj (bec) curved

recours [rəkur] nm recourse; **avoir r. à** (chose) to resort to; (personne) to turn to; **en dernier r.** as a last resort ▪ **recourir*** vi r. à (moyen, violence) to resort to; (personne) to turn to

recouvrer [rəkuvre] vt (santé, bien) to recover; (vue) to regain

recouvrir* [rəkuvrir] vt (revêtir, inclure) to cover (**de** with); (couvrir de nouveau) to re-cover

récréation [rekreasjɔ̃] nf Scol Br break, Am recess; (pour les plus jeunes) playtime

recroqueviller [rəkrɔkvije] se recroqueviller vpr (personne) to huddle up

recrue [rəkry] nf recruit ▪ **recrutement** nm recruitment ▪ **recruter** vt to recruit

rectangle [rɛktɑ̃gl] nm rectangle ▪ **rectangulaire** adj rectangular

rectifier [rɛktifje] vt (calcul, erreur) to correct; (compte) to adjust ▪ **rectification** nf (de calcul, d'erreur) correction

recto [rɛkto] nm front; **r. verso** on both sides

rectorat [rɛktɔra] nm Br ≃ local education authority, Am ≃ board of education

reçu, -e [rəsy] 1 pp de **recevoir** 2 adj (idée) received; (candidat) successful 3 nm (récépissé) receipt

recueil [rəkœj] nm (de poèmes, de chansons) collection (**de** of)

recueillir* [rəkœjir] 1 vt (argent, renseignements) to collect; (personne, animal) to take in 2 **se recueillir** vpr to meditate; (devant un monument) to stand in silence ▪ **recueillement** nm meditation

recul [rəkyl] *nm (d'armée, de négociateur, de maladie)* retreat; *(de canon)* recoil; *(déclin)* decline; **avoir un mouvement de r.** to recoil

reculer [rəkyle] **1** *vi (personne)* to move back; *(automobiliste)* to reverse, *Am* to back up; *(armée)* to retreat; *(épidémie)* to lose ground; *(renoncer)* to back down, to retreat; *(diminuer)* to decline; **faire r. la foule** to move the crowd back
2 *vt (meuble)* to move back; *(paiement, décision)* to postpone ▪ **reculé, -e** *adj (endroit)* remote

reculons [rəkylɔ̃] **à reculons** *adv* backwards

récupérer [rekypere] **1** *vt (objet prêté)* to get back, to recover; *(bagages)* to retrieve; *(forces)* to recover; *(recycler)* to salvage; *Péj (détourner à son profit)* to exploit **2** *vi (reprendre des forces)* to recover ▪ **récupération** *nf (d'objet)* recovery; *(de déchets)* salvage

recycler [rəsikle] **1** *vt (matériaux)* to recycle **2 se recycler** *vpr (personne)* to retrain ▪ **recyclage** *nm (de matériaux)* recycling; *(de personne)* retraining

rédacteur, -trice [redaktœr, -tris] *nmf* writer; *(de journal)* editor ▪ **rédaction** *nf (action)* writing; *(de contrat)* drawing up; *(journalistes)* editorial staff; *(bureaux)* editorial offices

redemander [rədəmɑ̃de] *vt* to ask for more; **il faut que je le lui redemande** *(que je pose la question à nouveau)* I'll have to ask him/her again

redémarrer [rədemare] *vi (voiture)* to start again

redescendre [rədesɑ̃dr] **1** *(aux avoir) vt (objet)* to bring/take back down **2** *(aux être) vi* to come/go back down

redevance [rədəvɑ̃s] *nf (de télévision)* licence fee

redevenir* [rədəvənir] *(aux être) vi* to become again

rediffusion [rədifyzjɔ̃] *nf (de film)* repeat

rédiger [rediʒe] *vt* to write; *(contrat)* to draw up

redire* [rədir] **1** *vt* to repeat **2** *vi* **avoir ou trouver à r. à qch** to find fault with sth

redoublant, -e [rədublɑ̃, -ɑ̃t] *nmf* pupil repeating a year *or Am* a grade

redoubler [rəduble] **1** *vt* to increase; *Scol* **r. une classe** to repeat a year *or Am* a grade **2** *vi Scol* to repeat a year *or Am* a grade ▪ **redoublement** *nm* increase (**de** in)

redouter [rədute] *vt* to dread (**de faire** doing) ▪ **redoutable** *adj (adversaire, arme)* formidable; *(maladie)* dreadful

redresser [rədrese] **1** *vt (objet tordu)* to straighten (out); *(économie, situation)* to put right; **r. la tête** to hold up one's head **2 se redresser** *vpr (personne)* to straighten up; *(pays, économie)* to recover ▪ **redressement** [-ɛsmɑ̃] *nm* **r. fiscal** tax adjustment

réduction [redyksjɔ̃] *nf* reduction (**de** in); *(rabais)* discount

réduire* [reduir] **1** *vt* to reduce (**à** to; **de** by); **r. qch en cendres** to reduce sth to ashes; **r. qn à qch** *(misère, désespoir)* to reduce sb to sth **2** *vi (sauce)* to reduce **3 se réduire** *vpr* **se r. à** *(se ramener à)* to come down to ▪ **réduit, -e 1** *adj (prix, vitesse)* reduced **2** *nm (pièce)* small room

réécrire* [reekrir] *vt* to rewrite

rééduquer [reedyke] *vt (personne)* to rehabilitate ▪ **rééducation** *nf (de personne)* rehabilitation; **faire de la r.** to have physiotherapy

réel, -elle [reɛl] *adj* real

réélire* [reelir] *vt* to re-elect

réévaluer [reevalɥe] *vt (monnaie)* to revalue; *(salaires)* to reassess

réexpédier [reɛkspedje] *vt (faire suivre)* to forward; *(à l'envoyeur)* to return

refaire* [rəfɛr] *vt (exercice, travail)* to do again, to redo; *(chambre)* to do up; *(erreur, voyage)* to make again; **r. sa vie** to make a new life for oneself; **r. du riz** to make some more rice

réfectoire [refɛktwar] *nm* dining hall, refectory

référence [referɑ̃s] *nf* reference; **faire r. à qch** to refer to sth

référer [refere] **se référer** *vpr* **se r. à** to refer to

refermer [rəfɛrme] *vt*, **se refermer** *vpr* to close or shut again

réfléchir [refleʃir] **1** *vt* (*image, lumière*) to reflect; **r. que…** to realize that… **2** *vi* to think (**à** *ou* **sur** about) **3 se réfléchir** *vpr* to be reflected ■ **réfléchi, -e** *adj* (*personne*) thoughtful; (*action, décision*) carefully thought-out; **tout bien r.** all things considered

reflet [rəflɛ] *nm* (*image*) & *Fig* reflection; (*lumière*) glint; **reflets** (*de cheveux*) highlights ■ **refléter 1** *vt* to reflect **2 se refléter** *vpr* to be reflected

réflexe [reflɛks] *nm & adj* reflex

réflexion [refleksjɔ̃] *nf* (*d'image, de lumière*) reflection; (*pensée*) thought, reflection; (*remarque*) remark; **faire une r. à qn** to make a remark to sb; **r. faite, à la r.** on second *Br* thoughts *or Am* thought

reflux [rəfly] *nm* (*de marée*) ebb; (*de foule*) backward surge

réforme [refɔrm] *nf* reform ■ **réformer** *vt* (*loi*) to reform; (*soldat*) to discharge as unfit

refouler [rəfule] *vt* (*personnes*) to force or drive back; (*étrangers*) to turn away; (*sentiment*) to repress; (*larmes*) to hold back

refrain [rəfrɛ̃] *nm* (*de chanson*) chorus, refrain

réfrigérateur [refriʒeratœr] *nm* refrigerator

refroidir [rəfrwadir] **1** *vt* to cool (down) **2** *vi* (*devenir froid*) to get cold; (*devenir moins chaud*) to cool down **3 se refroidir** *vpr* (*temps*) to get colder ■ **refroidissement** *nm* (*de température*) drop in temperature; (*de l'eau*) cooling

refuge [rəfyʒ] *nm* refuge; (*de montagne*) (mountain) hut

réfugier [refyʒje] **se réfugier** *vpr* to take refuge ■ **réfugié, -e** *nmf* refugee

refus [rəfy] *nm* refusal ■ **refuser 1** *vt*

to refuse (**qch à qn** sb sth; **de faire** to do); (*offre, invitation*) to turn down; (*proposition*) to reject; (*candidat*) to fail; (*client*) to turn away **2 se refuser** *vpr* (*plaisir*) to deny oneself; **se r. à faire qch** to refuse to do sth

regagner [rəgaɲe] *vt* (*récupérer*) to regain, to get back; (*revenir à*) to get back to

régaler [regale] **se régaler** *vpr* **je me régale** (*en mangeant*) I'm really enjoying it

regard [rəgar] *nm* (*coup d'œil, expression*) look; **jeter un r. sur** to glance at

regarder [rəgarde] **1** *vt* to look at; (*émission, film*) to watch; (*considérer*) to consider, to regard (**comme** as); (*concerner*) to concern; **r. qn fixement** to stare at sb

2 *vi* (*observer*) to look; **r. par la fenêtre** (*du dedans*) to look out of the window

3 se regarder *vpr* (*soi-même*) to look at oneself; (*l'un l'autre*) to look at each other

régénérer [reʒenere] *vt* to regenerate

régie [reʒi] *nf* (*entreprise*) state-owned company; *TV* (*organisation*) production management; (*lieu*) control room

régime [reʒim] *nm* (*politique*) (form of) government; (*de bananes*) bunch; **r. (alimentaire)** diet; **suivre un r.** to be on a diet

régiment [reʒimɑ̃] *nm* (*de soldats*) regiment

région [reʒjɔ̃] *nf* region, area ■ **régional, -e, -aux, -ales** *adj* regional

registre [rəʒistr] *nm* register

réglable [reglabl] *adj* adjustable ■ **réglage** *nm* (*de siège, de machine*) adjustment; (*de moteur, de télévision*) tuning

règle [regl] *nf* (**a**) (*principe*) rule; **en r.** (*papiers d'identité*) in order; **en r. générale** as a (general) rule (**b**) (*instrument*) ruler

règlement [regləmɑ̃] *nm* (**a**) (*règles*) regulations (**b**) (*de conflit*) settling; (*paiement*) payment; *Fig* **r. de**

comptes settling of scores ■ **réglementaire** adj in accordance with the regulations; Mil tenue r. regulation uniform ■ **réglementation** nf (règles) regulations ■ **réglementer** vt to regulate

régler [regle] **1** vt (problème, conflit) to settle; (mécanisme) to adjust; (moteur, télévision) to tune; (payer) to pay; **r. qn** to settle up with sb **2** (rue) to pay **3 se régler** upr se **r. sur qn** to model oneself on sb

réglisse [reglis] nf Br liquorice, Am licorice

règne [rɛɲ] nm (de souverain) reign; (animal, minéral, végétal) kingdom ■ **régner** vi (roi, silence) to reign (**sur** over); (prédominer) to prevail; **faire r. l'ordre** to maintain law and order

regorger [rəgɔrʒe] vi **r. de** to be overflowing with

regret [rəgrɛ] nm regret; **à r.** with regret; **avoir le r.** ou **être au r. de faire qch** to be sorry to do sth ■ **regrettable** adj regrettable ■ **regretter** [rəgrɛte] vt to regret; **r. qn** to miss sb; **je regrette, je le regrette** I'm sorry; **r. que...** (+ subjunctive) to be sorry that...

regrouper [rəgrupe] vt, **se regrouper** upr to gather together

régulariser [regylarize] vt (situation) to regularize

régulier, ère [regylje, -ɛr] adj (intervalles, visage) regular; (constant) steady; (légal) legal ■ **régularité** nf (exactitude) regularity; (constance) steadiness

réhabituer [reabitɥe] **se réhabituer** upr se **r. à qch/à faire qch** to get used to sth/to doing sth again

rein [rɛ̃] nm kidney; **les reins** (dos) the lower back

reine [rɛn] nf queen; **la r. Élisabeth** Queen Elizabeth

réinsertion [reɛ̃sɛrsjɔ̃] nf reintegration; **r. sociale** rehabilitation

réintégrer [reɛ̃tegre] vt (fonctionnaire) to reinstate; (lieu) to return to

rejaillir [rəʒajir] vi to spurt out

rejet [rəʒɛ] nm (refus) & Méd rejection ■ **rejeter** vt (relancer) to throw back; (offre, candidature, greffe, personne) to reject; (blâme) to shift (**on** to)

rejoindre* [rəʒwɛ̃dr] **1** vt (personne) to meet; (rue, rivière) to join; (lieu) to reach; (concorder avec) to coincide with **2 se rejoindre** upr (personnes) to meet up; (rues, rivières) to join up

réjouir [reʒwir] **1** vt to delight **2 se réjouir** upr to be delighted (**de** at; **de faire** to do) ■ **réjoui, -e** adj joyful ■ **réjouissance** nf rejoicing ■ **réjouissances** festivities

relâche [rəlɑʃ] nf faire r. Théât & Cin to be closed; Naut to put in (**dans un port** at a port); **sans r.** without a break

relâcher [rəlɑʃe] **1** vt (corde, étreinte) to loosen; (discipline) to relax; (prisonnier) to release **2** vi Naut to put into port **3 se relâcher** upr (corde) to slacken; (discipline) to become lax; (employé) to slack off

relais [rəlɛ] nm (dispositif émetteur) relay; Sport (**course de**) **r.** relay (race); **passer le r. à qn** to hand over to sb; **prendre le r.** to take over (**de** from); **r. routier** Br transport café, Am truck stop (café)

relancer [rəlɑ̃se] vt (lancer à nouveau) to throw again; (rendre) to throw back; (production) to boost; (moteur) to restart

relatif, -ive [rəlatif, -iv] adj relative (**à** to)

relation [rəlɑsjɔ̃] nf (rapport) relationship; (ami) acquaintance; **être en r. avec qn** to be in touch with sb; **avoir des relations** (amis) to have contacts; **r. (amoureuse)** (love) affair; **relations extérieures** foreign affairs; **relations internationales** international relations

relayer [rəleje] **1** vt (personne) to take over from; (émission) to relay **2 se relayer** upr to take turns (**pour faire** doing); Sport to take over from one another

relevé [rəlve] *nm* list; *(de compteur)* reading; **r. de compte** bank statement; *Scol* **r. de notes** list of *Br* marks *or Am* grades

relève [rəlɛv] *nf* relief; **prendre la r.** to take over (**de** from)

relèvement [rəlɛvmɑ̃] *nm (d'économie, de pays)* recovery; *(de salaires)* raising

relever [rəlve] **1** *vt (ramasser)* to pick up; *(personne)* to help back up; *(pays)* to revive; *(copies)* to collect; *(faute)* to pick out; *(empreinte)* to find; *(défi)* to accept; *(sauce)* to spice up; *(copier)* to note down; *(compteur)* to read; *(relayer)* to relieve; *(augmenter)* to raise; **r. la tête** to look up; **r. qn de ses fonctions** to relieve sb of his/her duties

2 *vi* **r. de** *(dépendre de)* to come under; *(maladie)* to be recovering from

3 se relever *vpr (après une chute)* to get up

relief [rəljɛf] *nm (de paysage)* relief; **en r.** in relief; *Fig* **mettre qch en r.** to highlight sth

relier [rəlje] *vt* to connect, to link (**à** to); *(idées, faits)* to link together; *(livre)* to bind

religion [rəliʒjɔ̃] *nf* religion ■ **religieuse** *nf (femme) nun; (gâteau)* cream puff ■ **religieux, -euse 1** *adj* religious; **mariage r.** church wedding **2** *nm (moine)* monk

relire* [rəlir] *vt* to reread

reliure [rəljyr] *nf (couverture)* binding; *(art)* bookbinding

reluire* [rəlɥir] *vi* to shine, to gleam; **faire r. qch** to polish sth up

remanier [rəmanje] *vt (texte)* to revise; *(ministère)* to reshuffle ■ **remaniement** *nm (de texte)* revision; **r. ministériel** cabinet reshuffle

remarier [rəmarje] **se remarier** *vpr* to remarry ■ **remariage** *nm* remarriage

remarquable [rəmarkabl] *adj* remarkable (**par** for)

remarque [rəmark] *nf* remark; **faire une r.** to make a remark

remarquer [rəmarke] *vt (apercevoir)* to notice (**que** that); *(dire)* to remark (**que** that); **faire r. qch** to point sth out (**à** to); **se faire r.** to attract attention

rembobiner [rɑ̃bɔbine] *vt*, **se rembobiner** *vpr* to rewind

rembourser [rɑ̃burse] *vt (personne)* to pay back; *(billet, frais)* to refund ■ **remboursement** [-əmɑ̃] *nm* repayment; *(de billet)* refund

remède [rəmɛd] *nm* cure, remedy (**contre** for) ■ **remédier** *vi* **r. à qch** to remedy sth

remémorer [rəmemɔre] **se remémorer** *vpr* to remember

remercier [rəmɛrsje] *vt (dire merci à)* to thank (**de** *ou* **pour qch** for sth); **je vous remercie d'être venu** thank you for coming ■ **remerciements** *nmpl* thanks

remettre* [rəmɛtr] **1** *vt (replacer)* to put back; *(vêtement)* to put back on; *(disque)* to put on again; *(différer)* to postpone (**à** until); *(ajouter)* to add (**dans** to); **r. qch à qn** *(lettre)* to deliver sth to sb; *(rapport)* to submit sth to sb; *(démission)* to hand sth in to sb; **r. qn en liberté** to set sb free; **r. qch en question** to call sth into question; **r. qch en état** to repair sth; **r. qch à jour** to bring sth up to date

2 se remettre *vpr* **se r. à qch** to start sth again; **se r. à faire qch** to start to do sth again; **se r. de qch** to recover from sth

remise [rəmiz] *nf* (**a**) *(de lettre)* delivery; **r. à neuf** *(de machine)* reconditioning; **r. en question** questioning; **r. en état** *(de maison)* restoration (**b**) *(rabais)* discount (**c**) *Jur* **r. de peine** reduction of sentence (**d**) *(local)* shed

remontée [rəmɔ̃te] *nf* **r. mécanique** ski lift

remonter [rəmɔ̃te] **1** *(aux être)* *vi* to come/go back up; *(niveau, prix)* to rise again, to go back up; *(dans le temps)* to go back (**à** to); **r. dans** *(voiture)* to get back in(to); *(bus, train)* to get back on(to); **r. à dix ans** to go back ten years

2 (*aux avoir*) *vt* (*escalier, pente*) to come/go back up; (*porter*) to bring/take back up; (*montre*) to wind up; (*relever*) to raise; (*objet démonté*) to put back together, to reassemble; **r. le moral à qn** to cheer sb up ■ **remonte-pente** (*pl* **remonte-pentes**) *nm* ski lift

remords [rəmɔr] *nm* remorse; **avoir des r.** to feel remorse

remorque [rəmɔrk] *nf* (*de voiture*) trailer ■ **remorquer** *vt* (*voiture, bateau*) to tow ■ **remorqueur** *nm* tug(-boat)

rempart [rɑ̃par] *nm* rampart; **remparts** walls

remplacer [rɑ̃plase] *vt* to replace (**par** with); (*professionnellement*) to stand in for ■ **remplaçant, -e** *nmf* (*personne*) replacement; (*enseignant*) substitute teacher, *Br* supply teacher; (*joueur*) substitute ■ **remplacement** *nm* replacement; **en r. de** in place of

remplir [rɑ̃plir] **1** *vt* to fill (up) (**de** with); (*formulaire*) to fill out, *Br* to fill in; (*promesse*) to fulfil **2 se remplir** *vpr* to fill (up) (**de** with)

remporter [rɑ̃pɔrte] *vt* (*objet*) to take back; (*prix, victoire*) to win

remuer [rəmɥe] **1** *vt* (*bouger*) to move; (*terre*) to turn over **2** *vi* to move; (*gigoter*) to fidget

rémunérer [remynere] *vt* (*personne*) to pay; (*travail*) to pay for ■ **rémunération** *nf* payment (**de** for)

renaître* [rənɛtr] *vi* (*personne*) to be born again; (*espoir, industrie*) to revive ■ **renaissance** *nf* rebirth; (*des arts*) renaissance

renard [rənar] *nm* fox

renchérir [rɑ̃ʃerir] *vi* (*dire plus*) to go one better (**sur** than)

rencontre [rɑ̃kɔ̃tr] *nf* (*de personnes*) meeting; (*match*) *Br* match, *Am* game; **aller à la r. de qn** to go to meet sb ■ **rencontrer 1** *vt* (*personne*) to meet; (*difficulté*) to come up against, to encounter; (*trouver*) to come across

2 se rencontrer *vpr* to meet

rendement [rɑ̃dmɑ̃] *nm* (*de champ*) yield; (*d'investissement*) return, yield; (*de personne, de machine*) output

rendez-vous [rɑ̃devu] *nm inv* (*rencontre*) appointment; (*amoureux*) date; (*lieu*) meeting place; **donner r. à qn** to arrange to meet sb; **prendre r. avec qn** to make an appointment with sb; **recevoir sur r.** (*médecin*) to see patients by appointment

rendormir* [rɑ̃dɔrmir] **se rendormir** *vpr* to go back to sleep

rendre [rɑ̃dr] **1** *vt* (*restituer*) to give back, to return (**à** to); (*jugement*) to deliver; (*armes*) to surrender; (*invitation*) to return; (*santé*) to restore; (*exprimer*) to render; (*vomir*) to bring up; **r. célèbre** to make famous; **r. la monnaie à qn** to give sb his/her change; **r. l'âme** to pass away; **r. les armes** to surrender

2 *vi* (*vomir*) to vomit

3 se rendre *vpr* (*criminel*) to give oneself up (**à** to); (*soldats*) to surrender (**à** to); (*aller*) to go (**à** to); **se r. à l'évidence** (*être lucide*) to face facts; **se r. malade** to make oneself ill

renfermer [rɑ̃fɛrme] *vt* to contain ■ **renfermé, -e 1** *adj* (*personne*) withdrawn **2** *nm* **sentir le r.** to smell musty

renforcer [rɑ̃fɔrse] *vt* to strengthen, to reinforce

renfort [rɑ̃fɔr] *nm* **des renforts** (*troupes*) reinforcements; *Fig* **à grand r. de** with (the help of) a great deal of

renfrogner [rɑ̃frɔɲe] **se renfrogner** *vpr* to scowl

renier [rənje] *vt* (*ami, pays*) to disown; (*foi*) to deny

renifler [rənifle] *vti* to sniff ■ **reniflement** [-əmɑ̃] *nm* (*bruit*) sniff

renne [rɛn] *nm* reindeer

renom [rənɔ̃] *nm* renown; **de r.** (*ouvrage, artiste*) famous, renowned ■ **renommé, -e** *adj* famous, renowned (**pour** for) ■ **renommée** *nf* fame, renown

renoncer [rənɔ̃se] *vi* **r. à qch** to give

sth up, to abandon sth; **r. à faire qch** to give up doing sth

renouer [rənwe] **1** *vt* (lacet) to tie again **2** *vi* **r. avec qch** (tradition) to revive sth; **r. avec qn** to take up with sb again

renouveau, -x [rənuvo] *nm* revival

renouveler [rənuvle] **1** *vt* to renew; (expérience) to repeat **2** **se renouveler** *vpr* (incident) to happen again, to recur; (cellules, sang) to be renewed ▪ **renouvelable** *adj* renewable ▪ **renouvellement** [-ɛlmã] *nm* renewal

rénover [renɔve] *vt* (édifice, meuble) to renovate ▪ **rénovation** *nf* (d'édifice, de meuble) renovation

renseigner [rãsɛɲe] **1** *vt* to give some information (**sur** about) **2** **se renseigner** *vpr* to make inquiries (**sur** about) ▪ **renseignement** [-əmã] *nm* piece of information; **renseignements** information; **les renseignements (téléphoniques)** *Br* directory inquiries, *Am* information; **demander des renseignements** to make inquiries

rentable [rãtabl] *adj* profitable ▪ **rentabilité** *nf* profitability

rente [rãt] *nf* (private) income; (pension) pension

rentrée [rãtre] *nf* **r. des classes** start of the new school year

rentrer [rãtre] **1** (aux **être**) *vi* (entrer) to go/come in; (entrer de nouveau) to go/come back in; (chez soi) to go/come (back) home; **r. en France** to return to France; **en rentrant de l'école** on my/his/her/etc way home from school; **r. dans qch** (pénétrer) to get into sth; (sujet: voiture) to crash into sth; **r. dans une catégorie** to fall into a category

2 (aux **avoir**) *vt* (linge, troupeau) to bring/take in; (chemise) to tuck in; (griffes) to retract

renverse [rãvɛrs] **à la renverse** *adv* (tomber) backwards

renverser [rãvɛrse] **1** *vt* (faire tomber) to knock over; (liquide) to spill; (piéton)

to run over; (tendance, situation) to reverse; (gouvernement) to overthrow **2** **se renverser** *vpr* (récipient) to fall over; (véhicule) to overturn

renvoi [rãvwa] *nm* (de marchandise, de lettre) return; (d'employé) dismissal; (d'élève) expulsion; (rot) belch, burp ▪ **renvoyer*** *vt* (lettre, cadeau) to send back, to return; (employé) to dismiss; (élève) to expel; (balle) to throw back; (lumière, image) to reflect

réorganiser [reɔrganize] *vt* to reorganize ▪ **réorganisation** *nf* reorganization

repaître* [rəpɛtr] **se repaître** *vpr Fig* **se r. de qch** to revel in sth

répandre [repãdr] **1** *vt* (liquide) to spill; (odeur) to give off; (chargement) to shed; (bienfaits) to lavish **2** **se répandre** *vpr* (nouvelle, peur) to spread; (liquide) to spill; **se r. dans** (fumée, odeur) to spread through ▪ **répandu, -e** *adj* (opinion, usage) widespread

reparaître* [rəparɛtr] *vi* to reappear

réparer [repare] *vt* (objet, machine) to repair, to mend; (faute) to make amends for; **faire r. qch** to get sth repaired ▪ **réparable** *adj* (machine) repairable ▪ **réparateur, -trice** **1** *nmf* repairer **2** *adj* (sommeil) refreshing ▪ **réparation** *nf* (action) repairing; (résultat) repair; (dédommagement) reparation; **en r.** under repair

repartir* [rəpartir] (aux **être**) *vi* (continuer) to set off again; (s'en retourner) to go back; (machine) to start again

répartir [repartir] *vt* (poids, charge) to distribute; (tâches, vivres) to share (out); (classer) to divide (up); (étaler dans le temps) to spread (out) (**sur** over) ▪ **répartition** *nf* (de poids) distribution; (de tâches) sharing; (classement) division

repas [rəpa] *nm* meal

repasser [rəpase] **1** *vi* to come/go back; **r. chez qn** to drop in on sb again **2** *vt* (montagne, frontière) to go across again; (examen) to take again, *Br* to resit; (film) to show again; (disque, *cassette)* to play again; *(linge)* to iron ■ **repassage** *nm* ironing

repêcher [rəpeʃe] *vt (objet)* to fish out

repeindre* [rəpɛ̃dr] *vt* to repaint

répercuter [repɛrkyte] **1** *vt (son)* to reflect; *(augmentation)* to pass **2 se répercuter** *upr (son, lumière)* to be reflected; *Fig* **se r. sur** to have repercussions on

repère [rəpɛr] *nm* mark; **point de r.** *(espace, temps)* reference point ■ **repérer 1** *vt (endroit)* to locate **2 se repérer** *upr* to get one's bearings

répertoire [repɛrtwar] *nm (liste)* index; *(carnet)* (indexed) notebook; *Théât* repertoire

répéter [repete] **1** *vt* to repeat; *(pièce de théâtre, rôle)* to rehearse; **r. à qn que...** to tell sb again that...
2 *vi (redire)* to repeat; *(acteur)* to rehearse
3 se répéter *upr (radoter)* to repeat oneself; *(événement)* to happen again ■ **répétition** *nf (redite)* repetition; *Théât* rehearsal, **r. générale** dress rehearsal

répit [repi] *nm* rest, respite; **sans r.** ceaselessly

replacer [rəplase] *vt* to replace, to put back

replanter [rəplɑ̃te] *vt* to replant

repli [rəpli] *nm (de vêtement, de terrain)* fold; *(d'armée)* withdrawal; *(de monnaie)* fall

replier [rəplije] **1** *vt (objet)* to fold up; *(couteau)* to fold away; *(ailes)* to fold; *(jambes)* to tuck up **2 se replier** *upr (objet)* to fold up; *(armée)* to withdraw

réplique [replik] *nf (réponse)* retort; *(d'acteur)* lines; *(copie)* replica; **sans r.** *(argument)* unanswerable ■ **répliquer 1** *vt* **r. que...** to reply that... **2** *vi* to reply; *(avec impertinence)* to answer back

répondre [repɔ̃dr] **1** *vi* to answer, to reply; *(avec impertinence)* to answer back; *(réagir)* to respond (**à** to); **r. à qn** to answer sb, to reply to sb; *(avec impertinence)* to answer sb back; **r. à**

(lettre, question, objection) to answer, to reply to; *(besoin)* to meet; **r. au téléphone** to answer the phone; **r. de qn/ qch** to answer for sb/sth
2 *vt (remarque)* to answer *or* reply with; **r. que...** to answer *or* reply that... ■ **répondeur** *nm* **r. (téléphonique)** answering machine

réponse [repɔ̃s] *nf* answer, reply; *(réaction)* response (**à** to)

reportage [rəpɔrtaʒ] *nm (article, émission)* report; *(métier)* reporting

reporter¹ [rəpɔrte] **1** *vt (objet)* to take back; *(réunion)* to postpone *(à* until); *(transcrire)* to transfer (**sur** to) **2 se reporter** *upr* **se r. à** *(texte)* to refer to

reporter² [rəpɔrter] *nm* reporter

repos [rəpo] *nm (détente)* rest; *(tranquillité)* peace

reposer [rəpoze] **1** *vt (objet)* to put back down; *(problème, question)* to raise again; *(délasser)* to rest, to relax; **r. sa tête sur** *(appuyer)* to lean one's head on
2 *vi (être enterré)* to lie; **r. sur** *(bâtiment)* to be built on; *(théorie)* to be based on; **laisser r.** *(liquide)* to allow to settle
3 se reposer *upr* to rest; **se r. sur qn** to rely on sb ■ **reposant, -e** *adj* restful, relaxing ■ **reposé, -e** *adj* rested

repousser [rəpuse] **1** *vt (en arrière)* to push back; *(sur le côté)* to push away; *(attaque, ennemi)* to beat off; *(offre)* to reject; *(dégoûter)* to repel **2** *vi (cheveux, feuilles)* to grow again

reprendre* [rəprɑ̃dr] **1** *vt (objet)* to take back; *(évadé, ville)* to recapture; *(activité)* to take up again; *(vêtement)* to alter; *(corriger)* to correct; **r. de la viande** to take some more meat
2 *vi (recommencer)* to start again; *(affaires)* to pick up; *(continuer de parler)* to go on, to continue
3 se reprendre *upr (se ressaisir)* to get a grip on oneself; *(se corriger)* to correct oneself; **s'y r. à deux fois** to have another go (at it)

représenter [rəprezɑ̃te] **1** vt to represent; (pièce de théâtre) to perform **2 se représenter** vpr (s'imaginer) to imagine ■ **représentant, -e** nmf representative ■ **représentatif, -ive** adj representative (**de** of) ■ **représentation** nf representation; Théât performance

répression [represjɔ̃] nf (d'émeute) suppression; (mesures de contrôle) repression ■ **répressif, -ive** adj repressive ■ **réprimer** vt (sentiment, révolte) to suppress

réprimander [reprimɑ̃de] vt to reprimand

reprise [rəpriz] nf (recommencement) resumption; (de l'économie) recovery; (de locataire) = money for fixtures and fittings (paid by outgoing tenant); (de marchandise) taking back; (pour nouvel achat) part exchange, trade-in; **faire une r. à qch** to darn sth; **à plusieurs reprises** on several occasions ■ **repriser** vt (chaussette) to darn

réprobateur, -trice [reprɔbatœr, -tris] adj disapproving

reproche [rəprɔʃ] nm reproach; **sans r.** beyond reproach ■ **reprocher** vt **r. qch à qn** to blame or reproach sb for sth

reproduire* [rəprɔdɥir] **1** vt (modèle, son) to reproduce **2 se reproduire** vpr (animaux) to reproduce; (incident) to happen again ■ **reproduction** nf (d'animaux, de son) reproduction; (copie) copy

reptile [rɛptil] nm reptile

repu, -e [rəpy] adj (rassasié) satiated

république [repyblik] nf republic ■ **républicain, -e** adj & nmf republican

répugnant, -e [repyɲɑ̃, -ɑ̃t] adj repulsive ■ **répugner** vi **r. à qn** to be repugnant to sb; **r. à faire qch** to be loath to do sth

réputation [repytɑsjɔ̃] nf reputation; **avoir la r. d'être franc** to have a reputation for being frank or for frankness ■ **réputé, -e** adj (célèbre) renowned (**pour** for)

requête [rəkɛt] nf request

requin [rəkɛ̃] nm (animal) shark

réquisitionner [rekizisjɔne] vt to requisition, to commandeer

rescapé, -e [reskape] **1** adj surviving **2** nmf survivor

réseau, -x [rezo] nm network

réservation [rezervasjɔ̃] nf reservation, booking

réserve [rezerv] nf (provision, discrétion) reserve; (entrepôt) storeroom; (de bibliothèque) stacks; (de chasse, de pêche) preserve; (restriction) reservation; Mil **la r.** the reserve; **en r.** in reserve; **sans r.** (admiration) unqualified; **sous r. de** subject to; **sous toutes réserves** without guarantee; **r. naturelle** nature reserve

réserver [rezerve] **1** vt to reserve; (garder) to save, to keep (**à** for); (marchandises) to put aside (**à** for); (sort, surprise) to hold in store (**à** for) **2 se réserver** vpr **se r. pour qch** to save oneself for sth ■ **réservé, -e** adj (personne, place, chambre) reserved

réservoir [rezervwar] nm (lac) reservoir; (cuve) tank; **r. d'essence** Br petrol orAm gas tank

résidence [rezidɑ̃s] nf residence; **r. secondaire** second home; **r. universitaire** Br hall of residence, Am dormitory ■ **résident, -e** nmf resident ■ **résidentiel, -elle** adj (quartier) residential ■ **résider** vi to reside; **r. dans** (consister en) to lie in

résidu [rezidy] nm residue

résigner [reziɲe] **se résigner** vpr to resign oneself (**à qch** to sth; **à faire** to doing) ■ **résignation** nf resignation

résistance [rezistɑ̃s] nf resistance (**à** to); Hist **la R.** the Resistance

résister [reziste] vi **r. à** (attaque, agresseur, tentation) to resist; (chaleur, fatigue, souffrance) to withstand; (mauvais traitement) to stand up to ■ **résistant, -e 1** adj tough; **r. à la chaleur** heat-resistant **2** nmf Hist Resistance fighter

résolu, -e [rezɔly] **1** pp de **résoudre 2**

adj determined, resolute; **r. à faire qch** determined to do sth ■ **résolution** *nf (décision)* resolution; *(fermeté)* determination

résonance [rezɔnãs] *nf* resonance

résonner [rezɔne] *vi (cri)* to resound; *(salle, voix)* to echo (**de** with)

résoudre* [rezudr] *vt* **1** *(problème)* to solve; *(difficulté)* to resolve; **r. de faire qch** to resolve to do sth **2 se résoudre** *vpr* **se r. à faire qch** to resolve to do sth

respect [rɛspɛ] *nm* respect (**pour/de** for) ■ **respectable** *adj (honorable, important)* respectable ■ **respecter** *vt* to respect; **r. la loi** to abide by the law; **faire r. la loi** to enforce the law ■ **respectueux, -euse** *adj* respectful (**envers** to; **de** of)

respirer [rɛspire] **1** *vi* to breathe **2** *vt* to breathe (in) ■ **respiration** *nf* breathing; *(haleine)* breath

responsable [rɛspɔ̃sabl] **1** *adj* responsible (**de qch** for sth; **devant qn** to sb) **2** *nmf (chef)* person in charge; *(d'organisation)* official; *(coupable)* person responsible (**de** for) ■ **responsabilité** *nf* responsibility; *(légale)* liability

ressaisir [rəsezir] **se ressaisir** *vpr* to pull oneself together

ressemblance [rəsɑ̃blɑ̃s] *nf* likeness, resemblance (**avec** to) ■ **ressembler 1** *vi* **r. à** to look like, to resemble **2 se ressembler** *vpr* to look alike

ressentir* [rəsɑ̃tir] *vt* to feel

resserrer [rəsere] **1** *vt (nœud, boulon)* to tighten; *Fig (liens)* to strengthen **2 se resserrer** *vpr (nœud)* to tighten

resservir* [rəservir] **1** *vi (outil)* to come in useful (again) **2 se resservir** *vpr* **se r. de** *(plat)* to have another helping of

ressort [rəsɔr] *nm (objet)* spring; **du r. de** within the competence of; **en dernier r.** as a last resort

ressortir* [rəsɔrtir] **1** *(aux être) vi (personne)* to go/come back out; *(film)* to be shown again; *(se voir)* to stand out; **faire r. qch** to bring sth

out; **il ressort de...** *(résulte)* it emerges from... **2** *(aux avoir) vi (vêtement)* to get out again

ressortissant, -e [rəsɔrtisɑ̃, -ɑ̃t] *nmf* national

ressource [rəsurs] **1** *nfpl* **ressources** *(moyens, argent)* resources; **être sans ressources** to be without means **2** *nf (possibilité)* possibility (**de faire** of doing); **avoir de la r.** to be resourceful; **en dernière r.** as a last resort

ressusciter [resysite] *vi* to rise from the dead

restant, -e [rɛstɑ̃, -ɑ̃t] **1** *adj* remaining **2** *nm* **le r.** the rest, the remainder; **un r. de viande** some leftover meat

restaurant [rɛstorɑ̃] *nm* restaurant

restaurateur, -trice [rɛstoratœr, -tris] *nmf (hôtelier, -ière)* restaurant owner; *(de tableaux)* restorer

restaurer [rɛstore] **1** *vt (réparer, rétablir)* to restore **2 se restaurer** *vpr* to have something to eat ■ **restauration** *nf (hôtellerie)* catering; *(de tableau)* restoration

reste [rɛst] *nm* rest, remainder (**de** of); **restes** remains (**de** of); *(de repas)* leftovers; **au r., du r.** moreover, besides

rester [rɛste] *(aux être) vi* to stay, to remain; *(calme, jeune)* to keep, to stay, to remain; *(subsister)* to be left, to remain; **il reste du pain** there's some bread left (over); **il me reste une pomme** I have one apple left; **l'argent qui lui reste** the money he/she has left; **il me reste deux choses à faire** I still have two things to do

restituer [rɛstitɥe] *vt (rendre)* to return (**à** to); *(argent)* to repay ■ **restitution** *nf (d'objet)* return

restriction [rɛstriksjɔ̃] *nf* restriction; **sans r.** *(approuver)* unreservedly

résultat [rezylta] *nm* result; **avoir qch pour r.** to result in sth ■ **résulter** **1** *vi* **r. de** to result from **2** *v impersonnel* **il en résulte que...** the result of this is that...

résumer [rezyme] **1** *vt (abréger)* summarize; *(récapituler)* to s *upr* to withdraw; (*de* from); (*mer*) to ebb

se résumer *upr* (*orateur*) to sum up; **se r. à qch** (*se réduire à*) to boil down to sth ■ **résumé** *nm* summary; **en r.** in short

rétablir [retablir] **1** *vt* (*communications, ordre*) to restore; (*vérité*) to re-establish; (*employé*) to reinstate **2 se rétablir** (*malade*) to recover ■ **rétablissement** *nm* (*d'ordre, de dynastie*) restoration; (*de vérité*) re-establishment; (*de malade*) recovery

retard [rətar] *nm* (*de personne*) lateness; (*sur horaire*) delay; **en r.** late; **en r. sur qn/qch** behind sb/sth; **rattraper ou combler son r.** to catch up; **avoir du r.** to be late; (*sur un programme*) to be behind (schedule); (*montre*) to be slow; **avoir une heure de r.** to be an hour late; **prendre du r.** (*personne*) to fall behind

retarder [rətarde] **1** *vt* (*faire arriver en retard*) to delay; (*date, montre, départ*) to put back; **r. qn** (*dans une activité*) to put sb behind **2** *vi* (*montre*) to be slow; **r. de cinq minutes** to be five minutes slow

retenir* [rətənir] **1** *vt* (*personne*) to keep; (*eau, chaleur*) to retain; (*cotisation*) to deduct (**sur** from); (*suggestion*) to adopt; (*larmes, foule*) to hold back; *Math* (*chiffre*) to carry; (*se souvenir de*) to remember; (*réserver*) to reserve; **r. qn prisonnier** to keep sb prisoner; **r. l'attention de qn** to catch sb's attention; **r. qn de faire qch** to stop sb (from) doing sth **2 se retenir** *upr* (*se contenir*) to restrain oneself; **se r. de faire qch** to stop oneself (from) doing sth; **se r. à qn/qch** to cling to sb/sth

retenue [rətəny] *nf* (*modération*) restraint; (*de salaire*) deduction; *Scol* (*punition*) detention

retirer [rətire] **1** *vt* to withdraw; (*faire sortir*) to take out; (*ôter*) to take off; (*éloigner*) to take away; (*aller chercher*) to pick up; **r. qch à qn** (*permis*) to take sth away from sb; **r. qch de qch** (*gagner*) to derive sth from sth **2 se retirer**

retomber [rətɔ̃be] *vi* to fall again; (*après un saut*) to land; (*intérêt*) to slacken; **r. dans** (*l'oubli*) to sink back into

retouche [rətuʃ] *nf* (*de vêtement*) alteration ■ **retoucher** *vt* (*vêtement, texte*) to alter; (*photo, tableau*) to touch up

retour [rətur] *nm* return; (*trajet*) return journey; **être de r.** to be back (**de** from); **à mon r.** when I get/got back (**de** from); **r. à l'envoyeur** return to sender; **match r.** return *Br* match or *Am* game

retourner [rəturne] **1** (*aux avoir*) *vt* (*matelas, steak*) to turn over; (*terre*) to turn; (*vêtement, sac*) to turn inside out; (*compliment*) to return; **r. qch contre qn** (*argument*) to turn sth against sb; (*arme*) to turn sth on sb **2** (*aux être*) *vi* to go back, to return **3 se retourner** *upr* (*pour regarder*) to turn round; (*sur le dos*) to turn over; (*dans son lit*) to toss and turn; (*voiture*) to overturn; *Fig* **se r. contre** to turn against

retrait [rətrɛ] *nm* withdrawal; (*de bagages, de billets*) collection; (*des eaux*) receding; **en r.** (*maison*) set back; **rester en r.** to stay in the background

retraite [rətrɛt] *nf* (*d'employé*) retirement; (*pension*) (retirement) pension; (*refuge*) retreat, refuge; (*d'armée*) retreat; **prendre sa r.** to retire; **être à la r.** to be retired; **r. anticipée** early retirement ■ **retraité, -e 1** *adj* retired **2** *nmf* senior citizen, *Br* (old age) pensioner

retraitement [rətrɛtmɑ̃] *nm*

retrancher [rətrɑ̃ʃe] **1** *vt* (*passage, nom*) to remove (**de** from); (*argent, quantité*) to deduct (**de** from) **2 se retrancher** *upr* (*soldats*) to dig in; *Fig* **se r. dans/derrière qch** to hide in/behind sth

retransmettre* [rətrɑ̃smɛtr] *vt* to broadcast ■ **retransmission** *nf* broadcast

rétrécir [retresir] **1** vt (vêtement) to take in **2** vi (au lavage) to shrink **3** se **rétrécir** vpr (rue) to narrow

rétroactif, -ive [retrɔaktif, -iv] adj retroactive

rétrograder [retrograde] **1** vt (fonctionnaire, officier) to demote **2** vi (automobiliste) to change down

rétrospectif, -ive [retrɔspektif, -iv] **1** adj retrospective **2** nf **rétrospective** retrospective

retrouver [rɑtruve] **1** vt (objet) to find again; (personne) to meet again; (forces, santé) to regain; (se rappeler) to recall; (découvrir) to rediscover **2** se **retrouver** vpr (être) to find oneself; (trouver son chemin) to find one's way (**dans** round); (se rencontrer) to meet; se **r. à la rue** to find oneself homeless

rétroviseur [retrɔvizœr] nm rear-view mirror

Réunion [reynjɔ̃] nf **la R.** Réunion

réunion [reynjɔ̃] nf (séance) meeting; (d'objets) collection, gathering; (jonction) joining; **être en r.** to be in a meeting; **r. de famille** family gathering

réunir [reynir] **1** vt (objets) to put together; (documents) to gather together; (fonds) to raise; (amis, famille) to get together; (après une rupture) to reunite; (avantages, qualités) to combine; **r. qch à qch** to join sth to sth **2** se **réunir** vpr (personnes) to meet; se **r. autour de qn/qch** to gather round sb/sth

réussir [reysir] **1** vt (bien faire) to make a success of; (examen) to pass **2** vi to succeed, to be successful (**à faire** in doing); **r. à un examen** to pass an exam ▪ **réussi, -e** adj successful ▪ **réussite** nf success; Cartes **faire des réussites** to play patience

revaloriser [rɑvalɔrize] vt (monnaie) to revalue; (salaires, profession) to upgrade

revanche [rɑvɑ̃ʃ] nf revenge; (de match) return game; **prendre sa r.** to get one's revenge (**sur** on); **en r.** on the other hand

rêve [rɛv] nm dream; **faire un r.** to have a dream

réveil [revɛj] nm (de personnes) waking; (pendule) alarm (clock); **à son r.** on waking

réveiller [reveje] **1** vt (personne) to wake (up); Fig (douleur) to revive; Fig (sentiment, souvenir) to revive **2** se **réveiller** vpr (personne) to wake (up); (nature) to reawaken; Fig (douleur) to come back ▪ **réveillé, -e** adj awake ▪ **réveille-matin** nm inv alarm clock

réveillon [revɛjɔ̃] nm (repas) midnight supper; (soirée) midnight party (on Christmas Eve or New Year's Eve) ▪ **réveillonner** vi to see in Christmas/the New Year

révéler [revele] **1** vt to reveal (**que** that) **2** se **révéler** vpr (personne) to reveal oneself; (talent) to be revealed; se **r. facile** to turn out to be easy ▪ **révélateur, -trice** adj revealing; **r. de qch** indicative of sth ▪ **révélation** nf (action, découverte) revelation; (personne) discovery; **faire des révélations** to disclose important information

revendiquer [rɑvɑ̃dike] vt to claim; (attentat) to claim responsibility for ▪ **revendication** nf claim

revendre [rɑvɑ̃dr] vt to resell

revenir* [rɑvɑnir] (aux être) vi (personne) to come back, to return; (date) to come round again; **le dîner nous est revenu à 50 euros** the dinner cost us 50 euros; **r. cher** to work out expensive; **r. à** (activité, sujet) to go back to, to return to; (se résumer à) to boil down to; **r. à qn** (forces, mémoire) to come back to sb; (honneur) to fall to sb; **r. de** (surprise) to get over; **r. sur** (décision, promesse) to go back on; (passé, question) to go back over; **r. sur ses pas** to retrace one's steps

revenu [rɑvɑny] nm income (**de** from); (d'un État) revenue (**de** from)

rêver [reve] **1** vt to dream (**que** that) **2** vi to dream (**de** of; **de faire** of doing

réverbère [reverber] nm street l-

révérence [reverɑ̃s] *nf (respect)* reverence; *(salut)* curtsey

rêverie [rɛvri] *nf* daydream

revers [rəvɛr] *nm (de veste)* lapel; *(de pantalon) Br* turn-up, *Am* cuff; *(d'étoffe)* wrong side; *(de pièce)* reverse; *(coup du sort)* setback; *(au tennis)* backhand; **d'un r. de la main** with the back of one's hand; *Fig* **le r. de la médaille** the other side of the coin

reverser [rəvɛrse] *vt (café, vin)* to pour more; *Fig (argent)* to transfer (**sur un compte**) into an account)

réversible [reversibl] *adj* reversible

revêtir* [rəvetir] *vt (de with)*; *(habit)* to don; *(caractère, forme)* to assume; **r. qn** *(habiller)* to dress sb (**de** in) ▪ **revêtement** *nm (surface)* covering; *(de route)* surface

rêveur, -euse [rɛvœr, -øz] **1** *adj* dreamy **2** *nmf* dreamer

revient [rəvjɛ̃] *nm* **prix de r.** *Br* cost price, *Am* wholesale price

revirement [rəvirmɑ̃] *nm (changement) Br* about-turn, *Am* about-face; *(de situation, d'opinion, de politique)* reversal

réviser [revize] *vt (leçon)* to revise; *(machine, voiture)* to service; *(jugement, règlement)* to review ▪ **révision** *nf (de leçon)* revision; *(de machine)* service; *(de jugement)* review

revivre* [rəvivr] **1** *vt (incident)* to relive **2** *vi* to live again; **faire r. qch** to revive sth

revoici [rəvwasi] *prép* **me r.** here I am again

revoilà [rəvwala] *prép* **la r.** there she is again

revoir* [rəvwar] *vt* to see (again); *(texte, leçon)* to review; **au r.** goodbye

révolte [revɔlt] *nf* revolt ▪ **révolter 1** *vt* to appal **2 se révolter** *upr* to rebel, to revolt (**contre** against)

révolu, -e [revɔly] *adj (époque)* past; **avoir trente ans révolus** to be over thirty

révolution [revɔlysjɔ̃] *nf (changement, rotation)* revolution ▪ **révolutionner** *vt (transformer)* to revolutionize

revolver [revɔlvɛr] *nm* revolver

revue [rəvy] *nf (magazine)* magazine; *(spécialisée)* journal; *(spectacle)* revue; *Mil* review; **passer qch en r.** to review sth

rez-de-chaussée [redʃose] *nm inv Br* ground floor, *Am* first floor

Rhin [rɛ̃] *nm* **le R.** the Rhine

rhinocéros [rinɔserɔs] *nm* rhinoceros

Rhône [ron] *nm* **le R.** the Rhône

rhumatisme [rymatism] *nm* rheumatism; **avoir des rhumatismes** to have rheumatism

rhume [rym] *nm* cold; **r. des foins** hay fever

ri [ri] *pp de* **rire**

ricaner [rikane] *vi (sarcastiquement) Br* to snigger, *Am* to snicker; *(bêtement)* to giggle

riche [riʃ] **1** *adj (personne, pays, aliment)* rich; **r. en** *(vitamines, minérai)* rich in **2** *nmf* rich person; **les riches** the rich ▪ **richesse** *nf (de personne, de pays)* wealth; *(d'étoffe, de sol)* richness; **richesses** *(trésor)* riches; *(ressources)* wealth

ricocher [rikɔʃe] *vi* to rebound, to ricochet ▪ **ricochet** *nm* rebound, ricochet; *Fig* **par r.** indirectly

ride [rid] *nf (de visage)* wrinkle ▪ **ridé, -e** *adj* wrinkled ▪ **rider 1** *vt (visage, peau)* to wrinkle; *(eau)* to ripple **2 se rider** *upr (visage, peau)* to wrinkle

rideau, -x [rido] *nm* curtain; *(métallique)* shutter; *Fig (écran)* screen (**de** of)

ridicule [ridikyl] **1** *adj* ridiculous, ludicrous **2** *nm (moquerie)* ridicule; *(absurdité)* ridiculousness; **tourner qn/qch en r.** to ridicule sb/sth ▪ **ridiculiser 1** *vt* to ridicule **2 se ridiculiser** *upr* to make a fool of oneself

RIEN [rjɛ̃] **1** *pron* nothing; **il ne sait r.** he knows nothing, he doesn't know anything; **r. du tout** nothing at all; **r. d'autre/de bon** nothing else/good; **r. de tel** nothing like it; **de r.!** *(je vous en*

prie) don't mention it!; **ça ne fait r.** it doesn't matter; **pour r. au monde** never in a thousand years; **comme si de r. n'était** as if nothing had happened

2 *nm (mere)* nothing, trifle; **un r. de** a little; **en un r. de temps** in no time

rieur, -euse [rijœr, -øz] *adj* cheerful

rigide [riʒid] *adj* rigid; *(carton)* stiff; *(éducation)* strict

rigole [rigɔl] *nf (conduit)* channel; *(filet d'eau)* rivulet

rigueur [rigœr] *nf (d'analyse)* rigour; *(de climat)* harshness; *(de personne)* strictness; **être de r.** to be the rule; **à la r.** if need be ■ **rigoureux, -euse** *adj (analyse)* rigorous; *(climat, punition)* harsh; *(personne, morale, neutralité)* strict

rillettes [rijɛt] *nfpl* potted minced pork

rimer [rime] *vi* to rhyme (**avec** with)

rincer [rɛ̃se] *vt* to rinse; *(verre)* to rinse (out)

ring [riŋ] *nm (boxing)* ring

riposte [ripɔst] *nf (réponse)* retort; *(attaque)* counterattack ■ **riposter 1** *vt* **r. que…** to retort that… **2** *vi* to counterattack; **r. à** *(attaque)* to counter; *(insulte)* to reply to

rire* [rir] **1** *nm* laugh; **rires** laughter; **le fou r.** the giggles **2** *vi* to laugh (**de** at); *(s'amuser)* to have a good time; *(plaisanter)* to joke; **r. aux éclats** to roar with laughter; **faire qch pour r.** to do sth for a joke *or* laugh

risible [rizibl] *adj* laughable

risque [risk] *nm* risk; **au r. de faire qch** at the risk of doing sth; **à vos risques et périls** at your own risk; **assurance tous risques** comprehensive insurance

risquer [riske] **1** *vt* to risk; *(question)* to venture; **r. de faire qch** to stand a good chance of doing sth **2** *se* **risquer** *vpr* **se r. à faire qch** to dare to do sth ■ **risqué, -e** *adj (dangereux)* risky; *(osé)* risqué

rivage [rivaʒ] *nm* shore

rival, -e, -aux, -ales [rival, -o] *adj & nmf* rival ■ **rivaliser** *vi* to compete (**avec** with; **de** in) ■ **rivalité** *nf* rivalry

rive [riv] *nf (de fleuve)* bank; *(de lac)* shore

riverain, -e [rivərɛ̃, -ɛn] **1** *adj (de rivière)* riverside; *(de lac)* lakeside **2** *nmf (près d'une rivière)* riverside resident; *(près d'un lac)* lakeside resident; *(de rue)* resident

rivière [rivjɛr] *nf* river

riz [ri] *nm* rice; **r. blanc/complet** white/brown rice; **r. au lait** rice pudding ■ **rizière** *nf* paddy (field), ricefield

RMI [ɛrɛmi] *(abrév* **revenu minimum d'insertion)** *nm Br* ≃ income support, *Am* ≃ welfare

RN *(abrév* **route nationale)** *nf Br* main road, A-road, *Am* (state) highway

robe [rɔb] *nf (de femme)* dress; *(d'ecclésiastique, de juge)* robe; *(pelage)* coat; **r. du soir** evening dress; **r. de chambre** *Br* dressing gown, *Am* bathrobe; **pomme de terre en r. des champs** jacket potato, baked potato

robinet [rɔbinɛ] *nm Br* tap, *Am* faucet

robot [rɔbo] *nm* robot; **r. ménager** food processor

robuste [rɔbyst] *adj* robust

roc [rɔk] *nm* rock

rocaille [rɔkaj] *nf (terrain)* rocky ground; *(de jardin)* rockery ■ **rocailleux, -euse** *adj* rocky, stony; *(voix)* harsh

roche [rɔʃ] *nf* rock ■ **rocher** *nm (bloc, substance)* rock ■ **rocheux, -euse** *adj* rocky

rock [rɔk] **1** *nm (musique)* rock **2** *adj inv* **chanteur/opéra r.** rock singer/ opera ■ **rockeur, -euse** *nmf (musicien)* rock musician

roder [rɔde] *vt (moteur, voiture) Br* to run in, *Am* to break in

rôder [rode] *vi* to be on the prowl ■ **rôdeur, -euse** *nmf* prowler

rognon [rɔɲɔ̃] *nm* kidney

roi [rwa] *nm* king; **fête des Rois** Twelfth Night

rôle [rol] *nm* role, part; *(de père)* job; **à tour de r.** in turn

romain, -e [rɔmɛ̃, -ɛn] **1** *adj* Roman **2** *nmf* **R., Romaine** Roman **3** *nf* **romaine** *(laitue) Br* cos (lettuce), *Am* romaine

roman [rɔmɑ̃] *nm* novel; *Fig (histoire)* story ▪ **romancier, -ère** *nmf* novelist

romanesque [rɔmanɛsk] *adj* romantic; *(incroyable)* fantastic

romantique [rɔmɑ̃tik] *adj* romantic

romarin [rɔmarɛ̃] *nm* rosemary

rompre* [rɔ̃pr] **1** *vt* to break; *(pourparlers, relations)* to break off **2** *vi (casser)* to break; *(digue)* to burst; *(fiancés)* to break it off **3 se rompre** *upr (corde)* to break; *(digue)* to burst

ronces [rɔ̃s] *nfpl (branches)* brambles

rond, -e¹ [rɔ̃, -ɔ̃d] **1** *adj* round; *(gras)* plump; *(chiffre* **r.** whole number **2** *adv* **10 euros tout r.** 10 euros exactly **3** *nm (cercle)* circle; **en r.** *(s'asseoir)* in a circle ▪ **rondement** *adv* briskly ▪ **rond-point** *(pl* **ronds-points)** *nm Br* roundabout, *Am* traffic circle

ronde² [rɔ̃d] *nf (de soldat)* round; *(de policier)* beat; *(danse)* round (dance); *Mus Br* semibreve, *Am* whole note; **faire sa r.** *(gardien)* to do one's rounds

rondelle [rɔ̃dɛl] *nf (tranche)* slice

ronfler [rɔ̃fle] *vi (personne)* to snore

ronger [rɔ̃ʒe] **1** *vt* to gnaw (at); *(ver, mer, rouille)* to eat into; **r. qn** *(maladie, chagrin)* to consume sb **2 se ronger** *upr* **se r. les ongles** to bite one's nails ▪ **rongeur** *nm* rodent

ronronner [rɔ̃rɔne] *vi* to purr

roquette [rɔkɛt] *nf Mil* rocket

rosace [rozas] *nf* rosette; *(d'église)* rose window

rosbif [rɔzbif] *nm* **du r.** *(rôti)* roast beef; *(à rôtir)* roasting beef; **un r.** a joint of roast/roasting beef

rose [roz] **1** *adj (couleur)* pink; *(situation, teint)* rosy **2** *nm (couleur)* pink **3** *nf (fleur)* rose ▪ **rosé, -e 1** *adj* pinkish **2** *adj & nm (vin)* rosé

roseau, -x [rozo] *nm* reed

rosée [roze] *nf* dew

rossignol [rɔsiɲɔl] *nm (oiseau)* nightingale

rôti [roti] *nm* **du r.** roasting meat; *(cuit)* roast meat; **un r.** a joint; **r. de bœuf** (joint of) roast beef

rotin [rɔtɛ̃] *nm* rattan

rôtir [rotir] *vti* to roast; **faire r. qch** to roast sth

roue [ru] *nf* wheel; **r. dentée** cogwheel; **être en r. libre** to freewheel; **les deux roues** two-wheeled vehicles

rouge [ruʒ] **1** *adj* red; *(fer)* red-hot **2** *nm (couleur)* red; **le feu est au r.** the (traffic) lights are at red; **r. à lèvres** lipstick

rougeur [ruʒœr] *nf* redness; *(due à la honte)* blush; *(due à l'émotion)* flush; **rougeurs** *(irritation)* rash, red blotches

rougir [ruʒir] **1** *vt (visage)* to redden **2** *vi (de honte)* to blush **(de** with); *(d'émotion)* to flush **(de** with)

rouille [ruj] **1** *nf* rust **2** *adj inv (couleur)* rust(-coloured) ▪ **rouillé, -e** *adj* rusty ▪ **rouiller 1** *vi* to rust **2 se rouiller** *upr* to rust

rouleau, -x [rulo] *nm (outil, vague)* roller; *(de papier, de pellicule)* roll; **r. à pâtisserie** rolling pin; **r. compresseur** steamroller

roulement [rulmɑ̃] *nm (bruit)* rumbling, rumble; *(de tambour, de tonnerre)* roll; *(ordre)* rotation; **par r.** in rotation; *Tech* **r. à billes** ball bearing

rouler [rule] **1** *vt (crêpe, ficelle, manches)* to roll up **2** *vi (balle)* to roll; *(train, voiture)* to go, to travel **3 se rouler** *upr* to roll; **se r. dans** *(couverture)* to roll oneself (up) in ▪ **roulant, -e** *adj (escalier)* moving

roulette [rulɛt] *nf (de meuble)* castor; *(de dentiste)* drill; *(jeu)* roulette

roulotte [rulɔt] *nf (de gitan)* caravan

Roumanie [rumani] *nf* **la R.** Romania ▪ **roumain, -e 1** *adj* Romanian **2** *nmf* **R., Roumaine** Romanian **3** *nm (langue)* Romanian

rousse [rus] *voir* **roux**

rousseur [rusœr] *nf* **tache de r.** freckle ▪ **roussi** *nm* **ça sent le r.** there's a smell of burning ■ **roussir 1** vt (brûler) to scorch, to singe **2** vi (feuilles) to turn brown

route [rut] nf road (**de** to); (itinéraire) way, route; Fig (chemin) path; **grand-r., grande r.** main road; **code de la r.** Br Highway Code, Am traffic regulations; **en r.** on the way, en route; **par la r.** by road; Fig **faire fausse r.** to be on the wrong track; **mettre qch en r.** (voiture) to start sth (up); **se mettre en r.** to set out (**pour** for); **une heure de r.** (en voiture) an hour's drive; **faire r. vers Paris** to head for Paris; **r. départementale** secondary road, Br B road; **r. nationale** Br main road, A-road, Am (state) highway

routier, -ère [rutje, -ɛr] **1** adj **carte/sécurité routière** road map/safety; **réseau r.** road network **2** nm (camionneur) (long-distance) Br lorry or Am truck driver; (restaurant) Br transport café, Am truck stop

routine [rutin] nf routine; **contrôle de r.** routine check ■ **routinier, -ère** adj **travail r.** routine work; **être r.** (personne) to be set in one's ways

rouvrir* [ruvrir] vti, **se rouvrir** vpr to reopen

roux, rousse [ru, rus] **1** adj (cheveux) red, ginger; (personne) red-haired **2** nmf redhead

royal, -e, -aux, -ales [rwajal, -jo] adj (famille, palais) royal; (cadeau, festin) fit for a king; (salaire) princely

royaume [rwajom] nm kingdom ■ **Royaume-Uni** nm **le R.** the United Kingdom

royauté [rwajote] nf (monarchie) monarchy

ruban [rybɑ̃] nm ribbon; (de chapeau) band; **r. adhésif** sticky or adhesive tape

rubis [rybi] nm (pierre) ruby; (de montre) jewel

rubrique [rybrik] nf (article de journal) column; (catégorie, titre) heading

ruche [ryʃ] nf beehive

rude [ryd] adj (pénible) tough; (hiver, voix) harsh; (rêche) rough

rue [ry] nf street; **être à la r.** (sans domicile) to be on the streets ■ **ruelle** nf alley(way)

ruer [rɥe] **1** vi (cheval) to kick (out) **2 se ruer** vpr (foncer) to rush (**sur** at) ■ **ruée** nf rush; **la r. vers l'or** the gold rush

rugby [rygbi] nm rugby ■ **rugbyman** [rygbiman] (pl **-men** [-mɛn]) nm rugby player

rugir [ryʒir] vi to roar ■ **rugissement** nm roar

rugueux, -euse [rygø, -øz] adj rough

ruine [rɥin] nf (décombres, destruction, faillite) ruin; **en r.** (bâtiment) in ruins; **tomber en r.** (bâtiment) to become a ruin ■ **ruiner 1** vt (personne, santé, pays) to ruin **2 se ruiner** vpr (perdre tout son argent) to ruin oneself; (dépenser beaucoup d'argent) to spend a fortune ■ **ruineux, -euse** adj (goûts, projet) ruinously expensive; (dépense) ruinous; **ce n'est pas r.** it won't ruin me/you/etc

ruisseau, -x [rɥiso] nm stream; (caniveau) gutter ■ **ruisseler** vi to stream (**de** with)

rumeur [rymœr] nf (murmure) murmur; (nouvelle) rumour

ruminer [rymine] **1** vt (herbe) to chew **2** vi (vache) to chew the cud

rupture [ryptyr] nf breaking; (de fiançailles, de relations) breaking off; (de pourparlers) breakdown (**de** in); (dispute) break-up; **être en r. de stock** to be out of stock

rural, -e, -aux, -ales [ryral, -o] adj (population) rural; **vie rurale** country life

ruse [ryz] nf (subterfuge) trick; **la r.** (habileté) cunning; (fourberie) trickery ■ **rusé, -e** adj cunning, crafty

Russie [rysi] nf **la R.** Russia ■ **russe 1** adj Russian **2** nmf **R.** Russian **3** nm (langue) Russian

rythme [ritm] nm rhythm; (de travail) rate; (allure) pace ■ **rythmé, -e** adj rhythmic(al)

Ss

S, s [ɛs] *nm inv* S, s

s' [s] *voir* **se, si**

sa [sa] *voir* **son³**

sable [sabl] *nm* sand; **sables mouvants** quicksands

sablé [sable] *nm* shortbread *Br* biscuit *or Am* cookie ■ **sablée** *adj f* **pâte sablée** shortcrust pastry

sablier [sablije] *nm* hourglass; *Culin* egg timer

saborder [saborde] *vt (navire)* to scuttle

sabot [sabo] *nm (de cheval)* hoof; *(chaussure)* clog; **s. de Denver** wheel clamp

saboter [sabote] *vt (machine, projet)* to sabotage ■ **sabotage** *nm* sabotage ■ **saboteur, -euse** *nmf* saboteur

sabre [sabr] *nm* sabre

sac [sak] *nm* bag; *(grand, en toile)* sack; **s. à main** handbag; **s. à dos** rucksack; **s. de voyage** travelling bag

saccade [sakad] *nf* jerk, jolt; **par saccades** in fits and starts ■ **saccadé, -e** *adj* jerky

saccager [sakaʒe] *vt (détruire)* to wreak havoc in

sachant, sache(s), sachent [saʃɑ̃, saʃ] *voir* **savoir**

sachet [saʃɛ] *nm (small)* bag; **s. de thé** teabag

sacre [sakr] *nm (de roi)* coronation ■ **sacrer** *vt (roi)* to crown

sacré, -e [sakre] *adj (saint)* sacred ■ **sacrement** *nm Rel* sacrament

sacrifice [sakrifis] *nm* sacrifice ■ **sacrifier 1** *vt* to sacrifice (**à** to) **2** *vi* **s. à la mode** to be a slave to fashion **3** *se*

sacrifier *vpr* to sacrifice oneself (**pour** for)

sacrilège [sakrilɛʒ] **1** *adj* sacrilegious **2** *nm* sacrilege

sadique [sadik] **1** *adj* sadistic **2** *nmf* sadist

safari [safari] *nm* safari; **faire un s.** to go on safari

safran [safrɑ̃] *nm* saffron

sage [saʒ] **1** *adj (avisé)* wise; *(tranquille)* good **2** *nm* wise man ■ **sage-femme** *(pl* **sages-femmes)** *nf* midwife ■ **sagesse** *nf (philosophie)* wisdom; *(calme)* good behaviour

Sagittaire [saʒiter] *nm* **le S.** *(signe)* Sagittarius

saigner [seɲe] *vi* to bleed; **s. du nez** to have a nosebleed ■ **saignant, -e** *adj (viande)* rare

saillant, -e [sajɑ̃, -ɑ̃t] *adj* projecting ■ **saillie** *nf (partie avant)* projection

sain, -e [sɛ̃, sɛn] *adj* healthy; *(nourriture)* wholesome, healthy; **s. et sauf** safe and sound

saint, -e [sɛ̃, sɛ̃t] **1** *adj (lieu)* holy; *(personne)* saintly; **s. Jean** Saint John; **la Sainte Vierge** the Blessed Virgin **2** *nmf* saint ■ **Saint-Esprit** *nm* **le S.** the Holy Spirit ■ **Saint-Sylvestre** *nf* **la S.** New Year's Eve

sainteté [sɛ̃tte] *nf (de lieu)* holiness; *(de personne)* saintliness

sais [sɛ] *voir* **savoir**

saisie [sezi] *nf (de biens)* seizure; *Ordinat* **s. de données** data capture, keyboarding

saisir [sezir] *vt* to take hold of; *(brusquement)* to grab; *(occasion)* to seize;

to grasp; *(comprendre)* to grasp; *Jur* to seize; *(viande)* to seal **2 se saisir** *upr* se **s. de qn/qch** to take hold of sb/sth; *(brusquement)* to grab sb/sth ■ **saisissant, -e** *adj (film)* gripping; *(contraste, ressemblance)* striking

saison [sɛzɔ̃] *nf* season; **en/hors s.** in/out of season; **en haute/basse s.** in the high/low season; **la s. des pluies** the rainy season ■ **saisonnier, -ère** *adj* seasonal

sait [sɛ] *voir* **savoir**

salade [salad] *nf (laitue)* lettuce; **s. verte** green salad; **s. de fruits** fruit salad; **s. niçoise** salade niçoise

salaire [salɛr] *nm (mensuel)* salary

salarié, -e [salarje] **1** *adj (payé mensuellement)* salaried **2** *nmf (payé mensuellement)* salaried employee; **salariés** *(de société)* employees

sale [sal] *adj* dirty; *(dégoûtant)* filthy ■ **salement** *adv (se conduire, manger)* disgustingly ■ **saleté** *nf (manque de soin)* dirtiness; *(crasse)* dirt; **saletés** *(détritus)* Br rubbish, Am garbage; **faire des saletés** to make a mess

saler [sale] *vt* to salt ■ **salé, -e** *adj (goût, plat)* salty; *(aliment)* salted

salir [salir] **1** *vt* to (make) dirty **2 se salir** *upr* to get dirty ■ **salissant, -e** *adj (travail)* dirty, messy; *(étoffe)* that shows the dirt

salle [sal] *nf* room; *(très grande, publique)* hall; *(de cinéma)* Br cinema, Am movie theater; *(d'hôpital)* ward; **s. à manger** dining room; **s. de bain(s)** bathroom; **s. de classe** classroom; **s. de concert** concert hall; **s. de jeux** *(pour enfants)* games room; *(de casino)* gaming room; **s. de spectacle** auditorium; **s. d'embarquement** *(d'aéroport)* departure lounge; **s. d'opération** *(d'hôpital)* operating *Br* theatre *or Am* room

salon [salɔ̃] *nm* living room, *Br* lounge; *(exposition)* show; **s. de coiffure** hairdressing salon; **s. de thé** tea room

salopette [salɔpɛt] *nf Br* dungarees, *Am* overalls

salubre [salybr] *adj* healthy ■ **salubrité** *nf* healthiness; **s. publique** public health

saluer [salɥe] *vt* to greet; *(en partant)* to take one's leave of; *(de la main)* to wave to; *(de la tête)* to nod to; *Mil* to salute

salut [saly] **1** *nm* greeting; *(de la main)* wave; *(de la tête)* nod; *Mil* salute; *(sauvegarde)* rescue; *Rel* salvation **2** *exclam Fam* hi!; *(au revoir)* bye!

salutaire [salyter] *adj* salutary

samedi [samdi] *nm* Saturday

SAMU [samy] *(abrév* service d'aide médicale d'urgence) *nm* emergency medical service

sanctifier [sɑ̃ktifje] *vt* to sanctify

sanction [sɑ̃ksjɔ̃] *nf (approbation, peine)* sanction ■ **sanctionner** *vt (approuver)* to sanction; *(punir)* to punish

sanctuaire [sɑ̃ktɥer] *nm* sanctuary

sandale [sɑ̃dal] *nf* sandal

sandwich [sɑ̃dwitʃ] *nm* sandwich

sang [sɑ̃] *nm* blood ■ **sang-froid** *nm* self-control; **garder son s.** to keep calm; **tuer qn de s.** to kill sb in cold blood ■ **sanglant, -e** *adj* bloody

sangle [sɑ̃gl] *nf* strap

sanglier [sɑ̃glije] *nm* wild boar

sanglot [sɑ̃glo] *nm* sob ■ **sangloter** *vi* to sob

sanguin, -e [sɑ̃gɛ̃, -in] *adj (tempérament)* full-blooded; **vaisseau s.** blood vessel

sanguinaire [sɑ̃giner] *adj* bloodthirsty

sanitaire [saniter] *adj (conditions)* sanitary; *(personnel)* medical; **règlement s.** health regulations

sans [sɑ̃] *(*[sɑ̃z] *before vowel and mute* h) *prép* without; **s. faire qch** without doing sth; **s. qu'il le sache** without him *or* his knowing; **s. cela, s. quoi** otherwise; **s. importance/travail** unimportant/unemployed; **s. argent/manches** penniless/sleeveless ■ **sans-abri** *nmf inv* homeless person; **les s.** the homeless ■ **sans-faute** *nm inv Fig* **faire un s.** not to put a foot wrong

■ **sans-gêne 1** *adj inv* ill-mannered **2** *nm inv* lack of manners ■ **sans-papiers** *nmf inv* illegal immigrant

santé [sɑ̃te] *nf* health; **en bonne/mauvaise s.** in good/bad health; **(à votre) s.!** *(en trinquant)* cheers!

saoul [su] *adj & nm* = **soûl**

• **saper** [sape] *vt* to undermine; **s. le moral à qn** to sap sb's morale

sapeur-pompier [sapœrpɔ̃pje] *(pl* **sapeurs-pompiers)** *nm* fireman, firefighter

saphir [safir] *nm* sapphire

sapin [sapɛ̃] *nm (arbre, bois)* fir; **s. de Noël** Christmas tree

Sardaigne [sardɛɲ] *nf* la S. Sardinia ■ **sarde 1** *adj* Sardinian **2** *nmf* **S.** Sardinian

sardine [sardin] *nf* sardine

sarrasin [sarazɛ̃] *nm (plante)* buckwheat

Satan [satɑ̃] *nm* Satan

satellite [satelit] *nm* satellite; **télévision par s.** satellite television

satiété [sasjete] *nf* **boire/manger à s.** to eat/drink one's fill

satin [satɛ̃] *nm* satin

satire [satir] *nf* satire **(contre** on**)** ■ **satirique** *adj* satirical

satisfaction [satisfaksjɔ̃] *nf* satisfaction; **donner s. à qn** to give sb (complete) satisfaction ■ **satisfaire*1** *vt* to satisfy **2** *vi* **s. à qch** *(conditions)* to satisfy sth; *(obligation)* to fulfil sth, *Am* to fulfill sth ■ **satisfaisant, -e** *adj* *(acceptable)* satisfactory ■ **satisfait, -e** *adj* satisfied **(de** with**)**

saturer [satyre] *vt* to saturate **(de** with**)** ■ **saturation** *nf* saturation; **arriver à s.** to reach saturation point

sauce [sos] *nf* sauce

saucisse [sosis] *nf* sausage; **s. de Francfort** frankfurter ■ **saucisson** *nm* (cold) sausage

sauf¹ [sof] *prép* except; **s. erreur** if I'm not mistaken

sauf², sauve [sof, sov] *adj* **avoir la vie sauve** to be unharmed

saumon [somɔ̃] **1** *nm* salmon **2** *adj inv (couleur)* salmon (pink)

sauna [sona] *nm* sauna

saupoudrer [sopudre] *vt* to sprinkle **(de** with**)**

saur [sɔr] *adj m* **hareng s.** smoked herring

saura, saurait [sora, sorɛ] *voir* **savoir**

saut [so] *nm* jump, leap; **faire un s.** to jump, to leap; **s. à la corde** *Br* skipping, *Am* jumping rope; **s. à l'élastique** bungee jumping; **s. en hauteur** high jump; **s. en longueur** long jump; **s. en parachute** parachute jump; *(activité)* parachute jumping

sauter [sote] **1** *vt (franchir)* to jump (over); *(mot, repas, classe, ligne)* to skip **2** *vi (personne, animal)* to jump, to leap; *(bombe)* to go off, to explode; *(fusible)* to blow; **faire s. qch** *(pont, mine)* to blow sth up; *(serrure)* to force sth; **s. à la corde** *Br* to skip, *Am* to jump rope; **s. en parachute** to do a parachute jump

sauterelle [sotrɛl] *nf* grasshopper

sautes [sot] *nfpl (d'humeur, de température)* sudden changes **(de** in**)**

sauvage [sovaʒ] *adj (animal, plante)* wild; *(tribu, homme)* primitive; *(cruel)* savage; *(farouche)* unsociable; *(illégal)* unauthorized ■ **sauvagerie** *nf (insociabilité)* unsociability; *(cruauté)* savagery

sauve [sov] *adj* voir **sauf²**

sauvegarde [sovgard] *nf* safeguard **(contre** against**)**; *Ordinat* backup ■ **sauvegarder** *vt* to safeguard; *Ordinat* to save

sauver [sove] **1** *vt (personne)* to save, to rescue **(de** from**)**; *(matériel)* to salvage **2 se sauver** *vpr (s'enfuir)* to run away; *(s'échapper)* to escape ■ **sauvetage** *nm (de personne)* rescue ■ **sauveteur** *nm* rescuer

sauvette [sovɛt] **à la sauvette** *adv (pour ne pas être vu)* on the sly; **vendre qch à la s.** to peddle sth illegally on the streets

sauveur [sovœr] *nm* saviour

savant, -e [savɑ̃, -ɑ̃t] **1** *adj (érudit)*

learned; *(habile)* clever **2** *nm (scientifique)* scientist

saveur [savœr] *nf (goût)* flavour

Savoie [savwa] *nf* la S. Savoy

SAVOIR* [savwar] **1** *vt* to know; *(nouvelle)* to have heard; **s.** lire/nager to know how to read/swim; **faire s. à qn que...** to inform sb that...; **à s.** *(c'est-à-dire)* that is, namely; **pas que je sache** not that I know of; **je n'en sais rien** I have no idea, I don't know; **en s. long sur qn/qch** to know a lot about sb/sth
2 *nm (culture)* learning, knowledge ■ **savoir-faire** *nm inv* know-how

savon [savɔ̃] *nm* soap ■ **savonnette** *nf* bar of soap ■ **savonneux, -euse** *adj* soapy

savourer [savure] *vt* to savour ■ **savoureux, -euse** *adj* tasty

savoyard, -e [savwajar, -ard] **1** *adj* Savoyard **2** *nmf* S., Savoyarde Savoyard

saxophone [saksɔfɔn] *nm* saxophone

scalpel [skalpɛl] *nm* scalpel

scandale [skɑ̃dal] *nm* scandal ■ **scandaleux, -euse** *adj* scandalous ■ **scandaliser 1** *vt* to scandalize, to shock **2 se scandaliser** *vpr* to be shocked *or* scandalized (**de** by)

Scandinavie [skɑ̃dinavi] *nf* la S. Scandinavia ■ **scandinave 1** *adj* Scandinavian **2** *nmf* S. Scandinavian

scanner 1 [skanɛr] *nm* scanner **2** [skane] *vt* to scan

scaphandrier [skafɑ̃drije] *nm* diver

sceau, -x [so] *nm* seal ■ **sceller** *vt (document)* to seal

scénario [senarjo] *nm* script, screenplay ■ **scénariste** *nmf* scriptwriter

scène [sɛn] *nf* (**a**) *(de théâtre)* scene; *(plateau)* stage; *(action)* action; **mettre qch en s.** *(pièce)* to stage sth; *(film)* to direct sth; Fig **sur la s. internationale** on the international scene (**b**) *(dispute)* scene; **faire une s.** to make a scene; **s. de ménage** domestic quarrel

sceptique [sɛptik] **1** *adj* Br sceptical, Am skeptical **2** *nmf* Br sceptic, Am skeptic

schéma [ʃema] *nm* diagram ■ **schématique** *adj* schematic

schizophrène [skizɔfrɛn] *adj & nmf* schizophrenic

scie [si] *nf (outil)* saw ■ **scier** *vt* to saw

sciemment [sjamɑ̃] *adv* knowingly

science [sjɑ̃s] *nf* science; *(savoir)* knowledge; **sciences humaines** social sciences; **sciences naturelles** biology ■ **science-fiction** *nf* science fiction ■ **scientifique 1** *adj* scientific **2** *nmf* scientist

scinder [sɛ̃de] **se scinder** *vpr* to split up (**en** into)

scintiller [sɛ̃tije] *vi* to sparkle; *(étoile)* to twinkle ■ **scintillement** *nm* sparkling; *(d'étoile)* twinkling

scission [sisjɔ̃] *nf (de parti)* split (**de** in); **s. de l'atome** splitting of the atom

sclérose [skleroz] *nf Méd* sclerosis; Fig ossification; **s. en plaques** multiple sclerosis

scolaire [skɔlɛr] *adj* **année s.** school year; **enfant d'âge s.** child of school age ■ **scolariser** *vt (enfant)* to send to school ■ **scolarité** *nf* schooling; **pendant ma s.** during my school years

scooter [skuter] *nm* (motor) scooter; **s. des mers** jet ski

score [skɔr] *nm* score

scorpion [skɔrpjɔ̃] *nm* scorpion; **le S.** *(signe)* Scorpio

Scotch® [skɔtʃ] *(ruban adhésif) Br* sellotape®, *Am* scotch tape® ■ **scotcher** *vt Br* to sellotape, *Am* to tape

scout, -e [skut] *adj & nm* scout

script [skript] *nm (écriture)* printing; *Cin* script

scrupule [skrypyl] *nm* scruple; **sans scrupules** *(être)* unscrupulous; *(agir)* unscrupulously ■ **scrupuleux, -euse** *adj* scrupulous

scruter [skryte] *vt* to scrutinize

scrutin [skrytɛ̃] *nm (vote)* ballot; *(élection)* poll; *(système)* voting system; **premier tour de s.** first ballot *or* round; **s. majoritaire** first-past-the-post voting system

sculpter [skylte] *vt (statue, pierre)* to sculpt; *(bois)* to carve; **s. qch dans qch** to sculpt/carve sth out of sth ■ **sculpteur** *nm* sculptor ■ **sculpture** *nf (art, œuvre)* sculpture

SDF [ɛsdeɛf] *(abrév* **sans domicile fixe)** *nm* person of no fixed abode

SE [sə]

se becomes **s'** before vowel or mute h.

pron personnel (**a**) *(complément direct)* himself; *(féminin)* herself; *(non humain)* itself; *(indéfini)* oneself, *pl* themselves; **il se lave** he washes himself; **ils** *ou* **elles se lavent** they wash themselves

(**b**) *(indirect)* to himself/herself/itself/oneself; **il se lave les mains** he washes his hands; **elle se lave les mains** she washes her hands

(**c**) *(réciproque)* each other; *(indirect)* to each other; **ils s'aiment** they love each other; **ils** *ou* **elles se parlent** they speak to each other

(**d**) *(passif)* **ça se fait** that is done; **ça se vend bien** it sells well

séance [seɑ̃s] *nf (de cinéma)* showing, performance; *(d'assemblée, de travail)* session

seau, -x [so] *nm* bucket

sec, sèche [sɛk, sɛʃ] **1** *adj* dry; *(fruits, légumes)* dried; *(ton)* curt; **frapper un coup s.** to knock sharply **2** *adv (boire)* Br neat, *Am* straight; *(frapper, pleuvoir)* hard **3** *nm* **à s.** dry; **au s.** in a dry place

sécession [sesesjɔ̃] *nf* secession; **faire s.** to secede

sèche [sɛʃ] *voir* sec

sécher [seʃe] **1** *vti* to dry **2 se sécher** *vpr* to dry oneself ■ **séchage** *nm* drying ■ **sèche-cheveux** *nm inv* hair dryer ■ **sèche-linge** *nm inv Br* tumble dryer, *Am* (clothes) dryer

sécheresse [seʃrɛs] *nf (d'air, de sol, de peau)* dryness; *(de ton)* curtness; *(manque de pluie)* drought

séchoir [seʃwar] *nm (appareil)* dryer; **s. à linge** clothes horse

second, -e¹ [səgɔ̃, -ɔ̃d] **1** *adj & nmf* second

2 *nm (adjoint)* second in command; *(étage) Br* second floor, *Am* third floor

3 *nf* **seconde** Rail second class; *Scol Br* ≃ fifth form, *Am* ≃ tenth grade; *Aut (vitesse)* second (gear) ■ **secondaire** *adj* secondary; **école s.** *Br* secondary school, *Am* high school

seconde² [səgɔ̃d] *nf (instant)* second

seconder [səgɔ̃de] *vt* to assist

secouer [səkwe] *vt* to shake; *(poussière)* to shake off; **s. qch de qch** *(enlever)* to shake sth out of sth; **s. la tête** *(réponse affirmative)* to nod *(one's head)*; *(réponse négative)* to shake one's head

secourir [səkurir] *vt* to assist, to help ■ **secourable** *adj* helpful ■ **secourisme** *nm* first aid ■ **secouriste** *nmf* first-aid worker

secours [səkur] *nm* help; *(financier, matériel)* aid; *Mil* **les s.** *(renforts)* relief; **au s.!** help!; **porter s. à qn** to give sb help; **roue de s.** spare wheel

secousse [səkus] *nf* jolt, jerk; *(de tremblement de terre)* tremor

secret, -ète [səkrɛ, -ɛt] **1** *adj* secret; *(cachottier)* secretive **2** *nm* secret; **en s.** in secret, secretly

secrétaire [səkretɛr] *nmf* secretary; **s. d'État** Secretary of State ■ **secrétariat** *nm (bureau)* secretary's office; *(d'organisation internationale)* secretariat; *(métier)* secretarial work

sectaire [sɛktɛr] *adj & nmf Péj* sectarian

secte [sɛkt] *nf* sect

secteur [sɛktœr] *nm (zone)* area; *Écon* sector; *Él* mains

section [sɛksjɔ̃] *nf* section; *(de ligne d'autobus)* stage; *Mil* platoon ■ **sectionner** *vt (couper)* to sever

séculaire [sekylɛr] *adj (tradition)* age-old

sécurité [sekyrite] *nf (absence de danger)* safety; *(tranquillité)* security; **S.**

sociale *Br* Social Security, *Am* Welfare; **en s.** *(hors de danger)* safe

séduire* [sedɥir] *vt* to charm; *(plaire à)* to appeal to; *(abuser de)* to seduce ■ **séduisant, -e** *adj* attractive ■ **séducteur, -trice** *nmf* seducer, *f* seductress ■ **séduction** *nf* attraction

ségrégation [segregɑsjɔ̃] *nf* segregation

seigle [sɛgl] *nm* rye; **pain de s.** rye bread

seigneur [sɛɲœr] *nm Hist* (noble, maître) lord; *Rel* **le S.** the Lord

sein [sɛ̃] *nm* breast; **donner le s. à** *(enfant)* to breastfeed; **au s. de** within

Seine [sɛn] *nf* **la S.** the Seine

séisme [seism] *nm* earthquake

seize [sɛz] *adj & nm inv* sixteen ■ **seizième** *adj & nmf* sixteenth

séjour [seʒur] *nm* stay; **s. linguistique** language-learning trip; **(salle de) s. living room** ■ **séjourner** *vi* to stay

sel [sɛl] *nm* salt; *Fig (piquant)* spice; **s. de mer** sea salt; **sels de bain** bath salts

sélectif, -ive [selektif, -iv] *adj* selective ■ **sélection** *nf* selection ■ **sélectionner** *vt* to select ■ **sélectionneur** *nm* selector

self [sɛlf] *nm* self-service restaurant

selle [sɛl] *nf (de cheval, de vélo)* saddle

selon [səlɔ̃] *prép* according to; **s. que...** depending on whether...

semaine [səmɛn] *nf* week; **en s.** in the week

semblable [sɑ̃blabl] *adj* similar *(à* to); **de semblables propos** such remarks

semblant [sɑ̃blɑ̃] *nm* **faire s.** to pretend *(de* faire to do)

sembler [sɑ̃ble] **1** *vi* to seem *(à* to); **il (me) semble vieux** he seems *or* looks old (to me); **s. faire qch** to seem to do sth **2** *v impersonnel* **il semble que...** it seems that...; **il me semble que...** it seems to me that...

semelle [səmɛl] *nf (de chaussure)* sole; *(intérieure)* insole

semer [səme] *vt (graines)* to sow; *Fig (poursuivant)* to shake off; *Fig* **semé**

de strewn with ■ **semence** *nf* seed

semestre [səmɛstr] *nm* half-year; *Univ* semester

séminaire [seminɛr] *nm Univ* seminar; *Rel* seminary

semi-remorque [səmirəmɔrk] *(pl* **semi-remorques)** *nm (camion) Br* articulated lorry, *Am* semi(trailer), trailer truck

semoule [səmul] *nf* semolina

sénat [sena] *nm* senate ■ **sénateur** *nm* senator

sénile [senil] *adj* senile

SENS [sɑ̃s] *nm* **(a)** *(faculté, raison, instinct)* sense; **avoir le s. de l'humour** to have a sense of humour; **avoir du bon s.** to be sensible; **bon sens** common sense

(b) *(signification)* meaning, sense; **ça n'a pas de s.** that doesn't make sense

(c) *(direction)* direction; *Aut* **s. giratoire** *Br* roundabout, *Am* traffic circle, *Am* rotary; **s. interdit** *ou* **unique** *(rue)* one-way street; **'s. interdit'** 'no entry'; **à s. unique** *(rue)* one-way; **dans le s. des aiguilles d'une montre** clockwise; **dans le s. inverse des aiguilles d'une montre** *Br* anticlockwise, *Am* counterclockwise

sensation [sɑ̃sɑsjɔ̃] *nf* feeling, sensation; **faire s.** to create a sensation

sensé, -e [sɑ̃se] *adj* sensible

sensible [sɑ̃sibl] *adj* sensitive *(à* to); *(douloureux)* tender, sore; *(perceptible)* perceptible; *(progrès)* noticeable ■ **sensibiliser** *vt* **s. qn à qch** *(problème)* to make sb aware of sth ■ **sensibilité** *nf* sensitivity

sensuel, -elle [sɑ̃sɥɛl] *adj* sensual ■ **sensualité** *nf* sensuality

sentence [sɑ̃tɑ̃s] *nf Jur (jugement)* sentence

sentier [sɑ̃tje] *nm* path

sentiment [sɑ̃timɑ̃] *nm* feeling; **avoir le s. que...** to have a feeling that... ■ **sentimental, -e, -aux, -ales** *adj* sentimental; **vie sentimentale** love life

sentinelle [sɑ̃tinɛl] *nf* sentry

sentir* [sãtir] **1** vt (douleur) to feel; (odeur) to smell; **s. le moisi** to smell musty; **s. le poisson** to smell of fish **2** vi to smell; **s. bon/mauvais** to smell good/bad **3 se sentir** vpr **se s. humilié** to feel humiliated

séparation [separasjɔ̃] nf separation; (départ) parting

séparer [separe] **1** vt to separate (**de** from) **2 se séparer** vpr (couple) to separate; (cortège) to disperse, to break up; **se s. de qn/qch** (donner, jeter) to part with sb/sth ■ **séparé, -e** adj (distinct) separate; (époux) separated (**de** from)

sept [sɛt] adj & nm inv seven

septante [sɛptãt] adj (en Belgique, en Suisse) seventy

septembre [sɛptãbr] nm September

septième [sɛtjɛm] adj & nmf seventh; **un s.** a seventh

sépulture [sepyltyr] nf burial; (lieu) burial place

séquelles [sekɛl] nfpl (de maladie) after-effects

séquence [sekãs] nf sequence

séquestrer [sekɛstre] vt **s. qn** to keep sb locked up

sera, serait [sǝra, sǝrɛ] voir **être**

Serbie [sɛrbi] nf la S. Serbia ■ **serbe 1** adj Serbian **2** nmf S. Serbian

serein, -e [sǝrɛ̃, -ɛn] adj serene

sérénade [serenad] nf serenade

sérénité [serenite] nf serenity

sergent [sɛrʒã] nm Mil sergeant

série [seri] nf series; (ensemble) set; **de s.** (article, voiture) standard; **fin de s.** discontinued line; **fabrication en s.** mass production; **numéro hors s.** special issue

sérieux, -euse [serjø, -jøz] **1** adj (personne, doute) serious; (de bonne foi) genuine, serious; (fiable) reliable; **de sérieuses chances de…** a good chance of… ■ **2** nm (application) seriousness; (fiabilité) reliability; **prendre qn/qch au s.** to take sb/sth seriously

seringue [sǝrɛ̃g] nf syringe

serment [sɛrmã] nm (affirmation solennelle) oath; (promesse) pledge; **prêter s.** to take an oath; **faire le s. de faire qch** to swear to do sth; Jur **sous s.** on or under oath

sermon [sɛrmɔ̃] nm (de prêtre) sermon ■ **sermonner** vt (faire la morale à) to lecture

séropositif, -ive [seropozitif, -iv] adj Méd HIV positive ■ **séronégatif, -ive** adj Méd HIV negative

serpent [sɛrpã] nm snake

serpenter [sɛrpãte] vi (sentier) to meander

serre [sɛr] nf greenhouse

serrer [sere] **1** vt (tenir) to grip; (nœud, vis) to tighten; (poing) to clench; **s. la main à qn** to shake hands with sb; **s. qn** (sujet: vêtement) to be too tight for sb **2** vi **s. à droite** to keep (to the) right **3 se serrer** vpr (se rapprocher) to squeeze up; **se s. contre** to squeeze up against ■ **serré, -e** adj (nœud, vêtement) tight; (gens) packed (together); (lutte) close ■ **serre-tête** nm inv headband

serrure [seryr] nf lock

serveur, -euse [sɛrvœr, -øz] **1** nmf waiter, f waitress; (de bar) barman, f barmaid **2** nm Ordinat server

serviable [sɛrvjabl] adj helpful, obliging

service [sɛrvis] nm service; (travail) duty; (pourboire) service (charge); (d'entreprise) department; (au tennis) serve, service; **un s.** (aide) a favour; **rendre s.** to be of service (**à qn** to sb); **être de s.** to be on duty; **faire son s. (militaire)** to do one's military service; **s. à café** coffee set; **s. (non) compris** service (not) included; **s. après-vente** aftersales service

serviette [sɛrvjɛt] nf (pour s'essuyer) towel; (sac) briefcase; **s. de bain/de toilette** bath/hand towel; **s. de table** napkin, Br serviette ■ **serviette-éponge** (pl **serviettes-éponges**) nf terry towel

servir* [sɛrvir] **1** *vt* to serve (**qch à qn** sb with sth, sth to sb); (*convive*) to wait on

2 *vi* to serve; **s. à qch/à faire qch** to be used for sth/for doing sth; **ça ne sert à rien** it's useless, it's no good or use (**de faire** doing); **s. de qch** to be used for sth, to serve as sth

3 se servir *vpr* (*à table*) to help oneself (**de** to); **se s. de qch** (*utiliser*) to use sth

serviteur [sɛrvitœr] *nm* servant

ses [se] *voir* **son²**

session [sesjɔ̃] *nf* session

set [sɛt] *nm* (*au tennis*) set; **s. de table** place mat

seuil [sœj] *nm* (*entrée*) doorway; *Fig* (*limite*) threshold; *Fig* **au s. de** on the threshold of

seul, -e [sœl] **1** *adj* (*sans compagnie*) alone; (*unique*) only; **tout s.** by oneself, on one's own, all alone; **se sentir s.** to feel lonely or alone; **la seule femme** the only woman; **un s. chat** only one cat; **une seule fois** only once; **pas un s. livre** not a single book; **seuls les garçons…** only the boys…

2 *adv* (**tout**) **s.** (*rentrer, vivre*) by oneself, alone, on one's own; (*parler*) to oneself

3 *nmf* **le s., la seule** the only one; **un s., une seule** only one, one only; **pas un s.** not a (single) one

seulement [sœlmɑ̃] *adv* only; **non s.... mais encore...** not only… but (also)…

sève [sɛv] *nf* (*de plante*) sap

sévère [sever] *adj* severe; (*parents, professeur*) strict ■ **sévérité** *nf* severity; (*de parents*) strictness

sévices [sevis] *nmpl* ill-treatment; **s. à enfant** child abuse

sexe [sɛks] *nm* (*catégorie, sexualité*) sex; (*organes*) genitals ■ **sexiste** *adj & nmf* sexist ■ **sexualité** *nf* sexuality ■ **sexuel, -elle** *adj* sexual

shampooing [ʃɑ̃pwɛ̃] *nm* shampoo; **s. colorant** rinse; **faire un s. à qn** to shampoo sb's hair

shooter [ʃute] *vti* (*au football*) to shoot

short [ʃɔrt] *nm* (pair of) shorts

SI¹ [si]

si becomes s' [s] before il, ils.

1 *conj* if; **si je pouvais** if I could; **s'il vient** if he comes; **si j'étais roi** if I were or was king; **je me demande si...** I wonder whether or if…; **si on restait?** (*suggestion*) what if we stayed?; **si oui** if so; **si non** if not; **si seulement** if only

2 *adv* (**a**) (*tellement*) so; **pas si riche que tu crois** not as rich as you think; **un si bon dîner** such a good dinner; **si bien que...** so much so that…

(**b**) (*après négative*) yes; **tu ne viens pas? – si!** you're not coming? – yes (I am)!

si² [si] *nm inv* (*note*) B

siamois, -e [sjamwa, -waz] *adj* Siamese; **frères s., sœurs siamoises** Siamese twins

Sicile [sisil] *nf* **la S.** Sicily

SIDA [sida] (*abrév* **syndrome immunodéficitaire acquis**) *nm* AIDS; **virus du S.** AIDS virus

sidérurgie [sideryrʒi] *nf* iron and steel industry

siècle [sjɛkl] *nm* century

siège [sjɛʒ] *nm* (**a**) (*meuble, centre*) & *Pol* seat; (*d'autorité, de parti*) headquarters; **s. social** head office (**b**) *Mil* siege; **faire le s. de** to lay siege to

siéger [sjeʒe] *vi* (*assemblée*) to sit

sien, sienne [sjɛ̃, sjɛn] **1** *pron possessif* **le s., la sienne, les sien(ne)s** (*d'homme*) his; (*de femme*) hers; (*de chose*) its; **les deux siens** his/her two **2** *nmpl* **les siens** (*sa famille*) one's family **3** *nfpl* **faire des siennes** to be up to one's tricks again

sieste [sjɛst] *nf* siesta; **faire la s.** to have a nap

siffler [sifle] **1** *vi* to whistle; (*avec un sifflet*) to blow one's whistle; (*gaz, serpent*) to hiss

2 *vt* (*chanson*) to whistle; (*chien*) to whistle at; *Sport* (*faute, fin de match*) to blow one's whistle for; (*acteur,* *pièce*) to boo; **se faire s.** (*acteur*) to be booed ■ **sifflement** [-əmɑ̃] *nm* whistling; (*de serpent, de gaz*) hissing

sifflet [sifle] *nm* (*instrument*) whistle; **sifflets** (*de spectateurs*) booing ■ **siffloter** *vti* to whistle

sigle [sigl] *nm* (*initiales*) abbreviation; (*acronyme*) acronym

signal, -aux [siɲal, -o] *nm* signal; **s. d'alarme** alarm signal; **s. lumineux** warning light; **s. sonore** warning sound

signalement [siɲalmɑ̃] *nm* description, particulars

signaler [siɲale] **1** *vt* (*faire remarquer*) to point out (**à qn** to sb; **que** that); (*par panneau*) to signpost; (*dire à la police*) to report (**à** to) **2 se signaler** *upr* **se s. par qch** to distinguish oneself by sth

signalisation [siɲalizasjɔ̃] *nf* (*sur les routes*) signposting; **s. routière** (*signaux*) road signs

signature [siɲatyr] *nf* signature; (*action*) signing

signe [siɲ] *nm* (*indice*) sign, indication; **en s. de protestation** as a sign of protest; **faire s. à qn** (*geste*) to motion (to) sb (**de faire** to do); (*contacter*) to get in touch with sb; **faire s. que oui** to nod (one's head); **faire s. que non** to shake one's head; **s. particulier** distinguishing mark; **s. astrologique** astrological sign

signer [siɲe] **1** *vt* to sign **2 se signer** *upr* to cross oneself

signification [siɲifikasjɔ̃] *nf* meaning ■ **significatif, -ive** *adj* significant, meaningful

signifier [siɲifje] *vt* to mean (**que** that)

silence [silɑ̃s] *nm* silence; *Mus* rest; **en s.** in silence; **garder le s.** to keep quiet or silent (**sur** about) ■ **silencieux, -euse 1** *adj* silent **2** *nm* (*de voiture*) *Br* silencer, *Am* muffler; (*d'arme*) silencer

silhouette [silwet] *nf* outline; (*en noir*) silhouette; (*du corps*) figure

sillonner [sijɔne] *vt* (*parcourir*) to criss-cross

similaire [similɛr] *adj* similar ■ **similitude** *nf* similarity

simple [sɛ̃pl] *adj* (*facile, crédule, sans prétention*) simple; (*fait d'un élément*) single; (*employé, particulier*) ordinary ■ **simplicité** *nf* simplicity

simplifier [sɛ̃plifje] *vt* to simplify ■ **simplification** *nf* simplification

simpliste [sɛ̃plist] *adj* simplistic

simuler [simyle] *vt* (*reproduire*) to simulate; (*feindre*) to feign

simultané, -e [simyltane] *adj* simultaneous

sincère [sɛ̃sɛr] *adj* sincere ■ **sincérité** *nf* sincerity; **en toute s.** quite sincerely

Singapour [sɛ̃gapur] *nm* Singapore

singe [sɛ̃ʒ] *nm* monkey; **grand s.** ape

singulariser [sɛ̃gylarize] **se singulariser** *upr* to draw attention to oneself

singulier, -ère [sɛ̃gylje, -ɛr] *adj* (*peu ordinaire*) peculiar, odd ■ **singularité** *nf* peculiarity

sinistre [sinistr] **1** *adj* (*effrayant*) sinister; (*triste*) grim **2** *nm* disaster; (*incendie*) fire; *Jur* (*dommage*) damage ■ **sinistré, -e 1** *adj* (*population, région*) disaster-stricken **2** *nmf* disaster victim

sinon [sinɔ̃] *conj* (*autrement*) otherwise, or else; (*sauf*) except (**que** that); (*si ce n'est*) if not

sinueux, -euse [sinɥø, -øz] *adj* winding

sinusite [sinyzit] *nf* sinusitis; **avoir une s.** to have sinusitis

siphon [sifɔ̃] *nm* siphon; (*d'évier*) trap, *Br* U-bend

sirène [sirɛn] *nf* (*d'usine*) siren; (*femme*) mermaid

sirop [siro] *nm* syrup; (*à diluer*) (*fruit*) cordial; **s. contre la toux** cough mixture

sismique [sismik] *adj* seismic; **secousse s.** earth tremor

site [sit] *nm* (*endroit*) site; (*pittoresque*) beauty spot; **s. touristique** place of interest; **s. classé** conservation area; *Ordinat* **s. Web** website

sitôt [sito] *adv* **s. que...** as soon as...; **s. levée, elle partit** as soon as she was up, she left; **pas de s.** not for some time

situation [sitɥɑsjɔ̃] *nf* situation, position; *(emploi)* position; **s. de famille** marital status ■ **situé, -e** *adj (maison)* situated (à in) ■ **situer 1** *vt (placer)* to situate; *(trouver)* to locate; *(dans le temps)* to set **2 se situer** *vpr (se trouver)* to be situated

six [sis] ([si] *before consonant,* [siz] *before vowel) adj & nm inv* six ■ **sixième** [sizjɛm] **1** *adj & nmf* sixth; **un s.** a sixth **2** *nf Scol Br* ≃ first form, *Am* ≃ sixth grade

sketch [skɛtʃ] *(pl* **sketches**) *nm* sketch

ski [ski] *nm (objet)* ski; *(sport)* skiing; **faire du s.** to ski; **s. alpin** downhill skiing; **s. de fond** cross-country skiing; **s. nautique** water skiing ■ **skiable** *adj (piste)* skiable, fit for skiing ■ **skier** *vi* to ski ■ **skieur, -euse** *nmf* skier

slalom [slalɔm] *nm Sport* slalom

slave [slav] **1** *adj* Slav; *(langue)* Slavonic **2** *nmf* **S.** Slav

slip [slip] *nm (d'homme)* briefs, underpants; *(de femme)* panties, *Br* knickers

slogan [slɔgɑ̃] *nm* slogan

Slovaquie [slɔvaki] *nf* **la S.** Slovakia

Slovénie [slɔveni] *nf* **la S.** Slovenia

SMIC [smik] *(abrév* **salaire minimum interprofessionnel de croissance)** *nm* guaranteed minimum wage

smoking [smɔkiŋ] *nm (veston, costume)* dinner jacket, *Am* tuxedo

SNCF [ɛsɛnseɛf] *(abrév* **Société nationale des chemins de fer français)** *nf* = French national railway company

snob [snɔb] **1** *adj* snobbish **2** *nmf* snob ■ **snobisme** *nm* snobbery

sobre [sɔbr] *adj* sober ■ **sobriété** *nf* sobriety

sociable [sɔsjabl] *adj* sociable ■ **sociabilité** *nf* sociability

social, -e, -aux, -ales [sɔsjal, -o] *adj* social ■ **socialisme** *nm* socialism ■ **socialiste** *adj & nmf* socialist

société [sɔsjete] *nf (communauté)* society; *(compagnie)* company; **s. anonyme** *Br* (public) limited company, *Am* corporation ■ **sociétaire** *nmf (membre)* member

sociologie [sɔsjɔlɔʒi] *nf* sociology ■ **sociologique** *adj* sociological ■ **sociologue** *nmf* sociologist

sœur [sœr] *nf* sister; *(religieuse)* sister, nun

sofa [sɔfa] *nm* sofa, settee

soi [swa] *pron personnel* oneself; **chacun pour s.** every man for himself; **chez s.** at home; **cela va de soi** it's self-evident (**que** that) ■ **soi-même** *pron* oneself

soi-disant [swadizɑ̃] **1** *adj inv* socalled **2** *adv* supposedly

soie [swa] *nf (tissu)* silk

soient [swa] *voir* **être**

soif [swaf] *nf* thirst (**de** for); **avoir s.** to be thirsty

soigner [swaɲe] **1** *vt* to look after, to take care of; *(sujet: médecin)* (malade, maladie) to treat; *(présentation, travail)* to take care over; **se faire s.** to have (medical) treatment **2 se soigner** *vpr* to take care of oneself, to look after oneself ■ **soigné, -e** *adj (personne, vêtement)* neat, tidy; *(travail)* careful

soigneux, -euse [swaɲø, -øz] *adj (attentif)* careful (**de** with); *(propre)* neat, tidy

soin [swɛ̃] *nm (attention)* care; *Méd* **soins** treatment, care; **avoir** *ou* **prendre s. de qch/de faire qch** to take care of sth/to do sth; **avec s.** carefully, with care

soir [swar] *nm* evening; **le s.** *(chaque soir)* in the evening(s); **à neuf heures du s.** at nine in the evening; **repas du s.** evening meal

soirée [sware] *nf* evening; *(réunion)* party

sois, soit¹ [swa] *voir* **être**

soit² **1** [swa] *conj (à savoir)* that is (to say); **s.... s....** either... or... **2** [swat] *adv (oui)* very well

soixante [swasɑ̃t] *adj & nm inv* sixty

■ **soixantaine** *nf* une s. (de) *(nombre)* (about) sixty; **avoir la s.** *(âge)* to be about sixty

soixante-dix [swasɑ̃tdis] *adj & nm inv* seventy ■ **soixante-dixième** *adj & nmf* seventieth

soixantième [swasɑ̃tjem] *adj & nmf* sixtieth

soja [sɔʒa] *nm (plante)* soya; **germes** *ou* **pousses de s.** beansprouts

sol¹ [sɔl] *nm* ground; *(plancher)* floor; *(territoire, terrain)* soil

sol² [sɔl] *nm inv (note)* G

solaire [sɔlɛr] *adj* solar; **huile s.** sun(-tan) oil

soldat [sɔlda] *nm* soldier

solde [sɔld] 1 *nm (de compte, à payer)* balance; **en s.** *(acheter)* in the sales, *Am* on sale; **soldes** *(marchandises)* sale goods; *(vente)* (clearance)sale(s) 2 *nf (de soldat)* pay

solder [sɔlde] 1 *vt (articles)* to clear, to sell off; *(compte)* to pay the balance of 2 **se solder** *vpr* **se s. par un échec** to end in failure ■ **soldé, -e** *adj (article)* reduced

sole [sɔl] *nf (poisson)* sole

soleil [sɔlɛj] *nm* sun; *(chaleur, lumière)* sunshine; **au s.** in the sun; **il fait s.** it's sunny

solennel, -elle [sɔlanɛl] *adj* solemn

solidaire [sɔlidɛr] *adj* **être s.** *(ouvriers)* to show solidarity (**de** with) ■ **solidarité** *nf (entre personnes)* solidarity

solide [sɔlid] 1 *adj (objet, état)* solid; *(amitié)* strong; *(nerfs)* sound; *(personne)* sturdy 2 *nm (corps)* solid ■ **solidité** *nf (d'objet)* solidity

soliste [sɔlist] *nmf Mus* soloist

solitaire [sɔlitɛr] 1 *adj (par choix)* solitary; *(involontairement)* lonely 2 *nmf* loner; **en s.** on one's own ■ **solitude** *nf* solitude; **aimer la s.** to like being alone

solliciter [sɔlisite] *vt (audience)* to request; *(emploi)* to apply for; **s. qn** *(faire appel à)* to appeal to sb (**de faire** to do) ■ **sollicitation** *nf* request

sollicitude [sɔlisityd] *nf* solicitude, concern

soluble [sɔlybl] *adj (substance, problème)* soluble

solution [sɔlysjɔ̃] *nf (de problème)* solution (**de** to); *(mélange chimique)* solution

sombre [sɔ̃br] *adj* dark; *(triste)* sombre, gloomy; **il fait s.** it's dark

sombrer [sɔ̃bre] *vi (bateau)* to sink; *Fig* **s. dans** *(folie, sommeil)* to sink into

sommaire [sɔmɛr] 1 *adj* summary; *(repas)* basic 2 *nm (table des matières)* contents

somme [sɔm] 1 *nf* sum; **faire la s. de** to add up; **en s., s. toute** in short 2 *nm (sommeil)* nap; **faire un s.** to have a nap

sommeil [sɔmɛj] *nm* sleep; **avoir s.** to feel sleepy; **être en plein s.** to be fast asleep ■ **sommeiller** *vi* to doze

sommelier [sɔmalje] *nm* wine waiter

sommer [sɔme] *vt* **s. qn de faire qch** to summon sb to do sth

sommes [sɔm] *voir* **être**

sommet [sɔme] *nm* top; *(de montagne)* summit, top

sommier [sɔmje] *nm (de lit)* base

sommité [sɔmite] *nf* leading light (**de** in)

somnambule [sɔmnɑ̃byl] *nmf* sleepwalker; **être s.** to sleepwalk

somnifère [sɔmnifɛr] *nm* sleeping pill

somnoler [sɔmnɔle] *vi* to doze

somptueux, -euse [sɔ̃ptɥø, -øz] *adj* sumptuous

son¹ [sɔ̃] *nm (bruit)* sound

son² [sɔ̃] *nm (de grains)* bran

son³, sa, ses [sɔ̃, sa, se]

sa becomes **son** [sɔ̃n] before a vowel or mute h.

adj possessif (d'homme) his; *(de femme)* her; *(de chose)* its; *(indéfini)* one's; **s. père/sa mère** his/her/one's father/mother; **s. ami(e)** his/her/one's friend

sondage [sɔ̃daʒ] *nm (de terrain)* drilling; **s. (d'opinion)** opinion poll

sonder [sɔ̃de] *vt (rivière)* to sound; *(terrain)* to drill; *Fig (personne, l'opinion)* to sound out

songe [sɔ̃ʒ] *nm* dream

songer [sɔ̃ʒe] **1** *vi* s. à qch/à faire qch to think of sth/of doing sth **2** *vt* s. que… to think that… ■ **songeur, -euse** *adj* thoughtful, pensive

sonner [sɔne] **1** *vi* to ring; (*cor, cloches*) to sound; **on a sonné (à la porte)** there's someone at the door **2** *vt* (*cloche*) to ring; (*domestique*) to ring for; (*cor*) to sound; (*l'heure*) to strike

sonnerie [sɔnri] *nf* (*son*) ring(ing); (*de cor*) sound; (*appareil*) bell; (*de téléphone*) *Br* ringing tone, *Am* ring

sonnette [sɔnɛt] *nf* bell; **coup de s.** ring; **s. d'alarme** alarm (bell)

sonore [sɔnɔr] *adj* (*rire*) loud; (*voix*) resonant; **effet s.** sound effect ■ **sonorité** *nf* (*de salle*) acoustics; (*de violon*) tone

sont [sɔ̃] *voir* **être**

sophistiqué, -e [sɔfistike] *adj* sophisticated

soporifique [sɔpɔrifik] *adj* (*médicament, discours*) soporific

sorbet [sɔrbɛ] *nm* sorbet

sorcellerie [sɔrsɛlri] *nf* witchcraft, sorcery ■ **sorcier** *nm* sorcerer ■ **sorcière** *nf* witch

sordide [sɔrdid] *adj* (*acte, affaire*) sordid; (*maison*) squalid

sort [sɔr] *nm* (*destin*) fate; (*condition*) lot; (*maléfice*) spell

sortant, -e [sɔrtɑ̃, -ɑ̃t] *adj* (*numéro*) winning; (*député*) outgoing

sorte [sɔrt] *nf* sort, kind (**de** of); **toutes sortes de** all sorts *or* kinds of; **en quelque s.** in a way, as it were; **de (telle) s. que tu apprennes** so that *or* in such a way that you may learn; **faire en s. que…** (+ *subjunctive*) to see to it that…

sortie [sɔrti] *nf* (*porte*) exit, way out; (*action de sortir*) leaving, exit, departure; (*promenade*) walk; (*de film, de disque*) release; (*de livre*) appearance; **être de s.** to be out; **s. de bain** bathrobe; **s. de secours** emergency exit

sortir* [sɔrtir] **1** (*aux* **être**) *vi* to go out, to leave; (*pour s'amuser*) to go out; (*film*) to come out; (*numéro gagnant*) to come up; **s. de** (*endroit*) to leave; (*université*) to be a graduate of; (*famille, milieu*) to come from; (*rails*) to come off; **s. de l'ordinaire** to be out of the ordinary

2 (*aux* **avoir**) *vt* to take out (**de** of); (*film, livre*) to bring out

3 se sortir *vpr* **s'en s.** (*malade*) to pull through

SOS [ɛsoɛs] *nm* SOS; **lancer un SOS** to send (out) an SOS

sosie [sɔzi] *nm* double

sottise [sɔtiz] *nf* foolishness; (*action, parole*) foolish thing

souche [suʃ] *nf* (*d'arbre*) stump; (*de carnet*) stub, counterfoil; (*de virus*) strain

souci [susi] *nm* (*inquiétude*) worry, concern; (*préoccupation*) concern (**de** for); **se faire du s.** to worry, to be worried ■ **se soucier** *vpr* **se s. de** to be worried *or* concerned about ■ **soucieux, -euse** *adj* worried, concerned (**de qch** about sth)

soucoupe [sukup] *nf* saucer

soudain, -e [sudɛ̃, -ɛn] **1** *adj* sudden **2** *adv* suddenly ■ **soudaineté** *nf* suddenness

Soudan [sudɑ̃] *nm* **le S.** Sudan

souder [sude] **1** *vt* (*par alliage*) to solder; (*par soudure autogène*) to weld; **lampe à s.** blowlamp **2 se souder** *vpr* (*os*) to knit (together) ■ **soudure** *nf* (*par alliage*) soldering; (*autogène*) welding

souffle [sufl] *nm* (*d'air, de vent*) breath, puff; (*respiration*) breathing; (*de bombe*) blast; **reprendre son s.** to get one's breath back ■ **souffler 1** *vi* to blow; (*haleter*) to puff; **laisser s. qn** (*se reposer*) to give sb time to catch his/her breath **2** *vt* (*bougie*) to blow out; (*fumée, verre*) to blow; (*faire exploser*) to blast; (*chuchoter*) to whisper

souffrance [sufrɑ̃s] *nf* suffering; **en s.** (*colis*) unclaimed

souffrir* [sufrir] *vi* to suffer; **s. de** to suffer from; **faire s. qn** (*physiquement*)

souhait [swɛ] *nm* wish; **à vos souhaits!** *(après un éternuement)* bless you! ■ **souhaitable** *adj* desirable ■ **souhaiter** *vt (bonheur)* to wish for; **s. qch à qn** to wish sb sth; **s. faire qch** to hope to do sth; **s. que...** *(+ subjunctive)* to hope that...

soûl, -e [su, sul] **1** *adj* drunk **2** *nm* **tout son s.** *(boire)* to one's heart's content ■ **se soûler** *upr* to get drunk

soulager [sulaʒe] *vt* to relieve (**de** of) ■ **soulagement** *nm* relief

soulever [sulve] **1** *vt* to lift (up); *(question)* to raise **2 se soulever** *upr (personne)* to lift oneself (up); *(se révolter)* to rise up ■ **soulèvement** [-ɛvmɑ̃] *nm (révolte)* uprising

soulier [sulje] *nm* shoe

souligner [suliɲe] *vt (d'un trait)* to underline; *(faire remarquer)* to emphasize

soumettre* [sumɛtr] **1** *vt (pays, rebelles)* to subdue; *(rapport, demande)* to submit (**à** to); **s. qn à** *(assujettir)* to subject sb to **2 se soumettre** *upr* to submit (**à** to) ■ **soumis, -e** *adj (docile)* submissive; **s. à** subject to ■ **soumission** *nf (à une autorité)* submission; *(docilité)* submissiveness

soupçon [supsɔ̃] *nm* suspicion; **au-dessus de tout s.** above suspicion ■ **soupçonner** *vt* to suspect (**de** of; **d'avoir fait** of doing) ■ **soupçonneux, -euse** *adj* suspicious

soupe [sup] *nf* soup; **s. populaire** soup kitchen ■ **soupière** *nf* (soup) tureen

souper [supe] **1** *nm* supper **2** *vi* to have supper

soupir [supir] *nm* sigh ■ **soupirer** *vi* to sigh

souple [supl] *adj (corps, personne)* supple; *(branche)* flexible ■ **souplesse** *nf (de corps)* suppleness; *(de branche)* flexibility

source [surs] *nf* (**a**) *(point d'eau)* spring; **prendre sa s.** *(rivière)* to rise (**à** at) (**b**) *(origine)* source

sourcil [sursi] *nm* eyebrow ■ **sourciller** *vi Fig* **ne pas s.** not to bat an eyelid

sourd, -e [sur, surd] **1** *adj (personne)* deaf (**à** to); *(douleur)* dull; **bruit s.** thump **2** *nmf* deaf person ■ **sourd-muet, sourde-muette** *(mpl* **sourds-muets,** *fpl* **sourdes-muettes)* **1** *adj* deaf-and-dumb **2** *nmf* deaf mute

sourire* [surir] **1** *nm* smile; **faire un s. à qn** to give sb a smile **2** *vi* to smile (**à** at)

souris [suri] *nf (animal)* & *Ordinat* mouse *(pl* mice)

sournois, -e [surnwa, -waz] *adj* sly, underhand

sous [su] *prép (position)* under, underneath, beneath; *(rang)* under; **s. la pluie** in the rain; **nager s. l'eau** to swim underwater; **s. le nom de** under the name of; **s. Charles X** under Charles X; **s. peu** *(bientôt)* shortly

sous-bois [subwa] *nm* undergrowth

sous-chef [suʃɛf] *(pl* **sous-chefs)** *nmf* second-in-command

souscrire* [suskrir] *vi* **s. à** *(payer, approuver)* to subscribe to ■ **souscription** *nf* subscription

sous-développé, -e [sudevlɔpe] *(mpl* **sous-développés,** *fpl* **sous-développées)** *adj (pays)* underdeveloped

sous-directeur, -trice [sudirɛktœr, -tris] *(pl* **sous-directeurs)** *nmf* assistant manager

sous-entendre [suzɑ̃tɑ̃dr] *vt* to imply ■ **sous-entendu** [suzɑ̃tɑ̃dy] *(pl* **sous-entendus)** *nm* insinuation

sous-estimer [suzɛstime] *vt* to underestimate

sous-jacent, -e [suʒasɑ̃, -ɑ̃t] *(mpl* **sous-jacents,** *fpl* **sous-jacentes)** *adj* underlying

sous-louer [sulwe] *vt (sujet: locataire)* to sublet

sous-marin, -e [sumarɛ̃, -in] *(mpl* **sous-marins,** *fpl* **sous-marines)** **1** *adj* underwater **2** *nm* submarine

sous-préfet [suprefɛ] *(pl* **sous-préfets)** *nm* subprefect ■ **sous-préfecture** *nf* subprefecture

soussigné, -e [susiɲe] *adj & nmf* undersigned; **je s.** I the undersigned

sous-sol [susɔl] (*pl* **sous-sols**) *nm* (*d'immeuble*) basement; *Géol* subsoil

sous-titre [sutitr] (*pl* **sous-titres**) *nm* subtitle

soustraire* [sustrɛr] **1** *vt* to remove; *Math* to take away, to subtract (**de** from); **s. qn à** (*danger*) to shield *or* protect sb from **2 se soustraire** *upr* **se s. à** to escape from; (*devoir, obligation*) to avoid ■ **soustraction** *nf Math* subtraction

soustraitant [sutretɑ̃] *nm* subcontractor

sous-vêtement [suvɛtmɑ̃] *nm* undergarment; **sous-vêtements** underwear

soutenir* [sutnir] *vt* to support, to hold up; (*candidat*) to back; (*thèse*) to defend; (*regard*) to hold; **s. que...** to maintain that... ■ **soutenu, -e** *adj* (*attention, effort*) sustained

souterrain, -e [suterɛ̃, -ɛn] **1** *adj* underground **2** *nm* underground passage

soutien [sutjɛ̃] *nm* support; (*personne*) supporter ■ **soutien-gorge** (*pl* **soutiens-gorge**) *nm* bra

soutirer [sutire] *vt* **s. qch à qn** to extract sth from sb

souvenir¹ [suvnir] *nm* memory, recollection; (*objet*) memento; (*cadeau*) keepsake; (*pour touristes*) souvenir; **en s. de** in memory of

souvenir²* [suvnir] **se souvenir** *upr* **se s. de qn/qch** to remember sb/sth; **se s. que...** to remember that...

souvent [suvɑ̃] *adv* often; **peu s.** seldom; **le plus s.** usually, more often than not

souverain, -e [suvərɛ̃, -ɛn] *nmf* sovereign ■ **souveraineté** *nf* sovereignty

soviétique [sɔvjetik] *Anciennement* **1** *adj* Soviet; **l'Union s.** the Soviet Union **2** *nmf* Soviet citizen

soyeux, -euse [swajø, -øz] *adj* silky

soyons, soyez [swajɔ̃, swaje] *voir* **être**

spacieux, -euse [spasjø, -øz] *adj* spacious, roomy

spaghettis [spageti] *nmpl* spaghetti

sparadrap [sparadra] *nm* (*pour pansement*) *Br* sticking plaster, *Am* adhesive tape

spatial, -e, -aux, -ales [spasjal, -o] *adj* **station spatiale** space station; **engin s.** spaceship, spacecraft

spécial, -e, -aux, -ales [spesjal, -o] *adj* special; (*bizarre*) peculiar ■ **spécialement** *adv* (*exprès*) specially; (*en particulier*) especially, particularly

spécialiser [spesjalize] **se spécialiser** *upr* to specialize (**dans** in) ■ **spécialisation** *nf* specialization ■ **spécialiste** *nmf* specialist ■ **spécialité** *nf Br* speciality, *Am* specialty

spécifier [spesifje] *vt* to specify (**que** that)

spécifique [spesifik] *adj* specific

spécimen [spesimɛn] *nm* specimen; (*livre*) specimen copy

spectacle [spektakl] *nm* (**a**) (*vue*) sight, spectacle (**b**) (*représentation*) show; **le s.** (*industrie*) show business ■ **spectateur, -trice** *nmf* spectator; (*au théâtre, au cinéma*) member of the audience; **spectateurs** (*au théâtre, au cinéma*) audience

spectaculaire [spektakylɛr] *adj* spectacular

spéculer [spekyle] *vi* to speculate ■ **spéculateur, -trice** *nmf* speculator ■ **spéculation** *nf* speculation

spéléologie [speleɔlɔʒi] *nf* (*activité*) *Br* potholing, caving, *Am* spelunking

sphère [sfer] *nf* (*boule, domaine*) sphere

spirituel, -elle [spiritɥɛl] *adj* (*amusant*) witty; (*pouvoir, vie*) spiritual

spiritueux [spiritɥø] *nmpl* (*boissons*) spirits

splendide [splɑ̃did] *adj* splendid ■ **splendeur** *nf* splendour

spontané, -e [spɔ̃tane] *adj* spontaneous ■ **spontanéité** *nf* spontaneity

sport [spɔr] *nm* sport; **faire du s.** to play *Br* sport *or Am* sports; **voiture/**

terrain de s. sports car/ground; **sports de combat** combat sports; **sports d'équipe** team sports; **sports d'hiver** winter sports; **aller aux sports d'hiver** to go skiing; **sports mécaniques** motor sports *(ort land, in the air, on water)* ■ **sportif, -ive 1** *adj (personne)* fond of *Br* sports or *Am* sports; *(esprit)* sporting; *(association, journal, résultats)* sports, sporting; *(allure)* athletic **2** *nmf* sportsman, *f* sportswoman

spot [spɔt] *nm (lampe)* spotlight; **s. publicitaire** commercial

square [skwar] *nm* public garden

squash [skwaʃ] *nm (jeu)* squash

squatter 1 [skwate] *vi* to squat **2** [skwatœr] *nm* squatter ■ **squatteur, -euse** *nmf* squatter

squelette [skəlɛt] *nm* skeleton

stable [stabl] *adj* stable ■ **stabiliser** *vt*, **se stabiliser** *vpr* to stabilize ■ **stabilité** *nf* stability

stade [stad] *nm Sport* stadium; *(phase)* stage

stage [staʒ] *nm (période)* training period; *(cours)* (training) course; **faire un s.** to undergo training; **être en s.** to be on a training course ■ **stagiaire** *adj & nmf* trainee

stagner [stagne] *vi* to stagnate

stand [stãd] *nm (d'exposition)* stand, stall; **s. de tir** *(de foire)* shooting range

standard [stãdar] **1** *nm (téléphonique)* switchboard **2** *adj inv (modèle)* standard ■ **standardiste** *nmf* (switchboard) operator

standing [stãdiŋ] *nm* standing, status; **immeuble de (grand) s.** *Br* luxury block of flats, *Am* luxury apartment building

station [stasjõ] *nf (de métro, d'observation, de radio)* station; *(de ski)* resort; *(d'autobus)* stop; **s. de taxis** *Br* taxi rank, *Am* taxi stand ■ **station-service** *(pl* **stations-service***)* *nf* service station, *Br* petrol or *Am* gas station

stationnaire [stasjɔnɛr] *adj* stationary

stationner [stasjɔne] *vi (être garé)* to be parked ■ **stationnement** *nm* parking

statistique [statistik] **1** *adj* statistical **2** *nf (donnée)* statistic; **la s.** *(science)* statistics *(sing)*

statue [staty] *nf* statue

statut [staty] *nm (position)* status; **statuts** *(règles)* statutes

steak [stɛk] *nm* steak

sténographie [stenɔgrafi] *nf* shorthand, stenography

stéréo [stereo] *nf* stereo; **en s.** in stereo ■ **stéréophonique** *adj* stereophonic

stéréotype [stereɔtip] *nm* stereotype ■ **stéréotypé, -e** *adj* stereotyped

stérile [steril] *adj* sterile; *(terre)* barren ■ **stérilisation** *nf* sterilization ■ **stériliser** *vt* to sterilize ■ **stérilité** *nf* sterility; *(de terre)* barrenness

stéthoscope [stetɔskɔp] *nm* stethoscope

steward [stiwart] *nm (d'avion, de bateau)* steward

stigmatiser [stigmatize] *vt (dénoncer)* to stigmatize

stimuler [stimyle] *vt* to stimulate ■ **stimulation** *nf* stimulation

stimulus [stimylys] *(pl* **stimuli** [-li]*)* *nm (physiologique)* stimulus

stipuler [stipyle] *vt* to stipulate (**que** that)

stock [stɔk] *nm* stock (**de** of); **en s.** in stock ■ **stockage** *nm* stocking ■ **stocker** *vt (provisions)* to stock

stop [stɔp] **1** *exclam* stop **2** *nm Aut (panneau)* stop sign; *(feu arrière)* brake light, *Br* stoplight ■ **stopper** *vti* to stop

stratagème [strataʒɛm] *nm* stratagem, ploy

stratège [strateʒ] *nm* strategist ■ **stratégie** *nf* strategy ■ **stratégique** *adj* strategic

stress [strɛs] *nm inv* stress ■ **stressant, -e** *adj* stressful ■ **stressé, -e** *adj* under stress

strict, -e [strikt] *adj (principes, professeur)* strict; *(tenue)* plain; **le s.**

minimum the bare minimum ■ **strictement** [-əmɑ̃] *adv* strictly; *(vêtu)* plainly

strident, -e [stridɑ̃, -ɑ̃t] *adj* shrill, strident

structure [stryktyr] *nf* structure ■ **structural, -e, -aux, -ales** *adj* structural ■ **structurer** *vt* to structure

studieux, -euse [stydjø, -øz] *adj* studious; *(vacances)* devoted to study

studio [stydjo] *nm (de cinéma, de télévision, de peintre)* studio; *(logement)* Br studio flat, Am studio apartment

stupéfait, -e [stypefɛ, -ɛt] *adj* amazed, astounded (**de** at *or* by) ■ **stupéfaction** *nf* amazement

stupéfier [stypefje] *vt* to amaze, to astound ■ **stupéfiant, -e 1** *adj* amazing, astounding **2** *nm* drug, narcotic

stupeur [stypœr] *nf (étonnement)* amazement; *(inertie)* stupor

stupide [stypid] *adj* stupid ■ **stupidité** *nf* stupidity; *(action, parole)* stupid thing

style [stil] *nm* style; **meubles de s.** period furniture ■ **stylé, -e** *adj* welltrained ■ **styliste** *nmf (de mode)* designer ■ **stylistique** *adj* stylistic

stylo [stilo] *nm* pen; **s. à bille** ballpoint (pen), *Br* biro®; **s. à encre, s.-plume** fountain pen

su, -e [sy] *pp de* **savoir**

subdiviser [sybdivize] *vt* to subdivide (**en** into) ■ **subdivision** *nf* subdivision

subir [sybir] *vt* to undergo; *(conséquences, défaite, perte, tortures)* to suffer; *(influence)* to be under; **faire s. qch à qn** to subject sb to sth

subit, -e [sybi, -it] *adj* sudden

subjectif, -ive [sybʒɛktif, -iv] *adj* subjective ■ **subjectivité** *nf* subjectivity

subjuguer [sybʒyge] *vt* to subjugate, to subdue; *(envoûter)* to captivate

sublime [syblim] *adj & nm* sublime

submerger [sybmɛrʒe] *vt* to submerge; *Fig (envahir)* to overwhelm; *Fig* **submergé de travail** snowed under with work

submersible [sybmɛrsibl] *nm* submarine

subside [sypsid] *nm* grant, subsidy

subsistance [sybzistɑ̃s] *nf* subsistence

subsister [sybziste] **1** *vi (chose)* to remain; *(personne)* to subsist **2** *v impersonnel* to remain; **il subsiste un doute** there remains some doubt

substance [sypstɑ̃s] *nf* substance; *Fig* **en s.** in essence ■ **substantiel, -elle** *adj* substantial

substituer [sypstitɥe] **1** *vt* to substitute (**à** for) **2 se substituer** *vpr* **se s. à qn** to take the place of sb, to substitute for sb ■ **substitution** *nf* substitution; **produit de s.** substitute (product)

substitut [sypstity] *nm (produit)* substitute (**de** for); *(magistrat)* deputy public prosecutor

subtil, -e [syptil] *adj* subtle ■ **subtilité** *nf* subtlety

subvenir* [sybvənir] *vi* **s. à** *(besoins, frais)* to meet

subvention [sybvɑ̃sjɔ̃] *nf* subsidy ■ **subventionner** *vt* to subsidize

subversif, -ive [sybvɛrsif, -iv] *adj* subversive ■ **subversion** *nf* subversion

suc [syk] *nm (gastrique, de fruit)* juice; *(de plante)* sap

succéder [syksede] **1** *vi* **s. à qn** to succeed sb; **s. à qch** to follow sth, to come after sth **2 se succéder** *vpr (choses, personnes)* to follow one another

succès [syksɛ] *nm* success; **s. de librairie** *(livre)* best-seller; **avoir du s.** to be successful; **à s.** *(auteur, film)* successful

successeur [syksɛsœr] *nm* successor ■ **successif, -ive** *adj* successive ■ **succession** *nf* succession (**de** of; **à** to); *(série)* sequence (**de** of); *(patrimoine)* inheritance, estate; **prendre la s. de qn** to succeed sb

succinct, -e [syksɛ̃, -ɛ̃t] *adj* succinct, brief

succomber [sykɔ̃be] *vi (mourir)* to die; **s. à** *(céder à)* to succumb to

succulent, -e [sykylã, -ãt] *adj* succulent

succursale [sykyrsal] *nf* (*de magasin*) branch; **magasin à succursales multiples** chain store

sucer [syse] *vt* to suck ■ **sucette** *nf* lollipop; (*tétine*) *Br* dummy, *Am* pacifier

sucre [sykr] *nm* sugar; (*morceau*) sugar lump; **s. en poudre, s. semoule** *Br* castor *or* caster sugar, *Am* finely ground sugar; **s. d'orge** barley sugar

sucrer [sykre] *vt* to sugar, to sweeten ■ **sucré, -e** *adj* sweet, sugary; (*artificiellement*) sweetened; *Fig* (*douceureux*) sugary, syrupy

sucrerie [sykrəri] *nf* (*usine*) sugar refinery; **sucreries** (*bonbons*) *Br* sweets, *Am* candy

sucrier [sykrije] *nm* (*récipient*) sugar bowl

sud [syd] **1** *nm* south; **au s.** in the south; (*direction*) (to the) south (**de** of); **du s.** (*vent, direction*) southerly; (*ville*) southern; (*gens*) from *or* in the south; **l'Afrique du S.** South Africa **2** *adj inv* (*côte*) south(ern) ■ **sud-africain, -e** (*mpl* **sud-africains,** *fpl* **sud-africaines**) **1** *adj* South African **2** *nmf* **S., S.-Africaine** South African ■ **sud-américain, -e** (*mpl* **sud-américains,** *fpl* **sud-américaines**) **1** *adj* South American **2** *nmf* **S., S.-Américaine** South American ■ **sud-est** *nm & adj inv* south-east ■ **sud-ouest** *nm & adj inv* south-west

Suède [syed] *nf* la S. Sweden ■ **suédois, -e 1** *adj* Swedish **2** *nmf* **S., Suédoise** Swede **3** *nm* (*langue*) Swedish

suer [sye] *vi* (*personne, mur*) to sweat ■ **sueur** *nf* sweat; (*tout*) **en s.** sweating

suffire* [syfir] **1** *vi* to be enough (**à** for); **ça suffit!** that's enough! **2** *v impersonnel* **il suffit de faire qch** one only has to do sth; **il suffit d'une goutte/d'une heure pour faire qch** a drop/an hour is enough to do sth **3 se suffire** *upr* **s. à soi-même** to be self-sufficient

suffisance [syfizãs] *nf* (*vanité*) conceit

suffisant, -e [syfizã, -ãt] *adj* (*satisfaisant*) sufficient, adequate; (*vaniteux*) conceited ■ **suffisamment** [-amã] *adv* sufficiently; **s. de** enough, sufficient

suffoquer [syfɔke] *vti* to choke, to suffocate

suffrage [syfraʒ] *nm Pol* (*voix*) vote; **s. universel** universal suffrage

suggérer [syɡʒere] *vt* (*proposer*) to suggest (**à** to; **de faire** que); **que** + *subjunctive* that) ■ **suggestif, -ive** *adj* suggestive ■ **suggestion** *nf* suggestion

suicide [sɥisid] *nm* suicide ■ **se suicider** *upr* to commit suicide

suie [sɥi] *nf* soot

suinter [sɥɛ̃te] *vi* to ooze ■ **suintement** *nm* oozing

suis [sɥi] *voir* **être, suivre**

Suisse [sɥis] *nf* la S. Switzerland; **S. allemande/romande** German-speaking/French-speaking Switzerland ■ **suisse 1** *adj* Swiss **2** *nmf* **S.** Swiss; **les Suisses** the Swiss ■ **Suissesse** *nf* Swiss *inv*

suite [sɥit] *nf* (*reste*) rest; (*continuation*) continuation; (*de film, de roman*) sequel; (*série*) series, sequence; (*appartement, escorte*) suite; (*cohérence*) order; **suites** (*séquelles*) effects; (*résultats*) consequences; **faire s. (à)** to follow; **donner s. à** (*demande*) to follow up; **par la s.** afterwards; **par s. de** as a result of; **à la s.** one after another; **à la s. de** (*derrière*) behind; (*événement, maladie*) as a result of; **de s.** (*deux jours*) in a row

suivant, -e [sɥivã, -ãt] **1** *adj* next, following; (*ci-après*) following **2** *nmf* next (one); **au s.!** next!, next person! ■ **suivant** *prép* (*selon*) according to

suivi, -e [sɥivi] *adj* (*régulier*) regular, steady; (*cohérent*) coherent; **peu/très s.** (*cours*) poorly/well attended

suivre* [sɥivr] **1** *vt* to follow; (*accompagner*) to go with, to accompany; (*cours*) to attend, to go to; **s.**

qn/qch des yeux *ou* **du regard** to watch sb/sth; **s. l'exemple de qn** to follow sb's example; **s. l'actualité** to follow events *or* the news **2** *vi* to follow; *(courrier, lettre)* to forward; **'à s.'** 'to be continued' **3 se suivre** *upr* to follow each other

sujet¹, -ette [syʒɛ, -ɛt] **1** *adj* **s. à** *(maladie)* subject to; **s. à caution** *(information, nouvelle)* unconfirmed **2** *nmf (personne)* subject

sujet² [syʒɛ] *nm* (**a**) *(question)* subject; *(d'examen)* question; **au s. de** about; **à quel s.?** about what? (**b**) *(raison)* cause; **sujet(s) de dispute** grounds for dispute (**c**) *(individu)* subject; **un brillant s.** a brilliant student

super [sypɛr] *nm (supercarburant)* Br four-star (petrol), Am premium *ou* high-test gas

superbe [sypɛrb] *adj* superb

supercherie [sypɛrʃəri] *nf* deception

supérette [sypɛrɛt] *nf* convenience store

superficie [sypɛrfisi] *nf* surface; *(dimensions)* area ■ **superficiel, -elle** *adj* superficial

superflu, -e [sypɛrfly] *adj* superfluous

supérieur, -e [sypɛrjœr] **1** *adj (étages, partie)* upper; *(qualité, air, ton)* superior; **à l'étage s.** on the floor above; **s. à** *(meilleur que)* superior to, better than; *(plus grand que)* above, greater than; **s. à la moyenne** above average; **études supérieures** higher *ou* university studies **2** *nmf* superior ■ **supériorité** *nf* superiority

supermarché [sypɛrmarʃe] *nm* supermarket

superposer [sypɛrpoze] *vt (objets)* to put on top of each other; *(images)* to superimpose

superproduction [sypɛrprodyksjõ] *nf (film)* blockbuster

superpuissance [sypɛrpɥisɑ̃s] *nf* Pol superpower

supersonique [sypɛrsonik] *adj* supersonic

superstar [sypɛrstar] *nf* superstar

superstitieux, -euse [sypɛrstisjø, -øz] *adj* superstitious ■ **superstition** *nf* superstition

superviser [sypɛrvize] *vt* to supervise

supplanter [syplɑ̃te] *vt* to take the place of

suppléer [syplee] *vi* **s. à** *(compenser)* to make up for ■ **suppléant, -e** *adj & nmf (personne)* substitute, replacement; **(professeur) s.** substitute *or* Br supply teacher

supplément [syplemɑ̃] *nm (argent)* extra charge, supplement; *(de revue, de livre)* supplement; **en s.** extra; **un s. de** *(information, de travail)* extra, additional ■ **supplémentaire** *adj* extra, additional

supplice [syplis] *nm* torture ■ **supplier** *vt* **s. qn de faire qch** to beg *or* implore sb to do sth; **je vous en supplie!** I beg *or* implore you!

support [sypor] *nm* support; *(d'instrument)* stand

supporter¹ [syporte] *vt (malheur, conséquences)* to bear, to endure; *(chaleur)* to withstand; **je ne peux pas la s.** I can't bear her ■ **supportable** *adj* bearable; *(excusable, passable)* tolerable

supporter² [syporter] *nm (de football)* supporter

supposer [sypoze] *vt* to suppose, to assume (**que** that); *(impliquer)* to imply (**que** that); **à s.** *ou* **en supposant que…** (+ *subjunctive*) supposing (that)… ■ **supposition** *nf* assumption, supposition

supprimer [syprime] **1** *vt* to get rid of, to remove; *(mot, passage)* to cut out, to delete; *(train)* to cancel; *(tuer)* to do away with; **s. des emplois** to axe jobs; **s. qch à qn** to take sth away from sb
2 se supprimer *upr (se suicider)* to do away with oneself ■ **suppression** *nf* removal; *(de mot)* deletion; *(de train)* cancellation; *(d'emplois)* axing

suprématie [sypremasi] *nf* supremacy

suprême [syprɛm] adj supreme

sur [syr] prép on, upon; (par-dessus) over; (au sujet de) on, about; **six s. dix** six out of ten; **un jour s. deux** every other day; **six mètres s. dix** six metres by ten; **s. votre gauche** to or on your left; **mettre/monter s. qch** to put/climb on (to) sth

sûr, -e [syr] adj sure, certain (**de** of; **que** that); (digne de confiance) reliable; (lieu) safe; (goût) discerning; (main) steady; **s. de soi** self-assured; **bien s.!** of course!

surcharge [syrʃarʒ] nf (**a**) (poids) excess weight; **s. de travail** extra work; **en s.** (passagers) extra (**b**) (correction) alteration; (à payer) surcharge ■ **surcharger** vt (voiture, personne) to overload (**de** with)

surchauffer [syrʃofe] vt to overheat

surcroît [syrkrwa] nm increase (**de** in); **de s., par s.** in addition

surdité [syrdite] nf deafness

surdose [syrdoz] nf (de drogue) overdose

surélever [syreleve] vt to raise

surestimer [syrɛstime] vt to overestimate; (tableau) to overvalue

sûreté [syrte] nf safety; (de l'État) security; (garantie) surety; (de geste) sureness; **être en s.** to be safe; **mettre qn/qch en s.** to put sb/sth in a safe place; **pour plus de s.** to be on the safe side

surexcité, -e [syrɛksite] adj overexcited

surf [sœrf] nm Sport surfing; **faire du s.** to surf, to go surfing ■ **surfer** vi **s. sur le Net** to surf the Net

surface [syrfas] nf surface; (étendue) (surface) area; **faire s.** (sous-marin) to surface; **(magasin à) grande s.** hypermarket; **de s.** (politesse) superficial

surfait, -e [syrfɛ, -ɛt] adj overrated

surgelé, -e [syrʒəle] adj frozen ■ **surgelés** nmpl frozen foods

surgir [syrʒir] vi to appear suddenly (**de** from)

surhomme [syrɔm] nm superman

■ **surhumain, -e** adj superhuman

sur-le-champ [syrləʃɑ̃] adv immediately

surlendemain [syrlɑ̃dəmɛ̃] nm **le s.** two days later; **le s. de** two days after

surligner [syrliɲe] vt to highlight ■ **surligneur** nm highlighter (pen)

surmener [syrməne] vt, **se surmener** vpr to overwork ■ **surmenage** nm overwork

surmonter [syrmɔ̃te] vt (être placé sur) to surmount; Fig (obstacle, peur) to overcome

surnaturel, -elle [syrnatyrɛl] adj & nm supernatural

surnom [syrnɔ̃] nm nickname

surpasser [syrpase] **1** vt to surpass (**en** in) **2 se surpasser** vpr to surpass oneself

surpeuplé, -e [syrpœple] adj overpopulated

surplomb [syrplɔ̃] nm **en s.** overhanging ■ **surplomber** vti to overhang

surplus [syrply] nm surplus

surprendre* [syrprɑ̃dr] vt (étonner) to surprise; (prendre sur le fait) to catch ■ **surprenant, -e** adj surprising ■ **surpris, -e** adj surprised (**de** at; **que** + subjunctive that); **je suis s. de te voir** I'm surprised to see you ■ **surprise** nf surprise; **prendre qn par s.** to catch sb unawares

surréaliste [syrrealist] adj (poète, peintre) surrealist

sursaut [syrso] nm (sudden) start ou jump; **se réveiller en s.** to wake up with a start ■ **sursauter** vi to jump, start

sursis [syrsi] nm (à l'armée) deferment; Fig (répit) reprieve; **un an (de prison) avec s.** a one-year suspended sentence

surtout [syrtu] adv especially; (avant tout) above all; **s. pas** certainly not

surveiller [syrveje] vt (garder) to watch, to keep an eye on; (contrôler) to supervise; (épier) to watch ■ **surveillance** nf watch (**sur** over); (de travaux, d'ouvriers) supervision; (de

police) surveillance ■ **surveillant, -e** nmf (de lycée) supervisor (in charge of discipline); (de prison) (prison) guard, Br warder

survenir* [syrvənir] vi to occur; (personne) to turn up

survêtement [syrvɛtmã] nm tracksuit

survie [syrvi] nf survival ■ **survivre*** vi to survive (à qch sth); **s. à qn** to outlive sb ■ **survivant, -e** nmf survivor

survoler [syrvɔle] vt to fly over; Fig (question) to skim over

susceptible [sysɛptibl] adj (ombrageux) touchy, sensitive; **s. de** (interprétations) open to; **s. de faire qch** likely ou liable to do sth; (capable) able to do sth ■ **susceptibilité** nf touchiness, sensitivity

susciter [sysite] vt (sentiment) to arouse; (ennuis, obstacles) to create

suspect, -e [syspɛ, -ɛkt] **1** adj suspicious, suspect; **s. de qch** suspected of sth **2** nmf suspect ■ **suspecter** vt (personne) to suspect (**de qch** of sth; **de faire** of doing)

suspendre [syspãdr] **1** vt (accrocher) to hang (up) (à on); (destituer, interrompre) to suspend **2 se suspendre** vpr **se s. à** to hang from ■ **suspendu, -e** adj **s. à** hanging from; **pont s.** suspension bridge

suspens [syspã] **en suspens** adv (affaire, travail) in abeyance; (en l'air) suspended

suspense [syspens] nm suspense

suspension [syspãsjɔ̃] nf (d'hostilités, d'employé, de véhicule) suspension

suspicion [syspisjɔ̃] nf suspicion

suture [sytyr] nf Méd **point de s.** stitch

SVP [ɛsvepe] (abrév **s'il vous plaît**) please

symbole [sɛ̃bɔl] nm symbol ■ **symbolique** adj symbolic; (salaire, cotisation, loyer) nominal; **geste s.** symbolic ou token gesture ■ **symboliser** vt to symbolize

sympathie [sɛ̃pati] nf (affinité) liking; (condoléances) sympathy; **avoir de la s. pour qn** to be fond of sb ■ **sympathique** adj nice; (accueil) friendly ■ **sympathiser** vi to get along well, Br to get on well (**avec** with)

symphonie [sɛ̃fɔni] nf symphony

symptôme [sɛ̃ptom] nm Méd & Fig symptom

synagogue [sinagɔg] nf synagogue

synchroniser [sɛ̃krɔnize] vt to synchronize

syndicat [sɛ̃dika] nm (d'ouvriers) (Br trade or Am labor) union; (de patrons) association; **s. d'initiative** tourist (information) office ■ **syndicaliste** nmf Br trade or Am labor unionist

syndiquer [sɛ̃dike] **1** vt to unionize **2 se syndiquer** vpr (adhérer) to join a (Br trade or Am labor) union ■ **syndiqué, -e** nmf (Br trade or Am labor) union member

syndrome [sɛ̃drom] nm Méd & Fig syndrome; **s. immunodéficitaire acquis** acquired immune deficiency syndrome

synthèse [sɛ̃tɛz] nf synthesis ■ **synthétique** adj synthetic

synthétiseur [sɛ̃tetizœr] nm synthesizer

Syrie [siri] nf la S. Syria ■ **syrien, -enne 1** adj Syrian **2** nmf **S., Syrienne** Syrian

système [sistɛm] nm (structure, réseau) & Anat system; Ordinat **s. d'exploitation** operating system ■ **systématique** adj systematic ■ **systématiquement** adv systematically

Tt

T, t [te] *nm inv* T, t

t' [t] *voir* **te**

ta [ta] *voir* **ton¹**

tabac [taba] *nm* tobacco; *(magasin)* *Br* tobacconist's (shop), *Am* tobacco store

table [tabl] *nf* (a) *(meuble)* table; *(d'école)* desk; **mettre/débarrasser la t.** to set *or Br* lay/clear the table; **être à t.** to be sitting at the table; **à t.!** food's ready!; **t. à repasser** ironing board; **t. de nuit/d'opération** bedside/operating table (b) *(liste)* table; **t. des matières** table of contents

tableau, -x [tablo] *nm* (a) *(peinture)* picture, painting; *(image, description)* picture; **t. de maître** *(peinture)* old master (b) *(panneau)* board; *(liste)* list; *(graphique)* chart; **t. (noir)** (black)board; **t. d'affichage** *Br* notice board, *Am* bulletin board

tabler [table] *vi* **t. sur qch** to count or rely on sth

tablette [tablɛt] *nf (de chocolat)* bar, slab; *(de lavabo)* shelf; *(de cheminée)* mantelpiece

tablier [tablije] *nm (vêtement)* apron; *(d'écolier)* smock

tabouret [taburɛ] *nm* stool

tache [taʃ] *nf* mark; *(salissure)* stain ■ **tacher** *vt*, **se tacher** *vpr (tissu)* to stain

tâche [taʃ] *nf* task, job; **tâches ménagères** housework

tâcher [taʃe] *vi* **t. de faire qch** to try or endeavour to do sth

tacheté, -e [taʃte] *adj* speckled (**de** with)

tact [takt] *nm* tact; **avoir du t.** to be tactful

tactique [taktik] **1** *adj* tactical **2** *nf* tactics *(sing)*; **une t.** a tactic

Tahiti [taiti] *nm* Tahiti ■ **tahitien, -enne** [taisjɛ̃, -ɛn] **1** *adj* Tahitian **2** *nmf* **T., Tahitienne** Tahitian

taillader [tajade] *vt* to gash

taille¹ [taj] *nf* (a) *(hauteur)* height; *(dimension, mesure)* size; **de haute t.** *(personne)* tall; **de petite t.** short; **de t. moyenne** medium-sized (b) *(ceinture)* waist; **tour de t.** waist measurement

taille² [taj] *nf* cutting; *(de haie)* trimming; *(d'arbre)* pruning ■ **tailler** *vt* to cut; *(haie, barbe)* to trim; *(arbre)* to prune; *(crayon)* to sharpen

taille-crayon [tajkrɛjɔ̃] *nm inv* pencil sharpener

tailleur [tajœr] *nm (personne)* tailor; *(costume)* suit

taire* [tɛr] **1** *vt* to say nothing about **2** *vi* **faire t. qn** to silence sb **3** **se taire** *vpr (ne rien dire)* to keep quiet (**sur qch** about sth); *(cesser de parler)* to stop talking, to fall silent; **tais-toi!** be quiet!

Taiwan [tajwan] *nm ou f* Taiwan

talc [talk] *nm* talcum powder

talent [talɑ̃] *nm* talent; **avoir du t.** to be talented ■ **talentueux, -euse** *adj* talented

talkie-walkie [talkiwalki] *nm (pl talkies-walkies)* *nm* walkie-talkie

talon [talɔ̃] *nm* (a) *(de chaussure)* heel; **(chaussures à) talons hauts** high heels, high-heeled shoes; **talons**

aiguilles stiletto heels (**b**) *(de chèque)* stub, counterfoil

tambour [tãbur] *nm (de machine, instrument de musique)* drum ■ **tambourin** *nm* tambourine

Tamise [tamiz] *nf* **la T.** the Thames

tamiser [tamize] *vt (farine)* to sift; *(lumière)* to filter

tampon [tãpɔ̃] *nm* (**a**) *(marque, instrument)* stamp; **t. encreur** ink pad (**b**) *(bouchon)* plug, stopper; *(de coton)* wad, pad; *(pour pansement)* swab; **t. hygiénique** tampon (**c**) *(de train)* and *Fig* buffer; **état t.** buffer state

tamponner [tãpɔne] **1** *vt (lettre, document)* to stamp; *(visage)* to dab; *(plaie)* to swab; *(train, voiture)* to crash into **2 se tamponner** *upr* to crash into each other ■ **tamponneuses** *adj fpl* **autos t.** Dodgems®

tandem [tãdɛm] *nm (bicyclette)* tandem; *Fig (duo)* duo

tandis [tãdi] **tandis que** *conj (simultanéité)* while; *(contraste)* whereas, while

tanière [tanjɛr] *nf* den, lair

tank [tãk] *nm* tank

tanker [tãkɛr] *nm (navire)* tanker

tanner [tane] *vt (cuir)* to tan ■ **tanné, -e** *adj (visage)* weather-beaten

TANT [tã] *adv (travailler)* so much (**que** that); **t. de** *(pain, temps)* so much (**que** that); *(gens, choses)* so many (**que** that); **t. de fois** so often, so many times; **t. que** *(autant que)* as much as; *(aussi fort que)* as hard as; *(aussi longtemps que)* as long as; **en t. que** *(considéré comme)* as; **t. mieux!** so much the better!; **t. pis!** too bad!, pity!; **t. soit peu pour toi!** good for you!; **t. soit peu** *(même)* remotely *or* slightly; **un t. soit peu** somewhat; **t. s'en faut** far from it

tante [tãt] *nf* aunt

tantinet [tãtinɛ] *nm & adv* **un t.** a tiny bit (**de** of)

tantôt [tãto] *adv* (**a**) **t....t....** sometimes... sometimes... (**b**) *(cet après-midi)* this afternoon

taon [tã] *nm* horsefly, gadfly

tapage [tapaʒ] *nm* din, uproar ■ **tapageur, -euse** *adj (bruyant)* rowdy; *(criard)* flashy

tape [tap] *nf* slap

taper [tape] **1** *vt (frapper)* to hit; *(marteler)* to bang; **t. qch à la machine** to type sth **2** *vi (soleil)* to beat down; **t. du pied** to stamp one's foot; **t. à la machine** to type; **t. sur qch** to bang on sth ■ **tapant, -e** *adj* **à huit heures tapantes** at eight sharp

tapis [tapi] *nm* carpet; **envoyer qn au t.** *(abattre)* to floor sb; **mettre qch sur le t.** *(sujet)* to bring sth up for discussion; **t. de bain** bath mat; **t. roulant** *(pour marchandises)* conveyor belt; *(pour personnes)* moving walkway

tapisser [tapise] *vt (mur)* to (wall)paper ■ **tapisserie** *nf (papier peint)* wallpaper; *(broderie)* tapestry

tapoter [tapɔte] **1** *vt* to tap; *(joue)* to pat **2** *vi* **t. sur** to tap (on)

taquin, -e [takɛ̃, -in] *adj* teasing ■ **taquiner** *vt* to tease ■ **taquineries** *nfpl* teasing

tard [tar] *adv* late; **plus t.** later (on); **au plus t.** at the latest; **sur le t.** late in life

tarder [tarde] **1** *vi (lettre, saison)* to be a long time coming; **sans t.** without delay; **t. à faire qch** to take one's time doing sth; **elle ne va pas t.** she won't be long **2** *v impersonnel* **il me tarde de le faire** I long to do it

tardif, -ive [tardif, -iv] *adj* late; *(regrets)* belated ■ **tardivement** *adv* late

tare [tar] *nf (poids)* tare; *Fig (défaut)* defect

targuer [targe] **se targuer** *upr* **se t. de faire qch** to pride oneself on doing sth

tarif [tarif] *nm (prix)* rate; *(de train)* fare; *(tableau)* price list, *Br* tariff; **plein t.** full price; *(de train, bus)* full fare ■ **tarification** *nf* pricing

tartare [tartar] *adj* **sauce t.** tartar sauce

tarte [tart] *nf (open)* pie, tart ■ **tartelette** [-əlɛt] *nf (small)* tart

tartine [tartin] *nf* slice of bread; **t. de**

confiture slice of bread and jam ■ **tartiner** *vt (beurre)* to spread; **fromage à t.** cheese spread

tas [tɑ] *nm* pile, heap

tasse [tɑs] *nf* cup; **t. à café** coffee cup; **t. à thé** teacup

tasser [tɑse] **1** *vt* to pack (**dans** into) **2 se tasser** *vpr (se serrer)* to squeeze up; *(sol)* to sink, to collapse; *(se voûter)* to become bowed

tâter [tɑte] *vt* to feel

tâtonner [tɑtɔne] *vi* to grope about ■ **tâtons** *adv* **avancer à t.** to feel one's way (along); **chercher qch à t.** to grope for sth

tatouer [tatwe] *vt (corps, dessin)* to tattoo; **se faire t.** to get a tattoo ■ **tatouage** *nm (dessin)* tattoo; *(action)* tattooing

taudis [todi] *nm* slum

taupe [top] *nf (animal, espion)* mole

taureau, -x [tɔro] *nm* bull; **le T.** *(signe)* Taurus ■ **tauromachie** *nf* bull-fighting

taux [to] *nm* rate; **t. de cholestérol** cholesterol level; **t. d'intérêt** interest rate; **t. de natalité** birth rate

taxe [taks] *nf (impôt)* tax; **t. à la valeur ajoutée** value-added tax ■ **taxation** *nf* taxation

taxer [takse] *vt (produit, personne, firme)* to tax; **t. qn de qch** to accuse sb of sth ■ **taxé, -e** *adj (produit)* taxed

taxi [taksi] *nm* taxi

Tchécoslovaquie [tʃekɔslɔvaki] *nf Anciennement* **la T.** Czechoslovakia ■ **tchèque** [tʃɛk] *adj* Czech; **la République t.** the Czech Republic **2** *nmf* **T.** Czech **3** *nm (langue)* Czech

te [tə]

t' is used before a word beginning with a vowel or h mute.

pron personnel (**a**) *(complément direct)* you; **je te vois** I see you (**b**) *(indirect)* (to) you; **il te parle** he speaks to you; **elle te l'a dit** she told you (**c**) *(réfléchi)* yourself; **tu te laves** you wash yourself

technicien, -enne [tɛknisjɛ̃, -ɛn] *nmf* technician ■ **technique 1** *adj* technical **2** *nf* technique ■ **technologie** *nf*

technology ■ **technologique** *adj* technological

teckel [tekɛl] *nm* dachshund

tee-shirt [tiʃœrt] *nm* tee-shirt

teindre* [tɛ̃dr] **1** *vt* to dye; **t. qch en rouge** to dye sth red **2 se teindre** *vpr* **se t. (les cheveux)** to dye one's hair

teint [tɛ̃] *nm (de visage)* complexion; **bon** *ou* **grand t.** *(tissu)* colourfast

teinte [tɛ̃t] *nf* shade, tint ■ **teinter** *vt* to tint; *(bois)* to stain

teinture [tɛ̃tyr] *nf* dyeing; *(produit)* dye ■ **teinturerie** [-rri] *nf (boutique)* (dry) cleaner's

TEL, TELLE [tɛl] *adj* such; **un t. livre/ homme** such a book/man; **de tels mots** such words; **t. que** such as, like; **t. que je l'ai laissé** just as I left it; **laissez-le t. quel** leave it just as it is; **en tant que t., comme t.** as such; **t. ou t.** such and such; **rien de t. que…** (there's) nothing like…; **t. père t. fils** like father like son

télé [tele] *nf Fam* TV, *Br* telly; **à la t.** on TV, *Br* on the telly

Télécarte® [telekart] *nf* phone card

télécommande [telekɔmɑ̃d] *nf* remote control ■ **télécommandé, -e** *adj* remote-controlled

télécommunications [telekɔmynikasjɔ̃] *nfpl* telecommunications

télécopie [telekɔpi] *nf* fax ■ **télécopieur** *nm* fax (machine)

téléfilm [telefilm] *nm* TV movie

télégramme [telegram] *nm* telegram

télégraphe [telegraf] *nm* telegraph ■ **télégraphique** *adj* **poteau/fil t.** telegraph pole/wire

téléguider [telegide] *vt* to operate by remote control

télépathie [telepati] *nf* telepathy

téléphérique [teleferik] *nm* cable car

téléphone [telefɔn] *nm* (tele)phone; **coup de t.** (phone) call; **passer un coup de t. à qn** to give sb a ring *or* a call; **au t.** on the (tele)phone; **avoir le t.** to be on the (tele)phone; **t. portable** mobile phone; **t. sans fil** cordless phone ■ **téléphoner 1** *vt (nouvelle)* to (tele)phone (**à** qn to) **2** *vi* to (tele)phone; **t. à** qn to (tele)phone sb, to call sb (up) ■ **téléphonique** *adj* **appel t.** telephone call

télescope [teleskɔp] *nm* telescope ■ **télescopique** *adj* telescopic

télescoper [teleskɔpe] **1** *vt (voiture, train)* to smash into **2 se télescoper** *vpr (voiture, train)* to concertina

télésiège [telesjɛʒ] *nm* chair lift

téléski [teleski] *nm* ski tow

téléspectateur, -trice [telespɛktatœr, -tris] *nmf* (television) viewer

télétravail [teletravaj] *nm* teleworking

téléviser [televize] *vt* to televise ■ **téléviseur** *nm* television (set) ■ **télévision** *nf* television; **à la t.** on (the) television; **regarder la t.** to watch (the) television; **programme de t.** television programme

télex [telɛks] *nm (service, message)* telex

telle [tɛl] *voir* **tel** ■ **tellement** *adv (si)* so; *(tant)* so much; **t. grand que...** so big that...; **crier t. que...** to shout so much that...; **t. de travail** so much work; **t. de soucis** so many worries; **tu aimes ça? – pas t.!** *(pas beaucoup)* do you like it? – not much *or* a lot!; **personne ne peut le supporter, t. il est bavard** nobody can stand him, he's so talkative

tellurique [telyrik] *adj* **secousse t.** earth tremor

téméraire [temerɛr] *adj* reckless ■ **témérité** *nf* recklessness

témoigner [temwaɲe] **1** *vt (gratitude)* to show (**à** qn (to) sb); **t. que...** *(attester)* to testify that... **2** *vi/ur* to give evidence, to testify (**contre** against); **t. de qch** *(personne, attitude)* to testify to sth ■ **témoignage** *nm Jur* evidence, testimony; *(récit)* account; **faux t.** *(délit)* perjury; **en t. de qch** as a token of sth

témoin [temwɛ̃] **1** *nm* **(a)** *Jur* witness; **être t. de qch** to witness sth **(b)** *(de relais)* baton **2** *adj* **appartement t.** *Br*

show flat, *Am* model apartment

tempérament [tãperamã] *nm (caractère)* temperament; **acheter qch à t.** to buy sth on *Br* hire purchase *or Am* on the installment plan

température [tãperatyr] *nf* temperature; **avoir de la t.** to have a temperature

tempérer [tãpere] *vt (ardeurs)* to moderate ■ **tempéré, -e** *adj (climat, zone)* temperate

tempête [tãpɛt] *nf* storm

tempêter [tãpɛte] *vi (crier)* to storm, to rage (**contre** against)

temple [tãpl] *nm (romain, grec)* temple; *(protestant)* church

temporaire [tãpɔrɛr] *adj* temporary

temporel, -elle [tãpɔrɛl] *adj* temporal; *(terrestre)* wordly

TEMPS¹ [tã] *nm (durée, période, moment)* time; *(étape)* stage; **en t. de guerre** in wartime, in time of war; **avoir le t.** to have (the) time (**de faire** to do); **il est t.** it is time (**de faire** to do); **il était t.!** it was about time (too)!; **il est (grand) t. que vous partiez** it's (high) time you left; **ces derniers t.** lately; **de t. en t.** [dətãzãtã], **de t. à autre** [dətãzaotr] from time to time, now and again; **en t. utile** [ãtãzytil] in due course; **en t. voulu** in due course; **en même t.** at the same time (**que** as); **à t.** *(arriver)* in time; **à plein t.** *(travailler)* full-time; **à t. partiel** *(travailler)* part-time; **dans le t.** *(autrefois)* in the old days; **avec le t.** *(à la longue)* in time; **tout le t.** all the time; **de mon t.** in my time; **t. d'arrêt** pause, break; **t. libre** free time

temps² [tã] *nm (climat)* weather; **il fait beau/mauvais t.** the weather's fine/bad; **quel t. fait-il?** what's the weather like?

tenace [tənas] *adj* stubborn, tenacious ■ **ténacité** *nf* stubbornness, tenacity

tenailles [tənaj] *nfpl (outil)* pincers

tenant, -e [tənã, -ãt] **1** *nmf* **le t. du**

titre *(champion)* the title holder **2** *nm (partisan)* supporter (**de** of)

tendance [tɑ̃dɑ̃s] *nf (penchant)* tendency; *(évolution)* trend (**à** towards); **avoir t. à faire qch** to tend to do sth, to have a tendency to do sth

tendre¹ [tɑ̃dr] **1** *vt* to stretch; *(main)* to hold out (**à qn** to sb); *(bras, jambe)* to stretch out; *(cou)* to strain, to crane; *(muscle)* to tense; *(arc)* to bend; *(piège)* to set, to lay; *(filet)* to spread; **t. qch à qn** to hold out sth to sb; *Fig* **t. l'oreille** to prick up one's ears

2 *vi* **t. à qch/à faire qch** to tend towards sth/to do sth

3 se tendre *upr (rapports)* to become strained ■ **tendu, -e** *adj (corde)* tight, taut; *(personne, situation, muscle)* tense; *(rapports)* strained

tendre² [tɑ̃dr] *adj (personne)* affectionate (**avec** to); *(parole, regard)* tender, loving; *(viande)* tender; *(bois, couleur)* soft; **depuis ma plus t. enfance** since I was a young child ■ **tendresse** *nf (affection)* affection, tenderness

teneur [tənœr] *nf (de lettre)* content; **t. en alcool** alcohol content (**de** of)

TENIR* [tənir] **1** *vt (à la main)* to hold; *(promesse, comptes, hôtel)* to keep; *(rôle)* to play

2 *vi (nœud)* to hold; *(neige, coiffure)* to last, to hold; *(résister)* to hold out; **t. à qn/qch** to be attached to sb/sth; **t. à faire qch** to be anxious to do sth; **t. dans qch** *(être contenu)* to fit into sth; **t. de qn** to take after sb; **tenez!** *(prenez)* here (you are)!; **tiens!** *(surprise)* well!, hey!

3 *v impersonnel* **il ne tient qu'à vous de le faire** it's up to you to do it

4 se tenir *upr (avoir lieu)* to be held; *(rester)* to remain; **se t. debout** to stand (up); **se t. droit** to stand up/sit up straight; **se t. par la main** to hold hands; **se t. bien** to behave oneself; **se t. à qch** to hold on to sth

tennis [tenis] **1** *nm* tennis; *(terrain)* (tennis) court; **t. de table** table tennis

2 *nmpl Br (chaussures)* tennis shoes

tension [tɑ̃sjɔ̃] *nf* tension; **t. artérielle** blood pressure; **avoir de la t.** to have high blood pressure

tente [tɑ̃t] *nf* tent

tenter¹ [tɑ̃te] *vt (essayer)* to try; **t. de faire qch** to try or attempt to do sth ■ **tentative** *nf* attempt

tenter² [tɑ̃te] *vt (faire envie à)* to tempt; **tenté de faire qch** tempted to do sth ■ **tentant, -e** *adj* tempting ■ **tentation** *nf* temptation

tenture [tɑ̃tyr] *nf (wall)* hanging; *(de porte)* drape, curtain

tenu, -e [təny] **1** *pp de* **tenir 2** *adj* **t. de faire qch** obliged to do sth; **bien/mal t.** *(maison)* well/badly kept

ténu, -e [təny] *adj (fil)* fine; *(différence)* tenuous; *(voix)* thin

tenue [təny] *nf* **(a)** *(vêtements)* clothes, outfit; **t. de soirée** evening dress **(b)** *(conduite)* (good) behaviour; *(maintien)* posture **(c)** *(de maison, d'hôtel)* running; *(de comptes)* keeping **(d)** **t. de route** *(de véhicule)* road-holding

ter [ter] *adj* **4 t.** ≃ 4B

terme [term] *nm* **(a)** *(mot)* term **(b)** *(date limite)* time (limit); *(fin)* end; **mettre un t. à qch** to put an end to sth; **à court/long t.** *(conséquences, projet)* short-/long-term **(c)** *(solution)* middle course **(d)** **en bons/mauvais termes** on good/bad terms (**avec qn** with sb) **(e)** *(loyer)* rent; *(jour)* rent day; *(période)* rental period

terminal, -e, -aux, -ales [terminal, -o] **1** *adj* final; *(phase de maladie)* terminal **2** *adj & nf Scol* **(classe) terminale** *Br* ≃ sixth form, *Am* ≃ twelfth grade **3** *nm (d'ordinateur, pétrolier)* terminal

terminer [termine] **1** *vt* to end; *(achever)* to finish, to complete **2 se terminer** *upr* to end (**par** with; **en** in) ■ **terminaison** *nf (de mot)* ending

terminologie [terminɔlɔʒi] *nf* terminology

terminus [tɛrminys] *nm* terminus
terne [tɛrn] *adj (couleur, journée)* dull, drab; *(personne)* dull ▪ **ternir 1** *vt (métal, réputation)* to tarnish; *(meuble, miroir)* to dull **2 se ternir** *vpr (métal)* to tarnish

terrain [tɛrɛ̃] *nm (sol) & Fig* ground; *(étendue)* land; *(à bâtir)* plot, site; *(pour opérations militaires) & Géol* terrain; **un t.** a piece of land; **gagner/ perdre du t.** *(armée) & Fig* to give/ gain/lose ground; **t. de camping** campsite; **t. de football/rugby** football/rugby pitch; **t. de golf** golf course; **t. de jeu(x)** *(pour enfants)* playground; *(stade) Br* playing field, *Am* athletic field; **t. de sport** *Br* sports ground, *Am* athletic field

terrasse [tɛras] *nf (balcon, plateforme)* terrace; *(toit)* terrace (roof); *(de café) Br* pavement *or Am* sidewalk area; **à la t.** outside

terrassement [tɛrasmɑ̃] *nm (travail)* excavation

terrasser [tɛrase] *vt (adversaire)* to floor; *Fig (accabler)* to overcome

terre [tɛr] *nf (matière, monde)* earth; *(sol)* ground; *(opposé à mer, étendue)* land; **terres** *(domaine)* land, estate; *Él Br* earth, *Am* ground; **la t.** *(le monde)* the earth; **la T.** *(planète)* Earth; **à ou par t.** *(tomber)* to the ground; *(poser)* on the ground; **par t.** *(assis, couché)* on the ground; **sous t.** underground; **t. cuite** (baked) clay, earthenware; **t. battue** *(de court de tennis)* clay ▪ **terre-à-terre** *adj inv* down-to-earth ▪ **terre-plein** *(pl* **terres-pleins)** *nm* (earth) platform; *(de route) Br* central reservation, *Am* median strip

terrer [tɛre] **se terrer** *vpr (fugitif, animal)* to go to earth

terrestre [tɛrɛstr] *adj (vie, joies)* earthly; **transport t.** land transportation

terreur [tɛrœr] *nf* terror ▪ **terrible** *adj* awful, terrible

terrien, -enne [tɛrjɛ̃, -ɛn] **1** *adj* landowning; **propriétaire t.** landowner **2** *nmf (habitant de la terre)* earthling

terrier [tɛrje] *nm (de lapin)* burrow; *(chien)* terrier

terrifier [tɛrifje] *vt* to terrify ▪ **terrifiant, -e** *adj* terrifying

terrine [tɛrin] *nf (récipient)* terrine; *(pâté)* pâté

territoire [tɛritwar] *nm* territory ▪ **territorial, -e, -aux, -ales** *adj* territorial

terroir [tɛrwar] *nm (sol)* soil; *(région)* region

terroriser [tɛrɔrize] *vt* to terrorize ▪ **terrorisme** *nm* terrorism ▪ **terroriste** *adj & nmf* terrorist

tertiaire [tɛrsjɛr] *adj* tertiary

tes [te] *voir* **ton¹**

test [tɛst] *nm* test ▪ **tester** *vt (élève, produit)* to test

testament [tɛstamɑ̃] *nm (document)* will; *Rel* **Ancien/Nouveau T.** Old/New Testament

testicule [tɛstikyl] *nm Anat* testicle

tête [tɛt] *nf* head; *(visage)* face; *(cerveau)* brain; *(de lit, de clou, de cortège)* head; *(de page, de liste)* top, head; *(au football)* header; **à la t. de** *(entreprise, parti)* at the head of; *(classe)* at the top of; **de la t. aux pieds** from head or top to toe; **t. nue** bare-headed; **en t.** *(d'une course)* in the lead; **Fig perdre la t.** to lose one's head ▪ **tête-à-tête** *nm inv* tête-à-tête; **en t.** in private

téter [tete] *vt (lait, biberon)* to suck; **donner à t. à qn** to feed sb ▪ **tétée** *nf (de bébé)* feed ▪ **tétine** *nf (de biberon) Br* teat, *Am* nipple; *(sucette) Br* dummy, *Am* pacifier

têtu, -e [tety] *adj* stubborn, obstinate

texte [tɛkst] *nm* text; *(de théâtre)* lines ▪ **textuellement** *adv* word for word

textile [tɛkstil] *adj & nm* textile

texture [tɛkstyr] *nf* texture

TGV [teʒeve] *(abrév* **train à grande vitesse)** *nm* high-speed train

Thaïlande [tailɑ̃d] *nf* **la T.** Thailand ▪ **thaïlandais, -e 1** *adj* Thai **2** *nmf* **T., Thaïlandaise** Thai

thé [te] *nm (boisson, réunion)* tea ▪ **théière** *nf* teapot

théâtre [teatr] *nm (art, lieu)* theatre; *(œuvres)* drama; **faire du t.** to act ■ **théâtral, -e, -aux, -ales** *adj* theatrical

thème [tɛm] *nm* theme

théologie [teɔlɔʒi] *nf* theology

théorie [teɔri] *nf* theory; **en t.** in theory

théorique [teɔrik] *adj* theoretical

thérapeutique [terapøtik] **1** *adj* therapeutic **2** *nf (traitement)* therapy ■ **thérapie** *nf* therapy

thermal, -e, -aux, -ales [tɛrmal, -o] *adj* **station thermale** spa

thermique [tɛrmik] *adj (énergie, unité)* thermal

thermomètre [tɛrmɔmɛtr] *nm* thermometer

Thermos® [tɛrmɔs] *nm ou f* Thermos® *(Br* flask *or Am* bottle)

thermostat [tɛrmɔsta] *nm* thermostat

thèse [tɛz] *nf (proposition, ouvrage)* thesis

thon [tɔ̃] *nm* tuna (fish)

thym [tɛ̃] *nm (plante, aromate)* thyme

Tibet [tibɛ] *nm* **le T.** Tibet

tic [tik] *nm (contraction)* twitch, tic; *Fig (manie)* mannerism

ticket [tikɛ] *nm* ticket

tiède [tjɛd] *adj* lukewarm, tepid; *(vent, climat)* mild ■ **tiédir** *vti (refroidir)* to cool down; *(réchauffer)* to warm up

tien, tienne [tjɛ̃, tjɛn] **1** *pron possessif* **le t., la tienne, les tien(ne)s** yours; **les deux tiens** your two ■ *nmpl* **les tiens** *(ta famille)* your family

tiens, tient [tjɛ̃] *voir* **tenir**

tiercé [tjɛrse] *nm (pari)* place betting *(on the horses)*; **jouer/gagner au t.** to bet/win on the horses

tiers, tierce [tjɛr, tjɛrs] **1** *adj* third **2** *nm (fraction)* third; *(personne)* third party ■ **Tiers-Monde** *nm* **le T.** the Third World

tige [tiʒ] *nf (de plante)* stem, stalk; *(barre)* rod

tigre [tigr] *nm* tiger ■ **tigresse** *nf* tigress

tilleul [tijœl] *nm (arbre)* lime tree; *(infusion)* lime blossom tea

timbre [tɛ̃br] *nm* (**a**) *(vignette)* stamp; *(pour traitement médicale)* patch (**b**) *(sonnette)* bell (**c**) *(d'instrument, de voix)* tone (quality) ■ **timbrer** *vt (lettre)* to put a stamp on; *(document)* to stamp

timide [timid] *adj (gêné)* shy; *(protestations)* timid ■ **timidité** *nf* shyness

tinter [tɛ̃te] *vi (cloche)* to tinkle; *(clefs, monnaie)* to jingle; *(verres)* to chink

tique [tik] *nf* tick

tir [tir] *nm (sport)* shooting; *(action)* firing, shooting; *(au football)* shot; **t. (forain)** shooting *or* rifle range; **t. à l'arc** archery

tirade [tirad] *nf (au théâtre)* & *Fig Br* monologue, *Am* monolog

tirage [tiraʒ] *nm* (**a**) *(de journal)* circulation; *(de livre)* print run; *Typ & Phot (impression)* printing (**b**) *(de loterie)* draw; **t. au sort** drawing lots

tirailler [tiraje] **1** *vt* to pull at; *Fig* **tiraillé entre** *(possibilités)* torn between **2** *vi* **j'ai la peau qui tiraille** my skin feels tight

tire [tir] *nf* **vol à la t.** pickpocketing

tirelire [tirlir] *nf Br* moneybox, *Am* coin bank

tirer [tire] **1** *vt* to pull; *(langue)* to stick out; *(trait, rideaux, conclusion)* to draw; *(balle)* to fire; *(gibier)* to shoot; *(journal, épreuves de livre, photo)* to print; **t. qch de qch** to pull sth out of sth; *(nom, origine)* to derive sth from sth; *(produit)* to extract sth from sth; **t. qn de qch** *(danger, lit)* to get sb out of sth **2** *vi* to pull (**sur** on/at); *(faire feu)* to shoot, to fire (**sur** at); *(cheminée)* to draw; **t. au sort** to draw lots; **t. à sa fin** to draw to a close **3** **se tirer** *vpr* **se t. de qch** *(travail, problème)* to cope with sth; *(danger, situation)* to get out of sth ■ **tiré, -e** *adj (traits, visage)* drawn ■ **tire-bouchon** *(pl* **tire-bouchons**) *nm* corkscrew

tireur [tirœr] *nm* gunman; **t. d'élite** marksman

tiroir [tirwar] *nm (de commode)* drawer

tisane [tizan] *nf* herbal tea

tisser [tise] *vt* to weave ■ **tissage** *nm* (*action*) weaving

tissu [tisy] *nm* material, cloth; *Biol* tissue

titre [titr] *nm* (*nom, qualité*) title; *Fin* security; (*diplôme*) qualification; (**gros**) **t.** (*de journal*) headline; **à t. d'exemple** as an example; **à t. exceptionnel** exceptionally; **à t. indicatif** for general information; **à juste t.** rightly; **t. de transport** ticket

titrer [titre] *vt* (*film*) to title; (*journal*) to run as a headline ■ **titré, -e** *adj* (*personne*) titled

tituber [titybe] *vi* to stagger

titulaire [tityler] **1** *adj* (*enseignant*) tenured; **être t. de** (*permis*) to be the holder of; (*poste*) to hold **2** *nmf* (*de permis, de poste*) holder (**de** of) ■ **titulariser** *vt* (*fonctionnaire*) to give tenure to

toast [tost] *nm* (*pain grillé*) piece or slice of toast; (*allocution*) toast; **porter un t. à** to drink (a toast) to

toboggan [tɔbɔɡã] *nm* (*d'enfant*) slide; *Can* (*traîneau*) toboggan; (*voie de circulation*) *Br* flyover, *Am* overpass

toc [tɔk] *nm* **du t.** (*camelote*) trash; **bijou en t.** imitation jewel

toi [twa] *pron personnel* (**a**) (*après une préposition*) you; **avec t.** with you; (**b**) (*sujet*) you; **t., tu peux** you may; **c'est t. qui...** it's you who... (**c**) (*réfléchi*) **assieds-t.** sit (yourself) down; **dépêche-t.** hurry up ■ **toi-même** *pron* yourself

toile [twal] *nf* (**a**) (*étoffe*) cloth; (*à voile, sac*) canvas; **une t.** a piece of cloth *or* canvas; *Théât & Fig* **t. de fond** backdrop; **t. cirée** oil cloth (**b**) (*tableau*) painting, canvas (**c**) **t. d'araignée** (spider's web), cobweb

toilette [twalɛt] *nf* (*action*) wash(ing); (*vêtements*) clothes, outfit; **faire sa t.** to wash (and dress); **les toilettes** (*W-C*) *Br* the toilet(s), *Am* the men's/ladies' room

toit [twa] *nm* roof ■ **toiture** *nf* roof(ing)

tôle [tol] *nf* sheet metal; **t. ondulée** corrugated iron

tolérer [tɔlere] *vt* (*permettre*) to tolerate ■ **tolérable** *adj* tolerable ■ **tolérance** *nf* tolerance ■ **tolérant, -e** *adj* tolerant (**à l'égard de** of)

tomate [tɔmat] *nf* tomato

tombe [tɔb] *nf* grave; (*avec monument*) tomb ■ **tombale** *adj f* **pierre t.** gravestone, tombstone ■ **tombeau, -x** *nm* tomb

tomber [tɔbe] (*aux être*) *vi* to fall; (*température*) to drop, to fall; (*vent*) to drop (off); **t. malade** to fall ill; **t. par terre** to fall (down); **faire t.** (*personne*) to knock over; (*gouvernement, prix*) to bring down; **laisser t.** (*objet*) to drop; *Fig* **laisser t. qn** to let sb down; **t. un lundi** to fall on a Monday; **t. sur qch** (*trouver*) to come across sth ■ **tombée** *nf* **la t. de la nuit** nightfall

tome [tɔm] *nm* (*livre*) volume

ton¹, ta, tes [tɔ̃, ta, te]

> **ta** becomes **ton** [tɔ̃n] before a vowel or mute h.

adj possessif your; **t. père** your father; **ta mère** your mother; **t. ami(e)** your friend

ton² [tɔ̃] *nm* (*de voix*) tone; (*de couleur*) shade, tone; *Mus* (*gamme*) key; (*hauteur de son*) pitch ■ **tonalité** *nf* (*timbre, impression*) tone; (*de téléphone*) *Br* dialling tone, *Am* dial tone

tondre [tɔ̃dr] *vt* (*mouton*) to shear; (*gazon*) to mow ■ **tondeuse** *nf* shears; (*à cheveux*) clippers; **t.** (*à gazon*) (lawn)mower

tonifier [tɔnifje] *vt* (*muscles, peau*) to tone up; (*personne*) to invigorate

tonique [tɔnik] **1** *adj* (*froid, effet*) tonic, invigorating **2** *nm* (*médicament*) tonic; (*cosmétique*) tonic lotion

tonnage [tɔnaʒ] *nm* (*de navire*) tonnage

tonne [tɔn] *nf* (*poids*) metric ton, tonne

tonneau, -x [tɔno] *nm* (**a**) (*récipient*) barrel, cask (**b**) (*acrobatie*) roll; **faire un t.** to roll over

tonner [tɔne] **1** *vi* (*canons*) to thunder; *Fig* (*crier*) to thunder, to rage (**contre**

against) **2** *v impersonnel* **il tonne** it's thundering ■ **tonnerre** *nm* thunder

tonus [tɔnys] *nm (énergie)* energy, vitality

top [tɔp] *nm (signal sonore)* beep

topographie [tɔpɔgrafi] *nf* topography

toque [tɔk] *nf (de fourrure)* fur hat; *(de jockey)* cap; *(de cuisinier)* hat

torche [tɔrʃ] *nf (flamme)* torch; **t. électrique** *nf* torch, *Am* flashlight

torchon [tɔrʃɔ̃] *nm (à vaisselle)* dish towel, *Br* tea towel

tordre [tɔrdr] **1** *vt* to twist; *(linge, cou)* to wring; *(barre)* to bend **2 se tordre** *vpr* to twist; *(barre)* to bend; **se t. de douleur** to be doubled up with pain; **se t. (de rire)** to split one's sides (laughing); **se t. la cheville** to twist *or* sprain one's ankle ■ **tordu, -e** *adj* twisted; *(esprit)* warped

tornade [tɔrnad] *nf* tornado

torpille [tɔrpij] *nf* torpedo ■ **torpiller** *vt (navire, projet)* to torpedo

torrent [tɔrɑ̃] *nm* torrent; *Fig* **un t. de larmes** a flood of tears; **il pleut à torrents** it's pouring (down) ■ **torrentiel, -elle** *adj (pluie)* torrential

torride [tɔrid] *adj (chaleur)* torrid

torse [tɔrs] *nm Anat* chest; **t. nu** stripped to the waist

tort [tɔr] *nm (dommage)* wrong; *(défaut)* fault; **avoir t.** to be wrong *(de faire* to do, in doing); **être dans son t.** ou **en t.** to be in the wrong; **faire du t. à qn** to harm sb; **à t.** wrongly; **à t. ou à raison** rightly or wrongly

torticolis [tɔrtikɔli] *nm* **avoir le t.** to have a stiff neck

tortiller [tɔrtije] **1** *vt* to twist; *(moustache)* to twirl **2 se tortiller** *vpr (ver, personne)* to wriggle

tortionnaire [tɔrsjɔnɛr] *nm* torturer

tortue [tɔrty] *nf Br* tortoise, *Am* turtle; *(de mer)* turtle

torture [tɔrtyr] *nf* torture ■ **torturer** *vt* to torture

tôt [to] *adv* early; **au plus t.** at the earliest; **le plus t. possible** as soon as

possible; **t. ou tard** sooner or later; **je n'étais pas plus t. sorti que...** no sooner had I gone out than...

total, -e, -aux, -ales [tɔtal, -o] *adj & nm* total; **au t.** all in all, in total; *(somme toute)* all in all ■ **totaliser** *vt* to total ■ **totalité** *nf* entirely; **la t. de** all of; **en t.** *(détruit)* entirely; *(payé)* fully

totalitaire [tɔtalitɛr] *adj (État, régime)* totalitarian

touche [tuʃ] *nf (de clavier)* key; *(de téléphone)* (push-)button; *(au football & au rugby)* throw-in; **téléphone à touches** push-button phone; **une t. de** *(un peu de)* a touch *or* hint of

toucher [tuʃe] *nm (sens)* touch; **au t.** to the touch **2** *vt* to touch; *(paie)* to draw; *(chèque)* to cash; *(émouvoir)* to touch, to move; *(concerner)* to affect **3** *vi* **t. à** to touch; *(sujet)* to touch on; *(but, fin)* to approach **4 se toucher** *vpr (lignes, mains)* to touch ■ **touchant, -e** *adj (émouvant)* moving, touching

touffe [tuf] *nf (de cheveux, d'herbe)* tuft ■ **touffu, -e** *adj (barbe, haie)* thick, bushy

toujours [tuʒur] *adv (exprime la continuité, la répétition)* always; *(encore)* still; **pour t.** for ever

tour¹ [tur] *nf (bâtiment)* & *Ordinat* tower; *(immeuble)* tower block, highrise; *Échecs* castle, rook

tour² [tur] *nm* **(a)** *(mouvement, ordre, tournure)* turn; *(de magie)* trick; *(excursion)* trip, outing; *(à pied)* stroll, walk; *(en voiture)* drive; **t. (de piste)** *(de course)* lap; **de dix mètres de t.** ten metres round; **faire le t. de** to go round; **faire le t. du monde** to go round the world; **faire un t.** *(à pied)* to go for a stroll or walk; *(en voiture)* to go for a drive; **à t. de rôle** in turn; **t. à t.** in turn, by turns **(b)** *Tech* lathe; *(de potier)* wheel

tourbillon [turbijɔ̃] *nm (de vent)* whirlwind; *(d'eau)* whirlpool; *(de sable)* swirl ■ **tourbillonner** *vi* to whirl

tourisme [turism] *nm* tourism; **faire du t.** to do some touring ■ **touriste** *nmf* tourist ■ **touristique** *adj* **guide/menu t.** tourist guide/menu; **route t.**, **circuit t.** scenic route

tourmenter [turmɑ̃te] **1** *vt* to torment **2 se tourmenter** *vpr* to worry

tournage [turnaʒ] *nm (de film)* shooting, filming

tournant [turnɑ̃] *nm (de route)* bend; *Fig (moment)* turning point (**de** in)

tourne-disque [turnədisk] (*pl* **tourne-disques**) *nm* record player

tournée [turne] *nf (de facteur, de boissons)* round; *(spectacle)* tour; **faire sa t.** to do one's rounds; **faire la t. de** *(magasins, musées)* to go to, *Br* to go round

tourner [turne] **1** *vt* to turn; *(film)* to shoot, to make; *(difficulté)* to get round; **t. qn/qch en ridicule** to ridicule sb/sth

2 *vi* to turn; *(tête, toupie)* to spin; *(Terre)* to revolve, to turn; *(moteur, usine)* to run; *(lait)* to go off; **t. autour de** *(objet)* to go round; *(maison, personne)* to hang around; *(question)* to centre on; **t. bien/mal** *(évoluer)* to turn out well/badly; **t. au froid** *(temps)* to turn cold

3 se tourner *vpr* to turn (**vers** to, towards)

tournesol [turnəsɔl] *nm* sunflower

tournevis [turnəvis] *nm* screwdriver

tourniquet [turnike] *nm (barrière)* turnstile; *(pour arroser)* sprinkler

tournoi [turnwa] *nm (de tennis)* & *Hist* tournament

tournoyer [turnwaje] *vi* to swirl (round)

tournure [turnyr] *nf (expression)* turn of phrase; **t. d'esprit** way of thinking; **t. des événements** turn of events

Toussaint [tusɛ̃] *nf* **la T.** All Saints' Day

tousser [tuse] *vi* to cough

TOUT, TOUTE, TOUS, TOUTES [tu, tut, tu, tut] **1** *adj* all; **tous les livres** all the books; **t. l'argent/le temps/le village** all the money/time/village; **toute la nuit** all night, the whole (of

the) night; **tous (les) deux** both; **tous (les) trois** all three

2 *adj indéfini (chaque)* every, each; *(n'importe quel)* any; **tous les ans/jours** every *or* each year/day; **tous les deux mois** every two months, every second month; **tous les cinq mètres** every five metres; **t. homme** [tutɔm] every *ou* any man

3 *pron* [tus] all; **ils sont tous là**, **tous sont là** they're all there

4 *pron m sing* **tout** everything; **dépenser t.** to spend everything, to spend it all; **t. ce qui est là** everything that's here; **t. ce que je sais** everything that *or* all that I know; **en t.** *(au total)* in all

5 *adv (tout à fait)* quite; *(très)* very; **t. simplement** quite simply; **t. petit** very small; **t. neuf** brand new; **t. seul** all alone; **t. droit** straight ahead; **t. autour** all around, right round; **t. au début** right at the beginning; **le t. premier** the very first; **t. au plus/moins** at the very most/least; **t. en chantant** while singing; **t. rusé qu'il est** *ou* **soit** however sly he may be; **t. à coup** suddenly, all of a sudden; **t. à fait** completely, quite; **t. de suite** at once

6 *nm* **le t.** everything, the lot; **un t.** a whole; **le t. est que…** *(l'important)* the main thing is that…; **pas du t.** not at all; **rien du t.** nothing at all; **du t. au t.** *(changer)* entirely, completely

toutefois [tutfwa] *adv* nevertheless, however ■ **tout-puissant, toute-puissante** *(mpl* **tout-puissants,** *fpl* **toutes-puissantes)** *adj* all-powerful ■ **tout-terrain 1** *(pl* **tout-terrains)** *adj* **véhicule t.** off-road *or* all terrain vehicle; **vélo t.** mountain bike **2** *nm* **faire du t.** to do off-road racing

toux [tu] *nf* cough

toxicomane [tɔksikɔman] *nmf* drug addict ■ **toxicomanie** *nf* drug addiction

toxique [tɔksik] *adj* poisonous, toxic

trac [trak] *nm* **le t.** *(peur)* the jitters; *(de candidat)* exam nerves; *(d'acteur)* stage fright; **avoir le t.** to be nervous

trace [tras] *nf (quantité, tache, vestige)* trace; *(marque)* mark; *(de fugitif)* trail; **traces** *(de bête, de pneus)* tracks; **traces de pas** footprints; **disparaître sans laisser de traces** to disappear without trace

tracer [trase] *vt (dessiner)* to draw; *(écrire)* to trace; **t. une route** to mark out a route; *(frayer)* to open up a route ■ **tracé** *nm (plan)* layout; *(ligne)* line

tract [trakt] *nm* leaflet

tractations [traktɑsjɔ̃] *nfpl* dealings

tracter [trakte] *vt* to tow

tracteur [traktœr] *nm* tractor

tradition [tradisjɔ̃] *nf* tradition ■ **traditionnel, -elle** *adj* traditional

traduire* [traduir] *vt* to translate (**de** from; **en** into) ■ **traducteur, -trice** *nmf* translator ■ **traduction** *nf* translation

trafic [trafik] *nm (automobile, ferroviaire)* traffic; *(de marchandises)* traffic, trade ■ **trafiquant, -e** *nmf* trafficker, dealer

tragédie [traʒedi] *nf (pièce de théâtre, événement)* tragedy ■ **tragique** *adj* tragic; **prendre qch au t.** *(remarque)* to take sth too much to heart

trahir [trair] *vt* **1** to betray; *(secret)* to give away; to betray; *(sujet: forces)* to fail **2 se trahir** *vpr* to give oneself away ■ **trahison** *nf* betrayal; *(crime)* treason

train [trɛ̃] *nm* **(a)** *(de voyageurs, de marchandises)* train; **t. à grande vitesse** high-speed train; **t. corail** express train; **t. couchettes** sleeper **(b)** **en t.** *(en forme)* on form; **être en t. de faire qch** to be (busy) doing sth **(c)** *(allure)* pace; **t. de vie** life style **(d)** *(de pneus)* set; *(de péniches, de véhicules)* string **(e)** **t. d'atterrissage** *(d'avion)* undercarriage

traînard, -e [trenar, -ard] *nmf Br* slowcoach, *Am* slowpoke

traîne [trɛn] *nf (de robe)* train

traîneau, -x [treno] *nm* sleigh, *Br* sledge, *Am* sled

traînée [trɛne] *nf (de peinture, dans le ciel)* streak

traîner [trene] **1** *vt* to drag; *(wagon)* to pull

2 *vi (jouets, papiers)* to lie around; *(s'attarder)* to lag behind, to dawdle; *(errer)* to hang around; *(subsister)* to linger on; **t. par terre** *(robe)* to trail (on the ground); **t. en longueur** to drag on

3 se traîner *vpr (avancer)* to drag oneself (along); *(par terre)* to crawl; *(durer)* to drag on ■ **traînant, -e** *adj (voix)* drawling

traire* [trer] *vt (vache)* to milk

trait [trɛ] *nm* line; *(en dessinant)* stroke; *(caractéristique)* feature, trait; **traits** *(du visage)* features; **d'un t.** *(boire)* in one gulp, in one go; **avoir t. à qch** to relate to sth

traite [trɛt] *nf (de vache)* milking; *(lettre de change)* bill, draft; **d'une (seule) t.** *(sans interruption)* in one go; **t. des Noirs** slave trade

traité [trete] *nm (accord)* treaty; *(ouvrage)* treatise (**sur** on); **t. de paix** peace treaty

traiter [trete] **1** *vt (se comporter envers, soigner)* to treat; *(problème, sujet)* to deal with; *(marché)* to negotiate; *(matériau, produit)* to treat, to process; **t. qn de tous les noms** to call sb all the names under the sun

2 *vi* to negotiate, to deal (**avec** with); **t. de** *(sujet)* to deal with ■ **traitement** [tretmɑ̃] *nm (de personne, de maladie)* treatment; *(de matériau)* processing; *(gains)* salary; **t. de données/de texte** data/word processing; **machine à t. de texte** word processor

traiteur [tretœr] *nm (fournisseur)* caterer; **chez le t.** at the delicatessen

traître [tretr] **1** *nm* traitor; **en t.** treacherously **2** *adj (dangereux)* treacherous; **être t. à une cause** to be a traitor to a cause ■ **traîtrise** *nf* treachery

trajectoire [traʒektwar] *nf* path, trajectory

trajet [traʒe] *nm* journey; *(distance)* distance; *(itinéraire)* route

tramer [trame] **se tramer** *vpr* **il se trame**

quelque chose something's afoot

trampoline [trãpolin] *nm* trampoline

tramway [tramwɛ] *nm Br* tram, *Am* streetcar

tranche [trãʃ] *nf (morceau)* slice; *(bord)* edge; *(partie)* portion; *(de salaire, d'impôts)* bracket; **t. d'âge** age bracket

tranchée [trãʃe] *nf* trench

trancher [trãʃe] **1** *vt* to cut; *(difficulté, question)* to settle **2** *vi (décider)* to decide; *(contraster)* to contrast (**sur** with) ▪ **tranchant, -e 1** *adj (couteau)* sharp; *(ton)* curt **2** *nm (cutting)* edge; *Fig* **à double t.** double-edged ▪ **tranché, -e** *adj (couleurs)* distinct; *(opinion)* clear-cut

tranquille [trãkil] *adj* quiet; *(mer)* calm, still; *(esprit)* easy; **avoir la conscience t.** to have a clear conscience; **soyez t.** don't worry; **laisser qn/qch t.** to leave sb/sth alone

tranquilliser [trãkilize] *vt* to reassure ▪ **tranquillisant** *nm* tranquillizer

tranquillité [trãkilite] *nf (peace and) quiet; (d'esprit)* peace of mind

transaction [trãzaksjõ] *nf (opération)* transaction; *Jur* compromise

transatlantique [trãzatlãtik] **1** *adj* transatlantic **2** *nm (paquebot)* transatlantic liner; *(chaise)* deckchair ▪ **transat** *nm (chaise)* deckchair

transcrire* [trãskrir] *vt* to transcribe ▪ **transcription** *nf* transcription; *(document)* transcript

transe [trãs] *nf* **en t.** *(mystique)* in a trance; *(excité)* very excited; **entrer en t.** to go into a trance

transférer [trãsfere] *vt* to transfer (**à** to) ▪ **transfert** *nm* transfer

transformer [trãsfɔrme] **1** *vt* to transform; *(maison, au rugby)* to convert; *(matière première)* to process; **t. qch en qch** to turn sth into sth **2 se transformer** *vpr* to change, to be transformed (**en** into) ▪ **transformateur** *nm* Él transformer ▪ **transformation** *nf* change, transformation; *(de maison)* alteration

transfuge [trãsfyʒ] *nmf* defector

transfusion [trãsfyzjõ] *nf* **t. (sanguine)** (blood) transfusion

transgresser [trãsgrese] *vt (ordres)* to disobey; *(loi)* to infringe

transi, -e [trãzi] *adj (personne)* numb with cold

transiger [trãziʒe] *vi* to compromise

transistor [trãzistɔr] *nm* transistor

transit [trãzit] *nm* transit; **en t.** in transit

transition [trãzisjõ] *nf* transition ▪ **transitoire** *adj (qui passe)* transient; *(provisoire)* transitional

transmettre* [trãsmetr] **1** *vt (message, héritage)* to pass on (**à** to); *Radio & TV (informations)* to transmit; *(émission)* to broadcast **2 se transmettre** *vpr (maladie, tradition)* to be passed on ▪ **transmetteur** *nm (appareil)* transmitter ▪ **transmission** *nf* transmission

transparaître* [trãsparetr] *vi* to show (through)

transparent, -e [trãsparã, -ãt] *adj* clear, transparent ▪ **transparence** *nf* transparency; **voir qch par t.** to see sth showing through

transpercer [trãsperse] *vt* to pierce

transpirer [trãspire] *vi (suer)* to sweat, to perspire ▪ **transpiration** *nf* perspiration

transplanter [trãsplãte] *vt (organe, plante)* to transplant

transport [trãspɔr] *nm (action)* transport, transportation (**de** of); *(moyens)* transport; **transports** *(moyens)* transport; **transports en commun** public transport; **moyen de t.** means of transport

transporter [trãspɔrte] *vt (passagers, troupes, marchandises)* to transport, to carry ▪ **transporteur** *nm* **t. (routier)** *Br* haulier, *Am* trucker

transposer [trãspoze] *vt* to transpose ▪ **transposition** *nf* transposition

trapèze [trapez] *nm (de cirque)* trapeze

trappe [trap] *nf (de plancher)* trap door

trappeur [trapœr] *nm* trapper

trapu, -e [trapy] *adj (personne)* stocky, thickset

traquer [trake] *vt* to hunt (down)

traumatiser [tromatize] *vt* to traumatize ■ **traumatisant, -e** *adj* traumatic ■ **traumatisme** *nm (choc)* trauma

travail, -aux [travaj, -o] *nm (activité, lieu)* work; *(à effectuer)* job, task; *(emploi)* job; *(façonnage)* working (**de** of); *(ouvrage, étude)* work, publication; *Écon & Méd* **travaux** work; *(dans la rue) Br* roadworks; *Am* roadwork; *(aménagement)* alterations; *Scol & Univ* **travaux pratiques** practical work; *Scol & Univ* **travaux dirigés** tutorial; *Scol* **travaux manuels** handicrafts; **travaux ménagers** housework

travailler [travaje] **1** *vi (personne)* to work (**à qch** on sth); *(bois)* to warp **2** *vt (discipline, rôle, style)* to work on; *(façonner)* to work ■ **travailleur, -euse 1** *adj* hard-working **2** *nmf* worker

travailliste [travajist] *Pol* **1** *adj* Labour **2** *nmf* member of the Labour party

travers [traver] **1** *prép & adv* **à t.** through; **en t. (de)** across **2** *adv* **de t.** *(chapeau, nez)* crooked; **j'ai avalé de t.** it went down the wrong way

traverser [traverse] *vt* to cross; *(foule, période, mur)* to go through ■ **traversée** *nf (voyage)* crossing

travesti [travesti] *nm (acteur)* female impersonator; *(homosexuel)* transvestite

travestir [travestir] *vt* to disguise

trébucher [trebyʃe] *vi* to stumble (**sur** over); **faire t. qn** to trip sb (up)

trèfle [trefl] *nm (plante)* clover; *Cartes (couleur)* clubs

treillis [treji] *nm* (**a**) *(treillage)* lattice(-work); *(en métal)* wire mesh (**b**) *(tenue militaire)* combat uniform

treize [trez] *adj & nm inv* thirteen ■ **treizième** *adj & nmf* thirteenth

tréma [trema] *nm* di(a)eresis

trembler [trɑ̃ble] *vi* to shake, to tremble; *(de froid, peur)* to tremble (**de** with); *(flamme, lumière)* to flicker; *(voix)* to tremble, to quaver; *(avoir peur)* to be afraid (**que** + *subjunctive* that); **t. pour qn** to fear for sb ■ **tremblement** [-əmɑ̃] *nm (action, frisson)* shaking, trembling; **t. de terre** earthquake ■ **trembloter** *vi* to quiver

tremper [trɑ̃pe] **1** *vt* to soak, to drench; *(plonger)* to dip (**dans** in); *(acier)* to temper **2** *vi* to soak; **faire t. qch** to soak sth; *Péj* **t. dans** *(participer)* to be mixed up in

tremplin [trɑ̃plɛ̃] *nm* springboard

trente [trɑ̃t] *adj & nm inv* thirty; **un t.-trois tours** *(disque)* an LP; **se mettre sur son t. et un** to get all dressed up ■ **trentaine** *nf* **une t. (de)** *(nombre)* (about) thirty; **avoir la t.** *(âge)* to be about thirty ■ **trentième** *adj & nmf* thirtieth

très [trɛ] ([trɛz] *before vowel or mute h*) *adv* very; **t. aimé/critiqué** *(with past participle)* much or greatly liked/criticized

trésor [trezɔr] *nm* treasure; **le T. (public)** *(service)* public revenue (department); *(finances)* public funds; **des trésors de patience** boundless patience ■ **trésorerie** [-rri] *nf (bureaux d'un club)* accounts department; *(gestion)* accounting; *(capitaux)* funds ■ **trésorier, -ère** *nmf* treasurer

tressaillir* [tresajir] *vi (frémir)* to shake, to quiver; *(de joie, de peur)* to tremble (**de** with); *(sursauter)* to jump, to start

tresse [tres] *nf (cordon)* braid; *(cheveux) Br* plait, *Am* braid ■ **tresser** [trese] *vt* to braid; *Br (cheveux)* to plait, *Am* to braid

trêve [trɛv] *nf (de combat)* truce

tri [tri] *nm* sorting (out); **faire le t. de** to sort (out); **(centre de) t.** *(des postes)* sorting office ■ **triage** *nm* sorting (out)

triangle [trijɑ̃gl] *nm* triangle ■ **triangulaire** *adj* triangular

tribord [tribɔr] *nm (de bateau, d'avion)* starboard

tribu [triby] *nf* tribe ■ **tribal, -e, -aux, -ales** *adj* tribal

tribunal, -aux [tribynal, -o] *nm Jur* court; *(militaire)* tribunal

tribune [tribyn] *nf (de salle publique)* gallery; *(de stade)* (grand)stand; *(d'orateur)* rostrum

tribut [triby] *nm* tribute (**à** to)

tricher [triʃe] *vi* to cheat ■ **tricherie** *nf* cheating, trickery ■ **tricheur, -euse** *nmf* cheat, *Am* cheater

tricolore [trikɔlɔr] *adj (cocarde)* red, white and blue; **le drapeau/l'équipe t.** the French flag/team

tricot [triko] *nm (activité, ouvrage)* knitting; *(chandail)* sweater, *Br* jumper; *(ouvrage)* piece of knitting; **en t.** knitted; **t. de corps** *Br* vest, *Am* undershirt ■ **tricoter** *vti* to knit

trier [trije] *vt (lettres)* to sort; *(vêtements)* to sort through

trilingue [trilɛ̃g] *adj* trilingual

trimestre [trimestr] *nm* quarter; *Scol* term; *Scol* **premier/second/troisième t.** *Br* autumn *or Am* fall/winter/summer term ■ **trimestriel, -elle** *adj (revue)* quarterly; **bulletin t.** end-of-term *Br* report *or Am* report card

Trinité [trinite] *nf* **la T.** *(fête)* Trinity; *(dogme)* the Trinity

trinquer [trɛ̃ke] *vi* to chink glasses; **t. à la santé de qn** to drink to sb's health

trio [trijo] *nm (groupe)* & *Mus* trio

triomphe [trijɔ̃f] *nm* triumph (**sur** over) ■ **triomphal, -e, -aux, -ales** *adj* triumphal ■ **triomphant, -e** *adj* triumphant ■ **triompher** *vi* to triumph (**de** over); *(jubiler)* to be jubilant

triple [tripl] **1** *adj* treble, triple; *Sport* **t. saut** triple jump **2** *nm* **le t.** three times as much (**de** as) ■ **tripler** *vti* to treble, to triple ■ **triplés, -es** *nmfpl* triplets

triste [trist] *adj* sad; *(sinistre)* dreary; *(lamentable)* unfortunate ■ **tristesse** *nf* sadness; *(du temps)* dreariness

trivial, -e, -aux, -ales [trivjal, -o] *adj* coarse, vulgar

troc [trɔk] *nm* exchange; *(système économique)* barter

trois [trwa] *adj & nm inv* three; **les t. quarts (de)** three-quarters (of) ■ **troisième** **1** *adj & nmf* third; **le t. âge** *(vieillesse)* the retirement years; **personne du t. âge** senior citizen **2** *nf Scol* **la t.** *Br* ≃ fourth year, *Am* ≃ eighth grade; *Aut (vitesse)* third gear

■ **troisièmement** *adv* thirdly

trombe [trɔ̃b] *nf* **trombe(s) d'eau** *(pluie)* rainstorm, downpour

trombone [trɔ̃bɔn] *nm (instrument)* trombone; *(agrafe)* paper clip

trompe [trɔ̃p] *nf (d'éléphant)* trunk; *(d'insecte)* proboscis; *(instrument de musique)* horn

tromper [trɔ̃pe] **1** *vt (abuser)* to fool (**sur** about); *(être infidèle à)* to be unfaithful to; *(échapper à)* to elude

2 se tromper *vpr* to be mistaken; **se t. de route** to take the wrong road; **se t. de jour** to get the day wrong ■ **tromperie** [-pri] *nf* deceit, deception ■ **trompeur, -euse** *adj (apparences)* deceptive, misleading; *(personne)* deceitful

trompette [trɔ̃pet] *nf* trumpet ■ **trompettiste** *nmf* trumpet player

tronc [trɔ̃] *nm (d'arbre)* & *Anat* trunk; *(boîte)* collection box

tronçon [trɔ̃sɔ̃] *nm* section ■ **tronçonner** *vt* to cut into sections

trône [tron] *nm* throne ■ **trôner** *vi Fig (vase, personne)* to occupy the place of honour

trop [tro] *adv (avec adjectif, adverbe)* too; *(avec verbe)* too much; **t. dur/loin** too hard/far; **t. fatigué pour jouer** too tired to play; **lire t.** to read too much; **t. de sel** too much salt; **t. de gens** too many people; **du fromage en t.** too much cheese; **un verre en t.** one glass too many; **t. souvent** too often; **t. peu** not enough ■ **trop-plein** *(pl trop-pleins) (excédent)* overflow; *(dispositif)* overflow pipe

trophée [trɔfe] *nm* trophy

tropique [trɔpik] *nm* tropic; **sous les tropiques** in the tropics ■ **tropical, -e, -aux, -ales** *adj* tropical

troquer [trɔke] *vt* to exchange (**contre** for)

trot [tro] *nm* trot; **aller au t.** to trot ■ **trotter** *vi (cheval)* to trot

trottoir [trɔtwar] *nm Br* pavement, *Am* sidewalk

trou [tru] *nm* hole; *(d'aiguille)* eye; *Fig* **t. de mémoire** memory lapse

trouble [trubl] **1** adj (liquide) cloudy; (image) blurred; (affaire) shady **2** adv **voir t.** to see things blurred **3** nm (désarroi) distress; (désordre) confusion; **troubles** (de santé) trouble; (révolte) disturbances, troubles

troubler [truble] **1** vt to disturb; (vue) to blur; (liquide) to make cloudy; (esprit) to unsettle; (projet) to upset; (inquiéter) to trouble **2** **se troubler** vpr (liquide) to become cloudy; (personne) to become flustered ■ **troublant, -e** adj (détail) disturbing, disquieting

trouer [true] vt to make a hole/holes in

troupe [trup] nf (de soldats) troop; (de théâtre) company, troupe

troupeau, -x [trupo] nm (de vaches) herd; (de moutons) flock

trousse [trus] nf (d'étui) case, kit; (d'écolier) pencil case; **t. à pharmacie** first-aid kit; **t. de toilette** toilet bag

trousseau, -x [truso] nm (de mariée) trousseau; **t. de clefs** bunch of keys

trouvaille [truvaj] nf (lucky) find

trouver [truve] **1** vt to find; **aller t. qn** to go and see sb; **je trouve que...** I think that...; **comment la trouvez-vous?** what do you think of her?
2 **se trouver** vpr to be; (être situé) to be situated; **se t. dans une situation difficile** to find oneself in a difficult situation; **se t. mal** (s'évanouir) to faint; **se t. petit** to consider oneself small
3 v impersonnel **il se trouve que...** it happens that...

trucage [tryka3] nm = **truquage**

truffe [tryf] nf (champignon, confiserie) truffle; (de chien) nose

truffer [tryfe] vt (remplir) to stuff (**de** with)

truite [truit] nf trout

truquer [tryke] vt (photo) to fake; (élections, match) to rig ■ **truquage** nm (de cinéma) (special) effect; (action) faking; (d'élections) rigging ■ **truqué, -e** adj (élections, match) rigged; **photo truquée** fake photo

trust [trœst] nm Com (cartel) trust

tsar [dzar] nm tsar, czar

tsigane [tsigan] **1** adj gipsy **2** nmf **T.** gipsy

tu¹ [ty] pron personnel you (familiar form of address)

tu² [ty] pp de **taire**

tuba [tyba] nm (instrument de musique) tuba; (de plongée) snorkel

tube [tyb] nm tube; **t. à essai** test tube

tuer [tɥe] **1** vt to kill **2** **se tuer** vpr to kill oneself; (dans un accident) to be killed ■ **tuerie** nf slaughter ■ **tueur, -euse** nmf killer

tulipe [tylip] nf tulip

tumeur [tymœr] nf tumour

tunique [tynik] nf tunic

Tunisie [tynizi] nf **la T.** Tunisia ■ **tunisien, -enne 1** adj Tunisian **2** nmf **T., Tunisienne** Tunisian

tunnel [tynel] nm tunnel; **le t. sous la Manche** the Channel Tunnel

turban [tyrbɑ̃] nm turban

turbulent, -e [tyrbylɑ̃, -ɑ̃t] adj (enfant) boisterous

Turquie [tyrki] nf **la T.** Turkey ■ **turc, turque 1** adj Turkish **2** nmf **T., Turque** Turk **3** nm (langue) Turkish

turquoise [tyrkwaz] adj inv turquoise

tuteur, -trice [tytœr, -tris] **1** nmf (de mineur) guardian **2** nm (bâton) stake, prop

tutoyer [tytwaje] vt **t. qn** to address sb using the familiar "tu" form ■ **tutoiement** nm = use of the familiar "tu" instead of the more formal "vous"

tutu [tyty] nm tutu

tuyau, -x [tɥijo] nm pipe; **t. d'arrosage** hose(pipe); **t. d'échappement** (de véhicule) exhaust (pipe)

TVA [tevea] (abrév **taxe à la valeur ajoutée**) nf VAT

type [tip] **1** nm (genre) type; Fig **le t. même de** the very model of **2** adj inv typical; **lettre t.** standard letter ■ **typique** adj typical (**de** of)

typographie [typografi] nf typography, printing

tyran [tirɑ̃] nm tyrant ■ **tyrannie** nf tyranny ■ **tyranniser** vt to tyrannize

tzigane [tzigan] adj & nmf = **tsigane**

Uu

U, u [y] *nm inv* U, u

UE [yø] (*abrév* **Union européenne**) *nf* EU

Ukraine [ykʀɛn] *nf* **l'U.** the Ukraine

ulcère [ylsɛʀ] *nm* ulcer

ULM [yɛlɛm] (*abrév* **ultraléger motorisé**) *nm inv Aviat* microlight

ultérieur, -e [ylteʀjœʀ] *adj* later, subsequent (**à** to) ■ **ultérieurement** *adv* later (on), subsequently

ultimatum [yltimatɔm] *nm* ultimatum; **lancer un u. à qn** to give sb or issue sb with an ultimatum

ultime [yltim] *adj* last; (*préparatifs*) final

ultramoderne [yltʀamɔdɛʀn] *adj* high-tech

ultrason [yltʀasɔ̃] *nm* ultrasound

ultraviolet, -ette [yltʀavjɔlɛ, -ɛt] *adj & nm* ultraviolet

UN, UNE [œ̃, yn] **1** *article indéfini* **(a)** (*devant voyelle*) an; **une page** a page; **un ange** [œ̃nɑ̃ʒ] an angel
2 *adj* one; **la page un** page one; **un kilo** one kilo; **un par un** one by one
3 *pron & nmf* one; **l'un** one; **les uns** some; **le numéro un** number one; **j'en ai un** I have one; **l'un d'eux, l'une d'elles** one of them; *Journ* **la une** the front page, page one

---

unanime [ynanim] *adj* unanimous
■ **unanimité** *nf* unanimity; **à l'u.** unanimously

uni, -e [yni] *adj* (*famille, couple*) close; (*couleur, étoffe*) plain

unième [ynjɛm] *adj* first; **trente et u.** thirty-first; **cent u.** hundred and first

unifier [ynifje] *vt* to unify ■ **unification** *nf* unification

uniforme [ynifɔʀm] **1** *adj* (*expression*) uniform; (*sol*) even; (*mouvement*) regular **2** *nm* uniform ■ **uniformément** *adv* uniformly ■ **uniformiser** *vt* to standardize ■ **uniformité** *nf* (*de couleurs*) uniformity; (*monotonie*) monotony

unilatéral, -e, -aux, -ales [ynilateʀal, -o] *adj* (*décision*) unilateral; (*contrat*) one-sided; (*stationnement*) on one side of the road/street only

union [ynjɔ̃] *nf* (*de partis, de consommateurs*) union, association; (*entente*) unity; (*mariage*) marriage; **l'U. européenne** the European Union; **u. monétaire** monetary union; **u. libre** cohabitation

unique [ynik] *adj* **(a)** (*fille, fils*) only; (*espoir, souci*) only, sole; (*prix, parti, salaire, marché*) single **(b)** (*exceptionnel*) unique; **u. en son genre** completely unique ■ **uniquement** *adv* only, just

unir [yniʀ] **1** *vt* (*personnes, territoires*) to unite; (*marier*) to join in marriage; (*efforts, qualités*) to combine **2 s'unir** *vpr* (*s'associer*) to unite; (*se marier*) to be joined in marriage; **s'u. à qn** to join forces with sb

unitaire [yniteʀ] *adj* (*prix*) per unit

unité [ynite] *nf* (*de mesure, élément, régiment*) unit; (*cohésion*) unity; **u. de longueur** unit of measurement

univers [ynivɛʀ] *nm* universe; *Fig* world ■ **universel, -elle** *adj* universal

université [ynivɛʀsite] *nf* university; **à**

l'u. *Br* at university, *Am* in college ■ **universitaire 1** *adj* **ville/restaurant u.** university town/refectory **2** *nmf* academic

uranium [yranjɔm] *nm* uranium

urbain, -e [yrbɛ̃, -ɛn] *adj* urban ■ **urbaniser** *vt* to urbanize ■ **urbanisme** *nm Br* town planning, *Am* city planning

urgent, -e [yrʒɑ̃, -ɑ̃t] *adj* urgent ■ **urgence** *nf* (*de décision, de tâche*) urgency; (*cas d'hôpital*) emergency; **d'u.** urgently; *Pol* **état d'u.** state of emergency; **(service des) urgences** (*d'hôpital*) *Br* casualty (department), *Am* emergency room

urne [yrn] *nf* (*vase*) urn; (*pour voter*) ballot box; **aller aux urnes** to go to the polls

Uruguay [yrygwe] *nm* **l'U.** Uruguay

usage [yzaʒ] *nm* (*utilisation*) use; (*coutume*) custom; (*de mot*) usage; **faire u. de qch** to make use of sth; **d'u.** (*habituel*) customary; **à l'u. de** for (the use of); **hors d'u.** out of order ■ **usagé, -e** *adj* (*vêtement*) worn; (*billet*) used ■ **usager** *nm* user

user [yze] **1** *vt* (*vêtement*) to wear out; (*personne*) to wear down; (*consommer*) to use (up) **2** *vi* **u. de qch** to use sth **3** **s'user** *vpr* (*tissu, machine*) to wear out; (*talons, personne*) to wear down ■ **usé, -e** *adj* (*tissu*) worn out; (*sujet*) stale; (*personne*) worn out; **eaux usées** dirty *or* waste water

usine [yzin] *nf* factory; **u. à gaz** gasworks; **u. métallurgique** ironworks

ustensile [ystɑ̃sil] *nm* implement, tool; **u. de cuisine** kitchen utensil

usuel, -elle [yzɥɛl] *adj* everyday

usure [yzyr] *nf* (*de pneu*) wear

usurper [yzyrpe] *vt* to usurp

utile [ytil] *adj* useful (**à** to)

utiliser [ytilize] *vt* to use ■ **utilisateur, -trice** *nmf* user ■ **utilisation** *nf* use ■ **utilité** *nf* usefulness; **d'une grande u.** very useful

utilitaire [ytiliter] *adj* utilitarian

utopie [ytɔpi] *nf* (*idéal*) utopia; (*projet, idée*) utopian plan/idea ■ **utopique** *adj* utopian

UV [yve] (*abrév* **ultraviolet**) *nm inv* UV

Vv

V, v [ve] *nm inv* V, v

va [va] *voir* **aller¹**

vacances [vakɑ̃s] *nfpl Br* holiday(s), *Am* vacation; **partir en v.** to go on *Br* holiday *or Am* vacation; **les grandes v.** the summer *Br* holidays *or Am* vacation ▪ **vacancier, -ère** *nf Br* holiday-maker, *Am* vacationer

vacant, -e [vakɑ̃, -ɑ̃t] *adj* vacant

vacarme [vakarm] *nm* din, uproar

vaccin [vaksɛ̃] *nm* vaccine; **faire un v. à qn** to vaccinate sb ▪ **vaccination** *nf* vaccination ▪ **vacciner** *vt* to vaccinate; **se faire v.** to get vaccinated (**contre** against)

vache [vaʃ] *nf* cow; **maladie de la v. folle** mad cow disease

vaciller [vasije] *vi* to sway; *(flamme, lumière)* to flicker

vagabond, -e [vagabɔ̃, -ɔ̃d] *nmf (clochard)* vagrant, tramp ▪ **vagabonder** *vi* to roam, to wander

vague¹ [vag] *adj* vague; *(regard)* vacant; *(souvenir)* dim, vague

vague² [vag] *nf (de mer) & Fig* wave; **v. de chaleur** heat wave; **v. de froid** cold spell *or* snap

vaille, vailles *voir* **valoir**

vain, -e [vɛ̃, vɛn] *adj (sans résultat)* futile; *(vaniteux)* vain; **en v.** in vain ▪ **vainement** *adv* in vain

vaincre* [vɛ̃kr] *vt (adversaire)* to defeat; *Fig (maladie, difficulté)* to overcome ▪ **vaincu, -e** *nmf* defeated man/woman; *(de match)* loser ▪ **vainqueur** *nm* victor; *(de match)* winner

vais [ve] *voir* **aller¹**

vaisseau, -x [veso] *nm Anat* vessel; *(bateau)* ship, vessel; **v. spatial** spaceship

vaisselle [vesel] *nf* crockery; **faire la v.** to do the washing up, to do the dishes

valable [valabl] *adj (billet, motif)* valid

valet [vale] *nm Cartes* jack; **v. de chambre** valet

valeur [valœr] *nf (prix, qualité)* value; *(mérite)* worth; **avoir de la v.** to be valuable; **mettre qch en v.** *(faire ressortir)* to highlight sth; **objets de v.** valuables

valide [valid] *adj (personne)* fit, able-bodied; *(billet)* valid ▪ **valider** *vt* to validate; *(titre de transport)* to stamp ▪ **validité** *nf* validity

valise [valiz] *nf* suitcase; **faire ses valises** to pack (one's bags)

vallée [vale] *nf* valley

valoir* [valwar] **1** *vi (avoir pour valeur)* to be worth; *(s'appliquer)* to apply (**pour** to); **v. mille euros/cher** to be worth a thousand euros/a lot; **il vaut mieux rester** it's better to stay; **il vaut mieux que j'attende** I'd better wait; **faire v. qch** *(faire ressortir)* to highlight sth; *(droit)* to assert sth **2** *vt* **v. qch à qn** *(ennuis)* to bring sb sth **3 se valoir** *vpr (objets, personnes)* to be as good as each other

valse [vals] *nf* waltz

valve [valv] *nf* valve

vampire [vɑ̃pir] *nm* vampire

vandale [vɑ̃dal] *nmf* vandal ▪ **vandalisme** *nm* vandalism

vanille [vanij] *nf* vanilla

vanité [vanite] *nf (orgueil)* vanity

■ **vaniteux, -euse** *adj* vain, conceited

vanter [vɑ̃te] 1 *vt* to praise 2 **se vanter** *vpr* to boast, to brag (**de** about, of)

vapeur [vapœr] *nf* **v. (d'eau)** steam; **cuire qch à la v.** to steam sth

vaporiser [vaporize] *vt* to spray ■ **vaporisateur** *nm (appareil)* spray

vaquer [vake] *vi* **v. à qch** to attend to sth; **v. à ses occupations** to go about one's business

varappe [varap] *nf* rock-climbing

variable [varjabl] 1 *adj* variable; *(humeur, temps)* changeable 2 *nf* variable ■ **variation** *nf* variation

varicelle [varisεl] *nf* chickenpox

varier [varje] *vti* to vary (**de** from) ■ **varié, -e** *adj (diversifié)* varied

variété [varjete] *nf* variety

variole [varjɔl] *nf* smallpox

vas [va] *voir* **aller**[1]

vase[1] [vɑz] *nm (récipient)* vase

vase[2] [vɑz] *nf (boue)* mud, silt

vaste [vast] *adj* vast, huge

Vatican [vatikɑ̃] *nm* **le V.** the Vatican

vaut [vo] *voir* **valoir**

veau, -x [vo] *nm (animal)* calf; *(viande)* veal

vécu, -e [veky] 1 *pp de* **vivre** 2 *adj (histoire)* real-life 3 *nm* real-life experience

vedette [vədεt] *nf* (**a**) *(acteur)* star; **être en v.** *(dans un spectacle)* to top the bill (**b**) *(bateau)* launch

végétal, -e, -aux, -ales [veʒetal, -o] 1 *adj* **huile végétale** vegetable oil 2 *nm* plant ■ **végétalien, -enne** *nmf* vegan ■ **végétarien, -enne** *adj & nmf* vegetarian ■ **végétation** *nf* vegetation

véhément, -e [veemɑ̃, -ɑ̃t] *adj* vehement ■ **véhémence** *nf* vehemence

véhicule [veikyl] *nm* vehicle; **v. tout-terrain** off-road or all-terrain vehicle

veille [vεj] *nf* (**a**) *(jour précédent)* **la v.** the day before (**de** qch sth); **la v. de Noël** Christmas Eve; **à la v. de qch** *(événement)* on the eve of sth (**b**) *(état)* wakefulness

veillée [veje] *nf (soirée)* evening

veiller [veje] 1 *vi* to stay up or awake;

v. à qch to see to sth; **v. à ce que...** (+ *subjunctive*) to make sure that...; **v. sur qn** to watch over sb 2 *vt (malade)* to sit up with

veine [vεn] *nf* Anat, Bot & Géol vein

véliplanchiste [veliplɑ̃ʃist] *nmf* windsurfer

vélo [velo] *nm* bike, bicycle; *(activité)* cycling; **faire du v.** to cycle, to go cycling; **v. tout-terrain** mountain bike ■ **vélomoteur** *nm* moped

velours [vəlur] *nm* velvet; **v. côtelé** corduroy ■ **velouté, -e** 1 *adj* velvety 2 *nm* **v. d'asperges** cream of asparagus soup

velu, -e [vəly] *adj* hairy

venaison [vənεzɔ̃] *nf* venison

vendange [vɑ̃dɑ̃ʒ] *nf (récolte)* grape harvest; *(raisin récolté)* grapes (harvested); **vendanges** *(période)* grape-harvesting time; **faire les vendanges** to harvest *or* pick the grapes ■ **vendanger** *vi* to pick the grapes ■ **vendangeur, -euse** *nmf* grape picker

vendre [vɑ̃dr] 1 *vt* to sell; **v. qch à qn** to sell sb sth, to sell sth to sb; **v. qch 10 euros** to sell sth for 10 euros; **'à v.'** 'for sale' 2 **se vendre** *vpr* to be sold; **ça se vend bien** it sells well ■ **vendeur, -euse** *nmf (de magasin)* Br sales or shop assistant, *Am* sales clerk; *(non professionnel)* seller

vendredi [vɑ̃drədi] *nm* Friday; **V. saint** Good Friday

vénéneux, -euse [venenø, -øz] *adj* poisonous

vénérable [venerabl] *adj* venerable

venger [vɑ̃ʒe] 1 *vt* to avenge 2 **se venger** *vpr* to get one's revenge (**de qn** on sb; **de qch** for sth) ■ **vengeance** *nf* revenge, vengeance

venin [vənɛ̃] *nm* poison, venom ■ **venimeux, -euse** *adj* poisonous, venomous

VENIR* [vənir] 1 *(aux être) vi* to come (**de** from); **v. faire qch** to come to do sth; **viens me voir** come and see me; **je viens/venais d'arriver** I've/I'd just arrived; **les jours qui viennent**

the coming days; **faire v. qn** to send for sb

2 *v impersonnel* **s'il venait à pleuvoir** if it happened to rain

vent [vɑ̃] *nm* wind; **il y a** *ou* **il fait du v.** it's windy

vente [vɑ̃t] *nf* sale; **en v.** *(en magasin)* on sale; **mettre qch en v.** to put sth up for sale; **v. aux enchères** auction (sale); **v. par correspondance** mail order

ventilateur [vɑ̃tilatœr] *nm (électrique)* fan ■ **ventilation** *nf* ventilation ■ **ventiler** *vt* to ventilate

ventre [vɑ̃tr] *nm* stomach, belly; **à plat v.** flat on one's face; **avoir du v.** to have a paunch; **avoir mal au v.** to have a sore stomach

ventriloque [vɑ̃trilɔk] *nmf* ventriloquist

venu, -e [vəny] **1** *pp de* **venir 2** *adj* **bien v.** *(à propos)* timely; **mal v.** untimely **3** *nmf* **nouveau v., nouvelle venue** newcomer; **le premier v.** anyone **4** *nf* **venue** *(de personne, de printemps)* coming

ver [vɛr] *nm* worm; *(larve)* grub; *(de fruits, de fromage)* maggot; **v. de terre** (earth)worm; **v. à soie** silkworm

véranda [verɑ̃da] *nf* veranda(h); *(en verre)* conservatory

verbe [vɛrb] *nm* verb

verdict [vɛrdikt] *nm* verdict

verdir [vɛrdir] *vti* to turn green ■ **verdure** *nf (végétation)* greenery

verger [vɛrʒe] *nm* orchard

verglas [vɛrgla] *nm Br* (black) ice, *Am* glaze ■ **verglacé, -e** *adj (route)* icy

véridique [veridik] *adj* truthful

vérifier [verifje] **1** *vt* to check, to verify; *(comptes)* to audit **2 se vérifier** *(pr)* to prove correct ■ **vérifiable** *adj* verifiable ■ **vérification** *nf* checking, verification; *(de comptes)* audit(ing)

véritable [veritabl] *adj (histoire, ami)* true, real; *(cuir, or, nom)* real, genuine; *(en intensif)* real

vérité [verite] *nf (de déclaration)* truth; *(sincérité)* sincerity; **en v.** in fact; **dire la v.** to tell the truth

verni, -e [vɛrni] *adj (meuble, parquet)* varnished

vernir [vɛrnir] *vt (bois)* to varnish; *(céramique)* to glaze ■ **vernis** *nm* varnish; *(pour céramique)* glaze; **v. à ongles** nail polish *or Br* varnish ■ **vernissage** *nm (d'exposition)* opening

verra, verrait [vera, verɛ] *voir* **voir**

verre [vɛr] *nm (substance, récipient)* glass; **prendre un v.** to have a drink; **v. de bière** glass of beer; **v. à bière/à vin** beer/wine glass; **v. de contact** contact lens ■ **verrière** *nf (toit)* glass roof

verrou [veru] *nm* bolt; **fermer qch au v.** to bolt sth; **sous les verrous** behind bars

verrouiller [veruje] *vt (porte)* to bolt; *(quartier)* to seal off

verrue [very] *nf* wart; **v. plantaire** verruca

vers[1] [vɛr] *prép (direction)* toward(s); *(approximation)* around, about

vers[2] [vɛr] *nm (de poème)* line; **des vers** *(poésie)* verse

versant [vɛrsɑ̃] *nm* slope, side

verse [vɛrs] **à verse** *adv* **la pluie tombait à v.** the rain was coming down in torrents

Verseau [vɛrso] *nm (signe)* Aquarius

verser [vɛrse] *vt* to pour (out); *(larmes, sang)* to shed; *(argent)* to pay (**sur un compte** into an account) ■ **versement** *nm* payment

version [vɛrsjɔ̃] *nf (de film, d'incident)* version; *Cin* **en v. originale** in the original language; **en v. française** dubbed *(into French)*

verso [vɛrso] *nm* back (of the page); **'voir au v.'** 'see overleaf'

vert, verte [vɛr, vɛrt] **1** *adj* green; *(pas mûr)* unripe; **aller en classe verte** to go on a school trip to the countryside **2** *nm* green; *Pol* **les Verts** the Greens

vertical, -e, -aux, -ales [vɛrtikal, -o] *adj & nf* vertical; **à la verticale** vertically

vertige [vɛrtiʒ] *nm (étourdissement)*

(feeling of) dizziness or giddiness; *(peur du vide)* vertigo; **vertiges** dizzy spells; **avoir le v.** to be or feel dizzy or giddy ▪ **vertigineux, -euse** *adj (hauteur)* giddy, dizzy

vertu [vɛrty] *nf* virtue; **en v. de** in accordance with ▪ **vertueux, -euse** *adj* virtuous

verveine [vɛrvɛn] *nf (plante)* verbena; *(tisane)* verbena tea

vessie [vesi] *nf* bladder

veste [vɛst] *nf* jacket, coat

vestiaire [vɛstjɛr] *nm (de théâtre)* cloakroom; *(de piscine, de stade)* changing room, *Am* locker room

vestibule [vɛstibyl] *nm* (entrance) hall

vestiges [vɛstiʒ] *nmpl (ruines)* remains; *(traces)* relics

veston [vɛstɔ̃] *nm (suit)* jacket

vêtement [vɛtmã] *nm* garment, article of clothing; **vêtements** clothes; **vêtements de sport** sportswear

vétéran [veterã] *nm* veteran

vétérinaire [veterinɛr] **1** *adj* veterinary **2** *nmf* vet, *Br* veterinary surgeon, *Am* veterinarian

vêtir* [vetir] *vt*, **se vêtir** *vpr* to dress

veto [veto] *nm inv* veto; **opposer son v. à qch** to veto sth

vêtu, -e [vety] *adj* dressed (**de** in)

vétuste [vetyst] *adj* dilapidated

veuf, veuve [vœf, vœv] **1** *adj* widowed **2** *nm* widower **3** *nf* widow

veuille(s), veuillent [vœj] *voir* **vouloir**

veut, veux [vø] *voir* **vouloir**

vexer [vɛkse] **1** *vt* to upset, to hurt **2 se vexer** *vpr* to get upset (**de** at)

VF [veef] *(abrév* **version française)** *nf* film **en VF** film dubbed into French

viable [vjabl] *adj (entreprise, enfant)* viable

viaduc [vjadyk] *nm* viaduct

viande [vjãd] *nf* meat

vibrer [vibre] *vi* to vibrate; *(être ému)* to be stirred (**de** with); **faire v. qn** to stir sb ▪ **vibrant, -e** *adj (hommage)* stirring ▪ **vibration** *nf* vibration

vice [vis] *nm (perversité)* vice; *(défectuosité)* defect

vice versa [vis(e)vɛrsa] *adv* vice versa

vicié, -e [visje] *adj (air, atmosphère)* polluted

vicieux, -euse [visjø, -øz] *adj (pervers)* depraved; *(perfide)* underhand

victime [viktim] *nf* victim; *(d'accident)* casualty; **être v. de** *(accident, attentat)* to be the victim of

victoire [viktwar] *nf* victory; *(en sport)* win ▪ **victorieux, -euse** *adj* victorious; *(équipe)* winning

vidange [vidãʒ] *nf (de véhicule)* emptying, draining; *(de véhicule)* oil change ▪ **vidanger** *vt* to empty, to drain

vide [vid] **1** *adj* empty **2** *nm (espace)* empty space; *(d'emploi du temps)* gap; *Phys* vacuum; **regarder dans le v.** to stare into space; **emballé sous v.** vacuum-packed; **à v.** empty

vidéo [video] *adj inv* & *nf* video ▪ **vidéocassette** *nf* video (cassette) ▪ **vidéoclip** *nm* video

vider [vide] *vt*, **se vider** *vpr* to empty ▪ **vide-ordures** *nm inv Br* rubbish or *Am* garbage chute ▪ **videur** *nm (de boîte de nuit)* bouncer

vie [vi] *nf* life; *(durée)* lifetime; **en v.** living; **à v., pour la v.** for life

vieil, vieille [vjɛj] *voir* **vieux**

vieillard [vjɛjar] *nm* old man; **les vieillards** old people ▪ **vieillerie** *nf (objet)* old thing ▪ **vieillesse** *nf* old age

vieillir [vjejir] *vi* to grow old; *(changer)* to age; *(théorie, mot)* to become old-fashioned **2** *vt* **v. qn** *(vêtement)* to make sb look old(er) ▪ **vieilli, -e** *adj (démodé)* old-fashioned ▪ **vieillissant, -e** *adj* ageing ▪ **vieillissement** *nm* ageing

vieillot, -otte [vjɛjo, -ɔt] *adj* old-fashioned

Vienne [vjɛn] *nm* ou *f* Vienna

viens, vient [vjɛ̃] *voir* **venir**

vierge [vjɛrʒ] **1** *adj (femme, neige)* virgin; *(feuille de papier, film)* blank; **être v.** *(femme, homme)* to be a virgin **2** *nf* virgin; **la V.** *(signe)* Virgo

Viêt-nam [vjɛtnam] nm le V. Vietnam ■ **vietnamien, -enne 1** adj Vietnamese **2** nmf V., Vietnamienne Vietnamese

vieux, vieille, vieux, vieilles [vjø, vjɛj]

vieil is used before masculine singular nouns beginning with a vowel or mute h.

1 adj old; **être v. jeu** (adj inv) to be old-fashioned; **se faire v.** to get old **2** nm old man; **les vieux** old people **3** nf **vieille** old woman

vif, vive [vif, viv] **1** adj (personne) lively; (imagination) vivid; (intelligence, vent, douleur) sharp; (intérêt, satisfaction) great; (couleur, lumière) bright; (froid) biting; (pas, mouvement) quick; **brûler qn v.** to burn sb alive **2** nm **entrer dans le v. du sujet** to get to the heart of the matter; **à v.** (plaie) open

vigilant, -e [viʒilɑ̃, -ɑ̃t] adj vigilant ■ **vigilance** nf vigilance

vigile [viʒil] nm watchman

vigne [viɲ] nf (plante) vine;■ (plantation) vineyard ■ **vigneron, -onne** [-ərɔ̃, -ɔn] nmf wine grower ■ **vignoble** nm vineyard; (région) vineyards

vignette [viɲɛt] nf (de véhicule) road tax sticker, Br ≃ road tax disc; (de médicament) label (for reimbursement by Social Security)

vigueur [vigœr] nf vigour; **entrer en v.** (loi) to come into force ■ **vigoureux, -euse** adj (personne) vigorous

vilain, -e [vilɛ̃, -ɛn] adj (laid) ugly; (peu sage) naughty

villa [vila] nf villa

village [vilaʒ] nm village ■ **villageois, -e** nmf villager

ville [vil] nf town; (grande) city; **aller/être en v.** to go (in)to/be in town; **v. d'eaux** spa (town)

vin [vɛ̃] nm wine ■ **vinicole** adj (région) wine-growing

vinaigre [vinɛgr] nm vinegar ■ **vinaigrette** nf (sauce) vinaigrette, Br French dressing, Am Italian dressing

vingt [vɛ̃] ([vɛ̃t] before vowel or mute h and in numbers 22–29) adj & nm inv twenty; **v. et un** twenty-one ■ **vingtaine** nf **une v. (de)** (nombre) about twenty ■ **vingtième** adj & nmf twentieth

viol [vjɔl] nm rape; (de lieu) violation ■ **violation** nf violation ■ **violer** vt (femme) to rape ■ **violeur** nm rapist

violent, -e [vjɔlɑ̃, -ɑ̃t] adj violent; (effort) strenuous ■ **violence** nf violence; **acte de v.** act of violence

violet, -ette [vjɔlɛ, -ɛt] **1** adj & nm (couleur) purple **2** nf **violette** (fleur) violet

violon [vjɔlɔ̃] nm violin ■ **violoncelle** nm cello ■ **violoncelliste** nmf cellist ■ **violoniste** nmf violinist

vipère [vipɛr] nf adder, viper

virage [viraʒ] nm (de route) bend

virer [vire] **1** vi to turn; **v. au bleu** to turn blue **2** vt Fin (somme) to transfer (à to) ■ **virement** nm Fin transfer

virgule [virgyl] nf (ponctuation) comma; Math (decimal) point; **2 v. 5** 2 point 5

viril, -e [viril] adj virile; (force) male ■ **virilité** nf virility

virtuel, -elle [virtɥɛl] adj potential; (image) virtual; **réalité virtuelle** virtual reality

virtuose [virtɥoz] nmf virtuoso

virulent, -e [virylɑ̃, -ɑ̃t] adj virulent

virus [virys] nm Méd & Ordinat virus

vis¹ [vi] voir **vivre, voir**

vis² [vis] nf screw

visa [viza] nm (de passeport) visa

visage [vizaʒ] nm face

vis-à-vis [vizavi] **1** prép **v. de** (en face de) opposite; (envers) towards **2** nm inv (personne) person opposite

viser [vize] **1** vt (cible) to aim at; (concerner) to be aimed at **2** vi to aim (à at); **v. à faire qch** to aim to do sth

visible [vizibl] adj visible ■ **visibilité** nf visibility

visière [vizjɛr] nf (de casquette) peak; (en plastique) eyeshade; (de casque) visor

vision [vizjɔ̃] *nf (conception, image)* vision; *(sens)* sight ■ **visionnaire** *adj & nmf* visionary ■ **visionner** *vt (film)* to view

visite [vizit] *nf* visit; *(personne)* visitor; *(examen)* inspection; **rendre v. à qn** to visit sb; **avoir de la v.** to have a visitor/visitors; **v. médicale** medical examination; **v. guidée** guided tour ■ **visiter** *vt (lieu touristique, patient)* to visit ■ **visiteur, -euse** *nmf* visitor

vison [vizɔ̃] *nm* mink

visqueux, -euse [viskø, -øz] *adj* viscous; *(surface)* sticky

visser [vise] *vt* to screw on

visuel, -elle [vizɥɛl] *adj* visual ■ **visualiser** *vt* to visualize

vit [vi] *voir* **vivre, voir**

vital, -e, -aux, -ales [vital, -o] *adj* vital ■ **vitalité** *nf* vitality

vitamine [vitamin] *nf* vitamin

vite [vit] *adv (rapidement)* quickly, fast; *(sous peu)* soon; **v.!** quick(ly)!

vitesse [vites] *nf* speed; *(de moteur)* gear; **à toute v.** at top full speed

viticole [vitikɔl] *adj (région)* wine-growing ■ **viticulteur** *nm* wine grower ■ **viticulture** *nf* wine growing

vitre [vitr] *nf (window)*pane; *(de véhicule, de train)* window ■ **vitrage** *nm (vitres)* windows ■ **vitrail, -aux** *nm* stained-glass window ■ **vitré, -e** *adj* **porte vitrée** glass door ■ **vitrier** *nm* glazier

vitrine [vitrin] *nf (de magasin)* (shop) window; *(meuble)* display cabinet

vivace [vivas] *adj (plante)* perennial ■ **vivacité** *nf* liveliness; *(d'imagination)* vividness; *(d'intelligence)* sharpness; *(de couleur)* brightness; *(emportement)* petulance; **v. d'esprit** quick-wittedness

vivant, -e [vivɑ̃, -ɑ̃t] **1** *adj (en vie)* alive, living; *(récit, rue, enfant)* lively; *(être, matière)* living **2** *nm* **de son v.** in one's lifetime; **les vivants** the living

vive[1] [viv] *voir* **vif**

vive[2] [viv] *exclam* **v. le roi!** long live the king!

vivement [vivmɑ̃] *adv* quickly; *(répliquer)* sharply; *(regretter)* deeply

vivier [vivje] *nm* fish pond

vivifier [vivifje] *vt* to invigorate

vivisection [vivisɛksjɔ̃] *nf* vivisection

vivre* [vivr] **1** *vi* to live; **elle vit encore** she's still alive *or* living; **faire v. qn** *(famille)* to support sb; **v. vieux** to live to be old; **v. de** *(fruits)* to live on; *(travail)* to live by **2** *vt (vie)* to live; *(aventure, époque)* to live through; *(éprouver)* to experience ■ **vivres** *nmpl* food, supplies

VO [veo] *(abrév* **version originale)** *nf* **film en VO** film in the original language

vocal, -e, -aux, -ales [vɔkal, -o] *adj* vocal

vocation [vɔkasjɔ̃] *nf* vocation, calling

vociférer [vɔsifere] *vti* to shout angrily

vœu, -x [vø] *nm (souhait)* wish; *(promesse)* vow; **faire un v.** to make a wish; **tous mes vœux!** best wishes!

vogue [vɔg] *nf* fashion, vogue; **en v.** in vogue

voici [vwasi] *prép* here is/are; **me v.** here I am; **v. dix ans** ten years ago; **v. dix ans que...** it's ten years since...

voie [vwa] *nf (route)* road; *(rails)* track, line; *(partie de route)* lane; *(chemin)* way; *(de gare)* platform; *(de communication)* line; *(moyen)* means, way; **pays en v. de développement** developing country; **v. sans issue** dead end

voilà [vwala] *prép* there is/are; **les v.** there they are; **le v. parti** he has left now; **v. dix ans** ten years ago; **v. dix ans que...** it's ten years since...

voile[1] [vwal] *nm (étoffe, coiffure)* veil ■ **voilé, -e** *adj (femme, allusion)* veiled; *(photo, lumière)* hazy ■ **voiler**[1] [vwale] **1** *vt (visage, vérité)* to veil **2** **se voiler** *vpr (personne)* to wear a veil; *(ciel)* to cloud over

voile[2] [vwal] *nf (de bateau)* sail; *(sport)* sailing; **faire de la v.** to sail ■ **voilier** *nm* sailing boat; *(de plaisance)* yacht

voiler [vwale] *vt*, **se voiler** *vpr* (roue) to buckle

VOIR* [vwar] **1** *vt* to see; **faire v.** to show sth; **v. qn faire qch** to see sb do/doing sth
2 *vi* to see; **fais v.** let me see, show me; **ça n'a rien à v. avec ça** that's got nothing to do with that
3 **se voir** *vpr* (soi-même) to see oneself; (se fréquenter) to see each other; (objet, attitude) to be seen; (reprise, tache) to show

voisin, -e [vwazɛ̃, -in] **1** *adj* (pays, village) *Br* neighbouring, *Am* neighboring; (maison, pièce) next (**de** to); (état) similar (**de** to) **2** *nmf Br* neighbour, *Am* neighbor ■ **voisinage** *nm* (quartier, voisins) *Br* neighbourhood, *Am* neighborhood; (proximité) closeness, proximity ■ **voisiner** *vi* **v. avec** to be side by side with

voiture [vwatyr] *nf* car; (de train) carriage, *Br* coach, *Am* car; **en v.!** (dans le train) all aboard!; **v. de course** racing/private car

voix [vwa] *nf* voice; (d'électeur) vote; **à v. basse** in a whisper; **à haute v.** aloud

vol [vɔl] *nm* (**a**) (d'avion, d'oiseau) flight; (groupe d'oiseaux) flock, flight; **attraper qch au v.** to catch sth in the air (**b**) (délit) theft; **v. à main armée** armed robbery

volaille [vɔlaj] *nf* **la v.** poultry; **une v.** a fowl

volatiliser [vɔlatilize] **se volatiliser** *vpr* to vanish into thin air

volcan [vɔlkɑ̃] *nm* volcano ■ **volcanique** *adj* volcanic

voler¹ [vɔle] *vi* (oiseau, avion) to fly ■ **volant** *nm* (de véhicule) (steering) wheel; (de badminton) shuttlecock; (de jupe) flounce ■ **volée** *nf* (de flèches) flight; (de coups) thrashing

voler² [vɔle] **1** *vt* (prendre) to steal (**à** from); **v. qn** to rob sb **2** *vi* (prendre) to steal

volet [vɔlɛ] *nm* (de fenêtre) shutter; (de programme) section, part

voleur, -euse [vɔlœr, -øz] *nmf* thief; **au v.!** stop thief!

volière [vɔljɛr] *nf* aviary

volley-ball [vɔlebol] *nm* volleyball ■ **volleyeur, -euse** *nmf* volleyball player

volontaire [vɔlɔ̃tɛr] **1** *adj* (geste, omission) deliberate; (travail) voluntary; (opiniâtre) *Br* wilful, *Am* willful **2** *nmf* volunteer ■ **volontairement** *adv* (spontanément) voluntarily; (exprès) deliberately

volontariat [vɔlɔ̃tarja] *nm* voluntary work

volonté [vɔlɔ̃te] *nf* (faculté, intention) will; (détermination) willpower; (souhait) wish; **bonne v.** willingness; **mauvaise v.** unwillingness; **à v.** (quantité) as much as desired

volontiers [vɔlɔ̃tje] *adv* gladly, willingly; **v.!** (oui) I'd love to!

volte-face [vɔltəfas] *nf inv* **faire v.** to turn round; *Fig* to do a U-turn

voltiger [vɔltiʒe] *vi* (feuilles) to flutter

volume [vɔlym] *nm* (de boîte, de son, livre) volume ■ **volumineux, -euse** *adj* bulky, voluminous

volupté [vɔlypte] *nf* sensual pleasure ■ **voluptueux, -euse** *adj* voluptuous

vomir [vɔmir] **1** *vt* to bring up, to vomit **2** *vi* to vomit, *Br* to be sick ■ **vomissements** *nmpl* **avoir des v.** to vomit

vont [vɔ̃] *voir* **aller¹**

vorace [vɔras] *adj* voracious

vos [vo] *voir* **votre**

vote [vɔt] *nm* (action) vote, voting; (suffrage) vote; (de loi) passing; *Br* **bureau de v.** polling station, *Am* polling place ■ **votant, -e** *nmf* voter ■ **voter 1** *vt* (loi) to pass; (crédits) to vote **2** *vi* to vote

votre, vos [vɔtr, vo] *adj possessif* your ■ **vôtre 1** *pron possessif* **le** *ou* **la v.**, **les vôtres** yours; **à la v.!** cheers! **2** *nmpl* **les vôtres** (votre famille) your family

voudra, voudrait [vudra, vudrɛ] *voir* **vouloir**

vouer [vwe] **1** *vt* (promettre) to vow (**à** to); (consacrer) to dedicate (**à** to) **2** **se**

vouer *vpr* **se v. à** to dedicate oneself to

VOULOIR* [vulwar] *vt* to want (**faire qch** to do); **je veux qu'il parte** I want him to go; **v. dire** to mean (**que** that); **je voudrais un pain** I'd like a loaf of bread; **je voudrais rester** I'd like to stay; **je veux bien attendre** I don't mind waiting; **voulez-vous me suivre** will you follow me; **si tu veux** if you like *or* wish; **en v. à qn** d'avoir fait qch to be angry with sb for doing sth; **v. du bien à qn** to wish sb well; **sans le v.** unintentionally

voulu, -e [vuly] *adj* (*requis*) required; (*délibéré*) deliberate, intentional

vous [vu] *pron personnel* (**a**) (*sujet, complément direct*) you; **v. êtes ici** you are here; **il v. connaît** he knows you (**b**) (*complément indirect*) (to) you; **il v. l'a donné** he gave it to you, he gave you it (**c**) (*réfléchi*) yourself, *pl* yourselves; **v. v. lavez** you wash yourself/yourselves (**d**) (*réciproque*) each other; **v. v. aimez** you love each other ▪ **vous-même** *pron* yourself ▪ **vous-mêmes** *pron pl* yourselves

voûte [vut] *nf* (*arch*) vault ▪ **voûté, -e** *adj* (*personne*) bent, stooped

vouvoyer [vuvwaje] *vt* **v. qn** to address sb as "vous" ▪ **vouvoiement** *nm* = use of the formal "vous" instead of the more familiar "tu"

voyage [vwajaʒ] *nm* trip, journey; (*par mer*) voyage; **aimer les voyages** to like *Br* travelling *or Am* traveling; **faire un v., partir en v.** to go on a trip; **être en v.** to be (away) *Br* travelling *or Am* traveling; **bon v.!** have a pleasant trip!; **v. de noces** honeymoon; **v. organisé** (package) tour ▪ **voyager** *vi* to travel

▪ **voyageur, -euse** *nmf Br* traveller, *Am* traveler; (*passager*) passenger; **v. de commerce** *Br* travelling *or Am* traveling salesman, *Br* commercial traveller ▪ **voyagiste** *nm* tour operator

voyant, -e¹ [vwajɑ̃, -ɑ̃t] **1** *adj* (*couleur*) gaudy, loud **2** *nm* (*signal*) (warning) light; (*d'appareil électrique*) pilot light

voyant, -e² [vwajɑ̃, -ɑ̃t] *nmf* clairvoyant

voyou [vwaju] *nm* hooligan

vrac [vrak] **en vrac** *adv* (*en désordre*) in a muddle; (*au poids*) loose

vrai [vre] *adj* true; (*réel*) real; (*authentique*) genuine ▪ **vraiment** *adv* really

vraisemblable [vresɑ̃blabl] *adj* (*probable*) likely, probable; (*crédible*) credible ▪ **vraisemblablement** *adv* probably ▪ **vraisemblance** *nf* likelihood; (*crédibilité*) credibility

vrombir [vrɔ̃bir] *vi* to hum ▪ **vrombissement** *nm* hum(ming)

VTT [vetete] (*abrév* **vélo tout terrain**) *nm inv* mountain bike

vu, -e¹ [vy] **1** *pp de* **voir 2** *adj* **bien vu** well thought of; **mal vu** frowned on **3** *prép* in view of; **vu que…** seeing that…

vue² [vy] *nf* (*sens*) (eye)sight; (*panorama, photo*) view; **en v.** (*proche*) in sight; (*en évidence*) on view; *Fig* (*personne*) in the public eye; **avoir qn/qch en v.** to have sb/sth in mind; **à v.** (*tirer*) on sight; (*payable*) at sight; **à première v.** at first sight; **à v. d'œil** (*grandir*) visibly; **de v.** (*connaître*) by sight; **v. d'ensemble** overall view

vulgaire [vylger] *adj* (*grossier*) vulgar; (*ordinaire*) common ▪ **vulgariser** *vt* to popularize ▪ **vulgarité** *nf* vulgarity

vulnérable [vylnerabl] *adj* vulnerable ▪ **vulnérabilité** *nf* vulnerability

Ww

W, w [dubləve] *nm inv* W, w

wagon [vagɔ̃] *nm (de voyageurs)* carriage, *Br* coach, *Am* car; *(de marchandises) Br* wagon, *Am* freight car ■ **wagon-lit** (*pl* **wagons-lits**) *nm* sleeping car, sleeper ■ **wagon-restaurant** (*pl* **wagons-restaurants**) *nm* dining *or* restaurant car

Walkman® [wɔkman] *nm* Walkman®, personal stereo

wallon, -onne [walɔ̃, -ɔn] **1** *adj* Walloon **2** *nmf* **W., Wallonne** Walloon

watt [wat] *nm Él* watt

w-c [(dublə)vese] *nmpl Br* toilet, *Am* bathroom

week-end [wikɛnd] (*pl* **week-ends**) *nm* weekend; **partir en w.** to go away for the weekend

whisky [wiski] (*pl* **-ies** *ou* **-ys**) *nm Br* whisky, *Am* whiskey

wysiwyg [wiziwig] *adj & nm Ordinat* WYSIWYG

Xx

X, x [iks] *nm inv* (*lettre, personne ou nombre inconnus*) X, x; **x fois** umpteen times

xénophobe [gsenɔfɔb] *adj* xenophobic ■ **xénophobie** *nf* xenophobia
xylophone [gsilɔfɔn] *nm* xylophone

Yy

Y, y¹ [igrɛk] *nm inv* Y, y

y² [i] **1** *adv* there; *(dedans)* in it/them; *(dessus)* on it/them; **elle y vivra** she'll live there; **j'y entrai** I entered (it); **allons-y** let's go **2** *pron* **j'y pense** I'm thinking about it; **je m'y attendais** I was expecting it; **ça y est!** that's it!

yacht [jɔt] *nm* yacht

yaourt [jaurt] *nm* yoghurt

Yémen [jemɛn] *nm* **le Y.** Yemen

yen [jɛn] *nm* yen

yeux [jø] *voir* **œil**

yoga [jɔga] *nm* yoga; **faire du y.** to do yoga

yog(h)ourt [jɔgurt] *nm* = **yaourt**

Yo-Yo® [jojo] *nm inv* yo-yo

Zz

Z, z [zɛd] *nm inv* Z, z
Zaïre [zair] *nm* **le Z.** Zaïre
zèbre [zebr] *nm* zebra
zèle [zɛl] *nm* zeal; **faire du z.** to overdo it ■ **zélé, -e** *adj* zealous
zéro [zero] *nm (chiffre)* zero, *Br* nought; *(de numéro de téléphone) Br* 0 [əʊ], *Am* zero; *(température)* zero; *Fig (personne)* nonentity; **deux buts à z.** *(au football) Br* two nil, *Am* two zero
zeste [zɛst] *nm* **un z. de citron** a piece of lemon peel
zigzag [zigzag] *nm* zigzag; **en z.** *(route)* zigzag(ging) ■ **zigzaguer** *vi* to zigzag

Zimbabwe [zimbabwe] *nm* **le Z.** Zimbabwe
zinc [zɛ̃g] *nm (métal)* zinc
zipper [zipe] *vt Ordinat* to zip
zodiaque [zɔdjak] *nm* zodiac; **signe du z.** sign of the zodiac
zone [zon] *nf* zone; **de seconde z.** second-rate; **z. industrielle** industrial *Br* estate *or Am* park; **z. fumeurs/non-fumeurs** smoking/no-smoking area
zoo [zo(o)] *nm* zoo ■ **zoologie** *nf* zoology ■ **zoologique** *adj* zoological; **parc z.** zoo
zoom [zum] *nm (objectif)* zoom lens